The World and Its People
ONE FLAG, ONE LAND

RICHARD C. BROWN
Former University Professor of History,
State University of New York College at Buffalo

HERBERT J. BASS
Professor of History, Temple University, Philadelphia, Pennsylvania

ANNOTATED
TEACHER'S
EDITION

SILVER BURDETT COMPANY

MORRISTOWN, NJ
Atlanta, GA • Cincinnati, OH • Dallas, TX • Northfield, IL
San Carlos, CA • Agincourt, Ontario

TABLE OF CONTENTS

Built on a solid factual foundation

The Silver Burdett social studies program THE WORLD AND ITS PEOPLE was developed to help pupils understand themselves and the world around them and to instill in them the knowledge and skills necessary for responsible citizenship. Built on a sold factual foundation, the program examines the pupils' world in an ever-widening circle. THE WORLD AND ITS PEOPLE begins with a study of self and family; expands to a study of neighborhood, community, state, region, nation, and world; and ends with a study of the history of the United States.

Instills knowledge and skills

Each book in the series reflects the following belief: *Pupils need to know, to appreciate, and to do.* A grasp of basic facts is essential in gaining an understanding of social studies. To that end, a wealth of material is provided. Lesson checkups, chapter and unit reviews, and chapter tests ensure the pupils' understanding of the text material. Opportunities for development of language, reading, and social studies skills are provided throughout the series through vocabulary study, skills development exercises, and other skills-related activities.

Encourages active learning

THE WORLD AND ITS PEOPLE involves *doing.* Pupils work with maps, charts, graphs, tables, and time lines as a vital part of the learning process. Pupils build models, conduct interviews, hold debates, and take part in a variety of other activities. In short, pupils are *active participants.*

Fosters responsible citizenship

THE WORLD AND ITS PEOPLE enables pupils to appreciate themselves, the world around them, and their role as citizens of the United States. Pupils learn to understand some of the important links between them and their families, community, state, region, nation, and world. In doing so, they develop an appreciation of historic and geographic factors and economic and political relationships that have shaped their world. Morever, pupils are given specific suggestions for assuming a responsible role — in a capacity commensurate with age and ability — in their community, state, region, nation, and world. THE WORLD AND ITS PEOPLE not only prepares pupils for the future but also helps them function meaningfully in the present.

An Expanding Horizons Approach That Teachers Like to Use

THE WORLD AND ITS PEOPLE is a social studies series that begins with the student's familiar world — self and family — and broadens into a study of neighborhoods, communities, states, regions, the United States, other countries around the world, and ends with an indepth study of the history of the United States.

PROGRAM COMPONENTS

- **PUPIL'S TEXT**
- **ANNOTATED TEACHER'S EDITION**
- **TEACHER'S PLANNING GUIDE**
- **WORKBOOK**
- **TEACHER RESOURCE PACKAGE**

ONE FLAG, ONE LAND
Is Organized to Excite Student Interest

● Students learn, in chronological order, about the birth and growth of our nation and the significant events that shaped our history.

● This highly exciting book meets the needs of students by presenting history — not as a dull listing of dates and events, but as a fascinating study of the men and women who lived and made the history.

Page 705

Page 139

KEY 1. Richard Stockton, N.J.; 2. Josiah Bartlett, N.H.; 3. Thomas Nelson, Jr., Va.; 4. George Clymer, Pa.; 5. Francis Lightfoot Lee, Va.; 6. John Penn, N.C.; 7. Abraham Clark, N.J.; 8. John Morton, Pa.; 9. George Ross, Pa.; 10. James Smith, Pa.; 11. Samuel Adams, Mass.; 12. Robert Treat Paine, Mass.; 13. Button Gwinnett, Ga.; 14. Robert Morris, Pa.; 15. Benjamin Harrison, Va.; 16. Carter Braxton, Va.; 17. John Hart, N.J.; 18. John Jamin Franklin, Pa.; 19. Roger Sherman, Conn.; 20. James Wilson, Pa.; 21. Va.; 22. Charles Thomson, (Secretary); 23. John Hopkins, R.I.; 24. Francis Hopkinson, N.J.; 25. William Ellery, R.I.; 26. Edward Rutledge, S.C.; 27. Benjamin. 28. Charles Carroll, Md.; 29. Richard Henry Lee, Va.; 30. George Read, Del.; 31. George Taylor, Pa.; 32. Stephen Hopkins, R.I.

Members of the Continental Congress prepare to approve the Declaration of Independence.

The Declaration of Independence
On June 7, 1776, Richard Henry Lee of Virginia introduced a resolution into the Second Continental Congress. Its main part stated that "these United Colonies ought to be free and independent states." For nearly a month the members of Congress debated Lee's resolution. They approved it on July 2, 1776. This was all that was needed to declare independence. However, Congress had chosen a committee to prepare a suitable statement to accompany Lee's resolution. It is this statement, explaining Congress' action, that became known as the **Declaration of Independence.**

139

he ended all remaining controls on the price of oil and gas, saying that this would encourage Americans to produce more oil.

The President felt that some of the regulations in the fields of conservation and pollution were too strict. His secretary of the interior, James Watt, allowed private companies to search for oil in protected wilderness areas and in nearly a billion acres of coastal waters as well. Watt also leased government-owned coalfields to private companies. However, Watt made important improvements in the country's national parks.

The Reagan administration was less active than earlier administrations in enforcing desegregation laws and laws dealing with racial and sex discrimination. Minority groups became very critical.

Dr. Sally Ride, America's first woman astronaut, was one of the crew of the Space Shuttle Challenger in 1983.

An offshore drilling rig searches for oil in waters along the coast of the United States.

Women's rights groups were angry because the President had opposed ERA. Supporters of the President pointed out that he was the first to appoint a woman, Sandra Day O'Connor, to the Supreme Court. He also named Jeane Kirkpatrick, a foreign policy expert, as ambassador to the United Nations. On the other hand there were no women, blacks, or Hispanics in the Reagan Cabinet and few in other high government positions.

The New Federalism   In addition to cutting out or reducing certain federal programs, Reagan proposed to shift other programs from the federal government to the states. These would include welfare and some health-care programs. Certain tax revenues would be transferred to

705

Clear Organization and Lively Content

 ONE FLAG, ONE LAND consists of 31 chapters. Brief chapter introductions focusing on individuals, families, or groups prepare students for the chapter content that follows.

 At the beginning of each chapter is a time line that shows some of the major events in American history.

Page 40

Page 41

CHAPTER
3 Outsiders Explore and Settle in America

Columbus Leads the Way

— VOCABULARY —

Far East	Vinland
Indies	colony
Vikings	New World

A man from Genoa   It was early in the morning of Friday, October 12, 1492. Rodrigo de Triana (rod rē′ gō də trē än′-ə) stood as lookout on the *Pinta*. The *Pinta*, the *Niña*, and the *Santa Maria* were the three ships in a tiny fleet commanded by Christopher Columbus. Each ship was less than 100 feet (30 m) in length.

Christopher Columbus was born in the old seaside city of Genoa (jen′ ō ə), Italy, in 1451. His father and his grandfather were weavers of woolen cloth. His mother was a weaver's daughter. But Columbus chose to go to sea.

Christopher Columbus had two brothers. Bartholomew (bär thol′ ə myü), the older, was tough, skillful, and loyal. He became a partner in the project that resulted in Columbus's voyages to America. The other brother was named Diego (dē ā′ gō). Though willing enough, Diego failed as a sailor and colonist in the New World. Later he became a priest.

The brothers had a sister named Bianchinetta (byäng′ kē net′ ə). She married a wine merchant in Genoa. Little more is known of Bianchinetta. In those days women had little choice to be anything other than a wife and mother, or perhaps a member of a religious order.

A plan for reaching the Indies   When Christopher Columbus was 25, he sailed with a fleet of merchant ships from the port of Genoa. Off the coast of Portugal, several French and Portuguese warships attacked the merchant vessels. They sank the ship on which Columbus was sailing. He saved himself by grabbing a large oar. Hanging onto it, he floated to the coast of Portugal, 6 miles (10 km) away.

Columbus stayed in Portugal for several years. There he sailed with and talked to many experienced sailors. At that time Europeans were talking of finding a water route to the **Far East**. There was a great demand in Europe for the silks, spices, and other products of eastern Asia. Trade with the Far East by way of land routes had proved to be slow, costly, and dangerous. A water route would be much better.

Some of the sailors that Columbus talked of reaching Asia by sailing south from Portugal and then east around Africa. In this way they hoped to reach the rich Asian islands called the **Indies**.

Gradually Columbus formed another plan. Like other thoughtful men of the

Several countries in the Americas have issued postage stamps honoring Columbus.

40

41

Special Interest Materials Complement the Basic Narrative

- The section How Americans Lived paints a picture of the day-to-day life of Americans at a particular time in history. Beginning with 1750, each 50-year interval in America's social history is highlighted, through 1950.

- The feature What's In a Name, which appears frequently throughout the text, responds to and builds on curiosity about names. This section provides information on many kinds of names in their historical context.

- At appropriate places throughout the book are special boxes on the Presidents of the United States. Each box includes a portrait and interesting information about the President's life and his administration.

Page 221

Page 484

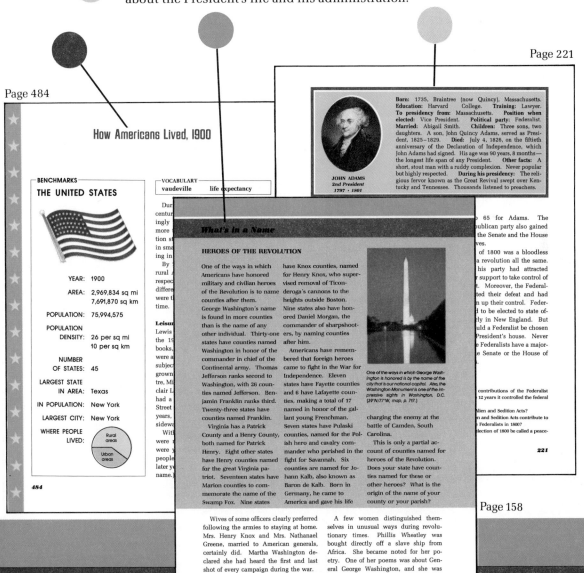

How Americans Lived, 1900

BENCHMARKS

THE UNITED STATES

YEAR:	1900
AREA:	2,969,834 sq mi
	7,691,870 sq km
POPULATION:	75,994,575
POPULATION DENSITY:	26 per sq mi
	10 per sq km
NUMBER OF STATES:	45
LARGEST STATE IN AREA:	Texas
IN POPULATION:	New York
LARGEST CITY:	New York
WHERE PEOPLE LIVED:	Rural areas / Urban areas

VOCABULARY
vaudeville   life expectancy

484

JOHN ADAMS
2nd President
1797 · 1801

Born: 1735, Braintree (now Quincy), Massachusetts. **Education:** Harvard College. **Training:** Lawyer. **To presidency from:** Massachusetts. **Position when elected:** Vice President. **Political party:** Federalist. **Married:** Abigail Smith. **Children:** Three sons, two daughters. A son, John Quincy Adams, served as President, 1825–1829. **Died:** July 4, 1826, on the fiftieth anniversary of the Declaration of Independence, which John Adams had signed. His age was 90 years, 8 months— the longest life span of any President. **Other facts:** A short, stout man with a ruddy complexion. Never popular but highly respected. **During his presidency:** The religious fervor known as the Great Revival swept over Kentucky and Tennessee. Thousands listened to preachers.

What's In a Name

HEROES OF THE REVOLUTION

One of the ways in which Americans have honored military and civilian heroes of the Revolution is to name counties after them. George Washington's name is found in more counties than is the name of any other individual. Thirty-one states have counties named Washington in honor of the commander in chief of the Continental army. Thomas Jefferson ranks second to Washington, with 26 counties named Jefferson. Benjamin Franklin ranks third. Twenty-three states have counties named Franklin.

Virginia has a Patrick County and a Henry County, both named for Patrick Henry. Eight other states have Henry counties named for the great Virginia patriot. Seventeen states have Marion counties to commemorate the name of the Swamp Fox. Nine states

have Knox counties, named for Henry Knox, who supervised removal of Ticonderoga's cannons to the heights outside Boston. Nine states also have honored Daniel Morgan, the commander of sharpshooters, by naming counties after him.

Americans have remembered that foreign heroes came to fight in the War for Independence. Eleven states have Fayette counties and 6 have Lafayette counties, making a total of 17 named in honor of the gallant young Frenchman. Seven states have Pulaski counties, named for the Polish hero and cavalry commander who perished in the fight for Savannah. Six counties are named for Johann Kalb, also known as Baron de Kalb. Born in Germany, he came to America and gave his life

One of the ways in which George Washington is honored is by the name of the city that is our national capital. Also, the Washington Monument is one of the impressive sights in Washington, D.C. (39°N/77°W, map, p. 717.)

charging the enemy at the battle of Camden, South Carolina.

This is only a partial account of counties named for heroes of the Revolution. Does your state have counties named for these or other heroes? What is the origin of the name of your county or your parish?

221

65 for Adams. The Republican party also gained the Senate and the House ...

of 1800 was a bloodless ... a revolution all the same. ... his party had attracted ... support to take control of ... . Moreover, the Federal-... their defeat and had ... up their control. Feder-... to be elected to state of-... rly in New England. But ... uld a Federalist be chosen ... President's house. Never ... Federalists have a major-... Senate or the House of ...

contributions of the Federalist ... 12 years it controlled the federal ...

Alien and Sedition Acts? ... n and Sedition Acts contribute to ... Federalists in 1800? ... election of 1800 be called a peace-

Page 158

Wives of some officers clearly preferred following the armies to staying at home. Mrs. Henry Knox and Mrs. Nathanael Greene, married to American generals, certainly did. Martha Washington declared she had heard the first and last shot of every campaign during the war.

A few women distinguished themselves in unusual ways during revolutionary times. Phillis Wheatley was bought directly off a slave ship from Africa. She became noted for her poetry. One of her poems was about General George Washington, and she was

158

A Practical Three-Part Lesson Format Structured to Save Time for Teachers

Each lesson opens with a list of key social studies vocabulary words that are defined in the Glossary. The words are in boldface where they first appear in the lesson, and difficult words are followed by phonetic respellings.

Every lesson is divided into parts identified by descriptive headings, which facilitate student comprehension.

Checkup questions at the end of every lesson provide students with immediate review of key points.

Page 204

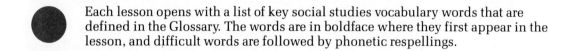

CHAPTER

9 The Federalist Period

The New Government Begins

VOCABULARY

inauguration
tariff
Cabinet
Judiciary Act of 1789
loose interpretation
strict interpretation
Bank of the United States

George Washington, our first President April 30, 1789, was a sunny day in New York City. A happy and curious crowd had gathered in front of the new Federal Hall. The crowd had come to see the first **inauguration** of a President of the United States. An inauguration is the ceremony that is held when one takes office.

A little after noon a group of people stepped onto the balcony of Federal Hall, overlooking Broad Street. Everyone recognized the tall white-wigged figure of George Washington. The crowd cheered as he appeared. Only a few recognized Robert Livingston, the chief judge of New York's highest state court. Livingston was there to read the oath of office, which the new President would take.

Not many on the street below the balcony heard the words. Still, they knew that George Washington was taking the President's oath of office. As soon as the

oath was administered, Livingston turned to the crowd. In a voice heard by all, he cried, "Long live George Washington, President of the United States!" The people below responded with a loud cheer. Washington bowed and the crowd cheered again. With the ceremony over, the group on the balcony moved inside Federal Hall. There Washington gave his first inaugural address to Congress.

Congress acts Most of the men in the first Congress had supported the Constitution. Nearly half of the 26 senators had taken part in the Constitutional Convention. Most of the others had worked to bring about ratification. James Madison led a powerful group in the House of Representatives. Like their leader, members of this group supported the new, stronger central government.

The new government badly needed money to meet its expenses. Some money—but not enough—would come from the sale of western lands. So, as one of its first actions, Congress passed a **tariff** bill. A tariff is a tax on goods brought from another country. The tariff of 1789 put a tax of from 5 to 15 percent on about 80 manufactured articles imported into the United States. For more than a century, tariffs supplied most of the money the government needed.

George Washington takes the oath of office as the first President of the United States.

204

Page 209

The newly chartered Bank of the United States set up its headquarters in Philadelphia.

ferson's view is known as the **strict interpretation** (or narrow interpretation) of the Constitution. According to this interpretation, the government could not charter a bank because the Constitution did not give the legislative branch the specific power to do so.

Actually, Congress had already passed a bill chartering the first **Bank of the United States**. President Washington, however, had cautiously held off signing the bill into law. He wanted to hear his Cabinet's views on whether the Constitution gave Congress the power to establish a bank. After listening carefully, Washington decided to accept Hamilton's argu-

ments. He signed the bank bill in 1791. It provided a charter for the Bank of the United States. Under its charter, which would last 20 years, the headquarters of the bank would be in Philadelphia. It could, however, set up branches in other parts of the country.

CHECKUP

1. How did the tariff of 1789 raise money for the new government?
2. What was the purpose of the President's Cabinet?
3. How did the Judiciary Act of 1789 establish a federal court system?
4. Why was Hamilton's debt plan adopted?
5. Explain the difference between Hamilton's and Jefferson's interpretation of the Constitution concerning the Bank of the United States.

209

A Better Map and Globe Skills
Program Encourages Student Achievement

The many maps included in the text reinforce the map skills learned in previous grades. The first chapter of ONE FLAG, ONE LAND is devoted to map and globe skills. An Atlas in the back of the book includes a variety of political maps. The series THE WORLD AND ITS PEOPLE includes more than 450 colorful maps.

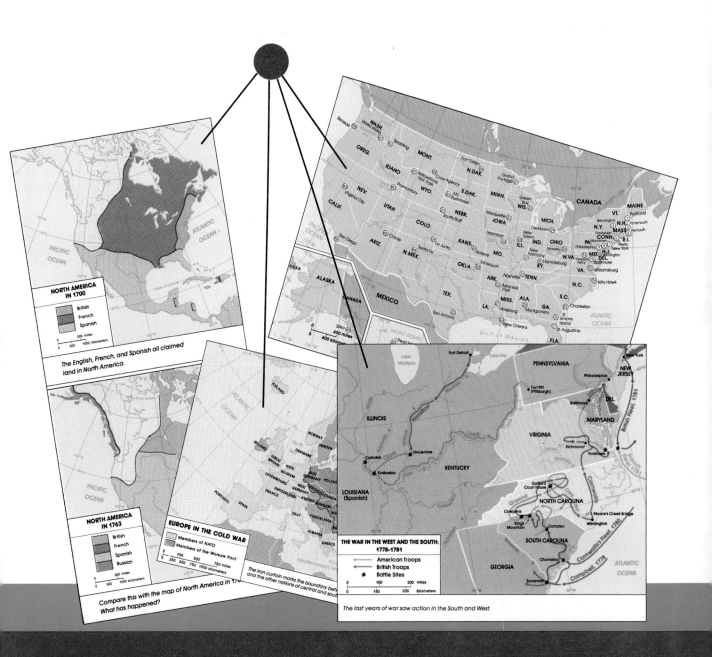

NORTH AMERICA IN 1700

British
French
Spanish

0   500 miles
0 500 1000 kilometers

The English, French, and Spanish all claimed land in North America.

NORTH AMERICA IN 1763

British
French
Spanish
Russian

0   500 miles
0 500 1000 kilometers

Compare this with the map of North America in 1700. What has happened?

EUROPE IN THE COLD WAR

Members of NATO
Members of the Warsaw Pact

0 250 500 750 miles
0 250 500 750 1000 kilometers

The iron curtain marks the boundary between and the other nations of central and south

THE WAR IN THE WEST AND THE SOUTH: 1778-1781

American Troops
British Troops
★ Battle Sites

0   100   200 miles
0 150 300 kilometers

The last years of war saw action in the South and West.

A Biographical Dictionary Helps Students Develop Skill in Using Reference Tools

A handy feature of ONE FLAG, ONE LAND is the Biographical Dictionary. This reference tool, which can be found in the back of the text, is a selective listing of over 200 significant persons in America's history.

Henry, Patrick (1738–1789). A Virginia Patriot in the Revolutionary War period. Noted for his fiery speeches. p. 119.

Page 724

Page 129

The First Continental Congress In Virginia, the House of Burgesses sent out a call for another meeting of delegates from each of the colonies. This meeting was meant to discuss colonial grievances against Great Britain. Committees of Correspondence spread the word. Fifty-five colonial leaders assembled in Philadelphia in September 1774. This time only Georgia failed to send delegates. This meeting in Philadelphia became known as the **First Continental Congress.**

Samuel Adams and Patrick Henry from Virginia met for the first time at the First Continental Congress in Philadelphia. No two men had done more to arouse resistance to British policies. George Washington was also there as a delegate to the Congress from Virginia. He listened as the other delegates debated for 7 weeks.

From these debates came several statements. One was a declaration of the rights of the colonists. Another was an appeal to the British king and the British people. The appeal asked for an end to all the harsh laws passed since the end of the French and Indian War. Before the delegates went home, they organized the **Continental Association.** One of its purposes was to unite the colonies in a refusal to sell anything to the British. The Continental Association was the first written agreement pledging the colonies to act together.

Another fiery speech In some of their declarations, delegates to the First Continental Congress had called themselves "His Majesty's most loyal subjects." Perhaps so, but already many of them wanted

In a spirited address before the Virginia House of Burgesses, Patrick Henry attacks the Stamp Act.

independence from Great Britain. And back in their home colonies, people were preparing to fight to defend their liberty if that became necessary. In Massachusetts the Committee of Public Safety was authorized to call out the militia to protect American lives, American property, and American rights.

The militia drilled openly in Massachusetts and the other colonies. Colonial leaders gathered powder, shot, and other military necessities. They stored these in secret places. At a meeting in Richmond, Virginia, on March 3, 1775, Patrick Henry made another fiery speech. At its conclusion came the inspiring words: "Is life so dear, or peace so sweet, as to be purchased at the price of chains and slavery? Forbid it, Almighty God! I know not what course others may take, but as for me, give me liberty or give me death!"

129

Coolidge · Houston

Coolidge, Calvin (1872–1933). Thirtieth President. p. 576.

Cooper, James Fenimore (1789–1851). An author who wrote novels about frontier people and American Indians. p. 283.

Cortés, Hernando (1485–1547). Spanish conqueror of the Aztec Indians. Established the Spanish empire in Mexico. p. 46.

Davis, Jefferson (1808–1889). Mississippi plantation owner and senator who became President of the Confederate States of America. p. 333.

Debs, Eugene V. (1855–1926). Labor leader. Head of the American Railway Union. p. 471.

Deloria, Vine, Jr. (1933–). A leader for equal rights for American Indians. p. 690.

Dewey, George (1837–1917). Commander of the United States Pacific fleet in 1898. Captured Manila in the Spanish-American War. p. 512.

Dix, Dorothea (1802–1887). A reformer who worked for better care and treatment of the mentally ill. p. 277.

Douglas, Stephen A. (1813–1861). Senator from Illinois. Proposed the Kansas-Nebraska bill. Defeated in the presidential election of 1860. p. 322.

Douglass, Frederick (1817?–1895). Former slave who became a leading abolitionist. Publisher of an abolitionist newspaper, *The North Star.* p. 271.

Drew, Charles (1904–1950). Black doctor who, during World War II, developed the first blood bank. p. 620.

Dulles, John Foster (1888–1959). Secretary of state in Eisenhower's Cabinet. p. 648.

Du Sable, Jean Baptiste Pointe (1745–1818). Black fur trader in New France. Ran a trading post near the place where Chicago was later built. p. 59.

Edison, Thomas Alva (1847–1931). Inventor of the electric light bulb, phonograph, motion-picture machine, and other devices. p. 434.

Eisenhower, Dwight D. (1890–1969). Thirty-fourth President. p. 661.

Emerson, Ralph Waldo (1803–1882). Writer and philosopher who lived in Concord, Massachusetts. p. 286.

Fillmore, Millard (1800–1874). Thirteenth President. p. 326.

Ford, Gerald (1913–). Thirty-eighth President. p. 698.

Ford, Henry (1863–1947). Manufacturer of the Model T and other Ford cars. Introduced the assembly-line method of making cars. p. 558.

Foster, Stephen (1826–1864). Composer of popular American songs. p. 286.

Franklin, Benjamin (1706–1790). Publisher, statesman, and scientist. Signer of Declaration of Independence. p. 84.

Frémont, John C. (1813–1890). Explorer and army officer in the Far West. p. 294.

Friedan, Betty (1921–). A leader in the movement for equal rights for women. p. 690.

Fulton, Robert (1765–1815). Invented the first practical steamboat in 1807. p. 288.

Garfield, James A. (1831–1881). Twentieth President. p. 386.

Garrison, William Lloyd. (1805–1879). Publisher of an abolitionist paper, *The Liberator.* p. 271.

Garvey, Marcus (1887–1940). Black leader who started a "back to Africa" movement. p. 564.

Gates, Horatio (1728?–1806). Revolutionary War general. Fought at battle of Saratoga. p. 149.

Glenn, John (1921–). First American to orbit the earth in space (1962). p. 2.

Glidden, Joseph (1813–1906). Invented barbed wire for fences used on the Great Plains. p. 419.

Goethals, George (1858–1928). Army engineer in charge of building the Panama Canal. p. 531.

Gompers, Samuel (1850–1924). Longtime head of American Federation of Labor. p. 462.

Gonzales, Rodolfo (1928–). Organized crusade for Justice for Mexican Americans. p. 693.

Gorgas, William C. (1854–1920). Army medical officer who put an end to yellow fever in Panama. p. 530.

Grant, Ulysses S. (1822–1885). Eighteenth President. p. 379.

Greeley, Horace (1811–1872). Influential editor of the New York Tribune. p. 280.

Greene, Nathanael (1742–1786). Revolutionary War general. Fought in North Carolina. p. 154.

Hamilton, Alexander (1755–1804). Secretary of the treasury in Washington's Cabinet. A leader in forming the policies of the Federalists. p. 162.

Harding, Warren G. (1865–1923). Twenty-ninth President. p. 574.

Harrison, Benjamin (1833–1901). Twenty-third President. p. 479.

Harrison, William Henry (1773–1841). Ninth President. p. 264.

Hay, John (1835–1905). Secretary of state in McKinley's Cabinet. p. 523.

Hayes, Rutherford B. (1822–1893). Nineteenth President. p. 385.

Hearst, William Randolph (1863–1951). Publisher of The New York Journal. p. 518.

Henry, Patrick (1736–1799). A Virginia Patriot in the Revolutionary War period. Noted for his fiery speeches. p. 119.

Hobby, Oveta Culp (1905–). Secretary of health, education, and welfare in Eisenhower's Cabinet. p. 659.

Homer, Winslow (1836–1910). An artist who painted landscapes and other subjects. p. 395.

Hoover, Herbert (1874–1964). Thirty-first President. p. 586.

Houston, Sam (1793–1863). Leader of the Texas army that defeated Mexican troops. Elected first president of the Republic of Texas. p. 301.

724

Meaningful Social Studies Activities Support the Teaching of Reading Skills

 Many of the Skills Development pages, which follow each Chapter Review, consist of questions and activities that develop reading and language arts skills through social studies content.

 ONE FLAG, ONE LAND can function as an extension of the teacher's individual reading program. Reading for meaning, outlining, descriptive writing, using the library, giving oral reports, and similar skills are developed.

Page 177

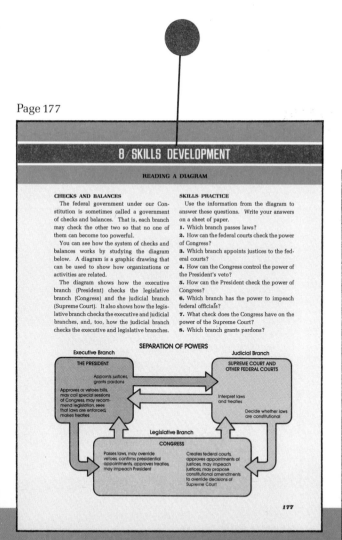

Page 533

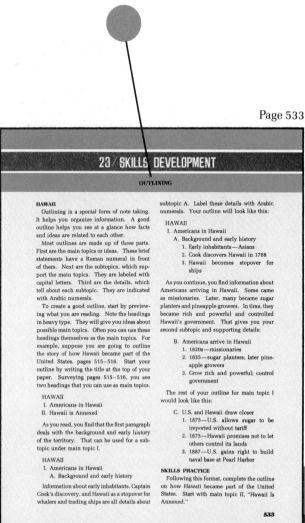

Chapter and Unit Reviews
Measure Growth and Reinforce Ideas

 Chapter Reviews present the chapter's main ideas, test vocabulary knowledge, ask recall and thinking questions, and suggest activities that require a minimum of teacher direction.

 At the end of each unit is a Unit Review page. This page is devoted to skills development. Among the skills developed in this section are the following: reading the text, reading a map, reading a picture, reading a cartoon, reading a time line, reading a chart, and reading a graph.

Page 510

22/CHAPTER REVIEW

KEY FACTS

1. Most Progressives wanted the government to regulate big business, break up trusts, and reform the banking system.
2. In a number of cities, reform movements took power out of the hands of political bosses and gave it to trained experts.
3. During the Progressive era, many states passed laws to protect workers.
4. The muckrakers, who wrote about corrupt government and unhealthy living and working conditions, influenced politicians to bring about reforms.
5. Theodore Roosevelt can be called the first modern President. With him began the tradition of an active federal government led by a strong chief executive.

VOCABULARY QUIZ

On a separate sheet of paper, write the word or phrase from the list to best complete each of the sentences below. There are two extra words or phrases.

public utility	commission
banking	Republican
city manager	direct primary
muckraker	recall
Progressive	conservation
income tax	arbitration

1. Voters in each party select their party's candidates in a _____.
2. The Bull Moose party was a nickname for the _____ party.
3. A company that sells water, gas, or electricity is a _____.
4. An elected official may be removed from office before his or her term is over by _____.

510

5. The creation of the Federal Reserve System brought about reforms in _____.
6. The form of government first used in Galveston, Texas, was the _____.
7. To protect the nation's natural resources, Theodore Roosevelt had an active program of _____.
8. A writer of the early 1900s who exposed abuses in business and government was called a _____.
9. The process of having a third party settle a disagreement between employers and employees is called _____.
10. An expert hired to run a city is called _____.

REVIEW QUESTIONS

1. Write a statement about each of the following, telling something important about his or her ideas or work: (a) Tom Johnson, (b) Ida Tarbell, (c) Florence Kelley, (d) Robert La Follette.
2. How were populism and progressivism alike? How were they different?
3. List two reforms brought about by each President: (a) Roosevelt, (b) Wilson, (c) Taft.
4. Explain how each of the following was meant to give more power to the people: (a) direct primary, (b) recall.

ACTIVITIES

1. Draw up a list of reforms you would support for your community. Choose one, write about the problem, and tell how it might be solved.
2. The Food and Drug Administration established by Theodore Roosevelt still exists. Find out about its activities. What drugs have been outlawed? What rules are there about labeling food?

Page 490

5/UNIT REVIEW

READING THE TEXT

Turn to pages 432 and 433. On those pages you are told about some of the factors that helped to bring about America's industrial growth. Read those pages carefully and then, on a sheet of paper, answer these questions.

1. In a sentence or two, explain what is meant by the title "A strong foundation."
2. List at least five resources that were factors in industrial growth.
3. In what two ways did increased population contribute to industrial growth?
4. Explain why a corporation was a favorite form of business organization during the period of industrial growth.
5. List eight factors that led to America's industrial growth in the late 1800s.

READING A MAP

Turn to page 414 and study the map titled "The United States: Developing the West." On a sheet of paper, write T if the statement is true and F if it is false.

1. The Chisholm Trail ran from San Antonio to Sedalia.
2. Pikes Peak was a mining camp in the Black Hills.
3. The Rocky Mountains ran through the Wyoming Territory.
4. A railroad line connected Cheyenne and Boise.
5. The three big cattle trails all went through Indian Territory.
6. Virginia City grew up on the edge of the Rocky Mountains.
7. A city located at 37°N/97°W is St. Louis.
8. Albuquerque is farther west than Santa Fe.

490

9. If one traveled from Sedalia to Abilene, he or she would be going east.
10. The western boundary of Nevada is the 110th parallel.

READING A PICTURE

Turn to page 428 and study the picture. On a sheet of paper, answer these questions.

1. What are the line of people doing at upper right?
2. Why are the buildings at upper left on wheels?
3. What, do you think, are these buildings used for?
4. For what purpose, do you think, are the wagons at left center used?

READING TIME LINES

In this unit there are four time lines, on pages 405, 425, 443, and 463. On a sheet of paper, list the following items and beside each write the correct date from the chapter time lines.

Homestead Act
Oklahoma land rush
Transcontinental railroad line completed
Peak year of immigration
Haymarket Riot
Decade of great city growth begins
Bryan's "cross of gold" speech
First modern skyscraper

Now make a time line on which these events are shown. First of all, decide what will be the beginning and ending dates and how many divisions your time line will have. Then label each event at the proper place on the time line.

Varied Workbook Activities Strengthen Student Skills

Concise directions to the student are clearly marked with a blue triangle (▶), allowing students to work with a minimum of teacher direction.

Workbook activities are based on information provided in pictures, drawings, maps, graphs, illustrations, word puzzles, and symbols as well as reading selections.

The lesson in the textbook on which the workbook exercise is based is clearly indicated. Sample pages shown are from the annotated Teacher's Edition of the workbook.

Page 4 (TE Workbook)

Page 148 (TE Workbook)

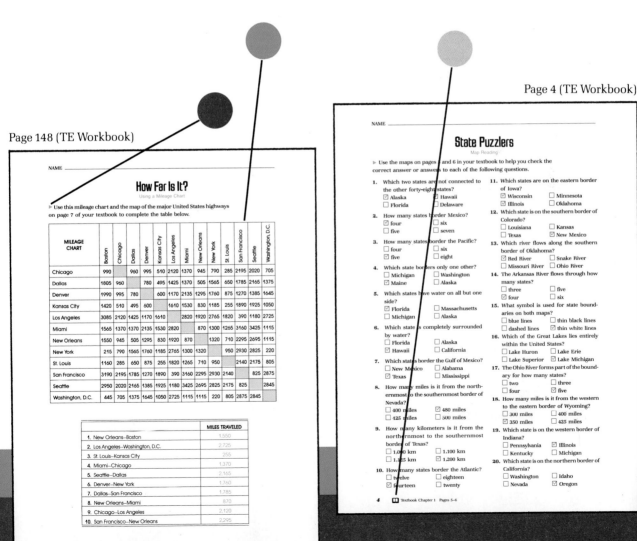

NAME _____

How Far Is It?
Using a Mileage Chart

▶ Use this mileage chart and the map of the major United States highways on page 7 of your textbook to complete the table below.

MILEAGE CHART	Boston	Chicago	Dallas	Denver	Kansas City	Los Angeles	Miami	New Orleans	New York	St. Louis	San Francisco	Seattle	Washington, D.C.
Chicago	990		960	995	510	2120	1370	945	790	285	2195	2020	705
Dallas	1805	960		780	495	1425	1370	505	1565	650	1785	2165	1375
Denver	1990	995	780		600	1170	2135	1295	1760	875	1270	1385	1645
Kansas City	1420	510	495	600		1610	1530	830	1185	255	1890	1925	1050
Los Angeles	3085	2120	1425	1170	1610		2820	1920	2765	1820	390	1180	2725
Miami	1565	1370	1370	2135	1530	2820		870	1300	1265	3160	3425	1115
New Orleans	1550	945	505	1295	830	1920	870		1320	710	2295	2695	1115
New York	215	790	1565	1760	1185	2765	1300	1320		950	2930	2825	220
St. Louis	1160	285	650	875	255	1820	1265	710	950		2140	2175	805
San Francisco	3190	2195	1785	1270	1890	390	3160	2295	2930	2140		825	2875
Seattle	2950	2020	2165	1385	1925	1180	3425	2695	2825	2175	825		2845
Washington, D.C.	445	705	1375	1645	1050	2725	1115	1115	220	805	2875	2845	

	MILES TRAVELED
1. New Orleans–Boston	1,550
2. Los Angeles–Washington, D.C.	2,725
3. St. Louis–Kansas City	255
4. Miami–Chicago	1,370
5. Seattle–Dallas	2,165
6. Denver–New York	1,760
7. Dallas–San Francisco	1,785
8. New Orleans–Miami	870
9. Chicago–Los Angeles	2,120
10. San Francisco–New Orleans	2,295

148 Textbook Chapter 29 Page 669

State Puzzlers
Map Reading

▶ Use the maps on pages 5 and 6 in your textbook to help you check the correct answer or answers to each of the following questions.

1. Which two states are not connected to the other forty-eight states?
   ☑ Alaska ☑ Hawaii
   ☐ Florida ☐ Delaware

2. How many states border Mexico?
   ☑ four ☐ six
   ☐ five ☐ seven

3. How many states border the Pacific?
   ☐ four ☐ six
   ☑ five ☐ eight

4. Which state borders only one other?
   ☐ Michigan ☐ Washington
   ☑ Maine ☐ Alaska

5. Which states have water on all but one side?
   ☑ Florida ☐ Massachusetts
   ☐ Michigan ☐ Alaska

6. Which state is completely surrounded by water?
   ☐ Florida ☐ Alaska
   ☑ Hawaii ☐ California

7. Which states border the Gulf of Mexico?
   ☐ New Mexico ☐ Alabama
   ☑ Texas ☐ Mississippi

8. How many miles is it from the northernmost to the southernmost border of Nevada?
   ☐ 400 miles ☑ 480 miles
   ☐ 425 miles ☐ 500 miles

9. How many kilometers is it from the northernmost to the southernmost border of Texas?
   ☐ 1,000 km ☐ 1,100 km
   ☐ 1,125 km ☑ 1,200 km

10. How many states border the Atlantic?
    ☐ twelve ☐ eighteen
    ☑ fourteen ☐ twenty

11. Which states are on the eastern border of Iowa?
    ☑ Wisconsin ☐ Minnesota
    ☑ Illinois ☐ Oklahoma

12. Which state is on the southern border of Colorado?
    ☐ Louisiana ☐ Kansas
    ☐ Texas ☑ New Mexico

13. Which river flows along the southern border of Oklahoma?
    ☑ Red River ☐ Snake River
    ☐ Missouri River ☐ Ohio River

14. The Arkansas River flows through how many states?
    ☐ three ☐ five
    ☑ four ☐ six

15. What symbol is used for state boundaries on both maps?
    ☐ blue lines ☐ thin black lines
    ☐ dashed lines ☑ thin white lines

16. Which of the Great Lakes lies entirely within the United States?
    ☐ Lake Huron ☐ Lake Erie
    ☐ Lake Superior ☑ Lake Michigan

17. The Ohio River forms part of the boundary for how many states?
    ☐ two ☐ three
    ☐ four ☑ five

18. How many miles is it from the western to the eastern border of Wyoming?
    ☐ 300 miles ☐ 400 miles
    ☑ 350 miles ☐ 425 miles

19. Which state is on the western border of Indiana?
    ☐ Pennsylvania ☑ Illinois
    ☐ Kentucky ☐ Michigan

20. Which state is on the northern border of California?
    ☐ Washington ☐ Idaho
    ☐ Nevada ☑ Oregon

4 Textbook Chapter 1 Pages 5–6

An Annotated Teacher's Edition Saves Teachers Time and Work

The high quality and diversity of annotations in the Teacher's Edition make ONE FLAG, ONE LAND easy to use. The annotations include questions, interesting facts, and supplementary information that enrich the subject matter.

Answers for Checkup questions, Chapter Review and Unit Review sections, and Skills Development pages are provided in a special section in the back of the book.

Assign several pupils to research the *Plessy* v. *Ferguson* and *Brown* v. *Board of Education of Topeka* cases. See if they can do a follow-up on what happened to Homer Plessy and Linda Brown after their cases had been decided.

Page 528

Page 663

Assign several pupils to research the *Plessy* v. *Ferguson* and *Brown* v. *Board of Education of Topeka* cases. See if they can do a follow-up on what happened to Homer Plessy and Linda Brown after their cases had been decided.

cases in the courts. Still, segregation remained. A half century earlier in the case of *Plessy* v. *Ferguson*, the Supreme Court had adopted the "separate but equal" rule (page 388). Most northern states did not have the Jim Crow laws that prevailed in the South, but segregation existed in the North as well. Unwritten laws, or custom, kept blacks living in separate neighborhoods, eating in separate restaurants, bathing at separate beaches, and in countless other ways living their lives apart from whites.

In practice, separate facilities were almost never equal. School buildings for black children, for example, were often old, poorly equipped, and supplied with out-of-date books. Even if the facilities were exactly equal, Marshall pointed out, "the very fact of segregation establishes a feeling of humiliation and deprivation in the group considered to be inferior."

Thurgood Marshall, who argued the Brown case before the Supreme Court, later became its first black member.

Attacking school segregation To end segregation, Marshall and the NAACP decided they must attack the "separate but equal" rule head on. The case they chose for this involved an 8-year-old black girl named Linda Brown in Topeka, Kansas. Linda lived just five blocks from a public school. However, this school was for whites only. Linda had to go to an all-black public school more than 20 blocks away. With help from the NAACP, Linda's father sued to allow his daughter to attend the all-white school. The case made its way through the courts to the Supreme Court of the United States. Handling the case for the NAACP, Marshall argued that the Court should reverse the decision reached in the case of *Plessy v. Ferguson*.

In May 1954 the Supreme Court gave its historic decision in the case of **Brown v. Board of Education of Topeka**. ". . . we conclude that in the field of public education the doctrine of 'separate but equal' has no place. Separate educational facilities are inherently [that is, by their very nature] unequal." The Court soon followed up this historic decision with an order that desegregation of public schools should begin promptly.

Resistance to desegregation Following the Brown decision, some states and cities promptly obeyed the order of the Supreme Court and ended school segregation. Much of the white South, however, resisted change. White citizens councils were formed to fight desegregation. They threatened those blacks and whites who challenged segregation with the loss of their jobs. The Ku Klux Klan came to

663

The need for a canal across Central America was dramatically shown during the Spanish-American War, when the United States battleship *Oregon* was sent from San Francisco to Santiago. The 12,000-mile (1,900-km) trip took 68 days, and the war was nearly over when the ship reached its destination.

THE CARIBBEAN AREA IN 1920

United States and Possessions

For many years the United States exerted strong control over the lands of the Caribbean areas.

States to take over the collection of **customs duties**. These are taxes that are paid on imported goods. Half the duties were then used to pay off debts; the other half went to run the government.

American customs collectors, backed by the power of the United States government, remained for many years. Like Cuba, the Dominican Republic was not a colony. But it was no longer completely independent either.

The Roosevelt Corollary helped turn the Caribbean Sea into an "American lake." Using the Roosevelt Corollary, the United States controlled the actions of many countries in the region. Under Presidents Taft and Wilson, intervention in the affairs of these countries increased. Often, United States Marines were sent in and stayed for many years. These interventions led to a great deal of ill will toward the United States.

528 Discuss this question: Why did American intervention lead to a great deal of ill will toward the United States?

Planning a canal A big reason why the United States wanted to control the Caribbean lands was to protect a future canal across the narrow neck of Central America. Such a canal would allow the United States Navy to travel quickly from one ocean to another. By eliminating the need to go around the tip of South America, a canal would take nearly 8,000 miles (12,800 km) off the trip between New York and San Francisco.

The idea of a canal across Central America was not a new one. In the 1880s Colombia granted a French company the sole rights to build a canal across Panama, which Colombia controlled. The company failed to carry out its plan but hoped to sell to the United States the rights to build a canal.

Many members of Congress favored a canal site farther north, in Nicaragua. However, at the time the site was under

A Distinctive Teacher's Planning Guide Offers an Abundance of Teaching Suggestions and Activities

 Chapter Projects suggest a variety of interesting approaches for launching the chapter.

 Lesson-by-lesson Teaching Suggestions provide easy-to-use guidelines for helping students develop social studies skills using material from the text.

 Frequent Supplementary Information sections offer helpful sidelights on topics related to the text.

 This symbol ★ designates activities expanded for use with pupils who have difficulty grasping the concepts and with pupils who need additional challenge.

Page 43

CHAPTER 9 PAGES 204–223

THEME
During the Federalist period the ideals of the Constitution were put to work in a practical way during the presidencies of George Washington and John Adams.

CHAPTER PROJECTS

1. In 1791 the District of Columbia, now Washington, D.C., was chosen as the permanent site for our nation's capital. In 1800 it became the seat of government. Washington, D.C., has grown from a swampy area along the Potomac River during George Washington's time to a fine capital city. Have pupils use an encyclopedia or other resource to find out about the following:

a. Why Washington, D.C., was chosen as the capital

b. What life was like in Washington, D.C., in 1800

c. How streets were named

d. Who Pierre L'Enfant, Andrew Elliott, and Benjamin Bannecker were

Pupils could also research and prepare a report on a famous building or attraction in or near the capital. Among the buildings and attractions in Washington, D.C., are the Capitol; the White House; the Library of Congress; the Supreme Court Building; the Washington, Jefferson, and Lincoln Memorials; the John F. Kennedy Center for the Performing Arts; Ford's Theatre; the Smithsonian Institution; the National Gallery of Art; the Museum of African Art; and the Bureau of Engraving and Printing. Attractions located near Washington, D.C., are Mount Vernon, Arlington National Cemetery, and the Marine Corps War Memorial.

2. Current Events. Divide the class into small groups and have each group choose one of the 13 Cabinet positions. Have them make a scrapbook of pictures and articles from newspapers and magazines showing the work of the Cabinet position they selected.

LESSON 1 PAGES 204–209

GOALS 1. To write a news report about the details of Washington's inauguration. 2. To use the *Reader's Guide to Periodical Literature* to find a newsmagazine account of a recent presidential inauguration. 3. To list some precedents established during Washington's presidency. 4. To use an almanac or other resource to find the titles of the 13 Cabinet positions and the names of the current occupants. 5. To identify whether present practices in the United States are a result of strict or loose interpretation of the Constitution.

TEACHING SUGGESTIONS

1. Writing a News Report. Have pupils pretend they are reporters covering Washington's inauguration. They should describe the scene and include imaginary interviews with Robert Livingston and members of the crowd in their report. Some pupils may wish to do a "live television coverage" report of this event, presenting the same information through oral reporting and interviews.

2. Using Reference Materials. In modern times Presidents get inaugurated amidst a great deal of pomp and pageantry. After showing pupils how to use the *Reader's Guide to Periodical Literature,* have them find an account in a newsmagazine (*Time, Newsweek,* or *U.S. News and World Report)* of a presidential inauguration in recent times. Have them make comparisons between Washington's inauguration and more recent ones.

3. Landslide Elections. Have pupils use an almanac or encyclopedia to discover presidential candidates who have won landslide elections. Point out that Washington was the only person to win unanimously. Ask: *Who came closest to that?* (James Monroe was unopposed in 1820, but one elector refused to vote for him, saying Washington alone should have the honor of unanimous victory.) Other landslides they may find are Roosevelt's in 1936 (over Alf Landon), Johnson's in 1964 (over Barry Goldwater), Nixon's in 1972 (over George McGovern), Reagan's in 1980 (over Jimmy Carter).

4. Establishing Precedents. Ask pupils if they know what a precedent is. (Something which serves as an example or rule) Then have pupils list

43

Page 47

based on the Alien and Sedition Acts. 4. To evaluate the accomplishments and reasons for failure of the Federalists. 5. To explain what was revolutionary about Jefferson's election in 1800. 6. To examine selected quotes from Thomas Jefferson.

TEACHING SUGGESTIONS

1. Defeated Incumbents. Explain to pupils the meaning of the word *incumbent.* Ask whether it would be an advantage or disadvantage to run as an incumbent. (Advantage of name recognition and successes, disadvantage of unpopular policies costing votes)

Next have pupils give reasons why John Adams may have lost in 1800, and then have them find names of other incumbent Presidents who have lost reelection bids. (John Quincy Adams, Martin Van Buren, Grover Cleveland, Benjamin Harrison, Herbert Hoover, Gerald Ford, Jimmy Carter)

SUPPLEMENTARY INFORMATION

Washington, D.C., in 1800. A visitor to the federal city of the United States in 1800 might have been surprised to find only a village, albeit one with great plans. When the government moved there in November 1800, the new city had a population of more than 2,500. It boasted more than 400 private homes, but there was a noticeable lack of boarding-houses and hotels.

Pierre L'Enfant's design for the city looked like a gridiron superimposed with radiating broad avenues. The main features of the city were the Executive Mansion and the Capitol. But neither of these buildings was completed by the end of 1800. Both houses of Congress and the Supreme Court met in the only completed section of the Capitol, the north wing.

Abigail Adams, wife of President John Adams, also came to the city in November 1800. She was dismayed to find the Executive Mansion had no heat, water, or bathrooms. In a letter to her daughter she mentioned that she used the large-audience room (today the East Room) to hang up the family wash. Despite the inconveniences she noted that Washington was "a beautiful spot, capable of every improvement and the more I view it the more I am delighted with it."

2. Finding Facts. Have pupils choose one of the three areas below and see if they can answer some or all of the related questions. Note that each area is a constitutionally mandated function.

a. Making money — *Why does the federal government control the making of money? Where are United States mints located? How are coins made? How is security insured? Where is paper money made? How is paper money made? How is security ensured? What happens to worn out money?*

b. Patents — *What are patents? Why does the federal government control patents? What are some unusual inventions for which patents have been given?*

c. Copyrights — *What are copyrights? What things are covered by copyrights? Where can you find copyright information in this text? What controversies have raged in recent years over copyrights of video materials?*

3. Evaluation. Have pupils evaluate the accomplishments and failures of Federalist government versus the promise of the Democratic-Republicans. In their evaluation they should include actual events in addition to perceptions. Then ask: *How would you have voted in the election of 1800 if faced with the choice between Adams and Jefferson?* The process that pupils will go through to answer this question closely resembles the process they should use when they participate in actual elections.

4. Discussion. Start a discussion with pupils about the presidential election of 1800, especially the deadlock between Thomas Jefferson and Aaron Burr, which resulted in 36 ballots to determine a winner. This election was called "revolutionary" by the text. Ask: *What is meant by the term revolution?* (Change) *What was revolutionary about the election of Thomas Jefferson?* (Answers will vary but should include the demise of the Federalists and the triumph of Jefferson's more egalitarian ideas.)

★5. Interpreting Quotations. Thomas Jefferson wrote extensively on a variety of topics, especially democracy. Discuss with pupils the meaning of the following quotes and whether they agree with Jefferson's beliefs.

a. "To consider the will of the society enounced by the majority of a single vote, as sacred as if unanimous . . . ."

b. "There is a natural aristocracy among men. The grounds of this are virtue and talents . . . ."

c. "If a nation expects to be ignorant and free, in a state of civilization, it expects what never was and never will be . . . . Where the press is free, and every man able to read, all is safe."

47

T15

PROGRAM CONTENT OUTLINE

MY WORLD AND ME

FAMILIES AND NEIGHBORHOODS

NEIGHBORHOODS AND COMMUNITIES

The World and Its People

COMMUNITIES AND RESOURCES

STATES AND REGIONS

PROGRAM CONTENT OUTLINE

THE UNITED STATES AND ITS NEIGHBORS

CANADA AND LATIN AMERICA

The World and Its People

EUROPE, AFRICA, ASIA, AND AUSTRALIA

PROGRAM CONTENT OUTLINE

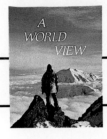

A WORLD VIEW

The World and Its People

ONE FLAG, ONE LAND

MAP AND GLOBE SKILLS
SCOPE AND SEQUENCE

SKILLS	MY WORLD AND ME	FAMILIES AND NEIGHBORHOODS	NEIGHBORHOODS AND COMMUNITIES	COMMUNITIES AND RESOURCES	STATES AND REGIONS	THE UNITED STATES AND ITS NEIGHBORS	CANADA AND LATIN AMERICA	EUROPE, AFRICA, ASIA, AND AUSTRALIA	A WORLD VIEW	ONE FLAG, ONE LAND
Globe	●	●	●	●	●	●	●	●	●	●
Continents and Oceans	●	●	●	●	●	●	●	●	●	●
Landform Identification	●	●			●	●	●	●	●	●
Shape Identification	●				●	●	●	●	●	●
Cardinal Directions		●	●	●	●	●	●	●	●	●
Legend (Key)		●	●	●	●	●	●	●	●	●
Symbols		●	●	●	●	●	●	●	●	●
Color		●	●	●	●	●	●	●	●	●
Political Boundaries		●	●	●	●	●	●	●	●	●
Pictorial		●	●	●	●	●	●	●	●	●
Abstract		●	●	●	●	●	●	●	●	●
Transition from Photo to Map		●	●	●	●	●	●	●	●	●
Comparative Size		●	●	●	●	●	●	●	●	●
Labels		●	●	●	●	●	●	●	●	●
Location		●	●	●	●	●	●	●	●	●
Inset Maps		●	●	●	●	●	●	●	●	●
Picture Maps	●	●	●							
Directional Arrows	●	●	●							
North Pole					●	●	●	●	●	●
South Pole					●	●	●	●	●	●
Floor Plan				●	●	●	●	●	●	●
Thematic Maps					●	●	●	●	●	●
Atlas					●	●	●	●	●	●
Intermediate Directions					●	●	●	●	●	●
Compass Rose					●	●	●	●	●	●
Latitude					●	●	●	●	●	●
Equator					●	●	●	●	●	●
Arctic Circle					●	●	●		●	●
Antarctic Circle					●	●	●	●	●	●

SKILLS

SKILLS	MY WORLD AND ME	FAMILIES AND NEIGHBORHOODS	NEIGHBORHOODS AND COMMUNITIES	COMMUNITIES AND RESOURCES	STATES AND REGIONS	THE UNITED STATES AND ITS NEIGHBORS	CANADA AND LATIN AMERICA	EUROPE, AFRICA, ASIA, AND AUSTRALIA	A WORLD VIEW	ONE FLAG, ONE LAND
Latitude (continued)										
Tropic of Cancer				●	●	●	●	●	●	●
Tropic of Capricorn				●	●	●	●	●	●	●
Longitude				●	●	●	●	●	●	●
Prime Meridian				●	●	●	●	●	●	●
Using a Coordinate System				●	●	●	●	●	●	●
Hemispheres				●	●	●	●	●	●	●
Shaded Relief				●	●	●	●	●	●	●
Scale				●	●	●	●	●	●	●
Elevation Tints				●	●	●	●		●	●
Mileage Chart				●	●	●	●	●	●	●
Subway Map				●					●	●
Railroad Map						●	●	●	●	●
Physical-Political Map					●	●	●	●	●	●
Road Map						●	●	●	●	●
Isolines (e.g., contour lines)					●	●	●	●	●	●
Profile Maps					●	●	●	●	●	●
Travel Routes						●	●	●	●	●
Historical Maps						●	●	●	●	●
Weather Map							●	●		●
Time Zones						●	●	●	●	
Projections							●	●	●	●
Diagrams			●	●	●	●	●	●		●
Graphs	●	●	●	●	●	●	●	●	●	●
Pictograph	●	●		●	●	●	●	●	●	●
Pie Graph			●	●	●	●	●	●	●	●
Bar Graph	●	●	●	●	●	●	●	●	●	●
Line Graph				●	●	●	●	●	●	●
Climograph					●	●	●	●	●	●

READING SKILLS
SCOPE AND SEQUENCE

SKILLS	MY WORLD AND ME	FAMILIES AND NEIGHBORHOODS	NEIGHBORHOODS AND COMMUNITIES	COMMUNITIES AND RESOURCES	STATES AND REGIONS	THE UNITED STATES AND ITS NEIGHBORS	CANADA AND LATIN AMERICA	EUROPE, AFRICA, ASIA, AND AUSTRALIA	A WORLD VIEW	ONE FLAG, ONE LAND
VOCABULARY BUILDING										
Understanding and defining words by:										
Using objects	●	●	●	●	●	●	●	●	●	●
Using illustrations	●	●	●	●	●	●	●	●	●	●
Using a glossary			●	●	●	●	●	●	●	●
Using a dictionary				●	●	●	●	●	●	●
Using context clues				●	●	●	●	●	●	●
Alphabetical Order	●	●			●	●	●	●	●	●
Synonyms/Antonyms	●	●			●	●	●	●	●	●
Prefix/Suffix					●	●	●	●	●	●
Acronyms/Abbreviations					●	●	●	●	●	●
Word Origins					●	●	●	●	●	●
DEVELOPING READING COMPREHENSION										
Understanding and identifying the main idea		●	●	●	●	●	●	●	●	●
Following directions	●	●	●	●	●	●	●	●	●	●
Understanding relationships	●	●	●	●	●	●	●	●	●	●
Understanding sequence	●	●	●	●	●	●	●	●	●	●
Understanding cause and effect	●	●	●	●	●	●	●	●	●	●
Recalling information	●	●	●	●	●	●	●	●	●	●
Recognizing attitudes and emotions	●	●	●	●	●	●	●	●	●	●
Understanding different literary forms		●	●	●	●	●	●	●	●	●
Understanding that facts support main idea			●	●	●	●	●	●	●	●

SKILLS

DEVELOPING READING COMPREHENSION (continued)

SKILLS	MY WORLD AND ME	FAMILIES AND NEIGHBORHOODS	NEIGHBORHOODS AND COMMUNITIES	COMMUNITIES AND RESOURCES	STATES AND REGIONS	THE UNITED STATES AND ITS NEIGHBORS	CANADA AND LATIN AMERICA	EUROPE, AFRICA, ASIA, AND AUSTRALIA	A WORLD VIEW	ONE FLAG ONE LAND
Identifying purpose for reading			•	•	•	•	•	•	•	•
Reading schedules and calendars			•	•	•	•	•	•	•	•
Identifying topic sentence				•	•	•	•	•	•	•
Distinguishing between the main idea and details				•	•	•	•	•	•	•
Skimming				•	•	•	•	•	•	•
Distinguishing between fact and opinion				•	•	•	•	•	•	•
Summarizing				•	•	•	•	•	•	•
Reading mileage charts				•	•	•	•	•	•	•
Reading time lines				•	•	•	•	•	•	•
Reading and interpreting facts from tables				•	•	•	•	•	•	•
Using details to support main idea					•	•	•	•	•	•
Distinguishing between relevant and irrelevant data						•	•	•	•	•
Paraphrasing							•	•	•	•
Recognizing and identifying author's or speaker's purpose							•	•	•	•
Understanding primary and secondary sources							•	•	•	•
Recognizing propaganda							•	•	•	•

LANGUAGE ARTS SKILLS
SCOPE AND SEQUENCE

SKILLS	My World and Me	Families and Neighborhoods	Neighborhoods and Communities	Communities and Resources	States and Regions	The United States and Its Neighbors	Canada and Latin America	Europe, Africa, Asia, and Australia	A World View	One Flag, One Land
WRITING SKILLS										
Letter Writing (personal)		●	●	●	●	●	●	●	●	●
Descriptive Writing	●	●	●	●	●	●	●	●	●	●
Narrative Writing	●	●	●	●	●	●	●	●	●	●
Report Writing	●	●	●	●	●	●	●	●	●	●
Letter Writing (business)	●	●	●	●	●	●	●	●	●	●
Book Reports				●	●	●	●	●	●	●
Writing a Diary				●	●	●	●	●	●	●
Outlining				●	●	●	●	●	●	●
Persuasive Writing						●	●	●	●	●
SPEAKING SKILLS										
Expressing a Point of View	●	●	●	●	●	●	●	●	●	●
Oral Reports		●	●	●	●	●	●	●	●	●
Debate						●	●	●	●	●
LIBRARY SKILLS										
Choosing References					●	●	●	●	●	●
Card Catalog					●	●	●	●	●	●
Encyclopedia						●	●	●	●	●
Newspapers and Magazines					●	●	●	●	●	●
Vertical File						●	●	●	●	●
Readers' Guide to Periodical Literature							●	●	●	●
Almanac							●	●	●	●

REASONING SKILLS
SCOPE AND SEQUENCE

SKILLS	MY WORLD AND ME	FAMILIES AND NEIGHBORHOODS	NEIGHBORHOODS AND COMMUNITIES	COMMUNITIES AND RESOURCES	STATES AND REGIONS	THE UNITED STATES AND ITS NEIGHBORS	CANADA AND LATIN AMERICA	EUROPE, AFRICA, ASIA, AND AUSTRALIA	A WORLD VIEW	ONE FLAG, ONE LAND
Identifying and expressing preferences and opinions	●	●	●	●	●	●	●	●	●	●
Generalizing		●	●	●	●	●	●	●	●	●
Making inferences	●	●	●	●	●	●	●	●	●	●
Drawing conclusions	●	●	●	●	●	●	●	●	●	●
Comparing and contrasting	●	●	●	●	●	●	●	●	●	●
Classifying	●	●	●	●	●	●	●	●	●	●
Interpreting cause and effect			●	●	●	●	●	●	●	●
Gathering information	●				●	●	●	●	●	●
Observing	●	●	●	●	●	●	●	●	●	●
Interviewing		●	●	●	●	●	●	●	●	●
Using primary sources					●	●	●	●	●	●
Using secondary sources					●	●	●	●	●	●
Polling						●	●	●	●	●
Identifying a problem					●	●	●	●	●	●
Identifying alternatives					●	●	●	●	●	●
Recognizing and identifying points of view					●	●	●	●	●	●
Defending a point of view					●	●	●	●	●	●
Predicting						●	●	●	●	●
Developing objectivity						●	●	●	●	●
Making or withholding judgment					●	●	●	●	●	●
Evaluating relevance of information						●	●	●	●	●

SOCIETAL SKILLS
SCOPE AND SEQUENCE

SKILLS	MY WORLD AND ME	FAMILIES AND NEIGHBORHOODS	NEIGHBORHOODS AND COMMUNITIES	COMMUNITIES AND RESOURCES	STATES AND REGIONS	THE UNITED STATES AND ITS NEIGHBORS	CANADA AND LATIN AMERICA	EUROPE, AFRICA, ASIA, AND AUSTRALIA	A WORLD VIEW	ONE FLAG, ONE LAND
LIFE SKILLS										
Telling time		●	●							
Reading a calendar		●	●							
Practicing pedestrian and bicycle safety	●	●	●							
Reading traffic signs	●	●	●			●	●	●	●	●
Recognizing warning signs and symbols	●	●	●			●	●	●	●	●
Knowing full name and address	●	●	●			●	●	●	●	●
Understanding the importance of good nutrition	●	●	●			●	●	●	●	●
Knowing fire drill procedure	●	●	●			●	●	●	●	●
Knowing when and how to call fire or police help	●	●	●			●	●	●	●	●
Practicing basic safety techniques in home and school	●	●	●			●	●	●	●	●
Knowing emergency telephone numbers		●	●			●	●	●	●	●
Using a telephone		●	●			●	●	●	●	●
Becoming aware of job opportunities		●	●	●	●	●	●	●	●	●
Budgeting and banking		●		●	●	●	●	●	●	●
Addressing an envelope		●	●	●	●	●	●	●	●	●
Using a telephone directory				●	●	●	●	●	●	●
Reading a schedule					●	●	●	●	●	●
Filling out forms and applications						●	●	●	●	●
Reading newspaper ads							●	●	●	●
HUMAN RELATIONS										
Developing personal friendships	●	●	●							
Developing respect for self	●	●	●		●	●	●	●	●	●
Developing respect for others	●	●	●		●	●	●	●	●	●
Working in groups	●	●	●		●	●	●	●	●	●
Recognizing interdependence among people	●	●	●	●	●	●	●	●	●	●

SKILLS

HUMAN RELATIONS (continued)

	MY WORLD AND ME	FAMILIES AND NEIGHBORHOODS	NEIGHBORHOODS AND COMMUNITIES	COMMUNITIES AND RESOURCES	STATES AND REGIONS	THE UNITED STATES AND ITS NEIGHBORS	CANADA AND LATIN AMERICA	EUROPE, AFRICA, ASIA, AND AUSTRALIA	A WORLD VIEW	ONE FLAG, ONE LAND
Understanding the importance of courtesy	●	●	●	●	●	●				
Recognizing other points of view					●	●	●	●	●	●
CITIZENSHIP AND VALUES										
Respecting our American heritage and beliefs		●	●	●	●	●	●	●	●	●
Understanding the democratic process		●	●	●	●	●	●	●	●	●
Understanding the role of the citizen in a democracy		●	●	●	●	●	●	●	●	●
Understanding and accepting the need for laws		●	●	●	●	●	●	●	●	●
Developing a respect for rules and laws	●	●	●	●	●	●	●	●	●	●
Appreciating ethnic heritage			●	●	●	●	●	●	●	●
Appreciating basic American values			●	●	●	●	●	●	●	●
Appreciating the dignity in all occupations	●		●	●	●	●	●	●	●	●
Developing pride in one's own work	●	●	●	●	●	●	●	●	●	●
Developing good work and job habits	●	●	●	●	●	●	●	●	●	●
Understanding the importance of responsibility	●	●	●	●	●	●	●	●	●	●
Participating in decision making	●	●	●	●	●	●	●	●	●	●
Understanding the importance of leisure time						●	●			
Respecting the rights of others while exercising one's own						●	●	●	●	●
Recognizing that responsibility and freedom are related						●	●	●	●	●
Recognizing and avoiding negative stereotypes						●	●	●	●	●

BOOKS, FILMSTRIPS, FILMS, RECORDS, MICROCOMPUTER COURSEWARE

Some of the books mentioned may be out of print. However, they may be available in your school or local library.

UNIT 1

BOOKS FOR STUDENTS

A Pictorial History of the American Indian. Oliver La Farge. Crown Publishers. (2)
Ishi: Last of His Tribe. Theodora Kroeber. New York: Bantam Books. (2)
This Way to Rainy Mountain. N. Scott Momaday. Albuquerque, N.M.: University of New Mexico Press. (2)
What We Find When We Look at Maps. John E. Oliver. New York: McGraw-Hill. (1)
When the Legends Die. Hal Borland. New York: Bantam Books. (2)
The World of Maps and Mapping: A Creative Learning Aid. Norman Thrower. New York: McGraw-Hill. (1)

BOOKS FOR TEACHERS

Mapping. David Greenhood. Chicago: University of Chicago Press. (1)

Maps and Their Makers: An Introduction to the History of Cartography. A.R. Crone. Hamden, Conn.: The Shoe String Press. (1)
The Oxford History of the American People, Vols. 1–3. New York: The New American Library. (2)

FILMSTRIPS

Age of Exploration. Chicago: Encyclopaedia Britannica Films. Series of 6 filmstrips. Color. (3)
Ancient American Indian Civilization. Chicago: Encyclopaedia Britannica Films. Series of 7 filmstrips. Color. (2)
Discovery and Exploration. New York: American Heritage Publishing Co. Series of 5 filmstrips. Color, sound. (3)
Finding Our Way with Maps and Globes. Burbank, Calif.: Walt Disney Educational Media Co. Set of 7 filmstrips. Records or cassettes, teacher's guide. Color. (1)

Indian Cultures of America. Chicago: Encyclopaedia Britannica Films. Series of 6 filmstrips. Color. (2)

FILMS (16 mm)

The English and Dutch Explorers. Chicago: Encyclopaedia Britannica Films. 11 min. Color. (3)
First Americans, Parts I & II. New York: NBC Films. Part I, 20 min; Part II, 32 min. Color. (2)
Indians of Early America. Chicago: Encyclopaedia Britannica Films. 22 min. Color. (2)
Marco Polo's Travels. Chicago: Encyclopaedia Britannica Films. 19 min. B/W. (3)
The Witches of Salem: The Horror and the Hope. New York: Learning Corporation of America. Color. (4)

RECORD

"Thanksgiving Chorale." *Silver Burdett Music 5,* 1985 ed., Record 4. (4)

UNIT 2

BOOKS FOR STUDENTS

Black Heroes of the American Revolution. Burke Davis. New York: Harcourt Brace Jovanovich. (7)
America's Paul Revere. Esther Forbes. Boston: Houghton Mifflin Co. (6)
Johnny Tremain. Esther Forbes. New York: Dell Publishing Co. (6)
A History of Women in America. Carol Hymowitz and Michaele Weissman. New York: Bantam Books. (7)
The American Revolution. Bruce Lancaster. New York: Doubleday & Co. (7)

BOOKS FOR TEACHERS

The Great Rehearsal: The Story of the Making

and Ratifying of the Constitution of the United States. Carl Van Doren. New York: The Viking Press. (8)
This Was America. Oscar Handlin. Cambridge, Mass.: Harvard University Press. (6)
The Story of the Declaration of Independence. Dumas Malone. New York: Oxford University Press. (7)

FILMSTRIPS

The American Revolution: Two Views. Pleasantville, N.Y.: Educational Audio Visual. (6)
Stories in American History Set 1: Johnny Tremain and the Boston Tea Party. Burbank, Calif.: Walt Disney Educational Media Co. (6)
Colonial America. New York: American Heritage Publishing Co. Series of 5

filmstrips. Color. (8)
Political Parties. Chicago: Society for Visual Education. Color. (9)

FILMS (16 mm)

Constitution: One Nation, Parts I & II. New York: Ford Foundation TV Workshop. 30 min. B/W. (8)
Thomas Jefferson. West Hollywood, Calif.: Handel Film Corporation. 34 min. Color. (9)
Defining Democracy. Chicago: Encyclopaedia Britannica Films. 18 min. B/W. (9)

RECORD

"America." *Silver Burdett Music 8,* 1985 ed., Record 2. (9)

UNIT 3

BOOKS FOR STUDENTS

The Age of Jackson. Arthur M. Schlesinger, Jr. Boston: Little, Brown & Co. (11)
The Dark and Bloody Ground: Stories of the American Frontier. Compiled by Phyllis R. Fenner. New York: William Morrow & Co. (10)
Heroines of the Early West. Nancy Ross. New York: Random House. (13)
The Lewis and Clark Expedition. Richard L. Neuberger. New York: Random House. (10)
On to Oregon. Honoré Morrow. New York: William Morrow & Co. (13)
Profiles in Courage. John F. Kennedy. New York: Harper & Row, Publishers. (11)

BOOKS FOR TEACHERS

A Diplomatic History of the American People. Thomas A. Bailey. East Norwalk, Conn.: Appleton-Century-Crofts. (11)
American Heritage Book of the Pioneer Spirit. New York: American Heritage Publishing Co. (10)
The Journals of Lewis and Clark. Edited by Bernard DeVoto. Boston: Houghton Mifflin Co. (10)

FILMSTRIPS

California, Texas and the Mexican War. New Haven, Conn.:Yale University Press Film Service. 40 frames. B/W. (13)
Inventions and Technology That Shaped

America, Part I: Colonial Times to Civil War. New York: Learning Corporation of America. Series of 6 filmstrips. Color, sound. (13)
The Jackson Years: The New Americans. New York: Learning Corporation of America. Series of 2 filmstrips. Color, sound. (11)
Mexico — The Land and Its History. International Communications Films. 75 frames. Color. (13)

FILMS (16 mm)

The Big Push West. New York: NBC Films. 25 min. Color. (13)
The Lewis and Clark Journey. Chicago: Coronet Films. 11 min. Color. (10)

The Railroad Builders. Chicago: Encyclopaedia Britannica Films. 14 min. Color. (12)
Saga of the Erie Canal. Chicago: Coronet Films. 10 min. Color. (12)
The Westward Movement. West Hollywood, Calif.: Handel Film Corporation. 15 min. Color. (13)

RECORDS
"Camptown Races." *Silver Burdett Music 5,* 1985 ed., Record 10. (12)
"Follow the Drinking Gourd." *Silver Burdett Music 8,* 1985 ed., Record 12. (12)
"Get on Board." *Silver Burdett Music 5,* 1985 ed., Record 9. (12)

"The Star-Spangled Banner." *Silver Burdett Music 5,* 1985 ed., Record 2. (10)
"Swing Low, Sweet Chariot." *Silver Burdett Music 8,* 1985 ed., Record 3. (12)

UNIT 4

BOOKS FOR STUDENTS
Abraham Lincoln: The War Years. Carl Sandburg. New York: Harcourt Brace Jovanovich. (14)
Appomattox. Burke Davis. New York: Harper & Row, Publishers. (14)
Reconstruction: The Great Experience. Allen W. Trelease. New York: Harper & Row, Publishers. (16)
Roots. Alex Haley. New York: Dell Publishing Co. (14)
Frederick Douglass: Slave — Fighter — Free Man. Arna Bontemps. New York: Alfred A. Knopf. (15)

BOOKS FOR TEACHERS
Document of American History. Henry S. Commager. East Norwalk, Conn.: Appleton-Century-Crofts. (15)
From Slavery to Freedom. John Hope Franklin. New York: Alfred A. Knopf. (14)
Ebony Pictorial History of Black Americans, Vol. I. Compiled by the editors of *Ebony* magazine. Chicago: Johnson Publishing Co. (14)

FILMSTRIPS
The Civil War. New York: American Heritage Publishing Co., Series of 5 filmstrips. Color, sound. (15)

A House Divided. Peoria, Ill.: Thomas S. Klise Co. 77 frames. Color. (15)
Picture History of the Civil War. Chicago: Encyclopaedia Britannica Films. Series of 8 filmstrips. Color. (15)
Slavery. New York: Zenger Productions. Series of 2 filmstrips. Color, sound. (14)

FILMS (16 mm)
Background of the Civil War. Film Associates of California. 20 min. Color. (15)
Black History: Lost, Stolen or Strayed. New York: CBS Films. 53 min. Color. (16)

RECORDS
"Pay Me My Money Down." *Silver Burdett Music 5,* 1985 ed., Record 3. (14)
"Oh, Swing Low." *Silver Burdett Music 8,* 1985 ed., Record 2. (14)
"Oh, Swing Low." *Silver Burdett Music 8,* 1985 ed., Record 2. (14)

MICROCOMPUTER COURSEWARE
The Road to Gettysburg. Available for use with Apple® II Plus, TRS-80®, and ATARI® computers. Educational Audio Visual, Pleasantville, New York. (15)
Battle of Shiloh. Available for use with Apple II® Plus, TRS-80®, and ATARI® computers. Educational Audio Visual, Pleasantville, New York. (15)

Lincoln's Decisions: Simulation. Available for use with Apple®, Commodore PET, and TRS-80® computers. Social Studies School Service, Culver City, California. (15)

FILMS (16 mm)
Andrew Carnegie and the Gospel of Wealth. New York: Learning Corporation of America. (19)
Growth of Big Business in America, 1865–1900. Chicago: Coronet Films. 15 min. B/W. (19)
Immigration in America's History. Chicago: Coronet Films. 11 min. B/W. (20)
Inventions in America's Growth, 1850–1910. Chicago: Coronet Films. 11 min. B/W. (19)
The Masses and the Millionaires: The Homestead Steel Strike. New York: Learning Corporation of America. (19)
The Railroad Builders. Chicago: Encyclopaedia Britannica Films. 14 min. Color. (19)
Trust and Trustbusters. New York: McGraw-Hill Inc. 25 min. Color. (21)

RECORDS
"Old Texas." *Silver Burdett Music 5,* 1985 ed., Record 8. (18)
"The Stars and Stripes Forever." *Silver Burdett Music 6,* 1985 ed., Record 13. (19)
"Streets of Laredo." *Silver Burdett Music 8,* 1985 ed., Record 3. (18)
"Sweet Betsy from Pike." *Silver Burdett Music 5,* 1985 ed., Record 12. (18)

UNIT 5

BOOKS FOR STUDENTS
The American West. Lucius Beebe and Charles Cliff. New York: E.P. Dutton. (18)
Bury My Heart at Wounded Knee: An Indian History of the American West. Dee Brown. New York: Holt, Rinehart & Winston. (18)
How the Other Half Lives. Jacob Riis. New York: Dover Publications. (20)
The Rise of the City. Edited by A.M.

Schlesinger and D.R. Fox. New York: Macmillan Co. (20)
Trail Driving Days. Dee Brown and Martin F. Schmitt. New York: Charles Scribner's Sons. (18)

BOOKS FOR TEACHERS
America. Alistair Cooke. New York: Alfred A. Knopf. (18)
The American People in the Twentieth Century. Oscar Handlin. Boston: Beacon Press. (20)
The Other America. Michael Harrington.

New York: Macmillan Co. (20)
The Way Our People Lived. William E. Woodward. New York: Pocket Books, Washington Square Press. (19)

FILMSTRIPS
America in the 1890s. Chicago: Coronet Films. Multimedia kit: 1 filmstrip (color, sound), 4 duplicating masters. (21)
The Rise of the Industrial Giants. New York: McGraw-Hill Films. Series of 2 filmstrips. Color, sound. (19)

BOOKS, FILMSTRIPS, FILMS, RECORDS, MICROCOMPUTER COURSEWARE

UNIT 6

BOOKS FOR STUDENTS

An Album of Black Americans in the Armed Forces. Donald L. Miller. New York: Franklin Watts. (24)
The First Book of World War I. L.L. Snyder. New York: Franklin Watt. (24)
The Making of a World Power. Paul Angle. New York: Fawcett Book Group. (22)
The Origins of the World War. Sidney Bradshaw Fay. New York: Macmillan Co. (24)

BOOKS FOR TEACHERS

All Quiet on the Western Front. Erich M.

Color, sound or audiotape. (22)
The Huddled Masses. Illinois: Thomas S. Klise Co. 2 filmstrips, record or cassette. (22)
World War I: The Great War. Illinois: Thomas S. Klise Co. 2 filmstrips, record and cassette. (24)

FILMS (16 mm)

Admiral Dewey's Victory at Manila. You Are There Series. New York: CBS, McGraw-Hill. 27 min. B/W. (23)
Hawaii's History: Kingdom to Statehood. Schumann Productions. 14 min. Color. (23)
Imperialism: The Lure of Empire. New York: Learning Corporation of America. (23)
U.S. Expansion Overseas, 1893–1917. Chicago: Coronet Films. 14 min. Color. (23)

Remarque. New York: Fawcett Book Group. (24)
The American People in the Twentieth Century. Oscar Handlin. Boston: Beacon Press. (22)
American Diplomacy: 1900–1950. George F. Kennan. Chicago: University of Chicago Press. (23)
Hurrah for Peace! Hooray for War! Steven L. Jantzen. New York: Alfred A. Knopf. (24)
The Influence of Seapower Upon History. Alfred T. Mahan. New York: Hill & Wang. (23)

FILMSTRIPS

America Becomes a Great Power. New York: Pathescope Educational Films. 61 frames.

UNIT 7

BOOKS FOR STUDENTS

The First Book of World War II. L.L. Snyder. New York: Franklin Watts. (27)
Roosevelt: The Soldier of Freedom. James M. Burns. New York: Harcourt Brace Jovanovich. (26)
The Great Crash, 1929. John Kenneth Galbraith. Boston: Houghton Mifflin Co. (26)
John F. Kennedy and PT-109. Richard Tregaskis. New York: Random House. (27)
Return to Hiroshima. Betty Jean Lifton. New York: Atheneum Publishers. (27)
Years of Decision, Vol. 1. Harry S. Truman. New York: Doubleday & Co. (27)

BOOKS FOR TEACHERS

The American Story: The Age of Exploration to the Age of the Atom. New York: Channel Press. (25)
Diplomatic History of the American People. Thomas A. Bailey. New York: Appleton-Century-Crofts. (24)
Great American Fighter Pilots of World War II. Robert D. Loomis. New York: Random House. (27)
We, the American Women: A Documentary History. Beth Millstein and Jeanne Bodin. Chicago: Science Research Associates. (25)

FILMSTRIPS

Hiroshima Decision: Was the Use of the

A-Bomb Necessary? New York: Zenger Productions. 35 frames. Color, sound. (27)
History of the United Nations. New York: McGraw-Hill Textfilms. 39 frames. Color. (28)
World War II: The Last Great War. Peoria, Ill.: Thomas S. Klise Co. 2 filmstrips. Cassette. (27)

FILMS (16 mm)

The Second World War: Triumph of the Axis. Chicago: Encyclopaedia Britannica Films. 24 min. B/W. (27)
World War II: 1939–1941. Chicago: Coronet Films. 16 min. B/W. (27)
World War II: 1942–1945. Chicago: Coronet Films. 17 min. B/W. (27)

UNIT 8

BOOKS FOR STUDENTS

America's Endangered Wildlife. George Laycock. New York: W.W. Norton & Co. (27)
Mary McLeod Bethune. Emma Gelders Sterne. New York: Alfred A. Knopf. (27)
Melindy's Medal. G. Faulkner and J. Becker. New York: Julian Messner. (27)
Puerto Rican Spirit: Their History, Life and Culture. Maria T. Babin. New York: Macmillan Co. (28)

BOOKS FOR TEACHERS

A Biographical History of Blacks in America.

Edgar A. Toppin. New York: David McKay and Company. (30)
The American Heritage History of the American People. Bernard A. Weisberger. New York: American Heritage Publishing Co. (28)
Chicano Manifesto. Armando Rendon. Edited by S.D. Stewart. New York: Macmillan Co. (29)
Puerto Rican Americans: The Meaning of Migration to the Mainland. J. Fitzpatrick. Englewood Cliffs, N.J.: Prentice-Hall. (29)
Feminism: The Essential Historical Writings. Edited by Miriam Schneir. New York: Random House. (29)
Megatrends. John Naisbitt. New York: Warner Communications. (29)

FILMSTRIPS

America, The Melting Pot: Myth or Reality? Current Affairs Filmstrips. 42 frames. Color, sound. (29)
Changing Role of Women. New York: Associated Press Special Reports. Series of 2 filmstrips. Color, sound. (29)
Martin Luther King, Jr. Peoria, Ill.: Thomas S. Klise Co. 83 frames. (29)
Power and Energy Crisis. New York: Associated Press Special Reports. Series of 2 filmstrips. Color. (31)

ONE FLAG, ONE LAND

The World and Its People

SERIES AUTHORS

Val E. Arnsdorf, Professor,
    College of Education, University of Delaware,
    Newark, Delaware

Herbert J. Bass, Professor of History,
    Temple University, Philadelphia, Pennsylvania

Carolyn S. Brown, Late Principal,
    Robertson Academy School, Nashville, Tennessee

Richard C. Brown, Former University Professor of
    History,
    State University of New York College at Buffalo

Patricia T. Caro, Assistant Professor of Geography,
    University of Oregon, Eugene, Oregon

Kenneth S. Cooper, Professor of History, Emeritus,
    George Peabody College for Teachers, Vanderbilt
    University, Nashville, Tennessee

Gary S. Elbow, Professor of Geography,
    Texas Tech University, Lubbock, Texas

Alvis T. Harthern, Professor of Education,
    University of Montevallo, Montevallo, Alabama

Timothy M. Helmus, Social Studies Instructor,
    City Middle and High School, Grand Rapids,
    Michigan

Bobbie P. Hyder, Elementary Education Coordinator,
    Madison County School System, Huntsville,
    Alabama

Theodore Kaltsounis, Professor and Associate Dean,
    College of Education, University of Washington,
    Seattle, Washington

Richard H. Loftin, Director of Curriculum and Staff
    Development,
    Aldine Independent School District, Houston, Texas

Clyde P. Patton, Professor of Geography,
    University of Oregon, Eugene, Oregon

Norman J. G. Pounds, Former University Professor
    of Geography,
    Indiana Univeristy, Bloomington, Indiana

Arlene C. Rengert, Professor of Geography,
    West Chester University, West Chester,
    Pennsylvania

Robert N. Saveland, Professor of Social Science
    Education,
    University of Georgia, Athens, Georgia

Edgar A. Toppin, Professor of History and Dean of
    the Graduate School,
    Virginia State University, Petersburg, Virginia

GRADE-LEVEL CONTRIBUTORS

Denice Decker, Teacher,
    Andrew Carnegie Intermediate School District,
    Sacramento, California

Lawrence N. Greer, Jr., Teacher,
    Beck Middle School, Greenville, South Carolina

Carol Hallman, Social Studies Coordinator
    West Clermont Local Schools, Cincinnati, Ohio

Dale A. Ketcham, Supervisor of Social Studies,
    Union Endicott Central School District, Endicott,
    New York

C. Monty Pope, Team Leader, Social Studies,
    Apollo Middle School, Antioch, Tennessee

ONE FLAG, ONE LAND

RICHARD C. BROWN   Former University Professor of History,
State University of New York College at Buffalo
HERBERT J. BASS   Professor of History,
Temple University, Philadelphia, Pennsylvania

CONSULTANTS

Edgar A. Toppin   Professor of History and Dean of the Graduate School,
Virginia State University, Petersburg, Virginia
Barbara S. Bass   Reading Specialist
Cheltenham School District, Cheltenham, Pennsylvania

SILVER BURDETT COMPANY   MORRISTOWN, NJ
Atlanta, GA • Cincinnati, OH • Dallas, TX • Northfield, IL • San Carlos, CA • Agincourt, Ontario

CONTENTS

ACKNOWLEDGMENTS

Page 39: By permission of the Smithsonian Institution Press from *Smithsonian Miscellaneous Collection, Vol. 80, No. 7.* "Aboriginal Indian Population North of Mexico," by James Mooney, Smithsonian Institution, Washington, D.C., 1928. Page 161: Excerpt adapted from THE AMERICAN HERITAGE BOOK OF THE REVOLUTION by Bruce Lancaster, 1958 American Heritage Publishing Co., Inc. Adapted by permission of American Heritage Publishing Co., Inc. Page 223: Excerpt from THE BOOK OF ABIGAIL AND JOHN, ed. by L. H. Butterfield, Cambridge, Mass.: The Belknap Press of Harvard University, Copyright © 1975 by the Massachusetts Historical Society. Reprinted by permission of the publishers. Page 599: Entry "platform" reprinted from the WORLD BOOK DICTIONARY by permission of J. G. Ferguson Publishing Company, Chicago, Illinois.

MAPS

ATLAS

GRAPHS

DIAGRAMS

TABLES

TIME LINES

SPECIAL INTEREST MATERIALS

END-OF-CHAPTER SKILLS DEVELOPMENT

A LETTER TO YOU FROM THE AUTHORS

Dear Student,

You are about to begin a study of our country's exciting history. One Flag, One Land does not contain the full story of this history. No book could tell everything that has happened in the past. Nor could a single book tell of all the groups or of all the individual men and women who have contributed to our country's history. So during the coming year and during future years, you should be on the lookout for books, movies, television programs, and vacation trips that can add details and color to information within the covers of One Flag, One Land.

There is still another reason this book contains less than the full story of our history. It is because our history is a never-ending story — at least we hope it will be. Each of you has another 60 years to live, on the average. That's 60 years of history that has yet to be written. You will contribute to that history in a great, a moderate, or a small way. It is impossible to escape making some kind of a contribution.

Knowledge of what American women and men have done in the past will shape the contribution you make. That contribution must fit in with the goals, the ideals, and the dreams of those who came before you. Yes, One Flag, One Land tells only part of a never-ending story. However, it will tell you where we have been, where we are today, and the direction we are likely to take in the future, since that future is influenced by the past.

Sincerely,

Richard C. Brown

Herbert J Bass

6.15.15

A New World Is Added to the Old

Each unit-opening page has the same time line, one that spans American history from prehistoric times to the present day. However, the time period that is covered in each unit is set off in blue. In the box below the time line are drawings of people and objects that are dealt with in the unit. Make use of the unit-opening pages to arouse the interest of pupils in the chapters they will be studying.

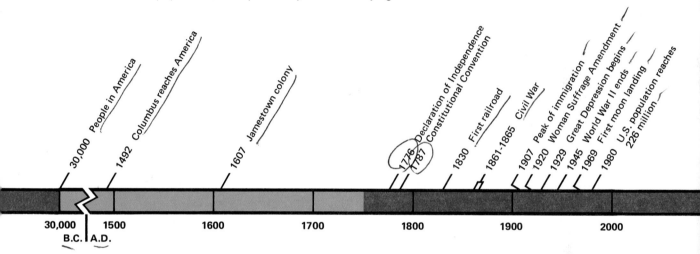

30,000 People in America
1492 Columbus reaches America
1607 Jamestown colony
1776 Declaration of Independence
1787 Constitutional Convention
1830 First railroad
1861-1865 Civil War
1907 Peak of immigration
1920 Woman Suffrage Amendment
1929 Great Depression begins
1945 World War II ends
1969 First moon landing
1980 U.S. population reaches 226 million

30,000 B.C.   A.D. 1500   1600   1700   1800   1900   2000

Above: Spanish explorer, explorer's or colonizer's ship, William Penn, colonial woman, Native American

1

CHAPTER

1 The United States Today

Maps Can Show It Whole

The bird lifts off "There was deafening handclapping and cheering as the bird gracefully lifted itself into the sky, its rocket belching from the lower end, soared through a few thin clouds, began a vapor trail, then disappeared into space history. . . ." That is the way Lucian C. Warren, a reporter, described the launching. It was May 5, 1961, when Commander Alan B. Shepard became the first American to penetrate outer space.

It was indeed a historic time. And yet it was only a new chapter in the continuing history of our country. This book is dedicated to helping you understand that history. Shepard's flight lasted 15 minutes. He landed in the Atlantic Ocean, 180 miles (288 km) from the launching pad in Florida.

The astronauts The first people chosen as **astronauts** in the United States space program became as close as the members of a large family. They trained together and ate, slept, and lived under the same roof. Three of them died together in an accident at Cape Canaveral (kə nav′ ə rəl) in January 1967.

In time, 25 of the first 30 astronauts were rocketed into space. John H. Glenn, later a senator from Ohio, was the first to **orbit**, or circle, the earth. His successful three-orbit flight took place on February 20, 1962. The flight lasted 4 hours, 55 minutes, and 23 seconds from blast-off to landing. During that time, Glenn's space capsule reached a height of 162 miles (260 km) and a speed of approximately 17,500 miles (28,158 km) per hour.

Other astronauts have reached heights equal to or greater than Glenn's. A dozen have had the thrill of walking on the moon. The first astronaut to set foot on the moon was Neil Armstrong in 1969. From the moon, astronauts have an unusual experience. In one glance they can see the *whole* United States.

Few of us will ever see the whole United States as astronauts can see it. But we can see our whole country in other ways. Maps can show the whole United States. Indeed, maps can show aspects of the United States that were invisible from space.

Political maps No astronaut can see the boundaries dividing our country into 50 states. You can, by looking at the map

The Space Shuttle Challenger is blasted aloft at the Kennedy Space Center in Florida.

Cape Canaveral in Florida is the site of the John F. Kennedy Space Center. Cape Canaveral was renamed Cape Kennedy in 1963 after President Kennedy's assassination, but in 1973 the name was changed back to Cape Canaveral in accordance with the wishes of the people of Florida.

THE METRIC SYSTEM OF MEASUREMENT

On page 2 you read that John Glenn's space capsule reached a height of 162 miles (260 km). The measurement 260 km (kilometers) is about the same as 162 miles. Kilometers and miles are both units of measure used to express distance or length. A kilometer is a unit of measure in the metric system. The system is called metric because it uses the meter in measuring length. A meter is 39.37 inches, or a little more than 1 yard.

The metric system is used to measure such things as distance, weight, area, and temperature. This system is in use or is being introduced in all the major countries of the world except the United States.

Someday the United States will probably "go metric" also, adopting the measurement system that is used so widely.

To get you ready for this change, both American and metric measurements are used in this book. When an American measurement appears, it is followed in parentheses ( ) by the metric measurement that is about equal to it. Inches are changed to centimeters (cm), feet and yards to meters (m), miles to kilometers (km), and acres to hectares (ha). Pounds are changed - to kilograms (kg), and quarts to liters (L). Pecks and bushels are also changed to liters. Degrees Fahrenheit (°F) are changed to degrees Celsius (°C).

on pages 716–717. It is a **political map.** A political map shows such things as national and state boundaries and the names and locations of towns and cities. Find your state on the map. Does it share a common boundary with other states? If so, which ones?

Can you find states on the political map that do not touch any of the other states? That touch only one other state? How many foreign countries share a common boundary with the United States? Some states have no water boundaries, only land boundaries. Find three states having only land boundaries with their neighbors. Then find a water boundary between two states.

The political map on pages 716–717 shows the capital city in each state. Could astronauts pick out your state's capital city as they orbited the earth? Probably not. But you can tell the location and the name of the capital city of each state by looking at the map on pages

Four state capitals bear Presidents' names: 716–717 again. How many states have capital cities named for United States Presidents? (See page 728 for a list of our Presidents.) You can find the answer to this question on a political map because you can see the *whole* United States.

Jackson, Mississippi; Jefferson City, Missouri; Lincoln, Nebraska; and Madison, Wisconsin.

Relief maps As the astronauts speed through space above the United States, they can perhaps make out certain landforms, such as mountain ranges. Whether they can or cannot, you can see them by means of the **relief map** on page 5. A relief map shows the **elevation,** or height, of the earth's surface. The elevation of land is expressed in feet or meters above or below sea level. Elevation is often shown by **contour lines,** as on the map on page 5. All points along a contour line are exactly the same distance above or below the level of the sea. Sometimes color is added between contour lines to show different elevations more clearly.

Alaska and Hawaii do not touch other states. Maine touches only one other state. Two foreign countries — Canada and Mexico — share a common boundary with the United States. Wyoming, Colorado, and Utah are among the states having only land boundaries. Most states have some water boundaries.

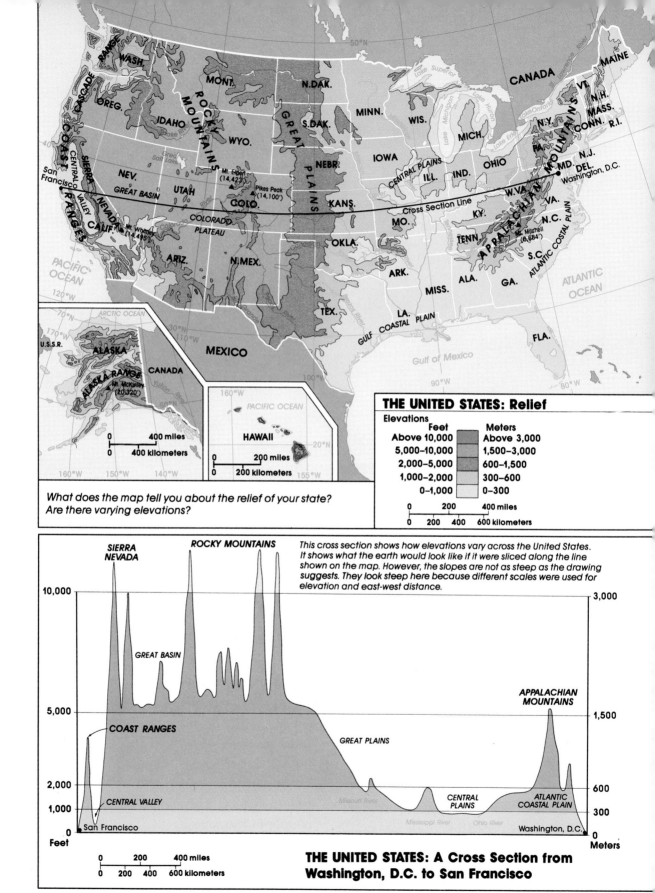

THE UNITED STATES: Relief

Elevations

	Feet	Meters
	Above 10,000	Above 3,000
	5,000–10,000	1,500–3,000
	2,000–5,000	600–1,500
	1,000–2,000	300–600
	0–1,000	0–300

0   200   400 miles
0   200   400   600 kilometers

What does the map tell you about the relief of your state? Are there varying elevations?

This cross section shows how elevations vary across the United States. It shows what the earth would look like if it were sliced along the line shown on the map. However, the slopes are not as steep as the drawing suggests. They look steep here because different scales were used for elevation and east-west distance.

THE UNITED STATES: A Cross Section from Washington, D.C. to San Francisco

SIERRA NEVADA

ROCKY MOUNTAINS

GREAT BASIN

COAST RANGES

CENTRAL VALLEY

GREAT PLAINS

CENTRAL PLAINS

APPALACHIAN MOUNTAINS

ATLANTIC COASTAL PLAIN

San Francisco

Washington, D.C.

Feet

10,000

5,000

2,000

1,000

0

Meters

3,000

1,500

600

300

0

Missouri River

Mississippi River

Ohio River

0   200   400 miles
0   200   400   600 kilometers

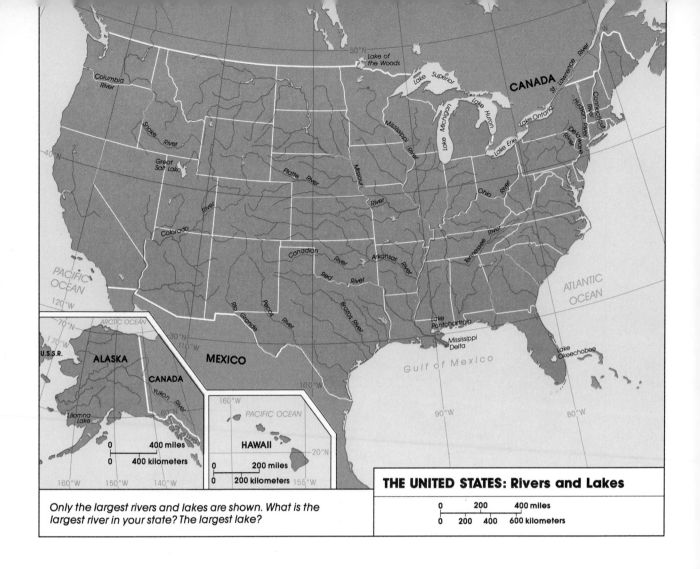

Only the largest rivers and lakes are shown. What is the largest river in your state? The largest lake?

THE UNITED STATES: Rivers and Lakes

Among the mountain ranges shown on the relief map on page 5 are the Appalachians and the Rockies. Can you find them? Which ocean is the Appalachian range closer to? The Rocky Mountains make up the largest range in the United States. Between the Appalachians and the Rockies, there are plains and plateaus. West of the Rockies are three other mountain ranges. What are their names?

Mountain ranges have been important in American history. They were barriers, or walls, that slowed for a time the movement of the American people. Nevertheless, as you will learn, these barriers were overcome as the United States spread from the Atlantic to the Pacific and on out into that ocean.

Rivers and lakes The map on this page shows the largest rivers and lakes in the United States. As you can see, the Mississippi River and its **tributaries**—rivers that run into the Mississippi—stand out as features of the land. During the entire span of human life in North America, the Mississippi River system has provided food and transportation for the people of the region.

In the northeastern quarter of the United States are the Great Lakes. Can you find the names of these five lakes on

6 Tell pupils that the word *HOMES* is a good memory device for recalling the names of the Great Lakes: *H* — Huron, *O* — Ontario; *M* — Michigan; *E* — Erie; *S* — Superior.

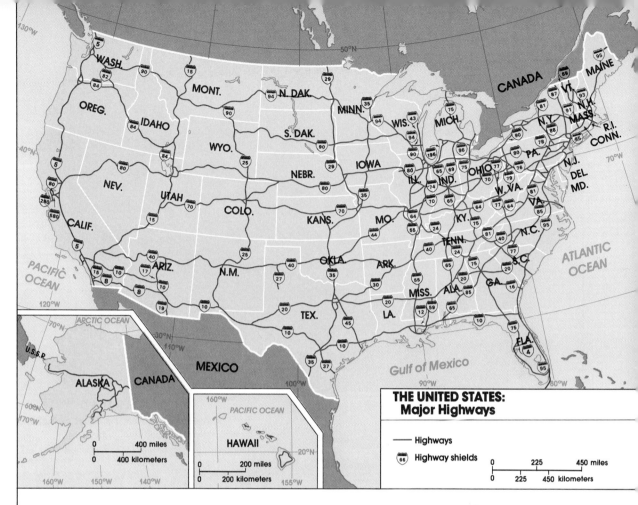

Are there interstate highways in your state? If so, through what cities do they run?

the map on page 6? Which is the only one entirely within the United States?

Lake Michigan

Our nation's extensive highway system Rivers and lakes provided a natural system of transportation in our land for thousands of years. But nineteenth-century Americans added to this natural system by building canals and railroads. In the twentieth century, Americans added an extensive highway system.

The map on this page shows our Interstate Highway System. Interstate highways are identified by route markers that look like red, white, and blue shields. The even-numbered interstates, such as 40, 70, and 80, run east and west. Those with odd numbers, such as 5, 25, and 95, are north-south routes. Find these routes on the map above.

The first interstates were begun in 1956. Today the system is 95 percent complete. At times of gasoline shortages some Americans have criticized the Interstate Highway System. These critics say it is not wise to spend large sums of money on a system that encourages travel by private automobile. It would be better, they say, to spend the money on **mass transit.** Mass transit is the carrying of people by buses, trains, and subways. How do *you* think the money should be

The Interstate Highway System is expected to be completed in the early 1990s. It will connect almost all cities that have populations over 50,000.

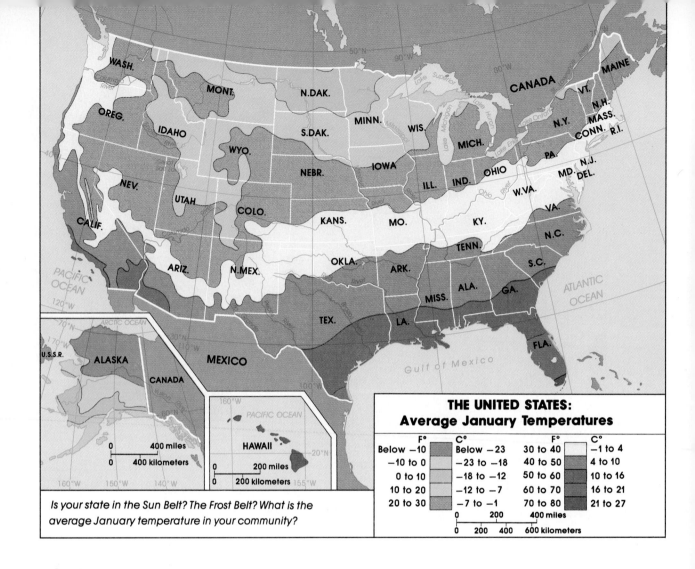

Is your state in the Sun Belt? The Frost Belt? What is the average January temperature in your community?

spent—for interstate highways or for mass transit?

No doubt you have been on interstate highways. Which ones have you traveled on? Which interstate is nearest to your community? Though you may have ridden on the interstates, have you ever had a train ride? Or a ride on a canal boat?

A nation of great variety   Any nation as large as the United States has great variety. Maps can demonstrate this variety. For example, the map above shows the average January temperatures in the United States. You can see how winter temperatures differ from one part of the country to another. In recent years large numbers of people have moved from the Frostbelt to the Sunbelt. Looking at the map, can you tell where these two belts are located?

On the map on page 9, note the area of very low annual **precipitation** (pri sip ə-tā′ shən), that is, water falling to earth as rain, snow, hail, sleet, or mist. For many years in the nineteenth century, this area in the West was labeled on maps *The Great American Desert*. It was thought to be almost unfit for human settlement. And yet today this area supports millions of people. What changed, do you think, so that people could live there?

Irrigation systems were built. Among the first settlers to build such systems were the Mormons, who farmed in the 1840s in what is now Utah.

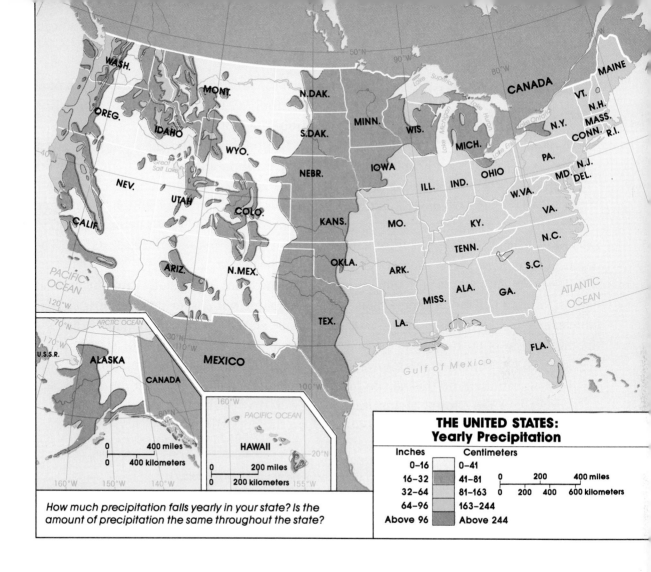

THE UNITED STATES: Yearly Precipitation

Inches	Centimeters
0–16	0–41
16–32	41–81
32–64	81–163
64–96	163–244
Above 96	Above 244

How much precipitation falls yearly in your state? Is the amount of precipitation the same throughout the state?

The many uses of maps   People who make maps are known as **cartographers** (kär tog´ ra fərz). They make a useful product. The maps in this history book will help to teach you how the United States began, how it grew, and how it got to be the nation it is today.

There are many other uses of maps. Drivers taking long-distance trips depend on road maps. There are state maps, city maps, maps of fairgrounds, maps of the world, and even maps of our universe. The seating plan of a theater, a baseball park, or a football stadium is a kind of map. A collection of maps is called an **atlas.**

Maps are a part of our lives. This is true whether we are in or out of school. The alert person will understand the many uses of maps and will know how to read them.

CHECKUP

1. What is shown on a political map of the United States? On a relief map?
2. In what ways have mountain ranges, rivers, and lakes influenced American history?
3. What waterways have provided a natural system of transportation in the United States?
4. How have Americans added to this natural system of transportation?
5. What different kinds of maps do people use in everyday life?

A collection of maps gets its name from Atlas, a god in Greek mythology. He is frequently pictured supporting the world on his shoulders.

Tables and Graphs Can Inform You

Learning from tables Information about our states can be presented, as you have seen, on a map. But for some information, a **table** is handier than a map. A table can be used to present many facts, as the one on the opposite page shows.

A map of the United States shows you Virginia's location. And the map on page 717 shows you the capital of Virginia is Richmond. Still, the map does not show you the area of the state or the state's population. Can you learn this information from the table?

By looking at the map you can guess that Virginia and Kentucky are about the same size. The table, on the other hand, shows you *exactly* which is larger. Which *is* larger, Virginia or Kentucky? What is the nation's largest state? The smallest?

How does your state rank in area as compared with other states? How large is your state? How many states have a larger population than your state? What state has the largest population? These and other questions can be easily answered with the information in the table on the opposite page.

Largest — Alaska; smallest — Rhode Island
Largest population — California

As the table tells you, Richmond is the capital, or seat of government, of Virginia. Below is the capitol, or building where Virginia's lawmakers meet. (38°N/77°W; map, p. 717)

FACTS ABOUT THE STATES

State	Area (sq. mi.) and Rank	Area (sq. km.)	Population (in thousands) and Rank	Capital City
Alabama	51,609(29)	133,667	3,943(22)	Montgomery
Alaska	586,400(1)	1,518,776	438(50)	Juneau
Arizona	113,909(6)	295,024	2,860(29)	Phoenix
Arkansas	53,104(27)	137,539	2,291(33)	Little Rock
California	158,693(3)	411,015	24,724(1)	Sacramento
Colorado	104,247(8)	270,000	3,045(27)	Denver
Connecticut	5,009(48)	12,973	3,153(26)	Hartford
Delaware	2,057(49)	5,328	602(47)	Dover
Florida	58,560(22)	151,670	10,416(7)	Tallahassee
Georgia	58,876(21)	152,489	5,639(12)	Atlanta
Hawaii	6,424(47)	16,638	994(39)	Honolulu
Idaho	83,557(13)	213,822	965(41)	Boise
Illinois	56,400(24)	146,076	11,448(5)	Springfield
Indiana	36,291(38)	93,994	5,471(14)	Indianapolis
Iowa	56,290(25)	145,791	2,905(28)	Des Moines
Kansas	82,264(14)	213,064	2,408(32)	Topeka
Kentucky	40,395(37)	104,623	3,667(23)	Frankfort
Louisiana	48,523(31)	125,675	4,362(18)	Baton Rouge
Maine	33,215(39)	86,027	1,133(38)	Augusta
Maryland	10,577(42)	27,394	4,265(19)	Annapolis
Massachusetts	8,257(45)	21,386	5,781(11)	Boston
Michigan	58,216(23)	150,779	9,109(8)	Lansing
Minnesota	84,068(12)	217,736	4,133(21)	St. Paul
Mississippi	47,716(32)	123,584	2,551(31)	Jackson
Missouri	69,686(19)	180,487	4,951(15)	Jefferson City
Montana	147,138(4)	381,087	801(44)	Helena
Nebraska	77,227(15)	200,018	1,586(35)	Lincoln
Nevada	110,540(7)	286,299	881(43)	Carson City
New Hampshire	9,304(44)	24,097	951(42)	Concord
New Jersey	7,836(46)	20,295	7,438(9)	Trenton
New Mexico	121,666(5)	315,115	1,359(37)	Santa Fe
New York	49,576(30)	128,402	17,659(2)	Albany
North Carolina	52,719(28)	136,542	6,019(10)	Raleigh
North Dakota	70,665(17)	183,022	670(46)	Bismarck
Ohio	41,222(35)	106,765	10,791(6)	Columbus
Oklahoma	69,919(18)	181,090	3,177(25)	Oklahoma City
Oregon	96,981(10)	251,181	2,649(30)	Salem
Pennsylvania	45,333(33)	117,412	11,865(4)	Harrisburg
Rhode Island	1,214(50)	3,144	958(40)	Providence
South Carolina	31,055(40)	80,432	3,203(24)	Columbia
South Dakota	77,047(16)	199,552	691(45)	Pierre
Tennessee	42,244(34)	109,412	4,651(17)	Nashville
Texas	267,339(2)	692,408	15,280(3)	Austin
Utah	84,916(11)	219,932	1,554(36)	Salt Lake City
Vermont	9,609(43)	24,887	516(48)	Montpelier
Virginia	40,815(36)	105,711	5,491(13)	Richmond
Washington	68,192(20)	176,617	4,245(20)	Olympia
West Virginia	24,181(41)	62,629	1,948(34)	Charleston
Wisconsin	56,154(26)	145,439	4,765(16)	Madison
Wyoming	97,914(9)	253,597	502(49)	Cheyenne
District of Columbia	69	178	631	
United States	3,539,289	9,166,758	231,534	Washington

Ask: Where does our state rank among the other states in area and population? What state is closest to ours in area? In population?

Learning from graphs Still another way to show information about the United States is by using a **graph**. Graphs are useful because they can pack a lot of information into a small space. On this page there are three different kinds of graphs. Each tells you something about the United States today.

Each kind of graph is named. One **bar graph** seen below shows the population of the United States by sex. Another bar graph shows the size of different age groups in the United States. The graph showing the racial makeup of the American population is called a **pie graph**. Why? The **line graph** shows the percentage of women in the labor force over 10-year periods from 1890 to 1980.

The statistics in these graphs were gathered by **demographers** (di mog′ rə fərz). A demographer is one who studies the characteristics of human populations. According to the demographers, which sex is more numerous today? About how many millions of people are in your age group? Which is the most numerous age group? About how many people are in this group?

Most numerous: 15–24 age group (42 million)

What facts does each graph tell you about the United States today?

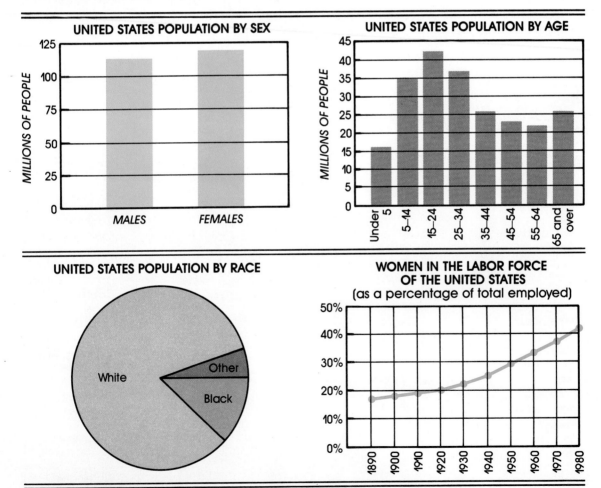

Have pupils make a pie graph, showing the makeup of the class by sex.

The pie graph divides the American population according to race. About how many white persons are there for every black person in the United States? What races are included in the group labeled *Other*? How does this group compare in size to the other groups? About 9 whites to 1 black. *Other:* Asians, Native Americans. Much smaller group — about 2½ percent of population.

The need to explain The line graph on page 12 shows that the percentage of women in the working force has grown over the years. *Why,* do you think, has the percentage grown? About what year did the percentage go above 40? About 1976

When you try to answer this question, you are going a step beyond the facts shown on the graph. You are getting into an *explanation* of the facts. Knowing the facts of history is not enough—the facts need to be explained.

Usually there is more than one explanation for a historical fact. Certainly there is more than one explanation for the increasing number and percentage of working women in the United States. The text of this history book, your teacher, outside sources, your fellow students, even you, yourself, will help to provide explanations for the facts you learn this year. We can make a formula that applies to this learning. It would go like this:

facts + explanation = understanding

CHECKUP

1. Explain the differences between tables and graphs.
2. What kinds of graphs are there?
3. What facts about the American population are revealed by the graphs in this chapter?
4. What is the formula leading to understanding in history?

The Months and Years Ahead

┌─VOCABULARY─────────────────┐
| |
| unit   benchmark |
| caption   fun factor |
| annotation |
└──────────────────────────┘

Why study history? Perhaps most of you have at least studied parts of American history in school before. You might well ask, "Why study it again?" There are good reasons. One excellent reason is that you are older than you were when, in a lower grade, you last learned about the history of your country.

We can compare your life to climbing a mountain. As you grow older, you reach a higher place than you occupied 3 or 4 years ago. Having now reached a higher level, you can see more than you could before. Things you were unable to understand several years ago now can be made clear to you.

Furthermore, good citizenship in our complex world requires almost constant study and thought. Patrick Henry, the great American patriot, once said: "I know of no way of judging the future but by the past." Learning about American history will make you a more alert and effective citizen.

No one studying American history can learn all there is to know about it. Men and women who devote a lifetime to studying American history still confess they have an incomplete knowledge of our past. Since no one can learn everything, teachers in the earlier grades had to choose those things they thought you could learn best at that time. Now you are older, so different things have been selected for you to learn.

You will find some familiar names and events in this year's work. But you are not about to study them *once more*. You are continuing your study at a higher level. As you continue your study, you will be practicing and improving learning skills that are immensely important to your future success.

To help you learn   Maps, tables, and graphs are *guides* to learning. This section is a guide, too. It describes the parts of this book so that you can find your way through it in the months ahead. It will help you make the best use of the book's features.

Look in the front part of this book at the pages that list the contents. They show that the 31 chapters of the book are divided into eight **units,** or major parts. Each unit deals with a period of time. The first unit contains five chapters. Most other units contain four chapters. Two units have three chapters.

Already you have learned about maps, tables, and graphs. They will help you learn about the history of your country during the coming year. You will find pictures and cartoons in this book. Each map, graph, picture, and cartoon has a **caption.** A caption is a description or explanation of the meaning of an illustration. As you study, be sure to read the captions.

Historical documents   You will find the Declaration of Independence and the Constitution printed in full in Unit 2. Along with the text of these historical documents are comments in the margins. These comments are called **annotations.** Annotations point out and explain important parts of these two great historical documents.

Parts of shorter historical documents are placed in appropriate sections in the text. Sometimes the documents are accounts of historical events written by persons who saw the event or took part in it. They add color and realism to your study of history.

Vocabulary and Checkup   You will note that each chapter is divided into sections. At the beginning of each section is a list of words or phrases. You may already know the meaning of some of these terms. Each word or phrase will appear in the section that follows and its meaning will be made clear. The word or phrase will also be explained in the Glossary, beginning on page 730. Thus, as the year goes on, you will find your own vocabulary increasing.

At the end of each section are questions labeled Checkup. They are designed to review your understanding of what you studied in that section.

At the end of each chapter you will find a list of key facts from the chapter, a vocabulary quiz, a series of review questions, and a number of suggested activities. Here again the purpose is to help you check up on what you have studied and to help you learn more about the material in the chapter.

Skills Development   Also at the end of each chapter you will find a Skills Development page. The exercise on that

Perhaps at this time you will want to schedule and order films, filmstrips, and other resources for the coming months. You may wish to use the manual to help you plan. Films and filmstrips as well as books and records are listed by unit in the manual.

page will help you learn about American history. In addition, the Skills Development pages will help you sharpen skills that are important for living in the twentieth century.

Knowing how to read a map, a table, or a graph is a skill. It is a skill you will make use of at different times during your life. Will you use a library only this next year? Of course not—or at least we hope not. So developing skills in using the library will benefit you now and later.

On the last Contents page, look over the list of skills you will get a chance to practice as you learn from this book. Which skills do you consider most important? Try to think of a way in which you might use each of these skills in the coming years.

How Americans Lived   At the end of several units is a section entitled How Americans Lived. These sections describe the way people lived at specific times, at 50-year intervals.

Within each of these sections is a feature called Benchmarks. A **benchmark** is a mark used by surveyors. It shows the elevation of the land at a certain point. A benchmark is used as a reference point in finding the elevation of other places. In this book the feature Benchmarks is also a reference point by which we can compare population, area, and other facts at different periods in our history.

The section How Americans Lived and the feature Benchmarks give a good picture of America and its people at a particular time in history. Since most people live as members of families, family life is emphasized in these sections.

This family is at a historic site, the Civil War battlefield at Gettysburg, Pennsylvania. (40°N/77°W; map, p. 352) The events that made Gettysburg a historic site are described on pages 351–352.

In fact, families are an important emphasis throughout this book. Perhaps there is no such thing as the "typical" American family. Nevertheless, no matter what their form, families have been and will remain a significant institution. Primarily through families, values are passed from generation to generation. In this book you will learn about important individuals in American history. In addition, you will learn about the families of some of these individuals.

Interesting people, events, places, and things are the subject of other feature material in this book. Throughout the text are boxes on the Presidents. They include a picture of each President and facts about his life. Still another feature is called What's in a Name? There is a lot of history wrapped up in the names of our states, our cities, and even our streets. Curiosity about names can be a fascinating hobby, one that you can follow throughout your life.

In the back of the book A number of valuable learning aids come near the end of the book. You will find the Biographical Dictionary interesting and useful. It lists alphabetically more than 225 people who have played significant roles in American history. Each person is described briefly. A page reference tells you where you can find more information about his or her activities.

Still another valuable aid is the Atlas. It contains a map of the world, maps of the major continents, and a map of the United States. You will want to refer to the Atlas often as you study our nation's history.

Finally, there is the Index. In the Index you can quickly find information about persons, places, and things that are dealt with in this book.

The fun factor Many Americans find a hobby in some aspect of the past. For them there is a **fun factor** in the study of history. Perhaps they restore antique automobiles or collect old stamps and coins. Perhaps they like to read good historical novels or biographies of famous people. They may concern themselves with the history of the state or community in which they live or the history of their own families.

Perhaps they travel to historic places. The map on page 17 shows 50 historic places in the United States. Each place is numbered and is identified and briefly described in the key below the map. The places listed are only a small fraction of the historic places in the United States. Practically every community has places of historic interest. What historic places are there in your community?

As you study American history this year, you will read about what happened at many of the places shown on the map. Have you visited any of these historic places? Have you visited other historic places? Doesn't a visit to a historic place mean more if you know what took place there?

There is history all around you. History is in the streets where you walk. It is in the place where you live. It is in your family, and in your place of worship, and in your school. In fact, there is a history to everything you see or read or touch. Keep this in mind in your study of American history. Perhaps this book will encourage you to develop a continuing interest in the past, present, and future of your country, the United States of America. If so, *One Flag, One Land* will have done what it was meant to do.

CHECKUP

1. How is this book divided?
2. What two significant historical documents appear in full and are annotated?
3. Why is there a Skills Development page at the end of each chapter?
4. What are the purposes of Benchmarks, boxes on the Presidents, and What's in a Name?
5. What learning aids are printed near the end of the book?

Ask the pupils to bring to class postcards, snapshots, and newspaper and magazine illustrations that show places of historic interest in your state. Have a committee arrange the pictures in a bulletin-board display.

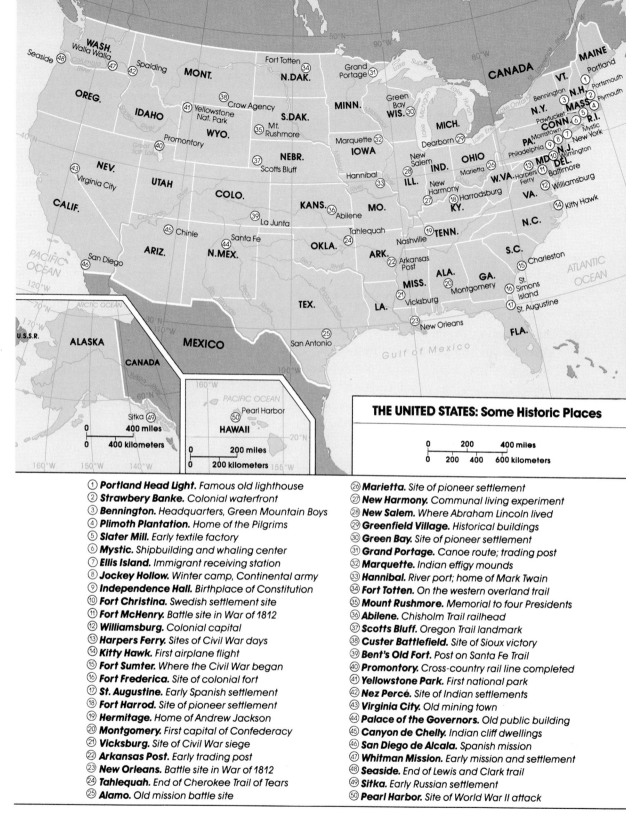

THE UNITED STATES: Some Historic Places

0   200   400 miles
0   200   400   600 kilometers

① **Portland Head Light.** Famous old lighthouse
② **Strawbery Banke.** Colonial waterfront
③ **Bennington.** Headquarters, Green Mountain Boys
④ **Plimoth Plantation.** Home of the Pilgrims
⑤ **Slater Mill.** Early textile factory
⑥ **Mystic.** Shipbuilding and whaling center
⑦ **Ellis Island.** Immigrant receiving station
⑧ **Jockey Hollow.** Winter camp, Continental army
⑨ **Independence Hall.** Birthplace of Constitution
⑩ **Fort Christina.** Swedish settlement site
⑪ **Fort McHenry.** Battle site in War of 1812
⑫ **Williamsburg.** Colonial capital
⑬ **Harpers Ferry.** Sites of Civil War days
⑭ **Kitty Hawk.** First airplane flight
⑮ **Fort Sumter.** Where the Civil War began
⑯ **Fort Frederica.** Site of colonial fort
⑰ **St. Augustine.** Early Spanish settlement
⑱ **Fort Harrod.** Site of pioneer settlement
⑲ **Hermitage.** Home of Andrew Jackson
⑳ **Montgomery.** First capital of Confederacy
㉑ **Vicksburg.** Site of Civil War siege
㉒ **Arkansas Post.** Early trading post
㉓ **New Orleans.** Battle site in War of 1812
㉔ **Tahlequah.** End of Cherokee Trail of Tears
㉕ **Alamo.** Old mission battle site

㉖ **Marietta.** Site of pioneer settlement
㉗ **New Harmony.** Communal living experiment
㉘ **New Salem.** Where Abraham Lincoln lived
㉙ **Greenfield Village.** Historical buildings
㉚ **Green Bay.** Site of pioneer settlement
㉛ **Grand Portage.** Canoe route; trading post
㉜ **Marquette.** Indian effigy mounds
㉝ **Hannibal.** River port; home of Mark Twain
㉞ **Fort Totten.** On the western overland trail
㉟ **Mount Rushmore.** Memorial to four Presidents
㊱ **Abilene.** Chisholm Trail railhead
㊲ **Scotts Bluff.** Oregon Trail landmark
㊳ **Custer Battlefield.** Site of Sioux victory
㊴ **Bent's Old Fort.** Post on Santa Fe Trail
㊵ **Promontory.** Cross-country rail line completed
㊶ **Yellowstone Park.** First national park
㊷ **Nez Percé.** Site of Indian settlements
㊸ **Virginia City.** Old mining town
㊹ **Palace of the Governors.** Old public building
㊺ **Canyon de Chelly.** Indian cliff dwellings
㊻ **San Diego de Alcala.** Spanish mission
㊼ **Whitman Mission.** Early mission and settlement
㊽ **Seaside.** End of Lewis and Clark trail
㊾ **Sitka.** Early Russian settlement
㊿ **Pearl Harbor.** Site of World War II attack

Have you visited any of the historical sites listed above? If so, which ones? What other places of historical interest have you visited?

KEY FACTS

1. Maps are valuable aids to learning. They can show large areas in a small space—for example, they can show the whole United States.

2. Maps can show many kinds of facts such as information about landforms, boundaries, cities and towns, rivers, highways, precipitation, and climate.

3. Maps can show us not only how things are in the present but how they were in the past.

4. Tables and graphs are effective tools for presenting certain kinds of information.

5. Learning about American history will make you a more alert and effective citizen.

6. There is history all around you.

VOCABULARY QUIZ

Using a separate sheet of paper, match each term with the correct definition.

a. precipitation   **f.** cartographer
b. atlas   **g.** unit
c. demographer   **h.** index
d. caption   **i.** contour lines
e. the Constitution   **j.** mass transit

e **1.** A historical document

a **2.** Any form of rain or snow

b **3.** A collection of maps

c **4.** A person studying the characteristics of human populations

d **5.** A description or explanation of a picture, map, or graph

j **6.** The carrying of people by buses, trains, or subways

f **7.** A person who makes maps

h **8.** An alphabetical listing of names, places, and subjects that are in a book

i **9.** A way of showing elevation on a map

g **10.** A division of a book

REVIEW QUESTIONS

1. What can maps show that cannot be seen by astronauts in space?

2. What differences are there between political maps and relief maps?

3. On which of these two kinds of maps would contour lines appear? The location and the name of a city?

4. What other kinds of information can be shown on maps?

5. Explain the kinds of information that can be shown on tables and graphs.

6. This book is organized to help you learn. Name at least six different parts of the book and briefly describe each.

ACTIVITIES

1. Bring to class a table or graph from a newspaper or magazine. Explain to the class what the table or graph shows.

2. In your school library or in a classroom reference book, look up the population of the five largest cities in your state. Round off the population of each to the nearer thousand. Using those figures, make a bar graph to show how the cities compare in population.

3. Draw a map showing the route you take from your home to your school. Draw it to show directions and distances.

4. Using a road atlas, show the route you would take for traveling by automobile from your community to one of the historic places shown on the map on page 17.

5. On page 16 you were told that many Americans find a hobby in some aspect of the past. Do you know of anyone who has such a hobby? If so, ask him or her to tell you about it. Then make a report to the class on this hobby.

I/SKILLS DEVELOPMENT

USING THE PARTS OF THIS BOOK

FINDING YOUR WAY

You have read that this book is organized to help you learn about your country's history. But knowing the book's organization cannot help you unless you know how to use its various learning aids.

The following exercise is meant to give you practice in using the parts of this book. By finding the answers to the questions, you will be sharpening skills that you will use many times in your study of American history. Moreover, you will often use these same skills in future years as you read magazines, newspapers, and books.

SKILLS PRACTICE

On a sheet of paper, write the answer to each of the following questions.

1. What is the title of the page in this book on which a listing of all the units and chapters starts?

2. What is the number of the unit in which you can find an account of World War II?

3. What time period does Unit 7 cover?

4. What chapter deals with each of the following topics? (**a**) Andrew Jackson's presidency (**b**) The rise of industry (**c**) The 1920s

5. On what page is a map showing all of the English colonies?

6. On what page is a graph showing the estimated Native American population in 1492?

7. Which is longer, the Declaration of Independence or the Constitution?

8. Which of these documents begins with the words "When, in the course of human events . . ."?

9. How many amendments are there to the Constitution?

10. How many vocabulary terms are there in the box at the beginning of Chapter 14?

11. How many other vocabulary boxes are there in Chapter 14?

12. In which of the four sections on a chapter review page are there statements that tell some of the main ideas of the chapter?

13. According to the time line on page 275 what took place in 1848?

14. What is the title of the section in which the Benchmarks charts are usually placed?

15. How many sections entitled How Americans Lived are there in the book?

16. In what year shown on the Benchmarks charts is the United States population listed as closest to 75 million?

17. How many presidential boxes are there in the book?

18. On what pages would you look to find a map of the world?

19. In the feature entitled Biographical Dictionary, find the home state of each of the following persons: (**a**) John C. Calhoun, (**b**) Henry Cabot Lodge, (**c**) Belva Lockwood

20. In the index, find the page numbers on which each of the following topics is described: (**a**) The siege of Vicksburg, (**b**) The impeachment of President Andrew Johnson, (**c**) The appointment of Sandra Day O'Connor to the Supreme Court.

CHAPTER

2 The Earliest Americans

Where Did They Come From?

VOCABULARY	
prehistoric	tribe
archaeologist	Folsom man
Ice Age	geologist
glacier	tree rings
Mongoloid	radioactivity
extinct	carbon 14

A flight toward the rising sun　　Fear of enemies behind them drove Omuk the Leader and his small band along. Out of the fog these enemies had come 2 days earlier. They were men and women dressed in furs, looking much like the people Omuk led. There were at least 100 of these enemies. But Omuk's band had no more than 20 fit fighters.

Omuk and his people had fled. The enemies had not followed for long. But they had taken over the good hunting grounds that Omuk and his followers had enjoyed. Now Omuk must find food for his people, or else they all would die. Already Amar, a woman carrying her baby, had sunk to her knees, unable to keep up. Others might soon become exhausted and fall behind.

The flight had led the band away from familiar landmarks. Now Omuk the Leader was lost. He kept the open water to the side of him as he moved on. Always he moved in the direction of the rising sun.

In their flight, Omuk and his band may have been the first people to enter America.

We do not know that there was really a man named Omuk or a woman named Amar. But we do know there were people like them in **prehistoric** times— that is, in those early years before there were written records. **Archaeologists** (är kē ol′ ə jists) say that the flight of this prehistoric band of people might well have taken place. Archaeologists are scientists who study objects, ruins, and other evidence of human life in the past.

A land bridge from Asia　　Omuk and Amar and others like them lived at a time known as the **Ice Age**. Long tongues of ice called **glaciers** had pushed down from the north to cover much of North America. Beneath the ice a narrow strip of land connected Siberia, in Asia, and Alaska, in North America.

As the Ice Age ended, the glaciers melted. In time, the water from the melting ice covered the land bridge. Today the land that Omuk and his band walked on is covered by the waters of the Bering Strait, which separates Siberia and Alaska.

Indians of the Pacific Northwest were adept at fishing and building boats.

There have been several ice ages. The last one, the one in which Omuk and Amar lived, is called the Pleistocene. Ice crept southward from the Hudson Bay region to the present-day Ohio and Missouri river valleys. The ice gouged depressions that filled with water and became the Great Lakes.

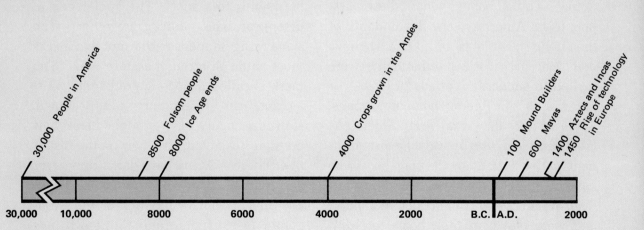

30,000 People in America

8500 Folsom people

8000 Ice Age ends

4000 Crops grown in the Andes

100 Mound Builders

600 Mayas

1400 Aztecs and Incas

1450 Rise of technology in Europe

30,000   10,000   8000   6000   4000   2000   B.C. A.D.   2000

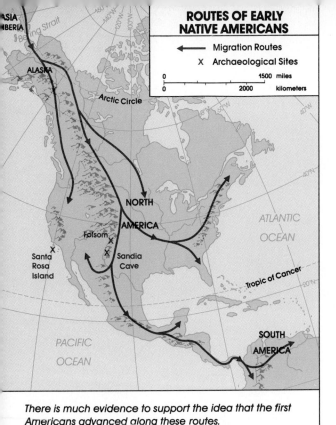

ROUTES OF EARLY NATIVE AMERICANS

← Migration Routes
X Archaeological Sites

0   1500 miles
0   2000   kilometers

There is much evidence to support the idea that the first Americans advanced along these routes.

Most scholars today accept the idea that the first people in America came across the land bridge from Asia. But there are other ideas advanced by some.

Some other explanations Could the ancestors of the American Indians have come from across the Atlantic Ocean? Some people believe that these first people in America were descendants of the ten lost tribes of Israel. Others believe that America's earliest inhabitants were related to ancient Egyptians or Greeks or perhaps to the Phoenicians or Romans. Some think that the first Americans crossed the Atlantic by way of a lost continent called Atlantis. It may be, some have said, that the ancestors of the American Indians were from Wales or Ireland and were blown in their boats to North America by an Atlantic storm.

Still others think that the first Americans crossed the Pacific Ocean by boat or raft from China, Japan, or the islands of Polynesia (pol ə nē′ zhə). There is indeed some physical evidence that they did come from an Asian land, whether by boat, by raft, or by the land bridge.

Physical evidence The American Indians are of the **Mongoloid** race. So are the people of China. The American Indians and the people of China differ in many ways. Yet there are some ways in which they are much alike.

Most Indians have a fold of skin along the inner edge of their eyes. So do Asiatic people of Mongoloid stock. This fold probably developed over thousands of years, passed along from generation to generation. Such a physical characteristic would help the people having it to survive. Certainly it would have helped Omuk as he narrowed his eyes to peer into the fog and snow along the Ice Age bridge.

Amar's baby probably had a bluish-black spot on the lower back. A large number of American Indian babies are born with this spot. The spot tends to disappear when they grow older. The same thing happens to the spot that marks most of the children of eastern Asia. The mark is called the Mongoloid spot.

American Indians vary in appearance. However, many have straight black hair on their heads but little hair on the rest of their bodies. Many have dark brown eyes and reddish or brownish-red skin. These are physical characteristics of the Mongoloid race. Indian and Chinese babies often resemble each other. This may be

The islands of Polynesia are in the central and south Pacific. They include New Zealand, the Hawaiian Islands, Samoa, the Cook Islands, the Ellice Islands, Tonga, and others. Have pupils locate these islands on a map.

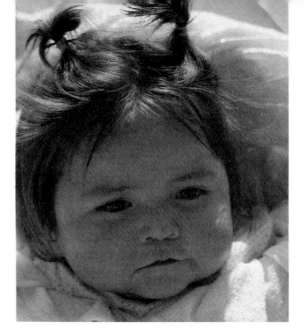

How do these pictures of an Indian baby (left) and a Chinese baby (right) support the theory that the ancestors of Native Americans came from Asia?

one more indication that the ancestors of the American Indians came from Asia.

How the first Americans lived   Omuk and his Ice Age descendants lived by hunting. They hunted animals that are now **extinct**—that is, kinds of animals that have died out. Among them were ancient bison and huge elephantlike animals called mammoths. No doubt the lives of these first Americans were harsh and short.

Nevertheless, these people increased in numbers. The first group to come across the land bridge was followed by others. However, the main increase came from the children born in the new land. Though many died young, enough lived to populate hundreds of places.

Moving southward   Omuk's people and their descendants roamed from place to place. Slowly they spread eastward and southward into the Yukon River valley, away from the coast. They moved southward from Alaska into western Canada. Finally they reached lands the glaciers had left uncovered. As time passed, some small bands joined into larger groups called **tribes.**

By the time the Ice Age ended, these early Americans had reached at least as far as present-day New Mexico. How do we know this? We know it partly through a find made by a bronco-riding black cowboy on a ranch in northeastern New Mexico. His name was George McJunkin.

The mystery of the buried bones   One day in the spring of 1926, George McJunkin was following the trail of some missing cows. The trail led him along the edge of Dead Horse Gulch. McJunkin saw some bones sticking out of the mud on the side of the gulch. Being a curious man, he got off his horse to take a closer look at the bones.

The bones the curious cowboy found were about the size of cow bones. But they were buried 20 feet (6 m) below the surface. This seemed strange to McJunkin. Even stranger was the flint spearhead he pried from a bone with his cattle knife. It had a groove, or channel, on each side and was different from any other spearhead that George McJunkin had ever seen. Why, he asked himself, were the animal bones and the flint spearhead buried so deep?

This also seemed strange to the people whom McJunkin told of his discovery. As the news spread, an expert on animal bones came to have a look. He found that the bones belonged to a kind of bison that had lived in North America during the last years of the Ice Age. The spearhead in one of the bones proved that human beings were living in New Mexico thousands of years ago.

Bones of other ancient bison were dug up at the site of McJunkin's discovery. Several more grooved flint spearheads were found. These discoveries were all made near the small town of Folsom. Therefore whoever made the flint spearhead and killed the bison became known as the **Folsom man.**

The spearhead with the carbon-dated bison bones shows that humans were in New Mexico during the Ice Age.

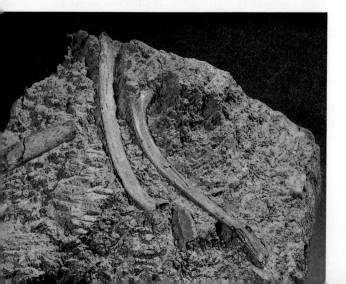

No human bones were found at the site of McJunkin's discovery. Scholars guessed that the bison bones might have come from a single hunt. Perhaps a herd of the ancient bison drank from a pool or lake that no longer exists. The Folsom people might have surprised the bison, killing them on the spot. They might then have cut up the dead animals and carried the meat back to their campsite. This would explain the absence of human bones near the bison bones.

How long in America? How long have people been in America? **Geologists** (jē ol′ ə jists) are scientists who learn about the earth and its history mostly through the study of rocks. They are able to tell much about the Ice Age but nothing that helps a great deal in dating the time that Omuk and his people crossed the land bridge from Asia. Nor are they able to give more than a very rough estimate of the time when the Folsom people lived.

Counting **tree rings** on the ends of logs or the stumps of trees is one way of time dating. Each tree ring shows a year's growth. Another method is counting the layers of soil or gravel laid down at the bottom of what was once a glacial lake. But the best method of time dating makes use of what scientists have discovered about living matter and **radioactivity.**

Carbon dating Scientists have discovered that all living things have a radioactive substance called **carbon 14.** In living matter the amount of carbon 14 is always the same. But when a living thing dies, the carbon 14 in it decreases at a fixed rate. Think of a kettle of water boil-

Over hundreds of years the first Americans and their descendants moved southward.

This picture is a detail from a mural in the George C. Page Museum in Los Angeles, California.

ing dry as the water turns to steam. This is much like the way that once-living matter "boils dry" as it gives off radioactivity.

It is known that a pound of carbon 14 will be reduced by radioactivity to half a pound in 5,568 years. In another 5,568 years it will weigh only a quarter of a pound. Even then it will continue to throw off radioactive rays. Delicate instruments can measure the amount of carbon 14 in anything that has been alive. By carbon dating we know that the bison at Dead Horse Gulch were speared about 10,000 years ago.

In Sandia Cave, near Albuquerque, New Mexico, hunters left the bones of ancient camels, mastodons, and small horses. All these animals have long been extinct. But by using carbon 14 dating, we find that hunters killed the camels, mastodons, and small horses about 25,000 years ago.

No one has ever found conclusive evidence of the date when the first people crossed the Ice Age land bridge from Asia. Probably no one ever will. Nevertheless, that crossing must have been made more than 25,000 years ago according to the evidence found in Sandia Cave. Other finds have pushed the date back even further. For example, charred mammoth bones found on Santa Rosa Island, off the coast of California, date back about 30,000 years.

The southward journey of the Ice Age people did not stop in New Mexico or California. They pushed on into Mexico and South America. In fact, there is proof that humans lived in Fell's Cave, near the southern tip of South America, from 8,000 to 10,000 years ago. If prehistoric people had spread so far across the American continents by that time, their date of entry must have been very early indeed.

CHECKUP

1. Name at least three points that are used as evidence that the first people in America came from Asia.
2. How did these early people meet their daily needs?
3. What did the discovery of Folsom man help to prove?
4. Explain how prehistoric bones are dated.

25

Agriculture Aids Native Americans

VOCABULARY

omnivorous	irrigate
agriculture	pueblo
terrace	drought

A great discovery   Leel the Clever One was the first to notice. First, you put seeds from plants into holes in the ground. Then, when spring came, plants like the ones the seeds came from grew from the earth. It was a great discovery. On this discovery was based the rise of great civilizations in the Americas.

The Ice Age had ended. Animals of the late Ice Age had become extinct. Early Americans had lived by killing these animals and eating their flesh.

Human beings in the Americas might have become extinct, too, had it not been for an important fact. Human beings are **omnivorous**—that is, they can eat plants as well as meat. They do not have to depend on meat alone. In the centuries following the end of the Ice Age, prehistoric Americans turned more and more to plants for food.

The beginning of agriculture   Even during the Ice Age, hunters had probably learned that many roots, berries, and nuts were good to eat. As the large animals vanished, tribes continued to move about. Their members lived by gathering these wild foods and by eating the flesh of such small animals as they were able to trap and kill. This was probably the time that Leel—or someone like her—began the practice of **agriculture**.

Agriculture is the planting of seeds and the care of growing plants. It also involves saving the very best of the plant

On slopes of the Andes Mountains, terraces make it possible to raise crops. Agriculture in the Americas is believed to have started in this region.

seeds to improve the next year's crop. It is believed that agriculture was first practiced in Asia and Africa. Leel and her tribe may have begun this practice in the Americas. They may then have taught it to others. Or clever people in several different tribes may have started agriculture in the Americas at about the same time.

From south to north   Where and when agriculture began in the Americas have been matters for debate. Most scholars now believe, however, that agriculture was first practiced in the Andes Mountain region of South America. This was the land of the people known as the Incas (ing' kəz). Crops were grown there at least 4,000 years ago. Some of the crops that the Incas grew were potatoes, peanuts, kidney beans, peppers, and tomatoes. So Leel the Clever One may have been the ancestor of an Inca.

The earliest movement of people in the Americas was almost certainly from north to south. But evidence shows that the practice of agriculture advanced from south to north. In the places where agriculture had been practiced the longest, the greatest civilizations arose.

The Incas   The Incas were at first a small tribe. By conquering their neighbors, they greatly expanded the region they controlled. They ruled over all the tribes in the area of present-day Peru and Ecuador and parts of Chile, Bolivia, and Argentina.

The Incas worked out their system of farming with great care. They then taught it to the peoples they conquered.

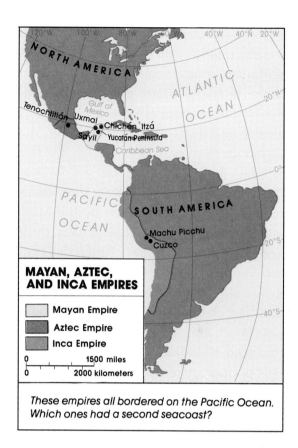

MAYAN, AZTEC, AND INCA EMPIRES

☐ Mayan Empire
◼ Aztec Empire
▨ Inca Empire

0 ——— 1500 miles
0 ——— 2000 kilometers

These empires all bordered on the Pacific Ocean. Which ones had a second seacoast?

On the steep sides of the Andes, the Incas cut **terraces**. On these narrow ledges, cut one above the other, like steps, they planted crops. Water from mountain streams **irrigated**, or supplied water to, the dry soil. By these means the Incas were able to raise food crops.

The Mayas   Farther to the north the Mayas (mä' yəz) lived in the jungles of Central America and southern Mexico. Their civilization flourished from 1,200 to 700 years before Europeans arrived in America. The Mayas built large cities, supported by croplands carved from the jungle. One of their main crops was corn. From this area, the cultivation of corn spread throughout North America and South America.

Corn is a truly American crop. It was unknown in Europe until Columbus, returning from America, reported on "a grain called maiz." **27**

About the year 900 the Mayan civilization declined for unknown reasons. But reminders of its greatness can still be seen in the jungles. There are ruins of temples, pyramids, and other stone buildings constructed during the great years of the Mayan empire.

The Aztecs   By the 1300s the Aztecs (az′ teks) ruled what is now central Mexico. Like the Mayas, the Aztecs built large and beautiful cities. The Aztec capital, Tenochtitlán (tä näch tē tlän′), stood on the site of today's Mexico City. Tenochtitlán had a population of about 300,000. The surrounding farmlands produced abundant food supplies.

The chart on this page shows the approximate number of Indians living in America when Europeans arrived. The largest numbers lived in the areas where agriculture was most advanced. Hunting and food gathering alone could not have supported such large populations. Even in what is now the United States, the most Indians lived where agriculture was well developed.

The Pueblo Indians   About 700 years ago Indian civilization in the American Southwest reached its height. Agriculture had come to this region from the south probably 2,000 years earlier. Still, it took centuries for farming to develop enough to support a large population.

Much of this population lived in **pueblos** (pweb′ lōz)—the Spanish word for "towns." Indian pueblos were, however, more like apartment houses than towns. At the highest point of Indian civilization in the Southwest, there were thousands of pueblos. They ranged from the Mexican state of Chihuahua (chē wä′ wä) in the south to Kansas and Colorado in the north. One of the most famous is called Pueblo Bonito (bə nēt′ ō). It stands empty today in Chaco (chäk′ ō) Canyon in New Mexico.

About 1,000 years ago Pueblo Bonito housed at least 1,500 people. Until a bigger apartment house was built in New York in 1882, Pueblo Bonito and some of the other pueblos were the largest dwellings ever built in North and South America.

What countries had the largest Indian population in 1492?

AN ESTIMATE OF THE AMERICAN INDIAN POPULATION IN 1492

Mexico

Peru

Rest of South America

Central America

United States and Canada

Each figure represents 1 million persons.

At Mesa Verde in Colorado, impressive pueblo ruins can be seen. (37°N/108°W; map, p. 36)

To support so many people, pueblo agriculture had to be well developed. Farmers raised corn, squash, and beans. They looked upon these vegetables as gifts from the gods they worshipped. They had no way of knowing what Leel the Clever One—or someone like her—had done thousands of years before and thousands of miles to the south.

Like farmers to the south, the Pueblo Indians irrigated their crops with water brought from distant streams. They raised cotton, too. From its fibers, cloth was woven and decorated with a variety of fancy designs.

At Mesa Verde (mā′ sə verd′ ē), in southwestern Colorado, pueblos were built along the sides of steep cliffs. Some of these dwellings were several stories high. They were probably built along the sides of cliffs as a means of protection from enemies.

Most pueblos in the Southwest were abandoned long before Europeans came to America. Invaders from the north may have driven the peaceful Pueblo Indians from their towns. Or changes in climate may have caused a **drought**, that is, a long period of dry weather. A lengthy drought could have hurt farming to the point of disaster. If so, people would have had to leave the pueblos to find other sources of food. And with the scattering, the Pueblo civilization would have declined.

CHECKUP

1. After the Ice Age ended, how did the source of food supplies change?
2. Where did agriculture in the Americas most likely originate? What were some of the crops that were grown?
3. Describe three early American civilizations south of the present-day United States.
4. What were the main features of the Pueblo Indian civilization?

The ruins shown above are inside Mesa Verde National Park and are viewed by thousands of tourists yearly.

The Mound Builders

A pile of earth   Aru the Strong carried the heavy earth-filled basket to the top of the ramp. After emptying the basket, he trod on the soil with his bare feet, making it solid. Aru did the same thing many times each day. He did it day after day, year after year. Was he a slave captured from a neighboring tribe? Was he a paid worker? Or did he carry the baskets as part of his religious duties?

No one knows exactly why Aru did this work. And yet we know what he was doing. He was helping to build a large earthen mound.

A unique civilization   The civilizations of the Incas, the Mayas, and the Aztecs flourished in areas south of what is now the United States. Still, within the area of the present-day United States, there were thriving native civilizations. You have already learned about the Pueblo Indians. Hundreds of miles to the east, another thriving civilization was that of the **Mound Builders**. This civilization developed in stages. Each stage was more advanced than the one that came before it.

Some Europeans saw at first hand the glories of the Aztec civilization. The high level of Inca civilization is also a matter of historical record. But no European ever saw the Mound Builders at the high point of their civilization. And they left no written records. They left only mounds such as Aru the Strong helped to build.

Mysterious mounds   When settlers moved into the river valleys of the United States in the eighteenth and nineteenth centuries, they saw in many of the valleys strange mounds of earth. Farmers and others who were puzzled by these piles of earth dug into them. One person who wondered about the mounds and the people who built them was Thomas Jefferson, later our third President. He **excavated**, or dug into, a mound on his Virginia farm.

Unlike Jefferson, most diggers were interested only in collecting **artifacts** from the mounds. Artifacts are objects that people have made. Among these objects are necklaces, tools, and pottery. Only a few of the diggers wondered why the mounds were built. But as time went on, the mysterious mounds attracted the attention of scholars.

In 1890 a group of scholars working for the Smithsonian Institution published a report on the mounds. The Smithsonian Institution, in Washington, D.C., is widely known for the scientific research it carries on. Its report on mounds was based on 10 years of study. The report described vast numbers of mounds in an area extending from Ontario, Canada, southward to the Gulf Coast of Florida, Mississippi, and Louisiana. The mounds are especially numerous in the Ohio and Mississippi river valleys. (See the map on page 36.) In the states of Illinois and Ohio, thousands of mounds have been counted.

Like Omuk and Amah (page 20) and Leel (page 26), Aru the Strong is an imaginary individual. But there were thousands of people whose names are not known who did the work attributed to Aru.

The Great Serpent Mound in Ohio takes the form of a snake. (39°N/84°W; map, p. 36)

Types of mounds   These mounds, built by several groups over hundreds of years, are of different types. The type found most often is the small round **burial mound.** These mounds nearly always contain skeletons and objects buried with them. Another numerous type is the **temple mound.** It is flat on top but sometimes has terraced sides. Clearly this kind of mound is used as a foundation for a wooden building or temple.

There are several other types of mounds besides the two main ones. **Geometric mounds** were built in the form of circles, squares, or parallel lines. Sometimes these geometric mounds enclose an area of 100 acres (40 ha) or more.

The **effigy mounds** are especially interesting. An effigy mound is built in the shape of a bird, snake, animal, or human being. The state of Wisconsin has many effigy mounds, and some can be seen in Indiana, Ohio, and other states. The Great Serpent Mound in southern Ohio and the Opossum Mound in Tennessee are famous effigy mounds.

The Mound Builders worked with a purpose. They had a reason for building each mound. Some experts believe that the custom of mound building came from the south, as did agriculture. There is some resemblance between the earthen temple mounds and the pyramids of the Mayas and Aztecs.

Tribes were building mounds at different times in different places. The years A.D. 1 to A.D. 1000 were a time of great building activity. Artifacts found in some of the mounds of those years showed that a lively trade took place

The Banjo-Playing Collector

In the nineteenth century, Cyrus Moore made a fortune in the cotton business. Having plenty of money, he was able to pursue his hobby of collecting Mound Builder treasures. Each winter Cyrus Moore had a houseboat built to order in either St. Louis or Cincinnati. Each spring he moved aboard his new boat with a crew of strong-armed diggers. In summer, Moore's houseboat was towed or floated along the banks of the Mississippi and its tributaries.

There were thousands of mounds near these rivers. Moore's diggers had plenty of sites for their busy shovels. The pottery, tools, ornaments, and other objects they found were cleaned and brought aboard the houseboat. While the diggers worked, Cyrus Moore sat on deck in a special chair, playing his banjo. He always played a lively tune when his men found something special.

Each fall the summer's collection was unloaded at New Orleans. Then the houseboat was sold. The next spring Moore and his crew went north to take over another new houseboat. Then they repeated the process of the previous summer. In this way Cyrus Moore built up a great collection. It was the envy of other collectors. Oddly enough, Moore displayed little curiosity about the

This pottery jar with handles representing the heads of birds came from a mound near a creek in the northwestern part of Florida.

Mound Builders or what had happened to them. He was mostly interested in collecting objects buried in their mounds—that, and playing his banjo.

among well-to-do tribes of Mound Builders. Among the materials and objects found in the mounds are copper from the Lake Superior region, shells from both the Atlantic and Gulf of Mexico coasts, and grizzly bear teeth from the area of the Rocky Mountains.

Cahokia City   Perhaps the most remarkable work of the Mound Builders stands today near Collinsville, Illinois, about 15 miles (24 km) east of St. Louis. Its name is Cahokia (kə hō′ kē ə) Mounds State Historic Site. It could just as well be called Cahokia City. The site includes a great number of different mounds. They were built by a skilled Indian civilization that mysteriously disappeared about 500 years ago.

Cahokia Mounds is known as the only prehistoric Indian city north of Mexico. At its height it had a population of up to 40,000 people. Probably 30,000 more Mound Builders lived in villages nearby.

At Cahokia Mounds the main mound is a flat-topped pyramid 1,080 feet (330 m)

By 1699, when French settlers came to southern Illinois, the population of Cahokia Mounds had dropped at about 2,000.

long, 710 feet (216 m) wide, and 100 feet (30 m) high. It covers 14 acres (6 ha). It is believed to have held a massive wooden building, used for religious purposes. It is known today as Monks Mound.

Surrounding Monks Mound are nearly 100 burial mounds. At the center of this old cemetery is the grave of a prominent ruler. Buried with him were attendants meant to serve him in the next world. Around the site of the Cahokia Mounds are the traces of a stockade that required 50,000 logs.

Imagine the length of time and the many baskets of earth it took to build the Cahokia Mounds! Mound Builders knew nothing about wheels, so they worked without wagons or wheelbarrows. They had no beasts of burden to haul earth from many miles away. All they had was the labor of thousands of persons like Aru the Strong.

Why did the custom of mound building die out? What happened to the highly organized tribes of Mound Builders? No one knows for certain. Perhaps they suffered the fate of other great civilizations of the past. Savage, warlike people have time and again invaded the lands of more civilized people and have overthrown them. This may have been what happened to the Mound Builders.

CHECKUP

1. Why do we know so little about the Mound Builders' civilization?
2. Describe four types of mounds.
3. Why are the Cahokia Mounds so remarkable? What knowledge would have made the Mound Builders' work easier?
4. What might have caused the Mound Builders' civilization to decline and finally disappear?

Environment Shapes the Way of Life

> **VOCABULARY**
>
> | | |
> |---|---|
> | culture | Western |
> | environment | civilization |
> | tepee | technology |
> | llama | |

Salmon bones Salma the Priest Woman buried the salmon bones carefully. It was her religious duty to do so. Salma was a member of the Makah (mä′ kä) tribe. The Makahs lived along the coast of what is now the state of Washington. The Pacific Ocean and the rivers that run into it made this good country for fishing.

Fishing for salmon and halibut was important to the Makahs. It touched upon every aspect of their **culture**. (The word *culture* means "the way of life of a people.") Salmon became almost sacred to the Indians of the Pacific Northwest. That is why Salma treated the bones of the fish so respectfully.

Many cultures When Europeans first came to America, there were at least 200 different Indian tribes in the territory that would become the United States. Each tribe had a distinctive culture that set it apart from other tribal groups.

Some tribes, however, shared certain ways of doing things with other tribes in the same area. This was because nearby tribes shared the same **environment**. *Environment* means "everything in an area —land, water, plants, animals, and climate." These physical surroundings are

33

important to any group. This is especially true of the Indians because they had few means of changing their physical surroundings.

The environment of the Makahs favored fishing, so salmon became an important part of their lives. In fact, *salmon* was the word for "fish" among several of the Indian tribes of the Northwest. In the dry Southwest, of course, fishing played little or no part in the lives of the tribes living there. You learned earlier in this chapter how the Pueblo Indians lived in their dry region.

Growing crops   At the time that Europeans came, most North American Indians knew how to grow a few crops. Corn, squash, and beans were the most common. But crops varied, depending on the climate where a tribe lived. Indians of the Southwest, for example, could grow cotton. In the Southeast, tobacco was grown.

Indians worked out ways to grow better crops. Eastern Indians used dead fish as fertilizer when planting corn or beans.

As a defense measure, eastern Indians often put up fences around their villages.

The Pueblo Indians and other tribes in the dry Southwest knew how to irrigate their fields.

Most Indian tribes stayed in the same place for only a few years. There was much moving about. A tribe suffering from unusual weather conditions would move to escape from drought, or too much rain or cold. Also, tribes would have to move if their ways of farming wore out the soil. Occasionally a tribe would lose its crops because of raids by stronger, more aggressive Indians. This might force them to move to a safer place.

Kinds of homes   Because certain Indian tribes often moved, they seldom built permanent homes. An exception is the pueblos, which you learned about earlier. Even though most pueblos were abandoned by the time the first Europeans came to America, a few are still used. People have lived in Oraibi (ō rī′ bē), a pueblo in Arizona, for more than 800 years. About 600 people still live there. Oraibi is thought to be the oldest continuously inhabited community in the United States.

In the Pacific Northwest, cedar trees were plentiful. So Indians there built their shelters of cedar boards or logs. They were fitted or tied together because the Indians had no metal nails.

In the wooded lands of the Northeast and the Great Lakes region, lodges were made from logs, branches, and the bark of trees. Deer hides might have been stretched over cracks to keep out the winter cold.

The area bordering the Gulf of Mexico had a hot, humid climate. Indians there

Plains Indians sometimes used dogs to draw loads. Two trailing poles were attached to the dog. Across the poles was placed a platform that carried the load.

carry. To make such shelters the women stitched buffalo hides together. Then they stretched the hides over a framework of poles. This form of dwelling was called a **tepee.**

The women not only provided the basic dwelling but also did the cooking. They prepared rich buffalo meat, using buffalo stomachs as cooking pots. To serve the food, they used ladles and spoons made from buffalo horns.

With the coming of Europeans to America, the buffalo became even more important in the lives of the Plains Indians. The use of horses and guns brought to America by the Europeans made buffalo hunting much easier. In later years the Plains Indians became almost totally dependent on the buffalo.

usually built their houses without walls so cooling breezes could enter. Poles supported roofs of wood, bark, thatch, or reeds.

Culture of the Plains Indians   At first, Indians living on the western plains hunted and farmed in much the same way as Indians to the east and south. But their culture changed as buffalo herds increased in numbers. The Indians trailed the herds and cleverly invented ways to bring down the big animals. Sometimes the Indians surrounded a herd and drove it over a cliff. At other times, a hunter wrapped himself in a buffalo skin and crept close enough to the herd to kill one or more animals with a bow and arrows.

Following the herds made it necessary to have shelters that were light and easy to

Culture of the eastern Indians   In the eastern region also, the Indians carried on farming. They cleared trees to make fields where they raised beans, corn, pumpkins, and squash. They fished in the streams, and those who lived near the ocean gathered shellfish.

The eastern Indians hunted deer. They ate venison, the meat of the deer. They made the hides into clothing and the antlers into arrow points. But they never became as dependent on deer as the Plains Indians became on buffalo. Yet, like the Plains Indians, the eastern Indians made the fullest possible use of the animals and natural materials of their environment.

What Indians lacked   Indians in the Americas had made different kinds of adjustments before the coming of the Europeans. Some tribes had risen to high

It has been said that the Plains Indians used every part of the buffalo except its bellow! For example, buffalo intestines became

bowstrings, bones were used as clubs, and hoofs were made into glue.

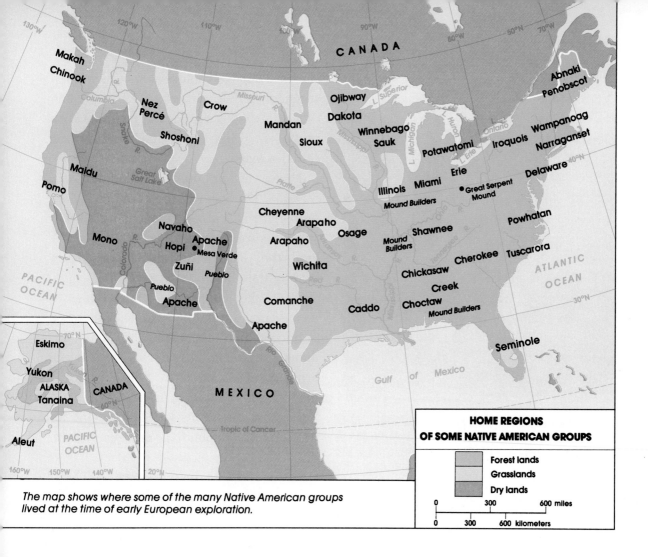

The map shows where some of the many Native American groups lived at the time of early European exploration.

HOME REGIONS OF SOME NATIVE AMERICAN GROUPS

Forest lands
Grasslands
Dry lands

0   300   600 miles

0   300   600 kilometers

levels of civilization. Others had remained at lower levels.

However, none of the tribes in early America had developed a written language. What they knew was passed on by word of mouth. The wheel was not known to the Native Americans. Nor was the secret of exploding gunpowder. Thus, Indians had no guns.

Except for the Incas, Indians lacked large animals for transportation or use as beasts of burden. In the Andes Mountains, the Incas had trained wild **llamas**. These animals were probably descendants of prehistoric camels. Like the small horses that once roamed the plains of North America, the camels had become extinct. But llamas were much less useful than the horses, oxen, and mules brought to America by the Europeans.

What Indians had   Still, the Indians had the knowledge and skills to enable them to survive in the Americas. Outsiders coming to these continents at first had to learn from the Indians.

American Indians had great respect for nature. Their religions differed from tribe to tribe, from culture to culture. But all the religions showed in many ways the Indians' respect for the natural wonders they saw about them.

36   Though tribes in early America had no written language, some of them kept records by drawing pictures on bark or animal skins.

American Indians had a long history in what came to be called the New World. Of course, to the Indians it was really a very old world. They had developed complex civilizations that had adapted to various environments in the Americas. Some of these civilizations, to be sure, had declined or vanished entirely. But so had high civilizations elsewhere.

A clash of civilizations   In Europe a new kind of civilization had grown up by the fifteenth century. It was a rising civilization, ready to expand its influence. This **Western civilization**, as it has been called, put a high value on **technology** (tek nol′ ə jē). Technology is the amount of scientific knowledge and the kinds of tools a people have. Some of this technology had been borrowed from cultures in Africa and Asia. Some had been invented or improved by Europeans.

Whatever the sources of technology, Western civilization was far more advanced than the Indian cultures of the Americas. In any conflict between the Indians and the European settlers, the Europeans' technology would give them a big advantage. In basic values, however, Indian civilizations were at least an even match for Western civilization.

Indian influences   Indeed, today there are many parts of the Americas showing a blend of Western and Indian civilizations. Thousands of names for cities, states, lakes, mountains, and rivers throughout the Americas are taken from Indian languages. Half the states in our nation have Indian names. Americans daily use such Indian words as *squash, to-*

bacco, chipmunk, skunk, moose, pecan, woodchuck, and *toboggan.* Phrases such as "walking Indian file" and "enjoying Indian summer" are frequently heard.

In spite of Western civilization's superior technology, the first explorers and European colonists had to learn from the Indians. Indians taught them how to plant, fish, and hunt in the Americas. Indian medicine men and women often were called on to doctor pioneer colonists when no white physicians were available. The Indian knowledge of herbs and plants as medicines was made use of by grateful pioneers.

Today we are still making use of Indian knowledge and skills. Indian jewelry designs are popular. Boy Scouts and Girl Scouts learn Indian woodcraft. Today's conservation movements owe much to Indian ideas of the relationship between human beings and nature. Books, movies, and television make use of Indian themes. Unfortunately, the way Indian history, culture, and characters are portrayed is often inaccurate. Sometimes it seems as if Western civilization overwhelmed the Indians. Actually, there is evidence all around us to show that the civilization of the Native Americans has had a lasting influence.

CHECKUP

1. In what ways did environment affect the culture of the North American Indians?
2. What development changed the way of life of the Indians on the western plains?
3. What did Indian civilizations lack in their clash with Western civilization?
4. What were the strengths of Indian cultures? What contributions have been made by Indians to modern American life?

Ask: What place-names in our state are of Indian origin? As the class responds, list the names on the chalkboard.

KEY FACTS

1. The first people on the American continents probably came from Asia on a land bridge thousands of years ago.

2. Carbon dating has proved to be the best method of finding out when ancient peoples were living in the Americas.

3. Agricultural skills to support large populations and complex civilizations in the Americas probably originated in the Andes region of South America and moved north.

4. The civilizations of the Pueblo Indians and the Mound Builders were among the more advanced of tribes living in what is now the United States.

5. A tribe's environment shaped its culture.

VOCABULARY QUIZ

On a separate sheet of paper, write **T** if the statement is true. Write **F** if it is false. If the statement is false, replace the underlined word or words to make the statement true.

T 1. The Ice Age bridge between Siberia and Alaska is now covered by water known as the Bering Strait.

T 2. A geologist is an expert in studying rocks.

F 3. Every living thing has a radioactive substance called earth beams. **carbon 14**

T 4. Human beings are omniverous.

F 5. The Aztecs lived in Peru. **Mexico**

F 6. In 1890 the Smithsonian Institution made a report on agriculture. **Indian mounds**

F 7. The Cahokia Mounds are an ancient Indian site in New Mexico. **Illinois**

F 8. An Indian tribe's culture can best be described as its ability to enjoy music. **way of life**

T 9. The wheel was unknown to America's prehistoric Indians.

F 10. Planting seeds and taking care of growing plants is known as technology. **agriculture**

REVIEW QUESTIONS

1. What significant fact, event, or achievement is associated with each of the following imaginary characters in this chapter?

a. Omuk the Leader
b. Leel the Clever One
c. Aru the Strong
d. Salma the Priest Woman

2. How have scientists contributed to the study of ancient human life in America?

3. Why has agriculture been important to the rise of concentrated populations and complex civilizations on the continents of North America and South America.

4. In what different ways did environment influence the way of life for the Pueblo Indians and Indians of the Northeast?

ACTIVITIES

1. American Indians had no written language using letters in an alphabet to make words as we do today. However, Indians communicated through pictures and symbols and in some cases through sign language. Make a sentence using words, and then try to communicate the same thought by using pictures.

2. Write an account of the way in which carbon dating might be used to learn how long ago a group of people occupied a cave.

3. Is there a dig in your area where scholars are trying to find objects that will let them know more about people who lived there long ago? If so, find out what has been found there, if possible, by actually making a visit to the dig.

USING A TABLE

NATIVE AMERICAN POPULATION

A table can be used to present many facts in a small space. The table below shows the estimated Native American, or Indian, population north of Mexico in the years when various regions were explored.

SKILLS PRACTICE

Using the table, answer the following questions on a sheet of paper.

1. In which area was the largest estimated Native American population? California

2. What was the estimated population of the Gulf States area in 1650? 114,400

3. What states are included, wholly or in part, in the Columbia River basin? Wash., Ore., Idaho

4. In what year were estimates of population made for New Mexico and Arizona? 1680

5. What area now in the United States had the smallest population? Central mountain

6. Was the population larger on the Northern Plains or the Southern Plains? Northern

7. In what area is Utah? Central mountain

8. When were estimates made in Alaska? 1740

NATIVE AMERICAN POPULATION NORTH OF MEXICO		
Area	Date	Estimated population
North Atlantic New England, New York, New Jersey, Pennsylvania	1600	55,600
South Atlantic Delaware, Maryland, Virginia, West Virginia, the Carolinas except Cherokee country	1600	52,200
Gulf States Georgia, Florida, Alabama, Mississippi, Louisiana, Arkansas, Tennessee, Cherokee country	1650	114,400
Central states Ohio Valley from Alleghenies to Mississippi; Chippewa in Canada	1650	75,300
The Plains Canada to Gulf		
Northern	1780	100,800
Southern	1690	41,000
Columbia River basin Washington, most of Oregon, northern half of Idaho	1780	89,300
California	1769	260,000
Central mountain Nevada, Utah, parts of surrounding states	1845	19,300
New Mexico and Arizona	1680	72,000
British America Eastern Canada, central Canada, British Columbia	1600–1780	190,950
Alaska	1740	72,600
Greenland	1721	10,000
Total		1,153,450

Outsiders Explore and Settle in America

Columbus Leads the Way

┌─VOCABULARY─────────────┐
Far East	Vinland
Indies	colony
Vikings	New World
└────────────────────────┘

A man from Genoa   It was early in the morning of Friday, October 12, 1492. Rodrigo de Triana (rod rē′gō də trē än′-ə) stood as lookout on the *Pinta*. The *Pinta*, the *Niña*, and the *Santa Maria* were the three ships in a tiny fleet commanded by Christopher Columbus. Each ship was less than 100 feet (30 m) in length.

Christopher Columbus was born in the old seaside city of Genoa (jen′ ō ə), Italy, in 1451. His father and his grandfather were weavers of woolen cloth. His mother was a weaver's daughter. But Columbus chose to go to sea.

Christopher Columbus had two brothers. Bartholomew (bär thol′ ə myü), the older, was tough, skillful, and loyal. He became a partner in the project that resulted in Columbus's voyages to America. The other brother was named Diego (dē ā′ gō). Though willing enough, Diego failed as a sailor and colonist in the New World. Later he became a priest.

The brothers had a sister named Bianchinetta (byäng′ kē net′ ə). She married a wine merchant in Genoa. Little more is known of Bianchinetta. In those days women had little choice to be anything other than a wife and mother, or perhaps a member of a religious order.

A plan for reaching the Indies   When Christopher Columbus was 25, he sailed with a fleet of merchant ships from the port of Genoa. Off the coast of Portugal, several French and Portuguese warships attacked the merchant vessels. They sank the ship on which Columbus was sailing. He saved himself by grabbing a large oar. Hanging onto it, he floated to the coast of Portugal, 6 miles (10 km) away.

Columbus stayed in Portugal for several years. There he sailed with and talked to many experienced sailors. At that time Europeans were talking of finding a water route to the **Far East.** There was a great demand in Europe for the silks, spices, and other products of eastern Asia. Trade with the Far East by way of land routes had proved to be slow, costly, and dangerous. A water route would be much better.

Some of the sailors that Columbus met talked of reaching Asia by sailing south from Portugal and then east around Africa. In this way they hoped to reach the rich Asian islands called the **Indies.**

Gradually Columbus formed another plan. Like other thoughtful men of the

Several countries in the Americas have issued postage stamps honoring Columbus.

The Portuguese attempt to find a route to the Indies by sailing south along Africa and then east started to meet with success with the voyage in 1488 of Bartholomeu Dias around the southern tip of Africa. Dias called it the Cape of Storms, but the Portuguese king renamed it the Cape of Good Hope.

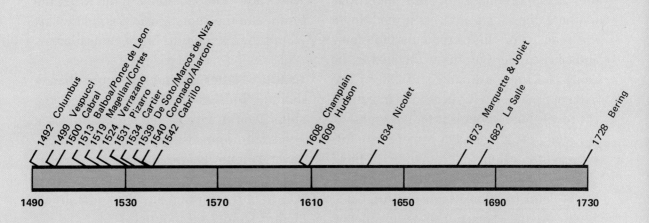

The United States stamp shown above was one of a set of 16 issued in 1892 to mark the 400th anniversary of Columbus's voyage of discovery. At that time, a full set cost $15.34. Today a full set in unused condition is priced at more than $17,000.

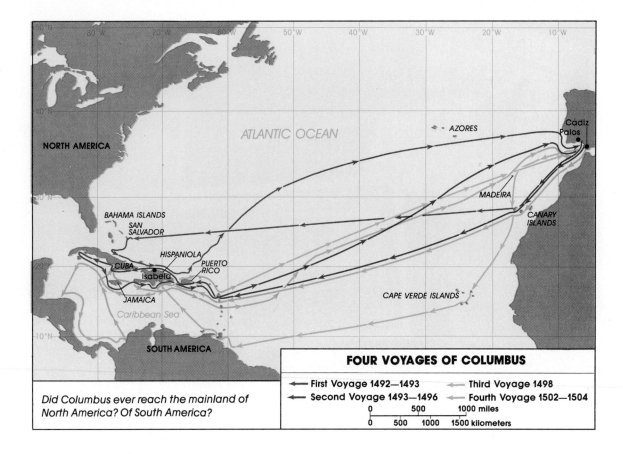

FOUR VOYAGES OF COLUMBUS

← First Voyage 1492—1493   ← Third Voyage 1498

← Second Voyage 1493—1496   ← Fourth Voyage 1502—1504

| 0 | 500 | 1000 miles |

| 0 | 500 | 1000 | 1500 kilometers |

Did Columbus ever reach the mainland of North America? Of South America?

time, he believed the world was round. If so, Columbus reasoned, he could reach the Indies by sailing west from Europe.

With the help of his brother Bartholomew, Christopher Columbus presented his plan to the king of Portugal. Much to the disappointment of the ambitious brothers, the king's advisers turned down the plan. For this reason Bartholomew and Christopher Columbus traveled to the court of King Ferdinand and Queen Isabella of Spain. They succeeded in getting approval there, though it took 6 years.

Finally the king and queen of Spain furnished the Columbus brothers with three ships. The little fleet sailed from the harbor of Palos (pä' lōs), Spain, on August 3, 1492. At the Canary Islands, about 800 miles (1,480 km) southwest of Spain, the ships made their first stop. The crews rested there and made needed repairs on their ships. They took on supplies for a long voyage before lifting anchor once more. This time they sailed directly westward. On September 9 the *Niña*, the *Pinta*, and the *Santa Maria* passed the last island then known to European sailors.

Land!   After sailing for more than a month, Rodrigo de Triana doubted the ships would ever reach land. But as a good sailor, he still kept watch carefully. Several hours before sunrise on October 12, he thought he saw something like a white cliff shining in the moonlight. "Land! Land!" he shouted.

Have pupils find the Canary Islands on the world map on pages 714–715.

Within a few minutes the captain of the *Pinta* also saw the land. He ordered a cannon fired as a signal that land had been sighted. As the three ships sailed closer together, Columbus called from the *Santa Maria* that the *Pinta* had won the prize as the first to sight land.

The rising sun clearly revealed an island in the distance. When Columbus went ashore he knelt down to kiss the soil. With tears of joy in his eyes, he named the island San Salvador, Spanish for "Holy Savior."

The West Indies   Columbus and his men stayed for a few months in the islands they had discovered. They believed these were the rich Indies near the coast of Asia. For this reason Columbus called the people there Indians.

After his first voyage Columbus sailed west from Spain three more times. On his third trip across the Atlantic, he began to suspect he had discovered a new continent. To this day, however, the islands he explored are known as the West Indies. Columbus also reached the coast of South America. However, he never saw any part of the mainland of what is now the United States.

Family fortunes   Columbus had an agreement with the Spanish rulers and businessmen who backed his first voyage. He was to be made admiral and also governor of the islands and continents he might discover. Moreover, these titles were to pass to his elder son and the son's heirs. In addition Christopher Columbus was to receive 10 percent of the profits from "pearls, precious stones, gold, silver, spices, and all other things" obtained as the result of his discoveries.

Had things worked out differently, Christopher Columbus might have been the richest man in the world. Instead he never received anything close to the 10 percent promised him. Disappointment, poverty, and ill health clouded his last years. He died in 1506, a bitter man.

Why we honor Columbus   Why do we honor Columbus as the discoverer of America? As you read in the last chapter, the first people to reach America were probably those who came from Asia by way of the Bering Strait land bridge. Nor was Columbus even the first European to reach America. Centuries before Columbus sailed, the **Vikings** had visited the North Atlantic islands of Iceland and Greenland. The Vikings were a bold, seafaring people who came from what are today the countries of Norway, Sweden, and Denmark. According to legends a Viking named Bjarni Herjulfson (byär'-nə hėr' yülf sən) set out for a small Viking settlement in Greenland but was blown off course. The storm blew his ship to a coast west of Greenland. In time he got back to Greenland with the exciting news of a land to the west.

A few years later another Viking, Leif Ericson (lāv er' ik sən), accidentally reached this new land. He and his crew spent a winter there. They called it **Vinland** ("land of vines") because of the wild grapes they found there. Still later, other Vikings tried to found a **colony** in Vinland. A colony is a settlement that is founded far away from the country that governs it.

The prize that Columbus awarded the *Pinta* as the first ship to sight land was 5,000 maravedis. A maravedi was a copper coin used in Spain. Today it would be worth less than a cent, but its purchasing power then was much greater. An ordinary seaman in Columbus's crew was paid 22 maravedis a day.   **43**

In a boat like this, Vikings crossed the Atlantic.

The Vinland colony was probably along the coast of New England or Canada. However, it was short-lived. In time even the Greenland colony of the Vikings was abandoned. The Viking discoveries were almost forgotten. But the voyage of Columbus in 1492 led directly to the exploration and colonization of the New World. That is why Columbus, even though others came before him, is called the discoverer of America.

Other early explorers   Soon after Columbus's third voyage, Pedro Cabral (kä-bräl′), a Portuguese sea captain, set out on a voyage down the coast of Africa. After storms blew his ship far off course, he landed on the coast of South America. Cabral claimed for Portugal the land we now call Brazil.

It was, however, the Spanish who led the way in exploring the mainland of the American continents. In 1513, Vasco Nuñez de Balboa (väs′ cō nü′ nyeth də bal bō′ ə) crossed the Isthmus of Panama. He became the first European to see the

Pacific Ocean from the shores of the New World. In the same year, Juan Ponce de Leon (wän pon′ sə dā lā on′) discovered the peninsula he named Florida.

These and other explorers soon suspected there was more land in the New World than anyone had first realized. Still they hoped there was a way around or through this land. Such a passage would make it possible to reach Asia by sailing west, as Columbus had believed.

In 1519 the Spanish King sent Ferdinand Magellan (mə jel′ ən) to look for a passage through the newly discovered lands. Magellan was Portuguese but had enlisted in the service of Spain. After crossing the Atlantic in five ships, Magellan's expedition spent the winter on the coast of South America. One ship was lost in a storm, but the other four sailed south in the spring. At the southern end of South America, they entered the strait that today bears Magellan's name.

In the stormy strait the crew of one ship seized control of the vessel and headed back to Spain. The other three ships sailed into the ocean that Magellan named the Pacific because it seemed so calm. For months they sailed across this broad ocean. Food supplies ran out, forcing the men to eat rats and to chew pieces of leather. At last they reached a group of islands, later named the Philippines for King Philip of Spain. On one of these islands Magellan was killed when he took part in a battle between rival Filipino groups.

The first voyage around the world
With the death of its commander, this voyage might have ended in the Philip-

During the 1960s the remains of a Viking settlement were discovered at L'Anse aux Meadows on the coast of Newfoundland.

Have pupils research the story of the fountain of youth.

AMERICA

Christopher Columbus not only lost the chance to become the richest man in the world—the lands to which he led the way were named for someone else.

Amerigo Vespucci (ä mə-rē′ gə ves pü′ chə) was a skillful navigator born in Florence, Italy. He took part in several Spanish and Portuguese voyages to the New World. In letters and other writings, he claimed to have been a member of an expedition that in 1499 discovered the mainland of a continent.

Martin Waldseemuller (vält zā mül′ ər), a German geographer and mapmaker, published some of Amerigo Vespucci's accounts in 1507. Along with the accounts Waldseemuller printed 12 pages of maps with the name "America" spread across each page. The maps showed all the discoveries made in the New World up to that time. Waldseemuller called the New World "the fourth continent," suggesting it be named for Amerigo Vespucci because he had discovered it.

Not many people agreed with Waldseemuller about the discovery. But the book and Waldseemuller's maps became so popular that people got into the habit of calling the New World "America."

Still the name of Columbus is remembered in a number of ways in the lands he discovered. The republic of Colombia in South America is named for him. Twenty-seven of the United States have counties, towns, or cities named Columbus or Columbia.

The District of Columbia is the site of our nation's capital. The mighty Columbia River drains a good part of the Pacific Northwest.

None of the United States celebrates an Amerigo Vespucci Day, but 40 states make Columbus Day a legal holiday. So Christopher Columbus is far from being forgotten as the European discoverer of America.

pines. But it did not. One ship, the *Victoria*, proceeded south, picked up a cargo of spices in the Indies, and then sailed westward across the Indian Ocean. After passing the Cape of Good Hope, at the southern tip of Africa, the ship turned north into the Atlantic. <u>In 1522 it reached Spain, 3 years after it set sail. The *Victoria* was the first ship to sail around the world.</u>

The voyage proved it was possible to reach Asia by sailing west from Europe. Even so, very few explorers wanted to suffer the hardships of such a lengthy voyage. In the years that followed, they devoted their attention to exploring and colonizing the American continents.

CHECKUP

1. What was the goal of Christopher Columbus on his famous voyage across the Atlantic?
2. How did the Native Americans come to be called Indians?
3. Since Columbus was not the first person to reach America, why is he called its discoverer? Who else might also be called America's discoverers?
4. Tell briefly what each of the following did in the era of exploration: Cabral, Balboa, Ponce de Leon, Magellan.

Have pupils trace on a globe the route followed by the *Victoria* on its record-breaking voyage.

The Spanish explorers have become known as the conquistadores, or conquerers. They were driven to explore by the hope of finding riches, the desire to win glory for themselves and their country, and, in some cases, the wish to Christianize the Indians. These goals are sometimes summarized as gold, glory, and God.

Spain's Empire in the New World

Spaniards conquer Aztecs and Incas
Columbus started Spain's first colony on the West Indian island of Hispaniola. Using this and other island bases, Spanish explorers and colonizers sailed to the mainland of North and South America. Within 100 years after Columbus's first voyage, Spaniards had explored, conquered, and colonized a great **empire** in the Americas. An empire is made up of the territories and peoples under the control of a powerful country.

Hernando Cortes (kôr tez') had learned to command troops in the Spanish conquest of the West Indies. In 1519 this Spanish explorer led an expedition to Mexico. It consisted of 600 men with 17 horses and 10 cannons. The Spaniards landed near present-day Vera Cruz and moved inland into the great empire of the Aztecs. The Spaniards' goals were to claim land for Spain, to seek gold and other treasure, and to develop trade.

The Spanish horses amazed the Aztecs. They had never before seen anything so large and swift. At first the Aztecs treated Cortes and his men like gods. But Cortes ordered the seizure of Montezuma (mon tē zü' mə), the Aztec ruler. Then Cortes forced the Indians to hand over their gold and silver ornaments. Even more, he made them dig new supplies of precious metals from deep mines.

Finally the Aztecs rebelled and drove the Spaniards from their capital city. But the Aztecs' victory was only temporary. More troops from the West Indies came to Cortes's aid, as did thousands of Indians who had been conquered by the Aztecs and who hated them. In the fighting that followed, Montezuma was killed, and the Spaniards again took the Aztec capital.

With the Aztec empire under his control, Cortes directed further conquests in Mexico. That land became one of the richest parts of Spain's empire in the New World. Later it became the base from which Spanish explorers moved north into what is now the United States.

In South America, another Spaniard, Francisco Pizarro (pə zär' ō), conquered the Inca empire of Peru. Pizarro commanded fewer than 200 men. Yet the Spaniards, mounted on horses and armed with swords and guns, attacked and killed thousands of Incas. Pizarro then seized the Incas' gold and silver. Most of these precious metals went into the royal treasury of Spain.

The ruthless plundering of the Aztec and Inca empires destroyed two powerful Native-American civilizations. With the flow of wealth from America, Spain became the richest and most powerful country in Europe for more than a century. The richest parts of Spain's New World empire lay in the West Indies, Mexico, and Peru. However, Spaniards also explored and colonized several parts of what is now the United States.

De Soto's march to the Mississippi
Another Spaniard, Hernando de Soto, led an expedition that landed in Florida

The ruins of Machu Picchu, high in the Andes of Peru, recall the days of the Inca empire. (13°S/73°W; map, p. 27)

in 1539. For 4 years the expedition marched through the wilderness. From Florida it moved north into present-day Georgia and the Carolinas. In 1541 the Spaniards reached the Mississippi River at a point south of the present location of Memphis, Tennessee.

De Soto died of fever while his expedition was camped on the banks of the Mississippi. One of his lieutenants led the surviving men west to the Brazos River in what is now Texas and then back to the Mississippi. After building boats and rafts, the Spaniards floated down the Mississippi to the Gulf of Mexico.

De Soto's expedition failed to find gold or any other wealth. Nearly half of the 600 Spanish soldiers died in the wilderness. However, the expedition made it possible for Spain to add the southeastern part of what is now the United States to the Spanish empire.

The search for the "golden cities" Tales of "golden cities" led Spanish explorers to the mountains, plains, and deserts of the American Southwest. Francisco Coronado entered this region in 1540 with a colorful army of 300 Spaniards and 1,300 friendly Indians.

Francisco Coronado and his men saw Indians living in pueblos. But these were not the golden cities they sought. To aid in the search, the expedition split up.

One group became the first Europeans to see the Grand Canyon of the Colorado River. Coronado himself led another group as far north as present-day Kansas and Nebraska. All he saw were grass-covered plains and large herds of buffalo, which he called "cows."

In disappointment Coronado led his expedition back to Mexico. He reported to the governor, "There is not any gold nor any other metal in all that country." For the next 60 years no one except missionaries entered the lands Coronado had explored. They brought Christianity to the Indians, who were gathered into communities called **missions.** In 1609 Spaniards started the city of Santa Fe, in the Rio Grande valley of what is now northern New Mexico.

Pacific coast exploration   While De Soto and Coronado explored by land, several Spanish sea captains explored the Pacific coast of North America. One of these was Hernando de Alarcon (ä lär-kon'). He tried to link up with Coronado's men by sailing up the Colorado River from the Gulf of California. The plan failed because neither Coronado nor Alarcon knew the vast extent of the American Southwest.

At about the same time, the Spanish government in Mexico ordered Juan Rodríguez Cabrillo (wän   rô thrē' gäth kä brē' yō) to explore the Pacific coast by sea. Cabrillo died along the way, but the two ships he had commanded sailed as far north as the present-day Oregon. Exploring parties from the ships went ashore, where they saw and talked with many tribes of Indians.

Spaniards gave the name California to the land they explored on the Pacific coast. The name came from an imaginary land described in a popular book of the time. But reports on the actual land were discouraging. There were no Aztec or Inca empires along the western coast of North America. Consequently nearly two centuries passed before Spain made serious efforts to colonize this northern fringe of its empire.

Spanish influence in the United States
Actually all those parts of the United States once claimed by Spain were on the fringes of the Spanish New World empire. And yet signs of Spanish influence are readily seen in the United States today. Centuries ago, lands in the American Southwest were often given as grants by the Spanish king. Some laws regulating the use of water in that dry region are Spanish in origin. Ranch-style houses,

The influence of Spanish colonial architecture is seen in many buildings in the American Southwest.

Several of the conquistadores died violently, and others fell out of favor with Spain's rulers. Few of them ever realized their dream of living out their lives as honored citizens of Spain.

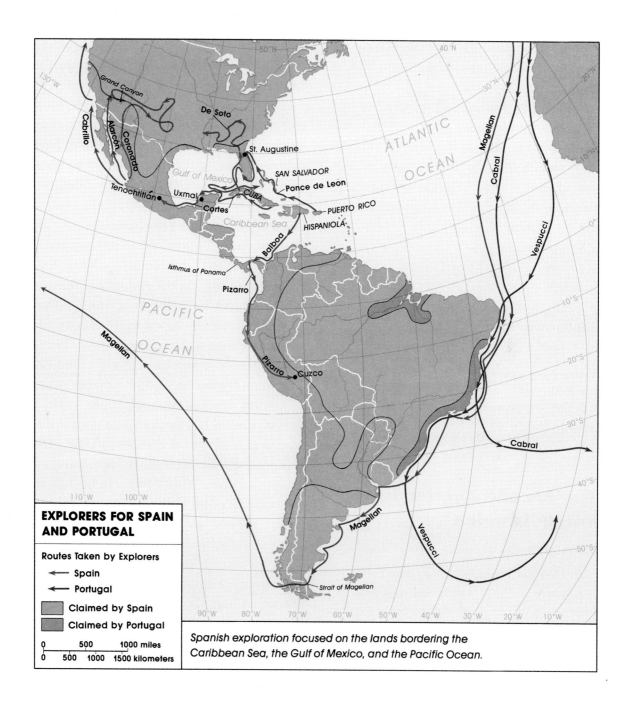

EXPLORERS FOR SPAIN AND PORTUGAL

Routes Taken by Explorers

← Spain

← Portugal

Claimed by Spain

Claimed by Portugal

| 0 | 500 | 1000 miles |
| 0 | 500 | 1000 | 1500 kilometers |

Spanish exploration focused on the lands bordering the Caribbean Sea, the Gulf of Mexico, and the Pacific Ocean.

churches, and public buildings in southwestern cities show the influence of Spanish colonial architecture.

We think of the cowboy as being typically American. But the **vaquero** (vä-kär′ ō), or Spanish cowboy, invented most of the equipment used on the range. The cowboy's hat and rope are commonly known by the Spanish words *sombrero* and *lariat*. **Longhorn cattle** were brought to the West by Spanish colonists, as were the ancestors of the cowboy's horse. Riding and roping contests called *rodeos* date from an old Spanish custom.

When Ponce de Leon sailed along the southeastern coast of North America, many flowers were in bloom. He named the land Florida, which is Spanish for "full of flowers."

Spaniards gave Florida its name. In Florida they established St. Augustine in 1565. Spain's worldwide empire lasted for more than four centuries. Today immigrants from former colonies of that empire are numerous in southern Florida, as they are in certain other parts of the United States. In the areas where these people live, the Spanish language is still widely spoken.

CHECKUP

1. Why did the empires of the Aztecs and the Incas come to an end?
2. How did each of the following contribute to Spain's New World empire? (a) Hernando de Soto (b) Francisco Coronado (c) Juan Rodríguez Cabrillo
3. Where is it possible to see Spanish influence in the United States?
4. In what ways does that influence show itself?

The French Empire in North America

┌─VOCABULARY─────────────────┐
| northwest passage | aristocrats |
| portage | bilingual |
└────────────────────────────┘

The search for a northwest passage The desire to find a water route to the Indies first sent French explorers to North America. Magellan's voyage had shown there was no short route through the southern continent. But perhaps there was such a route through the northern landmass. Several expeditions sailed from France in search of a **northwest passage** that would give trading ships access to the riches of the Far East.

Giovanni Verrazano (jô vä′ nə vär rə tzä′ nō), an Italian sea captain living in France, commanded the first of these expeditions. In 1524 he sailed from what is now North Carolina up to Newfoundland. Verrazano found no northwest passage, but he taught mapmakers something about the eastern coast of North America.

The French explore the interior Ten years after Verrazano's explorations, Jacques Cartier (kär tyā′) made the first of three voyages to North America. During these voyages he discovered the Gulf of St. Lawrence. He sailed up the broad St. Lawrence River as far as present-day Montreal. France based her claims to the St. Lawrence region on Cartier's discoveries.

Samuel de Champlain (sham plān′) started the first French colony along the St. Lawrence River at Quebec in 1608. He explored as far west as Lake Huron and as far south as New York State. In his honor the body of water along the boundary between present-day New York and Vermont is called Lake Champlain. Samuel de Champlain made 20 exploring trips to the region, gaining the title Father of New France. Champlain became the governor of France's first colony in the New World.

It was Champlain who sent Jean Nicolet (nik ō lə′) west to visit the Winnebago Indians of Wisconsin. Nicolet claimed the lands he saw for the king of France. Years later, Frenchmen returned to explore this land. Father Jacques Marquette (mär ket′), a missionary, and Louis Joliet (zhō lē ā′), a trader, reached the northern part of the Mississippi River in 1673. They traveled down it by canoe for a long way before turning back.

The name of the Italian sea captain who sailed for France is remembered in the name of one of the world's longest suspension bridges. The Verrazano-Narrows Bridge in New York spans the Narrows channel, which separates Brooklyn from Staten Island.

La Salle's expedition leaves Fort Frontenac on Lake Ontario to explore the Midwest. (44°N/77°W; map, p. 99)

It remained for another Frenchman, Robert de La Salle (lä sal), to go all the way down the Mississippi to the Gulf of Mexico. Before this, La Salle had explored the Ohio River country and claimed it for France. He traveled down the Mississippi in 1682. Grandly he also claimed all the land drained by that mighty river for France. La Salle named the land Louisiana in honor of King Louis XIV of France.

"Water highways"   At its greatest extent the French empire in North America stretched from the St. Lawrence River in the north to the Gulf of Mexico. In addition France claimed vast unsettled lands between the Appalachians and the Rocky Mountains. Water routes held together this far-reaching empire.

Travelers could go by canoe from Quebec, on the St. Lawrence, to New Orleans, on the Mississippi. Canoes had to be carried around rapids or for short distances from waterway to waterway. Such a task on land was called a **portage**, from the French word *porter*, which means "to carry." But the portages took far fewer miles than the waterways, where travel was easier. The St. Lawrence, the Great Lakes, the Ohio, and the Mississippi and its tributaries were "water highways" for the French empire in North America.

The fur trade   None of these water highways was a northwest passage through the North American continent. Still they permitted Frenchmen to carry on a rich business in furs. Sailors on fishing boats visiting the St. Lawrence region

51

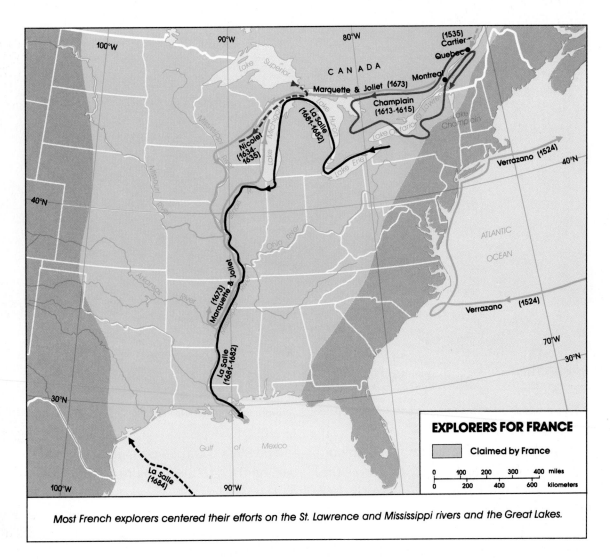

Most French explorers centered their efforts on the St. Lawrence and Mississippi rivers and the Great Lakes.

started the fur trade with the Indians. French fishers brought iron weapons, tools, and trinkets, which they bartered for furs.

Fur-bearing animals had become scarce in France. But it was the custom for French nobility and wealthy businessmen to wear clothing made of fur or decorated with fur. For these reasons the price of furs was high. Thousands of people living in the region called New France made their living from the fur trade.

French fur traders traveled long distances into the interior of the North Amer-ican continent. Often they lived for years with Indians, learning their languages and their ways. The French government tried to control traders by requiring each to have a license to trade furs. But many traders broke the law. They kept on the move, and few settled anywhere for long. They were not a firm basis upon which to build a lasting empire.

In an effort to attract permanent colo-nists, the French king granted land to **aristocrats,** or people of high social stand-ing. The aristocrats were supposed to find settlers and pay for their passage to

The most popular fur was that of the beaver. This soft, shiny fur was made into coats and hats. So many beavers were killed for their fur that by 1900 they were threatened with extinction. Laws today protect the beaver in both the United States and Canada.

New France. But this system failed. Settlers wanted to own the land they lived and worked on. The aristocrats wanted to rent their land, not to sell it. Moreover, the French government allowed only Roman Catholics to settle in New France, although there were Protestants and Jews who might have come. For these reasons most of France's New World empire remained unsettled. Probably no more than 100,000 people moved there from France.

French influence in America The most heavily settled parts of the French empire in North America were along the St. Lawrence River. Today this area is in Quebec, one of the provinces of Canada. The Canadian cities of Quebec and Montreal contain large numbers of French-speaking people. Indeed Canada is now a **bilingual** nation; that is, two languages—English and French—are officially used there. The widespread use of French in the province of Quebec stems from the time when eastern Canada was part of France's American empire.

Inside the United States, French colonial influence is less apparent. Two states with French names are Vermont, which means "green mountain," and Louisiana. Some large and small cities in the central United States also have French names. Among these are Detroit, Michigan; La Crosse, Wisconsin; Des Moines, Iowa; Terre Haute, Indiana; Bellefontaine, Ohio; St. Louis, Missouri; and Baton Rouge, Louisiana. A few buildings in New Orleans date from French colonial times. On the whole, however, only the French names are left to remind us that large parts of the United States were at one time within the New World empire of France.

CHECKUP

1. What were the early French explorers looking for in North America?
2. Where did each of the following explore?
   (a) Giovanni Verrazano
   (b) Samuel de Champlain
   (c) Marquette and Joliet
   (d) Jacques Cartier
   (e) Jean Nicolet
   (f) Robert de La Salle
3. How did water highways contribute to the French empire? To the fur trade?
4. Why was the French empire sparsely settled?
5. What reminds us today that France once claimed large parts of the United States?

The Netherlands, Sweden, and Russia Claim Land

VOCABULARY

Spice Islands	patroon system
patroon	tsar

Trade with the Spice Islands The Netherlands, sometimes known as Holland, was a great trading country in the seventeenth century. Its energetic Dutch merchants had a lively business with islands off the coast of Southeast Asia. They obtained such spices as cloves, pepper, and nutmeg from these islands. Traders called them the **Spice Islands.** To reach the Spice Islands, Dutch merchant ships took the long route around Africa and across the Indian Ocean. The voyage to the Spice Islands and the return to the Netherlands took at least two years and was very costly.

New Amsterdam quickly became a cosmopolitan city. Besides the Dutch it had Swedes, English, French Huguenots, Africans, Spaniards, and Jews. The first Jewish community in North America was in New Amsterdam. Many of these Jewish settlers had fled religious persecution in Spain and Portugal.

After a time the merchants became dissatisfied with this long, expensive route. They knew that Spanish, Portuguese, and French explorers were trying to find a shorter route by sailing west. So the Dutch merchants hired an English sea captain named Henry Hudson to look for a shorter route.

Hudson's explorations   Hudson first tried sailing northeast around northern Europe. After two unsuccessful attempts he decided this was impossible. Next he sailed west across the Atlantic in 1609. In his ship, the *Half Moon*, he explored the Atlantic coast of what is now the United States.

Henry Hudson's *Half Moon* entered three bays along the coast. Today they are known as New York Bay, Delaware Bay, and Chesapeake Bay. But none of these bays led to the northwest passage Hudson was looking for. However, he sailed up the river that flows into New York Bay. His *Half Moon* got as far as present-day Albany before turning back. Today the broad waterway is known as the Hudson River because of Henry Hudson's explorations.

Dutch colonies in North America Although Henry Hudson did not find a northwest passage, his explorations gave the Netherlands a claim to the land along the east coast of North America. Taking advantage of this claim, a Dutch trading company started a colony on Manhattan Island, near the mouth of the Hudson River. The company bought the island from Indians. Dutch settlers built a fort there, calling it Fort Amsterdam. Later it

became known as New Amsterdam, after the city of Amsterdam in the Netherlands.

The Dutch also built forts along rivers known today as the Connecticut and the Delaware. At the spot on the Hudson River that the *Half Moon* had reached in 1609, they built Fort Orange. It became a center for trade with the Iroquois Indians. But the Dutch were interested in more than trade. New Amsterdam was

In the Half Moon, *Henry Hudson sailed along America's eastern coast, searching in vain for a northwest passage that would lead to the Indies.*

made into a strong naval base. Dutch warships went out of New Amsterdam to capture Spanish vessels carrying gold and silver from America to Spain.

Settling farm families on the land was a lesser interest of the Dutch trading companies. Like the French the Dutch tried to promote settlement by giving away large grants of land. The **patroons** (pǝ-trüns′), or owners, of these large grants were supposed to rent the land to settlers whose passage they paid to New Netherland. This idea, known as the **patroon system**, failed because land was easy to get in North America. Most people wanted to own land rather than to rent it.

Dutch influence   Nevertheless the independent Dutch families that did settle on the land became some of the best farmers in America. Their style of barns and farmhouses can still be seen in the Hudson River valley. On Manhattan Island, Dutch merchants formed thriving business establishments. Three American Presidents—Martin Van Buren, Theodore Roosevelt, and Franklin D. Roosevelt—had ancestors who came to the Dutch colony in America.

There are some Dutch names still surviving in the New York City area. The Bowery section was originally *bouwerie,* meaning "a Dutch farm." The names *Harlem* and *Brooklyn* came from the Dutch towns Haarlem and Breucklen. At Christmastime Santa Claus, or Saint Nicholas, owes his appearance and name to Dutch customs brought to America. In the food category sauerkraut is a Dutch dish. In sports the Dutch were the first bowlers in America.

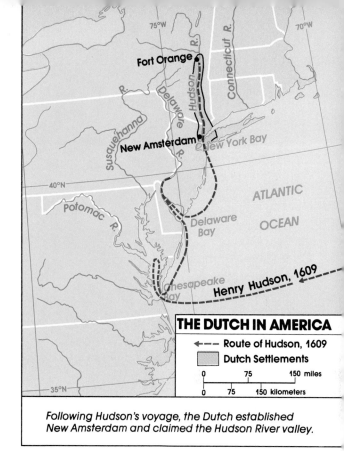

THE DUTCH IN AMERICA

←--- Route of Hudson, 1609

▨ Dutch Settlements

0   75   150 miles
0   75   150 kilometers

Following Hudson's voyage, the Dutch established New Amsterdam and claimed the Hudson River valley.

Sweden's little colony   On the Delaware River, near present-day Wilmington, a company chartered by the Swedish government started a colony in 1638. It was a small colony with only a few hundred settlers. However, they made—according to some historians—an important contribution to American frontier life.

The Swedish colonists came from a heavily forested region of northern Europe. Therefore they were skilled in cutting down trees and using logs for various purposes. So it is said Swedish colonists may have built the first log cabins in America. Perhaps other settlers learned how to build them from the Swedes. Such dwellings became so popular, especially on the frontier, that the log cabin is thought of as the typical dwelling of American pioneers.

The distinctively Russian style of this wooden church in Alaska is a reminder of the time when the Russian empire extended into North America.

Bering Strait. This is the region, you will recall, where a land bridge once existed and by which people came to America.

Bering's explorations revealed that Alaska was rich in furs, timber, and fish. Wealthy Russians, like the French, wore furs for warmth and to be stylish. Individuals and small companies traded in Alaskan furs until 1799. In that year the tsar of Russia granted the Russian American Company the right to take charge of all Russian interests in North America.

The tsar required the company not only to trade in furs but also to promote settlement and to teach Christianity to the Indians. Priests of the Russian Orthodox faith converted Indians to the Russian form of Christianity. Today older Alaskan towns, such as Kodiak and Sitka, still contain Russian Orthodox churches.

The land settled by the Swedish colonists was part of the Dutch claims. Still the Dutch in New Netherland left the little colony undisturbed until 1655. But in that year a Dutch force came from New Amsterdam and easily overcame the feeble resistance of the Swedish colonists.

Russia in North America At one time Russia, too, had claims to land in North America. Russia's claims came through the explorations of Vitus Bering in the waters between Siberia and Alaska. Bering was from Denmark but served Russia's **tsar** (zär), or ruler, as a sea captain. In 1728 and again in 1741, Bering explored the land and the waters east of Siberia. He discovered the passage between Alaska and Siberia that is today called the

Conflicting claims Not many Russians came to settle in Alaska. But the Russian army and navy built outposts down the west coast of North America. At one time Russians occupied a fort only 40 miles (64 km) north of San Francisco, California. This expansion of Russian claims alarmed Spanish officials. It caused them to add more settlements and military bases in California. Through these methods they hoped to halt the Russian advance down the west coast.

The west coast of North America was but one of the places where European powers had conflicting claims. Spain and France clashed over rival settlements in Florida and the Carolinas. New Orleans, at the mouth of the Mississippi, changed hands a number of times during the colonial period.

In fact nearly every part of what is now the United States was claimed by one or more European powers. The exception is our fiftieth state, Hawaii.

Hawaiian history Probably the Hawaiian Islands were uninhabited until about 1,700 years ago. At that time Polynesians crossed 2,000 miles (3,218 km) of the open Pacific in large canoes. A second wave came to settle in Hawaii 700 years later.

Spain, France, the Netherlands, and England began to explore the northern Pacific after they learned that the Russians had found riches there. Captain James Cook of England commanded one of these expeditions. He was the first European to sight the Hawaiian Islands. While returning from the North Pacific in 1778, Cook landed at one of these tropical islands. He called them the Sandwich Islands, in honor of the Earl of Sandwich, an English nobleman.

However, neither England nor any other European country ever planted a colony on these islands. They remained under native rule until 1898. Then, as you will learn, Hawaii became part of the American empire in the Pacific.

CHECKUP

1. Why did Dutch merchants hire Henry Hudson?
2. How did the Dutch promote settlement of their colony? How successful were they?
3. What contribution to American life may have been made by Swedish colonists?
4. Whose explorations gave Russia claims to Alaska?
5. What did the tsar require of the Russian American Company?
6. How does Hawaii's history make it unique among American states?

Africans in America

People from Africa Africans were among the early explorers of the Americas. Some of the Africans were servants. Some were slaves. Some were free.

Columbus had black sailors in his crews. Blacks marched with Balboa across the Isthmus of Panama in 1513. They helped build the first ships on the Pacific coast. Six years later, blacks dragged the heavy Spanish artillery that helped Cortes conquer the Aztecs. Blacks accompanied Pizarro in his conquest of Peru. In 1565, blacks assisted in building St. Augustine. Africans sailed up the St. Lawrence River with the French and helped to explore the Mississippi Valley.

"Little Steven" One black who wrote his name on the pages of history was Estevanico (əs tā bä′ nē kō) or "Little Steven." Estevanico served as an adviser to Hernando Cortes. As a guide he traveled through Florida, Mexico, and parts of Arizona, New Mexico, and Texas.

During an exploration of Florida in 1528, Estevanico and three companions were captured by Indians. They escaped but spent 8 years wandering before they reached the Spanish headquarters in Mexico. From Indians that Estevanico met during these wanderings, he first heard of **Cibola** (sē′ bə lə), the **Seven Cities of Gold**. These fabulous cities were said to be located somewhere north of Mexico.

The name Sandwich Islands is no longer used, but the Earl of Sandwich's name is remembered by the food that all of us eat on occasion. It goes back to the time when the earl, unwilling to leave a game of cards to eat dinner, ordered a servant to give him a piece of meat between slices of bread. **57**

Bright sunshine reflecting from pueblos and cliffs had a golden hue, and probably contributed to the legend that the Southwest had Seven Cities of Gold.

In 1539 the Spanish explorer Father Marcos de Niza (mar′ kōs də nē′ sä) led an expedition to search for the Seven Cities of Gold. Estevanico acted as a scout for the expedition, but he was more than that. He could talk with the Indians in their native language. As one member of the expedition later wrote, "He inquired about the roads we should follow, and the villages; in short, about everything we wished to know."

Unfortunately Estevanico's skills led to his death. Father Marcos sent him ahead of the main group to scout out the best way to the golden cities. Weeks later, a wounded Indian staggered into the Spanish camp with the news that Estevanico had been murdered by hostile Indians near the Seven Cities of Gold. Father Marcos's expedition fled back to Mexico.

No one knew if Estevanico had reached the golden cities. Nevertheless the story of Estevanico spurred De Soto, Coronado, and other Spanish explorers to search for these cities. Hundreds of years later the Zuni (zü′ nyē) Indians still told stories about a strange black man who had met his death as he approached their pueblos.

Blacks in New France　Blacks also joined in French explorations of the New World. Blacks paddled down the Mississippi River with Marquette and Joliet. At least 70 blacks served as farmers, carpenters, blacksmiths, brewers, and stonemasons in the French colony at Kaskaskia, Illinois. In 1720 a Paris banker named Phillipe Renault (rə nō′) brought both white and black laborers to work in the mines of New France.

Probably the best-known black in New France was Jean Baptiste Pointe du Sable (də sä′ bəl). A tall handsome man, he had been educated in Paris before coming to New France. Like many other French traders and trappers, du Sable married an Indian woman. The couple set up a trading post at the mouth of the Chicago River. The trading post expanded to include a house, a bakery, a dairy, a stable, a workshop, and a barn. The site is now within the modern city of Chicago.

In New Amsterdam There were 11 male African slaves at the founding of the Dutch colony of New Amsterdam in 1626. A few years later, women slaves were brought to the colony. Dutch merchants were prominent in the slave trade, but they often freed their slaves.

The Dutch freed a dozen slaves in New Amsterdam in 1644. In 1661 the first American slave **petition** (pə tish′ ən), or request, for freedom was sent to the governor of the colony. It was granted, giving the 12 slaves "their freedom on the same footing as other free peoples."

Ten million slaves The first African slaves in the New World had been brought to the Spanish colony of Hispaniola in the West Indies in 1501. From then until slavery finally was ended in the Americas, about 10 million slaves were brought to the New World. About three quarters of them were sent to the Portuguese colony of Brazil and to the Caribbean islands. In Brazil the slaves worked in the gold mines and in the fields, where sugarcane, coffee, and cotton were raised. In the West Indies slaves

Jean Baptiste Pointe du Sable, a French trader, built the first house on the site of what is now Chicago, Illinois. (42°N/88°W; map, p. 717)

worked to produce sugar and other crops. The slaves' lives were usually harsh and often short.

The English colonies in North America, the subject of our next chapter, received about 400,000 slaves directly from Africa. Other slaves, however, came to the English colonies after working for a time in the West Indies. As in all the colonies of the European powers, some slaves worked at skilled trades. But the great majority were unskilled laborers.

CHECKUP

1. How did Africans help build New World empires for the European powers?
2. How did Estevanico and Jean Baptiste Pointe du Sable contribute to American history?
3. How many Africans came to the New World as slaves?
4. Where were the majority of the slaves sent?

In 1518, King Charles V of Spain granted a license permitting the shipment of African slaves to the Spanish colonies. By 1560, Africans outnumbered Europeans in the larger Caribbean islands. From there, slavery spread to the region that would become the United States.

3/CHAPTER REVIEW

KEY FACTS

1. Columbus was not the first person to reach America, but his voyages led to the exploration and colonization of the Americas.

2. Within 100 years after Columbus's first voyage, Spain explored America, conquered native peoples, and colonized an empire that made Spain the richest nation in Europe.

3. Most of Spain's empire lay outside the present-day United States; nevertheless in those United States areas that were once part of Spain's empire, Spanish influence is still strong.

4. The French empire in North America was sparsely populated except in a few places, because it was based in large part on the fur trade.

5. The Netherlands, Sweden, and Russia had smaller holdings in North America than Spain and France.

VOCABULARY QUIZ

On a sheet of paper, match the letter with the number of the best definition.

a. aristocrats
b. vaquero
c. bilingual
d. northwest passage
e. patroon system
f. Vikings
g. empire
h. portage
i. the Indies
j. tsar

e **1.** An attempt to settle tenant farmers in New Amsterdam

c **2.** A country where two languages are officially in use

a **3.** People of high social standing

j **4.** Russia's ruler

d **5.** A shorter way to the Far East sought by European explorers

i **6.** Rich islands off the coast of Asia

b **7.** Spanish name for a cowboy

h **8.** Carrying boats from one waterway to another waterway

f **9.** A bold, seafaring people

g **10.** Territories and peoples under the control of a powerful country

REVIEW QUESTIONS

1. Why was Columbus a bitter man at the time of his death?

2. Why were the Spanish able to build such a rich empire in the New World?

3. What parts of America were claimed by the French?

4. Why did France have little success in attracting settlers to North America?

5. Where in the New World were there conflicting claims among the European empires?

6. For what is Estevanico remembered today?

7. How did Africans contribute to building European empires in the New World?

ACTIVITIES

1. Use the index to an atlas such as the Rand McNally Road Atlas to find counties or cities named for early explorers of the New World.

2. Besides those described in this chapter, what other signs of European colonial influence can you find in the United States? Look for these signs on maps, in the names of foods, in customs, and in words we commonly use.

3. Each of the explorers in this chapter has biographies or encyclopedia articles written about him. Find an unusual fact about each explorer and present it to the class.

3/SKILLS DEVELOPMENT

UNDERSTANDING CHRONOLOGY

PUTTING THINGS IN SEQUENCE

Chronology (krə nol′ ə jē) deals with time and putting things in sequence—that is, in the order in which they happened. It is especially important to understand chronology in history. A time line is a good way to put things in sequence. At the bottom of this page is a time line with dates marked below it, running from 1400 to 1800. Note that the time line is drawn to scale, with 1½ inches equalling 100 years.

Several explorations and settlements are described in Chapter 3. Some of these are listed below with the date when each event took place. Each event is identified by a letter at left.

SKILLS PRACTICE

On a sheet of paper draw a time line like the one below. Find the proper place on the time line for each event. Make a dot on the line for each event. Above the dot write the letter that identifies the event.

a. Vitus Bering explores in Alaskan waters. (1728 and 1741)

b. The Dutch conquer the Swedish colony. (1655)

c. Columbus sails from Palos, Spain, on his first voyage to America. (1492)

d. Captain Cook lands in Hawaii. (1778)

e. Balboa sees the Pacific Ocean. (1513)

f. Coronado explores the American Southwest. (1540)

g. Samuel de Champlain starts a French colony at Quebec. (1608)

h. The Russian American Company is chartered. (1799)

i. La Salle claims Louisiana for France. (1682)

j. Magellan begins his historic voyage. (1519)

k. Swedish settlers start a colony on the Delaware River. (1638)

By doing this exercise with the time line, you not only put events in sequence, but you also show the time span between events. You can see that the Spanish were the first to explore and colonize the Americas. The other powers established colonies here a century later. Finally, you can see that the whole process of exploring and colonizing in the New World and the Pacific occurred over a period of more than 3 centuries.

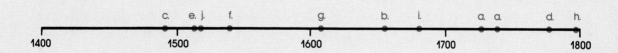

4 England Plants Colonies

Virginia Succeeds

A lively Indian girl   Her Indian name was Matoaka (mä tō ä′ kə). English colonists at Jamestown, however, knew her best as Pocahontas (pō kə hon′ təs). It meant "lively," and was a pet name given the young Indian girl by her father. He was known as Powhatan (pou ə tan′), chief of the Indian tribes living along the coast of Virginia.

Pocahontas was about 13 years old when the English colonists founded Jamestown in 1607. She is the subject of many legends—stories from the past that may or may not be true. One legend tells how she saved the life of Captain John Smith, the colonists' leader at Jamestown. He had gone too far into Indian territory and was captured. Chief Powhatan ordered Smith's head cut off. As John Smith later told it, Pocahontas covered his body with her own. She pleaded for his life. Her father gave in. He pardoned the English leader and sent him back to Jamestown in peace.

In 1613 the English colonists took advantage of Powhatan's great love for his daughter. They lured Pocahontas onto an English ship and carried her off to Jamestown. To get his daughter back, Powhatan had to return some English colonists his warriors had captured.

Pocahontas and John Rolfe   While Pocahontas was living at Jamestown, she met John Rolfe. Records from that time describe this colonist as "an honest gentleman and of good behavior." Pocahontas and John Rolfe fell in love. She became a Christian, baptized under the name of "the lady Rebecca." In April 1614, "the lady Rebecca" and John Rolfe were married.

About 2 years after their marriage, Mr. and Mrs. John Rolfe went to England. She was received as a princess there. King James I and Queen Anne welcomed her at their royal court. After a few months, however, John Rolfe got word to return to Virginia on business.

Before the Rolfes could leave, however, Pocahontas sickened and died. On March 21, 1617, she was buried in an English churchyard. Pocahontas and John

Reconstructed Jamestown looks much like the early village did.   (37°N/77°W; map, p. 70)

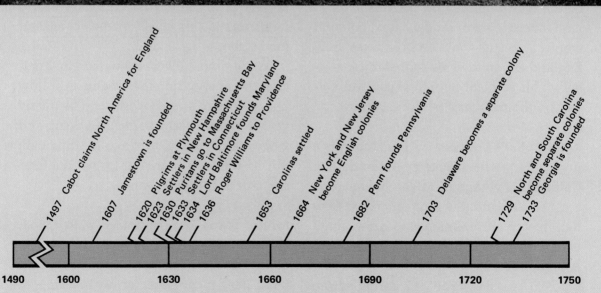

1497 Cabot claims North America for England

1607 Jamestown is founded

1620 Pilgrims at Plymouth

1623 Settlers in New Hampshire

1630 Puritans go to Massachusetts Bay

1633 Settlers in Connecticut

1634 Lord Baltimore founds Maryland

1636 Roger Williams to Providence

1653 Carolinas settled

1664 New York and New Jersey become English colonies

1682 Penn founds Pennsylvania

1703 Delaware becomes a separate colony

1729 North and South Carolina become separate colonies

1733 Georgia is founded

1490 1600 1630 1660 1690 1720 1750

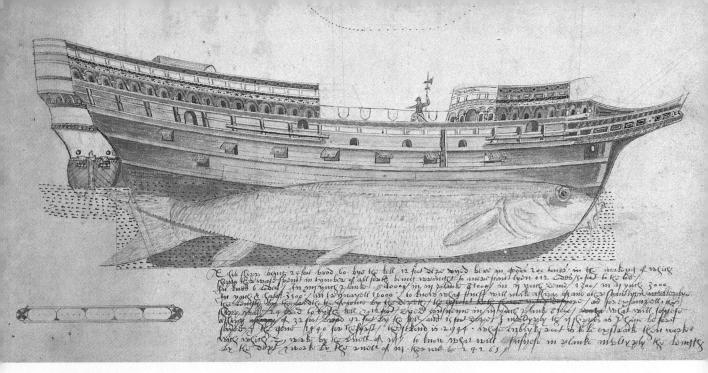

To meet the threat posed by Spain's fleet, the English built a faster and more seaworthy warship, designed to slip through the water as easily as a fish.

Rolfe had one son. They named him Thomas Rolfe. Eventually he returned to Virginia. Among his long line of descendants were the Randolphs, one of Virginia's most famous families.

Pocahontas, Powhatan, John Rolfe, and Captain John Smith all lived at the time England was struggling to start colonies in the New World. Unlike Spain, England entered late in the race for a colonial empire. Let us look back and see how England, in spite of its late start, was finally able to plant its first successful colony on the mainland of North America.

John Cabot's voyages   England was a poor but ambitious country at the time of Columbus's voyage in 1492. As the news reached England, the king and some English merchants wanted to know more about the land that lay across the North Atlantic. So they backed Giovanni Caboto (jō vän′ nē kä bō′ tō), an Italian sea captain who had taken the English form of his name—John Cabot.

Cabot made two voyages across the stormy North Atlantic. In 1497 he claimed "New Found Land" (now Newfoundland) for the English king. The next year Cabot sailed south along the North American coast, also claiming it for England. A century later England based its claims to this coast on the voyages of John Cabot.

At the time, however, England had neither the energy nor the wealth to follow up on Cabot's discoveries. For many years England was weaker than Spain and was careful not to provoke the Spanish. But as England's strength grew, England and Spain became rivals.

Spain plans an invasion   In 1587, Spain began a war against England. The next year King Philip of Spain ordered a large fleet to prepare for an invasion of

On his second voyage to America, Cabot commanded a fleet of five ships, only one of which made it back to England. Cabot himself was on one of the ships that was presumably lost in a storm.

England. He called this fleet the **Invincible Armada.** It consisted of 130 armed ships, carrying 8,000 sailors and 22,000 soldiers.

Queen Elizabeth I governed England at that time. She ruled her country brilliantly from 1558 until her death in 1603. She ruled so brilliantly, in fact, that those years are known as the Elizabethan Age. As the Spanish Armada sailed toward England, Queen Elizabeth rallied her subjects. "I have resolved to live or die amongst you," she told them. "I know I have but the body of a weak and feeble woman, but I have the heart of a king."

The defeat of the Armada Inspired by their queen, English sea captains, led by Sir Francis Drake, prepared to meet the Armada. Making use of their accurate cannons and superior sailing skill, they fought the larger Spanish ships from long range. In a running battle that lasted more than 4 days, 200 English ships drove the Invincible Armada away from England and into the North Sea. Strong storms there finished the work that the English cannons had begun. More than half of the ships and more than two thirds of the fighting men in the Armada were lost. The invasion attempt by Spain had been beaten back.

This crushing defeat was a blow to Spain. But it opened a door to England where there was mounting interest in colonization. No longer could Spain prevent other European countries from colonizing the east coast of North America. Soon England, France, the Netherlands, and Sweden began to plant colonies along the Atlantic coast.

Virginia Dare disappears Sir Walter Raleigh (rol′ ē) was one of Queen Elizabeth's favorite sea captains. He had hoped to plant English colonies in northern Ireland. But in 1587 he shifted his attention to North America. The spot he chose was Roanoke (rō′ ə nōk) Island, a short distance off the coast of what is now North Carolina.

Sir Walter Raleigh's colonists included men, women, and children. John White, in charge of the expedition, stayed only long enough to get the colonists settled. A week before White returned to England for more supplies, his daughter, Elizabeth White Dare, gave birth to his grandchild. Sir Walter Raleigh called his colony Virginia, and this was the name given to the little girl. Virginia Dare was the first English child born in what is now the United States.

England's war with Spain kept John White from returning to Virginia until 1590. When he did return to Roanoke, however, he found none of the colonists he had left there 3 years before. John White and other men kept looking for the missing people. There was no trace of what had happened except the word *Croatan* (krō ə tan′) carved on a post in the crude fort the colonists had built. This was the name of another island, held by Indians friendly to the colonists. To this day no one knows for sure what happened to Raleigh's **Lost Colony** and to little Virginia Dare.

Joint-stock companies In the failure of the Roanoke colony, Sir Walter Raleigh lost his entire fortune. His loss served as a lesson to others. Colonization was too

During the Elizabethan Age, Francis Drake was one of the daring sea captains who became known in English history as the "sea dogs." They attacked Spanish ships and raided Spanish coastal towns. Some pupils might find out more about Drake's exploits and report to the class.

risky and costly for one person to undertake. So the English formed **joint-stock companies** to obtain the large amount of money needed for starting colonies.

A joint-stock company was like a modern corporation. Many people could buy **stock**—that is, shares in the ownership of the company. If the company succeeded and made a profit, the stockholders would share in it. If the company failed, the stockholders lost only the amount that each had invested.

Hundreds of joint-stock companies were formed in England for the purpose of planting colonies. These companies started colonies in the West Indies, in Canada, and in what is now the United States. In 1606, rich English merchants organized the Virginia Company of London. Its goal was to start a colony on the coast of North America. Members of the group hoped that gold would be found in the colony. No member suspected that the company was about to plant a seed from which a mighty nation would take root and grow.

Jamestown survives   King James I of England gave a **charter** to the Virginia Company of London. A charter is a written agreement giving permission to settle or trade in a certain area. In December 1606 the *Susan Constant*, the *Godspeed*, and the *Discovery* sailed for North America. These three company ships carried 104 men and supplies. On May 24, 1607, the ships anchored near a sandy peninsula on the north shore of the James River. There the weary men built a village and a fort. They called it Jamestown in honor of their king.

From the beginning, everything seemed to go wrong at Jamestown. The settlement was in a low, swampy area, and the first flimsy shelters let rain leak in. So there was much sickness. In 1607 the settlers failed to get a crop planted, and food became scarce. Only 53 colonists lived through the first winter.

The story of Pocahontas saving John Smith's life may or may not be true. What is true is that John Smith saved Jamestown at this time. In the winter the desperate colonists elected the tough little captain as their leader. He saved the colony by forcing the colonists to do the necessary work and by getting food from the Indians who lived nearby.

The next year a gunpowder explosion injured Captain John Smith. He returned to England for medical attention. Without his leadership, Jamestown went through a winter so hard it was called the "starving time." At the end of this terrible time, the survivors were digging roots and catching snakes for food.

Things got even worse before they got better. Finally the Virginia Company reorganized in England. Once more the company sent colonists and supplies. The stockholders still hoped to make a profit from their colony. Their profit came from an unexpected source.

Profit from tobacco   The Spanish had brought tobacco from the New World to Europe. Its use had spread to England. The English liked best the mild tobacco from South America. They called this mild tobacco **oronoco** (ō rə nō′ kō) because it came from near the Orinoco River.

Two years before John Rolfe married Pocahontas, he managed to get some seeds of mild oronoco. He planted them in Virginia. John Rolfe's first crop sold for a good price in London. More and more Virginians started raising tobacco. A man with a small tobacco farm was called an oronoco because that was the kind of tobacco he raised.

When an oronoco planted new land, he did not cut down the trees that grew there. Instead, he **girdled** them. That is, he killed them by cutting through the bark all the way around the trunk. This let sunlight in through the leafless branches. The first crop on the new land was then planted among the dead trees.

Plantations and slave labor As time went on, some colonists developed larger farms for growing tobacco. Such large farms, devoted to growing a single crop, were called **plantations**. Tobacco gave Virginia a **cash crop**, that is, a crop grown for sale rather than for use by the farmer. This crop greatly improved the outlook for the success of the Virginia colony.

Tobacco growing also fastened the system of **slavery** on the colony. In 1619 the first Africans to arrive in English North America landed at Jamestown. The Dutch ship that brought them had been headed for a Caribbean island but was blown off course. The ship's captain exchanged the Africans for food and supplies. Records are unclear, but it appears that these first 20 Africans worked as servants rather than as slaves.

However, as more plantations grew up along the rivers of Virginia, there were increased demands for laborers to work in the tobacco fields. Already some Africans were working as slaves on the tobacco plantations of Spain's Caribbean

At Jamestown, casks of tobacco are rolled aboard a ship bound for England.

Late in the year 1618, 220 people came by ship from England to Virginia. They settled on a tract of land called Martin's Hundred. It lay along the James River.

On Martin's Hundred these settlers built a fort and a tiny village called Wolstenholme Towne. In 1622, Indians burned nearly all the buildings and killed or took hostage more than half the population living there. Though the survivors rebuilt and held on for several years, hard times and disease finally caused the settlement to be abandoned.

Martin's Hundred was almost forgotten for 350 years. All signs of settlement disappeared. Then, in the middle 1970s, a group of archaeologists started digging there. In four summers they dug up pieces of pottery and stoneware, clay tobacco pipes, and two small coins that had been minted in England in 1613. Military relics discovered at Martin's Hundred included two helmets with visors. These are the only such helmets ever found intact in the New World.

The archaeologists also found graves, the contents of which told a grim story of disease and violent death. In one grave was a skull split by a heavy blow. In another, four people had been hastily buried without coffins. This showed that they had probably died during an epidemic of some contagious disease. All in all, the discoveries at Martin's Hundred show evidence of the desperate, tragic lives of the early Virginians who lived in Wolstenholme Towne.

These face-covering helmets were unearthed at Martin's Hundred, near Jamestown. They are the only such helmets ever found in the New World.

For further information about and photographs of Martin's Hundred, see the issues of National Geographic magazine for June 1979 and January 1982.

colonies. The slave-labor system was then brought to the English colonies. By the latter part of the 1600s, slavery was firmly established in Virginia.

Two kinds of government In 1619 the Virginia Company allowed the colonists to elect members to a **House of Burgesses.** Burgess meant "free citizen" in England. So the House of Burgesses represented the free citizens of Virginia. It gave white male land-owning Virginians the chance to help make the laws under which they were to live. As such, the Virginia House of Burgesses was a first step in the English colonies toward **self-government**—the belief that people can and should rule themselves.

King James I of England hated tobacco. He called smoking it "a custom loathsome to the eye, hateful to the nose, harmful to the brain, and dangerous to the lungs." Perhaps this was reason enough to be suspicious of the colony from which so much English tobacco came. But an even greater reason for his suspicions was the elected House of Burgesses. King James mistrusted this tiny amount of self-government in Virginia and the leaders of the Virginia Company of London.

In 1624 King James took back the charter he had granted to the Virginia Company. Virginia was then made a **royal colony,** that is, a colony directly under the king's control. King James planned also to do away with the House of Burgesses. But he died in 1625. His successor, Charles I, permitted the House of Burgesses to meet.

Virginia remained a royal colony for the next 150 years. The English king appointed Virginia's governor and a council to advise the governor. In time the appointed governor and council were certain to clash with the elected House of Burgesses.

CHECKUP

1. Explain the parts played by John Smith and John Rolfe in making Virginia a success.
2. Why was the defeat of the Invincible Armada important to English colonization?
3. What are the known facts about the colony set up by Sir Walter Raleigh? What is still unknown?
4. How were joint stock companies helpful in planting English colonies in America?
5. What was the importance of the creation of the Virginia House of Burgesses?
6. What changes did King James I seek to bring about in the government of the Virginia colony? How successful was he?

The New England Colonies

┌─**VOCABULARY**─────────────────┐

Church of England	Puritan
Separatist	constitution
Pilgrim	Fundamental
Mayflower Compact	Orders

└────────────────────────────────┘

England's northern settlements After Jamestown the next successful English settlements were started far to the north. Massachusetts became the first of the New England colonies. Religion was of great importance in the early days of these colonies. In fact, religion was the major reason most of the first colonists came to New England.

In Virginia most of the colonists were members of the **Church of England,** which, by law, was England's official church. In New England, on the other

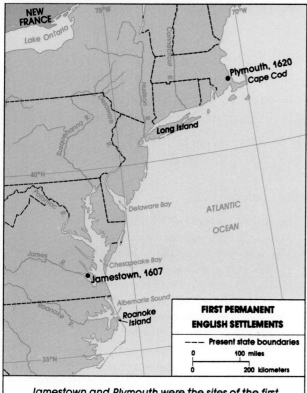

Jamestown and Plymouth were the sites of the first permanent English settlements in America.

more, this time to land that England claimed in America. Thus they earned the name of **Pilgrims**, meaning persons traveling on a religious journey. It is the name by which they are known in American history.

The Pilgrims were poor. They needed money for supplies and transportation. London merchants gave them money and supplied a ship called the *Mayflower*. In return the Pilgrims agreed to give the merchants a share of all the profits earned by the colony after 7 years in America.

The Pilgrims find a home　In September 1620 the *Mayflower* picked up Pilgrims from Leiden. Then the ship sailed to Plymouth, England, where more people boarded for the journey to America. In November the *Mayflower*, carrying about 100 passengers, reached the New England coast. It anchored in a bay at the end of Cape Cod, near the site of present-day Provincetown, Massachusetts. From there, exploring parties searched for a suitable spot to settle.

The Pilgrims had permission to settle on land owned by the Virginia Company of London. But Massachusetts was far north of Virginia. If they settled in Massachusetts, the Pilgrims would be living on land they had no right to occupy. For this reason Pilgrim leaders decided they needed some form of government for the colony, even before landing. While still on board ship, they drew up and signed a paper known as the **Mayflower Compact**.

"We whose names are underwritten . . ." So begin the few short sentences of the Mayflower Compact. The 41 men who signed it agreed to obey several sim-

hand, the first two groups to arrive had disagreements with the official church.

The travels of the Pilgrims　The first group to settle successfully in New England wanted to separate from the Church of England. Some of these **Separatists,** as they are sometimes called, left Scrooby, England, in 1608. They moved to Leiden, a town in the Netherlands, where they felt they could worship as they pleased. But during the next few years, the Separatists began to worry as they saw their children learning the Dutch language and Dutch ways.

These deeply religious people wanted to live where they could worship in their own way. And yet they wanted their children to grow up as English boys and girls. So they decided to move once

Legend has it that the Pilgrims' exploring party first stepped ashore onto a big boulder, know today as Plymouth Rock. It now stands under a large granite canopy.

ple rules and regulations. The Mayflower Compact was another step toward self-government in the English colonies. Because of the Mayflower Compact, adult males in the Pilgrim colony soon began meeting to make laws for their new colony.

The Pilgrims live quietly   Most of the Pilgrims had left England from the port of Plymouth. So it was decided to call the colony in New England by the same name. They built their first houses along what they called Leiden Street, after their temporary haven in the Netherlands. As at Jamestown, the first years at Plymouth were hard. By March 1621, 44 members of the original Mayflower company had died. Those who survived were mainly the young and fit. In fact, more than half the survivors were under 16 years of age.

It was then that an Indian named Samoset appeared. His greeting—"Much welcome, Englishmen"—startled the Pilgrims. They found that Samoset had learned English from sailors fishing near islands off the New England coast. His offer of friendship must have been one of the few pleasant moments for the Pilgrims during that first winter.

In the spring the Indian chief Massasoit (mas′ ə soit) and 60 of his men came to Plymouth. The Indians offered help and hospitality to the Pilgrims. Squanto, another Indian, showed them where to hunt and fish and how to raise corn. The Pilgrims harvested the corn and other crops in the fall. These became part of the first Thanksgiving Day dinner in the New England colonies.

By living quietly, working hard, and worshiping God in their own way, members of the Pilgrim colony survived in the wilderness. Thirty times in annual elections they chose William Bradford as their governor. He wrote *Of Plimoth Plantation*, a history of the Pilgrims in New England and how they got there.

The Pilgrim settlement of Plymouth was the first permanent colony in New England. Like Jamestown, Plymouth has been reconstructed. (42°N/71°W; map, p. 70)

What's In a Name?

NEW ENGLAND

John Smith had a spectacular career in early Virginia. Yet his contributions to the settlement of New England were possibly more important. In fact, he gave the name *New England* to what is now the northeastern part of the United States.

In 1614 a group of London merchants hired John Smith to explore the rocky coast that John Cabot had explored more than a century before. Smith brought back a valuable cargo of fish and furs. He talked of the value of the fishing places among the islands and along the coast.

John Smith left his mark on New England as well as on Jamestown.

After he got back to England, John Smith wrote a book about his voyage. He called his book *A Description of New England,* saying a part of that coast looked like Devonshire, in "old" England. He used the name *New England* many times in his book, so it became familiar. So, 6 years later, when King James I gave a charter to that land, the king wrote, "The same shall be called by the name New England in America."

The maps in Smith's book fastened another name on part of New England. He placed the location of an Indian town, and called the Indians who lived there Massachusetts. So New England and Massachusetts were already named by the time the Pilgrims and the Puritans got there.

The Puritans come to Massachusetts Bay Within a few years, other settlements were founded on the shores of Massachusetts Bay, to the north of Plymouth. Among these were several started by an energetic group known as the **Puritans.** Unlike the Pilgrims, the Puritans wanted to stay within the Church of England. But they wanted a more simple church organization, with the church governed by its worshipers rather than by bishops. Their desire to "purify," or reform, the church is why they were called Puritans.

There were other differences between Pilgrims and Puritans. While many Pilgrims were poor, most Puritans were prosperous. They were also generally better-educated than the Pilgrims. Moreover the Puritans came to America in much greater numbers than the Pilgrims. More than 1,000 came in 1630, the Puritans' first year in Massachusetts. In the next 13 years, more than 20,000 English people joined the Puritan settlements.

Before they left England, Puritan leaders organized the Massachusetts Bay Company with a charter from King Charles I. The charter, which the Puritans brought with them, served for many years as a **constitution** for the colony. A

The Puritans founded Boston in 1630, naming it after an English town in which many of them had lived. It soon became the capital of Massachusetts Bay Colony.

The Puritans believed that cooking on Sunday was a sin. A dish they often prepared on Saturday to be served for dinner on Sunday was baked beans. From this practice, Boston was nicknamed Beantown.

constitution is a set of basic laws by which people are governed. During all those years, the Puritan settlements prospered through fishing, fur trading, and shipbuilding. Still the Puritans never forgot that religious reasons had brought them to Massachusetts in the first place.

Religion's role   During the early years of the colony, Puritan ministers had a great deal of influence. They watched over their congregations to protect them from sin. The ministers' fiery sermons sometimes lasted for hours. In the Massachusetts Bay Colony, there was a close relationship between the Puritan church and the colonial government.

The ministers held no government offices, but only members of the Puritan church could vote and hold office. Only about one fifth of the adult white males had political rights as more and more non-Puritans came to Massachusetts. Newcomers who did not belong to the Puritan church were unable to vote.

In early colonial days, children often learned to read and write in a class in the teacher's home.

A belief in education   The Puritans are remembered for their belief in education. Because many Puritans had been well-educated in England, they put great effort into education in Massachusetts. In 1636 at Cambridge, near the prominent Puritan town of Boston, they started the first college in the English colonies. It soon became known as Harvard College. Today it is one of the most famous universities in the United States. The main purpose of Harvard College in its early years was to train Puritan ministers.

In 1647 the government of Massachusetts Bay Colony passed an education law. It required every town of more than 50 families to start a school in which children could learn to read and write. Puritans believed that all persons should know how to read so they could study the Bible. That was the main reason for the School Law of 1647. Because of it, Massachusetts set up the first public schools in the English colonies.

An expanding colony   It has been said of Massachusetts that "all earlier settlements [in New England] grew into it—all later colonies grew out of it." The first part of that statement refers to the Puritan colony's take-over of three other settled areas in New England.

In 1641 Massachusetts took control of settlements in New Hampshire. It remained part of Massachusetts until the king of England made New Hampshire a royal colony in 1679. In 1677 Massachusetts bought the land that is today the state of Maine. This land was a part of Massachusetts until 1820, when Maine became the twenty-third state of the

United States. And in 1691 the older Pilgrim colony at Plymouth merged with Massachusetts, its larger neighbor to the north.

The founding of Rhode Island The second part of the statement about Massachusetts is also true—that all later New England colonies grew out of it. Most Puritan leaders were capable men. Indeed, they were often brilliant. Sometimes, however, they were narrow-minded and unwilling to admit that others might also have good ideas.

In 1631 Roger Williams, a well-educated Puritan minister, came to Massachusetts. He soon began to disagree with other Puritan ministers. Williams believed that the Puritan church leaders had too much control over the Massachusetts government. He wanted to separate the church and the state, and he argued that all people should be free to worship in their own way. Also he felt that the Indians should be paid for the land on which the Puritans had settled.

Roger Williams expressed his views openly in sermons preached at Plymouth and Salem. Because of this, the General Court of Massachusetts ordered him to leave the colony. With the aid of friendly Indians, he made his way southward through dense forests. On the shores of Narragansett (nar ə gan' sət) Bay, Williams built a settlement he called Providence. Out of this settlement grew the colony of Rhode Island.

Other settlements on Narragansett Bay also offered refuge to persons disagreeing with the church leaders in Massachusetts. Among those who came was Anne

For her beliefs, Anne Hutchinson was put on trial by Puritan leaders and banished from Massachusetts.

Hutchinson, a highly intelligent and spirited woman. She was married to William Hutchinson. Twelve of their 15 children were born in England. The other three were born after the family moved to Massachusetts in 1636.

Anne Hutchinson had a deep interest in religion. It was this interest that eventually led her to move to Rhode Island. In her own home she had begun to hold religious meetings that were popular and well attended. But what she discussed there was different from what the Puritan church leaders taught. So they ordered her to leave Massachusetts.

Others followed Anne Hutchinson to Rhode Island, and by 1643 there were four settlements on Narragansett Bay. Rhode Island offered more religious freedom

74 Rhode Island is today the smallest state, but it has the longest official name: *State of Rhode Island and Providence Plantations.* The name dates back to a charter granted to the colony in 1663.

than any of the other English colonies. Its government provided for a firm separation of church and state. Rhode Island also became a thriving center of trade. Its merchants made Newport one of the busiest and wealthiest ports in the American colonies.

Connecticut's constitution   In 1636 the Reverend Thomas Hooker led a group out of Massachusetts. The minister and his followers left for at least two reasons. First they felt that their voice in the government of Massachusetts was not as strong as it should have been. But a second reason was to find better farmland than there was in Massachusetts.

Hooker and his followers found good land for crops in the broad Connecticut River valley. As time passed, this rich soil proved to be the most fertile in New England. Other people moved into the fertile river valley, settling in communities they named Windsor, Wethersfield, and Hartford.

Representatives from these towns organized the Connecticut Colony. In 1639 they drew up a document called **Fundamental Orders**. People living in the colony agreed to be governed by this constitution. Connecticut's Fundamental Orders have been called the world's first written constitution. It provided the settlers in Connecticut with one of the most democratic of all the governments in the American colonies.

Thus Rhode Island, Connecticut, and New Hampshire all grew out of Massachusetts in one way or another. These were the four New England colonies. Of the four, Rhode Island was the smallest and Massachusetts the largest in area and population. Second oldest of the English colonies, Massachusetts was a leader from the start.

CHECKUP

1. How did the Indians help the Plymouth colonists to survive?
2. Explain the differences between the Pilgrims and the Puritans.
3. What earlier settlements were taken over by the Puritan colony of Massachusetts Bay?
4. How did other New England colonies grow out of Massachusetts?

The Middle Colonies

┌─ VOCABULARY ─────────────────────┐

legislature   "holy experiment"
Quaker   pamphlet

└──────────────────────────────────┘

A soldier and a governor   Peter Stuyvesant (stī′ və sənt) served in the Dutch army. Fighting for the Dutch, he lost his right leg in a campaign against the French on the West Indian island of St. Martin. As a reward for his loyal service, he was made governor-general of the Dutch colony of New Netherland. He arrived in New Amsterdam, the capital of that colony, in 1647.

Peter Stuyvesant was a stern, energetic governor. He kept peace with neighboring Indian tribes. He settled a boundary dispute with the English colony of Connecticut. He drove the Swedes out of their colony in Delaware and he kept tight control of his own colony.

In spite of these successes, Peter Stuyvesant could do little more than fume and stomp his leg when an English fleet sailed

New York is today the largest city in the United States, but the population of New Amsterdam in 1664 — when the English seized it and renamed it New York — was only about 1,500.

Dutch New Amsterdam was renamed New York in 1664 when the English seized it. Its fine harbor soon made it a flourishing center of trade. (41°N/74°W; map, p. 79)

into the harbor of New Amsterdam in September 1664. By this time the English and the Dutch were not as friendly as they had been earlier in the seventeenth century. England had claimed *all* of the Atlantic coast north of Florida because of John Cabot's voyages. By 1664, English rulers were unwilling to have a Dutch colony between the New England colonies and England's southern colonies.

The English take over   King Charles II of England ordered the capture of the Dutch colony. An English fleet dropped anchor in New Amsterdam's harbor. The guns of the fleet's four warships were trained on the city. Peter Stuyvesant had the desire and courage to fight the English. But, having no munitions, he was forced to surrender. The colony was then renamed for the Duke of York, the king's brother. In this way New Netherland and New Amsterdam both got the name *New York*.

Even so, Dutch influence remained strong in New York. Dutch ships, along with those from other countries, sailed in and out of New York Harbor, as they had when the settlement was called New Amsterdam. Most Dutch farmers and traders stayed in the colony after the English took control. In fact, Peter Stuyvesant returned to live there after a brief visit to his homeland.

New Jersey and Delaware   Besides New York, two other English colonies came from the former Dutch possessions along the Atlantic coast. Among friends of the Duke of York were two English noblemen, Sir George Carteret and Lord John Berkeley. In gratitude for their friendship, the Duke of York gave them land across the Hudson River from New York.

They called the land New Jersey because Carteret had been governor of an English island named Jersey.

The two English noblemen cared little for their land in far-off America. They soon sold part of it. The remaining land changed owners a number of times. Nevertheless, small towns and farms eventually dotted the New Jersey landscape. After several changes in government, New Jersey became a prosperous royal colony.

The land Peter Stuyvesant took from the Swedes became the English colony of Delaware. The name came from Lord De La Warr, an early governor of Virginia. For many years Delaware was considered to be part of the neighboring colony of Pennsylvania. However, in 1703 the people of Delaware won the right to elect their own **legislature** or law-making body. After that, Delaware was counted as a separate English colony.

Peaceful Pennsylvania   William Penn was born into a wealthy English family. He was named for his father, an admiral in the English navy. Young William grew up as a member of the Church of England. For a time he served in the English navy. Then he took charge of several estates his father owned in Ireland.

A great change came in Penn's life when he joined the Society of Friends, or **Quakers.** At that time Quakers were persecuted in England because of their religious beliefs. Quakers refused to serve in England's army or navy. They would not swear oaths of loyalty to the king. Penn was in jail briefly because he accepted these Quaker beliefs.

The principles of toleration, peace, and liberty, on which William Penn founded his colony, attracted thousands of settlers to Pennsylvania.

But Penn's father was wealthy and had influence, and King Charles II owed him a debt. When Penn's father died, the king offered to pay the debt by giving young William some land in America. Penn agreed and in 1681 received a large land grant. The king named the land Pennsylvania, meaning "Penn's woods," in memory of Penn's father.

Pennsylvania, like Massachusetts, was a success almost from the beginning. William Penn thought of Pennsylvania as a **"holy experiment"** for furthering the Quaker way of life. He worked hard to make the experiment succeed. He insisted on paying the Indians for the land on which his colonists settled.

Penn named the chief settlement in his colony Philadelphia. The name meant "city of brotherly love." He encouraged

Quakers to come to Pennsylvania, but everyone who believed in God was welcome there. Only one other colony, Rhode Island, had as much religious freedom as Pennsylvania did.

Advertising attracts settlers   William Penn attracted settlers by advertising. His agents wrote and distributed **pamphlets** describing attractive features of the colony. These paper-covered booklets told of Pennsylvania's fertile soil, good government, peaceful Indians, and healthful climate.

Because the pamphlets were sent to different countries, people came from many places. Whether rich or poor, whether Quaker or not, they helped Pennsylvania grow. Some who came were wealthy merchants or landowners. Experienced farmers came from lands along the Rhine River in Europe. Families from northern Ireland and Scotland settled on the frontier in the western part of Pennsylvania.

Why "middle colonies"?   New York, New Jersey, Delaware, and Pennsylvania were in the middle of the English colonies. To the north were the New England colonies; to the south, the southern ones. Thus their location is one reason they were called the middle colonies.

But they were in the middle of the English colonies in other ways, too. New York and Pennsylvania were neither the largest nor the smallest colonies. Virginia and Massachusetts exceeded them in population, yet there were colonies in New England and the South that had fewer people. In terms of religious freedom, these colonies were in the middle.

None was as free in religious matters as Rhode Island. Nor was any as strict as Massachusetts.

The people of the middle colonies were a varied group. There were not as many English people as there were in New England. Though slavery was legal in all four of the middle colonies, there were far fewer blacks there than in the southern colonies.

The middle colonies were not as heavily agricultural as the southern colonies, though most of the residents were farmers. Only along the Hudson River in New York were any farms as big as Virginia's plantations. Yet the middle colonies were more agricultural than New England.

CHECKUP

1. How did New Amsterdam become New York?
2. What three English colonies grew from the former Dutch possessions in North America?
3. Explain how the colony of Pennsylvania was started.
4. For what reasons were settlers attracted to the Pennsylvania colony?
5. Name the four middle colonies. Why were they called the "middle colonies"?

The Southern Colonies

```
┌─ VOCABULARY ─────────────────────┐
│  proprietor          Toleration Act
│  proprietary         assembly
│    colony            indigo
│  Roman Catholic      squatter
│    Church            debtor
└──────────────────────────────────┘
```

A proprietor founds Maryland   Three of England's southern colonies were founded by **proprietors**. A proprietor

Have pupils write the words for a handbill that is to be circulated in Europe to attract settlers to Pennsylvania.

was a person to whom the king gave a large grant of land. William Penn was a proprietor, and Pennsylvania was a **proprietary colony.** Penn made money by selling his land to colonists. The proprietors who founded southern colonies hoped to do the same thing.

A few prominent families in England were members of the **Roman Catholic Church.** Since the Church of England was the official church, Roman Catholics had many restrictions placed on them. Nevertheless, King Charles I of England had several Roman Catholic friends. Among these was Lord Baltimore.

Because of their friendship <u>King Charles I gave Lord Baltimore a large grant of land to the north and east of Virginia.</u> Through this, Lord Baltimore became proprietor of the colony he called Maryland. He gave his colony this name in honor of Henrietta Maria (or Mary), the king's wife. In 1634, St. Marys became the first settlement in Maryland.

Like Virginia, Maryland became a tobacco-growing, slaveholding, plantation colony. Its land was fertile and its location made it easy to trade with England. So Maryland soon prospered.

A refuge for Roman Catholics Lord Baltimore wanted to make money by selling his land. He also had the idea of making his colony a refuge for Roman Catholics from England. Many of Maryland's first settlers were Catholics, but the majority were English Protestants. It seemed possible that the Protestant majority might impose the same restrictions in Maryland that Roman Catholics had experienced in England.

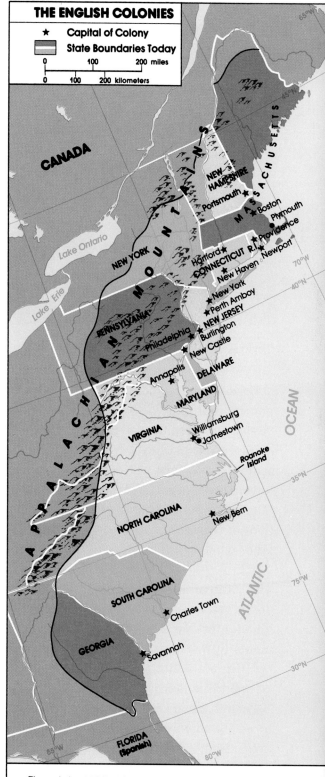

THE ENGLISH COLONIES

★ Capital of Colony

State Boundaries Today

0   100   200 miles
0 100 200 kilometers

CANADA

Lake Ontario

Lake Erie

NEW HAMPSHIRE
Portsmouth ★
MASSACHUSETTS
★ Boston
Plymouth
Providence ★
NEW YORK
Hartford ★ CONNECTICUT R.I. ★ Newport
★ New Haven
★ New York
★ Perth Amboy
NEW JERSEY
PENNSYLVANIA
Philadelphia ★ ★ Burlington
★ New Castle
DELAWARE
Annapolis ★
MARYLAND
APPALACHIAN MOUNTAINS
VIRGINIA
Williamsburg ★
★ Jamestown
Roanoke Island
NORTH CAROLINA
★ New Bern
SOUTH CAROLINA
★ Charles Town
GEORGIA
★ Savannah
FLORIDA (Spanish)

OCEAN
ATLANTIC

The original 13 English colonies stretched from the northern province of Massachusetts to Georgia.

Indians are welcomed to a church service in Maryland.

Lord Baltimore had appointed a governor to represent him in Maryland. In 1649 he ordered the governor to introduce a **Toleration Act** into Maryland's local **assembly**, or legislature. The governor followed orders, and the assembly passed the Toleration Act. It guaranteed freedom of worship to all Christians in Maryland, whether Protestant or Catholic.

The Carolina colonies   Until the 1660s there were several hundred miles of uncolonized land between Spanish settlements in Florida and the growing colony of Virginia. Both Spain and England claimed this land.

Earlier, Spanish missionaries had tried to establish missions along the coast of present-day South Carolina. However, Indians had driven them out. In 1653, colonists from Virginia settled in the disputed land. Ten years later it was the Spaniards' turn to be angry. It was then that they learned King Charles II had granted the land south of Virginia to eight English noblemen.

The eight noblemen became known as lords proprietors of Carolina. The name *Carolina* came from the Latin word for Charles. The lords proprietors were chiefly interested in the land nearest to the islands the English claimed in the West Indies. So they made their first settlement at what is today Charleston, South Carolina. They named it Charles Town, again in honor of the king who had given them the land.

The lords proprietors either gave or sold large plantations near Charleston to their aristocratic friends. Instead of tobacco, however, rice and **indigo** became the principal cash crops on these Carolina plantations. Indigo is a plant used to make a blue dye.

Both rice and indigo need sun and swampy land to grow successfully. These conditions created a great demand for slave labor to cultivate the crops. Most slaves brought to the Carolina mainland came from the West Indies. A century after Charleston got its start, there were twice as many black slaves as white people in South Carolina.

One Carolina becomes two   In 1729 the English government bought back all the land owned by descendants of the original lords proprietors of Carolina. At that time the colony was divided into North Carolina and South Carolina. There were several reasons for this.

Poor people from Virginia had drifted down into the unsettled northern part of

By 1740, Charles Town had become a busy seaport. (33°N/80°W; map, p. 79)

Carolina. In most cases they were **squatters.** This means that they settled on land to which they had no legal claim. There they raised families on the small farms they cleared from the wilderness.

These small farmers had left Virginia because the colony was controlled by plantation aristocrats. Now the farmers feared control by aristocrats from the southern part of Carolina. People in the northern and southern parts had little in common, so they often quarreled. Recognizing this, the English government wisely split the huge colony in two. Both North Carolina and South Carolina became royal colonies.

Georgia is last   Georgia was founded in 1733, the last of the 13 English colonies on the mainland of North America. There were two reasons for its existence. First, it was set up to protect prosperous South Carolina from raids by Spaniards and Indians in Florida. Second, it was thought of as a home for English **debtors** —people unable to pay the money they owed to others.

In England at that time, persons unable to pay their debts had to go to jail. A group of wealthy men in England thought this system was unfair. They asked King George II to release some of the male debtors so they could go to America and start new lives. The king agreed to this plan but asked that the debtors become part-time soldiers. They could then be used to prevent Spanish raids on South Carolina.

After the king gave the wealthy men a charter, one of them—James Oglethorpe —became the governor of the new colony. It was named Georgia to honor King George II. By the time Georgia was founded in 1733, Virginia was 126 years old. It had taken England a long time to plant her 13 colonies along the Atlantic coast of North America.

CHECKUP

1. How did the proprietors of colonies hope to profit from their holdings?
2. For what two purposes was Maryland founded?
3. How did the colonists in South Carolina differ from those in North Carolina?
4. Why was Georgia founded in 1733?
5. Name the five southern colonies.

Have pupils list the 13 colonies by name. Then beside each name have them write a sentence that tells something about the founding of the colony.   **81**

4/CHAPTER REVIEW

KEY FACTS

1. Between 1607 and 1733, England founded 13 colonies on the mainland of North America.
2. Virginia, the first successful colony, was the creation of a joint-stock company.
3. The Pilgrims and the Puritans started the colony of Massachusetts, from which three other New England colonies grew.
4. In 1664, England took over the Dutch possessions in North America and divided them into three middle colonies.
5. Pennsylvania, Maryland, and the two Carolinas were originally under the control of proprietors.
6. By the middle of the eighteenth century, England had four New England colonies, four middle colonies, and five southern colonies.

VOCABULARY QUIZ

Using a separate piece of paper, match the terms with the definitions.

a. joint-stock company
b. House of Burgesses
c. Pilgrims
d. Fundamental Orders
e. Puritans
f. Quakers
g. "holy experiment"
h. indigo
i. proprietor
j. debtors

d **1.** Said to be the first written constitution in the world
i **2.** Person to whom the king of England gave a large grant of land
a **3.** A means of combining people and money for a project
j **4.** Georgia founded to provide them with a new life
h **5.** A crop that was grown extensively in South Carolina
b **6.** The first representative government in the English colonies
e **7.** Largest group in the Massachusetts Bay Colony
g **8.** What William Penn considered his colony to be
c **9.** So named because they went on a religious journey to Massachusetts in 1620
f **10.** Group that refused military service in England

REVIEW QUESTIONS

1. Why was England slow in starting colonies in North America?
2. How did Virginians overcome difficulties to become the first successful English colony?
3. Why were the Puritans important in the New England colonies?
4. What were differences in the origins of New York and Pennsylvania?
5. Name the four New England colonies, the four middle colonies, and the five southern colonies.

ACTIVITIES

1. Make a chart showing (a) the name of each of the 13 colonies, (b) the date of establishment, (c) whether it was a New England colony, a middle colony, or a southern colony, and (d) a person or group closely associated with each colony.
2. Find the origins of the name for each of the 13 English colonies.
3. Using the map on page 79, choose a settlement in each of the 13 colonies and find the origins of each settlement's name.

FINDING INFORMATION

In school and out, a library can be used to find more information on a subject that interests you. In studying this chapter, perhaps you would like to know more about one of the English colonies or about a person connected with the colonies. Or later in the year you may want to know more about another aspect of American history. Possibly in later life after your school days are over, you may want or need to know something about a subject that concerns you.

Your school library or the public library in your community can be very helpful. To obtain the greatest benefit from a library, you must know how to use it. Most libraries are arranged the same way, with certain aids to finding what you want to know.

LIBRARY AIDS

Card catalogs in libraries contain cards for every book in the library. There probably is a card listing the book by *title*, another card filed under the name of the *author* or *authors*, and often a third card under the *subject* of the book.

For example, your library card catalog might have the book *Colonial Living* listed under its title; under the author's name (last name first), Tunis, Edwin; and under United States: Social Life and Customs—Colonial Times, the subject of the book.

Libraries have a reference section. It includes encyclopedias, almanacs, atlases, dictionaries, and other books of general interest.

One helpful reference book is called the *Dictionary of American Biography*. Its 22 volumes contain biographical information on more than 15,000 famous Americans. *Notable American Women* has biographical details for hundreds of famous American women in its four volumes. You will find many other helpful books in the reference section of your library.

Librarians are persons with special skills in finding the right source for information. Librarians also have many other duties, so they are usually quite busy. Although they are willing to help, you should first try to find what you need on your own.

SKILLS PRACTICE

You can sharpen your skill at using a library by choosing one of the topics below, or you may choose a topic suggested by your study of the preceding chapters in this book. After choosing a topic, go to the library and do enough research to write in your own words a short essay on your topic. At the end of your essay, be sure to list the sources you used. This list of sources is called a bibliography.

Plymouth Rock	Queen Elizabeth I
Colonial Williamsburg	Sir Walter Raleigh
	King Charles II
Anne Hutchinson	The Society of Friends
Captain John Smith	
William Penn	Philadelphia
Eliza Lucas Pinckney	Anne Bradstreet
James Oglethorpe	Chesapeake Bay

Why People Came to America

VOCABULARY

apprentice	promotional literature
craft	indenture

An arrival in Philadelphia   It was October 1723. A young man, hardly 17 years old, had just arrived in Philadelphia. He had left his home in Boston after a quarrel with his half brother. The young man walked along Second Street to a bakery where he bought three big, puffy bread rolls, too large to fit in his pockets. Carrying a roll under each arm and eating the third, he walked to Market Street. On the way he passed the home of Mr. Read.

Mr. Read's young daughter, Deborah, stood in the doorway of the home. She laughed at the awkward, ridiculous appearance of the young man. His name was Benjamin Franklin. During the next year, the girl and the young man got to know each other better. She began to think he looked less ridiculous and less awkward.

In 1730 Benjamin Franklin and Deborah Read were married. In the same year he became sole owner of a prosperous printing business. He also became owner of a newspaper. Franklin made The Pennsylvania Gazette one of the leading newspapers in the English colonies. He did so well in the printing business that he could retire at the age of 48 and devote the rest of his life to the service of his country.

Growing up in Boston   Josiah Franklin was Benjamin Franklin's father. He was of English birth, one of thousands who left their homeland in search of a better life in the colonies. His wife and three children came with him from England. The family settled in Boston where four more children were born to Josiah Franklin and his first wife. After she died, Josiah married Abiah Folger, by whom he had ten more children. Benjamin, born in January 1706, was the youngest son of this second marriage.

Josiah Franklin had been a silk dyer in England, but there was little demand for his trade in colonial Boston. So he worked as a soap-boiler and candle-maker. His youngest son went to the Boston Grammar School until he was 10 years old. For the next 2 years Benjamin helped his father at work.

Twelve-year-old Benjamin Franklin hated boiling soap and making candles. He wanted to go to sea on one of the merchant ships sailing from Boston's busy harbor. His father feared the boy would

By 1750 the wilderness in many colonies had given way to orderly fields and farms.

The painting on the opposite page shows Bethlehem, Pennsylvania, in 1757. The settlement was made by German immigrants.

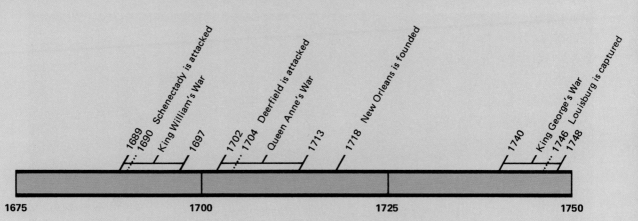

1689 Schenectady is attacked
1690 King William's War
1697
1702
1704 Deerfield is attacked
Queen Anne's War
1713
1718 New Orleans is founded
1740
King George's War
1746 Louisburg is captured
1748

1675
1700
1725
1750

One of Franklin's most successful ventures was the annual publication of *Poor Richard's Almanack*. This small pamphlet gave useful information about the weather, the solar system, and many other subjects. In many homes the only reading material was the Bible and *Poor Richard's Almanack*.

run away. To prevent that, his father made young Benjamin an **apprentice** to his older half brother James Franklin, a printer. An apprentice is one who learns a **craft**, or trade, by working with one who is skilled at it.

A quarrel between brothers Along with his printing business, James Franklin published a newspaper called the *New England Courant*. Some things he printed in his paper angered the Massachusetts General Court. The Court ordered him to give up the paper. Instead, he merely transferred ownership to Benjamin Franklin. Benjamin had written some pieces for the paper, so it was not strange that his brother gave the paper to him.

But the arrangement worked poorly. Before long, the half brothers quarreled. So at the age of 17, Benjamin Franklin decided to strike out on his own.

Benjamin Franklin's rise was one of the great success stories in eighteenth-century America. Yet he was not alone in climbing from poor beginnings to fame and fortune. The English colonies were booming. There were opportunities everywhere. Even those who did not climb as high as Franklin were generally better off in America than in Europe.

Advertising America People across the Atlantic learned about the opportunities in America through **promotional literature**. This literature was in the form of pamphlets, advertisements, books, and letters from people already in the English colonies. Much of the promotional literature was exaggerated and unreliable in terms of fact. But it dealt with the topics that most interested the people who were thinking of going to America. The promotional literature reflected the people's hopes and dreams of what they might find in the English colonies.

A young Welshman named Gabriel Thomas wrote a well-known piece of promotional literature. Thomas was a Quaker from a small town in Wales. He was among the first colonists in Pennsylvania, coming there by himself on a ship named the *John and Sarah* in 1681.

Benjamin Franklin's success as a publisher launched him on a career in public service.

Many other young unmarried persons came to the English colonies. But many families came, too. In fact, Gabriel Thomas's parents and sisters followed him to William Penn's colony.

Gabriel Thomas stayed 15 years in Pennsylvania. Then he returned to Wales and England for a visit. While there he published a little book with a big title, *An Historical and Geographical Account of the Province and Country of Pennsylvania.* . . . He wrote the book to inform and to encourage people thinking of coming to Pennsylvania.

Plentiful food There was plenty of food in Pennsylvania, Gabriel Thomas wrote. Wild turkeys weighed 40 or 50 pounds. There were red deer in the woods as well as pheasants, partridges, and pigeons. Likewise, there were "prodigious quantities" of fish waiting to be caught.

Gabriel Thomas's list of wild fruits must have made mouths water. And there were nuts and berries. If his readers needed further encouragement, they could have read: "Their sorts of grain are wheat, rye, pease, oates, barley, buckwheat, rice, Indian corn, Indian pease, and beans." In addition, there were root crops such as turnips, potatoes, carrots, and parsnips. All these fruits, grains, and vegetables were produced yearly in greater quantities than in England, according to Gabriel Thomas.

Gabriel Thomas described many other attractive features of Pennsylvania. Land was inexpensive. Government was just. Good schools were available. Indians were peaceful. The air and the climate were healthful. People could worship God almost as they pleased. And "poor people, both men and women, will get near three times more wages for their labor in this country than they can earn either in England or Wales."

Growing colonies After Gabriel Thomas wrote his book, he returned to Pennsylvania to live the rest of his life. Certainly some of what he wrote, even though exaggerated, was close to the truth about other English colonies. Pennsylvania's population grew rapidly in the eighteenth century, but so did that of the other colonies.

The pictures and captions on page 98 sum up the advantages of life in the English colonies. Hundreds of thousands of people felt they would be better off in the English colonies than in their homelands. They had to be willing to undergo great hardships, for the voyage to America was not an easy one.

The Atlantic voyage Usually the voyage across the Atlantic from England or a port on the European continent took from 7 to 12 weeks. It was not a pleasant journey. One man making the trip wrote, "There is on board these ships terrible misery, stench, fumes, horror, vomiting, many kinds of sea-sickness, fever, dysentery, headache, heat, constipation, boils, scurvy, cancer, mouth-rot, and the like, all of which come from old and sharply salted food and meat, also from very bad and foul water, so that many die miserably." It seems a miracle that anyone survived conditions like these, but hundreds of thousands did.

The flourishing appearance of Philadelphia midway through the eighteenth century is proof that Gabriel Thomas's enthusiasm for Pennsylvania was well founded. By 1750, Philadelphia was a thriving city of 13,000 people. (40°N/75°W; map, p. 79)

Most people coming to the colonies were too poor to pay their way across the Atlantic. To come to the colonies, a person would sign an **indenture**, or contract. The indenture pledged the person to work for a certain number of years after arriving in America. Usually the term of service was from 4 to 7 years.

Indentured servants The contract was held by the ship's captain. When he reached a port in the English colonies, he would sell the contract to someone wanting to buy the service of the person who had signed the indenture. Sometimes whole families would sign indentures to get to America. Occasionally husband, wife, and children would be separated when their contracts were sold to different purchasers.

The advantages of coming to America as an indentured servant usually outweighed the disadvantages of this arrangement. Upon becoming free at the end of the term of service, an indentured servant might receive new clothes, tools, money, or some land. Courts in America made masters treat their indentured servants well. Masters were forced to live up to the terms of the contract. It was not unknown for a woman servant to marry her master or one of his sons. There was no disgrace attached to coming to America as an indentured servant. In fact, at least half of the white people coming to the English colonies came as indentured servants.

CHECKUP

1. Why did Benjamin Franklin move to Philadelphia? What success did he have there?
2. Explain the purpose of promotional literature.
3. What attractions were there in Pennsylvania, according to Gabriel Thomas?
4. What hardships were involved for those coming by ship from Europe to America?
5. Describe the indenture system. Why did so many people make use of it?

The business of selling indentured servants became so profitable that it attracted the criminal and greedy. In English seaport cities, children were sometimes kidnapped for labor in the colonies. Some poor parents indentured their children so that the children would not go hungry.

A Variety of People

┌─VOCABULARY─────────────────┐
│ **Huguenots**   **frontier**   │
│ **textiles**   **population explosion** │
└────────────────────────────┘

The English were first   Until about 1700 most of the colonists came from England.   The Pilgrims and the Puritans came for religious reasons, at least in part.   But the great majority of colonists came because the English colonies offered better opportunities for getting ahead in life.   Younger sons with no chance to inherit the family farm came to find land in the colonies.   After the frequent wars of the 1600s and 1700s, thousands of discharged soldiers and sailors came to the colonies to find work.   Anyone unemployed in England could always try for a better life by coming to the colonies.

Yet even in the 1600s some non-English people came to the English colonies.   French Protestants, known as **Huguenots** (hyü′ gə notz), who were persecuted in their home country, came in small numbers.   They settled near the area of what is now Charleston, South Carolina, as well as in other colonial communities.   People of the Jewish faith, forced out of Spain and Portugal by religious persecution, found new homes at Newport, Rhode Island.   Thousands of Dutch people were added to the English population when New Amsterdam became New York in 1664.   Slaves from Africa or the West Indies and some free blacks could be found in all the colonies.   Still, in 1700 the great majority of people in the English colonies were of English descent.

German colonists   The first non-English people to migrate from Europe to the English colonies in large numbers were of German background.   Many of them came from the Upper Rhine Valley, where they had suffered from invading armies in time of war.   They came to America searching for a land where they could live in peace.   At first these German-speaking people settled in Pennsylvania because of the advertising distributed by agents of William Penn.   In time, some of them and their descendants migrated north into New York or south into Virginia, Maryland, and the Carolinas.

Wherever they settled, most German immigrants worked hard, obeyed the laws, and kept to themselves.   Most were farmers, though a few turned to industry, making **textiles**—that is, cloth—paper, or glass.   Some of them were the ancestors of the people that are today called the Pennsylvania Dutch.

Scots and Scots-Irish   During the 1700s about 300,000 people from Scotland and northern Ireland migrated to the English colonies in America.   Those from northern Ireland were descendants of Scots who had settled there 100 years before.   They were known as the Scots-Irish.

At first these people prospered by raising sheep and turning wool into heavy, warm cloth.   Late in the 1600s, the English government denied them the right to sell their cloth in England.   This destroyed the market that many of these colonists depended on.

Whether Scots or Scots-Irish, these people were usually poor.   By the time they got to the English colonies, good

The Pennsylvania Dutch are the descendants of German, not Dutch, immigrants. The German word meaning "German" is *deutsch* (pronounced doych). People misinterpreted the word as *Dutch.*   **89**

Many Scots-Irish were weavers of linen and woolen cloth. In 1699 the English forbade weavers to export cloth abroad. The law threw many of the Scots-Irish weavers out of work. This, along with the persecution they received for refusing to conform to the Anglican Church, encouraged the Scots-Irish to emigrate.

land near the coast was expensive. So the newcomers went to the **frontier**, that is, the western parts of the colonies where few people, if any, lived. They settled along the frontier of all the colonies, particularly in Pennsylvania, Virginia, North and South Carolina, and Georgia.

On the frontier, Scots and Scots-Irish cleared land, built homes, and put up churches. Often the frontier people quarreled with government officials who represented the more settled eastern part of the colonies. The frontier people wanted more protection from the Indians. Also they quarreled about taxes. Taxes collected from all residents of the southern colonies were used to support the official Church of England. Scots and Scots-Irish in Virginia especially resented this. They were Presbyterians, unwilling to be taxed to support the Church of England.

Black people in the colonies You read in the last chapter how the first blacks came to Jamestown in 1619. It seems likely that they were sold as indentured servants rather than slaves and in time earned their freedom. By 1700, however, slavery had fastened itself on the colonies. After that date, the number of black people brought to the colonies as slaves increased rapidly.

There were several reasons for this rapid increase. Slaves were considered more desirable than indentured servants because slaves did not have to be released after a certain time. Children of slave mothers were born into slavery, thus there was a natural increase in the number of slaves. Moreover, rapid growth of the plantation system in the 1700s created a need for laborers. And large profits could be made from the slave trade.

Life was not easy for the colonists who cleared land and built homes on the frontier.

Portuguese, Dutch, and English sea captains, as well as some from New England, took part in the slave trade. The sea captains bought the slaves at trading posts along the African coast. African chiefs whose tribes had taken captives from rival tribes sold these captives to the slave traders. The slave ships were crowded and filthy. A great many slaves died before reaching America.

Usually Africans were brought first to the West Indies. Many of them worked on the sugar plantations. Others were sold in the English colonies on the mainland. Slavery was legal in all the colonies, but by 1750 it was most closely associated with the South.

Of the colonies north of Maryland, New York had the most slaves. As the colonial period neared its end, there was probably 1 black out of every 8 New Yorkers. No more than 1 in every 50 New Englanders was black. Only in South Carolina were there more blacks than whites, although in colonial Virginia blacks and whites were nearly equal in number.

Not all blacks in colonial times were slaves. Whether slave or free, some blacks practiced a skilled trade such as that of a carpenter or blacksmith. Most slaves worked in the fields on plantations and farms, although a good number were house servants and cooks. The labor of blacks contributed greatly to the prosperity of the colonies in the 1700s.

What colonists brought No matter how poor they were, colonists brought a few possessions with them. Even more important, they brought the language, religious beliefs, and ideas of government

Making boots was a skilled trade in colonial Virginia.

they had known in their homeland. Since the English settled along the Atlantic coast before other Europeans, the colonies based their colonial governments on English models. The early comers from England brought English ideas of liberty and law to America. They introduced into most of the colonies the customs of the Church of England—or, as with the Puritans and Quakers, the customs of the offshoots of the official English church.

Because these were English colonies, English became the common language. But other languages were spoken in some colonial homes. One third of the population of Pennsylvania spoke German. In neighboring New York, the Dutch language held on long after the English government had taken over. Huguenots spoke French, and many educated English colonists spoke that language. Still, the language of business and government was English.

The largest company in the slave trade was the Royal African Company of London. In the colonies Newport, Rhode Island, was a center of the slave trade for many years, yet Rhode Island was also the first colony to ban the importation of slaves.

A leap in population   The 13 English colonies experienced a **population explosion** in the 1700s. By 1760 the population had climbed to more than 1.5 million. Immigration explained only part of this rapid increase. Families were quite large, so there were many native-born Americans. Josiah Franklin's family of 17 children by two wives was above average in number, but families with 10 or 12 children were not at all uncommon. A large family meant more hands to do the hard work that was necessary for the family to survive.

This population explosion had a number of effects. First, it meant the colonies expanded, especially along the western frontier. Second, the population explosion created scores of new towns, while at the same time it increased the population of the older ones. Third, farming, trade, and industry grew because there were more workers and more customers. Finally, the population explosion was an indication of the rising strength of the English colonies.

By 1760 the 13 colonies not only had survived but had grown and prospered. Many different kinds of people had started new lives there. The colonists had begun to have characteristics of their own. They were becoming different from the English.

CHECKUP

1. What groups of non-English people came to the colonies in large numbers during the 1700s?
2. Why did newcomers to the colonies generally go to the frontier?
3. Why did the number of slaves increase rapidly during the 1700s?

How Colonists Made a Living

┌─VOCABULARY─────────────────────┐

mahogany	hogshead
bread colonies	factor
sperm whale	commission
triangular trade route	mercantilism

└────────────────────────────────┘

A variety of occupations   Among the 1.5 million residents of the English colonies in 1760, there were many occupations. Most people lived in rural surroundings. Yet by no means did all colonists make their living by farming.

Gabriel Thomas listed occupations in Pennsylvania in which the pay was better than it was in England. His list will help you to see the many ways of making a living in the English colonies. Thomas's list of occupations includes blacksmith, carpenter (for houses and ships), bricklayer, mason, shoemaker, tailor, sawyer (one who saws boards), weaver, wool comber, potter, tanner (one who makes animal hides into leather), currier (one who makes leather goods), brickmaker, hatmaker, glazier (one who puts glass into place), cooper (one who makes wooden barrels, tubs, and pails), baker, butcher, brewer, silversmith, plasterer, wheelwright (one who makes wheels), millwright (one who builds mills), brazier (one who works with brass), gunsmith, locksmith, watchmaker and clockmaker, saddler, barber, printer, bookbinder, and rope maker.

There also were lawyers and physicians in the colonies. Thomas omitted them from his list, explaining, "Of lawyers and

Ask: Which of the occupations listed above no longer exist or are much less essential than in colonial times?

Most colonial communities had cooper shops where pails, tubs, and barrels were made.

physicians I shall say nothing, because this country is very peaceable and healthy.'' He also omitted surveyors, whose services were greatly in demand where so much land was bought and sold.

There were no real factories in the English colonies. They would come later. People working at crafts and trades generally had small shops. During the 1700s American cabinetmakers fashioned furniture as good as any made in England or France. They used such native woods as cherry, maple, or oak. Sometimes they made furniture from **mahogany**, a heavy hardwood shipped from the West Indies. Usually they worked from pattern books, following models of the master furniture makers of England. Often, however, the American craftworkers added distinctive touches of their own.

On plantation and farm   In the early days of each colony, almost all settlers were farmers. They raised the food needed for their own families and some of the materials from which clothing was made. But as life became a little easier, groups of colonies developed products for a thriving trade.

In Virginia, Maryland, and North Carolina, tobacco proved to be the most profitable crop. In South Carolina and Georgia the leading products were rice and indigo. These crops were grown mainly by slave labor on large plantations. Nevertheless, small farms contributed a share.

By the 1700s the middle colonies were known as the **bread colonies.** Much grain was raised there. Farmers in New York and Pennsylvania also sent large amounts of beer, beef, and pork to England and the West Indies. At the same time, Albany, New York, was a fur-trading center. Furs obtained through trade with Indians were collected in Albany. Then they were shipped to England or to one of the colonial cities to be made into hats, blankets, rugs, or clothing.

New England's rocky soil made farming difficult. However, forests and the

Ask: If you had lived in colonial times, what occupation would you have preferred to follow? Why?   **93**

sea offered opportunities for making a living. As a result, New Englanders turned to shipbuilding, fishing, and trade as their major occupations.

Oak trees, codfish, and whales An English ship's carpenter was among the early settlers at Plymouth. Soon afterward, six shipwrights (carpenters skilled in shipbuilding) settled at Salem, in the Massachusetts Bay colony. They brought pitch, tar, ships' ropes, and sailcloth with them from England. Oak trees in New England forests provided fine lumber for building ships. Before long, ships built in Massachusetts were sailing along the coast, from Maine to Virginia.

Because of the abundant supply of lumber, it cost only half as much to build ships in the colonies as it did in England. For this reason, English merchants bought many of the ships built in colonial ship-

yards. By 1665, some 300 ships built in New England sailed the seas. By 1720 Boston shipyards alone produced 200 ships a year, and Philadelphia shipyards launched nearly as many.

Hundreds of New Englanders made their living fishing for cod. Salted or dried codfish were packed in barrels and shipped out in great quantities. Many Massachusetts merchants made their fortunes from this business. A model of a codfish still hangs in the State House in Boston as a reminder of how much the fish meant to the colony.

The most adventurous of all who made their living from the sea were those going after the great whales. Sometimes the whales were caught close to the New England coast. The whales' fat was boiled down to make oil for lamps. In the early 1700s, whalers from Nantucket captured a kind of whale they had not heard of be-

Among those who made a living from the sea, the whalers were the most adventurous.

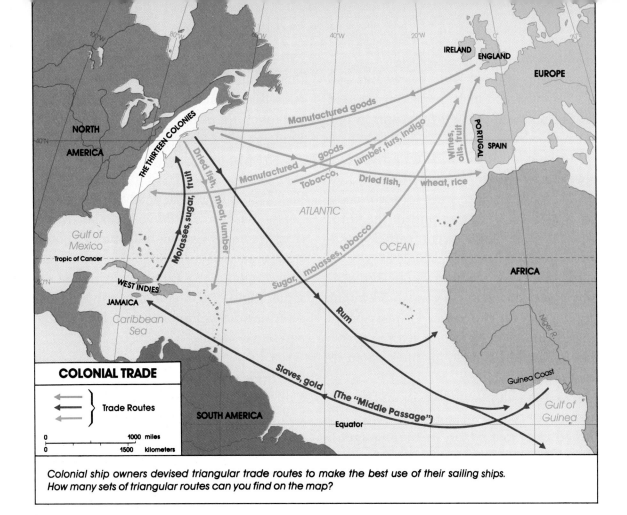

Trade Routes

0   1000 miles
0   1500 kilometers

Manufactured goods

Manufactured goods

Tobacco, lumber, furs, indigo

Dried fish, wheat, rice

Wines, oils, fruit

Dried fish, meat, lumber

Molasses, sugar, fruit

Sugar, molasses, tobacco

Rum

Slaves, gold (The "Middle Passage")

IRELAND ENGLAND
EUROPE
PORTUGAL SPAIN
NORTH AMERICA
THE THIRTEEN COLONIES
ATLANTIC   OCEAN
AFRICA
Gulf of Mexico
Tropic of Cancer
WEST INDIES
JAMAICA
Caribbean Sea
Niger R.
Guinea Coast
Gulf of Guinea
SOUTH AMERICA
Equator

Colonial ship owners devised triangular trade routes to make the best use of their sailing ships. How many sets of triangular routes can you find on the map?

fore. It was the **sperm whale.** A waxy substance from its head made excellent candles. Oil from its head burned with a clear, bright flame. Before long, whaling ships from New England ports sailed forth to every ocean of the world in search of the valuable sperm whale. A whaling ship would not return until it had its hold full of oil. A man signing on for a voyage on a whaler knew that he might not see his home port for 3, 4, or even 5 years.

Colonial trade   By the middle of the 1700s, the colonies were very active members of an Atlantic trading community. Generally this trade was carried on by merchants whose offices were in Boston, Philadelphia, or New York. However, every section of the colonies took part in trade. The southern colonies sold tobacco and rice. The middle colonies dealt in grain, livestock, and furs. New England specialized in lumber and fish, and, in addition, built many of the ships that carried colonial products to England, to the West Indies, and to countries bordering on the Mediterranean Sea.

Some New England merchants made fortunes through what became known as a **triangular trade route.** Rum made in New England was carried to Africa. There it was traded for African people sold into slavery. The slaves were carried to the West Indies where they were traded for molasses. This molasses was then brought back to New England and used in the making of more rum. Merchants and sea captains counted on making a good profit from each of the three stages in this triangular trade route.

In Virginia, ships sailed up a river to a plantation wharf. Slaves then rolled large barrels packed with tobacco along the wharf and into the hold of the ship. These large barrels were called **hogsheads**. Before the ship sailed, the owner of the plantation would give the ship captain an order for English goods. He might order a fine set of dishes. Or perhaps he would order cloth from which pretty dresses could be made for the women in his family.

When the ship anchored in an English harbor, its cargo of tobacco would be turned over to a **factor**, or trading agent, for sale. The factor kept part of the sale price as his **commission**, or payment for his services. He used some of the remainder to buy the items the plantation owner had ordered. Perhaps the same ship carried these items back to Virginia. Then it took on a cargo of tobacco, and the process would be repeated.

Trade with England   The English believed that colonies should exist for the benefit of the country that held them. This belief was part of a system called **mercantilism.** Under this system the colonies were to produce raw materials and send them to England. There they would be made into manufactured goods and sold back to the colonies. English leaders thus encouraged commerce and the development of colonial resources. But they had no intention of encouraging manufacturing in the colonies. Trying to protect their own industries, English leaders passed laws aimed at forcing the colonies to buy all their manufactured goods from England.

Increasingly, colonial leaders felt strong enough to try to get around these laws. Some manufacturing developed in Massachusetts and Pennsylvania. Moreover, smuggling manufactured goods from France or from other countries apart from England began to be a feature of colonial trade. Sooner or later, England and its American colonies were bound to disagree over trade.

Women's roles   Most women in colonial times worked in, or close to, their homes. Still, women's work was by no means confined to the traditional tasks of cooking, cleaning, and child care. Usually skilled craftsmen had their homes above or behind their shops. This made it possible for wives and children to help in the work. Wives waited on customers, perhaps leaving older children to care for the younger ones. Likewise, in the numerous taverns of the time, wives often served customers during busy hours.

On southern plantations, black men, women, and children held in slavery did nearly all the housework. The plantation owner's wife supervised them in the household tasks. She also supervised the spinning, weaving, and food preserving, while her husband directed the field work.

On the small farms where most colonial families lived, each member of the family had assigned tasks. The farm family functioned as a unit. There were so many tasks to be done that it was almost impossible for a single man or woman to survive

Be sure that all pupils understand the system called mercantilism. The belief that colonies should exist for the benefit of the mother country would prove to be a major issue in the events leading to the War for Independence.

Some pupils might like to report to the class on the achievements of Abigail Smith Adams and Mercy Otis Warren. Accounts of the lives of these two early feminists may be found in the *Dictionary of American Biography* and in *Notable American Women: A Biographical Dictionary.*

detail, Museum of Fine Arts, Boston

At a time when women's roles were generally confined to those of wife, mother, and keeper of the home, Abigail Smith Adams (left) and Mercy Otis Warren (right) spoke out for the rights of women. Both were natives of Massachusetts.

alone. Widows did not stay widows very long. Stories have been told of women receiving proposals on the way back from the cemetery following the burial of their husbands.

Colonial marriages took place at about the same average age as marriages today. The colonial town of Dedham, Massachusetts, has been closely studied. In Dedham, over a span of time, the average age of the first marriage for men was 25; for women, it was 22.

Before marriage, girls got years of instruction and practice in the duties of being a wife and mother. Older girls were expected to take over much of the care of younger brothers and sisters.

An extremely important role for colonial women was that of doctor-nurse. Physicians were few and far between and not very skilled anyway. In the home it was the role of the woman to care for the sick. Therefore, a woman had to learn the use of the few available medicines. She learned what herbs and roots were useful for treating certain illnesses. She splinted the broken bones and bound up the wounds of the adults and children in her home.

CHECKUP

1. Describe the variety of occupations available to colonial workers.
2. What products were most typical of the southern colonies? The middle colonies?
3. In what three ways did most New Englanders make their living?
4. Describe (**a**) a triangular trade route and (**b**) mercantilism.
5. Describe women's roles in colonial life in America in the 1700s.

97

ADVANTAGES OF LIFE IN THE ENGLISH COLONIES

GOOD OPPORTUNITIES FOR MAKING A LIVING

Land and work were easy to get in America. The English colonies were "long on land but short on people." There was more work to be done in the colonies than there were hands to do it.

MORE POLITICAL FREEDOM

All the colonies had some form of representative government, so colonists had a part in making their own laws. A higher percentage of people could vote and hold office there than in Europe.

MORE RELIGIOUS FREEDOM

People could worship as they pleased in nearly all the colonies. Religious groups that had been persecuted in Europe found new freedom in the English colonies in America.

MORE SOCIAL DEMOCRACY

Family background and social position made little difference in the colonies. The achievement of a satisfying way of life depended much more on initiative, ability, and perseverance.

MORE FREEDOM FOR WOMEN

Women played an important part in the development of the colonies. They had more freedom to work, to choose their own husbands, and to live their own lives than women in Europe had.

LESS GOVERNMENTAL INTERFERENCE

England's government was far away and did not interfere greatly with the growth of local governments. The burden of taxes was lighter in the American colonies than it was in the countries of Europe.

98   Ask: Were there disadvantages to life in the English colonies? If so, what might they have been?

Neighbors of the 13 Colonies

┌─VOCABULARY──────────────────┐
allies
└─────────────────────────────────┘

New France   To the north of the 13 English colonies lay New France. The population of New France had grown slowly. By 1700 New France had only 15,000 colonists in its vast territory. The population of the English colonies at that time was nearly 20 times larger.

Nevertheless, the French from the beginning had been aggressive fur traders, trappers, and fishermen. There had been minor clashes between French and English colonists for years. In addition, both the French and English governments claimed some of the same land in North America.

Colonial wars   Between 1689 and 1750 the colonists were drawn into three wars. Usually these wars started in Europe between France and England, or Great Britain. (The term *Great Britain* came into use in 1707 after the union of England and Scotland.) In North America these three wars were known as King William's War (1689–1697), Queen Anne's War (1702–1713), and King George's War (1740–1748). In each of these wars the colonists fought alongside British troops against the French. Both sides had Indian **allies**, or groups that fought with them against the enemy.

Frontier settlements in the colonies suffered in these wars. From their base in Canada, French soldiers and Indians attacked and wiped out the village of

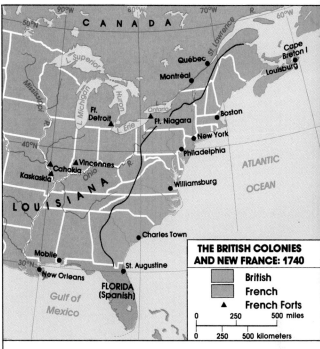

The boundaries between British and French areas are approximate. They were generally disputed.

Schenectady, New York, in 1690. In 1704 Indian allies of the French attacked the frontier town of Deerfield, Massachusetts, killing or capturing more than half the residents.

The British and the colonials fought back. In 1710, Port Royal, a French settlement in Nova Scotia, fell to the British and their allies. But an attempt to take Quebec and Montreal the next year was abandoned after ten British troopships were wrecked in the Gulf of St. Lawrence.

In the last of these three wars, New Englanders invaded Canada. With the help of a British fleet, the New England farmers and fishermen captured Louisburg. Louisburg was a French fort built on an island at the entrance to the Gulf of St. Lawrence. A few months later French and Indians raided towns in Maine.

British ships unload an attack force of New Englanders at Cape Breton Island in 1745. The force took the French fortress of Louisburg. (46°N/60°W; map, p. 99)

Other groups of French-led Indians burned Saratoga and Albany in New York.

The treaty of peace that ended King George's War gave Louisburg back to France. This angered people in New England, especially those who had taken part in the capture of the French fort.

In two of these colonial wars France and Spain were allies against Great Britain. In the south a mixed force of Carolinians and Indians seized and burned the town of St. Augustine in Spanish-held Florida. However, they were unable to capture the fort there.

Another expedition from Carolina marched across northern Florida toward French Louisiana. It destroyed 13 of the 14 Catholic missions that formed a link between Florida and Louisiana. But Choctaw Indians, allied with the French, turned back this invasion before it could reach any actual French settlements.

The capture of Louisburg in 1745 was an amazing military feat, carried out by a hastily assembled group of New England farmers and fishermen. Supported by the Royal Navy, the makeshift army landed near Louisburg and laid siege to the strongest French fortress in North America. Six weeks later the French surrendered.

French Louisiana   Nevertheless, the French government felt that Louisiana was in danger. A combination of British and colonial soldiers might invade and seize the rich fur-trading regions along the Mississippi River and its tributaries. To protect Louisiana, the French built a string of forts along the water routes that held together the vast territory. Forts at Detroit, Niagara, Kaskaskia, Cahokia, Vincennes, Mobile, and New Orleans were among these. The settlement that grew into the city of New Orleans was begun in 1718.

In addition to building forts, the French government transported colonists from Canada to settle in Louisiana. In these ways the French tried to make secure their control of Louisiana. Still, the British government and the American colonists saw the nearly empty land to the west of the Appalachian Mountains as a desirable place to expand.

The West Indies   Planting settlements on the West Indian islands followed much the same pattern as the colonization of the mainland of North America. For 100 years after Columbus's voyages, the Spanish were the major power in the Caribbean Sea. Beginning in the 1600s, however, England, France, and the Netherlands began to colonize some of the hundreds of islands in this sun-drenched sea.

In time, each of these European powers claimed one or more of the West Indian islands. Some of these islands changed hands during the colonial wars. Great naval battles took place in the West Indies as fleets from France and England fought each other.

Because of the sugar plantations located in the West Indies, some islands were at first considered more valuable than any of the mainland colonies. Providing owners of sugar plantations with slaves was a profitable business as well. You have already learned how a triangular trade route enriched some New England merchants. Much of the salted or dried cod shipped from New England went to the West Indies. There it became food for the African men and women who were forced to toil as slaves in the fields of the sugar plantations.

A strong base   It was, however, shortsighted to think of a West Indian island as being more valuable than one of the British mainland colonies. By the 1700s each of the colonies on the mainland of North America had a strong base of population and prosperity.

The two oldest colonies, Virginia and Massachusetts, were probably strong enough to be independent countries on their own. In fact, the people of each colony considered themselves to be independent of the other colonies. But all considered themselves to be parts of the British Empire. In 1750 it is doubtful that any colonist thought of being anything but a loyal subject of the British king.

CHECKUP

1. What part did American colonists play in the three colonial wars fought between 1689 and 1750?
2. How did the French government attempt to protect Louisiana against invasion and seizure?
3. Why were some West Indian islands considered so valuable?

Have pupils find the French forts mentioned above on the map on page 99.

KEY FACTS

1. The attractions of the English colonies were well advertised through promotional literature.

2. A great many settlers came to America through the indenture system.

3. In the 1700s, Germans, Scots and Scots-Irish, and Africans were the three largest non-English groups coming to the colonies.

4. Though most settlers in the English colonies were farmers, there was an increasing variety of occupations in the crafts and trades.

5. Between 1689 and 1750, colonists participated in three wars on the side of England.

6. By the middle of the 1700s, Great Britain's mainland colonies had achieved a strong base of population and prosperity.

VOCABULARY QUIZ

On a separate sheet of paper write the letter of the term next to the number of its description.

a. apprentice   **f.** factor
b. indenture   **g.** commission
c. Huguenots   **h.** triangular trade
d. frontier   route
e. promotional   **i.** hogshead
     literature   **j.** allies

f **1.** One who arranged for the sale of Virginia tobacco in England

a **2.** Usually a young person learning a trade from a master craftworker

c **3.** French Protestants

i **4.** A barrel used for shipping tobacco

d **5.** Western edge of settlement

j **6.** Groups that work together against a common enemy

b **7.** A contract pledging a person to serve for a specified number of years

e **8.** Written matter intended to persuade people to come to America

h **9.** Trade between New England, Africa, and the West Indies

g **10.** A payment for making a sale

REVIEW QUESTIONS

1. How did Benjamin Franklin's early life prepare him for the occupation he followed in Philadelphia?

2. In what ways was life in the English colonies more attractive than it was in the countries of Europe?

3. Why was there a population explosion in the English colonies during the 1700s?

4. What caused the system of slavery to become fastened on the colonies?

5. Who were the opposing groups in the colonial wars that took place between 1689 and 1750?

6. What actions did the French take to strengthen their control over the lands they claimed in North America?

ACTIVITIES

1. In his old age Benjamin Franklin started to write his *Autobiography* but never got much beyond his early years. Obtain a copy of his *Autobiography* and write a summary of an interesting incident described in it.

2. Choose one of the occupations listed by Gabriel Thomas. Explain what a person did in this occupation. How is the job done today?

3. Make a chart comparing jobs held by colonial women with jobs held by women today.

5/SKILLS DEVELOPMENT

USING CONTEXT CLUES

THE WAY THAT WORDS ARE USED

The following paragraphs are taken from *Colonials and Patriots*, a publication of the United States Department of the Interior, National Park Service (Washington, 1964). As you read the paragraphs, you will see that some words are underlined. These are words you may not know. However, you should be able to understand what they mean by the *context*; that is, the way in which the words are used with relation to words around them.

Cities and towns reflected the population boom. In 1700, Boston was the colonial metropolis with 7,000 people, and only Philadelphia came close, with 5,000. By 1775, however, Philadelphia's population had risen to 34,000, making her the largest city, and 11 other cities had passed the 5,000 mark. During the same period, colonial towns increased in number by 3½. But the urban centers could accommodate only a fraction of the mushrooming population.

In 1700, settlements dotted the seaboard from Penobscot Bay, in present Maine, southward to the Edisto River in South Carolina. They were not continuous, and only in the valley of the Hudson River had they penetrated inland more than 100 miles. Seventy years later, however, settlement had spread down the coast another 150 miles, to the St. Marys River, and inland 200 miles and more to the crest of the Appalachians. . . .

The westward movement flowed continuously but not evenly. Before 1754 it was slowed by the hostility of Indian tribes angered by the English invasion and incited by French and Spanish agents. . . .

SKILLS PRACTICE

Show that you understand the underlined words by matching each word repeated below with its correct meaning. Write your answers on a sheet of paper.

1. metropolis (major city, a large center of government)

2. urban (farm, city)

3. accommodate (occupy, take care of)

4. fraction (part, broken bone)

5. mushrooming (agricultural, increasing rapidly)

6. seaboard (coastal area, islands)

7. continuous (touching each other, separated from each other)

8. penetrated (entered, swung back and forth)

9. crest (highest ridge, farthest point)

10. hostility (hospitality, warlike action)

11. incited (stirred up, stopped)

Show how well you understand what you have read by answering the following questions.

12. Which colonial city was the second largest in 1700?   Philadelphia

13. How many cities had more than 5,000 people in 1775?   twelve, counting Philadelphia

14. Where were the southernmost colonial settlements in 1700?   in South Carolina

15. Where had colonial settlements reached the farthest inland in 1700? Hudson River valley

16. How far west had settlements reached by 1770?   the crest of the Appalachians

17. What had slowed the westward movement of the colonial people in some places before 1754?   the hostility of Indian tribes

18. Who had incited Indian tribes against the English? French and Spanish agents

How Americans Lived, 1750

Rural areas

Urban areas

In 1750 about 1.2 million people lived in the 13 British colonies on the mainland of North America. These people were of different races, religions, and social classes, and they lived in different geographical locations. So it is impossible to describe how *all* the colonial people lived in 1750. What we can do, however, is select certain people who were living at that time and see how they participated in some aspect of life. In other words, we will be looking at samples of American life as it was lived in 1750.

Going to school In the South and in the middle colonies, education was left for a long time to parents and to private schools. Only in New England was there anything like a school system. John Adams, later to be the second President of the United States, was 15 years old in 1750. What was school like for young John Adams?

John Adams was born in a plain frame house, which still stands in Quincy, Massachusetts. His father was a farmer and the village shoemaker. John Adams learned to read at home, like many New England boys of the time. Those not learning to read at home attended a **dame school**. These were small private schools

Young John Adams was an enthusiastic participant in the pleasures that boys in small northern towns indulged in — playing marbles in the spring, swimming and boating in the summer, and skating and sledding in the winter. Muscular and quick, young John was proud of his skill in wrestling.

taught by women in their homes. Usually 10 or 12 students attended.

The dame schools were somewhat like kindergarten today. Children were taught the alphabet and the simplest addition and subtraction. While mostly boys went to the dame schools, a few girls attended. It was probably the only formal education girls ever had. They were expected to become wives and mothers, and it was felt that they did not need much book learning to fill those roles. Instead, girls worked at home with their mothers, learning to cook, sew, and run the household.

John Adams started in **grammar school** at the age of 7. Grammar schools then were quite different from our schools today. Their sole purpose was to prepare boys to attend college. Girls did not go to grammar school in colonial times, and some boys who attended were judged un-

able to do college work. Preparing for college in grammar school, John Adams learned to speak and write Latin and Greek. These were the main subjects taught there, but grammar school students also learned advanced mathematics.

Most schoolhouses were freezing cold in winter. Benches were narrow and backless, yet students were expected to sit on them for 8 hours. Schoolmasters enforced rigid discipline. If a boy failed to recite correctly, the schoolmaster might whip him with a birch rod. The slightest disorder could bring the same punishment. And yet parents approved this discipline. They felt that a student who had never been whipped could not be learning much.

Having survived grammar school, John Adams left home to study at Harvard College. Life there was more of the same hard study. His living quarters were

As a Harvard freshman, John Adams studied Greek, Latin, logic, rhetoric, and physics.

Young John Adams studied at Harvard College, near Boston. (42°N/71°W; map, p. 79)

At the age of 21, Daniel Boone married 17-year-old Rebecca Bryan. She was as much a pioneer as her husband. Adept at handling a rifle, she guarded the cabin and children when Daniel was off on his frequent trips as a hunter, woodsman, and trailblazer.

cold, heated poorly by an open fireplace. Meals were usually meager—hardly enough for growing boys. Hours of study were long, with only an hour after the evening meal for relaxation. How could John Adams be anything other than happy when he graduated from Harvard in 1755!

Abigail Smith, the young woman John Adams married in 1764, had no formal education at all. She was 6 years old in 1750. What she learned after that, as she later wrote, she "picked up as an 'eager gatherer' rather than from systematic instruction." She picked up a good deal, for she was the daughter of a minister, himself a Harvard graduate. Conversation in the Smith home was lively, and books were plentiful.

Abigail Smith taught herself French. She also learned to write in a witty style, becoming one of the greatest letter writers of all time. Anyone who reads the love letters she exchanged with her future husband might think she was the Harvard graduate.

Building a house   Daniel Boone, the pioneer and frontier trailblazer, was a year older than John Adams, having been born near Reading, Pennsylvania, in 1734. While John Adams was preparing to enter Harvard in 1750, 16-year-old Daniel Boone and his family were moving from Pennsylvania to North Carolina.

Daniel Boone had become a hunter and trapper at the age of 12. This was not unusual—the largest wolf ever killed on the Pennsylvania frontier was shot by a 10-year-old boy. Boone and his family spent about a year in the Shenandoah Valley before settling at Buffalo Lick, on the north fork of the Yadkin River, in North Carolina. There in the wilderness they built their house of logs.

As was customary, the whole community came to help the Boones build their house. With sharp axes enough timber could be cut to finish the job in 3 days. This included the **clapboard** roof and the **puncheon** (pun' chan) floor. A clapboard is a narrow board that is thicker at one edge than the other. A puncheon is a log split in half lengthwise. For floors, puncheons were laid flat side up. Puncheons were also used to make tabletops and benches. Puncheon floors, tables, and benches were as smooth and splinterless as axes could make them.

The Boone family was only one of thousands of colonial families living in log houses. Most frontier cabins had only one room. Often they had only a dirt floor rather than a puncheon floor. Windows had no glass but were merely holes in the wall. At night wooden shutters closed them from the inside. Greased paper that let light in might later be stretched across the windows to keep out rain and snow.

Building a log cabin for shelter was one of the first tasks for families settling on the frontier.

Having been born in a log cabin came to be an asset for anyone seeking high office. It symbolized the dream of improving one's status.

George Mason and Ann Eilbeck had their portraits painted at about the time of their wedding in 1750. Each was a member of a prominent Virginia family.

A fireplace with a log chimney lined with mud or clay provided heat and was used for cooking. The family ate meals from wooden dishes called **table furniture**. There were plenty of trees in the forests. With wood and an ax, a frontier family could fashion many of the articles it needed.

Getting married On Wednesday, April 4, 1750, the Reverend John Moncure, an Anglican (Church of England) clergyman, performed the marriage of George Mason and Ann Eilbeck. At that time, only Anglican clergymen were licensed to perform legal marriages in the colony of Virginia, where the Church of England was recognized by law as the established, or official, church.

George Mason was a Virginia aristocrat. The Mason and Eilbeck families had been neighbors when George and Ann were children. After they were married, George ordered the building of a new home for the happy couple and the children they expected. Eventually there were nine Mason children living in this home, which George Mason called Gunston Hall.

Gunston Hall was no log cabin built in 3 days with the cooperation of independent members of the community. Started in 1755, it was finally completed in 1758. William Buckland directed the construction and personally designed the elaborate woodwork inside the house. Buckland was a skilled craftworker, brought from England as an indentured servant.

Eliza Lucas is believed to have been born on the island of Antigua. Have pupils locate Antigua on the inset map on page 714.

From Gunston Hall, <u>George Mason went on to become a leader in colonial politics and government.</u> Today visitors to Gunston Hall, near Lorton, Virginia, can see the colonial home and gardens of George Mason. It is remarkable that people in the 1750s could be living in houses as different as John Adams's plain frame house in Massachusetts, Daniel Boone's cabin on the North Carolina frontier, and George Mason's Gunston Hall in Virginia. Yet from homes like these came the heroes of early America.

Managing a plantation   Six years before 1750, Eliza Lucas had married Charles Pinckney, a prominent South Carolinian. Eliza was born in 1722 in the West Indies, the daughter of a British army officer. He owned a plantation called Wappoo, near Charleston, South Carolina. In 1738 he took Eliza there. Then he returned to England, leaving his daughter to manage Wappoo, though she was only 16 years old.

Eliza Lucas set out to learn all she could. Wappoo was a large plantation, with 20 slaves. But Eliza had to plan carefully to pay off its debts, for Wappoo was heavily mortgaged. <u>She ordered the planting of oak trees</u>, hoping they would grow into sturdy timber for ships of the British navy. <u>She experimented with growing indigo</u> from seeds her father sent from the West Indies, although indigo had never been grown successfully before in South Carolina.

Managing Wappoo kept Eliza Lucas busy. Still, along with her business duties, she found time for music and reading. In nearby Charleston she became popular because she was a witty girl with the ability to carry her part of the conversation in any gathering.

At the time of their marriage in 1744, Eliza gave Charles Pinckney some of the indigo plants grown successfully at Wappoo. Her husband later gave some of the seeds to neighbors. From this wedding gift came most of the indigo grown in South Carolina.

In 1750 Eliza Pinckney was living at Belmont, a plantation owned by her husband. She no longer had the responsibility of managing a plantation by herself. Nevertheless, she kept up her agricultural experiments. She found better ways to raise hemp and flax. She became interested in using silkworms to produce threads to be woven into silk cloth. Dresses made from this silk are still on exhibit in South Carolina.

George Mason and Ann Eilbeck Mason occupied Gunston Hall soon after their marriage.

The blue dye indigo is no longer made from plants like those that Eliza Pinckney grew. This dye today is synthetic, made from a coal-tar product.

Workers bring indigo plants from the fields to be made into blue dye.

Two sons were born to Eliza Pinckney and her husband before he died in 1758. As a widow with small children, she again had the responsibility of managing large properties. Few mothers in America in 1750 were able to give their sons the advantages Eliza Pinckney gave to hers, for she was a skillful manager in a prosperous land.

Both sons were given a fine education in England. Later they helped to make the Pinckney name famous in the history of South Carolina and the United States. Eliza Pinckney lived to see South Carolina become one of the original United States of America. By that time she was as well-known as her famous sons. George Washington, who knew Eliza Pinckney, asked for the honor of helping to carry her casket to the grave when she died in 1793 during a visit to Philadelphia.

In 1750 there were hundreds of thousands of women living in America. Not many managed plantations as Eliza Pinckney did. Still, they were good wives and mothers, as she was. And, like Eliza Pinckney, a great many talented women found time for other activities.

CHECKUP

1. How did schools in 1750 differ from today's schools? Why did girls receive so little formal education?
2. What was the house of the Boone family like?
3. How did the home of George Mason differ from that of the Boones?
4. What steps did Eliza Lucas take before and after her marriage to make the plantations that she lived on successful?

109

I/UNIT REVIEW

READING THE TEXT

Turn to page 37 and read the section titled "A clash of civilizations." Then, on a sheet of paper, write the answers to these questions.

1. What is technology?

2. What civilization put a very high value on technology?

3. Where did this kind of civilization grow up?

4. List some ways in which technology gave the settlers an advantage over the Native Americans.

5. Now list some ways in which Indian civilization influenced the Western civilization that the settlers brought to America.

READING A MAP

Turn to page 79 and look at the map titled "The English Colonies." Note the latitude and longitude lines. Remember that the latitude lines run east and west, and the longitude lines run north and south. In this book, north is always at the top of a map, and south is at the bottom. East is on the right side of maps in this book, west is on the left side.

On a sheet of paper, write the answers to these questions.

1. What colony extended farthest east? **Mass.**

2. What colony lay completely to the west of the 80°W longitude line? **Ga.**

3. In what direction would you be going if you traveled from Jamestown, Virginia, to Annapolis, Maryland? **North**

4. In what direction would you be going if you traveled from Hartford, Connecticut, to Providence, Rhode Island? **East**

5. In what direction would you be going if you traveled from Portsmouth, New Hampshire, to Boston, Massachusetts? **South**

READING A PICTURE

Turn to page 21 and carefully examine the picture showing activities of the Indians of the Pacific Northwest. On a sheet of paper, write answers to these questions.

1. What are the two Indians at the far left doing?

2. What tool have they fashioned to carry out their task?

3. What is the Indian standing by the tree doing?

4. What, do you think, is the purpose of the fire at the far right?

5. Why, do you suppose, did the Indians build such large canoes as the one shown in the center?

READING A TABLE

Turn to the table titled "Facts About the States" on page 11. Use the table to find out whether the statements that follow are true or false. On a sheet of paper, write **T** if the statement is true and **F** if it is false.

T **1.** Minnesota is bigger in area than Idaho.

F **2.** Maine has a larger population than New Mexico.

F **3.** The capital of the state of South Dakota is Bismarck.

F **4.** Two states are more than 1 million square kilometers in area.

F **5.** The state with the largest population also has the largest area.

Founding a New Nation

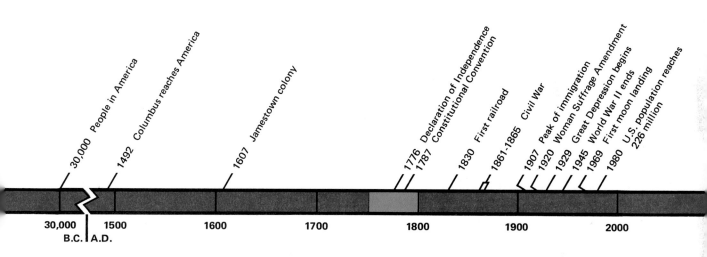

30,000 People in America

1492 Columbus reaches America

1607 Jamestown colony

1776 Declaration of Independence
1787 Constitutional Convention

1830 First railroad

1861-1865 Civil War

1907 Peak of immigration
1920 Woman Suffrage Amendment
1929 Great Depression begins
1945 World War II ends
1969 First moon landing
1980 U.S. population reaches 226 million

30,000   1500   1600   1700   1800   1900   2000
B.C. A.D.

Above: Constitutional Convention, Paul Revere, George Washington, Molly Pitcher and soldiers, Liberty Bell

CHAPTER

6 The Road to Independence

Chapter 6 might be organized around a central question: Could the American Revolution have been avoided by wiser British policy?

British Policy Changes

VOCABULARY

militia	Grenville Acts
French and Indian War	trade and navigation laws
Treaty of Paris (1763)	enumerated articles
Proclamation of 1763	warrant
prime minister	Quartering Act
Parliament	Stamp Act

The Reveres of Boston   Young Paul Revere, his mother, and his brothers and sisters were returning from a Boston cemetery known as the Old Granary. There, on a hot July day in 1754, they had witnessed the burial of Apollos Rivoire (ə pol′ əs rē′ vwär), the 52-year-old father of the family.

Apollos Rivoire had come to America from France in 1716 as a 13-year-old boy. He soon found that English-speaking people in Boston had trouble pronouncing his name. Moreover, people with French names were none too popular in New England because of the wars between France and Great Britain. So Apollos Rivoire began to call himself Paul Revere when he started in business as a silversmith.

The first Paul Revere in America married a Massachusetts girl named Deborah Hitchbourn. Her family was English and had been in Massachusetts almost from the beginning of the colony. Mr. and Mrs. Revere had nine children. The eldest boy was also called Paul Revere, after the English name his father had taken.

Young Paul learned the secrets of the silversmith's trade from his father. By the time he was 13, he could turn out a silver bowl, a tray, or a cup as well as any other mechanic in Boston. In those days a craftworker such as a silversmith or a blacksmith was known as a mechanic.

After his father's death Paul Revere took over added duties in the family business. His mother managed the silversmith's shop on Fish Street in Boston. But another person was now needed to turn out the articles of silver. So Paul taught the trade to his younger brother, Thomas. Then, in 1756, 21-year-old Paul Revere, convinced that the family could take care of business for a time, marched off to war.

George Washington's first mission   The war had begun in the frontier wilderness far to the south of Massachusetts. It was the fourth of the French-British conflicts in which the colonists took part. During the peaceful years following the third of these wars, aggressive Frenchmen had pushed south from the Great Lakes

Young George Washington, on horseback, directs his men in a bloody encounter with the French in the Pennsylvania wilderness as the French and Indian War gets under way.

Paul Revere's house, built about 1670, is the oldest building in central Boston. Revere lived in this house from 1770 to 1800. Visitors may see some of its original furnishings, plus momentos of Revere.

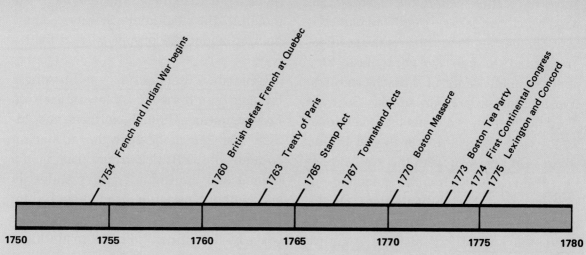

1754 French and Indian War begins

1760 British defeat French at Quebec

1763 Treaty of Paris

1765 Stamp Act

1767 Townshend Acts

1770 Boston Massacre

1773 Boston Tea Party

1774 First Continental Congress

1775 Lexington and Concord

1750   1755   1760   1765   1770   1775   1780

into the Ohio River valley. Alarmed by this action, Governor Robert Dinwiddie of Virginia decided to warn the French that they were invading British territory.

Young George Washington was the man Governor Dinwiddie chose to carry the warning to the French. Washington was a Virginian, 21 years old at the time, a landowner and surveyor and a member of the **militia** (mə lish′ ə). The militia was an organization made up of the able-bodied men in the colony. They could be called into military service in an emergency. George Washington returned from his wilderness journey with grim news. He reported that the French were determined to stay in the Ohio River valley and could not be removed except by force.

A setback at Fort Necessity In 1754 Governor Dinwiddie made Washington a lieutenant-colonel, in command of nearly 150 Virginia militiamen. His orders were to occupy a fort that had recently been built by Virginians near the headwaters of the Ohio River. Before Washington and his men reached the fort, they learned that the French had seized it, and had named it Fort Duquesne (dü kān′). As the soldiers proceeded through the wilderness, they met a small band of French soldiers. Washington ordered an attack. So were fired the first shots of what became known to the colonists as the **French and Indian War.** On one side were the government of France, the French colonists in America, and their Indian allies. On the other side were the government of England, the English colonists in America, and *their* Indian allies.

After the Virginians had driven off the French soldiers, Washington ordered his men to build a fort. He named it Fort Necessity. More French soldiers from Fort Duquesne soon arrived and surrounded flimsy Fort Necessity. Though Washington and his men fought bravely, the French finally made them surrender. Washington and his men were, however, allowed to march away without giving up their weapons.

Braddock's defeat In 1755 General Edward Braddock had come to America from England with a strong force of soldiers. His goal was to drive the French from the Ohio River valley. As Braddock set off toward Fort Duquesne, he ordered his men to cut a road through the woods and march over it as if they were on parade.

George Washington went with Braddock's army. Now a colonel, Washington commanded 450 colonial soldiers. Washington and others warned Braddock that his troops should be cautious in their advance. However, the British general refused to listen to the advice. He thought the colonial soldiers knew nothing about the proper way to fight a war.

General Braddock's stubbornness brought on a disaster. A few miles from Fort Duquesne, French soldiers and Indian warriors ambushed the advancing columns of the British army. That is, the French and the Indians struck suddenly and without warning from their hiding place in the thick woods. The bright red coats of the British soldiers made them easy targets. General Braddock himself

114

was mortally wounded. Colonel George Washington had two horses shot from under him. But in spite of these close calls, Washington was able to lead what was left of the defeated British army back to safety.

William Pitt's leadership   By 1756 the British leaders knew they were in for a long, hard fight. In 1757 William Pitt became Britain's secretary of state and took charge of the war planning. The brilliant Pitt realized the value to England of its North American colonies. He poured men and money into destroying France's New World empire. He replaced unsuccessful generals and admirals with more able men. His leadership soon paid off with victories in battle. British and American troops once more captured the great French fort at Louisburg in Canada. Fort Duquesne was captured and renamed Fort Pitt. From that fort the present-day city of Pittsburgh got its name.

Some of the greatest British victories were won in Canada. A combined British land and naval force advanced up the St. Lawrence River as far as Quebec. There, in 1759, General James Wolfe's army defeated a French army commanded by General Louis Montcalm. Both Wolfe and Montcalm lost their lives in the battle fought on the Plains of Abraham, outside the fortress of Quebec. The next year, the British easily captured Montreal, winning control over the settled parts of Canada.

British General Edward Braddock, mortally wounded, is taken from the scene of battle in a Pennsylvania forest. The French and their Indian allies ambushed Braddock's army.

Braddock's defeat left the long frontier of Pennsylvania, Maryland, and Virginia open to Indian attack.

Chicago Historical Society

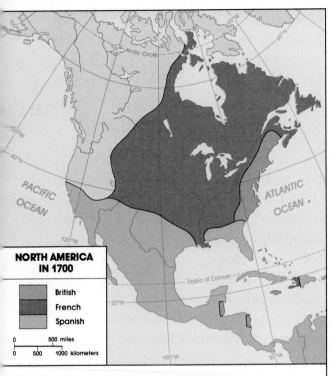

The English, French, and Spanish all claimed land in North America.

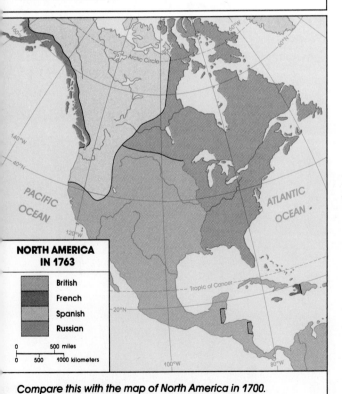

Compare this with the map of North America in 1700. What has happened?

Results of the French and Indian War

The peace treaty signed in Paris in 1763 changed the map of North America. Under the **Treaty of Paris,** France gave all of Canada and the part of Louisiana east of the Mississippi River to Great Britain.

Spain had helped France during the war. As a reward, France gave Spain the port of New Orleans at the mouth of the Mississippi and all of Louisiana west of the Mississippi. But since Spain was on the losing side, Spain was forced to give up its Florida holdings to the victorious British.

Thus Great Britain added more territory to its empire. But it was a costly victory. Now the British had an even larger empire to control. When the war ended, Great Britain had a large army and a large navy to support. In addition, it had a large war debt. Somehow the expenses of the army and the navy and the war debt would have to be paid.

The French and Indian War had important effects on the American colonists. During the war 25,000 of them had fought at one time or another alongside the British. Many of their leaders, like George Washington, had gained valuable military experience. Most of the 13 colonies had prospered during the war, as their farmers, shipbuilders, and merchants sold supplies to the British and sometimes to the French. Probably most importantly, the outcome of the war meant that France could no longer discourage the movement of Americans into the lands west of the Appalachians. Moreover, combined French and Indian raiders could no longer swoop down on settlements along the colonial frontier.

Plainly, the outcome of the war had greatly benefited the American colonists. In view of this fact, the British decided that the colonists should help pay for the war. Acting on this idea, the British government made a series of decisions that would have far-reaching effects in the American colonies.

The Proclamation of 1763   The first of these decisions had little to do with making the colonists pay for a share of the war. Advisers to King George III of Great Britain needed time to plan for governing the new British territory in North America. Also, they felt responsible for protecting settlers from Indian attacks, such as those led by Pontiac, the Ottawa Indian chief, in the spring and summer of 1763. For these reasons they persuaded the king to issue a royal order known as the **Proclamation of 1763.**

This proclamation prohibited settlers from entering the land west of the Appalachians. Thousands of colonists had planned to move into this region. Indeed, thousands were already there. Now these settlers were ordered to move back east of the mountains. It seemed to them that the western lands won from the French were to be reserved for the Indians. In addition, the Proclamation of 1763 said that only merchants licensed by a representative of King George III could trade with the Indians.

The Proclamation of 1763 aroused great resentment in the colonies. To many Americans the Proclamation of 1763 looked like an example of British greed. It seemed that only the British would profit from the lands won from France.

The Grenville Acts   George Grenville was **prime minister** of Great Britain after the French and Indian War. As prime minister, Grenville was the leader of **Parliament,** the British legislature. He was also chief adviser to King George III. In 1764, Grenville announced some new policies for Britain's American colonies. Known as the **Grenville Acts,** these policies caused quarrels between the government of Great Britain and the American colonies.

Grenville shaped his new policies with two goals in mind. First, he wanted his government to have tighter control over the American colonies. Second, he wanted to make the colonies pay a share of the large British war debt. To tighten control, a part of the Grenville Acts ordered stricter enforcement of **trade and navigation laws.** Parliament had passed these laws at one time or another for more than 100 years.

Some of these laws said that certain colonial products could be shipped only to England or to other English colonies. These listed products were known as **enumerated articles.** By the 1760s the list of enumerated articles included raw materials such as tobacco, indigo, cotton, furs, lumber, and sugar. Other laws regulated the sale of products manufactured in the colonies. For example, colonists could not make fur hats, ironware, or woolen goods to be sold outside the colony in which they were made.

Still other trade and navigation laws provided that only English or colonial ships could carry products to or from the colonies. Furthermore, products from other countries had to go through English ports before proceeding to the colonies. In the English ports these foreign products were taxed. This meant that they cost more in the colonies than if they had been shipped directly.

Before Grenville's time, British officials had seldom enforced the trade and navigation laws. Colonial merchants and manufacturers had conducted their business as if the laws did not exist. In 1764, however, the Grenville Acts provided for more British officials in America. These officials sometimes made searches for illegal goods without a **warrant** to do so. A warrant is a paper signed by a judge or other authorized person that gives officials the right to make a search or carry out other acts. But these officials broke into warehouses and even into private homes in their efforts to find goods that had been obtained illegally.

The Quartering Act   In March 1765 Grenville set forth another new policy, the **Quartering Act**. After the French and Indian War, about 7,000 British troops had remained in the colonies. The Quartering Act ordered colonial governments to furnish quarters—that is, a place to live—and provisions for these troops.

However, since the war was over, most Americans thought they no longer needed British soldiers to protect them. The colonists were shocked to learn that they were expected to pay for quartering and feeding these soldiers. Soon some colonists began to suspect that the British troops remained not to protect American colonists but to enforce British laws.

The Stamp Act   None of the Grenville Acts aroused so much anger as the **Stamp Act**, which became effective in 1765. It

Boston citizens protest the Stamp Act by seizing and burning stamped paper from England.

The idea of protesting is important in understanding this section. Select a current event that has been the subject of protest, and then discuss it. Include the methods of protest (letters to Congress, demonstrations, meetings). Compare these methods with colonial protest.

listed about 50 items which had to be printed on stamped paper or have official stamps glued to them. The Stamp Act list included newspapers, almanacs, pamphlets, marriage licenses, wills, deeds, and other legal documents. Special officials sold the stamps and stamped paper, turning the money over to the British government after keeping a small fee as their pay. The money raised by the Stamp Act was used to help pay for the British troops stationed in America.

American colonists resisted the stamp tax with a fury that amazed the British government. For many years people in Great Britain had paid a stamp tax at a rate nearly three times what the colonists were required to pay. But George Grenville and other British leaders failed to realize two very important things.

First of all, the Stamp Act set up an internal tax—that is, a tax collected *within* the colonies. Before the Stamp Act, only the colonial legislatures had passed laws providing for taxes within the colonies. Second, the Stamp Act affected nearly everyone in the colonies. No newspaper could be printed, no land could be legally sold, no couple could be married unless the stamp tax was paid. For these reasons, Americans resisted the Stamp Act in many different ways.

CHECKUP

1. Where and how did the French and Indian War begin?
2. What were the results of the war?
3. Why did Prime Minister Grenville announce new policies for the American colonies?
4. Explain why the colonists objected to (**a**) the Proclamation of 1763 (**b**) the trade and navigation laws (**c**) the Quartering Act (**d**) the Stamp Act.

American Colonists Resist

VOCABULARY

tyranny	Declaratory Act
Sons of Liberty	Townshend Acts
"taxation without representation"	writ of assistance
Stamp Act Congress	veto
repeal	governor's council
nonimportation agreements	

A fiery speech   Patrick Henry of Virginia was 29 years old when he was elected to the House of Burgesses in 1765. He represented the northern and western counties of Virginia. And he defended the rights of all Virginians against what he believed to be the illegal acts of the British government in their dealings with Virginia and the other colonies.

Consequently, though he was a very new member of the House of Burgesses in 1765, Patrick Henry spoke out against the Stamp Act. He called it an example of British **tyranny**—harsh and unfair government. In one fiery speech he came close to calling King George III a tyrant, or dictator. In the same speech he declared that the Virginia Assembly had "the sole exclusive right and power to levy taxes" upon the colony. This and other statements that he put forth in support of the colony's rights received wide publicity. From Boston, Massachusetts, to Charleston, South Carolina, Henry's statements became the basis for opposing the Stamp Act. Moreover, they made Patrick Henry well known, not only in Virginia but in all the other colonies.

The American colonists were familiar with paying external taxes. Customs duties, an external tax, were collected in colonial ports, and this charge increased the costs for consumer goods. **119**

At the port of London, customs officials inspected cargoes from colonial ships and collected the duties. British regulation of colonial trade was a source of continuing irritation to the colonists.

Violent actions   Some angry people in the American colonies did more than make speeches against the Stamp Act. They threatened violence to the stamp collectors. In many towns they organized secret societies known as **Sons of Liberty**, or by other quite similar names. On occasions they tarred and feathered stamp-tax collectors as well as colonists suspected of being too friendly to the new British policies.

In Boston a man named Samuel Adams organized the Sons of Liberty. The Sons paraded openly and held picnics and other social events, but they sometimes met secretly. There was an air of mystery about these private meetings.

One night in August 1765, a mob invaded the fine home of Thomas Hutchinson on Court Street in Boston. Thomas Hutchinson was lieutenant governor and chief justice of the colony of Massachusetts. His family had come early to the colony and had done well there.

Thomas Hutchinson was a troubled man. He was caught between loyalty to his colony and loyalty to the British government. He could understand the anger that Massachusetts people felt because of the stamp tax. But he was part of the official British colonial government, and he felt that Parliament had a right to pass the Stamp Act. Because Hutchinson held this last belief, his home was invaded and its furnishings destroyed. Only Samuel Adams and the mob's leaders knew for certain whether the Sons of Liberty were involved.

Other ways of resistance   Calmer leaders in all the colonies resisted the Stamp Act, but they did not favor the use of violence in opposing it. These leaders argued that only their colonial legislatures could levy taxes within the colonies. American colonists were not represented in Parliament. Therefore, these colonial leaders pointed out, the Stamp Act was a case of **"taxation without representation."**

Some colonial leaders thought the time had come to unite in opposition to the new British policies. In October 1765, delegates from nine colonies assembled in New York for what became known as the **Stamp Act Congress.** Leaders of the nine colonies talked about colonial problems and got to know each other better. Some resolutions passed officially by the Stamp Act Congress stated what the delegates believed were the rights of the American

Tarring and feathering was a common form of punishment in the colonial era. The person being punished was smeared with tar and covered with feathers. Sometimes that person was then tied to a rail and driven out of town.

colonists. Other resolutions listed objections to the new British policies. A final resolution asked the British government to **repeal** the Stamp Act—that is, to cancel or do away with it.

Stopping imports   Before they went home, delegates to the Stamp Act Congress urged colonial merchants to stop all imports from England until Parliament repealed the Stamp Act. This turned out to be the most effective way of resisting the hated tax. Merchants in the colonial ports signed **nonimportation agreements.** They pledged not to import any British goods.

It took only a short time for the sale of British goods to drop far below what it had been. In Great Britain, merchants and manufacturers became worried. Ship captains complained about losses in their carrying trade. Those hurt most asked Parliament for an end to the Stamp Act so that trade with the colonies could begin again.

Good news and bad news   In 1766 good news came to the American colonists. Parliament had given in to pressure from the British merchants. Also, British leaders had come to see that enforcing the Stamp Act would cost more than the money gained from it. So the act was repealed.

Americans celebrated when the good news came. They lit bonfires, they sang, and they cheered. They had come close to rebellion in their resistance to the Stamp Act. Now it seemed their troubles were over. Few were aware of the bad news that came along with the good news.

The bad news was the **Declaratory Act,** passed the same day Parliament repealed the Stamp Act. The Declaratory Act said that Parliament had the right to tax and to pass laws for the colonies "in all cases whatsoever." In other words, Parliament refused to accept the complaint of the colonists that "taxation without representation" was illegal.

Punishing the legislatures   The legislatures of New York and Massachusetts had refused to pay the expense of the Quartering Act. The next year Charles Townshend became the most powerful man in the British government. He resolved to punish these rebellious legislatures. First he turned to New York because the British army had its headquarters there. He ordered New York's legislature suspended, meaning it was forbidden to meet.

Later the British government suspended the colonial legislatures of Massachusetts and Virginia. The British government did this because of the legislatures' opposition to the Quartering Act and to some new taxes put on the colonies by Parliament.

The Townshend Acts   The new taxes were called the **Townshend Acts.** They placed taxes on glass, lead, paint, and tea imported from England by the colonial merchants. British leaders thought the colonists would willingly pay these duties because they were external taxes, collected *before* the goods were unloaded in colonial ports. Therefore, they were not internal taxes paid within the colonies as the stamp tax had been.

121

In 1768 the Massachusetts legislature helped to get common action against the Townshend Acts by issuing a Circular Letter calling on all the other colonial legislatures to join with them in protest against the measure.

However, the colonists did not accept this line of reasoning. In fact, Townshend's actions brought even more opposition than had the Stamp Act. Some colonial leaders believed that keeping the legislatures from meeting might end all self-government in the colonies. The colonists were upset, too, to learn that tax money raised by the Townshend Acts would be used to pay the salaries of the royal governors and other British officials in America. If this was done, colonial legislatures could no longer put pressure on officials by threatening to hold back their pay.

In making a stand against the Townshend Acts, colonial leaders used the same methods that had worked in fighting the Stamp Act. They declared the new taxes were "taxation without representation." They urged merchants to revive the nonimportation agreements. The Sons of Liberty in Boston and in other colonial ports threatened violence to merchants who imported British goods.

Many merchants had been alarmed by the violence at the time of the Stamp Act. For this reason, they were less willing to oppose the Townshend Acts. Some merchants paid the Townshend taxes and passed the cost along to those who bought goods from them. These merchants thought this was better than running the risk of arousing more violence. Other merchants avoided the new taxes altogether by smuggling the goods on which taxes were imposed. Smuggling means bringing in the goods secretly without paying taxes on them.

Years of turmoil If those who led the opposition to the Townshend Acts expected the British to give in, they were mistaken. More customs officials were sent to colonial ports to collect the Townshend taxes. The British army and navy received orders to help the tax collectors enforce the law. **Writs of assistance** were made legal in the colonies. These were documents giving an official who was looking for smuggled goods the right to enter and search a ship or building.

Between 1767 and 1770, Americans started to disagree among themselves, thus adding to the turmoil. Some colonists favored giving in to the British. Others wished to continue the resistance. None, however, spoke out openly

Samuel Adams worked tirelessly to arouse and keep alive colonial resistance to the British.

detail, Museum of Fine Arts, Boston

122

Colonial Government

Each of the 13 colonies had a governor. The table on this page shows the ways in which colonial governors were chosen. A colonial governor could appoint people to certain jobs in his colony. He commanded the armed forces of the colony. He was responsible for seeing that the laws were enforced. He could **veto**—that is, refuse to approve—acts that had been passed by the legislature of his colony.

By the 1760s each colony had a legislature, usually divided into two parts. One part—often referred to as the upper house—was made up of members appointed by the governor. For this reason the upper house in most colonies was known as the **governor's council.** Generally the other part of the legislature —or lower house—was called the assembly.

Voters elected the members of the assemblies. Only white men over 21 years of age could vote. To vote, a man also had to own a certain amount of property. These elected assemblies had been in existence for a long time. Over the years the powers of the assemblies had increased a great deal.

One source of power came from the assembly's control over taxes imposed within each colony. In several colonies the governor was paid his salary from these taxes. If a governor did something to displease the assembly, its members could vote to withhold his pay. Even though the assembly was the lower house, it was the most important part of self-government in a colony.

COLONIAL GOVERNORS IN 1767			
Colony	Type of Colony	Governor	How chosen
Massachusetts	Royal	Francis Bernard	Appointed by king
Connecticut	Self-governing	William Pitkin	Elected by voters
New Hampshire	Royal	John Wentworth	Appointed by king
Rhode Island	Self-governing	Stephen Hopkins	Elected by voters
New York	Royal	Henry Moore	Appointed by king
New Jersey	Royal	William Franklin	Appointed by king
Pennsylvania	Proprietary	John Penn	Chosen by proprietor
Delaware	Proprietary	*	
Maryland	Royal	Horatio Sharpe	Appointed by king
Virginia	Royal	Francis Fauquier	Appointed by king
North Carolina	Royal	William Tryon	Appointed by king
South Carolina	Royal	Charles Montagu	Appointed by king
Georgia	Royal	James Wright	Appointed by king

* Delaware, governed for many years as a part of Pennsylvania, did not have its own governor until 1777.

Ask pupils to name the three types of colonies that existed in America in 1767. Then ask: How were the governors chosen in each of these types of colonies?

for breaking the ties between the colonies and Great Britain. Most colonists still considered themselves to be loyal subjects of the king. In fact, they argued that Parliament was trying to take away a right that they held as English citizens—to be taxed only by legislatures they had helped to elect.

A change in British policy   Charles Townshend died in 1767, but the British government continued to follow his policies until 1770. However, in that year new British leaders decided to end the turmoil in the colonies. They repealed the Townshend Acts except the tax on tea. At the same time, the new British leaders allowed the suspended legislatures in New York, Massachusetts, and Virginia to meet again.

To Americans, this seemed like another victory. Most were tired of the uproar of the preceding 3 years. Therefore, when the British leaders gave in, a great wave of relief swept over the colonies.

Yet even after the repeal of the Townshend Acts, the Sons of Liberty and other groups continued to meet and talk about the ways in which British policies were harming the colonies. They kept alive the hatreds, worries, and disagreements.

CHECKUP

1. What methods were used by the colonists to resist the Stamp Act?
2. Why did the British repeal the stamp tax?
3. Explain the role of the governor and the legislature in colonial government. How could the assembly put pressure on the governor?
4. In what ways were the years between 1767 and 1770 years of turmoil?

Armed Conflict Begins

┌─**VOCABULARY**─────────────────────┐

Boston Massacre	Intolerable Acts
acquit	First
propaganda	Continental
	Congress
Committee of	
Correspon-	Continental
dence	Association
monopoly	minuteman
Boston Tea	
Party	

└────────────────────────────────────┘

Bloodshed in Boston   On the snowy evening of March 5, 1770, five men in Boston were shot down by British soldiers. Among the five was Crispus Attucks, a tall black man who had once been a slave in Framingham, Massachusetts. After gaining his freedom, Attucks worked for 20 years as a sailor. How did he happen to die in Boston?

The British government had sent two regiments of troops to Boston in 1768 to preserve law and order. To most colonists, these soldiers were unwelcome. Residents of Boston hooted and jeered at them and sometimes threw stones.

On the evening of March 5, a crowd gathered in front of the Boston Customs House, where a British soldier was standing guard. Some men and boys started throwing snowballs and chunks of ice at the soldier. As the crowd became more threatening, the soldier called for help. A British officer named Captain Preston and seven soldiers hastened to the aid of the guard.

The crowd, jeering and hooting, kept increasing in size. Some men waved clubs at the soldiers. As the crowd surged forward, redcoats and colonists

Ask pupils to discuss whether the defense of Captain Preston and the British soldiers by John Adams and Josiah Quincy was a courageous act.

were separated by no more than an arm's length. Suddenly a musket shot rang out. Whether the British soldier who fired did so out of panic or because he thought he had been ordered to fire, we do not know. But other soldiers then fired into the crowd. When the smoke from the British muskets cleared away, four men lay dead and one was seriously wounded.

Later it was said that Crispus Attucks had led an advance on the British troops. Killed along with him were Jonas Baldwell, also a sailor; Samuel Maverick, a lad of 17; and Samuel Gray. Patrick Carr died 4 days later from his wounds. The skirmish in which these men died became known in the colonies as the **Boston Massacre.** Accounts of the affair, often exaggerated, quickly spread throughout Massachusetts and the other colonies.

Captain Preston and the British soldiers were put on trial for murder. Two young Massachusetts lawyers, John Adams and Josiah Quincy, thought the soldiers deserved a fair trial and agreed to defend them. Adams and Quincy defended the accused men so skillfully that Captain

Paul Revere made this engraving of the Boston Massacre. Many prints were made from it.

You might wish to assign at this time the first item in the Activities section on page 132.

Preston and all but two of the soldiers were **acquitted**, or freed without punishment. The remaining two were convicted of manslaughter, a lesser charge than murder. They were branded on their hands and dishonorably discharged from the British army. In a few years the two young lawyers would be involved in the American Revolution. Twenty-six years later, John Adams would be elected President of the United States.

After the French and Indian War, Paul Revere had returned to silversmithing. He had also learned to make engravings from which pictures and diagrams could be printed. Whether he saw the shooting or not is uncertain. However, he made a diagram that was used at the trial. The diagram showed the positions of the soldiers and the persons killed. Revere also made a copper engraving from which prints were produced and sold. The prints were first-class pieces of **propaganda**. Propaganda is the spreading of ideas for the purpose of helping a cause. Revere's print showed a line of British soldiers firing into a crowd of innocent-looking people. Thousands of people learned to hate the British because of Paul Revere's version of what happened on the night of March 5, 1770.

A communications network Samuel Adams, a cousin of lawyer John Adams, acted quickly to spread the word of the Boston Massacre. Samuel Adams was now convinced that Americans could only keep their liberties by breaking away from the British Empire. He set about trying to convince others that such a break was necessary.

In Boston, Adams set up a **Committee of Correspondence.** Its members wrote letters to people in other colonies. In time, there were such committees in most towns from Massachusetts to Georgia. Letters from one group to another told of British acts that threatened colonial liberties. The letters suggested ways of dealing with these acts.

A tall, lanky redhead named Thomas Jefferson was active in organizing a Committee of Correspondence in Virginia. Virginia voters had elected him to the House of Burgesses in 1769. There he joined a group led by Patrick Henry in opposition to British policies. As you will learn later, Jefferson would play a major role in the colonies' search for liberty.

The Committees of Correspondence kept alive the sparks of colonial resistance to British policies. Moreover, they built unity among the leaders of this resistance. And they gave excellent training to the people who were about to make an American revolution.

The tax on tea When the British government repealed the Townshend taxes on various articles in 1770, it kept the tax on tea sold in the colonies. At that time more than 1 million Americans drank tea. The colonists continued to protest this tax. Many of them avoided it by buying tea that had been smuggled past tax collectors by colonial merchants and ship captains. But despite resentment over the tea tax, the period of relative calm beginning in 1770 continued until 1773. In that year the British government made a decision that marked another step along the road to revolution and war.

Contrast the personalities of Jefferson and Patrick Henry. Henry was a brilliant orator with little talent for writing. Jefferson was not a dynamic speaker but wrote in a clear and lucid style.

In 1773 the powerful British East India Company had 17 million pounds of unsold tea. Though it was a private company, it had a great deal of influence with Parliament. To help the company, Parliament granted it a **monopoly** on the sale of tea to the American colonies. In other words, only the British East India Company could sell tea to the colonies. The company arranged to sell the tea through its own agents rather than through colonial merchants. But the company did not raise the price on tea, as it could have done. Instead it lowered the price.

With tea now at lower prices, Parliament hoped the colonists would no longer object to the tea tax. The British leaders thought, too, that now it would not pay the colonists to risk smuggling tea. But Parliament was wrong in thinking how the colonists would act. The colonists were angered that only one group could sell tea. Those who had sold tea—and had obeyed the law in doing so—were upset over their loss of business. On the other hand, smugglers feared there would no longer be a profit in breaking the law. For many in America, it seemed as if cheap tea was being offered as a bribe to get them to pay the tax on it.

By this time the well-organized Committees of Correspondence had plans for united action. They warned that tea shipped by the British East India Company must not be unloaded. At Philadelphia and New York, determined colonists forced the tea ships to carry their cargoes back to British ports. At Annapolis, Maryland, both the tea and the vessel that had brought it from England were burned in the harbor.

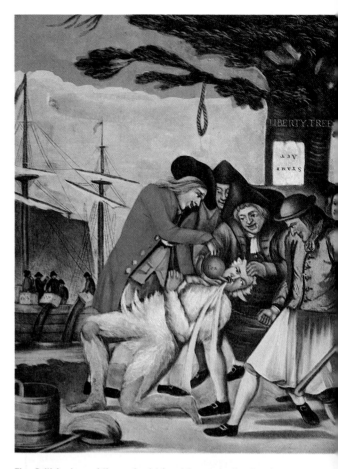

The British view of the colonists' resistance to the tea tax is reflected in this drawing. A tax collector, tarred and feathered, is forced to drink some tea.

The Boston Tea Party   The most famous "tea party" of all took place in Boston. In December 1773 three tea ships— the *Beaver*, the *Eleanor*, and the *Dartmouth*—were tied to Griffin's Wharf in Boston Harbor. One dark night more than a hundred men disguised themselves as Mohawk Indians. They slipped on board the three ships and dumped about $90,000 worth of tea into the harbor.

Thousands of people watched the **Boston Tea Party** from the shore. But no one seemed to know who the "Indians" were. Some of them certainly were Sons of Liberty.

The British response   In response to the Boston Tea Party, Parliament passed four laws to punish the people of Massachusetts. These laws so angered the colonists that they called them the **Intolerable Acts.**

One law ordered the closing of the port of Boston until the tea was paid for. Surely, British leaders thought, Boston merchants and sea captains would turn in the guilty persons or perhaps pay for the tea themselves. Parliament was mistaken. A second law reorganized the colonial government of Massachusetts. This law gave more power to the royal governor and took power away from the legislature.

A third law changed the Quartering Act, first passed in 1764. The new Quartering Act said that British soldiers could be housed in privately owned buildings, even in the homes of Massachusetts citizens. Thus it seemed to colonists that British soldiers could spy on and control the activities of private citizens. A fourth law allowed British officials to be tried in England for crimes they might have committed in the colonies. In this way, they might avoid facing hostile colonial juries and judges.

These laws helped to unite the 13 colonies. Several colonies sent messages of sympathy to Massachusetts, the principal victim of the Intolerable Acts. Some colonies sent food for the families of the hundreds of seafaring men and dock laborers thrown out of work by the law which closed the port of Boston.

Angered by the tea tax, Bostonians dump cases of tea into Boston Harbor. The artist has pictured the event in daylight; it actually occurred on a dark December night.

The First Continental Congress In Virginia, the House of Burgesses sent out a call for another meeting of delegates from each of the colonies. This meeting was meant to discuss colonial grievances against Great Britain. Committees of Correspondence spread the word. Fifty-five colonial leaders assembled in Philadelphia in September 1774. This time only Georgia failed to send delegates. This meeting in Philadelphia became known as the **First Continental Congress.**

Samuel Adams and Patrick Henry from Virginia met for the first time at the First Continental Congress in Philadelphia. No two men had done more to arouse resistance to British policies. George Washington was also there as a delegate to the Congress from Virginia. He listened as the other delegates debated for 7 weeks.

From these debates came several statements. One was a declaration of the rights of the colonists. Another was an appeal to the British king and the British people. The appeal asked for an end to all the harsh laws passed since the end of the French and Indian War. Before the delegates went home, they organized the **Continental Association.** One of its purposes was to unite the colonies in a refusal to sell anything to the British. The Continental Association was the first written agreement pledging the colonies to act together.

Another fiery speech In some of their declarations, delegates to the First Continental Congress had called themselves "His Majesty's most loyal subjects." Perhaps so, but already many of them wanted

In a spirited address before the Virginia House of Burgesses, Patrick Henry attacks the Stamp Act.

independence from Great Britain. And back in their home colonies, people were preparing to fight to defend their liberty if that became necessary. In Massachusetts the Committee of Public Safety was authorized to call out the militia to protect American lives, American property, and American rights.

The militia drilled openly in Massachusetts and the other colonies. Colonial leaders gathered powder, shot, and other military necessities. They stored these in secret places. At a meeting in Richmond, Virginia, on March 3, 1775, Patrick Henry made another fiery speech. At its conclusion came the inspiring words: "Is life so dear, or peace so sweet, as to be purchased at the price of chains and slavery? Forbid it, Almighty God! I know not what course others may take, but as for me, give me liberty or give me death!"

What's in a Name?

MILITIAMEN AND MINUTEMEN

None of the colonies had a professional army like that of Great Britain. But each of them had a militia, or a body of citizen soldiers. These men, bearing arms, could be called upon in times of danger. As tensions grew between the colonies and Great Britain, militiamen met more often for drill.

In Massachusetts the Committee of Public Safety was set up. This group had the power to call out the militia. However, many members of the militia lived on farms that were far apart. Often it took hours for all of the militiamen to come together.

So special groups were formed within the various militia units. They were made up of men who could be counted on to answer at once, ready to fight if need be. These special groups had to have some name. Since they were subject to instant call, someone labeled them **minutemen**, implying they could be ready in a minute. No one remembers who gave these

This statue of a minuteman at Lexington, Massachusetts, honors the brave men who stood their ground there against the British redcoats on the morning of April 19, 1775.

special units their name, but as minutemen they have entered history.

You might want to read a section of Ralph Waldo Emerson's "Concord Hymn" with your pupils.

The war begins General Thomas Gage was the British military governor of Massachusetts. His headquarters were in Boston. In 1775 he received orders to put down all signs of rebellion against King George III. Gage knew colonial leaders had stored military supplies at Concord, a small town about 20 miles (32 km) northwest of Boston. The British general was determined to seize the supplies. On the night of April 18, 1775, a force of about 700 British soldiers marched out of Boston, bound for Concord.

They were being watched. As they marched, Paul Revere, William Dawes, and Dr. Samuel Prescott rode ahead of them. These riders warned, "The British are coming!" Early the next morning part of the British forces reached Lexington, on their way to Concord.

On the village green at Lexington, about 70 Massachusetts militiamen had assembled. The British commander ordered them to disperse. Captain John Parker, commander of the militia, told his men: "Stand your ground. Don't fire unless fired upon, but if they mean to have a war, let it begin here."

Suddenly the sound and smoke of musket fire filled the morning air. Who fired the first shot is a mystery even today, but 8 militiamen were killed and several were wounded. After the brief skirmish, the militiamen withdrew and the red-coated British soldiers continued on their march toward Concord.

You may wish to assign to a few pupils the task of learning what happened to Revere, Dawes, and Prescott. If possible, assign this project before you teach the lesson so that pupils can report their findings to the class.

Massachusetts militiamen in large numbers had gathered at Concord. However, they were unable to keep the British from searching the town and destroying all the military supplies they could find. A small battle took place at the North Bridge in Concord and both sides suffered casualties. News of the fighting at Lexington and Concord had spread rapidly. Thousands of Massachusetts men picked up their muskets and hurried across the fields toward the sounds of battle. No one who heard the call to arms was too young or too old to go.

Around noon the outnumbered British force began the long march from Concord back to Boston. No one now opposed the British openly. Instead, colonial marksmen fired from farmhouse windows, and from behind stone walls, trees, and barns. Every Massachusetts man fought for himself, but the damage they did together was immense.

The exhausted British soldiers reached their camp near Boston after dark. For 24

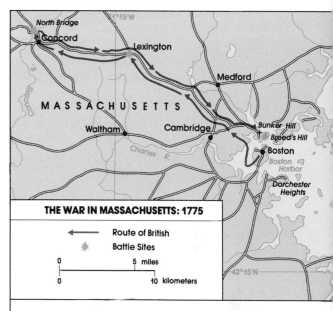

THE WAR IN MASSACHUSETTS: 1775

← Route of British
✳ Battle Sites

The British march to Concord touched off the War for Independence.

hours they had been on the march and much of that time under fire. Seventy-three British soldiers had been killed. More than 200 were wounded or missing. American casualties numbered 49 killed and 41 wounded. Though Americans did not know it at the time, the War for Independence had begun.

CHECKUP

1. Explain the circumstances of the Boston Massacre. What were the results?
2. How did colonial leaders keep in touch about their plans for resisting British policies after 1770?
3. Why did tea become important on the road toward independence?
4. What were the Intolerable Acts? Why did Americans give them that name?
5. Explain how and why fighting broke out at Lexington and Concord.

British soldiers fire a volley into the ranks of the minutemen assembled on Lexington green. This encounter marked the beginning of the War for Independence.

6/CHAPTER REVIEW

KEY FACTS

1. The American colonists fought side by side with the British against the French in the French and Indian War. Each side had Native American allies.

2. The Treaty of Paris (1763) saw France give all of Canada and the part of Louisiana east of the Mississippi to Britain.

3. After the French and Indian War, the British began new policies in an attempt to exert more control over their American colonies and to make those colonies help pay for the war.

4. Each new British policy led to a stronger colonial response until warfare erupted at Lexington and Concord in April 1775.

VOCABULARY QUIZ

On a separate sheet of paper write **T** if the statement is true and **F** if it is false. If the statement is false, change the underlined word or words to make the statement true.

F **1.** The Proclamation of 1763 <u>opened</u> the lands west of the Appalachian Mountains to settlement by the American colonists. **closed**

T **2.** In military terms, "<u>quarters</u>" refers to a place where soldiers stay.

T **3.** The stamp tax was an example of an <u>internal</u> tax.

F **4.** As a result of the French and Indian War, <u>France</u> won control over the settled parts of Canada. **Great Britain, or England**

T **5.** In most colonies, members of the upper house of the legislature were appointed by <u>the governor of the colony.</u>

F **6.** The repeal of the Townshend Acts saw all external taxes on the colonies lifted except the tax on <u>glass</u>. **tea**

T **7.** The militia was a <u>larger</u> group than the minutemen at the time of the War for Independence.

F **8.** The first shots of the War for Independence were fired on the village green in <u>Boston</u>. **Lexington**

T **9.** Smuggling means to <u>import</u> goods illegally.

F **10.** The lower house of the legislature in most colonies was called the <u>Parliament</u>. **assembly**

REVIEW QUESTIONS

1. How did Paul Revere's activities contribute to the movement directed toward colonial independence?

2. Name three ways in which the colonists opposed the Stamp Act and the Grenville Acts.

3. What was the British response to the Boston Tea Party?

4. What evidence is there that the colonies were becoming more united between 1753 and 1775?

ACTIVITIES

1. Using a biographical collection such as the *Dictionary of American Biography*, prepare written reports on the activities in the 1770s of one of the following:

Paul Revere   John Adams   Samuel Adams
Patrick Henry   Thomas   George Mason
              Jefferson

2. Paul Revere became well known to millions of people because of a poem written by the nineteenth-century poet Henry Wadsworth Longfellow. Obtain a copy of this poem, "Paul Revere's Ride." Have a committee choose members of the class to read the poem aloud, one student to a stanza.

132

STATING A POINT OF VIEW

PAUL REVERE'S ACCOUNT

On page 130 you read that Paul Revere, William Dawes, and Dr. Samuel Prescott rode to warn the militia and the minutemen on the night of April 18, 1775. Here is Paul Revere's account of that night, written 23 years later.

In the fall of 1774 and winter of 1775, I was one of upwards of thirty, chiefly mechanics, who formed ourselves into a committee for the purpose of watching the movements of the British soldiers . . . On Tuesday evening, the 18th, it was observed that a number of soldiers were marching toward the bottom of the Common . . . About 10 o'clock Dr. Warren sent in great haste for me and begged that I would immediately set off for Lexington. . . .

I went home, (got) my boots and coat (and) set off upon a very good horse. It was then about 11 o'clock and very pleasant. After I had passed Charlestown Neck . . . I saw two men on horseback under a tree. When I got near them, I discovered they were British officers. . . . I turned my horse very quick and galloped . . . for the Medford Road. The (British officer) who chased me . . . got into a clay pond . . . I got clear of him, and went through Medford (where) I awaked the captain of the minutemen; . . . I alarmed almost every house, till I got to Lexington. . . .

After I had been there about half an hour, Mr. Dawes came. We refreshed ourselves and set off for Concord. We were overtaken by a young Dr. Prescott, whom we found to be a high Son of Liberty. . . .

(On their way to Concord the three men ran into six British officers on horseback. Dawes and Prescott got away, but this time Revere was caught. The letter resumes.)

One of (the British officers) whom I afterwards found to be a Major Mitchell, of the 5th Regiment, clapped his pistol to my head, called me by name and told me he was going to ask me some questions, and if I did not give him true answers, he would blow my brains out.

(After questioning Revere, Major Mitchell turned him over to a sergeant, and the whole party rode back toward Lexington. The sergeant's horse was tired, and as they neared Lexington he took the horse Paul Revere was riding.)

I went across the burying-ground and some pastures and came to the Rev. Mr. Clark's house, where I found (John) Hancock and (Samuel) Adams. I told them of my treatment, and they concluded to go from that house towards Woburn. I went with them and a Mr. Lowell, who was a clerk to Mr. Hancock.

When we got to the house where they intended to stop . . . Mr. Lowell asked me to go to the tavern with him, to get a trunk of papers belonging to Mr. Hancock . . . While we were getting the trunk, we saw the British, very near . . . In their front was an officer on horseback. They made a short halt, when I heard a gun fired . . . then two guns, and then a continual roar of musketry, when we made off with the trunk.

SKILLS PRACTICE

This account is written from the point of view of Paul Revere. Would William Dawes or Dr. Prescott have a point of view markedly different from Revere's? Can you suggest ways in which Major Mitchell's point of view might conflict with Revere's?

Write an account of the night of April 18, 1775, from the point of view of Major Mitchell. Or write an account of that night from the point of view of Paul Revere's wife.

CHAPTER 7
The War For Independence

Washington Takes Command

┌─ VOCABULARY ─────────────────┐

Second Continental Congress

Continental army

Loyalist

Tory

Patriot

Common Sense

Declaration of Independence

└──────────────────────────────┘

Washington's Mount Vernon   George Washington was the eldest son of Augustine Washington and his second wife, Mary Ball Washington. When George was 11 years old, his father died. Young George then went to live with his elder half brother, Lawrence, who was 25 at the time.

Lawrence Washington was the owner of Mount Vernon, a large plantation on the Potomac River. After Lawrence's death in 1752, George Washington inherited the estate. Following his service in the French and Indian War, George Washington returned to Mount Vernon to live. Thereafter, he left the plantation only when service to Virginia or to the United States made his absence necessary. In 1759 he married a widow, Martha Dandridge Custis, who brought her two children with her to Mount Vernon.

Through his inheritance from his half brother, his marriage to a wealthy widow, and his own efforts, George Washington acquired thousands of acres of land. He worked hard at managing his plantation. In fact, Virginians recognized him as the best farmer in their colony. But Washington was something more than a good farmer and major landowner. In the American Revolution he was the indispensable man—the one person who was absolutely necessary during those critical times.

The Second Continental Congress On May 10, 1775, delegates from all 13 colonies came together in Philadelphia. The meeting became known as the **Second Continental Congress.** Until 1781 that group acted as a central government in the American fight for independence.

George Washington was a delegate from Virginia to the Second Continental Congress. He attended, wearing the uniform of the Virginia militia he had been chosen to command. At Philadelphia he was given a much larger command. On June 15, 1775, members of the Second Continental Congress chose him to take charge of the troops around Boston. They had gathered in Cambridge and other nearby towns after the fighting at Lexington and Concord.

General George Washington takes command of the Continental army in July 1775.

George Washington's admiration for his half brother Lawrence was an important influence during his early years. Lawrence had the polish of an English gentleman. He served as militia captain in Central America in a brief war between Britain and Spain. His war tales excited George's imagination.

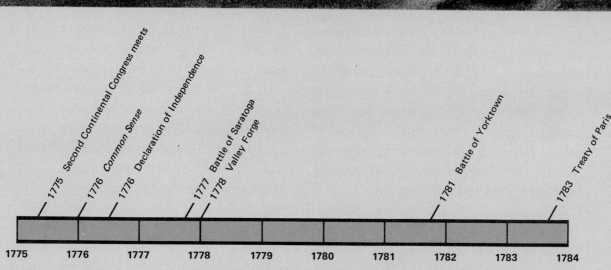

1775 Second Continental Congress meets
1776 *Common Sense*
1776 Declaration of Independence
1777 Battle of Saratoga
1778 Valley Forge
1781 Battle of Yorktown
1783 Treaty of Paris

| 1775 | 1776 | 1777 | 1778 | 1779 | 1780 | 1781 | 1782 | 1783 | 1784 |

The Continental army   The army Washington took command of was little more than a loosely organized group of poorly trained militia.   The enlistments of most of its members would run out in a few months.   And yet the Congress had named the militia the **Continental army.** Thousands served in its ranks for various periods of time, but George Washington remained its commanding general throughout the long years of the War for Independence.

The militia that made up the Continental army around Boston had fought one battle before Washington took command. Two months after Lexington and Concord, a large force of militia had taken up positions across the Charles River from Boston on Bunker Hill and Breed's Hill. Cannons could be fired from these hills across the river into Boston.   Actually, the militia had no cannons, but British General Thomas Gage did not know that. So he resolved to drive the militia from these hills.

The battle of Bunker Hill   A little after noon on June 17, 1775, British troops crossed the Charles River.   They marched in orderly ranks toward the trenches on Breed's Hill.   As they drew close, a withering blast of musket fire shattered the silence.   The British fell back, but then charged again.   Once more, the determined militia drove them back.   After reforming their ranks, the British infantry charged up the hill a third time.

This time the British were successful. The militia, with ammunition running low after 2 hours of fighting, had to withdraw.   Though most of the fighting took place on Breed's Hill, the struggle became known in history as the battle of Bunker Hill.   Even though the battle was a victory for the British, they suffered more than 1,000 casualties, compared to less than 400 for the Continental troops.   Moreover, the militiamen gained the confidence they badly needed.   Until their ammunition was nearly gone, they had stood up to the British regulars.

Cannons from Fort Ticonderoga Several months went by before the Continental army around Boston had any cannons.   These cannons came from Fort Ticonderoga (tī kon də rō′ gə), about 150 miles (240 km) northwest of Boston.   Fort Ticonderoga stood at the southern end of Lake Champlain.   That lake was an important link in the land-and-water route between Canada and the middle colonies.

At daybreak on May 10, 1775, Ethan Allen and a band of Vermont militiamen called the Green Mountain Boys won an almost bloodless victory there.   The attack was such a surprise that the British commander surrendered while still dressed in his nightclothes.   By capturing Ticonderoga, the militiamen gained a key fort. In addition, they captured valuable cannons and supplies of ammunition.

Under the direction of General Henry Knox, these cannons were started on their way to Boston.   They were dragged over snowy trails through the forests by teams of oxen.   Forty-three cannons and 16 mortars reached Boston on January 24, 1776. Early in March, units of the Continental army captured Dorchester Heights.   From there, Boston and most of the harbor were in range of General Knox's cannons.   Be-

Ethan Allen and the Green Mountain Boys joined forces with Benedict Arnold and his force of American militia at Fort Ticonderoga. Mention Arnold's later betrayal of the American cause. He became a general in the British army.

Ethan Allen, waving his sword, calls upon the British to surrender Fort Ticonderoga. The Green Mountain boys took the fort without loss of life. (44°N/75°W; map, p. 129)

cause of this threat, the British decided to give up Boston. In March their troops left on ships, sailing to Halifax in Canada. They never returned to Boston.

Loyalists and Patriots   About 1,000 civilians left Boston with the British troops. They were colonists who remained loyal to King George III, so they were called **Loyalists**. Sometimes they were called **Tories** because that was the name of the political party that supported the king.

The colonists who rose up against Great Britain are often called the **Patriots**. Most of them did not yet think of themselves as Americans. They thought of themselves as Virginians or New Yorkers or members of one of the other 11 English colonies.

The well-informed John Adams believed that only one third of the colonists were Patriots, that is, people actively supporting the Revolution. Adams said that one third remained loyal to Great Britain and so could be called Loyalists. In fact, during the Revolution about 40,000 Loyalists signed up to fight against the Patriots. Adams felt that the other third of the people remained neutral. This group did not care which side won.

Action in the Carolinas   There were large numbers of Loyalists in North Carolina and South Carolina. For this reason, British leaders thought it would be easy to put down any revolt there. In February

1776 a British fleet sailed toward Wilmington, North Carolina. At the same time, about 1,500 Loyalists marched to aid in the capture of Wilmington. They never got there, because a force of Patriots defeated the Loyalists in battle at Moore's Creek Bridge.

Without the help of land forces, the British fleet had little chance to capture Wilmington. So the fleet sailed farther south, to Charleston, South Carolina. The British ships shelled the defenses the Patriots had thrown up. These defenses were built with logs cut from the palmetto tree. British cannonballs were unable to penetrate these thick, tough logs. After failing in several attempts to capture Charleston, the British fleet sailed north to New York.

In Common Sense *Thomas Paine urged the colonies to seek freedom from British rule. His pamphlet induced many colonists to support the cause of independence.*

National Portrait Gallery, London

Patriots in South Carolina wanted people to remember how they had resisted the British fleet. So they put a palmetto tree as a symbol on their new state flag. To this day, South Carolina is known as the Palmetto State.

Paine's pamphlet   The Patriot leaders waited for more than a year before breaking their ties with Great Britain. Some favored a form of self-government that would keep them within the British Empire. Gradually, however, those favoring independence gained the upper hand.

Thomas Paine helped swing public opinion in favor of independence. He was a poor young writer from England who came to Philadelphia less than a year before fighting broke out at Lexington and Concord. In January 1776, Paine published a pamphlet called ***Common Sense.*** It was a best seller for its time, with sales of more than 120,000 copies.

Paine's pamphlet stated that it was only common sense for the colonies to declare their independence from Great Britain. "How is it that a continent should be ruled by an island?" he asked. *Common Sense* had an almost magical effect. It convinced thousands of doubtful men and women that independence from Great Britain was proper and logical. Abigail Adams wrote to her husband, John, at the Second Continental Congress in Philadelphia, "*Common Sense . . .* has come to clear our doubts and fix our course." George Washington wrote to a friend, "By private letters, which I have lately received from Virginia, I find Paine's *Common Sense* is working a wonderful change there in the minds of many men."

Point out the harshness of Paine's language in *Common Sense*. He referred to George III as "the royal brute of Great Britain" and described him as "the principal ruffian of some ruthless gang."

KEY 1. *Richard Stockton, N.J.;* **2.** *Josiah Bartlett, N.H.;* **3.** *Thomas Nelson, Jr., Va.;* **4.** *George Clymer, Pa.;* **5.** *Francis Lightfoot Lee, Va.;* **6.** *John Penn, N.C.;* **7.** *Abraham Clark, N.J.;* **8.** *John Morton, Pa.;* **9.** *George Ross, Pa.;* **10.** *James Smith, Pa.;* **11.** *Samuel Adams, Mass.;* **12.** *Robert Treat Paine.* *Mass.;* **13.** *Button Gwinnett, Ga.;* **14.** *Robert Morris, Pa.;* **15.** *Benjamin Harrison, Va.;* **16.** *Carter Braxton, Va.;* **17.** *John Hart, N.J.;* **18.** *John Adams, Mass.;* **19.** *Roger Sherman, Conn.;* **20.** *James Wilson, Pa.;* **21.** *Thomas Jefferson, Va.;* **22.** *Charles Thompson, (Secretary);* **23.** *John* *Hancock, Mass.;* **24.** *Francis Hopkinson, N.J.;* **25.** *William Ellery, R.I.;* **26.** *Edward Rutledge, S.C.;* **27.** *Benjamin Franklin, Pa.;* **28.** *Charles Carroll, Md.;* **29.** *Richard Henry Lee, Va.;* **30.** *George Read, Del.;* **31.** *George Taylor, Pa.;* **32.** *Stephen Hopkins, R.I.*

Members of the Continental Congress prepare to approve the Declaration of Independence.

The Declaration of Independence

On June 7, 1776, Richard Henry Lee of Virginia introduced a resolution into the Second Continental Congress. Its main part stated that "these United Colonies ought to be free and independent states." For nearly a month the members of Congress debated Lee's resolution. They approved it on July 2, 1776. This was all that was needed to declare independence. However, Congress had chosen a committee to prepare a suitable statement to accompany Lee's resolution. It is this statement, explaining Congress' action, that became known as the **Declaration of Independence.**

Emphasize the courage displayed by the men who signed the Declaration of Independence. The British saw these men as traitors. The punishment for this crime was to be hanged, drawn, and quartered.

139

A committee of five prepared the statement. Its members were Benjamin Franklin of Pennsylvania, John Adams of Massachusetts, Roger Sherman of Connecticut, Robert Livingston of New York, and Thomas Jefferson of Virginia. Jefferson was chosen as chairman.

When Thomas Jefferson came to Philadelphia to attend the Second Continental Congress, he rented rooms in the house of Mr. Graff, a bricklayer. After sessions of Congress each day, Jefferson spent the warm June nights working on the Declaration of Independence. Sometimes other members of the committee brought suggestions. It was Thomas Jefferson, though, who was most responsible for the words, phrases, and ideas in the historic document. Congress received the committee's report on June 28. All the delegates except those from New York approved the Declaration of Independence on July 4. That is why we celebrate Independence Day on that date.

The news spreads   Congress ordered the Declaration of Independence printed and sent to Patriot officials, military units, and the press. On July 8, outside the Pennsylvania State House, the declaration was first read to the public. During the celebration that followed, people cheered, bells rang, and soldiers paraded.

Within a month, more than 25 newspapers had spread the words of the Declaration of Independence from New England to South Carolina. Ships carried copies of the declaration to Europe. It was read with interest not only in the British court but also by government officials in countries on the European continent.

The importance of the declaration
The text of the Declaration of Independence is on pages 141–145. Although it is a short document, the effects of the declaration have been long and mighty. In 1776 it had an immediate effect on the undecided. They had to choose between loyalty to the Revolution and loyalty to Great Britain. Probably most importantly, the declaration gave foreign nations that were enemies of Great Britain the opportunity to harm Britain by helping the new United States of America gain independence.

Throughout the world the Declaration of Independence is the best-known American document. Colonial people everywhere have used its ideas in support of their own movements toward independence. Here in the United States it has been a source of inspiration for people fighting for equal rights for all Americans. In 1776, it put into words the reasons for peoples' willingness to fight for independence. Yet, declaring independence left much to be done. There remained the pressing task of winning the War for Independence.

CHECKUP

1. Who attended the Second Continental Congress? What role did this group play during the War for Independence?
2. Name three accomplishments of the Second Continental Congress.
3. What big battle was fought before Washington took command of the Continental army?
4. How did Thomas Paine contribute to the drive for independence?
5. Why do Americans celebrate on July 4?
6. After reading the Declaration of Independence on pages 141–145, state in your own words the main ideas that are put forth.

You might want to assign at this time the Skills Development activity at the end of this chapter. This activity develops pupils' ability to use and interpret historical materials.

The Declaration of Independence

In Congress, July 4, 1776

When, in the course of human events, it becomes necessary for one people to dissolve the political bands which have connected them with another, and to assume, among the powers of the earth, the separate and equal station to which the laws of nature and nature's God entitle them, a decent respect to the opinions of mankind requires that they should declare the causes which impel them to the separation.

We hold these truths to be self-evident; that all men are created equal, that they are endowed by their Creator with certain unalienable rights, that among these are life, liberty, and the pursuit of happiness. That to secure these rights, governments are instituted among men, deriving their just powers from the consent of the governed; that whenever any form of government becomes destructive of these ends, it is the right of the people to alter or to abolish it, and to institute new government, laying its foundation on such principles, and organizing its powers in such form, as to them shall seem most likely to effect their safety and happiness. Prudence, indeed, will dictate that governments long established should not be changed for light and transient causes; and accordingly all experience hath shown that mankind are more disposed to suffer while evils are sufferable, than to right themselves by abolishing the forms to which they are accustomed. But when a long train of abuses and usurpations, pursuing invariably the same object, evinces a design to reduce them under absolute despotism, it is their right, it is their duty, to throw off such government, and to provide new guards for their future security.

Such has been the patient sufferance of these colonies; and such is now the necessity which constrains them to alter their former systems of government. The history of the present king of Great Britain is a history of repeated injuries and usurpations, all having in direct object the establishment of an absolute tyranny over these states. To prove this, let facts be submitted to a candid world.

He has refused his assent to laws the most wholesome and necessary for the public good.

He has forbidden his governors to pass laws of immediate and pressing importance, unless suspended in their operation till his assent should be obtained; and when so suspended, he has utterly neglected to attend to them.

He has refused to pass other laws for the accommodation of large districts of people, unless those people would relinquish the right of representation in the legislature, a right inestimable to them, and formidable to tyrants only.

He has called together legislative bodies at places unusual, uncomfortable, and distant from the depository of their

Why the Declaration of Independence was issued The first paragraph (previous page) states that it has become necessary for the American colonists to break their political ties with Great Britain, and that it is only proper to explain why they are taking this step. (One reason was that Americans hoped to get help from other nations.)

The purposes of government The paragraph directly at left, beginning "We hold these truths . . .," is the very heart of the Declaration of Independence. It states that all men are born with equal claims to "life, liberty, and the pursuit of happiness." These rights, given by the Creator, are "unalienable," that is, they cannot be given away, nor can a government take them away.

The paragraph goes on to state that governments were created to protect these human rights. Whenever a government interferes with them, its citizens have the right as well as the duty to change or do away with it. A government must be based on the consent of the governed. Changing or doing away with a government will be carried out, however, only after events have proved that the government has abused its powers.

The charges against the British king Here the Declaration of Independence reviews the years between 1763 and 1776, stating that the colonists believed the king's government had many times denied their

public records, for the sole purpose of fatiguing them into compliance with his measures.

He has dissolved representative houses repeatedly, for opposing, with manly firmness, his invasions on the rights of the people.

He has refused, for a long time after such dissolutions, to cause others to be elected; whereby the legislative powers, incapable of annihilation, have returned to the people at large for their exercise; the state remaining, in the meantime, exposed to all the dangers of invasion from without and convulsions within.

He has endeavored to prevent the population of these states; for that purpose obstructing the laws for the naturalization of foreigners, refusing to pass others to encourage their migrations hither, and raising the conditions of new appropriations of lands.

He has obstructed the administration of justice, by refusing his assent to laws for establishing judiciary powers.

He has made judges dependent on his will alone for the tenure of their offices, and the amount and payment of their salaries.

He has erected a multitude of new offices, and sent hither swarms of officers to harass our people and eat out their substance.

He has kept among us, in times of peace, standing armies, without the consent of our legislatures.

He has affected to render the military independent of, and superior to, the civil power.

He has combined with others to subject us to a jurisdiction foreign to our constitution and unacknowledged by our laws, giving his assent to their acts of pretended legislation:

For quartering large bodies of armed troops among us;

For protecting them, by a mock trial, from punishment for any murders which they should commit on the inhabitants of these states;

For cutting off our trade with all parts of the world;

For imposing taxes on us without our consent;

For depriving us, in many cases, of the benefits of trial by jury;

For transporting us beyond seas, to be tried for pretended offenses;

For abolishing the free system of English laws in a neighboring province, establishing therein an arbitrary

basic human rights. King George III and his government are charged with committing a long list of misdeeds. Because of these acts, the declaration states that the king is no longer entitled to rule the American colonies. He no longer has the consent of the governed.

143

government, and enlarging its boundaries, so as to render it at once an example and fit instrument for introducing the same absolute rule into these colonies;

For taking away our charters, abolishing our most valuable laws, and altering fundamentally the forms of our governments;

For suspending our own legislatures, and declaring themselves invested with power to legislate for us in all cases whatsoever.

He has abdicated government here, by declaring us out of his protection and waging war against us.

He has plundered our seas, ravaged our coasts, burned our towns, and destroyed the lives of our people.

He is at this time transporting large armies of foreign mercenaries to complete the works of death, desolation, and tyranny already begun with circumstances of cruelty and perfidy scarcely paralleled in the most barbarous ages, and totally unworthy the head of a civilized nation.

He has constrained our fellow-citizens, taken captive on the high seas, to bear arms against their country, to become the executioners of their friends and brethren, or to fall themselves by their hands.

He has excited domestic insurrection among us, and has endeavored to bring on the inhabitants of our frontiers, the merciless Indian savages, whose known rule of warfare is an undistinguished destruction of all ages, sexes, and conditions.

In every stage of these oppressions we have petitioned for redress in the most humble terms; our repeated petitions have been answered only by repeated injury. A prince whose character is thus marked by every act which may define a tyrant is unfit to be the ruler of a free people.

Nor have we been wanting in attentions to our British brethren. We have warned them, from time to time, of attempts by their legislature to extend an unwarrantable jurisdiction over us. We have reminded them of the circumstances of our emigration and settlement here. We have appealed to their native justice and magnanimity; and we have conjured them, by the ties of our common kindred, to disavow these usurpations, which would inevitably interrupt our connections and correspondence. They, too, have been

The attempts to obtain justice These two paragraphs state that the American colonists have asked the British king for justice. They have also appealed to the British people. Yet neither the king nor the British people have responded to the colonists' pleas.

deaf to the voice of justice and consanguinity. We must, therefore, acquiesce in the necessity which denounces our separation, and hold them, as we hold the rest of mankind, enemies in war; in peace, friends.

We, therefore, the representatives of the United States of America, in General Congress assembled, appealing to the Supreme Judge of the world for the rectitude of our intentions, do, in the name and by the authority of the good people of these colonies, solemnly publish and declare that these United Colonies are, and of right ought to be, free and independent states; that they are absolved from all allegiance to the British crown, and that all political connection between them and the state of Great Britain is, and ought to be, totally dissolved; and that, as free and independent states, they have full power to levy war, conclude peace, contract alliances, establish commerce, and do all other acts and things which independent states may of right do. And, for the support of this declaration, with a firm reliance on the protection of Divine Providence, we mutually pledge to each other our lives, our fortunes, and our sacred honor.

The colonies declare their independence This final paragraph actually proclaims independence. It also lists those things that the new United States of America may do as an independent country.

In the last sentence the signers pledge their lives and all they own to support the cause of independence. This was a serious matter, for as Benjamin Franklin said, "Now we must all hang together, or we will all hang separately." Still, they took the risk and signed the document that proclaimed to the world the independence of the United States of America.

John Hancock, President
(MASSACHUSETTS)

NEW HAMPSHIRE
Josiah Bartlett
William Whipple
Matthew Thornton

MASSACHUSETTS
John Adams
Samuel Adams
Robert Treat Paine
Elbridge Gerry

NEW YORK
William Floyd
Philip Livingston
Francis Lewis
Lewis Morris

RHODE ISLAND
Stephen Hopkins
William Ellery

NEW JERSEY
Richard Stockton
John Witherspoon
Francis Hopkinson
John Hart
Abraham Clark

PENNSYLVANIA
Robert Morris
Benjamin Rush
Benjamin Franklin
John Morton
George Clymer
James Smith
George Taylor
James Wilson
George Ross

DELAWARE
Caesar Rodney
George Read
Thomas McKean

MARYLAND
Samuel Chase
William Paca
Thomas Stone
Charles Carroll
  of Carrollton

VIRGINIA
George Wythe
Richard Henry Lee
Thomas Jefferson
Benjamin Harrison
Thomas Nelson, Jr.
Francis Lightfoot Lee
Carter Braxton

NORTH CAROLINA
William Hooper
Joseph Hewes
John Penn

SOUTH CAROLINA
Edward Rutledge
Thomas Heyward, Jr.
Thomas Lynch, Jr.
Arthur Middleton

CONNECTICUT
Roger Sherman
Samuel Huntington
William Williams
Oliver Wolcott

GEORGIA
Button Gwinnett
Lyman Hall
George Walton

145

The Ups and Downs of War

---VOCABULARY---

mercenary	treaty of alliance
Hessian	privateer

The British attack   In the spring of 1776, word came that an overwhelming British force was moving to attack New York City. The British had assembled 32,000 soldiers and 500 ships for this attack. Washington's Continental army had only 19,000 men. Nevertheless, he ordered the army south from Boston to meet the expected British attack.

British troops landed first on Staten Island in July. Later, 20,000 more came ashore on Long Island. They easily defeated the poorly trained American soldiers. Under cover of darkness and fog, the retreating Americans escaped to New York City. It was at this time that Nathan Hale, a young Connecticut schoolmaster who had become a captain in the Continental army, volunteered to spy on British positions. Posing as a Dutch schoolmaster, he worked his way through the front lines. On his return with valuable information, Hale was captured, and a day later he was hanged as a spy. His last words are said to have been, "I only regret that I have but one life to lose for my country."

A long retreat   In September the advancing British drove the Continental army from New York City. After an indecisive battle at White Plains, General Washington ordered a retreat.

The Americans retreated all the way across New Jersey into Pennsylvania. This put the Delaware River between them and their foes. If General Howe's troops had followed more closely, they might have won the war at this time. Expiring enlistments, desertions, and sickness had shrunk the Continental army to no more than 5,000 men. Instead of

General Washington directs his troops at the battle of Princeton.   (40°N/75°W; map, p. 125)

crushing this remnant, however, Howe ordered his army into winter quarters. Most of the British troops were housed in New York and New Jersey. In Trenton and several other communities, Howe stationed German soldiers that had been hired by the British to fight for them. Soldiers hired by a government from outside its own country are known as **mercenaries.** These mercenaries were called **Hessians** because many of them came from the German state of Hesse.

A Christmas victory   On December 25, 1776, the Delaware River was in full flood. Heavy sheets of ice spun and whirled on its wild surface. Yet on Christmas night, boatloads of shivering American soldiers crossed the river. The Continental army was about to make a surprise attack on Trenton, New Jersey.

By four o'clock in the morning, the army had crossed. It then began marching the 9 miles (14 km) from the river to Trenton. The soldiers' wet muskets were useless, but Washington ordered, "Use the bayonet—I am resolved to take Trenton." This the Continentals did, capturing about 900 Hessians and seizing valuable supplies.

News of the Christmas victory spread through the country. It was good news, because it came after a series of near disasters for the fighting Americans. Even more encouraging news came 8 days later when Washington won another surprise victory at Princeton, New Jersey.

The plan to split the colonies   In spite of Washington's successes in New Jersey, British generals thought they

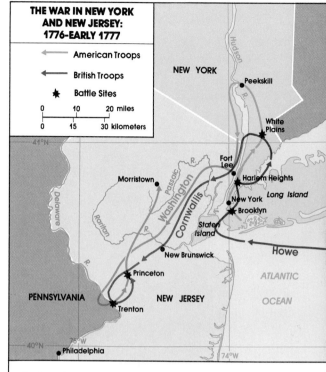

An American victory at Trenton climaxed the first full year of war.

could deliver a knockout blow in 1777. They planned a campaign to invade New York State and seize the rich Hudson River valley. If successful, this campaign would cut off New England from the rest of the United States. It would put all of New York under British control. And it would crush American spirits.

The campaign got under way as British General John Burgoyne (bər goin´) advanced south from Canada along the Lake Champlain route. Burgoyne had 7,000 men under his command. British Colonel Barry St. Leger (lej´ər) led a somewhat smaller force east from Lake Ontario toward Albany. The British plan also called for General Howe to send troops up the Hudson from New York City. All three forces were to meet near Albany.

General Howe made a grave tactical error by not capturing Washington and his men. As long as Washington was free, Americans felt the revolution would go on. At this point, Washington feared defeat. He wrote a relative, "I think the game is pretty near up…."

The Night Ride of Sybil Ludington

Two years after Paul Revere made his ride, a 16-year-old girl named Sybil Ludington also made a night ride for the cause of independence.

She lived in New York State, just across the line from Connecticut. One rainy night in April 1777, an exhausted man rode up to the Ludington home. He brought word to Colonel Henry Ludington, Sybil's father, that the British had captured Danbury, Connecticut. Now the British soldiers, drunk with liquor they had found there, were looting and burning homes.

Colonel Ludington, the militia commander, could see the red glow in the sky. Danbury was burning, but perhaps part of it could be saved if his men were assembled. But who could call for them to meet at his house? He would have to stay there and organize them. The exhausted messenger could go no farther. Besides, the messenger knew nothing of the country roads where the militiamen lived.

Then Sybil spoke up. "I'll go, Father," she said.

"It will be a hard ride," her father warned. "There will be dangers." But Sybil was already out the door, running toward the stable. It took no more than a minute to get Star, her big bay horse, saddled and bridled.

Sybil Ludington rode hard through the night. She pounded on doors, shouting for the militiamen to assemble at her father's house. By the time she got home the next morning, she had ridden 40 miles (74 km). Nearly every militiaman had responded. Colonel Ludington led them to join other

This statue of Sybil Ludington and her horse, Star, is near the route of her long night ride in April 1777.

forces who drove the redcoats out of Danbury.

Highway signs today mark the road that Sybil Ludington traveled more than 200 years ago. A statue of Sybil and Star stands on the shore of Lake Gleneida, in New York State, not far from where the spirited teenager set out on her ride.

But General Howe, instead of ordering an advance up the Hudson, took most of his troops by sea to a point near Philadelphia. By this time Philadelphia had become America's largest city and was the meeting place of the Continental Congress. Apparently Howe thought he could capture Philadelphia and still have time to take part in the Hudson Valley campaign.

Howe's troops did capture Philadelphia after defeating Washington's army in the battle of Brandywine. The Continental Congress had to flee, first to Lancaster, Pennsylvania, and then farther west to York. When the Americans tried to retake Philadelphia, the British beat them back at Germantown. But Howe's army was never able to take part in the Hudson Valley campaign.

Point out that despite General Howe's victory in Pennsylvania, his arbitrary change of plans and failure to meet Burgoyne caused a more serious British defeat. American confidence was restored with Burgoyne's defeat.

Saratoga   Meanwhile, General Burgoyne, advancing through the forests of New York State, was in trouble. His was an unusual army. It was made up of British soldiers, Canadians, Hessians, and Indian allies. Though Fort Ticonderoga surrendered to Burgoyne, he met stronger resistance as he moved farther south. American militia swarmed and stung like hornets along his army's flanks.

General Philip Schuyler (skī′lėr) and General Horatio Gates organized these militiamen into an able fighting force. General Washington sent a company of sharpshooters under Daniel Morgan to help the American northern army. In August, Americans turned back an expedition sent by Burgoyne to seize supplies stored at Bennington, Vermont. Nearly 1,000 of his men were killed, wounded, captured, or missing at the end of the battle of Bennington. To make matters worse, Burgoyne learned that American resistance had driven Colonel St. Leger's small army back to its base at Oswego.

In September the American militiamen turned back an attack by Burgoyne's desperate army at Saratoga, New York. Three weeks later the militiamen defeated the British once more. Now Burgoyne's army was nearly surrounded. His Indian allies had deserted him. Supplies were almost gone. Faced with these conditions, Burgoyne had no choice but to give up. He surrendered the remainder of his army on October 17, 1777.

British General Burgoyne surrenders to American General Gates at Saratoga in 1777. The battle at Saratoga was the turning point of the war. (43°N/74°W; map, p. 129)

The turning point   Burgoyne's surrender was the turning point in the War for Independence. Although there were hard years ahead, American spirits rose with this victory and the capture of a major British army. It seemed that the Americans now had a very good chance to win. With this in mind, the French government decided to help openly in the American struggle against the British.

For 2 years France had been secretly helping the Americans with money and supplies. But the French government had refused to openly join the new United States in fighting the British. Then came news of Burgoyne's surrender at Saratoga. Four months later, France and the United States signed a **treaty of alliance**. The next year Spain pledged its support to the American struggle for independence. In 1780 Holland joined the growing list of Great Britain's enemies.

Foreign aid   Wars cost money, and the Americans had trouble financing their struggle for independence. Congress was powerless to tax the states or individuals. Though the states voluntarily furnished a small amount of money, it was never enough. To pay for the war, Congress had to issue paper money and to borrow. Robert Morris, who served as American superintendent of finance, lent part of his own fortune when money was needed. Haym Salomon, an immigrant from Poland, lent so much money to Congress that he ruined himself financially.

Loans and gifts from other countries were part of the aid the Americans received during the war. France gave the most financial help. In some ways

America's fight for independence was another war between France and Great Britain. The two nations fought each other in several parts of the world. This kept Great Britain from giving its entire attention to putting down the American colonial rebellion. In addition, France furnished the United States with tons of equipment, thousands of soldiers, and the help of its large naval fleet.

Still, foreign aid did not end the War for Independence immediately. For 6 years after Burgoyne's surrender in 1777, the war continued. During these years Americans experienced many hardships and bitter disappointments.

Naval warfare   In 1775 Congress authorized the formation of an American navy. Though it had too few ships to fight as a fleet, single ships and their crews fought hard against the British. John Paul Jones was one of the outstanding naval officers. He specialized in sinking or seizing British merchant ships in their home waters. In 1779 Jones fought a now-famous naval battle with the British warship *Serapis*, off the English coast. Jones commanded the *Bonhomme Richard*. The first part of the fight went against him and his ship. But when the British commander asked if he wanted to surrender, Jones replied, "I have not yet begun to fight." With renewed determination, he ordered his crew to continue to fire and finally forced the captain of the *Serapis* to surrender.

In addition to the regular navy, Congress and some of the states authorized **privateers** to make war on British ocean commerce. Privateers were privately owned vessels especially built to attack and capture enemy merchant ships. About 1,000 American privateers sailed the high seas during the War for Independence. They captured nearly 600 British merchant ships. Because of damage done by privateers and the regular American navy, British merchants brought increasing pressure on Parliament to bring the war to an end.

Valley Forge   One of the hardest times for the Continental army came during the winter following Burgoyne's surrender. General Howe's British soldiers were warm, well-fed, and comfortable in Philadelphia. Conditions were different at Valley Forge, only a little more than 20 miles (32 km) from Philadelphia. The Continental army camped there for the winter of 1777–1778.

The Continental camp was on a low plateau, already cold and windswept when the troops arrived in December. Washington later said, "You might have tracked the army to Valley Forge by the blood of their feet." Ice and frozen ground had cut through the soldiers' worn shoes and boots. The men lived in tents until small huts were built at Valley Forge. But the huts were drafty, sunless, and damp inside, bringing on sickness and infection among the soldiers on the snow-covered plateau.

Food was always in short supply during that terrible winter. Soap was also scarce. Men could not wash their clothes or their bodies. This resulted in a tormenting itch. Thousands of men deserted, and more might have done so had they been strong enough to leave the

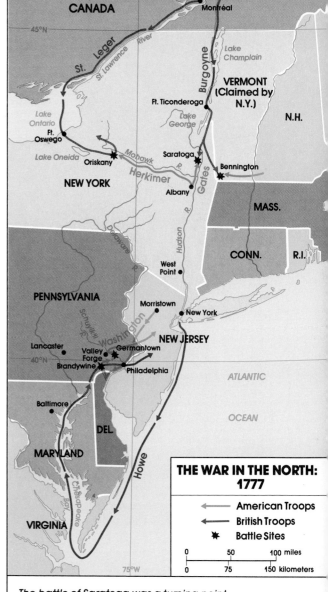

The battle of Saratoga was a turning point in America's fortunes.

camp. By spring the ranks of the Continental army had shrunk to fewer than 4,000 soldiers.

Without Washington's courage and strength of character, the Continental army might have disappeared completely. In the spring, news of the French alliance raised the spirits of the discouraged men. Fresh clothing, more plentiful food, and money to pay the soldiers brought an upsurge in morale. As

The Continental army endured much suffering at Valley Forge. (40°N/75°W; map, p. 129)

the army prepared for its summer campaigns, new recruits entered the camp. The ranks of the Continental army increased, and the fight for independence continued.

CHECKUP

1. Where did Washington take the Continental army after its defeats in New York?
2. Why were the victories at Trenton and Princeton important?
3. Why might Burgoyne's surrender at Saratoga be considered a turning point of the war?
4. What were the main achievements of American naval vessels in the War for Independence?
5. Explain why the winter of 1777–1778 was a hard time for the Continental army.

The United States Wins Independence

VOCABULARY

Northwest Territory	treason
	traitor
guerrilla	mutiny

War in the west In the fall of 1777 George Rogers Clark was a militia leader living at Fort Harrod in Kentucky. At that time Kentucky was still part of Virginia. Clark asked Governor Patrick Henry of Virginia to let him lead an expedition against the British in the west. The British were holding many of the forts once owned by France, near the Great Lakes. From these forts the British, aided by Loyalists and Indian allies, were making attacks on western settlements. Their goal was to take over the entire region that lay to the west of the Appalachian Mountains.

Patrick Henry liked the idea put forth by George Rogers Clark and made Clark a colonel. In May 1778, Clark took command of 175 militiamen from Virginia and Kentucky. They traveled down the Ohio River almost to the Mississippi, then marched northwestward. On July 4 the daring expedition captured Kaskaskia, originally a French settlement in the Illinois country. With the help of the French settlers, Colonel Clark's men took control of Cahokia, Vincennes, and other settlements in the region.

But the British had no intention of withdrawing from the Illinois country. Colonel Henry Hamilton, the British lieutenant governor at Detroit, led an attack on Vincennes, and recaptured it. But

George Rogers Clark's commitment to defeating the British in the west was so great that he used his own money to feed and pay his men. This left him penniless but saved the Northwest Territory.

British occupation of the former French fort lasted only a short time. In February 1779, George Rogers Clark gathered 150 men at Kaskaskia. He led them toward Vincennes, often through swamps and icy streams where the water was neck deep. His surprise attack left Colonel Hamilton with no choice but to surrender.

Clark's brilliant campaign left Americans in control of the vast territory north of the Ohio River from the Appalachian Mountains to the Mississippi River. When peace came at the end of the War for Independence, American diplomats could argue that this region, which would become known as the **Northwest Territory**, should be part of the new United States.

Action in New Jersey   While George Rogers Clark was winning in the west, New York and New Jersey became the scene of action in the east. General Henry Clinton replaced General Howe as commander of the British army in Philadelphia. Clinton learned that a French fleet was sailing for America and was probably headed for New York. Therefore, he decided to move his army to New York.

As the British marched across New Jersey, Washington ordered an attack at Monmouth. It was during this battle, fought under a blazing summer sun, that Mary Ludwig Hays, the wife of a soldier, won her place in American history. During the fighting, she carried water in a pitcher to the soldiers, who gratefully nicknamed her Molly Pitcher. Later, when her husband suffered a heat stroke, she took his place in a gun crew. Though the Continental army fought well at Monmouth, Clinton's army was able to continue its march to New York.

War in the south   Late in 1778, British officials decided that their main military effort should be in the southern colonies. The British believed that there were more Loyalists in the south than in the north. British leaders also felt they could use their naval strength to better advantage along the southern coast. British ships sailed from the north and, with the aid of Loyalists, captured the port of Savannah, Georgia. Within a year all of Georgia was under British control.

In 1780 Clinton's army and a British fleet forced the surrender of Charleston, South Carolina. The surrender of Charleston was the biggest American disaster of the entire War for Independence. More than 5,000 American soldiers and huge amounts of supplies were captured by the British. Many of the Patriot leaders in the area were seized.

General Clinton turned over command of the British southern campaign to General Charles Cornwallis in June 1780. Clinton sailed back to New York with 4,500 of his troops. But before sailing, he sent a long report to the British war office in London. In the report Clinton said, "I venture to assert that there are few men in South Carolina who are not our prisoners or in arms with us."

Guerrilla warfare in South Carolina   As it turned out, Clinton's report was an exaggeration. There were plenty of fighting Patriots left in South Carolina. Among them was Francis Marion, a genius at **guerrilla**, or hit-and-run, warfare.

Marion's exploits earned him the name *Swamp Fox* because he conducted surprise attacks from secret bases in the Carolina swamps. Andrew Pickens and Thomas Sumter carried out attacks similar to Marion's. The three guerrilla leaders struck British outposts, cut supply lines, and attacked small detachments of British troops and Loyalists. These tactics weakened the British southern campaigns by pinning down regular troops.

In October 1780 a hastily gathered force of 900 American frontiersmen won a decisive battle at Kings Mountain, on the western border between North Carolina and South Carolina. These frontiersmen trapped 1,100 Loyalists led by British Major Patrick Ferguson, on top of the mountain. Their marksmanship turned back bayonet charges by the Loyalists. Ferguson was killed and his entire force was either killed or captured.

The main American army in the Carolinas met with less success than did the guerrilla fighters and frontiersmen. After the army suffered a bloody defeat at Camden, South Carolina, Washington sent General Nathanael Greene of Rhode Is-

On the United States postage stamps below are shown six people of differing backgrounds who backed the American cause. Lafayette, from France; Kosciusko and Pulaski, from Poland; and Von Steuben, from Prussia, all served with Continental troops. Haym Salomon, a Jewish immigrant from Poland, ruined himself financially with loans to the Continental Congress. Philip Mazzei, an Italian, wrote many pieces supporting American independence.

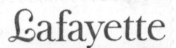

US Bicentennial 13c

Philip Mazzei
Patriot Remembered

USA irmail
40c

Haym Salomon   *Financial Hero*

land to take command. Greene promised no miracles. "We fight, get beat, rise, and fight again," he said. For a time, that is what happened. When Cornwallis pursued him, Greene took his army across the Dan River into Virginia. In the spring of 1781, Greene moved into the Carolinas again and captured a number of smaller British outposts. This convinced General Cornwallis that British control could not be restored in the Carolinas while Virginia remained a supply and training base for the Americans. So Cornwallis decided to lead his army into Virginia.

Treason and mutiny   While American fortunes rose and fell in the south, discouraging events took place in the north. In the fall of 1780, the news that General Benedict Arnold had committed **treason** shocked all Americans. The crime of treason is that of making war against or aiding the enemies of one's country. One who commits treason is called a **traitor**.

Arnold had shown great courage and ability as an army officer. He had helped to bring about Burgoyne's defeat at Saratoga. His ability had won him promotion to major general. Yet Arnold thought Congress had not rewarded him sufficiently. Besides, he was deep in debt.

In 1780 Washington placed Arnold in command of West Point on the Hudson River. This fort guarded against a British advance up the river from New York City. Arnold offered to turn this key fort over to the British in exchange for a large sum of money. The plot was discovered in time to keep West Point from being taken by the British, but Arnold himself escaped into British lines. Arnold's trea-

son was especially hard on Washington. He had trusted Benedict Arnold.

The year 1781 opened with more bad news for Washington. In their camp at Morristown, New Jersey, the Pennsylvania soldiers **mutinied**, that is, rebelled against their officers. The soldiers had not been paid for a year. They were half-naked and starving. Many claimed they had enlisted only for 3 years, not for as long as the war lasted. After killing one of their officers, they marched to Philadelphia to tell Congress of their troubles.

Washington feared the mutiny might spread. But he did not want to use force against men who had fought bravely in several campaigns. Finally the problem was settled by promising part of the back pay and releasing from service many of the men who claimed they had enlisted for only 3 years.

Surrender at Yorktown   As so often happened, good news came for Americans after a string of bad news. During the summer of 1781, Washington and the French General Rochambeau (rô sham bō′) were planning an attack on New York City. Then came word that Cornwallis had taken his army to Yorktown, Virginia. Yorktown was located on a small peninsula in Chesapeake (ches′ ə pēk) Bay. Cornwallis felt safe there as long as the British navy could reach him with more soldiers and supplies. But a French fleet, commanded by Admiral Francois de Grasse, sailed from the West Indies to drive British ships from Chesapeake Bay.

Washington and Rochambeau hurried their armies southward to join troops already in Virginia. Under Washington's

One reason for Benedict Arnold's financial difficulties and self-centered actions may have been the influence of his second wife, Margaret Shippen, a socially ambitious Philadelphian whom he married in 1778. **155**

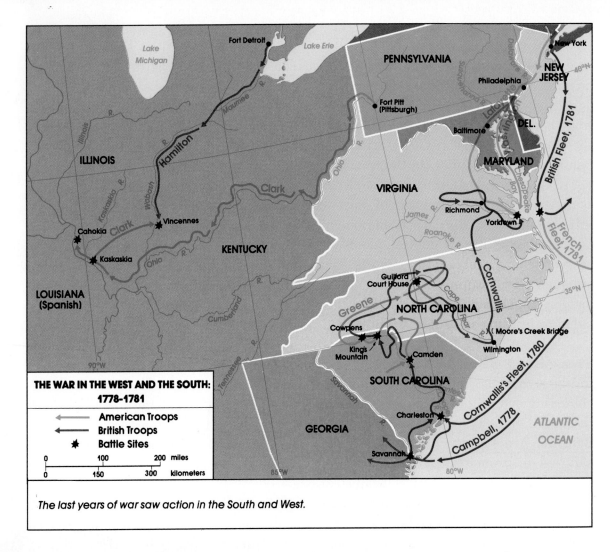

THE WAR IN THE WEST AND THE SOUTH:
1778-1781

← American Troops
← British Troops
★ Battle Sites

| 0 | 100 | 200 miles |
| 0 | 150 | 300 kilometers |

The last years of war saw action in the South and West.

command the combined armies surrounded Yorktown on land. With the French fleet blocking the mouth of Chesapeake Bay, Cornwallis was trapped. On October 19, 1781, he surrendered his force of about 8,000 soldiers and sailors. British military bands played "The World Turned Upside Down" as the formal surrender took place.

The War for Independence continued for more than a year after the surrender at Yorktown. But the British people and the British government were growing increasingly tired of the war. It was going against them in other parts of the world as well as in America.

The peace treaty   Formal negotiations for a peace treaty began at Paris in September 1782. It took more than a year before agreement was reached. The peace treaty was signed at Paris on September 3, 1783, and formally approved by the American Congress the following March.

Great Britain recognized the independence of the United States in the Treaty of Paris. The new country's boundaries were the Mississippi River on the west, Florida on the south, and the Great Lakes on the north. In the treaty, Congress agreed to recommend to the states that property that had been taken from Loyalists be returned.

Have pupils list each of the battles shown on the map above and accompany each item with the date and victor of that battle.

One result of the active role that women took in the revolution was the realization that schools were needed to enable women to obtain a better education. Academies and schools for women were established in many parts of the new nation.

The major role of women It would be wrong to think that it was only the fighting men of the American and French armies and navies who won independence for the new United States. Other groups made important contributions to victory. Women played a major role. Some managed farms and shops while their husbands, brothers, and fathers went off to war. Other women helped more directly by following the armies in the field or in camp. They washed, cooked, and sewed for the soldiers. They nursed the sick and cared for the wounded in makeshift hospitals.

In fact, women were considered an essential part of eighteenth-century armies. They traveled with the baggage trains of the armies and were issued rations, half the amount given to the soldiers. At Saratoga in October 1777, the voices of American women could be heard over the gunfire. They wailed for the safety of the soldiers or jeered at the enemy. When the sun set, they crawled through the wreckage of the battlefield, collecting from the dead any articles of clothing that their own men would need when winter came.

It was not unusual for women to work as part of a gun crew, as Molly Pitcher did. (See page 153.) Margaret Corbin, the 25-year-old wife of John Corbin, took over his position at a small cannon during the American retreat across New Jersey in November 1776. She was badly wounded. Congress, recognizing that her wounds would leave her crippled. awarded her a pension. It consisted of half a soldier's pay and "one compleat suit of cloaths" each year for the rest of her life.

Cornwallis's army surrenders in October 1781 at Yorktown. (37°N/77°W; map, p. 134)

What's in a Name

HEROES OF THE REVOLUTION

One of the ways in which Americans have honored military and civilian heroes of the Revolution is to name counties after them. George Washington's name is found in more counties than is the name of any other individual. Thirty-one states have counties named Washington in honor of the commander in chief of the Continental army. Thomas Jefferson ranks second to Washington, with 26 counties named Jefferson. Benjamin Franklin ranks third. Twenty-three states have counties named Franklin.

Virginia has a Patrick County and a Henry County, both named for Patrick Henry. Eight other states have Henry counties named for the great Virginia patriot. Seventeen states have Marion counties to commemorate the name of the Swamp Fox. Nine states have Knox counties, named for Henry Knox, who supervised removal of Ticonderoga's cannons to the heights outside Boston. Nine states also have honored Daniel Morgan, the commander of sharpshooters, by naming counties after him.

Americans have remembered that foreign heroes came to fight in the War for Independence. Eleven states have Fayette counties and 6 have Lafayette counties, making a total of 17 named in honor of the gallant young Frenchman. Seven states have Pulaski counties, named for the Polish hero and cavalry commander who perished in the fight for Savannah. Six counties are named for Johann Kalb, also known as Baron de Kalb. Born in Germany, he came to America and gave his life

One of the ways in which George Washington is honored is by the name of the city that is our national capital. Also, the Washington Monument is one of the impressive sights in Washington, D.C. (39°N/77°W, map, p. 717.)

charging the enemy at the battle of Camden, South Carolina.

This is only a partial account of counties named for heroes of the Revolution. Does your state have counties named for these or other heroes? What is the origin of the name of your county or your parish?

Wives of some officers clearly preferred following the armies to staying at home. Mrs. Henry Knox and Mrs. Nathanael Greene, married to American generals, certainly did. Martha Washington declared she had heard the first and last shot of every campaign during the war.

A few women distinguished themselves in unusual ways during revolutionary times. Phillis Wheatley was bought directly off a slave ship from Africa. She became noted for her poetry. One of her poems was about General George Washington, and she was

A research project relating to the tradition of naming places after heroes of the American Revolution might be assigned. Expand the research called for in the What's in a Name section above to include street names, parks, and public buildings in your community.

After the war, thoughtful Americans began to ask themselves whether it was right for people to make slaves of others. The Declaration of Independence stated that all men are created equal. Controversy over the slavery question grew under these circumstances.

invited to visit his headquarters at Cambridge in 1776. Deborah Sampson dressed in men's clothes, served as an American soldier, and won a pension from Congress. "Number 355" was a female American spy in New York. No one knew her name, but she was one of the most valuable agents the Americans had.

The help of other groups   Blacks also did essential work on the home front and with the fighting armies. Crispus Attucks, a black sailor, has been called "the first casualty of the American Revolution." (See page 125.) Once fighting began, blacks and whites together served in the militia and the Continental army. Peter Salem, Prince Hall, and Salem Poor were black militiamen at the battle of Bunker Hill. One historian has written that two thirds of a Rhode Island regiment at Yorktown were blacks. On the other side, some Loyalist regiments fighting for the British were made up entirely of American slaves who had been promised their freedom by the British if they would fight against their masters.

In New York most tribes in the Iroquois confederacy supported the British. But the Oneidas and some of the Tuscaroras aided the American cause. Jerusha Bingham Kirkland, wife of a New England missionary, influenced the Oneidas to favor the American side. She was held in the highest regard by the members of the tribe. In the west nearly all the Indians fought alongside the British. However, George Rogers Clark had Indian guides and some Indian support.

No single group could claim sole credit for the American victory. General George Washington might have been the "indispensable man," but it took the help of many others to achieve independence.

Washington returns to Mount Vernon   The Treaty of Paris allowed British troops to remain in New York until November 1784. In that month the last British soldiers left.

A few days later, General George Washington rode into the city with the governor of New York at his side. On December 4, Washington bade goodbye to his officers at Fraunces Tavern. His journey back to Mount Vernon was a triumphal procession, as cheering Americans honored the man who had done so much to win independence for their country. On the way, Washington passed through Annapolis, where Congress was meeting.

Two days before Christmas, 1784, Washington appeared before Congress to resign his commission as commander in chief. In doing so, he said, "I now take leave of all the employments of public life." But this was not to be. After a few years of peace and quiet at Mount Vernon, Washington would answer his country's call for service in another role.

CHECKUP

1. Why was George Rogers Clark's campaign in the west important to the United States?
2. What disastrous defeat did the Americans suffer in South Carolina? After that defeat, how did the Patriots in South Carolina fight back effectively?
3. Explain the two pieces of bad news that came to George Washington from West Point, New York, and from Morristown, New Jersey.
4. What events brought about the surrender of Cornwallis at Yorktown?
5. What were the provisions of the Treaty of Paris with respect to boundaries?

7/CHAPTER REVIEW

KEY FACTS

1. George Washington commanded the Continental army from 1776 to 1784.
2. Only about one third of the American people actively supported the Revolution.
3. The American cause experienced many setbacks before independence was finally won.
4. Foreign nations, particularly France, helped the United States in its struggle for independence.

VOCABULARY QUIZ

On a sheet of paper write the letter of the term next to the number of its definition. There are two extra definitions that will not match any of the terms.

a. treaty of alliance
b. Tory
c. privateer
d. guerrilla
e. Northwest Territory
f. mutiny
g. treason
h. mercenary
i. *Common Sense*
j. Patriot

f **1.** A rebellion against military leaders
2. A peace treaty between 2 countries who have been at war with each other
b **3.** A supporter of the king of England
h **4.** A soldier hired by a government from outside its own country
e **5.** A region lying west of the Appalachian Mountains
i **6.** A pamphlet
a **7.** An agreement by 2 or more countries to fight a common enemy
d **8.** A hit-and-run fighter
c **9.** A ship fitted for war
j **10.** A colonist who sought American independence from England
g **11.** Aiding the enemies of one's country
12. A region south of the Ohio River

REVIEW QUESTIONS

1. Why was George Washington the "indispensable man" in the American Revolution?
2. Why was the battle of Bunker Hill a valuable experience for the Continental troops even though they were defeated?
3. In what ways did the seizure of Fort Ticonderoga help the Continental cause?
4. What were the immediate effects of the Declaration of Independence? The long-term effects?
5. Why did foreign countries help the United States in its struggle for independence?
6. What finally brought the long War for Independence to an end?

ACTIVITIES

1. Among the many who fought for American independence were Ethan Allen, Marquis de Lafayette, John Paul Jones, Nathanael Greene, Casimir Pulaski, Daniel Morgan, George Rogers Clark, Molly Pitcher, and John Sullivan. Choose one of these or any other Patriot of the American Revolution and find out all you can about him or her in your library. Make a report to the class on that person.
2. On an outline map, make a dot where each of the following battles took place and label it.

Bunker Hill	Yorktown
Kings Mountain	Monmouth
Vincennes	Charleston
Bennington	Germantown
Saratoga	Trenton
Moore's Creek Bridge	Savannah

PRIMARY AND SECONDARY SOURCES

Documents, letters, artifacts, and books written by historians are some of the historical material available for the study of history. Historians must be able to evaluate a source by determining whether it is primary or secondary material. Knowledge of the type of source and its origin is very helpful in evaluating and understanding history.

Primary source material is composed of original documents, speeches, eyewitness accounts such as those recorded in letters or diaries, and artifacts including photographs and some paintings. Primary source materials are firsthand accounts, recorded at the time an event occurred.

Secondary source material is made up of generalizations by historians who have studied primary source materials. Secondary sources are not firsthand observations but are descriptions of events based on what others have written. This textbook is an example of secondary source material. However, it includes the use of primary source materials.

Below are two selections of historical material. Read the selections and see if you can distinguish the primary source material from the secondary source material.

1. . . . my situation is inexpressibly distressing, to see the winter fast approaching upon a naked army, the time of their services within a few weeks of expiring, and not provision yet made for such important events. Added to this, the military chest is totally exhausted; the paymaster has not a single dollar in hand: the commissary-general assures me he has strained his credit to the utmost for the subsistence of the army. The quarter-master general is precisely in the same situation; and the greater part of the army are in a state not far from mutiny . . . if the evil is not immediately remedied . . . the army must absolutely break up.

2. From his headquarters on the edge of Morristown Common, the commander in chief watched his army settle itself in long huts on the south slope of Thimble Mountain, ready to face still another winter in the field. Despite the lingering glow of Trenton and Princeton, the future must have appeared ominous to him, for all his neverfailing outward calm. Smallpox broke out, and Washington had to set up isolation areas and struggle with the then almost impossible problem of camp sanitation.

The first selection is part of a letter George Washington wrote to the Congress. It is a primary source. The second is a historian's description of the winter the Continental army spent in Morristown, New Jersey. It is a secondary source.

SKILLS PRACTICE

. On a sheet of paper, write **P** if the source is primary and **S** if it is secondary.

P **1.** Thomas Paine's pamphlet *Common Sense*

S **2.** The author's article on Valley Forge on page 151

P **3.** The Declaration of Independence

S **4.** A composition you might write about the signers of the Declaration of Independence

P **5.** The diary of a soldier during the American Revolution

P **6.** A letter written by Martha Washington to George Washington

S **7.** A picture painted last year of Benjamin Franklin

CHAPTER

8 Confederation and Constitution

The First Union of States

┌─VOCABULARY──────────────┐

confederation   Shays's
                        Rebellion
Articles of
    Confederation   Northwest
                        Ordinance
western land
    claims

└─────────────────────────┘

Helped by a hurricane A hurricane seldom turns out to be a stroke of good fortune. And yet a hurricane proved to be lucky for Alexander Hamilton, who was born in the British West Indies. His mother was the daughter of a French physician and plantation owner. His father was a Scottish trader.

When the boy was 11, his mother died. His father's business had gone to ruin, and young Alexander soon had to give up school. He was working as a clerk in a store in 1772 when, in the late summer, a hurricane swept across the West Indian island of St. Croix (kroi). In a letter the 15-year-old youth wrote of the damage done by the hurricane. The letter was so impressive that a local newspaper published it.

Several plantation owners read the letter. They decided the boy should be sent to the mainland for a college education. With their help, Alexander Hamilton came to New York. There he enrolled in what is now Columbia University. It was a step toward making him a builder of our nation. Had it not been for the hurricane of 1772, Hamilton could not have taken that step.

From aide to legislator The War for Independence interrupted Alexander Hamilton's college education. His skill at writing won him a position as secretary and aide to General George Washington. Later, at Yorktown, Hamilton commanded troops and led a daring charge against the British positions.

In 1780, Hamilton married Elizabeth Schuyler, daughter of General Philip Schuyler and a member of a prominent New York family. After the War for Independence ended, Alexander Hamilton practiced law in New York. Beginning in 1782 he served a term in Congress. However, he did not seek another term because he did not think the central government was strong enough.

The Articles of Confederation Plans for a new government had begun at the time of the Declaration of Independence. When Richard Henry Lee had introduced his resolution for independence in 1776, he had urged the Second Continental Congress to form a government for the 13 states. Lee wanted a **confederation**, that

Delegates to the Constitutional Convention bring their session to a successful ending.

Have pupils study the picture and pick out George Washington and Benjamin Franklin. Ask: Who were some of the other men at the Convention?

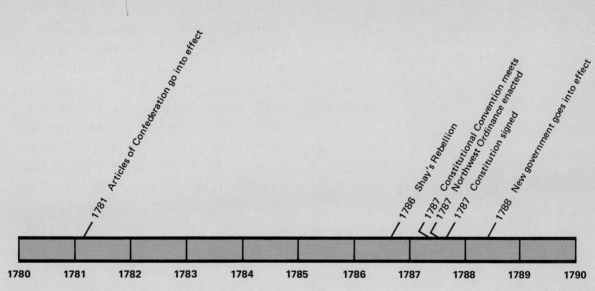

1781 Articles of Confederation go into effect

1786 Shay's Rebellion

1787 Constitutional Convention meets

1787 Northwest Ordinance enacted

1787 Constitution signed

1788 New government goes into effect

1780	1781	1782	1783	1784	1785	1786	1787	1788	1789	1790

After pupils have studied the time line, ask: In what year did the Articles of Confederation go into effect? (1781) **163**

is, a loose union of independent states organized to take action on a few—but only a few—matters.

After months of discussion, the delegates agreed in November 1777 on the **Articles of Confederation.** This document listed the powers of the central government and the powers of the states in the new United States of America.

The 13 states were slow to approve the Articles of Confederation. Some leaders felt the states should run their own affairs independently. They feared that any kind of central government would limit the power of the states.

There was one other major reason for delay. Several states claimed land west

This postage stamp appeared on the 200th anniversary of the drafting of the Articles of Confederation.

of the Appalachian Mountains. The Articles of Confederation provided that the new central government should control these lands. But some states were reluctant to give up their **western land claims.**

The western land claims States without claims or with weak claims to western lands thought the addition of such lands to other states would make them larger and stronger than the rest. Leaders in Maryland in particular feared this development. Therefore, they refused to approve the Articles of Confederation until all states agreed to yield their western land claims to the central government. Since all 13 states had to approve the Articles of Confederation before they became effective, Maryland's stand delayed the first union of the states.

One by one, the states agreed to give up their western land claims. New York was first, partly because its claims to western lands were weak. Virginia probably had the strongest claims of any state. But Virginia, too, promised to turn over its western lands to the central government. Maryland then was satisfied. In 1781 it

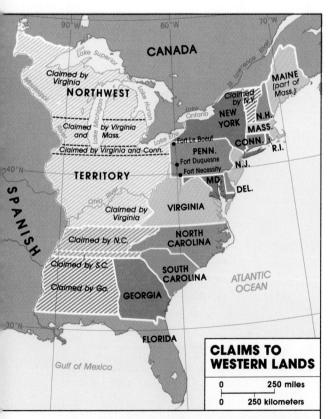

Which of the original states claimed land west of the Appalachians?

Have pupils check an atlas to see which five present states were carved out of the Northwest Territory.

became the last of the 13 states to approve the Articles of Confederation.

The Confederation government

The United States operated under the Articles of Confederation for 8 years. The government during that time differed greatly from our government today. Congress was the major part of the Confederation government. Depending on its population, each state had from two to seven representatives in Congress. However, each state had only one vote, so small states had as much power as larger ones in the Confederation Congress. Furthermore, it took a two-thirds majority, or 9 states, to pass important legislation. Thus any 5 states could block action by Congress.

The Confederation government had a president, but he was only a member of Congress elected each year to preside over its meetings. The Confederation government lacked a system of courts in which those who broke national laws could be tried.

Congress under the Articles of Confederation did have several important powers. It could wage war and make peace. Under its guidance the United States finally won independence in the peace treaty signed in Paris. In addition, the Confederation Congress could conduct negotiations between the United States and foreign countries. It could control trade with Indian tribes. It could, and did, organize a mail service. And it could borrow money in the name of the United States. Under this power, Congress borrowed heavily from foreign countries, not only during the War for Independence but also in later years.

Weaknesses of the Confederation

Because of its limited powers, the Confederation government had a difficult time. It lacked power to regulate trade and commerce among the states. Each state could, therefore, arrange its own trade regulations. The Confederation Congress could only *ask* the states for money. It had no power to compel payment of taxes. Confusion spread through the money system because each state issued its own coins. Some states issued paper money, which was unstable in value. Riots broke out in Rhode Island and New Jersey in 1786 because storekeepers would not accept paper money as payment for their goods.

In the same year a serious uprising took place in Massachusetts. Times were hard, and many farmers could not pay

The first president in the Confederation government was Samuel Huntington of Connecticut.

Obtain a current-year copy of the *Information Please Almanac* and turn to the new events section. From that section select events that concern actions by the federal government. Ask pupils to decide if the government under the Articles of Confederation had the power to perform these actions.

165

their taxes and other debts. When their lands were seized for overdue taxes, the farmers rebelled. Led by Daniel Shays, a Revolutionary War veteran, the farmers armed themselves. Violence broke out, and the Massachusetts militia had to be called out to put down what is known as **Shays's Rebellion.** Congress, lacking the power to keep order, stood by helplessly.

Congress was equally weak in its dealings with other countries. After the war, Great Britain refused to enact trade treaties with the United States. Moreover, it kept its soldiers on American territory at western forts and trading posts such as Detroit and Fort Niagara. This action was contrary to the Treaty of Paris. Still, the Confederation Congress could do little except protest.

Spain had been an ally of the United States for a time during the War for Independence. Nevertheless, after the war it denied western Americans the right to ship their products through the port of New Orleans. From France, Thomas Jefferson reported that the government there paid little attention to any action of the Confederation Congress. Thus, even though the Confederation Congress was authorized to deal with foreign countries, it had trouble gaining respect abroad for the new United States.

The Confederation's accomplishments
The Confederation government did accomplish some good things. It not only directed the War for Independence to a successful conclusion, but it held the country together for 6 years following that war. Its most lasting accomplishment was the passage of the **Northwest Ordinance** in 1787.

An ordinance is a law. The Northwest Ordinance set up a system for governing the Northwest Territory. The Northwest Ordinance provided a series of steps through which this territory could be divided into three, four, or even into five states. For residents of this territory and the later states, the ordinance guaranteed public support of education, trial by jury, and freedom of worship.

Significantly, the ordinance declared that any states made from the territory would be equal to any of the existing states in all respects. Finally, the law prohibited slavery in the territory and in the states that might be made from it.

A call for a stronger government
Except for the Northwest Ordinance, the accomplishments of the Confederation government were not very impressive.

THE NORTHWEST TERRITORY: 1787

| 0 | 200 | 400 miles |
| 0 | 300 | 600 kilometers |

The Northwest Territory was formed from land ceded by eastern states.

The first steps toward a stronger central government for the United States were taken at a conference in Annapolis, Maryland. (39°N/76°W; map, p. 79)

By 1787 many people in the United States believed the country needed a stronger central government. Among these were Alexander Hamilton and James Madison, a Virginian and a friend and follower of Thomas Jefferson.

Hamilton and Madison had already taken the lead in calling for a stronger central government. They had met with others holding the same views at a conference in Annapolis, Maryland, in 1786. Not all the states sent delegates to this meeting. The delegates were supposed to discuss matters of trade. Most agreed that trade problems arose from the weaknesses of the Confederation government.

Alexander Hamilton had a plan. He urged those attending the Annapolis meeting to ask Congress to hold in Philadelphia a convention of all the states. Its purpose, Hamilton said, would be to suggest changes in the Articles of Confederation. It seems likely, however, that Hamilton wanted those attending the meeting to decide on an entirely new government. Changes to the Articles of Confederation required the consent of all 13 states, and Hamilton undoubtedly knew this was impossible to get.

At first, Congress was reluctant to call the convention. But despite Congress' attitude, some states started to name delegates to a convention in Philadelphia. James Madison wisely persuaded the Virginia legislature to name George Washington as a delegate from that state. Washington's prestige was so great that Congress could hardly refuse any longer. Its members gave in and issued a formal call for a convention to meet in Philadelphia in May 1787.

CHECKUP

1. Why did it take so long for the states to adopt the Articles of Confederation?
2. What were the main powers of the government under the Articles of Confederation?
3. What were the weaknesses of this government?
4. Why is the Northwest Ordinance considered a major accomplishment of the Articles of Confederation government?
5. Who led the movement for a stronger central government?

The Constitutional Convention

```
┌─VOCABULARY────────────────────────┐
│  amendment          executive     │
│  Virginia Plan        branch      │
│  New Jersey Plan    judicial branch │
│  Great              three-fifths  │
│    Compromise         compromise  │
│  legislative                      │
│    branch                         │
└───────────────────────────────────┘
```

Independence Hall   Few places in the United States had more to do with our nation's beginnings than the red brick building that stands on Chestnut Street, between Fifth and Sixth Streets, in Phil-

The Constitutional Convention was held in the building now known as Independence Hall.

adelphia. Completed in 1748, it was designed to be the meeting place for the Pennsylvania legislature. In 1753 a tower was added, and hung in it was a "bell of about two thousand pounds weight," as the records show. Today we know it as the Liberty Bell. (See What's in a Name on page 172.)

The First and Second Continental Congresses and Congress under the Articles of Confederation met in this red brick building. Thomas Jefferson read his Declaration of Independence there, so it is now called Independence Hall. You will remember that the British held Philadelphia for a time during the War for Independence. For a while they housed soldiers in the red brick building. Later, after the battle of Germantown, they used it as a hospital.

The convention meets   Less than 10 years later, the red brick building became the meeting place for the convention called by Congress. In May of 1787, delegates began to drift into Philadelphia. They had differing instructions from their states. Some delegates were there only to suggest **amendments,** or additions, to the Articles of Confederation. Others believed they should write an entirely new constitution for the government of the United States. The view of the latter group won out as the convention began 4 months of debate in the sweltering heat of summer. Because its members wrote a new constitution, the meeting in Philadelphia in 1787 is known to history as the Constitutional Convention.

Fifty-five delegates from 12 states were at the opening meetings of the Constitu-

In the above picture a group of Indians stand before Independence Hall in Philadelphia.

tional Convention. Rhode Island refused to send any delegates. The convention unanimously chose George Washington of Virginia to preside over the meetings. James Madison of Virginia took notes of the proceedings. Delegates decided to bar the public from the meetings so that they could speak more freely. For this reason, much of what went on was known only to the delegates until Madison's notes were published 50 years later.

Distinguished and experienced men served as delegates to the Constitutional Convention. Most were prosperous, earning a good living as lawyers, merchants, bankers, or plantation owners. At 81, Benjamin Franklin was the oldest. James Madison of Virginia and Alexander Hamilton, who represented New York, were among the youngest. Madison was 36 and Hamilton was 4 years younger.

Four great American leaders were absent from the Constitutional Convention. Thomas Jefferson was in France and John Adams was in England. Both were serving as United States representatives to foreign governments. Samuel Adams was in Massachusetts, well satisfied with the central government under the Articles of Confederation. Patrick Henry stayed in Virginia, even though he had been chosen as a delegate. He suspected the convention would draw up a plan for a stronger central government, which he opposed.

The Great Compromise One problem faced by the delegates was the question of how states should be represented in the lawmaking body of the new central government. Virginia delegates got to the convention early. In the time before the convention opened, they drew up a plan. It was called the **Virginia Plan** or the Large States Plan. It proposed that states should be represented in the Congress according to population.

William Paterson of New Jersey took the opposite view. "New Jersey," he declared, "will never submit to a plan in which she could always be outvoted by a large state." His plan, in which the states would be represented equally in Congress, got the name of the **New Jersey Plan,** or Small States Plan.

Two months passed before the convention accepted the **Great Compromise,** which solved this problem. This arrangement is also sometimes called the Connecticut Compromise because Roger Sherman, a Connecticut delegate, played a major role in working it out.

At this point in the convention, there was already general agreement among the delegates that Congress should consist of two houses. The Great Compromise suggested that the states be represented according to population in one body, the House of Representatives. In the other body, the Senate, each state would be represented equally. In both the House of Representatives and the Senate, each member would have one vote. This solution satisfied both the small and the large states and the compromise was written into the new constitution.

The three branches of government The delegates did not want a central government that was all-powerful. It solved this problem by dividing power among three equal branches. One would be the **legislative branch,** a Congress that would

169

pass laws. A second branch, headed by a President, would execute, or carry out, the laws passed by Congress. This would be known as the **executive branch.** Third would be the **judicial branch,** which would set up courts to try those who disobeyed national laws.

Having decided this, the convention debated over the details. How long should the terms be for the various offices? Should a minimum age be required to serve as President or a member of Congress? Could a foreign-born person serve as an elected official in the new government? Settling these questions took time, but the answers were finally written into the new constitution.

The issue of slavery By the time of the Constitutional Convention, Massachusetts had ended slavery in its state constitution. Other northern states were thinking of doing the same. And, as we have seen, the Northwest Ordinance had prohibited slavery in the territory north of the Ohio and west of the Appalachians. Still, opposition from some southern delegates kept the convention from writing into the new constitution an end to slavery throughout the United States.

Slaves and slavery entered into debates in other ways, although they were not mentioned in the new constitution. Delegates had agreed that direct taxation should be divided among the states, according to population. Southern delegates did not want slaves counted for taxation purposes. If slaves were counted, southern states would be more heavily taxed. And yet southern delegates wanted slaves counted when the number

of members in the House of Representatives for each state was decided.

Another compromise was arranged to settle this problem. For every five slaves in a state, the constitution allowed three to be counted, both for the purpose of taxation and of representation in Congress. This solution was known as the **three-fifths compromise.**

The opposition of southern delegates made it impossible for the new constitution to end slavery in the United States. But ending the importation of slaves was another matter. Virginia and Maryland, as well as most of the northern states, had forbidden the importation of slaves by the time of the Constitutional Convention. However, delegates from South Carolina and Georgia said that their states would never approve a constitution that barred the importation of slaves into the entire United States. Nevertheless, they were willing to allow Congress to prohibit the importation of slaves after 20 years had passed. This agreement was still another compromise that helped the delegates to continue their work.

Writing the Constitution The delegates worked in the red brick building on Chestnut Street from May 1787 through the whole summer. By September they had agreed on the most important matters. They turned over to the Committee on Style the task of writing down what they wanted. The organization and the wording of the Constitution came from the work of this group. It was headed by Gouverneur Morris of Pennsylvania. He wrote the Preamble, or introduction, beginning "We the people of the United

Have pupils use current newspapers and newsmagazines to find examples of the workings of the system of checks and balances.

Gouverneur Morris, a delegate from Pennsylvania, prepared the final draft of the Constitution.

tion approved by the necessary number of states. (See pages 178–203 for the text of the Constitution.)

(See pages 178–203 for the text of the Constitution.)

CHECKUP

1. Describe in general terms the delegates to the Constitutional Convention. Why did they meet?
2. What three important compromises were written into the Constitution?
3. What was the function of each of the three branches of government under the Constitution?
4. How was the issue of slavery dealt with?

"A More Perfect Union"

┌─VOCABULARY─────────────────┐

ratify	Federalist papers
federal government	bill of rights
Federalists	electors
Anti-Federalists	federal republic

The task of winning state approval
Alexander Hamilton played only a small part in the Constitutional Convention. His legal work in New York kept him busy during much of the time the convention met. Even when he was present, he was always outvoted by the other two delegates from New York, Robert Yates and John Lansing. They opposed a stronger central government, fearing it would take away the power of their state. In fact, they refused to sign the Constitution.

So Hamilton knew that the task of those who favored the new Constitution would be difficult. In his own state the opposition was strong. Still, Hamilton knew the convention had done two things to make it easier to get the states to **ratify**, or approve, the Constitution.

States" and ending "do ordain and establish this Constitution for the United States of America." The new government was not to be a loose union of the states. It was to be a union of *the people.*

On September 17, 1787, the Committee on Style presented the Constitution to the 39 delegates still present. All these delegates, including George Washington as presiding officer, signed the document. Sixteen delegates had gone home for one reason or another. Some of them refused to sign because they disapproved of one part or another of the Constitution.

Drawing up and signing a new constitution was only one part of forming a stronger central government. There remained the task of getting the Constitu-

171

THE LIBERTY BELL

One of the most famous patriotic symbols of the United States is the Liberty Bell. But it has not always been known by that name. For many years it was called the State House Bell. The superintendents of the State House of the Province of Pennsylvania ordered it made in England in 1751. The bell was cast with a biblical quotation on its crown: "Proclaim liberty throughout all the land, unto all the inhabitants thereof."

The bell was hung in the steeple of the State House in Philadelphia. The bell cracked the first time it was rung, but it was repaired and its tone restored. When the British occupied Philadelphia in 1777, the State House Bell and other bells were hastily moved for fear that the British would melt them down for making cannons. The State House Bell was hidden for more than a year under the floor of a church in Allentown, Pennsylvania.

After the British left Philadelphia, the bell was returned to the State House. Until 1835 it was rung every year on July 4, the anniversary of the adoption of the Declaration of Independence. It was sometimes called Old Independence or the Bell of the Revolution. In 1837 someone recalled the quotation on the old bell. Supporters of the movement to free slaves quickly realized the significance of the quotation, "Proclaim liberty throughout the land. . . ." It was they who first called

The Liberty Bell is on display near Independence Hall in Philadelphia. It is seen each year by thousands of tourists who visit the city's many historic sites.

the old State House Bell the Liberty Bell.

The bell cracked again in 1835 while being rung during the funeral of John Marshall, the Chief Justice of the United States. The Liberty Bell is now kept on display in Philadelphia's historic area, a treasured symbol of our country's independence.

First, the convention had provided that when 9 states accepted the Constitution, it would go into effect for those states. This would certainly be easier than trying for approval by all 13 states. This meant, too, that once the new government was formed, it would be hard for the other 4 states to stay out of the union. Second, the delegates had directed that the Constitution be considered for approval by special conventions in each state, not by the state legislatures. Knowing these facts, Alexander Hamilton decided to work very hard in the state ratifying convention in New York.

Opposing views The group favoring the Constitution wanted a **federal government.** In such a government the powers are either shared or divided between the states and the central government. This group took the name of **Federalists.**

Their opponents had little choice but to take the name of **Anti-Federalists.** They had three main reasons for opposing the Constitution. First, they said the Constitution had no guarantees of certain rights or freedoms for the people of the United States. Second, they believed the new government would destroy the states by not sharing power with them. Third, they argued the new government would favor the rich, setting up a ruling class of wealth and power.

The last argument in particular appealed to people living on the frontiers, poorer people living in towns and cities, and to people with small businesses. But not all who opposed the Constitution were poor. Some wealthy plantation owners opposed it because they were powerful within their states. Several state officials, who feared that the central government would overshadow state governments, also opposed the Constitution. Patrick Henry in Virginia and Governor George Clinton in New York led the fight against ratification in their states.

The Federalist papers As New Yorkers prepared to elect delegates to their state convention, a series of articles began to appear in four New York newspapers. Eighty-five articles in all appeared, signed with the name "Publius." Alexander Hamilton wrote at least 45 of them and James Madison about 30. These articles became known as the **Federalist papers.** Later they were published in a book called *The Federalist.* They received this name because each article supported the Federalist arguments in favor of the Constitution.

The Federalist papers answered every question raised about the new Constitution. They explained each part of the document, showed how the new government would work, and praised the benefits that would come if the Constitution was approved. The articles were written to influence the vote in the New York state convention, but they were widely read in the other states, too. They helped to convince many people that the new Constitution was a good thing.

The vote in the state conventions Federalist leaders were well organized. They worked hard to get their supporters chosen to attend the state conventions. Small states favored the Constitution because it gave them equal representation in the Senate. Delaware was first to ratify. It did so by unanimous vote. In Pennsylvania the vote was closer but still in favor of ratification. New Jersey, Georgia, and Connecticut soon gave their approval. Thus five states had ratified the Constitution by the time the Massachusetts convention met.

Samuel Adams was still a respected leader in Massachusetts. At first he was against the Constitution. He said it did

Delaware's auto license plates proudly recall that it was the first state to ratify the Constitution. The state's convention approved the Constitution in December 1787.

Ask: Who consistently opposed ratification of the Constitution? (Patrick Henry, George Clinton)

not give enough liberty to the people. The Federalists promised to add a bill of rights. This satisfied Adams, and Massachusetts ratified the Constitution. Maryland and South Carolina followed. In June 1788, New Hampshire became the ninth state to approve the Constitution, putting the new government into effect.

Virginia and New York approve
Still, the new government could hardly work if Virginia and New York remained outside it. In Virginia the debates over ratification were at a very high level.

James Madison led the fight for ratification in Virginia, aided by the quiet support of George Washington. Hoping to gain the support of Thomas Jefferson, Madison wrote to him in France. Jefferson replied that, like Samuel Adams, he believed a bill of rights should be added to the Constitution. Madison took Jefferson's advice, promising to see that citizens' rights would be protected. Virginia's convention then voted approval.

In New York, Alexander Hamilton had persuaded the convention to delay voting until after Massachusetts and Virginia had voted. When those two states ratified, Hamilton argued that New York could hardly afford to stay out of the new government. The final vote in the New York convention showed 30 in favor of the Constitution and 27 opposed. Without Alexander Hamilton, the vote would surely have been different.

POWERS OF THE CENTRAL GOVERNMENT

Under Articles of Confederation	*Under the Constitution*
1. No executive branch to direct enforcement of the laws	1. An executive branch, headed by a strong President
2. No courts to try those accused of breaking the central government's laws	2. A system of federal courts, topped by a Supreme Court
3. No power to regulate interstate commerce (trade between the states)	3. Congress can regulate both foreign and interstate commerce.
4. No power to levy taxes	4. Congress has ample power to levy taxes.
5. No power to act directly against individuals or against states	5. Extensive executive and judicial powers to act against individuals and to some extent against states
6. Power to coin money (but did not use it)	6. Central government can coin money, but states cannot.
7. One vote in Congress for each state	7. Two votes in Senate for each state; membership in House based on population; each member has one vote.
8. Two-thirds majority (nine states) required in Congress to pass important legislation	8. Simple majority in both houses of Congress required to pass legislation, subject to presidential veto
9. All states must agree to amendments.	9. Amending process less difficult
10. The United States was a loose confederation of states.	10. The United States is a firm and enduring union of people.

A stronger government The word *revolution* means "a sudden and complete change." Sometimes the change is brought about by arms and war, as in the American Revolution. But revolution can happen in other ways, as the Federalists now proved.

In 14 months they had brought about a revolution. They had written the new constitution and 11 states had accepted it. This was a peaceful revolution but, all the same, a revolution, setting up a new and stronger government. The table on page 174 shows how the government was made stronger by the Constitution.

During the summer of 1788, the machinery for choosing a President and members of Congress under the Constitution was set in motion. Voters elected members of the House of Representatives directly, while state legislatures elected two senators each, as the Constitution provided. State legislatures also followed the Constitution by choosing people called **electors,** who in turn would choose the President. Most people assumed George Washington would become the first President under the new Constitution. And so he did, being named by a unanimous vote of the electors.

Partly through Alexander Hamilton's influence, New York City was named the temporary capital of the United States. In April 1789, George Washington left Mount Vernon once more to serve his country. Every village and city he passed through wanted to honor him—a great man on his way to becoming the first President of the United States. So numerous were the celebrations that it took Washington a week to reach New York.

Alexander Hamilton of New York played a major role in achieving approval for the new government.

Kings, queens, emperors, and others of noble rank ruled elsewhere in the world. But the people of the United States had created a new kind of government. That new government was a **federal republic.** It was *federal* because powers were shared by the states and the central government. It was a *republic* because it was based on the consent of the people, acting through their elected representatives.

CHECKUP

1 What were the Federalist papers?
2 What arguments were used by those who opposed the new Constitution? To whom did these arguments appeal?
3 Why did smaller states generally give approval to the Constitution?
4 How did Alexander Hamilton persuade the New York convention to approve the Constitution?
5 In what ways was the new government stronger than the old Confederation government?

KEY FACTS

1. The first union of the United States was set up by the Articles of Confederation. The Confederation government existed from 1781 to 1789.

2. The Northwest Ordinance was one of the chief accomplishments of the Confederation government.

3. Congress called a Constitutional Convention to meet in Philadelphia in 1787.

4. Delegates to this convention wrote the Constitution, which proposed a stronger central government.

5. Men known as Federalists successfully organized to get the Constitution ratified and a new government put into effect.

VOCABULARY QUIZ

Supply the correct words for the blanks below. All the words are in this chapter. Write the answers on a sheet of paper.

1. A loose union of states able to act only on certain matters is a ___confederation___.

2. An uprising that showed the weakness of the central government in 1786 was called ___Shays's Rebellion___.

3. A law forbidding slavery west of the Appalachian Mountains and north of the Ohio River was the ___Northwest Ordinance___.

4. A proposal at the Constitutional Convention that states be represented in Congress according to population was called the ___Virginia Plan___.

5. Under the Constitution, the President is chosen by people called ___electors___.

6. The three equal branches of government are the executive, the legislative, and the ___judicial___.

7. The three-fifths compromise in the Constitution had to do with the counting of ___slaves___.

8. Persons favoring the ratification of the Constitution were known as ___Federalists___.

9. An addition to the Constitution that was favored by Samuel Adams and Thomas Jefferson was the ___Bill of Rights___.

10. In a federal republic like ours, powers are shared by the central government and the ___states___.

REVIEW QUESTIONS

1. What evidence can you state that shows the Confederation government lacked respect at home and abroad?

2. Name three accomplishments of the Confederation government. Explain which one you believe to have been the most important.

3. What were the major differences between the central government under the Articles of Confederation and the central government under the Constitution?

ACTIVITIES

1. Take the point of view of a Federalist and write a speech in which you state why the United States needs a stronger central government than the Articles of Confederation have provided.

2. Take the role of one of the following: the owner of a small business in New York; the wife of a frontiersman; a poor girl in Charleston, South Carolina; a poor man in Williamsburg, Virginia; a sailor on a ship leaving Salem, Massachusetts. In front of the class, tell why you oppose or support a stronger central government in 1787.

READING A DIAGRAM

CHECKS AND BALANCES

The federal government under our Constitution is sometimes called a government of checks and balances. That is, each branch may check the other two so that no one of them can become too powerful.

You can see how the system of checks and balances works by studying the diagram below. A diagram is a graphic drawing that can be used to show how organizations or activities are related.

The diagram shows how the executive branch (President) checks the legislative branch (Congress) and the judicial branch (Supreme Court). It also shows how the legislative branch checks the executive and judicial branches, and, too, how the judicial branch checks the executive and legislative branches.

SKILLS PRACTICE

Use the information from the diagram to answer these questions. Write your answers on a sheet of paper.

1. Which branch passes laws?

2. How can the federal courts check the power of Congress?

3. Which branch appoints justices to the federal courts?

4. How can the Congress control the power of the President's veto?

5. How can the President check the power of Congress?

6. Which branch has the power to impeach federal officials?

7. What check does the Congress have on the power of the Supreme Court?

8. Which branch grants pardons?

SEPARATION OF POWERS

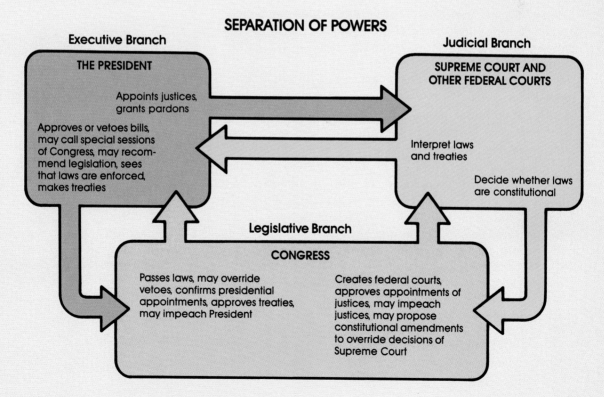

Executive Branch

THE PRESIDENT

Appoints justices, grants pardons

Approves or vetoes bills, may call special sessions of Congress, may recommend legislation, sees that laws are enforced, makes treaties

Judicial Branch

SUPREME COURT AND OTHER FEDERAL COURTS

Interpret laws and treaties

Decide whether laws are constitutional

Legislative Branch

CONGRESS

Passes laws, may override vetoes, confirms presidential appointments, approves treaties, may impeach President

Creates federal courts, approves appointments of justices, may impeach justices, may propose constitutional amendments to override decisions of Supreme Court

The Constitution of the United States of America

We the people of the United States, in order to form a more perfect union, establish justice, insure domestic tranquility, provide for the common defense, promote the general welfare, and secure the blessings of liberty to ourselves and our posterity, do ordain and establish this Constitution for the United States of America.

Preamble The Preamble is a beautifully written introduction stating the purposes for which the government under the Constitution is established.

ARTICLE I

SECTION 1.

All legislative powers herein granted shall be vested in a Congress of the United States, which shall consist of a Senate and House of Representatives.

SECTION 2.

The House of Representatives shall be composed of members chosen every second year by the people of the several States, and the electors in each State shall have the qualifications requisite for electors of the most numerous branch of the State legislature.

No person shall be a representative who shall not have attained to the age of twenty-five years, and been seven years a citizen of the United States, and who shall not, when elected, be an inhabitant of that State in which he shall be chosen.

Representatives and direct taxes shall be apportioned among the several States which may be included within this Union, according to their respective numbers, which shall be determined by adding to the whole number of free persons, including those bound to service for a term of years, and excluding Indians not taxed, three fifths of all other persons.* The actual enumeration shall be made within three years after the first meeting of the Congress of the United States, and within every subsequent term of ten years, in such manner as they shall by law direct. The number of representatives shall not exceed one for every thirty thousand, but each State shall have at least one representative; and until such enumeration shall be made, the State of New Hampshire shall be entitled to choose three, Massachusetts eight, Rhode Island and Providence Plantations one, Connecticut five, New York six, New Jersey four, Pennsylvania eight, Delaware one, Maryland six, Virginia ten, North Carolina five, South Carolina five, and Georgia three.

LEGISLATIVE BRANCH

Congress The lawmaking branch of the federal government is Congress. It is made up of two bodies—a Senate and a House of Representatives.

House of Representatives The writers of the Constitution intended this body to be closer than the Senate to the people. Its members are elected every 2 years.

Qualifications To be a member of the House of Representatives, one must be at least 25 years old, a United States citizen for 7 years, and a resident of the state from which elected.

Apportionment Each state, no matter how small its population, has at least one representative, but each member of the House no longer represents 30,000 people. If this were true today, the House of Representatives would have nearly 8,000 members! For some years, laws passed by Congress have limited the House of Representatives to 435 voting members.

NOTE: Items that have been changed or replaced are underlined.
* Changed by the Fourteenth Amendment

When vacancies happen in the representation from any State, the executive authority thereof shall issue writs of election to fill such vacancies.

The House of Representatives shall choose their speaker and other officers, and shall have the sole power of impeachment.

SECTION 3.

The Senate of the United States shall be composed of two senators from each State, chosen by the legislature thereof,* for six years; and each senator shall have one vote.

Immediately after they shall be assembled in consequence of the first election, they shall be divided as equally as may be into three classes. The seats of the senators of the first class shall be vacated at the expiration of the second year, of the second class at the expiration of the fourth year, and of the third class at the expiration of the sixth year, so that one third may be chosen every second year; and if vacancies happen by resignation, or otherwise, during the recess of the legislature of any State, the executive thereof may make temporary appointments until the next meeting of the legislature, which shall then fill such vacancies.*

No person shall be a senator who shall not have attained to the age of thirty years, and been nine years a citizen of the United States, and who shall not, when elected, be an inhabitant of that State for which he shall be chosen.

The Senate The states are equally represented in the Senate, with two senators from each state. A senator must be at least 30 years old, a United States citizen for 9 years, and a resident of the state from which elected. Senators serve a 6-year term, although only one third of them are elected every 2 years. The writers of the Constitution wanted the Senate to consist of experienced lawmakers; therefore, they arranged this rotating plan so that two thirds of the Senate will always consist of experienced lawmakers.

* Changed by the Seventeenth Amendment

The Vice President of the United States shall be president of the Senate, but shall have no vote, unless they be equally divided.

The Senate shall choose their other officers, and also a president pro tempore, in the absence of the Vice President, or when he shall exercise the office of President of the United States.

The Senate shall have the sole power to try all impeachments. When sitting for that purpose, they shall be on oath or affirmation. When the President of the United States is tried, the Chief Justice shall preside: and no person shall be convicted without the concurrence of two thirds of the members present.

Judgment in cases of impeachment shall not extend further than to removal from office, and disqualification to hold any office of honor, trust or profit under the United States: but the party convicted shall nevertheless be liable and subject to indictment, trial, judgment and punishment, according to law.

SECTION 4.

The times, places, and manner of holding elections for senators and representatives shall be prescribed in each State by the legislature thereof; but the Congress may at any time by law make or alter such regulations, except as to the places of choosing senators.

The Congress shall assemble at least once in every year, and such meeting shall be on the first Monday in December,* unless they shall by law appoint a different day.

The Vice President This is the only part of the Constitution that assigns duties or powers to the Vice President. However, recent Presidents have given their Vice Presidents important duties as aides.

Impeachment Both the House of Representatives and the Senate have roles in the process known as impeachment. The House of Representatives states the misconduct of which the federal official is accused. The Senate then acts as a court to determine if the official is guilty. If two thirds of the senators judge the official to be guilty, he is removed from office.

Elections and meetings Congress has decided that federal elections will take place in even-numbered years on the Tuesday after the first Monday in November. A new Congress now meets on January 3 after its election the preceding November.

* Changed by the Twentieth Amendment

SECTION 5.

Each house shall be the judge of the elections, returns and qualifications of its own members, and a majority of each shall constitute a quorum to do business; but a smaller number may adjourn from day to day, and may be authorized to compel the attendance of absent members, in such manner, and under such penalties as each house may provide.

Each house may determine the rules of its proceedings, punish its members for disorderly behavior, and, with the concurrence of two thirds, expel a member.

Each house shall keep a journal of its proceedings, and from time to time publish the same, excepting such parts as may in their judgment require secrecy; and the yeas and nays of the members of either house on any question shall, at the desire of one fifth of those present, be entered on the journal.

Neither house, during the session of Congress, shall, without the consent of the other, adjourn for more than three days, nor to any other place than that in which the two houses shall be sitting.

SECTION 6.

The senators and representatives shall receive a compensation for their services, to be ascertained by law, and paid out of the Treasury of the United States. They shall in all cases, except treason, felony and breach of the peace, be privileged from arrest during their attendance at the session of their respective houses, and in going to and returning from the same; and for any speech or debate in either house, they shall not be questioned in any other place.

No senator or representative shall, during the time for which he was elected, be appointed to any civil office under the authority of the United States, which shall have been created, or the emoluments thereof shall have been increased during such time; and no person holding any office under the United States shall be a member of either house during his continuance in office.

SECTION 7.

All bills for raising revenue shall originate in the House of Representatives; but the Senate may propose or concur with amendments as on other bills.

Every bill which shall have passed the House of Representatives and the Senate, shall, before it become a law, be presented to the President of the United States; if he approve he shall sign it, but if not he shall return it, with his objections to that house in which it shall have originated, who shall enter the objections at large on their journal, and proceed to reconsider it. If after such reconsideration two

Rules of procedure Congress makes nearly all its own rules of operation and controls its own membership. Both the Senate and the House of Representatives keep journals, which are published daily. In these journals, people can find out how their representatives voted on bills.

Pay and privileges Under the Articles of Confederation, each state paid its members in Congress. This caused trouble because state legislatures could withhold salaries if Congress did something that displeased them. The Constitution resolves this problem by stating that members of Congress will be paid from the national treasury. Several privileges are spelled out. They are intended to make members of Congress as free as possible from undue influence.

Lawmaking The main business of Congress is passing laws, but no bill can become a law unless the President signs it or unless Congress passes it over his veto.

181

thirds of that house shall agree to pass the bill, it shall be sent, together with the objections, to the other house, by which it shall likewise be reconsidered, and if approved by two thirds of that house, it shall become a law. But in all such cases the votes of both houses shall be determined by yeas and nays, and the names of the persons voting for and against the bill shall be entered on the journal of each house respectively. If any bill shall not be returned by the President within ten days (Sundays excepted) after it shall have been presented to him, the same shall be a law, in like manner as if he had signed it, unless the Congress by their adjournment prevent its return, in which case it shall not be a law.

Every order, resolution, or vote to which the concurrence of the Senate and House of Representatives may be necessary (except on a question of adjournment) shall be presented to the President of the United States; and before the same shall take effect, shall be approved by him, or being disapproved by him, shall be repassed by two thirds of the Senate and House of Representatives, according to the rules and limitations prescribed in the case of a bill.

Checks and balances The relationship between Congress and the President in making laws is a clear example of the checks-and-balances system in the United States Constitution.

SECTION 8.

The Congress shall have power to lay and collect taxes, duties, imposts and excises, to pay the debts and provide for the common defense and general welfare of the United States; but all duties, imposts and excises shall be uniform throughout the United States;

To borrow money on the credit of the United States;

To regulate commerce with foreign nations, and among the several States, and with the Indian tribes;

To establish a uniform rule of naturalization, and uniform laws on the subject of bankruptcies through the United States;

To coin money, regulate the value thereof, and of foreign coin, and fix the standard of weights and measures;

To provide for the punishment of counterfeiting the securities and current coin of the United States;

To establish post offices and post roads;

To promote the progress of science and useful arts by securing for limited times to authors and inventors the exclusive right to their respective writings and discoveries;

To constitute tribunals inferior to the Supreme Court;

To define and punish piracies and felonies committed on the high seas, and offenses against the law of nations;

To declare war, grant letters of marque and reprisal, and make rules concerning captures on land and water;

To raise and support armies, but no appropriation of money to that use shall be for a longer term than two years;

To provide and maintain a navy;

Powers of Congress This is one of the most important parts of the Constitution. The powers of the national government as exercised through Congress are listed here. This section shows that the makers of the Constitution wanted a national government strong enough to do the things they thought needed to be done. Among the most important powers given to the national government are the powers (**1**) to tax and spend for the general welfare, (**2**) to regulate interstate and foreign commerce, and (**3**) to wage war and to provide for the common defense.

To make rules for the government and regulations of the land and naval forces;

To provide for calling forth the militia to execute the laws of the Union, suppress insurrections and repel invasions;

To provide for organizing, arming, and disciplining the militia, and for governing such part of them as may be employed in the service of the United States, reserving to the States respectively the appointment of the officers, and the authority of training the militia according to the discipline prescribed by Congress;

To exercise exclusive legislation in all cases whatsoever, over such district (not exceeding ten miles square) as may, by cession of particular States and the acceptance of Congress, become the seat of the government of the United States, and to exercise like authority over all places purchased by the consent of the legislature of the State in which the same shall be, for the erection of forts, magazines, arsenals, dockyards, and other needful buildings; and

To make all laws which shall be necessary and proper for carrying into execution the foregoing powers, and all other powers vested by this Constitution in the government of the United States, or in any department or officer thereof.

Elastic clause The last paragraph in this section contains the famous "elastic clause." It permits Congress to make whatever other laws it thinks necessary to carry out its "enumerated powers" in the previous paragraphs of Section 8.

SECTION 9.

The migration or importation of such persons as any of the States now existing shall think proper to admit, shall not be prohibited by the Congress prior to the year one thousand eight hundred and eight, but a tax or duty may be imposed on such importation, not exceeding ten dollars for each person.

The privilege of the writ of habeas corpus shall not be suspended, unless when in cases of rebellion or invasion the public safety may require it.

No bill of attainder or ex post facto law shall be passed.

No capitation, or other direct,* tax shall be laid, unless in proportion to the census or enumeration herein before directed to be taken.

No tax or duty shall be laid on articles exported from any State.

No preference shall be given by any regulation of commerce or revenue to the ports of one State over those of another; nor shall vessels bound to, or from, one State be obliged to enter, clear, or pay duties in another.

No money shall be drawn from the Treasury, but in consequence of appropriations made by law; and a regular statement and account of the receipts and expenditures of all public money shall be published from time to time.

No title of nobility shall be granted by the United States: and no person holding any office of profit or trust under them, shall, without the consent of the Congress, accept of any present, emolument, office, or title of any kind whatever, from any king, prince, or foreign State.

SECTION 10.

No State shall enter into any treaty, alliance, or confederation; grant letters of marque and reprisal; coin money; emit bills of credit; make anything but gold and silver coin a tender in payment of debts, pass any bill of attainder, ex post facto law, or law impairing the obligation of contracts, or grant any title of nobility.

No State shall, without the consent of the Congress, lay any imposts or duties on imports or exports, except what may be absolutely necessary for executing its inspection laws: and the net produce of all duties and imposts laid by any State on imports or exports, shall be for the use of the Treasury of the United States; and all such laws shall be subject to the revision and control of the Congress.

No State shall, without the consent of Congress, lay any duty of tonnage, keep troops, or ships of war in time of peace, enter into any agreement or compact with another State, or with a foreign power, or engage in war, unless actually invaded, or in such imminent danger as will not admit of delay.

Forbidden powers This section contains several provisions to protect the people of the United States against injustice. A writ of *habeas corpus* requires that an arrested person be brought promptly before a court to determine if he is being held legally. A bill of attainder is a legislative act by which a person can be declared guilty of treason and executed without a trial. An ex *post facto* law is one that makes an act a crime after it has been committed. Therefore, it could turn an innocent person into a criminal.

Powers denied to the states One purpose of our Constitution is to limit the powers of the states and strengthen those of the national government. This section forbids the states to exercise any of those powers given to Congress. The states are also forbidden to do certain things that the national government is forbidden to do.

* Changed by the Sixteenth Amendment

ARTICLE II

SECTION 1.

The executive power shall be vested in a President of the United States of America. He shall hold his office during the term of four years, and, together with the Vice President chosen for the same term, be elected as follows:

Each State shall appoint, in such manner as the legislature thereof may direct, a number of electors, equal to the whole number of senators and representatives to which the State may be entitled in the Congress: but no senator or representative, or person holding an office of trust or profit under the United States, shall be appointed an elector.

The electors shall meet in their respective States, and vote by ballot for two persons, of whom one at least shall not be an inhabitant of the same State with themselves. And they shall make a list of all the persons voted for, and of the number of votes for each; which they shall sign and certify, and transmit sealed to the seat of the government of the United States, directed to the president of the Senate. The president of the Senate shall, in the presence of the Senate and House of Representatives, open all the certificates, and the votes shall then be counted. The person having the greatest number of votes shall be the President, if such number be a majority of the whole number of electors appointed; and if there be more than one who have such

EXECUTIVE BRANCH

President, Vice President The writers of the Constitution felt that the President's and Vice President's terms of office (4 years) should be different from the terms of members of Congress, and that the executive officers should be chosen in a different way. Therefore they set up a system of electors who were to choose the President and Vice President. However, hardly anything about the electoral system works today as the writers of the Constitution intended. For one thing, the Twelfth Amendment changed the method somewhat by requiring each elector to indicate separately his choice for President and Vice President. Furthermore, the rise of political parties changed the system markedly.

majority, and have an equal number of votes, then the House of Representatives shall immediately choose by ballot one of them for President; and if no person have a majority, then from the five highest on the list the said house shall in like manner choose the President. But in choosing the President, the votes shall be taken by States, the representation from each State having one vote; a quorum for this purpose shall consist of a member or members from two thirds of the States, and a majority of all the States shall be necessary to a choice. In every case, after the choice of the President, the person having the greatest number of votes of the electors shall be the Vice President. But if there should remain two or more who have equal votes, the Senate shall choose from them by ballot the Vice President.*

The Congress may determine the time of choosing the electors, and the day on which they shall give their votes; which day shall be the same throughout the United States.

No person except a natural-born citizen, or a citizen of the United States, at the time of the adoption of this Constitution, shall be eligible to the office of President; neither shall any person be eligible to that office who shall not have attained to the age of thirty-five years, and been fourteen years a resident within the United States.

In case of the removal of the President from office, or of his death, resignation, or inability to discharge the powers and duties of the said office, the same shall devolve on the Vice President, and the Congress may by law provide for the case of removal, death, resignation, or inability, both of the President and Vice President, declaring what officer shall then act as President, and such offer shall act accordingly, until the disability be removed, or a President shall be elected.

The President shall, at stated times, receive for his services a compensation, which shall neither be increased nor diminished during the period for which he shall have been elected, and he shall not receive within that period any other emolument from the United States, or any of them.

Before he enter on the execution of his office, he shall take the following oath or affirmation:—"I do solemnly swear (or affirm) that I will faithfully execute the office of President of the United States, and will to the best of my ability, preserve, protect and defend the Constitution of the United States."

SECTION 2.

The President shall be commander in chief of the army and navy of the United States, and of the militia of the several States, when called into the actual service of the

* Changed by the Twelfth Amendment

The electors Today each political party in a state selects people to be candidates for the position of electors. These people pledge that if they become electors, they will vote for the presidential and vice presidential candidates of their party.

When people vote in a presidential election today, they seem to be voting only for electors. Actually, however, they are voting for the President and Vice President since the voters know which candidates the electors are pledged to vote for.

Election day Congress has determined that presidential elections shall take place every 4 years on the Tuesday after the first Monday in November.

Salary The President's salary is now $200,000 a year, and he receives $50,000 for expenses. He pays income taxes on both sums. He also receives a sum not to exceed $100,000 a year for travel expenses. This fund is not taxed.

Military powers By making the President the Commander in Chief of the armed forces, the

United States; he may require the opinion, in writing, of the principal officer in each of the executive departments, upon any subject relating to the duties of their respective offices, and he shall have power to grant reprieves and pardons for offenses against the United States, except in cases of impeachment.

He shall have power, by and with the advice and consent of the Senate, to make treaties, provided two thirds of the senators present concur; and he shall nominate, and by and with the advice and consent of the Senate, shall appoint ambassadors, other public ministers and consuls, judges of the Supreme Court, and all other officers of the United States, whose appointments are not herein otherwise provided for, and which shall be established by law: but the Congress may by law vest the appointment of such inferior officers, as they think proper, in the President alone, in the courts of law, or in the heads of departments.

The President shall have power to fill up all vacancies that may happen during the recess of the Senate, by granting commissions which shall expire at the end of their next session.

SECTION 3.

He shall from time to time give to the Congress information of the state of the Union, and recommend to their consideration such measures as he shall judge necessary and expedient; he may, on extraordinary occasions, convene both houses, or either of them, and in case of disagreement between them with respect to the time of adjournment, he may adjourn them to such time as he shall think proper; he shall receive ambassadors and other public ministers; he shall take care that the laws be faithfully executed, and shall commission all the officers of the United States.

writers of the Constitution made sure that an elected representative of the people would control the military power of the nation. This is a basic principle of a free society. In the missile age, when Congress may not have time to declare war, the President has an awesome responsibility as head of the defense forces of the nation.

The President and Congress Congress makes the laws, but the President signs most of them before they go into effect. In addition, the President suggests needed legislation each year when he gives his State of the Union message to Congress.

SECTION 4.

The President, Vice President, and all civil officers of the United States, shall be removed from office on impeachment for, and conviction of, treason, bribery, or other high crimes and misdemeanors.

ARTICLE III

SECTION 1.

The judicial power of the United States shall be vested in one Supreme Court, and in such inferior courts as the Congress may from time to time ordain and establish. The judges, both of the Supreme and inferior courts, shall hold their offices during good behavior, and shall, at stated times, receive for their services, a compensation which shall not be diminished during their continuance in office.

SECTION 2.

The judicial power shall extend to all cases, in law and equity, arising under this Constitution, the laws of the United States, and treaties made, or which shall be made, under their authority;—to all cases affecting ambassadors, other public ministers and consuls;—to all cases of admiralty and maritime jurisdiction;—to controversies to which the United States shall be a party;—to controversies between two or more States;—between a State and citizens of another State;—between citizens of different States,—between

JUDICIAL BRANCH

Federal courts The President, with the consent of the Senate, appoints the judges for the federal courts. They are the only officials of the national government to hold office for life.

Cases in federal courts The Constitution names the kinds of cases to be handled in federal courts. Only a few are handled directly by the Supreme Court. Most of these kinds of cases start in a lower federal court. If the verdict is questioned, the case may go to a court of appeals, and it may in time be appealed again and reach the Supreme Court. The judgment of the Supreme Court is final.

EQUAL JUSTICE UNDER LAW

citizens of the same State claiming lands under grants of different States, and between a State, or the citizens thereof, and foreign States, citizens or subjects.

In all cases affecting ambassadors, other public ministers and consuls, and those in which a State shall be party, the Supreme Court shall have original jurisdiction. In all the other cases before mentioned, the Supreme Court shall have appellate jurisdiction, both as to law and fact, with such exceptions, and under such regulations as the Congress shall make.

The trial of all crimes, except in cases of impeachment, shall be by jury; and such trial shall be held in the State where the said crimes shall have been committed; but when not committed within any State, the trial shall be at such place or places as the Congress may by law have directed.

SECTION 3.

Treason against the United States shall consist only in levying war against them, or in adhering to their enemies, giving them aid and comfort. No person shall be convicted of treason unless on the testimony of two witnesses to the same overt act, or on confession in open court.

The Congress shall have power to declare the punishment of treason, but no attainder of treason shall work corruption of blood, or forfeiture except during the life of the person attainted.

ARTICLE IV

SECTION 1.

Full faith and credit shall be given in each State to the public acts, records, and judicial proceedings of every other State. And the Congress may by general laws prescribe the manner in which such acts, records, and proceedings shall be proved, and the effect thereof.

SECTION 2.

The citizens of each State shall be entitled to all privileges and immunities of citizens in the several States.

A person charged in any State with treason, felony, or other crime, who shall flee from justice, and be found in another State, shall on demand of the executive authority of the State from which he fled, be delivered up to be removed to the State having jurisdiction of the crime.

No person held to service or labor in the State, under the laws thereof, escaping into another, shall, in consequence of any law or regulation therein, be discharged from such service or labor, but shall be delivered up on claim of the party to whom such service or labor may be due.*

---

* Changed by the Thirteenth Amendment

One of the great powers of our federal courts is their right to declare an act of Congress or a state legislature unconstitutional, though this right is not specifically mentioned in any part of the Constitution.

Treason This crime is carefully defined. The last sentence in Section 3 says that if a person is convicted of treason, the taint of the crime cannot legally be passed on to his children or later descendants.

THE STATES

Relations among the states The Constitution insures that persons cannot escape a legal obligation by moving from one state to another. Also, citizens moving from one state to another shall be treated the same as are citizens of the state they have moved to.

SECTION 3.

New States may be admitted by the Congress into this Union; but no new State shall be formed or erected within the jurisdiction of any other State; nor any State be formed by the junction of two or more States, or parts of States, without the consent of the legislatures of the States concerned as well as of the Congress.

The Congress shall have power to dispose of and make all needful rules and regulations respecting the territory or other property belonging to the United States; and nothing in this Constitution shall be so construed as to prejudice any claims of the United States, or of any particular State.

SECTION 4.

The United States shall guarantee to every State in this Union a republican form of government, and shall protect each of them against invasion; and on application of the legislature, or of the executive (when the legislature cannot be convened) against domestic violence.

ARTICLE V

The Congress, whenever two thirds of both houses shall deem it necessary, shall propose amendments to this Constitution, or, on the application of the legislatures of two thirds of the several States, shall call a convention for proposing amendments, which, in either case, shall be valid to all intents and purposes, as part of this Constitution, when ratified by the legislatures of three fourths of the several States, or by conventions in three fourths thereof, as the one or the other mode of ratification may be proposed by the Congress; provided [that no amendment which may be made prior to the year one thousand eight hundred and eight shall in any manner affect the first and fourth clauses in the ninth section of the first article, and] that no State, without its consent, shall be deprived of its equal suffrage in the Senate.

ARTICLE VI

All debts contracted and engagements entered into, before the adoption of this Constitution, shall be as valid against the United States under this Constitution, as under the Confederation.

This Constitution, and the laws of the United States which shall be made in pursuance thereof; and all treaties made, or which shall be made, under the authority of the United States, shall be the supreme law of the land; and the

New states Without this section we might still be a nation of only 13 states. This permits Congress to admit new states to the Union. No state may be divided into two or more states without the consent of its people. This explains why the people of Massachusetts had to consent before Maine could become a state at the time of the Missouri Compromise. (See p. 251.)

AMENDMENTS

Changing the Constitution Two methods are provided for proposing amendments, but the second—that is, on the application of the legislatures of two thirds of the states—has never been used.

GENERAL PROVISIONS

The supremacy clause The second paragraph of Article VI is often called the supremacy clause. It makes clear that when national and state authority collide, state authority must give way, for the Constitution is the supreme law of the nation.

judges in every State shall be bound thereby, anything in the Constitution or laws of any State to the contrary notwithstanding.

The senators and representatives before mentioned, and the members of the several State legislatures, and all executive and judicial officers, both of the United States, and of the several States, shall be bound by oath or affirmation to support this Constitution; but no religious test shall ever be required as a qualification to any office or public trust under the United States.

ARTICLE VII

The ratification of the conventions of nine States shall be sufficient for the establishment of this Constitution between the States so ratifying the same.

Done in Convention by the unanimous consent of the States present the seventeenth day of September in the year of our Lord one thousand seven hundred and eighty-seven, and of the independence of the United States of America the twelfth. In witness whereof we have hereunto subscribed our names.

George Washington, President
(VIRGINIA)

MASSACHUSETTS
Nathaniel Gorham
Rufus King

NEW YORK
Alexander Hamilton

GEORGIA
William Few
Abraham Baldwin

DELAWARE
George Read
Gunning Bedford
John Dickinson
Richard Bassett
Jacob Broom

VIRGINIA
John Blair
James Madison

PENNSYLVANIA
Benjamin Franklin
Thomas Mifflin
Robert Morris
George Clymer
Thomas FitzSimons
Jared Ingersoll
James Wilson
Gouvernor Morris

NEW HAMPSHIRE
John Langdon
Nicholas Gilman

NEW JERSEY
William Livingston
David Brearley
William Paterson
Jonathan Dayton

CONNECTICUT
William Samuel
   Johnson
Roger Sherman

NORTH CAROLINA
William Blount
Richard Dobbs Spaight
Hugh Williamson

SOUTH CAROLINA
John Rutledge
Charles Cotesworth
   Pinckney
Charles Pinckney
Pierce Butler

MARYLAND
James McHenry
Daniel of
   St. Thomas Jenifer
Daniel Carroll

No religious test A person's religion shall never be used officially to keep him or her from holding office under the government of the United States.

RATIFICATION

Conventions All states had ratifying conventions in which they gave approval to the Constitution. The table below gives the date and the vote in each of the state conventions.

1787
Del.	Dec. 7	Unanimous
Pa.	Dec. 12	46–23
N.J.	Dec. 18	Unanimous

1788
Ga.	Jan. 2	Unanimous
Conn.	Jan. 9	128–40
Mass.	Feb. 6	187–168*
Md.	Apr. 28	63–11
S.C.	May 27	149–73
N.H.	June 21	57–46*
Va.	June 25	87–76*
N.Y.	July 26	30–27*

1789
| N.C. | Nov. 21 | 187–77 |

1790
| R.I. | May 29 | 34–22 |

*Strongly urged Bill of Rights

FIRST AMENDMENT—1791

Congress shall make no law respecting an establishment of religion, or prohibiting the free exercise thereof; or abridging the freedom of speech, or of the press; or the right of the people peaceably to assemble, and to petition the government for a redress of grievances.

The first ten amendments are known as the Bill of Rights. The First Amendment sets forth several basic rights and freedoms. Congress cannot interfere with freedom of religion or a person's right to speak freely. It cannot curb the right to print the truth. It cannot prevent citizens from meeting peaceably to discuss their problems and to ask the government to do something about them.

SECOND AMENDMENT—1791

A well-regulated militia, being necessary to the security of a free State, the right of the people to keep and bear arms, shall not be infringed.

THIRD AMENDMENT—1791

No soldier shall, in time of peace, be quartered in any house, without the consent of the owner, nor in time of war, but in a manner to be prescribed by law.

The Second and Third Amendments are not so pertinent today as they were in 1791. Today, for example, it is not likely that the national government would quarter soldiers in a private home.

FOURTH AMENDMENT—1791

The right of the people to be secure in their persons, houses, papers, and effects, against unreasonable searches and seizures, shall not be violated, and no warrants shall issue, but upon probable cause, supported by oath or affirmation, and particularly describing the place to be searched, and the persons or things to be seized.

The Fourth Amendment is still very important. It protects people against illegal invasions of their homes and against seizure of their property by government officials without a proper search-and-seizure warrant.

FIFTH AMENDMENT—1791

No person shall be held to answer for a capital or otherwise infamous crime, unless on a presentment or indictment of a grand jury, except in cases arising in the land or naval forces, or in the militia, when in actual service in time of war or public danger; nor shall any person be subject for the same offense to be twice put in jeopardy of life or limb; nor shall be compelled in any criminal case to be a witness against himself, nor be deprived of life, liberty, or property, without due process of law; nor shall private property be taken for public use without just compensation.

SIXTH AMENDMENT—1791

In all criminal prosecutions, the accused shall enjoy the right to a speedy and public trial, by an impartial jury of the State and district wherein the crime shall have been committed, which district shall have been previously ascertained by law, and to be informed of the nature and cause of the accusation; to be confronted with the witnesses against him; to have compulsory process for obtaining witnesses in his favor, and to have the assistance of counsel for his defense.

SEVENTH AMENDMENT—1791

In suits at common law, where the value in controversy shall exceed twenty dollars, the right of trial by jury shall be preserved, and no fact tried by a jury shall be otherwise reexamined in any court of the United States, than according to the rules of the common law.

Rights of persons accused of crimes The Fifth, Sixth, Seventh, and Eighth Amendments set forth the procedures that courts must follow regarding persons accused of crimes. Among the rights are trial by jury within a reasonable time, the services of a lawyer, and the right to call witnesses. If the accused person is found not guilty, he or she cannot be tried again for the same crime.

EIGHTH AMENDMENT—1791

Excessive bail shall not be required, nor excessive fines imposed, nor cruel and unusual punishments inflicted.

NINTH AMENDMENT—1791

The enumeration in the Constitution of certain rights shall not be construed to deny or disparage others retained by the people.

TENTH AMENDMENT—1791

The powers not delegated to the United States by the Constitution, nor prohibited by it to the States are reserved to the States respectively, or to the people.

ELEVENTH AMENDMENT—1795

The judicial power of the United States shall not be construed to extend to any suit in law or equity, commenced or prosecuted against one of the United States, by citizens of another State, or by citizens or subjects of any foreign State.

TWELFTH AMENDMENT—1804

The electors shall meet in their respective States, and vote by ballot for President and Vice President, one of whom, at least, shall not be an inhabitant of the same State with themselves; they shall name in their ballots the person voted for as Vice President, and they shall make distinct lists of all persons voted for as President and of all persons voted for as Vice President, and of the number of votes for each, which lists they shall sign and certify, and transmit sealed to the seat of government of the United States, directed to the president of the Senate;—The president of the Senate shall, in the presence of the Senate and House of Representatives, open all the certificates and the votes shall then be counted;—The person having the greatest number of votes for President shall be the President, if such number be a majority of the whole number of electors appointed; and if no person have such majority, then from the persons having the highest numbers not exceeding three on the list of those voted for as President, the House of Representatives shall choose immediately, by ballot, the President. But in choosing the President, the votes shall be taken by States, the representation from each State having one vote; a

Bail, penalties An accused person cannot be required to put up an unreasonable sum of money as bail if he or she is released from jail while awaiting trial. If found guilty, the accused person cannot be tried again for the same crime.

People's rights and reserved powers The people may retain rights that were not stated earlier. Moreover, any power that the Constitution does not forbid to the states is retained by them or by their people.

Election of President and Vice President This amendment was made necessary because of the rise of political parties during the 1790s. The amendment changed the details for electing a President through the electoral system.

In 1800 the most famous tie vote in American political history occurred. At that time, electors voted for two candidates without distinguishing between President and Vice President. The electors of the victorious party—the Democratic-Republicans—were pledged to vote for Thomas Jefferson and Aaron Burr. They cast their votes in this way, meaning that they wanted Jefferson to be President and Burr to be Vice President. It had been expected that at least one elector would vote for Jefferson and not for Burr, avoiding a tie. But none did, and each got 73 electoral votes.

quorum for this purpose shall consist of a member or members from two thirds of the States, and a majority of all the States shall be necessary to a choice. And if the House of Representatives shall not choose a President whenever the right of choice shall devolve upon them, *before the fourth day of March next following,** then the Vice President shall act as President, as in the case of the death or other constitutional disability of the President. The person having the greatest number of votes as Vice President shall be the Vice President, if such number be a majority of the whole number of electors appointed, and if no person have a majority, then from the two highest numbers on the list, the Senate shall choose the Vice President; a quorum for the purpose shall consist of two thirds of the whole number of senators and a majority of the whole number shall be necessary to a choice. But no person constitutionally ineligible to the office of President shall be eligible to that of Vice President of the United States.

THIRTEENTH AMENDMENT—1865

SECTION 1.
Neither slavery nor involuntary servitude, except as a punishment for crime whereof the party shall have been duly convicted, shall exist within the United States, or any place subject to their jurisdiction.

SECTION 2.
Congress shall have power to enforce this article by appropriate legislation.

Under the Constitution the election then had to be decided in the House of Representatives. At such times, each state had one vote. The Federalists still controlled the House of Representatives, and they saw the opportunity to keep Jefferson, whom they disliked, from becoming President. Only the personal influence of Alexander Hamilton kept the Federalists from making Burr President. To prevent such a mix-up from happening again, the Twelfth Amendment was adopted. It instructs electors to cast separate votes for the candidates for President and Vice President.

Slavery abolished The Thirteenth Amendment, added soon after the Civil War, prohibited slavery.

* Changed by the Twentieth Amendment

FOURTEENTH AMENDMENT—1868

SECTION 1.

All persons born or naturalized in the United States, and subject to the jurisdiction thereof, are citizens of the United States and of the State wherein they reside. No State shall make or enforce any law which shall abridge the privileges or immunities of citizens of the United States; nor shall any State deprive any person of life, liberty, or property, without due process of law; nor deny to any person within its jurisdiction the equal protection of the laws.

Rights of citizens The Fourteenth Amendment defines citizenship and forbids the states to interfere with the rights of citizens of the United States. Also added soon after the Civil War, this amendment protects citizens' rights against state action. Section 2 says that if a state denies the right to vote to any group, that state's delegation in Congress will be reduced.

SECTION 2.

Representatives shall be apportioned among the several States according to their respective numbers, counting the whole number of persons in each State, excluding Indians not taxed. But when the right to vote at any election for the choice of electors for President and Vice President of the United States, representatives in Congress, the executive and judicial officers of a State, or the members of the legislature thereof, is denied to any of the male inhabitants of such State, being twenty-one years of age, and citizens of the United States, or in any way abridged, except for participation in rebellion, or other crime, the basis of representation therein shall be reduced in the proportion which the number of such male citizens shall bear to the whole number of male citizens twenty-one years of age in such State.

Apportionment If a state denies voting rights to any group for any reason except for taking part in a rebellion or other crime, that state's delegation in Congress will be reduced.

SECTION 3.

No person shall be a senator or representative in Congress, or elector of President and Vice President, or hold any office, civil or military, under the United States, or under any State, who, having previously taken an oath, as a member of Congress, or as an officer of the United States, or as a member of any State legislature, or as an executive or judicial officer of any State, to support the Constitution of the United States, shall have engaged in

Dealing with rebels This section denies the privilege of serving in any public office to any former officeholder who took part in the rebellion of the 1860s. In 1898, Congress removed this limitation so that former Confederate officers could serve in the Spanish-American War.

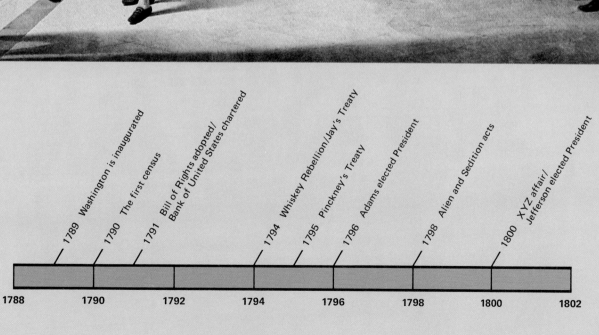

1789 Washington is inaugurated

1790 The first census

1791 Bill of Rights adopted/
Bank of United States chartered

1794 Whiskey Rebellion/Jay's Treaty

1795 Pinckney's Treaty

1796 Adams elected President

1798 Alien and Sedition acts

1800 XYZ affair/
Jefferson elected President

| 1788 | 1790 | 1792 | 1794 | 1796 | 1798 | 1800 | 1802 |

A list of the Presidents of the United States appears on page 728.

In Massachusetts, Virginia, and other states, Federalist leaders had promised to add a bill of rights to the Constitution. In the first Congress they worked hard to keep their promise. This meant amending—that is, making a correction or change in—the Constitution. Ten amendments were added in 1791, and these became the promised Bill of Rights. (See the Bill of Rights, starting on page 192.)

The President's Cabinet Congress knew that President Washington would need help to run the executive branch of government. So, within the executive branch Congress created the Departments of State, Treasury, and War. Each was headed by an official called a secretary.

Congress also authorized the office of attorney general to handle legal affairs. The chart on page 207 shows the duties of these officials and the names of the four men first appointed to these offices in the new government.

These four men soon became known as the President's **Cabinet**, which means "a group of advisers." It was Washington who began the practice of consulting with the heads of the major departments in the executive branch of the government. The Constitution says nothing about advisers to the President, but every President since Washington has had a Cabinet. The number of Cabinet members has increased over the years as Congress has added new departments to the executive branch.

At Washington's left are four Cabinet members: Henry Knox, Alexander Hamilton, Thomas Jefferson, and Edmund Randolph. See the table on page 207 for their offices and duties.

Have pupils use an almanac or another resource to list the 13 Cabinet positions and the people who now occupy them.

Samuel Osgood of Massachusetts became the first postmaster general under the Constitution. However, the office did not become a Cabinet post until 1829.

WASHINGTON'S FIRST CABINET		
Office	Official	Duties
Secretary of State	Thomas Jefferson	To conduct the relations of the United States with other nations
Secretary of the Treasury	Alexander Hamilton	To handle the government's finances
Secretary of War	Henry Knox	To take charge of all military matters
Attorney General	Edmund Randolph	To act as chief legal adviser to the executive branch

In making appointments to his Cabinet, a President tries to gain support from different parts of the country. Thomas Jefferson and Edmund Randolph were from Virginia, Henry Knox was from Massachusetts, and Alexander Hamilton was from New York. From Washington's day on, Presidents have sought geographical balance in their Cabinets.

Washington—and the Presidents following him—tried to have different points of view represented in the Cabinet. Edmund Randolph had attended the Constitutional Convention but in Virginia had opposed ratification of the Constitution. Thomas Jefferson was not so firmly in favor of a strong central government as Hamilton and Knox were.

The federal courts Article III of the Constitution states that the judicial branch of the federal government will consist of a Supreme Court and any lower courts Congress wishes to establish. Acting under this authority, Congress passed the **Judiciary Act of 1789.** This act provided for a Supreme Court with a chief justice and five associate justices. The Judiciary Act of 1789 also set up lower courts on two levels. At the lower level were 13 district courts, one for each state. There were three circuit courts at a higher level, between the district courts and the Supreme Court.

Since 1789, Congress has changed the number of associate justices on the Supreme Court as well as the number of district and circuit courts. Still, our federal court system today has the same framework as that set up by the Judiciary Act of 1789. Through this court system, justice is assured in the enforcement of federal laws.

Hamilton's debt plan Article VI of the Constitution required the new government to pay all debts contracted by the old government under the Articles of Confederation. Moreover, most of the states were still in debt for money they had borrowed during the War for Independence. The new federal government had no responsibility for the state debts. However, it arranged to pay these debts, too.

This came about through a plan proposed by Alexander Hamilton. In 1789, Congress asked him, as secretary of the treasury, to prepare a report on government finances. In his report, Hamilton suggested that the new government pay both the federal and the state debts. Hamilton argued that the federal government would be strengthened by taking responsibility for the state debts. People who had lent money to the states would look to the federal government for payment. Therefore, they would support the federal government and would work for its success.

The federal district Virginia and other southern states had paid nearly all their state debts. They had no quarrel with the plan to pay the federal debt. But their leaders were unwilling to have the federal government take over the task of paying the state debts. If this happened, southern leaders said, their citizens would be taxed to help pay the debts of northern states.

As it happened, Congress was trying to decide the location of a new capital at the same time that Hamilton's debt plan was being considered. This presented an opportunity for compromise. Thomas Jefferson knew that people in the South wanted the permanent capital of the United States in or near their part of the country. So he persuaded some Virginia congressmen to vote for Hamilton's plan. In return, Hamilton used his influence to place the new capital in a federal district between Maryland and Virginia. Philadelphia was to be the capital for 10 years. Then the United States government would move to Washington in the newly formed District of Columbia.

A national bank Alexander Hamilton and Thomas Jefferson were successful in working out a compromise on the debt question. On another matter, however, the two leaders disagreed. Hamilton proposed that the United States Congress charter a national bank, modeled on the Bank of England. A national bank, Hamilton said, should be owned partly by the government and partly by private individuals. It would be a safe place for the federal government to keep its money. Moreover, it could help the government borrow money.

Hamilton and Jefferson disagreed on the question of whether Congress had the power to charter a national bank. Hamilton said that the Constitution (Article I, Section 8) gave Congress the power to pass any laws necessary to carry out its listed powers. He argued that Congress clearly had the power to tax and spend for the general welfare. A bank, he said, would help Congress carry out this power. Therefore, Hamilton declared, Congress did have the power to charter a bank.

Hamilton's argument is known as the **loose interpretation** (or broad interpretation) of the Constitution. The makers of the Constitution could not possibly write in all the details of government. Therefore, they included a clause permitting Congress to create whatever agencies were "necessary and proper" to carry out the functions of government. This clause made a loose interpretation of the Constitution possible.

Jefferson, on the other hand, believed the federal government could do only what the Constitution specifically gave it the power to do. In his opinion, the Constitution should be interpreted exactly as it was written, not loosely or broadly. Jef-

208

During Washington's presidency three new states — Vermont, Kentucky, and Tennessee — entered the Union.

The newly chartered Bank of the United States set up its headquarters in Philadelphia.

ferson's view is known as the **strict interpretation** (or narrow interpretation) of the Constitution. According to this interpretation, the government could not charter a bank because the Constitution did not give the legislative branch the specific power to do so.

Actually, Congress had already passed a bill chartering the first **Bank of the United States.** President Washington, however, had cautiously held off signing the bill into law. He wanted to hear his Cabinet's views on whether the Constitution gave Congress the power to establish a bank. After listening carefully, Washington decided to accept Hamilton's arguments. He signed the bank bill in 1791. It provided a charter for the Bank of the United States. Under its charter, which would last 20 years, the headquarters of the bank would be in Philadelphia. It could, however, set up branches in other parts of the country.

CHECKUP

1. How did the tariff of 1789 raise money for the new government?
2. What was the purpose of the President's Cabinet?
3. How did the Judiciary Act of 1789 establish a federal court system?
4. Why was Hamilton's debt plan adopted?
5. Explain the difference between Hamilton's and Jefferson's interpretation of the Constitution concerning the Bank of the United States.

The Rise of Political Parties

A "fishing" trip   In the summer of 1791, Thomas Jefferson and his friend James Madison took a trip through the northern states. The two men said they were going on a "fishing and botanizing" journey. But it was neither fish nor rare plants that sent them north. They were looking for northern leaders opposed to the policies of Alexander Hamilton.

Jefferson and Madison found what they were looking for in New York. There they talked with Aaron Burr, an opponent of Alexander Hamilton. They talked, too, with George Clinton, who had long been governor of New York. Out of these talks grew an organization called a **political party.**

Political parties   A political party is an organization of people holding similar views on the policies a government should follow. The party members work to elect people of their choice to office and to shape government policies. The writers of the Constitution had not foreseen the development of political parties, and the Constitution makes no mention of them. Nevertheless, political parties have become important to all levels of government in the United States. Our first two political parties grew from the

WHAT POLITICAL PARTIES DO

1. Political parties select candidates for office by means of caucuses or conventions.
2. By nominating candidates, political parties offer the voters a choice at elections.
3. Political parties draw up *platforms*, which are statements of the stand the party takes on important issues.
4. Political parties collect money to finance their candidates' campaigns.
5. Candidates and other party leaders provide information to voters through speeches, written statements, and advertisements.
6. When elected to office, political parties' candidates direct the activities of the government.
7. When out of office, political parties' leaders act as watchdogs, checking to see that the party in power conducts the activities of the government properly.
8. Political parties make it possible for voters to express their wishes in a peaceful manner.

opposing views of Thomas Jefferson and Alexander Hamilton. As you have read, the two men had different opinions on the Bank of the United States. In time they differed on other questions, too.

Both Thomas Jefferson and Alexander Hamilton had many followers. Those with views similar to Hamilton's joined in what became known as the **Federalist party.** The leaders of this party had helped to write the Constitution. They believed in a strong central government and had worked hard to get the Constitution ratified. For more than 10 years, they had held most of the important offices in the government.

Jefferson's supporters were pro-French, while Hamilton's followers were pro-British.

Those persons who had been against ratification of the Constitution were called Anti-Federalists. In the 1790s many of them became followers of Thomas Jefferson. At that time his party was known as the **Democratic-Republican party**. Later it would shorten its name to the Democratic party.

Washington's second term   In 1792 President Washington wanted to retire to Mount Vernon. However, the infant republic still needed his steadying hand. So he consented to accept a second 4-year term. Once more he was chosen President of the United States with the unanimous vote of the electors.

During Washington's second term a crisis arose. Hamilton had persuaded Congress to put a tax on whiskey. He said the government needed the money such a tax would provide. The whiskey tax angered western farmers. Since they had difficulty getting their grain to eastern markets, the farmers distilled some of their corn and rye into whiskey. Jugs, kegs, and barrels of whiskey could be more eas-

ily carried over bad roads than could wagonloads of bulky grain.

Many western farmers refused to pay the whiskey tax because they felt it was an unjust burden on them. When the federal government sent tax collectors, the angry farmers threatened them with violence. Washington was alarmed by this threat, and in 1794 he called the militia of three states into federal service. With Alexander Hamilton in command, 15,000 men marched into western Pennsylvania. This display of force brought about the collapse of the **Whiskey Rebellion**, the name given to the farmers' brief resistance to the federal government.

The Whiskey Rebellion had two results. First, it showed that the federal government could enforce the laws that Congress had passed. Second, it convinced many western farmers that violence was a very poor way of opposing Federalist policies. Joining Jefferson's Democratic-Republican party was a better way. Perhaps they could change the government's policies by voting the Federalists out of office.

Angry farmers carry on a rail a whiskey-tax collector they have tarred and feathered.

Born: 1732, Westmoreland County, Virginia. **Education:** Private tutors and relatives. **Training:** Surveyor, militia officer, plantation owner. **To presidency from:** Virginia. **Position when elected:** Plantation owner. **Political party:** Belonged to no party. **Married:** Martha Dandridge Custis. **Children:** None, though his wife had two children by a former marriage. **Died:** 1799, from a cold and sore throat that doctors of the time could not cope with. **Other facts:** Tall, broad-shouldered, and muscular. Large land holdings made him one of the richest persons of his time. Yet he was so short of cash that he had to borrow money to travel to his inauguration. **During his presidency:** Saw the first successful balloon flight in America in Philadelphia in 1793.

GEORGE WASHINGTON
1st President
1789 · 1797

The election of 1796 No doubt George Washington could have been elected to a third term as President. However, he believed two terms were enough. He also believed that political parties would weaken the national government. In a farewell message to the country, Washington warned against the harmful effects of the "spirit of party." His advice came too late. Political parties were already in existence.

As the end of Washington's second term neared, the two political parties openly chose, or **nominated**, candidates for election to the presidency. Federalist leaders wanted to nominate Alexander Hamilton, but they feared he had too many enemies to be elected. Instead they chose John Adams of Massachusetts as the Federalist presidential candidate. For Vice-President they nominated Thomas Pinckney of South Carolina, the youngest son of Eliza Lucas Pinckney, whom you read about on pages 108–109.

Democratic-Republican leaders held a meeting to choose candidates for their party. Such a meeting of party leaders is called a **caucus**. From 1796 to 1832, parties used this method to choose those who ran for office. In 1796 the Democratic-Republican caucus named Thomas Jefferson as the party's presidential candidate. For Vice-President, they chose Aaron Burr of New York.

The election showed the growing power of the Democratic-Republican party. Although John Adams won the presidency, he received only three more electoral votes than Thomas Jefferson. The Constitution at that time stated that the person with the second highest number of electoral votes would be Vice-President. Therefore, Jefferson became Vice-President even though he and John Adams were members of different political parties.

CHECKUP

1. What were the first two political parties in the United States?
2. What were the main differences between these two parties?
3. What are the main functions of political parties in the United States?
4. How did the presidential election of 1796 show the growing strength of the Democratic-Republican party?

Treaties and Troubles

The last Federalist President   John Adams was one of the giants of the American Revolution. His writings had put forth many of the arguments in favor of revolution. Adams had helped draft the Declaration of Independence, had signed it, and had helped persuade the Second Continental Congress to approve it. He had served as his country's diplomatic representative abroad. He had been Vice-President during Washington's two terms as President. Very few Americans in 1796 had as much experience in politics and government as John Adams.

Nevertheless, John Adams won only a narrow victory over Thomas Jefferson. This was one reason why he did not have greater success as President. Another reason was his stubborn personality. John Adams refused to change his ways to make himself popular. Even though Federalists were in control of the Senate and the House of Representatives, President Adams had trouble with Congress.

President Adams's main troubles, however, were in dealing with other countries. In 1789, the year that George Washington was inaugurated for his first term, a revolution broke out in France. John Marshall, who later became Chief Justice of the United States, wrote in 1789, "In no part of the globe was this revolution hailed with more joy than in America."

At first, most Americans looked on the French Revolution with favor. But as time passed, the French Revolution took a violent turn, with much bloodshed. Events in France as well as in other countries became matters of great concern in the United States. The way the Federalists dealt with these problems turned out to be unpopular. The foreign relations of the United States during the years that the Federalists were in power helped make John Adams the last Federalist President.

The old treaty with France   You have learned that the United States and France signed a treaty of alliance in 1778. This was at a time when the United States was struggling for independence. France helped mightily in that struggle. In fact, without France's aid, the United States might not have been victorious in its War for Independence.

Fifteen years later, war broke out again between France and Great Britain. Because of the treaty of alliance, some Democratic-Republicans thought the United States should join France in this war against Great Britain. But Federalists argued that the treaty was no longer in force. They said that the revolution in France had changed the government that had signed the treaty. In addition, the Federalists feared the democratic spirit of the French Revolution.

President Washington knew the United States was too weak to get involved in another war so soon after its War for Independence. Therefore, he issued a **proclamation of neutrality**. This meant the United States would take no part in the war between France and Great Britain.

It also made plain that the treaty of alliance between France and the United States was no longer in effect.

Jay's Treaty   Though President Washington declared American neutrality, the French-British conflict still caused trouble for the United States. British war vessels seized or sank American merchant ships suspected of trading with France. The British **impressed** American sailors—that is, they took sailors off American ships and forced them to serve on British ships.

Moreover, as late as the 1790s, the British still held western forts and trading posts on American soil. In 1794 Washington sent John Jay of New York to Great Britain to try to arrange solutions to these problems. Jay had earlier been made the first Chief Justice of the United States. However, he had regarded this as an unimportant office and had resigned.

Jay succeeded in coming to an agreement with the British. In what became known as Jay's Treaty, Great Britain agreed to move out of the forts and trading posts on America's western lands. However, Jay was not able to solve all the problems that had caused trouble between the United States and Great Britain. There was nothing in Jay's Treaty about Great Britain's interference with American shipping. And the trade terms that were agreed on seemed to favor Great Britain.

The Democratic-Republicans and even some Federalists were unhappy with Jay's Treaty. President Washington was not pleased with it either. Still, he thought it might keep the United States out of war. So he presented it to the Senate for ap-

John Jay's treaty with Britain was so unpopular that he was burned in effigy by demonstrators.

proval, as the Constitution required. Ratification in the Senate turned into a fight between the two political parties. Finally, in 1794 the Senate ratified Jay's Treaty and President Washington signed it. Nevertheless, the split between Democratic-Republicans and Federalists had widened.

Pinckney's Treaty   The year after Jay's Treaty, Thomas Pinckney, also a Federalist, was sent to Spain to try to work out problems between Spain and the United States. France had turned over its holdings west of the Mississippi River to Spain 12 years before the American Revolution. As long as the colonists were confined to the region east of the Appalachians, it made little difference who laid claim to the wilderness region beyond the Mississippi. But as Americans moved into the lands beyond the mountains after the Revolution, trouble developed between the settlers of the region and the Spanish officials.

A major issue was the use of the Mississippi River as a water highway. Spain did not want the river opened to free navigation. It saw such an act as a threat to its landholdings in the heart of North America. To western farmers, however, use of the Mississippi was essential to getting their crops to market. The crops could be sent down the river on flatboats. Near the mouth of the river they could then be transferred to oceangoing vessels for shipment to ports on the Atlantic coast or in Europe.

Pinckney had more success than John Jay. The treaty he negotiated with Spain was widely popular. In **Pinckney's Treaty**, Spain granted Americans the right to travel on the Mississippi River. Even more important, the treaty allowed Americans to ship goods through the port of New Orleans, at the mouth of the Mississippi. For many a western farmer, the right to use the port was the difference between failure and success.

In addition, Pinckney's Treaty cleared up the disputed boundary between American and Spanish territory in the southeastern United States. Spain and the United States agreed to accept the 31st parallel as the northern boundary of Spanish Florida. Thomas Pinckney won such popularity through this treaty that Federalist leaders nominated him as their party's candidate for Vice-President of the United States in 1796.

Thomas Pinckney was the son of Eliza Lucas Pinckney, the woman who introduced the cultivation of indigo in America.

Trouble with France   Washington's proclamation of neutrality angered French leaders. They had expected the United States to aid them in their war against Great Britain because of the old treaty of alliance. In fact, the French ambassador had made plans to have French armed ships use American harbors.

America's relations with France reached their lowest point during John Adams's term as President. French officials insulted the American ambassador. They even threatened him with arrest unless he left France. Some Federalists thought Adams should ask Congress to declare war on France because of these insults. Adams refused to do that. Instead, he sent three special ambassadors to France with instructions to try for a peaceful solution to the difficulties.

The success of Thomas Pinckney of South Carolina in negotiating a treaty with Spain won him much praise.

The XYZ affair   When the three American ambassadors got to Paris, three French officials met them. The French officials suggested that the Americans pay them a bribe before negotiations could begin. The Americans refused and sent a report to President Adams about what had happened. Adams then reported the whole affair to Congress.

In his report to Congress, President Adams refused to name the French officials who had asked for the bribe. He identified them as X, Y, and Z. For this reason, the negotiations with France became known as the **XYZ affair.** When news of it reached the American public, demands for a declaration of war against France increased.

Adams stands firm   President Adams continued to withstand pressure to declare war. Still, he realized his duty to protect the United States against a possible invasion by French forces. He called George Washington out of retirement to take command of an army of volunteers. Alexander Hamilton was named second-in-command.

Congress established a Department of the Navy headed by Benjamin Stoddert of Maryland. Stoddert served with great ability as America's first secretary of the navy. He established several navy yards in which American warships were built. Some French and American naval vessels actually fought battles between 1798 and 1800, though there was no declaration of war.

During these years, President Adams stood firm. His patience was rewarded in 1800 when Napoleon Bonaparte came to power in France. Napoleon was willing to end the undeclared naval warfare. New American diplomatic representatives sent to France were treated with courtesy.

In 1800 France and the United States cancelled the troublesome treaty of alliance of 1778. To take its place, the two countries signed a trade treaty. By showing firmness and patience, John Adams had kept the United States out of war with France. Later, John Adams spoke of this as the greatest achievement of his term as President. However, some Federalist leaders never forgave him for his refusal to go to war with France.

CHECKUP

1. Why did President Washington issue a proclamation of neutrality?
2. What did Pinckney's Treaty and Jay's Treaty provide? Why was Pinckney's Treaty more popular with Americans than Jay's Treaty?
3. What kinds of troubles disturbed relations between the United States and France in the 1790s?
4. How were peaceful solutions to these troubles worked out?

The Federalist Record

VOCABULARY

White House	census
mint	Alien and
patent	Sedition Acts

The President's house   Abigail Adams was getting ready to move during the late winter of 1801. She and her husband, John Adams, had lived in the President's house only a few months. It was the first public building in Washington,

At the time that the Adams family moved to Washington, the capital was a little river port. Final selection of the site on the Potomac River was made by George Washington.

the new capital city. The cornerstone for the President's house was laid on October 13, 1792, by George Washington. President and Mrs. Adams moved in 8 years later. More than 20 years would pass before the President's house would be called the **White House.**

Some people complained about the size and the cost—$400,000—of the President's house. Abigail Adams had other complaints. "We had no fence, yard, or other conveniences," she wrote. The house stood on the edge of a swamp. It lacked bathrooms. Water had to be carried by hand from a distance of five city blocks. Several of the rooms were unfinished. Mrs. Adams dried clothes in one of the largest unfinished rooms.

Abigail Adams may have been happy to leave the President's house. It is doubtful that her husband was. John Adams thought he had done well in his 4 years as President. Nevertheless, the electors in 1800 preferred Thomas Jefferson and Aaron Burr, the candidates of the Democratic-Republican party for President and Vice-President. A new party with new policies was about to take over the federal government.

Perhaps the Federalists deserved better treatment from the voters. Their party had done a great deal for the infant United States. Their leaders had filled in the framework provided by the Constitution. Much of what they did for the first time has lasted to the present day.

The new national capital was built on an area of land between Maryland and Virginia.

After pupils have read the section "The Alien and Sedition Acts," ask: Which amendment was said to be violated by the Sedition Act?

Coins and inventions For 16 years following the Declaration of Independence, people in the United States used British and other foreign coins. It was the Federalists who first set up a system of American coins in 1792. Philadelphia was chosen as the home for the government's first **mint**, or place where coins are made. Some of the first United States coins were made from silverware given by George Washington.

The Federalists also started the issuing of **patents** to inventors. A patent is a document that gives an inventor the sole right to his or her invention for a certain number of years. No one else can make, use, or sell the invention without the inventor's permission. The first patent issued by the new patent office went to Samuel Hopkins. In 1790 Mr. Hopkins perfected a process for using potash in the manufacture of soap. Since 1790 about 4.5 million patents have been issued through the office the Federalists established.

Federalist achievements In spite of criticisms, Presidents Washington and Adams had kept the country out of war. Moreover, they had arranged treaties that solved problems existing between the United States and foreign countries. At the same time, Alexander Hamilton's financial policies had worked wonders for the credit of the United States government. During the 1790s, the government was able to borrow money from foreign countries at favorable rates of interest.

At home, the country had achieved a decent prosperity. In 1790 the government undertook the first **census,** or count of people, in the United States. Between the first census and the second census in 1800, the United States had increased its population by 35 percent. Foreign trade had tripled during the same 10-year period. With this kind of record during the first 12 years under the Constitution, why were the Federalists turned out of office? Why was Thomas Jefferson moving to the President's house in 1801?

One answer to these questions lay with the public image of the Federalist party. Somewhat unfairly it had the reputation of being a party for the wealthy. There were wealthy people in the Federalist party, but there were also many common people. At the same time, many of the rich favored the Democratic-Republicans, the party of Thomas Jefferson, who was himself a large landowner in Virginia.

The Alien and Sedition Acts No political party can remain in power for 12 years without losing some backing. The unpopular treaty that John Jay worked out with Great Britain created opposition to the Federalists. So did their whiskey tax, and the way the government crushed the Whiskey Rebellion. By 1798 the Federalist leaders knew their power was slipping. Some of them were willing to chance a war with France if, by doing so, they could retain their control over the federal government. When it became clear that Adams wanted peace, not war, desperate Federalists pushed the **Alien and Sedition Acts** through Congress.

The Federalist leaders thought these acts would weaken the Democratic-Republican party. Three of the acts applied to aliens, that is, people not yet citizens of the country in which they live.

218

What's in a Name?

FROM THALERS TO DOLLARS

Several questions had to be settled in the early 1790s before the Philadelphia Mint could start producing United States coins. Should the new coins be based on the British system of coinage—pounds, shillings, and pence? Or should the United States use an entirely new system? If a new system were used, what should be the worth of the various coins?

At this time Holland was a friend of the United States. Dutch bankers had lent the federal government a great deal of money. When it was decided to use an entirely new system for United States coins, it was also decided to name the basic unit after a Dutch coin, the thaler. Americans knew about this Dutch coin, but they pronounced its name in a way that sounded something like "dollar." In this way the Dutch coin known as the thaler became the American dollar.

The Mint Act of 1792 provided for coins valued at $10, $5, $2.50, $1, 50¢, 25¢, 10¢, 5¢, 1¢, and ½¢. Coins worth more than $1 were made of gold. The $1 coin and others down through 5¢ were made of silver. The 1¢ and ½¢ coins were made of copper. It may seem odd to have need of a ½¢ coin, but in those days even the penny had considerable purchasing power. And fractional pricing of goods was common. For example, apples might sell for 5½¢ a half dozen.

Today our coins are still based on their relationship to the dollar. The penny, or cent, is $1/100$ of a dollar. The dime is $1/10$ of a dollar. The quarter is ¼ (a quarter) of a dollar. The 50¢ piece is ½ of a dollar. And it all goes back to the days when Treasury officials chose the Dutch thaler as the basis for the money system of the United States.

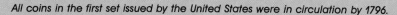

All coins in the first set issued by the United States were in circulation by 1796.

Ask: Which branch of government had the power to coin money and issue bank notes?

THE TWO POLITICAL PARTIES IN THE 1790s

	Federalist	Democratic-Republican
Political and governmental beliefs	1. The "best people" should control the government. 2. Strong national government 3. Favored loose interpretation of the Constitution 4. Restrictions on free speech and press	1. The average citizen is capable of choosing representatives to govern. 2. Limited national government, to preserve states' rights 3. Favored strict interpretation of the Constitution 4. Relatively free speech and press
Economic beliefs	1. Favored active government aid to business, finance, and commerce 2. Favored United States Bank to insure stable finances 3. Whisky tax necessary to finance governmental expenditures 4. Tariff necessary to insure revenue and protect industry	1. No special favors for business; farming preferred 2. Against Bank; thought it united national government and wealthy people against the poor 3. Rigid economy in government, to reduce taxes 4. No higher tariff than necessary to secure adequate revenue
Foreign affairs	1. Favored Great Britain because of commercial ties and because of fear of the French Revolution 2. Favored Jay's Treaty	1. Sympathized with goals of French Revolution 2. Opposed Jay's Treaty
Sources of strength	1. Strong in New England and seacoast areas 2. Very well organized 3. Supported by manufacturers, bankers, and merchants 4. Brilliant leadership under Alexander Hamilton	1. Strong in South, Southwest, and frontier areas 2. Grew better organized as average citizen became aware of issues of government 3. Supported by small farmers, tradesmen, and mechanics 4. Brilliant leadership under Thomas Jefferson

One of these three acts increased the waiting period before aliens could become citizens of the United States. Aliens now had to wait 14 years instead of 5 years before becoming naturalized citizens with the right to vote. Most naturalized citizens had been voting for Jefferson's party. This law, the Federalists thought, would slow the growth of the Democratic-Republican party and assure continued Federalist control of the government.

Naturalized citizens thought the Federalists were questioning their loyalty by passing the Alien Acts. Therefore, they supported the Democratic-Republican party more strongly than ever. Thus these acts did not have the effect that the Federalists had hoped.

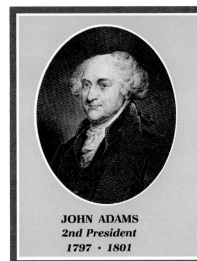

Born: 1735, Braintree (now Quincy), Massachusetts. **Education:** Harvard College. **Training:** Lawyer. **To presidency from:** Massachusetts. **Position when elected:** Vice President. **Political party:** Federalist. **Married:** Abigail Smith. **Children:** Three sons, two daughters. A son, John Quincy Adams, served as President, 1825–1829. **Died:** July 4, 1826, on the fiftieth anniversary of the Declaration of Independence, which John Adams had signed. His age was 90 years, 8 months—the longest life span of any President. **Other facts:** A short, stout man with a ruddy complexion. Never popular but highly respected. **During his presidency:** The religious fervor known as the Great Revival swept over Kentucky and Tennessee. Thousands listened to preachers.

JOHN ADAMS
2nd President
1797 · 1801

The Sedition Act was meant to silence criticism of Federalist officials. It called for the arrest and trial of anyone who spoke or published anything "false, scandalous, and malicious" about Congress or the President. Soon, 25 persons were arrested and tried for violations of the Sedition Act. All were either editors or publishers of papers opposing the Federalists. Ten were convicted, fined, and given prison sentences.

Thomas Jefferson and other Democratic-Republican leaders were quick to protest the Sedition Act. They pointed out that it clearly violated the First Amendment, which guaranteed freedom of speech and freedom of the press. After Jefferson became President, he pardoned the men convicted under the Sedition Act, and Congress returned their fines.

The election of 1800   The Federalists again nominated John Adams. However, many members of his own party refused to support him. The Democratic-Republicans once more nominated Thomas Jefferson. This time Jefferson won 73 electoral votes to 65 for Adams. The Democratic-Republican party also gained control of both the Senate and the House of Representatives.

The election of 1800 was a bloodless revolution but a revolution all the same. Jefferson and his party had attracted enough popular support to take control of the government. Moreover, the Federalists had accepted their defeat and had peacefully given up their control. Federalists continued to be elected to state offices, particularly in New England. But never again would a Federalist be chosen to live in the President's house. Never again would the Federalists have a majority in either the Senate or the House of Representatives.

CHECKUP

1. What were the contributions of the Federalist party during the 12 years it controlled the federal government?
2. What were the Alien and Sedition Acts?
3. How did the Alien and Sedition Acts contribute to the defeat of the Federalists in 1800?
4. Why might the election of 1800 be called a peaceful revolution?

KEY FACTS

1. The first Congress established a series of departments in the executive branch of the government and set up the federal court system.

2. Alexander Hamilton's financial plans put the credit of the United States on a firm and stable basis.

3. The disagreements of Alexander Hamilton and Thomas Jefferson on whether Congress could charter a national bank and on other matters resulted in the formation of the first political parties.

4. Federalists controlled the federal government for 12 years, from 1789 to 1801, making some mistakes but on the whole doing well for the country.

5. In foreign affairs the Federalists steered a careful course, avoiding war and attempting to solve disagreements by negotiations.

6. In 1800 the Federalists lost control of the federal government in what has been called a peaceful revolution.

VOCABULARY QUIZ

On a separate sheet of paper, fill each blank with the word or phrase that best completes the sentence.

1. Department heads who advised the President became known as the ___Cabinet___.

2. Alexander Hamilton strongly favored a ___loose___ interpretation of the United States Constitution.

3. The Whiskey Rebellion took place in the state of ___Pennsylvania___.

4. The Democratic-Republican party was the forerunner of today's ___Democratic___ party.

5. In the 1790s each party chose its candidates for President and Vice-President in a meeting called a ___caucus___.

6. In the 1790s, the Presidents and the Vice-Presidents were chosen by people called ___electors___.

7. At the time of a new war between France and Great Britain, President Washington issued a proclamation of ___neutrality___.

8. The XYZ affair made relations worse between the United States and ___France___.

9. An inventor has the sole right to his or her invention for a certain number of years by means of a ___patent___.

10. In 1795, Pinckney's Treaty settled the boundary between the United States and the Spanish territory of ___Florida___.

REVIEW QUESTIONS

1. Why did Congress add the first ten amendments to the Constitution?

2. What functions are performed by the President's Cabinet?

3. What were the chief differences between the Federalists and Democratic-Republicans?

4. What were the main provisions of Jay's Treaty and Pinckney's Treaty?

5. Why did Federalist leaders force the Alien and Sedition Acts through Congress?

ACTIVITIES

1. Make a chart that contrasts the good things the Federalists did with the mistakes they made.

2. Appoint two people in your class to act as Democratic-Republicans and two to act as Federalists. Have the four hold a panel discussion designed to recruit other members of the class for their party.

READING EYEWITNESS ACCOUNTS

LETTER OF ABIGAIL ADAMS

Eyewitness accounts are written by people who saw or who took part in the events they are writing about. Historical eyewitness accounts tell us a lot about events that happened long ago. These written accounts, in the form of diaries and letters, are also known as primary sources. They add color and interest to the study of history.

Some eyewitness accounts written during the eighteenth and nineteenth centuries show grammar and spellings that are different from those in use today. As you read the letter below, notice how some words are misspelled. In some cases they are errors. In others they reflect the style during that time.

In 1784 Abigail Adams sailed from the United States to join her husband, John Adams, in Europe. While on board the ship *Active*, Abigail wrote a letter to her sister Elizabeth. The following portion of that letter is an eyewitness account of Abigail's voyage.

This day 3 weeks I came on Board this Ship; and Heaven be praised, have hietherto had a favourable passage. Upon the Banks of Newfoundland we had an easterly Storm, I thought, but the Sailors say it was only a Brieze. We could not however sit without being held into our chairs, and every thing that was moveable was in motion, plates Mugs bottles all crashing to peices: the Sea roaring and lashing the Ship, and when worn down with the fatigue of the voilent, and incessant motion, we were assisted into our Cabbins; we were obliged to hold ourselves in, with our utmost Strength, without once thinking of closeing our Eyes, every thing wet, dirty and cold, ourselves Sick; you will not envy our Situation: yet the returning sone, a smooth sea and a mild Sky dispelld our fears, and raised our languid heads.

SKILLS PRACTICE

These words are misspelled in the passage above. On a sheet of paper, write the correct spelling for each word. If you do not know the correct spelling, use a dictionary.

1.	hietherto	hitherto
2.	favourable	favorable
3.	brieze	breeze
4.	peices	pieces
5.	voilent	violent
6.	cabbins	cabins
7.	closeing	closing
8.	sone	sun
9.	dispelld	dispelled

Answer the following questions about the eyewitness account. Write your answers on a sheet of paper.

1. What changes other than spelling would you make in Mrs. Adams's letter if you were to write it today?
2. How did Abigail Adams's description of the weather differ from the description of the sailors?
3. What tells you that the passengers were awake during the storm?
4. What was the weather like after the storm?

How Americans Lived, 1800

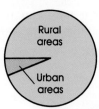
According to the census of 1800, there were 5,308,483 people in the United States of America. These Americans were spread unevenly across the land. Two thirds of them lived within 50 miles (80 km) of the Atlantic Coast. In this narrow band were all the American cities. In these cities were a few painting schools, music halls, and theaters. Much of what went on in these places was an imitation of European art, music, and drama. Moreover, there was as yet very little typically American literature.

Acting on the stage Many of the actors and actresses appearing in American theaters in 1800 had been trained in England. This was true of Elizabeth Arnold's mother, who brought her 8-year-old daughter to Boston in 1796.

When Elizabeth Arnold made her first stage appearance at the old Boston Theater, she was 9 years old. From then until her death at the age of 24 she sang, danced, and acted numerous roles in American theaters. At first, Elizabeth Arnold played young boys in Shakespeare's plays. Then she learned light comedy roles at which she was very successful. In Philadelphia in the spring of 1800 she

The first building constructed specifically to be a theater in the colonies was in Williamsburg, Virginia, in 1716. However, it was soon converted into the town hall. Other cities where playhouses came into operation in the early 1700s include Charleston, Baltimore, Philadelphia, and New York.

met Charles Hopkins. They were married in 1802, although Elizabeth was barely 15.

Charles and Elizabeth Hopkins joined a company of actors known as the Virginia Players. Not long afterward, Charles Hopkins died. Some time later the young actress married another member of the Virginia Players, David Poe.

After their marriage, Elizabeth and David Poe acted together in Richmond, Philadelphia, and New York. Then they settled down for 3 years of appearances at the Federal Street Theater in Boston. Their two sons were born in Boston. The younger, Edgar, was born in January 1809. A few months later the Poes moved to New York. At the Park Theater there, Elizabeth acted the Shakespearean roles of Ophelia in *Hamlet* and Desdemona in *Othello*.

Tragedy struck in New York. David Poe disappeared from the American stage. Perhaps he deserted his wife. Perhaps he became ill. At any rate, Elizabeth had to support two small children and possibly her husband. In the fall of 1811 she joined a theatrical company in Richmond, Virginia. Elizabeth Arnold Hopkins Poe died there the following December, possibly of pneumonia, and was buried in St. John's churchyard.

Mrs. Poe was a pleasing, versatile actress. During her short life, she enacted 201 varied roles besides numerous singing and dancing parts. Often she portrayed two or three characters in the same evening. Elizabeth Poe's troubled life did not stem from any lack of acting ability. Rather, what happened to her shows how unstable the acting profession was in the early 1800s.

Elizabeth Arnold Hopkins Poe appeared many times in stage productions at the Park Theater in New York.

John Allan, a Richmond merchant, and his wife took over the care of little Edgar Poe. As a young man, Edgar Poe took Allan as his middle name. Not even 3 years old when his mother died, he probably had no memory of her. Nor does the world remember much about Elizabeth Poe. However, the world does remember her brilliant son. Though his life was as tragic as hers, Edgar Allan Poe is remembered as one of America's greatest writers. Along with Washington Irving, James Fenimore Cooper, Nathaniel Hawthorne, and Herman Melville, Edgar Allan Poe created a distinctively American literature during the first half of the nineteenth century.

Some pupils might like to read some of Edgar Allan Poe's short stories, such as "The Tell-Tale Heart" and "The Gold Bug."

Studying law   Three members of the United States Senate came to dominate the political life of the nation in the early 1800s.   They were John C. Calhoun, of South Carolina; Daniel Webster, of Massachusetts; and Henry Clay, of Kentucky. Each of the three was a lawyer.

In those days young people preparing to be lawyers studied law differently from young people today.   Generally, they "read law" in the office of an experienced lawyer.   That is, they studied the collections of laws and other books kept in every lawyer's office.   John C. Calhoun was 18 in 1800.   The death of his father in 1796 had forced the 14-year-old boy to take on some family responsibilities. Nevertheless, he was able to go to Yale University, beginning in 1800.   After graduation he returned to South Carolina to read law in the office of a Charleston lawyer, Henry W. DeSaussure.

Daniel Webster of New Hampshire and Massachusetts

Daniel Webster was a sickly, highly emotional boy.   He had a good mind, however, and did well in his studies.   In his early teens he was shy and sensitive about his unfashionable clothes and clumsy manners.   Like Calhoun, Webster was also 18 in 1800.   But he was ahead of Calhoun in formal education, having only one more year to go before graduation from Dartmouth College, in his home state of New Hampshire.   Eventually Daniel Webster moved to Massachusetts to become a clerk in the law office of Christopher Gore.

Henry Clay was born in Hanover County, Virginia.   He was 5 years older than Calhoun and Webster.   As a boy, he was poorer than either of them.   His formal education was limited to 3 years in a backwoods school.   When he was 14, his

John C. Calhoun of South Carolina

Ask: How does one prepare to be a lawyer today as compared to the time of Calhoun, Webster, and Clay?

Ask: Why, do you suppose, is the study of law one avenue to a career in politics? Can you name politicians in our community or state who are lawyers?

family moved to Richmond, Virginia. Young Henry worked in a store and then as a clerk in one of Virginia's highest courts. He studied law in the office of the attorney general of Virginia, Robert Brooke. Within a year, Clay had learned enough law to earn his license to practice.

In 1797 Henry Clay moved to Lexington, Kentucky. At that time 220,000 people, including 40,000 slaves, lived in Kentucky. Five years earlier, Kentucky had become the first state west of the Appalachian Mountains to be admitted to the Union. By 1800 Clay had gained a fine reputation as an up-and-coming lawyer, though he was only 23 years old. Already he was in **politics**—taking part in the business of government. Calhoun and Webster became involved in politics just a few years later. Then, as today, the study of law was one avenue to a career in politics.

Henry Clay of Virginia and Kentucky

Setting up factories   Machines to spin and weave cotton fibers were developed in England before America's War for Independence. These developments were the beginning of what is known as the **Industrial Revolution**. The Industrial Revolution was the period of change brought about through the development of power-driven machines—the change from muscle power to machine power. The British government passed laws against taking these machines out of their country. If other countries got the machines, their factories would be competition for the factories in England.

However, the British government could not keep people from leaving England. A young man named Samuel Slater left England for the United States in 1789. He had studied and memorized all the details of the valuable spinning and weaving machines. In the United States, Slater settled in Rhode Island. At first he built machines for Almy and Brown, partners in a factory in Pawtucket. This was the first successful spinning mill in America. In 1798 Samuel Slater started his own company. By 1800 he had several factories making cloth.

Samuel Slater's factories employed many children who were no more than 10 years old. This seems harsh, but it was the tradition for children to work at home or on the farm. So, most people asked, why shouldn't children work in factories? When a machine was simple enough for children to operate, their parents were delighted. At first children seemed to thrive on the work.

Moreover, in Rhode Island's early factories, supervisors saw to it that the chil-

227

Slater's first mill was beside the Blackstone River in Pawtucket, Rhode Island. (42°N/71°W; map, p. 17)

dren were decently clothed and fed. Working children were read to and drilled in their ABCs as they tended the machines. As time went on, child-labor abuses crept into the factory system, and young women replaced the child workers. But in 1800 the infant textile industries of New England depended on hundreds of young workers who were hardly more than infants themselves.

A Yankee inventor   In 1800 a man whose name was already well-known was working in a Connecticut factory. He was Eli Whitney, inventor of the **cotton gin.**

After graduating from Yale in 1792, Whitney set out for Savannah, Georgia. On his way south he met Catherine Greene. She was the widow of General Nathanael Greene, a hero of the War for Independence. The job Eli Whitney expected in Savannah fell through. He gratefully accepted Mrs. Greene's invitation to live at Mulberry Grove, one of the plantations she owned.

Eli Whitney made himself useful at Mulberry Grove. He built and repaired all kinds of things for Mrs. Greene and her plantation manager. Impressed by his skill, Mrs. Greene asked him to make a machine that could strip seeds from the short-fibered cotton that was grown in

Georgia and other parts of the South. The time it took to remove the seeds by hand kept the crop from being profitable.

Eli Whitney worked in secret for 6 months to make a machine that would do what Mrs. Greene wanted. He called it a gin, short for *engine*. Though the cotton gin worked poorly at first, Mrs. Greene showed it to several neighbors. They immediately set out to build cotton gins for themselves. Later, someone stole Whitney's model from Mrs. Greene's barn.

On March 14, 1794, Whitney received a patent for an improved cotton gin. With the improved machine, one worker could clean 50 pounds (23 kg) of cotton in a day. By this time, however, it was too late for Whitney to profit because so many others were making cotton gins.

The invention of the cotton gin had a great effect on slavery. The production of cotton in the United States increased from 140,000 pounds (63,560 kg) in 1791 to 35,000,000 pounds (15,890,000 kg) in 1800. In the latter year, slaves made up almost 20 percent of the population of the United States. Yet only 10 years before, the slave-labor system had seemed to be on its way out. But the invention of the cotton gin changed that. As cotton plantations became more and more profitable, many more slaves were needed in the cotton fields, and the possibility of freedom for slaves became more and more remote.

Interchangeable parts   The invention of the cotton gin was not the only accomplishment of Eli Whitney. In 1789 he obtained a government contract to make 10,000 guns for the army in a Connecticut factory. Gunsmiths had been accustomed

Have some pupils do research on the beginnings of the Industrial Revolution in England and report their findings to the class. Have them identify the Luddites and explain the behavior of this group.

to making one gun at a time—lock, stock, and barrel—but Whitney proposed to mass-produce guns. Factory machines would make the same part of each gun exactly alike. For example, every one of 10,000 gun locks would be interchangeable with the other 9,999 gun locks. The method Whitney used is known as the system of **interchangeable parts.**

When Whitney's guns were assembled, some parts may have had to be finished by hand to make them fit. But Whitney's idea was sound and caught on. Improvements in the system were made by others.

Today we take it for granted that parts of machines are interchangeable. If a part wears out in an automobile or a washing machine, we can replace the worn-out part with a new one just like it. But before Eli Whitney set to work in his Connecticut factory, that was not so. The idea of interchangeable parts that Whitney promoted has played an important role in modern industrial development.

CHECKUP

1. What does the life of Elizabeth Poe tell us about the state of the American theater in 1800?
2. How did John C. Calhoun, Daniel Webster, and Henry Clay prepare themselves for a career in politics?
3. What factors led to the rise of textile mills in New England?
4. What were the effects of each of Eli Whitney's two accomplishments?

Eli Whitney's gun factory was in New Haven, Connecticut. (42°N/73°W; map, p. 79)

Yale University Art Gallery

2/UNIT REVIEW

READING THE TEXT

Turn to page 169 and read the section titled "The Great Compromise." Then, on a sheet of paper, write the answers to these questions.

1. What problem did the delegates to the Constitutional Convention face concerning the states and the new central government?

2. What was the Virginia Plan?

3. What was the New Jersey Plan?

4. What part did Roger Sherman play in finding a solution to the problem?

5. What were the terms that were agreed to in the Great Compromise?

READING A MAP

Turn to page 116 and look at the maps on that page. The top map shows North America in 1700 and the bottom map shows North America in 1763. In both of those years, European nations claimed most of North America. To identify the areas claimed by these countries, refer to the key in the lower left corner of each map. On a sheet of paper, answer the following questions.

1. Which country's claims are shown in green? In brown? green—Spain; brown—Britain

2. Did Britain or France claim more land in North America in 1700? France

3. Which of these two countries claimed more land in North America in 1763? Britain

4. Which European nations claimed land on the Pacific coast in 1763? Spain and Russia

5. In both years, what country claimed the most land in the southern part of North America? Spain

READING A PICTURE

Turn to page 125 and study the illustration on that page. This is a copy of an engraving made by Paul Revere. It is based on the events that took place on the evening of March 5, 1770, near the Boston Customs House. On a sheet of paper, answer these questions.

1. Who are the uniformed men lined up on the right?

2. Who are the people at the left?

3. Does the picture agree with the account you read on pages 124–125?

4. Do you think that Revere's engraving shows the events exactly as they took place? Why or why not?

5. How might a drawing made by a British witness to this event have possibly been different?

READING A TABLE

On page 123 is a table of colonial governors in 1767. This was 8 years before the outbreak of the War for Independence. On a sheet of paper, answer these questions about the colonial governments.

1. In royal colonies how was the governor chosen? Appointed by king

2. How many royal colonies were there? 9

3. Why were there only 12 governors in the 13 colonies? Del. and Pa. had same governor

4. In which colonies was the governor chosen by a proprietor? Pa. and Del.

5. In which colonies was the governor elected by the voters? Conn. and R.I.

The Nation Grows Bigger and Stronger

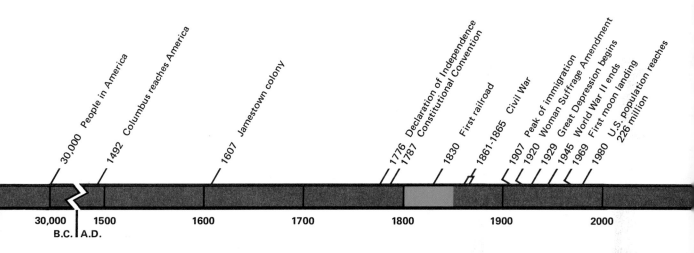

30,000 People in America

1492 Columbus reaches America

1607 Jamestown colony

1776 Declaration of Independence
1787 Constitutional Convention

1830 First railroad

1861-1865 Civil War

1907 Peak of immigration
1920 Woman Suffrage Amendment
1929 Great Depression begins
1945 World War II ends
1969 First moon landing
1980 U.S. population reaches 226 million

30,000 B.C. | A.D. 1500 | 1600 | 1700 | 1800 | 1900 | 2000

Above: Andrew Jackson, frontiersman, woman suffragists, covered wagon heading west

CHAPTER
10 The Frontier Moves West

Across the Appalachians

VOCABULARY

Wilderness Trail	salt lick
Fallen Timbers	flatboat
Treaty of Greenville	

Shooting Star   Warfare with invading whites was a family tradition with Tecumseh (tə kum′ sə), chief of the Shawnee (shô nē′) tribe. His father, also a chief, had died fighting frontiersmen in 1774 when Tecumseh was a boy of 6. Two older brothers later fell in battles with soldiers sent to open up western lands for settlement.

Tecumseh, whose name may be translated as Shooting Star, wanted to organize a great Indian alliance. He traveled through the western lands, urging Indians to unite. He and his one surviving brother helped a group of more than 1,000 Indians settle on the Wabash (wô′ bash) River in what is today the state of Indiana. Tecumseh argued that the white man's government had no right to buy land from a single tribe. The western lands belonged to all the tribes together, Tecumseh said. Indians and non-Indians alike felt the force of his personality. One white observer who heard him speak to an Indian gathering reported that Tecumseh "hurled out his words like thunderbolts."

The tide of settlement   Tecumseh and his brother had reason to fear the advancing tide of white settlement. In 1774 the first permanent settlement west of the Appalachians was made at Harrodsburg in the region called Kentucky. The next year Daniel Boone blazed the **Wilderness Trail** through Cumberland Gap. Thousands followed it into Kentucky. Thousands more came by way of the Ohio River.

In 1792, Virginia gave up its claim to that region, and Kentucky became the fifteenth state. Tennessee gained statehood in 1796. By 1800 more than 225,000 people lived in Kentucky and Tennessee, the first states to be formed west of the Appalachians. No state had yet been carved out of the Northwest Territory, but more than 50,000 people had settled there. Most of them were in Ohio, which would be admitted as a state in 1803.

The Treaty of Greenville   In 1794 General Anthony Wayne led an army into the Northwest Territory. At a place called **Fallen Timbers** in northwestern Ohio, Wayne's army defeated the Indians. Unable to resist any longer, the chiefs of 12 tribes signed the **Treaty of Greenville** a year later.

The Treaty of Greenville set up a boundary between Indian lands and the

Daniel Boone leads a party of pioneers through Cumberland Gap. (37°N/84°W; map, p. 238)

Depending on the point of view, Tecumseh can be seen as a great champion of his people or a bloodthirsty killer of brave pioneers. Pupils may form small teams to research Tecumseh's life and debate whether he was a hero or a villain.

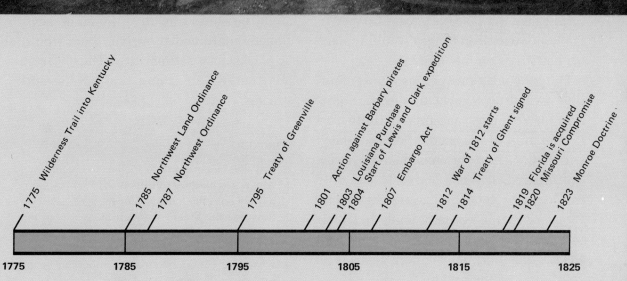

1775 Wilderness Trail into Kentucky

1785 Northwest Land Ordinance

1787 Northwest Ordinance

1795 Treaty of Greenville

1801 Action against Barbary pirates

1803 Louisiana Purchase

1804 Start of Lewis and Clark expedition

1807 Embargo Act

1812 War of 1812 starts

1814 Treaty of Ghent signed

1819 Florida is acquired

1820 Missouri Compromise

1823 Monroe Doctrine

1775   1785   1795   1805   1815   1825

It took a group of settlers working together about 4 days to erect a family's cabin. After the walls were finished, spaces were cut out for the door and chimney. Open cracks between the logs were filled in with mud or clay. Nevertheless, in rainy weather, the cabin roof generally leaked.

land on which newcomers could settle. By doing so, it encouraged settlement in Ohio. For years the treaty kept Indians and settlers apart and at peace. In time, though, the treaty was broken by settlers who invaded the Indian lands. This process occurred again and again as the settlers pushed their frontiers westward.

Frontier life   A pioneer family's first task was to clear the land. Food for the winter depended on getting a crop raised before the first frost. With axes and scythes, husband, wife, and older children cut trees and brush. Then, in ground slashed with a shovel or axe, they planted corn and a few vegetables. Sometimes a crude plow made the task easier.

A family's first shelter was probably a rough cabin, good enough to get them through the winter. During the next year they would improve their living quarters. Friends and neighbors might help in putting up a sturdier building. As time passed, more rooms would be added and other improvements made. Glass would take the place of greased paper in the windows. Iron hinges would replace leather straps on the doors.

Only the more prosperous pioneer families owned pigs, cows, or sheep. Squirrels, turkeys, deer, and other wildlife furnished most of the meat. Berries, honey, and maple syrup sweetened an otherwise dull diet. Salt was a necessity, not only to flavor the food but as a preservative. Pioneers in the western lands got their salt from natural springs or from **salt licks**. Salt licks are natural deposits of salt found on the ground.

Rivers and streams   Many pioneers in the lands west of the Appalachians had traveled at least part of the way by water to reach their new homes. Generally river travel was easier than travel by land since there were few roads west of the mountains. The western pioneers also used the rivers to get their surplus farm crops to market. They built **flatboats** and loaded them with grain and livestock. Then they set out on the long voyage down the Ohio and Mississippi rivers to New Orleans.

In New Orleans, merchants bought the farm products and the flatboats. The boats were broken up for lumber. Farm products and lumber might be shipped to the West Indies or Europe. Meanwhile, those who had ridden down river on the flatboats started on the long walk back to their homes. After the following year's harvest, many of them would again be making the long voyage by flatboat.

Rivers and streams were also sources of waterpower. The current of a stream could run a sawmill or a mill to grind grain. A store and blacksmith shop might be started nearby. Soon, as newcomers continued to arrive, there would be a sizeable settlement. Thus, towns often grew up along the rivers and streams.

CHECKUP

1. Why did Tecumseh want Indians to organize?
2. Why was it hard for Indians to stop settlers from moving onto the Indians' lands?
3. How was the Treaty of Greenville typical of the agreements signed by the American government and Indian tribes?
4. Why were rivers and streams important in the settlement of the western lands?

After they have read the section "Rivers and streams," have pupils name the functions of these waterways and then sketch or diagram the functions or choose one of the functions as the subject of a more detailed sketch.

Jefferson Buys Louisiana

---VOCABULARY---

cede

Louisiana
    Purchase

Lewis and Clark
    Expedition

Old Northwest

Old Southwest

Adams-Onís
    Treaty

A great bargain President Thomas Jefferson was much disturbed by rumors that reached the United States soon after he became President. It seemed that Napoleon Bonaparte, the French dictator, was interested in building a colonial empire in America to replace the one that France had lost in 1763. At that time, you will recall, France lost Canada to Great Britain and **ceded**, or gave up, Louisiana to Spain.

In 1801 it became known that Spain had secretly agreed to return Louisiana to France. The area then known as Louisiana stretched from the Mississippi River to the Rocky Mountains. It included the port of New Orleans. Pinckney's Treaty with Spain had given Americans the valuable right to ship goods through New Orleans. But would Napoleon honor that treaty? Or would he "put a cork in the bottle" and close the outlet to world trade that was of such importance for the western settlements?

To keep New Orleans open to American goods, Jefferson offered to buy the port. He instructed our representatives in France to offer Napoleon up to $10 million in payment for New Orleans. Much to Jefferson's amazement, the American representatives reported that Napoleon

Flatboats, like this one on the Ohio River, carried settlers west with their belongings.

Have pupils use the map below to answer the following questions: From what town did the Lewis and Clark Expedition start? (St. Louis) What is its latitude and longitude? (39°N/90°W) What important city near the mouth of the Mississippi was gained by the Louisiana Purchase? (New Orleans)

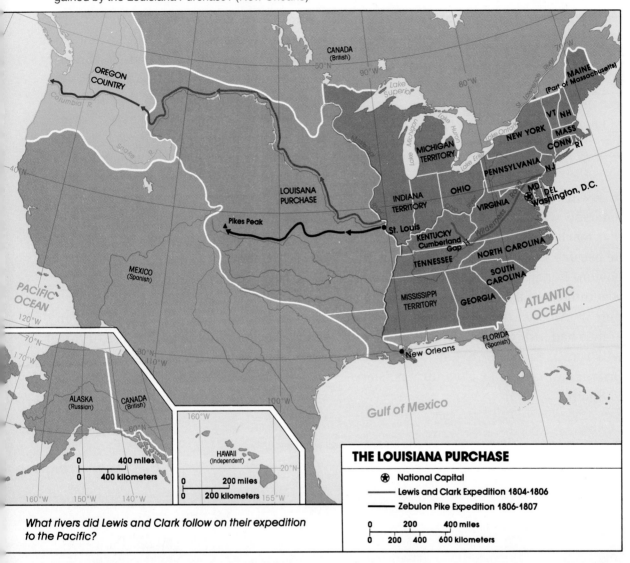

What rivers did Lewis and Clark follow on their expedition to the Pacific?

THE LOUISIANA PURCHASE

⊛ National Capital
⎯ Lewis and Clark Expedition 1804-1806
▬ Zebulon Pike Expedition 1806-1807

0   200   400 miles
0 200 400 600 kilometers

was willing to sell *all* of Louisiana for $15 million. Napoleon needed money for new wars in Europe and had given up plans to regain France's empire in North America.

The Constitution did not specifically give the President the power to buy land, but after much thought Jefferson decided to accept Napoleon's offer. The Senate approved. Thus, in 1803 the United States was doubled in size by the **Louisiana Purchase** at a cost of about three cents an acre.

The Lewis and Clark Expedition
Thomas Jefferson wanted to know more about the land acquired in the Louisiana Purchase. He was curious, too, about the land west of the Rocky Mountains, even though the United States had little claim to it. He decided to send an expedition to explore the entire region.

As commander of the expedition, Jefferson named Captain Meriwether Lewis of the United States Army. Lewis was an experienced explorer, but at the time was serving in Washington as Jefferson's private secretary. Lewis asked William Clark, the younger brother of George Rogers Clark, to share the leadership.

The **Lewis and Clark Expedition** consisted of 23 soldiers, 3 interpreters, and Clark's slave whose name was York. In the spring of 1804 the group left from the small fur-trading town of St. Louis. The expedition traveled in boats up the Missouri River. By autumn they reached Indian villages near the site of present-day Bismarck, North Dakota. After wintering with the friendly Mandan Indians, the expedition moved west toward the Rocky Mountains in the early spring of 1805.

The role of Sacagawea Living among the Mandans were a French-Canadian fur trader, Toussaint Charbonneau (tü san′ shär bô nō′), and his young Indian wife Sacagawea (sak ə je wē′ ə). When the expedition left Mandan country, Charbonneau went along as an interpreter and was accompanied by Sacagawea, carrying their newborn baby on her back. One reason why Sacagawea went along was probably her longing to see her own Shoshone (shō shō′ nē) people. Crow Indians had stolen Sacagawea from her Rocky Mountain home 5 years earlier, when she was about 12 years old. They had sold her to the Mandans, who, in turn had sold her to Toussaint Charbonneau.

Sacagawea has inspired many legends. It seems, however, that she served

Sacagawea, standing by Captain Lewis, converses in sign language with a party of Indians.

the expedition mainly as a peacemaker. Clark wrote of her, "Sacagawea reconciles all the Indians as to our friendly intentions—a woman with a party of men is a token of peace." When the expedition met up with a band of Shoshones, Sacagawea danced with joy. Soon she was reunited with her brother, who had become chief of the tribe.

Once through the mountains, the expedition built canoes and followed the Columbia River to the Pacific Ocean. The group spent the winter on the Pacific coast before heading back east. Charbonneau and Sacagawea returned to the Mandan village from which they had started. The rest of the expedition reached St. Louis on September 23, 1806. The whole country rejoiced, for the group had long been given up for lost. With the expedition ended, Clark wrote to Charbonneau that the "woman who accompanied you that long, dangerous, and fatiguing route to the Pacific Ocean and back deserved a greater reward for her attention and services than we had in our power to give her."

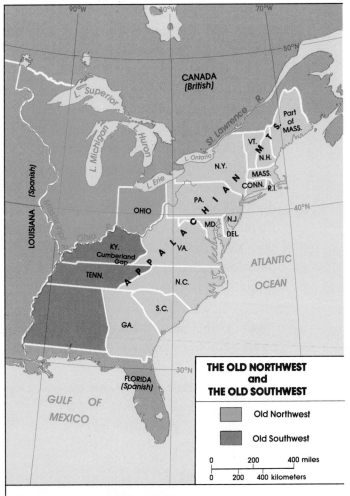

Why did the word *Old* come into use in describing the Northwest and Southwest?

Americans learn about the West   The journals of Lewis and Clark, published in 1814, created a growing fascination with the little-known lands along and beyond the Missouri River. Other adventurous Americans began to push into the Far West.

Major Zebulon Pike was an army officer who spent part of his career as an explorer. In a book published in 1810, he told of his journeys. On one expedition, he had explored the upper reaches of the Mississippi River. A second expedition had taken him into Colorado and New Mexico. A snowcapped mountain peak that he had observed in Colorado is today called Pikes Peak.

Americans added to their geographical knowledge by reading books or reports written by Pike and others. What they learned changed their way of speaking about different parts of their country. With the purchase of Louisiana from France, the Northwest Territory was no longer in the northwest corner of the United States. It was now called the **Old**

Northwest. Similarly, after the Louisiana Purchase, the area south of the Ohio River between the Appalachians and the Mississippi became the **Old Southwest.**

Some differences There were historic differences between the Old Northwest and the Old Southwest. Lands in the Old Northwest were surveyed and sold in accordance with an ordinance passed by the Confederation Congress in 1785. Surveyors divided the land in the Old Northwest into square townships, 6 miles (11 km) on each side. Within each township, surveyors marked off 36 sections. Each section was a square, 1 mile (1.6 km) on each side, and contained 640 acres (256 ha). Surveyors could later divide the sections into halves, quarters, or even smaller areas if necessary. Land marked off in this orderly way could be sold without disputes over boundaries.

In the Old Southwest there was no such orderly land policy. Boundary lines were irregular. A boundary might run from a large rock to a tall tree to a bend in a river to other points that were plainly visible. However, these landmarks disappeared or changed as time passed. This caused many arguments among southern neighbors concerning the boundaries of their properties.

The status of slavery marked another important difference between the Old Northwest and the Old Southwest. The Northwest Ordinance of 1787 barred slavery from that territory. Thus slavery was illegal in the states carved out of the Old Northwest: Ohio, Indiana, Illinois, Michigan, and Wisconsin. No such ordinance applied to the Old Southwest. Four states entirely east of the Mississippi were made from that region: Kentucky, Tennessee, Mississippi, and Alabama. In all of those states, slavery was legal.

Fixing the boundaries In the early 1800s Florida was owned by Spain. The boundary between the United States and Florida remained in doubt following the Louisiana Purchase. At that time, Florida was larger than the state of that name today. The simplest way to settle the

LAND SURVEY IN THE NORTHEAST TERRITORY

The system of survey devised for the Northwest Territory is used in most states west of the Appalachians. With this system any piece of land can be immediately identified. The 6-mile-square townships do not always conform with political townships.

In 1819, Spain also agreed to give up its claims to territory in the Pacific Northwest.

boundary question seemed to be for the United States to acquire all of Florida. This happened in three bites.

The first bite took place in 1810, and the second bite, in 1813. Then, in 1819, the **Adams-Onís Treaty** gave the United States the rest of Florida in return for a $5 million payment to Spain. Another part of the Adams-Onís Treaty fixed the boundary between the United States and Spanish territory in the New Southwest.

In the North, the boundary of the Louisiana Purchase was worked out between Great Britain (which owned Canada) and the United States in 1818. The boundary ran along the 49th parallel from the Lake of the Woods to the crest of the Rocky Mountains.

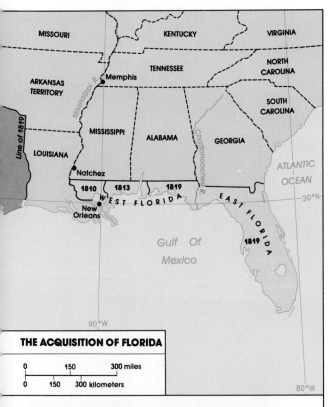

THE ACQUISITION OF FLORIDA

0   150   300 miles
0   150   300 kilometers

By acquiring Florida, the United States extended its southeastern boundary.

CHECKUP

1. How did Jefferson's offer to buy New Orleans result in the purchase by the United States of the entire Louisiana territory?
2. What parts of the Louisiana Purchase were explored by the Lewis and Clark Expedition?
3. How did Sacagawea help the expedition?
4. What were two important differences between the Old Northwest and the Old Southwest?
5. How and where were the boundaries of the Louisiana Purchase and Florida fixed?

The War of 1812

Mediterranean pirates   After the Revolution, American merchants sought new areas for trade. One of these areas was the region bordering on the Mediterranean Sea.

In the Mediterranean Sea, pirate ships became threats to merchant vessels from northern Europe and the United States. The pirate raiders came from harbors along the **Barbary Coast** of North Africa. The Barbary Coast included the shores of independent states called Morocco (mə rok' ō), Algeria (al jir' ē ə), Tunis (tü' nis), and Tripoli (trip' ə lē). To keep their ships from being captured, European governments had been forced to make payments to the Barbary Coast rulers. The United States had also made such payments until Jefferson became President.

In 1801 the ruler of Tripoli became dissatisfied with the amount of money the

Ask: What natural boundary divided East Florida and West Florida? (Chattahoochee River) At what line of longitude? (85°W)

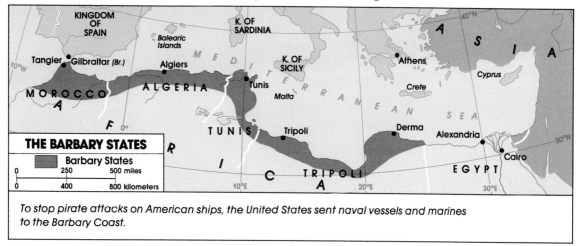

THE BARBARY STATES

Barbary States

0   250   500 miles
0   400   800 kilometers

To stop pirate attacks on American ships, the United States sent naval vessels and marines to the Barbary Coast.

United States had been paying. So he declared war. Jefferson sent a naval squadron and some marines into the Mediterranean. Finally, in 1805, this show of force caused Tripoli to make peace with the United States. Tripoli's ruler promised that pirates would stop interfering with American merchant ships.

Thomas Jefferson disliked war and the use of force. Still, he knew how important it was for American ships to sail the world's oceans and seas freely. Any interference with shipping would be harmful to America's overseas trade. Poor transportation made it hard to trade by land within the boundaries of the United States. Moreover, the United States at that time had few factories to manufacture necessary items. For these two reasons, foreign trade was vital to the prosperity of our country.

The rights of a neutral   In 1803 war broke out once more between France and Great Britain. President Jefferson declared America's neutrality as President Washington had done in 1793 when the same two countries had fought each other. Jefferson also asserted our **neutral rights.** He claimed that the United States, as a neutral country, had the right to trade with both France and Great Britain. Each of these countries disputed that claim, and each tried to keep American products from reaching the other.

French privateers seized or sank American merchant ships heading for England. British warships seized or sank American ships bound for France. In addition, the British began the practice of impressment. This meant they would seize a few sailors from ships they stopped or captured, claiming these sailors were deserters from the British navy. They would then impress these men into service for the British. In June 1807 the *Leopard,* a British warship, attacked the American naval vessel *Chesapeake* near the entrance to Chesapeake Bay. After a bloody battle British marines boarded the *Chesapeake* and impressed four sailors. News of this encounter shocked and angered the American people. Some demanded that the United States go to war against Great Britain.

Actually, both Great Britain and France were interfering with our neutral rights. Jefferson had no wish to fight either of

During the Barbary War, the commander of the American ship Intrepid *had it blown up in the harbor of Tripoli rather than let it fall into pirate hands. (33°N/13°E; map, p. 241)*

them and certainly not both. Instead, he decided to defend American rights by putting economic pressure on the two warring countries. This was done by a law that Jefferson got Congress to pass in December, 1807. It was called the **Embargo Act.**

The Embargo Act   An embargo is the act of a government to limit or stop trade with other countries. The new law said that American ships would not be allowed to sail to other countries. The law also said that foreign ships could not carry American goods to other countries. Jefferson thought that this law would make British and French leaders realize the importance of American trade. He hoped that the law would cause the leaders to change their attitudes. But, for the most part, the embargo failed. British

farmers raised ample supplies of food the next summer, making it unnecessary to rely on American corn or wheat. France proved able to get along well without American trade.

As the result of the Embargo Act, idle ships clogged American harbors. About 150,000 sailors, clerks, and dockworkers lost their jobs. Tons of cotton, tobacco, and grain piled up in seaport warehouses. Clearly, Jefferson's Embargo Act was hurting the United States more than it hurt Great Britain and France.

The embargo hit New England merchants and sea captains especially hard. Opponents in that region turned the word *embargo* around, calling Jefferson's policy "The O-grab-me Act." Federalist leaders in New England threatened to take their states out of the Union unless the hated law was repealed.

Tell pupils that Jefferson once wrote, "Peace is our passion." Ask them how the Embargo Act was appropriate to this philosophy. (It was an effort to apply economic rather than military pressure to achieve a purpose.) Ask: Why wasn't the Embargo Act successful?

Thomas Jefferson was one of the greatest statesmen and most brilliant leaders this country has ever had. Several pupils might be interested in writing a report on some facet of his career to be presented to the class.

THOMAS JEFFERSON
3rd President
1801 · 1809

Born: 1743, Albemarle County, Virginia. **Education:** College of William and Mary. **Training:** Lawyer, plantation owner, public official. **To presidency from:** Virginia. **Position when elected:** Vice President. **Political party:** Democratic-Republican. **Married:** Martha Wayles Skelton. **Children:** Five daughters, one son. **Died:** July 4, 1826, the same day that John Adams died. **Other facts:** Called "Long Tom" by some because of his height. A man of many interests. Played the violin, experimented in raising crops and flowers, and designed his lovely home, Monticello. **During his presidency:** In 1807, Robert Fulton's *Clermont*, the first commercially successful steamboat, went up the Hudson River from New York to Albany in 32 hours.

Madison becomes President   In 1809 Thomas Jefferson left the White House after serving two terms as President. He was succeeded by James Madison, who, like Jefferson, was a Virginian and a leader in the Democratic-Republican party. It seemed likely that Madison would carry out Jefferson's embargo policy and other peaceful means of protecting our neutral rights.

Three days before Jefferson left office, however, Congress repealed the Embargo Act. In its place, Congress passed a law permitting trade with any country except Great Britain and France. A year later Congress tried another plan. This plan allowed trade for one year with France and Great Britain. In addition, it provided that if either of them stopped interfering with our merchant ships, we would stop all trade with the other. But these plans did not work. Both Britain and France continued to harass American shipping.

"On to Canada!"   Impatient Americans were plainly unhappy with economic weapons. The elections in 1810 brought a number of eager young Democratic-Republicans from southern and western states into the House of Representatives. They won control of that body of Congress and chose Henry Clay of Kentucky as the Speaker of the House. Brilliant, intense John C. Calhoun of South Carolina was also one of the **War Hawks** as these hotheaded young men from the South and West came to be called.

The War Hawks were more than ready for a war with Great Britain. Their battle cry became "On to Canada!" That British colony looked defenseless now that Great Britain was involved in a great war with France. By declaring war on Great Britain and then invading Canada, the War Hawks believed the United States could add more territory into which American settlers could expand. In addition, an invasion of Canada might destroy bases from which Indians had been raiding frontier settlements throughout the Northwest Territory.

Still, the War Hawks were something more than land grabbers. Proud and patriotic, they resented the way in which Great Britain had violated the neutral

The War of 1812 has sometimes been called a needless war. Ask pupils to try to discover why this might have been true. (Two days before Congress declared war, Britain had decided to stop seizing American ships. The news of this change of policy arrived in America too late to stop the war.)

rights of the United States and had impressed American sailors. Urged on by the War Hawks' demands, President James Madison asked Congress in 1812 to declare war on Great Britain.

A poor beginning   Americans call this the War of 1812 because it began in that year. Canadians call it the War for Defense, however, because it began with American invasions across the Canadian border. In 1812 there were 8 million Americans and only 500,000 Canadians. Conquering Canada appeared to be an easy matter, especially since there were but a small number of British troops stationed there.

However, Americans soon found that their own troops had been hastily organized and were improperly trained, poorly supplied, and badly commanded. Consequently, three American attempts to invade Canada failed. The map below shows the battle sites of the war.

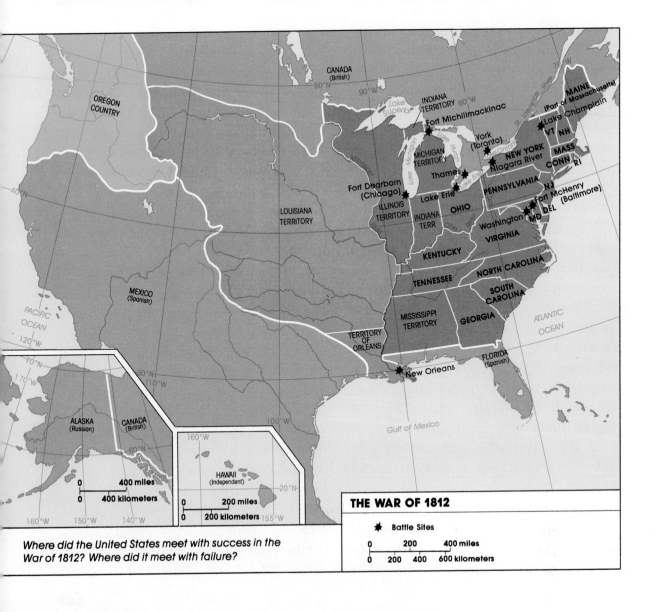

Where did the United States meet with success in the War of 1812? Where did it meet with failure?

THE WAR OF 1812

★ Battle Sites

0   200   400 miles
0   200   400   600 kilometers

The crews of Captain Perry's Lake Erie warships were made up of militiamen and northern blacks.

Naval victories   At the beginning of the War of 1812 the American navy had fewer than 20 ships. The British navy had more than 800. Even though many of these were busy against the French, Americans could not challenge mighty Britain in a sea battle between fleets. Still, in contests between single war ships, Americans won several victories. The most famous of these took place early in the war. It involved the American war vessel *Constitution* against the British *Guerrière*. Captain Isaac Hull commanded the *Constitution*. In a fierce sea battle Captain Hull and his crew left the *Guerrière* a burning wreck. In this encounter, the *Constitution* earned the nickname *Old Ironsides* because cannonballs seemed to bounce off its thick, oaken sides.

On Lake Erie, energetic Oliver H. Perry directed the building of some American warships. With these he defeated and captured a small British fleet. Now that Americans controlled the lake, the British and Canadians with their Indian allies could no longer hold Detroit. They retreated into Canada, followed by an army led by William Henry Harrison.

The death of Tecumseh   William Henry Harrison was the son of Benjamin Harrison, who was a signer of the Declaration of Independence and later the governor of Virginia. After joining the army, William Henry Harrison served in the Northwest Territory. By the Treaty of Fort Wayne in 1809, Harrison had obtained about 2½ million acres (1 million ha) of Indian land along the Wabash River. There in 1811 Harrison, who had

Tecumseh, the chief of the Shawnees, tried in vain to stem the tide of settlers moving westward.

become governor of Indiana Territory, had his first encounter with Tecumseh.

Tecumseh warned Harrison he would oppose occupation of the Indian lands. The Indian chief directed about 1,000 Indians to place themselves in a camp near the point where Tippecanoe Creek flowed into the Wabash. Harrison sent 900 American soldiers to Tippecanoe, where they then camped near the Indian settlement. In the spring of 1811 Tecumseh left for the south, attempting to persuade Creeks, Choctaws, and Chickasaws to join his alliance.

While Tecumseh was gone, his brother Tenskwatawa ordered the Indians to attack the Americans, thus touching off the battle of Tippecanoe. At its end, the Indians were defeated and were scattered. They had believed Tenskwatawa's claim that white men's bullets could not hurt them. Tecumseh returned to find his alliance shattered, his hopes all but destroyed. He went to Canada as the War of 1812 was beginning. The British greatly respected Tecumseh. They made him a brigadier general. As a British officer, Tecumseh led white soldiers and Indians in four major battles against the Americans.

Meanwhile, William Henry Harrison had become a general in the American army. Perry's victory on Lake Erie made it possible for Harrison's army to reach Canada by water. On October 5, 1813, his force of about 4,500 soldiers met the British and Indians in battle. On the north bank of the Thames River, Americans won a great victory. Tecumseh was killed in the battle. Perhaps the great Indian leader had felt the approach of death. Before the battle he had taken off his army uniform and dressed himself in his traditional Indian buckskins.

British invasions By 1814 the British had defeated Napoleon and his armies in Europe. This made it possible to send thousands of veteran British soldiers and sailors to fight against the United States. As a result, Americans in 1814 had to face invasions of American soil.

One invading army moved south from Montreal into the state of New York. Instead of marching through the forests, it tried to use the Lake Champlain water route. Near Plattsburg a hastily constructed American fleet commanded by Captain Thomas Macdonough met the British. After a desperate battle, the small American fleet turned the British back. In this way, New York was saved.

The burning of Washington A more successful British invasion took place in the Chesapeake Bay area. At Bladensburg, Maryland, British marines defeated American militiamen. On August 24, 1814, a British force of about 5,000 marched into Washington. President Madison and other government officials fled to the hills surrounding the city. The British set fire to the Capitol, where Congress met. They burned the President's House and nearly every other government building in Washington. Before leaving the President's House, Dolley Madison, the President's wife, hurriedly grabbed everything of worth she could, including a valuable portrait of George Washington.

Our national anthem After leaving Washington, the British marines boarded warships that sailed up Chesapeake Bay to Baltimore. There the guns of the British fleet bombarded Fort McHenry. Had the fort been captured or had it surrendered, Baltimore might have suffered the same fate as Washington. British cannon thundered throughout the day and night of September 13, 1814. On the morning of September 14, a man watching anxiously saw that "our flag was still there." He was Francis Scott Key, a prisoner on board one of the attacking ships.

Inspired by the American defense of Fort McHenry, Key promptly wrote the words to "The Star Spangled Banner." It was published as a poem, and later that year it was sung to the music of an old English tune. It took more than 100 years, however, before "The Star-Spangled Banner" was officially adopted as our **national anthem.**

At dawn Francis Scott Key observes the American flag still waving over Fort McHenry. (39°N/77°W; map, p. 244)

The battle of New Orleans A third British invasion in 1814 threatened the American ports on the Gulf of Mexico and the entire Mississippi River Valley. General Andrew Jackson of Tennessee commanded the American forces in the South. He had gained a reputation as an Indian fighter. When Jackson learned of the British plan to attack New Orleans, he hurried to the city's defense.

The defenders of New Orleans were a mixed group. They included regular army troops, militiamen from Kentucky and Tennessee, free blacks, and Choctaw Indians. For a time Jackson refused the help of Jean Laffite (zhän la fēt'), the leader of pirates who had preyed on merchant ships sailing in the Gulf of Mexico. But Laffite persuaded Jackson that the pirate cannons and cannoneers would be of great help against the British—and they were.

The decisive battle of New Orleans took place on January 8, 1815. Jackson's colorful army won an overwhelming victory. Americans rejoiced when they heard of it. Only later did they learn that the peace treaty ending the War of 1812 had been signed in Europe 2 weeks before the battle. No one in the United States knew it at the time because of the slowness of communications.

Peace without victory Negotiations to end the war had begun when American and British representatives met in Ghent (gent), Belgium, in August 1814. They signed the **Treaty of Ghent** in December of that year, although it was February 1815 before the news reached the United States. The treaty said nothing about American grievances, and no territory changed hands. The country forgot that the War Hawks had shouted "On to Canada!" at the beginning of the war. Even though the United States failed to gain territory, neither had it lost any. In spite of these inconclusive results, the Treaty of Ghent was so popular that the Senate approved it without a dissenting vote.

The truth was, the War of 1812 never had the support of the whole country at any one time. Blunders during the invasion attempts, failures in supplying the armies, and incompetent leaders had brought on storms of criticism. Opposition to the war was particularly strong in

Two heroes of the War of 1812, Andrew Jackson and William Henry Harrison, later became President. Ask pupils to find the names of other Presidents who were war heroes. (Among others, Zachary Taylor, Ulysses S. Grant, Theodore Roosevelt, Dwight Eisenhower, John F. Kennedy)

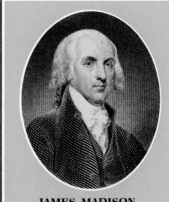

Born: 1751, Port Conway, Virginia. **Education:** College of New Jersey (now Princeton University). **Training:** Lawyer, public official. **To presidency from:** Virginia. **Position when elected:** Secretary of State. **Political party:** Democratic-Republican. **Married:** Dolley Payne Todd. **Children:** None, though his wife had one child from an earlier marriage. **Died:** 1836, the last surviving signer of the Constitution. **Other facts:** The smallest President, standing 5 feet 4 inches (1.6 m) tall and weighing about 100 pounds (45 kg). Often called "Father of the Constitution." **During his presidency:** Work began, in 1811, on building the National Road, leading west from Cumberland, Maryland. It was the chief road into the region west of the Appalachians.

JAMES MADISON
4th President
1809 · 1817

New England. Federalist leaders there declared that their section was suffering because of the war. They called it "Mr. Madison's War," indicating they wanted nothing to do with it.

Discontent in New England brought about a meeting of Federalist leaders at Hartford, Connecticut, in December 1814. At the meeting were 26 top leaders from five New England states. Some of the men at the **Hartford Convention** talked of having their states leave the Union. However, calmer views won out. The protests were soon forgotten with the joyful news that the war was over.

The war's results In spite of its indecisive ending, the War of 1812 had some important results. For one, the opposition of the Federalists to the war had made them seem unpatriotic. This badly weakened their political party. Their loss of strength was seen in the voting for President in 1816. James Monroe, the candidate of the Democratic-Republicans, received 183 electoral votes. Rufus King, his Federalist opponent, got only 34.

Moreover, the War of 1812 convinced Great Britain and other European countries that the United States could defend itself from outside attack. Europeans had a greater respect for and interest in the United States after the war ended. Among Americans the war created an increasing spirit of **nationalism**, or loyalty to their country as opposed to a single state or region. The power of the Indians in the Northwest Territory had been broken, and more settlers now moved into the region. Finally, the war made popular heroes of Andrew Jackson and William Henry Harrison. Later both of these men who had led troops in battle became Presidents of the United States.

CHECKUP

1. Why was foreign trade vital to the United States in the early nineteenth century?
2. How did Presidents Jefferson and Madison try to defend the neutral rights of the United States?
3. Who were the War Hawks? Why did they want to go to war against Great Britain?
4. Why can it be said that the Treaty of Ghent was a peace without victory?
5. What were the most important results of the War of 1812?

Have pupils review the results of the War of 1812. Point out that it was our least expensive war in terms of lives lost (2,260) and second least expensive in cost ($90 million). Ask: Did the results of the war justify these costs? Why or why not?

The Virginia Dynasty

An Era of Good Feeling James Monroe was the last of three Presidents who, as a group, have been called the **Virginia Dynasty.** A dynasty is a family or group that maintains power for a long period of time. Thomas Jefferson, James Madison, and James Monroe were not of the same family. But they were members of a group of great Virginians who headed the United States government during the first quarter of the nineteenth century.

You have read how James Monroe defeated Rufus King, the Federalist candidate for the presidency in 1816. In 1820 Monroe won a second term. The years during which he was President have been called the **Era of Good Feeling.** It appeared to be a period of calm in national politics. Democratic-Republicans had little opposition in national government. The Federalists' strength was mainly confined to New England. Soon the Federalist party would disappear completely.

The Burr-Hamilton duel Alexander Hamilton was the guiding light of the Federalist party in its early years. Had he lived, the Federalists might have challenged the Virginia Dynasty. Indeed, Hamilton himself might have been elected President. But Alexander Hamilton was killed in a duel with Aaron Burr at Weehawken, New Jersey, in July 1804.

The duel came as the result of a long series of private and public disputes between Hamilton and Burr. Finally Burr challenged Hamilton to a duel with pistols. Hamilton tried to avoid the duel, but Burr persisted. Each man fired one shot during the duel, with Burr's bullet plowing its way into Hamilton's stomach. Hamilton died the next day.

Burr's shot killed Hamilton, but it also wrecked Burr's political career. At the time he was Vice-President under President Thomas Jefferson. After the duel, Democratic-Republicans refused to nominate Aaron Burr for a second term as Vice-President.

Hamiltonian policies are adopted Though Alexander Hamilton died in 1804, his influence lived on. This came about because the Democratic-Republicans adopted some of the policies Hamilton had favored. Hamilton favored a Bank of the United States, and, as you will recall, the bank was chartered in 1791 for a period of 20 years. When its charter ran

On July 11, 1804, Alexander Hamilton was mortally wounded in a duel with Aaron Burr.

In 1806, Burr was arrested for treason. He was tried and freed. Pupils might try to find the story behind his arrest.

out, the Democratic-Republicans chartered a second Bank of the United States with powers similar to the first one.

As Secretary of the Treasury in the 1790s, Hamilton had urged that the United States adopt a tariff on imported goods. This would allow the government to collect a fee on all imports. Congress had passed tariff laws from the 1790s onward. However, until 1816, these were chiefly for **revenue**—that is, for money to pay the expenses of government. During the years of Jefferson's embargo and during the War of 1812, manufacturing increased in the northeastern United States. After the war, a flood of low-priced British manufactured goods threatened to destroy these budding industries by taking over their markets. To prevent this, Congress in 1816 approved a **protective tariff**, a policy that Hamilton had urged years before. The protective tariff raised duties high enough so that imported goods would not be sold at lower prices than American-made products. The effect in many cases was to keep foreign manufacturers from trying to sell their goods in the United States.

The Monroe Doctrine   Early in the nineteenth century, revolutions against Spanish rule broke out in many of Spain's colonies in South America and Central America. One after another, these Spanish colonies fought for their independence as the United States had done.

By itself, Spain had little chance of regaining its lost colonies. It might do so, however, with help from Austria, France, or Russia. At that time, Russia was claiming territory along the Oregon coast, terri-

tory also claimed by the United States. If Austria or France helped Spain, would they also help Russia in North America?

In 1823 President Monroe, following the advice of his Secretary of State, John Quincy Adams, decided to issue a warning to these European countries. His statement, known as the **Monroe Doctrine**, has been called the American "declaration of independence from Europe." The Monroe Doctrine promised European nations that they could keep whatever holdings they had in the Western Hemisphere as of 1823. However, they must not claim any additional territory in this hemisphere. Moreover, the United States would oppose any effort to extend the European system of rule by kings and queens to the Western Hemisphere. In return, the United States promised not to interfere in events in any European country.

The Missouri Compromise   The Monroe Doctrine was not the only important event during the Era of Good Feeling. The **Missouri Compromise** rivaled the Monroe Doctrine in importance. By 1819, 9 additional states had joined the original 13 in the Union, making a total of 22. These 22 states were evenly divided between 11 **slave states**—states in which slavery was legal—and 11 **free states**—states in which slavery was illegal. The 9 new states had been admitted with little or no controversy. It was different, however, in 1819, when Missouri asked to be admitted as a slave state.

Northerners opposed to slavery objected to the admission of Missouri as a slave state. The admission of Missouri would give the southern slave states two

Discuss the Monroe Doctrine. Ask: Did the United States have a legal right to speak for the affairs of Latin America? Is the presence today of a Communist government in Cuba a violation of the Monroe Doctrine?

JAMES MONROE
5th President
1817 · 1825

Born: 1758, Westmoreland County, Virginia. **Education:** College of William and Mary, from which he withdrew to join the Continental army. **Training:** Lawyer, public official. **To presidency from:** Virginia. **Position when elected:** Secretary of State. **Political party:** Democratic-Republican. **Married:** Elizabeth Kortright. **Children:** Two daughters, one son. **Died:** 1831, New York City. **Other facts:** A tall blue-eyed man of military bearing. Wounded in the battle of Trenton. In 1819, at Savannah, Georgia, the first President to ride on a steamboat. **During his presidency:** The first public high school in the United States opened in 1821 in Boston. The English Classical School admitted only boys for instruction in reading, writing, English grammar, and mathematics.

more votes in the Senate and therefore a majority. An additional danger, some northerners claimed, was that the admission of Missouri as a slave state might set a pattern. It might mean that all other states made from the Louisiana Purchase territory would become slave states.

Some southerners, on the other hand, argued that Missouri had a right to be admitted as a slave state if that is what its people wanted. Furthermore, they said the North had a larger population than the South. Therefore, the North had a majority in the House of Representatives. It would be only fair, they argued, to give the South a majority in the Senate by admitting Missouri as a slave state.

Feeling about the Missouri question ran high throughout the country as well as in Congress. Thomas Jefferson wrote from Monticello that the controversy alarmed him like "a fire bell in the night." Then in December 1819, Massachusetts agreed to give up its three northern counties. These counties then asked for admission to the Union as a free state, to be called Maine. This made possible what became known as the Missouri Compromise.

By the terms of the compromise, Missouri was admitted to the Union as a slave state and Maine as a free state. This preserved the balance between slave and free states in the Senate. In the Louisiana Purchase, slavery was prohibited north of the 36°30′ line, except in Missouri. It was agreed that Congress would make no laws excluding slavery from the territory south of that line.

By means of the Missouri Compromise, Congress avoided a dangerous confrontation between North and South. But the dispute, as you will see later, had been postponed, not resolved. A deadly confrontation was yet to come.

CHECKUP

1. Name four leaders who might be considered members of the Virginia Dynasty.
2. How did the Burr-Hamilton duel affect the future of the Federalist party?
3. What Hamiltonian policies came to be adopted by the Democratic-Republicans?
4. In the Monroe Doctrine, what did the United States demand of European nations? What did it promise in return?
5. What did North and South each give up in the Missouri Compromise? How was this a gain for the whole nation?

KEY FACTS

1. As the settlers moved westward, many Indians were forced off the lands they lived on.
2. President Thomas Jefferson's purchase of Louisiana from France more than doubled the size of the United States.
3. The War of 1812 between the United States and Great Britain came to an inconclusive end, but it brought about a growth in national pride.
4. The years soon after the War of 1812 became known as the Era of Good Feeling.
5. The Monroe Doctrine said that European powers must stay out of the Americas and that the United States would not interfere in European affairs.

VOCABULARY QUIZ

On a separate sheet of paper write **T** if the statement is true and **F** if it is false.

F **1.** Jefferson's goal in purchasing Louisiana was to move the United States boundary to the Pacific.
F **2.** The route that Lewis and Clark followed in Louisiana was called the Wilderness Trail.
T **3.** In the Old Northwest, the land was divided into square townships.
F **4.** The Adams-Onís Treaty fixed the northern boundary of the Louisiana Purchase.
F **5.** Presidents Jefferson and Madison supported the Embargo Act as a way of defeating the Barbary pirates.
T **6.** A feeling of *nationalism* means affection and support for the whole country rather than for a particular state or section.
F **7.** The Hartford Convention was called to support the War of 1812.
T **8.** The War Hawks were young members of the House of Representatives from the South and West.
T **9.** The Democratic-Republicans adopted a Federalist idea when they chartered the Second Bank of the United States.
T **10.** The Era of Good Feeling is most closely tied to the presidency of James Monroe.

REVIEW QUESTIONS

1. In what ways were rivers and streams used by frontier settlers?
2. Name two important differences between the Old Northwest and the Old Southwest.
3. List two complaints against Great Britain that helped bring on the War of 1812.
4. Why did President James Monroe issue the doctrine that bears his name?
5. How did the Missouri Compromise avoid a dangerous confrontation?

ACTIVITIES

1. Make a list of the states admitted from territory west of the Appalachians in the order of their admission between 1790 and 1825. Put S next to those that were part of the Old Southwest; N next to those admitted from the Old Northwest; and L next to those admitted from the Louisiana Purchase territory.
2. Much good historical fiction has been written about pioneers in the Old Southwest or the Old Northwest. Ask your teacher or your school librarian for suggestions, read an appropriate piece of historical fiction, and report on it in class.
3. In 1830 Oliver Wendell Holmes published a poem called "Old Ironsides." Appoint a committee to find a copy of this poem and to read it in class as a basis for discussion.

10/SKILLS DEVELOPMENT

UNDERSTANDING CAUSE AND EFFECT

WHAT HAPPENED AND WHY

When an event occurs, it sometimes causes something else to happen. For example, during a thunderstorm, lightning struck a tree. The tree fell across a road. This is called a cause-and-effect relationship. The cause of what happened was the storm. The effect was lightning striking the tree and the tree falling across the road. To understand cause and effect, you must ask what happened and why it happened. *What* happened tells you the effect. *Why* it happened tells you the cause.

Many events in history had a cause-and-effect relationship. In this chapter you have read how the Embargo Act of 1807 put a halt on American trade. It resulted in the loss of many jobs in the United States. The effect was the loss of jobs. The cause was the Embargo Act of 1807.

SKILLS PRACTICE

The following statements are about events mentioned in this chapter. Each statement is followed by three other statements. Each of the three statements is true, but only one gives the cause of the event. On a sheet of paper, write the letter of the statement that makes each sentence tell what happened and why.

1. The United States nearly doubled in size because
   a. of the purchase of Louisiana from France.
   b. Tennessee gained statehood in 1796.
   c. Ohio became a state.
2. European countries had a greater respect for the United States as a result of
   a. the Missouri Compromise of 1820.
   b. the Treaty of Greenville.
   c. the War of 1812.
3. General William Harrison was able to reach Canada by water because
   a. Daniel Boone blazed the Wilderness Trail.
   b. Wayne's army defeated the Indians at Fallen Timbers.
   c. Perry defeated the British at Lake Erie.
4. In 1816, Congress passed a protective tariff because
   a. the United States was flooded with British manufactured goods.
   b. salt was necessary to preserve food.
   c. pirate ships became a threat in the Mediterranean.
5. Canadians called the war that started in 1812 the War for Defense because
   a. slavery was illegal in the Old Northwest.
   b. the British began impressing seamen.
   c. it began with American invasion into Canada.

11 The Jacksonian Era

A New Kind of President

> VOCABULARY
>
> favorite son   Democrats
> sectionalism

Inauguration day   March 4, 1829, was Andrew Jackson's inauguration day. Immense crowds gathered in Washington to see the man from Tennessee take the oath of office as President of the United States. Jackson walked from his hotel down Pennsylvania Avenue to the Capitol. He walked bare-headed, hat in hand, to indicate he was "a Servant, in the presence of his Sovereign, the People," as one observer put it.

After Jackson had taken the oath and given his acceptance speech, an unruly crowd broke through the barriers. Everyone wanted to shake Jackson's hand. The new President had difficulty making his way to his horse. Mounting it, he rode to the White House. Behind him there followed a procession of carriages, wagons, and people on foot.

That afternoon the "presidential palace" witnessed a mob scene. Some 20,000 people came to the reception that honored President Andrew Jackson. Nothing like this had ever happened before. One person who attended had this to say: "Ladies fainted, men were seen

with bloody noses, and such a scene of confusion took place as is impossible to describe—those who got in could not get out by the door again and had to scramble through the windows. . . ."

In this way Andrew Jackson began his years as President of the United States. He was a new kind of President. Unlike Washington, Adams, and Jefferson, he was not a descendant of an old colonial family. Instead he was the son of an immigrant, raised on the frontier and grown to manhood in the newly opened lands west of the Appalachians.

Jackson's early years   Andrew Jackson's father was an immigrant from northern Ireland. He died shortly before his youngest son's birth at Waxhaw Settlement in South Carolina. During the War for Independence, Andrew's brother Hugh was killed and his brother Robert died of smallpox. His mother died in 1781, leaving him completely without family at the age of 14. For a time he studied law at Salisbury, North Carolina. In 1788 he crossed the mountains into Tennessee before that region became a state.

Jackson lived a busy and varied life in Tennessee. He was at different times a judge, a member of Congress, and a major general of the Tennessee militia. He sold

President-elect Andrew Jackson greets the people on his way to Washington in 1829.

Andrew Jackson's mother died after traveling to Charleston to nurse captured Patriots aboard prison ships in the harbor.

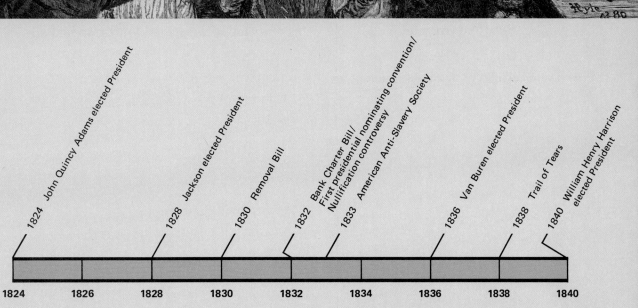

1824 John Quincy Adams elected President

1828 Jackson elected President

1830 Removal Bill

1832 Bank Charter Bill/
First presidential nominating convention/
Nullification controversy

1833 American Anti-Slavery Society

1836 Van Buren elected President

1838 Trail of Tears

1840 William Henry Harrison elected President

1824 1826 1828 1830 1832 1834 1836 1838 1840

land to settlers, had slaves, raised cotton and tobacco, kept packs of hunting dogs, and owned some of the finest racehorses in the United States. The home Jackson built outside Nashville was called the Hermitage. Andrew Jackson and his wife, Rachel, had no children of their own, but the Hermitage was like a home for several of his wife's nephews and nieces.

In 1814, Jackson led the Tennessee militia's campaign against the Creek Indians, defeating them at the battle of Horseshoe Bend. A few months later, as you have read, General Andrew Jackson defended New Orleans against the British invaders. After the United States acquired all of Florida, Jackson served as its first territorial governor for 6 months. With his rise to fame as the victor at New Orleans, Jackson began to be mentioned as a presidential candidate.

The election of 1824 The campaign for President in 1824 was unusual because all four leading candidates claimed to be members of the Democratic-Republican party. When the party failed to agree on a single candidate, each section of the country nominated a **favorite son**. A favorite son is a candidate favored by the delegates from one state or section. The South backed William H. Crawford of Georgia, who was serving at the time as President Monroe's secretary of the treasury. John Quincy Adams, son of our second President, was New England's favorite. The West offered two candidates. One was Henry Clay of Kentucky. Clay was the Speaker of the House of Representatives. The other was Andrew Jackson, the war hero from Tennessee.

In the voting, Jackson received 99 electoral votes. He had nearly as many popular votes as those of the next two candidates together. John Quincy Adams finished second with 84 electoral votes. Crawford had 41, and Clay had 37. Clearly, Andrew Jackson was the people's choice. However, no one of the four had a majority of the electoral votes.

The Constitution stated that if no one had a majority, the House of Representatives should choose the President from the three leaders in electoral votes. Henry Clay had finished fourth, so he had

Jackson became a popular hero after the battle of New Orleans. (30°N/90°W; map, p. 244)

John Quincy Adams was one of our most able and yet unpopular Presidents. Pupils might use library resources to research Adams's personality and the temper of the times and find reasons for Adams's unpopularity.

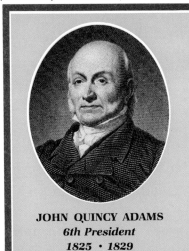

JOHN QUINCY ADAMS
6th President
1825 · 1829

Born: 1767, Quincy, Massachusetts. **Education:** In France and Holland and at Harvard College. **Training:** Lawyer, diplomat. **To presidency from:** Massachusetts. **Position when elected:** Secretary of state. **Political party:** National Republican. **Married:** Louise Catherine Johnson. **Children:** Three sons, one daughter. **Died:** 1848. The only man to serve in the House of Representatives after being President, he suffered a stroke on the floor of the House and died in the Speaker's Room. **Other facts:** Served at the age of 14 as private secretary to the first United States diplomat in Russia. As President, liked to swim in the Potomac River. **During his presidency:** Noah Webster published a dictionary of the English language, considered the finest of its time.

to drop out. However, as Speaker of the House, Clay could influence the choice. Crawford had suffered a stroke during the campaign, so Clay knew that Crawford was too sick to be President. Clay and Jackson disagreed on a number of points, even though both represented the West at the time. This left John Quincy Adams, whose political views were close to those of Henry Clay.

Thus Henry Clay gave his support to John Quincy Adams. As a result the House of Representatives chose the man from Massachusetts as the successor to President James Monroe. After his inauguration, Adams named Henry Clay as his Secretary of State. Jackson's supporters quickly charged that Adams and Clay had made a "corrupt bargain." By this, they meant that Clay had supported Adams in return for the office of secretary of state.

The second President Adams John Quincy Adams entered office under the handicap of the "corrupt bargain" charges. He was a "minority President," having received fewer than one third of the popular votes in the election of 1824.

His distinguished father, John Adams, had never been a popular President. The second President Adams was even less popular than his father had been.

John Quincy Adams had served brilliantly in diplomatic posts before he became President. Nevertheless he lacked political skill. He had none of the warmth that would attract support from the common people. Part of his failure as a President stemmed from these personal characteristics. He also had to combat the increasing **sectionalism** that was dividing the country. Sectionalism is the attaching of great importance to a single region, or section, of the country.

President John Quincy Adams believed that the national government, rather than the states, should build roads and make other internal improvements. He proposed to raise money for these internal improvements in two ways—by raising the tariff, and by increasing the price of public land. These policies were popular in New England and in other parts of the East. However, they failed to win support from the West and the South. Why, do you think, was this so?

Answers to question in column 2: A higher tariff would raise the prices the West and the South had to pay for manufactured goods. Most of the public land was in the West and the South, and many people moved there in order to buy land at low prices.

Jackson wins in 1828   It was almost certain that Andrew Jackson would win the presidency in 1828. John Quincy Adams was not popular, and his policies had failed to win wide support. However, Jackson's campaign managers took no chances. They worked hard to win votes for Jackson. As the election drew closer, they made sure that newspapers carried articles praising Jackson. They held meetings in every city and town where they could gather a crowd of people. With this help and with his standing as a war hero, Jackson won easily. He received more than 56 percent of the popular votes and more than twice as many electoral votes as Adams.

During the years of Adams's presidency, people who favored the strong national program supported by Adams and Clay had begun to call themselves National Republicans. On the other hand, Jackson's supporters had kept the name of Democratic-Republicans. When Jackson became President, however, they shortened the name to **Democrats.** Thus Andrew Jackson joined Thomas Jefferson as a founder of what is today the Democratic party. In this way the election of Andrew Jackson marked another step in the development of one of the two major political parties of today.

CHECKUP

1. In what ways was Andrew Jackson a "new kind of President"?
2. Why did Jackson's supporters charge that a "corrupt bargain" had been made?
3. Why was the administration of President John Quincy Adams generally unsuccessful?
4. What were the reasons for Jackson's easy victory in the election of 1828?

Section and Nation

VOCABULARY

nullify	Whigs
nullification	depression
secession	"Tippecanoe
Force Bill	and Tyler too"
Bank Charter Bill	

A sectional issue   During the presidential campaign, Jackson had been thought of as a sectional candidate from the West. During his two terms in office, however, he skillfully balanced sectional and national interests. Whenever sectional interests threatened national unity, Jackson struck hard.

The most serious sectional dispute during Jackson's presidency had to do with the tariff issue. In 1828, during John Quincy Adams's administration, Congress had raised the tariff again as a way of protecting eastern industries. Higher tariffs were unpopular in the South where, at that time, there was little industry. Higher tariffs meant that southerners had to pay more for manufactured products. Consequently the legislature of South Carolina protested this action by Congress. As part of its protest, the legislature supported a statement issued by John C. Calhoun. Calhoun said that a state could **nullify**—that is, cancel or veto — a national law within its own boundaries. The belief that a state could do this was called the **nullification** doctrine.

John C. Calhoun was Andrew Jackson's Vice President, but Jackson kept to himself his views on Calhoun's stand. Jackson did, however, use his influence to get

Have each pupil make up a ten-question objective test based on Lesson 1. Then have them exchange tests and answer the questions. Pupils should check the tests and discuss the answers with their partners.

American manufacturers of cloth made from sheep's wool were outspoken supporters of a high tariff.

Congress to pass a new tariff law in 1832. The new law brought the tariff rates down by a small amount. Yet the 1832 law continued to protect American industry.

The nullification controversy In 1832 a convention took place in Columbia, the capital of South Carolina. By a large vote, South Carolina leaders stated that the tariff acts of both 1828 and 1832 were "null, void, and no law." The people of South Carolina were authorized to refuse to pay the tariff duties after February 1, 1833. The convention went even further in its challenge to the national government. It added that any attempts by the national government to enforce the tariff acts in South Carolina "would be a just cause for the **secession** [withdrawal] of the state from the Union." The governor of South Carolina then asked for 10,000 volunteers to defend the state.

In 1830, Andrew Jackson had made a firm public statement that the Union *must* be preserved. Until 1832, however, he said nothing more about nullification. But when faced with South Carolina's challenge, he acted swiftly and decisively. First, he issued a statement strongly opposing the nullification doctrine. Then he let it be known that he would send 50,000 soldiers to South Carolina to enforce the tariff laws.

Bloodshed seemed certain to occur if neither side backed down. South Carolina appealed to the other states for help but got no promises of military assistance. John C. Calhoun realized his home state had gone too far. He turned to Henry Clay for help in arranging a compromise. Clay responded by supporting a law that would lower tariff rates annually over a period of 10 years.

Under Clay's plan, the tariff rates would by 1842 be nearly as low as they were in 1816. By a narrow margin, Congress passed the Compromise Tariff of 1833. At the same time, Congress passed the **Force Bill**. This authorized the President to use the army and navy, if necessary, to collect tariff duties.

The crisis ended It was now up to South Carolina to compromise. Once more a convention met in Columbia. This convention repealed the nullification of the tariffs of 1828 and 1832. But to show that it still supported the principle of nullification, the convention nullified the Force Bill. However, the national government now had no need to use force because South Carolina had accepted the Compromise Tariff of 1833.

Both sides claimed victory in this crisis. The fact was, though, that neither the state nor the national government had won completely. South Carolina had won a reduction in the tariff. When its convention nullified the Force Bill, South Carolina held to the principle of nullification. On the other hand, Jackson had kept the Union together without bloodshed. He had held fast against the threat of secession.

Other sectional issues   Should the national government pay for highways and other improvements? On that question, Jackson took the middle road. He backed measures providing funds for improvements that helped more than one state. For example, he favored funds for building the National Road that ran from Cumberland, Maryland, westward through several states. He refused, however, to support national government expenditures for improvements within a single state.

Before Jackson became President, Congress had lowered the price of public land to $1.25 an acre and permitted it to be sold in amounts as small as 80 acres (32 ha). During the Jacksonian era, new land laws made it even easier for people to buy cheap land in the West. If land could not be sold at $1.25 an acre, it could now be sold at less than that. By 1840 these laws made it possible for poor people to settle on government land and pay for it later. Some people thought government land should be given away free. Jackson never quite went that far, but he always favored a policy of cheap government land. By doing so, he favored the sectional interest of the West, along with the hopes of many eastern working people who dreamed of someday owning a little farm in the West.

The Second Bank   The Democratic-Republicans had adopted a Hamiltonian policy in 1816 by setting up the Second Bank of the United States. The national government kept its funds in the Second

Many Americans traveling west on the National Road stopped briefly at this inn.

Born: 1767, Waxhaw, South Carolina. **Educated:** Very little formal schooling. **Training:** Lawyer, soldier, landowner. **To presidency from:** Tennessee. **Position when elected:** Private citizen living on his estate, the Hermitage, near Nashville. **Political party:** Democratic. **Married:** Rachel Donelson Robards. **Children:** One adopted son. **Died:** 1845 at the Hermitage. **Other facts:** The first President to have been born in a log cabin. As a 13-year-old, served in the South Carolina militia in the War for Independence. Became an orphan at 14. Had a quick temper and as a young man fought several duels. Owned racehorses. The first President to ride on a railroad train. **During his presidency:** Cyrus McCormick invented a machine for reaping grain.

ANDREW JACKSON
7th President
1829 • 1837

Bank and in that bank's branches. This gave the Second Bank of the United States an advantage over other banks.

Thousands of people in the South and West disliked the Second Bank. They thought that the national government's funds should be spread out among other banks. Moreover, southerners and westerners blamed the Second Bank for the high interest rates they had to pay when they borrowed money. President Jackson also disliked the Second Bank. Still, he felt there was little he could do about it because the bank's 20-year charter would not run out until 1836.

However, Henry Clay hoped to defeat Jackson in the election of 1832, and he hit upon an idea that he thought would help him. Clay persuaded Nicholas Biddle, head of the Second Bank, to ask Congress for a new charter in 1832, 4 years before the old one ran out. Biddle did what Clay wished. Clay and his friends in Congress then passed the **Bank Charter Bill.** It was then sent to Jackson for him to sign.

Clay thought that this would cause great trouble for Andrew Jackson. If Jackson signed the bill, he would surely lose votes in the South and the West. But if he vetoed it, the Second Bank would use its influence against Jackson in the coming election. Actually, Henry Clay thought Jackson would never dare to veto the Charter Bill.

Jackson not only vetoed the Charter Bill, he also sent Congress a stinging message along with his veto. In this message he said he thought that the Second Bank was unconstitutional because Congress had no power to charter a bank in the first place. Moreover, said Jackson, the Second Bank was a monopoly. It was also un-American, Jackson concluded, because many of its stockholders were British.

End of the Bank Henry Clay's supporters in Congress could not pass the Bank Charter Bill over Jackson's veto. Furthermore, Jackson's veto message proved to be so popular with voters that he easily defeated Henry Clay in the election of 1832. After the election, Jackson ordered his secretary of the treasury to remove the national government's funds from the Second Bank and put them into state banks throughout the country.

Many in business who had borrowed money from the Second Bank had to repay it sooner than they had intended. Some of them went bankrupt and blamed Jackson for their troubles.

Like all strong Presidents, Andrew Jackson made enemies. The bankrupt business people were only a few of these enemies. Others opposed Jackson's belief that the President was as important as Congress because he represented all the people. Still others were angry when he said a President had as much right as the Supreme Court to declare an act of Congress unconstitutional.

The Whig party Because Andrew Jackson took on such presidential power,

This cartoon, critical of Jackson, pictures him treading on the Constitution of the United States.

his opponents started calling him King Andrew. They pointed out that Jackson had vetoed more acts of Congress during his first term than all previous Presidents together. So, in the early 1830s, Jackson's opponents started calling themselves **Whigs** after the party of that name that opposed the king in England.

A **depression** takes place when business slows down for many months and a large number of people lose their jobs. Near the end of Jackson's second term, a depression began. Because of this, the Whigs hoped they could beat Jackson's party, the Democrats, in 1836. However, the Whigs could not agree on one candidate, so they nominated four favorite-son candidates. They hoped that one would win a majority of the electoral votes. But if no one did, it would be up to the House of Representatives to make the choice from among the three leaders. If this happened, the Whigs believed that one of their candidates would have a good chance of winning.

Van Buren wins Perhaps Andrew Jackson could have been elected to a third term as President in 1836, for he was still very popular with the common people. But Jackson was old and tired. Moreover, by 1836 a tradition had grown that a President should serve only two terms. So Jackson retired to the Hermitage. While still in office, however, he was able to get the Democratic party to choose Martin Van Buren of New York as its presidential candidate in 1836. Van Buren had served as secretary of state during Jackson's first term and as Vice President in Jackson's second term.

Born: 1782, Kinderhook, New York. **Education:** Village school, read law. **Training:** Lawyer, public official. **To presidency from:** New York. **Position when elected:** Vice President. **Political party:** Democratic. **Married:** Hannah Hoes. **Children:** Four sons. **Died:** 1862, Kinderhook, New York. **Other facts:** Small, dapper, an elegant dresser. Served in the United States Senate and as governor of New York. The first President who was born a United States citizen—that is, after the Declaration of Independence. Considered to have been a master politician. Called "the Little Magician" by political enemies, who charged him with being a sly schemer. **During his presidency:** Mount Holyoke, the first permanent women's college, was established.

MARTIN VAN BUREN
8th President
1837 · 1841

The Whig candidates failed to get enough votes to throw the election into the House of Representatives, as they had hoped to do. Van Buren was elected quite handily. But as President, he received the chief blame for the severe depression that began even before he entered that office. As Vice President, Van Buren had helped Jackson defeat the bill to recharter the Second Bank of the United States. Now, as the depression deepened, many state banks failed. Depositors lost their money, factories closed down, and thousands of workers suffered from unemployment. In the South the price of cotton fell by 50 percent. Many western farmers lost their farms because they were unable to pay their debts.

The election of 1840 As the election of 1840 approached, the Whigs were sure they could win the presidency from Van Buren and the Democrats. All that was needed, the Whigs believed, was to agree on one candidate. Henry Clay was their real leader and Clay was certain he would be chosen as the Whig candidate. However, he had made some enemies within his party, and the Whig nominating convention chose William Henry Harrison. Harrison's electoral vote total had been the highest of all four Whig candidates in 1836. Like Jackson, William Henry Harrison was a hero of the War of 1812, leading Americans to victory in the battle of the Thames. And a year earlier, he had defeated the Indians at the battle of Tippecanoe. For Vice President the Whigs nominated John Tyler of Virginia. Formerly a Democrat, Tyler had joined the Whigs because he disagreed with President Jackson over nullification.

In 1840, the Whig party showed it had learned from the Democrats. The Whigs borrowed the methods the Democrats had used to win votes for Jackson. This time, however, the methods were used to win votes for William Henry Harrison. The Whigs described their presidential and vice presidential candidates with the clever slogan **"Tippecanoe and Tyler too."** Whig orators attacked Martin Van Buren, calling him an aristocrat who wore corsets. They said that Van Buren ate fancy French foods with golden teaspoons from golden plates.

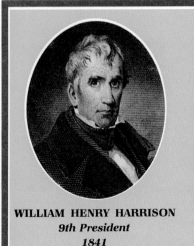

Born: 1773, Berkeley, Charles City County, Virginia. **Education:** Hampden-Sydney College. **Training:** Army officer, public official. **To presidency from:** Ohio. **Position when elected:** County clerk of Hamilton County, Ohio. **Political party:** Whig. **Married:** Anna Symmes. **Children:** Six sons, four daughters. **Died:** 1841, a month after his inauguration. Had made the longest inaugural speech on record (1 hour, 45 minutes) on a stormy winter day, catching a cold that brought on pneumonia. **Other facts:** A military hero of the War of 1812. Governor of Indiana Territory for 12 years. **During his presidency:** For the first time, copies of an inaugural address were carried by railroad. Philadelphians read Harrison's address the day it was delivered.

WILLIAM HENRY HARRISON
9th President
1841

Slogans, parades, and shouting drowned out any serious discussion of the issues. The Whigs refused to adopt a party platform explaining what they stood for. Instead, they shouted "Tippecanoe and Tyler too" and "Van, Van is a used-up man." When the votes were counted, the Whigs had won. Democrats complained that they had been shouted down, sung down, and lied down. Basically, however, the Democrats lost because of the depression that lasted through most of Van Buren's single term in office.

Whig leaders had hoped to persuade the newly elected President to follow their policies. However, the plans of the Whigs fell apart when Harrison died of pneumonia a month after his inauguration at the age of 68.

CHECKUP

1. How did the tariff issue turn into a nullification controversy in 1832?
2. What was the result of the nullification controversy between South Carolina and the national government?
3. Why did Jackson veto the Bank Charter Bill?
4. How did the Whigs win the presidential election of 1840?

Jacksonian Democracy

┌─**VOCABULARY**─────────────────────┐

political democracy   **spoils system**

nominating convention   **Kitchen Cabinet**

└────────────────────────────────────┘

Nominating conventions The years between 1824 and 1840 are often called the Jacksonian era. During that period Jackson's beliefs about freedom, democracy, and equality influenced every aspect of American life.

One of the most significant developments of the Jacksonian era was the expansion of **political democracy**. That is, more people than ever before took part in the process of choosing their leaders and influencing their government. One development of these years was the presidential **nominating convention**. Before this time, candidates for President, Vice President, governor, and lesser offices had been chosen by caucus. That is, a group of influential politicians would meet to choose their party's candidates in the next election. This was an undemocratic way

Ask pupils why, in their opinion, the depression during Van Buren's presidency was the main cause of his defeat in the election of 1840.

of choosing candidates because it put the power of nomination in the hands of very few people.

In 1832 the two major political parties held their first presidential nominating conventions. Andrew Jackson was chosen for a second term by Democratic delegates, who came from every state except Missouri. All party members could vote for delegates from their state to attend the nominating convention. This gave even the humblest members the feeling that they had a voice in choosing their party's candidates for the highest office in the national government.

Since 1832 each major party has held a nominating convention every 4 years. These are colorful meetings that generally draw a great deal of attention. They remind one of how American democracy grew during the time of Andrew Jackson.

More voters   There were other developments that showed a growing democratic spirit. When Indiana became a state in 1816 and when Illinois followed in 1818, their constitutions permitted all white men over 21 years of age to vote. Other states at that time required voters and officeholders to own property or to pay a certain amount of tax. Gradually the reform pioneered by Indiana and Illinois spread to the older states. By 1840 only a few states kept their property requirements for voting and holding office.

Before Jackson's time, some states had religious requirements for voting. To be eligible to vote, a man had to be a member of an approved church. By the end of the Jacksonian era, all religious requirements were removed. Because of this change, three times as many men voted for President in 1828 as had in 1824.

During Jackson's time, increasing numbers of voters cast ballots on election day.

The growth in political democracy never reached women, blacks, or Indians during the Jacksonian era. But for white male citizens there was a sizeable expansion of political rights in the years between 1824 and 1840.

Lively campaigns   Before the Jacksonian era, presidential campaigns were quiet, dignified affairs. In fact, not much campaigning was done. Things were different from 1828 on. Many voters needed excitement to get them to the polls. Busy with their farms or their town jobs, the voters had little time to read lengthy arguments for one candidate or another.

Jacksonian Democrats were the first to use slogans to attract voters. Democratic newspapers featured cartoons that any voter could understand. Parades, songs, and band concerts brought men out to support the Democratic party and its candidates. As you have read, the Whigs adopted these tactics in 1840. Since then, political campaigns in America have been generally lively and usually noisy. They seem to have to be that way to attract the average voter's attention.

Political organizations   Another development during Jackson's time was the strengthening of political-party organizations. After Jackson was defeated in 1824, those who had backed him started planning for victory in 1828.

At first these political organizations were small and simple. As time went by, however, they became large and lasting. Some of Jackson's supporters worked full time at the task. Only a few were wealthy enough to work without pay. Full-time workers were paid through dues or gifts of party members. Or they were given government jobs while still spending much of their time working for their political party. The practice of rewarding party members with government jobs came to be known as the **spoils system**.

The spoils system   The spoils system received its colorful name from Senator William Marcy of New York. In a speech to the Senate in January 1832, Marcy said, "They (the Jacksonians) see nothing wrong in the rule that to the victor belong the spoils (possessions) of the enemy."

Jackson and his political supporters preferred to call the practice "rotation in office." When Jackson became President, many employees of the national government had held their jobs for 25 years or

This Whig cartoon attacking the spoils system shows Jackson on a pig fattening on political fare.

Television is the newest way for political candidates to attract voter attention. Ask pupils how television has affected elections.

What's in a Name?

OLD HICKORY

Do you have a nickname, or do you know someone who does? A nickname may be a shortened form of a given name. Examples are "Bob" for Robert; "Debbie" for Deborah; "Steve" for Steven; "Bill" or "Will" for William. Or a nickname can be given because of a characteristic or physical feature a person possesses. "Red," "Skinny," "Slim," or "Curly" are nicknames of this type. Or a nickname may have some other origin.

Generally, nicknames are affectionate and are used for people we like and respect. Such was the case with Andrew Jackson, who had a number of nicknames. His friends and supporters affectionately called him "Old Andy" and "Old Hickory." Andrew Jackson seemed old to many Americans when he was inaugurated in 1829 at 61 years of age. And "Andy," of course, is a short name that is often used in place of Andrew.

Why did people call Andrew Jackson "Old Hickory?" The future President earned the nickname during the War of 1812 because of his toughness and endurance— characteristics associated with the wood of the hickory tree. He carried the nickname up to and through his presidency until his death. People gave these nicknames to Andrew Jackson because they liked and admired him. They felt he was one of them—a man of the people.

---

more. Some did their jobs well, but some were inefficient. Others regarded their jobs as lifetime appointments and thought they could serve the public in any way they wanted to.

Jackson favored short-term appointments to prevent the growth of a permanent office-holding group. Also, he believed in equality and thought one person had as much right to a government job as any other. Therefore, he saw nothing wrong with replacing some government employees with those who supported him politically. During his two terms in office, he "rotated" the employees in about one fifth of the positions available in the national government.

An old soldier himself, Jackson was reluctant to remove old soldiers from their government jobs. He refused to replace the aged postmaster in Albany, even though that postmaster was a supporter of Henry Clay. "I will not remove the old man," Jackson declared. "He carries a pound of British lead in his body." Neither would he rotate in office a veteran who had lost his leg on the battlefield, although the man had voted for Jackson's opponent. "If he lost a leg fighting for his country, that is vote enough for me," Jackson said.

To Jackson, rotation in office was a way of showing his faith in the intelligence and ability of the common man. Furthermore, his enemies greatly exaggerated the number of men he replaced with his own supporters. And, at least in the case of deserving war veterans, Jackson made exceptions to the spoils system. Still, he started a practice that went on for many years. It often put people who were not fit for their jobs into government posts.

After they have read "The spoils system," have pupils give reasons for or against the system as a way of governing. List their reasons on the chalkboard under two headings and allow time for class discussion on the various items.

267

Horace Mann was a leader in the public school movement. In Massachusetts he succeeded in getting state funding for better schoolhouses and equipment and was responsible for many other improvements in education. Under Mann's influence the first teachers' college was established in 1839.

Jackson's Cabinets Jackson well knew how strong sectional feelings were in the United States. When his first term began, he tried to please each part of the country. He chose a person from each section as a member of his Cabinet. Secretary of State Martin Van Buren of New York represented the East. John Eaton of Jackson's home state of Tennessee came from the West to serve as secretary of war. Jackson's first attorney general was John M. Barrien, from the southern state of Georgia. However, the keen-witted Van Buren was the only member of the official Cabinet that President Jackson relied on for advice. So within a few months Jackson stopped having regular Cabinet meetings.

The President had another group of advisers, however. The group included several politicians and newspapermen, some of whom held minor government jobs. Jackson's opponents called this informal group of advisers the **Kitchen Cabinet**, and pictured them sitting around Jackson's kitchen stove, chewing over political questions. The group probably did not actually meet in the kitchen. However, Jackson did rely on the group for advice because he knew its members were in close touch with ordinary people.

Equal opportunities In Jackson's time, democracy in America came to mean equal opportunity for all and special privileges for none. This was one of the ideas that led to the free public school system in the United States. There were schools in America as early as colonial times. Only a few of these were free, however, and they were free only to chil-

dren of poor parents. The poor parents had to sign an oath saying they were unable to pay the fees that other parents had to pay.

During the Jacksonian era, several states experimented with free public elementary schools. In 1834 Thaddeus Stevens, a member of the Pennsylvania legislature, pointed out that there were 100,000 voters in his state who were unable to read. Surely, he argued, this was sufficient reason to establish free public schools. New York City and Philadelphia had free elementary school systems in the 1830s. By that time Massachusetts had a state law requiring towns with more than 500 families to provide opportunities for high school education at public expense. All these schools were started to create equal opportunities for students. As Thaddeus Stevens expressed it: "Let them all fare alike in the . . . schools and be animated by a feeling of perfect equality."

Special privilege for none During the 1830s and 1840s, Jacksonian Democrats attacked what they called monopolies. To them, a monopoly was any business that had a special privilege. For example, Jackson called the Second Bank of the United States a monopoly because it had a charter giving it privileges no other bank possessed. Therefore, when Jackson destroyed the Second Bank, he took away a privilege it had and created equal opportunities for all banks.

Other businesses had special privileges in their charters. Many of these charters had been given to businesses by state legislatures during the early years of the United States. Often these special privi-

268

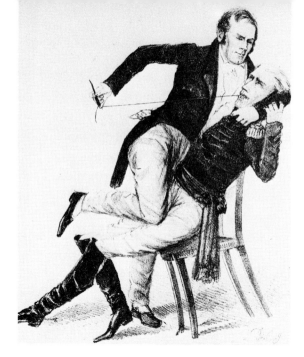

In this cartoon, Henry Clay is shown stitching the lips of the President together to silence him in the controversy over the Bank of the United States. Jackson held that the bank was a monopoly.

Inequalities in the Jacksonian Era

VOCABULARY

Trail of Tears   abolitionist
Black Hawk's War   women's rights

Indian removal   When Jacksonian Democrats spoke of equality of opportunity, they usually thought only of white men. They gave little thought to the unequal treatment of Indians, blacks, and women of whatever color.

By Jackson's time, Indians east of the Mississippi were no longer a danger to white settlements. Most eastern Indians lived peacefully on land granted to them by treaties with the national government. But many white people wanted to take this land away from the Indians. These people believed the Indians should be forced to live west of the Mississippi.

Congress gave in to the demands of these people in 1830 by passing the Removal Bill. This bill ordered Indians to give up their land east of the Mississippi River in exchange for lands west of the river. The Removal Bill had Jackson's backing. Even earlier, he had allowed people in Georgia to take land away from the Cherokees.

By treaties made earlier, Indians were not supposed to be removed without their agreeing to it. Also, they were supposed to be paid for any lands they gave up. However, the government made the eastern Indians move without any regard for their wishes. Furthermore, Jackson ignored the protests of many white people who protested the government's treatment of the Indians.

leges prevented new companies from competing with those already chartered. However, during Jackson's second term, states began to change their charter laws. The changes made it much easier for companies to get charters to do business of one kind or another. All the new charters were alike. None contained a special privilege for the chartered company. Thus, the emphasis on equality of economic opportunity in Jackson's time opened the door to free competition among businesses.

CHECKUP

1. How did the presidential nominating conventions help to give more political rights to people?
2. What led to an increase in the number of voters during the Jacksonian era?
3. How did political organizations and the spoils system get started in the Jacksonian era?
4. What two kinds of cabinets gave advice to Andrew Jackson? Why did Jackson pay more attention to one kind than the other?

Indian removal reached a tragic height in the 1830s. During that decade the Choctaw, Chickasaw, Seminole, Cherokee, and Creek peoples were forced from their southern lands. These Indians were known as the Five Civilized Tribes. The Cherokee in particular had accepted white people's culture by becoming Christians and inviting missionaries to live among them. One of their leaders, Sequoya, had created an alphabet for their language.

Nevertheless, the Cherokees were required to move. Under guard by the United States Army, about 15,000 of them set forth on what became known as the **Trail of Tears.** Heartbroken at being forced from their homes, they were herded westward in the fall and early winter of 1838. Rain and cold brought on sickness, and about 4,000 died before they reached Oklahoma.

Indian resistance Some southern Indians refused to move. Bands of Seminole, Cherokee, and Creek Indians resisted as white families waited to settle on their land. A few Indians managed to hide out near their homes. Others died of starvation or were hunted down and killed. Sometimes those removed to the western lands were killed by other Indians, who resented new intruders on their hunting grounds.

Indians of the Old Northwest also were moved west of the Mississippi during Jackson's time. Some of them refused to stay there. Under the leadership of the chieftain Black Hawk, a group of Indians tried to return to their former homes near Rock Island, Illinois, in 1832. Fighting broke out and the governor of Illinois called out the state militia. A large number of Sac and Fox Indians were killed in what became known as **Black Hawk's War.** Black Hawk himself was captured. Several months later he was sent on a trip to the East, which included a visit with President Jackson. "We did not expect to conquer the whites," Black Hawk told Jackson. "I took up the hatchet to revenge injuries which my people could no longer endure."

The Cherokees proceed on their forced march to Oklahoma over the Trail of Tears.

Philbrook Art Center, Tulsa, Oklahoma

Black inequality   There were between 2 and 3 million black people living in the United States during the Jacksonian era. Most of these people were slaves, but even free blacks were denied equality. Some Americans had protested against the evils of slavery in colonial times. During and soon after the American Revolution, most northern states had begun the process of ending slavery within their borders. By the time of the Jacksonian era, **abolitionists**—people who wanted to abolish slavery—were active in all parts of the nation.

As early as 1800, free black Americans in Philadelphia sent an antislavery petition to Congress. Individual white southerners like Levi Coffin, James G. Birney, Angelina Grimké, and her sister, Sarah, were early supporters of the antislavery movement. They joined northerners in working for *gradual abolition*, that is, ending slavery over a period of years. However, beginning about 1830 a group of northerners became *extreme abolitionists*. Probably William Lloyd Garrison of Massachusetts was the most widely known of the extreme abolitionists, who wanted to end slavery immediately. Garrison published a paper in Boston that he called *The Liberator*.

Frederick Douglass, a self-educated former slave, also published an abolitionist newspaper. He called it *The North Star* and suggested that slaves escaping from the South could use the North Star in the sky as a guide to freedom.

In 1833 abolitionist leaders organized the American Anti-Slavery Society. These leaders were influenced by the Jacksonian emphasis on equality as well as by humane concerns. As the movement spread, the American Anti-Slavery Society gained 200,000 members. Nevertheless, in spite of these efforts, slavery and racial discrimination continued.

Women's inequality   Equality between men and women had little meaning during the Jacksonian era. No male leader of the 1830s seriously argued that women should have the right to vote or to hold office. In fact, throughout the country the laws treated women as children, no matter how old they were. Most states refused women the right to own property. Women were denied entry into the professions of law, medicine, and the ministry.

Yet, at the same time, expanding prosperity freed some women from work in their homes. Immigrant girls and black servants often took over household duties in middle- and upper-class homes. This allowed women from these homes to work for causes they believed in. They became active in antislavery societies and in missionary work. From these activities grew a **women's rights** movement. It would be years before changes were made in the laws that denied equality to women. Nevertheless, the seeds for these changes and for many other reforms were planted in the days when Andrew Jackson was President.

CHECKUP

1. What groups did not gain equality during the Jacksonian era?
2. Why were eastern Indians removed to lands west of the Mississippi?
3. Give evidence to show that an antislavery movement began during the Jacksonian era.
4. In what ways were women denied equality during the Jacksonian era?

KEY FACTS

1. Andrew Jackson was elected as President in 1828 because of his friends' support and because of the widespread unpopularity of John Quincy Adams.

2. President Jackson tried to balance sectional interests with those of the nation as a whole, but he strongly opposed the nullification doctrine.

3. Jackson crushed the Second Bank of the United States because he regarded it as an un-American monopoly.

4. Jacksonian democracy expanded the role of the common man in American politics through presidential nominating conventions, lively campaigns, and permanent political organizations.

5. During the Jacksonian era, Indians, blacks, and women continued to be denied rights held by white males.

VOCABULARY QUIZ

On a separate sheet of paper, write the letter of the word or phrase that best completes each sentence.

1. A favorite-son candidate is one who is (**a**) seeking office for the first time, (**b**) the son of an officeholder, (**c**) favored by one state or region, (**d**) the oldest son in a family.

2. "Tippecanoe and Tyler too" was a slogan that helped to win the presidency for (**a**) Andrew Jackson, (**b**) Martin Van Buren, (**c**) William Henry Harrison, (**d**) John Tyler.

3. John C. Calhoun of South Carolina was chiefly responsible for (**a**) the Bank Charter Bill, (**b**) the Force Bill, (**c**) the doctrine of nullification, (**d**) the Indian Removal Bill of 1830.

4. The expansion of political democracy in Jackson's time resulted in (**a**) the election of a woman as governor of Indiana, (**b**) an increase in the number of voters, (**c**) a denial of voting rights to people who owned no land, (**d**) the Indian Removal Bill.

5. The practice that Democrats called "rotation in office" (**a**) originated in Georgia and Kentucky, (**b**) became known as the spoils system, (**c**) caused 90 percent of the national government's employees to lose their jobs, (**d**) ended when Jackson left office.

REVIEW QUESTIONS

1. Why were favorite-son candidates nominated by the Democratic-Republicans in 1824 and the Whigs in 1836?

2. What was Jackson's attitude toward each of the following? (a) the Second Bank of the United States (b) the doctrine of nullification

3. Why were permanent political organizations and the spoils system linked together?

4. What rights were denied to women during the Jacksonian era?

ACTIVITIES

1. Plan an automobile trip to the Hermitage, near Nashville, Tennessee. Use road maps to locate the routes you would follow. List these routes and the states you would pass through.

2. Draw a cartoon on one or more of the following subjects:

a. The Second Bank of the United States as seen by Jacksonian Democrats

b. A Whig view of "King Andrew"

c. John C. Calhoun's view of the protective tariff

USING SYNONYMS

WORDS THAT REPLACE OTHER WORDS

Usually there is more than one way to say the same thing. For example, one sentence in this chapter reads: A favorite son is a candidate favored by the delegates from one state or section. The underlined word could be replaced by a synonym without changing the meaning of the sentence. It would read: A favorite son is a candidate preferred by the delegates from one state or section. Synonyms are words or terms that mean the same thing.

SKILLS PRACTICE: Part I

Listed below is a series of statements mentioned in this chapter. Each statement is followed by three words. One of the words could be used in place of the underlined word without changing the meaning of the numbered statement.

On a sheet of paper, write the number of the statement and the word that could replace the underlined word.

1. Immense crowds gathered in Washington to see the man from Tennessee take the oath of office as President of the United States. (Small, Large, Angry)
2. Jackson had to combat the increasing sectionalism that was dividing the country. (help, start, fight)
3. The Tariff of 1832 retained the principle of protecting American industry. (kept, changed, started)

4. As the depression deepened, many state banks failed. (collapsed, expanded, increased in size)
5. Jackson favored short-term appointments to prevent the growth of a permanent office-holding group. (aid, stop, expand)

SKILLS PRACTICE: Part II

In the following statements think of a word that could be used in place of the underlined word without changing the meaning of the statement. On a sheet of paper, write the number of each statement and the word you think of. Use your dictionary if you need to look up any of the underlined words.

1. Andrew Jackson's mother died in 1781, leaving him completely without family at the age of 14.
2. Land laws passed during the Jacksonian era permitted some land to be sold at less than $1.25 an acre.
3. Most eastern Indians lived peacefully on land granted them by treaties with the national government.
4. In 1833, abolitionist leaders organized an American Anti-Slavery Society.
5. During the 1828 election, Jackson's campaign managers worked hard to attract the votes of the common man.
6. Immigrant girls and black servants often took over household duties in middle- and upper-class homes.

The Spirit of Reform

VOCABULARY

reform   suffrage
Declaration of   egalitarian
  Sentiments

A determined young woman   On July 14, 1848, there appeared in the *Seneca Falls Country Courier* the following unusual announcement:

> Woman's Rights Convention—a Convention to discuss the social, civil, and religious conditions and rights of woman, will be held in the Wesleyan Chapel, at Seneca Falls, N.Y., on Wednesday and Thursday, the 19th and 20th of July . . . commencing at 10 o'clock A.M. . . .

With this announcement Elizabeth Cady Stanton and Lucretia Mott called upon women to organize and work for rights that had been denied them. Lucretia Mott was an older woman, but Elizabeth Cady Stanton was a young mother with three children under 6 years of age. She and her husband lived near Seneca Falls. The care of her young children kept her from traveling, so the first organized women's rights convention in the United States had to come to her.

As a child, Elizabeth Cady sometimes hid in her father's law office. From her hiding place she heard pitiful stories of married women who had come to her father for help. Often they told of having their property and their children taken from them because of laws that favored men. When her only brother died, Elizabeth Cady's father cried because he had no more sons. Elizabeth resolved to prove to her father that a daughter was as good and as valuable as any son.

The determined girl became a skillful horseback rider. She learned to play chess and other games that many men thought to be above the mental powers of girls and women. She studied Greek, Latin, and mathematics. She begged to go to Union College, a men's school in Schenectady, New York. Instead she was sent to Emma Willard's Troy Female Seminary.

Wider interests   After graduating, Elizabeth Cady became interested in movements for **reform**. Reform is improving conditions by changing them. Elizabeth Cady heard about women's rights at the meetings she attended. Sometimes Henry Stanton, a journalist and reformer, spoke at these meetings. Though Stanton was 10 years older than Elizabeth Cady, the two soon learned they shared many of the same views. In May 1840, they were married.

Elizabeth Cady Stanton and her husband spent their honeymoon in London,

Elizabeth Cady Stanton addresses the first women's rights convention in 1848.

Women in the nineteenth century were considered by law to be minors. They could not vote. By law a woman could be beaten by her husband. Her property and earnings belonged to him. If she committed a crime, she was not always considered responsible. Divorce and child guardianship laws favored men.

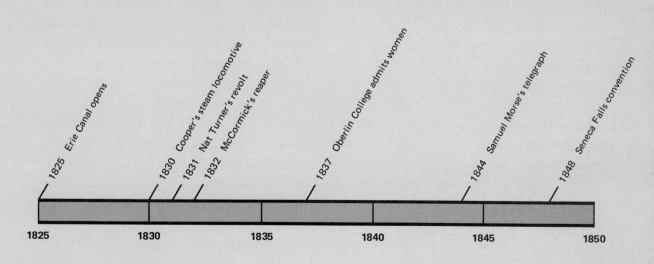

1825 Erie Canal opens

1830 Cooper's steam locomotive

1831 Nat Turner's revolt

1832 McCormick's reaper

1837 Oberlin College admits women

1844 Samuel Morse's telegraph

1848 Seneca Falls convention

1825   1830   1835   1840   1845   1850

England, where he was a delegate to a World's Anti-Slavery Convention. She found women delegates were barred from the convention. This seemed unfair and turned Elizabeth Cady Stanton's thoughts to the many ways that society discriminated against women. At the convention she met Lucretia Mott and the two resolved to work together for women's rights.

After returning to the United States, the Stantons lived for several years in Boston. Elizabeth Cady Stanton met other reformers there. She met the abolitionist Frederick Douglass; John Greenleaf Whittier, an abolitionist poet; and Lydia Maria Child, an author whose husband had protested against President Andrew Jackson's treatment of the Cherokee Indians (see pages 269–270).

"All men and women . . ." The damp climate around Boston turned out to be bad for Henry Stanton's health. The drier air of central New York seemed to be better for him. The Stantons moved to Seneca Falls in 1847 with their three small children. Later they had four more children.

The women's rights convention that met at Seneca Falls in July 1848 was attended by both men and women reformers. The convention issued a **Declaration of Sentiments**, written by Elizabeth Cady Stanton. She used the Declaration of Independence as her model, beginning her Declaration of Sentiments with the words "All men and women are created equal." She followed this with a long list of ways in which society discriminated against women.

At the end of her declaration came the demand that women be given **suffrage**— that is, the right to vote. Not all reformers believed this was a good idea at that time. But Frederick Douglass, among others, spoke in favor of it. Later women's rights conventions also demanded woman suffrage. Still, many years passed before women were granted the right to vote throughout the United States.

Some influential women reformers were missing from the Seneca Falls Convention. Susan B. Anthony, for example, was teaching school at the time. However, she joined Elizabeth Cady Stanton in 1851 as a crusader for women's rights. They made a good team. While Stanton stayed home and wrote speeches, Anthony traveled around delivering them and organizing local groups. As Mrs. Stanton's husband is said to have remarked to his wife, "You stir up Susan and she stirs up the world."

Sojourner Truth Elizabeth Cady Stanton and Susan B. Anthony knew and worked with another influential woman reformer of the time who went by the name Sojourner (sō jėr′ nə) Truth. Originally named Isabella Baumfree, she was a slave in a New York family of Dutch descent. When New York did away with slavery in 1828, she became a member of the African Zion Church and worked in religious causes in New York City.

A powerful woman with a magnificent voice, Isabella attracted large audiences. She spoke of her dreams and her visions as she traveled from town to town. In the 1840s she took the name Sojourner Truth

Isabella Baumfree changed her name to Sojourner Truth when she received what she felt was a call from God to become a preacher. Pupils might look up the definition of *sojourner* and consider why it was an appropriate name.

Sojourner Truth is a good subject for a biographical report.

Sojourner Truth, a former slave, worked tirelessly to help other black people gain their freedom.

and became one of the most sought-after speakers in the cause of abolitionism and other reforms.

The goals of reformers   Nearly all reformers of the time were abolitionists, people who wanted to abolish slavery. However, they often disagreed about the best way to end slavery and the speed of ending it. Moreover, the abolitionists were generally interested in other reforms besides the abolition of slavery. Whether black or white, male or female, they worked together to make the United States—and the entire world—a better place to live in.

Frederick Douglass was not only an abolitionist, but he also worked for women's rights. Susan B. Anthony spoke and wrote in favor of abolitionism, temperance in the use of alcoholic beverages, and the right of women to vote. William Lloyd Garrison borrowed some ideas from David Walker, a free black who urged slaves to revolt if their masters refused to free them. And Garrison argued as strongly for women's rights and better treatment of Indians as he did for the abolition of slavery.

A dedicated woman named Dorothea Dix worked during the 1830s and 1840s for better treatment of the mentally ill. At the time, these unfortunate people were put in prisonlike cells. They were chained, whipped, and left with very little care. Dorothea Dix investigated this shameful treatment of the mentally ill in several parts of the country.

Methods of reform   Though Dorothea Dix favored many reforms, she was most interested in improving the lot of the mentally ill. She visited jails and other places where mentally troubled people were held and were often cruelly treated. She then appeared before committees of state legislatures. She described the hopeless conditions she had seen. She called upon the committees to use the power of the state to improve the lives of the mentally disturbed. As a result of her investigations, state after state took mental patients out of jails and prisons. They were put into hospitals where they could be better cared for.

Many other reformers used methods like those of Dorothea Dix. They worked

Interested pupils might like to find out more about the dangers and opposition faced by some of these reformers and revolutionaries: Susan B. Anthony, Lucy Stone, Frederick Douglass, Elijah Lovejoy, Denmark Vesey, Gabriel Prosser, and Nat Turner.

Gradually the efforts of reformers working within the existing state systems began to succeed. In 1839, Mississippi was the first state to allow married women to control their own property. Other states followed with reforms. Pupils might research where and when these reforms took place.

inside the existing bodies of government. Those working for women's rights set out to bring about changes in state laws that discriminated against women. Abolitionists hoped to do away with slavery in the south by state action, as had been done by 1850 in all northern states. Temperance advocates petitioned for laws limiting the sale of liquor or prohibiting it completely. Sometimes reformers organized tiny political parties made up of those who believed reforms were needed.

Unlike Dorothea Dix, most reformers of the time spoke long and loud in public. Nearly all of them were skillful speakers. Going to a lecture was a favorite form of entertainment in those days. Sometimes a reformer's lecture might last two or three hours. Occasionally fights broke out between those who sympathized with the lecturer and those who opposed him or her. At first, women were denied the right to speak in public, but in time they won this right as well as other rights long denied them.

Thus reformers sought to convince others of the need for reform by lecturing to audiences. This was a slow method, however, and limited in the number of people it reached. A better way was to use the printed word. Consequently, many reformers wrote about the reforms they favored and had their arguments published in books, magazines, newspapers, or pamphlets.

Better education Until the 1840s most Americans opposed the idea of free public schools. However, when workers in the cities and other people without property got the right to vote, many who had opposed free public schools began to change their minds. Voters needed to be able to read and write. Factory owners realized that their workers might be more productive if they could read instructions and perhaps do a little simple arithmetic. Gradually, opposition lessened to the idea of free public schools.

Thanks to the leadership of Horace Mann, a lawyer and a member of his state's legislature, Massachusetts pioneered in providing free public schools. Mann persuaded the Massachusetts legislature to pass a law in 1842 that required every child to attend school for a certain length of time each year. To educate these children, Massachusetts provided free schools. The Massachusetts idea spread, as Horace Mann lectured all over the country in support of free public

After teaching school for 25 years, Dorothea Dix spent the rest of her life improving the lot of the insane.

schools. By the 1850s many states had free public education for children through the elementary school years. In the elementary schools of the time, youngsters studied reading, spelling, writing, arithmetic, and perhaps a little geography and history.

The new interest in education for all brought about the growth of some high schools, colleges, and universities. However, the idea of free high schools spread very slowly. The colleges and universities of the time were usually supported by churches or other private groups. College and university students were required to pay tuition. But the idea of tax-supported state universities was spreading. Michigan, Mississippi, Iowa, Indiana, Missouri, and Wisconsin had them by 1850.

Educational opportunities for girls and women increased during this time. By the 1820s Emma Willard had started schools for girls in Vermont and in Troy, New York. (The latter was the school in which Elizabeth Cady Stanton studied.) As the free public elementary schools spread, girls studied alongside boys in many states. Oberlin College in Ohio allowed four women to enroll in 1837, along with men students. Later, other western colleges and universities admitted women as well as men. Separate colleges for women were established at about the same time.

Oberlin was also the first college to admit blacks.

More reading material As more and more people learned to read, more and more books, magazines, and newspapers were published. Reformers furnished some of this reading material. Frederick Douglass had his paper, *The North Star*. William Lloyd Garrison published his abolitionist paper, *The Liberator*. During these years Elizabeth Cady Stanton wrote articles for a New York newspaper and for a women's rights magazine, the *Una*. But none of these reform newspapers had a large circulation.

One women's magazine of the time did have a large circulation. Louis Godey published the magazine called *Godey's Lady's Book*. Mrs. Sarah Hale became editor of the *Lady's Book* in 1837. She remained as the magazine's influential editor for 40 years and was largely responsible for its success. *Godey's Lady's Book* contained beautiful drawings of women's fashions of the time. It also contained editorials, written by Sarah Hale, favoring women's rights and other reforms.

Many more newspapers Americans of the 1830s and 1840s liked to read newspapers. In 1790 there were 92 newspapers in the United States, but only eight were published every weekday. Sixty years later there were more than 3,000 newspapers with 387 of them being dailies. One of these was *Freedom's Journal*, the first newspaper in the United States directed to black people. Samuel Cornish and John B. Russwurm began its publication in New York in 1827. Another successful New York paper was the *Sun*, published by Benjamin H. Day beginning in 1833. The *Sun* was a daily and sold for only one cent a copy.

Newspaper publication had spread widely throughout the United States by 1850. The Nashville *Union* and the Detroit *Free Press* both began publication in

What's in a Name

NEWSPAPERS

In this chapter you read of the rapid spread of newspaper publishing between 1825 and 1850. Did you ever wonder how these and later newspapers got their names? Undoubtedly Benjamin F. Day chose *Sun* for his New York newspaper's name to show that it came out each day, and in the morning. The Nashville *Union*'s name showed that its owners and publishers favored national interests of the United States over sectional interests of the

South. A *tribune* is a protector or champion of the people. Can you see why Horace Greeley would choose such a name for his New York *Tribune?*

It is difficult to see why the New Orleans *Picayune* was given that name. A picayune is something of little value or importance. Surely the owners would not want readers in New Orleans to think their paper was of little importance or value! No, the word *picayune* is from a French word meaning "a small

coin." So the people who chose the name of the New Orleans paper were trying to convey the idea that you could buy it for a very small price.

Today, because of mergers, many papers have two names. They are called the *Herald-Leader,* the *Advocate-Messenger,* or the *Courier-Express.* But you can be sure that each of these two names meant something originally and was chosen for a reason. How did your newspaper get its name?

1835. *The Telegraph and Texas Register* first appeared that same year in San Felipe, Texas. Later it became the Houston *Telegraph.* An influential southern paper, the New Orleans *Picayune* (pik ə-yün'), started in 1836. The Monterey *Californian* began in 1846 as the first newspaper in California. Three years later it changed its name to the *Alta Californian* and became the first daily newspaper in California. *Spectator,* Oregon's first paper, also started in 1846.

The 1830s and 1840s were years of very heavy immigration to the United States. Between 1841 and 1850 nearly 1,750,000 Irish and German people crossed the Atlantic to settle in America. These immigrants wanted to read news about their homelands and about the new country to

which they had come. By 1856 there were 56 German-language newspapers published in the United States.

In 1841 Horace Greeley started the *Tribune* as a daily newspaper in New York City. He was a brilliant editor and his paper rapidly gained national influence. Greeley fearlessly expressed his own views in *Tribune* editorials. He opposed slavery, believing it to be both immoral and uneconomical. He despised and feared monopoly of any kind. He supported labor unions, argued against capital punishment, and urged restrictions on the sale of liquor. In other words, Horace Greeley was an all-purpose reformer and he made the New York *Tribune* one of the great voices calling for reform throughout the land.

Before the *Sun* reduced its price to one cent, daily newspapers cost about six cents. Many people earned as li as a dollar a day and previously could not afford to buy a daily paper. Some pupils might use library resources do a report on the lurid "penny dreadful," the name some critics gave to the *Sun.*

Religion and reform   Many reforms of the time were based on the idea of dignity and equality of individuals. It was no accident that the women at the Seneca Falls Convention began their Declaration of Sentiments with the phrase "All men and women are created equal." Jacksonian democracy stressed "Equal opportunities for all; special privilege for none." Horace Greeley was known as an **egalitarian** because he favored *equal* political, economic, and legal rights for all American citizens.

Religious beliefs were also a source of reform during the 1830s and 1840s. Many male reformers were ordained ministers. Many women reformers, such as Sojourner Truth, were deeply religious. Some southern clergymen argued that the Bible sanctioned slavery, but an equal number of reformers pointed out that slavery was immoral. For black people, whether slave or free, religion was both a comfort and a guide.

Opposition to reform   It would be wrong to think that many Americans in the 1830s and 1840s were reformers or even to think that most people favored reform. A few brave women argued for the rights of all. Most women, however, kept busy with their traditional tasks in the home. Most men were too busy earning a living for themselves and their families to think much about reforms. Organized workers did back the movement for free public schools. Some also campaigned for a shorter working day. In 1834 a national federation of workers was formed. However, when hard times hit the country in 1837, this group broke up.

Outspoken opposition to slavery was dangerous in many parts of the country. Elijah Lovejoy, an abolitionist editor, had his printing press destroyed by a mob in Alton, Illinois. The Ohio Anti-Slavery Society sent him another press. When the mob came once more, Lovejoy was shot dead while trying to defend the new

Members of a mob, angered by antislavery editorials in Elijah Parish Lovejoy's newspaper, set fire to his printing plant in Alton, Illinois. (39°N/90°W; map, p. 299)

press. James G. Birney left his native state of Kentucky because of opposition to his antislavery views. After moving to New York, Birney was the presidential candidate of an Anti-Slavery party in 1840 and of the Liberty Party in 1844.

Slave revolts were punished with great severity. Nat Turner, a black preacher and leader, led a revolt in Southampton County, Virginia, in 1831. Fifty-one white persons were killed in a single day and night. Turner and his associates were hunted down, killed outright, or tried and hanged.

In Boston a mob threatened to hang William Lloyd Garrison because of his abolitionist views. Women reformers were often hooted at and jeered as they attempted to speak out against injustice. In fact, reformers in general had a hard time of it. What they asked for was change, and most people were against change.

Yet, even with the resistance that reformers met, the 1830s and 1840s are looked upon as one of the great reform periods in American history. By 1850 women enjoyed more rights than they had had 20 years earlier, more tax-supported schools were in existence, and more people were aware that slavery was a gigantic blot on the principles of dignity and equality.

CHECKUP

1. What situation brought about, in 1848, the first organized Women's Rights Convention?
2. Why could some men and women of the time be described as "all-purpose reformers"?
3. What methods did the reformers use?
4. How were better educational opportunities made available in the 1830s and 1840s?
5. Why was there opposition to reform?

An American Spirit in the Arts

VOCABULARY

Leatherstocking Tales	Hudson River School
	Concord group

Independence in the arts   The United States of America won political independence from Great Britain at the time of the American Revolution. Nearly 50 years passed, however, before Americans won independence in the arts. During those years American authors, painters, and sculptors generally followed European models. At that time, a Britisher might sneer as he or she asked, "Who reads an American book?"

The Britisher would have asked a good question. Some Americans had written books before that time. Other Americans had painted pictures and shaped statues. And yet there was no way to tell that these were American achievements. These works of art were only imitations of what Europeans had done before.

Ralph Waldo Emerson, one of America's great thinkers, urged an end to this artistic situation. In a speech at Harvard in 1837 he asked for an "intellectual Declaration of Independence." By this Emerson meant that Americans should stop relying on foreign models and should create stories, pictures, and statues based on American ideas and American scenes.

Irving and Cooper   At least two American writers had already done what Emerson asked. Under the pen name Diedrich Knickerbocker, Washington Irv-

Some pupils might borrow a library copy of *The Sketch Book* or an anthology that includes such *Sketch Book* tales as "Rip Van Winkle" and "The Legend of Sleepy Hollow." Pupils might write a story report on one of the tales, and the class might discuss what is particularly American about these tales.

One of Washington Irving's best-known tales is "The Legend of Sleepy Hollow," in which Ichabod Crane, a young schoolmaster, is pursued by a headless horseman.

ing in 1809 had published a history of New York. Actually, it was more a history of the old Dutch colony of New Amsterdam. Washington Irving later wrote *The Sketch Book*, a collection of stories about the early Dutch settlers in colonial America.

James Fenimore Cooper wrote of other American scenes and other kinds of Americans. In a series of novels called the **Leatherstocking Tales,** he created a character named Natty Bumppo. This character appeared at different times and in different places but was always the honest, brave, and true American frontiersman. Cooper's Indian characters, too, were always noble and uncorrupted

by civilization. Cooper's *Leatherstocking Tales* were immensely popular not only in the United States but also in Europe. In fact, some European authors began imitating *him*. They wrote stories about American Indians without ever having seen one.

American painters Several American artists had begun to depict American scenes by the time Ralph Waldo Emerson advocated an intellectual Declaration of Independence. Thomas Cole, Thomas Doughty, and Asher Durand were among these. They were members of a group called the **Hudson River School,** since they painted scenes along the Hudson

283

The Versatile Mr. Morse

Few people become famous in even one field. Samuel F. B. Morse became famous in two fields, painting and inventing. Like other young artists, he studied abroad for a time. Morse studied at the Royal Academy of London, between 1811 and 1815. Returning to America, Morse found that portraits were the only works of art which Americans would buy. So he became a portrait painter—and a good one.

Samuel F.B. Morse painted this picture of the House of Representatives meeting for an evening session in 1822. Morse is remembered today not so much for his artistry as for his invention of the telegraph.

Then tragedy struck. First, Morse's young wife died, then his parents. Saddened by these deaths, he found it difficult to paint. He went to Europe, hoping to rekindle the fires of his artistic skill. The treatment worked. On the voyage home he talked with a scientist who mentioned that electric impulses could travel any distance in an instant. This set Morse to thinking about the use of this force to send messages over long distances.

It took Samuel F. B. Morse many years to perfect his invention of the telegraph. But in 1844 Congress appropriated money to build a telegraph line between Washington and Baltimore. The first telegraph message was sent over that line. The telegraph proved to be a great aid to American enterprise, especially for railroads and newspapers. Telegraph lines ran along railroad lines around the country. By means of the telegraph, railroads could operate more efficiently and more safely. Newspapers could receive news from all parts of the country almost as events happened.

River. They were the first to concentrate on painting American scenes in a distinctive style of their own. The Hudson River School of artists painted landscapes. Other American artists became well known by painting people. George Caleb Bingham, for example, painted scenes of American frontier life. His *Daniel Boone Coming Through Cumberland Gap* was painted from imagination because Bingham was born long after the event shown in his picture. (This painting is shown on page 233.) Other scenes, however, Bingham saw and remembered from his early years in Missouri. Among these scenes of fron-

Have pupils contribute to a class scrapbook of great American inventions occurring between 1800 and 1850. Ask pupils to include a picture or sketch of each invention, the inventor's name, and the date of the invention.

tier life painted by George Caleb Bingham are *Jolly Flatboat Men, Raftsmen Playing Cards, Fur Traders Descending the Missouri,* and *Verdict of the People.*

American Indians of the early nineteenth century were painted from life by George Catlin. He traveled extensively west of the Mississippi in the 1830s and 1840s. There he recorded scenes of the West and the lives of western Indians. Catlin's *Bird's Eye View of the Mandan Village,* painted in 1832, shows the same scene the members of the Lewis and Clark Expedition might have witnessed some 30 years before.

American birds and animals were the subjects of John James Audubon's paintings. Though Audubon was born on the island of Santo Domingo, he lived most of his adult life in the United States. He had prints of his pictures fastened together and sold as huge books.

During the 1840s inexpensive copies of famous paintings became available. Demand increased as more Americans developed a taste for art. Most of the copies they bought were of paintings by European artists. However, prints sold by Nathaniel Currier and James M. Ives became very popular. They flooded the country with reproductions of pleasant scenes of American life.

Folk art Artistic creations that come from the common people are known as folk art. An example might be the lovely quilts handmade by nineteenth-century women. However, much of American folk art dating from that time is made of wood, which, of course, was readily available. With their sharp knives, many early nineteenth century men developed great skill in carving wood into all kinds of shapes.

Nearly every large sailing vessel had a wooden figurehead at its bow. Some of these figureheads were fine examples of folk art. Well-designed weathervanes, sign boards for country taverns, and kitchen utensils could also be considered to be folk art. The best of these objects are

This carving of Andrew Jackson, a fine example of folk art, once graced the prow of a sailing vessel.

in American museums today. They remind us of the skills and artistic sense that were part of the character of many Americans in the 1830s and 1840s.

Popular music Stephen Foster is probably the best-known of a small number of American composers whose songs are still sung a century and a half after they were written. He never earned much money from them, but Foster's compositions were very popular in his time. An Albany newspaper had this to say about Stephen Foster's song "Old Folks at Home," which appeared in 1851: "Sentimental young ladies sing it; sentimental young men warble it in midnight serenades . . . All the bands play it . . ." Among other Stephen Foster songs still sung by Americans today are "My Old Kentucky Home," "Camptown Races," and "O Susanna."

As folk art was created at this time, so was folk music. Examples of folk music are sea chanteys, songs sung by sailors as they worked together to raise ships' anchors and sails. Negro spirituals, sung in the fields or at religious services, are other examples of Americans creating their own folk music.

The Concord group By the 1840s a group of New England writers lived in and near the town of Concord, Massachusetts. Ralph Waldo Emerson was probably the most famous member of the **Concord group.** Henry David Thoreau, a close friend of Emerson's, would become well-known when he published *Walden* in 1854. In the book, Thoreau explained his ideas about living alone in a hut be-side Walden Pond, near Concord. *Walden* is famous as a criticism of American society at the time it was written.

Nathaniel Hawthorne lived in Concord for several years, where he was a neighbor of Emerson and Thoreau. Hawthorne first made a reputation for himself by publishing collections of short stories. He gained even greater fame later with two novels, *The Scarlet Letter* and *The House of the Seven Gables*. Both were about Puritan ideas during the time Massachusetts was a colony of Great Britain.

The poet Henry Wadsworth Longfellow was also a member of the Concord group. Longfellow used historical themes in many of his poems. Many Americans could quote all or parts of "The Midnight Ride of Paul Revere." Longfellow also wrote story-poems such as *The Song of Hiawatha, Evangeline,* and *The Courtship of Miles Standish.*

Like many American writers and poets, the Concord group borrowed some European ideas. But they mixed these borrowed ideas with their own thoughts and based their work in American locations. It made for a product that was distinctly American.

CHECKUP

1. What did Ralph Waldo Emerson urge American writers and artists to do?
2. What were the subjects of each of the following painters? (a) Asher Durand (b) George Caleb Bingham (c) George Catlin (d) John James Audubon
3. What were Nathaniel Currier and James M. Ives noted for?
4. What is folk art? Why was much of nineteenth century folk art made of wood?
5. For what were the members of the Concord group known?

The Spirit of American Enterprise

A canal boom The *Seneca Chief* was the lead boat in a fleet of boats gathered at Buffalo, New York, on the morning of October 26, 1825. Soon the *Seneca Chief* would begin the first triumphant trip along the Erie Canal to the Hudson River and then south to New York City. Work on the western end of the canal had begun only a little more than 2 years before. Now completed, it was "the longest canal made in the least time with the least experience for the least money . . . of any other in the world," according to one orator on that great day when the fleet set out from Buffalo.

Prominently displayed on the *Seneca Chief's* deck were two kegs, painted red, white, and blue. They contained "pure waters of Lake Erie," which were to be dumped into the Atlantic Ocean when the *Seneca Chief* got to New York City. The Erie Canal was nearly 400 miles (644 km) long, and it took the leading canalboat 8 days to get to New York City. Nevertheless, because of the Erie Canal, freight rates between Buffalo and New York dropped from $100 to $10 a ton within a few years. The new canal soon became the main artery of trade between the eastern seaboard and the West.

The success of the Erie Canal touched off a great boom in canal building. Before the completion of the Erie Canal, there were fewer than 100 miles (161 km) of canals in the United States. By 1840 more than 3,300 miles (5,310 km) of canals had been built. Completed canals linked Lake Erie and the Ohio River across several parts of Ohio and Indiana. Another canal would connect Lake Michigan and the Mississippi River by way of the Illinois River. The state of New Jersey financed the Delaware and Raritan Canal, which, when completed in 1838,

Traveling on the Erie Canal was a pleasant experience on a sunny summer day.

detail, Chicago Historical Society

The Erie Canal cost $7 million to build. But this money was paid off within 9 years. The canal helped make New York City the busiest seaport in America. The trip from Buffalo to New York had previously taken 20 days.

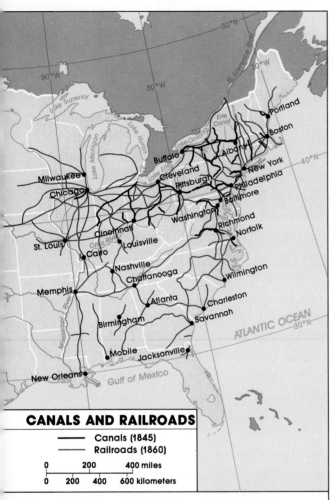

CANALS AND RAILROADS

——— Canals (1845)
——— Railroads (1860)

0   200   400 miles
0   200   400   600 kilometers

By 1860 a network of canals and railroads linked the major cities of the eastern half of the nation.

persuaded the owners to try his *Tom Thumb*, the first **steam locomotive** built in the United States. In its first trial a horse defeated the *Tom Thumb* in a race. Nevertheless, the owners of the Baltimore and Ohio were convinced that the steam locomotive was the best source of power for railroads.

Soon the Baltimore and Ohio, with its steam locomotives, became the first railroad in the United States to carry both passengers and freight. By 1850 there were many others. States, local communities, and private companies financed the 9,021 miles (14,515 km) of railroads built by that time. Railroads had several advantages over canals. Trains were faster than canalboats. Railroad tracks could be laid where it was difficult or even impossible to dig canals. During cold weather, canals might freeze over while railroads could operate in both summer and winter.

Railroads caught the fancy of Americans in ways that canals never could. Canalboats were pulled by horse or mule teams walking on a path beside the canal. Canal travel was smooth and safe but very slow. On the other hand, travel by rail was fast, exciting and sometimes dangerous. But the danger only added to the fascination of the railroads. As a New York man wrote in his diary in the summer of 1839:

> Imagine a locomotive rushing . . . whizzing and rattling and panting, with its fiery furnace gleaming in front, its chimney vomiting fiery smoke above, and its long train of cars rushing along behind like the body and tail of a gigantic dragon . . . and all darting forward at the rate of 20 miles an hour. Whew!

linked the waters of the Delaware River and the Atlantic Ocean. These canals were splendid examples of **American enterprise**—that is, the energy and the will of Americans to launch big new projects benefiting them and their country.

Steam railroads Railroads would soon surpass canals. The owners of the Baltimore and Ohio Railroad at first tried horses and sails to move their cars over rails. In 1830 Peter Cooper of New York

Steamboats While steam locomotives sped along the rails, **steamboats** traveled the rivers of America. Within a very few years after Robert Fulton's *Clermont* steamed up the Hudson in 1807, steamboats made their appearance on the Ohio and the Mississippi. In 1815 the *Enterprise* steamed from New Orleans to Louisville in the record time of 25 days.

Western steamboats were quite different from those on the eastern rivers and the oceans. Western rivers were generally broad and shallow. To navigate in these shallow waters, western boats carried their powerful engines above the waterline. Their huge paddle wheels dipped only slightly into the water. Dipping too deep might ground the boat on one of the many sandbars of the western rivers. Steamboats were important to the river towns. Without steamboats on the western rivers, Cincinnati, St. Louis, Louisville, Memphis, and Natchez could not have developed as rapidly as they did.

As important as steamboats were, they did not completely replace rafts and flatboats on the western rivers. Steamboats could travel upriver, against the current. But rafts and flatboats could be used for carrying cargo downstream. They were an inexpensive means of shipping. As late as the 1850s many families moved down the Ohio or the Mississippi on a slow-moving raft or flatboat.

This painting of a steamboat proceeding down the Mississippi River was the work of George Catlin. In the background is St. Louis, Missouri. (39°N/90°W; map, p. 236)

A transportation revolution   Canals, railroads, and steamboats brought about a transportation revolution in the United States. This transportation revolution had a number of effects. For one, it hastened the westward movement of the American people. They could move into western lands more rapidly and easily than their grandparents had moved across the Appalachians.

Even more important, this revolution made it possible for people in each part of the country to specialize in the manufacture of certain goods. Since it was now easier to exchange goods, no part of the country needed to be wholly self-sufficient. River steamboats carried western corn, wheat, and pork to southern markets, returning with rice, sugar, and hemp. The West and the Northeast exchanged many products by means of the Great Lakes-Erie Canal route. Southern cotton could be carried to New England textile mills by rail or by steamboat sailing along the coast.

The factory system   Early factories in the United States needed waterpower to turn their machinery. The small, swift rivers of southern New England proved ideal for this purpose. One such river was the Blackstone, which flowed from Worcester, Massachusetts, to Providence, Rhode Island. By 1840 it provided waterpower for 94 cotton mills, 22 woolen mills, and 34 machine shops and ironworks! With an abundance of waterpower, New England became the first great manufacturing region in the United States.

In an early textile factory, workers operate looms on which cotton cloth is made.

Yale University Art Gallery

Many young New Englanders carried the factory system into other parts of the country. By 1850, Ohio was important in the manufacture of woolen cloth. Cincinnati and St. Louis became important manufacturing and commercial centers through the leadership of sons and grandsons of men born in New England. Later other sons and grandsons led the way in making Chicago a great commercial and railroad center.

In 1850 the South was still primarily an agricultural region. Still, the spirit of American enterprise was as noticeable there as elsewhere in the United States. Important railroads ran through all the southern states. Richmond, Virginia, was the site of a flourishing iron works. And yet, in investment in industry the South had fallen behind the North. But, southern cotton helped to feed the northern factory system and helped to make the North a prosperous region.

Farm machinery   The spirit of American enterprise affected farms as well as factories in the years between 1825 and 1850. In Virginia, Cyrus Hall McCormick perfected a **mechanical reaper** in 1832. His father had tried to develop such a machine for 20 years. The son succeeded in part because he had the help of a black man, Joe Anderson. Before the McCormick reaper came into use, farmers had cut grain by hand at harvesttime. The first mechanical reaper pulled by horses could do the work of five men. Later it was improved even more.

McCormick's reaper was the first of a number of machines that revolutionized farming in the United States. In 1833

Interested pupils might find how farm machinery today differs from the machinery in use in 1850.

Spectators cheer as Cyrus McCormick oversees the successful testing of his reaper. Soon afterwards he was building and selling 1,000 reapers a year.

John Lane of Illinois fashioned a steel-bladed plow that was lighter and stronger than the iron or wooden plows then in use. In 1840 an improved grain drill for planting seed was developed. Later that same year a threshing machine was invented, and in 1850 a mechanical binder proved to be a great help to farmers.

CHECKUP

1. Why did the Erie Canal set off a canal boom in the United States?
2. What advantages did railroads have over canals?
3. Where were steamboats used widely in the early nineteenth century?
4. What were the effects of the transportation revolution in the United States?
5. Why did the factory system develop first in New England?
6. How did the spirit of American enterprise affect farm work between 1825 and 1850?

KEY FACTS

1. The 1830s and 1840s witnessed one of the greatest reform periods in American history.

2. Women's rights, the abolition of slavery, temperance, better treatment for the mentally ill, and free public schools were major areas of interest to reformers at this time.

3. An American spirit in the arts developed during this period as American writers and painters began to deal with American ideas and American scenes.

4. The growth of canals, railroads, and factories represented the spirit of American enterprise during the 1830s and 1840s.

5. These developments caused a transportation revolution that speeded up the westward movement of the American people and increased economic specialization in major sections of the country.

VOCABULARY QUIZ

On a separate sheet of paper write **T** if the statement is true and **F** if it is false.

T **1.** The Declaration of Sentiments was a statement in support of women's rights.

F **2.** The Concord group was composed of a group of American landscape painters.

T **3.** The reformers of the 1830s and 1840s all aimed to make the United States a better place in which to live.

F **4.** Woman suffrage is a term that referred to the mentally ill.

F **5.** Horace Mann was the founder of the Hudson River School.

T **6.** One who advocates equal rights is called an egalitarian.

F **7.** Washington Irving was best known as the author of the Leatherstocking stories.

T **8.** American enterprise may be defined as the energy and will of Americans to undertake new projects.

T **9.** Steamboats on western rivers were different from the steamboats on eastern rivers.

F **10.** Cyrus McCormick's first reaper was known as the *Tom Thumb*.

REVIEW QUESTIONS

1. What took place at the Seneca Falls Convention of 1848?

2. What methods did reformers use in their efforts to accomplish reforms?

3. How were educational opportunities for women improved during the 1830s and 1840s?

4. How did Jacksonian democracy and religious beliefs act as sources for reform ideas?

5. What American authors and painters were the first to use American themes?

6. What advances were made during this period in transportation and in manufacturing?

ACTIVITIES

1. Imagine that you were going west with your family in the 1830s by way of the Erie Canal. Keep a diary and make entries about your journey for a week. You may use an encyclopedia or other reference book to get further information on early travel by canalboat.

2. Choose one of the writers discussed in this chapter. In a library find a book or poem written by that writer. Pick out a poem or a selection from a novel, read it, and write a report on it. In the report, tell what the theme was in the selection, what period of history it dealt with, and whether or not it was based on American ideas and scenes.

RECOGNIZING ATTITUDES AND EMOTIONS

PERSUASIVE WRITING AND SPEAKING

You have just finished reading about the attempts by some people to bring about social change in America. Such people were called reformers. They wanted to better the conditions of life for others. Rights for women, abolishment of slavery, and better treatment of Indians and the mentally ill were just a few of their goals.

Many methods were used by reformers to further the causes in which they believed. They lectured at public meetings, appeared before committees of state legislatures, and wrote newspaper articles telling what they thought was wrong and what should be done about it. Not all people wanted social change, however. They, too, spoke out and wrote newspaper articles.

Below is an attitude regarding the issue of slavery. It was written by abolitionist William Lloyd Garrison, who wanted an immediate end to slavery.

1. I will be harsh as truth, and as uncompromising as justice. On this subject, I do not wish to think, or speak, or write with moderation. No! No! Tell a man whose house is on fire to give a moderate alarm; . . . tell the mother to gradually extricate her babe from the fire into which it has fallen—but urge me not to use moderation in a cause like the present. I will not equivocate, I will not excuse—I will not retreat a single inch —AND I WILL BE HEARD.

Dorothea Dix pleaded the cause of the mentally ill and those in prisons. The passage below is part of a speech Dix made before the Massachusetts legislature.

2. I come to present the strong claims of suffering humanity. I come to place before the Legislature of Massachusetts the condition of the miserable, the desolate, the outcast. I come as the advocate of helpless, forgotten, insane, and idiotic men and women; of beings sunk to a condition from which the most unconcerned would start with real horror; of beings wretched in our prisons, and more wretched in our almshouses (poorhouses).

I must confine myself to a few examples, but am ready to furnish other and more complete details, if required.

SKILLS PRACTICE

In each selection the writer's opinion and attitude toward a major issue of that time is being expressed. Today there are many other issues that people are concerned about. Prepare a newspaper editorial or a 3-minute speech about a current issue. You may choose an important issue in your community or one of the following: pollution, nuclear power plants, year-round school, or a candidate running for office. Explain why you feel strongly for or against the cause and why you want to persuade others to feel the same way that you do on this issue.

CHAPTER
13 Spanning the Continent

On to Oregon

---VOCABULARY---

Great American Desert	provisional government
mountain man	"Fifty-four forty or fight"
Oregon Trail	
covered wagon	49th parallel

Major Long's mistake   Major Stephen Long was chiefly responsible for a great mistake in American geography. In the 1820s this army officer led an exploring expedition in the lands between the Missouri River and the Rocky Mountains. The official maps of the expedition labeled the region the **Great American Desert.** Major Long wrote of this region: "It is wholly unfit for cultivation and . . . uninhabitable by people depending on agriculture for their subsistence."

For 50 years mapmakers copied Long's maps with their misleading labels. Settlers crossed the "desert" without stopping on their way to more desirable lands west of the Rockies. It was a long, hard journey. Water was scarce. Much of the land was a great treeless plain. Indians were a constant threat. Today these plains support millions of people. But to those pioneers it must have seemed as if they had indeed crossed a Great American Desert by the time they reached the Rockies.

Trails west   In one way, Major Stephen Long made a mistake. In other ways, however, his explorations helped the western pioneers. During his explorations he discovered routes through the trackless Great Plains. Another army officer, Captain John C. Frémont, also roamed through the West. He and his guide, Kit Carson, discovered suitable routes for the westward migration to follow.

It was Frémont's wife, Jessie Benton Frémont, who carried the story of her husband's explorations to people in the East. She took his official reports of two exploring expeditions of the 1840s and turned them into popular books. Persons planning to venture to the west coast eagerly read the books and studied the maps and the descriptions of the western trails.

By the early 1840s experienced and capable guides were ready to lead wagon trains of settlers and traders over the best routes into the far western lands. Many of these guides were men who had spent their early lives trapping and trading for furs in the Rockies. They have become known to history as the **mountain men.**

Mountain men   The mountain men were highly resourceful, wise in the ways of the wilderness. Many of them guided exploring expeditions that were sent out

During the 1840s, hundreds of families headed west, traveling by covered wagon.

Conestoga wagons, which are shown on page 295, were first manufactured in Conestoga, Pennsylvania. They were higher in the front and back so that goods would not roll out when traveling up or down hills. Pupils might make a model of this famous vehicle or of the prairie schooner.

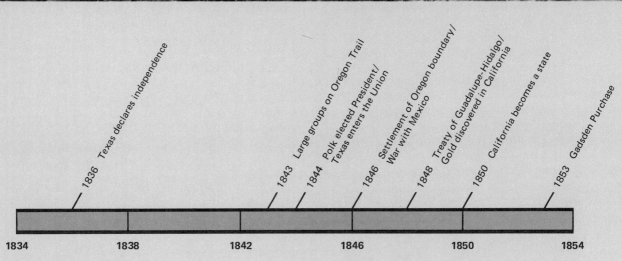

1836 Texas declares independence

1843 Large groups on Oregon Trail

1844 Polk elected President /
Texas enters the Union

1846 Settlement of Oregon boundary /
War with Mexico

1848 Treaty of Guadalupe-Hidalgo /
Gold discovered in California

1850 California becomes a state

1853 Gadsden Purchase

1834   1838   1842   1846   1850   1854

by the army. They led parties that had goods to trade with the Indians for furs. And they hired out as guides to the wagon trains of pioneers heading west.

Jim Bridger was a famous mountain man. He discovered many of the principal landmarks between the Rockies and the Sierra Nevada. Like most of the mountain men, Bridger got along well with the Indians. His first wife was the daughter of a chief of the Flathead tribe. They had two children before she died. His second wife was a Ute. She died in childbirth on July 4, 1849. It is said that Jim Bridger raised his motherless baby on buffalo milk.

James Beckwourth was another famous mountain man. He was born in Virginia, probably into slavery, but he grew up in St. Louis as a free man. After joining a fur-trading expedition to the Rocky Mountains, Beckwourth lived for 11 years with the Crow Indians. They gave him the name of Morning Star. Later, Beckwourth became an army scout and discovered a pass through the Sierra Nevada. This route through the mountains is today called Beckwourth Pass.

The Oregon country As early as 1792, American ships had visited the Oregon coast. Little more than 10 years later, the Lewis and Clark expedition gave the United States a further claim to the Oregon country. Great Britain also claimed the region. It based its claims on explorations made by men working for the Hudson's Bay Company. In 1818 a treaty between Great Britain and the United States allowed citizens of both nations to settle in Oregon. But no decision was made about which nation owned the country.

The Oregon country was much larger than the present state of Oregon. It extended west from the Rocky Mountains to the Pacific Ocean. Its northern boundary was recognized as 54°40′ north latitude. In the south the Oregon country touched the northern border of California. Both American and British fur traders helped spread the word about the richness of the land.

Christian missionaries also played a prominent part in attracting settlers to Oregon. In 1834, Jason Lee led a party of Methodist missionaries to the Oregon country. Father De Smet, a Jesuit missionary, also established several missions in Oregon. Marcus Whitman, a young New York doctor, was still another pioneer missionary. In 1836 he and his gen-

During the 1840s, Easterners poured into the fertile Oregon Country.

Fort Laramie was a busy trading post on the Oregon Trail. (41°N/106°W; map, p. 299)

tle wife, Narcissa Prentiss Whitman, built their mission near the site of present-day Walla Walla, Washington. The reports of the missionaries created great interest in the Oregon country.

"Oregon fever"   By the 1840s the interest in moving to this northwestern region was so intense that it began to be called "Oregon fever." People talked of the great crops of wheat one could raise in Oregon. Stories of the richness of the soil and the attractions of the climate were told and retold. One fanciful account declared that "out in Oregon the pigs are running about under the great acorn trees, round and fat, and already cooked, with knives and forks sticking in them so that you can cut off a slice whenever you are hungry."

After hearing tales like this, it is no wonder that thousands of people planned to move to the Oregon country. The first large group to travel the **Oregon Trail** left Independence, Missouri, in the spring of 1843. It included about 1,000 men, women, and children. They had loaded their household furnishings, tools, and other possessions into huge **covered wagons** pulled by oxen.

Starting from Independence, the trail to Oregon covered nearly 2,000 miles (3,218 km). The slow-moving caravans went northwest to the Platte River. They followed the river to Fort Laramie in present-day Wyoming. This was a place to stop for rest and for fresh supplies. Then they went on through the Rockies by way of South Pass to the Snake River. Here the settlers could make a choice. Those bound for California turned southwest. Those continuing on the Oregon Trail followed the Snake and the Columbia rivers. The trip usually took about 6 months.

Born: 1790, Greenway, Charles City County, Virginia. **Education:** College of William and Mary. **Training:** Lawyer, public official. **To presidency from:** Virginia. **Position when taking office:** Vice President. **Political party:** Whig. **Married:** (1) Letitia Christian, (2) Julia Gardiner. **Children:** Eight sons, six daughters. **Died:** 1862, Richmond, Virginia. **Other facts:** A tall, thin man, thoughtful and courteous. The first Vice President to succeed to the presidency through the death of a President. Elected a member of the House of Representatives of the Confederate States of America shortly before his death. **During his presidency:** Samuel F. B. Morse sent the first message by telegraph from Washington to Baltimore.

JOHN TYLER
10th President
1841 · 1845

Setting up a government Some farming had been done in Oregon near the fur-trading posts. However, French Prairie, in the rich valley of the Willamette River, was the first area settled solely for farming purposes. By 1841 about 65 American and 61 French-Canadian families were living in the Willamette Valley.

In 1843, settlers began to arrive in large numbers. Among them was George William Bush, a free black man who had fought with Andrew Jackson's army at the battle of New Orleans. Bush, with his wife and five children, arrived in Oregon in 1844. During that same year, American settlers in the Willamette Valley organized a **provisional government.** This was a temporary government set up as a first step toward making Oregon an official territory of the United States. The provisional government passed a law forbidding black people to settle in Oregon. But the law was never seriously enforced. In fact, George William Bush secured a homestead of 640 acres (259 ha) and is today recognized as one of the pioneer settlers of the American Northwest.

The Oregon question By 1844 several thousand Americans were living in the region that is today the states of Oregon and Washington. A lesser number of British citizens lived in the same region. Nevertheless, the Americans had made clear their dissatisfaction with joint ownership of the Oregon country between Great Britain and the United States. "Oregon fever" had brought on an "Oregon question."

Expansion was the chief issue in the presidential election of 1844. John Tyler had quarreled bitterly with the leaders of his own party, so the Whigs made Henry Clay their candidate. James K. Polk of Tennessee was the Democratic candidate. He declared that the United States should have all the Oregon territory that had been jointly occupied up to the 54°40′ boundary with Alaska. **"Fifty-four forty or fight!"** became a slogan of the campaign. Henry Clay avoided the issue of expansion entirely and lost the election.

But two years later, Polk changed his mind. As you will read later in this chapter, the United States was by then in-

Black trappers, explorers, and pioneers, such as George William Bush, James Beckwourth, and Jean Baptiste Point du Sable, helped open the West. Some pupils might use library resources to do a report on one of these Americans.

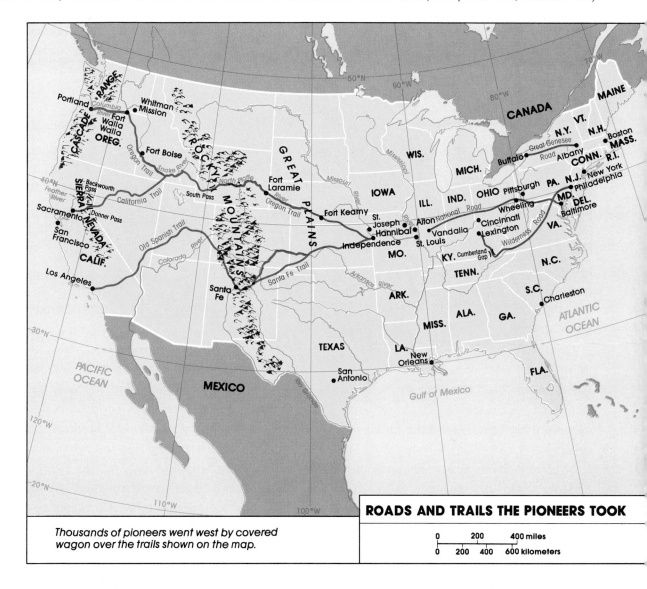

Thousands of pioneers went west by covered wagon over the trails shown on the map.

ROADS AND TRAILS THE PIONEERS TOOK

volved in a serious dispute that seemed likely to lead to war with Mexico. Faced with this dangerous situation, Polk decided to compromise on the Oregon question. The British, too, were ready to end the dispute. A treaty set the boundary at the **49th parallel** north latitude, an extension of the eastern boundary between the United States and British-controlled Canada. The northern boundary of the United States was now fixed from the Atlantic to the Pacific.

CHECKUP

1. How did the land between the Missouri river and the Rockies get the name *Great American Desert?* What was the effect of this name?

2. What contributions to settlement in the Oregon country were made by missionaries and the mountain men?

3. Describe the Oregon Trail and the methods of travel over it.

4. Why was the Willamette Valley the favored destination of many early pioneers in the Oregon country?

5. How did an "Oregon question" arise and how was it settled?

299

The Alamo was actually a group of buildings — a church, a monastery, and several outbuildings — surrounded by high walls. The Mexican attack began on February 23, 1836. On March 6, 1836, the Mexican troops were able to scale the walls and, in spite of fierce hand-to-hand fighting, the Alamo fell.

Texas: Republic and State

VOCABULARY
"Remember the Alamo!"	Republic of Texas annexation

The Austins   Moses Austin first got the idea of an American colony in Texas. He was a banker and lead-mine owner from Missouri. In 1821 he received permission from the Spanish government to bring Americans into Texas. However, Moses Austin died before any settlers came. His son, Stephen Austin, then led in the development of an American settlement along the Brazos River.

Meanwhile, Mexico had won its independence from Spain, and Texas became part of a northern Mexican state. At first Stephen Austin and other Americans in Texas got along well with the Mexican authorities. Land could be bought in Texas for 12½ cents an acre. This was much cheaper than government land in the United States at that time. Moreover, it was good land. It was well-watered with plenty of timber, and the Brazos River gave access to the Gulf of Mexico. One landowner wrote that the soil was so rich "even the weeds grow 20 feet tall."

Trouble in Texas   Most Americans in Texas had small farms. Some, however, had brought slaves with them in spite of Mexican laws against slavery. By 1835 the Americans in Texas—more than 30,000 of them—outnumbered the Mexicans living there. The Mexican government became alarmed and forbade any more Americans to settle in Texas. Some land grants were cancelled.

Americans in Texas started talking about making their territory either an independent country or a separate state of Mexico. Stephen Austin thought they should do neither. But he did go to the capital at Mexico City to protest the new policies of the Mexican government. When he got there, he was thrown in jail and held for 8 months. Mexican authorities charged him with secretly working for annexation of Texas to the United States.

At the Alamo   In the early 1830s, General Antonio López de Santa Anna established himself as dictator of Mexico. His solution to the problem of Texas was to place the area under military rule. Several armed clashes occurred in 1835 between Mexican soldiers and Texans. Early in the next year, General Santa Anna led a Mexican army against the rebellious Texas-Americans.

The Mexican army surrounded about 190 Texas volunteers in the Alamo, an old Spanish mission on the outskirts of San Antonio. From February 23 until March 6, 1836, the men in the Alamo held out, but finally all were killed in the Mexican attacks. While some Texans and Mexicans were dying at the Alamo, other Texans were meeting to declare independence from Mexico. They met at Washington, Texas, where they set up a temporary government under a constitution modeled on that of the United States. Though it was too late to save the Alamo's defenders, **"Remember the Alamo!"** became the rallying cry for a new Texas army. Within weeks this force was preparing to avenge the Alamo defeat.

300   Two of the Americans killed at the Alamo were the frontier hero and congressman Davy Crockett and Jim Bowie, the inventor of the Bowie hunting knife, which was humorously known as the Arkansas toothpick. Both of these men are colorful figures and interesting subjects for reports.

Texans—to the last man—defended the Alamo in San Antonio. (29°N/99°W; map, p. 303)

Texas becomes a republic Sam Houston commanded the Texas army. Houston was a former governor of Tennessee and a good friend of Andrew Jackson. Before Houston's army went into action, however, Santa Anna's men had wiped out a force of 300 Texans at Goliad. Houston's army soon had its revenge. On April 21, 1836, the army surprised Santa Anna near the San Jacinto (san jə sint′ ō) River. Texans went into battle crying "Remember the Alamo! Remember Goliad!" They quickly defeated the Mexican army and captured General Santa Anna himself.

Following his victory at the Battle of San Jacinto, Sam Houston was elected as the first president of the **Republic of Texas.** As a prisoner, General Santa Anna signed a treaty recognizing the in-dependence of Texas. Later, however, the Mexican congress refused to approve the treaty. Nevertheless, in 1837 President Andrew Jackson recognized Texas officially as an independent nation.

Texas joins the Union Many Texans wanted their republic to be added to the United States. Leaders in the South wanted the same thing. On the other hand, many Northerners opposed the **annexation** of Texas because it would mean another slave state in the Union. Indeed it might mean the addition of even more than one slave state, since Texas was large enough to be divided into a number of states.

The Texas issue, like the Oregon question, came to the fore in the presidential election of 1844. As you know, James K.

Many patriotic Americans, such as Abraham Lincoln, felt that the United States was unjust in fighting a war with Mexico in order to gain territory. After a careful reading of the text and some research in other sources, the class might form teams to debate the subject.

Polk, the Democratic candidate, spoke out in favor of taking the whole Oregon territory. He also favored the annexation of Texas. Polk's victory showed that the American people sided with him.

Three days before Polk was inaugurated, Congress voted to admit Texas as a state in the Union. However, Americans and Mexicans differed over the boundary between Mexico and the new American state. During the summer of 1845, President Polk angered the Mexican government by sending American troops into the disputed border area.

War with Mexico   The Mexican government also sent troops to the disputed area. With hostile soldiers facing each other along an uncertain border, a fight seemed sure to take place. It did take place in April 1846 when 1,600 Mexican cavalrymen surrounded 63 American soldiers and killed, wounded, or captured all of them. An angry President Polk told Congress, "Mexico has passed the boundary of the United States, has invaded our territory and shed American blood upon American soil." Congress then declared war on Mexico on May 13, 1846.

The Mexican army was poorly trained and poorly equipped. Still, at the beginning of the war, it was larger than the army of the United States. But eager volunteers from the southern states soon increased the size of the American forces. Of the 62,000 volunteers, about 49,000 were from Texas and the states of the lower Mississippi Valley.

General Winfield Scott leads his troops into Mexico City. (19°N/99°W; map, p. 303)

Chicago Historical Society

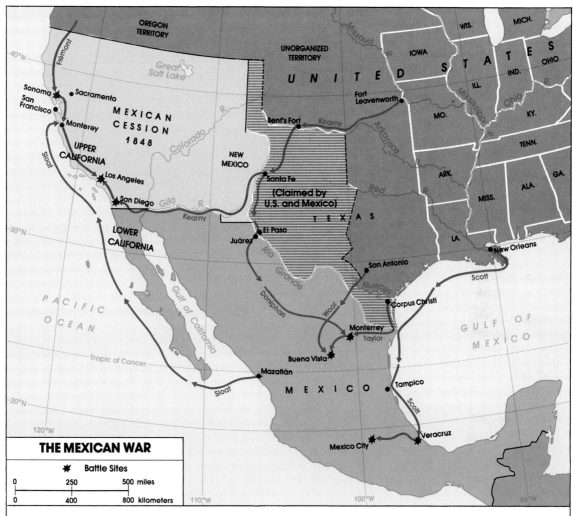

THE MEXICAN WAR

✸ Battle Sites

| 0 | 250 | 500 miles |
| 0 | 400 | 800 kilometers |

The Mexican War added an immense area of land to the United States. From this land came California, Nevada, and Utah, and parts of four other states.

During the Mexican War the American navy blockaded both coasts of Mexico. General Zachary Taylor led an invasion force into northern Mexico, winning victories at Monterey (mon tủ rā′) and Buena Vista (bwā′ nä vē′ stä). General Winfield Scott headed an American force that landed at Vera Cruz on Mexico's east coast. From there, Scott's soldiers fought their way to Mexico City. Armed with superior guns and led by able officers, the American army was the victor in every battle. In spite of their brave fighting, Mexican forces were overwhelmed. The war lasted less than 2 years.

CHECKUP

1. How did 30,000 Americans become settlers in Texas?
2. Why did Texas declare and win independence from Mexico?
3. What was James K. Polk's campaign of 1844 based on?
4. How did the annexation of Texas by the United States bring on a war with Mexico?

Have pupils find out about some of the problems that exist today between the United States and Mexico (paternalism, illegal immigration, economics) and discuss them in class. Pupils might also try to discover possible areas of common interest and cooperation.

303

A Southwestern Empire

"Old Rough and Ready"   Because of his success in the Mexican War, General Zachary Taylor became a presidential candidate in 1848. Running as a Whig, Taylor defeated the Democratic candidate, Lewis Cass. General Taylor's men had called him "Old Rough and Ready" during the Mexican War because he seldom wore an official uniform. Instead, he liked to slouch around in overalls and a farmer's straw hat. This reputation for informality and simplicity helped to make him a popular hero.

The War for Independence had produced George Washington as a military hero and President. The War of 1812 had made Andrew Jackson and William Henry Harrison popular generals and successful presidential candidates. Now the Mexican War had a similar result for General Zachary Taylor.

The peacy treaty   By far the most significant result of the Mexican War, however, was the expanse of land it brought to the United States. In 1848, representatives of the United States and Mexican governments signed the **Treaty of Guadalupe Hidalgo** (gwä′ dl üp ā hē däl′ gō), a village outside Mexico City. In the treaty, Mexico accepted the Rio Grande as the boundary of Texas. Mexico ceded to the United States the rest of the territory between Texas and the Pacific. Including Texas, the United States gained nearly half of Mexico's total territory. This expanse of land was an area even larger than the Louisiana Purchase.

For its part the United States agreed to pay Mexico $15 million for this land. In addition, the American government agreed to pay claims of American citizens against Mexico up to a total of $3.5 million. A few Senators opposed the treaty because they thought it was wrong to take Mexican territory through war. A few others opposed it because they wanted even more Mexican land added to the United States. But after some debate the United States Senate approved the Treaty of Guadalupe Hidalgo.

The land ceded to the United States by Mexico is called the **Mexican Cession.** From this vast area came the states of California, Utah, Nevada, and parts of Arizona, New Mexico, Colorado, and Wyoming. To straighten the border of the Mexican Cession, the United States paid Mexico $10 million in 1853 for a small strip of land. This is known as the **Gadsden Purchase** because James Gadsden was the American representative in Mexico at that time. New Mexico and Arizona eventually shared the Gadsden Purchase land.

With the Mexican Cession, the United States reached the Pacific Ocean in the Southwest. The occupation of Oregon had brought the United States to the shores of the Pacific in the Northwest. Many Americans in the 1830s and 1840s had said that it was **manifest destiny** for

One reason the Gadsden Purchase was made was the desire to obtain a route for a transcontinental railroad. Many Americans felt that the land slightly south of the Mexican border would be the most feasible. James Gadsden himself was a well-known South Carolina railroad man.

JAMES K. POLK
11th President
1845 · 1849

Born: 1795, Mecklenburg County, North Carolina. **Education:** University of North Carolina. **Training:** Lawyer, public official. **To presidency from:** Tennessee. **Position when elected:** In private law practice and business. **Political party:** Democratic. **Married:** Sarah Childress. **Children:** None. **Died:** 1849, Nashville, Tennessee. **Other facts:** Short, slight in build. Served seven terms in House of Representatives. The first "dark-horse" candidate for President. (A dark-horse candidate is one who is unexpectedly chosen as a compromise between strong candidates.) Declined to seek a second term. **During his presidency:** The first baseball game of record took place in Hoboken, New Jersey, in 1846, between the Knickerbockers and the New Yorks.

the western boundary of the United States to be the Pacific Ocean. By this they meant that fate had clearly intended for our country to stretch from ocean to ocean. Vigorous Americans made this possible by 1850, only 74 years after the Declaration of Independence created a new nation.

The Mormons   The Mexican Cession included over 500,000 square miles (1,295,000 sq km) of land. Probably no more than 100,000 people lived in this vast area. At least half of these people were Indians. The largest concentration of non-Indian population lived in or near the Salt Lake City area. Nearly all these people were **Mormons**, members of the Church of Jesus Christ of Latter Day Saints.

The Mormons had originated in western New York State among people who accepted the teachings of Joseph Smith. Smith's teachings were unpopular with many of his neighbors, so the Mormons were forced to move from time to time. After a mob killed Joseph Smith in Illi-

nois, Brigham Young became the new Mormon leader. He led the Mormons to the area of the Great Salt Lake. At the time, this area was outside the western boundaries of the United States. However, the Mexican Cession made it part of the territory of the United States.

The Mormons cross the frozen Mississippi River on the trip that took them to Utah's Great Salt Lake.

The Mormons used irrigation to insure productive farming in their semiarid area. Pupils might investigate their clever cooperative irrigation systems. The story of the success of their 1848 crops, which were saved from crickets by the seemingly miraculous appearance of gulls, is also fascinating.

The names of early settlements in California as well as many other Californian place-names are Spanish. You might have your pupils use a map of California to locate Spanish names, which they could then translate into English.

California   California had its first settlers from Spain and Mexico late in the history of Spain's empire in the New World. (See page 48.) Soldiers and missionaries were almost equally active in bringing Spanish civilization to the region. The part of the region that the Spanish called Baja (bä′ hä) California, or Lower California, was settled first. Gaspar de Portolá, a military man, led an expedition from there to Alta California, or Upper California, in 1769. Portolá and his men established **presidios**—military forts—at San Diego and Monterey. Later, other presidios were built farther north.

Father Junípero Serra (hü nē′ pā rō ser′-rä) led five Franciscan missionaries who were with Portolá's expedition. When Portolá returned to Mexico, Father Serra remained behind. His goal was to bring the Christian religion to the Indians. While he lived, 9 missions were set up, and in time there were 21 missions, stretching from San Diego to San Francisco. Father Serra was lame in one leg, but traveling from mission to mission, he worked tirelessly supervising the work with the Indians. He was the major force in securing Spain's hold on the lands of Upper California.

In 1821, Mexico gained its independence from Spain. California then became a part of Mexico. Not long afterwards, President Andrew Jackson offered

The founding of California's mission at Monterey is celebrated. (37°N/122°W; map, p. 303)

This painting was actually done about 100 years after the event it depicts. By that time, Monterey was a thriving community and not an isolated mission.

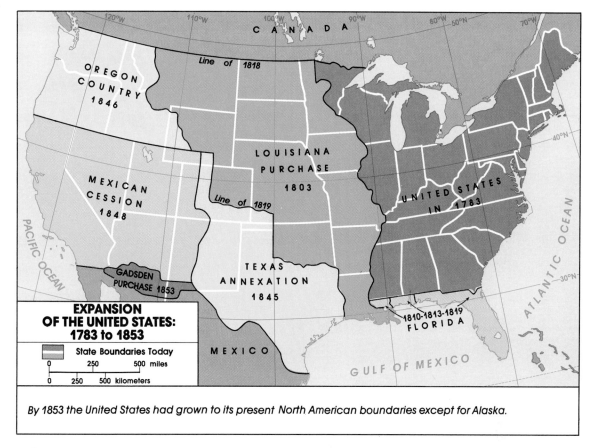

EXPANSION
OF THE UNITED STATES:
1783 to 1853

State Boundaries Today

0   250   500 miles

0   250   500 kilometers

By 1853 the United States had grown to its present North American boundaries except for Alaska.

to buy all or part of California from Mexico, but he was rebuffed. When James K. Polk became President, he too tried to buy California. For both Jackson and Polk, a major attraction was the magnificent harbor at San Francisco. Also, they feared that Mexico was too weak to challenge Russian claims to land on the west coast of North America. Probably no more than 50,000 people lived in California when the Mexican War broke out. Most of these were Indians. Fewer than a thousand settlers from the East lived there.

Nevertheless, these Americans wanted California to be part of the United States. They took the lead in a revolt against Mexican rule. President Polk may have encouraged this revolt. Captain John C. Frémont may also have had a hand in it.

He was in California on an exploring expedition with a small body of American soldiers at the time.

When the Mexican War began, a small American army commanded by General Stephen W. Kearny invaded New Mexico. Kearny's army captured Sante Fe without a fight and then marched on to California. Helped by American naval units, it soon brought all of Upper California under American control. When news of the Treaty of Guadalupe Hidalgo came, General Kearny worked to establish a territorial government for California.

Gold!   Early in 1848, workmen were building a sawmill for John Sutter, an early settler in California, on the American River, near Sacramento. They found

307

Forty-niners arriving in San Francisco lived in a tent city. (38°N/122°W; map, p. 303)

shiny bits of metal in the stream that supplied power for the sawmill. Soon the metal was recognized as gold. John Sutter tried to keep the discovery a secret, but the news spread rapidly. Before long, hundreds of Californians were on their way to Sutter's mill.

As the news reached the eastern United States and other parts of the world, the **California gold rush** began. It was 1849 before the real rush developed, so the gold seekers are usually known as **forty-niners.** About 50,000 persons started along the western trails in 1849, nearly all of them hurrying to the gold fields of California. Farmers abandoned their fields, workers flung down their tools, and clerks left their desks. The way was rough, and nearly 5,000 of the travelers died without reaching California.

Other eager forty-niners reached California by sea. Some took fast ships around Cape Horn, at the tip of South America, then sailed up the Pacific Coast to San Francisco. Others sailed to Panama, crossed the isthmus, and continued to California by ship from the Pacific side. This route was shorter and more popular, but it was also more difficult. The land on the isthmus was rough and covered by tropical jungles and swamps. Consequently, the California gold rush stimulated interest in building a canal across the Isthmus of Panama.

After gold was discovered on his holdings, Sutter's workers left and he lost his livestock and land. He was eventually given a yearly pension of $3,000 in recognition of his losses.

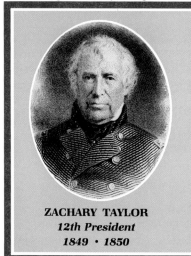

Born: 1784, Montebello, Orange County, Virginia. **Education:** Private tutors and relatives. **Training:** Army officer. **To presidency from:** Louisiana. **Position when elected:** Major general in United States Army. **Political party:** Whig. **Married:** Margaret Smith. **Children:** Five daughters, one son. **Died:** 1850, Washington, D.C. **Other facts:** Grew up on the Kentucky frontier. Spent almost all of his adult life in the army. A good military leader who never lost a battle. Called "Old Rough and Ready" by his soldiers. As President, sought advice from others but made his own decisions. **During his presidency:** As many as 500 ships were anchored in San Francisco Bay. Most were abandoned as passengers and crew rushed to the goldfields.

ZACHARY TAYLOR
12th President
1849 · 1850

A population boom By 1850 nearly 100,000 gold seekers had come to California. The mining camps contained a mixture of races and nationalities. One woman wrote home that her neighbors were French, Dutch, Scottish, Jews, Italians, Swedes, Chinese, and Indians. Men and women of Mexican Indian and of African ancestry had settled in California even before the discovery of gold. The numbers of all these, except Indians, now increased rapidly.

Most miners were men, though some families had come in search of gold. Whether men, women, or children, they lived at first under primitive conditions. Tents and lean-tos were the usual dwellings. A few miners even made their homes in barrels. Food and other supplies were expensive and hard to get. It was possible to "get rich quick," but most worked hard just to eke out a living. Some of the forty-niners grew discouraged and returned to their former homes. Nevertheless, enough remained to give California the necessary population to ask for statehood in 1850.

Slavery expansion? Not all Americans approved of the rapid expansion of the United States. Many Northerners believed that the annexation of Texas and the Mexican War that followed were plots of Southerners to add more slave territory to the Union. Some Northern leaders demanded that Congress prohibit slavery in the territories gained as the result of the war. Many Southerners were equally determined to make slavery legal in at least part of the Mexican Cession. As you will find out in the next unit, these and other sectional issues came to a head when California asked in 1850 to be admitted as the thirty-first state in the union.

CHECKUP

1. What were the major provisions in the Treaty of Guadalupe Hidalgo?
2. What did Americans mean when they spoke of *manifest destiny?*
3. Why were the Mormons concentrated around the Great Salt Lake area when the Mexican War began?
4. How did California become United States territory in 1848?
5. What changes did the discovery of gold bring to northern California?

In 1846, Representative David Wilmot of Pennsylvania presented a resolution to the House of Representatives stipulating that slavery would not be permitted in any of the land to be acquired from Mexico after the war. Although it was never passed, the so-called Wilmot Proviso became the focus of great controversy. **309**

13/CHAPTER REVIEW

KEY FACTS

1. By the 1840s, increasing numbers of settlers were moving westward in wagon trains across the Great Plains and through the Rocky Mountains.

2. A dispute between Great Britain and the United States over the Oregon country was settled by dividing it along the 49th parallel.

3. Texas won its independence from Mexico and later joined the United States.

4. Following the United States victory in the Mexican War, Mexico ceded to the United States a vast expanse of land in the Southwest.

5. The discovery of gold in California brought thousands of people to that region and hastened its development.

VOCABULARY QUIZ

On a separate sheet of paper, match each word or phrase with the correct description. There are two extra descriptions.

a. Great American Desert

b. covered wagon

c. provisional government

d. "Fifty-four forty or fight!"

e. manifest destiny

f. Mormons

g. forty-niners

h. Mexican Cession

i. mountain men

j. "Remember the Alamo!"

f **1.** Members of a religious group

2. Defenders at the Alamo

b **3.** Vehicle used on the western trails

a **4.** Mistaken description of land between the Missouri River and the Rocky Mountains

c **5.** A temporary ruling arrangement

6. The title of a book by Jessie Frémont

d **7.** A slogan relating to Oregon

e **8.** Something that many people felt was bound to happen according to fate

g **9.** California gold seekers

h **10.** All the land acquired by the Treaty of Guadalupe Hidalgo

j **11.** A slogan relating to Texas

i **12.** Guides for the western pioneers

REVIEW QUESTIONS

1. Why did pioneers in the West first settle along the Pacific coast rather than in the Great Plains area?

2. What were the main routes to the coast?

3. How did Texas win its independence?

4. Why and how did President Polk act to settle the Oregon boundary question?

5. What were the results of the war with Mexico?

ACTIVITIES

1. Imagine that you are a member of a wagon train from Independence, Missouri, traveling west on the Oregon Trail in the early 1840s. After your first week on the trail, write an account of what your daily life has been like. Describe what you have seen, what difficulties you have encountered, and how you feel about continuing on.

2. On an outline map of the United States, indicate with different colors (**a**) the Mexican Cession, (**b**) the Gadsden Purchase, (**c**) the part of the Oregon country that was acquired by the United States.

3. Choose a name from the list that follows and find out all you can about that person.

John C. Frémont   Marcus Whitman

Jessie Benton Frémont   Stephen Austin

Narcissa Whitman   James Beckwourth

Take notes on your reading and be prepared to report your findings to the class.

KEEPING A DIARY

WESTWARD MOVEMENT

Have you ever kept a diary? A diary is a written daily account of what one does and how one feels. On page 288, you read an entry from the diary of a New York man. He had just seen an early railroad train and was excited at the sight.

Below are selections from the diaries of two Americans who made the trip west. One went by ship and the other by wagon train.

The first entry is from the diary of Moses Cogswell, a young man from New Hampshire. Cogswell sailed from Boston to California. Like thousands of others, he was headed for California's gold fields. The following diary entry, written a month before the ship docked in San Francisco, told of the long, monotonous voyage.

> July 8, 1849
>
> A dead calm sun, exactly overhead. Prospect dark and dreary. Temper cross, body in perspiration. Mind, neither one thing or another. Occupation, learning Spanish. Companion, sick with the mumps. Food, potted meats and duff (a stiff flour pudding). Drink, lime juice and rain water. Novelty, a large shark. Ideas, none in the market. Friends, few and far between. Determination, to get gold. Hopes, again to see home . . . if any vessel makes a longer passage than we do, I pity them.

The next entry is from the diary of Susan Magoffin. In 1846, Magoffin and her husband led a trading caravan from Missouri to Santa Fe. Magoffin was then an 18-year-old bride. When she and her husband left Missouri, Santa Fe was part of Mexico. By the time they reached Santa Fe, General Kearny's army had captured the city. Magoffin's diary has this entry for the day of their arrival.

> August 31, 1846
>
> I have entered the city in a year that will always be remembered by my countrymen; and under the 'Star-Spangled banner,' too. The first American lady who had come under such auspices.

SKILLS PRACTICE

To find out more about the Santa Fe Trail and the California gold rush, look in an encyclopedia or in the following books: *The Santa Fe Trail* by Samuel Hopkins Adams (New York: Random House, Inc., 1951) and *California Gold Days* by Helen Bauer (Sacramento, Calif.: California State Department of Education, 1957). These and numerous other sources are available in most libraries.

Now write your own diary entries about the following situations.

1. Imagine you are Moses Cogswell. You have just completed the journey around Cape Horn and have finally arrived in California. It is your first day in the gold fields. Write a diary entry telling how it feels to be on land again. Describe what it's like on your first day of searching for gold.

2. Imagine you are Susan Magoffin. Try to feel as though you are actually on a wagon train. It is the last day on the trail before reaching Santa Fe. Tell how you feel after spending several months on the trail. Tell about your hopes and expectations for a new life in Santa Fe.

311

How Americans Lived, 1850

BENCHMARKS

THE UNITED STATES

YEAR:	1850
AREA:	2,940,042 sq mi
	7,614,709 sq km
POPULATION:	23,191,876
POPULATION DENSITY:	8 per sq mi
	3 per sq km
NUMBER OF STATES:	31
LARGEST STATE IN AREA:	Texas
IN POPULATION:	New York
LARGEST CITY:	New York
WHERE PEOPLE LIVED:	

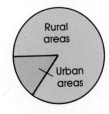

Rural areas

Urban areas

VOCABULARY

overseer   **steamboat pilot**

The Benchmarks box on this page shows that 23,191,876 people lived in the United States in 1850. Where a person lived was an important influence. But so was a person's age and race, whether that person was male or female, and whether he or she lived in a city or on a farm. <u>In 1850, fewer than one in six Americans were urban dwellers;</u> that is, living in towns or cities with a population of more than 2,500.

In a big eastern city   One city dweller in 1850 was Harriet Tubman. She lived in Philadelphia, Pennsylvania, the second most populous city in the United States. She had, however, not been there long. Harriet Tubman had been born into slavery on a Maryland plantation, one of 10 or 11 children in her family. Both sets of her grandparents had been brought in chains from Africa. From an early age Harriet Tubman was compelled to work at various tasks as maid, children's nurse, field hand, and cook.

In 1849, Harriet Tubman's master died. Rumors grew that his slaves were to be sold out of state, perhaps to masters of cotton plantations in Mississippi or Louisiana. Harriet, afraid of what might happen to her, decided to make a break for freedom. She escaped to Philadelphia, where she got a job in a hotel.

Pupils can find in an almanac the percentage of our nation's population that are urban dwellers according to the 1980 census. (79.2%) Ask: How does that compare to the situation in 1850?

Life in Philadelphia had much more variety than life on a Maryland plantation. The city's population was constantly growing and changing. In 1850, more immigrants came to the United States than in any single year before. The total of 370,000 included 164,000 from Ireland, 79,000 from the states of Germany, and 51,000 from Great Britain. Immigrants added many colorful customs to life in Philadelphia and other cities.

Life in Philadelphia in 1850 was also more fast-paced than life on a Maryland plantation. City people always seemed to be in a hurry. Vehicles drawn by horses and oxen jammed the streets. Their drivers shouted and yelled and cracked their whips. When a fire broke out in the city, volunteer fire companies raced each other to the scene. They often settled with their fists the question of which company got there first.

Chickens and hogs roamed throughout the city. They were the only garbage disposal system available in 1850, as they gobbled scraps thrown into the streets. Few American cities had good water systems in 1850, though Philadelphia was an exception. The city's water supply was pumped from the Schuylkill River.

In December 1850, Harriet Tubman set out on what was to be her major work for the next 10 years. She returned to Maryland and guided her sister and two children to freedom. Between periods of employment in the North, Harriet Tubman is believed to have made 19 dangerous trips into Maryland. The number of slaves she led from Maryland plantations to freedom is uncertain, but it may have been as many as 300.

By 1850, Philadelphia was a bustling city with large commercial buildings and cobblestoned streets.

On a cotton plantation   Life on a cotton plantation in Mississippi was different from life on a Maryland plantation, where tobacco was the chief crop. Probably fewer than one fourth of the families in Mississippi lived on farms large enough to be called plantations. Life on these plantations, however, was leisurely and elegant. The owner generally hired **overseers** to manage the slaves and take care of business matters.

Tutors came to educate the young sons and daughters of wealthy plantation owners. Still, there was time for plantation boys and girls to learn to ride well. As adults they would be expected to engage in fox hunting with hounds and horses. Such hunts were usually great social occasions enjoyed by young and old from neighboring plantations.

After the Fugitive Slave Law was passed in 1850, many slaves chose to escape to Canada, since under the new law they could not be sure of remaining free even in the nonslave states. Pupils might look up the provisions of this law.

When the sons of plantation owners reached college age, they often went to a northern school for further education, or perhaps to England. Their return home for vacation or after graduation frequently furnished the occasion for a series of parties. One plantation owner celebrated his son's homecoming with an evening party that included fireworks at 11 o'clock, supper at midnight, and dancing until dawn.

In a small midwestern city   In 1850, Mary Todd Lincoln was also an urban dweller. She was in her early 30s, about the same age as Harriet Tubman. Born in Kentucky, Mary Lincoln lived in Springfield, Illinois, with her husband, Abraham, and their growing family.

No photograph or drawing of the Lincoln family in 1850 is known to exist. The drawing below pictures the Lincoln family in the early 1860s when they were living in the White House.

Springfield was much smaller than Philadelphia. Yet it was a bustling, rapidly growing community. Thirteen years before, it had become the capital of Illinois.

By 1850, Mary and Abraham Lincoln and their sons Bob and Eddie were living in a two-story white frame house at the corner of Eighth and Jackson streets. An attached stable housed a horse and buggy. The family also had a cow that Lincoln milked. Not many years earlier this neighborhood had been open prairie. Now, frame and brick houses were going up as the population increased.

Like his wife, Abraham Lincoln was born in Kentucky, but his mother and father had taken him to Indiana when he was a little boy. His family was poor, so he had helped support the other members until striking out on his own at the age of 21. He moved to Illinois and supported himself in various ways while studying law. As a Whig, Abraham Lincoln served several terms in the Illinois state legislature. Between 1847 and 1849 he served one term in the House of Representatives in Washington as the only Whig congressman from Illinois. Deciding not to seek reelection, he returned to Springfield to resume his law practice.

Lincoln's office was on the public square, the center of activity in Springfield. Nearby were the courthouse, the jail, and shops in which blacksmiths, harness makers, and others carried on their trades. Except for a few places where planks had been laid down, the streets were black soil. In wet weather the mud was ankle-deep; in dry weather great clouds of dust hung in the air.

Refer pupils to pages 262–264 to review the material about the Whig party.

Abraham Lincoln's earlier life on the frontier was quite different from his life in Springfield. Pupils might try to find pictures relating to his life as a child and a young boy. Discuss differences in life-style depending on time and place.

The Lincoln family lived in this house in Springfield, Illinois. (40°N/84°W; map, p. 717)

Through the square there was a constant procession of horses carrying riders or pulling buggies. Oxen hauled creaking carts loaded with wheat, corn, and potatoes. Covered wagons were often seen proceeding farther west.

Though never rich, Abraham Lincoln was able to provide his family with a comfortable existence. In 1850 a third son, Willie, was born. But in late 1850, the death of their son Eddie brought grief to the Lincoln family. A similar grief was suffered by many American families in those days. For every 1,000 children born in 1850, at least 150 would die before the age of 1 year.

In a Mississippi River town   About 100 miles (160 km) west of Springfield, Illinois, lay the town of Hannibal, Missouri. Living there in 1850 was young Sam Clemens, who was 15 years old. Many years later, Samuel L. Clemens would remember Hannibal as a "sleepy little village." Actually while he was growing up there, it was a small but busy Mississippi River port with a population of about 3,000. It had a number of businesses: two slaughterhouses, four general stores, three sawmills, two planing mills, three blacksmith shops, two hotels, three saloons, a tobacco factory, a hemp factory, a tanyard, and a distillery.

Tell pupils that infant mortality is the number of children who die before the age of 1 out of every 1,000 born. Ask pupils to look up in an almanac the latest infant mortality statistics for the United States (11.2) and compare them to the 1850 figure above.

Pupils who have never read Mark Twain's *The Adventures of Tom Sawyer* or *Adventures of Huckleberry Finn* should take this opportunity to do so. They will appreciate the differences as well as the similarities in their own life-style with that of young people in nineteenth-century America.

Sam Clemens was a reluctant pupil at the three schools he attended until he was 13. The schools required their students to pay tuition, for there were no free public schools in Hannibal at the time. He also attended a country school during the summers he spent at his uncle John Quarles' farm. It was "a heavenly place for a boy," Samuel Clemens later wrote. And there was always the wide, mysterious Mississippi, an education in itself.

By 1850, Hannibal had become a main stop for many of the forty-niners as they headed west for the gold fields of California. Samuel Clemens later recalled that he and other boys he knew "would have sold our souls" to have gone with the forty-niners. But he was only 13. Besides, his father had died of pneumonia the year before. The boy now had to find a job to help support the family.

Sam Clemens became an apprentice printer at the age of 13. The printing office served as the boy's college. Type was set by hand in those days, so Sam Clemens had to read the written material in order to set it in type. In this way he absorbed information, studied ideas, learned history, and soaked up both good and bad literature.

Still, Sam Clemens found that life in the printing shop was often drudgery. So he fulfilled his boyhood ambition of becoming a Mississippi **steamboat pilot**, guiding the big riverboats on their routes up and down the Mississippi. He later became famous under the pen name of Mark Twain. Under that name he wrote *The Adventures of Tom Sawyer*, *Adventures of Huckleberry Finn*, and other books based on his memories of life in Hannibal, Missouri, in 1850 when he was 15.

In an Indian village While Mary Todd Lincoln was living much as most other middle-class American women, Cynthia Ann Parker was living a quite different life in the Indian Territory of Oklahoma.

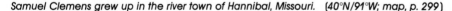

Samuel Clemens grew up in the river town of Hannibal, Missouri. (40°N/91°W; map, p. 299)

In 1850, Cynthia Ann Parker was living in a Comanche village much like this one.

In 1836, Cynthia Ann Parker, then 9 years old, had been captured by Comanche Indians when they attacked a settlement on the Texas frontier. The Quahadas, one of the Comanche bands, had adopted the little girl and treated her like one of their own.

By 1850, 23-year-old Cynthia Ann Parker had learned to set up a tepee, to preserve buffalo meat, and to tan and decorate animal skins for clothing. She had married Nocona, a noted Comanche war chief. One of their sons took his mother's family name and was known as Quanah Parker. Like his father, he became a noted chief and tried to unite several Indian tribes in resistance to the advancing tide of settlement. In time, however, Quanah Parker accepted white civilization and life in the Indian Territory of Oklahoma.

Cynthia Ann Parker refused all efforts to free her from her life with the Indians. The story of the "white Comanche" became a legend in the Southwest. She was living an unusual life in 1850, obviously different from that of most white American women. And yet it was a life much like that led by thousands of other American women—the Indian women of the Southwest.

CHECKUP

1. In what ways did life change for Harriet Tubman between 1849 and 1850?
2. What was life like on a large cotton plantation in Mississippi in 1850?
3. Compare the lives led by each of the following in 1850. (a) Mary Todd Lincoln, (b) Samuel Clemens, (c) Harriet Tubman
4. How did the life that Cynthia Ann Parker was leading in 1850 differ from that of most American women of the time?

3/UNIT REVIEW

READING THE TEXT

Turn to pages 264–265 and read the section titled "Nominating conventions." Then, on a sheet of paper, write the answers to the following questions.

1. What years have been given the name of Jacksonian Era? **From 1824 to 1840**
2. In what year was the first presidential nominating convention held? **1832**
3. Before that time, how did each of the parties choose its candidates for President and Vice President? **By caucus**
4. Which is the more democratic way of selecting candidates—the nominating convention or the caucus? **Nominating convention**
5. How often are presidential nominating conventions held? **Every 4 years**

READING A MAP

Turn to page 303 and study the map titled "The Mexican War." The map shows the routes taken by the United States military forces and shows the area acquired by the United States in the Treaty of Guadalupe Hidalgo. On a sheet of paper, answer the following questions.

1. From what port in the United States did Scott's army leave?
2. What was Scott's final destination?
3. Who were the leaders of the two forces that reached the Mexican city of Monterrey?
4. The area between what two rivers was claimed by both the United States and Mexico?
5. List the states that were carved out, in whole or in part, from the Mexican Cession. To help you make your list, you may compare this map with the one on page 307. The map on pages 716–717 will also be useful.

READING A PICTURE

Turn to page 247. Study the picture and recall what you read about the event shown. Write the answers to the following questions.

1. Who is the man at center? **Francis Scott Key**
2. What kind of ship is he on? **British warship**
3. In what harbor is the ship? **Baltimore**
4. What is the name of the structure from which the flag is waving? **Fort McHenry**
5. What time of day is it? **Dawn**

Now imagine that you are the man in the picture. On your paper write a paragraph describing your feelings at this moment.

READING A TIME LINE

Turn to page 233 and study the time line. On a sheet of paper, answer the following questions.

1. What years does the time line on page 233 cover? **1775 to 1825**
2. Into how many sections is this time line divided? **5**
3. How many years are in each section? **10**

On the same paper, beside the number of each statement below, write **T** if the statement is true and **F** if it is false.

F **4.** The Treaty of Ghent occurred before the Louisiana Purchase.
F **5.** The Treaty of Greenville ended the War of 1812.
F **6.** The year 1775 saw the Wilderness Trail go into Florida.
F **7.** The Lewis and Clark expedition set out 1 year before the Louisiana Purchase.
T **8.** Action was taken against the Barbary pirates before the Embargo Act went into effect.

The Nation Divides and Reunites

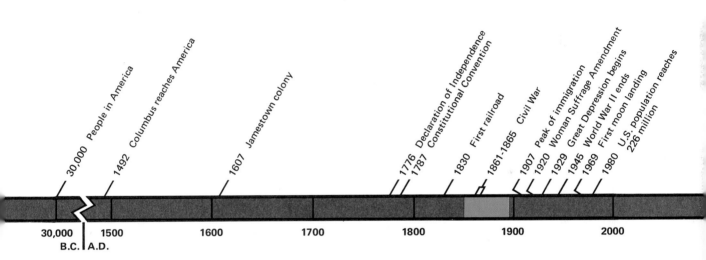

30,000 People in America

1492 Columbus reaches America

1607 Jamestown colony

1776 Declaration of Independence
1787 Constitutional Convention

1830 First railroad

1861-1865 Civil War

1907 Peak of immigration
1920 Woman Suffrage Amendment
1929 Great Depression begins
1945 World War II ends
1969 First moon landing
1980 U.S. population reaches 226 million

| 30,000 B.C. | A.D. | 1500 | 1600 | 1700 | 1800 | 1900 | 2000 |

Above: Abraham Lincoln, fleeing slaves, Robert E. Lee, Ulysses S. Grant, Harriet Beecher Stowe

CHAPTER

14 Rising Tensions

Another Compromise

VOCABULARY

Seventh of March speech

Compromise of 1850

Fugitive Slave Law

Underground Railroad

Three great senators Few of our leaders in government have had more effect on American history than three men sitting in the United States Senate in 1850. One was Henry Clay of Kentucky. Thirty years before, he had helped to arrange the Missouri Compromise, which settled a dangerous controversy between the North and the South.

Another of the three was John C. Calhoun of South Carolina. Since 1832 he had used his position within the Senate to protect the rights of the South. Daniel Webster was the third great senator. He was as popular in Massachusetts as John C. Calhoun was in South Carolina. Unlike Calhoun, Webster spoke always for a strong national government against the Southern doctrine of states' rights.

Henry Clay, John C. Calhoun, and Daniel Webster looked nothing alike. Clay was tall and graceful, with a high forehead and blue eyes. He smiled easily, spoke well, and charmed both men and women. Calhoun was dark-haired and of medium build. He was very serious and had a brilliant mind. Webster was short and stocky. His piercing dark eyes, heavy black brows, and broad forehead gave his face an impressive appearance. He was one of the great orators of the day, with a voice that was deep and musical.

For 30 years these three men had served their country. Over that period, they had dealt with the great issues of the times. On some occasions they had seen eye to eye; at other times, they had disagreed. Now, in 1850, they prepared to deal with an issue that could, if unresolved, bring on a dangerous confrontation between the North and the South. It would be the last time that these three giants of the Senate would come together. John C. Calhoun, suffering from tuberculosis, would die before the end of the year. Clay and Webster would die in 1852.

The California question As you learned in Chapter 13, the gold rush brought thousands of people into California. As a result, California was the first territory in the Mexican Cession to ask for admission as a state. Most of the gold seekers in California had come from the free-soil states, where slavery was illegal. Moreover, workers in the gold fields had no desire to face the competition of slave labor. For these reasons, California asked for admission as a free state.

Henry Clay urges the Senate to compromise the differences between North and South.

You may wish to assign reports on the following people: Henry Clay, Daniel Webster, John Calhoun.

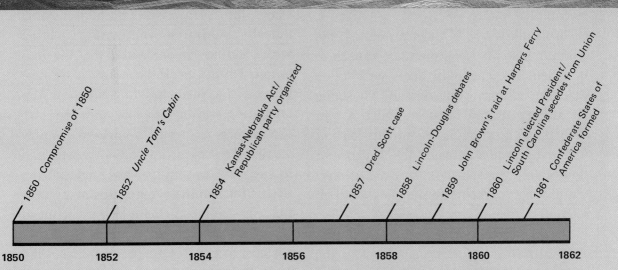

1850 Compromise of 1850

1852 *Uncle Tom's Cabin*

1854 Kansas-Nebraska Act/
Republican party organized

1857 Dred Scott case

1858 Lincoln-Douglas debates

1859 John Brown's raid at Harpers Ferry

1860 Lincoln elected President/
South Carolina secedes from Union

1861 Confederate States of
America formed

| 1850 | 1852 | 1854 | 1856 | 1858 | 1860 | 1862 |

lay is remembered as the Great Pacificator. On three occasions he arranged compromises to preserve the Union: the
lissouri Compromise, the tariff of 1833, and the Compromise of 1850. Review with pupils the compromises of 1820, 1833,
nd 1850 proposed by Clay. Have them consider the area of the United States that Clay represented. Ask: Why was he an
leal individual to suggest compromise?

321

In 1850 there were 15 slave states and 15 free states in the Union. The admission of California would destroy this balance. There were other questions involved, however. The status of slavery in all of the Mexican Cession had not yet been decided. If California became a free state, would this mean slavery would be barred from *all* of the Mexican Cession? To many Southerners, any attempts to bar slavery from the new territories threatened the welfare of the South. They felt that slavery must expand or the South would die. Many Northerners, on the other hand, felt that slavery must not be allowed to expand into new territory.

Clay's compromise Southern congressmen bitterly opposed the admission of California as a free state. Once more Henry Clay began working patiently on a compromise to save the Union. Stephen A. Douglas assisted Clay. Douglas was a young Democratic senator from Illinois. He was nicknamed the Little Giant— "little" because he was well below normal height, and "giant" because of his many accomplishments.

In January 1850, Clay presented his compromise plan in a dramatic speech to the Senate. The plan dealt with more than the California question and the status of slavery in the Mexican Cession. In fact, it was an attempt to deal with several unsolved issues between the North and the South. In his plan, Clay asked both Southerners and Northerners to give in on certain points.

There were six parts to the proposal:
(1) California would be admitted to the Union as a free state.

(2) The remainder of the Mexican Cession would be organized into two territories, Utah and New Mexico. Presumably the people of these territories could decide whether they wanted slavery when they applied for admission as a state.
(3) Some land in dispute between Texas and New Mexico would be awarded to New Mexico.
(4) Texas would receive $10 million from the national government for giving up its claims to this land.
(5) The buying and selling of slaves, but not slavery itself, would be prohibited in the District of Columbia.
(6) Congress would enact a strict law requiring that runaway slaves be returned to their masters.

Congress approves When the several parts of Clay's plan came before the Senate, John C. Calhoun made a dramatic appearance. Friends carried him into the meeting room on a stretcher. Too weak to speak himself, Calhoun had a younger Southern senator read his speech. In the speech, Calhoun agreed to the purpose of Clay's bill. However, Calhoun insisted that it should give even more protection to the South. He demanded that the government bring back the political balance between the North and the South and stop tampering with the slavery question.

Senators—indeed, the whole country—waited to hear what Daniel Webster had to say. He was from New England, the part of the country where antislavery feeling was strongest. Many people believed it would be political suicide for Daniel Webster to support the compromise. And yet, in what is called his **Seventh of March**

In discussing the Compromise of 1850 you might want to have pupils consider the following questions: Is compromise the best way to settle a dispute? Does it provide a permanent solution to the problem? Is avoiding a drastic solution a good reason for compromise? Was it right to compromise on the issue of slavery?

speech, Webster not only approved the compromise but pleaded with the whole country to do the same.

At the beginning of his speech, Webster said: "I wish to speak today, not as a Massachusetts man, nor as a Northern man, but as an American . . . I speak today for the preservation of the Union." Let Northerners make all reasonable compromises with the South, Webster pleaded. Plantations cannot possibly exist in the deserts, plains, and mountains of the Mexican Cession, he argued. Therefore, nature would make slavery unprofitable in that region and Congress would not need to make a law to prohibit it there.

It is doubtful that the compromise would have been approved without Webster's support. As it was, Congress approved the parts of the compromise, one by one. Most people in the country breathed a sigh of relief as Clay's plan became law in the **Compromise of 1850.** It appeared that this act had put an end to the controversy between the North and the South. Perhaps Calhoun could see farther ahead than others, however. When he died a few months later, it is said he murmured with his last breath, "The South, the poor South."

Review the Missouri Compromise. Ask: What changes have been made on the map of the United States since 1820?

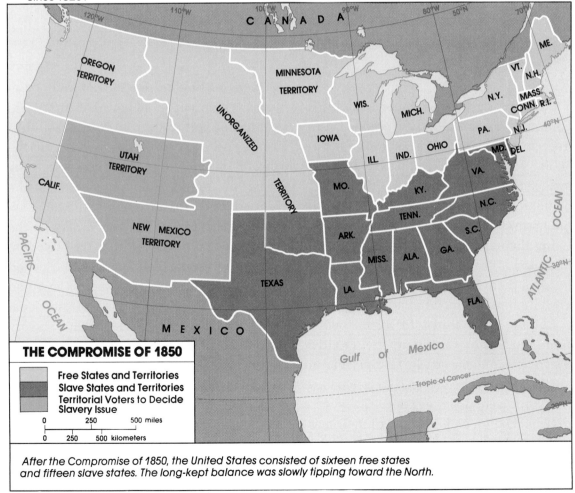

THE COMPROMISE OF 1850

- Free States and Territories
- Slave States and Territories
- Territorial Voters to Decide Slavery Issue

0   250   500 miles
0   250   500 kilometers

After the Compromise of 1850, the United States consisted of sixteen free states and fifteen slave states. The long-kept balance was slowly tipping toward the North.

Some Northerners wanted the Wilmot Proviso to be part of the Compromise of 1850. Assign a pupil to report to the class on the Wilmot Proviso.

323

Cotton plantations like this one on the Mississippi were dependent on slave labor.

A disaster for black people   John C. Calhoun was not alone in seeing future trouble because of the Compromise of 1850. For black people it was no compromise at all. It was a disaster. What did it matter if the slave sales were forbidden in the District of Columbia? White families living there could still keep slaves. And Southern officeholders could bring slaves to serve them in the capital city of a supposedly free, democratic nation.

But the chief threat for black people came from the passing of the **Fugitive Slave Law**, one part of the Compromise of 1850. Slaves who escaped to free soil in the North were no longer safe. They were to be picked up and returned to their masters. The new law provided bounties, or rewards, for the capture of escaped slaves. The law stated, too, that officials

in Northern towns and cities had to help in the return of fugitive slaves when asked to do so. Finally, the law said that those who knew of escaped slaves and did not report what they knew could be fined and even jailed.

Slave owners and many Northerners looked upon the new Fugitive Slave Law as a way of combatting the operations of the mysterious **Underground Railroad**. This was an informal system set up by antislavery people to guide fugitive slaves to safety. It was called "underground" because it was secret and "railroad" because escaping slaves were moved from one "station," or hiding place, to another. Those who guided the escaping slave from one station to another were called conductors.

Effects of the Fugitive Slave Law   Before 1850, escaped slaves needed only to get to free soil in the Old Northwest or in Pennsylvania. With the passage of the new Fugitive Slave Law, however, they were no longer safe anywhere in the United States. Furthermore, the new law made it necessary for free blacks in the North and in the South to carry "freedom papers" proving they were not escaped slaves. Consequently, many escaped slaves and free blacks went to the Canadian province of Ontario, where slavery had been illegal since the late 1700s.

Shortly after her own escape, Harriet Tubman found a home in St. Catherines, Ontario. Here, in the 1850s, she brought the slaves she led to freedom from Maryland. Other American blacks settled in Chatham and Wilberforce, Canada, to avoid the chance of being picked up as fugitive slaves. In addition, by settling there they escaped the kind of racial discrimination they experienced in the United States.

Within the northern United States, a number of fights and riots occurred when slave catchers tried to return blacks to their masters. For example, in 1854 in Boston, slave catchers seized Anthony Burns, an escaped slave. It took marines, cavalry, and artillery to hold back the thousands of people who tried to keep Burns from being returned to his Southern master. The attempt to free him failed. Nevertheless, a few months after his return to the South, Northern abolitionists purchased Anthony Burns from his master and sent him to Canada.

Besides guiding slaves out of the South, Harriet Tubman came to their aid in the North. In 1859, along with a crowd in Troy, New York, she helped to free Charles Nalle, a runaway slave who was being returned to the South.

The Fugitive Slave Law was only one part of the Compromise of 1850. But it made more problems than the other parts of the law had solved. For one thing, it caused many more people in the North to become abolitionists. Also, the northern reaction convinced many people in the South that people in the North did not intend to obey the law.

CHECKUP

1. What part did Henry Clay, John C. Calhoun, and Daniel Webster play in the Compromise of 1850?
2. What were the six provisions of the Compromise?
3. Why did blacks consider the Compromise of 1850 no compromise at all?
4. What was the Northern reaction to the Fugitive Slave Law? The Southern reaction?

Tensions Increase

┌─VOCABULARY─────────────────┐

Kansas-Nebraska bill	"bleeding Kansas"
popular sovereignty	Dred Scott case
Republican party	Confederate States of America

└────────────────────────────┘

New leaders President Zachary Taylor died suddenly in 1850. Vice-President Millard Fillmore succeeded him. However, the Whigs turned away from Fillmore in 1852. They nominated General Winfield Scott, who, like Taylor, was a hero of the Mexican War. In this election the Whigs, torn between Northern

Harriet Tubman (left) poses with two people she has guided to freedom over the Underground Railroad.

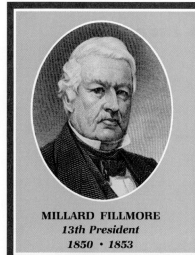

Born: 1800, Locke, New York. **Education:** Largely self-educated. **Training:** Lawyer, public official. **To presidency from:** New York. **Position when taking office:** Vice President. **Political party:** Whig. **Married:** (1) Abigail Powers, (2) Caroline Carmichael McIntosh. **Children:** One son, one daughter. **Died:** 1874, Buffalo, New York. **Other facts:** A handsome man more than 6 feet (1.8 m) tall, always well groomed. Apprenticed to a clothmaker at the age of 14; purchased his freedom at 19 for $30. Taught school briefly. Served in state government in New York and in United States Congress. Ran for President in 1856 as a third-party candidate but was defeated. **During his presidency:** Elisha Otis invented the first elevator for carrying passengers.

MILLARD FILLMORE
13th President
1850 · 1853

and Southern branches, lost and ceased to exist as a national political party. Franklin Pierce of New Hampshire, the Democratic candidate, was elected President.

A new group of political leaders was emerging on the American scene. Franklin Pierce was the first elected President to be born in the nineteenth century. William H. Seward, a Whig senator from New York, was 24 years younger than Henry Clay. James Henry Hammond, a senator from South Carolina in the 1850s, was 25 years younger than John C. Calhoun.

Stephen A. Douglas, the Little Giant from Illinois, attracted the support of young Democrats as early as 1852. The ambitious Douglas, born in Vermont, had moved west to Illinois at the age of 20. There he rose rapidly in the legal profession and in politics. He married a Southern girl who inherited 150 slaves from her father. Appointed to the Senate in 1847 and reelected in 1852, Senator Stephen A. Douglas had connections with three different sections of the country. It was felt by many that he might someday be his party's candidate for President.

A controversial bill In 1854, Douglas put forth the **Kansas-Nebraska bill.** Under the bill, two territories, Kansas and Nebraska, would be formed from the Louisiana Purchase land. Both lay north of the line drawn by the Missouri Compromise. The compromise had prohibited slavery north of that line. However, Douglas's bill said that the people of Kansas and Nebraska could decide whether they wanted to allow slavery. This would, of course, set aside the Missouri Compromise that had been the law since 1820.

Douglas called this idea **popular sovereignty**—in other words, "Let the people decide." He pointed out that this principle was followed when California asked for admission as a free state. Moreover, as Douglas pointed out, the Compromise of 1850 had left the status of slavery in the remainder of the Mexican Cession to be decided by the people living there.

Some people believe that Douglas sponsored the bill to attract Southern support for another try at the presidency in 1856. Others think that Douglas put forth the bill because it would help in a plan to build a railroad from Chicago to the West Coast. Such a railroad, to be financed partly by the national government, would encourage settlement of the sparsely settled lands north and south of the Missouri River. It would also enable Douglas to profit from his own landholdings along the proposed railway route.

The Kansas-Nebraska bill stirred up a storm of protest in the North. Northerners had come to regard the Missouri Compromise as almost sacred. They were shocked at this attempt to repeal the 34-year-old agreement. Southerners, on the other hand, saw the Kansas-Nebraska bill as an unexpected chance to add another slave state to the Union. The Kansas territory lay west of Missouri, a slave state. Presumably, people sympathetic to slavery would settle in Kansas and vote for its admission as a slave state.

Congress debated the Kansas-Nebraska bill with passion. Some members of Congress, fearing bloodshed, were carrying revolvers and knives. The halls of Congress mirrored the intense emotions aroused throughout the country for and against the bill. Nevertheless, with President Pierce's support, Douglas got the

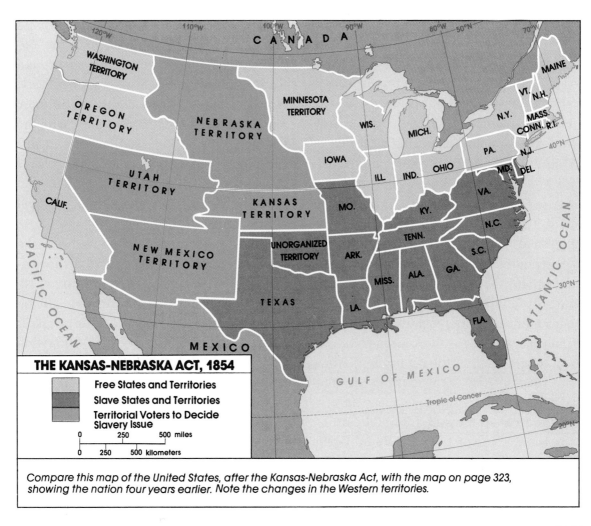

THE KANSAS-NEBRASKA ACT, 1854

Free States and Territories
Slave States and Territories
Territorial Voters to Decide Slavery Issue

0   250   500 miles
0 250 500 kilometers

Compare this map of the United States, after the Kansas-Nebraska Act, with the map on page 323, showing the nation four years earlier. Note the changes in the Western territories.

FRANKLIN PIERCE
14th President
1853 · 1857

Born: 1804, Hillsborough, New Hampshire. **Education:** Bowdoin College. **Training:** Lawyer, public official. **To presidency from:** New Hampshire. **Position when elected:** In private law practice. **Political party:** Democratic. **Married:** Jane Means Appleton. **Children:** Three sons. **Died:** 1869, Concord, New Hampshire. **Other facts:** Served in New Hampshire state legislature and later in Congress, in both House of Representatives and Senate. At age of 33 the youngest senator when he took his seat in 1838. Rose to rank of general in Mexican War. A dark-horse candidate for President, an office he had not sought. Made no speeches during his campaign. **During his presidency:** Japan for the first time opened ports to American ships.

Ask: Why did war break out in Kansas? Who were the opponents? What resulted from the conflict?

Kansas-Nebraska bill through Congress. In 1854 the President signed the controversial bill into law.

The Republican party   Senator Douglas had failed to understand that Northern opposition to the Kansas-Nebraska Act included people from three political parties. In Ripon, Wisconsin, a group of Whigs, unhappy Democrats, and members of a small Free-Soilers party met in a church early in March 1854. They talked about forming a new party. Someone suggested the name **Republican party.**

Four months later at a meeting in Jackson, Michigan, the name *Republican* was officially adopted. Across the Northern states more and more meetings took place from protests against the Kansas-Nebraska Act. Opposition to the act brought Abraham Lincoln back into politics. In 1856 he helped set up the new party in Illinois and called himself a Republican.

In the election of 1856, the Republicans chose the popular western explorer, John C. Frémont, as their presidential candidate. The Republican slogan of "Free soil, free speech, and Frémont" was shouted and carried on banners, in torchlight parades, and in hundreds of mass meetings. The Republican platform opposed any expansion of slavery and called for the repeal of the Fugitive Slave Law. However, the Democratic candidate, James Buchanan of Pennsylvania, won the election. Nevertheless, the Republicans did well. They had replaced the Whigs as a major political party and showed that they were an up-and-coming political organization.

Thus one result of the Kansas-Nebraska Act was opposition that caused the formation of the Republican party. Another result was open warfare in Kansas. If the vote of the people was to decide whether Kansas would be slave or free, each side was determined to have the majority. Armed men poured in from the North and the South.

Men favoring slavery formed one territorial government in Kansas. Men opposed to slavery formed another. Raids and murders took place as law and order broke down. John Brown, a fanatical abo-

Have pupils research the party platforms supported by Buchanan and John C. Frémont in the presidential election of 1856. Have them put the information into a chart. Ask: Based on his party platform, why, do you think, did James Buchanan win the election of 1856?

litionist, and his sons led an attack in which five proslavery settlers in Kansas were killed. Violence in **"bleeding Kansas"** added to the tensions now being felt in all parts of the country.

The Dred Scott case   Two days after President James Buchanan took office on March 4, 1857, the Supreme Court issued its decision in the **Dred Scott case.** Dred Scott, a slave, had been taken by his master from Missouri, a slave state, to Illinois, a free state. Then Dred Scott was taken to the Wisconsin territory, where slavery was forbidden by the Missouri Compromise. Later his master took him back to Missouri. Some antislavery people helped Dred Scott sue for his freedom on the grounds that he had been taken to live in a territory where slavery was prohibited by law.

The Dred Scott case raised a number of questions. Was a black person a citizen, with the right to sue in a federal court?

No, said the majority of the Supreme Court. The Court could have stopped there with its decision. But it decided to go further. Slaves were property, the Court said, and the Fifth Amendment to the Constitution protected property. Therefore Congress could not prohibit slavery in any of the territories. Therefore the Missouri Compromise of 1820 was unconstitutional.

The justices of the Supreme Court thought their decision would end the controversy over the expansion of slavery into the territories. They were badly mistaken. The Dred Scott decision pleased many Southern Democrats. It seemed to mean that all the territories of the national government were open to slavery and that not even a vote of the people living there could keep slavery out. Most Northern Democrats, however, were angry at the Dred Scott decision. They preferred Douglas's doctrine of popular sovereignty. Because of these differences, the

Violence erupts in "bleeding Kansas" as proslavery and antislavery groups clash.

Abraham Lincoln debates Stephen Douglas in 1858. Douglas stands directly behind Lincoln.

Dred Scott decision brought on a split between Northern and Southern Democrats.

Republicans and other opponents of slavery attacked the Dred Scott decision. Some Republicans announced they would defy the Supreme Court's decision. The Court, they said, had become the ally of Southern slaveholders. This defiance seemed to shock Southern leaders. First, Northerners had refused to obey the Fugitive Slave Law. Now they were defying the Supreme Court of the United States, the highest court in the land. How long, the Southern leaders asked, should the South remain united with the defiant North?

Seven debates   In 1858, Senator Stephen A. Douglas ran for another term as senator from Illinois. He seemed certain to be elected. To oppose Douglas, the Republicans nominated Abraham Lincoln. Lincoln boldly challenged the Little Giant to a series of debates. Seven Lincoln-Douglas debates were held in the late summer and autumn of 1858, each in a different Illinois city.

Although Douglas won the election to the Senate, the debates brought Lincoln to national attention. Moreover, in the debates, Lincoln forced Douglas to admit he was not wholly in favor of the Dred Scott decision. This admission would lose Douglas some Southern support in his campaign for the presidency 2 years later. Southern Democrats would not support any candidate who opposed the Dred Scott decision. Thus the Lincoln-Douglas debates widened the split in the Democratic party.

In class, have pupils read aloud portions of the 1858 debates between Lincoln and Douglas. They may be found in Commager's *Documents of American History* and *Annals of America*, Vol. 9. Ask: What was the political significance of the debates?

Slavery on the march   A month before the debates began, Abraham Lincoln made a speech to the Illinois State Republican convention. In the speech he said: "A house divided against itself cannot stand. I believe this goverment cannot endure permanently half slave and half free." Lincoln went on to say that it looked as if slavery would become legal throughout the United States. First, the Compromise of 1850 had allowed slavery to exist in the Mexican Cession territory if the people living there so desired. Second, the Kansas-Nebraska Act allowed slavery in territory where it had been prohibited by the Missouri Compromise. Third, the Dred Scott decision had said the Missouri Compromise was unconstitutional. If so, slavery would be legal in all of the Louisiana Purchase territory, and Congress was powerless to prevent its spread.

Moreover, Lincoln said, the Supreme Court's decision in the Dred Scott case meant something else. Scott had been taken by his master to live in Illinois. But the Court had ruled that this did not make Scott a free man. What was to prevent slaveholders from bringing thousands of slaves into Illinois or into any other free state to compete against the labor of free men?

Lincoln might also have told of aggressive men who were trying to expand slave territory in other directions. Some Southern leaders were urging that the United States buy Cuba from Spain. If Spain refused to sell, these leaders said, the island should be seized by force and made into a slave state. Other men wanted to seize territory in Central America in order to add it to the slave states in the Union. It seemed, indeed, as if slavery was steadily gaining ground in the 1850s.

John Brown's raid   By 1859 there were desperate men determined to end slavery by force, if necessary. John Brown was one of these men. Already he had committed murder in Kansas. "I have only a short time to live—only one death to die," he said then, "and I will die fighting for this (antislavery) cause." After fighting in Kansas, John Brown returned to the East. Eastern abolitionists greeted him as a hero and encouraged him in a plan he had devised.

Brown planned to establish a free state for escaped slaves and free blacks in the mountains of Maryland and Virginia. As a first step, Brown led a group of 19 men in a raid on the government arsenal—a storage place for weapons—at Harpers Ferry, Virginia. Brown's followers included five free blacks and Brown's own sons. They aimed to seize guns and ammunition stored in the arsenal. They hoped that slaves in the vicinity would rise up against their masters and come to Harpers Ferry for weapons.

Instead, marines commanded by Robert E. Lee of the United States Army surrounded the arsenal. Brown and his men were pinned down in the engine house. When Brown refused to surrender, the marines stormed the engine house and seized him. He was tried for treason, found guilty, and sentenced to death. His dream of a free state in the Southern mountains ended in a hangman's noose on December 2, 1859.

Democrats divide   In the presidential election of 1860, the Democratic party split into a northern and a southern wing. Northern Democrats chose Stephen A. Douglas as their candidate for President. Southern Democrats chose John Breckenridge of Kentucky. He had been Buchanan's Vice-President.

To complicate the voting further, a Constitutional Union party chose John Bell of Tennessee as its candidate. This party was made up mostly of former Whigs. Their old party had been torn apart by the slavery question.

Lincoln wins   Amid great excitement, the Republicans met in Chicago to choose

This campaign banner of 1860 supports the Republican ticket of Abraham Lincoln and Hannibal Hamlin.

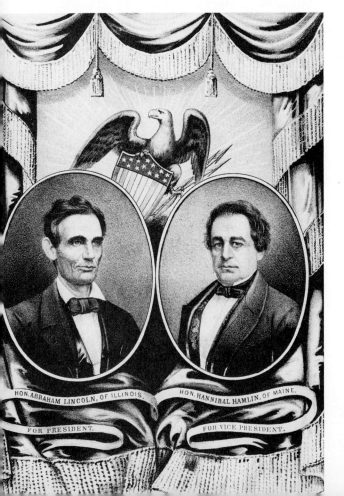

HON. ABRAHAM LINCOLN, OF ILLINOIS.

HON. HANNIBAL HAMLIN, OF MAINE.

FOR PRESIDENT.

FOR VICE PRESIDENT.

their candidate. The split in the Democratic party made almost certain the election of the Republican candidate, whoever he might be. It turned out to be Abraham Lincoln, who was chosen by the delegates on the third ballot.

The Republican platform made no threats toward slavery where it already existed. However, it made clear that Republicans would oppose the admission of any new slave states into the Union.

Furthermore, the Republican platform made many other attractive promises. To protect manufacturers and factory workers from foreign competition, it promised high protective tariffs. It promised a railroad to the Pacific and other internal improvements, paid for by the national government. It promised a Homestead Act providing free farms from the lands owned by the national government. It sought Republican votes from newcomers to the United States by promising more rights and benefits for recent immigrants.

Lincoln and the Republican party won an easy victory in the election of 1860. But the election showed it to be a sectional victory. Republicans got no electoral votes in ten Southern states. Leaders in these states had openly predicted they would secede from the Union if a Republican became President.

Secession begins   A month after Lincoln's election, a special convention in South Carolina voted to take that state out of the Union. Within two months, Mississippi, Florida, Alabama, Georgia, Louisiana, and Texas followed South Carolina's action. The seven seceding states formed the **Confederate States of**

Born: 1791, near Mercersburg, Pennsylvania. **Education:** Dickinson College. **Training:** Lawyer, public official. **To presidency from:** Pennsylvania. **Position when elected:** Minister to Great Britain during Pierce's administration. **Political party:** Democratic. **Married:** The only President never to have married. **Died:** 1868, Lancaster, Pennsylvania. **Other facts:** A distinguished-looking, white-haired man. Served in mounted troops in War of 1812. Had service in both bodies of Congress, where he staunchly supported Andrew Jackson. Held diplomatic posts in Russia and Great Britain. Secretary of state under Polk. **During his presidency:** Pony express riders carried the mail from St. Joseph, Missouri, to Sacramento, California.

JAMES BUCHANAN
15th President
1857 · 1861

America. Their first capital was at Montgomery, Alabama. In February 1861, Jefferson Davis of Mississippi was proclaimed the first President of the Confederacy.

James Buchanan remained as President of the United States until Lincoln's inauguration on March 4, 1861. He did little to stop the secession of the seven states except to hope that another compromise would be worked out. No compromise saved the Union this time, though several were suggested.

So Abraham Lincoln took his presidential oath "to preserve, protect, and defend the Constitution" with the Union already divided. Seven states had seceded. Eight more slave states were considering secession.

CHECKUP

1. Why did Senator Douglas sponsor the Kansas-Nebraska bill?
2. What were the main provisions of this bill?
3. What were the results of the Kansas-Nebraska Act?
4. Why did Southern and Northern Democrats react differently to the Dred Scott decision?
5. Why did the Lincoln-Douglas debates widen the split in the Democratic party?

North and South in 1860

┌─VOCABULARY─────────────────────┐
| *Uncle Tom's*   stereotype
| *Cabin*
| **foreign-born**
└────────────────────────────────┘

Slave states In 1860, "the South" generally meant those 15 states in which slavery was legal. Of these 15, Delaware is not usually thought of as part of the South, though slavery was legal there. Texas and Missouri were perhaps more western than southern at the time. Nevertheless, they are included as part of the South.

The 15 states of the South had a population of 12,240,000 in 1860. Of these, about 34 percent were black people. Of the blacks 251,000 were free and 3,950,-000 were slaves. Nearly all black people in the South in 1860 had been born there, since importation of slaves had been prohibited after 1808. Similarly, nearly all the white population was native-born. Fewer than 3 percent of white Southerners in 1860 had been born outside the United States. The whites were largely

Discuss with your pupils the different ways of life of people in the North and in the South. Have pupils write an essay describing how different life-styles can lead to different points of view and how different points of view can lead to conflict.

333

descended from English and Scotch-Irish people who had come to America during the seventeenth and eighteenth centuries.

Mostly farmers   It would be wrong to think of the South in 1860 as a region where all white families owned slaves. Fewer than a third of Southern families owned any slaves. Furthermore, most of the families with slaves owned fewer than ten. This was far less than the number needed to operate a cotton plantation.

Southern farmers without slaves were like Northern farmers in many ways. They often raised some corn and wheat, as Northern farmers did. Moreover, most Southern and Northern farmers lived in simple frame or log houses. But many a small Southern farmer dreamed of getting more land, buying slaves, and becoming the master of a large plantation.

Plantation owners   To most Southerners, the plantation owner's life was ideal. A plantation owner had a big house with fine furnishings imported from France or England. The owner's family enjoyed books, music, horses, dancing, good food, and, of course, house servants. Plantation owners as a group had most of the political power in the South. Southern officeholders usually came from the planter class or followed the wishes of that class.

Plantation owners also had great economic power. They provided the money that supported shopkeepers, warehousemen, lawyers, and cotton merchants. Indeed, by 1860 the culture and civilization of the South rested on plantations and on slavery.

Black Southerners   Many black people in the southern United States were descendants of Africans who had developed high civilizations before Columbus discovered America. Some Southern slaves were members of families that had been in America longer than the families of their owners. Conditions of slavery varied widely according to the slave's age, sex, and type of service. In general, household servants were treated better than field hands. Undoubtedly, slaves on cotton, rice, and sugar plantations of Mississippi, South Carolina, and Louisiana were more harshly treated than those in Virginia, Kentucky, and Missouri. Many slaves had skills with which to earn wages, but when their masters hired them out, the masters received the wages. Still, there is evidence to show that most masters did not mistreat their slaves. For one reason, slaves were property. A good field hand might be worth as much as $2,000.

There is plenty of evidence to show that slaves were not happy with their lot in life. Between 1830 and 1860, about 2,000 slaves escaped to the North each year. Many more thousands tried to escape, knowing they would be punished if caught. Slave revolts, work stoppages, and the destroying of tools and other property of their masters took place. The masters themselves offered evidence of the slaves' unhappiness. They agreed the greatest reward they could give their slaves was freedom.

The 251,000 free black people in the South in 1860 led uneasy lives. If they traveled, they had to carry papers to prove their freedom. They could neither vote

Ask pupils to identify the groups of whites that made up the class structure in the South. List them on the chalkboard. Then ask pupils to name reasons why each group would favor slavery. Ask: Why did Southern whites — both slaveholders, and nonslaveholders — favor slavery?

Have pupils comment on the two statements below.
Because of its effect on public opinion, *Uncle Tom's Cabin* has been called the greatest of American propaganda novels.
Senator Charles Sumner of Massachusetts declared that without this book Lincoln would not have been elected President.

nor hold office, though many were persons of talent and education. Law and custom limited their job opportunities. In spite of these restrictions, they paid the same taxes as whites and in some cases additional taxes because they were free blacks.

Uncle Tom's Cabin   Only 237,000 free blacks lived in the North in 1860. Therefore, more free black Americans lived in the South in 1860 than in the North. Many Northerners in 1860 had never seen a black person, free or slave. Whatever most Northerners knew about slavery came from what they had read or had heard from others.

In the early 1850s one of the most stirring books ever written aroused a great many Northerners against slavery. The book was **Uncle Tom's Cabin.** Its author was Harriet Beecher Stowe. She was the daughter of a Northern abolitionist minister and the wife of another. Much of what Mrs. Stowe wrote had been learned from her abolitionist friends. She had seen slaves only during a short visit to a plantation in Garrard County, Kentucky. Southerners complained that Harriet Beecher Stowe actually knew very little about slavery. They said that *Uncle Tom's Cabin* contained greatly exaggerated stories of cruelty to slaves. Yet millions of Northerners accepted these stories as the truth. After Mrs. Stowe's book appeared in 1852, many who had been unconcerned about slavery began to oppose it strongly.

The foreign-born   In 1860 there were 19 states in which slavery was illegal. These 19, along with the 7 territories and the District of Columbia, had a population of more than 19 million free people. This Northern population differed from that of the South in the number of **foreign-born.** Most immigrants to the United States settled in the North because they landed at

Slaves were sold as property at auctions that attracted many plantation owners.

Northern ports. Moreover, they avoided the South because there were fewer jobs there and because of the competition they would face from slave labor.

Minnesota's population in 1860 was 34 percent foreign-born. Many people from Norway and Sweden had settled in Minnesota. New York's population was about 26 percent foreign-born, with a mixture of immigrants from nearly every European country. The population of Massachusetts in 1860 was 21 percent foreign-born; of New Jersey, 18 percent.

Missouri with 14 percent of foreign-born had a higher percentage than any other state in the South. Louisiana came next with 11 percent, while 7 percent of the population of Texas in 1860 was foreign-born. But they were exceptions in the South. Only a little more than 1 percent of Alabama's population was foreign-born. Arkansas had less than 1 percent.

This poster, advertising the play Uncle Tom's Cabin, *shows Eliza fleeing across the ice of the Ohio River.*

Industry and commerce The most striking difference between the North and the South in 1860, however, was the amount of industry and commerce. More than 75 percent of all factories in the United States were in the North. Northern banks held 80 percent of all bank deposits in the country. The North had 70 percent of the nation's miles of railroads and 90 percent of the nation's industrial workers.

By 1860 there were differences in the way of life and the characteristics of people in the North and the South. Actually, the people of the North and the people of the South were more alike than they were different. But the differences were exaggerated and distorted because neither section had a true picture of the other section. Southerners thought Northern employers were "money grubbers" who were interested only in profits, and that Northern workers were "wage slaves," laboring in dark and dirty factories. Northerners, for their part, had decided by 1860 that most Southerners were "tyrants," living a life of luxury based on the toil of mistreated slaves.

Real disagreements As you learned in Chapters 11 and 12, Northern and Southern leaders had some real disagreements on matters of government and politics. Southern leaders wanted low tariffs to keep down the cost of manufactured goods. Northern leaders favored tariffs

Recall with pupils the different economic bases of the North and the South. Ask: Why, do you think, did people in the North feel themselves to be different from those in the South and vice versa?

UNCLE TOM'S CABIN

The title for Harriet Beecher Stowe's influential novel came from one of its main characters, Uncle Tom. In the novel, Uncle Tom lives in a slave cabin with his wife, Aunt Chloe, on a Kentucky plantation. Mr. Shelby, the plantation owner, is a kind man, but he has to sell one of his slaves because he is deep in debt. A New Orleans slave dealer named Haley buys Uncle Tom and also wants to buy Harry, the clever little son of Eliza, another of Mr. Shelby's slaves.

Eliza takes Harry and escapes across the floating ice in the Ohio River. She is helped in her flight north by white conductors on the Underground Railroad. After a time Eliza's husband, a slave on another Kentucky plantation, joins his wife and son in Canada. In the meantime, Uncle Tom is sold and falls into the hands of Simon Legree, the cruel master of a Mississippi plantation. Toward the end of the novel, Uncle Tom dies from a beating ordered by Simon Legree.

As you have read, many Southerners claimed the novel presented a false picture of slavery. But for many Northerners, Mrs. Stowe's novel was the only information they had about slavery. Yet far more people saw dramatized versions of Uncle Tom's Cabin than ever read the novel. Oddly enough, the play, presented by so-called Tom companies, was most popular 25 years *after* slavery had been ended.

In time the names of characters in Uncle Tom's Cabin became **stereotypes.** A stereotype is a mental picture of a whole group, exaggerated and often based on emotion. Any boss who showed little or no feeling for his employees might be called a Simon Legree. And any black man who refused to protest against ill-treatment and discrimination by whites risked being called an Uncle Tom by his fellow blacks.

---

high enough to protect Northern industries from foreign competition. Northern businessmen thought the national government should establish a national banking system. With such a system, business could be conducted on a national basis. Southerners wanted a national government that would not interfere with the powers of the states

By 1860, disagreements between the North and the South centered on two questions that overshadowed all others. First, should slavery be allowed to expand into new territories? And second, are the individual states more powerful than the Union? Southerners generally answered yes to both questions. An increasing number of Northerners were answering no.

CHECKUP

1. What were the major differences between the Southern and Northern people in 1860?
2. In what ways were the people of the two sections alike?
3. Why were plantations and plantation owners important in the South?
4. How did slaves show they were unhappy with their existence?
5. Why was Uncle Tom's Cabin an important book?

KEY FACTS

1. The Compromise of 1850 settled for a time certain issues between the North and the South, but the Fugitive Slave Law provoked further controversy.

2. The Kansas-Nebraska Act and the Dred Scott decision created new tensions between the North and the South.

3. The Republican party began in opposition to the Kansas-Nebraska Act in 1854 and elected its first President, Abraham Lincoln, in 1860.

4. Seven Southern states seceded and formed the Confederate States of America soon after Abraham Lincoln was elected President.

VOCABULARY QUIZ

On a separate sheet of paper, write **T** if the statement is true and **F** if it is false. If the statement is false, change the underlined term to make the statement true.

T **1.** Daniel Webster <u>supported</u> the Compromise of 1850 in his Seventh of March speech.

F **2.** The Fugitive Slave Law made it <u>easier</u> for slaves to escape to freedom. **harder**

F **3.** <u>Harriet Beecher Stowe</u> was a conductor on the Underground Railroad. **Harriet Tubman**

F **4.** The Kansas-Nebraska Act <u>was in agreement</u> with the Missouri Compromise.
was not in agreement

T **5.** Popular sovereignty meant that the people <u>in the territories</u> could decide whether they wanted slavery.

T **6.** When Abraham Lincoln and Stephen A. Douglas were candidates for the Senate in 1858, the winner was <u>Douglas</u>.

T **7.** Proslavery and antislavery forces battled for control in <u>Kansas</u>.

F **8.** <u>Dred Scott</u> led the raid at Harpers Ferry.
John Brown

F **9.** The Confederate States of America was formed <u>before</u> Lincoln was elected President. **after**

F **10.** Most foreign-born people in the United States in 1860 lived in the <u>South</u>. **North**

REVIEW QUESTIONS

1. What views did Clay, Calhoun, and Webster each have on the Compromise of 1850?

2. Why was the Fugitive Slave Law a disaster for black Americans?

3. Did the Kansas-Nebraska Act help or hinder Douglas's chances of becoming President?

4. Who won the Lincoln-Douglas debates?

5. Explain the circumstances and the results of the Dred Scott case.

6. Which of the four presidential candidates would you have voted for in the election of 1860? Why?

ACTIVITIES

1. The following headlines could have been found in newspapers of the 1850s. Arrange them in the order in which they happened.

6 DRED SCOTT DECISION ANNOUNCED

2 SENATOR CALHOUN DIES

7 JOHN BROWN HANGED FOR TREASON

3 STOWE'S BOOK A SENSATION

4 DOUGLAS INTRODUCES KANSAS-NEBRASKA BILL

5 BUCHANAN ELECTED PRESIDENT

1 CLAY SUBMITS COMPROMISE PLAN

9 SOUTH CAROLINA SECEDES

8 LINCOLN WINS PRESIDENCY

10 CONFEDERACY ORGANIZED

2. Choose one of the headlines above. Write a news story that might appear under the headline.

UNDERSTANDING A PICTURE

THE UNDERGROUND RAILROAD

There are many ways to learn about the past. One way is by studying pictures. The painting below is titled the "Underground Railroad." It shows escaping slaves arriving at the farm of Levi Coffin in Newport, Indiana.

The Underground Railroad was not really a railroad at all. It was a network of secret escape routes, set up by antislavery people, to help black slaves flee the South. Many people were involved in this organized attempt to help runaway slaves escape to Canada. Abolitionists, free blacks in the North and South, and slaves all played a part in the system. Escaping slaves were guided to homes or "stations" where they would stay in hiding during the day before traveling to the next station at night. Once they reached Canada, the slaves were assured of their freedom.

SKILLS PRACTICE

Study the painting. On a sheet of paper, write the answers to these questions.

1. How are the slaves in the picture being helped by the abolitionists?

2. By what means of transportation did these escaping slaves get to Coffin's farm?

3. What effect, if any, do you think the weather had on these slaves?

4. What, do you think, would happen to these slaves if they were caught?

5. Write a paragraph reconstructing the feelings of the escaping blacks and the abolitionists at this moment.

CHAPTER 15 The Civil War

The Early Years, 1861—1863

Ask pupils to research and write short essays comparing the personal qualities of Lincoln and Davis.

---VOCABULARY---

border states	Emancipation
ironclad	Proclamation

Lincoln and Davis   Abraham Lincoln traveled slowly toward Washington, D.C., by railroad for his inauguration on March 4, 1861. In order to reach the nation's capital, he had to pass through Maryland, a slave state. Rumors persisted that attempts would be made on Lincoln's life. His advisers urged him to leave the presidential train and enter Washington quietly, in disguise if necessary. Lincoln refused to do so, and completed the trip unharmed.

Jefferson Davis had served as President of the Confederate States of America for 16 days when Abraham Lincoln was inaugurated as President of the United States. Both men were born in Kentucky, Lincoln in 1809 and Davis the year before. Both left their native state as youngsters. Lincoln's family took him to Indiana, and he himself moved west to Illinois as a young man. After serving for 8 years in the Illinois state legislature and for one term in the United States Congress as a Whig, Lincoln returned to Springfield, Illinois, to resume his career as a lawyer.

Jefferson Davis's family took him to Mississippi. In that state he and his brothers became plantation owners and had great wealth and prestige. As a young man Jefferson Davis returned to Kentucky for part of his formal education. Then he graduated from the military academy at West Point but served only a short time in the regular army. Like many Southern plantation owners, Jefferson Davis combined political and military activities with management of his plantation. He commanded a regiment in the Mexican War, was wounded at the battle of Buena Vista, and earned a reputation for bravery. Later he was a Democratic senator from Mississippi and secretary of war in Franklin Pierce's Cabinet.

Fighting begins.   Soldiers of the Confederate States of America took over United States forts and arsenals in the South in February and March of 1861. In most cases, the commanders of the forts and arsenals gave up without a fight. But Major Robert Anderson did not. He commanded Fort Sumter in the harbor of Charleston, South Carolina. Confederate guns ringed the harbor.

This was the tense situation that Abraham Lincoln faced when he took office in March 1861. Should he order Major Anderson and his men to leave Fort Sumter

Union and Confederate troops meet in hand-to-hand combat at Gettysburg.

 Divide the class into small groups. Assign each group of pupils one segment of Lincoln's life, such as his youth, his early years in politics, President Lincoln and the Civil War, or his home life during his presidency. Ask each group to read at lea two biographical sources on the assigned segment of Lincoln's life and prepare a report to be given in class.

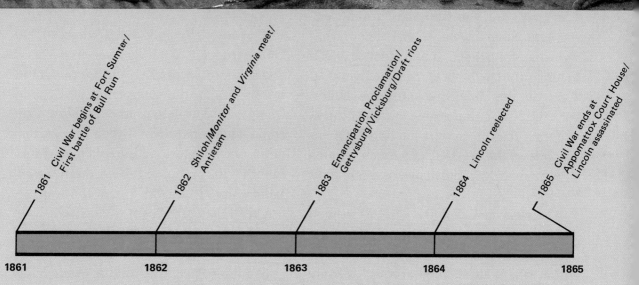

1861 Civil War begins at Fort Sumter/
First battle of Bull Run

1862 Shiloh/*Monitor* and *Virginia* meet/
Antietam

1863 Emancipation Proclamation/
Gettysburg/Vicksburg/Draft riots

1864 Lincoln reelected

1865 Civil War ends at
Appomattox Court House/
Lincoln assassinated

1861   1862   1863   1864   1865

341

or should he try to reinforce them? Lincoln knew that Anderson and his men were about to run out of food. At that point, he told South Carolina's authorities that he was sending supplies to the fort but no more soldiers.

The question of peace and war now lay with the Confederates. Jefferson Davis met with his Cabinet. In the discussions, those eager for war won out. Early in the morning of April 12, 1861, a fierce bombardment of Fort Sumter began. The fort surrendered a day later.

With war a reality, President Lincoln asked the North for 75,000 volunteers to put down what he called the "insurrection," or rebellion against the government of the United States. After this, Virginia, Arkansas, Tennessee, and North Carolina left the Union and joined the Confederate States of America. In view of Virginia's importance, the Confederates moved their capital from Montgomery, Alabama, to Richmond. The two capitals, Richmond and Washington, were less than 100 miles (160 km) apart.

War goals The war goals of the Confederate States were clear. They were fighting for their independence. To achieve independence, they had only to fight on the defensive until the Union realized it was impossible to defeat them. For this reason, except for two brief invasions of the North, Confederate armies fought mainly a defensive war on their own soil.

The war goals of the Union seemed more difficult to accomplish. The foremost goal was preserving the Union rather than abolishing slavery. There were at least two reasons for this. In southern Ohio, Indiana, and Illinois, there were many people who had economic and family ties with the South. Lincoln and his advisers knew these people would not fight for the abolitionists' goal of freeing the slaves, at least not at the beginning of the war.

Even more important was the need to keep the **border states** from seceding. In Delaware, Maryland, Kentucky, and Missouri, slavery was legal. If Lincoln announced that the war was being fought to end slavery, some or all of these states might join the Confederacy. As it turned out, none of the four did so. A large number of people in these states did favor the Southern cause. Yet all four furnished more soldiers for the Union than for the Confederacy.

By the end of 1862, it seemed certain that the border states would remain in the Union. After that, abolishing slavery became a second aim of the Union. Even later than that, however, it appeared that the Confederacy might achieve its goal of independence.

Bull Run By July 1861, some 30,000 Union troops had gathered around Washington. In western Virginia, Union troops under the command of General George B. McClellan had already won some small battles. Union supporters cried out for more action. "On to Richmond!" they shouted. Northern newspapers urged Lincoln to end the war.

On July 16, 1861, General Irvin McDowell led a Union army south toward Richmond. General P.G.T. Beauregard (bō' rə gärd) commanded a Confederate

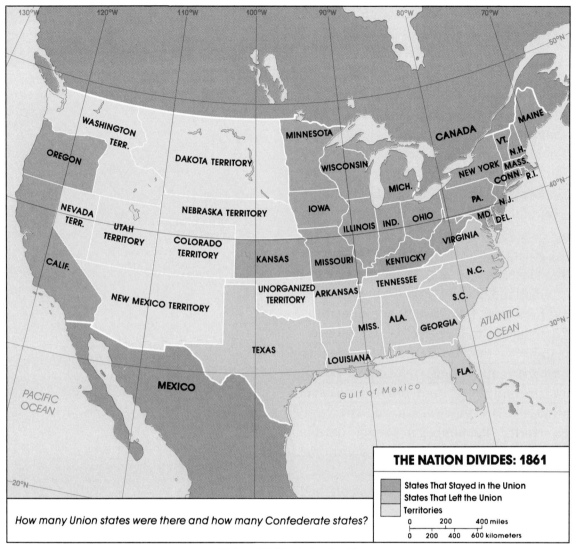

How many Union states were there and how many Confederate states?

THE NATION DIVIDES: 1861

States That Stayed in the Union
States That Left the Union
Territories

0   200   400 miles
0   200   400   600 kilometers

Union, 24; Confederate, 11

army stationed at Manassas Junction, Virginia. His troops met McDowell's on the banks of Bull Run, a nearby creek. At first the Union army drove the Confederates back and appeared to have the battle won. However, <u>one brigade of Confederate troops "stood like a stone wall."</u> They won for their commander, General Thomas J. Jackson, the nickname of "Stonewall" Jackson. And they saved the day for the Confederacy.

At this point in the battle, Confederate reinforcements arrived. Union troops began to withdraw. Hundreds of civilians had come south from Washington to watch the battle. They got caught up with the soldiers, turning the whole mass into a disorderly mob. The mob ran until it reached the safety of the Washington defenses.

<u>The disaster at Bull Run showed Union leaders that untrained troops could not be depended on.</u> Therefore, President Lincoln called General McClellan to take command of the Army of the Potomac. That was the name of the Union army

gathered around Washington. McClellan spent nearly a year training this army before again invading Virginia.

Grant fights   While McClellan trained the Army of the Potomac, General Ulysses Simpson Grant won several victories for the Union in Tennessee. In February 1862, he directed an advance up the Tennessee River. Union gunboats on the river helped capture Fort Henry. This opened the way into central Tennessee.

General Grant's Army of the Tennessee then marched to Fort Donelson, on the Cumberland River. Fort Donelson held out for a time, but Grant finally forced the Confederates to give up. When the commander of the fort asked for surrender terms, Grant replied, "No terms except an unconditional and immediate surrender." This made Grant well known in the North. People began saying that his initials, *U. S.*, stood for "Unconditional Surrender."

After Forts Henry and Donelson had fallen, Grant moved across Tennessee almost to the Mississippi state line. Near Shiloh (shī′ lō) a strong Confederate army made a surprise attack. The battle of Shiloh lasted 2 days, from April 6 to 7, 1862. It was by far the biggest battle of the war up to that time. Though it was counted as a Union victory, "Bloody Shiloh" cost Grant's army 13,000 men. The Confederates also lost heavily, with about 11,000 casualties.

Rumors that Grant had mismanaged his army persisted after the battle. Some people demanded that President Lincoln replace Grant as commander of the Army of the Tennessee. Lincoln refused.

During the Civil War, the Union army used observation balloons, such as the Intrepid. From the air, one could see and report on Confederate troop movements.

Ask: Why is a good general important?

Shaking his head, the President said, "I cannot spare this man. He fights." Grant not only fought, he won.

Ironclad ships   While armies fought on land, the United States Navy began to blockade Confederate ports. The blockade kept out supplies the Confederates needed from abroad. Only swift ships known as blockade runners could get through the tightening net of Union vessels. In March 1862, however, it looked as if the Confederates had found a way of breaking the Union blockade. They had captured a Union ship called the *Merrimac* and turned it into an **ironclad** by covering its sides and decks with iron.

With its new armor, the ironclad got a new name—the *Virginia*. Its mission was to break the Union blockade of Virginia's ports. On March 8, 1862, it rammed and sank one blockading vessel, drove another aground, and scattered the remainder of the ships blockading the coast of Virginia. Union guns fired without effect on the iron protecting the former *Merrimac*.

The next day a strange-looking vessel challenged the Confederate ironclad. Named the *Monitor*, the Union ship, too, was armored in iron. Instead of fixed guns, the *Monitor* had a revolving gun turret that looked like a round metal box stuck on a raft. John Ericsson, a Swedish immigrant, had developed the *Monitor* for the United States Navy.

The *Monitor* and the *Virginia* fired at each other for hours, until all their ammunition was gone. The *Monitor* had a little the better of the battle because the *Virginia* had to withdraw into the harbor at Norfolk for repairs. Later the Confederates sank the *Virginia* to keep the ship from falling into enemy hands when Union forces captured Norfolk.

Other countries had experimented with ironclad vessels before 1862. However, the *Monitor* and the *Virginia* fought the first battle between ironclads in the world's history. Though neither ship won a clearcut victory, their meeting proved that such vessels were practical. Even before their battle, the *Virginia* had shown that ships protected by sheets of

The Monitor *(right) battles the* Virginia *at Hampton Roads.* (37°N/75°W; map, p. 352)

The State of Kanawha

From the beginning of the United States, eastern and western Virginia were different. Western Virginia was mountainous and there were very few slaves there. The mountain people came to hate the rich slave owners of eastern Virginia. It seemed that the slave owners got their way in the state's politics and government.

Virginia seceded from the Union in April 1861. A short time later, representatives of Virginia's western counties met in Wheeling, an Ohio River town in the western part of the state. At the Wheeling Convention, these representatives set up the new state called Kanawha (kə nô′ wə) after another river in the region. Union troops were welcomed in Kanawha, which allied itself with the North.

The Congress of the United States approved the separation of 48 western counties from the rest of Virginia. In April 1862, Abraham Lincoln admitted the new state into the Union by presidential proclamation. However, by this time, the new state had the name of West Virginia.

Arrange for several pupils to present to the class the Constitution of the Confederate States of America.

iron were deadly to wooden vessels. However, the South was not able to make good use of this knowledge. It did not have enough resources to build more iron-clad ships. Union vessels, built of wood, kept up their blockade along the coast.

The peninsular campaign General McClellan seemed unwilling to order his well-trained Army of the Potomac into battle. He was overly cautious, always believing the opposing Confederate armies to be larger than they actually were. President Lincoln accused McClellan of having the "slows" and finally ordered him to advance on Richmond.

McClellan had a good plan for his attempt to capture Richmond. Instead of moving toward the Confederate capital by land, he had his troops ferried down the Potomac River and into Chesapeake Bay. The Army of the Potomac landed on a peninsula between the York and James rivers. From there McClellan ordered a slow advance toward Richmond.

In the peninsular campaign, as it was called, McClellan's army got within 5 miles (8 km) of Richmond. The army fought one indecisive battle during which Confederate General Joseph E. Johnston received a severe wound. General Robert E. Lee then took over the defense of Richmond.

Brilliantly assisted by Stonewall Jackson, General Lee drove McClellan's army back down the peninsula. But in the terrible Seven Days' Battle, from June 25 to July 1, 1862, the Confederates lost twice as many men as the Union army. Still, McClellan continued to retreat. The peninsular campaign was a failure.

Lee invades Maryland For nearly 3 years General Robert E. Lee commanded the Confederate Army of Northern Virginia. He built it into a remarkable fighting force with which he won a series of brilliant victories.

After McClellan's failure in the peninsular campaign, Lincoln replaced him as commander of the Army of the Potomac

After pupils have read the lesson, ask them to write newspaper headlines about each of the battles from 1861 to 1863.

with General John Pope. Pope, too, was a failure, defeated by Lee's Army of Northern Virginia at the second battle of Bull Run. In September 1862, Lee's confidence in the fighting ability of his army was at its height. It seemed a good time for an invasion of Maryland.

Lee hoped to accomplish two things. An invasion might cause Maryland, and perhaps other border states, to secede from the Union. Furthermore, by winning a victory in Maryland, Lee hoped that Great Britain and France might be induced to recognize the Confederate states as an independent nation. Surely, if this happened, Great Britain would help break the blockade and provide supplies.

To meet the danger in Maryland, President Lincoln put McClellan back in command of the main army in Lee's path. This army halted Lee's invasion in a bitter, bloody battle at Antietam (an tē′ təm) Creek, near Sharpsburg, Maryland, on September 17, 1862. However, McClellan failed to pursue Lee's army fast enough to please Lincoln. For this reason, Lincoln removed McClellan from command for the second and last time.

Emancipation   The battle of Antietam could best be described as a draw—neither a victory nor a defeat for the Union or the Confederacy. And yet this indecisive battle had far-reaching consequences. Had Lee won a decisive victory in Maryland, both Great Britain and France undoubtedly would have stepped in on the side of the Confederacy. Furthermore, though it was not a victory for the Union, Antietam gave Lincoln the result he needed before issuing his **Emancipation Proclamation.**

Both sides suffered a shocking number of casualties at Antietam.   (39°N/78°W; map, p. 352)

Since the beginning of the war, Lincoln had been cautious about including freedom for slaves as a Union war goal. As the war continued, however, antislavery Republicans urged him more and more to do something about slavery. In July 1862, Lincoln announced to the members of his Cabinet that he had decided to issue a proclamation freeing the slaves in the Confederate states. "Wait until the Union wins an important victory," Secretary of State William Seward advised Lincoln. Otherwise, Seward said, the proclamation would sound like a desperate effort to escape from defeat at the hands of the Confederacy.

President Lincoln followed Seward's advice as long as possible. He waited until 5 days after the battle of Antietam before issuing even a preliminary proclamation. Deciding Antietam had been the "victory" he needed, Lincoln acted. <u>On September 22, 1862, he announced his intention to free all slaves in the rebelling states on January 1, 1863, unless the slave owners freed them before that time.</u>

Slave owners in the unconquered parts of the Confederacy had no intention of freeing their slaves by January 1, 1863. So on New Year's Day, Lincoln issued the Emancipation Proclamation. It proclaimed all slaves "forever free" in those Confederate states still in rebellion. Still it freed no slaves in the border states nor in those areas of the Confederacy that had been overrun by the Union armies.

Important consequences Yet the Emancipation Proclamation had several important consequences. As Union armies pushed farther into the South, thousands of joyous slave families left the plantations to seek freedom behind Union lines. <u>More than 100,000 former slaves joined the Northern armies after the Emancipation Proclamation.</u> Many free blacks had joined before 1863. One of them, Martin L. Delany, became a major in the Union army. A social reformer, doctor, editor, and world traveler, Delany was the first black officer ever to reach that rank.

Major Martin Delany was the highest ranking black field officer in the Union army.

Ask: How did the Emancipation Proclamation influence the outcome of the war?

348

National Portrait Gallery, Smithsonian Institution

The Emancipation Proclamation had important effects on public opinion in the North and in Europe. Most antislavery people in the North welcomed the long-awaited proclamation of freedom. "God bless Abraham Lincoln," wrote Horace Greeley, the antislavery editor of the New York *Tribune*. In Great Britain the common people had favored the Union over the Confederacy since the beginning of the war. They greeted news of the Emancipation Proclamation with joy. After that, there was little chance that aristocratic British leaders would risk giving aid to the Confederacy.

Bad news In spite of the Emancipation Proclamation, bad news for the Union came from the eastern battlefields after Antietam. Lincoln continued to search for a man who would lead the Army of the Potomac to victory. For a time he settled on General Ambrose E. Burnside. Under Burnside's command, the Army of the Potomac attacked Lee's army at Fredericksburg, Virginia. The Confederates were dug in on the south side of the Rappahannock River, a strong position. Yet Burnside ordered a direct assault.

What took place on December 13, 1862, was a slaughter. The Army of the Potomac lost twice as many men as the Army of Northern Virginia but failed to drive the Confederates from the heights above Fredericksburg. The Union army then withdrew to winter quarters for rest, reinforcements, and more training. General Joseph Hooker, known as "Fighting Joe," replaced the incompetent Burnside.

In April 1863, the Army of the Potomac began still another invasion of Virginia. But Hooker had no more success in the spring than Burnside had the previous winter. Lee's Army of Northern Virginia won a battle at Chancellorsville that lasted 3 days, from May 2 to 4, 1863. At the end the Union army began another dismal retreat. The Confederate victory was a costly one, however. One of the 11,000 Confederate casualties was Stonewall Jackson, accidentally shot by his own men. An attempt to save his life by amputating his wounded arm failed, and Jackson died a few days later.

The news from Grant's Army of the Tennessee was nearly as bad as that from the Army of the Potomac. In Mississippi, Grant's men were still trying to take the Confederate stronghold of Vicksburg. In the North, the important Congressional elections in the fall of 1862 had gone against the Republicans. Northern Democrats gained more than 30 seats in the House of Representatives.

As the bad news continued, Northern opposition to the war mounted. Many people in the North were tired of the war and the awful loss of life it had brought. Few people realized that the momentum of the war was about to change.

CHECKUP

1. Who were the presidents of the Confederacy and of the Union as the war began?
2. Where and how did fighting between the Union and the Confederacy begin?
3. What were the war goals of the Confederacy? Of the Union?
4. Contrast the failures of the Army of the Potomac with the successes of the Army of Northern Virginia.
5. What were the results of Lincoln's Emancipation Proclamation?

The Last Years, 1863–1865

Grant and Lee   By 1863 the conflict between the North and the South ranged over a vast area and involved hundreds of thousands of men. New techniques of warfare were being used. European observers came to watch what was happening. They were amazed at the skill with which Union and Confederate generals used railroads, telegraph lines, and gigantic supply bases to move and support armies of 60,000 to 100,000 men.

Two opposing generals dominated the last years of this long war. General Ulysses S. Grant made use of the North's superior resources to lead the Union armies to eventual victory. Born in Ohio, Grant had graduated from the military academy at West Point. After serving in the Mexican War, he resigned from the army. In the 1850s he failed at farming and business near St. Louis, Missouri. When the war began, Grant was a 39-year-old clerk in his father's harness shop at Galena, Illinois. Because of his military experience, Grant received a commission as a colonel a few weeks after fighting started. He soon proved in Tennessee and Mississippi to be an able commander.

The Confederacy had given the task of defending its capital at Richmond to General Robert E. Lee and his Army of Northern Virginia. Robert E. Lee's father was Henry Lee, who had won the nick-

Of General Ulysses S. Grant, Lincoln said, "I cannot spare this man. He fights."

name of "Light Horse Harry" as a cavalry commander in the War for Independence. Later Henry Lee served as governor of Virginia. Robert E. Lee graduated from West Point and served in the Mexican War. Unlike Grant, Lee followed a professional military career afterwards. He was 54 when the war began. The United States War Department had offered him command of the Union armies. Robert E. Lee sadly refused the offer. He felt more loyalty to his home state than to the United States. When Virginia joined the Confederacy, so did Robert E. Lee.

Try to find several versions of Pickett's charge. Ask for volunteers to present the material. An excellent account of the action was published in *American Heritage*, December 1957. This account was written by Frank A. Haskell, an officer in the Union division that repulsed Pickett's troops.

Pennsylvania invaded   In the spring of 1863, General Lee planned another invasion of the North. This time he chose Pennsylvania as his target. Confederate hopes for foreign aid had nearly vanished. And yet a great victory on Northern soil might still convince France or Great Britain that open aid to the Confederate states would be to their benefit. Moreover, a victory in Pennsylvania might drive Northern morale even lower. Finally, Lee's Army of North Virginia needed clothes, food, shoes, horses, and other supplies. General Lee knew his troops could get these things from the prosperous farms and villages of central Pennsylvania.

In June 1863, Lee's army advanced into Pennsylvania. The Union Army of the Potomac moved northward also, keeping between the Confederate invaders and Washington. Toward the end of June, President Lincoln changed army commanders once more. This time he turned command of the Army of the Potomac over to General George G. Meade. Neither Meade nor Lee had planned to fight a great battle early in July. Nevertheless, on July 1, 1863, advance units of the Confederate and Union armies met, almost by chance, near the small town of Gettysburg, Pennsylvania.

Gettysburg   On the first day of the battle, the Confederate troops pushed the Union forces back through Gettysburg. The Union troops dug in on Cemetery Ridge, a long piece of high ground south of the town. During the night Generals Lee and Meade rushed their main armies toward Gettysburg. Lee positioned his troops and his headquarters on Seminary Ridge, about a mile northwest of the Union lines. After an attempt to outflank the Union Army failed, General Lee ordered a frontal attack on Cemetery Ridge. General George E. Pickett of Virginia led the attack that is known in history as **Pickett's Charge.** On the afternoon of July 3, some 15,000 Confederates marched toward the

Ask: What were the qualities that made Lee an outstanding military leader?

General Robert E. Lee, accompanied by some of his officers, makes plans for battle.

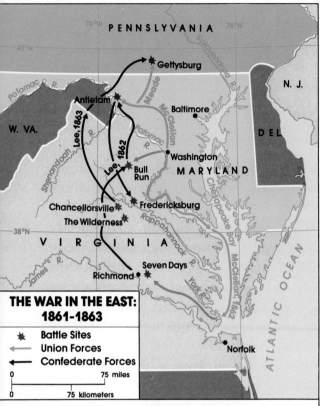

THE WAR IN THE EAST: 1861-1863

- ✳ Battle Sites
- ← Union Forces
- ◄ Confederate Forces

0 ——— 75 miles
0 ——— 75 kilometers

In the Eastern theater between 1861 and 1863, the Union forces failed to take Richmond, and the Confederates failed in their invasion of the North.

back on its home soil, fought on against the Northern forces for almost 2 more years.

Gettysburg is remembered for another reason. On November 19, 1863, Abraham Lincoln spoke at the dedication of the cemetery there. What he said in the **Gettysburg Address** has been called the perfect expression of the democratic faith of the American people.

LINCOLN'S GETTYSBURG ADDRESS

Four score and seven years ago our fathers brought forth on this continent a new nation, conceived in liberty and dedicated to the proposition that all men are created equal.

Now we are engaged in a great civil war, testing whether that nation, or any nation so conceived and so dedicated, can long endure. We are met on a great battlefield of that war. We have come to dedicate a portion of that field, as a final resting place for those who here gave their lives that that nation might live. It is altogether fitting and proper that we should do this.

But, in a larger sense, we cannot dedicate —we cannot consecrate—we cannot hallow—this ground. The brave men, living and dead, who struggled here, have consecrated it, far above our poor power to add or detract. The world will little note nor long remember what we say here, but it can never forget what they did here. It is for us the living, rather, to be dedicated here to the unfinished work which they who fought here have thus far so nobly advanced. It is rather for us to be here dedicated to the great task remaining before us— that from these honored dead we take increased devotion to that cause for which they gave the last full measure of devotion— that we here highly resolve that these dead shall not have died in vain—that this nation, under God, shall have a new birth of freedom—and that government of the people, by the people, for the people, shall not perish from the earth.

Union lines across a half mile of open ground as if on parade. Their bravery was wasted, however, as only a few managed to reach the Union center on Cemetery Ridge. These few were soon driven off by the determined resistance of the Union defenders.

Other battles of the war were bigger in number of soldiers taking part. Other battles had a higher percentage of casualties. Yet the fighting at Gettysburg over 3 days has become the best-known battle of the war. It is also often looked upon as the turning point. After this battle, Lee ordered his army to fall back into Virginia. He may have known then that the tide had turned. However, Lee's army,

Control of the Mississippi Almost from the beginning of the war, Union forces had tried to divide the Confederacy by capturing control of the Mississippi River. In the spring of 1862, a naval force commanded by Captain David Farragut forced New Orleans to surrender. Union gunboats then steamed up the Mississippi, capturing river ports along the way. At Vicksburg, Mississippi, Farragut's fleet was halted by fire from Confederate forts located on a high bluff in front of the city.

Now Grant swung into action. After his victory at Shiloh, Grant had captured Corinth in northeastern Mississippi. He then moved westward to Vicksburg. That city, Grant found, was so strongly defended that it could not be taken by storm. He therefore ordered his army to dig in and begin a siege of Vicksburg.

The siege provoked terrible hardships among both soldiers and civilians. For 6 weeks the city was under continual bombardment from Union artillery. Women and children were crowded into caves underlying Vicksburg. All supply routes into the city were cut by Grant's army. Finally, with food supplies exhausted, the Confederate garrison of 30,000 men surrendered on July 4, 1863. This gave the Union complete control of the Mississippi. Texas, Arkansas, and most of Louisiana were now cut off from the other states of the Confederacy by the Mississippi River.

The Anaconda Plan With the capture of Vicksburg, the Union was set to complete the strategic plan that it had devised early in the war. It was called the Ana-

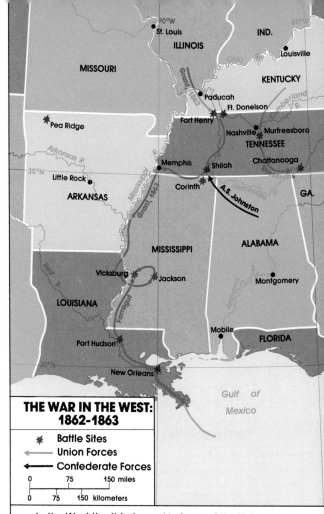

THE WAR IN THE WEST: 1862-1863

* Battle Sites
← Union Forces
← Confederate Forces

0   75   150 miles
0   75   150 kilometers

In the West the tide turned in favor of the Union. Vicksburg and Chattanooga were the sites of the most important Union victories.

conda Plan after the snake that wraps itself around its victims and crushes them.

The Anaconda Plan had four goals:

(1) To blockade the ports of the Confederacy to prevent trade with Europe
(2) To cut the Confederacy in two by capturing control of the Mississippi
(3) To cut the eastern half of the Confederacy in two by advancing up the Tennessee River and then southward into Georgia
(4) To capture Richmond

The Confederacy divided Following the capture of Vicksburg, Grant's army moved to southeastern Tennessee. At

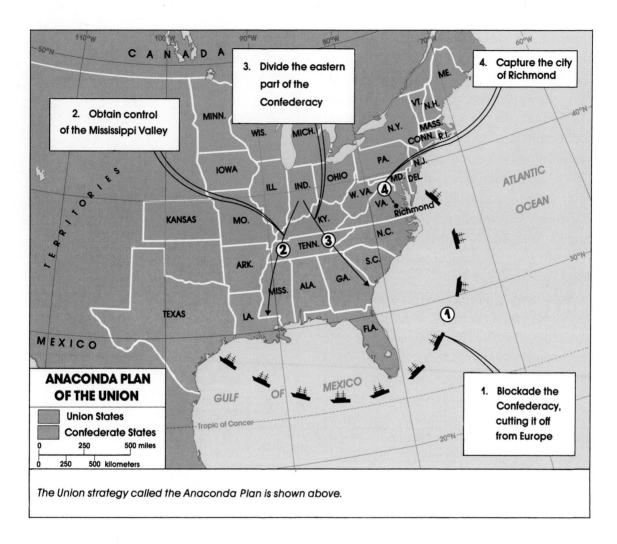

The Union strategy called the Anaconda Plan is shown above.

Chattanooga a Confederate army commanded by General Braxton Bragg guarded the gap that led through the southern mountains into Georgia. In a series of battles fought during November 1863, the Union army forced its way through the gap in the mountains. This advance made it possible to divide the eastern half of the Confederacy.

An army commanded by General William T. Sherman accomplished this division in 1864. First, the army fought its way from Chattanooga to Atlanta, Georgia. Atlanta fell to the Union forces in September 1864. Then, Sherman began his "march to the sea." Cutting his army loose from its supply bases, he advanced across Georgia to Savannah, on the Atlantic coast. Sherman's army left a path of total destruction behind it—uptorn rail lines, flattened bridges, burned factories and other buildings, and damaged crops. Shortly before Christmas the Union army reached and captured Savannah.

Richmond falls Under various commanders the Army of the Potomac had tried to capture Richmond. Early in 1864, Lincoln ordered Grant to come east and take command of all the Union armies.

Young boys, sometimes under 14 years of age, fought in the Civil War. Have some pupils do a report on these young people and what their duties were.

Soon after, Grant ordered another attempt to capture the Confederate capital with the hope this would bring the war to an end.

The Army of Northern Virginia resisted the steady advance of the Union forces toward Richmond. In May 1864 the opposing armies met in the bloody Wilderness campaign. A few days later they fought at Spotsylvania Court House. On June 1 the battle of Cold Harbor began.

In less than a month Grant lost over 60,000 men as he fought his way toward Richmond, but he kept on attacking. He knew Lee's losses were nearly as great and that the Union could bear such losses better than the Confederacy. Still, Grant was unable to pin a decisive defeat on the Army of Northern Virginia. Moreover, he was unable to capture Richmond in 1864. Instead of retreating, however, as previous Union commanders had, Grant moved his army south of Richmond. There he besieged the important railroad center of Petersburg. Gradually, the Union army tightened its control of the roads leading into and out of the Confederate capital. In the early spring of 1865, Lee was forced to abandon Richmond. He headed west in a desperate attempt to save his army. Union troops now took control of the Confederate capital.

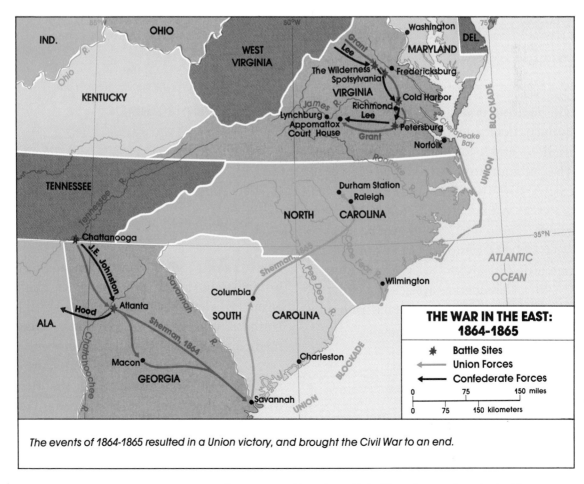

THE WAR IN THE EAST: 1864–1865

★ Battle Sites
← Union Forces
◄ Confederate Forces

0   75   150 miles
0   75   150 kilometers

The events of 1864-1865 resulted in a Union victory, and brought the Civil War to an end.

Confederate soldiers sadly furl their battle flags after Lee's surrender to Grant.

Have pupils arrange a news conference with Grant and Lee after the surrender of the Confederate troops.

The fighting ends   A week later, Lee's hungry, poorly clad, and worn-out army tried to break through the Union lines. The attempt to escape failed as Union troops surrounded the exhausted Confederates at Appomattox Court House, Virginia. There, on April 9, 1865, Lee surrendered his army to Grant and said a touching farewell to his valiant troops.

Other Confederate armies surrendered, one by one. On May 26, 1865, all organized resistance ended.

CHECKUP

1. What was the significance of the battle of Gettysburg?
2. How did the Union divide the Confederacy?
3. Why did Sherman's march to the sea divide the Confederacy a second time?
4. What was the Anaconda Plan?

The Home Fronts

```
┌─VOCABULARY──────────────────────┐
│  draft              War Democrat │
│  greenbacks         Peace Democrat│
│  Radical            Copperhead   │
│    Republican       Union party  │
└─────────────────────────────────┘
```

Draft laws   Both the Union and the Confederacy filled the ranks of their armies in a combination of ways. In the Union army, generous payments were made to men who would volunteer to serve. By 1863, however, more men were needed. So Congress passed the first draft law in United States history. The draft is the process by which men are selected for military service without their expressed consent.

Assign some pupils to report to the class on the draft riots of 1863. Ask: How did the draft policies of the Civil War differ from the present draft policies?

The draft law of 1863 was unfair. Men could hire substitutes or be excused from the draft by paying $300. New York City was the scene of an angry and destructive protest against the draft in July 1863. For several days, mobs ran loose in the city. Nearly 1,000 persons were killed or injured. Elsewhere in the North, minor riots also occurred in protest against the draft laws.

Like the Union, the Confederacy relied at first on volunteers. But since it had a smaller population, it began drafting men nearly a year earlier than the Union. The Confederate draft act passed in April 1862 also contained injustices. As in the Union, men with money could buy exemption from the draft or hire substitutes to go in their places. Owners of more than 15 slaves and those who supervised the work of that number could claim exemption from the Confederate draft. No widespread draft riots took place in the Confederacy. Still, exemptions for the wealthy caused hard feelings there, as they did in the North. Many Confederates said that this was "a rich man's war but a poor man's fight."

The fighting forces   More than 2.5 million men served in the Union ranks at one time or another during the course of the war. The Confederates had about half that many under arms. To fill the ranks, the Union had two sources that the Confederacy could not or would not use. More than 800,000 immigrants poured into the North during the war. Most of these immigrants were young men. Large numbers of them enlisted in the Union armies. In fact, about one-fourth of the Union forces were foreign-born. Even if immigrant ships wanted to dock in Confederate ports during the war, the Union blockade kept them from doing so.

Some Confederate leaders wanted to arm the slaves during the war, but this was never done. Officers in the Confederate army often brought slaves to serve them in camp. Slaves also were used to dig fortifications and to work in supply trains. Black men were not accepted in the Union army at first, but the situation changed after the Emancipation Proclamation was issued. By the end of the war, at least 200,000 black soldiers were enrolled in the Union army. Hardly a battle was fought in which there were not black troops. A good many received medals for actions on the battlefields. Nearly 40,000 black soldiers lost their lives in the war.

Both sides had Indians in their armies. The Five Civilized Tribes, living in what is now the state of Oklahoma, even had representation in the Congress of the Confederacy. About 5,500 Indians fought for the Southern cause. A Cherokee chief, Stand Watie, became a brigadier general in the Confederate army. Ely Parker, a Seneca, was one of about 4,000 Indians serving in the Union army. Parker, too, became a brigadier general. As Grant's military secretary, Parker wrote the copies of the surrender terms handed to Lee at Appomattox.

Women and the war   Women in both North and South helped their sides in many ways. Southern women managed plantations while their husbands were

Assign a small group of pupils to read an in-depth description of Clara Barton's experience during the Civil War. Have the group present their findings to the class in an oral report.

away. Other women in the South planted crops, worked in the Confederacy's few war factories, and cared for the sick and wounded in Confederate hospitals. Sally Tompkins, who ran a private hospital for the wounded in Richmond, was commissioned a captain—the only woman officer in the Civil War.

Northern women did much the same kind of war work—in factories, on farms, and in hospitals. Louisa May Alcott, the author of *Little Women* and other books, was a nurse during the war. So was Dorothea Dix, who had earlier done so much for the mentally ill. Clara Barton, later a founder of the American Red Cross, also cared for the Union's sick and wounded in wartime hospitals.

Women on each side acted as spies. Belle Boyd, barely 17 at the beginning of the war, became famous as a Confederate spy and messenger. Emma Edmonds served two years with the Army of the Potomac disguised as a man. Occasionally she put on women's clothes and acted as a spy behind the Confederate lines. In 1865, her book *Nurse and Spy in the Union Army* sold 175,000 copies.

Money matters. The Union and the Confederacy used similar methods to finance the war. Both governments sold bonds to their people and to investors in Europe. Both governments collected heavy taxes. Likewise, both issued paper money to help pay wartime expenses. The Union's paper money was called **greenbacks.** It fell in value and at one time the greenback dollar was worth 39 cents in comparison with gold. Confederate paper money was worth even less. A Confederate paper dollar was valued at only a little more than 1 cent at the end of the war.

Crew members of the ship Vermont *were among many blacks serving in the Union navy.*

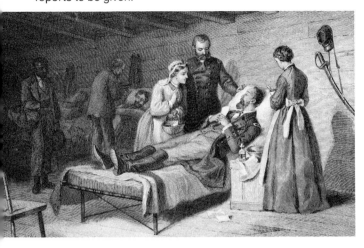

Two nurses and a doctor attend to the needs of a gravely wounded soldier in an army hospital.

In the presidential campaign of 1860, Republicans had promised to raise the protective tariff. With no Southern members in Congress to oppose the move, the tariff was raised a number of times during the war. The Union collected more than $300 million in tariff duties between 1861 and 1865.

The war cost the United States government about $15 billion to save the Union. It also revealed the need for a stronger central banking system. Congress filled this need in 1863 by passing the National Banking Act. It set up the first national system of banking since President Andrew Jackson destroyed the Second United States Bank more than 30 years before.

Most people in the Confederacy suffered badly from shortages in practically everything during the war. Food was plentiful in some parts of the South. However, breakdowns in the transportation system kept food and other supplies from being evenly distributed. The few factories in the South found it impossible to supply both military and civilian populations with shoes, clothing, and other necessities. And the tight Union blockade kept drugs and other medicines from reaching the South.

On the other hand, the North remained prosperous during the war. In fact, a great many people made money from the war. The economic problem in the North was rising prices, not shortages. Workers' wages rose less rapidly than prices. In 1864 the organized printers in New York City protested. They asked that their wages be raised to make up for the wartime inflation. "The average value of 16 dollars now paid is really only 8 dollars," they said, "and what printer is expected to support a family on that pittance. . . ?"

Wartime politics Abraham Lincoln had opposition as he directed the Union's war effort. The opposition came from within his own party as well as from the Democrats. Many Republicans doubted Lincoln's ability to bring the war to a successful conclusion. Lincoln's strongest critics within his own party became known as **Radical Republicans.** As President, Lincoln was able to control them, although they insisted he was too sympathetic toward the South.

Democrats in the Union kept up a vigorous opposition to the Republicans and to many of Lincoln's actions. Stephen A. Douglas died of typhoid fever in the year the war began. Had he lived, he might have kept the Northern Democrats united behind the effort to preserve the Union. As it was, only about a third of the Northern Democrats supported Lincoln's conduct of the war. Known as **War Democrats,** they opposed other Republican

359

Born: 1809, Hardin County (now Larue County), Kentucky. **Education:** Largely self-educated. **Training:** Storekeeper, public official, lawyer. **To presidency from:** Illinois. **Position when elected:** In private law practice. **Political party:** Republican. **Married:** Mary Todd. **Children:** Four sons. **Died:** 1865, assassinated at the age of 56 by John Wilkes Booth, a deranged actor. **Other facts:** His own description of himself: "in height, 6 feet 4 inches, nearly; lean in flesh, weighing on an average of 180 pounds; dark complexion, with coarse black hair and grey eyes." Traveled by flatboat down the Mississippi when he was 19. Postmaster for 3 years at New Salem, Illinois. **During his presidency:** A national income tax was enacted for the first time.

ABRAHAM LINCOLN
16th President
1861 · 1865

policies, such as high tariffs and a central banking system.

By 1864 the majority of Northern Democrats favored an immediate end to the long war. For this reason, they were known as **Peace Democrats.** Most of the Peace Democrats wanted the Union preserved. But they thought this should be done by discussion and compromise, not by war. A minority of Peace Democrats acted in ways that approached treason. They earned the name of **Copperheads** after the snake that is said to strike without warning.

As President of the Confederacy, Jefferson Davis faced opposition from Confederate state governors and other "states' righters." President Davis favored a strong central government for the Confederacy. At several critical times, Confederate state governors resisted orders from the central government at Richmond. In fact, some historians have written that the Confederacy died from an overdose of states' rights.

Lincoln reelected The Confederate constitution called for a single 6-year term

for its President. So Jefferson Davis did not have to face the task of a presidential election in the middle of the war. This was not the case, though, with Abraham Lincoln. Republicans looked to the War Democrats for support as the election year of 1864 came closer. In fact, the Republican party name was not used that year. A new **Union party** took the place of the Republican party. For a time it was not even certain that Lincoln would receive the presidential nomination of the Union party.

At its convention, however, the new party selected Lincoln without great opposition. The party's choice for Vice President was Andrew Johnson. He was a Democrat from Tennessee but had remained loyal to the Union when Tennessee joined the Confederacy. Andrew Johnson was nominated to attract votes from the War Democrats and from the border states.

Peace Democrats nominated General George B. McClellan. In their party platform, the Peace Democrats declared that the war was a failure and should be ended by recognizing the independence of the

Discuss the disagreement in the Northern states over the conduct of the war. Ask: What opposition did Lincoln face on the home front? Why is Lincoln considered by historians to have been a great President?

Confederate States of America. McClellan rejected this part of the Peace Democrats' platform. If he approved, he said, he could not face his old comrades-in-arms. Peace Democrats thought they had a good chance to win, for the war seemed to be going badly again for the Union in the summer of 1864.

By election time, however, the war was turning once more in the Union's favor. Lincoln had advised Northern voters, "Don't swap horses in the middle of the stream." The voters took his advice and returned him to office for a second term. But only a little more than a month after his second inauguration, Abraham Lincoln was assassinated.

Lincoln's assassination   On the night of April 14, 1865, President and Mrs. Lincoln attended a performance of *Our American Cousin*, a comedy, at Ford's Theater in Washington. An actor named John Wilkes Booth shot Lincoln as the President watched the play. Apparently Booth sought revenge for the defeated South by shooting the President of the United States.

The morning after Booth's attack, Lincoln died without regaining consciousness. Friends had carried him to a rooming house across from Ford's Theater. There the President breathed his last. After Lincoln's death, Northerners forgot the cruel things many of them had said about him. Crowds wept as a funeral train returned his body to Springfield, Illinois, for burial. Lincoln had left there only a little more than 4 years before.

CHECKUP

1. Why were there objections to the draft laws in both the Union and the Confederacy?
2. In filling the ranks of the army, what two sources available to the North were not used by the South?
3. How did women assist the war effort for the Union and for the Confederacy?
4. What was the chief economic problem in the North by 1864? In the South?
5. Why was the Union party formed for the presidential election of 1864? Who were the presidential and vice-presidential candidates of that party?

John Wilkes Booth shoots Abraham Lincoln at Ford's Theater in Washington.

KEY FACTS

1. In the Civil War the goal of the North was to preserve the Union. The goal of the South was to achieve independence.

2. The war that began at Fort Sumter in 1861 lasted 4 years. It ended in 1865 with the surrender of General Robert E. Lee to General Ulysses S. Grant at Appomattox Court House.

3. The Emancipation Proclamation, issued by Lincoln in 1863, freed no slaves immediately but resulted in the enlistment of about 200,000 black soldiers in the Union Army.

4. Abraham Lincoln was President of the United States during the war, and Jefferson Davis was President of the Confederate States of America.

5. The Civil War resulted in a tremendous number of casualties for both sides, and it left the South in economic ruin.

VOCABULARY QUIZ

On a separate piece of paper, write the letter representing the best completion for each of the statements below.

1. The border states (**a**) bordered on the Gulf of Mexico, (**b**) included Virginia, (**c**) remained within the Union, (**d**) joined the Confederacy.

2. The Emancipation Proclamation applied to (**a**) only those states still in rebellion against the United States, (**b**) all states in which slavery was legal, (**c**) the border states, (**d**) only Virginia, South Carolina, and Georgia.

3. The Anaconda Plan included (**a**) a naval blockade of Confederate ports, (**b**) releasing snakes in the Appalachian mountains of the South, (**c**) a refusal to invade Virginia, (**d**) all these things.

4. Draft acts (**a**) took place in the Union but not in the Confederacy, (**b**) took place in both the Union and the Confederacy, (**c**) were welcomed in both the Union and the Confederacy, (**d**) were fair to rich and poor alike.

5. A greenback was (**a**) a rookie soldier, (**b**) an old gold coin, (**c**) a Confederate sympathizer, (**d**) a piece of Union paper money.

REVIEW QUESTIONS

1. Compare the goals of the Union and the Confederacy at the beginning of the war.

2. How did the Union complete the four parts of the Anaconda Plan?

3. In what ways was the draft, used by both the Union and the Confederate armies, unfair?

4. Contrast the economic conditions in the Union and the Confederacy during the war.

5. Explain the circumstances and the results of the presidential election of 1864.

ACTIVITIES

1. On an outline map, locate the following:

Tennessee River	Chattanooga
James River	Cumberland River
Potomac River	Mississippi River
border states	Washington, D.C.
Richmond	Gettysburg
Atlanta, Georgia	Savannah, Georgia

2. After library research, prepare either a written or an oral report on one of the following topics:

Famous Generals of the Confederacy
Famous Generals of the Union
Women and the War
The War on the Water
Photography During the War
Medicine and the War
Black Soldiers in the War

USING THEMATIC MAPS

PLACE GEOGRAPHY ON THEMATIC MAPS

All maps give different kinds of information about places. Thematic maps show a particular kind of information. In this chapter are several thematic maps. Each shows military action in the Civil War.

Listed below are three exercises based on the thematic maps in this chapter. Each exercise refers you to a map. Look at each map to find the information needed to answer the statements. Use a sheet of paper for your answers—write **T** for true and **F** for false.

SKILLS PRACTICE: PART I

The map on page 352 shows troop movement in the eastern United States from 1861 to 1863. Use this map to help you find answers to these statements.

T **1.** The Confederate troops led by General Lee traveled north from Chancellorsville to Gettysburg, Pennsylvania.

T **2.** On their move to Bull Run, Union troops crossed the Potomac River near the city of Washington.

F **3.** After leaving Bull Run, Lee moved his troops south to Richmond.

T **4.** The Potomac River serves as a boundary between Maryland and Virginia.

SKILLS PRACTICE: PART II

The map on page 353 shows fighting in the West from 1862 to 1863. Use this map to help you find whether a statement is true or is false.

F **1.** The battles of Vicksburg and Port Hudson took place along the Alabama River.

T **2.** Union troops led by General Grant traveled south from Illinois to Fort Henry, Kentucky.

F **3.** Pea Ridge was the site of a major battle in Kentucky.

T **4.** The Union navy blockaded the port of New Orleans.

SKILLS PRACTICE: PART III

The map on page 355 shows the events in the East that brought the war to an end. Use the map to help you answer the following statements.

T **1.** After leaving Atlanta, Sherman led his troops across Georgia and then northward into South Carolina.

F **2.** The Pee Dee River separates South Carolina and Georgia.

T **3.** After being defeated at Atlanta, Hood's Confederate forces crossed the Chattahoochee River into Alabama.

T **4.** Appomattox Court House in Virginia is between the Roanoke and James rivers.

CHAPTER
16 Reconstruction

Restoring a Divided Nation

From tailor to President   Persons visiting Andrew Johnson's tailoring shop in Greeneville, Tennessee, in the early 1830s could see the stocky, broad-shouldered tailor sitting cross-legged as he sewed. He had been a poor boy, born in North Carolina and orphaned at an early age. Andrew Johnson had crossed the mountains to live in eastern Tennessee when he was 17. There he met Eliza McCardle, who was 15 years old at the time. The two were married the following year. They became the parents of five children.

Those early years were hard ones as Johnson struggled to make a living for himself and his family in his Greeneville tailoring shop. He was ambitious and a hard worker. At first, however, his lack of education handicapped him. He could read only a little and was unable to write more than his name. Anything beyond the simplest arithmetic was a mystery to Andrew Johnson at this time.

Eliza McCardle Johnson helped her husband in his tailoring shop. But she helped him with more than his sewing. She taught him to write. As he sewed, she read to him. In the evenings she worked to improve his knowledge of mathematics.

Andrew Johnson began his political career as a friend to working people in eastern Tennessee. First, he was mayor of Greeneville. Then, in succession, he became a member of the Tennessee legislature, a United States congressman, a governor, and a senator. After the Union army's advance into Tennessee in 1862, Abraham Lincoln made Johnson military governor of that border state. During his whole career, Andrew Johnson opposed the aristocratic slaveholders of Tennessee and the other Southern states.

As you read in Chapter 15, Andrew Johnson was chosen as Lincoln's Vice President in 1864. He became President when Lincoln was shot down in April 1865.

Some important questions   Historians call the years from 1865 to 1877 the time of **Reconstruction.** These were the years during which American leaders struggled with the task of rebuilding and restoring a divided nation.

Reconstruction involved a number of questions. How could the Confederate states be restored to the Union? How

The Reconstruction years saw the stationing of federal troops throughout the South. These occupation troops are outside their quarters on St. Louis Street in New Orleans.

Have pupils read a biography of Andrew Johnson and prepare a book report. You may wish to have them make a time line showing the major events in Johnson's life.

1862 Homestead Act

1865 Johnson becomes President/
Thirteenth Amendment

1866 Freedmen's Bureau set up/
Ku Klux Klan organized

1867 Reconstruction Act of 1867/
President Johnson impeached/
Alaska purchased

1868 Grant elected President/
Fourteenth Amendment

1870 Fifteenth Amendment

1872 Amnesty Act

1876 Hayes elected President

1877 Reconstruction ends

1862   1864   1866   1868   1870   1872   1874   1876   1878

could the war damage to the South be repaired? How could nearly 4 million slaves be helped to live full and useful lives as free persons? Who would control the Reconstruction process—the President or Congress?

The Lincoln-Johnson plan   In 1863, Lincoln had announced his plan for restoring the Union. The first step, according to the President's plan, was for a certain number of men in a Confederate state to take an oath of allegiance to the Union. This number was to be 10 percent of those voting in that state in the election of 1860. Persons taking the oath of allegiance pledged themselves to support the Constitution of the United States. They agreed to obey laws passed by the United States Congress and to honor the President's proclamations on slavery. When

At war's end, the state house in Richmond still stood, but all around it was a scene of total destruction.

10 percent had taken the oath of allegiance, they could organize a state government. The President would then recognize it as the true and loyal government of that state.

When Andrew Johnson became President, he followed the 10 percent plan with some additions. The state governments formed under the plan had to repeal their secession acts. They had to promise they would make no attempt to pay the Confederate war debt. Finally, they had to ratify the Thirteenth Amendment to the Constitution, which said: "Neither slavery nor involuntary servitude, except as a punishment for crime whereof the party shall have been duly convicted, shall exist within the United States, or any place subject to their jurisdiction." (See page 195.)

One by one, governments in the former Confederate states carried out the requirements of the **Lincoln-Johnson plan.** By late fall in 1865, all 11 states had been restored to the Union. This entitled them to elect members to the Congress of the United States.

Congress objects   But Congress also had its plans for Reconstruction. Some Republican members thought the Lincoln-Johnson plan was too easy on the South. Among those who thought so were the Radical Republicans. They had opposed Abraham Lincoln much of the time during the war. Now they took a tough stand toward the defeated South. At first they were only a small group in their party. But they gained the backing of others when the first postwar Congress met in Washington in December 1865.

Ask: How may Lincoln's death have changed the course of history?

The voters in the old Confederate states sent a number of distinguished ex-Confederates to the new Congress. Understandably, these voters had selected as leaders some of those who had led them in the past. Among those they chose to represent them in Washington were six former members of the Confederate Congress and four former generals in the army of the Confederate States of America.

And understandably many Northerners were alarmed by the presence of these former Confederates in the nation's Congress. Confederates had recently been engaged in an armed rebellion against the United States government. Were "rebels" to be welcomed into Congress and permitted to share in making laws as though nothing had happened in the preceding 4 years? The Radical Republicans were determined to prevent this.

The Republican congressional plan
Radical Republicans gained many allies as they prepared for a showdown with President Johnson on the question of who should control the process of Reconstruction. After the 11 Southern states had seceded, Republicans had controlled Congress. But the new Southern Congressmen, who were all Democrats, might join Northern Democrats and turn the Republicans into a minority in Congress. No Republican, whether Radical or not, wanted this to happen.

Consequently, in 1866 the Republicans in Congress offered their own program for Reconstruction. Under the Republican plan, it would be much harder for the Confederate states to resume their place in the Union. For one thing, the Republican congressional plan required the seceded states to approve the Fourteenth Amendment, as well as the Thirteenth, before reentering the Union.

The Fourteenth Amendment in its first section made all persons born or naturalized in the United States "citizens of the United States and of the state wherein they reside." The first section also prohibited any state from taking away "privileges or immunities" of citizens of the United States. Nor could any state deny to persons within its borders "the equal protection of the laws." Clearly, this section of the Fourteenth Amendment was designed to make black people United States citizens if they were born there, as almost all of them were. Furthermore, the Fourteenth Amendment attempted to protect them from illegal actions by states or individuals. Thus the amendment was one attempt to help the former slaves in their new status of freedom.

Other parts of the Fourteenth Amendment were directed more against Southern Democrats. The second section said that the number of members a state had in Congress could be reduced if that state did not allow its black citizens the right to vote. In its third section, the Fourteenth Amendment stated that those who had held offices in the South before the war could no longer serve in government if they had taken part in the rebellion. The amendment also said that the United States war debt would be paid. However, the Confederate war debt would *not* be paid. Finally, under the terms of the Fourteenth Amendment to the Constitution, no one who had held slaves would ever be paid for their loss.

Johnson and Congress struggle   President Johnson advised the 11 former Confederate states to reject the Fourteenth Amendment. He particularly opposed the section barring former Southern office-holders from again holding office if they had taken part in the rebellion. Where else, Johnson asked, could the South look for experienced leadership? Moreover, Johnson held that the Southern states had already been restored to the Union by accepting the Lincoln-Johnson plan.

In the summer of 1866, Tennessee ratified the Fourteenth Amendment and returned to the Union. The other 10 states of the former Confederacy refused. Radical Republicans declared that these Southern states needed to be treated harshly. For this reason, the congressional elections of 1866 were a contest between Johnson's "easy" Reconstruction program and the Radical Republicans' "hard" plan.

President Johnson fought for his control over the Reconstruction process. In August 1866 he went on a speaking tour through the North. Hecklers taunted the President almost everywhere he spoke. Angrily, the hotheaded Johnson responded with many tactless remarks. He had badly misjudged public opinion among the Northern voters. When the congressional elections were over, the Republicans, led by the Radicals, were still firmly in control of Congress and the Reconstruction process.

Not all Northern voters thought the same way, of course. Still, a large number thought the ex-Confederate states should be punished for having brought on a long,

This anti-Johnson cartoon pictures the President as a little boy who has unwisely involved himself in constitutional issues and meets with disastrous results.

costly, and bloody war. Many more felt that blacks deserved the same rights as white persons and that the Radical Republican program would guarantee equal treatment for all. Moreover, Northern industrialists feared that Southern Democrats in Congress would repeal economic benefits favored by the Republicans.

Some Northern businessmen saw a chance to get control of the South's natural resources by supporting a hard Reconstruction program. Republican politicians believed they could stay in power only if they supported the Radical program. That program would deny many white Southerners the right to vote or hold office. It would also permit eligible blacks to vote and they presumably would vote for Republicans out of gratitude.

Military occupation   For these reasons, Republicans swept to a big victory in the congressional elections of 1866. Radicals returned to Washington, set on passing their own Reconstruction bill. President Johnson vetoed it, but on March 2, 1867, Congress easily passed what was called the **Reconstruction Act of 1867.**

This act divided the former Confederate States of America, except for Tennessee, into five military districts. In each one a United States army general was in charge, with soldiers to carry out his orders. To get out from under military rule, a state had to accept the Fourteenth Amendment and had to guarantee black men the right to vote. Only then would Congress agree to accept that state's senators and members of the House of Representatives. However, United States troops might stay until Congress was satisfied that the state was "reconstructed." In some Southern states, military occupation continued until 1877. The presence of United States troops in those states caused a good deal of hard feelings toward the federal government.

Johnson impeached   After arranging for military occupation in the South, the Radical Republicans set out to deal with President Johnson. The House of Representatives **impeached** the President, that is, they accused him of "high crimes and misdemeanors" in 11 separate articles. The accusations against him were based on Radical Republican opposition to his policies, not on any actual crimes he had committed.

Ask: Why was Andrew Johnson impeached?

A Senate official serves President Johnson with a summons to appear for his impeachment trial.

As a basis for understanding the issues in the impeachment of President Andrew Johnson, several pupils should investigate and report on the Tenure of Office Act. Have one pupil state the terms of the law. Ask another to explain why it is a law no President could tolerate.

369

Born: 1808, Raleigh, North Carolina. **Education:** Largely self-educated. **Training:** Tailor, public official. **To presidency from:** Tennessee. **Position when taking office:** Vice President. **Political party:** Democratic, but elected Vice President on the ticket of the wartime Union party. **Married:** Eliza McCardle. **Children:** Three sons, two daughters. **Died:** 1875, Carter Station, Tennessee. **Other facts:** Apprenticed to a tailor at the age of 13. Married at 18 and taught to write by his wife. The only Southern senator who refused to secede with his state. The only President who was impeached. Later became the only former President to serve as a senator. **During his presidency:** The United States purchased Alaska from Russia for $7.2 million.

ANDREW JOHNSON
17th President
1865 • 1869

The Constitution provides that impeachment trials shall take place in the Senate with senators acting as a jury and the Chief Justice presiding. (See page 180.) Johnson's dramatic trial lasted from March 30 until May 16, 1868. Radicals were sure that the necessary two thirds —36—of the senators would vote for Johnson's conviction. But the final votes were 35 for conviction and 19 for acquittal. Thus the Radicals failed to convict Johnson by the margin of 1 vote. Seven Republicans joined 12 Democrats in voting Johnson not guilty.

Johnson was nearly powerless as he served out the remainder of his term. However, the Radical failure to remove him had far-reaching effects. It meant that the weapon of impeachment would not be freely or easily used in future conflicts between Congress and the President. Johnson's fight to save his presidency also helped to insure the future independence of the executive branch of government.

The Fifteenth Amendment For the presidential election of 1868, the Democrats chose Horatio Seymour, a former governor of New York, as their candidate. Republicans nominated General Ulysses S. Grant. Grant won a big margin in electoral votes with the help of black voters in the South. This convinced the Radical Republicans that they needed the votes of Southern blacks in future elections. Therefore, they proposed what, in 1870, became the Fifteenth Amendment to the Constitution.

The Fifteenth Amendment forbade any state to deny the right to vote because of "race, color, or previous condition of servitude." (See page 197.) Black voters in the South supported Grant's reelection to the presidency in 1872. It seemed as if the Radical program for Reconstruction had triumphed completely.

CHECKUP

1. What were the main features of the Lincoln-Johnson plan for Reconstruction?
2. Why did the Radical Republicans gain allies after the election of the first postwar Congress?
3. What were the results of Andrew Johnson's impeachment trial?
4. Why were the Thirteenth, Fourteenth, and Fifteenth Amendments added to the Constitution?

Had the Radical Republicans won, they might have established a congressional dictatorship. Suppose the separation of power between the executive and legislative branch had been dissolved. Ask: What might have been the results?

The Reconstructed South

┌─VOCABULARY─────────────────┐

Freedmen's   **scalawag**
  Bureau   **crop lien system**
black codes   **sharecropping**
Amnesty Act   **Ku Klux Klan**
carpetbagger   **New South**

└────────────────────────────┘

". . . the poor South." In 1850, John C. Calhoun had died murmuring, "The South, the poor South." The future he imagined had come true 15 years later. In 1865 the South was indeed poor, defeated, and nearly destroyed by war. Confederate dollars and bonds were worthless. Confederate war veterans straggled home, their uniforms in rags, their feet often bare. Home folks could do little for them but thank them for the sacrifices they had made.

The war had exhausted white Southerners. For most of them the South was a land of war ruins and war cripples. Their hopes and their fortunes were gone.

For black Southerners, Lincoln's assassination brought sadness and fear, for Lincoln had represented the end of slavery and great hope for future progress. But even after Lincoln's death, hope remained. Black people in the South knew they had many friends in Congress and many supporters among the Northern people, both white and black.

The Freedmen's Bureau Months before the end of the war, slaves freed by the Emancipation Proclamation had begun to help themselves. Thousands had enlisted in the Union army. Others stayed in the area where they had served

Setting up schools for former slaves was one accomplishment of the Freedmen's Bureau.

as slaves. In many cases they went to work on land abandoned by their former masters.

In 1865, Congress set up the **Freedmen's Bureau** to help the freed slaves. This was the first time that the national government had given aid to large numbers of people. The Freedmen's Bureau furnished food and supplies for thousands of poor people, both white and black. It found jobs for those without work and homes for those without shelter. Some of the bureau's work was poorly done. Still it did many good things.

It was the Freedmen's Bureau that organized efforts for the education of the freed slaves. In the five years of its existence, the Freedmen's Bureau built 4,300 schools and hired 3,300 teachers. General Oliver O. Howard headed the Freedmen's Bureau. He had fought at Gettysburg and had marched through Georgia with General Sherman. In 1867 he founded Howard University in Washington, D.C. Hampton Institute, Fisk University, and Atlanta University also were founded during the Reconstruction years to provide educational opportunities for black people.

Black codes In spite of aid given by the Freedmen's Bureau, Southern blacks had a rough time after the war. Many white Southerners could not or would not accept the new situation. As a visitor in the postwar South put it, freed blacks "received a hundred blows for every helping hand."

Some of these blows came from the state governments established under the Lincoln-Johnson plan. Legislators in these state governments passed laws that became known as **black codes.** The black codes differed from state to state. In general, however, they put restrictions on freed blacks that were not applied to Southern whites.

Some of the laws forbade former slaves from moving freely from one place to another. Other provisions of the black codes made it illegal for freedmen to possess firearms, to sit on juries, to vote, or to hold office. In some states, blacks were forbidden to own land and to testify against whites in court. Moreover, the black codes sometimes applied more severe penalties to blacks than to whites guilty of the same crimes.

White Southerners declared that these black codes were needed to put former slaves back to work and to keep them from roaming restlessly all over the South. On the other hand, many Northerners believed the black codes to be an attempt to restore slavery under another name. As it turned out, these controversial Southern laws were one of the main reasons for the Radical Republican victories in the congressional elections of 1866.

Ask: Were the black codes fair?

Reconstruction governments Under the Reconstruction Act, the army sent some 20,000 soldiers (along with some black militiamen) into 10 states of the South. Military governments took the place of those state governments set up under the Lincoln-Johnson plan. Under the direction of the army, new civilian governments were put in charge in these 10 states. It then became the job of these Reconstruction state governments to repair the war damage and to build a new social and political order in the South. Such a huge task would have challenged the wisdom and skill of the wisest leaders.

Unfortunately some leaders in these new state governments meant well but were lacking in wisdom and experience. Others were corrupt. The third section of the Fourteenth Amendment barred the South's most experienced leaders from participation in government until 1872. In that year, Congress passed the **Amnesty Act.** This allowed all but about 500 former Confederate officials to take part in state and national government again.

Carpetbaggers and scalawags   Until 1872, and to some extent even after that, many leaders of Southern state governments were **carpetbaggers.** Carpetbaggers were Northerners who came south after the war. They carried their belongings in luggage made of carpeting. This was the fashion of the times, since carpeting was durable. The carpetbaggers came for various reasons. Some sincerely wanted to help in the rebuilding of the South. Others were out to profit in any way they could from the unsettled conditions. Some of these people got leading positions in state governments.

Among others who gained positions of influence in the state governments were certain white Southerners who cooperated with the carpetbaggers. Some of these Southerners had the best of intentions. Others simply aimed to gain power for themselves. The old ruling class looked down on these people and called them **scalawags,** a scornful term used to describe mean, runty farm animals.

Cartoonist Thomas Nast pictured the carpetbagger as one who always saw the South's faults in the front bag but never saw his own faults in the other bag.

The new Southern state governments spent money for a variety of purposes, and they spent a lot of it. South Carolina's legislature, for example, spent large sums for rich furnishings in the new state capitol. Louisiana's carpetbag government increased the state debt by $34 million, an immense sum for the time. Still, much of the money spent by carpetbag governments went for good causes. The repair of war damages required large expenditures. So did construction of schools for Southern children. It might truthfully be said that the carpetbag governments of the Reconstruction period created a public education system for the South.

Black voters   The Fourteenth and Fifteenth Amendments made it possible for black men to vote and hold office in the South throughout the Reconstruction years. Blacks held offices from county sheriff to governor. Although black voters outnumbered white voters in several states for a time, only once—in South Carolina—did black people have a majority in a state legislature. That was only in one house and for only a few years.

Fourteen blacks served in the United States Congress during the Reconstruction years. Joseph Hayne Rainey of South Carolina was the first black to serve in the House of Representatives. As a member of that body from 1870 to 1879, he acted with ability and tact. Rainey was very effective in speaking for civil rights. He later became an agent for the Treasury Department.

Two black men were chosen as senators from Southern states during the Reconstruction years. Blanche K. Bruce had been a slave who escaped to the North.

He moved to Mississippi after the war and became a senator in 1874. Pinckney Pinchback was a senator from Louisiana and also served briefly as governor of the state.

The crop lien system   Of course, most Southerners made their living in other ways than politics after the war. The postwar South had a plentiful supply of land and labor, both black and white. Yet most small landowners lacked money for seed, tools, and mules to get the land back into production. Plantation owners had somewhat different problems. They had no money to pay people to work on their land, which had formerly been worked by slaves. Often plantation owners sold off part of their land in order to get money to farm what remained. Sometimes carpetbaggers bought this land at bargain prices.

The South Carolina legislature conducts the state's business during Reconstruction.

For plantation owners and small farmers alike, one solution to their problems lay in the **crop lien system**. Through this system, landowners got seeds, tools, and other necessities from a local merchant. In return, farmers gave the merchant a first lien on their crop, usually cotton. This meant repaying the merchant first when the year's crop was sold. Often the proceeds were only enough to cover part of the lien. Consequently, many Southern farmers remained in debt to some local merchant year after year until they had to give up their land.

Sharecropping   Another way for Southern farmers to get back into production was by **sharecropping**. Using this method, landowners would get people to farm the land in return for a share of the crop that was produced. Most landowners insisted that their sharecroppers raise only cotton or tobacco, both good cash crops. This made it difficult for the postwar South to develop more diversified agriculture.

Freed blacks were most prominent among the sharecroppers. As slaves they had owned no land. The Emancipation Proclamation and the Thirteenth Amendment gave them their freedom but nothing else. Thaddeus Stevens of Pennsylvania, a leader among Radical Republicans in Congress, thought that freed black families should be given 40 acres (16 ha) of land as an economic base. He favored breaking up large Southern plantations in order to distribute this land to freed blacks. But the promise of "40 acres and a mule" for each family of freed blacks never worked out.

Secret societies   During the early years of the Reconstruction governments, a number of secret societies came into being in the South. Three of these groups were the Order of the White Rose, the Knights of the White Camellia, and, most notorious of all, the **Ku Klux Klan**. In 1866 some Southern war veterans in Pulaski, Tennessee, formed the Klan. It spread rapidly to other Southern states. Its members met at night, disguised in white hoods and white robes. At first the Klan's goal was to drive carpetbaggers, scalawags, and blacks out of politics. Fearing the effects that the votes of black people would have, the Klan's chief role became one of keeping blacks from voting. Using threats and violence, the Klan destroyed the basis of the Republican party in the South.

As the Klan's actions became more brutal and violent, many responsible Southerners refused to have anything to do with the Klan and other secret societies. The Amnesty Act of 1872 weakened the secret societies further. After it was passed, most Southerners could work openly to reach their political goals. They could use legal methods to seek control of their state governments.

Home rule returns   Since the carpetbag governments were Republican, the Democratic party became the white Southerners' instrument for regaining control of their state governments. Democratic voters defeated the Republican carpetbag government in Virginia in 1869. It took longer in other states. Nevertheless, white Southern Democrats had taken control of all Southern states by 1877.

Have pupils imagine they are either a Southern plantation owner trying to rebuild the plantation, or a Northern representative of the Freedman's Bureau in the South. Have them write a letter to a friend describing some of their daily activities.

375

Ku Klux Klan members prepare to hang one of their foes. He was saved by government troops.

With the return of home rule, some Southern leaders tried to make the South an industrial region. By cooperating with Northern industrialists and bankers, Southerners hoped to create a **New South.** By this they meant a land in which manufacturing and commercial interests would play a larger part. This was a long time coming, however. It would be many years before industry was as important in the South as in the North.

CHECKUP

1. How did the future appear for white and for black Southerners at the end of the war?
2. How did the Freedmen's Bureau help Southern blacks? How did the black codes hinder them?
3. Explain how two systems were used to get Southern agriculture back into production.

The End of Reconstruction

┌─VOCABULARY─────────────────┐

Homestead Act	Tweed Ring
"Seward's Icebox"	Compromise of 1877

└────────────────────────────┘

Union veterans   Northern soldiers returned to a prosperous land that was almost wholly unscarred by war. Moreover, the United States government gave every veteran $235 in discharge pay, a warm blue uniform, and a ticket to the place where he had joined the army. In the North there were jobs nearly everywhere. Returning soldiers, seeking adventure and opportunity, could go west. Many did.

Have pupils give a short report on the history of the Ku Klux Klan.

In 1862 Congress had passed the **Homestead Act**. By this act, any citizen or person intending to become a citizen could get 160 acres (65 ha) of government land by meeting certain requirements. Such a person had to be a "head of family" and over 21 years of age. That person had to live on the land continuously for 5 years and pay a fee ranging from $26 to $34. When these requirements were met, the head of family owned the land.

The government assumed that anyone being a head of family would be male. However, there were women who registered for land under the Homestead Act. Many of them got their 160 acres (65 ha) independently, without the aid of men. It is said these women "sought economic freedom through land ownership . . . sought to earn a living by means other than those of school teacher, maid, or factory worker."

Confederate war veterans were ineligible for the benefits of the Homestead Act until most of them had their citizenship restored by the Amnesty Act of 1872. After that, many of them joined the Union veterans who had already settled on homesteads. Blacks could homestead after the adoption of the Fourteenth Amendment, which made clear their rights as citizens of the United States. Thousands of black families moved west to take up homesteads. Indeed, the Homestead Act was a major reason for the rapid settlement of the Great Plains region after the Civil War. Another reason was the extension of railroad lines. During the Civil War, Congress had passed a number of laws aiding the construction of western railroads.

Republicans triumphant Naturally, this kind of economic legislation won the support of a great many people for the Republican party. Republicans were also honored as the party that saved the Union, the party that had freed the slaves, and the party of Abraham Lincoln. All these reasons combined to make the Republican party dominant in national politics for many years after the Civil War.

Before the war, Democrats had been the expansionist party. They had added Texas and the Mexican Cession to the United States. After the war, Republicans became the party favoring the addition of more territory.

Alaska is purchased In 1867, Secretary of State William Seward had a chance to add a large new territory to the United States. This came about when Russia offered to sell the North Pacific region known as Alaska. Seward was very much in favor of expansion. However, he had some trouble in getting Congress to make the purchase. Few people had any idea of Alaska's great wealth of natural resources. Some members of Congress called that northern land "**Seward's Icebox.**"

Finally, however, Congress agreed to buy Alaska for $7.2 million. It turned out to be as great a bargain as Louisiana had been. Less than 100 years later, Alaska would become the largest state in the Union.

Grant's two terms In 1868, General Ulysses S. Grant had become another of the war heroes Americans have elected to the presidency. Grant ran the President's office like an army headquarters.

What's in a Name?

CORRUPT RINGS

The word *ring* has many meanings. During Grant's two terms as President, however, the word was used as the name for a group of persons acting outside the law in their own interests. There was, for example, the Whiskey Ring. This was a group of whiskey distillers, most of whom were in business in St. Louis. For years the Whiskey Ring worked hand in hand with United States officials to keep from paying certain taxes. During Grant's administration the Whiskey Ring even got help from Orville E. Babcock, the President's secretary. Babcock warned the swindlers whenever government inspectors were sent out to St. Louis from Washington.

The Whiskey Ring was only one of scores of corrupt rings operating in the North at all levels of government. The carpetbag governments in the South had no monopoly on corruption during those years. Perhaps the most notorious of all the corrupt rings was headed by William M. Tweed of New York City. The **Tweed Ring** used bribery, graft, and other forms of dishonesty to steal more than $50 million from the city treasury. Eventually "Boss" Tweed was arrested, put on trial for his illegal activities, and found guilty. He fled the United States to escape prison but was recognized by a Spanish immigration official. The Spanish official identified Tweed because Thomas Nast's cartoons (page 381) had made the "Boss" well known throughout the world. Tweed was sent back to New York to serve his prison sentence.

He, too, briefly considered the idea of expanding American territory. Soon after his inauguration he considered annexing the Dominican Republic in the Caribbean. The idea fell through, however.

Grant made some poor appointments to his Cabinet. Though Grant was honest himself, a number of his friends and associates turned out to be corrupt. Several scandals marked his second term in office. (See What's in a Name on this page.) Just as he began that term in 1873, a depression struck the country. Still, Grant was unable to understand Republican failure to nominate him for a third term in 1876.

Instead, the Republican convention nominated Rutherford B. Hayes, a congressman from Ohio. Hayes had a reputation for honesty. Moreover, he had reached the rank of major general during the Civil War and it was thought this would make him popular with Union war veterans. The Democrats chose Samuel J. Tilden, the governor of New York, as their candidate for the presidency. Tilden had won a national reputation by helping to smash the corrupt Tweed Ring.

A disputed election   At first it appeared that Tilden had won the election. He had 250,000 more popular votes than Hayes, and he was one electoral vote short of a majority. (See page 194.) However, 20 electoral votes were in dispute—19 in three Southern states and 1 in Oregon. The three Southern states—Florida, Louisiana, and South Carolina—were still under military occupation as part of the

Assign some pupils to report to the class on the disputed election of 1876.

Born: 1822, Point Pleasant, Ohio. **Education:** United States Military Academy. **Training:** Army officer. **To presidency from:** Illinois. **Position when elected:** General of the Army. **Political party:** Republican. **Married:** Julia Dent. **Children:** Three sons, one daughter. **Died:** 1885. **Other facts:** Fought in the Mexican War and served in remote western army posts. Resigned from the army in 1854. Worked at various jobs without much success until Civil War broke out. Was impoverished after leaving the presidency by failure of a banking firm. To support his family, wrote his memoirs, which became a financial success. **During his presidency:** Joseph Glidden's development of barbed wire solved the problem of fencing the cattle range.

ULYSSES S. GRANT
18th President
1869 · 1877

Radical Republican Reconstruction plan. Each of these states sent two sets of electors for the final count. One set favored Tilden, the other favored Hayes.

It was nearly time to inaugurate a new President before the dispute was settled. Tempers in the North and the South had become heated. Tensions between Republicans and Democrats had risen to the point that some people feared civil war might break out again. Clearly it was time for a compromise, so Congress appointed an electoral commission to settle the dispute. The Republicans made up the majority on this electoral commission. They decided that all of the disputed electoral votes should be awarded to Hayes. This gave Rutherford B. Hayes the necessary number of electoral votes to become President.

To bring about this result, however, Republicans had to make promises to Southern Democratic leaders. For one, soldiers would be withdrawn from those Southern states where they still remained. For another, Hayes promised to pick at least one Southerner for his Cabinet. Finally, leaders of the Republicans in Congress promised to supply money for internal improvements in the South. The day after Hayes took office, he appointed David M. Key of Tennessee to his Cabinet. In April, Hayes ordered the withdrawal of the last troops from the South.

These agreements between Republicans and Southern Democrats have sometimes been called the **Compromise of 1877**. The compromise did settle the crisis brought on by the disputed presidential election. But it had other results. It meant the end of Reconstruction under the Radical Republican plan. From 1877 on, the former Confederacy was again under the control of white Southern Democrats.

CHECKUP

1. Contrast the homecoming of the Union war veteran with that of the Confederate veteran.
2. How were Republicans able to remain the dominant political party for a generation following the war?
3. What kind of President was Ulysses S. Grant?
4. Why was the presidential election of 1876 so hotly disputed?
5. How was the dispute settled? What were the terms and the results of the settlement?

KEY FACTS

1. After the Civil War, American leaders were confronted with the task of rebuilding and restoring a divided nation.

2. The Radical Republicans controlled the program of Reconstruction but failed in their attempt to impeach President Johnson.

3. The Thirteenth, Fourteenth, and Fifteenth Amendments were added to the Constitution with the goal of giving black Americans the same rights enjoyed by white citizens.

4. The Reconstruction period ended in 1877 with the nation reunited but with many problems still unsolved.

VOCABULARY QUIZ

On a separate sheet of paper, match the letter with the number of the best definition. Two listed definitions will not be used.

a. Fourteenth Amendment
b. impeach
c. black code
d. carpetbagger
e. Homestead Act
f. Amnesty Act
g. sharecropping
h. "Seward's Icebox"
i. Tweed Ring
j. Ku Klux Klan

h **1.** Scornful term for Alaska

d **2.** A Northerner who went to the South after the war

i **3.** A group of corrupt politicians and businessmen in New York City

g **4.** A way of farming in the South after the Civil War

a **5.** A measure that made native-born Americans citizens

6. A white Southern Republican

c **7.** A state law restricting freed blacks

j **8.** A secret society whose goal was to maintain white control in the South

f **9.** A law that restored citizenship to most former Confederates

b **10.** To accuse an official of the national government of misconduct

11. One of the ways in which the Freedmen's Bureau helped former slaves

e **12.** A law that made government land available for citizens at low cost

REVIEW QUESTIONS

1. Contrast the Lincoln-Johnson plan with the Reconstruction Act of 1867.

2. Describe the purposes of the Thirteenth, Fourteenth, and Fifteenth Amendments to the Constitution.

3. What were the bad points and the good points of the Radical Reconstruction state governments in the South?

4. Why was a compromise necessary in order to settle the disputed election of 1876?

ACTIVITIES

1. Using information contained in this chapter, write a letter based on one of the following situations.

a. A Northern war veteran describes his plans for reentering civilian life.

b. A Southern veteran writes about his future plans.

c. A former slave tells how the Freedmen's Bureau helped him or her.

d. A Southerner describes the carpetbag government in his or her state.

e. Secretary of State Seward defends the purchase of Alaska in a letter to a member of Congress.

f. An observer describes Johnson's impeachment trial in a letter to a friend.

INTERPRETING POLITICAL CARTOONS

"BOSS" TWEED

A political cartoon is a drawing that makes a statement about a person, a subject of current public interest, or an important problem. Like a newspaper editorial, it tries to persuade people to see things a certain way. Sometimes a cartoonist will use a caricature to express a point of view. That is, the drawing will distort or exaggerate a person or thing.

The two cartoons below show Thomas Nast's view of William "Boss" Tweed. In 1869, Tweed became the leader of a powerful political group in New York City. Tweed's power lay in his influence on large numbers of immigrants to the city. Immigrants were sometimes helped by illegal means to gain citizenship, and they were given gifts of money. In return, they had to vote the way Tweed wanted.

Nast's cartoon attack on the Tweed Ring contributed much to its overthrow.

SKILLS PRACTICE

Study the cartoons and answer the questions that follow.

1. Why, do you think, is Tweed giving money to these people?
2. What tells you the money belongs to the taxpayers?
3. Why, do you think, is Tweed guarding the ballot box?
4. Explain the meaning of the phrase "In counting there is strength."

Bring to class a cartoon depicting a present-day subject and be prepared to explain it. Or you may want to draw a cartoon showing your opinion of a current subject.

THE BALLOT

IN COUNTING THERE IS STRENGTH

PUBLIC TREASURY

CHAPTER 17 The Gilded Age

Politics During the Gilded Age

VOCABULARY

Gilded Age   civil service

Two decades get a name   Samuel L. Clemens, better known as Mark Twain, married and settled down in Hartford, Connecticut, in 1872. One winter night he and his wife invited their neighbors, Mr. and Mrs. Charles Dudley Warner, to have dinner with them. Warner was a writer, too, though he never became as well known as Mark Twain. At the time, Charles Dudley Warner was editor of a local newspaper, the *Hartford Courant*.

During the dinner the husbands poked fun at the popular novels their wives had been reading. "Why don't you try to write a better one?" the wives challenged their husbands. Mark Twain and Charles Dudley Warner accepted the challenge. The next day they began work together on a novel they called *The Gilded Age*.

The two writers chose the name for their novel carefully. Something that is gilded is attractive and shiny on the surface. Underneath, however, the gilded object may be ugly and cheap. And that is the way the two writers looked at the years in which they lived. Their novel described the flashy, get-rich-quick society of the United States in the period after the Civil War. *The Gilded Age* pointed out that underneath the glittering surface lay corruption and false ideals.

Today the novel *The Gilded Age* is all but forgotten. It was never as popular as Mark Twain's later books *The Adventures of Tom Sawyer*, *Life on the Mississippi*, *Adventures of Huckleberry Finn*, and *A Connecticut Yankee in King Arthur's Court*. And yet the name of the novel has lasted. Historians often call the 20 years between 1870 and 1890 the **Gilded Age**.

Balanced parties   There was little difference between the Democratic and the Republican parties during these years. Leaders of both parties lived up to the compromise that settled the disputed election of 1876. That is, Republicans in the national government no longer interfered in local affairs in the South. Democrats had already kept their part of the bargain by allowing the Republican candidate, Rutherford B. Hayes, to become President of the United States.

National elections in the Gilded Age were quite close. Republicans won most of the presidential elections, but the Democrats controlled the House of Representatives nearly as often as Republicans controlled the White House. There were few real issues in these elections until the

Tennis became a stylish pastime for ladies and gentlemen during the Gilded Age.

Have pupils study the photograph on page 383. Ask: What were some of the other pastimes during the Gilded Age? You may wish to have pupils write reports on bicycling and baseball, two pastimes of the period.

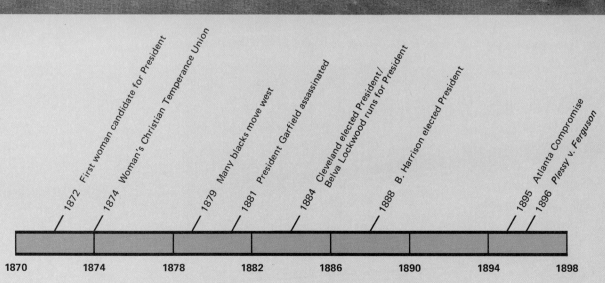

1872 First woman candidate for President

1874 Woman's Christian Temperance Union

1879 Many blacks move west

1881 President Garfield assassinated

1884 Cleveland elected President/
Belva Lockwood runs for President

1888 B. Harrison elected President

1895 Atlanta Compromise

1896 *Plessy v. Ferguson*

1870 1874 1878 1882 1886 1890 1894 1898

rise of a third party challenged the Democrats and the Republicans. (You will read about this third party in Chapter 21.) Also, both the Democratic and the Republican parties became and remained "white men's parties." Gradually, black men were kept from voting and holding office in the southern states, where white Democrats held control. Moreover, women were still denied political rights.

The Hayes presidency   The scandals of Ulysses S. Grant's administration disgusted many people. The long dispute over the presidential election of 1876 caused much doubt about politicians' honesty. Rutherford B. Hayes, however, conducted himself honorably as President. Some thoughtful people questioned the wisdom of withdrawing national troops from the southern states. Still, Hayes had made a bargain and he kept his part of it.

Lucy Webb Hayes, wife of the President, was a well-educated woman. Along with her husband she set an example of wholesome respectability. Her critics called her Lemonade Lucy because she refused to serve alcoholic beverages at social occasions in the White House. But this stand won her praise from the Woman's Christian Temperance Union.

President Hayes was conservative in most of his policies, though he did make some weak efforts toward reform of the **civil service**, the system under which people hold jobs in the offices of government. Since the days of Andrew Jackson, the spoils system had increasingly put unfit people into government jobs. One way to remedy this was to fill these positions through competitive exams. Nevertheless, most politicians wanted to appoint their party workers to the positions, and Hayes's attempts at reform failed. In fact, Hayes pleased neither reformers nor conservatives within the Republican party. As the end of his term approached, the frustrated President announced he would not seek reelection.

The election of 1880   When the Republican convention met at Chicago in 1880, the fight for the presidential nomi-

In keeping with the Compromise of 1877, federal troops depart from New Orleans.

Have pupils report to the class on the presidency of Rutherford B. Hayes, listing the highlights of his political career.

Born: 1822, Delaware, Ohio. **Education:** Kenyon College. **Training:** Lawyer, army officer, public official. **To presidency from:** Ohio. **Position when elected:** Governor of Ohio. **Political party:** Republican. **Married:** Lucy Webb. **Children:** Seven sons, one daughter. **Died:** 1893, Fremont, Ohio. **Other facts:** Practiced law in Cincinnati. Distinguished himself in Civil War. Wounded four times. Rose to rank of major general. Winner in most disputed presidential election in history. First President to visit the West Coast (San Francisco, 1880). First President to have a telephone in White House. Declined to seek a second term. **During his presidency:** A new transcontinental speed record by rail (3½ days) was set by the Lightning Express.

RUTHERFORD B. HAYES
19th President
1877 · 1881

nation was between Senator James G. Blaine of Maine and ex-President Grant, who had recently returned from a trip around the world. As the delegates cast ballot after ballot, it became apparent that neither Blaine nor Grant could win a majority. In order to break the deadlock, the delegates compromised. On the thirty-sixth ballot, they picked James A. Garfield of Ohio. Like Hayes, Garfield had been a general in the Civil War. Chester Alan Arthur, a New York City politician, was chosen as the Republican candidate for Vice President. The Democrats also chose a Civil War general—Winfield Scott Hancock of Pennsylvania—as their presidential candidate. Though the popular vote was very close, Garfield won by a sizeable margin in electoral votes.

Garfield and Arthur   James A. Garfield was a scholarly man. A graduate of Williams College, he could read and write Latin and Greek. To entertain his friends, he would write Latin with one hand and at the same time write Greek with the other. Yet he was an experienced politician and officeholder, having

served for 18 years as a congressman from Ohio. Garfield might have been a good President, but he got little chance to show what he could do. On July 2, 1881—less than 4 months after his inauguration—he was shot in the back by Charles J. Guiteau. Guiteau was a disappointed office seeker with a record of unstable behavior.

Garfield lived until September 19. After his death, Guiteau was tried for murder, convicted in spite of his plea of insanity, and hanged on June 30, 1882. By this time Chester A. Arthur was turning out to be an unexpectedly good President. Almost overnight he changed from a machine politician to an honest and efficient executive. Among other evidence of this change, Arthur supported a civil service law that did much to remedy the evils of the spoils system.

A Democratic President   In 1884, Grover Cleveland, the Democratic governor of New York, was elected President, defeating the Republican candidate, James G. Blaine. Cleveland was the first Democrat elected President since James Buchanan in 1856. Like Buchanan,

Born: 1831, Orange, Ohio.   **Education:** Williams College.   **Training:** Teacher, army officer, public official.   **To presidency from:** Ohio.   **Position when elected:** Member of Congress.   **Political party:** Republican.   **Married:** Lucretia Rudolph.   **Children:** Four sons, one daughter.   **Died:** September 19, 1881, about 10 weeks after he had been shot by a disappointed office-seeker in the railroad station in Washington, D.C.   **Other facts:** Taught Latin, Greek, and other subjects at Hiram College and later became college president.   In Civil War, one of the youngest generals in the Union army. A good linguist, campaigned speaking in German before German Americans.   **During his presidency:** Clara Barton founded the American Red Cross.

JAMES A. GARFIELD
20th President
1881

Grover Cleveland was a bachelor when he entered the White House, but in 1886 he married Frances Folsom of Buffalo, New York. Cleveland's bride was the daughter of his friend and law partner. Cleveland was the first and only President to be married in the White House.

Grover Cleveland was one of our hardest-working Presidents. By staying at his desk until 2 or 3 o'clock in the morning, he mastered the details of his job. He improved the civil service and opposed the high protective tariff favored by Republican leaders. In 1888, Benjamin Harrison, the Republican candidate, defeated Cleveland in his try for reelection. However, in 1892, Cleveland won from Harrison and entered the White House for a second term.

CHECKUP

1. How did the Gilded Age get its name?
2. On what matters were Republicans and Democrats in general agreement during the late 1870s and the 1880s?
3. Who were the Republican Presidents during the Gilded Age?
4. How did Grover Cleveland differ from the other Presidents of the Gilded Age?

Black People in the Gilded Age

VOCABULARY

Atlanta Compromise	"separate but equal"
civil rights	Jim Crow
segregated	exodus of 1879
Plessy v. *Ferguson*	

The Atlanta Compromise   It was a dramatic moment on a sunny September afternoon in 1895 at Atlanta, Georgia. That city was playing host to the Cotton States International Exposition, a miniature World's Fair. Booker T. Washington was about to give a speech at the exposition. He was the black president of Tuskegee Institute in Alabama, a school for manual training of young black men and women. Both whites and blacks recognized Booker T. Washington as a leading spokesman for his race.

The year 1895 was a year of important changes in the life of black Americans. Their great leader Frederick Douglass had died early in the year. In Washington the Supreme Court was considering the case

Have pupils research and write reports on one of the Presidents of the Gilded Age. Ask: Was the President you chose a good representative of the time? Why, or why not?

of Homer Plessy, a black man who had broken a segregation law in Louisiana. During the year, the lynchings of black people in southern states had averaged about four a week. Lynchings are murders committed by a mob. Some of these states were rewriting their constitutions to eliminate the civil and political rights of black people.

What would Booker T. Washington say about all this? What he said in his speech that September afternoon has been called the **Atlanta Compromise**. He advised his fellow blacks to give up temporarily their attempts for social equality with whites in return for the opportunity to develop their skills. They could thereby prepare themselves to earn a good living. Washington asked southern whites to provide economic opportunities by making use of the 8 million southern black people "whose habits you know. . . . You will find that they will buy your surplus land, make blossom the waste places in your fields, and run your factories. . . ." For both races he summed up the Atlanta Compromise by saying: "In all things that are purely social, we can be as separate as the fingers yet one as the hand in all things essential to mutual progress."

Civil rights   In 1868 the Fourteenth Amendment to the Constitution had defined citizenship. It had seemingly protected the rights of American citizens against harmful actions by state governments. The basic rights to which all American citizens are entitled are known as **civil rights**. These rights are set forth in several amendments to the Constitution. (See pages 192–203.)

Ask: Who speaks for black people today?

In 1875, Congress had passed the broad Civil Rights Act. It was one of the last attempts by Radical Republicans to enforce equality between blacks and whites. Among other things, the Civil Rights Act of 1875 prohibited racial discrimination in places of "public accommodation." These included hotels, railroad stations and passenger cars, steamboats, theaters, "and other places of public amusement." Sooner or later, the Civil Rights Act of 1875 was certain to be tested in the courts. The final test came in 1883 when six cases came before the United States Supreme Court. The court ruled in these six cases that the Civil Rights Act of 1875 was unconstitutional. The court's decision stated that the Fourteenth Amendment did not protect citizens against acts of discrimination by private individuals.

In a speech to an Alabama audience, Booker T. Washington stresses the value of vocational education in helping black people achieve equality of citizenship.

CHESTER A. ARTHUR
21st President
1881 · 1885

Born: 1830, Fairfield, Vermont. **Education:** Union College. **Training:** Teacher, lawyer, public official. **To presidency from:** New York. **Position when taking office:** Vice President. **Political party:** Republican. **Married:** Ellen Herndon. **Children:** Two sons, one daughter. **Died:** 1886, New York City. **Other facts:** Taught school and studied law. Showed early interest in politics and became leader of Republican machine in New York City. Appointed collector of New York Customs House. Despite reputation as machine politician, served honestly and well as President. Declining health kept him from seriously seeking 4 more years as President. **During his presidency:** The Brooklyn Bridge, then the world's largest suspension bridge, was completed in 1883.

This decision by the Supreme Court opened the way for an increasing amount of racial discrimination. With few exceptions, whites and blacks were **segregated**, that is, set apart, in the public school systems. Moreover, in 1896, racial segregation by state law received the approval of the Supreme Court.

A far-reaching decision   The case of *Plessy* v. *Ferguson* involved a law passed by the Louisiana state legislature in 1890. The law required that "all railway companies carrying passengers in their coaches in this state, shall provide equal but separate accommodations for the white and colored races." Homer Plessy, a black citizen of the United States, took a seat in a coach reserved for whites. He was arrested and took legal action against Louisiana on the grounds that the law violated his rights under the Fourteenth Amendment. The Ferguson named in the case was an official of the Louisiana state government.

In *Plessy* v. *Ferguson* the Supreme Court ruled that the Louisiana law did not violate the Fourteenth Amendment if the separate coaches for blacks and whites were equal. This and the decisions in the civil rights cases fastened racial segregation on the country. By law and by custom, all sorts of public facilities were segregated according to race. And all this was accepted as legal if the facilities were **"separate but equal."**

Political rights   Meanwhile, law and custom had begun to affect the political rights of black men. For a few years after home rule was restored in the South, black men had kept on voting and holding office. Most black voters favored the Republican party. They thought of it as the party that had given them freedom and the right to vote. This made it hard for black politicians to hold office in southern states. All of these states were under the control of white Democrats.

Yet state legislatures did have as members a few black Republicans during the Gilded Age. Likewise, there were southern blacks in every Congress but one during the 1870s and 1880s. However,

Have several pupils report to the class on the Supreme Court decisions in the cases of *Plessy* v. *Ferguson* and *Brown* v. *Board of Education of Topeka.* Ask: How are they similar? How are they different?

more political restrictions were being placed on them. By the latter years of the Gilded Age, some southern states were considering laws that would keep blacks from voting.

Second-class citizenship By the end of the Gilded Age, the Fourteenth and Fifteenth Amendments had little meaning for black Americans. White southerners had not at first defied these amendments when home rule was given back to the South. Instead, they had experimented for years before arriving at a new system of relationships between whites and blacks. This new system separated the two races in nearly all social situations.

To describe the new system, the term **Jim Crow** came into use. Jim Crow waiting rooms, Jim Crow water fountains, and many other "separate but equal" facilities were described by this name. (The term came from a black song-and-dance man who, in his act on the stage, called himself Jim Crow.) In time this system would bar blacks from voting or holding office in southern states. By the 1890s the Supreme Court had given its approval to key features of the new system. It was accepted in the North as well as in the South.

Booker T. Washington accepted this new system as a temporary situation in his Atlanta speech. Some black people criticized Washington for his acceptance of what amounted to second-class citizenship. Nevertheless, Washington continued to emphasize to black Americans the need for vocational education, for more wealth, and for more experience as ways of achieving equality of citizenship.

One or more pupils can read *The Strange Career of Jim Crow* by C. Van Woodward and give a report to the class.

The exodus of 1879 Not many blacks lived in the northern states during the Gilded Age. For this reason, most northerners thought of race relations as only a southern problem. Some blacks did leave the South during these decades. For example, Benjamin Singleton, a former slave, led an emigration of black people from the South to the West in what has been called the **exodus of 1879.**

The exodus of 1879 involved thousands of people. Poor black farmers organized committees, donated their savings, and hired agents to arrange the journey to the West. Most of them settled in either Kansas or Nebraska, where they founded several communities. In most cases the new black residents were accepted, although a group of black migrants from Mississippi was driven out of Lincoln, Nebraska. On the other hand, Tom

W.E.B. Du Bois, an outstanding scholar on the problems of black people in American society, agreed only in part with Booker T. Washington's views. Du Bois felt that the first step toward achieving equality was to remove the obstacles that had been thrown up in many states to prevent black people from voting.

The Shores family, shown in front of their sod house and barn, made a new life for themselves in Nebraska.

Cunningham, a black man, became a police officer in Lincoln. And M. O. Ricketts, an ex-slave, graduated with honors from the medical school of the University of Nebraska in 1884. Dr. Ricketts was later twice elected to the state legislature of Nebraska.

CHECKUP

1. What were the main features of the Atlanta Compromise?
2. Explain the meaning of the Supreme Court's decisions in the civil rights cases and in *Plessy v. Ferguson*.
3. Why could black Americans be considered "second-class citizens" by the end of the Gilded Age?

Women in the Gilded Age

┌─VOCABULARY─────────────┐
│ sweat shop   │
└────────────────────────┘

A woman for President?   Who was the first female candidate for the office of President of the United States? There are at least two claimants to this honor, both well known during the Gilded Age. The earliest was Victoria Woodhull, a lady whose actions created controversy at the time. In 1870, Mrs. Woodhull and her sister were stockbrokers in New York City. They were proud of their success in what was thought of as a man's business. Victoria Woodhull believed women were capable of doing anything. So she announced herself as a candidate for President of the United States in an election that was still 2 years off.

Soon after her announcement, Victoria Woodhull started a weekly newspaper to publicize her candidacy. The newspaper also advocated other reforms she believed in, including woman suffrage. Woodhull tried to get the National Woman Suffrage Association to support her candidacy but was refused. Undaunted, she held her own convention, which declared her to be the presidential candidate of the Equal Rights party. The convention nominated Frederick Douglass for Vice President. The surprised black leader declined the honor, preferring to support Ulysses S. Grant in the election of 1872.

In the unlikely event that Mrs. Woodhull had won the election, her inauguration would have been delayed for 6 months. Only then would she have reached the age of 35, required by the Constitution for the presidency. As it turned out, her Equal Rights party was unable to get on the ballot in any state, so she got no votes at all.

Twelve years later, a handful of women met in California. They formed the National Equal Rights party and nominated Belva Lockwood, a New York lawyer, for President. Her platform called for equal rights for all, including blacks, women, Indians, and immigrants; regulation of the sale of liquor; uniform marriage and divorce laws in all the states; and universal peace.

Have pupils imagine what it would have been like to be a black person emigrating from the South to the West in 1879. Have them write several entries in a journal describing how they feel about their new life in the West.

Suffrage denied   Belva Lockwood ran a dignified campaign that aroused much public interest. However, Susan B. Anthony and many other women's leaders were against her candidacy. They thought it would bring ridicule to the entire woman suffrage movement. Nevertheless, Mrs. Lockwood received 4,140 votes, scattered among six states. None of these votes came from women, for women were still not allowed to vote in a national election.

After the Civil War, Susan B. Anthony and Elizabeth Cady Stanton were shocked that male ex-slaves were given the right to vote, when the right was still denied to women. For the next 50 years, women's organizations made suffrage their chief goal. Their efforts were handicapped for a time by personality and policy clashes, making it difficult to form a united front. For two decades there were two different national organizations seeking woman suffrage.

Other reforms   While suffrage remained the chief goal, women's organizations also worked for other reforms. The temperance movement got new life at the beginning of the Gilded Age through a women's antisaloon crusade that started in Ohio. It led to the formation of the Woman's Christian Temperance Union (WCTU) in 1874. Frances Willard assumed leadership of the organization 5 years later. She committed the organization to a wide range of reforms that appealed to millions of American women.

Women were leaders in bringing the sorry plight of American Indians to the attention of the nation. Early in the Gilded Age, Mary Bonney and Amelia Quinton started the first national organization devoted to improving conditions for the Indians. A few years later, their organization became known as the Women's National Indian Association. This association supported 50 missions working to Christianize and assist western Indians.

In 1879 Susette La Flesche Tibbles, the daughter of an Omaha Indian chief, made a lecture tour through the East. She used her Indian name, Bright Eyes, and wore Indian costumes when she spoke. The Indian girl was an effective speaker. She induced many influential people to support the cause of the American Indian. Among these was Helen Hunt Jackson, a writer whose critical history of the government's shameful treatment of Indians appeared in 1881 as a book called *A Century of Dishonor*. Three years later, Mrs. Jackson published *Ramona*, a romantic novel of Indian and Spanish families in California. It achieved a wide popular success.

In 1884, Belva Lockwood was a presidential candidate.

Opportunities for women Going to college was the great adventure for ambitious young women of the Gilded Age. In the Midwest they went to one of the state universities that were starting to open their doors to women. In the East they could go to one of the new women's colleges offering a liberal-arts education similar to that of the men's colleges. From this group of college-educated young women came most of the women's leaders of the next generation.

By the beginning of the Gilded Age, there were three medical schools for women. The University of Michigan's medical school also admitted women along with men. After graduation, however, women had great difficulty in practicing medicine. No established hospital would take them as students, interns, or staff members. The best-trained women in the medical profession had to go to Europe for higher degrees.

For women it was easier to practice law than to practice medicine. Most women lawyers in the Gilded Age were the wives of lawyers. They prepared for admission to the bar by reading law with their husbands. After passing their bar exams, they usually joined their husbands in practice. The early women lawyers were devoted to the cause of women's rights. Except for politicians' wives, these lawyers were the first women to become active in party politics. This was long before women had the right to vote.

Writing for pay was one way in which women earned money and fame during the Gilded Age. Some of the best women writers of the time produced children's books of high quality. Louisa May Alcott, for example, drew on her own childhood experiences to create realistic youthful characters living in familiar home settings. *St. Nicholas Magazine*, for boys and girls, printed good books as serials.

These students are attending a class in one of the first medical schools for women.

THE TELEPHONE

Alexander Graham Bell was born in Scotland. He came to Canada in 1870, and a year later he moved to Boston, where he was a teacher of the deaf. In 1874, Bell conceived a theory for reproducing the human voice by electrical means. Two years later he turned his theory into fact, as the first understandable sentence was transmitted over a short distance. In 1876, assisted by drawings made by Lewis Howard Latimer, a black American electrical engineer and draftsman, Alexander Graham Bell received patents for what he named a telephone.

Why did he call his invention a telephone? *Tele* is classical Greek for "from afar" or "far away." Americans were already familiar with it as part of Samuel F. B. Morse's telegraph. The second part, *phone,* also Greek, means "sound" or "speech." Thus *telephone* is a Greek name. It is a better name (or at least shorter) than "an instrument for transmitting speech from far away," which is what it means in English. Can you guess why we today have such a word as *television?*

The invention of Alexander Graham Bell that received a patent in 1876 has taken many forms over the years. The model that is shown above is one of the earliest dial phones. Telephones like this were usually fastened to the wall.

Mary Mapes Dodge edited the magazine for many years after it started publication in 1873. She insisted on high standards for *St. Nicholas Magazine,* and many of the most capable female and male authors wrote for it.

Work for girls and women

Teaching was the preferred occupation for women who worked outside the home during the Gilded Age. Indeed, teaching in the elementary schools was on its way to becoming associated primarily with women. At the same time, two inventions created jobs for hundreds of thousands of girls and women.

A number of people are associated with the invention of the typewriter. Christopher L. Sholes is generally credited with making the first practical typing machine. By the 1870s, typewriters were being used in thousands of offices. Increasingly, women were being hired as typists. The number of male clerks and stenographers decreased as more and more women took their place.

From the beginning, women worked at the switchboards made necessary by the invention of the telephone. Thousands of them learned to say "Number, please" as part of their first jobs. Female sales clerks in department stores were replacing male clerks during the Gilded Age, and many women were replacing men in business offices. But the hours for female sales clerks were long and the

Women usually operated the switchboards made necessary by the invention of the telephone.

pay was low. Moreover, they were given the routine clerical jobs, while male clerks were often promoted to positions as managers.

Jobs in mills and factories were less pleasant and usually no better paid. Immigrant girls in particular filled these positions. In the garment trade, **sweat shops** were common. These were shops where workers were employed under unhealthy conditions for long hours with poor wages. Immigrant girls also went into domestic service, working as cooks and maids.

Whether immigrants or native-born Americans, most women during the Gilded Age thought of marriage and a family as their eventual goal. In 1870 there were more than 1.9 million girls and women working at jobs outside their homes. Twenty years later this number had more than doubled to 4 million. Of this number, only about one eighth were married, with a husband present in the home. Nearly three fourths of the females working outside the home in 1890 were young and single.

The Arts in the Gilded Age

Two poets Presidents during the Gilded Age served with little distinction. For black people, the Gilded Age was a time of shrinking opportunities. Though some doors opened for women during the 1870s and 1880s, women failed to win the right to vote. And yet American contributions to the arts were numerous and significant in those years. For example, two of America's greatest poets lived and wrote during the Gilded Age.

Walt Whitman was the older of the two. *Leaves of Grass*, his great collection of poetry, first appeared in 1855, but it was revised and expanded up to the time of Whitman's death in 1892. *Leaves of Grass* reflects the poet's love of life and of America. Some critics scorned Whitman's writings. They said that what he wrote did not look or sound like poetry. Nevertheless, one judgment of Walt Whitman states: "As a maker of phrases, a master of rhythms, a weaver of images . . . he is beyond the reach of criticism."

Walt Whitman was a man very much involved with the world. Emily Dick-

In his poems Walt Whitman sang the praises of America and democracy. Have pupils read several of his poems aloud in the class.

inson was the opposite. Her poems focus on the inner self. A stern father dominated Emily. Nevertheless, she lived a normal early life. But as time passed, Emily became increasingly withdrawn.

No one knows when she began writing poetry. Only two of her poems were published before her death in 1886. However, the poems she wrote in her Amherst, Massachusetts, home were preserved by her sister and later published. Most of Emily Dickinson's poems did not have titles. They are identified by numbers, such as "1263," written about 1873, which contains the lines "There is no Frigate [sailing ship] like a Book/To take us Lands away. . . ."

A trio of painters   Among the American painters active during the Gilded Age were three masters. One of these, George

Poet Emily Dickinson focused on the inner self.

Poet Walt Whitman created rhythms and images.

Inness, was a follower of the Hudson River School in his early career (see page 283). However, he later went beyond these painters, developing his own style. His painting *The Coming Storm* is so realistic that viewers might wonder why the boy in the foreground has failed to run for cover. And yet Inness could paint softly. His *June*, finished in 1882, brings thoughts of the beauty seen in that lovely month.

Winslow Homer, another great American painter, went through three different styles and subjects during his career. He first became well-known as an illustrator and painter of Civil War scenes. After that, he shifted to landscapes and pictures of rural people working and playing. Like other American painters of the time, he traveled abroad. Winslow Homer returned from England in 1882

395

The Coming Storm *by George Inness catches the feel of a sultry summer afternoon.*

and began a third style of painting. This included scenes showing the drama of the sea. Homer's *Eight Bells, The Gulf Stream,* and *A Summer Squall* are among the sea pictures for which he is chiefly famous.

Thomas Eakins was a third great American painter during the Gilded Age. Eakins was unusual because he studied anatomy at a medical college. Knowledge gained in this way made him a master at drawing the human figure at rest or in action. Eakins demonstrated this skill in many fine pictures, including *The Swimming Hole, Between Rounds,* and *Max Schmitt in a Single Scull.*

The writers   Mark Twain not only helped give the name of the Gilded Age to the 1870s and 1880s, he did his best work during those years. He made Tom Sawyer, Becky Thatcher, and Huckleberry Finn immortal characters. As a writer and a lecturer, Mark Twain was head and shoulders above the others of the time.

Mark Twain drew upon his boyhood experiences on the Mississippi in some of his most popular books. In others he told of his western experiences during the 1860s. For several years he had worked as a newspaper reporter in the mining camp of Virginia City, Nevada, and later in San Francisco. In his writ-

Mark Twain was considered to be one of the country's best satirists. Ask: What is a satire? Have pupils bring in examples of satire from current newspapers. (One example might be an article by Erma Bombeck or Art Buchwald.)

ings that made use of these backgrounds, he could be considered a **local colorist.**

Local colorists were authors who set their tales in a specific region of the United States. They tried to make the scenes, the characters, and the dialogue in their stories typical of that region. Bret Harte became one of the best known of the western local colorists with his stories of the California mining country. Joel Chandler Harris wrote scores of novels and stories of southern life, although he is chiefly identified as author of the Uncle Remus tales. Mary Noailles Murfree became well-known under the pen name Charles Egbert Craddock with her first and best book, *In the Tennessee Mountains,* published in 1884. And Sarah Orne Jewett, who wrote under her own name, produced hundreds of stories based in the seacoast towns of Maine. Her novel *The Country of the Pointed Firs* is a classic.

Mark Twain had a close association with another classic of the Gilded Age,

Winslow Homer's painting Eight Bells *shows two seafaring men on a ship's deck, probably at noon, using an instrument to "shoot the sun"—that is, determine the ship's location. The title refers to the way that a ship's bell marks the hours.*

Marietta Holley is largely forgotten today as an author, but her humorous novels were very popular 100 years ago. They dealt with two country characters, Josiah Allen and his wife, Samantha. In the novels, Josiah is pictured as a typical male chauvinist of the time, one who believes that males are always superior to females. Samantha is portrayed as a practical wife whose common-sense arguments for women's rights often leave Josiah speechless.

Josiah Allen believes the only right a woman needs is the right to marry. All women should be put on a pedestal, he says. Samantha, a hefty woman, wants to know how one as big as she is going to get up on a pedestal in the first place. Then, she asks, how is she going to get down to take care of the children, get back up, then climb down again to prepare supper?

At another time Josiah says that Samantha's tombstone should read "Wife of Josiah Allen," as was the custom in those days. A list of his accomplishments could then be put on the tombstone to honor her. Samantha points out that he might die first, in which case she would have "Josiah Allen, husband of Samantha Allen" put on his tombstone. Josiah gets very upset at this. After some thought he announces that if she is going to do that, he is not going to die.

Samantha comments humorously on woman suffrage, temperance, and other issues. In 1892 Marietta Holley wrote *Samantha on the Race Problem* in which Samantha ridicules white American attitudes toward black people.

The common-sense views about women's rights that Samantha Allen put forth in discussions with her husband, Josiah, amused the many readers of Marietta Holley's popular novels.

The American Publishing Company brought out the first Samantha Allen book in 1873. During the Gilded Age and later, Marietta Holley's Samantha Allen rivaled Mark Twain's Tom Sawyer and Huckleberry Finn in popularity. Samantha's comments helped to advance the ideas of women reformers. In time their ideas would become everybody's ideas.

---

the *Personal Memoirs of U. S. Grant.* The great general—but less than great President—had fallen on hard times in the 1880s. Business losses plunged him into bankruptcy. A series of illnesses and, finally, cancer of the throat brought him near to death. There was a real possibility that Grant might die leaving his family in poverty.

Friends came to Grant's rescue. He was taken to a house at Mount McGregor, near Saranac, New York. There, Grant grimly set to work on his memoirs. Mark Twain was then in business as a publisher. He received the final pages of Grant's account only a few days before the tough old general's death. *Personal Memoirs of U. S. Grant* became one of the most successful of all American books. From the sale of the book, Grant's family received nearly $450,000. This sum, a fortune for the time, assured that the general's family would be financially secure.

The musicians   One of the outstanding musicians of the Gilded Age was John Philip Sousa. When only 6 years old, he entered a conservatory to study violin and harmony. He received a solid musical education.

In John Philip Sousa's day, almost every city park contained a bandstand. On summer evenings, crowds of people attended band concerts. Band music fascinated John Philip Sousa. He learned to play all the instruments used in the military bands of the time. In 1880, Sousa became the leader of the United States Marine Corps band. After 12 years as leader, he left the Marine Corps to develop a band of his own.

Sousa turned out to be more than a band leader. He became a composer of marches, a form of music very popular in those days. Sousa's marches are still played today. Among them are "Washington Post March," "Semper Fidelis," "El Capitan," "High School Cadets," and the thrilling "Stars and Stripes Forever." His band toured the United States, played in the capitals of European countries, and made a trip around the world. John Philip Sousa's band and his musical compositions earned for him the title of the March King.

John Philip Sousa's marches came at a time when a great wave of patriotism was covering the scars left by the Civil War. Mark Twain and Charles Dudley Warner

Concerts by the United States Marine Band under the direction of John Philip Sousa were eagerly awaited events in cities all over the world.

were only partly right about the Gilded Age. There was a superficial gilding of life during the 1870s and 1880s, but underneath there was strength, not weakness; steel, not tin. During the Gilded Age the United States was laying the foundations for greatness.

CHECKUP

1. How did the poetry of Walt Whitman and Emily Dickinson differ?
2. Give one fact about the paintings of each of the following artists: George Inness, Winslow Homer, Thomas Eakins.
3. Why does the term *local colorist* fit Mark Twain?
4. For what is musician John Philip Sousa chiefly remembered?

KEY FACTS

1. The 1870s and 1880s were sometimes referred to as the Gilded Age because the surface glitter of American society concealed much corruption and ugliness.

2. National elections were close during the Gilded Age because the two major parties were balanced, with few differences after the end of Reconstruction.

3. During the Gilded Age, most black Americans were gradually pushed into the status of second-class citizens through custom and by new laws in some states.

4. More and better opportunities in education and careers became available to women, but the right to vote was still to be won.

5. American contributions to literature, painting, and music were substantial during the Gilded Age.

VOCABULARY QUIZ

On a separate sheet of paper, write the letter representing the best completion of each of the following statements.

1. The Atlanta Compromise approved **(a)** the goals of the Ku Klux Klan, **(b)** sharecropping and the crop lien system, **(c)** temporary social segregation of blacks and whites, **(d)** the removal of Army troops from the South.

2. The exodus of 1879 referred to **(a)** the departure of carpetbaggers from the South, **(b)** the Cotton States International Exposition. **(c)** the book written by Ulysses S. Grant, **(d)** a migration of southern black people into Kansas and Nebraska.

3. Civil rights for United States citizens include **(a)** the right to assemble peacefully, **(b)** the right to trial by jury, **(c)** the right of free speech, **(d)** all of these.

4. In the case of *Plessy* v. *Ferguson* the Supreme Court approved the doctrine of **(a)** civil rights, **(b)** woman suffrage, **(c)** racially segregated, but equal, public facilities, **(d)** none of these.

5. The Gilded Age saw **(a)** the employment of larger numbers of women outside the home, **(b)** the appointment of a woman to the Supreme Court, **(c)** the passage of a national woman suffrage law, **(d)** the nomination of a woman for President by one of the two major parties.

REVIEW QUESTIONS

1. What were the main features of the Atlanta Compromise? Why did Booker T. Washington accept it?

2. Explain how black people became second-class citizens during the Gilded Age.

3. Describe the employment opportunities open to women during the Gilded Age.

4. Explain the chief contributions of each of the following to the arts during the Gilded Age: **(a)** Emily Dickinson, **(b)** Thomas Eakins, **(c)** John Philip Sousa.

ACTIVITIES

1. Using information contained in this chapter and in the *Dictionary of American Biography*, do a report on the Civil War activities of each of the men who became President during the Gilded Age.

2. Have a "literature day" in class. On that occasion, read selections from the poetry or fiction of several writers described in this chapter.

3. Prepare a bulletin board with copies of pictures painted by the artists discussed in this chapter.

DISTINGUISHING BETWEEN FACT AND OPINION

THE GILDED AGE

Some statements people make are statements of *fact*. Others are statements of *opinion*. There are ways to tell the difference. A statement of fact is true—it can be proven. A statement of opinion is what a person thinks or feels. The two statements below show the difference:

1. A touchdown in football counts six points. (Fact)

2. Football is a rougher game than hockey. (Opinion)

You can prove the first statement by reading a rule book or watching the scoreboard at a football game. The second statement is difficult to prove because it says what the person thinks or feels.

SKILLS PRACTICE

Below are facts and opinions about events during the Gilded Age. After reading each statement, mark on a sheet of paper whether the statement is fact or opinion. Write **O** for opinion and **F** for fact.

F **1.** In 1876 the United States celebrated the one-hundredth anniversary of the signing of the Declaration of Independence.

O **2.** A world's fair, held in Philadelphia as part of the celebration, was less interesting than the Cotton States International Exposition held in Atlanta in 1895.

O **3.** As President, Rutherford B. Hayes was more honest than Chester A. Arthur.

F **4.** Thousands of young women got jobs as telephone operators and typists during the Gilded Age.

O **5.** Women were more suitable than men as telephone operators and typists because of their nimble fingers, pleasant voices, and attention to details.

F **6.** After the return of home rule to the South, the Republican party withered and nearly died out in the southern states.

O **7.** Southern states would have been better off if national army troops had remained in the South.

O **8.** Booker T. Washington was correct in 1895 when he said economic opportunities were more useful than political rights for black Americans in the South.

O **9.** Emily Dickinson would have written better poetry if she had gotten out into the world more.

F **10.** The writings of local colorists were popular in the United States during the last decades of the nineteenth century.

4/UNIT REVIEW

READING THE TEXT

Turn to pages 322 and 323. These pages describe events in Congress in 1850, a critical year. After you have read these pages, write the answers to the following questions.

1. What person was chiefly responsible for the Compromise of 1850? **Henry Clay**

2. What new state was admitted into the Union under this measure? **California**

3. Was it a slave state or free state? **Free**

4. Who would decide whether the rest of the Mexican Cession would have slavery? **The people**

5. Did Daniel Webster support the plan? **Yes**

6. Would Texas receive more land? **No**

7. Where would the slave trade be prohibited yet slavery would be allowed? **D.C.**

8. Who was the Little Giant? **Stephen Douglas**

9. Who said, "I speak today for the preservation of the Union"? **Daniel Webster**

10. Who on his deathbed said, "The South, the poor South"? **John C. Calhoun**

READING A MAP

Turn to page 355 and study the map titled "The War in the East, 1864—1865." On a sheet of paper, write **T** if the statement is true and **F** if it is false.

F 1. After leaving Savannah, Sherman's army marched north to Charleston.

F 2. The distance from Chattanooga to Atlanta is approximately 160 miles.

T 3. Sherman's army crossed the Savannah, Pee Dee, and Cape Fear rivers.

F 4. The armies of Grant and Lee met at Petersburg before they met at Spotsylvania.

F 5. Lynchburg, Richmond, and Appomattox Court House are all on the James River.

READING PICTURES

Turn to pages 396 and 397. On each page is a copy of a painting by an artist of the late 1800s. Study the pictures and then on a sheet of paper answer the following questions.

1. What is happening in the painting shown on page 396?

2. How has the artist suggested that a storm is coming?

3. What is happening in the painting on page 397?

4. How can you tell that the painting shows a scene aboard a ship?

5. Tell which painting you like more. Why?

READING PRESIDENTIAL BOXES

In Chapter 17 are boxes with facts about three Presidents: Rutherford B. Hayes (page 385), James A. Garfield (page 386) and Chester A. Arthur (page 388). On a sheet of paper, beside the number of each statement, write **T** if the statement is true and **F** if it is false.

T 1. Hayes, Garfield, and Arthur were all members of the Republican party.

F 2. All three came from Ohio.

T 3. Garfield and Hayes were generals in the Union army in the Civil War.

T 4. Hayes was the only one of the three to serve a full term.

F 5. Arthur had the largest family.

F 6. Hayes sought a second term.

F 7. The Brooklyn Bridge was completed during Garfield's presidency.

F 8. All three Presidents were lawyers.

T 9. Garfield was assassinated.

F 10. Hayes and Arthur served their terms in office successively.

Laying the Foundation for Greatness

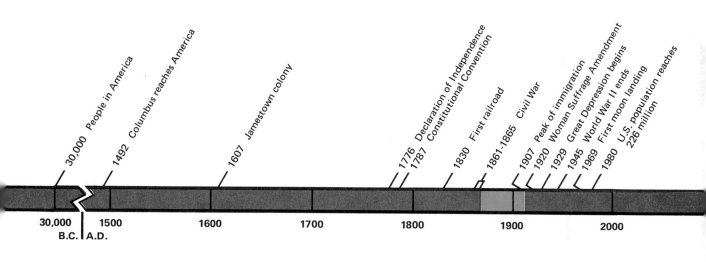

30,000 People in America
1492 Columbus reaches America
1607 Jamestown colony
1776 Declaration of Independence
1787 Constitutional Convention
1830 First railroad
1861-1865 Civil War
1907 Peak of immigration
1920 Woman Suffrage Amendment
1929 Great Depression begins
1945 World War II ends
1969 First moon landing
1980 U.S. population reaches 226 million

30,000 B.C. | A.D. 1500 | 1600 | 1700 | 1800 | 1900 | 2000

Above: Statue of Liberty, Andrew Carnegie, cowboy on the range, arriving immigrants **403**

CHAPTER
18 The Last Frontier

The Indians' Last Stand

VOCABULARY
reservation   Dawes Act
nomadic

A bitter choice   As dawn broke on September 30, 1877, Chief Joseph and his group of Nez Percé (nez pérs) Indians prepared to leave camp at Snake Creek, near the Bear Paw Mountains in the Montana Territory. Another 40 miles (64 km), just another 40 miles, and they would reach the Canadian border. Then they would be beyond the reach of the United States Army, which was pursuing them.

Before they could break camp, 600 soldiers on horseback appeared on the surrounding hills and began their charge. Quickly the Indian warriors drew themselves into a line of defense. All day the battle raged. The army lost more men than the Indians, but the Nez Percé lost several of their best leaders.

The next day a storm blew in. Cold rains and snow fell for 2 days. One Indian woman later remembered, "Children cried with hunger and cold. Old people suffering in silence. Misery everywhere." The Nez Percé were trapped and greatly outnumbered. Their three remaining chiefs—Joseph, Looking Glass, and White Bird—now had the bitter choice: Should they surrender and give up their independence? Or should they fight on, with defeat almost certain?

Ask: Which choice would you make if you were faced with this situation?

The plight of the Nez Percé   The events that had brought Chief Joseph's people to the encampment at Bear Paw had begun 22 years earlier. The Nez Percé lived in a valley where today's states of Oregon, Idaho, and Washington meet. There they farmed and raised cattle. They lived in bands of a few hundred, each band under its own chief.

In 1855 the United States government decided to make room for white settlers by requiring the various Indian tribes of the Northwest to move onto **reservations** —public land set aside by the government for the Indians' use. The Nez Percé agreed to accept a reservation of 10,000 square miles (25,900 sq km). In exchange, they received about $200,000 worth of goods.

This agreement lasted just 8 years. In 1863, as more whites moved in, the United States government decided that the Nez Percé reservation must be cut down from 10,000 to 1,000 square miles (2,590 sq km). Some of the Nez Percé chiefs yielded to government pressure. Five others, however, refused to move their bands onto the smaller reservation. One of these chiefs was Joseph's father.

At roundup time a cowboy was called upon to test his riding and roping skills.

The retreat of Chief Joseph and his people is still taught at West Point as an example of a classic retreat maneuver. Chief Joseph had learned about military tactics by watching soldiers at drill when he was young.

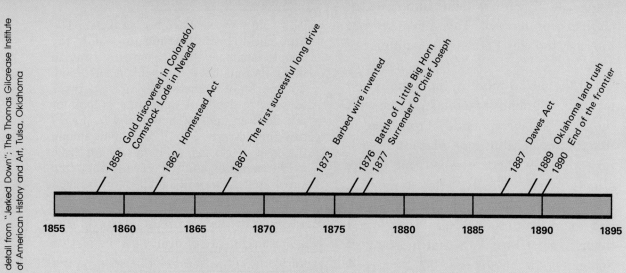

1858 Gold discovered in Colorado/Comstock Lode in Nevada

1862 Homestead Act

1867 The first successful long drive

1873 Barbed wire invented

1876 Battle of Little Big Horn

1877 Surrender of Chief Joseph

1887 Dawes Act

1889 Oklahoma land rush

1890 End of the frontier

1855 1860 1865 1870 1875 1880 1885 1890 1895

405

The name *Nez Percé* means *"pierced nose."* It was given to this tribe by a French interpreter who saw some of the tribe members with decorative shells in their noses.

Matters stayed that way for the next 14 years. Then, in 1877, the United States Army ordered the resisting chiefs to take their people onto the reservation or face war.

A desperate flight By that time, Joseph had succeeded his father as chief of his band. Chief Joseph was a peace-loving man. He believed that war would mean disaster for the Nez Percé. With great sadness, he decided that his band must move onto the reservation as ordered.

Before they could do so, warriors from another band of Nez Percé murdered 18 white settlers. Chief Joseph knew what this would mean. The army would surely strike back at all Nez Percé, even his own band who had nothing to do with the killings. His people, fearing for their lives, prepared to flee. There was nothing for the Nez Percé to do now but get ready to fight if attacked.

The Nez Percé numbered only about 150 fighting men and another 550 women, children, and old men. Against them were 2,000 soldiers and hundreds of civilian volunteers. This force set out to crush the Nez Percé in the summer of 1877.

For the next 3 months, the Indians fled through mountains and thick forests, with the army in close pursuit. From time to time, bitter fighting took place, but each time the Nez Percé slipped out of the army's grasp. Finally, after 3 months, nearly 1,700 miles (2,735 km) of travel, and many battles, the Nez Percé found themselves at Bear Paw that morning of September 30, 1877.

National Portrait Gallery, Smithsonian Institution

Chief Joseph, the great leader of the Nez Percé, was finally forced to move his people onto a reservation.

The surrender of Chief Joseph By October 4, Chief Joseph knew his situation was hopeless. Of the 150 warriors who had started out with him in June, only 79 had survived. There was nothing to do but surrender. The next day he did so, with these moving words:

It is cold and we have no blankets. The little children are freezing to death. My people, some of them, have run away to the hills and have no blankets, no food; no one knows where they are—perhaps freezing to death. I want time to look for my children and see how many of them I can find. Maybe I shall find them among the dead. Hear me, my chiefs. I am tired; my heart is sick and sad. From where the sun now stands, I will fight no more forever.

Broken treaties In the story of the Nez Percé, the fate of nearly all the Native Americans in the West can be seen. First

Ask: Why, do you think, did Chief Joseph feel that flight was the only alternative for his band of people, even though they had had nothing to do with the murder of the 18 white settlers? If the murders had not taken place, what do you think would have happened to the Nez Percé on the reservation?

George Catlin, an artist who studied Indians and drew sketches and paintings depicting their lives, said that the Indian could use his horse as an extra shield while "riding at fullest speed, carrying with him his bow and his shield, and also his long lance." The Indian skillfully fired arrows at the enemy, either over the horse's back or under its neck.

came the arrival of white settlers onto the Indians' ancient lands. A period of conflict between settlers and Indians followed. Pressed by the settlers, the United States government would make a treaty with Indian chiefs, reserving certain areas of land for their people in exchange for signing over the rest. As settlers' demands for land increased, these treaties were often broken. Indians were forced onto even smaller and poorer lands. Many resisted. War between the Indians and the United States Army would follow, and eventually the Indians were defeated.

On the Great Plains   The final chapter of the tragedy of the Native Americans was played out on the vast stage of the Great Plains. This region lies between 100° west longitude and the Rocky Mountains, from Canada all the way to Mexico.

By the 1860s this was the last great unsettled area in the United States. The reason is its climate. The 100° west line of longitude cuts through the center of the Dakotas, Nebraska, and Kansas, and then runs through Oklahoma and Texas. Lands to the east of this line usually get plenty of rain. To the west, rainfall generally drops below 20 inches (50 cm) a year, in some places below 10 inches (25 cm). Wind sweeps over the flatlands, which are bitterly cold in the winter and like a furnace in the summer. This is the region, you will recall, that Major Stephen Long called the Great American Desert.

Following the buffalo   On these dry lands and in the neighboring Rocky Mountains lived perhaps 250,000 Indians. Most of the Plains Indians were **nomadic,** that is, they did not live in permanent villages but traveled across the plains, following the herds of buffalo across the endless grasslands. For these Indians, the buffalo provided food, clothing, tepees, blankets, and tools.

In the late 1700s the Plains Indians started using horses, which had multiplied and spread northward since the

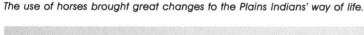

The use of horses brought great changes to the Plains Indians' way of life.

Plains Indians on snowshoes pursue buffalo whose flight is hindered by deep snow.

Spanish had brought them to Mexico in the sixteenth century. With horses the Plains Indians became more efficient hunters. Their warriors also became more efficient fighters, first against each other, later against the whites.

Warfare on the plains   Until the 1840s the United States government regarded the plains region as one big Indian reservation. Soon, however, the traders, miners, and settlers who crossed the plains demanded protection against the Indians. The government then built army posts along the main trails. It also decided to gather the tribes onto a number of large reservations scattered through the West. This would leave the rest of the land for the whites. At Fort Laramie in 1851, the Plains Indian chiefs signed treaties agreeing that their tribes would move onto these reservations. The reservation land was to belong to the Indians "forever," and the government guaranteed that no one would disturb their way of life.

The new policy did not last long. In the Colorado Territory "forever" turned out to be 10 years. News of a gold discovery brought thousands of miners into this area in 1858. In 1861 the government forced the Indians to sell most of Colorado. For the next 3 years, there was bloody fighting involving Indians, settlers, and the army. It ended only because nearly all of the Indians were killed. In other parts of the West, the pattern of events was much the same.

Decline of the Plains Indians   The warfare between the Plains Indians and the army and white settlers was not always one-sided. For a time, the Indians were able to hold their own. They were skilled horsemen and fighters. While on horseback, an Indian warrior could fire 20 to 30 arrows in the time it took a soldier or settler to reload his muzzle-loading rifle. In time, however, new weapons like the repeater rifle and the Colt six-shooter shifted the advantage to the whites.

Another thing that weakened the Plains Indians' ability to resist was the destruction of the buffalo herd. The buffalo, you will remember, was the Plains Indians' chief source of food, clothing, and shelter. In 1860 there had been 12 or 13 million buffalo on the Great Plains. During the

408

Review the parts of the buffalo with pupils.

next 10 years, workers laying railroad track across the plains killed many of these animals. Many more were killed for sport by hunters.

In 1871 it was discovered that buffalo hides could be made into valuable leather. Now the hides could be sold in the East at a good profit. That sealed the herd's fate. Over the next 3 years, 9 million buffalo were killed. By 1878 the great herd was almost wiped out, and by 1900 there were less than 50 buffalo left in the entire country!

A new policy   In the late 1860s the government announced that all Plains Indians were to be removed to two large reservations. One was in the Black Hills of South Dakota, the other in present-day Oklahoma. Here they were to give up their nomadic ways and become farmers. Worn down by war, the chiefs of the major tribes agreed to this plan in 1867 and 1868.

Many Plains Indians moved onto the two reservations, but a good many others refused. For the next 7 years, there was war. Finally, after more than 200 battles with the army, the Indians were forced onto the reservations.

For a short period there was quiet. Then in 1874, gold was discovered on the Black Hills reservation of the Sioux (sü) Indians. For a time the army pushed back the thousands of miners who kept trying to enter the reservation. In 1875 the army gave up, and miners poured in.

Angered by yet another broken promise, Indians took to arms. Many left their reservations and went to the nearby Montana Territory. When they refused the army's order to return, fighting broke out. Now and then, the Indians won a big victory. One came in June 1876, when a large force of Sioux and their Cheyenne allies, under Chiefs Crazy Horse and Sitting Bull, wiped out Colonel George Custer and his 264 men near the Little Bighorn River in Montana. But within a year Indian resistance on the northern plains was crushed. Most of Sitting Bull's people were captured, and Sitting Bull himself was forced to flee to Canada.

Pupils may want to watch the television listings for a showing of the movie *Custer's Last Stand*.

Custer's troopers fought to the last man near the Little Bighorn.   *(46°N/107°W; map, p. 17)*

Custer, a West Point graduate from Ohio, became the Union Army's youngest general at age 23. Custer thought that the Native Americans' "cruel and ferocious nature far exceeds that of any wild beast of the desert." Ask: Do you think Custer had an accurate perception of Native Americans? Why Not?

The Dawes Act   By 1887 most Plains Indians were on reservations. In that year Congress passed the **Dawes Act**, which was aimed at making Indians accept the ways of white Americans. The law permitted each head of a reservation family to own land for farming.

The plan did not work out well. For one thing, it tried to force Indians to give up their tribal ways. Most Indians did not want to do this. Also, most Indians were ill-prepared for farming. So for the almost 50 years that the Dawes Act was in effect, the standard of living of Native Americans dropped.

CHECKUP

1. What led to the long flight of the Nez Percé? Why did Chief Joseph surrender?
2. What brought about the years of warfare between Indians and the United States Army on the Great Plains?
3. What developments weakened the Plains Indians in their ability to resist?
4. What did the Dawes Act aim to do? Why did it not work out well?

The Mining Frontier

> VOCABULARY
>
> | | |
> |---|---|
> | "Pikes Peak or Bust!" | Comstock Lode |
> | Centennial State | vigilantes |

The rush to Colorado   Even as the Indians of the plains and the Rocky Mountains were being overcome, other people rushed to take over these areas. First among them were the miners. Earlier you read how the discovery of gold in 1848 brought thousands to California.

California was only the first of many gold rushes in the West. In the summer of 1858 came the report that gold had been discovered near Pikes Peak in the Colorado Territory. With the melting of the winter snows, the rush to Colorado was on. Within a year 100,000 people set out for the territory with the cry **"Pikes Peak or Bust!"**

A good many gave up and returned home before ever reaching Pikes Peak. For most who made it, a more accurate cry would have been "Pikes Peak *and* Bust!" It turned out that there was little gold and silver there, and what was found was quickly mined out. Many who had rushed to Colorado returned to their homes. Some, however, found work nearby in the new town of Denver. Still others settled down to farm or to raise cattle.

Later discoveries of silver and gold in the 1870s brought other miners to the Colorado Territory. In 1876, the population had grown large enough to enable Colorado to become a state. It was known as the **Centennial State** because it entered

The trip to Pikes Peak was long and difficult, and the hopes of most gold seekers were never realized.

the Union on the one-hundredth anniversary of the nation.

The Comstock Lode   In 1858, the same year gold was found in the Colorado Territory, two Irish immigrants named Pete O'Reilly and Pat McLaughlin made an even greater find in what is now western Nevada. Unfortunately for them, they didn't realize it. Neither did Henry Comstock, a lazy, bragging blusterer who had talked them into sharing their claim with him.

O'Reilly and McLaughlin were mining in Six Mile Canyon, on the eastern slope of the Sierra Nevadas, when they hit upon a vein of bluish ore. Two wealthy Californians who saw the ore quickly realized its value. They offered O'Reilly and McLaughlin a few thousand dollars each for their claim. The two miners were glad to sell. Comstock held out for more. When he got $11,000 from the Californians, he was sure he had made the deal of a lifetime. One can only imagine how all three felt when their discovery turned out to be the richest silver find in western mining history. It became known as the **Comstock Lode**. A lode is a vein of rich ore lying in the cracks of the rock. It would yield $300 million in silver over the next 20 years.

The discovery of silver touched off the usual rush of miners and others to the region. Thousands staked claims, but only about a dozen became rich. Most of the ore in Six Mile Canyon lay far below the surface. Machinery and expensive mining methods were needed to get it out, and that required a large investment. Thus, it was large mining companies,

Discovery of the Comstock Lode brought a rush of miners to the eastern slope of the Sierra Nevadas.

rather than small individual miners, that took most of the silver from the ground. Indeed, a great many who come to mine on their own wound up working for the mining companies.

The Comstock strike, and others that followed, brought enough people to Nevada for it to become a state in 1864, the year of President Lincoln's reelection.

The life and death of a mining town News of a big strike could turn a mining camp into a good-sized town in days. Hundreds of people would rush in to stake their claims. Then, small-business owners would arrive to sell food, tents, tools, clothing, and other goods to the miners. One such person was in San Francisco. A 20-year-old immigrant from Germany named Levi Strauss sold pants made out

ver is harder than gold and softer than copper. Wire that is finer than a strand of human hair can be made from silver. It is nished by air that contains sulfur. The United States today supplies about three fifths of the world's silver. Idaho, Arizona, vada, Colorado, Montana, and Utah are leading silver-mining states.

of a tough cotton fabric called denim. Today *Levi's* is a household name for these pants.

Women as well as men arrived. In one mining town a woman from Boston cleared a profit of $11,000 in 1 year by baking and selling pies. Other women ran boardinghouses and small hotels.

Soon a string of wooden stores lined the town's main street. Among them were many gambling houses and saloons. But some of those buildings might also house banks, hotels, newspaper offices, and even theaters.

Mining towns, which sprang up hundreds of miles from settled communities, had no organized law or law officials at first. To deal with the numerous outlaws and thieves, the people of the towns usually made their own laws and formed committees to enforce those laws. The committee members, known as **vigilantes** (vij ə lan' tēz), would hunt down the worst offenders. Those who were declared guilty of crimes were likely to be hanged. "Frontier justice" was harsh but effective.

The richest and most showy mining town in the West was Virginia City, near the Comstock Lode. Mark Twain, the famous American writer, was at that time a reporter for a newspaper in Virginia City. His description of this bustling city gives us something of its flavor during the boom period:

> The sidewalks swarmed with people. . . . The streets themselves were just as crowded with . . . wagons, freight teams, and other vehicles. . . . Joy sat on every countenance, and there was glad, almost fierce, intensity in every eye, that told of money-getting schemes. . . . Money was as plenty as dust. . . . There were . . . fire companies, brass bands, banks, hotels, theaters, . . . wide open gambling palaces, . . . street fights, murders, . . . riots, a whiskey mill every fifteen steps, . . . a dozen breweries, and half a dozen jails and station houses in full operation. . . .

Most mining towns blazed brightly for a brief time, and then, like a comet in the sky, were gone. After the gold or silver was mined out, most miners pulled up stakes and moved on. Even Virginia City, the richest mining town of them all, was eventually left to gather dust as the Comstock Lode played out.

The mining frontier moves In the 1860s a number of smaller strikes were made in the mountains of the West. The last great gold rush was in the Black Hills of South Dakota. This rush gave birth to

In 1861 there was no livelier community in the country than Virginia City, Nevada. (39°N/120°W; map, p. 414)

Calamity Jane and Wild Bill Hickok lived in Deadwood during its heyday. Some pupils might want to do research on Deadwood and report to the class.

Cowboys prepare for a roundup of horses that have spent the winter on the open range.

Deadwood, the last and maybe the most colorful of all the mining towns.

By the 1880s the day of the gold rush and the prospectors had passed. Few became rich. But in their search for instant wealth, they helped to settle the West. Each new gold rush brought men and women who ran the stores, farmed the land, and started schools, churches, and newspapers. When the mining frontier passed on, many of these people stayed to raise families and build up the country.

CHECKUP

1. With what event is the phrase "Pikes Peak or Bust!" connected?
2. What was the Comstock Lode?
3. How did the discovery of gold or silver affect life in the place of the discovery?
4. What lasting results did a gold or silver rush have on a region?

Ask: If gold was discovered in a remote area of North America today and people were allowed to stake claims, would you go? Why?

The Cattle Kingdom

┌─ **VOCABULARY** ─────────────────┐
| long drive | cowboy |
| cow town | open range |
└──────────────────────────────────┘

A vast grazing ground   If thousands were drawn to the mountain regions of the West by gold, other thousands were drawn to the Great Plains by its grasslands! For hundreds of years the grass of these plains provided food for millions of buffalo. With the buffalo fast disappearing, men realized that cattle could be grazed on this same grass and then sold for good prices.

Thus the cattle kingdom came into being. Its greatest years were between the middle 1860s and the mid-1880s. At its height the cattle kingdom stretched from Texas north to the Canadian border and from Kansas west to the Rockies.

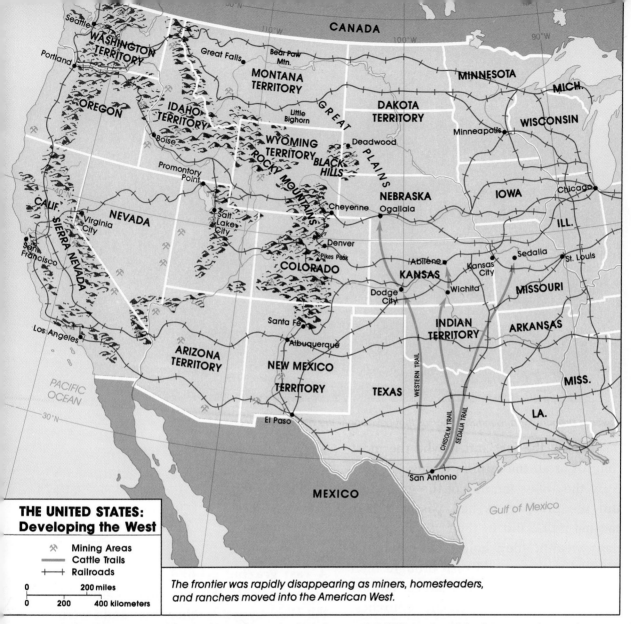

THE UNITED STATES:
Developing the West

⚒ Mining Areas
━━ Cattle Trails
╁━━╁ Railroads

0   200 miles
0   200   400 kilometers

The frontier was rapidly disappearing as miners, homesteaders, and ranchers moved into the American West.

Ask: What are some of the products that people obtain from cattle? (Milk, beef, veal, leather, soap, glue, and some medicines)

The growth of cattle ranches   Cattle were introduced into the Western Hemisphere by the Spanish early in the sixteenth century. Over the next 300 years, they multiplied and roamed freely in northern Mexico and Texas. <u>By the middle of the nineteenth century, there were some 5 million head of cattle in Texas alone.</u> These longhorns, as they were called, belonged to no one. They were for the taking. A few bold men did just that, starting large ranches.

<u>The rich market for beef, however, was not in lightly settled Texas but in the cities of the East.</u> Cattle that brought $3 or $4 each in Texas could be sold for $40 or more in the East. Every Texas rancher knew that; the problem was how to get the cattle there.

Railroads presented the best way. A railroad line had been completed as far west as Sedalia, Missouri, before the Civil War. That was still about a thousand miles (1,609 km) from the Texas ranches.

The longhorn lost its popularity to the Hereford and Aberdeen Angus breeds because those breeds of cattle grew faster and were more profitable. The longhorn is used in crossbreeding today.

Cowboys on a New Mexico range drink coffee and swap stories beside the chuck wagon.

But if the cattle could be herded to Sedalia, they could be shipped east quickly and cheaply by rail.

The long drive   In 1866, the year after the Civil War ended, several Texas ranchers organized the first **long drive.** The plan was to bring the herds together in the autumn and drive them northward to Sedalia, grazing them along the way.

Unfortunately, the ranchers chose a poor route. Much of the trail led through wooded areas where the cattle were hard to control. Parts of the route ran into fenced-in farms and crossed through Indian territory. To add to everything else, heavy rains turned the trails to mud.

Most of the 260,000 cattle that started the trip died or were lost or stolen. Still, for the cattle that reached Sedalia, ranchers got $35 a head. It was clear that the idea of the long drive was a good one. What was needed was a better route.

The next year a new route was chosen farther to the west. It ran from Texas across open, unsettled plains to a new rail line running into Abilene, in western Kansas. In 1867, some 75,000 cattle were driven north to Abilene and shipped to Chicago and other cities at a large profit. The long drive was a success, and Abilene became the first great **cow town.** As railroads pushed westward, other cow towns also grew up in Kansas—Wichita, Ellsworth Falls, and Dodge City. During the years of the cattle kingdom, about 6 million cattle were driven to these towns from Texas.

The western cowboy   Out of the cattle kingdom came America's most romantic figure, the **cowboy.** Celebrated in story and song, the western cowboy captured the imaginations not only of the people in America but also of the world. He remains a favorite subject for movies and television.

Most cowboys were young men, many of them in their teens. A good number had fought in the Civil War. Perhaps one in every three or four was Mexican. Quite a few others were blacks who had left the South in search of a new life after the Civil War.

Louis L'Amour and Zane Grey are celebrated authors of many books about the life of the cowboy. For extra credit interested pupils might enjoy reading novels by these authors and sharing the stories with the class. Another choice might be *The Log of a Cowboy*, written by an actual cowboy, Andy Adams.

Image Makers of the West

Few easterners ever saw the West. Their ideas about that region were formed in two ways. Many easterners had read western "dime novels"—paperbacked adventure stories sold on newsstands for 10 cents—and had seen shows based on western frontier life.

The first dime novel about the West came out in the 1860s. Over the next 30 years, publishers produced more than 2,200 of these stories, each one highly exaggerated. Taking on a half-dozen gunmen at a time was all in a day's work for characters like Arizona Joe, Denver Dan, and Lariat Lil.

Before long a few westerners saw the possibilities for making money by doing shows for eastern audiences. The first and most famous of these showmen was William F. "Buffalo Bill" Cody. Cody had worked as a rider for the pony express, a scout, a cowhand, and a buffalo hunter. After touring small cities and towns for several years with a small show about adventure in the West, Cody created the first great outdoor western show in 1883. Buffalo Bill's Wild West show featured riding and shooting contests, a stagecoach robbery, lots of gunfighting, and plenty of whooping Indians. After playing to huge crowds in the United States for several years, Cody took his show to England, where it was also a big hit.

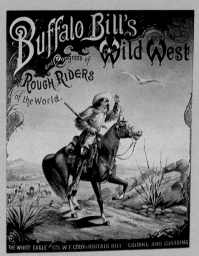

Posters like the one above advertised the coming of Buffalo Bill's Wild West show to dozens of towns and cities. The show was a great success wherever it appeared.

It was showmen like Buffalo Bill Cody, together with writers of dime novels, who fixed the image of the cowboy's glamorous life in the minds of many people.

If you live in an area where there are rodeos, you may want to arrange a class trip to a show.

The cowboy on our television screens lives a life of high adventure, but a cowboy's life was actually a far cry from that. For the most part it was filled with dull routine. For perhaps 8 or 9 months of the year, the cowboy's main job was to ride back and forth along the boundary of his employer's ranch, keeping the cattle from wandering off or being stolen. Twice a year he joined in a cattle roundup. The spring roundup was for branding newborn calves with the owner's special mark. In the fall roundup, cowboys sorted out the cattle by brand and separated those that were ready for market from the rest of the herd.

On the trail   Then began the long drive, in which several ranchers might combine their herds. The leader of the drive was the trail boss. For every thousand cattle on the drive, the trail boss took along six cowhands. Two rode at the front of the herd, two in the rear, and one on each side to keep the cattle from wandering off.

Ask: What aspects of a cowboy's life would you like? What aspects would you dislike?

Each cowboy might need eight or ten horses, so an extra hand was brought along to take care of them. And, of course, each group needed a cook with a chuck-wagon.

Once on the trail, cowboys spent up to 18 hours a day in the saddle, day after day, in all kinds of weather. With the herd covering only 15 miles (24 km) a day, the drive lasted 2 to 3 months.

The cowboy's greatest worry was a stampede. Lightning, thunder, or any other noise that frightened the cattle could set them off. It was then that the cowboy called on all his skills. Failure to head off a stampede could mean loss of the herd. It could even mean serious injury or death to himself or his comrades. For this mostly dull and sometimes dangerous work, the cowboy received about $30 a month—a dollar a day!

Yet, hard as it was, there was something that attracted men to this work. Perhaps the cowboy who set down his recollections of a lifetime explained best what it was:

> All in all, my years on the trail were the happiest I ever I lived. There were many hardships and dangers but . . . most of the time we were solitary adventurers in a great land as fresh and new as a spring morning. . . .

The open range　As ranchers learned that their animals could survive the winters on the northern plains, the cattle kingdom moved north. The United States government, which owned the range land, charged no rent. Thus, cattle ranchers grazed their herds absolutely free. Little wonder, then, that by 1880, 4.5 million head of cattle grazed on the **open range.**

Nat Love, nicknamed Deadwood Dick, was a cowboy famous for his riding, roping, and shooting skills.

For a time, cattle ranchers shared the open range, with each honoring the others' claims. After a while, some of the larger operators began to expand their claims to grazing lands and to mark off scarce watering places as their own. This led to many small-scale wars among the ranchers.

Challenges to the free use of the public grasslands came from others as well. By the 1880s, cattle ranchers no longer had

417

the open range to themselves. Sheep-herders and farmers moved in. Before long the cattle owners were battling with these newcomers over use of the land.

Even so, the 1870s and early 1880s were a time of great prosperity for the cattle kingdom. By this time, ranchers had bred the Texas longhorn with eastern stock to produce a better quality of beef. Eastern and European markets paid high prices for these cattle.

Bad times But this prosperity did not last. Soon there were more cattle than the market demanded. So prices fell sharply. The winter of 1885–1886 was the bitterest in memory. Many cattle died. Then came a hot, dry summer, which killed much of the grass. The winter of 1886–1887, even worse than the previous one finished off nearly 90 percent of the cattle. Ranchers were ruined.

This disaster marked the end of open-range ranching. Thereafter, those who raised cattle followed more settled ways. They acquired land of their own and raised smaller herds. The cowboy, master of the open range, became a ranch hand, fixing fences, harvesting hay for winter feed, and doing other chores. By the end of the 1880s, the cowboy had passed into folklore, and the day of the cattle kingdom was over.

CHECKUP

1. What problem had to be overcome before cattle ranching could be profitable?
2. What was the long drive?
3. Where were cow towns founded? Why?
4. What was the life of the cowboy like?
5. Why did the prosperous days of the cattle king-dom end?

The Farmers' Frontier

┌─VOCABULARY─────────────────────┐
  dry farming   sod house
└────────────────────────────────┘

The farmers arrive Even as cattle ranchers were conducting their first long drives in the 1860s, some farmers were beginning to move onto the Great Plains. This trickle became a flood in the 1870s.

For years, farmers had avoided the area that Stephen Long had called the Great American Desert. Why did they now rush there to settle? There were three reasons. First, there was a change in the weather pattern. For 8 years in a row, rainfall on the plains had been above average. Second, private land companies and rail-roads, which owned a great deal of land in the West, advertised heavily to attract settlers.

The third reason was that the Home-stead Act of 1862 encouraged settlement. In Chapter 16 you read that many veterans of the Union and Confederate armies moved west and acquired land under the terms of the act. Thousands of other Americans got free land, too. A good number of settlers from Germany, Nor-way, and Sweden also moved onto the plains at this time.

Problems the homesteaders faced Farmers who settled on the Great Plains found a climate and land different from anything they had known in the East or Europe. Summer temperatures reached 110°F (43°C). There was no wood for buildings, fencing, and fuel. The tough sod of plains grass would not yield to the old-style eastern plow.

Alert pupils to the fact that they will be reading about the building of the transcontinental railroad in Chapter 19, on pages 429–430. Ask: Why, do you think, did the railroads encourage farmers to settle on the Great Plains?

Lack of water was the biggest problem. One way to get water was to sink a well 200 to 300 feet (60 m to 90 m) deep and build a windmill to pump the water to the surface. But at a drilling cost of $2 per foot, plus the cost of building the windmill, few early settlers could afford to have a well.

Instead, settlers had to learn new ways of farming. They adopted a method known as **dry farming**. This involved turning the soil over immediately after a rain. This moved the wet surface soil nearer to the roots while it slowed down evaporation. Farmers also learned to space plants farther apart so that the roots would not compete for the scarce water. Consequently, farmers found that to raise crops successfully on the dry plains, they needed more than the 160 acres (65 ha) that the Homestead Act gave them. The shortage of water also led farmers to experiment with new strains of wheat that were more resistant to drought.

Barbed wire and new machines Other problems were solved by inventions. Farmers had to fence in their land to keep range cattle and sheep from trampling their crops, but wood was scarce and expensive on the plains. To fence a 160-acre farm with wood from the East might cost as much as $1,000. In 1873 an Illinois farmer named Joseph Glidden invented barbed wire, and within a few years its cost was low enough for nearly all farmers to use it.

An invention by James Oliver in 1877 helped farmers with their first and hardest task, plowing up the tough prairie sod. This was the chilled-iron plow, made of

This Union Pacific poster announces the opening of the nation's first transcontinental rail line.

an extra-strong kind of iron. Mechanical seed drills replaced the back-breaking work of planting seeds in rows. By the

1880s a single worker using a new machine called a combine could cut the wheat, rake it up, tie it in a bundle, separate the grains from the stalks, and bag the grain—150 pounds (68 kg) of it in 20 seconds!

By the end of the nineteenth century, the Great Plains, once thought of as a desert, was the country's chief producer of grain. Four of America's five leading wheat-growing states in 1900 were wholly or in part on the plains.

Life on the Great Plains   If farming on the Great Plains was difficult, living there was even more so. For most families the first house was made from blocks of sod. After rain or melting snow softened the hard soil, settlers cut the sod into blocks. Piled one upon another, the blocks of sod could make a surprisingly tight building. With their thick walls, **sod houses** were warm in winter and cool in summer. They were very small, however. They were also dirty, and in rainy weather, walls and ceilings leaked.

Newcomers to the plains found it difficult to adjust to the weather. Summer heat could be nearly unbearable at times. Winter snows and bitter cold could keep people cooped up in their one-room houses for days at a time.

Probably the hardest thing about life on the Great Plains was the loneliness. Farms were far apart. For many years there were not even small villages nearby to break up the isolation.

Such conditions might have been easier to bear if settlers could have been sure that their farms would be successful. Of course, there were no guarantees. A few dry years could bring the end of a dream to a farm family. A field of golden grain one day could be gone the next, eaten by a swarm of grasshoppers. These insects appeared on the plains every few years

A homesteader with a team of yoked oxen turns over the thick sod of the plains.

in such numbers as to darken the sky. One settler, reporting on the grasshopper plague that swept over a large part of the plains in 1873, wrote:

> So thick were the grasshoppers in the cornfield of which both of us had been so proud, that not a spot of green could be seen. And within two hours of the time that they had come, not a leaf was left in all that field.

The Oklahoma land rush   With all these difficulties, it may seem a wonder that anyone at all came to live and farm on the Great Plains. But come they did, and in ever-increasing numbers.

One part of the Great Plains, in fact, was the scene of the most spectacular land rush in the country's history. This was Oklahoma. This land, long known as the Indian Territory, had been set aside for Indian reservations. But settlers who pushed west eyed the land for themselves. The tribes were forced to sell most of it to the United States government. Two million acres (810,000 ha) of it were then divided into homesteads of 160 acres (65 ha), to be given away beginning at noon on April 22, 1889—first come, first served.

By the morning of April 22, about 100,000 would-be homesteaders lined up at the Oklahoma border. With the crack of the starter's gun at noon, the settlers bolted into Oklahoma like locusts descending on a field of wheat. In just hours, nearly all 2 million acres were claimed. New towns sprang up even faster than they had on the mining frontier. At noon on April 22, the town of Guthrie didn't exist. Before the sun had set, Guthrie had a population of 15,000.

Land seekers used every available form of transportation to rush into Oklahoma on April 22, 1889.

Oklahoma City went from zero population to 10,000 in the same few hours.

Thus, in the last part of the nineteenth century, the promise of land continued to be a powerful lure to the West, just as it had been all through American history. So rapidly was the West settled that in 1890 the Census Bureau announced that there no longer was a clearly defined frontier, the imaginary line that marked off the limit of western settlement. There was still plenty of unsettled land to the east of that line, but by 1890 the last frontier had passed. Americans would find their new frontiers elsewhere.

CHECKUP

1. Why did large numbers of farmers move onto the Great Plains in the 1870s?
2. What problems did newcomers to the Great Plains encounter?
3. How did they deal with these problems?
4. How was the settlement of Oklahoma different from that of other states?

KEY FACTS

1. Although the United States government promised the Indians that the land would be forever theirs, ranchers and miners eventually took over much of it.

2. The United States Army protected white settlers in the West with open warfare on Indian tribes.

3. Discovery of silver and gold in the West led to the growth of towns, cities, and states.

4. The long drive and the railroad made it possible to bring western cattle to the eastern United States for sale.

5. Farmers who settled on the Great Plains had to learn different methods of farming to grow crops in this dry region.

VOCABULARY QUIZ

Write **T** if the statement is true and **F** if it is false. If the statement is false, change the underlined term to make the statement true.

F **1.** Public land set aside for cattle ranchers to use was called a reservation. **Indians**

F **2.** The first shelter for most white settlers on the Great Plains was a tepee. **sod house**

T **3.** Most Plains Indians were nomadic.

F **4.** "Pikes Peak or Bust!" was a slogan of miners bound for Nevada. **Colorado**

T **5.** The Comstock Lode was the richest silver find in western mining history.

F **6.** Because it became a state in 1876, Oklahoma is called the Centennial State. **Colorado**

T **7.** Groups who enforced the law in early mining towns were known as vigilantes.

F **8.** Abilene, Kansas, was the first great mining camp. **cow town**

F **9.** A law aimed at making Indians accept the ways of white Americans was the Homestead Act. **Dawes Act**

T **10.** Cowboys on the long drive drove cattle north from Texas to railroad lines in Kansas and Missouri.

REVIEW QUESTIONS

1. How did the discovery of gold and silver affect the Indians in the West?

2. How were the Plains Indians forced to change their way of life after 1887?

3. What is the source for each phrase?

"I will fight no more forever."
"Pikes Peak or Bust!"
"The Great American Desert"

4. What factors led to the downfall of the cattle kingdom?

5. What effect did cattle ranching have on farmers?

6. Describe some of the hardships of the farming family on the Great Plains.

ACTIVITIES

1. You own cattle and want to hire cowboys. Write an advertisement describing the job. Include hours of work, duties, and pay.

2. For a time, Chief Joseph agreed that the Nez Percé should move to the reservation. Some of his followers agreed with this view; others opposed it. Take either point of view and write an argument to convince the others.

3. Describe the conflict between the Native Americans and the army from the point of view of:

(a) An easterner who has moved west to start a farm.

(b) A 13- or 14-year old Indian who has lived on the plains all his or her life.

(c) An army private who is assigned to protect white settlers.

SKIMMING

RAPID READING

People use different rates of reading for different purposes. You read a telephone book at a rate different from that which you use when reading a textbook. You read an adventure story at a different rate than either. You read the directions for assembling a bicycle at still another rate.

The rate you use with the telephone book is called *skimming*. When you skim, you are not concerned with reading all the information on the page but only with finding specific information quickly. Thus, you skim a dictionary or an index to find a certain word. You skim a newspaper to find out whether your favorite team won or lost.

Skimming is useful in studying, too. Suppose you needed to find some very specific information (such as a name, a location, or a date) on a page in this book. You could read the whole page carefully, but skimming is much more efficient. Skimming is also useful for previewing material. Before you start to read a chapter thoroughly, go through its pages quickly. Look for headings, pictures, graphs, maps, and charts. These will give you a general idea of what the chapter covers. This is important because the more you know about what is coming up, the more you will understand about it. In other words, previewing prepares you to get more from the slower, more careful reading that you will be required to do later.

SKILLS PRACTICE

Number a sheet of paper from 1 to 6. Skim the index of your textbook to locate these words and write down the page numbers.

1. Appalachian Mountains
2. Continental army
3. Cowboys
4. Incas
5. Iron Curtain
6. Sam Houston

Skim the passage below to find the following information:

a. the names of two Indian tribes
b. the territory where fighting occurred
c. the name of the army colonel who led the attack
d. the year of the attack

In 1861, the government forced the Arapaho and Cheyenne tribes to sell most of the Colorado Territory. The tribes were moved onto poor land in the southeastern corner of the territory. Some members of the tribes resisted. They lashed out and attacked the settlers. That brought in the army. For the next 3 years, there was fighting. The grim climax came in 1864, when Colonel Chivington led an attack upon an Indian camp. Colonel Chivington ignored Chief Black Kettle's attempt to surrender. In a few hours, nearly all the 500 men, women, and children in the camp were killed.

CHAPTER
19 The Rise of Industry

Carnegie and Steel

┌─ VOCABULARY ─────────────────┐
│ steelmaking   Bessemer furnace │
└──────────────────────────────┘

The Carnegies come to America   Even before the machines came to the town of Dunfermline, Scotland, making a living had not been easy for William Carnegie. After they arrived, it was impossible. Carnegie was a skilled worker, a hand-loom weaver of linen cloth. Just about the time his first child, Andrew, was born in 1835, the first power loom in Dunfermline was put into operation. Others followed, putting hundreds of handweavers like William Carnegie out of work.

In 1848, William and Margaret Carnegie and their two sons, Andy and Tom, left Scotland to seek new opportunities in America. Arriving in New York, they continued on to the area of Pittsburgh, Pennsylvania, where their relatives were already living.

It was necessary for both parents and 13-year old Andy to find work immediately. Andy's first job was as a bobbin boy in a textile mill. When the bobbins, or spools, on the spinning machines were full of cotton thread, Andy replaced them with empty ones. The job required no skill, and it paid accordingly: $1.20 a week. That came to 20 cents a day, 6 days a week, working from sunrise to sunset.

An ambitious young man   After a short while at this job and others like it, Andy became a messenger in a Pittsburgh telegraph office. When he was not delivering telegrams, he watched the telegraph operators at work. Soon, Andy mastered that skill, and at the age of 16 he was hired as an operator at $4 a week. In a short time he became one of the best in the country. In the evenings Andy went to school to learn bookkeeping, and on his own he read the important English, Scottish, and American writers of the day.

In 1853, Andrew Carnegie caught the eye of Thomas A. Scott, a leading official of the Pennsylvania Railroad Company. Scott hired the young man as his personal telegrapher and secretary. His starting pay was to be $35 a week. "I couldn't imagine what I could ever do with so much money," Carnegie later recalled.

For the next 12 years, Andrew Carnegie worked for Scott and the Pennsylvania Railroad Company. During these years he learned all he could about the ways of the business world. As his responsibilities increased, his income did, too. He invested it wisely, usually with Scott's advice. By the time he was 33 years old, Andrew Carnegie had an income of $50,000 a year. He could easily have retired from work, had he wished. But that did not fit in with the ambitious

The rise of industry in America was closely linked to new uses for iron and steel.

424   Ask: What were the new uses for iron and steel in America? (Iron rails, locomotives, iron bridges, steel beams for buildings)

Weir, FORGING THE SHAFT, Metropolitan Museum of Art

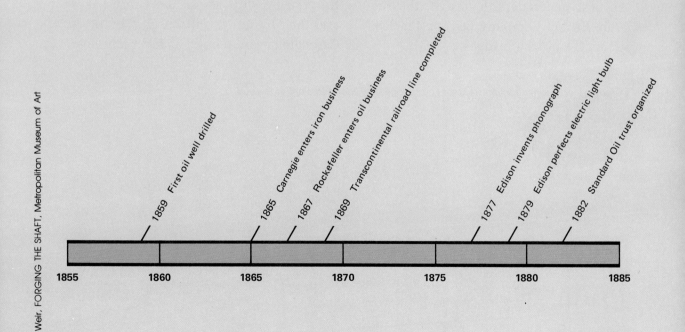

1859 First oil well drilled

1865 Carnegie enters iron business

1867 Rockefeller enters oil business

1869 Transcontinental railroad line completed

1877 Edison invents phonograph

1879 Edison perfects electric light bulb

1882 Standard Oil trust organized

1855   1860   1865   1870   1875   1880   1885

Carnegie was very pleased with the bridges made by his company; other "bridges had given way under wind pressure," but Keystone bridges were strong and sturdy. Carnegie commented, "There has been no luck about it. We used only the best material and enough of it…. We were our own severest inspectors, and would build a safe structure or none at all."

young man's plans. America was just entering a period of great economic expansion, and Carnegie was determined to have a part in it.

The iron business   Carnegie saw his opportunity in the iron business. Pittsburgh, located close to the coalfields of Pennsylvania, was the center of America's small iron industry. The demand for weapons and other war goods during the Civil War and for rails for the railroads had given the industry a big boost. In 1865, Carnegie left the Pennsylvania Railroad and soon after entered the iron business. He invested in one company that made iron rails and in another that made locomotives. But his shrewdest move was to buy the Keystone Bridge Company, a maker of iron bridges.

"I saw," said Carnegie later, "[that with railroads growing] it would never do to depend further upon wooden bridges for permanent railway structures." Using the best materials and design, the Keystone Bridge Company became the leading maker of iron bridges.

Moving into steelmaking   Carnegie soon decided to shift from iron to **steelmaking** and devoted all his efforts to it. The advantages of steel over iron had long been known. Steel is stronger, easier to work with, and less likely to break. But until the middle of the nineteenth century, making steel was slow and expensive. It took several weeks just to turn 50 pounds (23 kg) of iron into steel. Then an American named William Kelly and an Englishman named Henry Bessemer, working independently, discovered how to make steel quickly and cheaply. By the 1870s, **Bessemer furnaces** in English steel mills turned 30,000 pounds (13,620 kg) of pig iron into steel in a matter of minutes.

A visit to a Bessemer furnace in England convinced Carnegie that the future of industrial growth lay with steel. By this time, railroads had reached into upper Michigan and Minnesota, where large deposits of rich iron ore had been found in the 1840s. It was now possible to bring this ore by ship across the Great Lakes and then by rail to Pittsburgh. In 1873, Carnegie began to build a steel plant near

Carnegie's company supplied steel for Eads Bridge over the Mississippi at St. Louis.

Pittsburgh. Two years later the J. Edgar Thompson Works, the largest and best steel plant in America, opened. Carnegie named the plant for the president of the Pennsylvania Railroad, figuring that this bit of flattery would win the railroad's business. He was right.

The Thompson steel plant opened in 1875. That was a depression year in America. Nonetheless, Carnegie's company prospered. An excellent salesman, Carnegie convinced many railroad companies of the advantages of steel rails over iron. Among other things, steel rails lasted 20 times longer than iron rails. Orders poured in.

Carnegie was hardly alone in the steel business in the United States. In fact, in 1880 there were more than 1,000 companies, large and small, that made iron or steel. Many, however, were unable to compete and fell by the wayside. Carnegie bought up a number of others. By the 1890s, Carnegie's steel companies made nearly as much steel as all the remaining companies put together.

Why Carnegie prospered How was Carnegie able to achieve this record?

(1) *Efficiency* Carnegie was always ready to use the newest and most efficient methods to make steel. This helped him to keep costs down. He lowered costs still more by buying and running his own iron and coal mines. He also bought the railroads and ships to carry these materials to his mills.

(2) *Reinvesting profits* Carnegie put most of his profits back into the business. That is how he could buy the newest machinery and acquire his own iron-ore mines.

From an immigrant bobbin boy, Andrew Carnegie progressed to become the nation's foremost steelmaker.

(3) *Skilled management* Carnegie was an excellent judge of talent. He chose the ablest men he could find to run his companies. He once joked that his tombstone should read, "Here lies the man who was able to surround himself with men far cleverer than himself."

(4) *Foresight and imagination* Carnegie was able to see changes coming and adjust to them. For example, the 1880s were boom years for railroad building. In that decade some 70,000 miles (112,630 km) of track were laid. Carnegie's company made most of these rails and profited greatly. But Carnegie also realized that the railroad boom would end. And he saw that there would soon be a great demand for steel in the construction of

427

Carnegie's mills made most of the rails that construction crews laid across the plains.

the nation's growing cities. So in 1887, even as orders for rails kept coming in, Carnegie shifted much of his production from steel rails to steel beams for buildings. As a result, when the demand for this steel became strong, he was far ahead of his rivals.

Steel leads the way   Led by Carnegie, the steel industry in the United States grew rapidly. In 1867, when Carnegie was just beginning in the iron business, fewer than 20,000 tons (18,140 t) of steel were produced in the United States. In 1875, the year his new steel plant opened, the United States production still trailed far behind England. Twenty-five years later, United States steelmakers turned out more than 10,000,000 tons (9,070,000 t) of steel, more than any other country in the world. And Andrew Carnegie's mills made more steel than any other company in the world.

In 1901, Carnegie decided to sell his steel business to a new corporation formed by the great American banker J. P. Morgan. The new firm was the United States Steel Corporation. For his companies, Carnegie received nearly a half-billion dollars. He spent the rest of his life giving away most of his fortune to a variety of worthy causes.

Andrew Carnegie's achievements in the steel industry were an important factor in America's industrial growth. The two advanced side by side. Just as Carnegie rose to become the world's greatest steelmaker during the last 30 years of the nineteenth century, so the United States rose to become the world's greatest producer of manufactured goods.

CHECKUP

1. Why did the Carnegie family leave Scotland?
2. How did Andrew Carnegie prepare himself in order to get ahead of others?
3. Why did Carnegie shift from making iron to making steel?
4. What were four factors that led to success for Carnegie in the steel industry?

Education, public libraries, and world peace were the focal points of Carnegie's philanthropic activities. The Carnegie Corporation of New York is a foundation that supports the "advancement and diffusion of knowledge and understanding." The Carnegie Endowment for International Peace supports programs on international relations and arms control.

Refer pupils to the map on page 414. Have them locate the first transcontinental rail line, which ran from Omaha, Nebraska, approximately along the 42°N parallel to San Francisco. Then have them look at a physical map of the United States to note the geographical obstacles faced by the workers.

Railroads

VOCABULARY
subsidy

Railroads expand   One of the main factors in America's changing face was the railroad. In Chapter 12 you read about the first railroads in the United States. By the start of the Civil War, there were 30,000 miles (48,270 km) of railroad track in the country. In the last 40 years of the century, American railroads expanded greatly. By 1900 there was more than six times as much track—193,000 miles (310,000 km). Before the Civil War most of the tracks were in the Northeast. By 1900, railroads reached into every corner of the country.

To encourage railroad building, especially in areas where few people lived, the federal and state governments helped the railroad companies with loans and with gifts of land or money called **subsidies.** Railroad companies received more than 180 million acres (72.9 million ha) of land from state governments and the federal government.

Not all railroad companies received government help, however. In fact, most of the railroads built in the United States were built without any government aid.

The transcontinental railroad   The most spectacular railroad building took place in the West. In 1862, Congress passed a law designed to fulfill the dream of linking the Atlantic and Pacific coasts by rail. At that time, railroads reached only a third of the way across the continent. Under this act of Congress, a new company called the Union Pacific was to start building westward from Omaha, Nebraska. This railroad would link up with one being built eastward from Sacramento, California, by a second company, the Central Pacific. Altogether the new line would run for nearly 1,800 miles (2,896 km), almost entirely through unsettled territory. For each mile of track that was laid, a company would receive a gift of 10 square miles (26 sq km) of land,

The expanding Erie Railroad pictured some of its trains in this advertisement.

plus a large loan of money. With such handsome encouragement, each company raced to lay all the track it could.

The transcontinental railroad was the grandest construction project of the age. At one time more than 20,000 workers were employed, most of them Chinese, Mexican, and Irish immigrants. The difficulties they faced were enormous. To build around and sometimes through the mountains, Chinese workers on the Central Pacific had only pickaxes and shovels. Crews laying track across the plains even had to face Indian attacks. Under blazing summer sun and in the below-zero cold and snows of winter, work went on.

After 7 years the two lines met at a tiny place called Promontory Point, Utah. On May 10, 1869, a ceremony was held to mark the historic occasion. Leland Stanford, Jr., president of the Central Pacific,

drove a golden spike into the final railroad tie, and the telegraph flashed the news to a cheering nation: "One, two, three—done!" (Actually, the message should have been, "One, two, three, four—done!" On his first swing Stanford missed everything, bringing howls of laughter from the watching work crews.)

In the next 15 years, three more transcontinental rail lines were built, all with subsidies from the federal government. A fifth, built without federal subsidies, was completed 10 years after that.

Railroads help settle the West   Transcontinental railroads contributed to the rapid settlement of the West. Railroad companies wanted people to move west and use their rail lines for shipping crops and for travel. Also, as the population in the West increased, railroad land-

Pupils can find Promontory Point, Utah, on the map on page 414.

The first transcontinental railroad was completed when rail lines from east and west came together at Promontory Point, Utah.   (42°N/113°W; map, p. 17)

holdings would become more valuable. Therefore, <u>railroad companies promoted western settlement</u>, by advertising in the eastern United States and in Europe as well. Many thousands of those who settled in the West were influenced to do so by the railroads.

Railroads led to rapid settlement in other ways as well. Without railroads it would have been impossible to have large-scale farming in the West, for there would have been no way to ship crops to market. Also, railroads made moving west faster and safer than ever before.

In winter, railroad locomotives were sometimes brought to a halt by deep drifts of snow.

Railroads help the economy grow
Railroads contributed to the growth of an industrial economy in many ways. <u>The railroad industry was the largest employer in the United States.</u> In 1900 more than 1 million people worked for railroads. Railroads also created a demand for other goods. In 1880, for example, three fourths of all the steel made in the United States was used to make steel rails. Thus the steel industry was given a great boost by the railroads. Most important, railroads carried raw materials and finished goods cheaply from one part of the country to another. Railroads also helped some businesses grow to be very large. Here is an example of how this happened.

Suppose A and B are manufacturers of stoves. Their cities are 100 miles (160 km) apart. Company A sells its stoves for $60 each, including a small profit. Company B, which is more efficient, can sell a stove of the same quality for $40.

When transportation was by horse-drawn wagon, we'll say that shipping one stove cost $1 a mile. You can see that each company will sell its stoves in its own city. Even though B's stoves are cheaper, they can't compete with A's stoves in A's city, for it will cost $100 to get them there.

But see what happens when the railroad arrives and lowers the cost of shipping. One stove can now be shipped, let us say, at 10 cents a mile. Now Company B can sell stoves in A's city more cheaply than A can ($40 for the stove plus $10 for shipping). Company A will now be forced out of business.

Since Company B is selling more stoves, it can afford newer and better machinery. That will lower its costs. It will also be buying larger amounts of raw materials and therefore can buy them at a lower price. Down comes the price still more, perhaps to $30 a stove. Company B might also be able to get lower rates from the railroads because it is such a big customer. Now B can compete in cities still farther away. As it takes over the markets of other stove makers, Company B will grow still larger.

CHECKUP

1. What help did railroad companies receive from governments when they built their lines?
2. What problems confronted the workers who built the first transcontinental railroad?
3. Give two ways in which railroads contributed to the settlement of the West.
4. Give three ways in which railroads helped bring about the growth of an industrial economy.

Other Factors for Industrial Growth

> VOCABULARY
>
> capital   corporation

A strong foundation The steel industry and the railroads were two factors that led to America's industrial growth in the late nineteenth century. But there were a number of other factors. One was that a foundation had already been laid before the Civil War. You read earlier how a factory system was established and spread through the Northeast. By the time of the Civil War, textiles, shoes, and many other goods were being made in factories. You also learned how the construction of canals, steamboats, and finally railroads created a transportation system that could move these goods swiftly and cheaply.

The Civil War gave a boost to manufacturing. Not only was iron needed for weapons, but with more than 2 million men under arms, there was a great demand for uniforms, boots, and other supplies.

Thus at the end of the war, the United States was ready to embark on its great industrial expansion.

Resources and population Another factor leading to industrial growth in the United States was its wealth of natural resources. In Pennsylvania, West Virginia, Ohio, Kentucky, and Illinois were large deposits of coal, the main source of fuel in industrial countries of the time. Later, other large coal deposits would be found in the western states. Between 1865 and 1900, coal production rose from 3 million tons (2.7 million t) to nearly 200 million tons (180 million t).

You have already read about the great discoveries of iron ore in Michigan and Minnesota. In the West, the mining frontier produced not only gold and silver but also such important metals as copper, lead, and zinc. As a result, in just 15 years America's output of lead ore increased threefold, and the output of copper ore increased eightfold. Oil, which was used for lighting and lubrication (its use as a fuel would come later) was found in Pennsylvania in 1859 and later in Ohio and West Virginia. Thus there was plenty of oil even before the great discoveries in Texas and other states of the West and the South.

A third important factor in America's industrial growth was its rapidly increasing population. Between 1860 and 1910, America's population tripled. This meant there were more people to buy the products of its factories. Just as important, the population increase provided an abundant supply of labor to make those products. A large part of the increased

The drilling of oil wells like this gusher in Pennsylvania was a big factor in America's industrial growth.

new companies often made use of the form of business organization known as a **corporation.** A corporation—like the joint-stock company that you read about in Chapter 4—makes it possible to pool the capital of many individuals. The corporation sells stock, or shares of ownership, in the business to these people. If the business does well, stockholders share in the profits. If it does poorly, stockholders may lose what they invested, but they cannot be held responsible for the corporation's losses beyond that amount. The corporation was already in wide use in America before the Civil War. After the war most of the large businesses that speeded America's industrial development were corporations.

Capital came from foreign countries, too. Just as Americans sought profitable investments in American industry, so did wealthy people, companies, and banks in countries like England and France. All in all, 10 times as much capital was invested in American industries—from all sources—in 1900 as was invested just 35 years before.

Two other factors contributed greatly to America's industrial growth: new inventions and business leaders. After examining these, you will see how all these factors came together to create a great industrial nation.

population were immigrants, and it was they and their children who made up the majority of the workers in America's mines and factories.

Capital A fourth important factor in America's industrial growth was **capital** —that is, money in the form of savings. Building factories, buying machines, mining ores, and laying railroad track take a great deal of money. A growing number of Americans had some capital to invest, but few could set up a large business by themselves. Those who wished to start

CHECKUP

1. How did the Civil War affect industrial growth?
2. What natural resources found in the United States were important for industrial expansion?
3. In what two ways did increased population help industrial expansion?
4. Why is capital such an important factor in helping industries grow?

Inventors and Business Leaders

┌─VOCABULARY─
  electricity   rebate
  oil refinery   trust
└

A rash of inventions Americans had always been an inventive people, but the last half of the nineteenth century was an especially inventive time. One way to show this is by looking at figures from the United States Patent Office. This is the office with which inventors register their inventions. In 1850 the Patent Office issued 833 patents for inventions. Twenty-five years later the number leaped to 14,169. And in 1900 no fewer than 24,644 new inventions were given patents.

Most of the thousands of new inventions made only minor adjustments to the machines used to make or do things —a better valve here, a new gear there. Taken together, they added up to big gains in efficiency and cost. In some cases, a single invention led to great gains by itself. George Westinghouse's invention of the air brake in 1869 made it safe for trains to travel faster by allowing them to stop more quickly.

A few inventions were so important that they created whole new industries and changed the way people worked, lived, and communicated with each other. One example was Alexander Graham Bell's invention of the telephone in 1876. (The emperor of Brazil, trying out Bell's invention when visiting the United States, shouted in amazement, "It talks!") Less than 15 years later, a half-million phones

The invention of the typewriter changed office work in many ways and opened up new jobs for women.

were in use in the United States, and thousands of women were working as telephone operators. Christopher Sholes' invention of the typewriter in 1867 also changed the way people worked. Within a half-dozen years, the Remington Company was producing typewriters in large numbers. This machine changed office work in the United States, and as you read earlier, it also opened up new jobs for women.

Thomas Alva Edison The man whose inventions most changed the way Americans lived—and created whole new industries—was Thomas Alva Edison. Edison was a person who was endlessly curious all his life. Illness kept his school career from starting until he was 8 years old. It ended just 3 months later when his father could no longer pay the

Bell was only 29 when his telephone patent was granted in 1876. He also developed a method for making phonograph records on wax discs, a metal detector, an electric probe for surgery, and he supported the advancement of aviation.

school fees. Young Edison's mother, a former schoolteacher, taught him a few subjects at home, but for the most part the boy educated himself. He read all the science books he could. At the age of 10, he set up a laboratory in the basement of the Edison home. There he spent many hours on experiments.

Two years later young Edison got a job selling newspapers and candy on a train. He persuaded the train conductor to let him set up a chemistry lab in the baggage car. That venture ended when some chemicals spilled and set fire to the wooden floor of the car.

While still a teenager, Edison learned to operate a telegraph. It was in this work that his curiosity began to turn to **electricity**. By 19, he was already thinking of a career as an inventor. That was not as wild an idea as it might sound. At the time, there were only about 200 trained engineers in the United States, and very few of these engineers knew much about electricity.

For the next few years, Edison worked for a company on the New York Stock Exchange. The company received prices of stocks on a machine called a stock ticker and reported the prices to customers. Edison came up with inventions that improved the stock ticker and was able to sell his inventions for $40,000. He was then able to quit his job and, at the age of 23, give his full attention to inventing in his Newark, New Jersey, shop.

During the next 5 years, Edison averaged about 40 inventions a year. One was the mimeograph machine. He also figured a way to send four messages at once over a single telegraph wire.

In his New Jersey laboratory, Thomas Edison developed dozens of new devices and processes.

The Wizard of Menlo Park   In 1876, Edison built a larger laboratory at Menlo Park, New Jersey. He hired a team of people to help him in the business of inventing. He expected, he said, to turn out "a minor invention every 10 days and a big thing every 6 months or so." And he did. The next year Edison invented the phonograph and created an entirely new industry.

Already known as the Wizard of Menlo Park, Edison set out to build a practical

The year 1876 marked the one-hundredth anniversary of the Declaration of Independence. To celebrate the event, the United States gave itself a birthday party in Philadelphia, the birthplace of the nation. The party was a world's fair called the Centennial Exhibition. Those who planned the exhibition determined that it would be the biggest, fanciest, and most awe-inspiring show on earth, fit for a glorious and growing nation.

The Centennial Exhibition was just that. Main Hall, which stretched for a third of a mile, was the world's largest building. In Machinery Hall stood a symbol of the new industrial age—a giant steam engine, 40 feet tall, which supplied the power that ran 800 other machines in the hall. All in all, there were some 200 buildings sprawled over several hundred acres. Fifty countries entered exhibits, making this one of the largest world's fairs.

The most popular building was Machinery Hall. There one could see all the latest machines and inventions from all over the world—everything from the type-

One of the spectacular exhibits at the Centennial Exhibition was the Corliss engine, the largest steam engine up to that time.

writer and the telephone to the Westinghouse air brake and the railroad sleeping car. Americans noted with pride that machines from their own country compared well with those from the most advanced countries in the world.

The Centennial Exhibition opened on May 10, 1876, and ran for 6 months. During that time 10 million people—more than one in every five Americans—visited the exhibition. It was one of the most successful birthday parties of all time.

electric light bulb. After countless experiments he succeeded in 1879. Three years after that, he built the first central power plant for producing electricity and carrying it into homes and offices. This was the Pearl Street power station in New York City. Again, an entire new industry was created, and the way people lived, worked, and relaxed was changed. Numerous other inventions followed, including the motion-picture machine and the storage battery. Each of these inventions, and others as well, led to new industries.

John D. Rockefeller had almost complete control of the oil industry in the United States for many years.

John D. Rockefeller　The final factor that contributed so greatly to America's industrial growth was the rise of a number of able business leaders. They came from many backgrounds, but all had in common an ability to organize, imagination, a willingness to take risks, and a driving ambition to win wealth and power. Andrew Carnegie is one good example. Another is John D. Rockefeller. What Carnegie was to steel, Rockefeller was to oil.

John D. Rockefeller was born in 1839 in upstate New York. Serious-minded and religious, he decided early in life on a business career. After high school he studied bookkeeping at a small business college in Cleveland, Ohio. In 1859, at the age of 20, he and a friend went into business, trading in grains and meat. The business was successful from the start, thanks to Rockefeller's shrewdness and his careful attention to detail. He boldly borrowed from banks to expand the business. When the Civil War broke out, the firm was in a position to make large profits selling supplies to the Union army.

The new oil industry　By this time Rockefeller had become interested in the new but booming oil industry. People had long known of areas in western Pennsylvania where oil seeped through rock and floated on the creeks. A few people bottled and sold the oil as medicine, but otherwise it had no value. In the 1850s, Benjamin Silliman, a chemistry teacher at Yale University, showed that "Pennsylvania rock oil" could be refined —that is, changed by a simple method— into usable products like kerosene for lighting lamps. (Interestingly, at this time no one knew of any use for one of the other products that came from refining oil, and it was thrown away. That product was gasoline.)

Silliman's findings showed that oil could be valuable if someone could find a way to get it out of the ground in quantity. In 1859, Colonel E. L. Drake drilled the first oil well at Titusville, Pennsylvania, and a new industry was founded. People flocked to the region to drill for oil. It was the gold rush all over again, except that this time the treasure was "black gold," or oil. The crude oil was shipped to nearby Cleveland, where a few men had started **oil refineries**. At an oil refinery, crude oil is separated into its parts.

Controlling oil refining This was the part of the oil business that John D. Rockefeller entered in 1867, at the age of 27. His was one of perhaps 30 refineries that competed with each other in Cleveland.

The entire oil industry—from drilling to refining to distributing the kerosene to customers—was marked by fierce competition. Rockefeller saw that if he could gain control of refining, he could control the whole industry. He would be able to name the price he would pay the drillers for their crude oil. He could also name the price at which he would sell the refined oil to distributors. In 1870, Rockefeller formed the Standard Oil Company with the aim of gaining control of the refining business. Within 2 years he was

able to buy out most of the other refineries in Cleveland. A few years after that, he reached out to gain control of large refineries in New York, Philadelphia, Baltimore, and Pittsburgh.

How did Rockefeller accomplish this? For one thing, he was an efficient producer. Like Andrew Carnegie in steel, he plowed back profits into the business to pay for expansion. He used the latest methods and machinery. He saved money by manufacturing his own barrels, building his own warehouses, and buying his own pipelines, which carried oil from the wells to his refineries. Thus he was able to refine oil for less.

He was also able to ship for less. As the largest shipper of oil, Rockefeller forced railroads into secret deals to give him **rebates**—that is, to pay back to him a portion of the freight rates they charged him. Thus, in Ohio, Rockefeller could ship oil for only 10 cents a barrel, whereas his competitors had to pay 35 cents. After a time, he demanded that the railroads also give him a share of the freight charges his competitors paid! The railroads had to agree or lose Rockefeller's business.

With such advantages, Rockefeller could sell oil for less than his competitors. He gave other companies a choice: sell out to him at a fair price, or be driven out of business. Standard Oil was quite willing to sell oil at a loss for as long as it would take to drive another company out of business. With methods such as these, Rockefeller controlled 90 percent of the refining business in the United States by 1879. This was practically a monopoly, that is, complete control of an industry by a single company.

This Pennsylvania oil field brought vast wealth to John D. Rockefeller and others.

Among the many refineries controlled by Rockefeller was this one in New Jersey.

The trust In 1882, Standard Oil adopted a new form of organization called a **trust**. This allowed the company to control many other corporations without actually owning them. In a trust, stockholders of different companies turn over their stocks to a single group of trustees. These trustees guard against overproduction and insure good profits by seeing that the companies do not compete with each other. The profits are shared by all the stockholders. Using the trust form, Standard Oil brought 39 more oil companies under its control.

Soon trusts were formed in the tobacco, leather, sugar, and other industries. Businesses grew bigger. In 1900 two thirds of all manufactured goods in the United States were being produced by a handful of giant corporations.

In 1892 the Ohio Supreme Court dissolved the Standard Oil trust.

Benefits—and dangers—of big business
Large businesses could bring important benefits to the American people. They were often able to make goods more efficiently, at a lower cost than small companies could. This was important for several reasons. It meant that American-made goods could compete in foreign markets against goods made in other countries. Selling more goods abroad meant more jobs for American workers. At home, big businesses could sell their goods to American consumers for less.

But did they? Sometimes, yes. Even while making large profits, John D. Rockefeller passed on his lower costs to the buyers. Many trusts and monopolies, however, did not. In fact, one of the main reasons for forming the trust was to raise prices without fear of competition. This, then, was one reason why many Americans in the late nineteenth century became concerned about the growth of big business.

There were other reasons. Big corporations threatened to put an end to both competition and opportunity in business. People also feared big business's growing power in politics. By the last part of the century, therefore, there was a growing popular demand to control the growth and the behavior of big business.

CHECKUP

1. List five inventions that contributed to industrial growth in the latter years of the nineteenth century.
2. Name three of Thomas Edison's inventions that led to new industries.
3. How did John D. Rockefeller get control of the oil industry?
4. What benefits did big business bring to the American people? In spite of this, why did many Americans become concerned about the growth of big business?

his later years, Rockefeller became involved in philanthropy. He gave away about $550 million in his lifetime through tablishing foundations and helping found the University of Chicago. The Rockefeller Foundation deals with problems of nger, overpopulation, and international conflicts. It also works to improve education, provide opportunities for minorities, d protect the environment.

KEY FACTS

1. Andrew Carnegie in the steel industry and John D. Rockefeller in the oil industry were two of the business leaders that contributed to America's industrial growth.

2. By 1900, railroads reached every corner of the United States.

3. Factors that spurred industrial growth in the United States included improved transportation, a supply of natural resources, increasing population, capital for investment, new inventions, and bold business leaders.

4. The inventions of Thomas Edison and Alexander Graham Bell changed life in America and the rest of the world.

5. In the late nineteenth century, many giant companies were eliminating competition.

VOCABULARY QUIZ

Fill in each blank correctly. Choose your answer from the terms following each sentence below.

1. Bell and Edison were famous <u>inventors</u>.
investors   inventors   business leaders

2. When railroads returned money to Rockefeller in secret deals, he received <u>rebates</u>.
dividends   stock   rebates

3. A Bessemer furnace might be found in a <u>steel plant</u>.
textile factory   steel plant   oil refinery

4. A gift of financial aid from the government to a person or company is a <u>subsidy</u>.
rebate   stock   subsidy

5. Money used to produce goods is called <u>capital</u>.
deposit   capital   resource

6. One who invests money in a corporation to own part of it receives <u>stock</u>.
stock   rebates   inventions

7. An inventor is given the exclusive right to his invention for a certain time through a <u>patent</u>.
share   profit   patent

8. Having complete control of the supply of certain goods is a <u>monopoly</u>.
trustee   monopoly   corporation

9. A form of business organization that allows a company to control many other companies is a <u>trust</u>.
refinery   patent   trust

10. A form of business organization that makes it possible to pool the capital of many individuals is a <u>corporation</u>.
subsidy   refinery   corporation

REVIEW QUESTIONS

1. Does a patent encourage or discourage inventions? Explain how.

2. How did the government encourage the building of railroads?

3. List the steps that Rockefeller took to create a monopoly.

4. How did railroads affect the economy?

ACTIVITIES

1. Thomas Edison received hundreds of patents on inventions. Which ones, do you think, most affect the lives of people? Explain.

2. List all the electrical appliances in your home. Ask your parents to check off the ones in their homes when they were growing up. Ask your grandparents or other older people to check off the ones they had as children.

3. In folk-song books, look for these railroad songs: "Casey Jones," "I've Been Working on the Railroad," "Drill, Ye Tarriers, Drill," "John Henry." What are the messages expressed in these songs?

FRAMING QUESTIONS

SETTING PURPOSES FOR READING

Have you ever seen a pamphlet that gives information in the form of questions and answers? Presenting information in this way takes advantage of two important facts about reading. First, you get more out of reading when you read for a purpose, that is, for specific information. Second, the best way to get specific information is to ask a question that directs you to it.

How does reading for a purpose help you get more from your reading? Notice how this question has set a purpose for reading what comes next. Reading for a purpose helps you focus on the material. When you know what you are reading for, you concentrate better. You read more efficiently because you are looking for specific information to answer your question. You can better understand what you are reading. And you can recall what you have read.

What can you do when a purpose has not been set for you? You can set one for yourself. In this textbook you have noticed headings and subheadings in boldface type. These headings are signals to tell you what lies ahead. To set purposes for your reading, simply turn these headings into questions. When you frame questions, you create your own study guide. For example, in the subheading "The Carnegies come to America" on page 424, these are some questions that might come to mind: Who were the Carnegies? Why were they important? Why did they come to America? What did they do in America? When did they come to America?

SKILLS PRACTICE

On a sheet of paper, make up some questions from the subheadings below. Some subheadings may lead to four or five good questions, whereas others may lead to only one or two.

1. Why Carnegie prospered
2. Steel leads the way
3. Railroads expand
4. The transcontinental railroad
5. Railroads help settle the West
6. Railroads help the economy grow
7. A rash of inventions
8. The new oil industry
9. Controlling oil refining
10. Benefits—and dangers—of big business

To practice your skills, do the same for the next chapter. First use your skimming skill to preview the chapter. Then write out your questions. When you start reading for the answers to those questions, you will find that you are reading with better focus, greater efficiency, more understanding, and easier recall.

Ask pupils why *skyscraper* came to be the word used to refer to tall buildings. They might enjoy making up other words that could be used to describe tall buildings.

The Growth of Cities

VOCABULARY

architect   streetcar
skyscraper

Birth of the skyscraper When the Home Insurance Company hired William Le Baron Jenney to design a new office building in Chicago in 1882, the company did not know he was about to change the face of the American city. Jenney was an **architect**—a designer of buildings. He was born in 1832 and had studied in Boston and in Paris, France. During the Civil War he had served as an engineer in the Union army on the staff of General Ulysses S. Grant. Jenney later moved to Chicago, which offered great opportunities for an architect. At a time of rapidly growing cities, Chicago was one of the fastest growing cities in the country. Not even a great fire in 1871, which left much of the city in ashes, slowed Chicago's growth for long. Its population, which was 290,000 in 1870, had already reached a half million by 1880. New buildings were rising everywhere.

William Le Baron Jenney and other architects who designed office buildings had two main considerations. One was that the buildings had to be very tall. This was necessary because of the high price of land in the downtown area. A second consideration was creating plenty of window space to allow daylight into the offices, since electric lighting was not in wide use at the time.

The problem in those days was that the whole weight of a building, including the floors and the inner walls, was supported by its outside walls. Therefore, the taller a building, the thicker its walls had to be at the bottom. And if many spaces had to be left for windows, the walls would have to be even thicker. As a result, few office buildings were more than five or six stories high.

Jenney's solution was to design the new building with a skeleton of iron and steel—the same steel that Carnegie and others were making into rails for the railroads. This strong metal skeleton, rather than the outer walls, would carry the weight of the building. With this design Jenney could make his building taller without having to make the lower walls so thick. And since the building's walls merely provided a cover around the frame, he could put in as many windows as he wished.

Jenney's Home Insurance building was completed in 1885. It was 10 stories high, taller than all but a few buildings of the time. More important, Jenney had developed a design that would one day

One of the many American cities that experienced rapid growth in the late 1800s was Atlanta, Georgia, a center of trade and transportation. (34°N/84°W; map, p. 717)

Review examples of compound words with pupils. Compound words such as *skyscraper, streetcar,* and *railroad* were often used to describe new inventions in America.

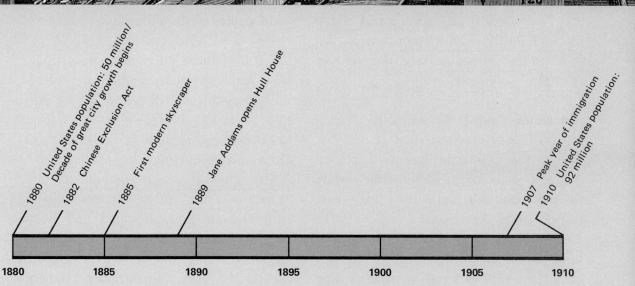

1880 United States population: 50 million/
Decade of great city growth begins

1882 Chinese Exclusion Act

1885 First modern skyscraper

1889 Jane Addams opens Hull House

1907 Peak year of immigration

1910 United States population: 92 million

| 1880 | 1885 | 1890 | 1895 | 1900 | 1905 | 1910 |

After pupils have finished reading Chapter 20, have them come back to the time line and develop a unit-inclusive time line on poster paper. They can add events from Chapter 21 when they have completed that chapter. This procedure will allow for a review of major events in the middle to late 1800s.

allow the construction of buildings many times higher than the Home Insurance building. The modern **skyscraper** had been born.

". . . a proud, soaring thing" If Jenney was the father of the modern skyscraper, Louis Sullivan helped make the design America's greatest contribution to architecture. Sullivan was 24 years younger than Jenney. Like Jenney, he was born in Massachusetts, studied there and in Paris, and moved to Chicago to embark upon his career. By the time he was 26, Sullivan was one of that city's most successful architects.

Sullivan believed that the American city should develop its own kind of architecture, different from anything else in the world. The new American building, he wrote, "must be tall, every inch of it tall . . .. It must be every inch a proud, soaring thing." Following Jenney's work, Sullivan designed a number of tall buildings, not only in Chicago but also in New York, Buffalo, and St. Louis. He became the most important American architect of his time. As a result of the work of Sullivan and his followers, the look of the American city was forever changed.

Americans move to the city Skyscrapers were evidence that in the last half of the nineteenth century America was fast becoming urban. In 1790, when the new country's first census was taken, only 1 in 20 Americans lived in cities. Even in 1860, only 1 in 6 did. But 40 years later, the number was 1 in 3. In 1860 there were still only 16 cities with a

The Flatiron Building in New York was one of the skyscrapers that changed the appearance of cities.

population of 50,000 or more. But by 1910 there were more than 100 such cities.

Some of these cities were truly huge. New York's population, which was a half-million people in 1850, grew to 3.4 million in 1900. Philadelphia went from 121,000 to 1.5 million in that time, and Chicago from 29,000 to 1.3 million.

The greatest single decade of city growth was the 1880s. In that 10-year period some cities doubled and even tripled their populations. Kansas City, Missouri, went from 60,000 to 132,000; Omaha, Nebraska, from 30,500 to 140,000;

According to the 1980 census these figures show the population of the following cities: New York — 7,071,639; Philadelphia — 1,688,210; Chicago — 3,005,072; Kansas City — 448,159; Omaha — 314,255.

and Minneapolis, Minnesota, from 47,000 to 164,000. Places that were hardly larger than villages and small towns at the start of the decade were busy cities by its end. Birmingham, Alabama, went from 3,000 to 26,000; Duluth, Minnesota, from 3,300 to 33,000; and Seattle, Washington, from 3,500 to 42,000.

Why cities grew Location had a good deal to do with the growth of these cities. Many were on important water routes. Fine harbors for oceangoing ships fostered the growth of some important commercial and shipping centers. These trade centers included cities like Boston, New York, Philadelphia, and Baltimore on the Atlantic seaboard, New Orleans along the Gulf of Mexico, and San Francisco and Seattle on the Pacific coast. Other cities, located on inland rivers and canals, served as collecting and processing points for goods produced in the countryside. St. Louis on the Mississippi River and Buffalo at the western end of the Erie Canal are examples.

As important as water transportation was to the growth of cities, railroads became even more important in the last half of the nineteenth century. For example, the location of Minneapolis on the Mississippi River had always given the city good water transportation. But the great growth of Minneapolis came in the 1880s when railroads tied the city to the rich wheatlands of the West and made it into a center for flour milling. In the same way, Chicago increased greatly in size when it became a major railroad center.

Railroads not only made some cities larger, they also created new ones. Kansas City, Missouri, was founded when a railroad company decided to run a line through that town rather than through nearby Fort Leavenworth.

The Industrial Revolution contributed to the growth of cities. People flocked to cities for jobs in the new factories. Many cities owed their growth to a single large industry. In Pittsburgh and Birmingham it was steel. In Cleveland it was oil refining. Milwaukee had beer; Omaha had meat packing; Minneapolis and St. Paul, wheat milling. After the turn of the century, Detroit had automobiles. Of course, very large cities like New York, Philadelphia, and Chicago had many industries—they were centers for railroads, manufacturing, banking, and trade.

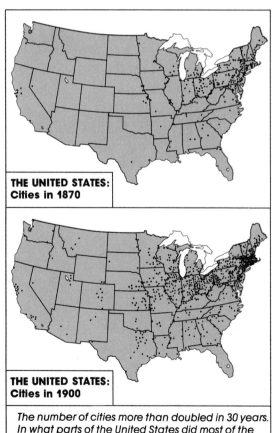

THE UNITED STATES: Cities in 1870

THE UNITED STATES: Cities in 1900

The number of cities more than doubled in 30 years. In what parts of the United States did most of the new cities appear? What caused this growth?

Cities spreading out   Transportation developments in the late nineteenth century changed not only the size of the cities but also their shape. Early cities were "walking cities"—that is, most people got around in them on foot. In the walking city, factories and warehouses, shops, and offices were in the center of the city, and most people lived near their place of work. Even the owners usually lived close to their factories. A walking city almost never measured more than 3 or 4 miles (5 or 6 km) from one end to the other—about the distance one might walk in an hour. When population increased in the walking city, more people simply crowded into the same space.

Then in the mid-1800s the street railway, or horsecar, made its appearance. These cars, drawn by horses along a track, could carry people about twice as fast as they could walk. In the late 1880s, electric **streetcars** replaced the horsecars and moved people even faster.

Streetcars made it possible for people to live farther from the center of the city. Cities spread out. By 1900, larger cities might measure 8 or 10 miles (13 or 16 km) from one end to another. People who could afford it began to move out from the center of the city. Poorer workers and newcomers to the city were left to occupy the older downtown neighborhoods.

CHECKUP

1. What change in design made it possible to have taller office buildings with ample window space?
2. How did American cities change during the 1880s?
3. Give three reasons why cities changed in the late nineteenth century.
4. What made it possible for cities to spread out?

With the introduction of electric streetcars, people began to move out from the center of the cities.

Natives and Strangers

From America's countryside   In 1860 about 6 million people lived in America's cities. In 1900, some 30 million did. Where did these millions of new city dwellers come from? One main source was America's countryside.

During the late 1800s, 40 percent of the townships in the United States saw their population decline. Most of this decline took place because many rural people moved to the cities. All in all, between 1880 and 1910 about 11 million people who were born in rural areas moved to cities. The traffic was almost entirely one-way—for every 20 who left the farm for the city, only 1 city dweller moved to a farm. In some parts of New England and the Midwest, entire villages were abandoned.

A small but growing part of this movement was made up of black people leaving the rural South. At first, black farmers and their families moved into southern states, where there had been a large number of free blacks before the Civil War. In the late nineteenth century, however, southern blacks began to move to northern and western cities.

Why did farm people go to the city? There were several reasons. For one thing, during the last three decades of the 1800s, farm prices had been low, and farmers had had a hard time making a living. Many even lost their farms.

Perhaps more important was the hope of escaping the long hours, the hard work, and the loneliness of farm life. Kate Sanborn, a New England farm woman, explained what life was like on many eastern farms:

It's all work, with no play and no proper pay. . . . and how can the children consent to stay on, starving body and soul? *That* explains the 3,318 abandoned farms in Maine at present. And the farmers' wives! What monotonous, treadmill lives! Constant toil, with no wages, no allowance, no pocket money, no vacations, no pleasure trips to the city nearest them. . . . Someone says that their only chance for social life is in going to some insane asylum!

By comparison, the city seemed a place of glamour and excitement. There were

This painting entitled Homesteader's Wife *suggests the loneliness of farm life.*

"Homesteader's Wife" by Harvey Dunn; South Dakota Memorial Art Center Collection, Brookings

447

From 1845 to 1847, Ireland's potato crop, the main source of food for poor farmers, failed due to a fungus called late blight. About 750,000 Irish people died from starvation and disease during those years. To make matters worse, the winter of 1846–1847 was very severe. Emigration to the United States was a source of hope for the Irish.

theaters, sports, and various other entertainments. There were shops with goods from around the world. There were variety and crowds and the latest marvel of the age, electric lighting. (Even 50 years later, 90 percent of America's farms would still have no electricity.)

Perhaps most of all, there was economic opportunity. For some, no doubt, their view was colored by popular literature, with its stories of winning fame and fortune in the city. Most, however, were more realistic. They hoped simply for jobs that would give them a little better life.

From overseas The second main source of population for America's growing cities was Europe. Immigrants from Europe's farms and villages had been swelling the population of American cities since the 1820s. In the 1840s and 1850s alone, more than a million Irish arrived. They were fleeing a terrible potato famine as well as harsh British rule. Altogether, about 2 million Irish came to the United States between 1820 and 1860. Another 1.5 million immigrants came from Germany, and three quarters of a million more were from England, Scotland, and Wales. Thousands of others arrived from France, the Netherlands, and the Scandinavian countries.

Those who had been skilled workers—tailors, carpenters, weavers, and the like—found a demand for their services in the cities and settled there. Most of the immigrants, though, were farming people. To them, America promised plentiful land and a good life in farming. Although thousands did become farmers, the great majority of these immigrants, too, wound up in the cities.

Most were far too poor to buy a farm. They had to find work quickly, and they could do this in the cities. They were unskilled. All they had to sell was their muscle power. They took whatever work they could get at whatever pay they were offered.

Immigrants did much of the labor for such jobs as the laying of trolley-car tracks.

What's in a Name?

HOT DOGS

Among the foods Germans brought to America was the meat sausage. In St. Louis in the 1880s, one of these German immigrants, Antoine Feuchtwanger, began to sell these sausages to the public in a new way—in a roll. Feuchtwanger came from Frankfurt, Germany, and was therefore known as a Frankfurter. So his new sausage sandwich came to be called that, too.

Call it what you will—frankfurter, red hot, or hot dog—this vendor's fare has long been a favorite food for Americans.

As America's first hot "fast food," frankfurters were popular at picnics, baseball games, beaches, and wherever else people went for outdoor entertainment. It was at baseball games that the frankfurter began to be called a hot dog. The change came in two steps. In a New York baseball park in the 1890s, vendors called attention to their hot fast food by shouting, "Get your red hots! Red hots!" For a time, frankfurters came to be called red hots. The change from *red hots* to *hot dogs* came about 10 years later. T.A. Dorgan, a popular newspaper cartoonist, had eaten many a red hot at ball games. But one day in 1906 he was suddenly struck by how much the frankfurter looked like the long body of a dachshund, a short-legged German dog. German sausage, German dog; red hots, hot dog—it clicked. He drew a cartoon showing the red hot as a dachshund in a bun and called it "Hot dog!" And it has been this ever since.

A rising tide The wave of immigration before the Civil War was just a taste of what was to come. Between 1865 and 1914, 25 million immigrants entered the United States. Most were from Europe, but some came from Asia and other countries in the Americas.

For the first part of this time period, most immigrants came from the same countries in northern and western Europe that had sent the earlier immigrants. Beginning in the 1880s, however, large numbers began to arrive from eastern and southern Europe. These included people from Russia, Poland, Austria-Hungary, Italy, Greece, and Romania. Immigration from this part of Europe came to be called the **New Immigration**, and the name given to immigration from the countries in northern and western Europe was the

On a ship entering New York Harbor, immigrants get their first glimpse of a new homeland.

Old Immigration. By the 1890s the number of New Immigrants entering each year passed the number of Old Immigrants. In 1907, the peak year of immigration, 80 percent of the 1.2 million people who left their countries to enter the United States were New Immigrants.

These immigrants came to America for many different reasons. Most were peasants—poor farming people. In their countries, population was growing fast, and there was simply not enough land to go around. Some young men left so they would not have to serve in the army. Many thousands, like the Poles and the Slovaks, were being forced to live under foreign rule. Armenians fled Turkish persecution. More than a million Jews fled persecution in Russia.

Mary Antin was one of those Jews whose family fled Russia. In her autobiography she described what it was like to experience a **pogrom.** A pogrom is an anti-Jewish riot. Such riots in Russia were usually encouraged by the Russian government.

> They [the peasants] would set out to kill the Jews. They attacked them with knives and clubs and scythes and axes, killed them or tortured them, and burned their homes.

In 1891, when Mary was 10, her father went to America. After 3 years he had saved enough to send for his wife and six children. Once in America, Mary enjoyed the benefits of a free public education. She later went on to college and became a social worker and a writer. She

Review the definition of *immigrant* with pupils. Ask: Even though we do not usually refer to the early colonists of Plymouth and Jamestown as immigrants, were they immigrants? Which group of Americans are usually considered the original inhabitants of America? (Indians)

called her autobiography *The Promised Land*, for she believed that her life story proved "what a real thing is this American freedom."

Not all who came to America in the New Immigration planned to stay. Some —perhaps as many as one in three—came to earn money to return and buy farmland in their native country.

The New Immigrants New Immigrants poured into cities in even greater numbers than did the Old Immigrants. They found jobs in the new factories of industrial America. They worked in steel mills, meat-packing plants, and textile factories. They made cigars in crowded workshops or sometimes in their own homes. Women did domestic work and also labored in the garment industry.

By 1910, foreign-born people made up 40 percent of New York City's population, 36 percent of Chicago's, and 34 percent of San Francisco's. Together with their children these people made up more than three fourths of the population of those cities, and of Detroit and Cleveland as well. More Italians lived in New York City than in Rome, and more Greeks lived there than in any city in Greece except Athens. More Poles lived in Chicago than in any Polish city except Warsaw. In a strange twist of history, the rapid growth of urban America around the turn of the century was largely the result of the coming of European peasants!

Loaded down with family possessions, European immigrants come ashore in New York.

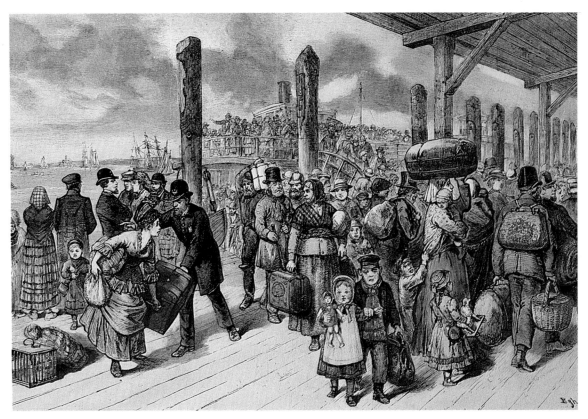

By 1900 there was a thriving Chinese community in San Francisco, California.

Immigrants from Asia added to the foreign-born population of several western cities. Chinese had been arriving on the West Coast since the days of the California gold rush. Many thousands of them were hired to build the Central Pacific Railroad in the 1860s. The Chinese population spread throughout the West in both large and small cities, and large neighborhoods of Chinese people formed in Los Angeles and San Francisco.

Japanese immigrants did not arrive much before the end of the 1800s. They came in smaller numbers, about 70,000 in all. Most took up farming or fishing, but a number found work in industry or opened small shops in some of the cities of California.

The New Immigrants gave American cities a foreign flavor. Like earlier immigrants, they sought the comfort and security of living with their own kind. They clustered in neighborhoods where they continued to speak their own languages, follow their familiar customs, and wear their traditional dress. These neighborhoods became known by such names as Little Italy and Greektown. Foreign-language newspapers appeared by the dozen.

The hardest jobs   There was a popular saying about America in Europe: "The streets are paved with gold." One person wrote that upon arrival in the United States, immigrants quickly learned three things: "First, that the streets were not paved with gold; second, that the streets were not paved at all; and third, that they [the immigrant workers] were expected to pave them."

Immigrants of the late nineteenth and early twentieth centuries were mostly unskilled workers. Fewer than 1 in 10 had a trade, or work skill. Fewer still could speak English. Add to this the discrimination they often met, and it is not hard to understand why immigrants wound up with the hardest and the lowest-paid jobs. These immigrants, along with the descendants of black slaves, provided much of the physical labor that built modern America.

In particular, immigrants from southern and eastern Europe filled the bottom ranks of heavy industry. In the Carnegie

452

steel mills in Pittsburgh, for example, more than 11,000 of the 14,000 common laborers in 1907 were from eastern Europe. Irish, Chinese, Mexican, and Italian immigrants dug tunnels and laid track for the railroads. The women did domestic work and held jobs in canneries, mills, and clothing factories. Their hours were long and their wages were low.

Even so, most immigrants found themselves better off in America than in the Old Country. And in time, many were able to improve their positions. As new waves of immigrants arrived and took the poorest jobs, those who had earlier held these jobs moved up the ladder. Also, many immigrants and their children were able to learn skills and to advance.

Should immigration be curbed?
Some Americans grew worried about the large number of immigrants entering the United States. These Americans disliked and feared the foreign ways of the newcomers. Would these new immigrants adopt American ways and values? Or would they weaken the character of America? Further, America was, for the most part, a Protestant country. These new immigrants were mainly Catholic, Greek and Russian Orthodox, and Jewish. Some American workers complained that the immigrants worked for low pay and would either take away their jobs or lower the wage level for all. All in all, said those who believed these things, America could be preserved only by limiting the

Canneries provided jobs for immigrant women, though the work was often seasonal.

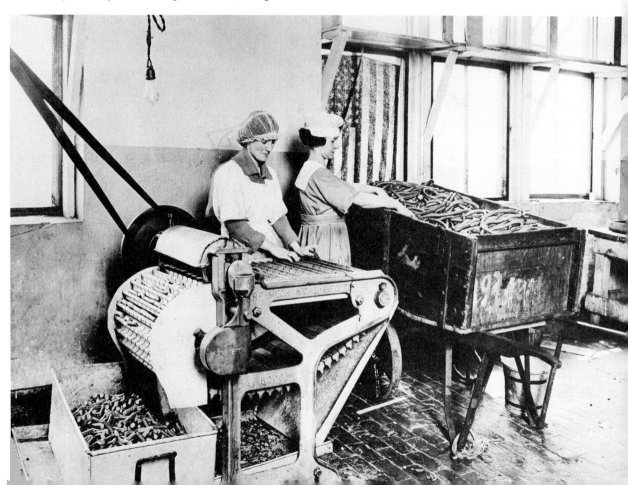

number of foreigners entering the United States or by ending immigration altogether. Those who favored this course were known as **nativists**.

Nativism won its first victory in the Chinese Exclusion Act of 1882. This was an act of Congress that ended further immigration of Chinese people. Nativists were not able to limit the flow of European immigrants at that time. However, their demands continued to be heard, and they would finally succeed in the 1920s.

CHECKUP

1. What were the two main sources of new city dwellers in the late nineteenth century?
2. What led each of the two main groups of newcomers to settle in cities?
3. What was the Old Immigration? What was the New Immigration?
4. What kind of jobs were filled to a large degree by immigrants?
5. Why did some Americans worry about the large number of immigrants entering the country?
6. What people were excluded from immigration in 1882?

Coping with Growth

Growing pains With populations doubling and even tripling in a decade, how could cities hope to keep up with the need for services? The answer was that, try as they might, they could not. Take street paving, for example. In 1890, after 10 years of mushrooming growth, not a single one of Minneapolis's 200 miles (320 km) of streets had been paved. Only 100 (161 km) of New Orleans's 500 miles (805 km) were paved. In Chicago, the nation's second largest city, two thirds of the streets were still dirt in 1900.

One can imagine the difficulty of getting around on such streets, whether by horse and wagon, bicycle, or foot. In dry weather, wagons raised clouds of choking dust. In rainy weather, the streets became rivers of mud.

In northern cities, winter was often the best season for travel. The frozen streets were covered with snow that soon packed down to make a smooth roadway for sleighs.

After Chicago was swept by fire in 1871, a third of the city was a wasteland.

Crowded cities meant crowded buildings. And since most of these buildings were made of wood, the chance of a fire sweeping away a whole section of a city was greatly increased. Many cities experienced that fate. The worst fire of the century occurred in Chicago in 1871. Within days, a third of the city—17,000 buildings—was destroyed, more than 300 persons were dead, and 90,000 were left homeless.

Crime increased in the crowded cities. Robbery, assault, and even killing were on the rise. In some notorious sections, like Hell's Kitchen in New York and the Barbary Coast in San Francisco, the rule of law was almost unknown.

Yet another serious urban problem was **sanitation**—making clean and healthful conditions. When cities were smaller, garbage was thrown into the streets and alleys, sometimes to be eaten by pigs that were permitted to roam freely. In the mushrooming cities of the late 1800s, other means were needed to get rid of the garbage that piled up and dirtied both the air and the water. Outhouses and cesspools were no longer sufficient for disposing of sewage when hundreds of people lived in a single building.

Tackling the problems   To cope with such problems, cities had to change their ways. They had always depended upon volunteer fire fighters to battle the blazes and volunteer police to protect the population against crime. Now they began to organize professional fire departments, train fire fighters, and buy fire engines that could pump water to the roofs of most city buildings. They organized professional police departments to protect citizens. They arranged to collect garbage on a regular schedule.

he summer of 1871 was unusually dry in Chicago. According to the story passed along, a cow kicked over a lighted lantern nd set the barn on fire. Strong winds and dry wooden buildings helped the fire to spread rapidly through the city. People ed to Lake Michigan to save themselves. The fire caused at least $200 million in damage.

Sometimes, though, in trying to solve one problem, cities made another problem worse. In 1900 most cities had built water systems that piped water into homes and offices. They also built underground sewage systems to replace outdoor toilets and cesspools. The problem was that the sewage pipes often led into the same lakes and rivers from which the city drew its water supply. It was little wonder, then, why such waterborne diseases as typhoid fever and cholera were widespread.

The housing problem   The city's greatest failure was its inability to provide good housing for its people. The housing problem was especially bad in large cities.

New York, the biggest city, had the biggest problem. There the poor, especially the immigrants, were packed into **tenements.** These were mostly four-to-six-story wooden apartment buildings, often in run-down condition. As the population increased, each building had to house more people. For example, a five-story tenement at 36 Cherry Street was already crowded with 500 people in 1865. Twelve years later, 800 lived in the same building.

Jacob Riis   A newspaper reporter named Jacob Riis (rēs) did more than any other person to make Americans aware of what life in a tenement was like. Riis was an immigrant himself. He came to America from Denmark in 1870 at the age of 21. He tried his hand at such jobs as farming, coal mining, brickmaking, and peddling before landing a job with a New York newspaper in 1877. For the next 15 years, Riis worked as a police reporter for two of the city's great newspapers, the *Tribune* and the *Evening Sun.*

Time and again his reporting on accidents and crime brought him into the city's slums. The young reporter became outraged by the conditions he saw there. He began to write articles about the life of the poor, and especially of children in these slums.

In 1890, Riis wrote a book called *How the Other Half Lives.* At one point he invites the reader to enter a typical tenement with him:

> . . . the hall is dark, and you might stumble over the children pitching pennies back there. . . . Here where the hall turns and dives into utter darkness is a step. . . . All the fresh air that ever enters these stairs

Jacob Riis, a crusading newspaper reporter, sought to improve life for the poor people of the slums.

In their crowded quarters a tenement family earns a living making artificial flowers.

comes from the hall door that is forever slamming, and from the windows of dark bedrooms. . . . The sinks are in the hall- way, that all tenants may have access—and all be poisoned alike by their summer stenches.

In many of these buildings, there was no running water. To get water for cooking or bathing, tenants had to take their buck- ets to a public pump in the street. Toilets were in the backyards. Riis reported how diseases raced unchecked through the tenements, taking a high toll among chil- dren. Of 138 children born in one tene- ment, 61 died at an early age, most of them before they were a year old.

Through his writings Jacob Riis got the tenement block known as Mulberry Bend torn down and replaced by a park. But there were hundreds of tenement blocks in New York City, with 2.5 million people living in them.

Jane Addams and Hull House   The plight of the city's poor stirred the con- sciences of many. Some reformers took on the task of making life better for them. One of the most famous of these was Jane Addams. She was born into a comfort- able family in a small Illinois town in 1860. She was part of the first generation of American women to attend college. After her graduation Jane Addams looked for a career in which she could be of ser- vice to others. She found it on a trip to England. There, in London, she visited what was known as a **settlement house.** In this building, services of various kinds were provided for the poor people of the neighborhood.

On her return to America, Jane Addams resolved to open a settlement house. She and a college friend, Ellen Gates Starr, rented an old, run-down mansion in a poor section of Chicago. The old building was repaired and in 1889, Hull House was opened to the people of the neighborhood—most of them Italian, Greek, Polish, Jewish, and Russian immigrants.

Helping the urban poor Hull House served as a neighborhood center. Here the poor received medical care, got help in finding jobs, and took lessons in English. There was a kindergarten class for the young and there were social clubs for the elderly. Young people took lessons in music and drama, and learned job skills as well. Jane Addams and her fellow settlement workers lived among the people they were serving. They re-

Jane Addams provided many services for the poor in the settlement house she founded in Chicago.

spected the immigrants' customs and values even as they helped them move into the mainstream of American life.

Hull House became a model for settlement houses in other cities. Some 70 others were established in cities such as New York, Boston, and Detroit in the 1890s and early 1900s.

Settlement houses showed what could be done to help the urban poor. Yet the settlement houses alone could not possibly take care of the millions of needy people. It was clear that many more changes would be needed for America to cope with the problems accompanying its tremendous growth.

Governing the cities City governments were poorly suited to cope with the problems of growth. In fact, one observer called America's city governments "the worst in Christendom—the most expensive, the most inefficient, and the most corrupt."

The problem was that these governments were designed in an earlier age, when cities were smaller and problems were simpler. Mayors had little power because in earlier times it was thought unwise to give much power to one person. What power there was in government usually lay with the city council. This body was made up of 12 to 24 people, each of whom was mainly interested in his own neighborhood rather than in the needs of the city as a whole. Yet there were great tasks to be done—roads to be paved; street railways to be built; public buildings to be constructed; gas, water, and electricity to be provided; and the health of the people to be protected.

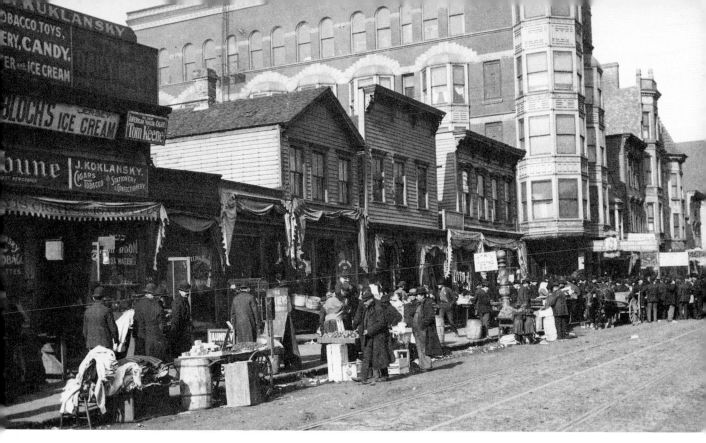

Open-air markets, like this one in Chicago, were often found in immigrant neighborhoods.   Chicago Historical Society

The political machine   Stepping into this situation was the **political machine.** *Machine* was simply the name given to a political organization that ran smoothly, from the ward politicians at the bottom to the boss at the top.   The machine elected its friends.   In awarding contracts for paving roads, constructing city buildings, and providing public utilities, officials acted as the boss told them to.   Those who received the contracts paid the machine and the boss handsomely.   There were always those who were willing to offer thousands in payoffs in order to make millions in profit.

The machine was able to elect its people because it won the support of immigrants.   From the boss to the ward workers, the machine understood the problem of immigrants when few others seemed to care.   It met the newcomers at the boat and helped them find their first jobs.   It provided them with food and coal in hard times.   It helped out when their children had brushes with the law.   It joined their ethnic celebrations.   It helped them with their citizenship papers.   In return, the grateful immigrants gave the machine their support on election day.   From the point of view of the immigrants, casting their ballots for the machine candidates was a fair exchange.

CHECKUP
1. Name four problems faced by the growing cities of the late nineteenth century.
2. How did they try to meet these problems?
3. What approaches did Jacob Riis and Jane Addams take to helping the urban poor?
4. What were some good and bad things about the political machines that grew up in the cities?

Ask: What kind of problems are city governments facing today? Do you think political machines are controlling some cities today? Why? (You might want pupils to bring in current newspaper articles about American cities.)   **459**

KEY FACTS

1. As the population of cities increased in the nineteenth century, land became more scarce and valuable. This led to the building of skyscrapers.

2. Cities developed in places where there was good water and rail transportation.

3. The increase in urban population was due both to the movement of farm dwellers to the city and the arrival of immigrants from other countries.

4. The rapid growth of cities created problems of health and safety.

5. The political machine gave aid to immigrants in exchange for their votes.

VOCABULARY QUIZ

On a separate sheet of paper, write **T** if the statement is true and **F** if it is false. If the statement is false, change the underlined term to make the statement true.

F **1.** An office building of many stories with a skeleton of iron and steel is called a tenement. **skyscraper**

F **2.** People who design office buildings are called social workers. **architects**

T **3.** In the late 1880s, city transportation was improved by the introduction of the electric streetcar.

F **4.** In the 1880s, people coming from eastern and southern Europe to the United States were called the Old Immigration. **New Immigration**

T **5.** Many immigrants from Russia had experienced anti-Jewish riots called pogroms.

T **6.** In the late 1800s a major urban problem was sanitation.

F **7.** Americans who felt that immigration should be greatly reduced were known as political bosses. **nativists**

T **8.** A city building where various services were provided for the poor was a settlement house.

T **9.** A political machine got votes for its candidates by helping immigrants.

F **10.** During the 1880s, great population gains were made in rural areas. **urban or city**

REVIEW QUESTIONS

1. Name some of the problems of growing cities in the late years of the nineteenth century. How did people try to solve them? Which of these problems do we still have?

2. How did the Old Immigration and the New Immigration differ?

3. Why did immigrants settle in neighborhoods where people of their own kind lived? What were the advantages? What were the disadvantages?

ACTIVITIES

1. Most people in the United States are either immigrants or the descendants of immigrants. Make a chart of the backgrounds of your own family. Compare your list with the lists of your classmates. How many different countries have you and your classmates listed?

2. Emma Lazarus wrote a poem entitled "The Great Colossus." The last verse is inscribed on the pedestal of the Statue of Liberty. Find this poem in your library and copy the last verse. What is the message it conveys to immigrants?

3. Describe what you think were the attitudes of the following toward immigrants: (**a**) an employer looking for cheap labor, (**b**) an American concerned about keeping his job, (**c**) a nativist, (**d**) the boss of a political machine in a big city.

20 / SKILLS DEVELOPMENT

MAKING INFERENCES

**DRAWING CONCLUSIONS
FROM EVIDENCE**

Read the following paragraph and answer the questions below.

One can imagine the difficulty of getting around on such streets, whether by horse and wagon, by bicycle, or on foot. In dry weather, wagons raised clouds of choking dust. In rainy weather, the streets became rivers of mud. Whatever the weather, the long skirts that women wore were constantly getting dirty.

1. Is this paragraph about a city of today?
2. Are the streets paved or unpaved?
3. What problems might a horse-drawn wagon have after several days of rain?

Nowhere above does it state that the place is not a city of today or that the streets were unpaved. You probably figured out those facts by using clues, or bits of evidence, you found in the paragraph. You also brought to your reading the knowledge that a heavy wagon will sink in mud. That information helped you to answer the third question.

The process of drawing conclusions from bits of evidence is called *making inferences.* It is an important learning skill. It helps you make the most of the information you have. When you make inferences, you combine the new information with what you already know to draw conclusions. The more evidence you have and the more information you bring to your reading, the more likely it is that you will make correct inferences.

SKILLS PRACTICE

Read the document below carefully. It is New York's Regulations for Teachers in 1872.

1. Teachers each day will fill lamps, clean chimneys and clean wicks.
2. Each teacher will bring a bucket of water and a scuttle of coal for the day's session of school.
3. Make your pens carefully. You may whittle nibs for the individual tastes of the pupils.
4. Men teachers may take one evening a week for courting purposes, or two evenings a week if they attend church regularly.
5. After ten hours in school, teachers should spend the remaining time reading the Bible or other good books.
6. Women teachers who marry or engage in unseemly conduct will be dismissed.
7. Each teacher who smokes, uses liquor in any form, frequents pool or public halls, or gets shaved in a barber shop, will give good reason to suspect his worth, intentions, integrity, and honesty.
8. Each teacher should lay aside from each pay a goodly sum of his earnings for his benefit during his declining years so he will not become a burden on society.
9. The teacher who performs his labors faithfully and without fail for five years will be given an increase of twenty-five cents per week in his pay providing the Board of Education approves.

Now on a sheet of paper, write one thing you can infer from the regulations about each of the following subjects.

1. Differences in attitude toward female and male teachers
2. Freedom of teachers to do as they wished outside of school
3. Teachers' salaries
4. Retirement pay for teachers
5. Care of school buildings
6. What is considered "correct behavior"

461

The word *strike* provides an excellent example of a word with a large number of meanings, both as a verb and as a

Industrialism Changes the Ways of Work

┌─ VOCABULARY ─────────────────┐
labor union   blacklist
strike
└──────────────────────────────┘

A 10-year-old worker   Samuel Gompers learned at first hand about unions and employers early in his working career.   Samuel was born in England in 1850. He attended school for a few years but had to drop out to help bring in income for his family. He took up his father's trade, cigar making. At the age of 10, Samuel was a full-time member of the English working class.

In 1863 the Gompers family moved to the United States. They hoped to escape a life of poverty in England. As it turned out, they simply exchanged their London slum for one on New York's Lower East Side. In their cramped apartment, Samuel and his father rolled tobacco leaves into cigars from early morning until night. After a year, Samuel began to work in the cigar-making shops of New York City. The hours were long and the pay low, but Samuel liked his job.

Belonging to a union   In 1864 the cigar makers formed a **labor union**. A labor union is an organization formed by a group of workers to bargain for higher pay and better working conditions. The 14-year-old Samuel joined the union, though he did not take an active part in it. One day his union called a **strike**—that is, they stopped working in an attempt to gain better wages and working conditions. But the strike was unsuccessful, and the workers finally returned to their jobs without gaining anything.

For Samuel Gompers, however, that was not the end of the matter. Gompers's employer fired him and others who had taken part in the strike. The employer also sent the names of the strikers to other employers, warning them against hiring these troublemakers. Such a list of names is known as a **blacklist.**

For a year and a half, the young Gompers could not work at his trade in New York. He took what jobs he could find in small cigar-making shops in New Jersey. The experience of being blacklisted was one part of Samuel Gompers's education on unions.

A second part came in the factory itself. In cigar factories, workers sitting at long tables did all the work by hand. In a number of such shops, workers took turns reading aloud newspapers, magazines, and books. Other workers chipped in to make up for the work time the reader lost. As the workers rolled the

During the Pullman strike of 1894, the United States cavalry escorts a train loaded with meat as it moves out of the Chicago stockyards past angry strikers.

noun. First review the differences between verbs and nouns with pupils. List on the chalkboard all the meanings pupils can think of for *strike*, separating verb and noun meanings. Then ask pupils to find in a dictionary any definitions they might have missed. Be sure they understand the use of *strike* in this chapter.

1867 The Grange is formed

1869 Knights of Labor started

1873 Depression begins

1877 Baltimore and Ohio Railroad strike

1886 AFL formed/Haymarket Riot

1887 Interstate Commerce Act

1890 Sherman Antitrust Act/
Populist party founded

1892 Homestead strike

1894 Pullman strike

1896 Bryan's "cross of gold" speech

1865   1870   1875   1880   1885   1890   1895   1900

When pupils have finished the chapter, have them add the events on this time line to their large unit time line.   **463**

cigars, they discussed political, social, and economic questions.

It was in these discussions that Gompers first began to think deeply about the problems of labor in an industrial society. He wondered how workers could protect themselves and improve their work conditions. He finally concluded that workers were most likely to make gains by organizing themselves into unions.

Gompers now began to take an active part in the cigar-makers' union. He organized a new branch and was elected as its president at the age of 25. Gompers then turned his efforts to making the national cigar-makers' union stronger.

Samuel Gompers was determined to prove that labor unions could bring about better working conditions.

Machines replace skilled workers
Gompers and others came to their conclusions about unions because industrialism had made great changes in the way people worked. In earlier times, goods like clothing, shoes, and furniture were made by skilled workers in their own homes or in small shops. These workers took pride in the products they made, and they were respected for their skills. Often they worked for themselves, setting their own hours. If they worked for someone else, their employer was usually a skilled worker, too. He knew their families. He worked out agreements with them about wages and conditions of work.

All this changed as small workshops gave way to factories. No longer did one worker make a product from beginning to end. Instead, the work was broken down into many separate steps. Each step was performed by a different worker who always did the same task. For example, in a shoe factory, a worker might stitch soles or nail heels—over and over, all day long. The routine became dull and monotonous. It was hard to take pride in one's work any longer.

In many fields, machines began to do the jobs that skilled workers had done before. "You can take a boy fresh from the farm," said one worker with 30 years experience, "and in 3 days he can manage a machine as well as I can." Many machines were run by young boys and girls, some of them only 7 or 8 years old. Young women, fresh from the farms of the nearby countryside, were also hired. So, too, were unskilled immigrants. All were paid very low wages. Skilled workers could not compete with goods made by lower-paid workers in factories. Many had to give up their trades. Some became factory hands themselves.

Ask: What life experiences would you have missed if you had had to go to work when you were 7 or 8 years old? Do you think you would have been a better person if you had had work experience? Why, or why not?

When Florence Kelley was 12 years old, her father took her to visit a steel mill and a glass factory. She never forgot the sight of 7- and 8-year-old boys working by the intensely hot furnaces. From that time on, the welfare of children became her lifelong work.

Industrialism changed the America of the 1800s in many ways. For instance, at the start of the century, 9 of every 10 Americans made their living by farming, and many of the others were self-employed. By the end of the century, half of all American workers worked for wages.

Working conditions   In the factories of the nineteenth century, working conditions were poor. Buildings were dimly lighted and badly ventilated. Hours were long. It was not unusual for workers to put in 12 to 15 hours a day. They were often not protected from dangerous machinery. A single slip, a moment of inattention, could cost a life or a limb.

Work was even more dangerous for the millions who worked in the mines, on railroads, and in lumbering. In 1891, on railroads alone, more than 7,000 workers were killed and another 33,000 were injured. By 1900 the United States had one of the highest accident rates among industrial countries. Each year, more than 20,000 were killed and 10 times that number were injured. There was no pay for those who couldn't return to work, no health insurance, and no pension for the family of a worker who was killed.

Women and children work, too
Women worked the same long hours and under the same unsafe conditions. Women made up 20 percent of the work force in manufacturing near the end of the century. They made up the largest part of the work force in the garment industry—the making of dresses and other clothing. However, they usually received less pay than men.

Children were widely employed in factories in the late 1800s. The girl shown below in a textile factory probably worked at least 12 hours a day, 6 days a week.

In 1904, Florence Kelley organized the National Child Labor Committee to better protect working children and to seek national legislation against child labor. Finally, in 1912, Congress established the Children's Bureau. In their first project, the Children's Bureau discovered that a quarter of a million infants under a year old were dying each year.

Children made up another important part of the industrial work force. Nearly a quarter-million children worked in factories and mines in the 1880s. Within 10 years that number more than doubled. Boys and girls between 10 and 14 years of age worked 10 to 12 hours a day. In the South especially, where new textile factories were opening in the 1890s, the number of child workers shot upward. Children under 10 years old worked the 12-hour night shift in some southern cotton mills. Their bosses kept the children from falling asleep at their machines by throwing cold water on them from time to time.

One reformer of the time caught the unfairness of child labor in these bitter lines:

The golf links lie so near the mill
That almost every day
The laboring children can look out
And see the men at play.

A sweatshop operator threatens a young woman at a sewing machine, possibly for working too slowly.

As companies grew larger, employers no longer knew those who worked for them. Not surprisingly, many began to think of their workers simply as a cost of production. One New England manufacturer said that he felt the same about his workers as he did about his machines. "So long as they can do my work for what I choose to pay them, I keep them, getting out of them all that I can." When factories built up a surplus of goods from time to time, many owners thought nothing of laying off workers for months.

CHECKUP

1. What early experiences taught Samuel Gompers about labor unions?
2. In what ways were skilled workers affected by the growth of industrialism?
3. How did the increasing use of machines affect safety conditions for wage earners?
4. Describe the conditions under which children worked in factories in the late 1800s.

Workers Organize

┌─ VOCABULARY ─────────────────┐
trade union	anarchist
Knights of Labor	American Federation of Labor
boycott	
└──────────────────────────────┘

The first unions How could workers improve their lot in this new world of work? Certainly not by acting alone. An individual worker, especially one who was unskilled and could be easily replaced, had no chance to bargain for better wages or better hours with an employer. Some workers began to see that if they banded together in a union, they might make employers listen to their demands. If the employer refused to bargain with them, they could strike.

These were the views held by Samuel Gompers. That is why he became so active in his cigar-makers' union in the 1870s. By that time, unions had already been on the scene in America for many years. In the 1820s and 1830s, workers formed a number of **trade unions.** A trade union is one whose members work at a single skilled trade, like printing, baking, or carpentry. However, these early trade unions were weak and unsuccessful. Only a few struggled on into the 1860s.

In 1866 an ironworker named William Sylvis tried to bring all trade unions together into a single organization, the National Labor Union (NLU). The NLU favored an 8-hour day, but its leaders did not believe in strikes. They talked grandly about workers owning factories and mines and being their own employers. NLU leaders also proposed many long-range social reforms.

Most workers, however, were interested in more immediate goals, such as better wages and hours. After Sylvis died in 1869, the organization he built came apart. When the NLU turned to politics and was badly defeated in the election of 1872, most of its members left. The NLU soon disappeared.

The depression of 1873 The 1870s were troubled times for workers. A depression began in 1873 and lasted for 6 years. Workers lost jobs. Others had to accept pay cuts. There was much frustration and anger.

Faced with a fifth wage cut in 3 years, Baltimore and Ohio Railroad workers walked off the job in 1877. The strike spread to railroad lines as far west as St. Louis. In some cities, violence occurred. Dozens were killed or injured, and property worth millions of dollars was destroyed. President Rutherford B. Hayes was forced to call out troops to restore order.

The Knights of Labor During this time, another labor organization was slowly growing. This was the **Knights of Labor.** The organization was started in 1869 to unite "all who toiled"—skilled and unskilled, men and women, black and white—into one big union. Even employers could join. The only people who could not join were gamblers, liquor dealers, bankers, and lawyers.

The Knights of Labor wanted equal pay for men and women, an 8-hour working day, health and safety measures in factories and mines, and an end to child labor. Like the National Labor Union, the Knights of Labor opposed strikes. They also favored some long-range social reforms. One, for example, was a demand for free public land for settlers in the West.

Terence V. Powderly The Knights of Labor grew rapidly after Terence V. Powderly became its head. Powderly had not even known about unions until he was 21 years old. He was born in Pennsylvania in 1849, the son of poor Irish immigrants. At 13 he left school to start working. Some years later, while working in a machine shop in Scranton,

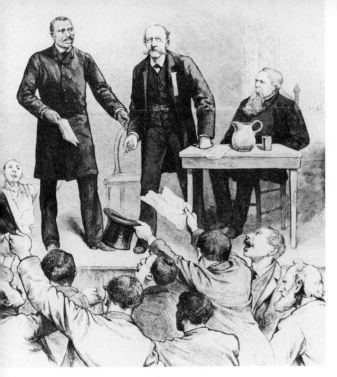

At a Knights of Labor convention, delegate Frank Farrell (left) introduces Terence Powderly.

Pennsylvania, he heard a leader of the coal miners give a talk about unions. Powderly joined the union of skilled machinists, and soon afterwards was elected president of his branch.

Powderly's union activities got him in trouble with his employer. When the depression of 1873 hit, Powderly was one of the first to lose his job. He was also blacklisted and could not find work for some time. A year later, he was shocked at the sight of the charred bodies of coal miners who were killed in a mine explosion. These experiences, he related later, led him to resolve "to improve the conditions of those who work for a living."

Powderly then became a member of the Knights of Labor. He was an exciting speaker and inspired many others to join the group. In 1879 he was elected to head the union. He took office with the pledge, "Labor first, last, and all the time."

Boycotts and strikes   Powderly did not want the Knights of Labor to strike. He thought unions were not strong enough to win strikes. He favored the use of **boycotts** instead. A boycott is an organized campaign in which people refuse to buy goods or services from or have any dealings with a particular group or company. The Knights of Labor used boycotts successfully a number of times.

The union also used the strike, despite their leader's opposition to it. In fact, successful strikes led to the biggest period of growth for the Knights of Labor. After one successful strike against a powerful railroad, membership jumped from 100,000 to 700,000 in a year.

The strike was a two-edged sword, however. When the group lost a big strike later on, workers dropped out almost as rapidly as they had earlier joined.

The Haymarket Riot   The Knights of Labor suffered a crippling blow in 1886. During a strike for an 8-hour day at the McCormick Harvesting Machine Company in Chicago, workers clashed with police. One worker was killed and several others were injured. **Anarchists**—radicals who wanted to do away with all government—called a protest rally at Haymarket Square the next day. The rally was orderly. As police moved in near the end, someone—to this day no one knows who—threw a bomb, killing seven people. Eight anarchists were tried and convicted; four were executed.

The Knights of Labor had nothing at all to do with the rally at Haymarket Square, but they became connected with the violence in the minds of many Ameri-

Ask: Many people were angry about labor conditions in the late 1800s. What makes some people, like Gompers and Powderly, stand up and do something to change unsatisfactory conditions while other people do nothing but complain?

During a strike in Chicago in 1886, a bomb explodes at a mass meeting. Though anarchists were convicted for the crime, many people blamed the Knights of Labor.

cans. Public opinion turned against the union. More members dropped out. Although the Knights of Labor continued to exist for a number of years, they were never effective after the violent events of the Haymarket rally.

Gompers and the AFL   Like many other members of trade unions, Samuel Gompers's cigar makers were also members of the Knights of Labor. But Gompers and the trade unionists did not share many of Powderly's beliefs. They had no patience with the vague, long-term reform goals of Powderly's group. They believed that unions should seek gains for their members in the present, rather than try to reform society in a distant future. Unions should concentrate on "bread-and-butter" issues such as wages, hours, and safety in the workplace. Gompers also believed that the strike was an important weapon for labor.

The best chance for success, Gompers said, lay in organizing skilled workers. A strike of skilled workers would be more successful than one of unskilled workers, who could easily be replaced by an employer. The workers should be organized by their special skills. Workers who did the same kind of work in the same industry were more likely to share the same problems, agree on common goals, and stick together to reach them.

In 1886, Gompers and other trade union leaders organized the **American Federation of Labor** (AFL). Members were not individual workers but rather the trade unions the workers belonged to. The AFL was a union of unions. It helped promote the unions' organizing work and settled problems that might arise among them. Gompers was elected the first president of the AFL. He was reelected every year except one until his death in 1924.

Opposing the unions   Employers resisted unions every step of the way. Their views were summed up by the mine owner who said, "I . . . will employ no one that belongs to any labor organization, and will at once discharge . . . any man who has anything to do with any labor organization." Companies used blacklists and other methods to keep unions from getting started. Workers who went on strike risked their jobs, for employers might hire others to take their place. Some companies even hired private armies to do battle with strikers.

A strike in 1892 showed how bitter the struggle between workers and employers had become—and how hard it was for unions to win. In that year, the Carnegie steel plant at Homestead, Pennsylvania, announced a wage cut. The ironworkers' union went out on strike. The company brought in 300 armed men from a detective agency to battle the strikers. Men on both sides were killed. After several months, the strike was broken and the union crushed. The company took back only 10 percent of the strikers, and fired and blacklisted the rest.

470

The Pullman strike   Two years later, the unions suffered another setback. Workers for the Pullman Company went on strike in Illinois. This company manufactured railroad cars. George Pullman, the owner, cut wages five times in 1 year when business slowed down. However, he refused to lower the rent he charged workers who lived in his company-owned houses. When several workers went to see him about this, Pullman fired them. Angry workers went on strike. They were joined by members of the American Railway Union, a union of railroad workers. In Chicago, the railroad workers refused to handle trains that included Pullman cars. Railroads across the country came to a standstill.

The United States government stepped in. Trains carried the mails, so the government got a court to order the workers not to interfere with the mails. President Grover Cleveland sent 2,000 troops to Chicago to see that the order was obeyed. This touched off violence. Men were killed; property was destroyed. As a re-

For his part in the Pullman strike, Eugene Debs, the president of the American Railway Union, was jailed.

sult, the strike was broken. The leader of the American Railway Union, Eugene V. Debs, spent 6 months in jail for disobeying a court order.

Despite such setbacks, organized labor made steady gains. By 1904, union membership rose to 2 million workers. The AFL accounted for most of these people. Gompers's approach to unionism proved to be the most effective for its time. Under Gompers's leadership, labor unions came to be accepted.

CHECKUP

1. Why were trade unions formed?
2. What means did Terence Powderly favor to advance the cause of labor?
3. How did the Haymarket Riot affect the Knights of Labor?
4. Why were the McCormick Harvesting and Pullman strikes regarded as setbacks to labor unions?

Farmers Organize

```
┌─ VOCABULARY ──────────────────┐
│  Grange              Populist  │
│  cooperative         platform  │
│  Interstate          initiative│
│     Commerce Act     referendum│
│  Sherman             free coinage│
│     Antitrust Act       of silver│
│  Farmers'            gold standard│
│     Alliance                   │
└────────────────────────────────┘
```

Mary Lease speaks for the farmers "We were told two years ago," the tall, slim woman said to the gathering of Kansas farmers, "to go to work and raise a big crop, that was all we needed. We went to work and plowed and planted;

Mary Lease of Kansas was an effective spokeswoman for the hard-pressed farmers of America.

the rains fell, the sun shone, nature smiled, and we raised the big crop they told us to; and what came of it?" All of her listeners, she was aware, knew the answer all too well. "Eight-cent corn, ten-cent oats, two-cent beef, and no price at all for butter and eggs—that's what came of it. Then," she added bitterly, "the politicians said we suffered from overproduction."

Mary Lease knew about the hardships of western farmers firsthand. The daughter of Irish immigrants, she had moved to Kansas from the East at age 20, taught school briefly, and married a young pharmacist. The couple decided to try their hand at farming. For 10 years they struggled to make a go of it. Finally the debts, the falling prices, and the loneliness of farm life were just too much. The Leases gave up.

Mary Lease then took up the cause of the debt-ridden farmers of Kansas, even though she was no longer one of them. As a public speaker she had a deep, powerful voice, and as her words show, she knew how to express her thoughts. When farmers decided to form a political party to seek solutions to their problems in 1890, they welcomed Mary Lease's help. That year she made 160 speeches. Two years later, in the presidential election, she traveled through the West and the South seeking support for the party's candidates. In one state she spoke to eight different groups in a single day.

She was not always favorably received. A southern newspaper wrote that "the sight of a woman traveling around the country making political speeches . . . [is] simply disgusting." Such comments, however, did not stop Mary Lease.

The farm problem   Mary Lease was one of hundreds who spoke out about the sorry condition of many farmers in the 1880s and 1890s. For two centuries, part of the American dream had been to farm one's own land. Millions were now doing that; but something had gone wrong with the dream.

Most of the problem resulted from the industrialism that was changing so much else in American life. Before industrialism, most farms in the United States,

New machines and improvements to old machines brought about a dramatic rise in crop production. This steam-powered machine threshed thousands of bushels of wheat daily.

The Farmers' Department Store

No. 13. THE ONWARD.
Our Drive Price $42.25
Retails everywhere at $75.00 and upwards.

Our Drive Price $42.95.

No. 14.
THE FORWARD.

For farm families the mail-order catalog furnished delightful reading.

While city dwellers shopped in large department stores, most farm families in the late nineteenth century were limited to the country store. There, choices were few and prices were often high. A growing number, however, had already begun to buy goods in a different way—by mail order.

Mail-order merchants at first relied upon advertisements in the small newspapers and magazines that many farmers bought. By the 1890s, however, the larger companies such as Montgomery Ward and Sears, Roebuck and Company were sending out catalogs that described thousands of items for sale.

The illustrated catalog quickly became the farmers' department store. For weeks after it arrived, family members feasted their eyes on items from watches and clothing to baby carriages, bicycles, sewing machines, and farm wagons.

Buying from catalogs became widespread in rural areas after 1900. Sears, Roebuck and Company printed 300,000 catalogs in 1897, but 30 years later the company distributed 65 million! By then, Sears was the largest retail seller of goods in the world.

Not only were mail-order catalogs found in nearly every farm home. In many one-room schoolhouses, children practiced reading and spelling from the catalogs. For practice in arithmetic, they filled out make-believe orders and added up the cost of the items. To some the catalog was known as "the wish book," to others simply as "the big book." By any name, mail-order catalogs helped to bridge the gap between city and country and to make farmers' lives better.

except for some southern cotton and tobacco plantations, were small. The farm family raised a variety of crops and animals for its own needs, and sometimes a little more for sale. Farmers did not plant many acres.

Inventions like the mechanical reaper began to make changes as early as the 1830s. In the last half of the nineteenth century, improvements on old tools and machines, and the invention of new ones frequently made it possible for a farmer to plant and harvest many more acres. For example, a single farmer could produce nearly 20 times as much wheat with a day's labor in the 1890s as he could 50 years earlier.

New machines, however, were expensive. It only paid to use them on large farms. So farmers bought more land. They also specialized in a single crop, which they sold for cash. As this happened, farming became more and more a business.

In November 1860 a reporter for a magazine wrote "...There are now...within a range of ten miles... twelve of these steam threshers running steadily during the threshing season.... (Threshing) is done by men who purchase a threshing machine and go from farm to farm threshing each man's crop for so much per bushel."

The business of farming Farmers, like other business people, now had to consider several factors if they were to succeed. One was the price they got for their product. A second was the cost of producing it. A third was the cost of getting it to market. In the last part of the nineteenth century, all three factors and more worked against the American farmer.

Take the first factor, price. Price is largely determined by supply and demand. A poor harvest reduces supply and causes prices to rise. A good harvest increases supply and causes prices to fall. But in the late nineteenth century, trains and steamships—the products of industrialism—began to carry crops swiftly and cheaply from one part of the world to another. Thus, grain grown on newly opened farmlands in Russia, Canada, Australia, and several South American countries competed with grain grown on the Great Plains. Price was now determined by supply and demand in the whole world, not just in the United States.

Most farmers did not understand the full meaning of that fact. They had always lived by the simple idea that the harder they worked and the more crops they grew, the more money they would earn. And so in the late nineteenth century, American farmers tripled the production of wheat and corn, and more than doubled the production of cotton. That increased world supply, and prices fell still more.

As for costs of production, the price of farm machinery was high. Taxes on land and farm buildings were high. And when the farmers borrowed money to buy more land or to see them through hard times, they found that interest rates were high, too. Charges of 17 to 25 percent a year were common in the West. In the South, where many farmers had to buy supplies on credit from storekeepers, interest ran from 40 to 100 percent a year.

Transportation costs, the third factor in determining whether or not farmers would make money, were also high. Railroads set freight rates low on routes where there was competition, and high where there was none. The latter was usually the case in farming country. One railroad charged five times as much to carry freight west of Chicago as to carry it east of that city. West of Chicago, there was no competition; east of Chicago, there was. Some farmers had to pay to the railroads half what they received for their crops. They also paid high charges for storing their crops in warehouses and grain elevators. Many of these were owned by the railroads.

A final problem that farmers experienced is harder to pinpoint but just as important. It was the feeling that they were not sharing in the progress of the nation. They felt left behind. Once they had been the ideal citizens, the backbone of the republic. Now they felt that city folks looked down on them as "hicks" and "hayseeds."

The Grangers Faced with these many problems, farmers began to organize. In 1867, Oliver H. Kelley, a clerk in the United States Department of Agriculture, founded an organization commonly called the **Grange**. The purpose of the

At one Grange convention a Granger said, "We propose meeting together, talking together, working together, buying together, and in general acting together for our mutual protection and advancement as occasion may require."

At an outdoor meeting in Illinois in 1873, members of the Grange gather to talk over their problems and to devise ways of solving them. Their discussion centered on low prices for their crops and high prices for farm machinery and transportation.

organization was to bring farm families together for social and educational gatherings. Soon, however, farmers were talking about their common problems and how to deal with them.

In a number of midwestern states, Grangers—members of the Grange— pooled their money and formed **cooperatives.** A cooperative is an organization that is owned and operated for the benefit of those who use its goods and services. Grangers set up factories to make machinery, built their own warehouses, and formed their own insurance companies. Grangers also got the legislatures in Illinois, Iowa, Minnesota, and Wisconsin to pass laws regulating railroad rates. These laws were known as Granger laws.

The Granger movement did not prosper for long, however. A number of the cooperatives failed, leaving Grange members with huge debts. With the return of better crop prices in the late 1870s, interest and membership in the Grange fell.

Regulating interstate commerce   The Granger laws, too, became less effective as the result of several later decisions of the Supreme Court. In the most important of these, the Court said that a state's Granger law could apply only to traffic that was entirely within that state. Once

Of Grange meetings, Hamlin Garland (*A Son of the Middle Border*) recalled, "It was grand, it was inspiring — to us, to see those long lines of carriages winding down the lanes…till…all the granges…were united in one mighty column advancing on the picnic ground…. Each of these assemblies was a most grateful relief from the sordid loneliness of the farm…."

the traffic crossed state lines, it was interstate commerce, or trade between two or more states. Under the Constitution, only Congress had the power to regulate interstate commerce. This decision came in 1886.

The following year, Congress used that power and passed the **Interstate Commerce Act.** This law forbade railroads to charge unfair rates, give rebates to favored shippers, and charge more for short distances than for long ones. The law also set up an Interstate Commerce Commission (ICC) to see that the law was carried out. However, Congress did not give the ICC enough power to do its job. For many years the law did not work well. Nonetheless, the Interstate Commerce Act was an important first—it marked the first time the federal government regulated business.

Regulating the trusts   An attempt to stop the growth of trusts and monopolies proved no more effective. This was the **Sherman Antitrust Act** of 1890. The Sherman act declared that trusts and other ways of restricting trade were illegal.

However, the law's wording was vague, and companies found ways to get around it. When the government did occasionally charge a business with wrongdoing, the courts usually sided with the business. After a while the law was hardly used. The number of trusts and monopolies continued to grow.

Farmers enter politics   The 1880s were hard times for the farmers. Many had to give up their farms. One response

to the hard times were the **Farmers' Alliances**, which were organized throughout the West and the South. More than 2.5 million farmers joined. They believed that neither of the main political parties—Republicans or Democrats—would help farmers. So in 1890 the alliances entered politics. They elected many people to local and state offices, and to the United States Congress. It was in this election campaign that Mary Lease made the bitter speech you read earlier in this chapter.

Encouraged by this success, the alliances, together with some reformers and labor leaders, formed a national party which they called the People's party, or **Populists.**   At its convention in 1892, the new party chose General James Weaver of Iowa, a Civil War veteran, to run for President.

This cartoon ridicules the People's, or Populist, party. The party is pictured as a leaky balloon, patched together by various small political groups.

Born: 1837, Caldwell, New Jersey. **Education:** Public school to age 14. Later read law. **Training:** Lawyer, public official. **To presidency from:** New York. **Position when first elected:** Governor of New York. **Political party:** Democratic. **Married:** Frances Folsom. **Children:** Three daughters, two sons. **Died:** 1908. **Other facts:** A big, good-humored man who weighed 260 pounds (118 kg) when he became President. Called "Uncle Jumbo" by his relatives. The only President married in the White House. Daughter Esther was the only child of a President to be born in the White House. The only President to serve two terms that were not successive. **During his presidency:** The Statue of Liberty was unveiled in New York Harbor.

GROVER CLEVELAND
22nd and 24th President
1885 · 1889, 1893 · 1897

What the Populists wanted The bitterness and despair of Populists can be seen in the language of their **platform**, or statement of party goals. "We meet in the midst of a nation brought to the verge of moral, political, and material ruin," the platform began. "Corruption dominates the ballot box. . . . The fruits of the toil of millions are boldly stolen to build up colossal fortunes for a few. . . ." The platform added that "government injustice" had turned the population into "two great classes—tramps and millionaires."

The platform went on to propose major changes. These included

• the government ownership of railroads, telegraphs, and telephones, which would be run "in the interests of the people"

• the secret ballot

• the direct election of senators by the voters. At that time senators were chosen by the state legislatures.

• the **initiative** and **referendum.** The initiative allows the people themselves to propose a law by signing a petition. If enough people sign, the legislature must examine the proposal and vote on it. The referendum allows the people to vote directly on a proposed law. Their vote is final.

• a shorter workday for those laboring in factories and mines

• government-run savings banks where people could safely deposit money without using the hated banks

• a graduated income tax. Those with large incomes would pay a greater percentage of their earnings than those with small incomes.

• the **free coinage of silver**

The last proposal, the free coinage of silver, needs explanation. Until 1873 the United States government had minted both silver and gold dollars. In that year the government stopped making silver coins. At just about that time, much silver was found in new mines in Nevada and Colorado. Populists wanted the government to allow silver to be coined again. The idea was that if *both* gold and silver dollars circulated, the supply of money would be increased. This would cause prices to rise. Farmers would get higher prices for their crops and could pay their debts more easily. Not surprisingly, silver mine owners also wanted the government to buy silver and coin it.

The Populists made a good showing for a new party in the 1892 election. President Benjamin Harrison, a Republican, was seeking reelection against the Democrat Grover Cleveland, a former President himself. Cleveland was elected, but Populist James Weaver received a million votes (about 9 percent of all the votes cast) and carried four western states. Populists also elected three governors and a number of United States senators and representatives.

Another depression   No sooner did Grover Cleveland become President for the second time, in 1893, than a depression began. Banks and businesses failed. Farm prices dropped still further and more farmers lost their farms. In the cities, 20 percent of the workers were unemployed, and many who still had jobs took wage cuts. Anger and frustration built up. There were hundreds of strikes. Many were accompanied by violence. The largest was the Pullman strike that you read about earlier.

Like many other Americans of the time, President Cleveland held to the belief that there was nothing government could or should do in a depression. The job of helping those who were suffering from unemployment belonged to private charities and local government, he said. Not everyone agreed. Charities and local governments were running out of money. Some proposed that the federal government hire unemployed men to build roads. But this proposal was never seriously considered.

Even in the best of times, farm families had to work hard—as this painting suggests—to wrench a living from the soil. But the margin between profit and loss was very small. When crop prices dropped in 1893, many families had to give up their farms.

Born: 1833, North Bend, Ohio.   **Education:** Miami (Ohio) University.   **Training:** Lawyer, public official. **To presidency from:** Indiana.   **Position when elected:** United States senator.   **Political party:** Republican. **Married:** (1) Caroline Lavinia Scott, (2) Mary Lord Dimmick.   **Children:** Two daughters, one son.   **Died:** 1901, Indianapolis, Indiana.   **Other facts:** Recruited and commanded an Indiana regiment in Civil War. Called "Little Ben" by his men because he was 5 feet 6 inches (170 cm) tall.   While he was President, electric lights were installed in the White House.   **During his presidency:** James Naismith, a physical-education teacher at what is now Springfield (Massachusetts) College, started the game of basketball, using two peach baskets and a soccer ball.

BENJAMIN HARRISON
23rd President
1889 · 1893

Cleveland also strongly opposed coining silver.   Most business people shared this opposition.   They said that coining silver would cheapen the dollar and be bad for business.   Bankers said it would be unfair to be paid back in dollars worth less than the ones they had loaned out. Many wage earners also were opposed to coining silver and adding to the money supply.   They feared that if prices rose, their wages would buy less.

With each passing month of hard times, the money question came to overshadow all others.   The country was divided on the question.   Westerners and southerners in the President's own Democratic party disagreed with him.   They favored silver.

Gold or silver?   For the presidential election of 1896, the Republican party chose William McKinley of Ohio as its candidate.   The Republican party came out firmly against the free coinage of silver.   It favored the **gold standard**—that is, that the money supply of the country should be based on gold only.

At the Democratic convention, those who favored silver were in the majority. The debate in the convention over the money question produced the party's candidate for President, William Jennings Bryan of Nebraska.   Born and raised in Illinois, Bryan had moved to Nebraska to open a law practice with a college friend. He soon became active in politics.   He was an excellent speaker with a beautiful, clear voice that carried a great distance. That was an important quality for a speaker in the days before microphones. In 1890 he was elected to Congress and served two terms.   By 1894 he had decided to seek the presidency.   He spent the next 2 years making speeches around the country to become better known. Still, by the time of the Democratic convention in 1896, few thought the 36-year-old Bryan had much chance for the nomination.   He was too young and too inexperienced, said the party leaders, to become the Democratic candidate.

But Bryan had planned carefully.   As he rose to make his speech in favor of silver, a friend passed him a note that read, "This is a great opportunity." Bryan scribbled a quick reply: "You will not be disappointed."

What followed was one of the most famous speeches in American history. Bryan declared that he was speaking for the small farmers of the nation who "are fighting in the defense of our homes, our families, and prosperity."

> You come to us and tell us that the great cities are in favor of the gold standard; we reply that the great cities rest upon our broad and fertile prairies. Burn down your cities and leave our farms, and your cities will spring up again as if by magic; but destroy our farms and the grass will grow in the streets of every city in the country.

At the end of what has become known as the "cross of gold" speech, Bryan threw down the challenge to the opponents of silver.

This cartoon, critical of Bryan and his supporters, pictures them as dummies manipulated by a ventriloquist who represents the silver mine owners.

Having behind us the producing masses of this nation and the world, supported by the commercial interests, the laboring interest, and the toilers everywhere, we will answer their demand for a gold standard by saying to them: You shall not press down upon the brow of labor this crown of thorns, you shall not crucify mankind upon a cross of gold.

With that, the convention went wild. The Democrats had found their leader. They supported the free coinage of silver, and William Jennings Bryan was named their candidate for President.

The dramatic election of 1896 Populists now faced a problem. To join the Democrats in support of Bryan would mean the end of the Populists as a separate party. But if they ran their own candidate, that would split the free-silver vote and give the election to the Republicans. In the end, the Populists supported Bryan.

The campaign of 1896 was one of the most dramatic in our history. Bryan, the youngest man ever to run for President, traveled 18,000 miles (28,800 km) and gave 600 speeches. He was the first ever to wage this kind of active campaign. On the other hand, contributions from business people and bankers who feared free silver gave the Republicans the largest amount of campaign funds ever collected up to that time. In some businesses, employers ordered their workers either to vote for McKinley or lose their jobs.

Bryan won support from the farmers of the South and the West, but he did not do well among either workers or the urban middle class. McKinley won the election.

McKinley was born in Ohio in 1843. His election in 1896 was said to represent a victory of newer, industrial America over older, agricultural America.

After his dramatic "cross of gold" speech, William Jennings Bryan is carried off the floor of the convention hall on the shoulders of his jubilant supporters.

Soon after the 1896 election, the economy improved. Poor harvests in Europe led to higher farm prices. Gold was found in Alaska, adding to the money supply. Business picked up. Farm protest quieted down, and the Populist party lost its appeal. It broke up into small factions, and soon the party disappeared from the political scene.

The Populists, however, made an important contribution. They were the first American party to favor using the power of the federal government to deal with social and economic problems. Many of their ideas in time became law.

CHECKUP

1. How did the growth of industrialism bring on a farm problem in the 1880s?
2. What steps did the Grange take to improve the lot of farmers?
3. List five goals of the People's party, or Populists.
4. What was the issue with regard to silver in the 1896 election?
5. Who were the candidates in that election, and who won?

Ask pupils to compare the drama of the 1896 election to the most recent presidential election.

481

21/CHAPTER REVIEW

KEY FACTS

1. In the late 1800s, many children between the ages of 10 and 14 worked 12 hours a day in mines and factories.

2. Workers organized labor unions in an effort to get higher wages and better working conditions.

3. Farmers in the late 1800s produced more than ever before, but they earned less. This was because the prices of farm products fell while the costs of machinery and transportation remained high.

4. Farmers and reformers founded the People's, or Populist, party to seek remedies for their problems through politics.

5. In the early 1890s the United States experienced a severe depression.

VOCABULARY QUIZ

On a separate piece of paper, match each word or phrase with the correct description. There are two extra descriptions.

a. anarchist **f.** Grange
b. blacklist **g.** cooperative
c. strike **h.** initiative
d. boycott **i.** platform
e. trade union **j.** referendum

1. An organization of all workers, both skilled and unskilled, in an industry

b **2.** The names of workers who were not to be given jobs

f **3.** A social organization for farm families

i **4.** A statement of a political party's goals

e **5.** An organization of skilled workers

c **6.** The stopping of work to get an employer to agree to workers' demands

g **7.** An organization that buys and sells for the benefit of its members

j **8.** The right of the people to vote directly for or against laws

d **9.** The refusal to deal with a particular group or company

10. An organization headed by Mary Lease

a **11.** A person who wants to do away with government

h **12.** The right of the people to introduce new laws

REVIEW QUESTIONS

1. What problems or abuses were each of the following laws supposed to correct? **(a)** Sherman Antitrust Act, **(b)** Interstate Commerce Act, **(c)** Granger laws

2. How did industrialism change the way that people worked? What were the advantages of industrialism? What problems did industrialism create?

3. Name and explain five of the proposals put forth in the Populist platform.

4. How did the amount of wheat grown in other countries in the late 1800s affect wheat farmers in the United States?

5. What effect did the Haymarket Riot and the Pullman strike have on union membership?

ACTIVITIES

1. In an encyclopedia or other reference book, find the origin of Labor Day. Be prepared to report your findings to the class.

2. In an almanac find the number of people in the labor force for the past 10 censuses. Make a line graph to show how the number of workers has changed.

3. In your library look up the story of Jacob Coxey and Coxey's army. How is this story related to the depression of the 1890s?

WRITING A DESCRIPTION

FOR MORE VIVID WRITING

When you write a description, you want the reader to *see* exactly what you are describing. You also want the reader to be interested in what you write. One way to make your writing more interesting and vivid is to use adjectives and adverbs. Study the following examples:

a. The boy worked at the factory.
b. The young boy worked long hours at the noisy, windowless factory.

Which sentence is more interesting and vivid? In the first example you were given information. In the second a picture was created for you. The writer used adjectives to help you see this picture.

Another way to make your writing more interesting and vivid is to vary sentence beginnings. This keeps your writing from becoming monotonous. Try to begin one sentence with a phrase or clause that answers *who*. Begin another with a phrase or clause that answers *when*. Other sentences could tell *where*, *why*, or *how*. Often it won't be possible to use *all* these sentence beginnings in every paragraph. But following this guideline will bring variety to your writing.

SKILLS PRACTICE

Read the following paragraph.

In the early morning the young lad trudges wearily to the badly ventilated factory. Because his family needs his income, he cannot go to school. He spends twelve hours each day at a large noisy machine. Next to him, another exhausted boy is about to fall asleep. By throwing cold water on him, the foreman keeps the boy awake.

On a sheet of paper, list all the adjectives and adverbs. For example, in the first sentence these words are *early*, *young*, *wearily*, *badly*, and *ventilated*. Then write the phrase or clause that tells *who*, *when*, *where*, *how*, and *why*.

Study the picture on this page, and note as many details as you can. Using the suggestions above, write a paragraph describing the picture for someone who cannot see it.

How Americans Lived, 1900

THE UNITED STATES

YEAR: 1900

AREA: 2,969,834 sq mi
7,691,870 sq km

POPULATION: 75,994,575

POPULATION
DENSITY: 26 per sq mi
10 per sq km

NUMBER
OF STATES: 45

LARGEST STATE
IN AREA: Texas

IN POPULATION: New York

LARGEST CITY: New York

WHERE PEOPLE
LIVED:

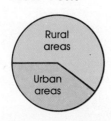

vaudeville   life expectancy

During the last half of the nineteenth century, the United States became increasingly industrial and urban. Although more than half of the American population still lived on farms, in villages, and in small towns, the number of people living in cities was increasing rapidly.

By 1900, the ways of life in urban and rural America had grown apart in many respects. One example of the growing differences between city and countryside were the way residents spent their leisure time.

Leisure time in a small town   Sinclair Lewis was a famous American writer in the 1920s and 1930s. His best-known books, such as *Main Street* and *Babbitt*, were about small-town America. It was a subject that Lewis knew firsthand, having grown up in the small town of Sauk Centre, Minnesota. In 1900, when Harry Sinclair Lewis was 15 years old, Sauk Centre had a population of about 2,200. Main Street would not be paved for another 24 years, and residents walked on wooden sidewalks.

Within 10 miles (16 km) of Sauk Centre were more than 30 lakes. These lakes were year-round playgrounds for young people like Harry Lewis. (It was only in later years that he started using his middle name.) In warm weather the young folks

The town that Sinclair Lewis called Gopher Prairie in his novel *Main Street* was based on Sauk Centre. In the book Carol Kennicott, the principal figure, tries to improve the quality of life in what Lewis satirically portrayed as a dull and cultureless town.

swam, fished, and floated on rafts they had made from logs. There was duck hunting in autumn, and ice skating in winter. On the nearby hills, young people sledded.

Although it was small, the village of Sauk Centre offered both its young and adult residents a good many public entertainments. In 1900, many professional entertainers toured America's small towns. At the Sauk Centre opera house, residents could watch a play, listen to a lecture, hear a dramatic reading, or attend a concert. The concert might be anything from a choral group or military band to a lone performer playing tunes on musical glasses. The opera house was also the site of occasional sporting events, such as wrestling matches.

Entertainments such as these were not late-night activities. In Sauk Centre, as in nearly all other small towns in 1900, there were no streetlights. People were usually in bed at 9:00 or 10:00 P.M. and up again at 4:00 or 5:00 A.M.

Then there was the circus. A writer who grew up in a small midwestern town later recalled, "From the time the 'advance man' flung his highly colored posters over the fence till the coming of the glorious day, we thought of little else." With its acrobats, animal acts, clowns, and death-defying feats on the trapeze and the high wire, the circus gave the people of Sauk Centre and of a hundred other villages and towns across the land their most exciting day of the year.

Mostly, however, residents of Sauk Centre provided their own entertainment. There were frequent dances: school dances, a fireman's dance, and special dances run by the town's social clubs. Even people like Harry Lewis who couldn't dance went along anyway to look on. And there were picnics, county fairs, and gun-shooting contests. Baseball was popular among Sauk Centre residents. During the warm weather, one could always find pickup games going on.

Leisure time in the city By 1900, city people had more leisure time than ever before. This was due to the invention of labor-saving machinery. In 1860 the average worker was on the job 6 days a week and put in 66 hours of labor. In

In areas where winters were cold, ice skating was a popular pastime in both small towns and cities.

Ask: What forms of entertainment did small towns have in 1900 that are different in kind or in degree from the entertainment available today?

1900 the number of hours per week for the average worker was under 60. Many city dwellers now worked 5½ days a week, or even 5 days.

How did city people use their new leisure time? Certainly they provided some of their own entertainment, as their country cousins did. Young people skated and sledded in winter, and in summer one could find a baseball game on nearly every vacant city lot. However, as cities became more crowded, there were fewer empty lots. Local governments found it necessary to create playgrounds as special areas for recreation.

The most popular sport in America in 1900 was bicycling. Probably 2 million Americans owned bicycles in that year. Both men and women bicycled, sometimes together on a "bicycle built for two." Because it was difficult to ride a bicycle on the unpaved, bumpy, and often muddy streets of villages, cycling was especially popular in the cities. In 1900, many bicyclists were members of cycling clubs. These groups put pressure on local and state government to provide more paved roads.

However, by 1900, entertainment in cities was becoming more and more an organized activity—even a business. City people were becoming spectators rather than participants. Professional baseball was already a big business in 1900. Occasionally, crowds as large as 50,000 watched National League teams play. In 1901, a new league, the American League, was formed, and 2 years later the champions of each league played in the first World Series. (The Boston Red

At the turn of the century, bicycling was the favorite sport of Americans.

Ask: Why, do you suppose, is bicycling not so widespread as an organized sport as it was in 1900?

Socks won over the Pittsburgh Pirates.) College football was also a popular sport. In addition to the thousands who watched the games, millions more followed them through the sports page of their newspapers—a feature that had been added to the papers in the 1880s.

Those who lived in large cities could choose from many stage plays, musical comedies, and concerts every night of the week. In 1900 the most popular theater entertainment was the **vaudeville** show. Vaudeville shows were variety shows that included song-and-dance acts, comedy, magic shows, animal acts, juggling, and the like.

In 1900 there was even something new called the moving picture. Thomas Edison had invented the moving picture in the 1880s. For the next 10 years or so, curious Americans put their nickels in a "peep-show" machine to see the flickering images. By 1900 a few promoters were using moving-picture projectors to put these images onto a large screen in front of seated audiences. It was a hint of things to come.

Medical care in a rural area   There were also growing differences between rural and urban America in the kind and quality of medical care available.

What kind of training did the country doctor of 1900 have? If he was an older man (nearly all doctors were men), he had learned medicine as a young man by working a year or two for a doctor—who himself had probably learned medicine the same way. No license was needed to practice medicine, and there were no examinations to pass. Young doctors in

The peep show was the forerunner of motion pictures.

1900 were more likely to have gone to medical school—but not to college. Normally, one went straight from high school to medical school. Most medical schools were little more than two or three classrooms, with no laboratories. The course of study was 2 years. Students spent half of each year attending lectures and the other half getting on-the-job experience in a hospital.

In small towns, villages, and farm areas, patients did not visit doctors. Doctors visited patients. There was no good medical reason for going to a country doctor's office, for he had little special equipment there. A doctor could carry all his instruments and medicines in his small black bag.

One of the first motion pictures that told a story was *The Great Train Robbery*. It lasted 11 minutes and showed a robbery and the chase and capture of the robbers. This movie created a sensation when it was first shown in 1903.

Ask: Why, do you suppose, did doctors in 1900 regularly make house calls? Why do very few doctors do it today?

A country doctor Sinclair Lewis's father's career as a doctor in small-town Minnesota was typical. Dr. Edwin Lewis began his practice of medicine in Ironton. Dr. Lewis visited all his patients in their homes. For house calls less than 3 miles away, he usually walked. For those more than 3 miles distant, he rode on horseback. Once a week Dr. Lewis rode to the neighboring town of Melrose, which had no doctor of its own.

After moving to Sauk Centre, Dr. Lewis opened an office on the town's main street. However, he continued to visit most of his patients in their homes. The main change from his Ironton days was that he now traveled by horse and buggy rather than on horseback.

The country doctor was truly a family doctor. That meant that he attended not only the sick person but also everyone else who was in the household. He checked the pulse, looked at the tongue and throat, observed the general appearance, and asked questions about each person's health. Although mercury thermometers had been invented some years before, the average doctor considered them unnecessary and rarely used them.

For many sick patients there was little that a doctor could do to help them. In the first place, not one doctor in a thousand could perform the scientific tests that would show whether the patient had an infection, such as tuberculosis or pneumonia, two of the most feared killers of the time. Second, there were no medicines to combat infections. For fever, pain, or general weakness, doctors ordered bed rest and a tonic. The tonic usually contained large amounts of alcohol or opium, and sometimes both!

In rural areas, a doctor was often paid for his services "in kind." This meant that patients might pay him with firewood, oats for his horses, bushels of wheat, or even days of work in his field or stable. Practicing medicine in rural America was not the easiest way to earn a living in 1900. Few country doctors earned large incomes.

A country doctor in the mountains of eastern Tennessee attends a young patient in her home.

Medical care in the city City doctors had a number of things in common with country doctors in 1900. City doctors, too, were mainly family doctors; and they had no better medicines than did the country doctor. However, by 1900, some important differences between medical practice in the city and the countryside had appeared.

One difference was in training. An increasing number of city doctors had gone to college and had studied basic science before going to medical school. And at least at some of the better medical schools, scientific training was increased.

Although city doctors treated many of their patients in their homes, a growing number were keeping office hours by 1900. This was mainly so that they could make use of new medical equipment, such as the X-ray machine.

Also, there were enough patients in the city to allow some doctors to specialize in certain illnesses. By 1900 a number of them were doing so. This meant that patients who could afford it could receive treatment from a doctor familiar with the latest methods for their special health problems.

Every city had at least one hospital, but that was not an advantage to most city dwellers. This was because in 1900, hospitals were mainly for the poor. Such patients were treated by doctors who donated their time or by young medical students getting their training. As the patients got better, they were expected to work in the wards, helping others.

People who could afford private doctors did not use hospitals. Women nearly always gave birth in their own homes. In 1900, even surgery like removing an appendix took place in the patient's home. In fact, nearly 20 years later, a magazine for doctors carried an article explaining how to hook up an automobile battery to a portable electric light for performing nighttime surgery in the patient's home.

Even with the improved medical knowledge of 1900, however, common

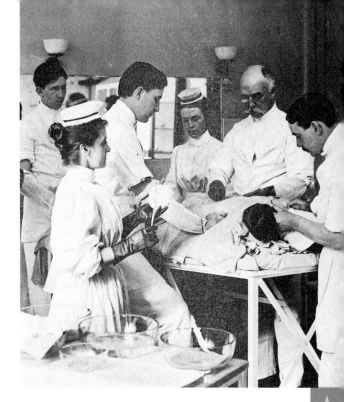

A surgeon, aided by nurses and other doctors, performs an operation in a city hospital in 1901. Observing the operation are several medical students.

diseases still took many lives. The highest death rate was among infants less than 1 year old. The second largest was among children from 1 to 5 years old. They usually died from such diseases as measles, whooping cough, scarlet fever, and diphtheria. In 1900 there were neither cures nor vaccines for these diseases. Overall, the average life expectancy was 47 years. This is a far cry from today's life expectancy in America—70 years for men and 77½ years for women.

CHECKUP

1. What did people in rural areas do for recreation in 1900?
2. How did leisure-time activities differ for a city dweller?
3. Compare the ways that doctors in rural and urban areas performed their duties in 1900.
4. Why was life expectancy in 1900 so much different from what it is today?

5/UNIT REVIEW

READING THE TEXT

Turn to pages 432 and 433. On those pages you are told about some of the factors that helped to bring about America's industrial growth. Read those pages carefully and then, on a sheet of paper, answer these questions.

1. In a sentence or two, explain what is meant by the title "A strong foundation."

2. List at least five resources that were factors in industrial growth.

3. In what two ways did increased population contribute to industrial growth?

4. Explain why a corporation was a favorite form of business organization during the period of industrial growth.

5. List eight factors that led to America's industrial growth in the late 1800s.

READING A MAP

Turn to page 414 and study the map titled "The United States: Developing the West." On a sheet of paper, write **T** if the statement is true and **F** if it is false.

F **1.** The Chisholm Trail ran from San Antonio to Sedalia.

F **2.** Pikes Peak was a mining camp in the Black Hills.

T **3.** The Rocky Mountains ran through the Wyoming Territory.

T **4.** A railroad line connected Cheyenne and Boise.

T **5.** The three big cattle trails all went through Indian Territory.

F **6.** Virginia City grew up on the edge of the Rocky Mountains.

F **7.** A city located at 37°N/97°W is St. Louis.

T **8.** Albuquerque is farther west than Santa Fe.

F **9.** If one traveled from Sedalia to Abilene, he or she would be going east.

F **10.** The western boundary of Nevada is the 110th parallel.

READING A PICTURE

Turn to page 428 and study the picture. On a sheet of paper, answer these questions.

1. What are the line of people doing at upper right?

2. Why are the buildings at upper left on wheels?

3. What, do you think, are these buildings used for?

4. For what purpose, do you think, are the wagons at left center used?

READING TIME LINES

In this unit there are four time lines, on pages 405, 425, 443, and 463. On a sheet of paper, list the following items and beside each write the correct date from the chapter time lines.

Homestead Act 1862
Oklahoma land rush 1889
Transcontinental railroad line completed 1869
Peak year of immigration 1907
Haymarket Riot 1886
Decade of great city growth begins 1880
Bryan's "cross of gold" speech 1896
First modern skyscraper 1885

Now make a time line on which these events are shown. First of all, decide what will be the beginning and ending dates and how many divisions your time line will have. Then label each event at the proper place on the time line.

Becoming a World Leader

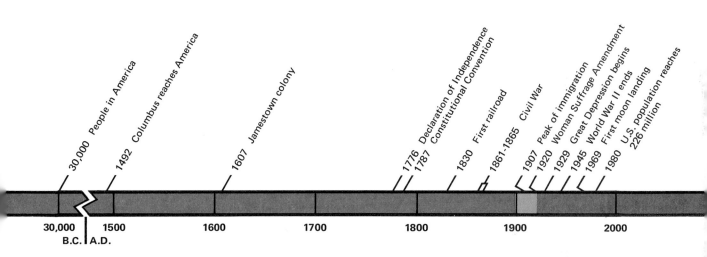

30,000 People in America

1492 Columbus reaches America

1607 Jamestown colony

1776 Declaration of Independence

1787 Constitutional Convention

1830 First railroad

1861-1865 Civil War

1907 Peak of immigration

1920 Woman Suffrage Amendment

1929 Great Depression begins

1945 World War II ends

1969 First moon landing

1980 U.S. population reaches 226 million

| 30,000 B.C. | A.D. 1500 | 1600 | 1700 | 1800 | 1900 | 2000 |

Above: Panama Canal, Woodrow Wilson, army nurses, Theodore Roosevelt, doughboy of World War I

22 The Progressive Movement

Working for Reform

┌─ VOCABULARY ─────────────────┐
public utility muckraker
direct primary commission
recall   government
Progressive   city manager
 movement
└──────────────────────────────┘

La Follette fights a party machine The turning point of Robert La Follette's career was probably the day of his meeting with Senator Philetus Sawyer. La Follette had recently been defeated for reelection to Congress, where he had served three terms. He had come home to Madison, Wisconsin, to practice law.

Sawyer was a millionaire, a United States senator, and the boss of the Wisconsin Republican party. He was involved in a lawsuit in which he stood to lose $300,000. The judge in the trial was Robert La Follette's brother-in-law. According to La Follette, Sawyer offered him a bribe "to fix things" with his brother-in-law. La Follette angrily refused the bribe and told the public what had happened. With that, Sawyer vowed that La Follette, a Republican, would never again have the support of the party.

That meeting took place in 1891. For the next 9 years, Robert La Follette began to understand what it meant to have a political party controlled by one man. In 1896 he decided to seek the Republican nomination for governor. Denied the backing of the regular organization, La Follette built support of his own. He championed popular issues such as regulating the railroads and the **public utilities**—those companies that sold water, gas, and electricity to the public. He won support from many young Republicans who were unhappy with the party machine.

At the party's convention, La Follette thought a majority of the delegates were for him. They were at first, but Sawyer's forces bribed enough of them to win the nomination for their own man. In 1898 the organization again blocked La Follette's bid for the nomination.

La Follette brings about reforms After that, La Follette added to his list of reforms the **direct primary**. In a direct primary, voters in each party choose the party's candidates directly, instead of having a convention of delegates choose them.

La Follette was finally nominated and elected in 1900, and he was twice reelected. During his three terms as governor, the legislature passed many reform laws. It adopted the initiative, the referendum, the direct primary, and the **recall**.

In 1897 at a county fair in Wisconsin, Robert La Follette demands Progressive reforms.

In the late 1800s the Wisconsin Republican party was closely tied to the state's railroad and lumbering interests.

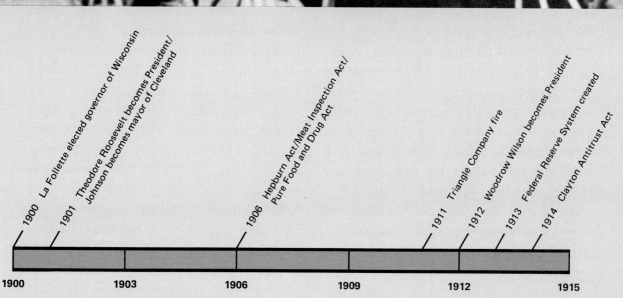

1900 La Follette elected governor of Wisconsin

1901 Theodore Roosevelt becomes President/
Johnson becomes mayor of Cleveland

1906 Hepburn Act/Meat Inspection Act/
Pure Food and Drug Act

1911 Triangle Company fire

1912 Woodrow Wilson becomes President

1913 Federal Reserve System created

1914 Clayton Antitrust Act

1900   1903   1906   1909   1912   1915

Robert La Follette, Sr., poses with his family. Young Bob (standing) became a senator like his father.

(By using the recall, voters may remove an official from office.) All these measures were meant to take away some power from the bosses and return it to the people.

The legislature also passed a workmen's compensation law, which made payments to those hurt on the job while working. It created commissions to regulate railroads and the utility companies. It taxed the railroads on the value of their properties so that for the first time they paid a fair share of taxes. It adopted a state income tax. It made a start on conserving the state's natural resources.

La Follette believed in using experts in government instead of politicians. Madison, the state capital, was also the home of the state university, and Governor La Follette called in professors to study problems and give him advice. He appointed university experts to office. When he set up commissions to regulate business or do other special jobs that required detailed knowledge, he hired experts to serve on them. La Follette's reforms and his use of experts came to be known as the Wisconsin Idea. The program spread. Soon many other states also had reform governors.

Later, "Fighting Bob" La Follette was elected to the United States Senate, where he served for 19 years. In a poll in 1950, the Senate named him one of the five greatest members ever to serve in that body.

Florence Kelley combats child labor

For Florence Kelley the turning point came much earlier in life. In 1871, when she was 12, her father took her to visit a glass factory. Mr. Kelley thought she would be impressed by the up-to-date method of production. What struck Florence, however, and what she remembered all her life, was the sight of boys younger than she working by the hot furnaces. The welfare of children became a lifelong interest of Florence Kelley.

In 1891, she started working at Hull House, Jane Addams's settlement house in Chicago. Florence Kelley made studies of the working conditions of women and children in the neighborhood. Her work led the Illinois legislature to pass a law in 1893 prohibiting child labor and setting an 8-hour day for women. Kelley was given the job of enforcing the law, but she was given no real power to do so. Four years later she was still reporting the large number of accidents that happened when tired child workers got caught in machinery. Bitterly, she wrote that "killing children by machinery has not yet been made a crime in Illinois."

Soon afterwards, Florence Kelley became head of an organization devoted to ending child labor. She played an important part in getting almost every state to adopt a child labor law between 1900 and 1914.

Each state law, however, applied only to businesses that operated entirely within the state. Under the United States Constitution, only the federal government could make laws to regulate businesses that operated in two or more states. In a time when businesses were growing larger, more and more companies were hiring children as workers. Kelley therefore took the lead in forming a national committee to seek a federal child labor

law. Because of the work of this committee, Congress twice passed child labor laws. Each time, however, the Supreme Court ruled them unconstitutional. Not until the 1930s would there finally be a federal child labor law.

Florence Kelley also championed laws to limit working hours and set minimum wages for women. Many states adopted such laws between 1900 and 1915.

The Progressive movement Robert La Follette and Florence Kelley worked in different fields, but they had much in common. They were both concerned about the problems and the injustices that had developed as America became a more industrialized society. They both believed that dedicated, trained people could find ways to make things better. And both believed that government could and should be used to remedy these problems and injustices.

Florence Kelley (third from left), *who had been chief factory inspector for Illinois for several years, poses with others who had also served as factory inspectors.*

La Follette and Kelley were part of a large number of men and women who became interested in reform—changing things for the better—around the turn of the century. They included business people and teachers, doctors and lawyers, social workers and clergy. In politics they were Republicans, Democrats, and independents. These people came to be known as Progressives. Together, they made up the **Progressive movement,** a wave of reform that swept the country in the early 1900s.

Progressives sought some of the same changes Populists had, like the initiative, referendum, and direct election of senators, but the two movements were quite different. Populists were from farms and small towns. Their programs reflected the interests of rural America. Most Progressives were city dwellers. They focused on problems of urban and industrial life. Some were mainly concerned with improving housing or health. Others sought to get rid of sweatshops. Some worked to give the people a greater say in government and to make government, especially in the cities, more honest and efficient. Still others wanted to limit the power of great corporations and regulate them in the public interest.

The muckrakers A group of writers played an important part in the Progressive movement. In popular magazines and books, they called attention to what was wrong and stirred the public to action. President Theodore Roosevelt once said that they were like a character in a well-known novel who spent all his time raking up the muck, or dirt on the floor. The image stuck, and thereafter these writers were known as **muckrakers.**

One of the muckrakers was Lincoln Steffens, who exposed the corruption of governments in many American cities. Another was Ida Tarbell. She spent 5 years gathering facts on the methods John D. Rockefeller used to drive out competition and create a monopoly.

Tom Johnson reforms Cleveland Those who knew Tom Johnson during his business career would not have guessed he would one day be the greatest reform mayor in America. Johnson was a millionaire. He had made his money in steel mills and in street railways in Indianapolis, Detroit, and Cleveland. During the first 40 years of his life, he showed no interest in politics. He seemed content to expand his street-railway business and add to his fortune.

Ida Tarbell, one of the muckrakers, exposed the methods used by John D. Rockefeller to create an oil monopoly.

The word *muckraker* was inspired by the man with the muckrake in John Bunyan's *Pilgrim's Progress.*

Tom Johnson (right), a businessman turned politician, brought honest, efficient government to Cleveland.

Then, Johnson read a book called *Progress and Poverty* in which Henry George, an economist, wrote about poverty and its causes. Johnson was moved. He began a new career as a reform politician.

In 1901, Johnson was elected mayor of Cleveland. One of the first things he did was open up government to the people. He held public meetings in a circus tent. There, citizens and city officials discussed ideas for dealing with Cleveland's problems. For many years, those with friends in government had paid lower taxes than other citizens. Johnson put a stop to that. He got the city council to tax the utility companies and to make the street-railway companies lower their fares.

Johnson knew that few politicians had the knowledge to run a department of public health, to plan housing and parks, or to manage a school system. So he brought in experts to run the city departments. By the time Johnson left office in 1908, the muckraker Lincoln Steffens called Cleveland "the best-governed city in the United States."

Cleveland was but one of many cities in which reform forces won control of the government. In Detroit, New York, San Francisco, and other cities, strong reform mayors fought corruption.

New forms of city government Progressives also brought about two changes in the form of city government. The first came about by accident. In 1900 a hurricane and tidal wave destroyed much of Galveston, Texas. The outdated and inefficient city government could not cope with the emergency. Therefore the state appointed a commission of five experts. Each commissioner took over one or more city departments, such as the police, fire, and water departments. Together, the commissioners ran the city. The people of Galveston were so pleased with the results that they changed their form of government permanently. Thus **commission government** was born. By 1914 more than 400 cities had adopted it.

The second new form of government was the **city manager** system. Under this system, elected commissioners appointed an expert, who used modern business methods to run the city. This took much of the politics out of city government and bypassed the political machine. The city manager system was first used in Staunton, Virginia, in 1908. It soon spread to other small and medium-sized cities.

Have pupils find out the form of government their city or town has. You might like to ask someone from the local government to speak to the class.

497

The Wisconsin Idea spreads   Wisconsin was only one of a number of states in which Progressives brought reform. In Oregon, New York, Missouri, Iowa, California, New Jersey, and other states, Progressive governors battled the political machines and cleaned up corruption. Many states adopted the initiative, referendum, direct primary, and direct election of senators. In 1913 the Seventeenth Amendment provided for the direct election of senators in all states.

Progressive states set up commissions like those in Wisconsin to regulate rates charged by railroads and public utilities. They also adopted many of the laws that Florence Kelley championed. In addition to child-labor and maximum-hour laws, those states provided for workmen's compensation and gave pensions to families of workers who were killed or seriously injured on the job.

These Wyoming women are voting in a state election in 1888. It was 1910, though, before the woman suffrage movement made headway throughout the nation.

During the Progressive Era, women made important gains in their effort to win the right to vote. Four states had given women the right to vote by 1896, but not another state was added to the list for the next 13 years. Starting in 1910, however, the women's movement began to achieve success. In the next 5 years, seven more states granted women full voting rights.

CHECKUP

1. Name and explain five reforms that came about in Wisconsin under the leadership of Robert La Follette.
2. What reforms did Florence Kelley work for?
3. How did the Progressive movement differ from the Populist movement?
4. Explain the contribution that each of the following made to the reform movement: Lincoln Steffens, Ida Tarbell, Tom Johnson.

The First Modern President

```
┌─ VOCABULARY ─────────────────────┐
│  arbitration      conservation    │
│  square deal      Bull Moose party│
└───────────────────────────────────┘
```

A man with a zest for living   Progressivism arrived on the national level with the presidency of Theodore Roosevelt. As a youth growing up on Long Island, New York, he was sickly and weak. Theodore—or Teddy, as his family referred to him—had an iron will, however. Through exercise and determination he grew strong. When he went to college, he took up boxing—even though he was so nearsighted he could hardly see without his glasses.

Theodore read widely, a habit he carried throughout his life. He was one of

There are many biographies of Roosevelt. Ask interested pupils to read one of them and prepare a book report.

the best-read and best-informed persons ever to serve as President. He also wrote a dozen books, on subjects from botany to American history. He had a zest for living and seemed to be interested in everything.

A career in politics   What most interested Roosevelt, however, was politics and power. Very early in his life, he decided that he wanted to be "a member of the governing class." He joined the local Republican club in New York and was soon chosen to run for the state legislature. He won and at 23 was its youngest member.

It was at this time that Roosevelt, who came from a well-to-do family, gained his first understanding of the life of the working poor. While investigating working and housing conditions among New York's immigrants, Roosevelt visited workers who were making cigars in their own homes. He later wrote:

> I have always remembered one room in which two families were living. . . . There were several children, three men, and two women in this room. The tobacco was stowed about everywhere, alongside the foul bedding, and in a corner where there were scraps of food. The men, women, and children in this room worked by day and far on into the evening, and they slept and ate there.

In 1884, Roosevelt's wife died, just 2 days after giving birth to their first child. On the same day, his mother died. Roosevelt was shattered. He gave up politics and left New York. He bought a ranch in the Dakota Territory. For the next 2 years this eastern city dweller lived the life of a ranch hand.

On his ranch in the Dakota Territory, young Teddy Roosevelt dressed like and lived the life of a cowboy.

In 1886, Roosevelt returned to the East and politics. He ran for mayor in New York City but was defeated. He was later appointed to the United States Civil Service Commission, on which he served 3 years. Then he served as police commissioner of New York, and after that as assistant secretary of the navy in Washington. He left this position to serve as a colonel in the Spanish-American War, as you will read in the next chapter.

Into the White House   Returning from the war as a national hero, Roosevelt was elected governor of New York. He proved to be an effective reform governor. He was so effective, in fact, that the boss of the state's Republican party wanted to get rid of this reformer. He arranged for

WILLIAM McKINLEY
25th President
1897 · 1901

Born: 1843, Niles, Ohio. **Education:** Attended Allegheny College, but illness forced his withdrawal. **Training:** Lawyer, public official. **To presidency from:** Ohio. **Position when elected:** Governor of Ohio. **Political party:** Republican. **Married:** Ida Saxton. **Children:** Two daughters, who died in infancy. **Died:** September 14, 1901. Shot 9 days earlier by an anarchist at the Pan-American Exposition in Buffalo, New York. **Other facts:** In the Civil War, served for a time under Colonel Rutherford B. Hayes, another future President. Devoted to his invalid wife. The first President to use the telephone extensively in his campaign. **During his presidency:** Thousands of Americans rushed to the Klondike region of Canada in search of gold.

Roosevelt to be nominated for Vice President in 1900. William McKinley was the party's choice for a second term as President. One Republican leader who was unhappy with the nomination of Roosevelt warned, "Don't you realize that there's only one life between this madman and the White House?"

McKinley and Roosevelt were elected. Only a few months after President McKinley began his new term, he was shot by a crazed man. He died soon afterward. Thus at the age of 42, Theodore Roosevelt became the youngest President of the United States. "Now look," said the Republican leader who had warned about Roosevelt, "that . . . cowboy is in the White House."

Regulating big business Like other Progressives, Roosevelt believed that government must play a larger role in regulating big business. Early in his presidency he took action against the Northern Securities Company. This company, formed in 1901, controlled all the long-distance railroad lines in the northwestern part of the country. With no competition,

it could charge customers whatever it wished.

Roosevelt said the company violated the Sherman Antitrust Act (see page 476). The Supreme Court agreed and ordered that the company be broken up. This was the first time the antitrust law had really been enforced. Roosevelt later brought action against Standard Oil, the American Tobacco Company, and more than 40 other large business combinations.

These actions earned Roosevelt the nickname the Trustbuster. Roosevelt himself would have been the first to say that the name was not accurate. He was not against all big businesses. In fact, he felt that growth was a perfectly natural development in modern business. There was a difference, however, between "good trusts" and "bad trusts." The latter were the ones that had been formed by illegal methods or that took unfair advantage of the public. Bad trusts, said Roosevelt, should be broken up. The others should be regulated by the federal government.

The coal-mining strike In another early action, Roosevelt used his power

The anarchist who shot McKinley was named Leon Czolgosz (chôl′ gôsh).

Roosevelt was a favorite of political cartoonists. His rimless glasses, bushy moustache, and energetic personality were easy to capture in caricature. One cartoon, showing him with a bear cub, prompted a new toy — the Teddy bear.

as President to settle a strike in the coal-mining industry. Mining was probably the most dangerous job in America. Every year, explosions and cave-ins took the lives of several thousand workers. Black lung, a disease caused by coal dust settling into the lungs, shortened the lives of thousands of miners. Hours were long and the work was backbreaking. For their labor, coal miners averaged about $600 a year. A miner's income was less than the amount an average-sized family needed to live on in 1900.

In the spring of 1902, miners asked the owners of the mines for a wage increase, an 8-hour day, and recognition of their union. The owners refused, and the men walked out. The strike dragged on into the fall with neither side budging. Owners would not even talk with union leaders.

With winter nearing and with some cities fearing a fuel shortage, the President stepped in. He called representatives of both sides to the White House and asked them to settle their differences. The miners were willing, but the owners were not. One owner still refused to talk to the union leader. Roosevelt later wrote that "if it wasn't for the high office I hold, I would have taken him by the seat of the breeches and . . . chucked him out the window."

Roosevelt eventually succeeded in getting the two sides to agree to **arbitration.** This meant that a third party would listen to both sides and propose a fair settlement, which the owners and the miners would have to accept. The strike then ended.

Roosevelt was not the first President to step into a major strike. Earlier Presidents, however, had sided with business and had sent in troops to break the strikes. Roosevelt was the first to take into account labor's viewpoint and to insist on a settlement fair to both sides.

Theodore Roosevelt became known as the Trustbuster. However, these alphabetical cartoons were part of a booklet published by the Democrats, who felt that the President had not acted vigorously enough in prosecuting the trusts.

Some of your pupils might like to try their hand at making their own political cartoons, using either historical or current issues.

501

The Day the Air Age Began

Of the many inventions in the early 1900s, few would prove as important as the airplane. Yet oddly, the first flight of a manned, heavier-than-air flying machine passed almost unnoticed.

The inventors of this airplane were Orville and Wilbur Wright, owners of a small bicycle shop in Dayton, Ohio. In the late 1890s the Wright brothers became interested in the possibilities of flying. After trying out their theories with large box kites and gliders, they built a passenger-carrying glider in 1900. To test it, the Wrights chose the beach at Kitty Hawk, North Carolina.

The glider worked beautifully. For the next 2 years, the brothers experimented with different wing shapes and made other improvements. Finally, they added a small gasoline engine.

On December 17, 1903, with Orville at the controls, they made the first successful flight — 12 seconds long! Taking turns, the Wrights made three more flights that day. The longest lasted 57 seconds, during which the plane traveled 852 feet (260 m).

The Wright brothers were now ready to tell the world. But the world did not seem ready to listen. In the next 2 days, only six newspapers in the country carried the story!

The nation's press had missed the significance of what had happened at Kitty Hawk on December 17, 1903. For that was the day the air age began.

The air age begins in 1903 as the Wright brothers plane lifts off the beach at Kitty Hawk, North Carolina. (36°N/76°W; map, p. 17)

Roosevelt won the 1904 election with a 2.5 million-vote plurality, the largest margin of victory to that time.

This was in line with Roosevelt's idea that government should use its power to see that everyone—business, labor, and the public—was treated fairly. Government should make certain that everyone received a **square deal**, said Roosevelt. This term became his slogan.

Further reforms　In 1904, Theodore Roosevelt was elected by a landslide to a full term as President. He promptly sought stronger laws to regulate the railroads. The Interstate Commerce Act of 1887 had never been effective. Pressed by the President, Congress passed the Hepburn Act in 1906. This law gave the Interstate Commerce Commission new powers to set rates.

Roosevelt also induced Congress to pass the Meat Inspection Act. Conditions in the meat-packing business in the United States were disgraceful. The plants were filthy. Companies passed along spoiled and diseased meat to con-

The Meat Inspection Act had the support of some of the largest packing companies, particularly those that exported meat to Europe. Exported meat had to meet stringent standards. Companies that didn't export meat didn't have to worry about standards, which gave them a competitive edge in pricing.

Dr. Harvey Wiley, chief chemist of the Department of Agriculture, was an important supporter of the Pure Food and Drug Act. He campaigned hard for the act and provided much of the necessary documentation. The General Federation of

THEODORE ROOSEVELT
26th President
1901 · 1909

Born: 1858, New York, New York. **Education:** Harvard College. **Training:** Writer, public official. **To presidency from:** New York. **Position when taking office:** Vice President. **Political party:** Republican. **Married:** (1) Alice Lee, (2) Edith Carow. **Children:** Four sons, two daughters. **Died:** 1919, Oyster Bay, New York. **Other facts:** An energetic man who loved the outdoors. Hiked, swam, rode horseback, and boxed. The youngest man (42 years, 10 months) to become President. The first President to ride in an automobile (1902), to go underwater in a submarine (1905), and to ride in an airplane (1910). **During his presidency:** An earthquake struck San Francisco in April 1906, destroying most of the city and killing some 700 people.

Women's Clubs, the *Ladies' Home Journal,* the AMA, and the Grange were also active supporters.

sumers. In 1906 a writer named Upton Sinclair wrote *The Jungle,* a novel exposing these conditions. The book caused a sensation. After reading it, Roosevelt sent investigators to find out if Sinclair's charges were true. Roosevelt then used his influence with Congress to pass a law that required federal inspection of meat before it could be sold. Another new law—the Pure Food and Drug Act—required truthful labeling of medicines.

Conservation Roosevelt gave strong support to **conservation**, that is, the protection of natural resources. The conservation movement had begun in the late 1800s. Forests were being cut at a shocking rate, and practices in both the lumbering and mining industries were wasteful. Acting under a law of Congress, Roosevelt set aside 150 million acres (60.7 million ha) of land to add to the national forests. This was three times as much land as had been set aside by earlier Presidents. He also saw to it that the government held on to millions of acres of mineral-rich land for the future. And

he created five new national parks. Most important of all, he brought the need for conserving our natural resources to the attention of the people.

Theodore Roosevelt has been called the first modern President. He began the tradition of an active federal government led by a strong chief executive. Without those changes, little reform could ever have been brought about on the federal level of government.

Taft becomes President Following his victory in the 1904 election, Roosevelt had announced that "under no circumstances will I be a candidate for or accept another nomination." Now, in 1908, many supporters urged him to run again. He was still very popular, and he probably could have won reelection. Roosevelt, however, was determined to keep his word, and he refused all urgings that he run again.

At the same time, the President wanted to be sure that his policies would be continued. He believed the best person to do this was his friend William Howard Taft, who was the secretary of war. With

WILLIAM H. TAFT
27th President
1909 • 1913

Born: 1857, Cincinnati, Ohio. **Education:** Yale College, Cincinnati Law School. **Training:** Lawyer. **To presidency from:** Ohio. **Position when elected:** Secretary of war. **Political party:** Republican. **Married:** Helen Herron. **Children:** Two sons, one daughter. **Died:** 1930, Washington, D.C. **Other facts:** Weighed more than 300 pounds but played tennis and golf and was an excellent dancer. Threw out the first ball at beginning of major-league baseball season in 1910, starting a practice that lasted many years. The only person to have served both as President and as Chief Justice. **During his presidency:** Robert E. Peary led the first expedition to the North Pole (1909) and Roald Amundsen's expedition resulted in discovery of the South Pole (1911).

Roosevelt's support, Taft won the Republican nomination and the election. His Democratic opponent was William Jennings Bryan of Nebraska. It was Bryan's third attempt to win the presidency, and again he failed.

Taft's record   Taft was no doubt sincere when he promised to carry out Roosevelt's policies. Indeed, progressivism did make some gains under Taft. Congress passed a new law further strengthening the Interstate Commerce Commission. Congress approved and sent on to the states for their approval one constitutional amendment for an income tax and another for the direct election of senators. These became the Sixteenth and Seventeenth Amendments in 1913 (see pages 197 and 198). All these measures had Taft's support. The President also started almost 80 new antitrust suits, nearly twice as many as Roosevelt had begun.

Yet Progressives distrusted Taft. He ignored them in making appointments to office. At the start of his term, he asked Congress to lower the tariff. Instead, Con-

gress passed a bill to raise it. Taft signed the bill into law anyway, even though Progressives urged him to veto it. Then he further angered Progressives by calling that law "the best tariff bill that the Republican party ever passed." On conserva-

Taft is here pictured as the crown prince, perched on King Teddy's shoulder. Later their friendship cooled.

tion, another favorite cause with Progressives, Taft's clumsy handling of the issue made it appear that he was against conservation when he was really in favor of it. Before long, Taft and the Progressives in his party were criticizing each other.

A cooling friendship   Meanwhile, the friendship between Roosevelt and Taft had cooled. Roosevelt felt that Taft had failed to keep his promise to carry out Roosevelt's policies. Taft felt that he had supported Progressive reforms and that Roosevelt was criticizing him unfairly.

In 1912, Roosevelt announced that he would battle Taft for the Republican nomination. "My hat is in the ring," proclaimed the former President. Roosevelt was still popular with the public, but Taft supporters controlled the Republican convention. When Taft got the nomination, Roosevelt and many of his Progressive followers walked out of the convention.

The Bull Moose party   A short time later, Roosevelt supporters formed a new party and nominated their hero for the presidency. Roosevelt accepted, saying that he felt "as fit as a bull moose." The name of the party was the Progressive party, but now many people simply called it the **Bull Moose party.**

The platform of the new party aimed to make political life more democratic. It favored the initiative, referendum, direct primary, and woman suffrage. To improve the lot of workers in an industrial society, the platform promised an 8-hour day, minimum wages for women, a federal child labor law, workmen's compensation, and unemployment insurance. It

The Progressive party called its platform the New Nationalism.

The cartoonist pokes fun at Theodore Roosevelt's attempts to drum up interest in the Bull Moose party.

also favored regulating businesses to promote safety.

The split between Taft and Roosevelt supporters gave the Democratic party a golden opportunity. The party nominated Governor Woodrow Wilson of New Jersey for President in 1912, and Wilson became the Democrats' first President-elect since Grover Cleveland.

CHECKUP

1. What steps did President Theodore Roosevelt take to regulate big business?
2. How did he settle a strike in the coal-mining industry?
3. What did Roosevelt do concerning conservation of natural resources?
4. How did the split between Roosevelt and Taft affect the election of 1912?

Ask: Why did the Taft-Roosevelt split allow Wilson to be elected?

505

The Wilson Presidency

A boy who dreamed of glory   The story of Woodrow Wilson's youth, one person wrote, "is the story of a boy who dreamed of winning glory by great speeches that would move people. . . ." Many a young person has no doubt shared that dream. Few, however, could have worked with such determination as Woodrow Wilson did to make it come true.

Woodrow Wilson was born in Virginia in 1856. As a teenager he memorized the speeches of great orators and delivered them in a forest or in an empty building. He continued to develop his skill with language in college, becoming not only a fine speaker but an excellent writer as well. His goal in life, he wrote a friend, was to have "a commanding influence in the councils . . . of my country."

From professor to governor   Wilson became a college professor and later president of Princeton University in New Jersey. His chance to enter politics came in 1910. The Democratic party in New

In 1912, Woodrow Wilson poses with his first wife and their three daughters. At that time Wilson was serving as governor of New Jersey.

506

Jersey was marked by scandal. It needed a candidate for governor whose honesty was beyond question. Wilson, a college president, was a perfect choice. He was nominated and elected.

Wilson became one of the leading Progressive governors in the nation. He stood up to the Democratic machine and refused to support its boss for the United States Senate. Under his leadership, New Jersey adopted far-reaching reforms. These included a direct primary law, workmen's compensation, regulation of utilities and railroads, and a law to clean up corrupt election practices. This record won attention all over America and helped Wilson win the Democratic nomination for President in 1912.

Wilson's views on trusts   In the campaign of 1912, Wilson and Roosevelt were the two chief candidates, with Taft trailing far behind. One of the main issues on which Wilson and Roosevelt differed was the method of handling the trusts. Roosevelt, you remember, did not believe that a company was automatically bad because it was big. In fact, he felt that large business combinations were a natural development of modern business. The correct way for the federal government to deal with them was to accept them but regulate them so they would serve the public interest.

Woodrow Wilson, on the other hand, believed that all trusts were bad because they shut out competition. He said that government should break up trusts and prevent new ones from forming. His strong belief in competition also led Wilson to favor lowering the tariff. Congress passed the Underwood Tariff Act in 1913. This law lowered the tariff on hundreds of imported items. It was the first law to lower the tariff since the Civil War.

It was expected that lowering the tariff duties would result in less income for the United States government. To make up for this loss, Congress added an income tax to the law. This was made possible by the Sixteenth Amendment, which had been added to the Constitution earlier that year.

Reforming the banking system   Next, Wilson asked Congress to reform banking. The banking system then in effect had been designed 50 years earlier. Since that time, the country's needs had changed greatly. Furthermore, control of banking lay in the hands of a few powerful bankers. Wilson and many Progressives believed it was wrong for a few individuals to have such power over the economy of the country.

With Wilson's leadership, Congress created the **Federal Reserve System**. The law divided the country into 12 banking districts, with a Federal Reserve Bank in each district. The Federal Reserve Bank did not do business with the public. It provided certain services for the private banks in its district, and it had power to regulate certain practices.

Heading the whole system was a Federal Reserve Board in Washington, D.C. Its members were appointed by the President. Through their decisions they could affect the supply of money in circulation and the rate of interest that borrowers would pay. Thus they had a large influence on the economy of the nation. As

Wilson called his trustbusting program the New Freedom.

a result, banking in the United States remained a private business, but the federal government now supervised it.

Dealing with the trusts   During the 1912 election, Wilson had promised to break up trusts.   As President, he found it difficult to devise a law that would do this. The result was that he proposed two separate laws.

One was the **Clayton Antitrust Act.** This law prohibited companies from gaining control of other companies in the same industry.   It also stopped them from engaging in certain business practices *if* these practices reduced competition. That was a big if, however.   In most cases, it was hard for the government to prove that a company's practices had really reduced competition.   Usually the courts sided with business.

The second law was the Federal Trade Commission Act.   This law was close to Roosevelt's views about how to deal with trusts.   It created a federal commission to regulate big business.   The President appointed five commissioners.   They had the power to investigate businesses. They could order businesses to stop "harmful practices," such as false advertising.   But telling a trust not to do certain things was very different from breaking it up.   All in all, Wilson found that regulating the trusts was a difficult problem. Of all the reforms that Wilson supported, he was least successful in this area.

Wilson's other reforms   President Wilson backed several laws to help farmers.   The Federal Farm Loan Act of 1916 provided low-interest loans to farmers. Another measure set up a network of trained agricultural agents to advise farmers on the growing and marketing of crops.

The President also supported two important laws involving labor.   One was the Adamson Act.   This set an 8-hour workday for railroad employees.   This was the first time the federal government had made a law about the length of the workday in a private business.   A second law was the Keating-Owen Child Labor Law of 1916.   This law attempted to end child labor by punishing companies that used it.   Any product made by children under 14, said the law, could not be shipped across state lines.   However, in 1918 the Supreme Court ruled this law unconstitutional.

In this cartoon the policeman (Clayton Antitrust Law) is ready to use his club on the robber (dishonest trusts). Unlike Roosevelt, Wilson considered all trusts bad.

508

Wilson signs the first federal child labor act, later declared unconstitutional.

Rating the Progressives How successful were the Progressives? Did they really accomplish their goals of achieving greater democracy, regulating business in the public interest, and protecting people against the ills of an industrial society?

The record is mixed. City governments became more honest and provided better services to their citizens. Yet political machines and bosses did not disappear. They often found ways to use the new laws to regain power. Businesses continued to grow bigger and more powerful, despite state and federal laws aimed to curb them. Laws on child labor and woman labor made a start toward protecting workers in an industrial society, but their effect was limited.

Still, the Progressive movement brought about important changes. It showed how experts could make government more efficient and better. It ended forever the idea that government had no responsibility to deal with large social problems. It established the principle that business had responsibilities to the public. And finally, it established the idea that the federal government should play an active role in improving American life. Those changes would become the foundation for much that followed in the twentieth century.

CHECKUP

1. How did Woodrow Wilson's views on trusts differ from the views of Theodore Roosevelt?
2. How does the Federal Reserve System influence the economy?
3. How did the Clayton Antitrust Act and the Federal Trade Commission Act attempt to deal with trusts?
4. What important changes did the Progressive movement bring to American life?

KEY FACTS

1. Most Progressives wanted the government to regulate big business, break up trusts, and reform the banking system.

2. In a number of cities, reform movements took power out of the hands of political bosses and gave it to trained experts.

3. During the Progressive era, many states passed laws to protect workers.

4. The muckrakers, who wrote about corrupt government and unhealthy living and working conditions, influenced politicians to bring about reforms.

5. Theodore Roosevelt can be called the first modern President. With him began the tradition of an active federal government led by a strong chief executive.

VOCABULARY QUIZ

On a separate sheet of paper, write the word or phrase from the list to best complete each of the sentences below. There are two extra words or phrases.

public utility	commission
banking	Republican
city manager	direct primary
muckraker	recall
Progressive	conservation
income tax	arbitration

1. Voters in each party select their party's candidates in a __direct primary__.

2. The Bull Moose party was a nickname for the __Progressive__ party.

3. A company that sells water, gas, or electricity is a __public utility__.

4. An elected official may be removed from office before his or her term is over by __recall__.

5. The creation of the Federal Reserve System brought about reforms in __banking__.

6. The form of government first used in Galveston, Texas, was the __commission__.

7. To protect the nation's natural resources, Theodore Roosevelt had an active program of __conservation__.

8. A writer of the early 1900s who exposed abuses in business and government was called a __muckraker__.

9. The process of having a third party settle a disagreement between employers and employees is called __arbitration__.

10. An expert hired to run a city is called a __city manager__.

REVIEW QUESTIONS

1. Write a statement about each of the following, telling something important about his or her ideas or work: (**a**) Tom Johnson, (**b**) Ida Tarbell, (**c**) Florence Kelley, (**d**) Robert La Follette.

2. How were populism and progressivism alike? How were they different?

3. List two reforms brought about by each President: (**a**) Roosevelt, (**b**) Wilson, (**c**) Taft.

4. Explain how each of the following was meant to give more power to the people: (**a**) direct primary, (**b**) recall.

ACTIVITIES

1. Draw up a list of reforms you would support for your community. Choose one, write about the problem, and tell how it might be solved.

2. The Food and Drug Administration established by Theodore Roosevelt still exists. Find out about its activities. What drugs have been outlawed? What rules are there about labeling food?

TAKING NOTES

THEODORE ROOSEVELT

As you read textbooks, you will find it helpful to take notes on the material. Writing down important information in this shortened form helps you in three ways. First, it gets you to think about which facts are more important and which are less important. Second, it helps you remember what you read. Third, it helps you review quickly what you read.

What should you include in your notes and what should you leave out? A simple rule that will help you make that judgment is to keep in mind the purpose of your reading. For example, look at the following paragraph.

> Theodore Roosevelt's colorful personality brought him a great deal of newspaper coverage. His Rough Rider hat and large gleaming teeth became familiar to millions through newspaper photographs and political cartoons. Roosevelt skillfully used this press coverage to win support for his proposals. Often, he went to the people to get Congress to act. An example occurred in 1906. Certain leaders of Congress were blocking Roosevelt's bill for federal inspection of meat. Roosevelt had a report about the unsanitary conditions in meat-packing plants. He gave part of it to the newspaper. When people read it, they were outraged. Roosevelt then warned the congressmen who were blocking the bill that if Congress did not act, he would publish the rest of the report, which was even more shocking. The public, he warned, would blame the congressmen who opposed it. With that, the leaders dropped their opposition and the Federal Meat Inspection Act was passed.

It may be interesting that Roosevelt often wore cowboy hats and that he had large gleaming teeth. If your purpose in reading the para-

In this cartoon, President Theodore Roosevelt is shown wearing his Rough Rider hat. Roosevelt was a favorite subject for editorial cartoonists.

graph is to get information for a report on "Clothes That Presidents Wear," or "The Dental Features of Presidents," those are facts you would want in your notes. But if your purpose for reading is to understand the Progressive era, or presidential power, your notes would probably look like this:

TR—colorful personality—much newspaper coverage. TR used press to pressure Cong.—example: 1906—Cong. block bill to inspect meat. TR gave press part of report on unsanitary cond.—public outraged—TR threatened to publish the rest—leaders gave in —passed Fed. Meat Inspec. Act.

SKILLS PRACTICE

To get some practice in note taking, turn back and take notes on the section "Regulating Big Business" on page 500.

511

America Looks Outward

┌─VOCABULARY─────────────────┐
│ overseas empire   imperialist │
└────────────────────────────┘

Have pupils look up the vocabulary words in the Glossary before they read the lesson.

To the Philippines Sailing by the light of a pale moon, the United States Asian fleet entered the quiet waters of Manila Bay in the Philippine Islands. It was midnight on April 30, 1898. Farther down the bay, closer to the shore, the Spanish fleet lay waiting. Commodore George Dewey, commanding the American fleet, knew that fighting would begin at dawn. For now, though, he gave the order for his men to get some sleep at their guns.

Dewey's force was a small one, six warships in all. But all of them were armored and fitted with modern rapid-fire guns that could hit a target 5 miles (8 km) away. They were part of the modern navy that the United States had been building since the late 1880s.

At 61, George Dewey was a part of the old navy as well as the new. Born in Montpelier, Vermont, in 1837, he entered the United States Naval Academy in 1854. During the Civil War he served in the Union fleet that won control of the Mississippi River from Confederate forces. In the years that followed the war, the navy entered a long period of decline. Old wooden ships were not replaced, even though some European countries were building steel ships. During this period, Dewey said that America's navy was the "laughingstock of the nations." By the 1890s, however, ships of the new steel navy were entering service.

By 1898, George Dewey had risen to the command of America's small Pacific fleet. Trouble was then starting with Spain, and Dewey's fleet was ordered to Hong Kong, a British possession on the coast of China. This put the American ships only 1,000 miles (1,600 km) from the Philippine Islands, which were under Spanish control. On April 25, 1898, the order came from Washington: "Proceed at once to the Philippine Islands. Commence operations . . . against the Spanish fleet."

The battle of Manila Bay At 4:00 A.M. on May 1, Dewey's men were awakened for coffee. As the American fleet steamed farther into the bay, Spanish guns on shore opened fire. Fortunately the shells fell harmlessly into the water. By 5:40 A.M. the American ships had closed to within 3 miles (4.8 km) of the Spanish fleet. Turning to his captain, Dewey ordered: "You may fire when ready, Gridley."

It was a one-sided contest. Spain's ancient wooden vessels were no match

Eventually Dewey was made Admiral of the Navy. He was the only American to hold this title.

American troops, at war with Spain, advance near Santiago, Cuba. (20°N/76°W; map, p. 521)

Dewey's fleet had been ordered to Hong Kong so that it would be able to prevent the Spanish fleet from leaving the Philippines and going to the aid of the fleet in Cuba.

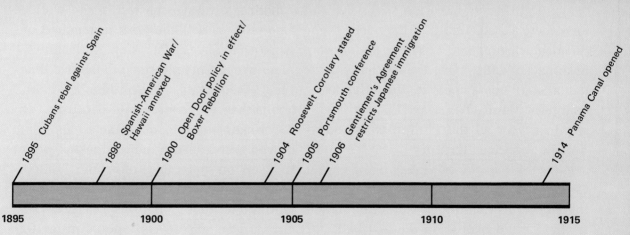

1895 Cubans rebel against Spain

1898 Spanish-American War/
Hawaii annexed

1900 Open Door policy in effect/
Boxer Rebellion

1904 Roosevelt Corollary stated

1905 Portsmouth conference

1906 Gentlemen's Agreement
restricts Japanese immigration

1914 Panama Canal opened

| 1895 | 1900 | 1905 | 1910 | 1915 |

Black troops were very much a part of the fighting in Cuba. They still had white officers however. In the regiment pictured here — the 9th and 10th Colored Cavalry — officers wore red sashes. The soldiers in red pants are Spanish. This action took place at the battle of Cuasimas, near Santiago, on June 24, 1898.

513

Have pupils find the Philippine Islands on the map on page 522.

An American fleet under the command of Commodore Dewey enters Manila Bay. (14°N/121°W; map, p. 522)

for America's steel ships. By noon, the Spanish surrendered. They had lost 8 ships and 381 men; Dewey had lost not a ship nor a man in the brief encounter. Manila Bay was Dewey's, and within a year all the Philippine Islands became American territory.

Changes in American thinking   Adding land to its holdings was nothing new for the United States. In the first half of the nineteenth century, large territories were added by purchase, by diplomacy, and by war. But all that land was on the North American continent and had bordered the United States. The Philippines lay across the Pacific Ocean, some 7,000 miles (11,200 km) from the western coast of the United States. At the time Dewey set sail for Manila Bay, most Americans had never heard of the Philippine Islands. Probably not 1 person in 100 could have pointed to them on a map.

How did it come to pass, then, that the American flag was raised over this land in 1898? For the answer, we must look at changes that had been taking place in America and in American thinking. During the years after the Civil War, most Americans showed little interest in affairs outside their own borders. Restoring the Union, settling the West, and adjusting to industrialization took up the country's energies. One New York newspaper in the 1880s even called on the government to bring home its ministers—representatives to other countries—and abolish the foreign service!

During these years, however, other forces were attracting the interest of some Americans toward the rest of the world. One of these was the great production of America's farms, factories, and mines. A number of people came to believe that the United States was producing more goods than its people could consume. If Americans were to continue to be employed and if farms and businesses were to keep on making profits, the United States would have to find markets in other lands for its goods. Bankers and investors also looked abroad for opportunities to invest in railroads, mines, and factories.

514

Some Americans had other reasons for urging their country to look outward. They watched with envy as Great Britain, France, Germany, and other European countries created **overseas empires**—that is, extended their control over distant lands. America was also a great power, they declared. It, too, should have colonies. Those who held such views were called **imperialists.**

Looking to the Pacific   Some Americans had been looking outward for many years. Merchants from New York, Philadelphia, Boston, and other ports in the Northeast had been sending trading ships to China since the 1780s.

In the 1850s, trade also began with Japan. For more than 200 years, Japan had shut itself off almost completely from

Japanese officials meet Matthew Perry on his arrival in Japan. His visit helped open Japan to trade.

contact with other lands. In 1853, Commodore Matthew Perry arrived in Japan with a fleet of four warships. Perry carried a letter from the President of the United States, asking that trade be opened between the two countries. The Japanese were distrustful, and Perry went home empty-handed. He returned next year, however, and this time a trade treaty was signed. The Japanese agreed to open several ports to American trading ships.

Trade with the Far East led to American interest in the islands of the Pacific. By the late nineteenth century, steam was rapidly replacing sails on oceangoing ships. Steamships making long trading voyages from the United States to the Far East or to Australia needed island stopovers where they could take on a new supply of coal. For the same reason, the new steam warships needed island bases.

Thus the United States became interested in Samoa, a group of islands in the South Pacific about 2,500 miles (4,000 km) from Australia. In 1878, local rulers gave the United States the right to build a naval base in Samoa. Britain and Germany also had claims in the islands. Arguments among the three countries almost led to war. In 1899, however, it was agreed that Samoa would be divided between the United States and Germany, with Great Britain receiving land in Africa and elsewhere in the Pacific.

Americans in Hawaii   Imperialists were even more interested in another territory in the Pacific. This was Hawaii, a group of islands about 2,000 miles (3,200 km) west of San Francisco. Asian peoples had been living on these islands

The three nations set up a protectorate in Samoa, guaranteeing the independence and neutrality of the islands while giving the United States the right to keep its naval base at Pago Pago.   **515**

for hundreds of years when the English explorer Captain James Cook first came upon them in 1788. From then on, whalers and trading ships sailing between Asia and the United States used the islands as a stopover for taking on fresh food and supplies.

In the 1820s, missionaries went to Hawaii to convert its people to Christianity. Soon, other Americans went to live there. In 1835 an American company started a sugarcane plantation in Hawaii. Before long, planters were recruiting people from Japan and other lands in Asia to work on these plantations. Later, planters raised pineapples as well as sugarcane. The American sugar planters grew rich and powerful. Hawaii had a native king, but the real power to govern passed into the hands of the planters.

In 1875 the United States agreed to allow sugar from Hawaii to enter the country without paying a tariff. In return, Hawaii promised never to allow any country other than the United States to control its territory. Twelve years later King Kalakaua (kä lä′ kä′ ü ä), the ruler of Hawaii, gave the United States the right to build a naval base at Pearl Harbor. The United States and Hawaii were drawing closer together.

Hawaii is annexed   Meanwhile, sugarcane growers in Louisiana were unhappy about having to compete with sugar from Hawaii. In 1890 they got Congress to put tariff duties back on Hawaiian sugar. The tax made Hawaiian sugar more expensive than sugar grown in the United States. Sales dropped, and the islands faced hard times.

Americans in Hawaii had an answer to this problem: Let the United States annex Hawaii. Once it was part of the United States, the sugar tariff would no longer apply.

Queen Liliuokalani (lē lē ü ō kä lä′ nē), Hawaii's new ruler, had a different answer to the problem. It was "Hawaii for the Hawaiians." She scrapped the old constitution and announced a new one that gave her almost complete power.

Fearing for their property, the sugar planters decided to overthrow the queen. To help them, the American minister to Hawaii sent in marines from American ships in the harbor. The queen was re-

Queen Liliuokalani, who ruled between 1891 and 1893, was the last of the Hawaiian monarchs.

moved from power. Then the victorious planters formed a republic and asked that it be made part of the United States. American imperialists were delighted. It appeared that Hawaii was about to come under American control.

President Grover Cleveland, however, opposed imperialism. He sent a representative to Hawaii to find out what had happened there. When the report came back that Americans had been behind the revolt and that American armed forces had wrongly been used, Cleveland refused to go along with annexation. For the next 5 years, the islands remained an independent republic under the control of the American planters. Hawaii was finally annexed during the war with Spain.

The Venezuela boundary dispute Closer to home, the United States was flexing its muscles. For many years, Venezuela and Great Britain had argued over the boundary between Venezuela and the British colony of Guiana in South America. When gold was discovered in the area, the argument became more heated. Venezuela asked the United States to step in and arbitrate the dispute. The British, however, felt their claim was right. They refused to arbitrate.

In 1894, President Cleveland's secretary of state, Richard Olney, told the British that the Monroe Doctrine gave the United States the right to step into any dispute between European and South American countries when it threatened the peace of the Western Hemisphere. When Britain rejected Olney's claim, American anger rose and there was talk of war. The British were startled by this reaction.

They had no desire to go to war with the United States over an unimportant territory thousands of miles away. In 1897 they agreed to arbitration. Two years later the matter was settled. American influence in Latin America was increased, and the Monroe Doctrine was given new importance.

Ask: What was the Monroe Doctrine?

CHECKUP

1. How did American thinking about an overseas empire change in the late 1800s?
2. What brought about United States contact with the following areas in the Pacific? (a) China, (b) Japan, (c) Samoa
3. How did Hawaii come to be a part of the United States?
4. What part did the United States play in a boundary dispute in South America?

War and Empire

VOCABULARY

yellow journalism	Teller Amendment
diplomacy	Rough Riders
"Remember the Maine!"	

Rebellion in Cuba It was the war with Spain in 1898 that announced America's arrival as a world power. The war broke out over events in Cuba, an island 90 miles (144 km) off the coast of Florida. This island, together with Puerto Rico, some 500 miles (800 km) east of Cuba, were all that was left of Spain's once-great empire in the New World.

The people of Cuba had tried many times to rid themselves of Spanish rule, but each time they were beaten down. In 1895, Cubans once more rose up against Spain. In hit-and-run attacks, rebels

517

swept down from their camps in the mountains to burn sugar plantations and sugar mills. To crush the uprising, Spain sent a tough general by the name of Weyler (we′ ē ler) to Cuba. Weyler's plan was simple and cruel. Rebels were receiving food and supplies from people living in the countryside. By cutting off this support, the Spanish believed they could end the rebellion. Weyler ordered thousands of Cubans moved off the sugar plantations and farms and herded them into a few towns surrounded with barbed wire. Spanish troops then burned plantations, crops, and buildings.

Meanwhile, death stalked the camps. More than 100,000 Cubans died of starvation and disease. Weyler's nickname, "the Butcher," was well earned.

Yellow journalism Americans followed events in Cuba through their newspapers. Two New York newspapers, Joseph Pulitzer's *World* and William Randolph Hearst's *Journal,* were locked in a war of their own. Each sought to be the largest-selling newspaper in America. To win readers, they made use of sensational headlines and exaggerated news stories. Such reporting came to be called **yellow journalism.**

The war in Cuba was just what the *World* and the *Journal* needed to sell newspapers. Pulitzer and Hearst each tried to outdo the other in printing the most shocking tales of Spanish cruelty, often with little care for truth. Each hoped for the United States to go to war with Spain over Cuba. On one occasion, Hearst sent a famous artist named Frederic Remington to Cuba to send back drawings

In this cartoon, President McKinley is trying to restrain the forces that are making use of yellow journalism to push the United States into war.

of the cruel warfare on the island. After a short time Remington sent a telegram to Hearst: "Everything is quiet. There is no trouble here. There will be no war. I wish to return." Hearst replied: "Please remain. You furnish the pictures and I'll furnish the war."

Sympathy for the rebels Stories of the cruelty in Cuba stirred the conscience of Americans. There was growing talk of America's "responsibility" to step in and stop the killing. In Congress, there was open sympathy for the rebels. Some officials, including Assistant Secretary of the Navy Theodore Roosevelt, urged that the United States join the fight. Roosevelt's aim was not only to help Cuba but to gain colonies through war.

Discuss the effects of propaganda (in this case the stories of atrocities in the *World* and the *Journal*) on public opinion.

Early investigations blamed the Spanish for the explosion of the *Maine*. Recent investigation, however, shows that the explosion came from inside the ship, which indicates that the Spanish could hardly have been responsible. One popular theory blames Cuban rebels who wanted to involve the United States in their cause.

However, President William McKinley opposed war. He hoped to end the violence and Spanish misrule through **diplomacy**, that is, peaceful negotiations between the governments involved. The President protested to Spain about General Weyler's "uncivilized and inhuman" conduct. A new government in Spain did remove Weyler in 1897. When Spain's rulers spoke of possibly granting Cuban self-rule within the Spanish empire, it seemed that war might be avoided.

"Remember the *Maine*!"   Then came two events in February 1898 that pushed the United States toward war. The first involved a letter that the Spanish minister to the United States wrote to a friend in Havana, Cuba. The letter was stolen by a Cuban rebel and published in the New York *Journal*. In the letter the minister, Dupuy Delôme (dü pü ē′ dē lōm′), called McKinley "weak" and said the President would do anything, including going to war, to be popular with the public. Americans were angered by this insult to their President.

The second and more important event came a week later. The United States had sent the battleship *Maine* to Cuba to protect Americans there. The ship was lying at anchor in Havana Harbor on the night of February 15 when suddenly an explosion ripped it apart. The ship sank, and 260 American sailors serving on the *Maine* lost their lives.

No one has ever discovered who caused the explosion. Most Americans, however, immediately blamed the Spanish and demanded action. The *Journal's* headline read: "WAR! SURE! *MAINE* DESTROYED BY SPANISH." Soon on city streets and in villages the cry **"Remember the *Maine*!"** was on everyone's lips.

A mysterious explosion rocks the Maine *in Havana Harbor.*   (23°N/82°W; map, p. 521)

McKinley and his advisers also feared that failure to act would give the Democrats a major issue in the upcoming presidential election.

The United States goes to war   Ten days after the explosion, Assistant Secretary of the Navy Theodore Roosevelt sent a cable to Commodore George Dewey. "Keep full of coal," instructed Roosevelt. "In the event of declaration of war by Spain, your duty will be to see that Spanish squadron does not leave the Asiatic coast . . . . then [prepare for] offensive operations in Philippine Islands."

McKinley could no longer resist the public pressure for action. On April 11, 1898, he laid the question before Congress. One week later, Congress passed a resolution that recognized Cuban independence and allowed the President to use armed force if necessary to make the Spanish leave the island. One part of this resolution was known as the **Teller Amendment**. It said that America would not seek to take Cuba for itself.

Spain replied by declaring war on the United States on April 24. The next day, Congress declared war on Spain. Dewey steamed out of Hong Kong Harbor bound for Manila Bay.

Manila surrenders   The war in the Pacific was over quickly. A few weeks after Dewey's smashing victory. Filipinos, led by 29-year-old Emilio Aguinaldo (ā mē′ lyō ä gē näl′ dō), rose up against Spanish rule. They had done this 2 years earlier, but the Spanish had put down their revolt.

Now the rebels declared independence and set up a new government. They won several victories over the Spanish. Rebels already controlled much of the land and had surrounded Spanish forces in Manila by the time American troops arrived.

Emilio Aguinaldo fought to free the Philippine Islands, first from Spain and then from America.

Americans joined in the siege. Manila surrendered August 12. Meanwhile, United States forces also captured the Spanish-controlled islands of Wake and Guam (gwäm) in the Pacific.

Success in Cuba   The American navy was equally successful in the Atlantic. Near the end of May, Spain's Atlantic fleet sailed into the harbor of Santiago, the main Spanish military post in Cuba. American warships quickly took up positions just outside the harbor.

The American army's first efforts were disorganized. It had trouble matching men with the right equipment. In its main training center at Tampa, Florida, thousands of men drilled under the hot sun in woolen winter uniforms.

In late June, about 17,000 Americans made the crossing from Tampa to Cuba. They landed on the southern coast of the island, a few miles east of Santiago. Al-

Refer pupils to the picture on page 513. Some of the men in the picture have been overcome by the heat.

though Spain had about 200,000 troops in Cuba at the time, Spanish generals did not take advantage of their number. The Americans landed without a fight.

During the following days the army fought and won battles at El Caney and San Juan (sən hwän) Hill. At the center of the fighting at San Juan Hill was Colonel Theodore Roosevelt. When the war started, Roosevelt resigned from his desk job with the navy to take part in the fighting. Roosevelt led a cavalry regiment known as the **Rough Riders.** The regiment was an odd collection of cowboys, ranchers, miners, Native Americans, and eastern college students.

With American troops pinned down by enemy fire, Roosevelt ordered a charge up San Juan Hill. Mounted on horseback, the colonel recklessly led the charge amid a hail of bullets. Most of his Rough Riders advanced on foot. They were

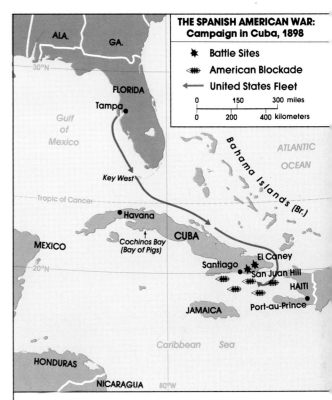

THE SPANISH AMERICAN WAR:
Campaign in Cuba, 1898

Major battles fought at El Caney and San Juan Hill were important to the outcome of the war.

Army field hospitals cared for the sick and wounded during the campaign in Cuba. To the rear of the medical officer (center), stretcher bearers can be seen.

joined by two regiments of black soldiers from the regular army. Despite heavy casualties the Americans took the hill.

The victories at El Caney and San Juan Hill opened the way to Santiago. Admiral Cervera, commander of the Spanish fleet, knew his position was hopeless. If he stayed in Santiago Harbor, the fleet would face a rain of shells from American guns on shore. If he made a dash for open sea, he would surely be caught and destroyed by the waiting United States fleet. Cervera wished to surrender, but his government foolishly ordered him to fight. On July 3 the Spanish fleet sailed out of the harbor to its doom. In 4 hours, Admiral William Sampson's American fleet sank or ran aground every one of Spain's ships.

521

Have pupils find Havana, Santiago, and Tampa on the map.

Hay's comment was part of a letter to Roosevelt. He said, "It has been a splendid little war; begun with the highest motives, carried on with magnificent intelligence and spirit, favored by that fortune which loves the brave."

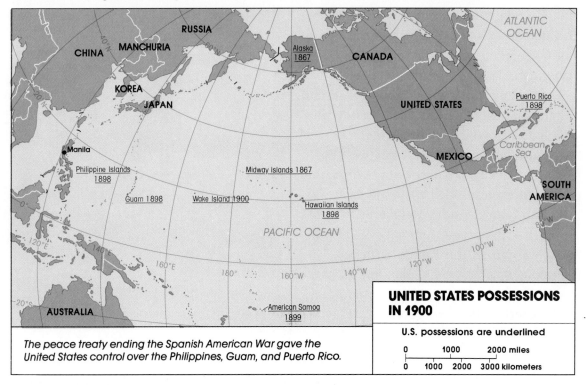

UNITED STATES POSSESSIONS IN 1900

U.S. possessions are underlined

The peace treaty ending the Spanish American War gave the United States control over the Philippines, Guam, and Puerto Rico.

The United States gains an empire Three weeks later, on July 25, American troops under General Nelson A. Miles landed in Puerto Rico. They met little opposition and soon took the island.

By August 12 the war was over. In the final peace treaty, Spain agreed to leave Cuba and to hand over Puerto Rico to the United States. The United States also acquired the Philippine Islands and Guam. Thus in less than 4 months of fighting, the United States gained an empire. No wonder John Hay, one of the imperialists, called the war with Spain "a splendid little war."

Other views Not all Americans favored having an overseas empire. For several months the issue was debated in the Senate and throughout the land. Americans had once had to fight for in-dependence from colonial rule, said some. Was it right, they asked, for the United States now to take other lands as colonies? They declared that ruling other peoples without their consent went against the ideas of the Declaration of Independence. These critics added that it was unwise to try to rule a people having a different culture than our own.

In the end, however, national pride carried the day. The United States Senate approved the peace treaty, and America had an empire.

Many in the Philippine Islands thought that the end of Spanish rule would be the start of Philippine independence. When they found this was not to be, the Filipinos under Aguinaldo rose up against the Americans. It took 70,000 American troops nearly 3 years to put down the rebellion at a cost of $600 million—more

522

Interested pupils could do some research on Emilio Aguinaldo and report their findings to the class.

than the cost of the war with Spain. In the bitter guerrilla warfare, American troops sometimes used the same harsh treatment against the Filipinos that the Spanish had used against the Cubans.

CHECKUP

1. What activities by the Spanish in Cuba in the mid-1890s aroused the sympathy of Americans?
2. How was the United States pushed toward war with Spain in February 1898?
3. What role did each of the following play in the war with Spain? (a) Commodore George Dewey, (b) Colonel Theodore Roosevelt
4. List the terms of the peace treaty ending the Spanish-American War.
5. Why did some Americans oppose the building of an overseas empire?

American Interests in Asia and the Caribbean

```
┌─VOCABULARY────────────────────┐
│ sphere of          protectorate    │
│    influence       intervene       │
│ Open Door policy   Roosevelt       │
│ Boxer Rebellion       Corollary    │
│ Gentlemen's        customs duties  │
│    Agreement                       │
└────────────────────────────────┘
```

The Open Door policy   One reason imperialists wanted to keep the Philippine Islands was that they are close to China. China, with its 400 million people, it was believed, would become a great market for American goods. The imperialists also saw great investment opportunities in developing China's natural resources and in building its railroads.

As it happened, that door was fast closing to Americans at the very time the United States gained the Philippines. All through the nineteenth century, European

powers had taken advantage of the weakness of the Chinese government to create **spheres of influence** in China. A sphere of influence is an area of a country where another nation has gained special trading privileges and other rights solely for itself. The nation that secures those rights will then usually keep out traders and investors from other countries. After Japan defeated China in a war in 1895, more spheres of influence were carved out.

American businesses asked the United States government to do something to keep them from being shut out of China. In 1899, therefore, Secretary of State John Hay sent messages to each of the great trading powers. He asked them to agree to an **Open Door policy** in China. This meant that all nations should have an equal opportunity to trade with China, even within another country's sphere of influence.

None of the six governments that Hay wrote to was really happy with his idea. However, none flatly said, "No." So Hay announced to the world that all six had "accepted" his proposal.

The Boxer Rebellion   Business people, missionaries, and others usually came to live in their country's sphere of influence, bringing with them their foreign ways. Many Chinese objected to this. Thousands of them joined secret societies whose goal was to drive the "foreign devils" out of China. The largest society was one whose Chinese name meant "Righteous and Harmonious Fists." Westerners called them Boxers because they practiced exercises that looked as if they were boxing.

The six countries Hay wrote to were France, Germany, Great Britain, Italy, Japan, and Russia.

523

The international army that defeated the Boxers was made up of troops from Austria, France, Germany, Great Britain, Italy, Japan, Russia, and the United States.

In June 1900 the Boxers rose up in rebellion. They killed hundreds of foreigners as well as hundreds of Chinese Christians, and they destroyed a great deal of foreign property. The Boxers also laid siege to the hundreds of foreigners in the capital city of Peking (pē king ').

An international army from eight countries, including the United States, was sent to rescue their citizens. In August the army arrived at Peking, defeated the Boxers, and freed those who were trapped.

The United States feared that some countries would use the **Boxer Rebellion** as an excuse to carve out more spheres of influence for themselves in China. Secretary Hay stated that the United States was against such threats to China's independence. He persuaded the powers to accept money from China instead of territory to pay for the losses caused by the Boxers. China agreed to pay $33.3 million. The United States received $24 million but returned $20 million to be used to send Chinese students to school in America.

War between Japan and Russia   After Commodore Perry opened Japan to foreign trade, that country imported not only Western goods but Western ideas. Within a few decades, it modernized and industrialized its economy. By 1900, Japan was an important power in Asia.

Like the other powers, Japan sought to extend its control over other lands. It soon became a rival of Russia for control

During the Boxer Rebellion, an international army rescued foreigners trapped in China. Here American forces mount an attack in Peking.   (40°N/104°E; map, p. 522)

of Korea and Manchuria, an area of north-eastern China. (See map, page 522.) In 1904, Japan and Russia went to war.

Japan had the better of the fighting, both on land and on sea. But after a year, Japan began to run out of money and re-sources. The Japanese government asked President Roosevelt to help arrange a peace.

Roosevelt steps in   Roosevelt agreed to try to end the war. He hoped for a peace that would leave neither country with too much power. He knew that if one became too powerful, that country might take over more of China and end the Open Door policy. In 1905, Roosevelt brought repre-sentatives of Japan and Russia together at Portsmouth, New Hampshire. With great skill he got the two sides to agree to peace.

Through his peacemaking efforts, Roo-sevelt had hoped to win greater influence for the United States with Japan. In fact, however, the opposite occurred. Japan did get control over Korea and a sphere of influence in half of Manchuria. But many Japanese thought their country should have received more land. Further, many expected that Russia would be made to pay a large amount of money to Japan for Japan's loss of life and property during the war. When the treaty gave Japan no money, the Japanese public blamed Roosevelt.

The Gentlemen's Agreement   Rela-tions between the two countries were worsened by the poor treatment of Asian immigrants in California, including the Japanese. Californians feared that Asian immigrants working for low pay would take away jobs from Americans. They passed state and local laws that discrim-inated against Asians. In 1906 the San Francisco school board ruled that Asian children could not go to the regular public schools with whites. This was a blow to Japanese pride, and Japan protested.

President Roosevelt was concerned about further damage to America's rela-tions with Japan. He invited San Fran-cisco's mayor and members of its school board to the White House and got them to cancel their order to segregate the Asian children. At the same time, Roosevelt got Japan to agree not to let more workers leave Japan for the United States. This arrangement was known as the **Gentle-men's Agreement.**

Unfortunately the agreement did not end discrimination against Asians on the West Coast. Lawmakers in California, Washington, and other states passed laws forbidding people of Japanese descent to own land. These laws were meant to keep them from owning farms.

Tour of the Great White Fleet   Presi-dent Roosevelt did not want Japan or any-one else to think that he had settled the school board incident out of fear. Roose-velt believed the United States should have a powerful navy. During his presi-dency, more modern ships were added to the navy. The President announced that the new American fleet—16 modern bat-tleships—would sail around the world and make friendly calls at the ports of many nations. He called the tour a good-will cruise. His clear purpose, however, was to make a dramatic show of America's new naval strength.

On its world cruise from 1907 to 1909, the "Great White Fleet" visited ports on four continents. Other nations were impressed with the strength of the United States Navy.

During its 14-month voyage, the Great White Fleet, as it was called, visited many countries. Everywhere, including Japan, it received a warm welcome. The tour succeeded as Roosevelt had hoped. It showed American goodwill, and it showed off American naval muscle.

". . . carry a big stick" Theodore Roosevelt was fond of quoting a West African saying: "Speak softly and carry a big stick; you will go far." To Roosevelt this meant that the United States should be prepared to use force in dealing with other countries to achieve its goals. Nowhere was this policy followed more openly than on the islands in, and the lands around, the Caribbean Sea. In the Caribbean area, Roosevelt rarely spoke softly, but he did carry a big stick.

The pattern of American control of the Caribbean area was set in Cuba. In enter-ing the war against Spain, Congress had promised not to annex Cuba. That promise was kept. However, American troops remained on the island for 3 years. The United States helped build schools and restore the Cuban economy.

In 1902 the United States and Cuba signed a treaty, and American troops left. However, the treaty placed certain limits on Cuba's independence. It required Cuba to give naval bases to the United States. It also gave the United States the right to send troops into Cuba to preserve Cuban "independence." In fact, American troops did return in 1906 when there was a threat of civil war in Cuba. They remained for 3 years, and a few years later they returned yet another time. Thus, though Cuba was not a colony of the United States, it was not completely independent either. A country in such a position is called a **protectorate.**

The ships of the fleet were painted white for the tour, hence the nickname. When the fleet returned home, the ships were again painted in the traditional gray.

It was during the time that the United States occupied Cuba that Walter Reed carried out his investigations of yellow fever. As a result of his work, the army was able to eliminate the disease in Cuba.

The Roosevelt Corollary   Several Latin American countries were not paying off large debts they had incurred by borrowing from Europeans. Roosevelt believed that the countries had an obligation to pay their debts. At the same time, he did not wish European countries to use their armies and navies to collect what was owed them. Roosevelt feared that they might use the debts as an excuse to take control of a small country and gain a foothold in the Western Hemisphere.

In 1904, Roosevelt announced his solution to this problem. The United States, he said, would see that Latin American countries paid their debts, preserved order, and protected life and property. If necessary, the United States would act as a police power and **intervene**, or step in, to do this.

This plan came to be known as the **Roosevelt Corollary**, or addition, to the Monroe Doctrine. That doctrine, you will remember, said that foreign countries may not intervene in the countries of the Western Hemisphere. Under the Roosevelt Corollary, the United States would keep other countries from intervening—by intervening itself.

United States intervention   The Roosevelt Corollary was first used in 1905 in the Dominican Republic, a small nation on an island in the Caribbean Sea. The Dominican Republic had a debt of $32 million, which was owed mostly to Europeans. European countries were threatening to use force to collect the debts. President Roosevelt got the Dominican Republic to agree to allow the United

This cartoon pictures Theodore Roosevelt as an arbitrator of disputes among nations. Some saw his strong foreign policy as an attempt to police the world.

The need for a canal across Central America was dramatically shown during the Spanish-American War, when the United States battleship *Oregon* was sent from San Francisco to Santiago. The 12,000-mile (1,900-km) trip took 68 days, and the war was nearly over when the ship reached its destination.

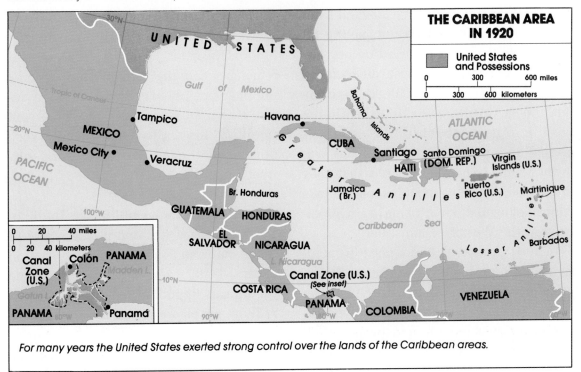

THE CARIBBEAN AREA IN 1920

United States and Possessions

For many years the United States exerted strong control over the lands of the Caribbean areas.

States to take over the collection of **customs duties.** These are taxes that are paid on imported goods. Half the duties were then used to pay off debts; the other half went to run the government.

American customs collectors, backed by the power of the United States government, remained for many years. Like Cuba, the Dominican Republic was not a colony. But it was no longer completely independent either.

The Roosevelt Corollary helped turn the Caribbean Sea into an "American lake." Using the Roosevelt Corollary, the United States controlled the actions of many countries in the region. Under Presidents Taft and Wilson, intervention in the affairs of these countries increased. Often, United States Marines were sent in and stayed for many years. These interventions led to a great deal of ill will toward the United States.

Planning a canal   A big reason why the United States wanted to control the Caribbean lands was to protect a future canal across the narrow neck of Central America. Such a canal would allow the United States Navy to travel quickly from one ocean to another. By eliminating the need to go around the tip of South America, a canal would take nearly 8,000 miles (12,800 km) off the trip between New York and San Francisco.

The idea of a canal across Central America was not a new one. In the 1880s Colombia granted a French company the sole rights to build a canal across Panama, which Colombia controlled. The company failed to carry out its plan but hoped to sell to the United States the rights to build a canal.

Many members of Congress favored a canal site farther north, in Nicaragua. However, at the time the site was under

Discuss this question: Why did American intervention lead to a great deal of ill will toward the United States?

discussion, a volcano in Nicaragua erupted. The threat an active volcano might pose to the canal was a factor in swinging members of Congress in favor of the Panama route.

In 1903, representatives of the United States and Colombia worked out an agreement. The United States would rent a strip of land across Panama, a part of Colombia, and would build a canal there. In return, Colombia would receive the sum of $10 million, plus a yearly payment of $250,000 for 99 years. The United States would pay the French company $40 million for the building rights.

However, Colombia's senate refused to approve the treaty. Its members didn't see why the French company that failed should get $40 million when Colombia, the owner of the land, got only $10 million. They thought Colombia should get at least $25 million.

A revolt in Panama   Probably an agreement could have been worked out with a bit of patience. But President Roosevelt was eager to "make the dirt fly"—that is, to start building a canal. He was angered by Colombia's refusal to go along. A revolt of Panamanians who also wanted a canal built allowed the impatient Roosevelt to have his way.

Panamanians had revolted against Colombian rule many times in the past without success. This time, however, they succeeded. President Roosevelt knew of the plan in advance. He sent a United States warship to keep Colombian troops from landing in Panama to put down the uprising. The revolt occurred on November 3, 1903. It lasted hardly a day and

In the early 1900s a smoking volcano was pictured on a Nicaraguan postage stamp. By chance, that volcano erupted while Congress was debating the site for a proposed canal through Central America. To persuade Congress to turn down the Nicaraguan route, the leading stockholder in the French company that controlled the Panama route sent a copy of the stamp to every congressman. Soon afterwards, Congress chose the Panama route over the one that went through Nicaragua.

was practically bloodless. At the cost of a single life, Panama won its independence. Within 2 weeks the new government signed a treaty with the United States. The United States was allowed to rent—"forever"—a strip of land 10 miles (16 km) wide in which to build its canal that would link the Atlantic and the Pacific oceans.

Throughout Latin America there was widespread resentment over the treaty. Latin Americans felt that their powerful northern neighbor had bullied and cheated Colombia. In 1921, Congress tried to make up for the damage in relations by voting a payment of $25 million to Colombia.

Digging the canal   Bad relations or not, work on the canal went forward. At first, the principal task was to control

A Doctor Helps Build a Canal

The Panama Canal was the greatest engineering achievement of the age. Everything about it was colossal. One person figured out that if all the earth removed from the canal's path was loaded onto railroad cars, the cars would circle the globe four times. Fifty million sacks and barrels of cement went into making the canal locks. This was enough cement to build a wall 8 feet (2.4 m) wide, 12 feet (3.7 m) high, and 300 miles (480 km) long!

Yet for several years an obstacle no larger than a half inch stood in the way of this colossal work. That obstacle was the mosquito, the carrier of deadly yellow fever and malaria. In the unsuccessful attempt by the French to build a canal in the 1880s, many workers had died from these diseases.

The job of ridding Panama of yellow fever and malaria was given to Colonel William C. Gorgas, an army medical officer. Earlier, Gorgas had wiped out yellow fever in Havana, Cuba, in just a few months. There he directed squads of workers to clean out every gutter, drain, and other place with standing water where mosquitoes could breed.

At first, those in charge of the canal project refused to believe there was any connection between mosquitoes and disease. They denied Gorgas the needed supplies and workers. Later, a new chief engineer who supported Gorgas was appointed. Within 2 years, Colonel Gorgas stamped out yellow fever in the Canal Zone and began to bring malaria under control as well. Work could now go forward on building the great "path between the seas."

William Gorgas surveys a body of water where disease-carrying mosquitos could breed.

Construction of the Panama Canal took 10 years and cost $375 million.
When the canal was built, its locks were big enough for any ship afloat. Today there are many ships that are too large to pass through them.

disease (see the opposite page). As soon as yellow fever was curbed, the digging of the canal began in earnest.

In 1907, Colonel George Goethals, an army engineer, was put in charge of the construction project. The canal's route of 50 miles (80 km) ran through jungle, swamps, and mountainous land. Over 40,000 workers were employed in building what was called "the big ditch." Most of them came from the West Indies. In August 1914, 10 years after the first shovelful of earth was turned, the first ship passed through the new Panama Canal. Although the United States controlled the canal, it was open to ships of all nations.

CHECKUP

1. Why did John Hay promote the Open Door policy?
2. How did President Theodore Roosevelt try to improve relations between Japan and the United States?
3. How did the Roosevelt Corollary help turn the Caribbean Sea into an "American lake"?
4. How was the United States able to get control of land for a canal across Central America?
5. What difficulties had to be overcome in building the Panama Canal?

In 1977 the United States and Panama signed a treaty giving Panama control of most of the Canal Zone. The Senate ratified the treaty in 1978. By the terms of the treaty, Panama will assume complete control of both the canal and the Canal Zone on December 31, 1999.

KEY FACTS

1. American anger over Spanish cruelty in Cuba, combined with the sinking of the *Maine*, led America into war with Spain in 1898.

2. The United States emerged from its victorious war against Spain with an overseas empire.

3. The United States tried to preserve trading opportunities with China and to keep that country from being carved up by other powers with the Open Door policy.

4. Under Presidents Roosevelt, Taft, and Wilson, the United States intervened in the affairs of many countries bordering the Caribbean Sea and controlled their policies.

VOCABULARY QUIZ

On a separate sheet of paper, write **T** if the statement is true and **F** if it is false. Then rewrite the sentences you have marked false to make them true statements.

F **1.** Imperialists were opposed to extending control over distant lands.

F **2.** Venezuela asked the United States to arbitrate its dispute with Germany concerning its boundary lines.

T **3.** Yellow journalism was the reporting of events in such a way as to make the stories more sensational.

F **4.** "Remember the *Maine!*" became a slogan after the battleship was blown up at Manila.

F **5.** The Boxer Rebellion came about as an effort to get foreigners out of Japan.

F **6.** George Dewey led a cavalry regiment known as the Rough Riders into battle at San Juan Hill in Cuba.

T **7.** The United States government pressed for the Open Door policy so that it could have an equal opportunity to trade with China.

T **8.** The United States made the Gentlemen's Agreement with Japan that would allow Japanese children to attend public schools if the Japanese prohibited more workers from coming to the United States.

F **9.** The Roosevelt Corollary encouraged European countries to come into the Western Hemisphere.

T **10.** Customs duties are taxes that are paid on goods imported from another country.

REVIEW QUESTIONS

1. What reasons did imperialists give in favor of overseas expansion? What reasons did anti-imperialists give in opposing it?

2. Why did sugar planters in Hawaii want the United States government to annex Hawaii?

3. What factors in the United States and Cuba led to the war with Spain?

4. What was the Open Door policy, and why did the United States favor it?

5. What effect did the Roosevelt Corollary have on relations between the United States and the small nations in the Caribbean?

6. Why was the building of the Panama Canal important to the United States?

ACTIVITIES

1. In your library, find out the status of Puerto Rico and of the Philippines today with regard to the United States.

2. Read about William C. Gorgas and Walter Reed. Find out how their activities affected the building of the Panama Canal.

3. Investigate the recent change in the status of the Panama Canal. Find out if all Americans were in favor of this change.

4. Learn the song "Aloha Oe" written by Queen Liliuokalani.

OUTLINING

HAWAII

Outlining is a special form of note taking. It helps you organize information. A good outline helps you see at a glance how facts and ideas are related to each other.

Most outlines are made up of three parts. First are the main topics or ideas. These brief statements have a Roman numeral in front of them. Next are the subtopics, which support the main topics. They are labeled with capital letters. Third are the details, which tell about each subtopic. They are indicated with Arabic numerals.

To create a good outline, start by previewing what you are reading. Note the headings in heavy type. They will give you ideas about possible main topics. Often you can use these headings themselves as the main topics. For example, suppose you are going to outline the story of how Hawaii became part of the United States, pages 515–516. Start your outline by writing the title at the top of your paper. Surveying pages 515–516, you see two headings that you can use as main topics.

HAWAII
I. Americans in Hawaii
II. Hawaii is Annexed

As you read, you find that the first paragraph deals with the background and early history of the territory. That can be used for a subtopic under main topic I.

HAWAII
I. Americans in Hawaii
  A. Background and early history

Information about early inhabitants, Captain Cook's discovery, and Hawaii as a stopover for whalers and trading ships are all details about

subtopic A. Label these details with Arabic numerals. Your outline will look like this:

HAWAII
I. Americans in Hawaii
  A. Background and early history
    1. Early inhabitants—Asians
    2. Cook discovers Hawaii in 1788
    3. Hawaii becomes stopover for ships

As you continue, you find information about Americans arriving in Hawaii. Some came as missionaries. Later, many became sugar planters and pineapple growers. In time, they became rich and powerful and controlled Hawaii's government. That gives you your second subtopic and supporting details:

  B. Americans arrive in Hawaii
    1. 1820s—missionaries
    2. 1835—sugar planters; later pineapple growers
    3. Grow rich and powerful; control government

The rest of your outline for main topic I would look like this:

  C. U.S. and Hawaii draw closer
    1. 1875—U.S. allows sugar to be imported without tariff
    2. 1875—Hawaii promises not to let others control its lands
    3. 1887—U.S. gains right to build naval base at Pearl Harbor

SKILLS PRACTICE

Following this format, complete the outline on how Hawaii became part of the United States. Start with main topic II, "Hawaii Is Annexed."

533

CHAPTER

24 World War I

Europe Goes to War

> **VOCABULARY**
> militarism   Western Front
> mobilize

A day for celebrating   There was a joyous air in the Bosnian town of Sarajevo (sär′ ə ya′ vō) on the morning of June 28, 1914. Bosnia was a territory of the Austro-Hungarian Empire, but most of its people were Serbs. On this day, Sarajevo would be celebrating the victory, many years before, of the Serbian people over the Turks. To mark the occasion, there would also be a visit from Archduke Franz Ferdinand, the heir to the Austro-Hungarian throne, and his wife, Sophie. The day was a special one for the royal couple, too; it was their fourteenth wedding anniversary. The streets of Sarajevo were gaily decorated, and everything was made ready for the visit of the man who would be the next emperor of Austria-Hungary.

Austria-Hungary was a large hodge-podge of an empire in central and eastern Europe. It was made up of many peoples —Austrians, Hungarians, Czechs, Slovaks, Slovenes, Serbs, Italians, Croatians, Poles, and others. Many of these peoples did not want to be in the Austro-Hungarian Empire. They wanted to live in independent countries of their own. For example,

Have pupils find Sarajevo on the map on page 538.

the Serbs in Bosnia wanted their territory to become part of the neighboring country of Serbia. Naturally, Austria-Hungary wanted to keep control of Bosnia. In fact, one of the reasons for the visit of Archduke Franz Ferdinand was to soothe the Serbs in the empire.

Death in Sarajevo   A group of seven young men in Sarajevo that morning had other ideas. They were members of a secret society called Union or Death. Its goal was to unite Bosnia with Serbia. Armed with guns and homemade bombs, this group of seven scattered through the crowd to wait for the archduke's procession to pass by.

Shortly after 10:00 A.M. the archduke's motorcar rolled down the street past the first member of the group. He froze. The second, standing a few steps away, threw a bomb that barely missed the car but injured a dozen spectators. The next four also had opportunities but failed to seize them.

The seventh man, Gavrilo Princip (prēn′ tsēp), did not fail. The driver of the archduke's car made a wrong turn, bringing it down the street on which Princip was standing. As the car came within 5 feet (1.5 m) of him, Princip fired two shots, killing both the archduke and his wife.

Members of a German U-boat crew watch a vessel go down after being torpedoed. Submarine warfare was a major factor in bringing the United States into World War I.

Princip was born in 1895. He was a high school student at the time of the assassination. He and some of his compatriots were caught, tried, and sentenced. Princip was in prison when he died of tuberculosis in 1918.

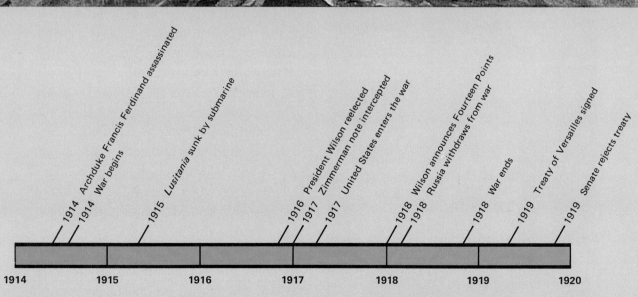

1914 Archduke Francis Ferdinand assassinated
1914 War begins
1915 Lusitania sunk by submarine
1916 President Wilson reelected
1917 Zimmerman note intercepted
1917 United States enters the war
1918 Wilson announces Fourteen Points
1918 Russia withdraws from war
1918 War ends
1919 Treaty of Versailles signed
1919 Senate rejects treaty

1914   1915   1916   1917   1918   1919   1920

Ask: How long did World War I last? (4 years) In what year was the peace treaty signed? (1919) When did the United States enter the war? (1917)

Those two shots set off a chain of events that led to one of the most destructive wars in history. Nearly every country in Europe became involved in what soon was called the Great War. It is known today as the First World War. Before it was over, 10 million soldiers and another 10 million civilians were killed. About 20 million more were badly injured. In countries like France and Germany, a whole generation of young men was wiped out. Property worth billions of dollars was destroyed.

How could this killing in a distant corner of Europe lead to such a horrifying result? To understand this, we must understand what had been happening in Europe during the previous 35 years.

The murder of Archduke Franz Ferdinand and his wife in Sarajevo on June 28, 1914, touched off events that led to World War I. (43°N/18°E; map, p. 538)

Imperial rivalries   The late nineteenth century was the great age of imperialism, or empire building. European powers added to their colonial holdings by raising their flags over many lands. Russia and Austria-Hungary, two of the great land powers, extended their control over neighboring peoples. Britain, France, Germany, Italy, and others added to their empires or created new ones by carving out colonies in Asia and Africa.

Colonies were important to European countries for several reasons. Colonies provided a supply of raw materials for those countries' expanding industries as well as markets for their manufactured goods. Bankers could invest in colonies and get a good, safe return on their money. Also, exercising control over others gave a satisfying feeling of power and pride to the peoples and governments of the imperialist countries. The race for colonies led to growing rivalry among the European powers.

Nationalism and armies   Among the great powers of Europe, nationalism was on the rise. Nationalism is a very strong feeling of loyalty toward one's country. Nationalism was also strong among subject peoples of Austria-Hungary. Many people were fiercely proud of their national heritage and expressed their loyalty to it. Sometimes, however, nationalism turned into a chip-on-the-shoulder attitude toward others and added fuel to old grudges and hatreds. Such strong feelings could easily lead to war.

The rise of nationalism and the drive for colonies was accompanied by **militarism**, that is, an emphasis on armies,

Franz Ferdinand's wife was Countess Sophie Chotek, Duchess of Hohenberg.

navies, and military power. Each country believed that a large army was an expression of national greatness. It also provided the means to protect oneself against others. Britain, an island nation, had the world's largest navy. Germany had an army of 4.5 million soldiers; France, an army of 4 million; and Russia, an army of more than 6 million. Europe was an armed camp.

The growth of alliances   Countries did not depend only upon their own armies and navies to protect themselves. They formed alliances with others. By 1914 there were two major alliances in Europe. Germany, Austria-Hungary, and Italy formed the Triple Alliance. These countries were also known as the Central Powers because they occupied the center of Europe. The other major alliance was the Triple Entente (än tänt´), made up of Russia, France, and Great Britain. Later they were known as the Allies. There were other alliances, too. Britain promised to protect Belgium from attack. Russia was the protector of Serbia.

With rivalries growing, nations arming themselves heavily, and a system of alliances involving every major power, peace in Europe rested on shaky ground. In fact, between 1900 and 1914, war almost broke out five different times. No wonder an American visiting Europe said that the continent was like a powder keg. "It requires only a spark to set the whole thing off," he predicted.

The shots fired in Sarajevo provided that spark. This is what followed. Austria-Hungary blamed Serbia for the death of its future emperor and declared war.

Mounted troops of Austria and Germany take part in training exercises in 1909.

Russia **mobilized,** or assembled, its army and prepared for war to protect Serbia. Germany knew what that would mean: If Russia attacked Austria-Hungary, Germany was bound by treaty to come to its ally's defense. That would automatically bring in France on the side of *its* partner, Russia. Germany would then face the situation it most dreaded, a war on both its eastern and western borders.

Germany therefore jumped the gun and declared war on both Russia and France. Germany's armies crashed into neutral Belgium, hoping to circle around the main French armies and knock France out of the war quickly. This brought Belgium's protector, Great Britain, into the war. In a week's time, much of Europe was at war.

Later that fall, Turkey came in on the side of the Central Powers. Bulgaria did

Have pupils find on the map on page 538 the countries named above.

537

the same in 1915. Italy, which had held back from joining the Central Powers, also entered the war in 1915 but on the side of the Allies. The lineup of sides was completed, and the continent of Europe was in flames.

A new kind of warfare Germany's plan to quickly defeat France almost succeeded. However, German troops were stopped just 15 miles (24 km) from Paris in the battle of the Marne. A French plan for a quick knockout of Germany was no more successful. With that, fighting in the west settled into a stalemate.

In those first months of the war, loss of life was staggering. Each side lost a half-million men. The main reason was a new weapon, the machine gun. A single gun could mow down hundreds of soldiers crossing an open field. Armies therefore learned to fight defensively. A soldier's shovel proved to be as important as his gun, as each side dug trenches, or long ditches, for protection. The men lived in these muddy trenches for months at a time, through rain and miserable cold. All the while, huge guns fired across the battle lines without letup. This line of trenches, running 400 miles (640 km) across Belgium and France, was known as the **Western Front.**

On the Western Front In trench warfare a typical battle consisted of soldiers of one side rushing out—"going over the

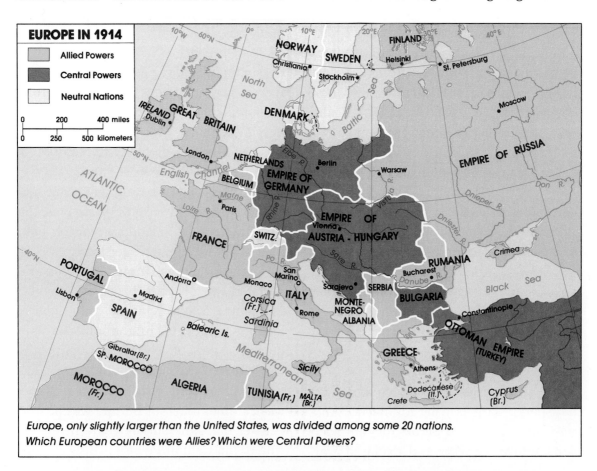

Europe, only slightly larger than the United States, was divided among some 20 nations. Which European countries were Allies? Which were Central Powers?

Allies: Finland, Russia, Romania, Serbia, Montenegro, Greece, Italy, France, Belgium, Luxembourg, Great Britain, Portugal, Algeria; *Central Powers:* Germany, Austria-Hungary, Bulgaria, Ottoman Empire

From 1914 to 1918, armies on both sides of the Western Front lived in trenches.   Separating the armies was a stretch of lifeless earth called no-man's land.

This photograph shows a French trench on the Alsace Front in 1916.

top"—and trying to break through the enemy's line of trenches. If they succeeded, they could pour men through the gap and attack the enemy's line of trenches from the rear. But barbed wire, machine guns, and poison gas made such attempts costly. In 1915 alone, the French lost 1.5 million men. For 3½ years, battle lines on the Western Front hardly moved.

On the Eastern Front, fighting between Russia and the Central Powers was equally fierce. The Russian armies defeated the Austro-Hungarian forces in a number of battles. On the other hand, German armies were successful in taking over huge chunks of Russian territory.

CHECKUP

1. What happened in Sarajevo in June 1914 that had far-reaching consequences?
2. Why were European countries competing for colonies at this time?
3. What were some results of the rise of nationalism in Europe?
4. How was the warfare of World War I different from that of earlier wars?

America's Reaction

┌─VOCABULARY─────────────────┐
│ **international**   *Lusitania*   │
│   **law**   *Sussex* **Pledge**   │
│ **submarine**   │
└────────────────────────────┘

A call for neutrality   Americans were shocked by the news that Europe was at war. Most, however, shared the view expressed by one newspaper: "Luckily we have the Atlantic between us and Europe. It is their war, not ours." President Wilson also said that this was a war "with which we have nothing to do." The President asked that all Americans be neutral "in thought as well as in action."

Being neutral in thought was hard for many. Nearly one in every three Americans either was born in Europe or had parents born in Europe. Many still had relatives in the countries now at war. A good many Americans of German background sided with Germany. Many Irish Americans were opposed to anything that was British.

Have interested pupils investigate the new strategies and weapons used in World War I and find out more about their role in World War I. Possible topics are trench warfare, airplanes, dirigibles, tanks, machine guns, flame throwers, submarines, and poison gas.

Most Americans, however, leaned toward Great Britain and the Allies. Not only were many Americans of British origin, but they spoke the same language and shared many traditions. Many high officials in the United States government were pro-Ally. Also, Germany's invasion of neutral Belgium turned a great many Americans against Germany. Still, for all these feelings, nearly all Americans wanted the United States to stay out of the fighting.

Violating America's rights   As the war progressed, Americans found it more and more difficult to follow a neutral course. The reason had to do with the violation of America's neutral rights on the seas. As a neutral nation, the United States had certain rights under **international law.** International law is the body of rules that countries agree to follow in controlling their relations with each other. One right held by neutral nations was to trade with both sides, except in weapons and similar war goods. But part of the war plan of each side was to keep supplies from reaching its enemy.

The British, with the largest navy in the world, used several means to do this. They dropped explosive devices called mines in the North Sea, making it dangerous for any ship to try to sail to German ports. They also announced a blockade of all German ports. This meant that no ships, no matter what they were carrying or what country they were from, would be allowed to enter the ports. The British navy stopped and searched American ships on the high seas for war goods. This was legal under international law, except that the British used their own definition of war goods. Their list included anything they thought might be of help to the enemy—oil, metals, even cotton and food. British warships sometimes forced American cargo ships into British ports for weeks at a time.

These actions angered the United States. President Wilson protested them strongly. The British continued them but were careful not to go so far with their actions as to cause a break in relations with America.

Submarine warfare   Britain's powerful navy kept German warships bottled up in port for most of the war. Germany, therefore, could not use its surface fleet to keep supplies from reaching its enemy. To do this, it came to rely on a new weapon, the **submarine.** The submarine, a warship that could operate under water, proved to be very effective. However, it could only be effective by breaking the rules of war agreed upon under international law.

The reason was this: International law required that before sinking an enemy merchant or passenger ship, the commander of a warship must allow time for passengers and crew to get off safely. Passengers and crew were considered to be civilians, and civilian life was to be spared.

These rules were made in an age when all warships were fast, heavily armed surface vessels. Giving warning before sinking a merchant ship or passenger ship cost nothing but a little time. Because the safety of passengers was assured, even citizens of neutral countries had the right to travel on ships of warring nations. The submarine, however, was a small weak vessel that depended upon surprise. If it came to the surface to give warning, it could easily be sunk by its intended

In 1915 the German Embassy warned travelers about the dangers of sailing on British ships in wartime.

OCEAN STEAMSHIPS.

CUNARD

EUROPE VIA LIVERPOOL
LUSITANIA

Fastest and Largest Steamer
now in Atlantic Service Sails
SATURDAY, MAY 1, 10 A. M.
Transylvania, Fri., May 7, 5 P.M.
Orduna, - - Tues.,May 18, 10 A.M.
Tuscania, - - Fri., May 21, 5 P.M.
LUSITANIA, Sat., May 29, 10 A.M.
Transylvania, Fri., June 4, 5 P.M.

Gibraltar–Genoa–Naples–Piraeus
S.S. Carpathia, Thur., May 13, Noon

NOTICE!

TRAVELLERS intending to embark on the Atlantic voyage are reminded that a state of war exists between Germany and her allies and Great Britain and her allies; that the zone of war includes the waters adjacent to the British Isles; that, in accordance with formal notice given by the Imperial German Government, vessels flying the flag of Great Britain, or of any of her allies, are liable to destruction in those waters and that travellers sailing in the war zone on ships of Great Britain or her allies do so at their own risk.

IMPERIAL GERMAN EMBASSY

WASHINGTON, D. C., APRIL 22, 1915.

victim. Yet firing its torpedoes without warning was almost certain to take the lives of innocent civilians—including people from neutral nations.

On February 4, 1915, Germany declared the waters around the British Isles to be a war zone. German submarines would sink without warning all enemy ships in that zone. The German government warned neutral ships that they entered the war zone at their own risk. "It may not always be possible to save crews and passengers," said the German announcement.

President Wilson was shocked and angry. The United States, he told the German government, would hold Germany responsible for any loss of American lives or ships.

The *Lusitania* is sunk   Wilson did not have to wait long for his words to be tested. On May 7, 1915, the British passenger liner *Lusitania* was torpedoed without warning off the coast of Ireland. Within 15 minutes the ship sank, carrying 1,198 passengers—128 of them Americans—to a watery grave.

The sinking of the *Lusitania* led to a major crisis between the United States and Germany. Some enraged Americans, including former President Theodore Roosevelt, called for war. President Wilson followed a more cautious course. He demanded that Germany apologize, make payment to the families of the victims, and end its use of the submarine.

Germany replied, correctly, that the *Lusitania* had been carrying arms and ammunition. The Germans also pointed out that they had placed ads in New York

The term *U-boat* comes from the German *U-boot*, which is short for *unterseeboot*, meaning "undersea boat."

The Allies also used submarines during World War I, although not as extensively as the Germans.

A U-boat victim, the Lusitania *sank off the Irish coast with the loss of 1,198 lives.*

newspapers warning Americans to stay off the ship. Wilson, however, declared that none of this excused the loss of life. He insisted that Germany yield.

After a time, Germany accepted responsibility for the loss of American lives and agreed to pay damages. It also promised not to sink unarmed passenger ships without warning. This outcome was regarded as a victory for President Wilson.

The *Sussex* Pledge   That was not the end of submarine warfare, however. The German pledge covered only passenger ships. Over the following months, German submarines sank many British and French merchant ships.

Then in the spring of 1916, a German submarine torpedoed the French passenger ship *Sussex*, injuring several American passengers. This time, Wilson warned that if Germany continued to attack ships without warning, the United States would break off diplomatic relations. This would be a most serious step because it was just one step short of war.

Germany gave in and issued the *Sussex* **Pledge.** Its submarines would no longer torpedo either passenger ships or merchant ships without warning. Once again, it appeared that Wilson had won a victory for American principles without going to war.

Preparedness   A growing number of Americans came to believe that while the United States must work for peace, it must also prepare for the possibility of war. They favored a program of preparedness. To defend the country, said supporters of preparedness, the army and navy must be built up.

Wilson's stand resulted in the resignation of Secretary of State William Jennings Bryan. He believed that it was wrong for the United States, as a neutral nation, to treat German violations of international law differently from British violations.

A good many Americans disagreed. Instead of keeping us out of war, they said, having a larger army and navy would tempt the United States to get into the war. Moreover, argued some, preparedness would just put money into the pockets of those who profited from war.

Wilson wins a second term In 1916, Wilson sought a second term as President. His Republican opponent was Charles Evans Hughes, a justice of the Supreme Court and a former Progressive governor of New York. Wilson had won the support of many Progressives through his championing of Progressive laws in his first term. Now his supporters came up with the slogan "He kept us out of war." The slogan proved to be effective, and Wilson was the winner in a close election.

Wilson knew that the longer the war in Europe dragged on, the harder it would be to keep America from being drawn into it. Earlier he had tried several times to get the two sides to end the war. Following his reelection in 1916, he tried once more. Neither side, however, was ready to settle for anything less than a clear victory.

In January 1917, Wilson made a speech before the United States Senate in which he gave his own ideas on a fair peace settlement. He called for a "peace without victory," one with neither a winner nor a loser. "Only a peace between equals can last," he said. The President also came out in favor of a general association of nations to keep the peace.

A fateful decision Even before Wilson's speech, however, Germany's leaders had made a fateful decision. They believed that Germany could win the war if it could cut off all supplies from the United States to the Allies. They believed they now had enough submarines to do this. Therefore, Germany announced that it would no longer be bound by the Sussex Pledge. All ships, including those of neutral nations, that entered the waters around the British Isles from January 31 on would be torpedoed without warning.

Germany knew that this action would probably bring the United States into the war. However, German leaders believed it would take a year before American military forces could go into action in Europe. By then, the submarine warfare, combined with an all-out attack on the Western Front, would have knocked out the British and the French.

President Wilson promptly announced the breaking off of diplomatic relations with Germany. Still, he hoped to avoid war. However, events soon forced him to act.

A Wilson campaign button in 1916 links the President with efforts to keep America at peace with the world.

At a special session on April 2, 1917, Wilson asks Congress to declare war on Germany.

The Zimmerman telegram In February, German submarines sank three American ships. Then came startling information from the British government. British agents had intercepted a secret telegram from Germany's foreign secretary, Arthur Zimmerman, to the German minister to Mexico.

Should war break out between Germany and the United States, the German diplomat was instructed by Zimmerman to offer Mexico the opportunity to ally itself with Germany. In exchange for Mexico's support, Germany would help Mexico "to reconquer the lost territory in Texas, New Mexico, and Arizona." This was the territory awarded the United States after the Mexican War. (See page 304.) When the United States government released this telegram to the newspapers on March 1, the American public was furious. Especially angry were the people of the Southwest. Then in March, German submarines sank five more American ships.

The United States goes to war Wilson could delay no longer. On April 2, 1917, he called Congress into special session and asked it to declare war on Germany. He said:

> The world must be made safe for democracy. . . . We have no selfish ends to serve. We desire no conquest, no dominion. We seek no . . . material compensation for the sacrifices we shall freely make. We are but one of the champions of the rights of mankind.

On April 6, 1917, Congress declared war on Germany. The United States had entered the Great War.

CHECKUP

1. Why did most Americans lean toward the Allies from the very outbreak of the Great War?
2. In what ways did the British violate America's neutral rights on the seas?
3. Why did German submarine warfare make it more difficult for the United States to stay neutral?
4. How did the Zimmerman telegram help bring the United States into the war?

Discuss the decision to enter the war. Ask: What choices did the United States have in 1917? What happened to the neutrality proclaimed by the United States? Should the United States have honored the German blockade and not shipped goods to Britain? Could the United States have stayed out of the war?

Waging the War

┌─VOCABULARY─────────────────┐

Selective Service   convoy
   Act
                    armistice
ration

└────────────────────────────┘

Filling the ranks   Now came the gigantic task of gearing up for war. The first step was to create an army. Americans had a long tradition of being opposed to a large standing army. At the time America entered the war, the regular army numbered only 75,000 men. In May 1917, Congress passed the **Selective Service Act.** This law required men between the ages of 21 and 30 to register for the draft. Later the age limits were widened to 18 and 45.

Before the war ended, 24 million men had registered, and nearly 3 million were drafted. Another 2 million volunteered or were in National Guard units called up for duty. Altogether 4.8 million Americans entered the service. This number included thousands of women who enlisted in the Nurse Corps of the army and the navy.

A new role for government   On entering the war, the United States was shocked to learn that the Allies were short of ammunition, clothing, and food. America would have to supply food and other supplies not only for its new army but for the Allies as well.

Throughout American history, decisions about what and how much to produce had always been made by private businesses. They decided on the basis of the demand for the goods and the opportunity for profit. Now, however, the federal government took on a greater role. To increase industrial production and cut down waste, the government created the War Industries Board. Bernard Baruch, a Wall Street financier, headed the board. The War Industries Board had sweeping powers. If there was not enough steel for both trucks and guns, the board decided how many of each should be made and which companies should make them.

Urged on by the War Industries Board and by large government contracts, factories ran day and night. Shells, rifles, uniforms, and other military supplies poured out of America's factories.

A need for workers   With more than 4 million men in uniform, there was a shortage of workers for making steel, running railroads, digging coal, and operating machines. To make the best use of the workers that remained, the government created the War Labor Board. The labor board saw to it that workers were available where they were needed. The board also urged management to recognize unions and bargain fairly with them. In return, it won from labor leaders like Samuel Gompers of the AFL a "no strike" pledge. Gompers strongly supported the war effort.

Two groups helped to fill the gap created by workers leaving for the service. A million additional women took jobs outside the home during the war. They did work that had never before been open to them. They made guns and ammunition, drove trucks, operated streetcars, and supervised assembly lines.

A second large new group of industrial workers was made up of southern blacks.

545

Women examine and pack shells in an ammunition factory in Connecticut during World War I.

Hundreds of thousands left the rural South for jobs in the factories of northern cities. In some communities the newcomers met with hostility, as they crowded into whatever housing was available. These families were part of the first great wave of black migration from the South to the North, and from farms to cities.

Increasing food supplies   To increase production of food and also to cut down consumption at home, the government created the Food Administration. President Wilson appointed Herbert Hoover to head it. Wilson could not have found a better person for the job. Herbert Hoover was born and raised on a small Iowa farm. He was orphaned at the age of 10. He worked his way through Stanford University, where he studied engineering, and became a mining engineer.

Hoover's work took him to distant lands—Australia, Russia, Africa, Latin America, and China. He was among the Americans trapped in Peking, China, during the Boxer Rebellion of 1900. His skills as an engineer and an organizer of large projects made him a millionaire before he was 40.

Hoover was living in London when the war in Europe broke out. He quickly offered his services to do welfare work among the victims of war. As head of the Belgian War Relief, he organized the feeding of 10 million starving Belgian and French people.

When the United States entered the war, Herbert Hoover lent his brilliant organizing talents to his own country. Under Hoover the Food Administration encouraged farmers to grow more by offering a high price for all the wheat they could produce. Hoover also got Americans to cut down consumption of food by observing "wheatless Mondays" and "meatless Tuesdays." Americans were also urged not to waste food. When eating apples, they were told to be "patriotic to the core." The government also **rationed**, or limited the consumption of, certain goods, such as sugar, so that there would be enough for the troops.

Safeguarding shipping   All the goods of America's farms and factories would be of no help in the war effort if they could not be delivered safely to Europe. When the United States entered the war, German submarines were sinking ships twice as fast as they could be replaced.

Admiral William Sims of the United States Navy proposed the use of a **convoy system**. In a convoy, freighters and troop carriers travel in a large group, escorted

With Hoover's wide connections and expertise in metal mining, he could have made a fortune during the war. Instead, he decided to put his organizational skills into welfare work among victims of the war.

on all sides by destroyers. These are small, fast warships that are equipped to fight off submarines.

Sims had to spend several weeks convincing the British navy that his convoy plan would work. Then he had to win over his fellow admirals in the United States Navy. They wanted to hold back their warships for other possible naval action. But Sims finally convinced them that convoying was an essential task.

Convoys proved to be very successful. In just 6 months, shipping losses were cut by two thirds. Most important, <u>not a single one of the 2 million American troops that were ferried to Europe was lost to the submarine.</u>

Pershing heads the army   The job of shaping the draftees and volunteers into a fighting army went to General John J.

Herbert Hoover, head of the Food Administration during the war, also directed relief programs in Europe.

Pershing. Pershing had had a varied career in the army. He had spent boring years in isolated outposts in the West. He had taught military science at the University of Nebraska and at West Point. He had served behind a desk in Washington and had fought in Cuba and the Philippines during the war with Spain. His commanding officer in the fighting in Cuba said he was "the coolest man under fire I ever saw."

Pershing got his nickname, Black Jack, from commanding for a time the Negro Tenth Cavalry, an outstanding unit. He and these troops liked and respected each other, and Pershing carried his nickname proudly throughout his career.

In 1917, with more than 30 years of service, Pershing wanted a bigger challenge. He was quite open about his ambitions. When the United States broke diplomatic ties with Germany, Pershing told a group of newspaper reporters, "That means that we will send an expedition abroad. I'd like to command it. Each of you must know some way in which you can help me. Now tell me how I can help you so that you can help me."

As it turned out, Pershing needed no help from the reporters. He had already come to the notice of President Wilson. One month after the United States entered the war, Pershing was called to the White House. "General, we are giving you some very difficult tasks these days," said the President. "Perhaps so, Mr. President," replied Pershing, "but that is what we are trained to expect." That is all that was said. A few weeks later, <u>Wilson appointed Pershing to command the American Expeditionary Force (AEF).</u>

The Yanks are coming   The first American soldiers set foot in France in June 1917. Their numbers, however, were small and increased but slowly through the fall and winter. Not until the spring of 1918, a year after the United States entered the war, did large numbers of American soldiers arrive. Then they came in a flood.

A sizable number of these troops were black Americans. Altogether nearly 370,000 blacks were in service. Although they, too, were part of the fight to "make the world safe for democracy," they faced discrimination at every turn. However, they fought hard and courageously. Many were honored by the French government for their bravery under fire.

Russia leaves the war   American forces arrived none too soon. Events in the east had changed the military picture dramatically. The war had gone badly for Russia. Its government was very inefficient. Its army was plagued by shortages of guns, ammunition, clothing, and food.

In March 1917 the Russians overthrew their tsar, or emperor, and set up a democratic government. That government was in turn overthrown by the Communists

The first American troops arrived in France on June 26, 1917.

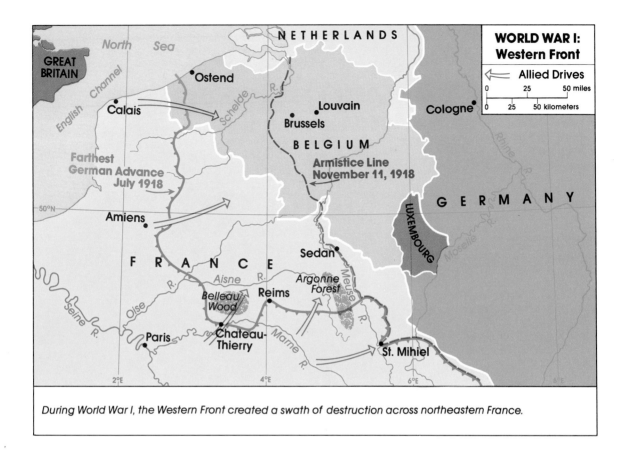

During World War I, the Western Front created a swath of destruction across northeastern France.

6 months later. Communist leaders were determined to get Russia out of the war even if it cost territory. They made peace with Germany in March 1918.

With Russia's withdrawal from the war, Germany could shift troops from the Eastern Front to the Western Front. Bolstered by these new arrivals, German forces began a great offensive in the spring of 1918. Once again, as in the early weeks of the war, they hammered French and British troops back toward Paris. But this time, when Allied armies rallied to check the German advance, American troops were at their side.

American troops in action Americans saw their first important action of the war in May, when they captured the town of Cantigny (kän tēn yē′) at one end of the Allied line. In June some 30,000 American troops helped the French turn back a German drive at Chateau-Thierry (sha tō tye rē′), some 56 miles (90 km) from Paris. Then, despite heavy losses, Pershing's troops took Belleau (be lō′) Wood.

In July and August came what many believe was the turning point of the war. The Germans attacked once more along the Marne River. With 85,000 American troops holding down one end of the line, the Allies stopped the Germans. Then the Americans started a counterattack. General Pershing later wrote that this attack "turned the tide of the war."

From this point on, it was the Allied and American forces that were on the offensive. In early September, American

549

What's in a Name?

DOUGHBOYS

Fighting men pick up nicknames easily, especially in wartime. During the War for Independence, there were minutemen. By the 1830s, marines were being called "leathernecks," from the black leather collar that was part of their uniform. And in the Civil War, Northern soldiers were called "blues" and Southern soldiers "grays," after the colors of their uniforms.

In World War I the nickname for an infantryman, or foot soldier, was "doughboy." No one can say for sure where the nickname came from. One possibility is that it came from a brass button that earlier soldiers wore on their uniforms. The buttons were called doughboys because they had the same shape as biscuits by that name that used to be served to sailors. Another explanation is that the infantry used to wear white belts that they cleaned with a kind of clay, or "dough." Whatever the origin of the word, just about everyone called an infantryman a doughboy.

Doughboys take a brief rest before advancing near Saint Mihiel.

troops, now more than half a million strong, drove back the Germans at Saint Mihiel (san mē yel′). Later that month the Americans fought a bloody battle in the Argonne Forest, pushing the Germans back. By the end of September, more than 1.2 million Americans were in action.

The Great War ends The Central Powers now knew their cause was hopeless. One by one they surrendered—Bulgaria in September, Turkey in October, Austria-Hungary in November. Germany finally asked for an **armistice**, or cease-fire, and on November 11, 1918, the shooting stopped. The Great War was over.

The United States had played an important part in achieving the victory over Germany. It had provided food and supplies when they were desperately needed. The British and French had suffered terrible losses during 4 years of fighting. Their troops were tired and discouraged. The arrival of fresh troops from America gave a great lift to Allied morale and helped the British and the French to fight on. In the end, it was the knowledge that several million more American troops could be thrown into battle that convinced the Germans they could not win.

CHECKUP

1. What steps were taken to produce war goods?
2. How did the government increase the production of food and curb consumption at home?
3. In getting goods and troops to Europe, how was the threat of submarine warfare met?
4. In what ways did the American Expeditionary Force help win the Great War?

Making the Peace

VOCABULARY
Fourteen Points	**League of Nations**
self-determination	**reparations**

Wilson's peace program President Wilson had called the Great War the "war to end all wars." He gave much thought to the kind of peace terms that could fulfill that hope.

In January 1918, Wilson outlined a peace known as the **Fourteen Points.** He asked for the following:

(1) An end to secret treaties

(2) Freedom of the seas

(3) An increase in trade among nations

(4) A reduction in the size of armies and navies

(5) A move toward the end of colonialism

(6) The removal of German troops from Russia

(7) The removal of German troops from Belgium

(8) The removal of German troops from France and the return of Alsace-Lorraine to France

(9) Changes in Italy's borders according to the nationalities of people living in border areas

(10) Limited self-government for the peoples of Austria-Hungary

(11) The removal of German troops from the Balkans with Serbia gaining access to the sea

(12) Independence for Turkey but with the opportunity for other groups under Turkish rule to have self-government

(13) Independence for Poland

(14) Creation of an association of nations

A goal of several of the Fourteen Points was for each nationality group to be able to live in its own country, under a government chosen by its own people—in short, to be able to practice **self-determination.** Wilson's fourteenth point was, to him, the most important one. The President called for all countries of the world to form the **League of Nations.** The foremost goal of this international organization would be to insure that the nations of the world would never again wage war.

Other plans Europe's victorious powers, however, had other plans. Each country—France, Great Britain, and Italy —burned with revenge and wanted to punish Germany.

Each, fearing for its future security, wanted to leave Germany too weak ever to make war again. Each wanted to take over territory that was part of Germany or Austria-Hungary, to take over Germany's colonies, or do both. And each wanted to make Germany pay for the entire cost of the war. Such payments are called **reparations,** since they are for repairing the damage caused by the enemy.

The Paris Conference Paris, France, was chosen as the place where delegates from 32 nations would meet in January 1919 to draw up a peace treaty. President Wilson decided to attend himself. No President had ever gone to Europe during his term of office. But Wilson felt that only he could get his goals written into the treaty. All the major decisions at the conference were made by the Big Four— Wilson and the prime ministers of Great Britain, Italy, and France.

The Big Four were David Lloyd George of Great Britain; Vittorio Orlando of Italy; Georges Clemenceau of France; and Wilson.

The peace treaty was completed 4 months later. It was signed in the Palace of Versailles (ver sī'), and was therefore called the Treaty of Versailles. But it was not the "peace without victory" that Wilson had hoped for. It was a victor's peace, dictated to defeated Germany. Nor was it a peace based completely on the Fourteen Points. Wilson had to accept many compromises. France not only recovered territory lost to Germany in an earlier war, but it also occupied valuable mining areas in Germany. Great Britain and France took over many of Germany's overseas colonies. Germany was allowed to keep only a small army and a small navy. Finally, the treaty laid the entire blame for the war on Germany and required that it pay reparations to the Allies. The amount became a staggering $56 billion.

Wilson did win on a number of points. Many boundaries in Europe were re-drawn. The Polish and Czech peoples each got their own country. Serbs were united in a new country, Yugoslavia, though this country contained other national groups as well. Most important to Wilson, the countries who drew up the peace terms accepted his plan for the League of Nations. They made the international peace-keeping organization a part of the Treaty of Versailles.

The task of winning approval Wilson now faced the task of winning his country's approval of the peace treaty. The Constitution requires that a treaty must be approved in the United States Senate by a two-thirds vote.

The most controversial part of the treaty was the plan for the League of Nations. A number of senators had already announced that they opposed having the United States join the League of Nations.

World leaders meet at Versailles to sign the peace treaty ending World War I.

In 1921 the United States and Germany made a separate treaty. An index treaty, its provisions merely referred to those of the Treaty of Versailles, which were either accepted or rejected by the United States. Provisions accepted were those with

Born: 1856, Staunton, Virginia. **Education:** Princeton University. **Training:** Lawyer, teacher, university president, public official. **To presidency from:** New Jersey. **Position when elected:** Governor of New Jersey. **Political party:** Democratic. **Married:** (1) Ellen Louise Axson, (2) Edith Bolling Galt. **Children:** Three daughters. **Died:** 1924, Washington, D.C., following a stroke in 1919 that made him an invalid. **Other facts:** An outstanding scholar. A professor at Bryn Mawr, Wesleyan, and Princeton. Also coached the football team at Wesleyan. Became president of Princeton University. The first President to hold a doctoral (Ph.D.) degree. **During his presidency:** The United States purchased Denmark's Virgin Islands for $25 million.

WOODROW WILSON
28th President
1913 · 1921

respect to colonies, disarmament, reparations, and responsibility for the war.

They said that this would break America's long tradition of isolation. Among them were William Borah of Idaho, Robert La Follette of Wisconsin, and Hiram Johnson of California.

Other senators would go along with a league only if certain of its powers were changed. These foes of Wilson were led by Republican Senator Henry Cabot Lodge of Massachusetts. Lodge pointed out that the Constitution of the United States gives Congress the sole power to declare war. But Article X of the league's constitution said that the league would protect member countries against attack. Did not this require the United States to go to war, even without Congress' approval? Wilson said it did not. But Lodge and others wanted that guaranteed in writing. Wilson refused to compromise.

The Senate votes down the treaty In September 1919, Wilson took his case directly to the people. In 3 weeks his train took him to 29 cities in the Midwest and Far West. He seemed to gain new strength from the thousands who turned out to hear him at each stop. But it was not really

so. In Pueblo, Colorado, the health of the 63-year-old President gave out. He collapsed and was rushed back to Washington. There he suffered a stroke. For months, President Wilson was bedridden.

With Wilson's illness went the last hope for his cause. The forces that favored United States entry into the League of Nations had lost their leader. In November 1919, the Senate voted against the Treaty of Versailles, with the League of Nations. Several months later, supporters of the League of Nations tried again. More senators voted for the treaty this time, but still not enough for approval. The United States never became a member of the League of Nations.

CHECKUP

1. Tell what at least five of Wilson's Fourteen Points dealt with.
2. What peace terms did Europe's victorious powers want?
3. Why might the Treaty of Versailles be called "a victor's peace"?
4. What task awaited Wilson upon his return to the United States?
5. Why did Wilson fail to win approval for the peace treaty?

Wilson traveled 8,000 miles (13,000 km) and delivered 40 speeches.

KEY FACTS

1. Among the causes of the Great War that started in Europe in 1914 were nationalism, militarism, and a web of rival alliances.

2. The sinking of American ships by German submarines was a major reason why the United States went to war in 1917 on the side of the Allies against the Central Powers.

3. American troops and supplies helped bring about an Allied victory in 1918.

4. The Treaty of Versailles placed the blame for the war on Germany, forced Germany to give up territory, reduced its military forces, and made it pay for the cost of the war.

5. President Woodrow Wilson persuaded the countries represented at the peace conference to create the League of Nations, but he could not persuade the Senate that the United States should join.

VOCABULARY QUIZ

On a sheet of paper write the letter of the term next to the number of its definition. There are two extra definitions that will not match any of the terms.

a. armistice
b. convoy
c. self-determination
d. mobilize
e. nationalism
f. reparations
g. ration
h. submarine
i. Sussex Pledge
j. Western Front

d **1.** To assemble armed forces for war
e **2.** Strong feelings of loyalty to one's country
c **3.** A group's ability to live in its own country under a government of its own choosing
j **4.** A line of trenches running across Belgium and France
h **5.** A warship that operates under water
6. To supply arms to a country's military force
b **7.** A group of ships escorted for safety by destroyers
i **8.** An agreement by the German government that its submarines would not torpedo ships without warning
9. A law requiring draft registration
a **10.** A cease-fire
g **11.** To limit the consumption of certain goods
f **12.** The payment for damages caused by war

REVIEW QUESTIONS

1. How did each of the following help bring on the Great War? (**a**) alliances, (**b**) nationalism, (**c**) militarism

2. What effect did the Zimmerman telegram have on American public opinion?

3. Name at least three agencies that were set up to aid the war effort on the home front.

4. What strategy was devised to combat submarine warfare?

5. Who were the Big Four? How did Wilson's views on peace differ from those of the European victors?

ACTIVITIES

1. Find out the origin of Armistice Day. By what name is it called today?

2. Look up and learn some of the wartime songs. Two of them are "Over There" and "Oh, How I Hate to Get Up in the Morning."

3. In your library, look up the stories of two heroes of World War I, Sergeant Alvin York and Captain Eddie Rickenbacker. Write a paragraph about each, telling what he did.

4. Find out where the Tomb of the Unknown Soldier is and why it was built. Be ready to report your findings to the class.

Another interesting research topic would be the campaigns of Colonel T.E. Lawrence, the English officer who was called Lawrence of Arabia.

RECOGNIZING PROPAGANDA

WORLD WAR I POSTERS

"Propaganda," someone has written, "is a good word with a bad reputation." One dictionary defines it as "the spreading of ideas, information, or rumor for the purpose of helping or injuring . . . a cause. . . ." The purpose of propaganda is to influence people to believe certain ideas or to take certain courses of action.

Attempts to influence can take many forms, such as symbols, slogans, cartoons, and posters. When Smokey Bear warns people to be careful with matches because "only you can prevent forest fires." that is propaganda. Smokey is a symbol that uses a slogan.

In this case the propaganda is truthful. It promotes a good cause. Why then does the word *propaganda* have a bad reputation? The answer is that in the twentieth century, some groups and governments have used propaganda to spread lies and to promote evil causes. Adolf Hitler, the dictator of Nazi Germany, rose to power in the 1930s by using propaganda. He once wrote, "The great masses of the people will more easily fall victims to a great lie than a small one."

SKILLS PRACTICE

During World War I, propaganda was used by all sides. Posters were an effective way of appealing to the public. Study the posters and answer the questions.

1. What is the message of the poster on the left? The poster on the right? Answers will vary.

2. What emotion are the posters trying to arouse in the American people? Patriotism

3. How does the poster on the left try to appeal to all Americans? Answers will vary.

6/UNIT REVIEW

READING THE TEXT

Turn to pages 536 and 537. Read those pages and as far as "A new kind of warfare" on page 538. On those pages you are told what conditions brought about the Great War, or World War I, as we call it today. On a sheet of paper answer the questions that follow.

1. Why did European powers compete for colonies in the late nineteenth century?
2. When is nationalism a good feeling? Under what conditions is it a bad feeling?
3. Why did the big countries of Europe build large armies at this time?
4. How did alliances increase the threat of war?
5. How could Europe be compared at this time to a powder keg?

READING A MAP

Turn to page 528 and study the map titled "The Caribbean Area in 1920." On a sheet of paper, answer the questions that follow.

1. What independent countries lay in Central America between Colombia and Mexico?
2. What possessions did the United States have in the Caribbean Sea?
3. What city is at 19°N/96°W?
4. About how far is it in miles from Havana to Tampico?
5. With what country does the Dominican Republic share an island?

READING CARTOONS

In this unit there are several political cartoons about Theodore Roosevelt. Three of these cartoons are on pages 504, 505, and 527.

Study each of these cartoons and then on a sheet of paper answer these questions.

1. How is Roosevelt pictured in the cartoon on page 504? Write a sentence or two telling what the cartoonist is saying about Theodore Roosevelt.
2. How is Roosevelt's role different in the cartoon on page 505? What is this cartoonist saying about Roosevelt?
3. What is Roosevelt pictured as in the cartoon on page 527? In a sentence or two, tell the meaning that the cartoonist is conveying in his drawing.
4. Do you think these cartoonists all picture Roosevelt favorably? If not, which one do you think is most critical of him? Why do you think so?

READING PRESIDENTIAL BOXES

Theodore Roosevelt, William H. Taft, and Woodrow Wilson were all Presidents during the era of the Progressive movement. Study the presidential boxes on pages 503 (Roosevelt), 504 (Taft), and 553 (Wilson). On a sheet of paper, write the name of the President that fits each of the descriptions below.

1. Served as Chief Justice Taft
2. Born in Virginia Wilson
3. A Yale graduate Taft
4. The youngest President Roosevelt
5. A college president Wilson
6. Loved the outdoors Roosevelt
7. A Democrat Wilson
8. Served as Vice President Roosevelt
9. Was not a lawyer Roosevelt
10. Held a Ph.D. degree Wilson

Prosperity, Depression, and War

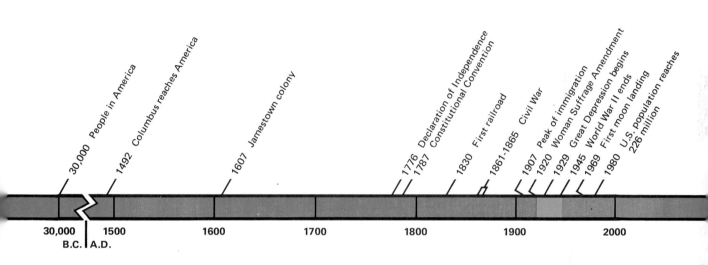

30,000 People in America

1492 Columbus reaches America

1607 Jamestown colony

1776 Declaration of Independence
1787 Constitutional Convention

1830 First railroad

1861-1865 Civil War

1907 Peak of immigration
1920 Woman Suffrage Amendment
1929 Great Depression begins
1945 World War II ends
1969 First moon landing
1980 U.S. population reaches 226 million

30,000
B.C. | A.D.   1500   1600   1700   1800   1900   2000

Above: Defense-plant worker, B-27 bomber, baseball player, early automobile, Franklin D. Roosevelt

CHAPTER
25 The Golden Twenties

A Time of Prosperity

> **VOCABULARY**
> assembly line   consumer credit
> consumer goods

A born tinkerer   What was it, a man asked Henry Ford in 1908, that made him tick? What was the ambition that drove him? Ford was already a successful manufacturer of cars and a millionaire. Ford replied to his questioner that his "life desire" was to produce cars at the rate of one a minute.

In 1908 that seemed like an impossible goal. More than 1,400 cars a *day*? Why, many of the 60 or so automobile manufacturers of that time didn't make that many in an entire *year*! Even if a car maker could produce more, who would buy them? Cars were expensive.

Still, if anyone could achieve the goal, it was Henry Ford. No one had contributed more than he to the young business of making automobiles. Henry Ford was born on a farm near Dearborn, Michigan, in 1863. He hated farm life from the moment he did his first farm chore. What interested him was machines. Henry Ford was a born tinkerer. One day he was given a watch. By the following morning he had taken it apart and put it together again.

At 16, Henry moved to Detroit to become a machinist. For the next dozen years, he worked in various machine shops. He seemed to drift along with no goals other than to tinker with watches and engines. Eventually he took a job as a mechanic with the electric company.

A "horseless carriage"   Meanwhile, European inventors were experimenting with a new product, the automobile. Then, in 1892, an American, Charles Duryea, invented the first American automobile in Springfield, Massachusetts. It was a carriage powered by a 1-cylinder gasoline engine.

Duryea's invention fired Henry Ford's imagination. For the next 4 years, he spent all his spare time building a "horseless carriage" of his own in a small shed behind his home. He made most of the parts by hand, including the 2-cylinder gasoline engine. Mounted on four bicycle wheels, the machine had no brakes. It could only go forward.

At 2:00 A.M. on a spring night in 1896, Ford took his invention out for a trial. The gasoline engine sputtered and the ride was jerky, but it worked! In the next few years, Henry Ford built several other cars. Soon he was driving them in daylight, much to the amusement and puzzlement of the people of Detroit.

Hundreds of cars fill a parking lot at a Massachusetts beach resort in 1925. The automobile brought about great changes in people's leisure activities.

Pupils should understand that the automobile was not the invention of one person. Mechanically minded tinkerers in several countries were attempting at about the same time to perfect a horseless carriage. The automobile that took shape in the 1890s and early 1900s drew upon the achievements of many inventive people.

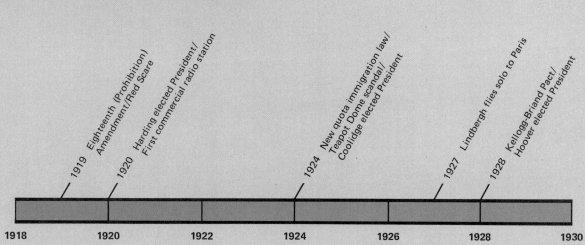

1919 Eighteenth (Prohibition) Amendment/Red Scare

1920 Harding elected President/ First commercial radio station

1924 New quota immigration law/ Teapot Dome scandal/ Coolidge elected President

1927 Lindbergh flies solo to Paris

1928 Kellogg-Briand Pact/ Hoover elected President

1918 1920 1922 1924 1926 1928 1930

559

Between 1908 and 1928 the Model T Ford was by far the most widely sold car in the United States. In fact, about half of the automobiles purchased by Americans over that period of time were Tin Lizzies.

Birth of the Model T   In 1903, Ford and several investors formed the Ford Motor Company. At first, like Ransom Olds, David Buick, and other carmakers of the time, Ford built racing and luxury cars. After a few years, however, he came up with a simple yet revolutionary idea. Instead of producing cars for the rich, he would build a car that ordinary people could afford. To keep down costs, the car would be simple in design, and it would be available in only one color—black.

Thus was born the famous Model T—the car Americans affectionately called the Tin Lizzie. Introduced in 1908, the Model T sold for $850, far less than other cars at the time. Ford sold nearly 6,000 cars the first year. Six years later the Ford Motor Company made a quarter of a million Model Ts and still could not keep up with the demand. Ford was the biggest car manufacturer in the world.

More efficient factories   Meanwhile, Henry Ford steadily made his factories more efficient. In the early days, a few skilled workers—jacks-of-all-trades—assembled each car. Ford hired engineers to study the assembly process and break it down into small, simple steps. Then he assigned separate workers to do each of these steps. As he explained:

> The man who puts in a bolt does not put on the nut; the man who puts on the nut does not tighten it. On operation number 34 the budding motor gets its gasoline. . . . On operation number 44 the radiator is filled with water, and on operation number 45 the car drives out.

Ford achieved a big breakthrough in 1914 when he introduced the moving **assembly line** to car making. "We began taking the work to the [workers], instead of the [workers] to the work," he later wrote. Heavy parts were put on a moving belt which was driven by an electric motor. Workers remained in one place,

Henry Ford (center), standing by the 15 millionth Ford, looks fondly at the first one.

performing their tasks on each partly built car as it passed slowly by. This saved more motions and was even more efficient. In just a few months, Ford cut the amount of time needed to make a single Model T from 14 hours to 93 minutes.

Putting America on wheels As production leaped ahead, Ford kept lowering the price of his car. And as he lowered the price, he sold still more cars. In 1916 he sold nearly 600,000 Fords at $360 each —less than half the price of 8 years earlier. By that time a new car rolled off Ford's assembly lines every 3 minutes.

In 1920, Henry Ford got his life desire. Ford factories produced a car every minute of the day. Even that amazing record paled next to the one Ford Motor Company achieved 5 years later—one car every 10 seconds! Furthermore, Ford lowered the price of the Model T to $260.

By the 1920s, other carmakers were also using the methods pioneered by Ford. General Motors went further than Ford and gave the public a large choice in models and colors. Millions of Americans owned cars.

The automobile brings changes The automobile changed the way people worked and played. People could live farther from their places of work than before. This speeded the growth of suburbs around large cities. People could shop in places far from their own neighborhoods—even as far away as neighboring cities. They could travel long distances to places of interest or perhaps to places that were not special at all. "Going for a spin" in the family car

In the 1920s, advertisements in magazines and newspapers helped create a market for automobiles.

became a favorite form of entertainment.

The automobile had a good deal to do with making the 1920s a decade of prosperity. Auto factories employed hundreds of thousands of workers. Hundreds of thousands more worked to make the steel, glass, rubber, paint, and other materials that went into making cars. New businesses such as gas stations, tourist cabins, and roadside restaurants sprang up. Local, state, and federal governments spent billions of dollars on roads, bringing profits to construction companies and jobs to many workers. Altogether the automobile industry created about 4 million jobs.

Ask: What are the advantages of consumer credit to a buyer? What are the disadvantages?

The growth of industries   No form of business benefited more from the automobile than did the oil industry. In 1901, drillers struck oil at Spindletop, Texas, and opened a whole new era. This discovery was followed by others in Texas, California, and other western states. By 1930 the oil industry had become 16 times larger than it was in 1901. It was the automobile with its demand for billions of gallons of gasoline that made this growth possible.

The boom times of the 1920s were due to more than just the automobile. Other industries contributed. Construction of new homes, office buildings, and factories reached an all-time high in the 1920s. The electrical industry also grew rapidly. In 1900 only a few city homes and apartments had electricity. By 1930, nearly all did. That, in turn, gave a big lift to the manufacture and sale of new electric household appliances such as refrigerators, washing machines, vacuum cleaners, irons, toasters, and radios.

A flood of consumer goods   In the 1920s, America's factories poured out **consumer goods**—things that people want and use. Manufacturers increased productivity by installing new electrical machinery. They also followed Henry Ford's pioneering use of moving assembly lines and other time-saving methods.

Manufacturers and store owners made use of two "inventions" of earlier times to help sell this flood of goods. One was advertising. Although a few products had been advertised for many years, it was in the 1920s that advertising became big business. In that decade, companies spent $3 billion on advertising. Advertising created a desire for goods.

The second invention, **consumer credit,** made it possible to satisfy the desire. Using consumer credit, buyers could enjoy the use of a product immediately while paying only part of its price at the time of purchase. The rest was paid for in small monthly installments. Half of all consumer goods and 60 percent of all cars were bought "on time"—that is, using credit—during the 1920s.

Prosperity—but not for all   Not all Americans shared in the prosperity of the 1920s. In "sick" industries such as coal mining, cloth manufacturing, and shipbuilding, many workers were laid off. Also, although skilled workers generally did well, wages of the unskilled rose

The vacuum cleaner and other appliances powered by electricity came into widespread use in the 1920s.

The high cost of tractors and other farm machinery was one reason why many farmers found themselves in debt at a time when most Americans were well-off.

hardly at all. Unskilled workers included most blacks, Mexican Americans, and recent immigrants. Black people continued to leave the rural South for the cities of the North and the West.

Most farmers also missed out on the prosperity of the 1920s. To produce more crops during World War I, farmers had borrowed money to buy more land. The land was expensive, and payments were high. Farmers didn't mind, however, because they were receiving very good prices for their crops. After the war, crop prices fell. However, farmers still had to make the same high payments for their land. Other costs remained high, too. Many farmers went deep into debt. A good many lost their farms.

Yet even with these and other exceptions, the 1920s were good times for the country as a whole. Americans enjoyed the highest standard of living the world had ever known. Economic experts saw no reason why good times should not continue. It was, said some, a golden age; America had entered the New Era.

Ask: Why did many farmers have a hard time in the 1920s? Are farmers better off today? Why or why not?

CHECKUP

1. What methods used by Henry Ford led to his success in making automobiles?
2. What changes did the automobile bring to the way Americans lived?
3. What ideas were used widely in the 1920s to increase the sale of goods?
4. What groups did not share in the prosperity of the 1920s?

Social Tensions and Social Change

┌─VOCABULARY─────────────────┐
Red Scare   quota
radical   **Harlem
                     Renaissance**
└────────────────────────────┘

A rise in prejudice   American society underwent important changes in the 1920s. It also experienced many tensions. World War I had stirred feelings of hatred and intolerance. These feelings did not die out when the war ended. With the enemy gone, they fastened upon other targets—racial minorities, political ideas, and immigrants.

Many blacks had served their country in the war "to make the world safe for democracy." They expected that when they returned home they would enjoy more fully the rights of Americans. But in the South, where most blacks lived, the threat of violence was never far below the surface. In fact, in 1919, the first postwar year, more than 70 blacks were lynched. Many of them were war veterans.

Black people who went north during and after World War I also met with racial prejudice as they competed with whites for jobs and housing. In 1917, whites in East St. Louis, Illinois, attacked blacks, touching off a riot that took the lives of 39 blacks and 10 whites. Two years later in Chicago, white youths killed a young black for swimming into an area that whites had reserved for themselves. For 6 days, rioting raged in Chicago. Thirty-eight people were killed, more than 500 were injured, and 1,000 more were left homeless as their houses burned.

Marcus Garvey   The rough treatment directed at black people gave rise to black protest and resistance. One of the most widely followed black leaders was Marcus Garvey, who had been born in Jamaica. Garvey founded the Universal Negro Improvement Association. He preached a message of racial pride and even of racial superiority. He wrote about the achievements of the people of Africa in past times. He said that blacks should return to Africa to create their own society.

Garvey asked his followers for money to buy ships that would carry them back. However, the ships that Garvey bought were broken-down tubs, unfit for an ocean voyage. Garvey was sent to jail for using the United States mail to defraud, or trick, people into giving money to his "back to Africa" movement. Many of his followers, however, believed he was really sent to prison for his ideas. After 2 years, Garvey was freed and deported, or sent out of the country, to his native Jamaica. Although some important black leaders like W. E. B. DuBois had no use for Garvey, he gave hope and pride to many black people.

The Red Scare   In 1917, as you read earlier, Communists overthrew the government of Russia. Soon after, they proclaimed the goal of spreading communism throughout the world. In 1919 a

Though Marcus Garvey failed in his "back to Africa" movement, he gave pride and hope to black people.

Have pupils find Jamaica on the map on page 714. Ask: What is its capital? (Kingston) About how far is its capital from Miami? (550 miles [1,019 km])

handful of people created the American Communist party. In that same year a small band of anarchists set off a number of bombs. Many Americans took these scattered acts of terrorism to be the start of a campaign to overthrow the government. They began to see every problem in American life, such as labor strikes, as the work of Communist plotters. This fear of Communist plots came to be called the **Red Scare.**

Many favored a crackdown on people who believed that America's system of government and type of economy should be scrapped. People with such extreme political views were often referred to as **radicals.** More than half the states passed laws that would punish radicals for their beliefs. In Washington, D.C., Attorney General A. Mitchell Palmer added to the Red Scare by talking about plots to destroy America. On New Year's Day 1920 Palmer directed raids on private homes and meeting places in 33 cities. Police rounded up about 6,000 people.

Palmer claimed these people were a danger to the country. Most, however, were guilty of nothing more than being foreign-born. Nearly all were later released. However, Palmer did arrange to send nearly 500 back to the countries they came from.

Sacco and Vanzetti   In time the Red Scare died out. But strong feelings against foreigners and radicals continued. In 1920, Nicola Sacco and Bartolomeo Vanzetti were accused of killing a man carrying a factory payroll in Braintree, Massachusetts. Both men were Italian immigrants. Both were also anarchists.

During the time of the Red Scare, Attorney General Mitchell Palmer directed raids in 33 cities.

The evidence against them was not very strong, but they were found guilty anyway and sentenced to death. Many believed that Sacco and Vanzetti did not get a fair trial. All appeals failed, and in 1927 they died in the electric chair.

Limiting immigration   For many years a movement to limit the number of immigrants entering the United States had been growing. In the 1920s, Congress limited the number of people from Europe who could enter the United States in any given year to 150,000. Each country in Europe was assigned a **quota,** that is, a share of the total number. Countries in southern and eastern Europe, where the New Immigrants came from, got much smaller

Lindbergh Flies Across the Atlantic

On May 21, 1927, the crew of a fishing boat in the Atlantic was startled to hear the pilot of a low-flying airplane call out, "Which way to Ireland?" If these men did not know who the pilot was, they were among the few in Europe and America who didn't. For Charles A. Lindbergh had captured the imagination of millions with his daring attempt to become the first flier to cross the Atlantic alone without stopping.

Lindbergh was a tall, shy 25-year-old with experience as an airmail pilot and stunt flier. When a wealthy New Yorker announced a prize of $25,000 for the first person to fly the Atlantic, Lindbergh was determined to try for it.

With help from a group of St. Louis businessmen, he bought a single-engine plane, which he named the *Spirit of St. Louis.*

For weeks Lindbergh prepared for his flight. He removed extra weight from the plane and figured out almost to the exact gallon the amount of gasoline he would need to reach Paris, France.

Finally, on May 19, 1927, came word that bad weather over the Atlantic had cleared. The next morning, Lindbergh took off from a New York airfield. He took no parachute and no radio. For the next 33 1/2 hours, millions followed the flight of the so-called Lone Eagle through special reports in the news-

Charles Lindbergh and his mother pose by the plane that the young aviator flew across the Atlantic.

papers and over radio. Finally, at 10:21 P.M. on May 21, 1927, the *Spirit of St. Louis* touched down in Paris, France. "Lucky Lindy" had done it—and in doing so, he became the greatest hero of the decade.

quotas than those in northern and western Europe. Asian and African nations got no quotas at all.

The new immigration laws did not apply to those who lived in the Western Hemisphere. Immigration from Canada, Mexico, and some other Latin American lands increased during the 1920s.

The Ku Klux Klan revives   One especially ugly expression of the desire to "save" America from foreign influences and radical ideas was the Ku Klux Klan (KKK). The original Ku Klux Klan had been aimed against blacks in the South during Reconstruction (p. 375). The new Klan was started in 1915. It was still anti-black, but it was now also anti-Catholic, anti-Jewish, and anti-immigrant. Using threats of violence, Klan members tried to drive all of these groups from their communities.

The KKK grew rapidly. By 1924 it claimed over 4 million members. It had great influence in several state legislatures in the Midwest. Its members boldly held marches in the streets of many towns and cities, including the nation's capital.

By 1925, however, Americans began to turn against the Klan's use of threats and violence. Membership and influence fell sharply within a few years.

Women gain more independence Among the most important changes in American society were those affecting women. The large role women played in the war effort brought wider support to the movement for full woman suffrage. That movement was crowned with success in 1920 when the Nineteenth Amendment was added to the Constitution. Women gained the vote in time to cast ballots in the presidential election of that year.

Since many new inventions cut down the time needed for housework, women were freer to take jobs outside the home. Women had long worked in factories and in household jobs as cooks, servants, and so forth. Now more of them found work as schoolteachers and nurses, in offices and at department-store counters. By 1930, women made up 22 percent of the work force.

Women, especially young women, sought the same freedoms that men had. This desire to break away from traditional roles was signaled by dramatic changes in their appearance and behavior. To the horror of many parents, young women bobbed, or cut short, their hair. They wore knee-length skirts. They danced new dances like the Charleston. They were called flappers.

Of course these changes were not true of all women—not even a majority. For most, life continued much as it had before the 1920s. This was especially the case in small towns and rural areas.

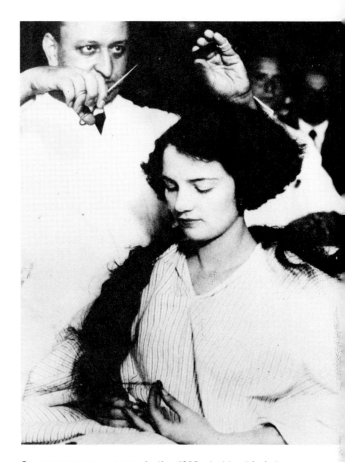

For many young women in the 1920s, bobbed hair became a mark of independence.

Movies, sports, and cars Many Americans began to live differently. The home became less important as the center of family life. Three things took people out of the homes more and more: moving pictures, sporting events, and the car.

Moving pictures had grown steadily in popularity since their invention in the 1890s. By the 1920s, going to the "movies" was America's favorite form of entertainment. Actors like Rudolph Valentino, Mary Pickford, and Charlie Chaplin became idols to millions. In 1927 came the first talking picture, *The Jazz Singer*. "Talkies" revolutionized the moving-picture industry. Movies soon became even more popular. By 1930, about 100 million people went to the movies every week.

The 1920s were also a golden age for sports. Large crowds turned out to watch their favorite college football and professional baseball teams. Nearly 100,000 people packed Soldiers' Field in Chicago to watch Jack Dempsey and Gene Tunney fight for the heavyweight boxing cham-

pionship. Every sport had its own heroes. In baseball it was the Babe—George Herman Ruth, the great home-run slugger. In college football, it was Red Grange of Illinois and the Four Horsemen of Notre Dame. Bobby Jones in golf and Bill Tilden and Helen Wills in tennis also became sports legends. Gertrude Ederle became the first woman to swim the English Channel.

Sports Heroes of the 1920s

GERTRUDE EDERLE

BABE RUTH

HELEN WILLS

RED GRANGE

Most important, the car undercut the home as the center of family life. Sons and daughters were forever asking to borrow the car for the evening—or so it seemed to many parents. Dinner, once the time when the whole family ate together, became simply the third meal of the day, eaten whenever and wherever it was convenient to do so.

The radio craze One new form of entertainment promoted family togetherness. That was the radio. Soon after the first commercial station, KDKA of Pittsburgh, took to the air in 1920, a radio craze swept the country. By 1923, some 500 radio stations were broadcasting. In 1926 the first national radio network, the National Broadcasting Company, was founded.

By the end of the decade, nearly half of all American families owned a radio. Families gathered around the radio to listen to their favorite programs—music, comedy shows, adventure programs, and the evening news. By broadcasting sporting events, the radio promoted the great interest in sports in the 1920s.

Prohibition Still another important change in American society in the 1920s was prohibition. This was the effort to prohibit the sale and drinking of alcohol. The effort to control drinking in America went back nearly a hundred years, to the 1830s. Women and religious groups took the lead. It was argued that liquor was the cause of crime, family breakup, and other social evils. Late in the nineteenth century, the leading organization in fighting "Demon Rum" was the Woman's Christian Temperance Union (WCTU).

Station KDKA of Pittsburgh, on the air in 1920, was the United States' first commercial radio station.

The prohibition movement made headway in the twentieth century. By World War I, about half the states had banned the sale of liquor and beer. Most of these were rural states. In 1919 the Eighteenth Amendment was added to the Constitution, prohibiting the manufacture, sale, or transportation of liquor throughout the United States. Thus began what many Americans called the Noble Experiment.

Prohibition did result in a decline in drinking. But it also led to some unfortunate results. Millions of people simply refused to obey the law. Some bought liquor from bootleggers—people who made it illegally or smuggled it into the country. Some bought it at speakeasies—bars where alcoholic drinks were illegally sold. Some brewed their own liquor at home.

What's In a Name?

THE TWENTIES

No decade has been given more names than the 1920s. Some Americans called these years the Golden Twenties. Those who did so were thinking of prosperity. To others this was "the dry decade"— the era of prohibition.

One of the labels most often given to this decade is the Roaring Twenties. The decade was "roaring," many believed, because everything was wide open—there were bootleggers, gangsters, and lawlessness. "Roaring" also referred to the noises of the 1920s—the roar of machines in factories, of car and truck traffic, and of crowds at sporting events.

Another name for the 1920s is the Jazz Age. Jazz is a style of music that was created by black people in New Orleans in the late nineteenth century. A blend of African and European influences, jazz is America's special contribution to the world of music. By the 1920s, jazz had spread far from its birthplace and was very popular in much of the United States. Both black and white musicians played it. Jazz became a symbol of the free and easy spirit of the times.

Of course, no single label can capture a decade. Certainly, to quiet, conservative Calvin Coolidge, the 1920s was not the Jazz Age. Those who lost farms or held low-paying jobs didn't think of the era as the Golden Twenties. Yet each of the labels attached to the 1920s does show us something about the flavor of those years.

Without public support, enforcement of prohibition was nearly impossible. The federal government assigned 2,000 agents to enforce the law. However, it would have taken a hundred times that many to prevent liquor from illegally entering the country along the thousands of miles of borders and coastline. Further, bootleggers and speakeasies often were able to operate because they "bought protection" from the law by paying off dishonest public officials and police.

Perhaps worst of all, prohibition contributed to the growth of organized crime. Bootlegging was a $2 billion-a-year business, and rival crime organizations fought it out on the streets for control of bootlegging in several American cities.

By the end of the 1920s it was clear that prohibition was not working. In 1933 the Twenty-First Amendment was adopted, thereby repealing the Eighteenth Amendment, which had been approved 14 years earlier.

Literature of the 1920s The 1920s produced some of America's greatest literature. Many of the writers of the time were disillusioned by World War I. They felt that the dying and suffering of millions had all been for nothing. This was the theme of Ernest Hemingway in two of his greatest novels, *The Sun Also Rises* and *A Farewell to Arms.*

Other writers focused on what they saw as shortcomings in American society. Sinclair Lewis wrote about the narrowness of small-town life in *Main Street* and *Babbitt.* Flappers and speakeasies were the subject of much of F. Scott Fitzgerald's writing. But Fitzgerald also criticized the emphasis on material success that he saw in the 1920s.

The decade also produced important poetry. Robert Frost's poems dealt with the more traditional side of American life. Those of Edna St. Vincent Millay, however, spoke with the voice of the modern world. "I burn my candle at both ends," she wrote about the decade's pursuit of pleasure.

Black poets like Langston Hughes, Claude McKay, and Countee Cullen spoke of the despair of black people in white America. "If We Must Die" and "To My White Friends," two of McKay's poems, told how it felt to be discriminated against.

The writings of these and other black writers were part of an important body of literature that came out of Harlem, New

Poet Countee Cullen wrote movingly about the status of black people in America.

Love, death, and the yearnings of youth were among the themes pursued by poet Edna St. Vincent Millay.

Some pupils may like to find a poem by one of the poets of the 1920s and read it aloud before their classmates.

York's large black community, during the 1920s. Much of it dealt with the African roots of American blacks. And much delivered the message of racial pride. "I am a Negro—and beautiful," read a line in one of Langston Hughes's poems. This flowering of black literature was part of a larger black cultural movement that is called the **Harlem Renaissance,** or revival.

CHECKUP

1. In what ways did racial prejudice show itself following World War I?
2. How did each of the following contribute to tension in the early 1920s: (a) the Red Scare, (b) Sacco and Vanzetti, (c) the Ku Klux Klan?
3. How did life change for women in the 1920s?
4. What effects did the following items have on American life in the 1920s: (a) sports, (b) radio, (c) prohibition?

The Political Scene

VOCABULARY

| Teapot Dome | Kellogg-Briand |
| merger | Pact |

Harding and normalcy   By the time of the 1920 election, the American people had grown tired of World War I, the League of Nations, and Woodrow Wilson's idealism. They wanted to get back to normal living and to enjoy the fruits of the nation's material progress.

Warren Harding of Ohio, the Republican candidate for President, caught the national mood perfectly. Americans, said Harding, wanted "not heroics but healing, not nostrums but normalcy." Harding was elected by one of the largest margins ever.

The federal government had grown greatly during wartime. As President, Harding aimed to reduce both federal spending and federal power. He especially believed that government should not interfere with business through regulation. If business were allowed to manage its own affairs, the country would prosper. Harding summed up his beliefs when he said, "What this country needs is less government in business and more business in government." His ideas were very different from those of the Progressives, who believed that government should regulate business in the public interest.

Harding supported most of the goals of business. To protect American products from foreign competition, he favored a high tariff. In 1922, Congress passed the Fordney-McCumber Tariff Act. This law set tariff duties higher than ever before.

A time of corruption   Harding was a friendly, likable man. With his strong, handsome face and gray hair, some said that he "looked like a President." But he had serious weaknesses. He was a poor judge of people. And he could not say no to friends.

For a few top positions in his Cabinet, Harding chose people of very great ability.

In 1920 millions of women voted for the first time in a presidential election.

Many political cartoons appeared in newspapers at the time of the scandals in the Harding administration. Some have been reprinted in history books and cartoon collections. Have a committee find some of these cartoons and exhibit them to the class.

He made Herbert Hoover his secretary of commerce. Charles Evans Hughes, a former governor, Supreme Court justice, and candidate for President, was the new secretary of state. Andrew Mellon became secretary of the treasury. He was a millionaire banker and industrialist.

For too many other posts, however, Harding chose his old Ohio pals and card-playing friends. They turned his administration into one of the most corrupt in American history. Attorney General Harry Daugherty, an Ohio friend, took bribes to give pardons, paroles, and liquor permits. He was tried but was able to avoid a jail term. Charles Forbes, head of the Veterans Administration, sold $250 million worth of government property to private buyers at ridiculously low prices in exchange for payments from the buyers. Forbes did go to jail.

Teapot Dome   The biggest of the Harding scandals was **Teapot Dome**. Teapot Dome was a hill in Wyoming, under which lay a large deposit of oil. The federal government owned this land. When Wilson was President, he had reserved the oil there and at Elk Hills, California, for the use of the United States Navy. Wilson put these sites under navy control.

When Harding became President, he made an old friend, Albert Fall, the secretary of the interior. Fall got the President to transfer control of Teapot Dome to his own department. Then, in exchange for a large bribe, Fall allowed several oil companies to drill oil wells there. The companies made fortunes before the scheme was discovered. Fall became the first Cabinet officer to be sent to jail.

Attorney General Harry Daugherty tries to hide the skeletons in his closet from the American people.

While on a trip to Alaska and the West Coast, Harding took ill suddenly and died in August 1923. None of these scandals had yet come to light, and the people mourned Harding as a good and beloved President. Before he died, however, Harding had begun to learn how his friends had betrayed him and the public. Speaking to a friend, Harding said, "In this job I am not worried about my enemies. I can take care of them. It is my friends who are giving me trouble."

Coolidge follows Harding   Vice President Calvin Coolidge was vacationing at his father's farm in Vermont when news of Harding's death came. Late at night by the light of a flickering kerosene lamp, Coolidge was sworn in as Harding's successor by his father, a local justice of the peace.

Born: 1865, Corsica (now Blooming Grove), Ohio. **Education:** Ohio Central College. **Training:** Newspaper editor and publisher. **To presidency from:** Ohio. **Position when elected:** United States senator. **Political party:** Republican. **Married:** Florence Kling De-Wolfe. **Children:** None. **Died:** 1923, in San Francisco, California, while returning from a trip to Alaska. **Other facts:** A friendly, generous man but weak-willed. A good speaker. Editor and an owner of newspaper, the *Marion Star*. A compromise choice for the Republican presidential nomination. The first President to visit Alaska. The first President to broadcast over the radio. **During his presidency:** The Unknown Soldier of World War I was buried at Arlington National Cemetery.

WARREN G. HARDING
29th President
1921 · 1923

The setting was a fitting place for Coolidge's term to begin. To most people, Coolidge stood for the simple values of rural America—thrift, honesty, and hard work. He was one of the few Presidents in our history who saved money from his presidential salary. He won the people's trust by removing many of Harding's corrupt friends from office.

Coolidge was a colorless man. He earned the nickname Silent Cal because he said so little in public. But silent or not, he seemed to be what the public wanted. In 1924 he ran for election to a full term of office with the slogan "Keep Cool With Coolidge." Times were prosperous, and Coolidge won easily.

Coolidge's policies   Coolidge shared Harding's views on government economy, taxes, and business. He kept government spending down. During Harding and Coolidge's terms, the national debt was reduced from $24 billion to $16 billion.

Coolidge and Secretary of the Treasury Mellon favored cutting taxes on high incomes. They said this would free more money for investment, making the econ-omy grow and creating more jobs. Congress did lower taxes on the wealthy. It also eliminated some taxes on business.

Coolidge also believed that government should not interfere with the dealings of business. "The business of America is business," he said. In the Progressive era, Presidents Roosevelt, Taft, and Wilson had used the antitrust laws to break up trusts. They had given new power to the Interstate Commerce Commission and created new agencies like the Federal Trade Commission to regulate business. Coolidge did nothing of this nature.

Big business gets bigger   With the government ignoring the antitrust laws, big business got bigger. There were thousands of **mergers**, in which two or more companies combined to make a single company. Most of American business was being controlled by fewer large firms. By 1929 nearly half the business wealth in the country was owned by just 200 companies. The other half was shared by nearly 400,000 smaller companies. In some industries, competition just about disappeared.

Coolidge's taciturn nature has given birth to many stories, which may or may not be true. For example, at a state dinner a lady guest is said to have told Coolidge, "I have made a bet, Mr. President, that I can get you to say more than two words." Coolidge replied, "You lose."

Few Americans seemed to mind. Times were good, and most believed that business enterprise had made them so. Goods, goods, and more goods flowed from the factories to an eager consuming public. The United States, it was said, was the first country in the history of the world to solve the problem of scarcity of goods. It was only a matter of time before the nation's plenty would be enjoyed by every last American.

Labor unions decline   The story of American labor unions in the 1920s was quite different. During World War I the government had backed their efforts to organize workers, and union membership rose. So did wages. Right after the war, however, unions lost strikes in such industries as steel, coal, and textiles.

In the next few years, unions lost other big strikes in the meat-packing and railroad industries. As a result, most of labor's wartime gains were wiped out.

During the 1920s, employers used the blacklist and other means to keep unions out of their companies. Some companies also offered new benefits to workers, such as paid vacations, health care, and recreational programs. In this way, employers spread the benefits of capitalism to their workers while also weakening the appeal of unions. For these and other reasons, unions lost members in the 1920s.

An agreement on reducing navies   Although the United States did not join the League of Nations, it promoted steps to maintain world peace. In 1921 the United States took the lead in heading off a naval arms race among several countries. It invited the leading naval powers to attend a conference in Washington, D.C.

Secretary of State Hughes startled the conference with a bold proposal. Each country, Hughes said, should build no new warships for the next 10 years. They should also scrap some ships already in

Secretary of State Hughes (fifth from left) *poses with delegates to the naval conference.*

CALVIN COOLIDGE
30th President
1923 · 1929

Born: 1872, Plymouth, Vermont. **Education:** Amherst College. **Training:** Lawyer, public official. **To presidency from:** Massachusetts. **Position when taking office:** Vice President. **Political party:** Republican. **Married:** Grace Goodhue. **Children:** Two sons. **Died:** 1933, Northampton, Massachusetts. **Other facts:** A shy, close-mouthed man with a dry wit. Practiced law in Northampton, Massachusetts. Held local and state offices. Elected governor of Massachusetts in 1918. The first President whose inaugural address was broadcast by radio. After his retirement from public service, wrote a daily newspaper column. **During his presidency:** The first woman governor, Nellie Tayloe Ross of Wyoming, took office in 1925.

service. In 1922, Japan, Great Britain, the United States, France, and Italy signed a treaty accepting Hughes's plan.

The Kellogg-Briand Pact   In 1928 the United States and France invited countries to sign a treaty in which they agreed not to use war "as an instrument of national policy." This meant that they agreed to settle disputes by peaceful means only.

The treaty was called the **Kellogg-Briand Pact.** Frank Kellogg was the secretary of state under President Coolidge. Sixty-two countries signed the Kellogg-Briand Pact. If it worked, it would mean the end of war among these countries. However, the treaty had no provisions for enforcement. It amounted to nothing more than good intentions.

Improving relations with Latin America
The United States also took steps to improve its relations with Latin American countries. These countries resented United States interference in their affairs.

In 1917, Mexico adopted a new constitution. Under it, the government was to take over ownership of mines and oil owned by foreign companies. American companies owned many of these properties. They appealed to the United States government to protect their interests. For several years, relations between Mexico and the United States grew steadily worse.

However, neither country wanted war. In 1927, President Coolidge appointed Dwight Morrow as the new ambassador to Mexico. Morrow helped arrange a compromise between the Mexican government and the United States business interests. He also helped the two countries understand each other better.

In 1928 the United States also agreed that it would no longer use the Roosevelt Corollary as a reason for intervening in Latin American countries. However, the United States continued to keep troops in several countries. When rebels took up arms against the government in Nicaragua in 1927, President Coolidge sent in marines once again. This time, however, the United States arranged to end the fighting and to hold an election. Even though the side favored by the United States lost, the marines were withdrawn.

Relations with Mexico reached a low point in 1916 when an American military force went into Mexico in pursuit of Pancho Villa, a bandit chieftain whose band had raided Columbus, New Mexico. Have some pupils do research on Villa and the expedition to Mexico, and report their findings to the class.

The war debts   During World War I the United States loaned billions of dollars to the Allies.   After the war, these countries said that the United States should not demand repayment.   America, they said, should treat these loans as its contribution to the war effort.   The Allies held that they had made their contribution in blood and destroyed property.

The United States, however, insisted that the debts be repaid.   The Allies could use the reparation payments they were receiving from Germany to help pay the debts.   This caused some bad feelings between the United States and European countries.   Also, if the Allies had to use their money to pay the war debts, they would have less money left over with which to buy American goods.   During the 1930s, nearly every country stopped paying its war debts.

Hoover becomes President   In 1927, Calvin Coolidge caught the country by surprise with a one-sentence announcement: "I do not choose to run for President in 1928."   The Republican party then turned to Herbert Hoover as its candidate.

Democrats countered with Alfred E. Smith, a reform governor in New York.   It would have been hard to find a greater contrast between two candidates.   Both started life as poor boys; however, Hoover was raised on an Iowa farm, and Smith grew up in New York City.   Hoover had a career as a mining engineer and businessman; Smith was a career politician.   Hoover was Protestant; Smith was Catholic, the first to run for the presidency.   On prohibition, Hoover was a "dry," Smith a "wet," that is, he favored repeal of the pro-

In 1928 the rival candidates were Herbert Hoover and Alfred E. Smith, acclaimed here on campaign buttons.

hibition amendment.   Smith seemed to stand for everything that rural and small-town Americans were against.   Hoover won the election of 1928 by a wide margin.

In one of his speeches during the campaign, Herbert Hoover said:

> We in America are nearer to the final triumph over poverty than ever before in the history of any land; . . . given a chance to go forward with the policies of the last 8 years, we shall soon, with the help of God, be in sight of the day when poverty shall be banished from this nation.

Most Americans shared Hoover's belief that prosperity could be made permanent.   Who could know that Hoover's words would soon be used to mock him?

CHECKUP

1. Give proof of this statement: "President Harding was a poor judge of people."
2. What policies did President Coolidge follow?
3. What steps were taken in the 1920s to maintain world peace?
4. Who were the candidates in the presidential election of 1928, and how did they differ?   What was the outcome?

KEY FACTS

1. American manufacturers produced record numbers of cars, household appliances, and other consumer goods in the decade of the 1920s.

2. Minority groups felt increased prejudice and were among those who did not share fully in the prosperity of the 1920s.

3. A fear of foreign influence led to the Red Scare after World War I and to laws restricting immigration.

4. Cars, movies, and sporting events made the home less important as the center of family life in the 1920s.

5. Many of the attempts of Progressives to regulate business were reversed during the presidencies of Harding and Coolidge.

VOCABULARY QUIZ

To fill the blank in each statement, unscramble the words that follow it. Write your answers on a sheet of paper.

1. During the 1920s a revival of arts and culture in the black community in New York City was called the _Harlem Renaissance_.

lamHre nsniaaceeRs

2. A hill in Wyoming that lay over a large oil deposit became the name of a scandal during the Harding administration. The scandal was called _Teapot Dome_.

etTpoa mDeo

3. An arrangement in which workers construct a car by adding parts as it is carried along a moving belt is an _assembly line_.

baeslmys nlie

4. The 1920s saw the manufacture of a flood of items that people wanted or needed. These items were called _consumer goods_.

eoucmrsn osogd

5. When people buy goods with a small payment at the time of purchase and pay the rest on monthly installments, they are using _consumer credit_.

omrecsnu dietrc

REVIEW QUESTIONS

1. How did consumer credit affect the buying habits of Americans?

2. In what ways did the mass production of inexpensive automobiles affect American life?

3. Which industries and groups of people missed out on the prosperity of the 1920s?

4. How did the Red Scare affect attitudes toward each of the following? (a) labor unions, (b) foreigners, (c) immigration

5. What were the desirable and the undesirable effects of prohibition?

6. What were the attitudes of Presidents Harding and Coolidge toward business?

ACTIVITIES

1. Find out why the following people were the subject of many newspaper articles in the 1920s. Then write a sentence about each one that tells why he or she was famous.

Admiral Byrd	Sacco and Vanzetti
Babe Ruth	Gertrude Ederle
Al Capone	Charles Lindbergh
Ty Cobb	Ernest Hemingway
Gene Tunney	Bobby Jones
Rudolph Valentino	Rudy Vallee

2. Look up and read one poem by Langston Hughes and one by Robert Frost. How do the subjects of these poems differ?

3. Find a photograph, drawing, or map of your town or city before the coming of the automobile. Compare it with your community today.

MAKING TABLES AND GRAPHS

PRESENTING STATISTICAL INFORMATION

"During the 1860s about 2,314,000 immigrants came to America. For the next two decades, immigration rose, climbing to 2,812,000 in the 1870s and 5,246,000 in the 1880s. After slipping to 3,687,000 in the next 10-year period, immigration reached 8,795,000 in the first decade of the new century. Thereafter, it fell to 5,735,000 between 1911 and 1920 to 4,107,000 in the next 10-year period. From 1931 to 1940, immigration plunged to just 528,000."

Did you find it difficult to absorb all that information? Sometimes when statistical information is presented in sentence form, it is hard to picture clearly. That is why tables and graphs are so useful. They allow us to present statistics in a manner that is clear and easy to read and understand.

To make a table showing the information above, you would set up two columns. The one on the left would be for decades: 1861–1870, 1871–1880, and so on. The one on the right would be for the number of immigrants in each decade. So, for the years from 1861 to 1880, your table would look like this:

Decade	Number of Immigrants
1861–1870	2,314,000
1871–1880	2,812,000

SKILLS PRACTICE

Copy the table that was started above. Using the statistical information at the top of the page, complete the table up to 1940.

The information in your table can also be shown effectively on a line graph. Using a sheet of graph paper, place points along the bottom line for the decades. The first point will be for 1861–1870, the next point for 1871–1880, and so on. On the vertical line to the left, enter points for the number of immigrants. Moving upward, the first point will be 1 million people, the second point 2 million people, and the third point 3 million people.

For 1861–1870, follow the line for that date upward, past 2 million but below 3 million. Place a dot on the line about where you think 2,314,000 should be. Next, follow the line for 1871–1880 upward, placing a dot about where you think 2,812,000 should be. Now connect the dots. So far, your line graph should look like the graph below.

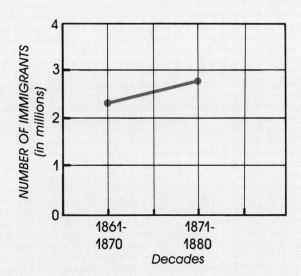

SKILLS PRACTICE

Using the information in the first paragraph, complete the line graph to 1940. Remember to connect the dots at the end of your work.

CHAPTER 26

The Great Depression and the New Deal

The Great Depression

VOCABULARY
stock market	speculation
dividend	inventory

Crash! The New York Stock Exchange is one of the world's great marketplaces. This is the **stock market**—the place where shares of stock in corporations are bought and sold. On Thursday, October 24, 1929, the stock market opened as usual at 10:00 A.M. Within minutes, however, it was clear that this would be no ordinary day. Stock prices were tumbling. Panic set in. People scrambled wildly to sell their shares before prices went still lower. At the close of business, a record number of shares had been traded. Those who kept track of sales were hours behind in recording them.

On Friday and Saturday the price of stocks remained steady. But on Monday the slide began again. Then on Tuesday, October 29—known forever after as Black Tuesday—everything fell apart. Prices plunged. No buyers at all could be found for some stocks. At the end of the day, 16 million shares had been sold, and billions of dollars in values had been wiped out. Persons who counted themselves wealthy only a week before had now lost everything.

This was the stock market crash of 1929. It was the beginning of the Great Depression.

A craze to get rich Why did the stock market crash happen? As you read in the last chapter, business boomed in the 1920s. Many corporations made large profits. Those people who held stock, or shares of ownership, in these profitable companies also did well. They received high **dividends**, or earnings, from their investment. Others wanted to buy these shares. With more people wanting to buy than to sell, the price of stocks went up.

As stock prices rose, some people thought they could use the stock market to get rich. Their idea was simple. They forgot about dividends and the true value of a company. They just bought stocks. With stock prices going up, they thought there would always be someone else to buy from them at a higher price. This kind of buying, with the hope of a quick profit, is called **speculation**. In fact, it is hardly different from gambling.

Worse still, some people speculated with borrowed money. They bought stock on margin. This meant that they paid as little as 10 percent in cash for the stock. When the stock went up and they sold it, they would pay off the loan out of

During the Great Depression, politicians in New York City hand out loaves of bread and cans of milk to some of the many people in need of food.

The people who negotiate contracts in the buying and selling of stock are called brokers. In George Washington's time, these traders in New York carried on their business in the shade of a big, old tree on Wall Street. That street is still the center of the financial district.

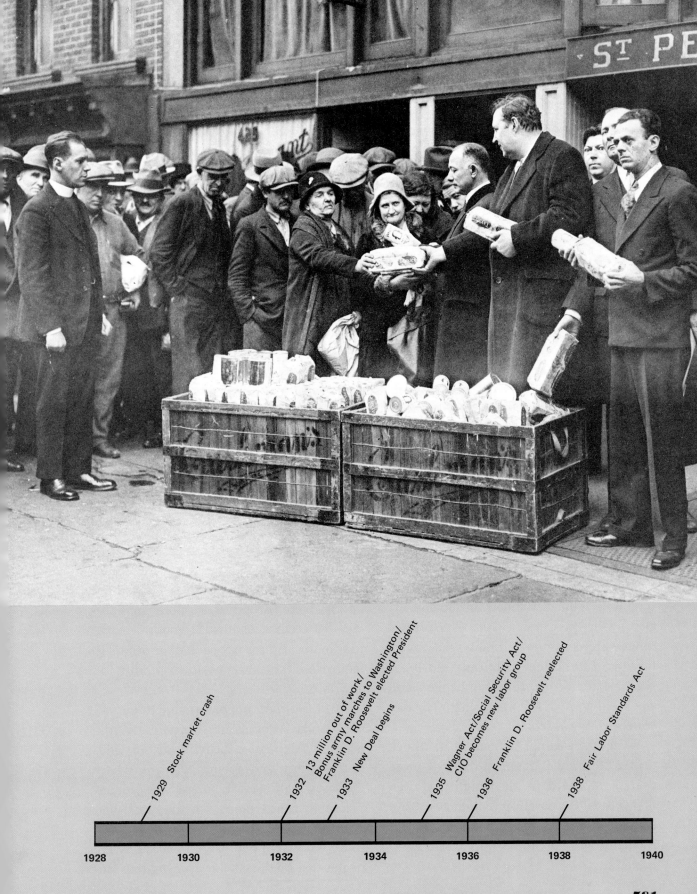

St PE

1929 Stock market crash

1932 13 million out of work/
Bonus army marches to Washington/
Franklin D. Roosevelt elected President

1933 New Deal begins

1935 Wagner Act/Social Security Act/
CIO becomes new labor group

1936 Franklin D. Roosevelt reelected

1938 Fair Labor Standards Act

1928   1930   1932   1934   1936   1938   1940

their profit. Few thought about how they would pay off the loan if the price of the stock went down.

Actually, only about 1 in every 100 Americans owned stock in the 1920s. Fewer than half of these people, plus some banks, engaged in speculation. But there were enough speculators to send stock prices moving rapidly upward, beginning in 1927. In the months that followed, people talked excitedly about "getting rich quick."

The downward plunge   All speculative crazes come to an end sooner or later. This one did in September 1929. For the next month, stock prices drifted downward. Some realized that the boom was over and decided to sell their stocks. Now there were more sellers than buyers. Prices slipped a little further. That led other shareholders to decide to sell. Down still more went the prices. Soon those who had bought on margin were forced to sell to pay off the loans they had made. By then, the prices of stocks were tumbling.

This is what happened on October 24 and again on October 29. The plunge downward continued. In 3 weeks, investors lost $30 billion. Not only did those who speculated go broke, but bankers and stockbrokers who loaned them money were also big losers.

Even that was not the end of it. Stock prices continued downward for 3 more years. A share in the mighty United States Steel Corporation, which cost $262 before the crash, brought just $22 in 1932. By that time some stocks were worth nothing at all.

A depression spreads   The stock market crash of 1929 was followed by a depression that spread over the country. However, the crash was not the main cause of this depression. That cause lay in certain weaknesses of the American economy, weaknesses that were hidden during the prosperous 1920s. A basic trouble was that Americans could not buy as much as they produced. Wages of workers increased in the 1920s, but production of goods increased even more. Even with consumer credit, ordinary people did not have enough money to buy all the cars, refrigerators, washing machines, and vacuum cleaners that were made.

Nor could all the goods be sold abroad. The high tariff prevented Europeans from selling much in the United States. Therefore, Europeans could not earn money with which to buy American goods. Also, after making payments on the war debts, European countries did not have much money left over for buying goods.

By early 1929 the economy was slowing down. Car sales were off. Homebuilding was down. Sales of consumer goods were dropping. Store **inventories**—the stock of unsold goods—began to pile up. Stores cut back their orders to factories. Factories cut down production and laid off workers.

With ordinary people unable to buy all the goods America was producing, the economy depended heavily on the well-to-do to buy and spend. Here is where the stock market crash entered the picture. Those who lost money in the crash had nothing left to spend. Even those well-to-do who were not "in the market" were frightened by the crash. Fearing that bad

582

times might be coming, they stopped spending and investing. That simply helped to bring on the bad times they feared.

The crash contributed to the depression in other ways, too. Banks that had loaned money to speculators or had invested in stocks lost a great deal of money. If people asked for their savings back all at once, the banks would be in trouble. That is what happened. Between 1929 and 1932, more than 4,000 banks failed. When a bank failed, depositors lost all their savings.

Conditions get worse   Soon after the stock market crash, President Hoover met with leaders of business and industry. He called upon them to keep people employed and not to cut wages. He urged cities, states, and businesses to go ahead with their plans for new construction. Hoover's idea was to keep people earning money. They could then continue to buy goods and keep others working.

Many companies did try at first to keep up employment and spending. But business got worse. Factory managers began to lay off some workers and to cut the wages of others. Workers without jobs could not buy goods, so still more factories had to cut their output. Thousands of firms, large and small, went out of business. Meanwhile, cities and states were running out of money. They had to put off building roads and schools.

Unemployment spread. In 1930, 4 million were out of work. The number rose to 8 million in 1931. In 1932, 13 million—one in every four workers—were without jobs. In Cleveland, 50 percent were unemployed. In several cities the percentage was even higher.

With no money and no place to live, many "took to the road" or "rode the rails"—that is, hopped onto freight trains.

Ask: Why might the depositors in the picture be unable to withdraw their savings?
Worried depositors, fearing a bank failure, wait to withdraw their savings.

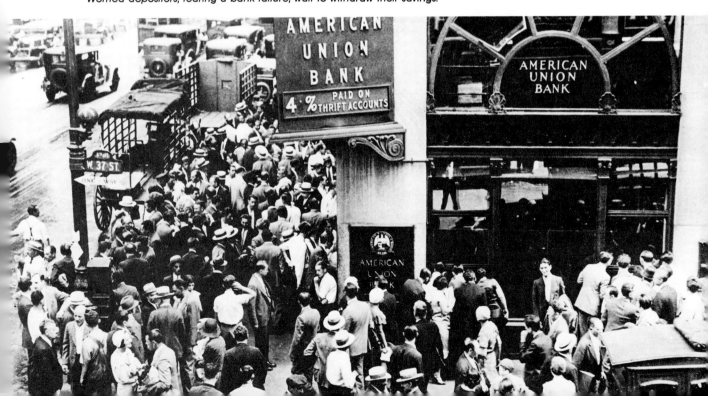

They went from city to city looking for work. At one time, more than 2 million were wandering in this way.

Desperate people   In the cities, "soup kitchens" were set up. People patiently stood in line for hours for some free bread and a cup of watery soup. Small groups of desperate people could always be found near the back doors of restaurants, searching through the barrels of garbage for food.

On the edge of cities and in empty lots, clusters of shacks sprang up. One-room shacks made from wooden packing cases, cardboard, and flattened tin cans housed whole families. Those who blamed the President for the sad state of affairs called these clusters of shacks "Hoovervilles." Others, sleeping on park benches, called

Selling apples was the only source of income for some of the unemployed during the depression.

the newspapers with which they covered themselves "Hoover blankets."

Farmers were worse off than ever. Farm prices had not been good in the 1920s. Between 1929 and 1932, they collapsed altogether. A bushel of wheat that sold for $1.03 in 1929 brought only 33 cents in 1932. Cotton, 19 cents a pound in 1929, was 6 cents a pound in 1932. The price of corn was so low that farmers burned it for fuel rather than sell it. Many could not pay their debts. They lost their farms.

Fighting the depression   President Hoover tried to fight the depression. Under one of his programs, the federal government helped farmers by buying and storing some of their crops. However, this did not succeed in keeping farm prices from falling further. Hoover also proposed the Reconstruction Finance Corporation (RFC) in 1931. The RFC made loans to banks, insurance companies, farm mortgage associations, and railroads to keep them going.

However, Hoover drew the line at involving the federal government in the economy much farther than that. He was opposed to having the federal government provide direct relief—that is, money or jobs—to the unemployed. He believed that providing relief was the job of private charities and local and state governments. If the federal government provided relief directly to the needy, these citizens, Hoover felt, would become too dependent on the government. They would lose their self-reliance. However, private charities had never before had to cope with so many needy people. They

Have pupils put themselves in the place of the apple seller pictured. Have them write a paragraph or two describing their feelings.

did not have enough money for the job. And many city governments did not have the money to help.

The bonus army World War I veterans had been promised a bonus, or sum of money, for service to their country. The bonus was to be paid in 1944. The depression threw many of these men out of work. They felt they should get the bonus right away, when they needed it most. More than 15,000 veterans marched on Washington, D.C., to make their demands heard. In tents and hastily built shacks, they camped near the Capitol.

When Congress refused their demands, most of the veterans gave up and returned home. However, about 2,000 veterans, wives, and children remained. Fearing they would cause trouble, President Hoover ordered the army to remove them. Led by General Douglas MacArthur, soldiers used tear gas to drive out the campers, and then set their shacks afire. Pictures of the fleeing veterans appeared in papers all over the country. President Hoover's popularity sank lower than ever.

Getting ready for the 1932 election Faced with the worst depression in the nation's history, Republicans knew they had an uphill fight to win the 1932 election. They picked Hoover to run again. The Democratic choice was Governor Franklin D. Roosevelt of New York.

The day after the Democratic convention in Chicago chose Roosevelt as its candidate, he made a dramatic break with tradition. Until then, candidates did not attend conventions. It was customary for a delegation from the party to call on the

In May 1932, many World War I veterans marched on Washington, D.C., to demand immediate payment of a promised bonus. Some veterans' families also marched.

candidate at his home and tell him of his nomination—which he had known about all the time, of course. But Roosevelt flew from Albany, New York, to Chicago to accept the nomination in person.

He intended for his trip to be a symbol. "Let it be from now on the task of our party to break foolish traditions," he said to the wildly cheering convention.

CHECKUP

1. What caused the stock market crash of 1929?
2. What weaknesses in the American economy helped bring on the Great Depression?
3. How were businesses and farmers affected by the depression?
4. What steps did President Hoover favor to fight the depression?

The Republicans again chose Charles Curtis of Kansas as Hoover's running mate. Curtis was partly of Kaw Indian ancestry. The Democrats picked John Nance Garner, a Texas congressman known as Cactus Jack, as their candidate for Vice President. **585**

Born: 1874, West Branch, Iowa. **Education:** Stanford University. **Training:** Mining engineer, public official. **To presidency from:** California. **Position when elected:** Secretary of commerce. **Political party:** Republican. **Married:** Lou Henry. **Children:** Two sons. **Died:** 1964. **Other facts:** Orphaned at age 9. Worked his way through college. Directed mining projects in many countries. Was in China during Boxer Rebellion and supervised building of defenses. Organized food relief in Belgium during World War I and directed relief programs in Europe following World War II. In late 1940s headed a commission to streamline government. **During his presidency:** Amelia Earhart made the first solo flight by a woman across the Atlantic Ocean.

HERBERT HOOVER
31st President
1929 • 1933

The New Deal

---VOCABULARY---

New Deal
bank holiday
fireside chat

Social Security Act
collective bargaining

Another Roosevelt Judging by his family background and upbringing, Franklin D. Roosevelt seemed a most unlikely person to be breaking with traditions. The Roosevelts had lived in America for nine generations, since the middle of the seventeenth century. Franklin grew up with all the advantages of wealth. He attended private schools and traveled to Europe eight times before he was 14 years old. He was a distant cousin of President Theodore Roosevelt, and he married the President's niece, Eleanor. But unlike Theodore, who headed a Republican administration, Franklin was a Democrat.

Franklin Roosevelt had entered politics in 1910 as a Democratic member of New York's state legislature. He then served in Woodrow Wilson's administration as assistant secretary of the navy. Mainly because he carried the famous Roosevelt name, the Democratic party nominated him for Vice President in 1920. However, the Roosevelt name proved to be of little help in the first postwar election. That was the year of Republican Warren Harding's landslide victory.

Roosevelt's life was changed when he was stricken with polio in 1921. For many months he was bedridden. Never again was he able to walk without the aid of crutches and braces. At the age of 39, his political career seemed ended. But with encouragement and help from his wife, Eleanor, Franklin Roosevelt fought back. Some believe that the experience gave him a deeper understanding of less fortunate people who had to struggle every day with life's setbacks.

After several years of rebuilding his muscles, Roosevelt renewed his activity in politics. Eleanor attended meetings for him and helped to keep his name before the public. In 1928, Roosevelt was elected governor of New York. He proved to be able and popular, and in 1930 he was reelected by a large margin.

Ask: Why are there many fewer cases of polio today than at the time when Franklin D. Roosevelt was stricken with it? Have some pupils do research on Jonas Salk and Albert Sabin and report their findings to the class.

Over the years the state of the economy has often been the most important factor in determining the winner of a presidential election. If times are prosperous, the party already in office is usually returned. If times are bad, the party in office is usually defeated.

The election of 1932   Franklin Roosevelt was conservative in many ways. However, during this terrible depression he believed that times called for change and for new ideas. When campaigning for the Democratic presidential nomination in 1932, he said:

> The country demands bold, persistent experimentation. It is common sense to take a method and try it. If it fails, admit it frankly and try another. But above all, try something.

In accepting the Democratic nomination, Roosevelt told the delegates, "I pledge you, I pledge myself, to a new deal for the American people." The phrase **New Deal** came to stand for Roosevelt's administration.

President Hoover believed that his own policies were best for the nation. He warned that if Roosevelt and the Democrats were elected, "the grass will grow in the streets of a hundred cities, a thousand towns; the weeds will overrun the fields of millions of farms." But the American people wanted a change. In the election of 1932, Roosevelt got 23 million votes to Hoover's 16 million. Roosevelt was the victor in 43 of the 48 states.

Dealing with the banking crisis   By the time Roosevelt was inaugurated on March 4, 1933, the depression had worsened. Unemployment climbed toward the 15-million mark. Despite this, Roosevelt struck a note of confidence as he addressed the nation by radio. "This great nation will endure as it has endured, will revive and prosper," he said. He assured his listeners that "the only thing we have

Franklin D. Roosevelt poses with his wife Eleanor (left) and his mother on the day of his 1933 inauguration.

to fear is fear itself." He said that the nation wanted "action, and action now."

President Roosevelt's first action dealt with the banking crisis. As the depression continued, more and more banks had failed, and those who had deposited money in the banks lost all their savings. By early 1933, people were in a panic. They rushed to banks to take out their savings. This caused still more banks to run out of money and close.

Hours after taking the oath of office, President Roosevelt declared a **bank holiday.** All banks in the country would be

587

Today about 97 percent of the deposits in United States banks are insured. If an insured bank closes and cannot pay its depositors, the Federal Deposit Insurance Corporation (FDIC) pays the sum due a depositor up to $100,000 for each account.

closed. He then called Congress into a special session to pass an emergency banking bill. The bill provided that government experts would examine the records of each bank and allow only the healthy ones to reopen. It was passed and signed into law in just 8 hours.

On Sunday evening, March 12, Roosevelt spoke to the American people over the radio in the first of his many **fireside chats**—radio reports to the American people. In a reassuring voice he explained what the government was doing about the banking crisis. "I can assure you," he said confidently, "that it is safer to keep your money in a reopened bank than under your mattress."

When the banks opened Monday morning, people were again standing in line. This time, however, most of them were putting money in. In a few days, most of the banks were open again. The banking crisis had passed.

Later, Congress approved insurance for deposits up to a certain amount. Even if a bank should fail, depositors would get their money back.

The first hundred days   Franklin D. Roosevelt—FDR, as the newspapers began to call him—moved quickly to follow up this first success. In the spring of 1933, he sent to Congress a flood of ideas for dealing with the depression. Con-

President Franklin D. Roosevelt talks to the nation in one of his fireside chats.

gress acted on them in record time. In the first hundred days of the New Deal, 15 major laws were passed. Most of them dealt with the 3 R's of the New Deal— relief, recovery, and reform. Relief meant providing immediate help for the millions in need. Recovery meant helping businesses, farmers, and workers recover from the depression and get back to prosperity. Reform had to do with long-term change. The aim of reform was not only to prevent future depressions but also to better the lives of more Americans.

One of the first and most successful programs of the hundred days was the Civilian Conservation Corps (CCC). This program combined unemployment relief and conservation. The CCC hired 250,000 men between the ages of 18 and 25 to work on conservation projects in rural areas. They were all from needy families. These young men built wildlife shelters, fought forest fires, built reservoirs, stocked streams with fish, and planted trees. For this they received, in addition to room and meals, $30 a month. Of this, they were required to send $25 home to their families. Recruits could stay in the CCC for up to 2 years. Before the program ended in 1942, more than 2.5 million young men took part in it.

Other New Deal programs provided money and jobs for the unemployed. Under the Federal Emergency Relief Act (FERA), Congress sent $500 million to the states to give to the needy. The Public Works Administration (PWA) spent $3 billion over several years for hiring people to build roads, bridges, dams, and government buildings. This was the first time the federal government hired

A CCC crew undertakes a land conservation project.

the unemployed directly. In still another program, the New Deal created temporary jobs for 4 million people to get them through the winter of 1933–1934.

Programs like the CCC, the FERA, and the PWA had several aims. By giving money to the needy and jobs to the unemployed, these programs provided relief. They were also meant to aid recovery, for as those who received the money spent it, they would make jobs for others.

Aid for agriculture   The New Deal's main effort to assist the farmers was the Agriculture Adjustment Act (AAA). Since overproduction had caused farm prices to fall, would not cutting down production cause farm prices to rise again? This was the idea behind the AAA.

There may be someone in your class whose grandfather or other elderly relative served as a young man in the CCC. If so, have the pupil interview that person about his experience and report to the rest of the class.   **589**

In this program the government paid farmers *not* to plant crops on a part of their fields. Another program helped farmers get low-interest loans to help them meet their mortgage payments. This would help them keep their farms.

Helping business and workers The main effort to bring about recovery in industry was the National Industrial Recovery Act (NIRA or NRA). Employers claimed that companies would hire back workers and start up production if they were allowed to ignore the antitrust laws. Then instead of having to compete, they could cooperate. They could prevent overproduction by agreeing to produce only a certain amount. They could prevent price-cutting and insure a profit by agreeing on how much to charge. The NIRA gave business the right to do these

In the early years of the New Deal, most businesses displayed the blue eagle, emblem of the NRA.

things. In exchange, business was required to do certain things for its workers. Companies had to pay a fair minimum wage, agree on maximum hours, end child labor, and allow their workers to form unions.

The NIRA was hailed as a great experiment when it went into effect in June 1933. Parades and rallies were held to whip up public support. Businesses that pledged cooperation displayed the NIRA symbol—a blue eagle with the words *We Do Our Part.*

However, industrial recovery was disappointing. In a short time, both business and labor were complaining that the program was not working well for them. By the spring of 1935, it was clear that the NIRA was failing. The Supreme Court ended it by declaring that the law was unconstitutional.

The Tennessee Valley Authority The most sweeping reform of the hundred days was the creation of the Tennessee Valley Authority (TVA). This was an attempt to plan the economic development of a whole region. The Tennessee Valley runs through parts of seven states in the Southeast. The 3.5 million people living in this region were among the poorest in the country. Their land was worn out by erosion. Frequent floods added to their misery.

To control flooding, the TVA built 20 dams on the Tennessee River and the streams that feed it. At many of these dams, waterpower produced electricity at low rates for the whole area. The TVA also planted millions of trees to keep the soil from washing away during rains.

Be sure that pupils understand that *unconstitutional* means "not in agreement with the Constitution." One reason why the NIRA was declared unconstitutional was that, in the view of the Supreme Court, the act delegated lawmaking power to the President when it rightfully belonged to Congress.

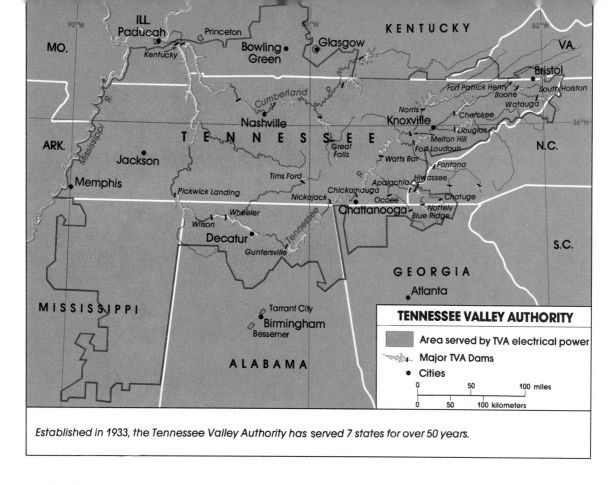

Established in 1933, the Tennessee Valley Authority has served 7 states for over 50 years.

The TVA was a remarkable success. Cheap electricity attracted business to the region. The standard of living was raised. Even so, some said that the government should not be in the business of producing electricity. They felt that the government was competing unfairly with private electric companies.

Americans approve   The first 2 years of the New Deal brought encouraging signs. The number of unemployed people, though still high, had been reduced by 4 million. Farmers were doing better. Perhaps most important, people seemed to have renewed faith in their government to help them.

Not everyone agreed that FDR was on the right track, however. Some believed that the New Deal was moving too slowly and not doing enough to restore prosperity. Others felt that it was changing too much too quickly. The latter group included many business people. They complained about the growth of government and government regulations.

However, in 1934 the majority of Americans gave a clear signal that they approved of the New Deal. In the congressional elections they elected more Democrats to Congress than ever before.

Other new laws   Encouraged by this show of support, Roosevelt proposed many other new laws in 1935 and 1936. One law set up the Works Progress Administration (WPA). The WPA was an emergency program that gave jobs to 35 million unemployed. During the next half-dozen years, the WPA built or improved thousands of school buildings, more than 800 airports, and a half-million miles of roads and highways.

The law also hired writers to write, actors to act, artists to paint, and musicians to play. It brought art, theater, and musical concerts to people in large and small communities.

Social security President Roosevelt regarded the **Social Security Act** as the most important act of his administration. For the first time, the government provided help for people in their old age.

A large audience watches a play put on outdoors by a unit of the WPA theater group.

During their working years, workers paid a tax into a special fund. This tax was matched by their employers. When the workers retired, they would receive monthly payments from this fund.

The law had two other parts. One provided help for workers who became blind, crippled, or handicapped in other ways and could no longer work. It also helped children with no means of support. The second part provided for unemployment insurance. Workers who lost their jobs would receive payments for a number of weeks while they looked for work.

The Wagner Act Another major law, the Wagner Act, dealt with labor relations. You will recall that one part of the NIRA gave workers the right to form unions. But the Supreme Court ruled that the NIRA was unconstitutional, and the law was thrown out.

President Roosevelt then gave his backing to a bill sponsored by Senator Robert Wagner of New York. This bill gave workers the right to join unions and practice **collective bargaining**. In collective bargaining a union represents the workers and bargains for them with the employer for better wages, hours, and working conditions. The Wagner Act also prohibited employers from interfering with the efforts of workers to form unions.

The election of 1936 When Roosevelt ran for reelection in 1936, he could point to many gains in the fight against the depression. He and the Democratic party overwhelmed the Republican party and its candidate, Governor Alfred Landon of Kansas. Roosevelt won more than

The operation of the social security system has been very much in the news in recent years. Have pupils find out why this issue has come to the fore in Congress and among the public.

60 percent of the votes and carried every state except Maine and Vermont.

At the start of his second term in 1937, FDR was at the height of his popularity. Yet hardly a year later the New Deal was in retreat, and Roosevelt was on the defensive against his critics. What had happened?

The Supreme Court controversy The President himself created opposition to his administration by trying to change the membership of the Supreme Court. You read earlier that the Court declared the NIRA unconstitutional. It also ruled that many other New Deal laws were unconstitutional. Roosevelt feared that if the Court went on to declare such laws as the Wagner Act and the Social Security Act unconstitutional, much of the New Deal would be undone.

All the justices on the Supreme Court were elderly. Roosevelt believed that many of them held old-fashioned ideas about the Constitution. He asked Congress to give him power to appoint one new justice for every old one who did not retire at the age of 70. This would have allowed Roosevelt to appoint 6 new justices immediately.

Roosevelt's proposal led to a storm of protest. He was accused of trying to pack the Court with his own supporters. The plan made Roosevelt appear power-hungry. Furthermore, the Court undercut Roosevelt's arguments when it ruled that both the Wagner Act and the Social Security Act were, in fact, constitutional. The court-packing plan was not adopted and Roosevelt lost much of his support from the public.

President Roosevelt's Supreme Court plan inspired this cartoon, showing a reorganized court with six new justices, all in Roosevelt's image.

Decline of the New Deal Then late in 1937 the economy went into a tailspin again. Farm prices fell, and unemployment climbed. New Deal policies were blamed. Opposition grew in Congress, and from that time on, few Roosevelt proposals were enacted. However, Roosevelt's foes were unable to do away with the reforms carried out earlier.

The last important social reform approved by Congress was the Fair Labor Standards Act of 1938. This law created the first national minimum wage, set the maximum hours of work per week at 40, and abolished child labor. By the end of 1938, the New Deal was over.

CHECKUP

1. How did President Franklin Roosevelt deal with the banking crisis?
2. Name the program each abbreviation refers to: CCC, PWA, AAA, NIRA, TVA. What did each program do?
3. What was done under the Social Security Act?
4. What factors brought the New Deal period to an end?

Though President Roosevelt failed in his attempt to enlarge the Supreme Court, he did succeed within a short time of achieving his goal of changing the makeup of the Court. Four justices retired within a period of months, and Roosevelt filled the vacancies with people who supported his policies.

593

Hard Times

Getting along   Most Americans were scarred by the depression in one way or another. Millions who had once earned a living for their families now felt shame and a loss of self-respect because they could not find a job. Millions more who still had jobs lived in constant fear of losing them. With the future so uncertain, young people postponed marriage. Families cut down expenses. They did without the daily newspaper, put off repairs on the car, and decided against using the doctor or the dentist. They found inexpensive ways to entertain themselves. Families gathered around the table to play the newest game, Monopoly. Or they listened to the radio, which brought entertainment into their homes. The main expense for entertainment outside their homes was the 15¢ admission to the movies. Eighty-five million Americans saw a movie every week and, at least for a while, escaped from the realities of the depression.

With few jobs available, young people stayed in school and continued their education. A special New Deal program, the National Youth Administration, provided part-time work for many students.

The plight of the farmers   Poverty in rural America was just as serious. Hundreds of small-farm owners lost their land, their buildings, everything. By the end of the Great Depression, nearly half of all farmers were tenant farmers— those who worked land that belonged to someone else. In the South, sharecroppers and migrant workers struggled along on less than $300 a year.

Among the people hit hardest were those who lived on the western part of the Great Plains. This was a belt of land that stretched from South Dakota through Kansas, Colorado, and Oklahoma, and on down to the plains of Texas and northeastern New Mexico. For several years this region experienced terrible droughts. The soil turned to dust. Beginning in 1933, high winds swept the dust across the open plains, whipping it into great clouds that darkened the sky. One observer reported:

> When the wind died and the sun shone forth again, it was on a different world. There were no fields, only sand drifting into mounds . . . In the farmyard, fences, machinery, and trees were gone, buried. The roofs of sheds stuck out through drifts deeper than a man is tall.

That winter, dust from western farms settled on the white snow that blanketed New England farms 1,000 miles away. Dust storms continued for several years, giving to the region the name **Dust Bowl.** One farmer, watching a storm from his window, said that he was "counting the Kansas farms as they came by."

With their farms gone, thousands piled their old trucks and cars high with mattresses, furniture, pots and pans, and a suitcase or two and headed west. There they hoped to make a fresh start. Many wound up in California and became migrant workers, living in roadside camps.

The desperation and the hopes of the migrant victims of the Dust Bowl were captured by John Steinbeck in his prize-winning novel *The Grapes of Wrath.*

Packed in an old car with all their belongings, a Dust Bowl family heads for California.

Blacks and the New Deal   Black people especially were hit hard by the Great Depression. In good times they could at least get certain low-level jobs that whites did not want. But in the depression even these jobs were in demand, and many of them went to whites. The unemployment rate among blacks was twice that of whites.

About 80 percent of black Americans still lived in the South, and most of these were in rural areas. There, two thirds of the black farmers who raised cotton made no money at all from their crops. Many of them survived mainly by raising vegetables and hunting rabbits and other small game.

Overall, however, the relief and welfare programs of the New Deal helped millions of black people. In addition, President Roosevelt appointed a number of blacks to important positions in government. He named William Hastie to a federal judgeship and Robert Weaver to an important post in the Interior Department. Mary McLeod Bethune became a special advisor on minority affairs. These officials and others came to be known as the Black Cabinet. They often met together and spoke up for the interests of black people.

Also, Eleanor Roosevelt worked to end discrimination against blacks and other minorities. In 1939 the Daughters of the American Revolution refused to let a black opera singer, Marian Anderson, sing in their concert hall. Mrs. Roosevelt promptly resigned from the organization and arranged for Anderson's concert to be given on the steps of the Lincoln Memorial. Over 75,000 people attended to show their support. Some regard the Anderson concert as one of the first modern civil rights demonstrations.

Most black people clearly felt they had gained from the New Deal. In 1928 the

Mary McLeod Bethune chats with a group of schoolgirls.

great majority of black voters supported the Republican party. But in 1936 a large majority voted for the Democrats.

Mexican Americans in the depression The number of immigrants from Mexico had grown in the 1920s. Most worked on farms in the Southwest.

Some federal and state officials decided to reduce the number of people seeking jobs by sending Mexicans back to Mexico. Between 1930 and 1940, between a quarter million and a half million—no one knows for sure—were forced to go back to Mexico. Most were Mexican citizens. However, some of the younger people had been born in the United States and were American citizens.

Indians in the depression Of all the minorities, Native Americans had the hardest time during the depression.

Their unemployment rate was three times that of the nation as a whole. They had lower income—an average of only $48 a year—had less schooling, and died younger than other Americans. Most New Deal relief and recovery programs did not help them.

However, the New Deal made an important change in government policy toward the Indians. The old policy of breaking up Indian lands and giving the land to individual Indians to farm had proved to be a failure. It was also destroying Indian culture. The Indian Reorganization Act of 1934 ended the breakup of Indian reservations into small pieces of land. It also allowed the tribes to have more say over their future and brought them greater cultural pride.

Women in the depression Women, too, could point to some gains during the New Deal. President Roosevelt appointed Frances Perkins as secretary of labor. She was the first woman Cabinet officer. Secretary Perkins was responsible for the report that led to the Social Security Act. Eleanor Roosevelt worked tirelessly to advance women's rights. Partly due to her influence, President Roosevelt appointed more than 100 women to high positions.

For the great majority of American women, however, nothing much changed during the depression and the New Deal. They continued to face job discrimination. For example, women made up 80 percent of the schoolteachers, but less than 2 percent of the principals and superintendents were women. In some school systems, women teachers who

596

Frances Perkins was secretary of labor for 12 years. She then served for 7 years on the United States Civil Service Commission.

Secretary of Labor Frances Perkins visits a construction site in California.

married were forced to give up their jobs. In general, women continued to earn less money than men for the same type of work.

Labor in the depression   During the depression, one of the big changes in America was the growth of unions. The American Federation of Labor had long been based on the idea of trade unionism. (See page 470.) Trade unions, however, left out the millions who worked on factory assembly lines and in other jobs that did not call for special skills. Some union leaders thought workers in the same industry, whatever the job, should be brought into one union, called an **industrial union**. John L. Lewis, head of the United Mine Workers, was one who favored this course.

Most AFL leaders were opposed to industrial unionism, however. In 1935,

Lewis and others broke away from the AFL and formed what later came to be called the **Congress of Industrial Organizations** (CIO). They organized workers in America's basic industries—steel, autos, rubber, textiles, and so on. Usually, employers agreed to recognize these unions and bargain with them only after long and bitter strikes. But by the end of the 1930s, some 8.5 million American workers belonged to unions—an increase of 100 percent in 5 years. And America's major industries were unionized.

CHECKUP

1. Why was the western part of the Great Plains hit so hard by the depression?
2. What steps were taken to help black people under the New Deal?
3. How did other minority groups fare under the New Deal?
4. What changes came about in labor unions during the 1930s?

In the labor-management conflict that marked the early days of the CIO, the sit-down strike was introduced. Instead of walking off the job, strikers sat down at their machines and took over factories. Though illegal, the sit-down tactic helped bring about recognition for CIO unions.

KEY FACTS

1. A stock market crash, caused by reckless speculation, ushered in the worst depression in the nation's history.

2. In the first hundred days in office, Franklin D. Roosevelt sent Congress a flood of proposals for providing relief, recovery, and reform, and Congress quickly adopted them.

3. By providing social security, unemployment insurance, and jobs for the unemployed, the federal government accepted a major responsibility for the welfare of its citizens.

4. Despite the success of a number of its programs, the New Deal failed to bring an end to the depression.

VOCABULARY QUIZ

Write the sentences below on a sheet of paper and fill in the blanks. To help you, the first letter of the word or words to be filled in is shown.

1. Stocks are bought and sold at a s tock m arket .

2. If a corporation earns profits, d ividends may be paid on the stock.

3. The merchandise, or goods, that a store has on hand to sell is its i nventory .

4. When nominated for President, Franklin D. Roosevelt promised "a N ew D eal for the American people."

5. In 1933 the four days during which all banks were closed for inspection were called a b ank h oliday .

6. A drought on the Great Plains caused a large part of that region to become known as the D ust B owl .

7. Roosevelt called each of his radio reports to the American people a f ireside c hat .

8. A program that provided funds for workers who were retired, blind, crippled, or handicapped was called s ocial s ecurity .

9. When union representatives negotiate with employers for better wages and working conditions, they are involved in c ollective b argaining .

10. In the 1930s, John L. Lewis and others organized workers into i ndustrial u nions .

REVIEW QUESTIONS

1. How did each of the following help bring on the Great Depression? **(a)** speculation, **(b)** overproduction of goods, **(c)** a high tariff, **(d)** surplus farm crops

2. How did Hoover's approach to the depression differ from Roosevelt's?

3. Name at least five major laws passed during the New Deal. What did each do?

4. Why did Roosevelt want to change the number of Supreme Court justices? What was the result of his proposal?

5. What happened to farmers who lived in the Dust Bowl?

6. How did the CIO differ from the AFL?

ACTIVITIES

1. Find out how the Twentieth Amendment to the Constitution changed elections. Be prepared to report your findings to the class.

2. In your community, interview people who lived through the Great Depression. Ask them what they remember about it. Record your information. Compare it with the information your classmates collect.

3. Two songs that were popular during the Great Depression are "Brother, Can You Spare a Dime?" and "Happy Days Are Here Again." Find the words to the songs. What point is each song trying to make?

26/SKILLS DEVELOPMENT

USING THE DICTIONARY

DEFINITIONS

Most words have more than one meaning and can be used in many different contexts. Think of the many ways you can use the word *run*. You run, or move rapidly, from one place to another. Politicians run for office. Workers run machines. One who spends more than he or she earns will soon run into debt. A baseball player crossing home plate scores a run. Some dictionaries have more than 50 definitions of *run*.

When you look up a word in a dictionary, you can expect to find many definitions. The one you will want is the one that will make sense in your sentence. For example, look at this sentence using the word *platform*. "The Republican party platform in 1924 favored high tariffs, lower taxes, and a continuation of prohibition." Here is one dictionary's definition of *platform*.

> **plat·form** (plat′ fôrm), *n*. **1.** a raised level surface or structure formed with planks, boards, or the like. **2.** the walk between or beside the tracks of a railroad station. **3.** *U.S.* the floor beyond the inside doors at either end of a railroad passenger car; vestibule. **4.** a piece of raised flooring, in a hall or in the open air, from which a speaker addresses his audience. **5.** a plan of action or statement of principles adopted by a political group, especially a political party at a convention where candidates are nominated.

How many definitions of *platform* do you see? Which is the correct definition for the sentence?

SKILLS PRACTICE: Part 1

Many terms used in Chapter 26 have several meanings. Find the number of definitions your dictionary gives for each of the seven words in the list. Then write the correct definition for each word when referring to each of the terms in parentheses.

1. Depression (the economy, a psychiatrist, a road)
2. Strike (a gold miner, a baseball player, a labor union)
3. Crash (an airplane, the stock market, an uninvited guest)
4. Reservation (a Native American, a person on vacation)
5. Recovery (the economy, a patient, a football game)
6. Cabinet (a carpenter, the President of the United States)
7. Stock (a cattle ranch, an investor, a department store)

SKILLS PRACTICE: Part II

Select four of the words above and use them in sentences. Make sure your sentences show that you understand the definition of the word.

CHAPTER
27 World War II

The Rise of the Dictators

```
┌─VOCABULARY──────────────────┐
│ totalitarian    Axis powers │
│ dictator        Neutrality Acts │
│ demilitarize                │
└─────────────────────────────┘
```

A general offers a challenge   To the congressman from Virginia, the witness's ideas about the use of airplanes in warfare were just a lot of theory, and the congressman said so. The witness was General William "Billy" Mitchell of the Air Service of the United States Army. Mitchell had claimed that with an airplane he could "destroy or sink any ship in existence." Now, in 1921, he was testifying before a committee of Congress. Making a claim was one thing, continued the doubting congressman. Proving it was another. This was the opportunity Mitchell had waited for. "Give us the warships to attack and come watch it," he challenged.

Mitchell had joined the army at the age of 18. He became interested in the military use of the airplane and in 1916 learned to fly. After watching British night bombers take off on strikes behind enemy lines in World War I, Mitchell wrote: "I am sure the future will see operations conducted in this way by thousands of planes." He himself later led two such operations.

After the war, General Mitchell tried to persuade top military leaders that the airplane would change warfare. The target, he said, would no longer be the enemy's armies but his industries, supplies, transportation, and cities. By dealing crippling blows beyond the battlefield, airplanes would leave the armies helpless. As for battleships, the airplane made them outdated. To develop air power for the next war, Mitchell said, an air force command separate from the army and the navy was needed.

Most generals and admirals, however, saw the airplane as just another weapon to be used by the army and the navy in their regular operations. Unable to persuade his superiors, Billy Mitchell took his case to the public. He gave speeches, wrote magazine articles, and testified before Congress. Now, in 1921, he would have the chance to prove his case.

A German battleship that was surrendered after World War I was towed to a point 60 miles (96 km) off the Virginia coast. The battleship was supposed to be unsinkable. With members of the Cabinet and Congress watching, Mitchell's planes swooped down and dropped their bombs. Some 20 minutes later, the battleship lay at the bottom of the ocean.

Mitchell fails to convince   Many military leaders were still not convinced. The

American bombers bound for German-held territory take off from an airfield in England.

World War I saw the beginning of aerial warfare. At first, planes were used for observation purposes—for spotting enemy forces. Then rival pilots started firing from open cockpits with pistols and rifles. Soon machine guns were installed in the planes. Pilots then engaged in air battles known as dogfights.

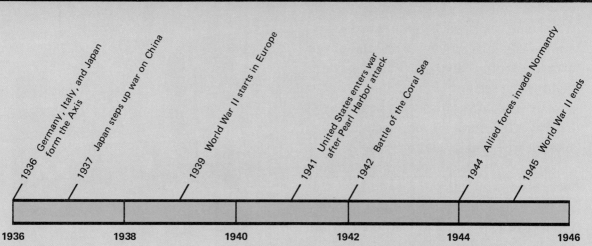

1936 Germany, Italy, and Japan form the Axis

1937 Japan steps up war on China

1939 World War II starts in Europe

1941 United States enters war after Pearl Harbor attack

1942 Battle of the Coral Sea

1944 Allied forces invade Normandy

1945 World War II ends

1936 1938 1940 1942 1944 1946

test was not under true battle conditions, they noted. Regarded as a troublemaker, General Mitchell was sent away on a long inspection tour to other countries. In 1924, after visiting the Far East, Mitchell wrote a report predicting a Japanese attack on the naval base at Pearl Harbor in Hawaii. Waves of planes launched from aircraft carriers would strike some morning at about 7:30, he wrote. The army said that Mitchell's report was "unsound" and put it aside. Mitchell continued to publicly criticize the leadership of the army and the navy. In 1925 he was suspended from duty for 5 years. A year later he chose to resign from the army. He died 10 years later.

Democracy loses out   At least part of Billy Mitchell's message was finally heeded by the United States. The nation did not spend much for arms in the 1920s and 1930s, but the army and the navy did begin to give greater attention to the need for bombers and aircraft carriers. It was well that they did, for in the 1930s the world was once again becoming a dangerous place. In many countries, democracy was being replaced by **totalitarian** governments—governments with total power over the people. In a democracy, government is the servant of the people. Under a totalitarian government the people exist to serve the state. Free elections, free speech, free press—all are ended.

Most of the totalitarian governments were headed by a **dictator**, or all-powerful ruler. These dictators rose to power by promising jobs and national glory to the people. They glorified war and the use of force.

Fascists, Nazis, and Communists   In Italy there was depression and unemployment after World War I. The government was weak. Many Italians also felt that their country did not receive all it should have had from the peace treaty. Taking advantage of these grievances, a former schoolteacher, writer, and soldier named Benito Mussolini (bə nē′ tō mü sə lē′ nē) and his Fascist (fash′ ist) party took power in 1922. Calling democracy "a rotting corpse," Mussolini established a dictatorship in Italy.

In Germany a weak democratic government set up after the war could not weather the storm of the depression. Also, many Germans felt bitter about the peace terms that had been forced upon

Benito Mussolini of Italy and Adolf Hitler of Germany destroyed democracy and set up dictatorships.

Discuss with the class the differences between totalitarian and democratic governments. You may wish to list differences on the chalkboard. The discussion will furnish a good opportunity to review the Bill of Rights on pages 192–194.

them. Adolf Hitler, a former army corporal, blamed Germany's defeat on enemies within the country—weak, old leaders; Communists; and especially Jews. Hitler was a man consumed by hatred. One historian has written, "He hated the Jews, he hated democracy, he hated the Christian religion in which he was reared . . .." In the 1920s he developed a twisted philosophy that proclaimed the German people to be a "master race" that would one day control all of Europe.

In the 1920s, few paid much attention to Hitler and his followers, called Nazis. With the start of a depression in 1930, however, his message began to attract Germans. In 1933, Hitler became chancellor, or prime minister, of Germany. Within a year he threw out the German constitution and made himself dictator. He began to build up Germany's military forces, even though this was forbidden by the Treaty of Versailles. He took Germany out of the League of Nations. And he passed laws taking away most of the legal rights of German Jews.

Following the Communist revolution of 1917, Russia changed its name to the Union of Soviet Socialist Republics (U.S.S.R.), or the Soviet Union. Its head, V. I. Lenin, proclaimed the Communist goal of worldwide revolution. After Lenin's death in 1924, Joseph Stalin succeeded him as the Russian dictator.

On the other side of the world in Japan, generals and admirals were gaining control of the government. Japan was a growing industrial nation. To get the coal, oil, and other raw materials it needed and also to win glory, Japan's military sought control of eastern Asia.

The Axis powers   Japan was the first to break the peace. In 1931 its army invaded Manchuria, a northern province of China. In less than a year, Manchuria was brought under Japanese control. The League of Nations made only a weak protest. Japan responded by withdrawing from the league.

Four years later, in 1935, Mussolini invaded the North African country of Ethiopia. Again, the league failed to stop an attack. Ethiopia was soon conquered, and Mussolini pulled Italy out of the league, which, it was now plain to see, could not curb aggression.

In 1936 it was Hitler's turn. He sent German troops into the Rhineland, a part of Germany that bordered on France. Un-

War broke out in Asia when Japanese troops invaded the province of Manchuria in northern China.

Hitler and his followers were members of the National Socialist German Workers Party. The word *Nazi* is a shortening of the German words meaning "National Socialist." After Hitler got power, he gave himself the title of Führer (leader).

603

der the Treaty of Versailles, the Rhineland was to have remained **demilitarized**—that is, no soldiers were to be stationed in the Rhineland. Again, nations protested but to no avail.

Until 1936 each of these militaristic nations acted on its own. In that year, Mussolini and Hitler signed a treaty of alliance. Mussolini boasted that from that moment on, the world would turn on the axis between Rome and Berlin, the capitals of the two countries. For this reason, Italy and Germany were called the **Axis powers.** Later that year the two countries signed a treaty of cooperation with Japan. Eventually the three became military allies as well, forming the Rome-Berlin-Tokyo axis.

America tries to stay neutral   Americans watched these events with growing concern. They were determined to have no part of another war. The Americans had shed their blood in the last one, yet the world was no safer for democracy. Further, with a worldwide depression, European countries had stopped paying their war debts to the United States. That led to more bad feelings.

Between 1935 and 1937, Congress passed several laws intended to keep America from being drawn into war. They were called the **Neutrality Acts.** One law prohibited the sale of arms to countries at war. Another forbade Americans to lend money to warring countries or to travel on their ships. A third law said that countries at war could not buy goods from the United States on credit. They must pay in advance and then carry the goods away in their own ships.

604   The single country that continued to pay war debts to the United States during the depression was Finland.

The Good Neighbor policy   Meanwhile, the United States improved relations with the other countries of the Western Hemisphere. President Hoover had made a start on this with a goodwill tour of Latin America. President Roosevelt continued along the same path. His policy, he said, would be one of "the good neighbor—the neighbor who . . . respects himself, and because he does so, respects the rights of others."

United States troops were withdrawn from Nicaragua and from Haiti, the last two Latin American countries in which they had been stationed. The United States also gave up its right to intervene in Cuba as it had been allowed to do by the 1902 treaty. And it joined other Western Hemisphere countries in agree-

Under the Good Neighbor policy, Uncle Sam exchanges a hearty handshake with a Latin American friend.

ing that "no state [nation] has a right to intervene in the internal or external affairs of another." From these changes the United States reaped a harvest of goodwill. When war finally came, almost every country in the hemisphere stood side by side with the United States.

The road to war Meanwhile the armies of the dictators continued to march. In 1937, Japan started a full-scale war against China. Japanese planes destroyed railroads, supplies, and cities, just as General Mitchell had predicted. In Europe, Hitler pushed ahead with his goal of conquest. He claimed that his only aim was to bring together all German people under one flag. In 1938, Nazi troops took over the German-speaking country of Austria without a fight.

Later that year, Hitler demanded that Czechoslovakia hand over a part of its country called the Sudetenland (sü dāt′ n land). About 3 million German-speaking people, plus many others, lived there. Czechoslovakia prepared to fight. The leaders of France and Britain knew that if war came, their countries would be drawn in. In September 1938 they met with Hitler and bowed to his demands. Left alone, Czechoslovakia had no choice but to yield. We know today from German records that if Britain and France had not given in, German generals were planning to remove Hitler from power.

Hitler had told Britain and France that the Sudetenland would be the last territory he would demand in Europe. But 6 months later he seized the rest of Czechoslovakia without firing a shot.

On a street adorned with swastika flags, German troops enter a city in Czechoslovakia.

On September 17, 1939, Russian troops drove into Poland from the east. By the end of the month, Polish resistance to the invading armies was crushed, and Germany and Russia divided Poland between them.

Britain and France now saw that they must rearm quickly. When Hitler now demanded territory from Poland, Britain and France promised to come to Poland's aid if Germany attacked. Hitler was not to be stopped, however. He first took action to make sure that if Britain and France went to war against Germany, he would not have to fight Russia at the same time. In August 1939, Germany and the Soviet Union—who had been sworn enemies—stunned the world by signing a treaty not to attack each other. In a secret part of the deal, they agreed to divide Poland between them.

Hitler's troops, invading Poland, advance amid the wreckage inflicted by German dive bombers.

Now the way was clear. On September 1, German planes, tanks, and troops attacked Poland. Two days later, Britain and France declared war on Germany. World War II had begun.

CHECKUP

1. How did the totalitarian governments of the 1930s differ from democratic governments?
2. What aggressive actions had Japan, Italy, and Germany taken by 1936?
3. What did Congress do to try to keep the United States out of war?
4. What events brought on war in Europe?

The United States Enters the War

VOCABULARY

blitzkrieg	D-Day
isolationist	concentration camp
lend-lease	
Atlantic Charter	holocaust
pacifist	island-hopping

France falls Hitler's armies moved with such swiftness and force in September 1939 that their attack was called a **blitzkrieg**, which is German for "lightning war." Planes struck cities, railroads, and highways, as well as at Polish troops. Tanks rolled over Polish positions before Poland's army could adjust. In less than a month, Poland fell. Soon after, the Soviet Union invaded Finland and took a large piece of that territory.

During the fall and winter, a quiet settled over the battlefronts. But in the spring of 1940, Nazi armies struck again with fury. In April, Denmark and Norway were invaded. In May, Hitler's armies attacked Holland and Belgium without warning and conquered both in a few days. From Belgium the Germans wheeled into northern France. The sudden attack trapped the British and French armies with their backs to the sea, at a place called Dunkirk. They were saved only by the greatest rescue operation in history. In boats of every size and description, Englishmen from coastal villages crossed the English Channel and ferried the soldiers to England.

There was now no way to save France. Early in June, Italy invaded France from the south. On June 22, France surrendered. Britain now stood alone, the last democracy among Europe's major powers.

The American response   The swiftness of Hitler's victories in Europe shocked Americans. At President Roosevelt's urging, Congress spent billions to build up the country's military strength. It also passed the country's first peacetime draft law.

Meanwhile a debate grew over aid to Britain. On one side were those who said that the best way to protect the United States was to help Britain with all aid short of going to war against the Axis powers. This was President Roosevelt's belief. On the other side were those who said that helping Britain would probably draw the United States into war. Those who held this view were called **isolationists.** The leading isolationist group was the America First Committee. Its speakers, such as Charles A. Lindbergh, argued that America should stay out of the conflict and create a "Fortress America" that the Axis would not attack.

Members of the America First Committee demonstrate against American involvement in World War II.

As the country rearmed, the presidential election of 1940 took place. Roosevelt ran for a third term and won reelection easily.

Lend-lease   By the end of 1940, Britain was running out of money with which to buy arms from the United States. President Roosevelt proposed that the United States lend Britain the weapons it needed. Congress passed this program, called **lend-lease,** in the spring of 1941. By summer the United States was also sending lend-lease aid to Russia. This was because Hitler, ignoring the treaty he signed in 1939, suddenly attacked the Soviet Union in June.

Ask: Do you think you would have been an isolationist or would you have favored Great Britain had you been an American citizen in 1939? Explain your answer.

Early in 1941, President Roosevelt declared, "We look forward to a world founded upon four essential human freedoms." The four freedoms were (1) freedom of speech and expression; (2) freedom to worship God in one's own way; (3) freedom from want—that is, poverty; and (4) freedom from fear.

Later that summer, President Roosevelt and Winston Churchill, the British prime minister, met on a ship off Newfoundland. There they drew up the **Atlantic Charter,** a statement of war aims for the Allies. The two agreed that their countries would work for the defeat of "Nazi tyranny," for a lasting peace, and for the right of all peoples to choose their own form of government. By this time, American naval vessels were protecting American and British merchant ships as they carried war goods across the Atlantic Ocean. In the fall these American warships and German submarines were firing at each other. The United States was edging closer and closer to war.

The attack on Pearl Harbor When war came, however, it was not in the Atlantic but the Pacific. In Asia, Japanese armies had been on the move for several years. When they marched into Indochina in July 1941, President Roosevelt acted to stop all American trade with Japan. This included the sale of oil, which Japan badly needed. Tensions rose between the two countries.

That fall, representatives from each side tried to settle their differences. However, Japanese military leaders had already decided on war. In the predawn hours of Sunday, December 7, 1941, bombers and fighter planes took off from Japanese aircraft carriers and headed for

Japan's surprise attack on the United States naval base at Pearl Harbor, Hawaii, on December 7, 1941, brought America into World War II. (21°N/158°W; map, p. 613)

the American naval base at Pearl Harbor, in Hawaii. At 7:55 A.M.—almost precisely the time that Billy Mitchell had predicted—they struck. Catching the American forces completely by surprise, the Japanese planes dealt a crippling blow to America's Pacific fleet and air force. They sank or damaged 19 warships, including 8 battleships, and destroyed 150 planes, more than half of the air force in the Pacific. Only luck spared the American aircraft carriers. They happened to be at sea when the Japanese attack came. There were more than 4,000 American casualties in the Pearl Harbor attack.

The next day, Congress declared war on Japan. Three days later, Germany and Italy joined their Axis partner and declared war on the United States.

The grand alliance   On New Year's Day, 1942, the United States broke a tradition that extended far back by making an alliance with other nations. On that day, 26 countries including the United States signed the Declaration of the United Nations. They pledged to fight until victory was gained.

The Allies who would carry most of the fighting were, of course, the United States, the Soviet Union, and Great Britain. It was also clear that the role of the United States would be far larger than it was in World War I. America would supply most of the military equipment. It would also have to build a great fighting force of its own. Eventually, more than 15 million men and women served in the United States armed forces.

A grim outlook   For the first half year after America entered the war, the outlook for the Allies was grim. In the Pacific, Japan marched from one success to another. By the summer of 1942, its armies controlled large parts of China, the Southeast Asian mainland, the Philippines, the Dutch East Indies, and nearly every island in the western Pacific. In addition, the Japanese navy dealt a crushing defeat in February to a combined United States-British fleet in the battle of the Java Sea.

On the other side of the world, the outlook was equally poor. In Europe, German armies had taken Greece and Yugoslavia and had driven hundreds of miles into the Soviet Union. In North Africa, German and Italian armies under General Erwin Rommel, "the Desert Fox," pushed British forces back across the desert into Egypt. The Axis forces were a victory away from smashing through to the Suez Canal and to the oil fields of the Middle East.

Europe first   The United States had to develop a plan for fighting a war in both Asia and Europe. From the beginning, America's military leaders decided on a strategy of "Europe first." The main effort would be to defeat Germany.

The first task was to bring German submarines under control. For the first year of the war, submarines sank Allied ships faster than they could be replaced. To combat the submarines, naval vessels and airplanes convoyed ships. Scientists also developed new antisubmarine weapons. Meanwhile, lights burned at night in American shipyards, where ships were being turned out in record numbers. By 1943 the Allies were winning the battle of the Atlantic.

In the fall of 1942, the tide of battle on land also began to turn in favor of the Allies. On the eastern front the Russians held firm at Stalingrad, and then counterattacked. Hitler's armies were defeated with the loss of a quarter of a million men and the capture of another 100,000. The battle of Stalingrad was one of the decisive battles in history. From then on, the German armies in Russia fell back.

General Dwight Eisenhower   In the west, Allied armies also took the offensive. Commanding the American forces in Europe was a man from a family of

These American generals—Marshall, Arnold, and Eisenhower—played major roles in the Allied victory.

Ask: Why, do you think, was the decision made to direct the first major war effort against Germany rather than against Japan? Was this a wise decision? Why or why not?

WORLD WAR II:
Europe and North Africa

- ▨ Axis Powers and occupied areas
- ← Allied Drives
- ▨ Neutral Nations

0   250   500 miles
0   250   500 kilometers

In May, 1945 Allied forces pushed deep into Germany. Within days the war in Europe was brought to an end.

pacifists—people who oppose war—and who had never been in combat himself. Dwight Eisenhower turned out to be one of the great generals of the war.

Dwight Eisenhower was born in Texas and grew up in Abilene, Kansas. Dwight, or Ike, as he was nicknamed, went to the United States Military Academy at West Point, much to the distress of his pacifist family. In the peacetime army of the 1920s and 1930s, Eisenhower rose slowly, but he impressed the army's top leaders. When America entered World War II, General George C. Marshall, chief of staff of the army, promoted Eisenhower over 366 officers who were senior to him.

Marshall appointed him to command American forces in Europe. Eventually he would assume command of all Allied troops in western Europe.

Eisenhower's first job, however, was to plan the invasion of North Africa. In November 1942, some 300,000 Allied troops landed in Morocco and Algeria. Only days before the landing, more than 1,600 miles (2,560 km) to the east, British general Bernard Montgomery won a brilliant victory at El Alamein (el al ə mān′) in Egypt and began to drive the Axis armies back to the west. Caught between the British and the Americans, the Axis forces surrendered in May 1943.

Code names were used to designate the landing beaches in Normandy on D-Day. American troops went ashore on Omaha and Utah beaches, near the base of the Cherbourg Peninsula. The British forces landed farther east on Gold, Juno, and Sword beaches.

The advance into Europe Two months later, Allied forces from North Africa invaded Sicily, an Italian island in the Mediterranean Sea. After 38 days of fierce fighting, the island fell. During this time the Italian people drove the dictator Mussolini from power. Near the end of the war, he was caught and executed by Italian patriots.

Sicily became the jumping-off place for an invasion of southern Italy on September 3. In less than a week, the new Italian government not only surrendered but changed sides and joined the Allies. However, German troops quickly occupied most of Italy, and Allied armies were able to move north only slowly and at great cost.

Growing Allied air power carried the war home to the German people. By early 1944, fleets of British and American bombers attacked German cities almost around the clock. Only occasional bad weather spared German factories, railroads, oil refineries, and civilian populations from the pounding. The enemy's ability to supply its armies was slowly being destroyed. Never did Billy Mitchell appear more to be a prophet.

The Normandy invasion All the while, the Allies continued to build for **D-Day**—the date that would be chosen for the invasion of western Europe. Mountains of supplies and thousands of planes and ships were assembled in England for this operation. Before dawn on June 6, American, British, Canadian, and French forces in southern England crossed the English Channel and landed on the beaches of Normandy in France. They were supported in the D-Day land-

The largest fleet ever assembled approaches a landing beach in Normandy on D-Day.   Omaha Beach

Born: 1882, Hyde Park, New York. **Education:** Harvard College. **Training:** Lawyer, public official. **To presidency from:** New York. **Position when elected:** Governor of New York. **Political party:** Democratic. **Married:** Eleanor Roosevelt, a distant cousin. **Children:** Five sons, one daughter. **Died:** 1945, Warm Springs Georgia, 3 months after the beginning of his fourth term. **Other facts:** Served as assistant secretary of the navy under Wilson. Crippled by polio at age of 39. The first President to appear on television. First President to serve more than two terms. **During his presidency:** Grand Coulee Dam on the Columbia River in Washington was completed. It is still the largest concrete dam and the greatest single source of waterpower in the United States.

FRANKLIN D. ROOSEVELT
32nd President
1933 · 1945

ings by 4,000 ships and 11,000 planes overhead—one of the greatest military operations in history. The invasion of Europe had begun.

The 176,000 men who landed that first day grew to a million in a few weeks. In late July they broke through the German defenses and pushed inland. Before the end of August, Paris was freed. By the end of September, French and Belgian soil was all but cleared of German troops. In eastern Europe, Soviet troops were clearing their land of Hitler's armies as well.

In December 1944 the Germans threw everything they had into a last desperate effort to avoid defeat. In the Battle of the Bulge, they attacked westward into Belgium and Luxembourg with the aim of splitting the Allied armies. Though German troops created a bulge 60 miles (96 km) deep in the Allied line, they could not break through. The German threat ended, and Allied armies went back on the attack.

In March 1945 the Allies crossed the Rhine River. British and American forces advanced toward Berlin from the west; Russian troops poured in from the east. In April, American and Russian troops met in northern Germany. A week later the Soviet army entered Berlin. Germany surrendered on May 8—V-E (Victory in Europe) Day. Hitler's dream of an empire that would last a thousand years lay in ashes. Hitler himself escaped punishment by committing suicide before he could be captured.

Concentration camps During 1943 and 1944, reports about mass killings of Jews and political enemies by the Nazis had been coming out of Europe. In the final months of the war, Allied troops came upon the grisly evidence of Nazi madness. In more than a dozen places in Poland, Austria, and Germany, they found **concentration camps,** which had been set up for the efficient slaughter of human beings. Even men hardened by war grew sick at the sight of the torture rooms and the gas ovens in which bodies were turned to ash. Six million Jews were put to death. Possibly as many as 6 million

The war crimes trial in Europe was held at Nuremberg, which had been the annual meeting place of Hitler's Nazi party. Four judges—one each from Britain, France, Russia, and the United States—presided at the trial. Nazi leaders were charged with war crimes, crimes against peace, and crimes against humanity.

others, including Poles, gypsies, and political foes, were also killed. This mass killing came to be called the **holocaust.**

After the war, the Allies put a number of top Nazis on trial for their war crimes. Ten were hanged; others received long prison terms.

Two crucial battles   In the Pacific the Japanese tide was first checked and then reversed in two big naval battles in 1942. In the first, a British-American force met the Japanese in May in the battle of the Coral Sea. This battle introduced something new into naval warfare. Ships of the opposing navies did not fire on each other—in fact, they were not even in sight of each other. All the fighting was done by planes launched from aircraft

carriers. Neither side could claim victory, but Japan's advance toward Australia was halted.

The second battle occurred in June near Midway Island in the central Pacific, not far from Hawaii. The United States Navy had intercepted Japanese messages that stated an invasion fleet was headed toward Midway. The Americans, under the command of Admiral Chester W. Nimitz, were ready and handed the Japanese a stinging defeat.

From one island to the next   From that time on, Japan was thrown on the defensive. In August 1942, American marines landed on Guadalcanal, one of the Solomon Islands, near Australia. Fierce fighting raged for 6 months, but

Smoke rises from the United States aircraft carrier Yorktown *under attack from Japanese torpedo bombers at the battle of Midway Island.*   (28°N/177°W; map, p. 617)

the United States troops took the island. For the next 2 years, Allied forces, mainly American, fought their way back through the islands of the Pacific toward Japan. Allied sea, air, and land forces attacked only certain islands while bypassing and cutting off the supplies of other Japanese-held islands. This strategy was called island-hopping.

In the central Pacific, naval and marine forces under Admiral Nimitz advanced in this manner through the Gilbert, Marshall, and Mariana islands. The Japanese defended every island fiercely, but despite heavy losses, Allied forces proved equal to the task. By the fall of 1944, the southern part of Japan was within range of land-based bombers operating from the islands of Guam and Saipan. The following spring, the capture of the islands of Iwo Jima and Okinawa brought American planes within 750 miles (1,200 km) of Tokyo itself. American planes rained destruction on that and other Japanese cities almost daily.

General Douglas MacArthur Meanwhile, a second fighting force in the southwest Pacific advanced toward Japan. This was under the command of General Douglas MacArthur. Unlike Dwight Eisenhower, Douglas MacArthur was raised to be a military man from birth. His father was a general who had commanded American forces in the Philippines after the United States acquired them from Spain. At West Point, MacArthur made the best 4-year record in the history of the academy. During World War I, he fought with reckless courage and rose to the rank of general. Under President Hoover, MacArthur became chief of staff, the youngest man ever to hold the army's highest position.

MacArthur retired from the United States Army in the 1930s. He was in the Philippines helping to train an army and design a defense for the islands when war threatened. President Roosevelt recalled him to active duty and made him commander of the combined American and Philippine force.

"I shall return" MacArthur's troops were hopelessly outnumbered and outgunned when Japan invaded the Philippines in December 1941. Several months later, as his army retreated, MacArthur escaped to Australia on a submarine. "I shall return," he vowed.

Starting in late 1942, General MacArthur moved northward from Australia toward Japan. In a series of brilliant campaigns, Allied forces island-hopped closer to the Philippines. On October 20, 1944, Americans landed on the island of Leyte (lā′ tē) in the Philippine Islands. Wading ashore, MacArthur announced dramatically, "People of the Philippines: I have returned."

Just 3 days later, Japan made a desperate attempt to stop the American advance. It threw most of its remaining warships into battle against American ships and planes in the Leyte Gulf in what was the largest battle in naval history. Japan's navy was crushed, and with that defeat Japan was through as a naval power.

As Japan was being driven back toward its home islands, the United States had a change in leadership. President Roosevelt had been elected President for a

615

fourth term in 1944. Even then, his health was failing. On April 12, 1945, while vacationing at Warm Springs, Georgia, he suffered a stroke and died almost instantly. Vice President Harry Truman became President.

The atomic bomb It fell to President Truman to make one of the most historic decisions of the war and perhaps of all human history. That was the decision to drop an atomic bomb on Japan. In 1939 the famed scientist Albert Einstein wrote a letter to President Roosevelt. Scientists, he told the President, had learned how to split the atom, releasing unimaginable energy. This made possible the building of the most destructive weapon the world had ever known.

Roosevelt promptly organized a top-secret effort to build an atomic bomb.

General MacArthur wades ashore at Leyte Island. With him are members of his staff and Filipino officers.

This was known as the Manhattan Project. On July 16, 1945, on a desert near Alamogordo, New Mexico, the first atomic bomb in history was tested successfully.

Most of President Truman's scientific advisers urged him to use the bomb against Japan. Some, however, disagreed. They feared that unleashing this new force might have terrible consequences for the future of humankind. In the end, Truman made his decision on military grounds. Military leaders believed that the Allies would have to invade Japan to defeat it. Such an invasion could cost a half-million American casualties—killed and wounded. Truman decided that if the atomic bomb could end the war quickly, it should be used.

World War II ends On July 26 the President warned Japan to surrender or face "prompt and utter destruction." When no reply came, a lone American bomber dropped an atomic bomb on the Japanese city of Hiroshima on August 6. The bomb wiped out nearly the whole city. At least 70,000 people were killed instantly; tens of thousands of others later died from the after-effects of the blast. A new and dangerous era of human history had been ushered in. Two days later the Soviet Union entered the war against Japan. When Japan still did not surrender, a second bomb was dropped on Nagasaki on August 9. Five days later, Japan gave up. The formal surrender was signed on September 2, 1945.

The war had been costly. The loss of human life was appalling. There were more than 400,000 dead in the American forces. Altogether, World War II took

Ask: Do you think that the United States was justified in using the atomic bomb in World War II? Why or why not?

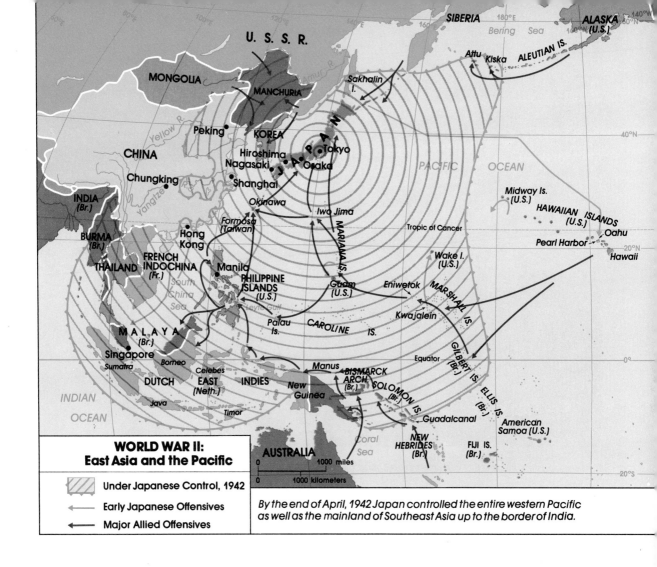

**WORLD WAR II:
East Asia and the Pacific**

	Under Japanese Control, 1942
←	Early Japanese Offensives
◄—	Major Allied Offensives

By the end of April, 1942 Japan controlled the entire western Pacific as well as the mainland of Southeast Asia up to the border of India.

perhaps 60 million lives around the world. Large parts of Europe and Asia lay in ruins. People could only hope that out of the death and destruction of war would somehow come a better world.

CHECKUP

1. How did the United States help the Allies prior to America's entering the war?
2. Why was the outlook grim for the Allies in the first year of war?
3. What was the Allied strategy in Europe? In the Pacific?
4. What events in World War II do each of the following names refer to: El Alamein, Normandy, Stalingrad, the Bulge, the Coral Sea, the Leyte Gulf, Hiroshima?

The Home Front

┌─VOCABULARY─────────────────┐
│ **total war**   **relocation** │
│   **center** │
└────────────────────────────┘

Total war   In 1939, before the start of World War II, a government report declared: "War is no longer simply a battle between armed forces . . . . It is a struggle in which each side strives to bring to bear against the enemy . . . the power of every . . . resource at its command. The conflict extends from the soldier in the front line to the citizen in the remotest hamlet . . . ."

Of the 60 million lives lost in World War II, perhaps 20 percent were victims of the holocaust. Have some pupils report on the meaning of the word *genocide*.

These youngsters helped the war effort by planting their own vegetable gardens.

That prediction turned out to be accurate. In no other war was America's whole population so fully involved as in World War II. In no other war were the country's material resources so completely devoted to the goal of victory. Homemakers saved cooking fats to be made into explosives. Schoolchildren collected scrap iron and newspapers for recycling. Everywhere, people sacrificed willingly. Those few who did not were harshly reminded by others, "Don't you know there's a war on?" This is what was meant by **total war**.

A production miracle American industry held one of the keys to victory. A government agency, the War Production Board (WPB), helped organize the changeover from peacetime manufacturing to making goods for war. The WPB also saw that war industries received the raw materials they needed. Production of refrigerators, stoves, washing machines, and other consumer goods was halted. In Detroit, auto factories stopped making cars and turned out airplanes, tanks, and military trucks. In hundreds of cities and towns, factories ran 24 hours a day. Scientists, meanwhile, developed substitutes for scarce materials. With the Japanese army in control of the sources of natural rubber in the Far East, scientists developed synthetic rubber.

The result was a production miracle. In 1939 the United States built fewer than 6,000 planes. When President Roosevelt set a goal of 50,000 planes a year in 1940,

Between 1941 and 1945 the production of synthetic rubber in the United States jumped 130 times! The factories that produced synthetic rubber were built by the United States government. In 1955 they were sold to private companies.

there were many doubters. A top Nazi general sneered, "The Americans can't build planes, only electric ice boxes and razor blades." But by 1944 the United States was producing not 50,000 planes a year but nearly *double* that number. In fact, in that year the United States produced twice as many goods as the Axis powers combined. World War II was won on the production lines as well as on the battlefields.

Rationing   With the United States helping to feed, clothe, and arm its allies as well as its own armed forces, some goods were in short supply at home. To make sure that everyone got a fair share of these scarce goods, the government rationed them, that is, limited the amount that each person could buy.

The Office of Price Administration (OPA) issued small books of ration stamps. For a long list of items, including sugar, coffee, butter, meat, canned goods, fats and oils, fuel oil, gasoline, tires, and shoes, one had to produce ration stamps as well as money. The OPA also set the prices of all goods except farm products.

Millions of jobs   The demand for goods created millions of jobs. At the same time, the armed forces took more than 15 million people out of the labor force. The result was that in just a few years the nation went from unemployment to full employment. In fact, in some industries, as well as in farming, there was a labor shortage. Incomes rose, as workers received added pay for working overtime. Farmers shared in the gen-

eral prosperity as prices for their crops rose.

Wartime created new opportunities for women. Six million additional women entered the work force—an increase of 50 percent in just a few years. Many worked at jobs that had before been closed to them. They worked in steel mills and in shipyards. They operated cranes, moved freight on the docks, and cut trees in the forests. In many defense factories, nearly half the workers were women. Some 300,000 women worked in the aircraft industry alone.

Blacks in the war   Just before the country entered the war, A. Philip Randolph, head of the Brotherhood of Sleeping Car Porters, threatened a march on Washington with 150,000 blacks unless

General Benjamin O. Davis, the first black to become a general, decorates his son, a combat pilot.

These fliers are members of a group of women pilots who, among other things, ferried war-planes to overseas bases and towed gliders and targets in training exercises.

the President moved against racial discrimination in industry. This prompted President Roosevelt to issue an order banning discrimination in defense plants. This order improved work opportunities for blacks. So did the mounting demand for workers in wartime industries. Thus, <u>many blacks left the South for jobs in the war factories of the North.</u>

As in World War I the arrival of large numbers of blacks in northern cities led to racial tensions. In 1943 there were race riots in a number of cities. The worst was in Detroit, where 34 people died. In many areas, black people continued to meet with discrimination.

In the military, too, discrimination against blacks was still the rule rather than the exception. A million black men and women served in the armed forces, but nearly all of them were in segregated units. Nonetheless, there were some signs that the barriers of race were weakening. The marine corps for the first time accepted black volunteers, and some 17,000 proudly served in the war. Many more black servicemen rose to become officers than in World War I. <u>More than 80 black fighter pilots were decorated for their actions in combat.</u>

Although still denied equal rights, blacks made their contribution to the war effort on the home front and in battle. <u>The contribution of a black doctor named Charles Drew saved thousands of lives.</u> Dr. Drew developed the blood bank, in

620 Black soldiers played an essential role in the army's drive across France in 1944. They manned the trucks bringing gasoline, food, and other supplies to the fast-moving tank columns. The truck battalions, shuttling between Normandy supply depots and the battlefront, were nicknamed the Red Ball Express.

American-born children of Japanese immigrants are called Nisei (nē′ sā′). Commenting on the heroism of the Nisei soldiers in World War II, General Joseph Stilwell declared, "The Nisei bought an awfully big hunk of America with their blood."

which blood was collected and was stored for the use of those who had been wounded in battle.

Japanese Americans   One minority group, the Japanese Americans, fared badly during the war. Most Japanese Americans lived on the West Coast. Many residents there had long held a prejudice against this minority. To this prejudice was now added the fear that people of Japanese ancestry might help the enemy in an attack upon the Pacific Coast. A demand arose for those of Japanese ancestry to be removed from

General Mark Clark presents awards for heroism to members of the Japanese American 442nd combat team.

the West Coast. Some military leaders joined the chorus, and President Roosevelt bowed to the pressure. In February 1942 he ordered the army to move some 110,000 people of Japanese background to **relocation centers** further inland. These relocation centers were crowded, hastily built camps where the residents lived behind barbed wire and under armed guard during the war. Some 70,000 of the 110,000 who were forced to give up their homes, businesses, and jobs had been born in the United States and were American citizens.

The whole episode was a shameful one, not fitting for a democratic society. There was never any evidence of disloyalty on the part of the Japanese Americans. In fact, when it was finally decided to accept Japanese Americans into service in 1943, thousands of them signed up. One of their groups, the 442nd Regimental Combat Team, was the most decorated combat force in the army. Its motto, "Go for broke," accurately described the reckless bravery of its members in combat in Italy and France. After the war some of the Japanese Americans were paid by the government for the loss of their property. However, the payments they received were at most no more than 20 percent of their losses.

CHECKUP

1. How did World War II differ from earlier wars?
2. How did American industry help the Allies win World War II?
3. How did the government meet the problem of shortages of many kinds of goods?
4. What contributions did black people and Japanese Americans make? What obstacles did they face?

27/CHAPTER REVIEW

KEY FACTS

1. Dictators who glorified the use of force and war threatened world peace in the 1930s.
2. The United States tried to stay on a neutral path, but after Hitler's troops overran Europe in 1940, the United States gave massive aid to Britain.
3. The United States entered World War II in December 1941 after Japan attacked Pearl Harbor in Hawaii.
4. World War II started badly for the United States in both Asia and Europe, but within a year the United States and its allies were on the offensive in both regions.
5. World War II ended in 1945 after two atomic bombs were dropped on Japan.
6. World War II was won on the production lines as well as on the battlefields.

VOCABULARY QUIZ

Using a separate piece of paper, match the terms with the phrases below.

a. blitzkrieg
b. concentration camps
c. demilitarize
d. dictator
e. holocaust
f. isolationists
g. Neutrality Acts
h. pacifists
i. rationing
j. totalitarian

j **1.** Describing a form of government that has total power over its people
d **2.** A person who has total power in governing a country
c **3.** To remove armed troops from a region
g **4.** Laws intended to keep the United States out of war
a **5.** A German word meaning "lightning war"
f **6.** People who wanted the United States to remain apart from affairs in other countries
b **7.** Areas where Hitler's government imprisoned and killed Jews and "political enemies"
h **8.** People opposed to all war
i **9.** Limiting the sale of articles in short supply so that they can be shared fairly
e **10.** The attempt by Hitler and his government to wipe out the Jewish people

REVIEW QUESTIONS

1. What was the Good Neighbor policy? What countries did it affect?
2. How did the following factors lead to the rise of dictatorships in Europe: (**a**) economic conditions, (**b**) nationalism?
3. Why did Hitler sign a pact with Russia in 1939? Did he keep the agreement?
4. How did America's view of the war in Europe change after the fall of France?
5. What action did the United States government take toward Japanese Americans living on the West Coast? Why?
6. Why did President Truman decide to drop the atomic bomb on Japan? Why did some of his advisers oppose it?

ACTIVITIES

1. Interview your grandparents and other people of that generation to find out what they can recall about what they were doing at the time of the announcement of the attack on Pearl Harbor and what their feelings were.
2. From interviews and from books about World War II, find out how civilians helped the war effort. Learn about (**a**) victory gardens, (**b**) air-raid wardens, (**c**) war bonds, (**d**) collecting paper, rubber, and scrap metal.
3. In your library, find the story of Anne Frank, who lived during World War II. Report to the class on her experiences.

UNDERSTANDING AUTHORS' POINTS OF VIEW

RELOCATION OF JAPANESE AMERICANS

If two people write about the same event, they study the same evidence and look at the same documents, newspapers, diaries, and letters. Yet they can arrive at totally different conclusions. How is that possible?

It is possible because every writer has a point of view. Perhaps the writers are working in different time periods. Perhaps they come from different backgrounds. Most likely they have had different experiences. They have developed different ideas about society and about which things are more important and which are less important. In other words, they weigh evidence differently.

Here are two passages about the relocation of Japanese Americans during World War II. The first passage was written by John J. McCloy in 1942, just after the removal was completed. McCloy was assistant secretary of the army, and it was the army that carried out the removal.

> I wonder if anyone realizes the skill, speed and humanity with which the evacuation of the Japanese has been handled by the Army on the West Coast? I am struck with the extreme care that has been taken to protect the persons and goods and even the comforts of each individual. Certainly an organization that can do a humane job like this and still be a fine fighting organization is unique—and American. I hope other countries that have similar problems will not overlook how an answer has been found in this country.

More than 30 years later, two historians, Leonard Dinnerstein and David M. Reimers, wrote about the same event this way:

> The hasty removal meant considerable hardship and suffering. Given only five days' notice of the evacuation, those interned could take only what they could carry; the government took over and held in storage all other belongings. In addition to the financial losses the conditions in the relocation centers were miserable. At first, the Japanese were placed in temporary quarters, including a hastily converted race track, which lacked basic facilities. Eventually, the government built ten camps, but they were mostly located in barren desert country, hot in the summer and cold in the winter. The surroundings were drab and unattractive, complete with barbed wire, military police, and, in some cases, machine guns. One Nisei intern later wrote of the camp in Arizona, "I must say this scorching Hell is a place beyond description and beyond tears."

SKILLS PRACTICE

Compare the writers' points of view in the two passages. How might McCloy's position have influenced his point of view? Dinnerstein and Reimers wrote 30 years later. How might the passage of three decades have affected their point of view?

How Americans Lived, 1950

THE UNITED STATES

YEAR: 1950

AREA: 2,974,726 sq mi
7,704,540 sq km

POPULATION: 150,697,361

POPULATION
DENSITY: 51 per sq mi
20 per sq km

NUMBER
OF STATES: 48

LARGEST STATE
IN AREA: Texas

IN POPULATION: New York

LARGEST CITY: New York

WHERE PEOPLE
LIVED:

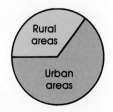

VOCABULARY
workweek

At the midpoint of the twentieth century, the American people were prospering. After providing for the necessities of life, they had more money left over than ever before to spend as they wished. Thanks to the great inventiveness and productivity of American industry, they also had more free time than ever before. In 1900 the average **workweek** was just under 60 hours. In 1950 it was about 40 hours. In the home the electric vacuum cleaner, the washing machine and clothes dryer, and the steam iron cut down the amount of time spent on housework. So did the new frozen foods, which could be cooked in minutes. Never before, then, did so many people have so much free time and so much money with which to enjoy it.

The age of television   How did Americans use their new leisure time in 1950? A good part of it was spent in front of a small box that brought flickering images on a bluish screen into their living rooms. In 1950 the age of television was just bursting upon America. Back in 1946, at the end of World War II, television had been only a novelty. There were about 7,000 sets in the entire country—about 1 for every 20,000 people. Telecasts were shown only between 5 P.M. and 10 P.M. In that year, barely a few thousand people in just five cities could watch heavyweight

In 1936, telecasts began on a very limited basis in New York City. The first program was a cartoon of Felix the Cat. During World War II, these programs came to a stop and were not resumed until after the war.

Have pupils ask relatives and other older people what they remember about the early days of television, what programs they watched, and what changes occurred in how their leisure time was spent. Have pupils report their findings to the class.

boxing champion Joe Louis defend his title against challenger Billy Conn.

Just 4 years later, in 1950, millions watched the New York Yankees defeat the Philadelphia Phillies in the World Series. There were television sets in nearly 4 million homes—1 for every 40 people. And Americans were buying new TV sets at the rate of 20,000 a day! Ten years later these Americans would own 50 million television receivers.

In just a few years, television had changed the entertainment habits of Americans. People went out in the evening less and less. Instead, they spent their leisure time watching television. The average American watched 3 hours of television every day—over 20 hours a week. On Tuesday evening most sets were tuned to comedian Milton Berle's show. He was soon called Mr. Television. Westerns were also a favorite. Most Americans couldn't seem to see enough programs about the Wild West.

Television takes over Meanwhile, other forms of entertainment suffered. Since the 1930s "big bands" such as those of Benny Goodman, Harry James, the Dorsey brothers, and Count Basie had toured the country, playing in theaters and dance halls. In 1950 they were playing to smaller and smaller audiences, as people stayed home to watch television.

The moving-picture industry was also hard-hit by the competition of television. In 1946 an average of 82 million Americans went to the movies each week. In 1950 the number fell to 60 million. The movie industry tried to fight back with ads such as these: "Don't be a living room captive." "Step out and see a great movie!" In 1952 the industry introduced the wide screen in the hope of bringing people back to the box office. Another 10 years would go by before Hollywood studios stopped fighting television and began to make movies for showing on TV screens.

In 1950, television was a new and fascinating form of entertainment for Americans.

TV's effect on the family   Noting how whole families gathered to watch evening programs, some observers suggested that television was becoming an important force for drawing families together once again. However, others pointed out that in earlier days, families had provided their own entertainment. They talked with each other. They joined in games, songs, and storytelling. Now, few words passed among them as they watched the entertainment provided by the television set.

In fact, television was undermining even family mealtime conversation. In 1954 the frozen "TV dinner" was introduced in markets around the country. At about the same time came the "TV table," a small metal tray on folding legs. Now in many homes, family members sat in front of the television, eating their separate dinners on their separate tables, and hardly exchanging a word.

More leisure time   Americans also spent much of their free time playing and traveling. In earlier days, time off from work—and there was not much of that—was thought of as a time for rest to prepare for the next day's work. By 1950, that attitude had changed dramatically. Now, time off from work was thought of as time for enjoyment. For example, in the 1950s, Americans spent as much money for leisure goods as they did for housing. Back in 1933, 5 million people had fishing licenses. But 20 years later, 15 million did. The number of hunting

In the 1950s, families were finding more time for leisure and relaxation.

licenses similarly increased. The boating industry also boomed in the 1950s. By the middle of the decade, there was one boat for every 30 Americans. Americans were not only working fewer hours in 1950, but they were also getting longer periods for vacations. Before World War II, fewer than half of all American companies gave paid vacations to their workers. By the early 1950s, nearly all of them did. Most of these vacations were at least 2 weeks long. And there were also many more "long weekends" of 3 and sometimes 4 days.

Millions of travelers   To a growing number of Americans in 1950, a vacation meant going someplace, not relaxing at home. And so they picked up by the millions, packed into the family car, and traveled. By the middle of the 1950s, about 70 million Americans—nearly 1 in every 2—were taking at least one automobile vacation each year. Many of them spent part of their vacations in a state or national park. Others went from city to countryside or from countryside to city. Everywhere, it seemed, Americans were on the road. Hotels, motels, gas stations, and restaurants did a growing business.

A smaller but growing number of Americans in 1950 were using their vacations to travel to other countries. In the past this kind of travel had been only for the rich. But wartime service overseas had encouraged an interest in foreign travel. And higher income, lower transportation costs, and faster travel made it possible for many ordinary people to visit other lands.

After World War II, most people who traveled overseas went by airplane rather than by ship.

The airplane was the most important factor. Before the war nearly all overseas travelers went by steamship. In 1950, however, air passengers outnumbered those who traveled by sea for the first time. In that year more than 670,000 Americans traveled to other countries. Just a few years later the number passed 1 million, and it has continued to rise.

CHECKUP

1. How did the average workweek change between 1900 and 1950?
2. In what respects did the coming of television affect family life?
3. By 1950, how had vacations changed from earlier times?
4. What businesses grew and profited from Americans' vacation activities?

7/UNIT REVIEW

READING THE TEXT

Turn to pages 582–583 and read the section entitled "A depression spreads." The text tells how the United States was plunged into the Great Depression. Then on a sheet of paper, write **T** if the statement is true and **F** if it is false.

F **1.** The main cause of the depression was the stock market crash.

F **2.** A cause of the depression was a scarcity of goods.

F **3.** Europeans were buying American goods at such a rate that there were not enough goods for our own people.

T **4.** Most Americans did not have enough money to buy the goods being produced.

F **5.** In 1929, stores sold goods so fast that they could not keep their inventories up.

T **6.** Factories were forced to lay off workers.

T **7.** After paying some war debts, European countries lacked money to buy American goods.

T **8.** People who had money feared that times might get worse and stopped spending.

F **9.** Banks were the only part of the economy that prospered between 1929 and 1932.

T **10.** Stores cut back their orders to factories.

READING A MAP

Turn to page 610 and study the map titled "World War II: Europe and North Africa." On a sheet of paper, write the answers to the following questions.

1. In what countries were each of these battles fought?

Stalingrad **Soviet Union**   Normandy **France**

The Bulge **Belgium**   El Alamein **Egypt**

Salerno **Italy**

2. What country was the main goal of Allied drives, both from east and west? **Germany**

3. In their invasion of Europe from Africa, what island did the Allied powers use as a stepping-stone? **Sicily**

4. What were the two northernmost countries occupied by the Axis powers? **Norway and Finland**

5. List the neutral countries in Europe.
Spain, Portugal, Ireland, Sweden, Switzerland, Turkey (partly in Europe)

READING PICTURES

In Chapter 26 are several pictures that show people who suffered as a result of the Great Depression. Look at the pictures on pages 583, 584, 585, and 595. On a sheet of paper, do the following:

1. In a sentence or two for each picture, tell how the Great Depression has hurt the person or persons who are shown.

2. Put yourself in the place of a person in one of the pictures. Imagine how you would feel. Write a paragraph expressing your feelings about what the depression has done to you, how you are trying to solve your problems, and what your hopes are for the future.

READING CHARTS

Compare the Benchmark charts on pages 484 and 624. Then on a sheet of paper, answer the following questions.

1. By about how many million did the population increase between 1900 and 1950? **75**

2. How many states were added in that time? **3**

3. How did the population distribution change between 1900 and 1950? **Became more urban**

4. Which state was largest in area in 1900? In 1950? **Texas, in both years**

5. What state and city were largest in population in each of those years? **New York State and New York City, in both years**

America in a Changing World

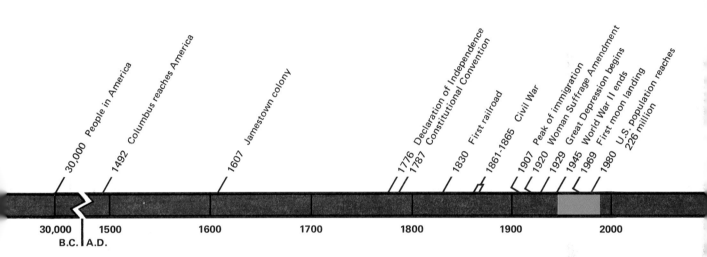

30,000 People in America

1492 Columbus reaches America

1607 Jamestown colony

1776 Declaration of Independence

1787 Constitutional Convention

1830 First railroad

1861-1865 Civil War

1907 Peak of immigration

1920 Woman Suffrage Amendment

1929 Great Depression begins

1945 World War II ends

1969 First moon landing

1980 U.S. population reaches 226 million

| 30,000 B.C. A.D. | 1500 | 1600 | 1700 | 1800 | 1900 | 2000 |

Above: Justice Sandra Day O'Connor; Martin Luther King, Jr.; proponents of Equal Rights Amendment; war in Vietnam; Cesar Chavez; Space Shuttle

28 The Cold War

An End to Wartime Cooperation

VOCABULARY

United Nations	Truman Doctrine
iron curtain	Marshall Plan
cold war	North Atlantic
containment	Treaty Orga-
	nization

Truman becomes President   "Last night the moon, the stars, and all the planets fell on me," Harry Truman told reporters on April 13, 1945. He was describing how he felt after learning that President Roosevelt had died suddenly, and that he—Harry Truman, Vice President of the United States—was now President.

Harry Truman had never expected to wind up in the White House. He was born in Independence, Missouri, in 1884. After graduating from high school, he held a number of minor jobs before taking over the operation of the family farm outside of town.

During World War I, Harry Truman served in France with the United States Army and rose to the rank of major. Six weeks after he returned home, he married Bess Wallace, whom he had known since childhood. Truman and a friend became partners in a men's clothing store, but after a few years the business failed.

Meanwhile, Truman became involved in local politics. He held local office until 1934, when he was elected to the United States Senate. His reputation for hard work and loyalty to his party earned him the Democratic nomination for Vice President in 1944. And now, less than a year later, he was President. The burden of making decisions that would affect the whole world rested on him.

Fortunately, Truman was able and willing to make decisions. On his presidential desk he placed a sign that said "The buck stops here." He also had a favorite saying for officials who were afraid to make decisions for which they might be criticized. "If you can't stand the heat," Truman said, "get out of the kitchen."

The United Nations   One of President Truman's first acts was to welcome delegates from 50 nations to a conference in San Francisco on April 25, 1945. Early in the war the United States, Great Britain, and the Soviet Union had agreed that an international organization should be formed after the war to keep the peace. Since then, many of the details had been worked out. Those who gathered in San Francisco drew up the final charter, or constitution, of the **United Nations.** In 2 months their work was done. All 50 nations signed the completed charter.

The conference shown in the picture on page 631 took place following the shooting of several German citizens by Russian troops. *During the cold war, Americans and Russians confer at a checkpoint on the border of the United States and Soviet zones in divided Berlin.* (52°N/13°E; map, p. 611)

The drafting of the UN charter took place between April 25 and June 26, 1945.

YOU ARE LEAVING
THE AMERICAN SECTOR

ВЫ ВЫЕЗЖАЕТЕ ИЗ
АМЕРИКАНСКОЙ ЗОНЫ

VOUS SORT
DU SECTEUR

1945 United Nations charter drawn up

1947 Truman Doctrine

1948 Marshall Plan/Berlin blockade

1949 NATO formed

1950 War in Korea begins

1953 Korean War ends

1957 Eisenhower Doctrine

1961 Peace Corps formed/
Berlin Wall erected/
Cuban missile crisis

| 1944 | 1947 | 1950 | 1953 | 1956 | 1959 | 1962 |

THE UNITED NATIONS AND ITS AGENCIES

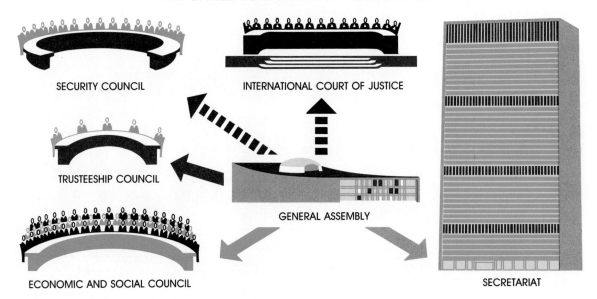

SECURITY COUNCIL

INTERNATIONAL COURT OF JUSTICE

TRUSTEESHIP COUNCIL

GENERAL ASSEMBLY

ECONOMIC AND SOCIAL COUNCIL

SECRETARIAT

The United Nations works through dozens of different agencies. The five main ones are shown in relation to the central body, the General Assembly. Solid arrows point to agencies over which the General Assembly has direct responsibility and control. The Security Council, while working with the General Assembly, is not governed by it. The 15 judges on the International Court of Justice are elected, but not controlled, by the General Assembly and the Security Council. The Economic and Social Council supervises the work of a number of the United Nations' specialized agencies.

As of the beginning of 1984 there were 158 nations represented in the General Assembly of the UN.

The main bodies of the new international organization were the General Assembly and the Security Council. In the General Assembly every nation, regardless of size, had an equal voice. However, the General Assembly had no power to act on important issues. That was left to the Security Council, a group of 11 members that dealt with major questions like threats to world peace. The council had 5 permanent members—the United States, Great Britain, the Soviet Union, France, and China. Each of these nations could veto a decision of the council. Other countries would take turns filling the remaining 6 seats. (Later the total membership of the council was raised to 15.) Other parts of the United Nations included the International Court of Justice, the Economic and Social Council, and the Secretariat, which handled the day-to-day business of the organization.

Decisions at Yalta   Even as the United Nations charter was being signed, disagreements were arising between the wartime allies. Most of the big decisions President Truman had to make grew out of the breakdown of cooperation with America's wartime ally, the Soviet Union. That cooperation had reached its high point in February 1945. By then the end of the war in Europe was in sight. The Big Three leaders—President Roosevelt, British Prime Minister Winston Churchill, and Soviet leader Joseph Stalin—met at Yalta in the Soviet Union to make decisions about the postwar world.

The UN charter is considered a multilateral treaty of the United States that is binding on American policies and activities. You may wish to have a group of pupils report on the specialized agencies of the UN. Many of them have become controversial.

Have a pupil read and report to the class on the "United Nations Participation Act," document number 565 in A. Commager's *Documents of American History*.

All three leaders wanted a peace that would end Germany's power to make war. They agreed that until a final peace treaty was made, Germany would be divided into four parts, or zones. An army from each of the Big Three powers would occupy a zone, with a French army occupying the fourth. The German capital of Berlin, located inside the Soviet zone, would also be divided into four parts.

The three leaders agreed on free elections in the Eastern European countries, which Soviet troops were then occupying. In addition, Stalin promised to enter the war against Japan within 3 months after Germany's final defeat. In return the Soviet Union would get control of certain territories in Asia.

Soviet actions   By the time Harry Truman became President, it was clear that the Soviet Union was not keeping its word about free elections. In Poland, Russian troops placed a Communist government in power against the wishes of the people. Over the next 3 years, they did the same in other countries of Eastern Europe—Yugoslavia, Romania, Bulgaria, Hungary, and Czechoslovakia.

The Soviets justified their action by pointing out that Germany had invaded their country twice in a generation, at a cost of millions of Russian lives. Each time, they said, the invasion route had been through Poland and Eastern Europe. To protect themselves in the future, the Soviets declared, they must have "friendly governments" on their borders. To Stalin this meant Communist governments. The United States, Great Britain, and other countries, however, saw Stalin's moves in Eastern Europe as an effort to expand the Soviet empire and to spread communism.

Europe's iron curtain   In Germany, cooperation ended soon after the war. A part of the Yalta agreement stated that

After the war in Europe ended, leaders of the Big Three powers—Britain's Clement Attlee, America's Harry Truman, and Russia's Joseph Stalin—met at Potsdam, near Berlin. Disagreements between Russia and the Western nations soon hardened into the cold war.

EUROPE

Black Sea 30°E

Istanbul

Bosporus

Sea of Marmara

Dardanelles

40°N

ASIA

Aegean Sea

STRATEGIC WATERWAYS

0 50 100 miles

0 50 100 kilometers

The Sea of Marmara and the two straits of the Bosporus and the Dardanelles connect the Black and Aegean seas.

Churchill's "iron curtain" speech was delivered at Westminster College, Fulton, Missouri, on March 5, 1946.

called **containment.** This meant that wherever the Soviet Union pressured to expand its territory or influence, the United States would use equal pressure to contain or limit it, doing so by diplomatic, economic, or military means.

One region in which the Soviets were trying to make gains was the eastern Mediterranean. In Greece they backed the Communist side in a civil war. In neighboring Turkey the Soviets tried to get the government to give them a share of control over the Dardanelles. This is a narrow waterway that connects the Black Sea to the Mediterranean Sea. (See map, this page.) Control of this entrance to the Mediterranean had been a goal of Russia's leaders for more than 200 years. The Soviets also demanded that Turkey allow them to build naval bases in that region. If the Soviet Union succeeded in Greece and Turkey, it would control the whole eastern Mediterranean.

the four occupying powers would run Germany as a single economic unit. This meant that goods and money would move freely from one zone to another. However, the Russians kept their zone separate from the others. The Soviets also cut off their zone of occupation in Berlin from the other three.

In a speech in March 1946, Winston Churchill said that the Soviets had lowered across the center of Europe an **iron curtain,** cutting off Eastern Europe and its people from Western Europe. From behind this iron curtain came reports of denial of freedom, persecution of church leaders, prison camps, and death.

Thus, less than a year after the victory over Hitler, the great alliance was in shreds. Each side filled the air with charges and threats. Each side used every means short of actual fighting to advance its own goals and to harm the interests of the other side. This struggle came to be called the **cold war.**

Containment To keep the Soviet Union from getting control of more territory, the United States followed a policy

The Truman Doctrine President Truman decided to act. In March 1947, he asked Congress to send $400 million in military aid to Greece and Turkey. He also declared that the United States would support peoples who were resisting attempts by Communists to take over their countries. This policy became known as the **Truman Doctrine.** Strengthened by this American aid, both Greece and Turkey were able to defend themselves. Russian expansion and Communist influence in the region were contained.

The Marshall Plan The countries of Western Europe also needed help, but of a different kind. Their economies had not

Have a group of pupils read and report to the class on the following documents from A. Commager's *Documents of American History:* no. 564, "Truman's Statement on the Fundamentals of American Foreign Policy" and no. 574, "The Truman Doctrine".

During the 462 days of the Berlin airlift, or Operation Vittles, the U.S. Air Force flew 277,000 missions to Berlin's Tempelhof Airport. At the height of the airlift, a plane was arriving every 3½ minutes.

recovered from the ruin of war. Poverty was widespread. Many feared that this poverty would be a breeding ground for communism. These countries needed money not for weapons but for farm equipment, factories, and machines to get their economies going again.

In June 1947, Secretary of State George C. Marshall proposed that the United States provide this help. President Truman backed the idea, which became known as the **Marshall Plan.** Congress passed it in 1948. In the next 3 years, the United States put $12 billion into the Marshall Plan. By 1950 the countries of Western Europe were back on their feet.

Blockade and airlift The United States, Great Britain, and France decided to combine their three occupation zones in Germany into one and allow the unified zone to have its own government.

The Soviets were opposed. In June 1948 they blocked all roads, railroads, and canals connecting Berlin to the western part of Germany. Their aim was to make the Western powers give up their plans for a separate West German government or else be forced out of Berlin.

President Truman never considered getting out of Berlin. "We are going to stay, period," he said. To keep food, fuel, and other supplies flowing into the city, the United States organized an airlift. For the next 10 months, American and British pilots flew cargo planes into West Berlin. At the height of the airlift, planes landed with supplies every 3 or 4 minutes. Meanwhile in the United States, Congress enacted a new peacetime draft to rebuild the army, which had been mostly disbanded after World War II.

The Berlin airlift was successful. The Russians called off the blockade in May

Have a pupil report to the class on the career of General George C. Marshall.

Amid the war ruins, children watch a plane bringing supplies to blockaded Berlin.

What's in a Name?

THE THIRD WORLD
The term *Third World* was coined at the height of the cold war. In that conflict the United States and the Western democracies stood on one side, and the Soviet Union and its satellites in Eastern Europe stood on the other. People called the first group of nations the Western World, or Free World, and the second group the Communist World.

During these same years, the colonial empires of such countries as Great Britain, Holland, and France crumbled. Dozens of countries in Asia and Africa became independent. These "emerging nations" did not consider themselves a part of the cold war struggle. Since they were not a part of either the Free World or the Communist World, it was said that they formed the Third World.

In later years the term *Third World* took on a new meaning. Today a Third World country is one with an underdeveloped economy. Thus, almost all the countries of Africa, Asia, South and Central America, and many of the countries in the Middle East are called Third World countries—whatever their feeling may be about the Free World and the Communist World.

1949. That fall the Federal Republic of Germany (West Germany) came into being with a democratic government. Soon after, the Soviets created the German Democratic Republic (East Germany) with a Communist government. Thus what was at first the temporary division of Germany became permanent.

NATO Many leaders in the United States and Western Europe feared that the Soviet Union might decide to use its military power in Europe. President Truman believed that the best way to curb the Soviets was for all the countries to stand together. Truman said that the United States would be willing to help defend Western Europe. In April 1949 the United States and 11 other countries formed the **North Atlantic Treaty Organization,** usually referred to as NATO. Three other countries joined later. The NATO countries agreed that an attack on

any one of them would be considered an attack on all.

The United States Senate approved the treaty, and President Truman named General Dwight Eisenhower to be NATO's first commander. Eisenhower promptly went to Europe to start the work of organizing the military forces of the many NATO countries into a common defense.

Prompt action was felt to be even more necessary after September 1949. In that month came the startling news that the Soviet Union had successfully tested an atomic bomb.

CHECKUP

1. What are the main bodies of the United Nations?
2. What did the Big Three leaders agree to at Yalta?
3. How did the Soviet Union and the United States stop cooperating after World War II?
4. What were the goals of the following: (**a**) the Truman Doctrine, (**b**) the Marshall Plan, (**c**) the Berlin airlift, (**d**) the North Atlantic Treaty Organization?

The original members of NATO were Belgium, Canada, Denmark, France, Iceland, Italy, Luxembourg, the Netherlands, Norway, Portugal, the United Kingdom, and the United States.

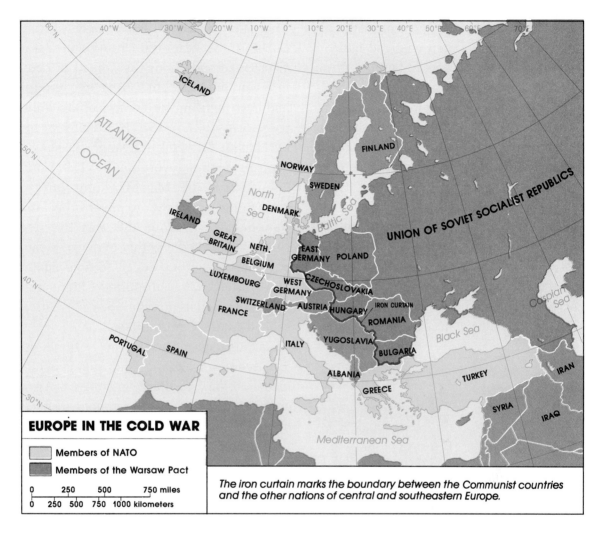

EUROPE IN THE COLD WAR

- Members of NATO
- Members of the Warsaw Pact

| 0 | 250 | 500 | 750 miles |
| 0 | 250 | 500 | 750 | 1000 kilometers |

The iron curtain marks the boundary between the Communist countries and the other nations of central and southeastern Europe.

A Hot War and a New President

┌─VOCABULARY─────────────────┐
| stalemate | summit conference |
| coexistence | Eisenhower Doctrine |
└────────────────────────────┘

Gains for democracy Japan, unlike Germany, was not divided after the war. The United States had the only occupying forces in Japan. General Douglas MacArthur, who was in charge of American forces in Japan, actually governed the country for several years. He carried out important reforms. MacArthur ordered some large landholdings to be divided among poor farm workers. He saw to it that women gained certain rights. In 1947, Japan adopted a new constitution, which made the country a democracy. The constitution promoted civil rights and gave women the right to vote for the first time. In 1951 the United States and other countries signed a treaty with Japan, ending the occupation.

Elsewhere in Asia the postwar years saw the end of Europe's colonial empires. One after another, Asian lands that had been ruled by European countries for centuries became independent. Many started

General MacArthur issued his orders through the Japanese emperor. The great respect the Japanese people had for their ruler was one reason the occupation went so smoothly.

out with democratic governments, although these were often changed later.

The United States was in favor of these colonies becoming independent and ruling themselves. It welcomed these countries into the family of nations. In fact, the United States set an example for other countries by granting independence to its own colony, the Philippines. In 1934, Congress had passed a law promising the Philippines their independence in 10 years. The war delayed this timetable, but on July 4, 1946, the United States made good on its word. The Philippines became independent, with an elected president and legislative body.

The American flag comes down and the flag of the independent Philippines goes up in Manila on July 4, 1946.

The Communists take over China During these years the United States was also concerned about the spread of communism in Asia. In China two groups had been fighting for control of the country since 1927. The Nationalists, led by Chiang Kai-shek (chyäng′ kī shek′), controlled the government. The Communists, led by Mao Tse-tung (mä′ ō dzu dung′), sought to overthrow the Nationalists. During the war the two sides had worked together to defeat Japan, but afterwards they began to fight again. The United States supported Chiang and the Nationalists. The Soviet Union backed Mao's Communists.

Despite American aid the Nationalists lost ground. Chiang and his generals made serious military mistakes. Also, corruption in the government caused much of the population to turn against the Nationalists. Meanwhile, the Communists promised land reform, meaning that they would take land away from the big landowners and give it to the peasants who had worked on the land. In 1949, Mao's forces drove the Nationalists off the mainland of Asia onto the nearby island of Formosa, now called Taiwan (tī wän′). That fall, Mao proclaimed a new Chinese government, the People's Republic of China.

The division of Korea One of the wartime agreements of the Allies was that the Asian land of Korea, long ruled by Japan, should be a free and independent country. At the end of World War II, the United States and Russia agreed that their troops would take over Korea from the surrendering Japanese army. Russia would occupy the area north of 38° north latitude. American troops would move into Korea south of that line.

This division was supposed to be temporary. However, the cold war made it permanent. The United Nations called for elections to unify the country, and in 1948 an election under UN supervision was held in the south. However, the Russians would not allow the United Nations to run an election in the north. In North Korea the Russians set up a separate Communist government called the People's Republic of Korea. They also trained and equipped a strong North Korean army. Then Russian troops left. Soon afterwards, the United States also pulled its troops out of the area now called the Republic of Korea, or South Korea. <u>Each government in Korea claimed to be the rightful government for the whole country.</u>

War in Korea On June 25, 1950, the North Korean army invaded South Korea. President Truman believed that North Korea must not be allowed to get away with this aggression. He ordered American naval and air forces to help South Korea. He also asked the United Nations to take action. The Security Council did, calling upon member nations to come to South Korea's aid. Eventually, 19 member nations sent troops. The United States sent the largest number by far. <u>General Douglas MacArthur was named commander of all UN forces in Korea.</u>

At first everything went North Korea's way. Communist troops drove the UN forces back to the southernmost tip of South Korea. Finally in August the UN

In the war in Korea, soldiers of an Australian regiment supporting the UN fire on Communist positions.

line held firm. Then in mid-September, General MacArthur staged a brilliant surprise landing by sea at the port of Inchon, far behind the North Korean line. At the same time, UN troops to the south went on the attack. North Korean troops retreated. UN forces drove them back across the 38th parallel, overran most of North Korea, and pushed on toward the Yalu River, Korea's border with China. By fall, victory and the unification of the two Koreas seemed assured.

China enters the war Then came a sudden new development. In October, China began warning the UN troops not to move any closer to its borders. The warnings were ignored by General MacArthur, who believed the Communist warning to be a bluff. He assured President Truman that the UN forces could

Sixteen nations sent troops to Korea. At their greatest strength the UN and South Korean forces numbered 1,109,000 (590,000 South Koreans, 480,000 Americans, and 39,000 from other countries). The North Korean army had about 260,000 soldiers. The Communist Chinese sent 780,000 troops.

easily handle any Chinese troops that might attack. But MacArthur had made a serious error in judgment. In late November 1950 a quarter-million Chinese troops poured across the Yalu. They drove the UN army back near the 38th parallel, where the UN forces finally held.

General MacArthur now wanted to bomb China, blockade its coast, and transport Chiang Kai-shek's armies from Formosa to the mainland to fight the Communists. President Truman and his military advisers, however, disagreed. They did not want to widen the war. They believed MacArthur's policies "would involve us in the wrong war, at the wrong place, at the wrong time, and with the wrong enemy." MacArthur continued to insist on his views. When he challenged Truman publicly, the President removed him from command. The war now settled into a **stalemate**, that is, a situation in which neither side could win. Peace talks, started in 1951, soon stalled.

In October 1950, President Truman and General Mac-Arthur conferred at Wake Island. (19°N/167°E; map, p. 715)

The Korean War ends   Many Americans were frustrated. In the presidential election of 1952, they turned against the party in power, the Democrats. The Republican nominee was Dwight Eisenhower, the popular war hero, and he won easily. During the campaign, Eisenhower had promised, if elected, "I will go to Korea." People hoped that he would find a way to end the war. Eisenhower did go to Korea immediately after his election. However, the war continued for another 7 months.

In the summer of 1953, the two sides finally agreed to a cease-fire. The boundary between North and South Korea was set very close to where it had been when the war started. To many Americans this was an unsatisfactory end to a war that had cost nearly 54,000 American lives. However, America's efforts had succeeded in stopping North Korea from taking over South Korea by force.

Curbing communism in Southeast Asia
The policy of containment was continued in the 1950s under President Eisenhower. Soviet expansion in Europe had been checked. But Eisenhower and Secretary of State John Foster Dulles were concerned about the spread of communism in Southeast Asia. Dulles believed that if one Southeast Asian country fell to communism, nearly all the others would also fall. He thought that an organization like NATO was needed for this region of the world.

In 1954 the United States, Great Britain, and France joined five Southeast Asian countries—Australia, New Zealand, Pakistan, Thailand, and the Philip-

Have your pupils compile a chronological fact sheet on the Korean War using standard reference materials.

On May 5, 1960, the USSR announced that an American U2 (Lockheed high-altitude plane), flying 1,200 miles inside the Soviet Union, had been shot down on May 1. On May 7, Premier Khrushchev revealed that the pilot, Francis Gary Powers, was alive and had confessed to being a spy for the Central Intelligence Agency (CIA). The United States confirmed that it

DIVISION OF KOREA

- ☐ North Korea
- ■ South Korea
- ----- Cease-fire line July 1953

The end of the war left Korea divided into Communist and non-Communist republics.

bomb by the Soviet Union, matching the bomb the United States had built a year earlier. Now both sides had a weapon a thousand times more powerful than the bomb that wiped out Hiroshima. As President Eisenhower said, nuclear war would be "suicide" for the human race. Russia's leaders spoke of the need for **co-existence**, that is, living together in peace.

In 1955, President Eisenhower met with leaders of the Soviet Union and other countries in Geneva, Switzerland, in a **summit conference.** This is a meeting of the top leaders of the major powers. For the first time since the wartime conferences 10 years before, heads of the United States and Russian governments met face-to-face. They talked about ways to prevent an arms race between the two countries. Although no agreements were reached, each side was convinced that the other really wanted to avoid war. This desire to work for peace came to be called "the spirit of Geneva."

The U-2 incident   During the following years, contacts between the two countries increased. Another summit conference was scheduled for Paris in May 1960. But just 2 weeks before the summit meeting, an American airplane flying over the interior of the Soviet Union was shot down. As the plane crashed to the ground, hopes for the summit conference crashed with it.

The airplane was a high-flying American spy plane called a U-2. The captured pilot admitted he had been spying on Soviet military bases. Arriving in Paris, the Soviet premier, Nikita Khrushchev (krüsh chôf′), demanded that the United

pines—to form the Southeast Asia Treaty Organization (SEATO). However, this treaty was different from the NATO treaty. Although members agreed to help each other in case of attack, they did not promise to go to war to do so.
In 1977, SEATO was dissolved.

A relaxation of tensions   During the 1950s, cold war tensions relaxed a bit. Three things that took place in 1953 brought about this development. One was the end of the fighting in Korea. The second was the death of Russia's dictator, Joseph Stalin. The men who took his place in the Soviet Union were more willing to try to reach an agreement with the leaders of Western countries. The third event was the development of a hydrogen

This meeting of Soviet Premier Khrushchev and President Eisenhower took place before the U-2 incident.

States stop such flights and apologize. President Eisenhower said the U-2 flights would be stopped, but he refused to apologize. Khrushchev left Paris, and the summit was cancelled.

The Middle East   Another region of concern to the United States was the Middle East. Geographically, this area is of great importance. It is a link that connects three continents—Africa, Europe, and Asia. Its vast deposits of oil make it important economically as well. Following World War II, strong feelings of nationalism had been awakened among the Arab peoples of this region. These feelings were heightened by the creation of the new state of Israel.

In the late 1800s a handful of Jews from Europe started a movement to set up a Jewish nation in their old, biblical home of Palestine. Jewish settlement in Palestine grew in the early 1900s. Before

World War II, the Jewish population reached nearly a half million. Arabs became alarmed. They looked upon Palestine as theirs. They feared that the coming of more Jews would lead to a separate Jewish state.

The founding of Israel   After World War II, Jews who escaped the holocaust were determined to have a land of their own. Thousands went to Palestine. In 1947, the United Nations voted to divide Palestine into two countries, one Arab and one Jewish. Jews accepted the plan, but Arabs opposed it. Finally, on May 14, 1948, Jews proclaimed the founding of their new nation, which they called Israel. Immediately, neighboring Arab countries sent their armies to join the Arab population of Palestine in fighting Israel. Despite the odds, Israel managed to hold its own in the fighting. Hundreds of thousands of Arab residents fled Palestine during the fighting and became refugees in other Arab lands.

After 8 months, both sides accepted a bid by the United Nations to stop the war. Dr. Ralph Bunche, an American, headed the United Nations team that worked out the truce, or cease-fire. Dr. Bunche was later awarded a Nobel Peace Prize for his work. Although the fighting ended, Arabs were still determined to reclaim all of Palestine.

The Suez war   In the 1950s, Colonel Gamal Abdel Nasser came to power in Egypt. He wanted to end Western influence in his country and was determined to destroy Israel. Starting in 1955 he encouraged raids across the border

Use a world map to point out the countries of the Middle East. Help pupils understand the complex problems of the region, especially the controversy that has developed between Israel and the Arab nations since 1948.

into Israel. The next year he seized control of the Suez Canal from Great Britain.

Israel wanted to end the raids on its land. The British and the French wanted to regain control of the canal, through which much of their trade flowed. The three countries agreed on a plan. In October 1956, Israeli forces launched an attack against the Egyptians. In 4 days they smashed Nasser's armies and swept across the Sinai (sī′ nī) Peninsula to the Suez Canal. British and French troops also landed to take control of the canal.

Both the Soviet Union and the United States opposed this action. The two countries supported a United Nations resolution that stopped the fighting and got the three invading armies to withdraw. A UN peacekeeping force took their place.

The Eisenhower Doctrine President Eisenhower feared that the Soviet Union might gain influence in the Middle East after the Suez war. In 1957 he announced a policy that extended containment to this region. Eisenhower said that the United States would defend countries in the Middle East against armed attack by Communist countries. The United States also offered economic help to the countries of the region. This policy became known as the **Eisenhower Doctrine.**

The Eisenhower Doctrine was used for the first time in 1958. The government of Lebanon was threatened with revolution by forces backed by both the Soviet Union and Egypt. It asked for help. President Eisenhower sent United States marines into Lebanon, and the rebellion quickly ended.

CHECKUP

1. What changes took place in the government of China after World War II?
2. What action did the United States take after the North Korean army invaded South Korea?
3. What events during the 1950s helped to ease the cold war?
4. In what ways did the United States become involved in the Middle East in the 1950s?

Dr. Ralph Bunche, shown here with U Thant, a United Nations official, won the Nobel Peace Prize in 1950.

New Threats, New Hopes

┌─ VOCABULARY ─────────────────┐

| Peace Corps | exile |
| Alliance for Progress | hot line |

└──────────────────────────────┘

President Kennedy President Eisenhower was succeeded in the White House by John F. Kennedy. Kennedy had long been interested in international affairs. In 1940, while still a student in college, he wrote a thesis about why England was

643

not prepared for World War II. This thesis was published as the book *Why England Slept?* Shortly before the United States entered that war, Kennedy joined the navy. In 1943 the torpedo boat he commanded was sunk by a Japanese warship. Kennedy swam 3 miles (4.8 km) to an island, towing an injured crew member by holding a strap of the man's life jacket in his teeth. In later years, when asked how he became a war hero, Kennedy replied, "It was involuntary. They sank my boat."

After the war, John F. Kennedy was elected to Congress, where he served for the next 14 years. He continued his interest in foreign affairs, supporting the Marshall Plan and NATO. In 1960, Senator Kennedy received the Democratic nomination for President and in a close election defeated the Republican candidate, Vice President Richard Nixon.

President Kennedy's inaugural address dealt mainly with foreign affairs. He made clear that he would continue the policy of containment. "Let every nation know," he said, " . . . that we shall pay any price, bear any burden, meet any hardship, . . . in order to assure the survival and the success of liberty." At the same time, Kennedy declared that he wanted to find peaceful solutions to problems. "Let us never negotiate out of fear," said the new President. "But let us never fear to negotiate."

The Peace Corps   President Kennedy brought several new ideas to American foreign policy. One that turned out to be extremely successful was the **Peace Corps**. Under this program, American men and women with skills in such varied fields as medicine, carpentry, teaching, farming, and engineering volunteered to go to countries seeking help in these areas.

The Peace Corps members lived among the people, learning to understand their language and to appreciate their ways. The Americans helped farmers increase

In 1960, presidential candidates Kennedy and Nixon met in four televised debates.

An American Peace Corps volunteer, an expert in child care, works with women in Sri Lanka (formerly Ceylon).

their crops, assisted in building water and sewage systems, taught basic skills, and in other ways helped to raise standards of living. Within 4 years the United States government was sending 10,000 volunteers to serve in 46 countries. Peace Corps volunteers created much goodwill toward the United States.

The Alliance for Progress Another of Kennedy's programs was the **Alliance for Progress.** This was a plan for building up the economies of countries in the Western Hemisphere, helping their poor people, and making democratic government stronger. Latin American governments, the United States government, and private investors joined to provide the needed capital. In 1961 all the countries of the hemisphere, except Cuba, joined the alliance. During the next 4 years, Latin American countries put $22 billion into the program, and the United States added another $4 billion.

The results, however, were disappointing. Although the economies of some countries did grow, the military and upper classes that controlled the governments dragged their feet on reform. The poor remained poor, and the governments did not become more democratic. Later, Congress cut its spending for the alliance.

The Bay of Pigs In January 1959 a Cuban revolution led by Fidel Castro overthrew the dictator who ruled Cuba. At first, many Americans were friendly toward Castro. But when he executed political opponents and seized American-owned property in Cuba, opinion turned against him. Castro also developed close ties with the Soviet Union. Thousands of Cubans fled and settled in the United States. Many of these **exiles** were determined to return and overthrow Castro.

In 1960, President Eisenhower approved a secret plan to train and arm these exiles for an invasion of Cuba. Our government believed that the Cuban people would support the invaders and rise up against Castro.

Kennedy learned of this plan after becoming President. He had doubts about its wisdom, but he allowed it to go forward. However, he ruled out the use of United States troops and planes. In April 1961 about 1,400 anti-Castro Cubans landed at the Bay of Pigs on the southern coast of Cuba. It became clear very quickly that the United States government and the Cuban exiles had misjudged the situation badly. There was no popular uprising. Within a few days, all the invaders were killed or captured. This misadventure was a serious setback for the

United States in Latin America and the rest of the world. At the same time it drove Castro more firmly into the Soviet camp.

The Berlin wall   Tensions between the Soviet Union and the United States increased after a meeting between President Kennedy and Premier Khrushchev a few months later in Vienna, Austria. The Soviets had never given up the goal of getting the Western powers out of Berlin. The wartime allies had never agreed on a peace treaty with defeated Germany. When Eisenhower was President, Khrushchev threatened that his country would make a separate peace treaty with East Germany. He said that would end any rights that the Western powers had to be

In the summer of 1961, East Germans began building a cement-block wall between East and West Berlin.

in Berlin. Eisenhower declared that the Western nations would not accept this and would remain in West Berlin, and Khrushchev dropped the threat.

Khrushchev now made the same threat to Kennedy, and Kennedy gave the same reply. The United States would not abandon the people of West Berlin. The two sides disagreed on other issues as well. It was a grim President Kennedy who returned to Washington. Determined to show the Soviet Union that the United States would stand firm, he doubled the number of men drafted. The President also asked Congress to increase spending for weapons.

One reason the Russians wanted the Western powers out of Berlin was that more than 4,000 people were escaping each week from Communist East Germany into the West. Many of these slipped out by way of West Berlin. This fact told the world that life behind the iron curtain was hardly the paradise that Soviet propaganda made it out to be.

On the morning of August 13, 1961, Berliners awoke to find that the East German government was putting up a barbed wire fence between East Berlin and West Berlin. Later a cement-block wall replaced the fence. Guards with "shoot-to-kill" orders patrolled the wall. The wall made escape from East Berlin nearly impossible, but it was also a reminder to the world of the differences between a Communist state and a free society. Kennedy sent American troops into West Berlin as a sign that the Western powers would remain in Berlin. Gradually, tensions eased in Germany. The Berlin wall, however, stands to this day.

On October 21, President Kennedy went on television to announce a strict quarantine on all offensive military equipment shipped to Cuba by the Soviet Union. He asked the U.S. armed forces to prepare for any eventualities. On October 24, the deadline for the quarantine passed without incident. Soviet ships approaching Cuba turned back.

The Cuban missile crisis A year later, Russia offered a still more serious challenge to the United States. In October 1962 an American spy plane took photographs showing that the Soviets were secretly building missile bases in Cuba. From these bases, missiles could carry nuclear bombs to much of the eastern and southern United States. For several days, President Kennedy discussed possible moves with his advisers. Then he went on television to inform the American people of the threat. He ordered the navy to stop any ship bound for Cuba with weapons. He demanded that Khrushchev remove the missiles already in Cuba and tear down the missile bases.

For 6 days the world stood on the brink of war. No one knew whether the Soviet ships on their way to Cuba would challenge the navy's blockade. American planes carrying live nuclear bombs took off and awaited orders. Behind the scenes, messages passed back and forth between Kennedy and Khrushchev. As the Russian ships neared the blockade, Khrushchev decided not to challenge the United States. The ships turned back. The crisis was over. In the end, Russia removed the missiles and bases. In return the United States promised not to invade Cuba.

Steps to avoid war One result of the Cuban missile crisis was that both sides realized they must avoid such dangerous showdowns. In 1963 they installed a **hot line**—a special communications system between the White House and Moscow—so that the leaders could talk immediately in a crisis. In the same year, the United

A United States naval ship inspects a Russian freighter to see if it is carrying missiles to Cuba.

States and the Soviet Union—along with Great Britain—worked out a treaty to ban the testing of nuclear weapons above ground, under water, and in space. Underground tests were still allowed. Over a hundred nations joined in signing the treaty.

In a speech that year, President Kennedy summed up the new awareness of the danger of nuclear war and of the need for the two sides to work for peace. "Our most basic common link," he said, "is that we all inhabit this small planet. We all breathe the same air. We all cherish our children's future. And we are all mortal."

CHECKUP

1. What new ideas did President Kennedy bring to foreign policy?
2. Why was the Bay of Pigs affair a setback for the United States?
3. Why was the Berlin wall built?
4. How was the Cuban missile crisis resolved?

28/CHAPTER REVIEW

KEY FACTS

1. Less than a year after victory over the Axis powers, the United States and the Soviet Union were involved in a cold war.

2. To keep the Soviet Union from expanding the territory under its control, the United States adopted a policy of containment.

3. When Communist North Korea invaded South Korea in 1950, United Nations forces, most of which were supplied by the United States, came to the aid of South Korea.

4. During John F. Kennedy's presidency the United States and Russia disagreed over events in Berlin and Cuba.

VOCABULARY QUIZ

On a separate piece of paper, write the number of the statements below. Next to each number write the word or phrase that best completes the statement.

Peace Corps
cold war
North Atlantic Treaty Organization
containment
United Nations

Alliance for Progress
Truman Doctrine
summit conference
Marshall Plan
iron curtain

1. The organization founded in 1945 to help keep the peace was the ___United Nations___.

2. Winston Churchill accused the Russians of lowering an ___iron curtain___ across Europe.

3. By 1946 the United States and the Soviet Union were engaged in a conflict called the ___cold war___.

4. To prevent the spread of communism, the United States adopted a policy of ___containment___.

5. United States military aid to Greece and Turkey was part of the ___Truman Doctrine___.

6. The United States helped the countries of Western Europe recover from the effects of war through the ___Marshall Plan___.

7. The United States joined with countries of Western Europe in a defense group called the ___North Atlantic Treaty Organization___

8. In 1955, President Eisenhower met with the leaders of the Soviet Union and other countries at Geneva in a ___summit conference___.

9. American volunteers who went to under-developed countries to help people were members of the ___Peace Corps___.

10. A program started under Kennedy to help countries in the Western Hemisphere was called the ___Alliance for Progress___.

REVIEW QUESTIONS

1. What areas of the world were affected by each of the following: (a) the Truman Doctrine, (b) the Marshall Plan, (c) the Alliance for Progress, (d) the Eisenhower Doctrine?

2. What changes were brought about in Japan after World War II?

3. What part did the United Nations play in the Korean War?

4. Explain the background and the outcome of each of the following: (a) the Bay of Pigs invasion, (b) the Cuban missile crisis.

ACTIVITIES

1. Make a list of the countries that are in the North Atlantic Treaty Organization today. Locate each on a globe or world map.

2. Several United Nations agencies are usually referred to by abbreviated names. Find out the full title of each of the following agencies: (a) UNESCO, (b) UNICEF, (c) WHO.

3. Find out what each of the agencies does. Report your findings to the class.

READING FOR SEQUENCE

THE COLD WAR

Understanding sequence—the order in which events occur—is necessary to understand history. That is because events that occur later in time almost always depend upon earlier events. For example, take these three events:

Columbus discovers America.
The English start colonies in America.
American colonies rebel against England.

Clearly the founding of colonies in America depended on someone first discovering the country. The revolution could happen only after there were colonies to rebel. Without knowing the correct sequence of these events, you could not make head nor tail of America's early history.

Sequence is not the same as cause and effect. Just because one event occurred before another does not mean that the first event caused the second event to happen. Columbus did not cause the English to start colonies in the New World a hundred years later. But the two events are related, and knowing their sequence helps you to understand how.

As you read, it is important to recognize the sequence of events. Writers provide various aids to help you follow sequence. Of course, the best aids are dates. But be alert also for signal words that tell *when* something happened. Some common signal words are *first, later, then, next, earlier, finally, during this time,* and so on.

SKILLS PRACTICE: Part I

Read the section "War in Korea" on pages 639–640. Locate and write down all the signal words, including dates, found in that section.

SKILLS PRACTICE: Part II

Even when there are no signal words, you will be able to put events in the correct order by reading carefully. For example, these four events are listed in the order in which they are mentioned in the section "Soviet actions" on page 633.

3 **1.** Russian troops placed a Communist government in power in Poland.

4 **2.** Russian troops placed Communist governments in power in other countries of Eastern Europe.

1 **3.** Germany invaded Russia twice through Poland and Eastern Europe.

2 **4.** The wars cost millions of Russian lives.

Read the section "Soviet actions" on page 633. On a sheet of paper, copy the four events listed above in the order in which they actually happened.

CHAPTER
29 A Changing Nation

The Consumer Society

VOCABULARY
GI Bill of Rights   Sunbelt
Green Revolution

Wartime housing Before World War II, the company of Levitt & Sons of Long Island, New York, was not much different from a thousand other builders of homes. The company was started during the Great Depression. By the end of the 1930s, it was building about 50 homes a year on Long Island. This area was a suburb of New York City, and homes there were fairly expensive. Levitt & Sons, like other home builders in those days, built only a few houses at a time.

Then came the war. With building materials and labor in short supply, the construction of private homes fell off sharply. However, there was a great need for temporary low-cost housing near the nation's mushrooming military bases and booming war industries. The Levitt company won a contract to build such housing at the naval base in Norfolk, Virginia. To complete the 2,300 dwelling units quickly, Levitt adopted some of the mass-production methods of factories.

Homes for veterans When the war was over, there was a mood of uncertainty in the country. Some feared a return to the depression of the 1930s. Many builders were cautious about starting too many new homes. However, some builders like Levitt saw the situation differently. Millions of war veterans would be returning home and starting families. They would need housing. Furthermore, Congress had passed a law in 1944 called the Servicemen's Readjustment Act, or the **GI Bill of Rights**. One part of this law allowed veterans to borrow money at low interest rates to buy homes. Other government programs begun during the New Deal also made borrowing for home buying easier. To Levitt all this added up to a great demand for inexpensive homes, suitable for families just starting out.

Levitt bought 1,400 acres (567 ha) of land near the town of Hicksville, Long Island. Hicksville is a few miles east of Queens, a part of New York City. Land near Hicksville was cheaper than land in the city. That would help keep down the cost of a house. Also, Levitt knew that suburbs had been growing for many decades. To many people the suburbs meant a better life—open space, clean air, and a good environment for raising a family.

Building whole communities Levitt's plan was to build not just a handful of homes but an entire community. Levittown, as the community was called,

Levittown's population grew from about 450 in 1947 to 60,000 by the late 1950s.

After World War II, the community of Levittown was built on potato fields on Long Island, not far from New York City. Hundreds of war veterans bought homes there.

Have pupils research and report to the class on the government programs to help veterans who served in World War II and more recent wars. Such benefits have included education and training at government expense, guaranteed loans, and job counseling.

1944 GI Bill of Rights

1947 Taft-Hartley Act

1948 Harry S. Truman elected President

1952 Dwight Eisenhower elected President

1954 Supreme Court orders public schools desegregated

1958 First American satellite in orbit

1960 John F. Kennedy elected President

1963 Civil rights march on Washington/ President Kennedy assassinated

1944   1948   1952   1956   1960   1964

More than 7.8 million World War II veterans and more than 2.3 million Korean War veterans studied under the GI Bill. Educational aid was also given to about 7 million Vietnam veterans.

651

would have 6,000 one-family houses plus its own shopping centers, parks, schools, and churches. Each house would come complete with kitchen appliances and would have a front yard and a back yard. Veterans would rent for a year at $65 a month. After that they could buy the house for $8,000. No down payment would be needed, and the monthly payment would actually be lower than the rent. Levittown was a bold experiment in mass production.

Building began in 1947. To keep costs down, Levitt applied the mass-production methods it had developed at the Norfolk navy base. All the houses had to be the same. The housing site became a huge assembly line. Work crews, each with its own specialty, went from house to house, putting in plumbing, installing stairs, and nailing on shingles. At each house, trucks dropped off the exact materials that the next work crew would need — pipes, roofing materials, paint. Soon the company was building 150 houses a week! Before the end of 1949, Levittown was completed, and every one of its houses was rented or sold.

Levitt went on to build other Levittowns. One in Bucks County, Pennsylvania, near Philadelphia, had 17,000 homes. A third, in New Jersey, had 12,000. These communities made Levitt the largest home builder in the East. Meanwhile, other builders were using Levitt's idea in Park Forest, Illinois; Orange County, California; and dozens of other places all over America. In fact, the postwar years marked the start of the greatest period of home building in American history.

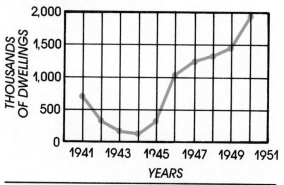

NEW HOUSING UNITS STARTED IN THE UNITED STATES 1941–1950

(The great majority of these units were one-family houses.)

Why were so few houses built from 1942 through 1945?

An increasing, shifting population This building boom was connected to three major developments in postwar America. First, there was a great increase in population. The growth of America's population had slowed down sharply during the Great Depression and the war. After the war, however, there was a "baby boom." This created a demand for housing.

Second, the building boom was connected to great shifts of population within the United States. The first shift was from the farm to the city. In 1940 nearly 1 in every 4 Americans lived on a farm. Thirty years later, fewer than 1 in 20 did.

This shift resulted mainly from advances in agriculture known as the **Green Revolution.** American scientists developed new varieties of rice, wheat, soybeans, and corn that produced many times more food than older varieties had. With better fertilizers, better insect control, and more efficient farm machinery, production increased dramatically. In 1950 a single farm worker could raise enough food to feed 15 people. In 1970 the same worker could feed 45 people. Fewer people were needed on farms, and millions left the land.

A second great population shift was from the city to the suburbs. You have read something about this shift already. After World War II about a million people each year joined the movement to the suburbs. By the early 1960s more Americans lived in the suburbs than in cities. Cars and new roads made it possible for people to live in the suburbs and work in the city. In time, business and industry moved to the suburbs. Huge shopping centers were also built. Soon many people were working in the suburbs as well as living there.

So rapidly did suburbs grow that by the 1960s and 1970s some suburbs had become like the cities their residents had sought to escape. It was often hard to tell where the city ended and the suburbs began. Traffic jams were a part of every rush hour. Noise and pollution increased. So did crime and taxes. At the same time, suburbs offered fewer opportunities for cultural experiences like theaters and concerts than did cities.

Shifts between the North and the South
A third population shift was from the northern and eastern parts of the United States to the West and the South. This area, roughly the southern third of the country, is known as the **Sunbelt**. The climate is sunny and warm much of the year, and winters are mild. People moved to the Sunbelt for many different reasons. Many of these people were senior citizens who wanted a warmer climate. Younger people were attracted by the different style of living in this region. As the textile industry moved south and the oil, gas, space, and defense industries in the Sunbelt states grew, people were drawn there by job opportunities.

The Sunbelt, with its warm climate and mild winters, has attracted many older Americans.

As a result, whole towns sprang up in California and Florida in areas where orange trees had grown only a few years before. New cities—"boom towns," they were often called—appeared in Arizona, New Mexico, Texas, and the Gulf Coast states. Small cities became great ones. By 1980, five of the ten largest cities in the United States—San Antonio, Houston, Dallas, Los Angeles, and San Diego—were in the Sunbelt.

A fourth major population shift was the movement of black Americans from the South to the North. As late as the 1930s, about 80 percent of the black population still lived in the southern states. So great was the migration during and after World War II that by 1960 more than half the black population lived outside the South. Most lived in cities of the North, the Midwest, and the West. This was the only population shift that did not create a demand for new housing. Most blacks moved into older housing in the central cities.

The demand for consumer goods The third major development in the building boom was the period of prosperity that the United States experienced from 1945 to 1970. It was the longest period of prosperity in the nation's history. This prosperity was based mainly upon the demand for consumer goods.

During the war, Americans had made good money but found few things to spend it on. They put their money into savings or bought United States war bonds. At the end of the war, therefore, they had saved billions. When factories again started to make cars, stoves, refrig- erators, and other goods, consumers snapped them up as fast as they came off the assembly lines. This postwar demand for goods lasted for several years, providing high employment and good wages.

The baby boom also created a demand for consumer goods, from food and clothing to washing machines and toys. Later, as the postwar babies became teenagers, it meant a demand for other goods like hi-fis, records, and tape recorders.

More goods, more jobs The growing population meant that city and state governments had to spend more for schools, roads, hospitals, and police and fire services. This meant still more jobs. More jobs meant more people who could afford to buy homes. And that, in turn, meant more sales of kitchen appliances, lawn mowers, and tool kits.

As people moved to the suburbs, owning a car became more and more a necessity. In the prosperous 1920s, manufacturers considered it a good year when they sold 3 million cars. In the 1950s and 1960s, there were few years when they failed to sell twice that many.

New consumer goods created whole new industries. Television is an example. In 1946 only 6,000 television sets were made in America. By 1950 American manufacturers were producing more than 7 million a year. Television created jobs for people who made the sets, sold them, repaired them, and created programs for them.

Purchases of consumer goods were made easy by plenty of consumer credit. In 1950 the newest thing in consumer credit, the credit card, was introduced at

Assign a group of pupils to make a listing of consumer goods that are available today in the computer field. Ask another group to draw up a list of capital goods in the same field. Be sure they understand the difference between them. Capital goods are used to make other goods. Consumer goods satisfy human wants and needs directly. After the class has

gas stations. Credit cards spread quickly to other businesses.

In addition to the growing market at home, the United States found a large market overseas for its goods. Europe's economies were shattered by the destruc-

Workers leaving a factory head for their cars. Jobs were plentiful in the prosperous postwar years.

tion of World War II. For many years, therefore, United States factories would be the chief suppliers of goods to that continent.

Thus, despite several recessions, the country was producing twice as many goods and services in 1970 as in 1945. Americans were earning more money and enjoying more goods than ever before.

CHECKUP

1. Why was there a building boom in the United States after World War II?
2. List four population shifts that occurred in the postwar years.
3. Why was the period following World War II a time of prosperity?

Postwar Politics and Policies

┌─ VOCABULARY ─────────────┐
inflation   censure
closed shop   space satellite
└──────────────────────────┘

A smooth changeover When the fighting ended in World War II, Americans everywhere wanted to get back to normal living quickly. Most of the 12 million men and women still in the service were anxious to return home. Factory owners wanted to shift back to making peacetime products.

Considering the size of the task, the changeover from wartime to peacetime progressed fairly smoothly. Within a year, 9 million men and women exchanged their uniforms for civilian clothes. The GI Bill of Rights not only aided veterans in buying homes, but it helped them go to college, train for jobs, and start businesses. Eventually, 8 million veterans took advantage of the opportunity for advanced education. Both they and the nation benefited from the knowledge and skills they gained. Factory owners, too, made the return to civilian production quickly. Less than 5 months after the shooting stopped, more than 90 percent of the war industries were back to making peacetime goods.

Rising prices The main problem of the early postwar years turned out to be **inflation,** or rising prices. Factories could not keep up with the demand for consumer goods. When demand is greater than supply, prices rise. Also, workers wanted wage increases to make up for the rise in living costs. There were many strikes. When employers agreed to raise wages, they covered their higher costs by charging more for their products. This raised the cost of living, leading to still more demands for higher wages.

President Truman tried to hold down inflation by continuing wartime price controls. But prices rose anyway. In 1946 nearly all price controls were removed. Prices continued to rise for a time before finally leveling off.

The Taft-Hartley Act The postwar strikes angered many Americans. They felt that labor unions had grown too powerful. In 1947, Congress passed the Taft-Hartley Act. This law outlawed the **closed shop.** A closed shop is one in which the company agrees to hire only people who already belong to a union. It also allowed the President to stop certain strikes. When the President felt a

Barrow in The Jacksonville Times-Union

"MAN IN THE MIDDLE"

TAFT-HARTLEY LAW

CONGRESS

WAGNER ACT

After World War II, there were many strikes. Congress had to consider how best to balance the powers of employers with those of the labor unions. The Wagner Act of New Deal days and the Taft-Hartley Act of 1947 were both attempts at establishing that balance.

strike threatened the country's welfare, he could call for an 80-day cooling-off period. President Truman vetoed this bill, but Congress passed it over his veto.

President Truman had many other disagreements with Congress. He sought laws to protect the civil rights of blacks and other minorities. As you know, civil rights are those rights guaranteed to all Americans by the Constitution—for example, the right to vote and the right to a fair trial. Truman also asked for laws to prevent discrimination in hiring. Congress did not act on his proposals. On his own, however, President Truman gave orders to end segregation in the armed forces.

The election of 1948 In 1948 the Democratic party nominated Harry Truman to run for a full term as President.

Initiate a class discussion on the "wage-cost push" theory of inflation, which developed in the 1950s. Higher wages brought higher operating costs. This in turn forced producers to raise prices to consumers. This cycle is known as creeping inflation.

His opponent was Thomas E. Dewey, a successful and popular governor of New York. Some of President Truman's decisions had made him unpopular with various groups of voters. Most people— including most Democrats—expected the Republicans to win easily after 16 years of Democratic rule.

Harry Truman surprised them all. He took his campaign directly to the people. Truman traveled 31,000 miles (49,600 km) and made more than 350 speeches. People admired the President's down-to-earth manner. By comparison, Dewey avoided talking about issues and seemed stiff and formal. On election day, Truman had the support of farmers and organized labor, and he won.

The Fair Deal   After his victory, President Truman called for laws that would bring New Deal reforms such as social security and the minimum wage to Americans still not covered by them. He also called for new programs in education, health care, agriculture, and low-income housing. Truman called his program the Fair Deal.

Congress gave Truman some of what he asked for. It extended social security coverage to 10 million more workers, and it raised the minimum wage. It also passed a housing act under which the federal government cleared slums and built housing for low-income families. But Congress turned down Truman's other ideas.

On the day after the 1948 election, an elated Harry Truman shows a newspaper which, in its early edition, mistakenly reported that his Republican opponent had won.

HARRY S. TRUMAN
33rd President
1945 · 1953

Born: 1884, Lamar, Missouri. **Education:** High school. **Training:** Farmer, soldier, public official. **To presidency from:** Missouri. **Position when taking office:** Vice President. **Political party:** Democratic. **Married:** Bess Wallace. **Children:** One daughter. **Died:** 1972, Kansas City, Missouri. **Other facts:** Operated the family farm for 15 years. Joined the National Guard and served in Europe in World War I. Held local offices in Missouri and elected to United States Senate, where he won a reputation as an investigator of waste and corruption in defense spending. Enjoyed playing piano and taking early morning walks. **During his presidency:** The atomic age began with the testing of an atomic bomb at Alamogordo, New Mexico, in July 1945.

Cold war politics During the years of the cold war, some Americans began to question whether communism was spreading at home. In 1946, officials in Canada discovered a Soviet spy ring that was stealing atomic secrets. Were Communists and their sympathizers in the United States also in positions where they might harm the nation? In 1947, responding to growing pressure from people in the government and outside it, President Truman ordered a check on the loyalty of all federal employees. In the next 4 years, more than 3 million federal workers were investigated and cleared. Two hundred twelve were fired as possible "security risks."

Meanwhile, committees of Congress and of several state legislatures looked for evidence of Communist influence. A new Red Scare was building throughout the country. The attorney general of the United States warned that Communists "are everywhere—in factories, offices, butcher shops, on street corners, in private business . . .." The charge that Communists had become well established caused great worry.

McCarthy's rise and fall Republican Senator Joseph R. McCarthy of Wisconsin took advantage of these fears to gain fame and power. Early in 1950 he rocketed to public attention with the claim that there were over 200 "known Communists" in the State Department. For the next 4 years, McCarthy held the headlines with charges that there were Communists in universities, in government, in business, and even in the military. He accused Presidents Roosevelt and Truman of "20 years of treason." He called George C. Marshall, the great wartime general and author of the Marshall Plan, a traitor. McCarthy never proved any of his charges. However, many people, worried by communism, believed at first that he was doing patriotic work.

In 1954 a Senate committee investigated McCarthy's charge of Communist influence in the United States Army. The committee's hearings were televised. Millions of Americans saw McCarthy's bullying ways for the first time, and he lost a lot of support. Later that year the Senate **censured**, or condemned, him for his behavior. McCarthy's influence fell

When McCarthy was later asked to name State Department employees, his list of 200 had shrunk to nine. Six of the nine had never worked for the department and the three others had positions that could not influence policy.

sharply after that. When the Democrats took control of the Senate in 1957, McCarthy lost his committee chairmanship. He died later that year.

Eisenhower's program McCarthy's fall came while Dwight Eisenhower was President. McCarthy had once said that President Eisenhower had allowed himself to be tricked by Communist lies. However, that was a charge that few Americans believed. Eisenhower was one of the best-liked and most trusted Presidents in history. During his campaigns, millions expressed their feelings by wearing "I Like Ike" buttons.

Eisenhower called his program Modern Republicanism. Although some members of his party wanted to repeal the reforms of the New Deal, Eisenhower accepted them. During his two terms of office, Congress again raised the minimum wage and brought millions of additional workers into the social security system. Eisenhower favored both actions. He also created the Department of Health, Education, and Welfare and named Mrs. Oveta Culp Hobby to head it. Mrs. Hobby was only the second woman to serve in the Cabinet. During these years the federal government also provided increased funds for medical research, hospitals,

In 1954 hearings, Senator Joseph McCarthy of Wisconsin makes his charge of Communist influence in the United States Army. At the table is Joseph Welch, the army counsel.

Oveta Culp Hobby is sworn in by Chief Justice Fred Vinson as federal security administrator. Later she became the secretary of health, education, and welfare.

and urban renewal. Further, Eisenhower proposed the Highway Act of 1956, under which most of today's interstate highways were built.

On the other hand, Eisenhower disagreed with New Deal programs like the Tennessee Valley Authority. (See page 590.) He believed that private companies, rather than the government, should develop electric power. He also favored less government regulation of business and industry.

The space age opens   It was during Eisenhower's presidency that the space age opened. On October 4, 1957, the Soviets put the world's first **space satellite,** which they called Sputnik, into orbit around the earth. One month later they launched Sputnik 2, which carried a live dog. This Soviet achievement was a blow to American prestige. It appeared that the Russians had beaten America at its own game—science and technology. More importantly, Russia's success in putting a space satellite into orbit around the earth increased concern for America's security against attack.

President Eisenhower and Congress responded by providing more funds for America's space program and by setting up the National Aeronautics and Space Agency (NASA) to direct it. They also adopted the National Defense Education Act (NDEA). One aim of this act was to produce more scientists and science teachers by providing funds for their training.

Meanwhile the United States speeded up its space efforts. In 1958 the first American satellite was lifted into orbit. However, the United States would remain behind the Soviet Union in the space race for some time. In 1961, Yuri Gagarin, a Russian, became the first person to orbit the earth.

The election of Kennedy   In 1960, John Kennedy won the presidency in the closest race of the twentieth century so far. He won by 118,000 popular votes— a bare one tenth of 1 percent more than his Republican opponent, Richard Nixon, received. This was the first "television election"—the first campaign to be waged mainly on television and the first that was probably decided by it. Kennedy and Nixon engaged in a series of four televised debates. Before the debates, polls showed Kennedy trailing by a wide margin. However, voters were favorably impressed by his showing in the debates. After them, Kennedy pulled even with Nixon. He became the first Catholic to become President and the youngest man ever elected to that position.

Appoint a group of pupils to compile a chronological fact sheet about the National Aeronautics and Space Administration (NASA). This agency, created in 1958, was in charge of the research and exploration of outer space. Overshadowing all other NASA undertakings was the manned spaceflight program. In May 1961, President

Born: 1890, Denison, Texas. **Education:** United States Military Academy. **Training:** Army officer. **To presidency from:** New York. **Position when elected:** General of the army at the time of his nomination. **Political party:** Republican. **Married:** Mamie Doud. **Children:** Two sons. **Died:** 1969, Washington, D.C. **Other facts:** Served as an army officer in Panama, the Philippines, and the United States. Commanded Allied forces for the invasion of Europe in World War II. Later became president of Columbia University, and then commander of NATO forces in Europe. The first President licensed to pilot an airplane. **During his presidency:** The crippling disease of infantile paralysis was conquered when Dr. Jonas Salk invented an antipolio vaccine.

DWIGHT D. EISENHOWER
34th President
1953 · 1961

President Kennedy called his program the New Frontier. At his urging, Congress provided funds to retrain unemployed workers and to help depressed areas. Congress also responded to Kennedy's call for a space program that would "land a man on the moon" before 1970. Kennedy also proposed plans for medical care for the aged, greater protection of civil rights, and federal aid to education.

The assassination of President Kennedy
President Kennedy did not live to see these proposals become law. On November 22, 1963, he went to Dallas, Texas, to deliver a speech. Crowds lined the streets to greet the President's motorcade as it passed by. Kennedy rode in an open car. Suddenly, shots rang out. Two bullets struck the President. By the time he could be brought to a hospital, Kennedy was dead.

Within hours, police arrested a man named Lee Harvey Oswald and charged him with the crime. Two days later, as Oswald was being moved from one jail to another, a Dallas nightclub owner named Jack Ruby stepped from a group of report-

ers and shot Oswald. Millions of shocked Americans watched the murder on their television sets.

A special commission headed by Chief Justice Earl Warren was appointed to get to the bottom of the Kennedy assassination. After a 9-month study, the group

John F. Kennedy was a member of the Senate when he posed for this picture with his wife and daughter.

Kennedy set as a national goal a manned landing on the moon "before this decade is out." In July 1969 two Americans set foot on the moon's surface.

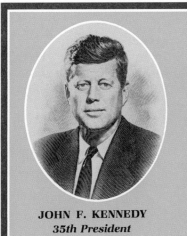

Born: 1917, Brookline, Massachusetts. **Education:** Harvard College. **Training:** Author, public official. **To presidency from:** Massachusetts. **Position when elected:** United States senator. **Political party:** Democratic. **Married:** Jacqueline Bouvier. **Children:** One daughter, one son. **Died:** November 22, 1963, shot by an assassin in Dallas, Texas. **Other facts:** As naval officer in South Pacific in World War II, decorated for heroism. Served in both houses of Congress. Received Pulitzer Prize for his book *Profiles in Courage*. The first Roman Catholic to become President. **During his presidency:** A civil rights march brought 200,000 people to Washington, D.C., in a demonstration of the demands of black people for equal rights.

JOHN F. KENNEDY
35th President
1961 • 1963

concluded that Lee Oswald had acted alone. But doubts remained. Many said the commission had failed to follow all the leads and had left many questions unanswered. In 1979 a committee of the House of Representatives conducted another study of Kennedy's murder. One group of experts used a new method to analyze the tape recording that contained the sounds of the gunshots. They concluded that the shots came from more than one rifle. However, other experts disagreed with these findings. Where did the truth lie? And if there was more than one rifle, who fired it? Each new answer seemed only to produce a puzzling new question.

CHECKUP

1. What troubles did inflation cause in the years right after World War II?
2. How did Senator McCarthy come into prominence in the early 1950s? Why was he censured by the Senate?
3. With what President is each of the following programs associated: (a) the New Frontier, (b) Modern Republicanism, (c) the Fair Deal?
4. Why was the launching of Sputnik a blow to America? How did the United States react?

The Struggle for Equal Rights

VOCABULARY

Brown v. *Board   nonviolent
    of Education   resistance
    of Topeka*   sit-in

Continuing segregation Like most black Americans of his day, Thurgood Marshall had personal experience with segregation. The grandson of a slave, Marshall was born in Baltimore, Maryland, in 1908. In 1930 he was denied admission to the law school of the University of Maryland because of his race. Instead he attended the law school at all-black Howard University in Washington, D.C. After his graduation he went to work for the National Association for the Advancement of Colored People (NAACP) and soon became head of its legal department. The NAACP was the leader in the struggle against those practices and laws that denied blacks their full rights as Americans.

In the 1930s and 1940s, the NAACP and Thurgood Marshall won many important

The Kennedy assassination shocked the nation. Have pupils interview family members and neighbors about their reactions to it. Many will recall exactly what they were doing when they heard the news. Some may have been watching television coverage from Dallas when it happened.

Assign several pupils to research the *Plessy* v. *Ferguson* and *Brown* v. *Board of Education of Topeka* cases. See if they can do a follow-up on what happened to Homer Plessy and Linda Brown after their cases had been decided.

cases in the courts. Still, segregation remained. A half century earlier in the case of *Plessy* v. *Ferguson*, the Supreme Court had adopted the "separate but equal" rule (page 388). Most northern states did not have the Jim Crow laws that prevailed in the South, but segregation existed in the North as well. Unwritten laws, or custom, kept blacks living in separate neighborhoods, eating in separate restaurants, bathing at separate beaches, and in countless other ways living their lives apart from whites.

In practice, separate facilities were almost never equal. School buildings for black children, for example, were often old, poorly equipped, and supplied with out-of-date books. Even if the facilities were exactly equal, Marshall pointed out, "the very fact of segregation establishes a feeling of humiliation and deprivation in the group considered to be inferior."

Thurgood Marshall, who argued the Brown *case before the Supreme Court, later became its first black member.*

Attacking school segregation To end segregation, Marshall and the NAACP decided they must attack the "separate but equal" rule head on. The case they chose for this involved an 8-year-old black girl named Linda Brown in Topeka, Kansas. Linda lived just five blocks from a public school. However, this school was for whites only. Linda had to go to an all-black public school more than 20 blocks away. With help from the NAACP, Linda's father sued to allow his daughter to attend the all-white school. The case made its way through the courts to the Supreme Court of the United States. Handling the case for the NAACP, Marshall argued that the Court should reverse the decision reached in the case of *Plessy* v. *Ferguson*.

In May 1954 the Supreme Court gave its historic decision in the case of ***Brown v. Board of Education of Topeka***. ". . . we conclude that in the field of public education the doctrine of 'separate but equal' has no place. Separate educational facilities are inherently [that is, by their very nature] unequal." The Court soon followed up this historic decision with an order that desegregation of public schools should begin promptly.

Resistance to desegregation Following the Brown decision, some states and cities promptly obeyed the order of the Supreme Court and ended school segregation. Much of the white South, however, resisted change. White citizens councils were formed to fight desegregation. They threatened those blacks and whites who challenged segregation with the loss of their jobs. The Ku Klux Klan came to

663

life again, threatening violence to stop desegregation. Southern leaders and officeholders threw up roadblocks.

In Arkansas the governor used National Guard troops to keep nine black students from entering Little Rock's Central High School. To enforce the desegregation order of the Court, President Eisenhower had to send federal troops to Little Rock. Even so, desegregation in the South went at a snail's pace. Six years after the Supreme Court ruled segregated schools unconstitutional, 99 percent of the black students in ten southern states were still in segregated schools.

In 1955 the refusal of Rosa Parks to give up her seat led to the end of segregation on buses.

The Montgomery bus boycott   With change coming only slowly through the courts, black people turned to more direct ways to end Jim Crow laws and practices. In Montgomery, Alabama, in December 1955, a black woman named Rosa Parks boarded a bus at the end of a day's work and took a seat near the front. At that time, buses in Montgomery, as in nearly all other southern cities, were segregated by law. Whites sat in the front, and blacks sat in the back. On that December day, all the seats in the bus were soon filled. When a white man entered, the driver ordered Mrs. Parks to give him her seat and move to the back. Rosa Parks refused, and the driver had her arrested.

Montgomery blacks then began a boycott of the city's buses, refusing to ride them. The boycott was led by a young minister named Martin Luther King, Jr. Dr. King believed that blacks should refuse to obey unjust laws. But he also believed that as Christians they must do so without violence and without hate. "If

we are arrested every day," he told his followers, ". . . if we are trampled over every day, don't let anyone pull you so low as to hate them. We must use the weapon of love." Even after he was jailed for a while and after his home was bombed, King told his followers to stick to the path of **nonviolent resistance**, and they did.

Meanwhile the NAACP and Thurgood Marshall challenged Montgomery's bus law in the courts. A little more than a year after Rosa Parks was ordered to give up her seat, the Supreme Court ruled that Montgomery's bus segregation law was unconstitutional.

The victory over segregation in Montgomery made Dr. King a national figure. In 1957 he helped to form a new organization called the Southern Christian Leadership Conference (SCLC) to fight for civil rights. The SCLC adopted King's philosophy of nonviolent resistance.

Ask your pupils to use the library to draw up a calendar of events of the civil rights movement from the time of the Supreme Court decision of 1954 to the present. Ask: Have black Americans gained or lost civil rights? What were the most important changes?

Sit-ins   King's example and leadership inspired black college students in the South to stage **sit-ins** to force department stores to desegregate their lunch counters. In a sit-in, students took seats in a section reserved for whites. They expected to be treated roughly, but they were committed to nonviolence. Some carried small cards in their pockets with reminders such as

Don't strike back or curse if abused.
Don't laugh out.
Show yourself courteous and friendly at all times.
Sit straight and always face the counter.
Remember love and nonviolence.

Eventually, police would arrest those taking part in the sit-ins. Blacks would then boycott the stores. Faced with the loss of business in other parts of their stores, many owners gave in and desegregated their lunch counters. The first sit-in was in 1960. In the next several years, thousands of students, both black and white, took part in sit-ins. By 1963 these demonstrations led to the desegregation of lunch counters, hotels, and theaters in 300 southern cities.

Freedom Riders   Still other nonviolent fighters for civil rights chose as their target the segregated bus stations of the South. Blacks and whites called Freedom Riders rode together from town to town on interstate buses. Inside the bus stations they refused to obey the signs that marked the segregated waiting rooms, water fountains, and toilets. Often they were met by riots and beatings. Their quiet dignity won attention and support for their cause.

In May 1961, United States Attorney General Robert F. Kennedy called on the

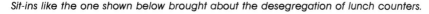

Sit-ins like the one shown below brought about the desegregation of lunch counters.

By sending federal troops to Mississippi in 1962 the Kennedy administration established itself as a friend and supporter of civil rights. Ask: Could it have done more than it did?

Interstate Commerce Commission to ban segregation in stations used by interstate buses. A few months later it did so.

President Kennedy acts   Still, progress came slowly. In the fall of 1962, President Kennedy had to send 5,000 troops to the all-white University of Mississippi to protect the right of James Meredith, a black air force veteran, to attend the school. In Birmingham, Alabama, the following spring, nonviolent marchers led by Dr. King were met by violence.

In June 1963, President Kennedy decided to give a televised address to the nation on the subject of civil rights. Although the year marked the one-hundredth anniversary of the Emancipation Proclamation, black people were still being denied the full measure of rights that America promised to all its citizens. "Are we to say to the world," Kennedy asked, "and, much more importantly, to each other that this is a land of the free except for Negroes?" The President announced that he would ask Congress to pass a strong civil rights bill.

A march on Washington   Civil rights leaders decided to hold a march on Washington to urge Congress to pass the bill.

More than 200,000 people gathered at the Lincoln Memorial in Washington in August 1963 to hear Dr. Martin Luther King, Jr., make a stirring plea for racial equality.

In 1964, Dr. Martin Luther King, Jr., receives the Nobel Peace Prize in Oslo, Norway, for leading the blacks' struggle for equality by nonviolent means.

On August 28, 1963, more than 200,000 Americans, black and white, gathered at the Washington Monument and the Lincoln Memorial. Dr. King made a moving address to them and to the millions watching on television. "I still have a dream," said Martin Luther King. "It is a dream deeply rooted in the American dream."

> I have a dream that one day . . . the sons of former slaves and sons of former slave-owners will be able to sit down together at the table of brotherhood . . ..

The rally ended with the singer Mahalia Jackson leading the singing of "We Shall Overcome," a hymn that had become the theme song of the civil rights movement.

Still, as the one-hundredth year after the Emancipation Proclamation drew to a close, Kennedy's civil rights bill had not been passed by Congress. And with the death of the President who proposed it, the task of getting that bill through Congress and enacted into law would have to be carried out by a new President, Lyndon Johnson.

CHECKUP

1. What far-reaching decision affecting public schools was made in 1954 by the Supreme Court?
2. What was the immediate effect of this decision?
3. Why did a bus boycott take place in Montgomery, Alabama?
4. In what other ways was the struggle for civil rights for black people carried on in the 1950s and early 1960s?

KEY FACTS

1. The 25 years following World War II marked the longest period of prosperity the United States has ever known.

2. This prosperity was based mainly on the demand for consumer goods.

3. Four great shifts in population occurred in the years after World War II: from farms to cities, from cities to suburbs, from the North to the Sunbelt, and—for many black people—from the South to the North.

4. During the 1950s and early 1960s, progress was made toward desegregating American society, but much remained to be done.

VOCABULARY QUIZ

Fill in each blank correctly. Choose your answer from the terms following each sentence.

1. The Green Revolution brought about advances in ____agriculture____.

education   agriculture   war

2. A law that helped ____war veterans____ to continue their education, buy homes, and start businesses was the GI Bill of Rights.

farmers   immigrants   war veterans

3. The area in the United States that is known as the Sunbelt is in the ____South and the West____.

North and the West   North and the East
South and the West

4. When there is inflation, the cost of living ____rises____.

rises   drops   is unchanged

5. A business that has a closed shop hires only members of a ____union____.

union   minority group   family

6. When Senator McCarthy was censured by the Senate, he was ____condemned____.

praised   condemned   investigated

7. Sputnik, which was sent up by the Russians, was the world's first ____space satellite____.

jet plane   space satellite   missile

8. To induce department stores to desegregate lunch counters, both black and white college students took part in ____sit-ins____.

riots   sit-ins   road marches

9. The case of *Brown* v. *Board of Education of Topeka* resulted in the order to desegregate ____public schools____.

buses   public beaches   public schools

10. In dealing with segregation, Martin Luther King, Jr., was committed to a policy known as ____nonviolent resistance____.

containment   nonviolent resistance
open door

REVIEW QUESTIONS

1. What advances were made in agriculture during the postwar years?

2. How did the country's rapid growth in population contribute to new job opportunities and economic growth?

3. What brought about rising prices in the years following World War II?

4. What did the Taft-Hartley Act do?

5. Which proposals in President Truman's Fair Deal program were passed into law?

ACTIVITIES

1. Find out if any of your grandparents or other members of your family are veterans of World War II. Ask them if they benefited from the GI Bill of Rights and, if so, in what way. Report your findings to the class.

2. Find out about the personal acts of courage of the following people in their efforts to gain civil rights for all: (**a**) Rosa Parks, (**b**) James Meredith, (**c**) Martin Luther King, Jr.

READING A MILEAGE CHART

FINDING ROAD MILES

In this chapter you read how the number of cars bought by Americans increased. You also read how the population shifted from one part of the United States to another. With this movement of people, cars became more and more of a necessity. People used cars to get from the suburbs to jobs in the city. With better roads and highways, people were able to travel easily by car from one city to another.

When you travel by car, you want to know the distance between one place and another. A mileage chart is a quick and easy way to tell distance. The chart below shows the number of road miles between some cities in the United States.

Suppose you want to find the distance between St. Louis and Miami. Put a finger of your left hand on *Miami* on the left side of the chart. Now find *St. Louis* at the bottom of the chart. Put a finger of your right hand on *St. Louis*. Move both fingers, one across and one up, until they meet at 1265. That is the number of road miles between the two cities.

SKILLS PRACTICE

Use the mileage chart to answer the following questions.

1. How many miles is it from Denver to New Orleans? **1295**

2. Which city is closer to New York, Seattle or San Francisco? **Seattle**

3. Which two cities are closest together? **Boston, N.Y.**

4. Which two cities are farthest apart? **Miami, Seattle**

5. How far would you have to drive from Chicago to Kansas City? **510 miles**

MILEAGE CHART	Boston	Chicago	Dallas	Denver	Kansas City	Los Angeles	Miami	New Orleans	New York	St. Louis	San Francisco	Seattle	Washington
Chicago	990		960	995	510	2120	1370	945	790	285	2195	2020	705
Dallas	1805	960		780	495	1425	1370	505	1565	650	1785	2165	1375
Denver	1990	995	780		600	1170	2135	1295	1760	875	1270	1385	1645
Kansas City	1420	510	495	600		1610	1530	830	1185	255	1890	1925	1050
Los Angeles	3085	2120	1425	1170	1610		2820	1920	2765	1820	390	1180	2725
Miami	1565	1370	1370	2135	1530	2820		870	1300	1265	3160	3425	1115
New Orleans	1550	945	505	1295	830	1920	870		1320	710	2295	2695	1115
New York	215	790	1565	1760	1185	2765	1300	1320		950	2930	2825	220
St. Louis	1160	285	650	875	255	1820	1265	710	950		2140	2175	805
San Francisco	3190	2195	1785	1270	1890	390	3160	2295	2930	2140		825	2875
Seattle	2950	2020	2165	1385	1925	1180	3425	2695	2825	2175	825		2845
Washington, D.C.	445	705	1375	1645	1050	2725	1115	1115	220	805	2875	2845	

CHAPTER 30 A Time of Shocks

Lyndon Johnson and the Great Society

VOCABULARY

Civil Rights Act of 1964	Great Society
	ghetto

A rising politician At the time of John F. Kennedy's death, Congress had passed few of the major laws he had asked for. The task of getting Kennedy's program enacted fell to his successor, Lyndon B. Johnson. It could not have been left in more skilled political hands. No one knew better how to get a bill through Congress. Even as a child, Lyndon Johnson had been fascinated by politics. His father served for a time in the Texas state legislature, and young Lyndon often went to the state capitol with him to watch the lawmakers in action. He also loved visiting the voters in his father's district during election campaigns.

After graduating from college and teaching for a year, the 24-year-old Johnson went to Washington to serve as secretary to a Texas congressman. In 1937 he won election to Congress himself. After 11 years in the House of Representatives, Johnson was elected to the Senate in 1948 by the narrow margin of 87 votes. Fellow senators quickly recognized his talents. In just 4 years, Democratic senators elec-

ted him their leader. He became one of the most powerful men in Washington.

Johnson tried for the Democratic nomination for President in 1960, but he lost out to John F. Kennedy. However, when Kennedy invited him to run as the vice presidential candidate, Johnson accepted. Now, 3 years later, he was President.

The Civil Rights Act of 1964 Johnson took advantage of the country's grief over Kennedy's death to get several of the late President's ideas passed into law. In urging Congress to pass Kennedy's civil rights bill, he said, "No memorial . . . could more eloquently honor President Kennedy's memory." Because of Johnson's able work with Congress, this bill became the **Civil Rights Act of 1964.**

The law ended racial discrimination in hotels, restaurants, theaters, and other businesses that serve the public. It also gave the federal government more power to speed up the desegregation of public schools and other public institutions. As a result, schools in the South were desegregated more rapidly. In addition, the act prohibited race and sex discrimination in hiring and attempted to protect the voting rights of blacks. These last parts of the law proved difficult to enforce. Still this act was the most important civil rights law since Reconstruction days.

Johnson took the presidential oath aboard Air Force One at Love Field in Dallas. The oath was administered by Federal Judge Sarah T. Hughes, an old friend of the President.

Aboard the presidential plane, Lyndon Johnson takes the oath as President a few hours after the assassination of John F. Kennedy. In the right foreground is Mrs. Kennedy.

Have some pupils investigate and report to the class on the similarities of the Kennedy and Lincoln assassinations and their aftermaths. Pupils will be fascinated with the number of coincidences that have been discovered.

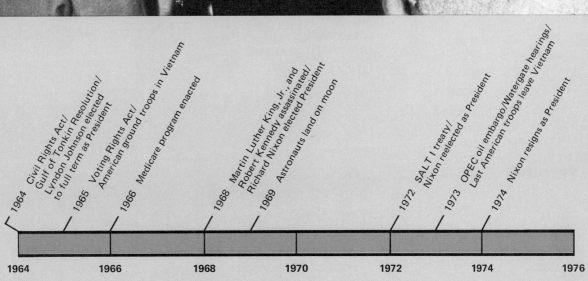

1964 Civil Rights Act/
Gulf of Tonkin Resolution/
Lyndon Johnson elected
to full term as President

1965 Voting Rights Act/
American ground troops in Vietnam

1966 Medicare program enacted

1968 Martin Luther King, Jr., and
Robert Kennedy assassinated/
Richard Nixon elected President

1969 Astronauts land on moon

1972 SALT I treaty/
Nixon reelected as President

1973 OPEC oil embargo/Watergate hearings/
Last American troops leave Vietnam

1974 Nixon resigns as President

1964   1966   1968   1970   1972   1974   1976

The Job Corps offers its services in more than 100 centers scattered throughout the United States. It encourages young people between 16 and 22 to finish high school and offers training in such trades as carpentry and bricklaying. The great majority of those who finish the course find jobs, join the armed services, or return to school.

The Great Society   Less than a year after becoming President, Lyndon Johnson ran for a full 4-year term. He overwhelmed his Republican opponent, Senator Barry Goldwater of Arizona, by more than 16 million votes and carried all but five states.

In addition to getting Kennedy's proposals enacted, Lyndon Johnson put forth his own program. " . . . We have the opportunity," he said, "to move not only toward the rich society but the **Great Society.**" To Johnson, the Great Society was one that cared for its aged and its underprivileged, one that broadened opportunities for all, and one that promoted racial justice. Achieving these goals would call for a greatly increased role for the federal government.

As part of his Great Society program, Lyndon Johnson called for a "war on poverty." Congress provided money to local communities to provide relief and jobs for the poor. It set up a food stamp program for needy families. It started the Job Corps to help workers train for better jobs and high school students find summer work. It created Head Start, a program for preschool children. Another program, Volunteers in Service to America (VISTA), was a kind of Peace Corps at home. It enlisted volunteers to help people in poor areas to improve their living conditions. Other programs helped low-income tenants with rent payments and built more public housing.

Two important parts of the Great Society were Medicare and aid to education. Medicare provided health care for the aged through the social security system. Through the program of aid to education, schools for the first time received large

A VISTA volunteer (right) discusses a corn crop with Navajo farmers in New Mexico.

amounts of federal money. In addition, cities received help for improving public transportation and for rebuilding old neighborhoods. States received money to help build new hospitals. Not since the New Deal had so many important laws been passed in such a short time.

The space program   The government also provided added support for the space program. That program had already passed two important milestones. In 1961, Alan Shepard became the first American to enter space when he rode a rocket 117 miles (188 km) into space from Cape Canaveral, Florida. In 1962, John Glenn became the first American to orbit the earth. These achievements were part of a series of rocket launches called Project Mercury.

Now the space program pressed on with the next steps toward putting a man on the moon. Project Gemini, another series of launches, included a "space walk." This program was followed by Project Apollo. Apollo included a launch in 1968 in which a team of astronauts orbited the moon and returned to earth safely.

A change in immigration   Congress also passed a new immigration law in 1965. The act changed the old quota system that had favored immigrants from northern and western Europe. Countries outside the Western Hemisphere were limited to a total of 170,000 immigrants a year, with no more than 20,000 from any one country. Another 120,000 could enter the United States from countries in the Western Hemisphere.

After this law went into effect, the main sources of immigration to the United States changed. Since 1965 most immigrants have come from Mexico and from such Asian countries as the Philippines, Korea, and Vietnam.

More blacks in government   Even after the Civil Rights Act of 1964, southern blacks found it difficult to vote. This was because many local officials used various methods to keep them from registering. Therefore, President Johnson got Congress to pass the Voting Rights Act of 1965. This law said that when local officials refused to do the job of registering voters fairly, federal officials would step in and do it.

This law proved to be effective. In less than a year, the number of southern blacks who were registered to vote jumped by 40 percent. Soon more blacks were seeking office. In 1983 some 5,400 blacks held office in the United States, and half of them were in the South. Blacks became mayors of such great cities as Cleveland, Atlanta, New Orleans, Detroit, Los Angeles, Chicago, and Philadelphia.

In addition, President Johnson appointed blacks to major posts in the federal government. Robert Weaver, a housing expert, became the first black Cabinet officer when he was named to head the Department of Housing and Urban Development. Thurgood Marshall was named to the Supreme Court, the first black to serve on that body.

Rioting in the ghettos   The civil rights movement brought great changes to much of America and especially to the South.

Robert Weaver, the first black Cabinet member, poses with President Lyndon Johnson, who appointed him.

However, the laws of the 1960s had little to do with the daily problems of millions who lived in black **ghettos** of northern, midwestern, and western cities. A ghetto is a section of a city in which members of a minority group live. The reality of their lives was crowded, run-down housing; drug dealers; crime; and high unemployment, especially among young people.

Many ghetto dwellers felt they were treated unfairly by white landlords, merchants, and the police. In 1965, anger boiled over in Watts, the black ghetto of Los Angeles. For 6 days, black residents rioted, burning property and looting stores. Before the riot finally ended, 28 black people were dead, hundreds of white-owned buildings were destroyed, and the homes of many black residents lay in ashes.

Watts turned out to be but the first of many ghetto riots. Between 1965 and 1967 there were riots in more than 70

cities. Those in the summer of 1967 were the worst in American history. In Detroit, block after block was leveled.

After the Detroit rioting, President Johnson appointed a special commission to study the causes of the riots. The commission was headed by Governor Otto Kerner of Illinois. The report of the Kerner Commission warned, "Our nation is moving toward two societies, one black, one white—separate and unequal."

President Johnson tried to get Congress to pass additional civil rights legislation. But by this time, resistance among many whites to more civil rights laws was growing. This resistance was called *white backlash*. Congress did pass a Fair Housing Act in 1968, forbidding discrimination in renting or selling houses. But it did not pass any other civil rights laws.

In April 1968, Martin Luther King went to Memphis, Tennessee, to support a sanitation workers' strike. Many workers believed they were being paid poorly because they were black. Only a few years before, King had received the Nobel Peace Prize as a champion of nonviolence. At Memphis he urged the workers to seek their goals without practicing violence. On April 4, Dr. King was shot and killed. During the next week, blacks in more than 100 cities exploded in anger at the killing of their leader.

CHECKUP

1. What did the Civil Rights Act of 1964 provide for?
2. Name and describe five of Lyndon Johnson's Great Society programs.
3. How was immigration changed by the law passed in 1965?
4. Why did riots occur in many cities in the middle years of the 1960s?

Ask pupils to explain the warning of the Kerner Commission: "Our nation is moving toward two societies, one black, one white—separate and unequal." Then ask: Has this statement become more or less true since it was made in 1967? Can you give specific examples to back your opinion?

The Vietnam War remains an emotional issue in our society. There are those who believe that it was the biggest mistake in our history. Others believe that the United States could have won the war. Invite speakers from both sides to address your class and let your pupils make judgments.

Vietnam

┌─ VOCABULARY ─────────────────┐
domino theory   Vietnamization
Gulf of Tonkin
   Resolution
└──────────────────────────────┘

Turmoil in Indochina   During Lyndon Johnson's presidency the United States became deeply involved in a war thousands of miles from home. The war deeply divided the American people. It was not a war that Johnson wanted. Yet step by step, the decisions he made drew the United States further into it. And in the end, the war in Vietnam (vē et näm′) wrecked his presidency.

The Southeast Asian countries of Vietnam, Laos (lä′ ōs) and Cambodia (now known as Kampuchea) are part of an area once called Indochina. Indochina was a French colony from the mid-1800s to World War II, when the Japanese took it over. After the war, France tried to regain control. But the people of Indochina wanted to be free of foreign rule. Ho Chi Minh (hō chē min′), a Vietnamese Communist, was a leader of the independence movement. His group, the Vietminh (vē et min′), fought against the French for the next 8 years, from 1946 to 1954. Ho's rebels received aid from the Soviet Union and Communist China. The United States helped the French with millions of dollars in arms and supplies.

In the spring of 1954, the Vietminh delivered a crushing defeat to the French armies. The following month the major European powers and representatives of the peoples of Indochina met in Geneva, Switzerland. It was agreed that the French would withdraw from Indochina and that the area would be divided into three countries—Laos, Vietnam, and Cambodia. Vietnam would, temporarily, be further divided into two parts. Communists led by Ho would control North Vietnam, the area north of 17° latitude. South Vietnam, the part below 17°, would be controlled by an anti-Communist government. After 2 years, Vietnam would hold national elections to unite the country under a single government.

The elections never took place. The South Vietnam government was headed by a strong anti-Communist named Ngo Dinh Diem (əngō dēn dyem). Fearing that the Communists would win the election, Diem refused to go through with it. Instead, he declared South Vietnam to be an independent country, with himself as its president.

Ho Chi Minh, a leader in the fight against France, set up a Communist government in North Vietnam.

In support of South Vietnam   The United States became the chief supporter of the anti-Communist South Vietnamese government. This was during the height of the cold war, and the policy of the United States was to contain Soviet communism and influence. President Eisenhower likened the countries of Southeast Asia to a row of standing dominoes. If one was knocked over, the others—Cambodia, Laos, Thailand, and others—would each fall in turn. If the United States was to contain communism, it must keep the first domino, South Vietnam, from falling. This belief came to be known as the **domino theory.**

Following this idea, the United States sent millions of dollars in military aid and supplies to South Vietnam. President Eisenhower also sent 600 Americans to help train South Vietnam's troops. Russia and China, meanwhile, continued to aid North Vietnam.

Unfortunately, Diem's government began to lose the support of the people in South Vietnam. Communist guerrillas, called the Vietcong (vē et kông'), moved into the countryside. North Vietnam sent supplies to the Vietcong. By the early 1960s, while John F. Kennedy was President, some of North Vietnam's troops had also moved south to fight beside the Vietcong. Kennedy increased American aid during his 3 years in office. He also sent more military and civilian advisers. By the end of 1963, there were nearly 17,000 American advisers in South Vietnam. Some of them were accompanying South Vietnamese troops into battle.

By the time Lyndon Johnson became President, the South Vietnamese were almost completely dependent upon American military and economic aid. Still the fighting went badly for them. A new government of military leaders replaced that of Diem, but this did not help. President

In preparation for a move, United States troops assemble on a beach in Vietnam.

Johnson's advisers warned that without a great increase in American help, South Vietnam would lose.

The Gulf of Tonkin Resolution   In August 1964, the United States Navy reported that North Vietnamese torpedo boats had fired on two American destroyers in the Gulf of Tonkin (tän′ kin) off North Vietnam. President Johnson asked Congress to approve a resolution allowing him to "take all necessary measures" to turn back "any armed attack against the forces of the United States and to prevent further aggression." This was known as the **Gulf of Tonkin Resolution.** Congress passed it overwhelmingly.

American involvement now increased rapidly. In February 1965, Johnson ordered American bombers to start bombing North Vietnam. In April he ordered American troops into combat. More men were drafted into the army. By 1968, there were more than 500,000 American troops in Vietnam.

Opposition to the war grows   All through 1966 and 1967, there were many predictions of victory. But victory did not come. At first a majority of the American people supported America's involvement. However, as the war dragged on and the number of American dead and wounded mounted, opposition grew. In the beginning, opponents of the war were mostly young people. Later, however, they included people of all ages.

Many believed that the war was a civil war among the Vietnamese people and should be settled by them. Others objected to supporting the South Vietnamese

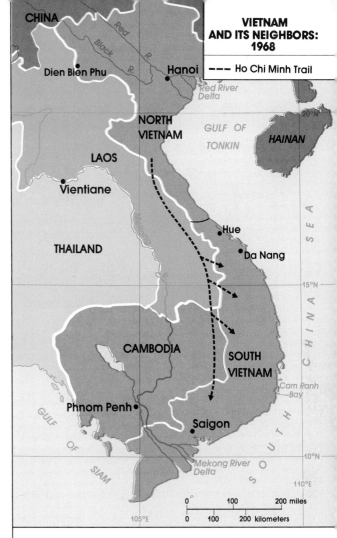

After the French withdrew, Vietnam was split into Communist and non-Communist areas.

government, which was a dictatorship. Although many thousands of young men volunteered for service, other thousands went to prison or moved to other countries rather than fight in what they believed was an unjust war. Not since the Civil War had the American people been so divided.

The Tet offensive   At the end of January 1968, on the Vietnamese New Year's holiday called Tet, the Communists launched a big offensive throughout South Vietnam. They attacked 30 major

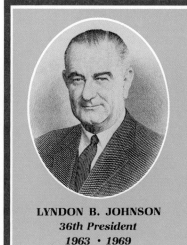

Born: 1908, near Stonewall, Texas. **Education:** Southwest Texas State Teachers College. **Training:** Teacher, public official. **To presidency from:** Texas. **Position when taking office:** Vice President. **Political party:** Democratic. **Married:** Claudia "Lady Bird" Taylor. **Children:** Two daughters. **Died:** 1973, San Antonio, Texas. **Other facts:** A star debater in high school. Taught public speaking and debating as a high school teacher. Entered politics as secretary to a Texas congressman. At age 44 became leader of his party in the Senate, the youngest man ever chosen for that position. **During his presidency:** In 1965 the federal government for the first time embarked on a major program of aid to elementary and secondary schools.

LYNDON B. JOHNSON
36th President
1963 · 1969

cities, taking a number of them. There was even fighting at the gates of the United States embassy in Saigon, the capital city.

American and South Vietnamese forces recovered and hit back. During the following months, they wiped out most of the gains of the Tet offensive, and the North Vietnamese and Vietcong suffered heavy losses. Yet the Communists still controlled much of the countryside. It was clear that the United States government's rosy statements about an early end to the war with the Communist forces were not correct.

A troubled period   Opposition to the war in the United States grew stronger. Early in 1968, two Democratic senators, Eugene McCarthy of Minnesota and Robert F. Kennedy of New York, announced that they would oppose Lyndon Johnson for the party's nomination for President. At the end of March, President Johnson told the nation in a televised speech that the United States would stop bombing North Vietnam and would seek to settle the war through peace talks. He

ended the speech with the surprise announcement that he would not run for reelection.

The nation was in for further shocks. In June 1968, Senator Kennedy was shot and killed by a Jordanian immigrant who opposed his support for Israel. This was just 2 months after Martin Luther King was gunned down and less than 5 years after Kennedy's brother, President John F. Kennedy, was murdered.

In the summer of 1968, Democrats met in Chicago to choose their candidate. With antiwar demonstrators battling police outside the convention hall, the Democrats chose Vice President Hubert H. Humphrey to run for President. Meanwhile the Republican party chose former Vice President Richard Nixon to run again. Humphrey had long been a popular Democrat, but he lost support because the public connected him with Johnson's war policies. A third party candidate, Governor George Wallace of Alabama, drew millions of votes by appealing to many who opposed the civil rights movement. In the November election, Nixon won by a narrow margin.

Assign pupils to do research in the library and to give brief reports to the class on each of the following people who played parts in the Vietnam War: Ho Chi Minh, Lyndon Johnson, General William Westmoreland, Henry Kissinger, Nguyen Van Thieu, and Eugene McCarthy.

Vietnamization During the presidential campaign, Nixon promised to end the war in Vietnam "with honor," while assuring that South Vietnam would remain independent and non-communist. In 1969 he announced his plan to do this. He called his plan **Vietnamization.** The United States would train and equip South Vietnamese troops to take over the fighting. This would free American troops to withdraw gradually from Vietnam. Meanwhile, the United States would provide air support for the troops and would renew the bombing of North Vietnam. President Nixon announced that the first 25,000 troops would leave Vietnam by the end of August 1969.

During the next 3 years, the United States carried out this plan for winding down the war. By the end of 1972, fewer than 25,000 American troops re-

American doctors and medics in Vietnam did not confine their services to members of the armed forces.

mained in Vietnam. At the same time, the United States Air Force continued its heavy bombing of North Vietnam.

Moving into Cambodia Meanwhile, President Nixon ordered bombing attacks on Vietcong supply lines and bases in Cambodia, a neutral country. The President kept these bombings secret from Congress and the American public. Then in April 1970 he revealed that he had sent troops into Cambodia to search out and destroy Vietcong bases there.

The news that the war had been widened led to new and angrier protests at home, especially at colleges. At Kent State University in Ohio, National Guard troops shot and killed four students during an antiwar demonstration. Police killed two students in another protest at Jackson State College in Mississippi.

Meanwhile, Congress cut off funds for any further operations in Cambodia. It also voted to repeal the Gulf of Tonkin Resolution. But neither of these actions could now have any effect upon the war.

The war ends In 1972, President Nixon sent his national security adviser, Henry Kissinger, to meet secretly with representatives from North Vietnam. These meetings finally led to a cease-fire in January 1973. The United States agreed to pull its remaining military forces out of Vietnam. The North Vietnamese agreed to return all American prisoners of war. Less than 2 months later, the last American troops left Vietnam. The war had cost over 57,000 American lives. Another 300,000 Americans had been wounded.

679

The Vietnam War was the longest in American history. It cost $139.9 billion. Only World War II was more costly. The Communists lost at least 937,000 soldiers, but they gained control of South Vietnam, Laos, and Cambodia (Kampuchea).

Vietnamization succeeded in getting American troops out of Vietnam. However, it did not succeed in keeping South Vietnam independent. Fighting between North and South Vietnam soon broke out again. In the spring of 1975, South Vietnamese forces suddenly crumbled, and North Vietnam troops overran the entire country. At the same time, Communists in Cambodia took control of that country. Thousands fled from South Vietnam, with more than 100,000 coming to America.

CHECKUP

1. How did Vietnam come to be divided along the 17th parallel north?
2. How did the United States become involved in Vietnam?
3. In what ways did the war in Vietnam divide the American people?
4. What were the results of the war?

The Rise and Fall of Richard Nixon

VOCABULARY

détente   perjury

Reducing tensions   When Richard Nixon became President, he said that the great powers were moving "from an era of confrontation"—that is, facing each other with hostility—"to an era of negotiation." Some people doubted that Nixon meant what he said. After all, during the cold war, Nixon was known as a strong anti-Communist who was against compromising with the Russians. However, Nixon surprised his critics by negotiating with Communist countries. He and Henry Kissinger sought to reduce tensions with the Soviet Union and lessen the chances of nuclear war. This policy was called **détente** (dā tänt'), which is a French word that means "relaxing of tensions."

In 1969 the United States and the Soviet Union started talks aimed at limiting nuclear arms. The meetings were called the Strategic Arms Limitation Talks (SALT). After more than 2 years, the two sides agreed to put a limit on building offensive weapons for a 5-year period. In 1972, President Nixon journeyed to Moscow to sign this agreement, which became known as the SALT I treaty. Nixon and the Soviet leader, Leonid Brezhnev (brezh' nef), also signed agreements to cooperate in health research, the exploration of space, and protection of the environment. Though the SALT I treaty did not end the arms race, it was a forward step.

A new China policy   No action of President Nixon's surprised more people than his reversal of the United States's policy toward the People's Republic of China.

In 1972, President Richard Nixon and Soviet leader Leonid Brezhnev reached agreement on several issues.

The Moon Landing

"Tranquility Base here. The *Eagle* has landed." The words of Commander Neil A. Armstrong crackled across 240,000 miles (384,000 km) of space to planet Earth. The date was July 20, 1969, the time 4:17 P.M., Eastern Daylight Time. Some 6 1/2 hours later, Armstrong stepped out of the space capsule *Eagle* and onto the surface of the moon. Back on Earth a billion people watched the scene on television.

The next day, Armstrong and Edwin E. "Buzz" Aldrin, Jr., explored the moon's surface, collected rocks, and performed experiments. After 21 1/2 hours they rejoined astronaut Michael Collins on the orbiting spaceship for the return of Apollo 11 to Earth.

The space voyage of Armstrong, Aldrin, and Collins was one of the greatest feats of exploration in history. It was also one of the great feats of science. For 8 years, thousands of scientists, engineers, and workers had teamed up to make their moment of triumph possible.

The moon landing was a victory for the United States in the space race with the Soviet Union. Commander

Astronaut Buzz Aldrin stands by the American flag planted on the moon during the historic trip of Apollo 11 in July 1969.

Armstrong, however, viewed the achievement in broader terms. As he first set foot on the moon, he said, "That's one small step for a man, one giant leap for mankind."

Throughout the 1950s and 1960s, the United States regarded Mao's government as an enemy and had no dealings with it. We continued to recognize the Nationalist government on Taiwan as the legal government of China. The People's Republic was equally hostile toward the United States.

However, during these same years, relations between China and Russia, the two large Communist countries, chilled. By the late 1960s, China felt that Russia, not the United States, was its greatest enemy. It sought to improve relations with the United States. Nixon had been one of the strongest foes of the Chinese Communists. However, he decided it was now in America's interest to improve relations with that country. For 20 years the United States had refused to agree that the People's Republic of China should replace the Nationalists as China's representative in the United Nations. In 1971, the United States eased its opposition, and the government of the People's Republic was awarded China's UN seat.

A few months later, in February 1972, President Nixon visited Peking (pē king'), the capital of the People's Republic of China. There he and the Chinese leaders took the first steps toward restoring normal relations between the two countries. They agreed to allow cultural exchanges and a limited amount of trade. However, they continued to disagree on the future of Taiwan. While agreeing that Taiwan was part of China, the United States defended the right of the Nationalists to rule it. Following this "opening up" of China, many Americans and Chinese traveled to each other's countries to visit, study, and do business.

War in the Middle East   The Middle East continued to be a threat to world peace in the 1960s and 1970s. With Egyptian President Gamal Abdel Nasser calling on Arabs to wage a "holy war" against Israel, fighting once again broke out in June 1967. Israel was victorious in the Six Day War against Egypt, Jordan, and Syria. Israeli forces captured the Sinai Peninsula and the Gaza Strip from Egypt, drove the Syrians off the Golan Heights, and gained control of the West Bank of the Jordan River.

Despite a cease-fire, real peace was nowhere in sight. By the late 1960s the Arab states were being rearmed by the Soviet Union, their chief supplier of weapons. The United States, meanwhile, provided Israel with jet planes and other weapons.

When Nixon became President, the United States tried to improve its relations with the Arab nations. Although still supporting Israel, the Nixon administration said it would follow a more "even-handed" policy between Israel and the Arabs, not favoring one over the other. Nixon's reasons for the policy were these: First, he hoped to use American influence to prevent another war, for there was danger that the superpowers might be drawn into such fighting. The second reason was that Arab countries supplied Western nations and the United States with much of their oil. It was important to assure that this supply would continue and that

A young Iranian herds his sheep near one of the many pipelines that carry oil to Middle Eastern ports. There it is loaded on tankers for transport to many nations.

is pressured into returning it to Egypt. (3) On June 5, 1967, Israel attacks Egypt, beginning the third Arab-Israeli war (the Six Day War). Israel occupies the West Bank of the Jordan and the Sinai. (4) A Syrian-Egyptian attack in October 1973 begins the fourth Arab-Israeli war. Jointly sponsored American and

the large investment of American oil companies in the region was protected.

On October 6, 1973, the Jewish holy day of Yom Kippur, Egypt and Syria suddenly attacked Israel. Using arms supplied by the Soviets, they were able to drive back the Israelis, who suffered heavy losses in men and weapons. However, an emergency shipment of arms from the United States helped the Israelis turn the tide of battle. Israeli forces drove into Egypt before Russia, the United States, and the United Nations induced them to accept a truce. During the following months, Henry Kissinger, who was now secretary of state, played a key role in getting Israel and Egypt to pull back their forces. United Nations troops were placed between them.

An oil embargo   To punish the United States for helping Israel, some Arab countries placed an embargo on oil shipments to the United States and several other Western countries during the war. Although fighting ended in November, they kept the embargo on for another 4 months, causing shortages of gasoline and heating oil. Meanwhile, the Arab and other oil-producing countries raised oil prices sharply, from $2 to $11 a barrel, in less than a year. These countries were members of the Organization of Petroleum Exporting Countries (OPEC), which they had joined with the aim of getting better prices for their oil. The embargo gave them their opportunity.

A slowing economy   During President Nixon's first years in office, the economy slowed down. Unemployment rose.

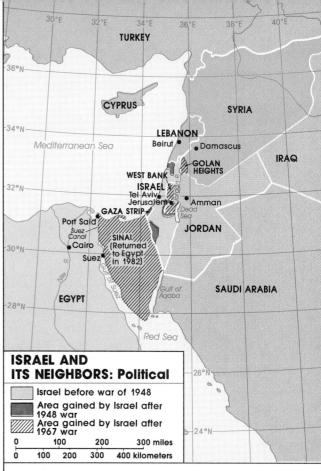

ISRAEL AND
ITS NEIGHBORS: Political

- Israel before war of 1948
- Area gained by Israel after 1948 war
- Area gained by Israel after 1967 war

0   100   200   300 miles
0 100 200 300 400 kilometers

The state of Israel was created out of the part of the Middle East once known as Palestine.

Most people didn't realize it at the time, but this slowdown marked the end of the 25-year era of prosperity that followed World War II. For the next decade or more, there would be little growth in the economy, and the problem of unemployment would continue.

These problems were accompanied by inflation. Heavy government spending for the war in Vietnam and for new social programs helped cause a big rise in prices. In 1971, Nixon tried to end the inflation by putting a 90-day freeze on wages and prices. This was followed by wage and price controls like those used during World War II. These measures slowed

Soviet cease-fire resolutions passed by the UN Security Council stop the fighting. (5) In 1978 President Carter succeeds in organizing the Camp David talks between Egypt and Israel. In March 1979 an Egyptian-Israeli peace treaty is signed. (6) Continuing PLO and terrorist attacks cause Israel to invade Lebanon four times in 1975, 1978, 1980, and 1982.

683

Students register to vote after the voting age was dropped to 18 during the Nixon administration.

By the time Nixon took office, great progress had been made in desegregating schools in the South. In some parts of the North, however, progress was slow. There, no Jim Crow laws existed. But some city school boards kept schools segregated by drawing school boundaries along racial lines. To end segregation, federal courts, therefore, began to order the busing of students from one school district to another. Many people favored busing as a tool to end segregation, but many others were opposed. President Nixon was one of these. He asked Congress to stop the courts from ordering busing. Congress refused, however, and court-ordered busing continued.

The Watergate break-in In 1972, Richard Nixon ran for reelection against Democrat George McGovern. The President's foreign-policy successes won him much support. Nixon won one of the greatest election victories in history, carrying every state but one.

Less than 2 years after his victory, Nixon resigned from office in disgrace. His troubles began when five burglars were caught breaking into the offices of the Democratic National Committee in Watergate, a group of apartment and office buildings in Washington, D.C. Police learned that the five were working with two other men who had ties to Nixon's reelection campaign committee and to the White House. The burglars were looking for documents that would help bring about the defeat of the Democrats in the fall campaign.

President Nixon was not involved in the plan for the break-in. However, when

inflation for a time. However, when the controls were removed a year later, prices climbed again.

Revenue sharing and busing President Nixon also proposed a plan to share the federal government's revenues with the states. Under this plan adopted by Congress, the federal government each year gave a sum of money to each state to use as it saw fit in dealing with its problems. The President also proposed laws to start cleaning up air and water pollution. However, he was not in favor of many of the social programs begun under Lyndon Johnson, and he tried to reduce federal support for them.

Jr., broke into the office of Ellsberg's psychiatrist and photographed documents. In May 1972, members of the group broke into the headquarters of the Democratic National Committee in the Watergate complex in Washington, D.C. to gather information. They were caught and arrested, and Hunt's White House

he learned what happened, he tried to cover up the connection between the people in his administration and the crime. He blocked an FBI investigation, and he approved the payment of "hush money" to the burglars so they wouldn't talk. He also seems to have promised to get them out of jail after a short time if they would remain silent. The President told his staff to stonewall investigators—that is, to tell them nothing. Under the law, such attempts to block justice are crimes.

All this was done secretly. Publicly, the President dismissed the matter as a "third-rate burglary." He said his administration had nothing to do with it. However, a few newspaper reporters began to dig up the facts. Then in January 1973, the five Watergate burglars and the two who directed them were tried and found guilty. Six of the men stuck to their story that they had acted on their own. But the seventh admitted to Judge John Sirica that the burglary had been approved by people high up in the White House. Now the Senate set up a special committee, headed by Senator Sam Ervin of North Carolina, to investigate. Still denying any connection with Watergate, President Nixon appointed a Harvard law professor, Archibald Cox, as a special government prosecutor to investigate.

The Senate hearings The televised Senate hearings began in May 1973. John Dean, a former Nixon aide, told the committee that Nixon officials were connected not only with the Watergate burglary but with other illegal activities aimed at opponents of the President. He said that the President had taken part in covering up the facts.

In the spring of 1973 the televised hearings of a special Senate committee set up to investigate the Watergate affair held the attention of Americans everywhere.

phone number was found on two of the burglars. A White House cover-up began immediately. A congressional committee investigating the charges was able to prove President Nixon's involvement in the cover-up almost from the beginning.

RICHARD M. NIXON
37th President
1969 · 1974

Born: 1913, Yorba Linda, California. **Education:** Whittier College. **Training:** Lawyer, public official. **To presidency from:** New York. **Position when elected:** Member of a New York City law firm. **Political party:** Republican. **Married:** Thelma "Pat" Ryan. **Children:** Two daughters. **Other facts:** A naval officer in the Pacific in World War II. Served in both houses of Congress. As Vice President under Eisenhower, toured nearly 60 countries. Defeated in run for presidency in 1960 but elected in 1968. Only President ever to resign from office. Did so when faced, in 1974, with almost certain impeachment for his part in Watergate scandal. **During his presidency:** The Twenty-sixth Amendment to the Constitution lowered the voting age from 21 to 18.

Who was telling the truth? For a time it seemed there might be no way to find out. Then a witness revealed that President Nixon had secretly tape-recorded all conversations in his White House office. Everyone quickly realized that the tapes probably held answers to the key questions: How much did the President know? When did he know it? Was John Dean's testimony truthful?

For the next year, there was a tug-of-war over the tapes. On one side were the Senate committee, special prosecutor Cox, and Judge Sirica. On the other was President Nixon. Nixon claimed that a President had the right to keep his records confidential. He called this right "executive privilege." He ordered Cox, his own appointee, to stop asking for the tapes and other records. When Cox continued to press for them, Nixon ordered him dismissed. This touched off such a storm of public criticism that Nixon finally turned over a few tapes to Judge Sirica. This did his cause no good, for one of the tapes had a gap of 18½ minutes. Experts said the tape had been deliberately erased.

Agnew resigns In the midst of all these troubles, Americans received another shock to their faith in their government. A separate investigation turned up evidence that Vice President Spiro Agnew had taken bribes as governor of Maryland and had also cheated on his income taxes. Agnew then resigned from office.

Under the Twenty-fifth Amendment to the Constitution, which had been added in 1967, President Nixon named Gerald Ford to serve as Vice President. Ford was a leading Republican member of the House of Representatives.

Nixon resigns Meanwhile, the Watergate cover-up was falling apart. In the spring of 1974, former Attorney General John Mitchell, two of Nixon's closest aides, and four other White House officials were charged with obstructing justice and with **perjury**, or lying under oath. They were later convicted and sent to prison.

The House Judiciary Committee began hearings on whether Nixon should be impeached—that is, charged with crimes that could lead to his removal from office. The committee demanded more tapes. Nixon refused to turn them over. Instead, he gave the committee written copies of some of the tapes. But the copies left out the material the committee was seeking. The Judiciary Committee then recommended that the House of Representatives impeach Nixon for obstructing justice and misusing presidential power.

A few days later, the Supreme Court ruled that President Nixon must give up the tapes. Nixon now admitted that the tapes showed he had been part of the cover-up almost from the start. Faced with almost certain impeachment and conviction, Nixon resigned as President on August 9, 1974. Gerald Ford became President. He was the first to serve in that office who had not been elected either President or Vice President.

Ford succeeds Nixon   On taking office, Gerald Ford told the American people, "Our long national nightmare is over. Our Constitution works." Ford was referring to the system of checks and balances in the American government. A President had abused the power of his office; the courts and Congress had risen up to check him. The Constitution did, indeed, work.

President Ford himself did much to restore public confidence in the government. He was an open, honest, and friendly man. However, he angered many people when he granted Richard Nixon a full pardon for any crimes he might have committed as President. Ford said it was important for the nation to put Watergate behind it and to look ahead to dealing

Gerald Ford, who succeeded Richard Nixon as President, is sworn in by Chief Justice Warren Burger.

with its problems. Many Americans, however, felt that if Nixon had broken the law, he should stand trial like any other citizen. In the end, more than 50 people in the Nixon administration were fined or sent to jail for their part in Watergate.

The Watergate scandal was the last in the series of shocks that Americans experienced in the 1960s and 1970s—assassinations, war, inflation, an oil embargo. As they prepared to celebrate the two-hundredth birthday of their nation in 1976, Americans hoped that the time of shocks was finally over.

CHECKUP

1. What change did President Nixon bring about in our policy toward China?
2. What events in the Middle East brought on an oil embargo?
3. What was the purpose of each of the following programs: (a) revenue sharing, (b) busing?
4. What event touched off the Watergate affair?
5. Why did President Nixon resign?

KEY FACTS

1. Under President Lyndon Johnson's leadership, Congress enacted the most sweeping reforms since the New Deal.

2. Important gains were made in civil rights during the 1960s, yet many black Americans continued to live in poverty.

3. The United States became deeply involved during the 1960s in a costly and unpopular war in Vietnam.

4. President Richard Nixon's foreign policy brought improved relations with the Soviet Union and the People's Republic of China.

5. President Nixon's part in the Watergate scandal wrecked his presidency and caused him to resign from office.

VOCABULARY QUIZ

On a sheet of paper write the letter of the term next to the number of its definition. There are two extra definitions that will not match any of the terms.

a. ghetto

b. Vietnamization

c. Civil Rights Act of 1964

d. domino theory

e. détente

f. Great Society

g. Project Apollo

h. Gulf of Tonkin Resolution

i. perjury

j. Medicare

c **1.** A law that, among other things, prohibited racial discrimination in businesses serving the public.

h **2.** An act that gave the President authority to take military action in Vietnam

b **3.** A plan that permitted American troops to withdraw gradually from Vietnam

i **4.** Lying under oath

5. A project in which volunteers help people in poor areas

f **6.** What Johnson called his reform program

a **7.** A crowded area where minorities live

e **8.** A relaxing of tensions between the United States and Communist countries

9. Talks between the United States and the Soviet Union on limiting arms

d **10.** The idea that the fall of one Southeast Asian country to communism would cause others to fall

j **11.** An act providing health care for the aged

g **12.** A program aimed at putting an astronaut on the moon

REVIEW QUESTIONS

1. What effect did the Voting Rights Act of 1965 have?

2. How did the continuing war in Vietnam affect Lyndon Johnson's political career?

3. Tell what each of the following stands for: **a**) OPEC, **b**) SALT, **c**) VISTA.

4. How did the oil embargo affect Americans?

5. Tell how each of the following terms was related to the Watergate affair: **a**) executive privilege, **b**) hush money, **c**) stonewall, **d**) "third-rate burglary," **e**) 18½-minute gap.

ACTIVITIES

1. Interview family, friends, and others to learn what kinds of protest took place during the war in Vietnam. You may also use your library for finding out about this period.

2. List the many ways in which Americans conserved oil during and after the embargo.

3. Find out when and why the Twenty-fifth Amendment was added to the Constitution.

4. Make a chart in which you show the important steps in the United States space program from 1957 to 1969.

30/SKILLS DEVELOPMENT

CLASSIFYING

GROUPING ITEMS AND IDEAS

Classifying means "grouping things according to what they have in common." For example, look at this list.

airplane
covered wagon
Model T
the *Clermont*
transcontinental railroad

These five items have been taken from different periods in history. However, you will quickly see that they have something in common. They are all means by which people travel from one place to another. They could be classified as means of transportation.

Often, items or things will fit more than one classification. For example, here is a list of laws and programs mentioned in Chapter 30.

Civil Rights Act of 1964
VISTA
Medicare
Voting Rights Act of 1965
Job Corps
Fair Housing Act of 1968

You might classify these items under the heading *Laws and Programs of the Johnson Presidency*. Three of these items—Civil Rights Act of 1964, Voting Rights Act of 1965, and Fair Housing Act of 1968—could be classified as civil rights laws. You might put VISTA and Job Corps under the heading *Aid to the Needy*.

Why classify? Classifying helps you to see connections. Making connections helps you to understand and to remember.

SKILLS PRACTICE

On a sheet of paper write the following headings.

a. Space Program 1, 7, 8, 12, 14
b. Vietnam War 4, 9, 10
c. Watergate 3, 10, 15
d. Civil Rights Movement 5, 13, 16
e. Johnson's "Great Society" 2, 6, 11

Classify the items below by writing the number of the item under the correct heading. Some items may fit under more than one heading. If you need help, skim back through Chapter 30.

1. Apollo
2. Medicare
3. Archibald Cox
4. Tet offensive
5. Martin Luther King, Jr.
6. Head Start
7. Project Mercury
8. Gemini
9. Vietnamization
10. Richard Nixon
11. Food stamp program
12. John Glenn
13. Kerner Commission
14. Cape Canaveral
15. John Sirica
16. Thurgood Marshall

31 America Today and Tomorrow

The Struggle for Equality Broadens

VOCABULARY

migrant	Women's Liberation movement
barrio	
commonwealth	termination

"Changing the situation"   Cesar and Helen Chavez (chä′ vās) made an important decision in 1962. Although they had eight children to support, they agreed that Cesar should give up his good-paying steady job and spend all his time organizing California's poor **migrant** farm workers—people who traveled from one farm to another to find work planting, cultivating, and harvesting crops. Most of these farm workers were, like Cesar and Helen Chavez, Mexican Americans. They received very low pay and had bad working conditions. As Cesar later explained, "It's easier for a person just to escape . . . poverty, than to change the situation [that creates poverty]." Cesar and Helen decided to try to "change the situation."

At about the same time, a woman living in a suburb of New York City was also trying to change the situation. Her name was Betty Friedan (frē dan′), and she was writing a book. From childhood onward, Friedan wrote, females were taught to think of themselves only as wives and mothers. Males, on the other hand, were taught that they would do "man's work" and become the leaders in business and politics. Such teaching about sex roles, wrote Betty Friedan, had limited women's chances to reach their full potential as human beings. Her book, *The Feminine Mystique*, came out in 1963.

Just a few years later, Vine Deloria, Jr., decided that he, too, must change the situation. Deloria had been born on the Pine Ridge Indian Reservation in South Dakota and was a member of the Standing Rock Sioux (sü) tribe. He decided to become a lawyer so that he could help small Indian tribes and communities like the Standing Rock Sioux gain their rights. While still in law school, Deloria wrote a book called *Custer Died For Your Sins*. It reminded white America of its treatment of Indians over the centuries. It also declared the Indians' goal of preserving their way of life.

Cesar Chavez, Betty Friedan, and Vine Deloria, Jr., were three people from different backgrounds, and from different walks of life. But all three had a single goal—to change the situation. Along with leaders like Martin Luther King, Jr., and representatives of other minorities, they were part of the struggle to achieve equal rights for all. They wanted to help fulfill the promise of America.

The Statue of Liberty, symbol of American democracy, stands on Liberty Island in New York Harbor. It was a gift to the United States from the people of France.

Assign individual pupils to research and report to the class on the careers of Cesar Chavez, Betty Friedan, Vine Deloria, Jr., and other leaders in the 1960s who struggled for greater equality in American society.

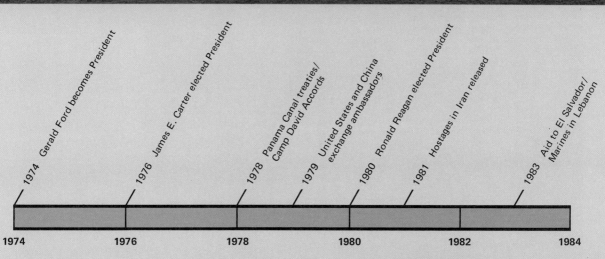

1974 Gerald Ford becomes President

1976 James E. Carter elected President

1978 Panama Canal treaties/
Camp David Accords

1979 United States and China
exchange ambassadors

1980 Ronald Reagan elected President

1981 Hostages in Iran released

1983 Aid to El Salvador/
Marines in Lebanon

1974   1976   1978   1980   1982   1984

In 1903 a poem by Emma Lazarus was inscribed in the pedestal of the statue. Have a pupil report on the poet and read her poem to the class. Use the poem to begin a class discussion on equality of opportunity in America.

Mexican Americans—a great migration

In the United States today there are some 20 million Spanish-speaking Americans, sometimes called Hispanics. They came originally from lands that were long ago colonized by Spain. These lands include Mexico, Puerto Rico, Cuba, and other countries in Central and South America and in the Caribbean Sea. Hispanics are the second largest minority in the United States. They are also the fastest-growing minority group.

The largest group of Spanish-speaking Americans are the Mexican Americans. They number some 11 or 12 million. Most live in the southwestern states. However, there are also large Mexican American communities in other parts of the country.

Some Mexican Americans are descended from families that lived in the American Southwest even before that land became part of the United States. Most, however, are part of the great migration from Mexico that began after 1900. This migration became especially large after 1940.

Many of the newcomers became migrant workers on large farms in California and Texas. These were the people Cesar Chavez decided to organize in 1962. He formed a union later known as the United Farm Workers (UFW). Chavez, like Martin Luther King, believed in nonviolence, and he insisted that his followers accept this principle.

In 1965 the farm workers went on strike against the grape growers in California. The strike lasted for 5 years, but in the end the UFW won improved wages and working conditions. In doing so, its members found a new dignity and self-respect.

Cesar Chavez talks to a group of migrant farm workers in California.

Today, although many Mexican Americans still work on farms, more than four out of five live in cities. In the cities as on the farms, they have experienced discrimination. Unemployment is high, and those who do find work often get the poorest-paying jobs. Many of these people live in poverty.

Most Mexican Americans in cities live in a separate neighborhood, which is called a **barrio.** Many people in the barrios continue to speak their native language and cling to their familiar culture, as many other immigrant groups have done. The Spanish language and culture have been a source of strength and of pride. At the same time they have led to some of the disadvantages that Mexican Americans have met in work and in education. Jobs that call for use of the English language are not open to those who speak only Spanish. Many have difficulty in school, where the language of instruction is English. This has led to debates about whether it is better to teach lessons in Spanish or to insist that students learn English. In an increasing number of schools today, both languages are being used. (Point out that *barrio* is the Spanish word for "neighborhood.")

Toney Anaya, a Mexican American, greets his supporters following his election as governor of New Mexico.

Mexican Americans make gains
Mexican Americans have begun to organize to improve their position and gain full rights. In 1965, the same year that Cesar Chavez led the farm workers out on strike, Rodolfo Gonzales (gon zä´ läs) started the Crusade for Justice in Denver, Colorado. The aim of the crusade was to gain full civil rights, increase job opportunities, and provide needed social services for Mexican Americans. In 1970, Mexican Americans in Texas started a political party called *La Raza Unida*, or "The United Race." Soon some of its candidates were winning election to local office in towns in Texas and other states in the Southwest.

Most Mexican Americans, however, worked for their goals through the two major political groups, the Democrats and the Republicans. By the 1980s, Mexican Americans were gaining a larger part in government. Several served in Congress. In New Mexico, Toney Anaya was the first Mexican American to be elected governor of an American state. In 1981, Henry Cisneros of San Antonio, Texas, became the first Mexican American mayor of a large city. As more Mexican Americans voted, they could expect to elect more candidates who would pay attention to their needs and wishes. They would also build on the gains already made toward winning equal rights and ending discrimination.

One of the founders of *La Raza Unida* was Jośe Angel Gutiérrez, a civil rights leader who felt that the Democratic and Republican parties ignored the needs of Mexican Americans. Have a pupil report to the class on Gutiérrez and his party.

693

The United States acquired Puerto Rico in 1898 after the Spanish-American War. Congress set up civil government on the island in 1900. Puerto Ricans became United States citizens in 1917. In 1952, Puerto Rico adopted its own constitution and became the self-governing Commonwealth of Puerto Rico, associated with the United States by its own desire.

Puerto Ricans to the mainland   The second largest Hispanic group is the Puerto Ricans. As you know, the island of Puerto Rico is part of the United States. Therefore, Puerto Ricans are American citizens whether they live on their home island or on the United States mainland. Puerto Rico has its own constitution, and its people govern themselves. Yet it is not a state but is called a **commonwealth.**

Since the 1940s Puerto Rico has made great strides in improving its economy. Even so, poverty and unemployment remain. Beginning after World War II, many Puerto Ricans decided to leave *la isla verde*—"the green island"—to look for work on the mainland. Today about 2 million people of Puerto Rican descent live on the mainland. A majority live in New York City, with most of the remainder in other cities of the Northeast. Like Mexican Americans, most Puerto Ricans live in barrios and cling to their native language and culture. And as in the case of Mexican Americans, this has been both an advantage and a disadvantage.

Puerto Ricans are slowly improving their position. Each year, larger numbers than before are going to college and getting good jobs. As more Puerto Ricans register to vote, they also gain political power. In 1970, Puerto Ricans in New York elected Herman Badillo (bä dē yō) to Congress, where he served for four terms. Puerto Ricans are also now serving in state legislatures and in many offices in their own communities.

Women seek equality   There are more women than men in the United States. Women are a majority group, not a minority group. Yet women have suffered from some of the same discrimination that minorities have known.

Although many women entered the work force in the 1950s and 1960s, they continued to find barriers to many fields. Few were promoted to high-level jobs— those that carried not only higher pay but also power to make important decisions. Women often were paid less than men for the same work. Rarely did a woman hold an important job in federal, state, or local government.

In 1966 some 300 women and men formed the National Organization for Women (NOW). They named Friedan as NOW's president. NOW's first goal was to help both men and women become more aware of the unequal treatment of women and to change their thinking about it. Action could then follow. Soon other groups also organized to promote equality for women. Some concentrated on the

Betty Friedan, Rosalynn Carter, and Betty Ford stand together in support of equal rights for women.

Since women outnumber men in the United States, it may seem odd to think of women as a minority group. Yet women workers suffer the same economic discrimination as other minority groups. Many fill the lowest paying jobs in industry. Black, Puerto Rican, and Mexican women are the most economically handicapped.

issue of jobs and pay. Others aimed at getting more women elected and appointed to public office. Still others focused on other areas of discrimination. Together, these efforts came to be called the **Women's Liberation movement**, or Women's Lib. Of course, not all women agreed with the goals of these groups. Many women said they felt entirely satisfied as wives and mothers and had no wish to change. Still, Women's Lib spoke for a growing number of women.

Led by NOW and other such groups, women made important gains in the 1960s and 1970s. They were aided by several laws and actions of the federal government. The Civil Rights Act of 1964 forbade discrimination not only on the grounds of race but also on the grounds of sex. By the early 1970s the government was actively enforcing this provision. By that time the federal government was also requiring that schools and colleges receiving federal money and companies doing business with the government must set goals for hiring qualified women and minorities. Another law of this period, the Equal Employment Opportunity Act of 1972, required employers to give equal pay to men and women for equal work.

Women's political goals   During the 1970s, thousands of women were elected and appointed to public office at all levels of government. Women served as governors and mayors and in the House of Representatives and the Senate. A growing number were appointed as judges. In 1981, Sandra Day O'Connor became the first woman justice of the Supreme Court of the United States.

Justice Sandra Day O'Connor swears in Margaret Heckler as secretary of health and human services in President Ronald Reagan's Cabinet. Beside Mrs. Heckler are her daughter and President Reagan.

The women's movement failed, however, to gain its political goal. This was an amendment to the Constitution that would ban all discrimination based on sex. In 1972, Congress passed the Equal Rights Amendment. It read: "Equality of rights under the law shall not be denied or abridged by the United States or by any state on account of sex." However, before the amendment could become part of the Constitution, three fourths of the states had to accept it. Many quickly did so.

Before long, an opposition was organized. Some of it came from women. One group, called Stop ERA, was headed by an Illinois woman named Phyllis Schlafly. Schlafly and others argued that ERA was not needed because women already had equal rights under the law. Adding this amendment, they said, might lead to more harm than good for women. They predicted it would weaken marriages and damage family life. They declared it

By 1975, 35 of the 38 states needed had ratified the proposed Equal Rights Amendment. But only one state did so after 1975. In 1978, Congress extended the deadline for ratification from March 22, 1979, to June 30, 1982.

The American Indian Movement (AIM) was militant and used tactics of direct confrontation in seeking full rights for Indians. The Wounded Knee protest caused much destruction of property and lost AIM the support of moderate Indians and many other people.

would wipe out legal protections in other laws that women had won over the years. Some feared it would lead to women being drafted into the army. Opponents succeeded in blocking ERA in a number of states. When the deadline for ratifying ERA came on June 30, 1982, only 35 states—3 short of the needed 38—had approved.

The struggle of Native Americans
You will remember that in 1934, Congress encouraged tribal landowning and tribal life for American Indians. In the early 1950s, however, the government changed its Indian policy once more. The new plan was called **termination.** *Terminate* means "to end." Under this plan, the federal government would end the reservation system. Lands would be divided among members of the tribe. The federal government would end the special health and education services it had long provided. Native Americans were to be encouraged to move to the cities, where they would enter the mainstream of American life.

Termination made things worse, not better, for most Native Americans. Many who left the reservations for the cities could not find jobs. They also found it hard to adjust to the "cement prairies" and strange ways of living. President Eisenhower ended the new policy soon after it started.

Many Indian leaders wanted the government to restore the reservation system and to provide more assistance in housing, education, and health. They believed, as Vine Deloria did, that tribal life should be strengthened so that Indians could preserve their cultural heritage. They also wanted Indians to choose their own people to run their reservations.

To work for these goals, a number of Native Americans organized the American Indian Movement (AIM) in 1968. Some AIM members believed that only dramatic actions could win attention to the plight of their people. In 1972 a number of them took over the offices of the Bureau of Indian Affairs in Washington, D.C., for several days. The next year, armed AIM members took over the village of Wounded Knee, South Dakota, for more than 2 months. They demanded the return of lands taken from Indians over the centuries. They chose this spot for their action because Wounded Knee was the

Russell Means, the president of AIM, and Wallace White Elk were among those who demonstrated in the takeover of the village of Wounded Knee, South Dakota, in 1973.

Assign two pupils to research and report to the class on AIM leaders Russell Means and Wallace White Elk. Ask: *How did the tactics of the AIM leaders differ from those used by Cesar Chavez and Martin Luther King, Jr.?*

site of a battle in 1890 in which almost 200 Indians were killed by federal troops.

By the 1980s, Native Americans could point to a few gains. An act of Congress in 1975 gave them a greater voice in running their own reservations. They won several court cases in which they sued to get land returned to them. But for most Indians, life remained a struggle. The average Indian family continued to live in poverty and poor health.

Black Americans The year 1978 was the tenth anniversary of the death of Dr. Martin Luther King, Jr. It was also the tenth anniversary of the Kerner Commission's report on ghetto riots. A new study was made to see whether the situation of black Americans had changed much during that 10 years. The study reported important and dramatic changes in the position of many blacks. "As a whole, the nation's 25 million blacks have gained enormously in the last decade. . . . Many urban blacks, perhaps 30 percent, have worked their way into the middle class and have moved to the suburbs or to better housing within the cities." However, the study continued, for the millions left in the ghettos, the situation had not improved and may even have become worse. People lived in poverty, with little hope for the future.

These trends continued into the 1980s. By the middle of the decade, the percentage of blacks who went to college had caught up with that of whites. Black men and women were now entering fields that had long been closed to them. However, unemployment among black teenagers, mainly those who were not finishing

Vine Deloria, Jr., a Sioux Indian from South Dakota, has been a leader in the struggle for Indian rights.

school and not getting job training, was running between 40 and 50 percent. And on the average it remained true that blacks earned only a little more than half as much as whites.

In the mid-1980s, then, it was clear that the struggle to win equal rights and to improve the lives of all Americans was not yet ended. But it was equally clear that very great gains had been made and that the America of the 1980s was far different from the America of the 1950s.

CHECKUP

1. What two large Hispanic groups are included in the United States population?
2. In what ways are these groups similar? In what respects are they different?
3. What gains have women made in recent years?
4. What are the goals of Indian leaders for improving the lot of their people?
5. How did the position of black people in American society improve in the 1970s?

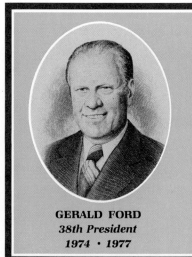

GERALD FORD
38th President
1974 · 1977

Born: 1913, Omaha, Nebraska. **Education:** University of Michigan. **Training:** Lawyer, public official. **To presidency from:** Michigan. **Position when taking office:** Vice President. **Political party:** Republican. **Married:** Elizabeth "Betty" Bloomer. **Children:** Three sons, one daughter. **Other facts:** A star football player in high school and college. Coached boxing and was an assistant football coach for 3 years at Yale. A naval officer in World War II. Served 13 terms in House of Representatives. Became Vice President by action of the President and Congress under the Twenty-third Amendment after resignation of Spiro Agnew in 1973. **During his presidency:** The United States in 1976 observed its bicentennial with celebrations in many communities.

The Carter Administration

VOCABULARY

solar energy	human rights
Camp David accords	SALT II
	hostage

A President from Georgia   In 1976, Gerald Ford decided to seek a full term as President. The Democrats chose a former governor of Georgia as their candidate. He was James Earl Carter, Jr., who preferred to be known as Jimmy Carter. An outsider to Washington politics, Carter campaigned as one who wanted to restore the people's faith in their government after Watergate. Continued unemployment and his pardon of Nixon cost Ford the support he needed. In a close election, Carter won the presidency.

President Carter appointed to his Cabinet and other high offices more women and members of minority groups than had any other President. He also took steps to protect the environment and reform the civil service system.

However, Carter and his aides did not work well with Congress. Thus, despite the fact that the President was intelligent and hard-working, he was not able to get Congress to accept a great many of his recommendations.

Providing for energy   When Carter took office in 1977, the country was importing half the oil it consumed, at a cost of many billions of dollars each year. Carter wanted to make the country less dependent on foreign oil. He proposed programs for conserving oil and gas, increasing the use of coal and nuclear power, and experimenting with **solar energy**—that is, harnessing the power of the sun. These goals were to be accomplished under the new Department of Energy. Congress created the new department, but it passed only a watered-down version of the President's energy plan.

Meanwhile, an accident occurred in 1979 at the nuclear power plant at Three Mile Island near Harrisburg, Pennsylvania. No one was injured, but most experts agreed that a disaster was only narrowly avoided. As a result of increasing public opposition to nuclear energy and high construction costs, most power com-

The Three Mile Island disaster was the worst nuclear accident in the United States. A hydrogen bubble formed in an overheated reactor, causing fear of a core meltdown. The worst fear did not occur, but the scare caused 3 days of panic.

panies put aside plans to build nuclear plants. Thus, in the 1980s it was clear that for many years to come, America would depend mainly on oil, gas, and coal for its energy.

The problem of inflation During President Carter's term, inflation became a more serious problem. From 1977 to 1981, oil-exporting countries raised the price of oil by a staggering 250 percent. That added to the cost of many other goods and services. Labor unions, trying to keep up with the cost of living, sought higher wages for their members. Businesses raised prices.

President Carter tried several ways to deal with inflation, but nothing worked. By 1980 the annual rate of inflation climbed to more than 12 percent. Meanwhile, interest rates rose sharply. This made it more costly for both businesses and consumers to borrow money. As a result, economic growth slowed down.

The Panama Canal treaties In foreign affairs, President Carter achieved some important successes. However, he also experienced some setbacks.

The United States' control of the Panama Canal and the Canal Zone had been a sore point with the people of Panama for many years. After anti-American riots in Panama in 1964, President Johnson opened talks with Panama to work out a new treaty. These talks continued under Presidents Nixon, Ford, and Carter. Finally, two treaties were agreed upon. Under them the United States and Panama would run the canal jointly until the year 2000, after which it would be turned over

An American aircraft carrier loaded with planes proceeds through the Panama Canal. (9°N/80°W; map, p. 528)

to Panama. The United States would retain the right to defend the canal.

Some Americans complained that the United States was "giving away" the canal. However, the Senate approved both treaties in 1978.

The Camp David accords President Carter's biggest foreign policy success came in the Middle East. For 30 years, Arab countries had been united in their determination to destroy Israel. But in 1977, President Anwar Sadat (sa dät′) of Egypt suddenly offered to make peace. He made a dramatic visit to Israel.

Peace talks between Sadat and Israeli Prime Minister Menachem Begin (mə näk′ əm bā′ gin) began soon afterwards, but they stalled. Fearing that the chance for peace might slip away, President Carter

In the Panama Canal treaties the Canal Zone was transferred to Panama's control. It became the Colon Free Zone. Until the year 2000 the canal is to be run by a joint United States–Panamanian body called the Panama Canal Commission.

offered to help. He invited Sadat and Begin to meet with him at Camp David, the presidential vacation home in Maryland. After 2 weeks of difficult negotiations, the three leaders produced the **Camp David accords.** These agreements provided a set of principles on which peace between Israel and Egypt would be founded, and held out a hope of general peace in the Middle East.

In March 1979, Israel and Egypt signed the peace treaty. Fittingly, Sadat and Begin proposed that the signing take place in the White House, in honor of President Carter's key role in achieving the treaty. Israel returned the Sinai Peninsula to Egypt. Egypt recognized the state of Israel and agreed to normal relations between the two countries.

Unhappily the Camp David accords did not lead to general peace in the region. Many Arab countries were angry with Egypt for making peace with the enemy. The Palestine Liberation Organization (PLO), an armed group of Palestinians based outside of Israel, continued to demand a return to their homeland and the destruction of Israel. The PLO continued to make terrorist attacks inside Israel and on Israelis living or traveling in other countries.

In 1981 a number of Egyptian soldiers who were members of an extreme religious group assassinated President Sadat. However, Egypt continued to honor its peace treaty under Sadat's successor.

Unrest in Central America President Carter believed that the United States should promote **human rights** around the world. This meant that we should not support governments that prevented free speech, denied fair trials, and killed or jailed their political opponents. The sad

During the Camp David talks, President Carter meets with President Anwar Sadat of Egypt (left) and Prime Minister Menachem Begin of Israel (right).

Sadat was assassinated by Moslem extremists on October 6, 1981, while watching a military parade. Egyptian-Israeli relations were strained in December 1981 when Israel's Parliament annexed the Golan Heights.

fact was that many governments, both Communist and non-Communist, did exactly those things.

In Central America, President Carter found it difficult to stick to this human rights policy. In most countries of this region, governments were controlled by a handful of wealthy families who owned most of the land. Nicaragua, for example, had been ruled by the Somoza family since the 1930s. The Somozas used their power to amass wealth running into hundreds of millions of dollars. But they did little for the masses of peasants and city dwellers who lived in poverty.

In several Central American countries, rebels used a guerrilla warfare against their governments in the 1970s. The rebels usually included both Communists and non-Communists. Often the rebels received support from the Communist government of Cuba. The governments that were under attack used ruthless methods against not only the rebels but also against anyone else who dared to criticize them. Thousands were killed or imprisoned and tortured.

What should the United States policy be? On one hand, Carter did not want to support governments that denied human rights to their people. On the other hand, rebel victory might lead to the spread of communism in the region. In practice the United States gave military and economic aid to the governments while trying to get them to stop their violations of human rights.

In Nicaragua, rebels calling themselves Sandinistas succeeded in overthrowing the rule of Anastasio Somoza in 1979. At first the Sandinistas included both Com-

During military exercises in Central America, an American advisor instructs a Salvadoran soldier.

munists and non-Communists. The United States hoped that the new government would be democratic and that it would not try to stir up more revolution in the region. It did not turn out that way, as Communists gained the upper hand.

Before long the Sandinistas, along with Cuba, were aiding guerrillas fighting the government in neighboring El Salvador. There the government had made some efforts to give land to poor farmers. But at the same time the army and private "death squads" roamed the country, killing not only rebels but also thousands of innocent victims. Again, President Carter tried to get the government to change its behavior while providing arms and military advisers to train government troops to fight the rebels.

SALT II   In 1979, American and Soviet negotiators agreed on a new treaty to limit the arms race. The treaty was called **SALT II**. However, when SALT II was sent to the Senate for approval, there was opposition. Some senators felt that it gave more to the Soviets than to the United States.

Any chance that the Senate might approve SALT II was taken away in December 1979 when the Soviet Union invaded Afghanistan, an Asian neighbor. The Soviets invaded when it appeared that the people of Afghanistan might overthrow their pro-Soviet government. To protest the Soviet action, President Carter withdrew SALT II from the Senate. He also cut off grain sales to Russia and he announced that the United States would boycott the 1980 Olympic Games that were to be held in Moscow.

None of these acts caused the Soviet Union to pull its army out of Afghanistan. However, Russia's soldiers were resisted by Afghan fighters, who took to the mountains. Four years after entering Afghanistan, Russia's army was still bogged down. Some people called Afghanistan "the Soviet Union's Vietnam."

Elsewhere in Asia, Carter followed the course begun by Nixon toward China. In 1979 the United States and the People's Republic of China exchanged ambassadors for the first time in 30 years.

American hostages in Iran   Carter's greatest success in foreign policy was the fashioning of the Camp David accords, aimed at bringing peace to the Middle East. But the Middle East was also the scene of his greatest failure. In the oil-rich nation of Iran, the United States had long supported a pro-Western ruler named Shah (Emperor) Mohammed Reza Pahlavi (pä′ lä vē). The shah was trying

to turn his ancient land into a modern industrial and military power. However, he met great opposition from traditional Moslems. The clergy believed that the shah's modernization went against Moslem teachings. The shah added to his problems by using secret police to torture and murder those who opposed him. Meanwhile, his family and friends created vast fortunes for themselves.

In January 1979, the shah was driven from his throne. A new government headed by a Moslem religious leader, Ayatollah Ruhollah Khomeini (hō mā ni′) took power. Khomeini's government was strongly anti-American because of our support of the shah.

For a time the shah lived in Mexico, and then in Panama, safe from the demand

Americans who had been held hostage in Iran deplane in West Germany on their way home after their release.

Have a group of pupils create a time-table of events connected with the Iranian hostage crisis from November 1979 to January 1981.

Born: 1924, Plains, Georgia. **Education:** United States Naval Academy. **Training:** Naval officer, farmer. **To presidency from:** Georgia. **Position when elected:** Private citizen. **Political party:** Democratic. **Married:** Rosalynn Smith. **Children:** Three sons, one daughter. **Other facts:** During 7 years in the navy, served on battleships and submarines. Helped develop the first nuclear-powered submarines. Resigned from navy after father's death to manage family farm and peanut warehouse. Governor of Georgia from 1970 to 1975. After his term as President, taught and wrote. Enjoyed hobby of woodworking. **During his presidency:** The Panama Canal Zone, governed by the United States since 1903, came to an end, becoming a part of Panama.

JAMES EARL CARTER, JR.
39th President
1977 · 1981

of Iran that he be returned to that country to stand trial for crimes against the people. Then in October 1979, President Carter allowed the shah to enter a hospital in the United States for treatment of cancer. A few days later, on November 4, angry revolutionary students seized the American Embassy in Iran's capital city of Tehran. The students took more than 50 Americans in the embassy as **hostages**, who would not be released until the United States had handed over the shah and all his wealth.

The United States refused to yield to the demands. The shah returned to Panama and later went to live in Egypt, where he died some months later. Not until Carter's last day in office did Iran finally agree to release the Americans.

CHECKUP

1. What problems inside the United States confronted President Carter?
2. How was the status of the Panama Canal changed?
3. What steps did President Carter take to bring peace to the Middle East?
4. Why did unrest in Central America present a difficult problem for the United States?
5. Why were Americans taken hostage in Iran?

Reagan and the New Federalism

┌─ **VOCABULARY** ─────────────
federal budget   **martial law**
deficit   **missile**
New Federalism
└─────────────────────────────

The election of 1980   In 1980 the Democrats nominated Jimmy Carter for a second term. Republicans chose Ronald Reagan to run against him. Reagan was a popular former governor of California and a leader of the conservative wing of his party.

During the campaign, Reagan spoke of the need to restore respect for America throughout the world. He said that America's military power had been allowed to slip and must be rebuilt. He also favored reducing government restrictions on businesses and individuals. In the election, Reagan won a landslide victory, receiving 483 electoral votes to Carter's 49.

Reagan's economic program   At the age of 69, Ronald Reagan was the oldest person to be elected President. He proved

On March 30, 1981, President Reagan narrowly escaped assassination by John Hinkley, Jr., who was later declared to be insane.

to be one of the most successful in winning the support of Congress for his programs. Following Reagan's recommendations, Congress cut $35 billion out of the **federal budget** that President Carter had proposed for 1981. The federal budget is the estimate of the amount of money that the government will take in and the amount that it will spend over a 12-month period. Most of the cuts made by Congress were in social programs. These included aid to cities, public housing, public health, education, and welfare. Critics said these cuts would fall mainly upon the poor. The President replied that his program would still provide a "safety net" for the "truly needy."

The President also got Congress to pass an income-tax cut for individuals, totaling 25 percent over 3 years. This was the largest tax cut in America's history. There were also tax cuts for business. Reagan said that these cuts would provide money for people to invest in factories and equipment. American industry could then become more productive and competitive with other countries. Tax cuts would also leave Americans with more money to spend on goods and services. This would help the economy to grow and provide more jobs.

Another major part of President Reagan's program was a large increase in military spending. Reagan believed that the United States had fallen behind the Soviet Union in several kinds of weapons.

Budget deficits President Reagan promised that his program would bring down inflation and also lead to a balanced federal budget. The budget is balanced when the amount that the government receives in taxes and the amount that it spends are equal. For 12 years in a row, there had been a federal budget **deficit**—that is, the government spent more than it took in.

Despite the President's predictions, the economy got worse instead of better during his first 2 years in office. Unemployment rose to nearly 11 percent, the highest since the Great Depression. Companies went out of business at a near-record rate. The federal budget deficit climbed to more than $100 billion in Reagan's first year and nearly $200 billion in his second, shattering all previous records. Meanwhile, interest rates soared to an all-time high. Critics had a name for the President's economic program; they called it Reaganomics.

On the other hand, with less demand for goods and services, the rate of inflation fell. By the end of 1982, it was down to 5 percent a year.

In 1983, the economy improved greatly. Automobile factories, retail stores, and others reported rising sales. New jobs were created. By the end of 1983, the number of people without jobs had dropped below 9 percent. Those who favored Reagan's course of action said that the drops in inflation and unemployment showed that his program was working. However, there were still worries over government spending. Budget deficits seemed likely to remain near $200 billion a year for several more years.

Relaxing regulations President Reagan also sought to reduce federal regulation of business. After 1 week in office,

Have a group of pupils use periodicals in the library to report to the class on aspects of President Reagan's domestic and economic programs. Ask: What is meant by the term Reaganomics?

he ended all remaining controls on the price of oil and gas, saying that this would encourage Americans to produce more oil.

The President felt that some of the regulations in the fields of conservation and pollution were too strict. His secretary of the interior, James Watt, allowed private companies to search for oil in protected wilderness areas and in nearly a billion acres of coastal waters as well. Watt also leased government-owned coalfields to private companies. However, Watt made important improvements in the country's national parks.

The Reagan administration was less active than earlier administrations in enforcing desegregation laws and laws dealing with racial and sex discrimination. Minority groups became very critical.

Dr. Sally Ride, America's first woman astronaut, was one of the crew of the Space Shuttle Challenger in 1983.

An offshore drilling rig searches for oil in waters along the coast of the United States.

Women's rights groups were angry because the President had opposed ERA. Supporters of the President pointed out that he was the first to appoint a woman, Sandra Day O'Connor, to the Supreme Court. He also named Jeane Kirkpatrick, a foreign policy expert, as ambassador to the United Nations. On the other hand there were no women, blacks, or Hispanics in the Reagan Cabinet and few in other high government positions.

The New Federalism In addition to cutting out or reducing certain federal programs, Reagan proposed to shift other programs from the federal government to the states. These would include welfare and some health-care programs. Certain tax revenues would be transferred to

705

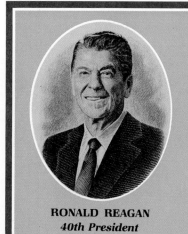

Born: 1911, Tampico, Illinois. **Education:** Eureka College. **Training:** Radio announcer, actor, public official. **To presidency from:** California. **Position when elected:** Private citizen. **Political party:** Republican. **Married:** (1) Jane Wyman, (2) Nancy Davis. **Children:** Two daughters, two sons. **Other facts:** A play-by-play sports announcer for radio stations in Iowa. Became an actor in motion pictures and played in more than 50 films, many of them westerns. Made training films for United States Army Air Forces in World War II. Served for 6 years as president of film performers' union. Twice elected governor of California. Likes to spend weekends at California ranch. **During his presidency:** The Space Shuttle Columbia was shot into orbit for the first time.

RONALD REAGAN
40th President
1981 ·

the states to help them pay the costs. The President believed that this would strengthen state governments. He called his plan the **New Federalism.**

Most state governors were very cautious about the plan. They feared it would cost more than their states could afford. Some also felt that the programs were the proper responsibility of the federal government. As of the end of 1983, the New Federalism had not been adopted.

Relations with the Soviet Union In many parts of the world, the United States still faced problems. Even though Israel and Egypt were at peace with each other, the Middle East remained a danger spot. In Central America, poverty and rebellions against dictatorships caused troubles that Communists tried to take advantage of.

President Reagan believed that the Soviet Union was behind much of the trouble in the world. During his first 3 years in office, America and Russia moved farther apart. While Reagan ended Carter's ban on grain sales to the Soviet Union, he discouraged the sale of certain

other goods by both the United States and its allies in Europe. He claimed that these goods were strengthening the Soviets' military abilities. The President succeeded in limiting American trade but not that of the European countries.

Events in Poland contributed to the worsening relations with Russia. In 1980, Polish workers started a labor union called Solidarity. Solidarity won great popular support as it championed greater freedom for the Polish people. Alarmed by these challenges to a Communist government, Russia's leaders warned that if the Polish government didn't put a stop to Solidarity, they would. In December 1981 the Polish government declared **martial law,** that is, rule by the military. The army put down Solidarity with the use of force and jailed its leaders.

The United States led the Western nations in denouncing this action. It showed, they said, the real attitude of Communists toward freedom. In a speech some time later, Reagan called the Soviet Union an "evil empire." Soviet leaders replied with their own charges against the United States.

Assign a group of pupils to report to the class on events in Poland from 1981 to the present. Their report should include biographical information on Lech Walesa, the Solidarity leader. Use the report to compare labor unrest in a Communist country with labor unrest in the United States.

Ask your pupils to draw up a chronology of the major events in American-Soviet relations between 1981 and 1984. Ask: Has there been a worsening of relations between the two countries? Have changes in Soviet leadership affected relations?

The arms race In such an atmosphere, progress toward a new agreement to limit the arms race was all but impossible. Indeed, in 1983, at the President's urging, Congress approved funds to start building a new kind of **missile**. A missile is a weapon—launched from the ground, sea, or air—that can be directed on a target many miles away. Each of the new missiles would carry ten separate nuclear warheads.

For several years the Soviet Union had been placing medium-range nuclear missiles near its European border. These missiles could reach targets in NATO countries in 10 minutes. To respond, NATO agreed to install similar United States missiles by December 1983 unless Russia removed its missiles. Talks produced no results. Despite large demonstrations in Western Europe against the American missiles, NATO governments went ahead with their plans.

This installation in North Dakota is one of the missile sites set up as part of our country's defense system.

Relations reached a new low in September 1983 when the Soviets shot down a Korean airliner, killing 269 people, including 60 Americans. The plane had strayed into Soviet airspace. Later evidence pointed to the likelihood that the Soviets had mistaken the civilian airliner for a spy plane. However, refusing to admit such an error, they insisted that the plane was on a spy mission and that they had a right to shoot it down. The Soviets were condemned by nearly all non-Communist nations for this act.

Trouble in Central America President Reagan made the country of El Salvador a test case of his determination to have no more governments in Central America that were unfriendly to the United States. In that country, rebel groups that included Communists threatened to overthrow the government. The United States had reason to believe that the Soviet Union and Cuba were sending arms to the rebels by way of Nicaragua.

The United States increased its aid to El Salvador and also sent 50 military advisers to help train its army. Many Americans, including some in Congress, were uncomfortable with this policy. They said that the government of El Salvador continued to violate human rights and killed thousands of its own people each year. They also feared that the United States might be drawn into war, as had happened in Vietnam. President Reagan, however, believed that stopping the spread of communism in the region must come before our human rights policy. He assured Americans that we would not take a direct part in the fighting.

Meanwhile the United States took strong action against two other countries in the region. The administration and Congress provided millions of dollars to Nicaraguan rebels who were fighting to get rid of the Sandinista government of that country. And in October 1983, American forces overthrew the Communist government in the tiny Caribbean island nation of Grenada.

Involvement in Lebanon   In the Middle East, attention shifted to the troubled nation of Lebanon. In the mid-1970s a civil war between the country's Christian and Moslem groups threatened to tear the country apart. Syrian troops, entering Lebanon supposedly to restore peace, remained to occupy a large part of the country. Meanwhile, the Palestine Liberation

In 1983, American marines and soldiers overthrew the Communist government of Grenada, a small island in the Caribbean Sea. (12°N/62°W; map, p. 714)

Organization used southern Lebanon as a base for attacks on Israeli settlements.

Determined to drive the PLO from its borders, Israel invaded Lebanon in June 1982. Israeli forces drove all the way to Beirut, the capital city and headquarters of the PLO. Western countries finally arranged a cease-fire, but the PLO had to agree to leave Lebanon.

A new Lebanese government then requested the United States, France, and Italy to send small peacekeeping forces to Beirut. The hope was to give the new Lebanese government time to get established, end the fighting among Moslems and Christians, and get Syrian and Israeli forces out of the country. Israel signed a treaty promising to withdraw its troops if Syria would. Syria, however, refused. Fighting soon flared again.

The danger to the small peacekeeping force was underlined when a fanatical Moslem group blew up a United States marine barracks in October 1983, killing 239 Americans. President Reagan made clear that the United States would not abandon its efforts to bring about peace in the troubled Middle East.

Two important anniversaries   Midway through the 1980s, Americans would observe two important anniversaries. The first, in 1986, would be the 100th anniversary of the official opening of the Statue of Liberty, symbol of American freedom (see box). The next year, 1987, would mark an even more significant event. The Constitution of the United States, the great charter of American government and the world's oldest written constitution, would be 200 years old.

The Statue of Liberty

On July 4, 1884, the people of France presented a gift to the United States. It was a gigantic statue of a woman, 151 feet (46 m) high and weighing 450,000 pounds (204,000 kg). In one hand the woman held high a great torch. In the other was a tablet bearing the date of the Declaration of Independence. So huge was the statue that it had to be shipped from France in 214 crates.

The crates arrived in New York in 1885. The following year the statue was assembled on a pedestal on a tiny island in New York Harbor, and in 1886 it was officially opened to the public.

The French sculptor, Frédéric Auguste Bartholdi, named his work *Liberty Enlightening the World*. To Americans and to millions the world over, however, it became known simply as the Statue of Liberty.

For the next century the Statue of Liberty stood in the harbor as both a symbol of American liberty and a welcome to newcomers to these shores. But the years took their toll on the great statue. Rust weakened its iron framework. Air pollution wore thin the copper covering on the uplifted hand and torch.

To make the necessary repairs, the statue had to be closed to the public in 1984. Private citizens raised $25 million to pay for the work, which would take at least a year to complete. In 1986 the Statue of Liberty would be open to visitors again — on time for its 100th anniversary and ready to begin its second century as the symbol of American freedom.

Workers prepare to assemble the Statue of Liberty in 1886. It was so huge that it had to be shipped from France to America in many separate parts.

Anniversaries are a time of celebration. They are also a time for taking stock. As Americans looked upon their country, they found much to be deeply satisfied about. America had grown from a handful of tiny settlements on the Atlantic coast and in the Southwest to become a great nation. Its economy produced more goods and services than any other nation on earth. Its 230 million people were among the freest and most prosperous in the world. For most of them, as for millions of people in other countries around the globe, America remained the land of opportunity.

Yet Americans also saw that there was more to be done before the promise of America would be fully realized. Even

Use the two anniversaries mentioned in the text to begin a class discussion on how the United States has kept the promises contained in the Constitution and symbolized in the Statue of Liberty. Ask: Has America truly been a land of freedom and equality of opportunity? What remains to be done?

709

as the great majority of Americans enjoyed a high standard of living, 15 percent—one in every seven—still lived in poverty in 1983. Even with the major advances toward equality for all—equal rights and equal opportunity—there were still many for whom the goal remained a distant dream. Gleaming new buildings rose in a hundred downtowns, but housing, public transportation, streets, and much else in the cities needed renewal or replacement. America's industries, too, were in need of attention. Once the most efficient in the world, many of its factories had become outdated. Other challenges lay ahead as well—the challenge of protecting the environment, the challenge of developing new sources of energy, and the challenge of maintaining a high standard of living for a rising population (see Benchmarks in the adjoining column). Lying ahead, too, was the greatest challenge of all—that of finding the way to peace in the dangerous nuclear age.

In preparing themselves to meet these challenges, Americans could find strength in their past. Although the challenges of an earlier day were different, they had seemed no less difficult at the time. The knowledge that Americans had met those challenges gave reason for confidence as the United States entered its third century as a nation.

BENCHMARKS

THE UNITED STATES

YEAR: 2000

AREA: 3,539,289 sq mi
9,166,758 sq km

POPULATION: 267,461,600

POPULATION
DENSITY: 76 per sq mi
29 per sq km

NUMBER
OF STATES: 50

LARGEST STATE
IN AREA: Alaska

IN POPULATION: California

LARGEST CITY: New York

WHERE PEOPLE
WILL LIVE:

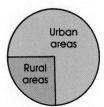

Urban areas

Rural areas

Population figures based on projections by United States Bureau of the Census

CHECKUP

1. What was President Reagan's approach to each of the following: (a) taxation, (b) military spending, (c) regulation of business?
2. What proposals were made under the New Federalism program?
3. Why was there a worsening of relations between the United States and the Soviet Union?
4. How did the United States become involved in the following regions: (a) Central America, (b) Lebanon?

31/CHAPTER REVIEW

KEY FACTS

1. In recent years most minority groups have made important gains, but the struggle for equality continues.

2. President Carter helped to bring about peace between Egypt and Israel, but elsewhere in the Middle East his policies were less successful.

3. President Reagan's domestic program marked a big change in the approach of the federal government to America's problems.

4. Relations between the United States and the Soviet Union continued to be the overriding matter of concern in our country's foreign policy.

VOCABULARY QUIZ

On a sheet of paper, write **T** if the statement is true and **F** if it is false. Then rewrite each false statement to make it true.

F **1.** Migrant workers are usually employed in factories.

T **2.** Puerto Rico is an American commonwealth and has its own constitution.

F **3.** The plan of termination increased special health and education services for Native Americans.

T **4.** President Carter's proposal for experimenting with solar energy was aimed at decreasing America's need for oil.

F **5.** The Camp David accords, which were signed by Carter, Sadat, and Begin, established peace between Israel and Syria.

T **6.** The SALT II treaty was aimed at limiting the arms race between the United States and the Soviet Union.

F **7.** The Iranians agreed to return the American hostages on President Carter's first day in office.

F **8.** If the federal budget has a deficit, it means that the government has taken in more money than it has spent.

F **9.** Under Reagan's New Federalism, welfare and health-care programs were to be shifted from the states to the federal government.

F **10.** Under martial law, the government of France arrested many Solidarity leaders.

REVIEW QUESTIONS

1. Why can it be said that it is both an advantage and a disadvantage for Mexican Americans and Puerto Ricans to hold onto their native Spanish language?

2. What arguments were given for and against the Equal Rights Amendment?

3. In what respects was the Middle East the scene of both success and failure for President Carter?

4. How did President Reagan's domestic programs differ from those of President Carter?

5. Under Presidents Carter and Reagan, what was United States policy in Central America?

ACTIVITIES

1. Find out what is meant by the phrase *affirmative action*. How is it related to Hispanics, blacks, and women?

2. Compare Presidents Carter and Reagan with regard to the following: (**a**) background before entering politics, (**b**) career in politics before becoming President, (**c**) success in winning support in Congress for their programs.

3. In your library find an account of the battle of Wounded Knee in 1890. After reading it, write an account of the battle as the soldiers' commanding officer might have written it. Then write an account as one of the Native Americans at the battle might have reported it.

UNDERSTANDING PREFIXES

GREEK AND LATIN PREFIXES

You have probably used the expression "It's Greek to me!" about something you did not understand. Actually, you know more Greek than you think—and Latin, too. Many of the words in the English language come from these two languages. So do many of the prefixes. A prefix is the unit of speech that is attached to the beginning of a word and modifies, or changes, the word's meaning. For example, the prefix *auto* comes from the Greek word meaning "self." An autobiography is a biography by oneself. An autograph is a signature by one's own hand.

A common prefix from Latin is *bi*, meaning "two." Someone who is bilingual speaks two languages. A bicycle is a two-wheeler. If you know what a three-wheeler is called, you will know another prefix that comes from Latin.

Prefixes modify words in many ways. Some change words into negatives. *Disapprove* means "to not approve." Something that is *mislabeled* is wrongly labeled. If something is *unpleasant*, it is not pleasant.

Some prefixes describe when something happened. *Prewar* means "before the war."

Postwar means "after the war." Other prefixes have to do with size and amount. America is a *multi-cultural* society—it is made up of many cultures.

Following are some commonly used prefixes and their meanings. Some are negative prefixes. Others tell where, when, how many, or how much.

Prefix	Meaning
bi	two
dis	away, apart, opposite
non	not
un	not
mis	wrongly
inter	between
sub	under
tri	three
multi	many
pre	before

SKILLS PRACTICE

Skim back through Lessons 1 and 2 of Chapter 31 and write as many words as you can find that have these or other frequently used prefixes.

8/UNIT REVIEW

READING THE TEXT

Turn to page 652 and read the section entitled "An increasing, shifting population." Continue on as far as the section entitled "More goods, more jobs" on page 654. Then, on a sheet of paper, write the answers to the following questions.

1. List the three major developments to which the building boom in postwar America was connected.

2. List the four great population shifts that took place in the United States from about 1940 to about 1970.

3. Which of these population shifts resulted mainly from the Green Revolution?

4. What part of the United States is known as the Sunbelt?

5. Five of the nation's ten largest cities in 1980 were in the Sunbelt. List them.

READING A MAP

Turn to page 637 and study the map titled "Europe in the Cold War." On a sheet of paper, write the answers to the following questions.

1. Name the two opposing military groups in Europe. NATO and Warsaw Pact nations

2. In addition to the United States and Canada, how many members does NATO have? 13

3. How many countries belong to the Warsaw Pact? 7

4. Which NATO nations border on Warsaw Pact countries? West Germany, Norway, Greece, Turkey

5. List the European countries that do not belong to either NATO or the Warsaw Pact. Switzerland, Ireland, Sweden, Finland, Austria, Yugoslavia

READING A PICTURE

Turn to page 691 and look at the picture of the Statue of Liberty. For almost a century this statue in New York Harbor has welcomed immigrants to America. It stands on Liberty Island in New York Harbor. Beneath the statue is Fort Wood, an old military installation shaped like an 11-point star.

Imagine that you are an immigrant on a ship sailing up New York Bay. You are getting your first glimpse of the Statue of Liberty and of your new country. On a sheet of paper, write a paragraph or two telling your feelings at this moment. Tell what the sight of the Statue of Liberty means to you. Write what your hopes and dreams for the future are.

READING A CHART

Turn to page 632 and study the chart entitled "The United Nations and Its Agencies." This global organization, with headquarters in New York City, has more than 150 member nations. On a sheet of paper write the answers to the following questions.

1. What is the central body of the United Nations called? General Assembly

2. What agencies does the central body directly control? Tr. Council, Ec. and Soc. Council, Secr't

3. Which United Nations groups are not controlled by the central body? Sec. Council, Court

4. How many member nations does the Security Council have? 15

5. Which of these agencies has the smallest membership? Trusteeship Council

Atlas

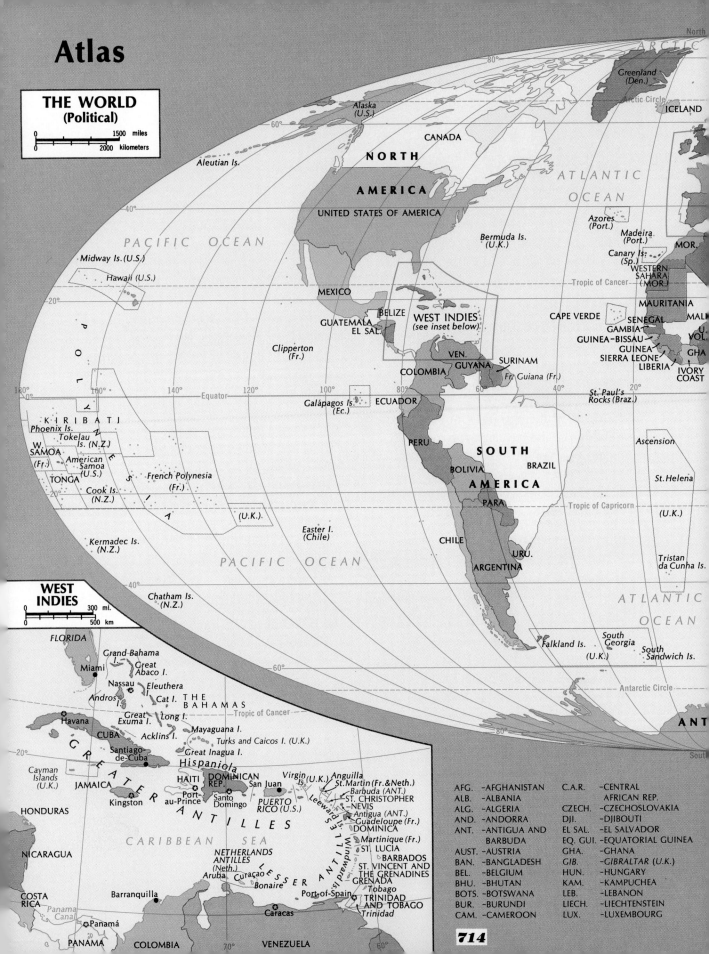

THE WORLD
(Political)

0 — 1500 miles
0 — 2000 kilometers

Labels on the world map

ARCTIC

Greenland (Den.)

Arctic Circle

ICELAND

Alaska (U.S.)

CANADA

NORTH

AMERICA

ATLANTIC

OCEAN

UNITED STATES OF AMERICA

Azores (Port.)

Madeira (Port.)

MOR.

Bermuda Is. (U.K.)

Canary Is. (Sp.)

WESTERN SAHARA (MOR.)

Tropic of Cancer

PACIFIC OCEAN

Midway Is. (U.S.)

Hawaii (U.S.)

MEXICO

WEST INDIES (see inset below)

CAPE VERDE

MAURITANIA

MALI

SENEGAL

GUATEMALA

BELIZE

EL SAL.

GAMBIA

GUINEA-BISSAU

GUINEA

U. VOL.

GHA.

SIERRA LEONE

LIBERIA

IVORY COAST

Clipperton (Fr.)

VEN.

GUYANA

SURINAM

COLOMBIA

Fr. Guiana (Fr.)

St. Paul's Rocks (Braz.)

Equator

Galápagos Is. (Ec.)

ECUADOR

P O L Y N E S I A

KIRIBATI

Phoenix Is.

Tokelau Is. (N.Z.)

W. SAMOA

American Samoa (U.S.)

TONGA

French Polynesia (Fr.)

Cook Is. (N.Z.)

(U.K.)

Easter I. (Chile)

Kermadec Is. (N.Z.)

PERU

SOUTH

AMERICA

BRAZIL

BOLIVIA

Ascension

St. Helena

Tropic of Capricorn

PARA.

(U.K.)

Tristan da Cunha Is.

CHILE

URU.

ARGENTINA

Chatham Is. (N.Z.)

PACIFIC OCEAN

ATLANTIC

OCEAN

Falkland Is. (U.K.)

South Georgia

South Sandwich Is.

Antarctic Circle

ANT

WEST INDIES

0 — 300 mi.
0 — 500 km

FLORIDA

Grand Bahama I.

Great Abaco I.

Miami

Nassau

Eleuthera

Andros

Cat I.

THE BAHAMAS

Tropic of Cancer

Havana

Great Exuma I.

Long I.

Mayaguana I.

CUBA

Acklins I.

Turks and Caicos I. (U.K.)

Santiago-de-Cuba

Great Inagua I.

Hispaniola

Cayman Islands (U.K.)

HAITI

DOMINICAN REP.

Virgin Is. (U.K.)

Anguilla

St. Martin (Fr.&Neth.)

JAMAICA

San Juan

Barbuda (ANT.)

Kingston

Port-au-Prince

Santo Domingo

PUERTO RICO (U.S.)

Leeward Is.

ST. CHRISTOPHER-NEVIS

Antigua (ANT.)

Guadeloupe (Fr.)

DOMINICA

HONDURAS

Martinique (Fr.)

ST. LUCIA

NICARAGUA

NETHERLANDS ANTILLES (Neth.)

BARBADOS

ST. VINCENT AND THE GRENADINES

Aruba

Curaçao

Bonaire

GRENADA

Tobago

Port-of-Spain

TRINIDAD AND TOBAGO

Trinidad

COSTA RICA

Barranquilla

CARIBBEAN SEA

GREATER ANTILLES

LESSER ANTILLES

Windward Is.

Panama Canal

Panamá

Caracas

PANAMA

COLOMBIA

VENEZUELA

Abbreviations

AFG.	-AFGHANISTAN	C.A.R.	-CENTRAL AFRICAN REP.
ALB.	-ALBANIA		
ALG.	-ALGERIA	CZECH.	-CZECHOSLOVAKIA
AND.	-ANDORRA	DJI.	-DJIBOUTI
ANT.	-ANTIGUA AND BARBUDA	EL SAL.	-EL SALVADOR
		EQ. GUI.	-EQUATORIAL GUINEA
AUST.	-AUSTRIA	GHA.	-GHANA
BAN.	-BANGLADESH	GIB.	-GIBRALTAR (U.K.)
BEL.	-BELGIUM	HUN.	-HUNGARY
BHU.	-BHUTAN	KAM.	-KAMPUCHEA
BOTS.	-BOTSWANA	LEB.	-LEBANON
BUR.	-BURUNDI	LIECH.	-LIECHTENSTEIN
CAM.	-CAMEROON	LUX.	-LUXEMBOURG

714

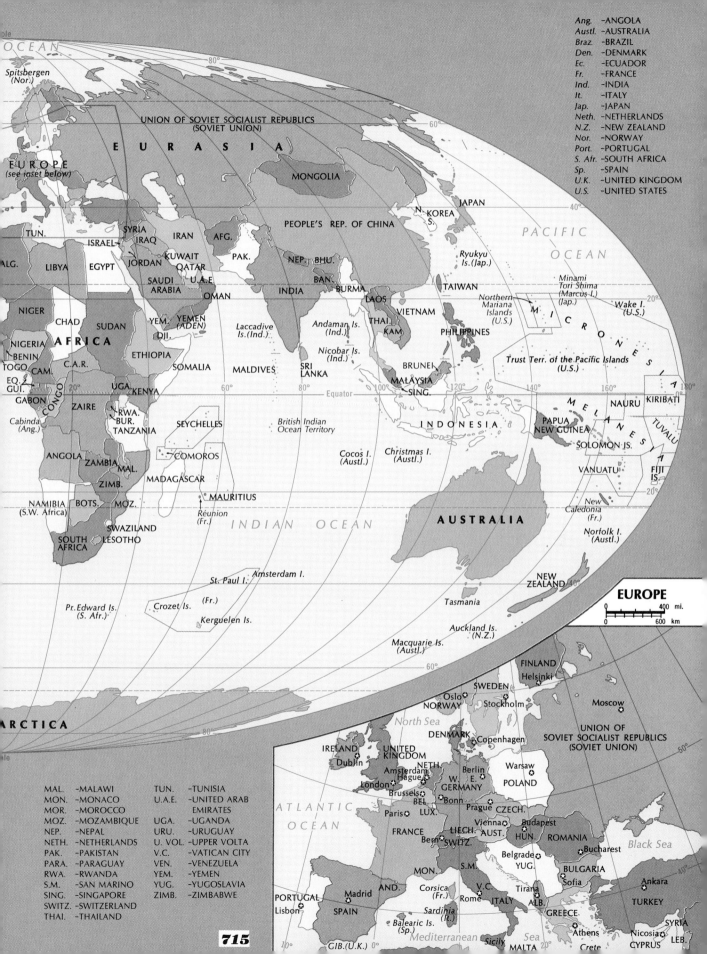

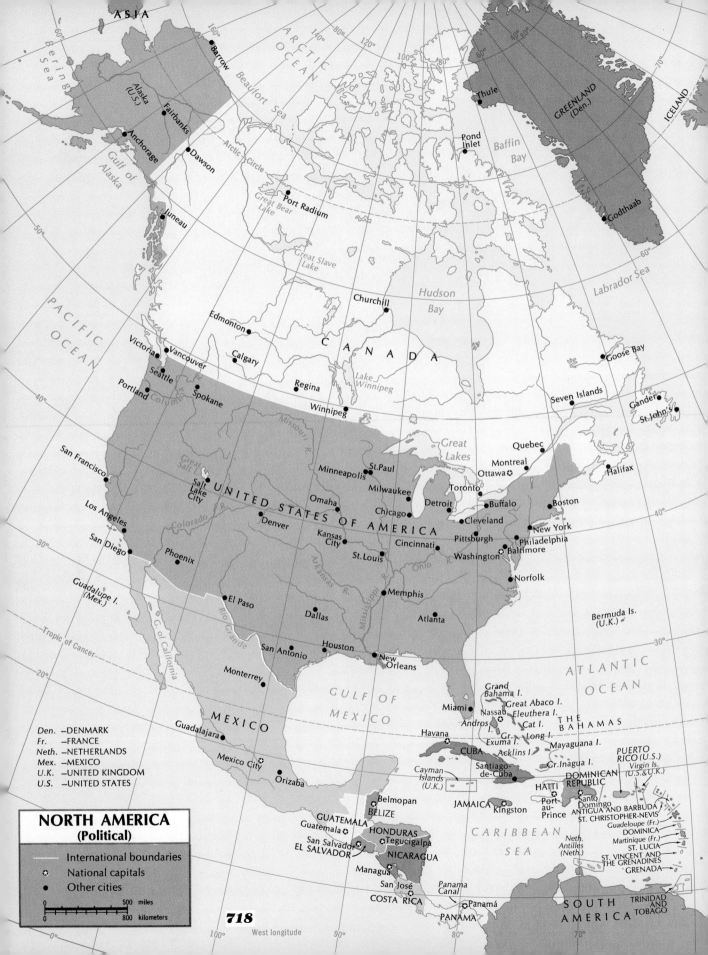

ASIA

ARCTIC OCEAN

Bering Sea

Barrow

Alaska (U.S.)

Beaufort Sea

Fairbanks

Anchorage

Dawson

Gulf of Alaska

Juneau

Arctic Circle

Great Bear Lake

Port Radium

Great Slave Lake

Thule

GREENLAND (Den.)

ICELAND

Pond Inlet

Baffin Bay

Godthaab

PACIFIC OCEAN

C A N A D A

Hudson Bay

Labrador Sea

Churchill

Edmonton

Calgary

Victoria

Vancouver

Seattle

Goose Bay

Lake Winnipeg

Regina

Seven Islands

Portland

Spokane

Winnipeg

Gander

St. John's

Columbia R.

Missouri R.

San Francisco

Great Salt Lake

Salt Lake City

UNITED STATES OF AMERICA

Minneapolis

St. Paul

Milwaukee

Great Lakes

Quebec

Montreal

Ottawa

Halifax

Omaha

Chicago

Detroit

Toronto

Buffalo

Boston

Los Angeles

Denver

Colorado R.

Kansas City

St. Louis

Cincinnati

Cleveland

Pittsburgh

New York

Philadelphia

San Diego

Phoenix

Arkansas R.

Ohio R.

Washington

Baltimore

Guadalupe I. (Mex.)

Rio Grande

El Paso

Memphis

Norfolk

Dallas

Atlanta

Bermuda Is. (U.K.)

Tropic of Cancer

San Antonio

Houston

Mississippi R.

Monterrey

New Orleans

G. of California

MEXICO

GULF OF MEXICO

ATLANTIC OCEAN

Miami

Grand Bahama I.

Great Abaco I.

Nassau

Eleuthera I.

THE BAHAMAS

Guadalajara

Andros I.

Cat I.

Long I.

Den. —DENMARK
Fr. —FRANCE
Neth. —NETHERLANDS
Mex. —MEXICO
U.K. —UNITED KINGDOM
U.S. —UNITED STATES

Havana

Gr. Exuma I.

Mayaguana I.

PUERTO RICO (U.S.)

Mexico City

CUBA

Acklins I.

Virgin Is. (U.S.&U.K.)

Orizaba

Santiago-de-Cuba

Gr. Inagua I.

Cayman Islands (U.K.)

DOMINICAN REPUBLIC

Belmopan

HAITI

Santo Domingo

ANTIGUA AND BARBUDA

BELIZE

JAMAICA

Port-au-Prince

ST. CHRISTOPHER-NEVIS

GUATEMALA

Kingston

Guadeloupe (Fr.)

Guatemala

HONDURAS

Tegucigalpa

CARIBBEAN SEA

Neth. Antilles (Neth.)

DOMINICA

Martinique (Fr.)

San Salvador

EL SALVADOR

NICARAGUA

ST. LUCIA

ST. VINCENT AND THE GRENADINES

Managua

GRENADA

San José

Panama Canal

SOUTH AMERICA

TRINIDAD AND TOBAGO

COSTA RICA

Panamá

PANAMA

NORTH AMERICA
(Political)

International boundaries

✪ National capitals

● Other cities

500 miles

0 800 kilometers

718

West longitude

80° Barranquilla
Cartagena
Maracaibo
Valencia Caracas
Barquisimeto
Cúcuta
San Cristóbal
Medellín Bucaramanga
Bogotá
Malpelo I. (Col.)
Cali COLOMBIA

VENEZUELA

Orinoco R.

Port-of-Spain
TRINIDAD AND TOBAGO

Georgetown
GUYANA
SURINAM
Paramaribo
Cayenne
Fr. Guiana (Fr.)

Col. —COLOMBIA
Fr. —FRANCE
U.K. —UNITED KINGDOM

Quito
ECUADOR
Guayaquil
Iquitos

Equator
Amazon R.
Manaus
Belém
São Luís
Fortaleza

Trujillo
PERU

Recife
Maceió

B R A Z I L

Callao Lima
Cuzco
Arequipa
Lake Titicaca
La Paz
Sucre
BOLIVIA

Salvador

Brasília
(Federal District)

PACIFIC OCEAN

Chuquicamata
Antofagasta

PARAGUAY
Asunción

Belo Horizonte

Rio de Janeiro
São Paulo Niterói
Santos
Curitiba

Tropic of Capricorn

San Felix I. (Chile) San Ambrosio I. (Chile)

Tucumán

Paraná R.

Córdoba
Santa Fe
Paraná
Rosario

Pôrto Alegre

CHILE

URUGUAY

ATLANTIC OCEAN

Valparaíso
Santiago
Juan Fernández Is. (Chile)
Concepción

Buenos Aires
La Plata
Montevideo
Río de la Plata

Mar del Plata

ARGENTINA
Bahía Blanca

Strait of Magellan

Falkland Is. (U.K.) (Malvinas Is.)

719

Punta Arenas

West longitude

SOUTH AMERICA
(Political)

——— International boundaries
✪ National capitals
● Other cities

0 ————— 500 miles
0 ————— 800 kilometers

ATLANTIC OCEAN
Madeira Is. (Port.)

PORTUGAL
Lisbon

SPAIN
Madrid
Valencia
Balearic Is. (Sp.)
Barcelona

Bordeaux
FRANCE
Paris
2
Brussels
5
London
UNITED KINGDOM
Glasgow
IRE.
Dublin
Amsterdam
Hamburg
Hannover
W. GER.
Bonn
Berlin
E. GER.
14
4
12
Munich
18
Bern
11
Vienna
3
Prague
7
Wrocław
POLAND
Warsaw
Kaliningrad

Marseilles
Nice
13
Corsica
Milan
16
ITALY
Rome
Naples
Sardinia
Palermo
Sicily

DEN.
Copenhagen
North Sea
Bergen
Oslo
NORWAY
Narvik
Göteborg
Stockholm
SWEDEN
Helsinki
FINLAND
Tallinn
Riga
Leningrad
Murmansk
Archangel

Spitsbergen (Nor.)
ARCTIC OCEAN
North Land
Novaya Zemlya
Barents Sea

MALTA
Valetta
Mediterranean Sea

Tirana
1
YUG.
Belgrade
Budapest
ROM.
Bucharest
Sofia
BUL.
GREECE
Athens
Crete (Gr.)
Izmir
Ankara
TURKEY

Istanbul (Constantinople)
Black Sea
Krasnodar

Moscow
Kiev
Kharkov
Odessa
UKRAINE
Saratov
Kazan
Perm
Sverdlovsk
Ufa
Chelyabinsk
Kuibyshev
Magnitogorsk
Orenburg
Volgograd

UNION OF SOVIET (SOVIET UNION)
Omsk
Tomsk
Novosibirsk
Ob R.
Yenisey R.
Volga R.

E U R O P E
A S

CYPRUS
Nicosia
Beirut
10
SYRIA
Damascus
ISRAEL
Jerusalem
Amman
JOR.
Sinai Pen.
IRAQ
Baghdad
Basra
Abadan
9
Kuwait
Euphrates R.
Tigris R.
Tehran
IRAN (PERSIA)

Caspian Sea
Baku
Aral Sea
TURKESTAN
Tashkent
Urumchi
SINKIANG

AFGHANISTAN
Kabul
Islamabad
Jammu and Kashmir
Lahore
TIBET
PAKISTAN
Karachi
Hyderabad
Delhi
New Delhi
NEP.
Katmāndu
Ganges R.
Indus R.

BAN. —BANGLADESH
BHU. —BHUTAN
BUL. —BULGARIA
DEN. —DENMARK
GER. —GERMANY
IRE. —IRELAND
JOR. —JORDAN
KAM. —KAMPUCHEA
NEP. —NEPAL
ROM. —ROMANIA
YUG. —YUGOSLAVIA
1—ALBANIA
2—ANDORRA
3—AUSTRIA
4—BAHREIN
5—BELGIUM
6—BRUNEI
7—CZECHOSLOVAKIA
8—HUNGARY
9—KUWAIT
10—LEBANON
11—LIECHTENSTEIN
12—LUXEMBOURG
13—MONACO
14—NETHERLANDS
15—QATAR
16—SAN MARINO
17—SINGAPORE
18—SWITZERLAND

AFRICA
Red Sea
Mecca
SAUDI ARABIA
Manama
4
Riyadh
15
Doha
Dubai
UNITED ARAB EMIRATES
Empty Quarter
Masqat
OMAN
YEMEN (SAN A)
San'a
YEMEN (ADEN)
Aden
Madīnat ash Sha'b
Socotra (Yemen [Aden])
Arabian Sea

Ahmadabad
INDIA
Bombay
Hyderabad
Madras

Laccadive Is. (Ind.)
MALDIVES
Male
Colombo
SRI LANKA

INDIAN OCEAN

East longitude

720

New Siberian Is.

a
i
r
e
b
S

Yakutsk

Lena R.

SOCIALIST REPUBLICS

Krasnoyarsk

Irkutsk

Magadan

Kamchatka Pen.

Bering Sea

Aleutian Is. (U.S.)

Sea of Okhotsk

Kuril Islands (U.S.S.R.)

Khabarovsk

Amur R.

MANCHURIA

Harbin

Vladivostok

Sapporo

Ulan Bator

MONGOLIA

INNER MONGOLIA

Shenyang

Fushun

N. KOREA

Pyongyang

Seoul

S. KOREA

Pusan

Sea of Japan

JAPAN

Tokyo
Yokohama

Kyoto
Kobe Nagoya
Osaka

Gr. —GREECE
Ind. —INDIA
Jap. —JAPAN
Nor. —NORWAY
Port. —PORTUGAL
Sp. —SPAIN
U.K. —UNITED KINGDOM
U.S. —UNITED STATES
U.S.S.R.—SOVIET UNION

Great Wall

Peking

Dairen

Tientsin

Taiyuan

Hwang Ho

Tsingtao

Kitakyushu

Lanchow

Sian

Nanking

Shanghai

East China Sea

PEOPLE'S REPUBLIC OF CHINA

Wuhan

Chengtu

Chungking

Yangtze R.

Ryukyu Is. (Jap.)

Lhasa

Thimbu
BHU.

Brahmaputra

BAN.
Dacca

Calcutta

Kunming

Canton

Macao
(Port.)

Hong Kong
(U.K.)

Taipei

TAIWAN

Mandalay

BURMA

Hanoi

Rangoon

Bay of Bengal

Andaman Is. (Ind.)

Nicobar Is. (Ind.)

Vientiane LAOS

THAILAND

Bangkok

KAM.

Phnom Penh

Hue

Da Nang

VIETNAM

Mekong R.

Ho Chi Minh City

South China Sea

Manila

PHILIPPINES

Davao

Diajapura

PAPUA NEW GUINEA

Lae

EURASIA (Political)

International boundaries

Indefinite or temporary boundaries

National capitals

Other cities

0   800 mi.
0   1200 km

PACIFIC OCEAN

Bandar Seri Begawan
6

Manado

IRIAN JAYA

New Guinea

Port Moresby

Medan

Kuala Lumpur
17

M A L A Y S I A

Borneo

Pontianak

Samarinda

Bandjermasin

Celebes

Ujung Pandang

I N D O N E S I A

Timor

Arafura Sea

Coral Sea

Sumatra

Palembang

Jakarta
Bandung

Surabaja

Java

A U S T R A L I A

721

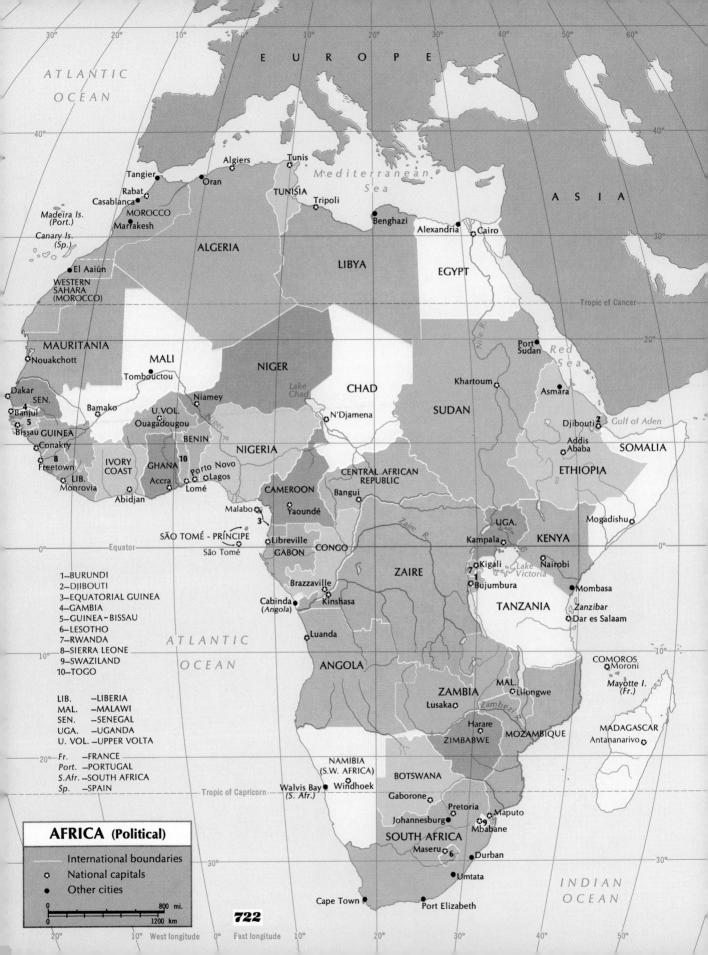

AFRICA (Political)

— International boundaries
✺ National capitals
• Other cities

1—BURUNDI
2—DJIBOUTI
3—EQUATORIAL GUINEA
4—GAMBIA
5—GUINEA-BISSAU
6—LESOTHO
7—RWANDA
8—SIERRA LEONE
9—SWAZILAND
10—TOGO

LIB. —LIBERIA
MAL. —MALAWI
SEN. —SENEGAL
UGA. —UGANDA
U. VOL.—UPPER VOLTA

Fr. —FRANCE
Port. —PORTUGAL
S.Afr.—SOUTH AFRICA
Sp. —SPAIN

0   800 mi.
0   1200 km

722

ATLANTIC OCEAN

EUROPE

ASIA

Mediterranean Sea

Tangier
Algiers
Tunis
Rabat
Oran
Casablanca
MOROCCO
Marrakesh
Tripoli
Benghazi
Alexandria
Cairo

Madeira Is. (Port.)
Canary Is. (Sp.)

El Aaiún
WESTERN SAHARA (MOROCCO)

ALGERIA
TUNISIA
LIBYA
EGYPT

Tropic of Cancer

MAURITANIA
Nouakchott

MALI
Tombouctou

NIGER
Lake Chad

CHAD

SUDAN
Khartoum

Port Sudan
Red Sea

Asmara

Dakar
SEN.
Banjul
Bissau
GUINEA
Conakry

Bamako
Niamey
U. VOL.
Ouagadougou
BENIN
NIGERIA
N'Djamena

Djibouti 2 Gulf of Aden
Addis Ababa
SOMALIA
ETHIOPIA

Freetown 8
LIB.
Monrovia
IVORY COAST
GHANA
Accra
10
Porto Novo
Lagos
Lomé
Abidjan

CAMEROON
Yaoundé
Bangui
CENTRAL AFRICAN REPUBLIC

Malabo
3
SÃO TOMÉ - PRÍNCIPE
São Tomé
Libreville
GABON
CONGO
Brazzaville
Kinshasa
Cabinda (Angola)

ZAIRE
Zaïre R.

UGA.
Kampala
Kigali 7
1 Bujumbura

KENYA
Nairobi
Lake Victoria
Mogadishu

Mombasa
Zanzibar
Dar es Salaam
TANZANIA

Equator

ATLANTIC OCEAN

Luanda

ANGOLA

ZAMBIA
Lusaka
Zambezi

MAL.
Lilongwe

COMOROS
Moroni
Mayotte I. (Fr.)

MADAGASCAR
Antananarivo

Harare
ZIMBABWE
MOZAMBIQUE

NAMIBIA (S.W. AFRICA)
Walvis Bay (S. Afr.)
Windhoek

BOTSWANA
Gaborone

Tropic of Capricorn

Pretoria
Johannesburg
Maputo
Mbabane 9
SOUTH AFRICA
Maseru 6
Durban
Umtata

Cape Town
Port Elizabeth

INDIAN OCEAN

30° West longitude 0° East longitude

BIOGRAPHICAL DICTIONARY

The page references tell where further information about each person can be found in the text.

Adams, Abigail (1744–1818). Wife of President John Adams. Her letters show her keen interest in public affairs. p. 216.

Adams, John (1735–1826). Second President. p. 221.

Adams, John Quincy (1767–1848). Sixth President. p. 257.

Adams, Samuel (1722–1803). A Revolutionary War Patriot. Leader of Sons of Liberty. p. 120.

Addams, Jane (1860–1935). Organized Hull House, a settlement house for helping the poor, in Chicago in 1889. p. 457.

Alcott, Louisa May (1832–1888). An author of books for children and young people. p. 392.

Anderson, Marian (1902–   ). A concert singer who helped lessen discrimination against black people in the field of music. p. 595.

Anthony, Susan B. (1820–1906). A leader in the movement for women's rights. p. 276.

Armstrong, Neil A. (1930–   ). Astronaut, and first person to land on the moon. p. 681.

Arthur, Chester A. (1829–1886). Twenty-first President. p. 388.

Attucks, Crispus (1723?–1770). A black sailor killed in 1770 in the Boston Massacre. p. 124.

Austin, Stephen (1793–1836). Leader of Americans who settled in Texas when the region was a part of Mexico. p. 300.

Barton, Clara (1821–1912). A nurse in Union hospitals during the Civil War. Later founded the American Red Cross. p. 358.

Beckwourth, James (1798–1867?). A free black from St. Louis. Became a mountain man and guide in the West. p. 296.

Bell, Alexander Graham (1847–1922). Inventor of the telephone (1876). p. 393.

Bethune, Mary McLeod (1875–1955). A black educator. Was an adviser on minority affairs in Franklin Roosevelt's administration. p. 595.

Black Hawk (1767–1838). Chief of the Sac Indians of Illinois. Led his people in fighting the whites in Black Hawk's War. p. 270.

Boone, Daniel (1734–1820). Frontiersman who blazed the Wilderness Trail for early settlers traveling to Kentucky. p. 106.

Bradford, William (1590–1657). Governor of the English colony at Plymouth, in New England. He wrote a history of the Pilgrim settlement. p. 71.

Bridger, Jim (1804–1881). Mountain man and guide in the western mountains. p. 296.

Brown, John (1800–1859). Fanatical abolitionist. Attacked proslavery settlers in Kansas. Led raid at Harpers Ferry, Virginia. p. 328.

Bryan, William Jennings (1860–1925). Unsuccessful Democratic candidate in presidential elections of 1896, 1900, and 1904. p. 479.

Buchanan, James (1791–1868). Fifteenth President. p. 333.

Bunche, Ralph (1904–1971). Diplomat. Head of United Nations group that arranged a truce between Israel and the Arabs in 1949. p. 642.

Burr, Aaron (1756–1836). Anti-Federalist follower of Jefferson. Vice President, 1801–1805. Killed Alexander Hamilton in a duel. p. 212.

Bush, George William (? – ?). A free black who was one of the pioneer settlers in the Oregon country. p. 298.

Cabot, John (1450–1498). Italian sea captain who explored for England. He made a voyage to Newfoundland and another voyage along the North American coast. p. 64.

Calhoun, John C. (1782–1850). Senator from South Carolina. Champion of the South and of states' rights. p. 226.

Carnegie, Andrew (1835–1919). Built iron and steel industry in late 1800s. Bought up steel companies and combined them. Profited from growth of railroads and growth of cities. p. 424.

Carter, James Earl "Jimmy" (1924–   ). Thirty-ninth President. p. 703.

Cartier, Jacques (1491–1557). French explorer. Made three voyages to North America. Explored the St. Lawrence River region. p. 50.

Champlain, Samuel de (1567?–1635). French explorer and colonizer. Founded Quebec in 1608. Called the Father of New France. p. 50.

Chavez, Cesar (1927–   ). A leader for equal rights for Mexican Americans. Organized union for migrant workers. p. 690.

Clark, George Rogers (1752–1818). Revolutionary War colonel. Captured British forts north of the Ohio River. p. 152.

Clark, William (1770–1838). One of leaders of the Lewis and Clark expedition, which explored the land gained by the Louisiana Purchase. p. 237.

Clay, Henry (1777–1852). Representative and senator from Kentucky. He proposed the Missouri Compromise and the Compromise of 1850. p. 226.

Clemens, Samuel L. (1835–1910). A writer of books, using the name Mark Twain. Grew up in Hannibal, Missouri. Was a Mississippi steamboat pilot. p. 315.

Cleveland, Grover (1837–1908). Twenty-second and twenty-fourth President. p. 477.

Clinton, George (1739–1812). Anti-Federalist governor of New York in the late 1700s. Vice President from 1809–1812. p. 210.

Cody, William F. "Buffalo Bill" (1846–1917). A scout, cowboy, and buffalo hunter. Later made tours with his Wild West show. p. 416.

Columbus, Christopher (1451–1506). Native of Genoa, Italy. Sailing in the service of Spain, reached the West Indies in 1492. His voyages led to the exploration and colonization of the Americas. p. 40.

Howard, Oliver O. (1830–1909). Head of the Freedmen's Bureau, which helped freed slaves. Founded Howard University. p. 372.

Hudson, Henry (? –1611). English sea captain who explored for the Netherlands. Claimed lands in eastern America for the Dutch. p. 54.

Hughes, Charles Evans (1862–1948). Republican candidate in presidential election of 1916. Later was secretary of state and Chief Justice of the Supreme Court. p. 543.

Hughes, Langston (1902–1967). A poet who was part of the Harlem Renaissance. p. 571.

Humphrey, Hubert H. (1911–1978). Vice President under Lyndon Johnson. p. 678.

Hutchinson, Anne (1591–1643). A leader for freedom of religion. Put out of Massachusetts, she moved to Rhode Island. p. 74.

Irving, Washington (1783–1859). An author who wrote history and stories of the Dutch people in New York. p. 282.

Jackson, Andrew (1767–1845). Seventh President. p. 261.

Jackson, Helen Hunt (1830–1885). An author who wrote about the government's treatment of Indians. p. 391.

Jackson, Thomas J. "Stonewall" (1824–1863). Confederate general in the Civil War. p. 343.

Jay, John (1745–1829). First Chief Justice of the Supreme Court. Arranged Jay's Treaty with Great Britain. p. 214.

Jefferson, Thomas (1743–1826). Third President. p. 243.

Jenney, William Le Baron (1832–1907). An architect whose design led to skyscrapers. p. 442.

Johnson, Andrew (1808–1875). Seventeenth President. p. 370.

Johnson, Lyndon B. (1908–1973). Thirty-sixth President. p. 678.

Johnson, Tom (1854–1911). Reform mayor of Cleveland in the early 1900s. p. 496.

Johnston, Joseph E. (1807–1891). Confederate general in the Civil War. p. 346.

Jones, John Paul (1747–1792). Revolutionary War naval officer. Sank or seized British merchant ships. p. 150.

Joseph (1840?–1904). Nez Percé Indian chief who surrendered to U.S. Army in 1877. p. 404.

Kelley, Florence (1859–1932). Reformer who worked for laws regulating child labor. p. 494.

Kelley, Oliver H. (1826–1913). Founded the Grange, a farm organization, in 1867. p. 474.

Kellogg, Frank (1856–1937). Secretary of state in Coolidge's Cabinet. p. 576.

Kennedy, John F. (1917–1963). Thirty-fifth President. p. 662.

Key, Francis Scott (1779–1843). Author of the words of "The Star-Spangled Banner." p. 246.

King, Martin Luther, Jr. (1929–1968). A leader in civil rights movement, using nonviolent methods. Awarded Nobel Peace Prize. p. 664.

Kissinger, Henry (1923–). National security adviser in the Nixon administration. Later the secretary of state in Nixon's Cabinet. p. 679.

Knox, Henry (1750–1806). Revolutionary War general and first secretary of war. p. 136.

La Follette, Robert (1855–1925). Governor of Wisconsin and senator from Wisconsin. Accomplished many reforms in government. p. 492.

Lease, Mary (1850–1933). An effective spokeswoman for farmers in 1890s. p. 471.

Lee, Jason (1803–1845). Leader of a group of missionaries to the Oregon country in 1834. p. 296.

Lee, Robert E. (1807–1870). Leading Confederate general in the Civil War. p. 346.

Lewis, John L. (1880–1969). Head of United Mine Workers. Helped to form CIO. p. 597.

Lewis, Meriwether (1774–1809). One of leaders of Lewis and Clark expedition, which explored the land gained by the Louisiana Purchase. p. 236.

Lewis, Sinclair (1885–1951). Author of novels and plays dealing with life in the early 1900s. p. 484.

Lincoln, Abraham (1809–1865). Sixteenth President. p. 360.

Lindbergh, Charles A. (1902–1974). The first aviator to fly alone across the Atlantic. p. 566.

Lockwood, Belva (1830–1917). A New York lawyer and a candidate for President in 1884. p. 390.

Lodge, Henry Cabot (1850–1924). United States senator from Massachusetts. Opposed American membership in League of Nations. p. 553.

Long, Stephen (1784–1864). Explored the northern Great Plains in the 1820s. Called this region the Great American Desert. p. 294.

MacArthur, Douglas (1880–1964). General in United States Army. In World War II, commanded forces in the Philippines and the southwest Pacific. Commanded United Nations forces in Korean War. p. 615.

McCarthy, Joseph R. (1908–1957). Senator from Wisconsin who accused many in the government of being Communists in 1950s. Censured by the Senate for his methods. p. 658.

McClellan, George B. (1826–1885). Union general in the Civil War. At one time headed the Army of the Potomac. p. 342.

McCormick, Cyrus Hall (1809–1884). Inventor of a mechanical reaper, the first of many machines that changed farming. p. 291.

McGovern, George (1922–). Democratic candidate in presidential election of 1972. p. 684.

McKinley, William (1843–1901). Twenty-fifth President. p. 500.

Madison, James (1751–1836). Fourth President. p. 248.

Magellan, Ferdinand (1480?–1521). Explorer for Spain. Sailed around South America and across the Pacific. Killed in the Philippine Islands, but one of his ships returned to Spain in 1522, the first ship to sail around the world. p. 44.

Mann, Horace (1796–1859). A leader in getting Massachusetts to provide the first free public elementary schools. p. 278.

Marion, Francis (1732?–1795). A guerrilla fighter in South Carolina in the Revolutionary War. Known as the Swamp Fox. p. 153.

Marshall, George C. (1880–1959). Chief of staff of the army in World War II. Secretary of state in Truman's Cabinet. Proposed Marshall Plan of economic aid for Europe. p. 635.

Marshall, John (1755–1835). Federalist leader in Virginia. Chief Justice of the Supreme Court from 1801 to 1835. p. 213.

Marshall, Thurgood (1908–   ). Lawyer who won case against segregation in public schools. Later was first black to be appointed a justice of the Supreme Court. p. 662.

Mason, George (1725–1792). Prominent Virginian. A leader in government. p. 107.

Meade, George G. (1815–1872). Union general in command at battle of Gettysburg. p. 351.

Millay, Edna St. Vincent (1892–1950). A poet who wrote in the first half of 1900s. p. 571.

Mitchell, William "Billy" (1879–1936). General in Air Service of U.S. Army. Called for greater use of military airplanes. p. 600.

Monroe, James (1758–1831). Fifth President. p. 251.

Morris, Gouveneur (1752–1816). Delegate from Pennsylvania to Constitutional Convention. p. 170.

Morse, Samuel F. B. (1791–1872). An artist and inventor of the telegraph. p. 284.

Mott, Lucretia (1793–1880). Leader in women's rights movement. p. 274.

Nimitz, Chester W. (1885–1966). Admiral in World War II. Commanded naval forces in the central Pacific. p. 614.

Nixon, Richard M. (1913–   ). Thirty-seventh President. p. 686.

O'Connor, Sandra Day (1930–   ). First woman justice of the Supreme Court. p. 695.

Oliver, James (1823–1908). Invented the chilled-iron plow for use on the Great Plains. p. 419.

Paine, Thomas (1737–1809). Author of *Common Sense,* the 1776 pamphlet that urged the colonists to declare their independence. p. 138.

Parker, Cynthia Ann (1827?–1864). A white woman captured by Comanche Indians when she was a child. Married a Comanche and remained with the Indians in Oklahoma. p. 316.

Paterson, William (1745–1806). Delegate from New Jersey to Constitutional Convention. p. 169.

Penn, William (1644–1718). Quaker who established the colony of Pennsylvania and the city of Philadelphia. Called the colony a "holy experiment." p. 77.

Perkins, Frances (1882–1965). Secretary of labor in Franklin Roosevelt's Cabinet. The first woman to hold a Cabinet post. p. 596.

Pershing, John J. (1860–1948). Army general who Commanded the American Expeditionary Force in World War I. p. 547.

Pickett, George E. (1825–1875). Confederate general in the Civil War. Led an attack at battle of Gettysburg. p. 351.

Pierce, Franklin (1804–1869). Fourteenth President. p. 328.

Pinckney, Eliza Lucas (1722–1793). Managed a plantation in South Carolina. Experimented in growing indigo. p. 108.

Pinckney, Thomas (1750–1828). Statesman who arranged Pinckney Treaty, a pact with Spain. Son of Eliza Lucas Pinckney. p. 214.

Pitcher, Molly (1754?–1832). Wife of a Revolutionary War soldier. Took part in battle of Monmouth. Real name Mary Ludwig Hays. p. 153.

Pizarro, Francisco (1470?–1541). Spanish explorer. Conquered the Incas in Peru. p. 46.

Poe, Elizabeth Arnold (1787?–1811). Actress and singer. Mother of Edgar Allan Poe. p. 224.

Polk, James K. (1795–1849). Eleventh President. p. 305.

Powderly, Terence V. (1849–1924). Labor leader. Head of Knights of Labor. p. 467.

Pulitzer, Joseph (1847–1911). Publisher of the newspaper The New York *World.* p. 518.

Rainey, Joseph Hayne (1832–1887). First black member of House of Representatives. Was a member of Congress from South Carolina. p. 374.

Randolph, A. Philip (1889–1979). Civil rights leader during and after World War II. p. 619.

Randolph, Edmund (1753–1813). Attorney general in Washington's Cabinet. p. 207.

Reagan, Ronald. (1911–   ). Fortieth President. p. 706.

Revere, Paul (1735–1818). Silversmith in Boston. An active Patriot before and during the Revolutionary War. p. 112.

Riis, Jacob (1849–1914). Newspaper reporter in New York City. He wrote about the terrible living conditions in tenements. p. 456.

Rockefeller, John D. (1839–1937) Formed Standard Oil Company in 1870. Gained control of the oil refining industry. p. 437.

Roosevelt, Eleanor (1884–1962). Worked for the benefit of blacks and other minorities. Head of United Nations Commission on Human Rights. Wife of Franklin Roosevelt. p. 595.

Roosevelt, Franklin D. (1882–1945). Thirty-second President. p. 613.

Roosevelt, Theodore (1858–1919). Twenty-sixth President. p. 503

Sacagawea (1787?–1812). Shoshone Indian woman. A valuable member of the Lewis and Clark expedition. p. 237.

Scott, Winfield (1786–1866). Army general who took Mexico City in the Mexican War. p. 303.

Sequoya (1770?–1843). A leader of the Cherokee Indians. Devised an alphabet for writing their language. p. 270.

Seward, William (1801–1872). Secretary of state in Lincoln's Cabinet. Purchased Alaska from Russia. p. 348.

Shepard, Alan (1923–   ). First American to ride a rocket into space (1961). p. 2.

Sherman, Roger (1721–1793). Delegate from Connecticut to Constitutional Convention. Proposed the Great Compromise. p. 169.

Sherman, William T. (1820–1891). Union general in the Civil War. Led march through Georgia. p. 354.

Sholes, Christopher L. (1819–1890). Inventor of the first practical typewriter (1867). p. 434.

Sims, William (1858–1936). Admiral in the United States Navy in World War I. p. 546.

Sinclair, Upton (1878–1968). A writer who exposed conditions in the meat-packing business. p. 503.

Sirica, John (1904–   ). Judge for the trial in the Watergate scandal in the Nixon administration. p. 685.

Slater, Samuel (1768–1835). Brought knowledge of machines for spinning and weaving cotton from England to Rhode Island. Started textile factory system. p. 227.

Smith, John (1580–1631). Leader of the English colony at Jamestown, Virginia. Explored the coast of New England. p. 62.

Sousa, John Philip (1854–1932). Composer of popular marches in the late 1800s. p. 399.

Stanton, Elizabeth Cady (1815–1902). Organized first women's rights convention at Seneca Falls, N.Y., in 1848. p. 274.

Steffens, Lincoln (1866–1936). Journalist who exposed corruption in city governments. One of the muckrakers. p. 496.

Stevens, Thaddeus (1792–1868). Congressman from Pennsylvania. A leader of Radical Republicans in Reconstruction years. p. 375.

Stowe, Harriet Beecher (1811–1896). Author of the antislavery book *Uncle Tom's Cabin*. p. 337.

Sullivan, Louis (1856–1924). An architect. Designed tall city buildings. p. 444.

Sylvis, William (1828–1868). Labor leader. Head of National Labor Union. p. 467.

Taft, William Howard (1857–1930). Twenty-seventh President. p. 504.

Tarbell, Ida (1857–1944). One of the muckrakers. Exposed the methods used by John D. Rockefeller. p. 496.

Taylor, Zachary (1784–1850). Twelfth President. p. 309.

Tecumseh (1768?–1813). Chief of the Shawnee Indian tribe. Organized Indians west of the Appalachians against white settlers. p. 245.

Tilden, Samuel J. (1814–1886). Governor of New York. Democratic candidate in disputed presidential election of 1876. p. 378.

Truman, Harry (1884–1972). Thirty-third President. p. 658.

Truth, Sojourner (1797?–1883). A black reformer who worked for abolitionism and women's rights. p. 276.

Tubman, Harriet (1820?–1913). A slave on Maryland plantation who escaped to Philadelphia. She returned south many times to lead other slaves to freedom. p. 312.

Twain, Mark (1835–1910). See Samuel L. Clemens.

Tweed, William M. "Boss" (1823–1878). Head of a corrupt ring in New York City. p. 378.

Tyler, John (1790–1862). Tenth President. p. 298.

Van Buren, Martin (1782–1862). Eighth President. p. 263.

Wagner, Robert (1877–1953). Senator from New York. Author of Wagner Act, which dealt with labor relations. p. 592.

Wallace, George (1919–   ). Alabaman who was third-party candidate in the presidential election of 1968. p. 678.

Warren, Earl (1891–1971). Chief Justice of the Supreme Court from 1953 to 1969. Head of commission to investigate assassination of President Kennedy. p. 661.

Washington, Booker T. (1856–1915). A black educator and a spokesman for black Americans. p. 386.

Washington, George (1732–1799). First President. p. 212.

Weaver, James (1833–1912). Populist candidate in presidential election of 1892. p. 476.

Weaver, Robert (1907–   ). Secretary of housing and urban development in Lyndon Johnson's Cabinet. First black Cabinet member. p. 673.

Webster, Daniel (1782–1852). Senator from Massachusetts. A noted orator who supported a strong national government. p. 226.

Whitman, Walt (1819–1892). A poet who wrote during the last half of the 1800s. p. 394.

Whitney, Eli (1765–1825). Inventor of the cotton gin. He also helped develop the system of interchangeable parts. p. 228.

Williams, Roger (1603?–1683). Puritan minister. An advocate of religious freedom, he started the first settlement in Rhode Island. p. 74.

Wilson, Woodrow (1856–1924). Twenty-eighth President. p. 553.

Young, Brigham (1801–1877). Mormon leader who started a settlement near the Great Salt Lake in 1847. p. 305.

PRESIDENTS AND VICE-PRESIDENTS OF THE UNITED STATES

President	Birth-death	State*	Term	Party	Vice-President
George Washington	1732–1799	Va.	1789–1797	None	John Adams
John Adams	1735–1826	Mass.	1797–1801	Federalist	Thomas Jefferson
Thomas Jefferson	1743–1826	Va.	1801–1805	Democratic-	Aaron Burr
			1805–1809	Republican	George Clinton
James Madison	1751–1836	Va.	1809–1813	Democratic-	George Clinton
			1813–1817	Republican	Elbridge Gerry
James Monroe	1758–1831	Va.	1817–1825	Democratic-Republican	Daniel D. Tompkins
John Quincy Adams	1767–1848	Mass.	1825–1829	National Republican	John C. Calhoun
Andrew Jackson	1767–1845	Tenn.	1829–1833	Democratic	John C. Calhoun
			1833–1837		Martin Van Buren
Martin Van Buren	1782–1862	N.Y.	1837–1841	Democratic	Richard M. Johnson
William H. Harrison	1773–1841	Ohio	1841	Whig	John Tyler
John Tyler	1790–1862	Va.	1841–1845	Whig	....
James K. Polk	1795–1849	Tenn.	1845–1849	Democratic	George M. Dallas
Zachary Taylor	1784–1850	La.	1849–1850	Whig	Millard Fillmore
Millard Fillmore	1800–1874	N.Y.	1850–1853	Whig	....
Franklin Pierce	1804–1869	N.H.	1853–1857	Democratic	William R. King
James Buchanan	1791–1868	Pa.	1857–1861	Democratic	John C. Breckinridge
Abraham Lincoln	1809–1865	Ill.	1861–1865	Republican	Hannibal Hamlin
			1865		Andrew Johnson
Andrew Johnson	1808–1875	Tenn.	1865–1869	Democratic	....
Ulysses S. Grant	1822–1885	Ill.	1869–1873	Republican	Schuyler Colfax
			1873–1877		Henry Wilson
Rutherford B. Hayes	1822–1893	Ohio	1877–1881	Republican	William A. Wheeler
James A. Garfield	1831–1881	Ohio	1881	Republican	Chester A. Arthur
Chester A. Arthur	1830–1886	N.Y.	1881–1885	Republican	....
Grover Cleveland	1837–1908	N.Y.	1885–1889	Democratic	Thomas A. Hendricks
Benjamin Harrison	1833–1901	Ind.	1889–1893	Republican	Levi P. Morton
Grover Cleveland	1837–1908	N.Y.	1893–1897	Democratic	Adlai E. Stevenson
William McKinley	1843–1901	Ohio	1897–1901	Republican	Garret A. Hobart
			1901		Theodore Roosevelt
Theodore Roosevelt	1858–1919	N.Y.	1901–1905	Republican	
			1905–1909		Charles W. Fairbanks
William H. Taft	1857–1930	Ohio	1909–1913	Republican	James S. Sherman
Woodrow Wilson	1856–1924	N.J.	1913–1921	Democratic	Thomas R. Marshall
Warren G. Harding	1865–1923	Ohio	1921–1923	Republican	Calvin Coolidge
Calvin Coolidge	1872–1933	Mass.	1923–1925	Republican	....
			1925–1929		Charles G. Dawes
Herbert C. Hoover	1874–1964	Calif.	1929–1933	Republican	Charles Curtis
Franklin D. Roosevelt	1882–1945	N.Y.	1933–1941	Democratic	John N. Garner
			1941–1945		Henry A. Wallace
			1945		Harry S. Truman
Harry S. Truman	1884–1972	Mo.	1945–1949	Democratic	....
			1949–1953		Alben W. Barkley
Dwight D. Eisenhower	1890–1969	N.Y.	1953–1961	Republican	Richard M. Nixon
John F. Kennedy	1917–1963	Mass.	1961–1963	Democratic	Lyndon B. Johnson
Lyndon B. Johnson	1908–1973	Texas	1963–1965	Democratic	....
			1965–1969		Hubert H. Humphrey
Richard M. Nixon	1913–	N.Y.	1969–1973	Republican	Spiro T. Agnew
			1973–1974		Agnew/Ford
Gerald R. Ford	1913–	Mich.	1974–1977	Republican	Nelson R. Rockefeller
James Earl Carter	1924–	Ga.	1977–1981	Democratic	Walter Mondale
Ronald Reagan	1911–	Calif.	1981–	Republican	George Bush

*State of residence at election

Our Presidents

First on the list is Washington,
Virginia's proudest name;
John Adams next, the Federalist,
From Massachusetts came.

Three sons of old Virginia
Into the White House go;
'Tis Jefferson and Madison,
And then comes James Monroe.

Massachusetts for one term sent
Adams called John Q;
And Tennessee, a Democrat,
Brave Jackson staunch and true.

Martin Van Buren of New York
And Harrison we see;
And Tyler of Virginia,
And Polk of Tennessee.

Louisiana, Taylor sent;
New York, Millard Fillmore;
New Hampshire gave us Franklin Pierce
When Fillmore's term was o'er.

The Keystone State, Buchanan sent;
War thunders shook the realm—
Abe Lincoln wore a martyr's crown,
And Johnson took the helm.

Then U.S. Grant of Illinois
Who ruled with sword and pen;
And Hayes, and Garfield who was shot,
True, noble Buckeye men.

Chester Arthur from New York,
And Grover Cleveland came;
Ben Harrison served just four years,
And Cleveland ruled again.

McKinley, shot at Buffalo,
The nation plunged in grief;
And Teddy Roosevelt of New York
Served seven years as chief.

Taft of Ohio followed him.
Then Woodrow Wilson came,
New Jersey's learned Democrat;
War set the world aflame.

And when the tide of strife and hate
Its baneful course had run,
The country went Republican
And Warren Harding won.

No duty would he shirk,
He died while on a western trip;
Coolidge of Massachusetts then
Assumed the leadership.

California's Hoover served one term.
Then, gripped by Depression's fears,
Voters chose Roosevelt of New York,
Who was President for thirteen years.

When Roosevelt died in office,
Harry Truman of Missouri stepped in;
Then Eisenhower of Kansas
Known for his grit and grin.

Massachusetts sent John Kennedy,
Killed before his term was done.
His V.P., Johnson of Texas,
Was sworn in on Air Force One.

Richard Nixon of California
Resigned after Watergate,
Making Gerald Ford of Michigan
The country's chief of state.

Carter of Georgia served four years,
Plagued by crisis and inflation.
Voters then chose Ronald Reagan
To lead their troubled nation.

Each President serves the people
And each has been quick to see
That the voters and their ballots
Guard this country's liberty.

Isabel Ambler Gilman
Barbara Thompson Howell

729

GLOSSARY

The page references tell where each entry first appears in the text.

KEY TO PRONUNCIATION

a	hat, cap					zh	measure, seizure
ā	age, face	i	it, pin	ou	house, out	ə	represents:
ã	care, air	ī	ice, five	sh	she, rush		a	in about
ä	father, far	ng	long, bring	th	thin, both		e	in taken
ch	child, much	o	hot, rock	ŦH	then, smooth		i	in pencil
e	let, best	ō	open, go	u	cup, butter		o	in lemon
ē	equal, see	ô	order, all	ů	full, put		u	in circus
ėr	term, learn	oi	oil, voice	ü	rule, move		

This Key to Pronunciation is from *Scott, Foresman Intermediate Dictionary*, by E.L. Thorndike and Clarence L. Barnhart. Copyright © 1983, by Scott, Foresman and Company. Reprinted by permission.

abolitionist (ab ə lish′ ə nist). Person opposed to slavery and in favor of ending it. p. 271.

acquit (ə kwit′). To set free; to declare not guilty. p. 126.

Adams-Onis Treaty (ad′ əmz ō nis′ trē′ tē). Treaty signed in 1819 between the United States and Spain that gave Florida to the United States and decided the boundary between the United States and Spanish territory in the Southwest. p. 240.

agriculture (ag′ rə kul chər). Raising crops and livestock; farming. p. 26.

Alien and Sedition Acts (ā′ lē ən and si dish′ ən akts). Four laws enacted by the Federalists in 1798 in response to French actions and with the hope of destroying the Republican party. p. 218.

Alliance for Progress (ə lī′ əns fôr prog′ res). United States program started under President Kennedy to help countries in the Western Hemisphere. p. 645.

allies (al′ īz). Groups or nations that unite for a special purpose. p. 99.

amendment (ə mend′ mənt). Formal change or addition. p. 168.

American enterprise (ə mer′ ə ken en′ tər prīz). Energy and will of Americans to undertake big new projects to benefit themselves and their country. p. 288.

American Federation of Labor (ə mer′ ə ken fed ə rā′ shən ov lā′ bər). Organization of trade unions that was established in the 1880s. Its goal was to organize workers by crafts and skills. p. 470.

Amnesty Act (am′ nə stē akt). Bill passed after the Civil War that allowed most Confederate officials to once again take part in state and national government. p. 373.

Anaconda Plan (an ə kon′ də plan). Strategic plan devised by the Union to defeat the South in the Civil War. It was named after the snake that wraps itself around its victims and crushes them. p. 353.

anarchist (an′ ər kist). Person who wants to do away with all government and laws. p. 468.

annexation (an ək sā′ shən). Taking a country or other territory and making it part of one's own country. p. 301.

annotation (an ə tā′ shən). Note added to point out or explain something in a text. p. 14.

Anti-Federalist (an tē fed′ ər ə list). Opponent of a federal government. p. 173.

apprentice (ə pren′ tis). Person bound by contract to a skilled worker for the purpose of learning a trade or craft. p. 86.

arbitration (är bə trā′ shən). Settlement of a dispute by an impartial person or group. p. 501.

archaeologist (är kē ol′ ə jist). Scientist who studies objects, ruins, and other evidence of human life from the past. p. 20.

architect (är′ kə tekt). Person who designs and draws plans for buildings. p. 442.

aristocrat (ə ris′ tə krat). Person of high social standing. p. 52.

armistice (är′ mə stis). Cease-fire, or halt to fighting, by agreement between warring nations. p. 550.

Articles of Confederation (är′ tə kəlz ov kən fed ə rā′ shən). Document that listed the powers of the central government and the powers of the states in the period immediately following the Revolutionary War. p. 164.

artifact (är′ tə fakt). Any object made by a person. p. 30.

assembly (ə sem′ blē). Legislative branch of a government, usually the lower of two lawmaking bodies. p. 80.

assembly line (ə sem' blē līn). Process by which several workers construct a product by each adding different parts as it moves past them. p. 560.

astronaut (as' trə nôt). Pilot or crew member who travels in a spacecraft into space. p. 2.

Atlanta Compromise (at lan' tə kom' prə mīz). Strategy suggested by Booker T. Washington in a speech in 1895. He advised blacks to give up attempts to achieve social equality and instead strive for opportunities to develop skills. p. 387.

Atlantic Charter (at lan' tik chär' tər). Statement signed by the United States and Great Britain in 1941 expressing their aims for an end to World War II. p. 608.

atlas (at' ləs). Collection of maps. p. 9.

Axis powers (ak' sis pou' ərz). Name given to Italy, Germany, and Japan, the countries that fought against the Allies in World War II. p. 604.

Bank Charter Bill (bangk chär' tər bil). Bill proposed by Henry Clay in 1832 to issue a new charter for the Second Bank of the United States. p. 261.

bank holiday (bangk hol' ə dā). Four-day period in 1933 when President Franklin Roosevelt closed all banks in the country. p. 587.

Bank of the United States (bangk ov thə yü nī' tid stāts). National bank chartered in 1791 to issue bank notes, lend money to the government, and serve as a place for deposit of the government's money. p. 209.

Barbary Coast (bär' bər ē kōst). Coast of North Africa. p. 240.

bar graph (bär graf). Drawing or graph that represents different amounts by bars of different lengths. p. 12.

barrio (bär' rē ō). Separate neighborhood in a city where mainly Spanish-speaking people live. p. 693.

benchmark (bench märk). Reference point used by surveyors to determine differences in elevation; reference point used to compare facts. p. 15.

Bessemer furnace (bes' ə mėr fer' nis). Process discovered by Henry Bessemer in the 1800s to make steel quickly and cheaply. p. 426.

bilingual (bī ling' gwəl). Knowing and using two languages. p. 53.

bill of rights (bil ov rīts). Statement of the basic rights of the people of a state or nation; first ten amendments to the Constitution of the United States, which state the basic rights held by citizens of the United States. p. 174.

black codes (blak kōds). Acts passed in the legislatures of Southern states after the Civil War to place restrictions on freed blacks. p. 372.

Black Hawk's War (blak hôks wär). War in 1832 between the United States and the Sauk and Fox Indians led by Chief Black Hawk. p. 270.

blacklist (blak' list). List of people who are disapproved of or are to be punished. p. 462.

"bleeding Kansas" (blē' ding kan' səs). Nickname given to the Kansas Territory in the 1850s because of the fighting that erupted there over the slavery issue. p. 329.

blitzkrieg (blits' krēg). German word meaning "lightning war," used to describe a type of warfare that is rapid and very violent. p. 606.

border states (bôr' dər stāts). States between the North and the South that stayed in the Union during the Civil War. p. 342.

Boston Massacre (bôs' tən mas' ə kər). Skirmish in 1770 between a mob of colonists and 10 British soldiers in Boston in which 5 colonists were killed. p. 125.

Boston Tea Party (bôs' tən tē pär' tē). Event on the night of December 16, 1773, during which chests of tea belonging to the British East India Company were thrown into Boston Harbor by patriotic colonists disguised as Indians. p. 127.

Boxer Rebellion (bok' sər ri bel' yən). Uprising against foreigners in China in 1900. p. 524.

boycott (boi' kot). Organized campaign in which people refuse to have any dealings with a particular group or business in order to force a change. p. 468.

bread colonies (bred kol' ə nēz). Name given to the middle colonies in the 1700s because of the amount of grain raised there. p. 93.

Brown *v.* Board of Education of Topeka (broun *v.* bôrd ov ej ù kā' shən ov tō pē' kə). Supreme Court case that decided the "separate but equal" doctrine should not apply to schools and that led to the order for the desegregation of public schools. p. 663.

Bull Moose party (bùl müs pär' tē). Another name for the Progressive party led by Theodore Roosevelt in the presidential election of 1912. p. 505.

burial mound (ber' ē al mound). Round mound or pile of earth used as a burial place by Native Americans. p. 31.

Cabinet (kab' ə nit). Group of advisers to the President of the United States. p. 206.

California gold rush (kal' ə fôrn' yə gōld rush). Period of time when many people hurried to California to search for gold. p. 308.

Camp David accords (kamp dā' vid ə kôrds'). Treaty signed in March 1979 in the United States by Israel and Egypt, aimed at establishing peace in the Middle East. p. 700.

capital (kap' ə təl). Money that people or companies invest in factories, machines, or other businesses. p. 433.

caption (kap' shən). Description or explanation accompanying an illustration. p. 14.

carbon 14 (kär′ bən 14). Substance found in all living things, used by archaeologists and geologists in dating materials. p. 24.

carpetbagger (kär′ pit bag′ ər). Name given to Northern whites who moved to the South after the Civil War. p. 373.

cartographer (kär tog′ rə fər). Person who makes maps. p. 9.

cash crop (kash krop). Crop grown for sale rather than for use by the farmer. p. 67.

caucus (kô′ kəs). Meeting of party leaders to choose candidates for public office. p. 212.

cede (sēd). To give up or surrender something. p. 235.

censure (sen′ shər). To find fault with; to condemn. p. 658.

census (sen′ səs). Government count of the number of people in a country. p. 218.

Centennial State (sen ten′ ē əl stāt). Nickname given to Colorado, which became a state in 1876, the one-hundredth anniversary of the United States. p. 410.

charter (chär′ tər). Written permission from a government giving a group of people the right to settle or trade in a certain area. p. 66.

Church of England (chèrch ov ing′ gland). Official church of England. p. 69.

Cibola (sib′ ō lə). Region north of Mexico, believed by the early Spanish explorers to contain vast treasures. p. 57.

city manager (sit′ ē man′ i jər). A person appointed by a city's commissioners to run the city government. p. 497.

civil rights (siv′ əl rīts). Basic rights to which all American citizens are entitled. p. 387.

Civil Rights Act of 1964 (siv′ əl rīts akt ov 1964). Law that prohibited discrimination because of a person's color, race, national origin, religion, or sex. p. 670.

civil service (siv əl sèr′ vis). System under which people are appointed to jobs in the offices of government. p. 384.

clapboard (klap′ bôrd). Thin, narrow board, thicker at one edge than the other. p. 106.

Clayton Antitrust Act (klā′ tun an′ tē trust akt). Law passed to prohibit companies from engaging in practices that reduce competition. p. 508.

closed shop (klōzd shop). Place of work that hires only union members. p. 656.

coexistence (kō ig zis′ tans). Living together in peace. p. 641.

cold war (kōld wôr). Prolonged struggle for power between nations. It is diplomatic and economic rather than military. p. 634.

collective bargaining (kə lek′ tiv bär′ gə ning). Process during which a union represents the workers and bargains for them with the employer. p. 592.

colony (kol′ ə nē). Place that is settled at a distance from the country that governs it. p. 43.

commission (kə mish′ ən). Part of the sale or business done that is paid to the person who did it. p. 96.

commission government (kə mish′ ən guv′ ərn mənt). Form of city government in which an expert is appointed to run each department. p. 497.

Committee of Correspondence (ka mit′ ē ov kôr ə spon′ dəns). Colonial group whose members maintained contact with and sent news through letters to other such groups prior to the War for Independence. p. 126.

Common Sense (kom′ ən sens). Pamphlet published by Thomas Paine in January 1776 in which he urged the colonies to declare their independence from Great Britain. p. 138.

commonwealth (kom′ ən welth). Nation, state, or other political unit that has its own authority but is voluntarily united with another; officially used to describe Puerto Rico. p. 694.

Compromise of 1850 (kom′ prə mīz ov 1850). Plan proposed in 1850 by Senator Henry Clay to end the North-South controversy. p. 323.

Compromise of 1877 (kom′ prə mīz ov 1877). Agreement that settled the disputed presidential election of 1876 and ended the period of Reconstruction. p. 379.

Comstock Lode (kum′ stok lōd). Richest vein of silver in the West, discovered in 1859 in what is today Nevada. p. 411.

concentration camp (kon sən trā′ shən kamp). Camp where political prisoners, prisoners of war, refugees, or members of an ethnic group are held by order of the government. p. 613.

Concord group (kon′ kôrd grüp). Group of American writers who lived near Concord, Massachusetts, in the 1800s. p. 286.

Confederate States of America (kən fed′ ar it stāts ov ə mer′ ə kə). Name taken by the southern states that withdrew from the United States in 1860 and 1861 and organized their own government. p. 332.

confederation (kən fed ə rā′ shən). Loose grouping of states, with some powers held by a central government, but most retained by the states. p. 162.

Congress of Industrial Organizations (kong′ gris ov in dus′ trē al ôr gə nə zā′ shənz). Group of labor unions formed in 1938 and organized according to industries. It merged with the AFL in 1955. p. 597.

conservation (kon sər vā′ shən). Managing natural resources in such a way as to prevent their waste or complete destruction. p. 503.

constitution (kon stə tü′ shən). Set of basic laws by which a nation, state, or group of people is governed. p. 72.

consumer credit (kən sü′ mər kred′ it). Device by which one can buy goods with a small payment at the time of purchase and pay the rest in monthly installments. p. 562.

consumer goods (kən sü′ mər gu̇dz). Things that are made or grown by producers and used by people. p. 562.

containment (kən tān′ mənt). Act of confining a political or military force within its current geographical boundaries. p. 634.

Continental army (kon tə nen′ təl är′ mē). Military force established by Continental Congress in the War for Independence. It was commanded by George Washington. p. 136.

Continental Association (kon tə nen′ təl ə sō sē ā′ shən). A group of delegates from each colony formed to unite the colonies against the British. p. 129.

contour line (kon′ tu̇r līn). Line on a map that is the same distance above or below sea level. p. 4.

convoy (kon′ voi). To travel together for protection. p. 546.

cooperative (kō op′ ə rā tiv). Organization owned and operated for the benefit of those who use its goods and services. p. 475.

Copperheads (kop′ ər heds). Democrats opposed to the policy of Abraham Lincoln in the Civil War. p. 360.

corporation (kôr pə rā′ shən). Group of people who pool their capital to set up a business and who own shares of stock in it. p. 433.

cotton gin (kot′ ən jin). Machine used to separate the cotton fiber from its seeds. p. 228.

covered wagon (kuv′ ərd wag′ ən). Wagon with a canvas top, widely used by Westward-bound pioneers. p. 297.

cowboy (kou′ boi). Person whose main job is to look after cattle on a ranch. p. 415.

cow town (kou toun). Town on a railroad line that grew because cattle were driven there for shipment. p. 415.

craft (kräft). Trade or type of work that requires special skill. p. 86.

crop lien system (krop lēn sis′ təm). System in which landowners could buy supplies on credit by giving shopkeepers a lien on their crops. This was a pledge to repay the shopkeeper when the crops were sold. p. 375.

culture (kul′ chər). Way of life of a group of people, including their customs, traditions, and values. p. 33.

customs duties (kus′ təms dü′ tēs). Taxes paid on imported goods. p. 528.

dame school (dām skül). Small private elementary school run by a woman in her home. p. 104.

Dawes Act (dôz akt). Law passed in 1887 that permitted Indians to own land on reservations for farming. p. 410.

D-day (d-dā). June 6, 1944, the day the Allies began the invasion of France in World War II. p. 612.

debtor (det′ ər). Person who owes something, usually money, to another person. p. 81.

Declaration of Independence (dek lə rā′ shən ov in di pen′ dəns). Document that stated the reasons why the American colonies desired to be independent of British control. p. 139.

Declaration of Sentiments (dek lə rā′ shən ov sen′ tə mənts). Document that declared women's equality with men. It listed ways in which society discriminated against women. p. 276.

Declaratory Act (di klar′ ə tor ē akt). Act by which Parliament declared that it had the authority to tax and pass laws in the colonies. p. 121.

deficit (def′ ə sit). Situation in which more is spent than is taken in. p. 704.

demilitarize (dē mil′ ə tə rīz). To remove armed troops from an area. p. 604.

Democrat (dem′ ə krat). Member of one of the two main political parties in the United States. The party was derived from the Democratic-Republican party. p. 258.

Democratic-Republican party (dem ə krat′ ik ri pub′ lə kən pär′ tē). Political party of the early 1800s, which was made up of Anti-Federalists. It was the forerunner of today's Democratic party. p. 211.

demographer (di mog′ rə fər). One who studies the characteristics of human populations. p. 12.

depression (di presh′ ən). Economic condition in which business is very bad and large numbers of people are unemployed. p. 262.

détente (dā tänt′). Relaxing of tensions, especially between nations or political groups. p. 680.

dictator (dik′ tā tər). Ruler having complete and uncontrolled authority over a nation. p. 602.

diplomacy (də plō′ mə sē). Handling of important dealings between nations. p. 519.

direct primary (də rekt′ prī′ mer ē). System by which members of a party vote to select their party's candidates. p. 492.

dividend (div′ ə dend). Money that stockholders receive as their share of the company's profits. p. 580.

domino theory (dom′ ə nō thir′ ē). Idea that if one country falls to the Communists, the next or neighboring country will inevitably fall in turn. p. 676.

draft (draft). Process by which men are selected for military service without their expressed consent. p. 356.

Dred Scott case (dred skot cās). United States Supreme Court case that upheld the right of the master to his slave as property and declared the Missouri Compromise of 1820 unconstitutional. p. 329.

drought (drout). Long period of dry weather with no rain. p. 29.

dry farming (drī fär' ming). Techniques used in farming areas that have little water. p. 419.

Dust Bowl (dust bōl). Area in the Great Plains in which soil erosion, caused by a long period of drought and poor farming methods, resulted in severe dust storms. p. 594.

effigy mound (ef' ə jē mound). Mound or pile of earth built in the shape of an animal or human being. p. 31.

egalitarian (i gal ə tār' ē ən). Person who believes all people are equal and have the same social, political, and economic rights. p. 281.

Eisenhower Doctrine (ī' zən hou ər dok' trən). Statement issued by President Eisenhower declaring that the United States would offer economic aid to the countries of the Middle East and defend them from attack by Communist countries. p. 643.

elector (i lek' tər). One of the people chosen by the state legislature to elect the President. p. 175.

electricity (i lek tris' ə tē). Form of energy. It can produce light, heat, motion, and magnetic force. p. 435.

elevation (el ə vā' shən). Height of the earth's surface, usually expressed in feet or meters above or below sea level. p. 4.

Emancipation Proclamation (i man sə pā' shən prok lə mā' shən). Proclamation issued by President Lincoln on January 1, 1863, that declared all slaves in the rebelling states to be free. p. 347.

Embargo Act (em bär' gō akt). Law passed in 1807 that forbade American ships and foreign ships from carrying American goods to other countries. p. 242.

empire (em' pīr). Territories and peoples under the control of a powerful nation. p. 46.

enumerated articles (i nü' mə rāt əd ar' tə kəlz). List of colonial products that could be shipped only to England or to other English colonies. p. 117.

environment (en vī' rən mənt). Everything in an area that affects the growth and development of living things, including land, water, plants, animals, and climate. p. 33.

Era of Good Feeling (ir' ə ov gùd fē' ling). Period following the War of 1812 (during the presidency of James Monroe) when the United States experienced peace and unity. p. 249.

excavate (eks' kə vāt). To dig into or to uncover by digging. p. 30.

executive branch (eg zek' yə tiv branch). Part of the government that is headed by the President and is responsible for carrying out laws passed by Congress. p. 170.

exile (eg' zīl). Person forced to leave his or her country. p. 645.

exodus of 1879 (ek' sə dəs ov 1879). Emigration of black people from the South to the West. p. 389.

extinct (ek stingkt'). No longer existing. p. 23.

factor (fak' tər). Person who does business for another; a trading agent. p. 96.

Fallen Timbers (fô' lən tim' bərz). Name of a region in the Northwest Territory where the Indians were defeated by American soldiers in a battle by the same name. p. 232.

Far East (fär ēst). Countries of eastern Asia and Southeast Asia. p. 40.

Farmers' Alliance (fär' mərz ə lī' əns). Regional organizations of farmers formed in the 1880s to help solve their problems. p. 476.

favorite son (fā' vər it sun). Candidate favored by the delegates or people from one state or section. p. 256.

federal budget (fed' ər əl buj' it). Estimate of the amount of money that the United States government will take in and spend over a 12-month period. p. 704.

federal government (fed' ər əl guv' ərn mənt). Form of government in which power is divided between the national government and the governments of the states. p. 172.

Federalist (fed' ər ə list). Person who supported the principle of federal government. p. 172.

Federalist papers (fed' ər ə list pā' pərz). Series of articles written in support of the Constitution. p. 173.

Federalist party (fed' ər ə list pär' tē). Political party in the United States that believed in a strong central government and favored the ratification of the Constitution. p. 210.

federal republic (fed' ər əl ri pub' lik). Government of the United States, in which powers are shared by the states and central government. It is based on the consent of the people through elected representatives. p. 175.

Federal Reserve System (fed' ər əl ri zerv' sis' t m). Federal system of banks consisting of 12 Federal Reserve banks, which provide services for the private banks in their district. p. 507.

"Fifty-four forty or fight" (fif' tē fôr fôr' tē ôr fīt). A campaign slogan used in the presidential election of 1844 by Americans who were for the expansion of America as far north as 54°40'. p. 298.

fireside chat (fīr' sīd chat). Name given to the reports President Roosevelt gave over the radio to the American people. p. 588.

First Continental Congress (ferst kon tə nen' təl kong' gris). Meeting in September 1774 of delegates from the American colonies assembled in Philadelphia to discuss colonial grievances against Great Britain. p. 129.

flatboat (flat' bōt). Large boat with a flat bottom. For carrying goods on a river or canal. p. 234.

Folsom man (fōl' səm man). Person of a prehistoric culture thought to have lived in North America at the end of the most recent Ice Age. p. 24.

Force Bill (fôrs bil). Law passed in 1833 giving the President authorization to use the army and navy to collect tariff duties. p. 259.

foreign-born (fôr' ən bôrn). Born in another country. p. 335.

forty-niners (fôr tē nī' nərz). Name given to gold seekers who came to California in the gold rush of 1849. p. 308.

49th parallel (49*th* par' ə lel). Parallel established as the boundary between the Oregon country and British-controlled Canada. p. 299.

Fourteen Points (fôr' tēn points). American terms of peace outlined by President Wilson to end World War I. p. 551.

free coinage of silver (frē koi' nij ov sil' vər). Campaign issue in presidential elections of the 1890s. Populists and some others wanted the government to coin silver again. p. 477.

Freedmen's Bureau (frēd' mənz byùr' ō). Governmental agency set up in 1865 to help freed slaves. p. 372.

free state (frē stāt). State in which slavery was illegal. p. 250.

French and Indian War (french and in' dē ən wôr). War fought in North America from 1754 to 1763 between Great Britain and France and their Indian allies. p. 114.

frontier (frun tir'). Farthest unsettled edge of a country. p. 90.

Fugitive Slave Law (fyü' jə tiv slāv lô). Law requiring that runaway slaves be picked up and returned to their masters. p. 324.

Fundamental Orders (fun də men' təl ôr' dərz). Constitution drawn up by the Connecticut Colony in 1639. It has been called the world's first written constitution. p. 75.

fun factor (fun fak' tər). Any one of the causes that result in having enjoyment or fun. p. 16.

Gadsden Purchase (gadz' den pèr chəs). Strip of land purchased by the United States from Mexico in 1853 for $10 million. Today it is the southern parts of New Mexico and Arizona. p. 304.

Gentlemen's Agreement (jen' təl mənz ə grē' mənt). Agreement between the United States and Japan that would allow Japanese children to attend public schools if the Japanese would not let more workers come to the United States. p. 525.

geologist (jē ol' ə jist). Scientist who learns about the earth by studying rocks and rock formations. p. 24.

geometric mound (jē ə met' rik mound). Mound or pile of earth built in the form of a circle, a square, or parallel lines. p. 31.

Gettysburg Address (get' ēz bərg ə dres'). Speech given by President Lincoln on November 19, 1863, at the site of the battle of Gettysburg. The occasion was the ceremony dedicating a part of the battlefield as a cemetery for those who had died in the battle. p. 352.

ghetto (get' ō). Section of a city where members of a minority group live. It is usually crowded and run-down. p. 674.

GI Bill of Rights (jē ī bil ov rīts). Bill that provided government aid to the veterans of World War II. p. 650.

Gilded Age (gil' did āj). Name given to the years following the Civil War, describing a flashy, get-rich-quick society. p. 382.

girdled (gér' dəld). Killed trees by cutting through the bark all the way around the trunk. p. 67.

glacier (glā' shər). Large body of ice formed from snow that moves slowly down a mountain or valley and spreads outward over a large area of land. p. 20.

gold standard (gold stan' dərd). Belief that the money supply of a country should be based on gold only. p. 479.

governor's council (guv' ər nərz koun' səl). Upper house in the legislature of most colonies. Members of the council were appointed by the governor. p. 123.

grammar school (gram' ər skül). Public elementary school, usually attended by boys, to prepare children for college. p. 105.

Grange (grānj). Organization of farmers who sought to improve their situation. p. 474.

graph (graf). Special kind of drawing that uses pictures, circles, bars, or lines to give facts and compare things. p. 12.

Great American Desert (grāt ə mer' ə ken dez' ərt). Name given by an exploration expedition in the 1820s to the lands between the Missouri River and the Rocky Mountains. p. 294.

Great Compromise (grāt kom' prə mīz). Connecticut Compromise; a proposal that created two houses of Congress, one in which states would be represented by population, and one in which states would be represented equally. p. 169.

Great Society (grāt sə sī' ə tē). Program favored by President Lyndon B. Johnson for improving the domestic welfare of all people in the United States. p. 672.

greenback (grēn' bak). Paper money printed on green paper that was issued by the Union to help pay war expenses. p. 358.

Green Revolution (grēn rev ə lü′ shən). Advances in agriculture that led to an increase in production. p. 652.

Grenville Acts (gren′ vil akts). Economic policies proposed by George Grenville in 1764 to tighten British control over the American colonies. p. 117.

guerrilla (gə ril′ ə). Member of an armed band that carried on hit-and-run warfare apart from a country's uniformed forces. p. 153.

Gulf of Tonkin Resolution (gulf ov tän′ kin rez ə lü′ shən). Act that allowed the United States government to take military action in Vietnam. p. 677.

Harlem Renaissance (här′ ləm ren ə säns′). Revival of arts and culture in the black community in New York City in the 1920s. p. 571.

Hartford Convention (härt′ fərd kən ven′ shən). Meeting in 1814 of New England's Federalist leaders in Hartford, Connecticut, at which they discussed their discontent with the War of 1812. p. 248.

Hessian (hesh′ ən). German soldier hired to fight for the British in the American War for Independence. p. 147.

hogshead (hogz′ hed). Large barrel. p. 96.

holocaust (hol′ ə kôst). Great or complete destruction; the mass extermination of European Jews by the Nazis during World War II. p. 614.

"holy experiment" (hō′ lē ek sper′ ə ment). Colony of Pennsylvania, set up by William Penn as a refuge for Quakers. p. 77.

Homestead Act (hōm′ sted akt). Law passed in 1862 that offered citizens the opportunity to acquire 160 acres of government land for a small fee provided they lived on it and farmed it for 5 years. p. 377.

hostage (hôs′ tij). Person who is seized by another person or group and is held captive in order for the captors to obtain a demand. p. 703.

hot line (hot līn). Direct telephone line between the United States and the Soviet Union, offering immediate communication in an emergency. p. 647.

House of Burgesses (hous ov bėr′ jis əs). Representative assembly in colonial Virginia. A step toward self-government. p. 69.

Hudson River School (hud′ sən riv′ ər skül). Group of American artists of the 1800s who painted scenes of areas along the Hudson River. p. 283.

Huguenot (hyü′ gə not). French Protestant of the sixteenth or seventeenth century. p. 89.

human rights (hyü′ mən rīts). Basic rights to which all humans are entitled. p. 700.

Ice Age (īs āj). Most recent time that the Northern Hemisphere was covered by glaciers. p. 20.

impeach (im pēch′). To charge a public official with doing something illegal while in office. p. 369.

imperialist (im pir′ ē ə list). Person who favors the policy of extending the rule of one country over other countries or lands. p. 515.

impress (im pres′). To seize by authority for public use. p. 214.

inauguration (in ô gyə rā′ shən). Ceremony to put someone in office. p. 204.

indenture (in den′ chər). Contract by which a person agrees to work for a certain period of time in exchange for free passage to a foreign land. p. 88

Indies (in′ dēz). Name used in the fifteenth and sixteenth centuries to refer to India and nearby lands. Europeans also used the name to refer to newly discovered lands in the Western Hemisphere. p. 40.

indigo (in′ də gō). Plant from which blue dye is made. p. 80.

Industrial Revolution (in dus′ trē əl rev ə lü′ shən). Period of great change in the way people worked and lived. It was brought about by the development of power-driven machines. p. 227.

industrial union (in dus′ trē əl yün′ yən). Union made up of all the workers in one industry. p. 597.

inflation (in flā′ shən). Economic condition in which the value of money decreases and the price of goods increases. p. 656.

initiative (i nish′ ē ə tiv). Right of citizens outside the legislature to introduce new laws. p. 477.

interchangeable parts (in tər chānj′ jə bəl partz). Parts that are made exactly alike and are capable of being used in place of each other in manufactured products. p. 229.

international law (in tər nash′ ə nəl lô). Body of rules that countries agree to follow in controlling their relations with each other. p. 540.

Interstate Commerce Act (in′ tər stāt kom′ ərs akt). Law passed in 1886 that determined the rates railroads could charge shippers. It also set up the Interstate Commerce Commission (ICC) to see that the law was carried out. p. 476.

intervene (in tər vēn′). To come between two people or groups to help settle a disagreement. p. 527.

Intolerable Acts (in tol′ ər ə bəl akts). Four laws passed by Parliament to punish the people of Massachusetts for the Boston Tea Party. p. 128.

inventory (in′ vən tôr ē). Stock of unsold goods. p. 582.

Invincible Armada (in vin′ sə bəl är mäd′ ə). Large fleet of ships sent by King Philip of Spain in 1587 to invade England. p. 65.

ironclad (ī′ ərn klad). Ship protected by iron plates. p. 345.

iron curtain (ī′ ərn kėr′ tən). Imaginary wall or line separating the countries of Eastern Europe from the other nations. p. 634.

irrigate (ir′ ə gāt). To bring water to crops, usually through canals, ditches, or pipes. p. 27.

island-hopping (ī′ lənd hop′ ing). Allied plan for fighting the Japanese in the Pacific during World War II. The Allies seized key islands and bypassed others. p. 615.

isolationist (ī sə lā′ shə nist). Person who favors the policy of his or her nation keeping to itself and not having political or economic relations with other nations. p. 607.

Jay's Treaty (jāz trē′ tē). Treaty signed in 1794 that resolved several problems that existed between the United States and Great Britain. p. 214.

Jim Crow (jim krō). Phrase used to describe the system of separate but equal facilities for black people. p. 389.

joint-stock company (joint stok kum′ pə nē). Company organized so that many people own stock in the company. The stockholders share the profits and lose only what they invested, should the company fail. p. 66.

judicial branch (jü dish′ əl branch). Part of government that decides the meaning of laws and sets up courts to try those who disobey laws. p. 170.

Judiciary Act of 1789 (jü dish′ ē er ē akt ov 1789). Act passed by Congress in 1789 that set up the basic framework of the federal court system, including the Supreme Court, 3 circuit courts, and 13 district courts. p. 207.

Kansas-Nebraska bill (kan′ zəs nə bras′ kə bil). Bill creating the territories of Kansas and Nebraska from the land of the Louisiana Purchase. p. 326.

Kellogg-Briand Pact (kel′ ôg brē än′ pakt). Treaty signed in 1928 in which many countries agreed to settle disputes by peaceful means. p. 576.

Kitchen Cabinet (kich′ ən kab′ ə nit). Group of advisers to the President, including several politicians and newspaper people who President Jackson considered to be closer to the ordinary people than his Cabinet members were. p. 268.

Knights of Labor (nīts ov lā′ bər). Organization started in 1869 to unite all skilled and unskilled workers into one union. p. 467.

Ku Klux Klan (kü kluks klan). Secret society formed by Southern whites after the Civil War to maintain white supremacy. p. 375.

labor union (lā′ bər yün′ yən). Group of workers joined together for the purpose of protecting the interests of its members. p. 462.

League of Nations (lēg ov nā′ shənz). Organization formed in 1920 to promote cooperation among nations and maintain peace following World War I. p. 551.

Leatherstocking Tales (leŦH′ ər stok ing tālz). Series of novels written by James Fenimore Cooper about an American frontiersman. p. 283.

legend (lej′ ənd). Story passed down over many years that may or may not be true. p. 62.

legislative branch (lej′ is lā tiv branch). Part of government responsible for making laws. p. 169.

legislature (lej′ is lā chər). Body of government responsible for making laws. p. 77.

lend-lease (lend lēs). Policy of making a loàn of goods or services to an ally and receiving goods or services in return. p. 607.

Lewis and Clark Expedition (lü′ is and klärk eks pə dish′ ən). Expedition running from 1804 to 1806 that explored the western lands. p. 237.

life expectancy (līf ek spek′ tən sē). Average age to which a person usually lives. p. 489.

Lincoln-Johnson plan (ling′ kən jon′ sən plan). Plan by which Confederate states were readmitted into the Union. p. 366.

line graph (līn graf). Graph that shows information by means of a line that connects points. p. 12.

llama (lä′ mə). South American animal that is related to the camel but is smaller and has no hump. p. 36.

local colorist (lō′ kəl kul′ ər ist). Author who writes a tale set in a specific region of the United States and makes the scenery, characters, and dialogue typical of that region. p. 397.

long drive (lông drīv). Herding large numbers of cattle from ranches over the plains to a rail line for shipment east. p. 415.

longhorn cattle (lông′ hôrn kat′ əl). Breed of cattle that has long horns and is raised for beef. It is descended from cattle brought to America by the Spanish. p. 49.

loose interpretation (lüs in tėr prə tā′ shən). Belief that Congress has certain implied powers that are not exactly stated in the Constitution. p. 208.

Lost Colony (lôst kol′ ə nē). English colony founded on Roanoke Island off the coast of North Carolina in 1587. The settlers of this colony later disappeared without a trace. p. 65.

Louisiana Purchase (lü ē zē an′ ə pėr′ chəs). Region of land the United States bought from France in 1803. It extended from the Mississippi River west to the Rocky Mountains and from Canada south to the Gulf of Mexico. p. 236.

Loyalist (loi′ ə list). Colonist who was a supporter of Great Britain and King George III. p. 137.

Lusitania (lü si tā′ nē ə). British passenger ship sunk without warning in May 1915 by a German submarine. p. 541.

mahogany (mə hog′ ə nē). Heavy reddish-brown hardwood used in making furniture. p. 93.

manifest destiny (man′ ə fest des′ tə nē). Belief held in the 1840s that the territorial expansion of the United States to its natural limits was right and inevitable. p. 304.

Marshall Plan (mär′ shəl plan). United States program for aiding the economic recovery of Europe after World War II. p. 635.

martial law (mär′ shəl lô). Military rule imposed during troubled times instead of the usual civil authority. p. 706.

mass transit (mas tran′ sit). Way of moving a great number of people from one place to another at the same time. Trains, subways, buses, and airplanes are types of *mass transit*. p. 7.

Mayflower Compact (mā flou′ ər kom′ pakt). Document drawn up and signed by the Pilgrims aboard ship by which they agreed to make laws as needed for the colony's good and to obey these laws. p. 70.

mechanical reaper (mə kan′ ə kəl rē′ pər). Machine that cuts grain or harvests a crop. p. 291.

mercantilism (mėr′ kən ti liz əm). Economic system by which a government controls agriculture, industry, and commerce so that the country sells more goods than it buys and thereby increases the money wealth of the nation. p. 96.

mercenary (mėr′ sə ner ē). Soldier serving in the army of a foreign country for wages. p. 147.

merger (mėr′ jer). Process by which two or more companies combine to make a single company. p. 574.

Mexican Cession (mek′ sə kən sesh′ ən). Land given to the United States by Mexico as part of the Treaty of Guadalupe Hidalgo. p. 304.

migrant (mī′ grənt). Person who travels from one place to another to find work. p. 690.

militarism (mil′ ə tə riz əm). Policy of placing emphasis on the military power of a country. p. 536.

militia (mə lish′ ə). Organized military force made up of able-bodied citizens, not regular soldiers, that is usually called upon in emergencies. p. 114.

mint (mint). Place where coins are made by government authority. p. 218.

minuteman (min′ it man). Member of an army of citizens ready to fight the British at "a minute's notice" during the War for Independence. p. 130.

missile (mis′ əl). Self-propelled rocket that can be launched from the ground, sea, or air to hit a target many miles away. p. 707.

mission (mish′ ən). Settlement consisting of a church, other buildings, and land for the purpose of teaching Christianity to nonbelievers. p. 48.

Missouri Compromise (mə zùr′ ē kom′ prə mīz). Compromise by which Missouri was admitted to the Union as a slave state and Maine was admitted as a free state. p. 250.

mobilize (mō′ bə līz). To assemble the armed forces and prepare for war. p. 537.

Mongoloid (mong′ gə loid). Person belonging to the race characterized by yellow skin, slanting eyes, prominent cheekbones, and straight dark hair. p. 22.

monopoly (mə nop′ ə lē). Sole control of an entire industry. p. 127.

Monroe Doctrine (mən rō′ dok′ trən). Statement issued by President Monroe in 1823 declaring that European nations should not interfere with American nations or try to claim additional territory in the Western Hemisphere. p. 250.

Mormon (môr′ mən). Member of the Church of Jesus Christ of Latter-day Saints, whose beliefs are based on the teachings of Joseph Smith. p. 305.

Mound Builders (mound bil′ dərz). Group of prehistoric Indians who lived in central and eastern North America, especially in the Ohio River and Mississippi River valleys. They built mounds of earth as burial places or as the foundation for a wooden building. p. 30.

mountain man (moun′ tən man). Fur trapper who lived in the mountains, was wise in the ways of the wilderness, and played an important part in the expansion of the United States in the 1800s. p. 294.

muckraker (muk′ rāk ər). Person who writes about wrongdoing in business and politics. p. 496.

mutiny (myü′ tə nē). Open rebellion against the person or people in authority, such as soldiers rebelling against their officers. p. 155.

national anthem (nash′ ə nəl an′ thəm). A country's official patriotic song. p. 246.

nationalism (nash′ ə nə liz əm). Feeling of loyalty to one's country. p. 248.

nativist (nā′ tə vist). Person who wanted to reduce or end immigration. p. 454.

Neutrality Acts (nü tral′ ə tē akts). Several laws passed by Congress between 1935 and 1937 to keep America out of war. p. 604.

neutral rights (nü′ trəl rīts). Rights associated with being neutral, or not taking sides in a quarrel or war. p. 241.

New Deal (nü dēl). Policies introduced by President Franklin D. Roosevelt in the 1930s to fight the Great Depression and improve the economic and social welfare of the United States. p. 587.

New Federalism (nü fed′ ər ə liz əm). Name given to President Reagan's domestic program, which reduced and eliminated certain federal programs and shifted other programs from the federal government to the states. p. 706.

New Immigration (nü im ə grā′ shən). People coming to the United States from eastern and southern Europe, beginning in the 1800s. p. 449.

New Jersey Plan (nü jėr′ zē plan). Small States plan; the proposal that all states should be represented equally in Congress. p. 169.

New South (nü south). A South in which manufacturing and commercial interests would play a more important role. p. 376.

New World (nü wėrld). Western Hemisphere. p. 44.

nomadic (nō mad′ ik). Moving from place to place. p. 407.

nominate (nom′ ə nāt). To choose a person as candidate for office. p. 212.

nominating convention (nom′ ə nāt ing kən ven′ shən). Meeting of party members from all states to nominate the presidential candidates. p. 264.

nonimportation agreements (non im pôr tā′ shən ə grē′ mənts). Agreements signed by colonial merchants, who pledged not to import any British goods until Parliament repealed the Stamp Act. p. 121.

nonviolent resistance (non vī′ ə lənt rē zis′ təns). Refusal to obey laws that one believes to be unjust, but without resorting to violence. p. 664.

North Atlantic Treaty Organization (nôrth at lan′ tik trē′ tē ôr gə nə zā′ shən), *or NATO* (nā′ tō). Alliance of 14 non-Communist countries formed for joint military defense. p. 636.

Northwest Ordinance (nôrth west′ ôr′ də nəns). Law passed in 1787 that set up a system for governing the Northwest Territory. p. 166.

northwest passage (nôrth west′ pas′ ij). Nonexistent water route sought by early explorers to provide a shortcut from Europe to Asia and the East Indies through North America. p. 50.

Northwest Territory (nôrth west′ ter′ ə tôr ē). Territory north of the Ohio River from the Appalachian Mountains to the Mississippi River. It now forms Ohio, Indiana, Illinois, Michigan, Wisconsin, and part of Minnesota. p. 153.

nullification (nul ə fə kā′ shən). Belief that a state could nullify, or declare void, a national law within its own boundaries. p. 258.

nullify (nul′ ə fī). To cancel or veto. p. 258.

oil refinery (oil ri fī′ nər ē). Industrial plant where gasoline and other products are separated from the crude oil that is taken out of the ground. p. 438.

Old Immigration (ōld im ə grā′ shən). People coming to the United States from the countries in northern and western Europe starting in the 1700s. p. 450.

Old Northwest (ōld nôrth west′). Name given to Northwest Territory after the purchase of Louisiana from France. p. 238.

Old Southwest (ōld south west′). Name given to the area south of the Ohio River between the Appalachians and the Mississippi River after the Louisiana Purchase. p. 239.

omniverous (om niv′ ər əs). Eating both plants and animals. p. 26.

Open Door policy (ō′ pən dôr pol′ ə sē). All nations having the same opportunities and privileges, even within another country's sphere of influence. p. 523.

open range (ō′ pən rānj). Government-owned lands in the northern plains on which cattle ranchers grazed their herds for free. p. 417.

orbit (ôr′ bit). To travel a circle around the earth. p. 2.

Oregon Trail (ôr′ ə gən trāl). Route from Missouri to Oregon used by settlers moving to the Northwest in the 1800s. p. 297.

oronoco (ôr ə nō′ kō). Mild tobacco from an area in South America near the Orinoco River. p. 66.

overseas empire (ō vər sēz′ em′ pīr). Lands controlled by distant countries. p. 515.

overseer (ō′ vər sē ər). Person hired to supervise others or their work. p. 313.

pacifist (pas′ ə fist). Person opposed to war who favors settling all disputes between nations by peaceful means. p. 611.

pamphlet (pam′ flit). Paper-covered booklet. p. 78.

Parliament (pär′ lə mənt). Lawmaking body in Great Britain. p. 117.

patent (pat′ ənt). Document giving an inventor the right to be the only person to make or sell his or her invention for a certain period of time. p. 218.

Patriot (pā′ trē ət). Person who loves and loyally supports his or her country. In the struggle against the British, a person who fought for the independence of the American colonies. p. 137.

patroon (pə trün′). Owners of large grants of land received from the Dutch government in colonial times. p. 55.

patroon system (pə trün′ sis′ təm). System by which Dutch government gave away large grants of land in North America to promote settlement. p. 55.

Peace Corps (pēs kôr). Agency of the United States government that sends volunteers with various skills to other countries to help improve conditions. p. 644.

Peace Democrat (pēs dem′ ə krat). Northern Democrat opposed to the Civil War. p. 360.

perjury (pėr′ jər ē). Act of lying while under oath. p. 686.

petition (pə tish′ ən). Formal request to someone in authority for a privilege or a right; often a written document containing the signatures of the people making the request. p. 59.

Pickett's charge (pik′ its chärj). Famous charge led by the Confederate general Pickett during the battle of Gettysburg. p. 351.

pie graph (pī graf). Graph drawn in the shape of a circle that represents an amount. A slice or section of the graph shows a part of the whole. p. 12.

"Pikes Peak or Bust!" (pīks pēk ôr bust). Cry used by the thousands of people rushing to Colorado Territory after gold was discovered there in 1858. p. 410.

Pilgrim (pil' grəm). Person who travels on a religious journey. Specifically, one who settled in Plymouth colony in 1620. p. 70.

Pinckney's Treaty (pingk' nēz trē' tē). Treaty signed in 1795 that settled the dispute between the United States and Spain over the western and southern boundaries of the United States and the issue of navigation on the Mississippi River. p. 215.

plantation (plan tā' shən). Large farm on which one main crop is grown. p. 67.

platform (plat' fôrm). Statement of goals or plan of action of a group. p. 477.

Plessy v. Ferguson (ples' ē v. fèr' gə sən). Case in which the Supreme Court ruled that the "separate but equal" policy did not violate the Fourteenth Amendment. p. 388.

pogrom (pō' grəm). Organized massacre of a group of people, especially of Jews. p. 450.

political democracy (pə lit' ə kəl di mok' rə sē). People taking part in the process of choosing leaders and influencing their government. p. 264.

political machine (pə lit' ə kəl mə shēn'). Smoothly run political organization. p. 459.

political map (pə lit' ə kəl map). Map that shows national and state boundaries and the names and locations of towns and cities. p. 4.

political party (pə lit' ə kəl pär' tē). Organization of people who hold similar views on policies a government should follow and who choose candidates for public office and work to get them elected. p. 210.

politics (pol' ə tiks). Art or science concerned with guiding or influencing government. p. 227.

popular sovereignty (pop' yə lər sov' rən tē). Doctrine existing before the Civil War that gave people living in a new territory the right to decide by vote whether they wanted slavery in their territory. p. 326.

population explosion (pop yə lā' shən ek splō' zhən). Rapid increase in the number of people in an area. p. 92.

Populist (pop' yə list). Member of the People's party, a national political party formed in the 1880s. p. 476.

portage (pôr' tij). Carrying boats or provisions for short distances on land, from one body of water to another, or around a falls or rapids. p. 51.

precipitation (pri sip ə tā' shən). Moisture that falls to the earth's surface in the form of rain, snow, sleet, hail, fog, or mist. p. 8.

prehistoric (prē his tôr' ik). Time before there were written records. p. 20.

presidio (pri sid' ē ō). Military post or fort in an area under Spanish or Mexican control. p. 306.

prime minister (prīm min' ə stər). Chief minister in certain governments. p. 117.

privateer (prī və tir'). Privately owned armed ship built to attack and capture enemy merchant ships. In the War for Independence, privateers joined the United States in fighting the British. p. 150.

proclamation of neutrality (prok lə mā' shən ov nü tral' ə tē). Statement that the United States would take no sides in the war between Britain and France. p. 213.

Proclamation of 1763 (prok lə mā' shən ov 1763). Royal order issued by the king of Great Britain that prohibited colonists from settling on land west of the Appalachians. p. 117.

Progressive movement (prə gres' iv müv' mənt). Period of reform in the United States in the early 1900s. p. 496.

promotional literature (prə mō' shə nəl lit' ər ə chər). Literature in the form of a pamphlet, advertisement, book, or letter used to develop interest in a person, product, or plan. p. 86.

propaganda (prop ə gan' də). Plan or method for spreading ideas to further a cause. p. 126.

proprietary colony (prə prī' ə ter ē kol' ə nē). Colony granted by the British government to a person or persons who then have full power of ownership and may appoint the governor and other officials. p. 79.

proprietor (prə prī' ə tər). Person who received a large grant of land from the king. p. 78.

protective tariff (prə tek' tiv tar' if). Tax on imports so that imported goods cannot be sold at lower prices than domestic goods. p. 250.

protectorate (prə tek' tər it). Place or country under the protection of another country. p. 526.

provisional government (prə vizh' ə nəl guv' ərn mənt). Temporary government. p. 298.

public utility (pub' lik yü til' ə tē). Company that offers a service to the public, such as selling water, gas, and electricity. p. 492.

pueblo (pweb' lō). Spanish word for "town." p. 28.

puncheon (pun' chən). A split log. p. 106.

Puritan (pyùr' ə tən). Member of a group who wanted a more simple church organization in the Church of England in the 1600s. p. 72.

Quaker (kwā' kər). Member of a Christian group called the Society of Friends. Quakers favor simple religious services and are opposed to war. p. 77.

Quartering Act (kwôr' tər ing akt). Act issued by the British in 1765 that ordered the colonial governments to furnish quarters and provisions for British troops in the colonies. p. 118.

quota (kwō' tə). Fixed or limited number. p. 565.

radical (rad' ə kəl). Person who favors extreme changes or reforms, especially in politics. p. 565.

Radical Republican (rad' ə kəl ri pub' lə kən). Member of Lincoln's party who believed he was too sympathetic toward the South. p. 359.

radioactivity (rā dē ō ak tiv' ə tē). Property of some elements by which they give off energy as a result of the spontaneous decay of the nuclei of their atoms. p. 24.

ratify (rat' ə fī). To approve. p. 171.

ration (rash' ən). To limit the amount of something that someone can buy or use. p. 546.

rebate (rē' bāt). To pay back part of the money paid. p. 438.

recall (rē' kôl). Procedure by which the people can vote to remove an elected official from office before his or her term has ended. p. 492.

Reconstruction (rē kən struk' shən). Name given to the period following the Civil War (1865–1877). p. 364.

Reconstruction Act of 1867 (rē kən struk' shən akt ov 1867). Bill placing Southern states under military rule until Reconstruction was complete. p. 369.

Red Scare (red skãr). Fear of Communist plots in America after the Russian Revolution in 1917. p. 565.

referendum (ref ə ren' dəm). Process by which citizens vote directly to pass or reject a proposed law. p. 477.

reform (ri fôrm'). To change conditions with the hope of making them better. p. 274.

relief map (ri lēf' map). Map that shows the elevation, or height, of the earth's surface. p. 4.

relocation center (rē lō kā' shən sen' tər). Camp where groups of people are sent to live on government orders. p. 621.

"Remember the Alamo!" (ri mem' bər ŦHə al' ə mō). Battle cry used to raise an army to fight for the independence of Texas. p. 300.

"Remember the Maine!" (ri mem' bər ŦHə mān). Popular slogan in the United States in 1898, after the battleship *Maine* was blown up at Havana. p. 519.

reparations (rep ə rā' shənz). Payment or other compensation for wrong or injury; payments made by a defeated country for damages inflicted during war. p. 551.

repeal (ri pēl). To cancel or do away with. p. 121.

Republic of Texas (ri pub' lik ov tek' səs). Independent nation formed in 1836 after the Texas victory over Mexico. p. 301.

Republican party (ri pub' lik ən pär' tē). One of the two major political parties in the United States. Formed in the mid-nineteenth century by opponents of slavery. p. 328.

reservation (rez ər vā' shən). Public land set aside, or reserved, by the government for the use of Native Americans. p. 404.

revenue (rev' ə nü). Money coming in. p. 250.

Roman Catholic Church (rō' mən kath' ə lik chėrch). A Christian church that recognizes the pope in Rome as its head. p. 79.

Roosevelt Corollary (rō' zə velt kôr' ə ler ē). Policy announced in 1904 that stated the United States would intervene in the Latin American republics to see that their debts were paid. p. 527.

Rough Riders (ruf rī' dərz). Cavalry regiment, led by Theodore Roosevelt, that was recruited for the war with Spain in 1898. p. 521.

royal colony (roi' əl kol' ə nē). Colony directly under the control of the king. p. 69.

salt lick (sôlt lik). Natural deposits of salt found on the ground. p. 234.

SALT II (sôlt tü). Treaty between the United States and the Soviet Union to limit weapons. p. 701.

sanitation (san ə tā' shən). Making clean and healthful conditions, especially in terms of water supply, garbage, and sewage. p. 455.

scalawag (skal' ə wag). Term used in the South after the Civil War to describe a white Southerner who sided with the new state governments. p. 373.

secession (si sesh' ən). Formal withdrawal from an organization. p. 259.

Second Continental Congress (sek' ənd kon tə nen' təl kong' gris). Body of delegates from the 13 colonies that acted as a central government during the Revolutionary War. p. 134.

sectionalism (sek' shə nə liz əm). Policy of placing great importance on a single section or region of a country. p. 257.

segregated (seg' rə gā ted). Set apart. p. 388.

Selective Service Act (si lek' tiv sèr' vis akt). Law passed by Congress in 1917 that required all men of a certain age to register for the draft. p. 545.

self-determination (self di tèr mə nā' shən). People choosing their form of government. p. 551.

self-government (self guv' ərn mənt). Belief that people can and should rule themselves. p. 69.

"separate but equal" (sep' ər it but ē' kwəl). Policy of separating blacks from whites in public facilities, such as schools and waiting rooms, while maintaining equal facilities for each. p. 388.

Separatist (sep' ə rə tist). Person wishing to separate from the Church of England; a Pilgrim. p. 70.

settlement house (set' əl mənt hous). City building where various kinds of services are provided for the poor people of a neighborhood. p. 457.

Seven Cities of Gold (sev' ən sit' ēz ov gōld). Cities north of Mexico that were believed by early Spanish explorers to contain vast treasures. p. 57.

Seventh of March speech (sev' enth ov märch spēch). Speech given by Daniel Webster in which he expressed approval for Clay's compromise. p. 322.

"Seward's Icebox" (sü' ərdz īs' boks). Name given to Alaska by several members of Congress. p. 377.

sharecropping (shâr' krop ing). Farming land for the landowner in return for a share of the crop produced. p. 375.

Shays's Rebellion (shāz' ez ri bel' yən). Uprising of farmers in Massachusetts after their lands were seized for overdue taxes. Viewed by many as proof of the need for a stronger central government. p. 166.

Sherman Antitrust Act (shėr' mən an tē trust' akt). Law passed in 1890 that declared trusts and any other ways of restricting trade to be illegal. p. 476.

sit-in (sit' in). Form of protest in which a group of people remains seated for a long period of time in a public place. p. 665.

skyscraper (skī' skrā pər). Very tall building. p. 444.

slavery (slā' vər ē). System in which one person is owned by another. p. 67.

slave state (slāv stāt). State in which slavery was legal. p. 250.

Social Security Act (sō' shəl si kyür' ə tē akt). United States government program started in 1935 to provide pensions to retired persons and their dependents. p. 592.

sod house (sod hous). Small house made from bricks of sod. p. 420.

solar energy (sō' lər en' ər gē). Power from the sun. p. 698.

Sons of Liberty (sunz ov lib' ər tē). Secret societies formed by American colonists who were discontent with British interference in the colonies. p. 120.

space satellite (spās sat' ə līt). Object made by people that is launched by rocket into space and circles the earth. p. 660.

speculation (spek yə lā' shən). Buying or selling when there is a large risk, in hope of making a profit. p. 580.

sperm whale (spėrm hwāl). Large whale with teeth and a square head. It is valuable for its oil. p. 95.

sphere of influence (sfir ov in' flü ens). Area or country where another nation has gained special privileges and rights for itself. p. 523.

Spice Islands (spīs ī' ləndz). Islands off the coast of Southeast Asia, important in the fifteenth and sixteenth centuries for spices such as cloves, nutmeg, and pepper. p. 53.

spoils system (spoilz sis' təm). Practice of rewarding party members with government jobs. p. 266.

"square deal" (skwâr dēl). Phrase used by Theodore Roosevelt to describe his idea of government, in which everyone was treated fairly. p. 502.

squatter (skwot' ər). Person who settles on land without owning it or paying any rent. p. 81.

stalemate (stāl' māt). Situation in which neither side can win. p. 640.

Stamp Act (stamp akt). Act passed in 1765 that required the use of stamps in the American colonies on all legal documents and other papers, including almanacs, newspapers, pamphlets, and wills. p. 118.

Stamp Act Congress (stamp akt kong' gris). Meeting in 1765 of delegates from nine colonies to discuss colonial problems. p. 120.

steamboat (stēm' bōt). Boat moved by steam power. p. 289.

steamboat pilot (stēm' bōt pī' lət). Person who guided a riverboat on its way up or down the river. p. 316.

steam locomotive (stēm lō kə mō' tiv). Locomotive that moves by the steam generated in its own boiler. p. 288.

steelmaking (stēl' mā king). Making steel, a metal made by mixing iron and carbon. p. 426.

stereotype (ster' ēə tīp). Mental picture of a whole group that is exaggerated or oversimplified and often based on emotion. p. 337.

stock (stok). Share in the ownership of a company. p. 66.

stock market (stok mär' kit). Place where shares of stock in corporations are bought and sold. p. 580.

streetcar (strēt' kär). Car that runs by electricity on rails in the streets and carries passengers. p. 446.

strict interpretation (strikt in tėr prə tā' shən). Belief that the federal government could do only what the Constitution specifically gave it the power to do. p. 209.

strike (strīk). Job stoppage by workers to get an employer to agree to their demands. p. 462.

submarine (sub' mə rēn). Ship that can operate under water. p. 540.

subsidy (sub' sə dē). Gift of land or money from the government. p. 429.

suffrage (suf' rij). Right to vote. p. 276.

summit conference (sum' it kon' fər əns). Meeting of the top leaders of the major powers to consider common problems. p. 641.

Sunbelt (sun′ belt). Southern and western parts of the United States. p. 653.

Sussex *Pledge* (sus′ iks plej). Agreement by the German government stating that German submarines would no longer torpedo passenger ships or merchant ships without warning. p. 542.

sweatshop (swet′ shop). Business in which workers were employed under unhealthy conditions for long hours with poor wages. p. 394.

table (tā′ bəl). Information organized in a brief form or list. p. 10.

table furniture (tā′ bəl fėr′ nə chər). Wooden dishes used for meals. p. 107.

tariff (tar′ if). Tax on imports or exports. p. 204.

"taxation without representation" (tak sā′ shən wiTH′ out rep ri zen tā′ shən). Issue in the American colonies when Parliament levied taxes in the colonies without the approval of the colonial legislature. p. 120.

Teapot Dome (tē′ pot dōm). Name of a hill in Wyoming that lay over an oil deposit reserved for the navy; leasing of the oil field became the subject of a scandal during the 1920s. p. 573.

technology (tek nol′ ə jē). Amount of scientific knowledge and kinds of tools a people have. p. 37.

Teller Amendment (tel′ ər ə mend′ mənt). Part of the resolution passed by Congress that recognized Cuban independence. It said America would not take over Cuba. p. 520.

temple mound (tem′ pəl mound). Mound or pile of earth that is flat on top and was used as a foundation for a wooden building or temple. p. 31.

tenement (ten′ ə mənt). Apartment building in a city, usually with poor safety and sanitary conditions. p. 456.

tepee (tē′ pē). Tentlike shelter used by certain tribes of Native Americans. The tepee was made of buffalo skins stitched together, draped over poles, and secured to the ground. p. 35.

termination (tėr mə nā′ shən). Ending of something. p. 696.

terrace (ter′ əs). Flat surface on the side of a steep hill or mountain, constructed to make crop-growing possible. p. 27.

textile (teks′ təl). Woven fabric or cloth. p. 89.

three-fifths compromise (thrē fifths kom′ prə mīz). Agreement reached at the Constitutional Convention that said for every five slaves owned, three would be counted for the purposes of taxation and representation in Congress. p. 170.

"Tippecanoe and Tyler, too" (tip ē kə nü′ and tī′ lər tü). Campaign slogan used by the Whig party in the presidential election of 1840 to get their candidates, William Henry Harrison and John Tyler, elected. p. 263.

Toleration Act (tol ə rā′ shən akt). Law passed in 1649 guaranteeing freedom of worship to all Christians in Maryland. p. 80.

Tory (tôr′ ē). Name sometimes given to colonists who supported Great Britain and King George III; named after the political party in Great Britain that supported the king. p. 137.

totalitarian (tō tal ə tār′ ē ən). Government that has total power over its people. p. 602.

total war (tō′ təl wär). War in which all of a nation's resources are used to further the national goals. p. 618.

Townshend Acts (toun′ zend akts). British law that placed taxes on glass, lead, paper, paint, and tea imported from England by colonial merchants. p. 121.

trade and navigation laws (trād and nav ə gā′ shən lôz). Laws passed by Great Britain that established the trade policies for the American colonies. p. 117.

trade union (trād yün′ yən). Group whose members work at a single skilled trade. p. 467.

Trail of Tears (trāl ov tėrz). Name given by the Cherokees to their journey from Georgia to Oklahoma after they had been forced off their land by the United States government. p. 270.

traitor (trā′ tər). Person who aids the enemies of his or her country. p. 155.

treason (trē′ zən). Act of aiding the enemies of one's country. p. 155.

treaty of alliance (trē′ tē ov ə lī′ əns). Treaty signed by France and the United States in 1778 in which France pledged its support to the Americans in their struggle for independence from Great Britain. p. 150.

Treaty of Ghent (trē′ tē ov gent). Treaty signed in 1814 between the United States and Great Britain, ending the War of 1812. p. 247.

Treaty of Greenville (trē′ tē ov grēn′ vil). Treaty signed in 1795 after the Indians' defeat at Fallen Timbers. It set up a boundary between Indian lands and land open to American settlers. p. 232.

Treaty of Guadalupe Hidalgo (trē′ tē ov gwä də lüp′ə hi dal′ gō). Treaty signed in 1848 between Mexico and the United States that ended the Mexican War. p. 304.

Treaty of Paris (1763) (trē′ tē ov par′ is). Peace treaty that ended the French and Indian War. p. 116.

tree rings (trē ringz). Circles or rings in the trunk of a tree that show each year's growth. p. 24.

triangular trade route (trī ang′ gyə lər trād rüt). The course of trading ships between three points—for example, the West Indies, Africa, and the United States. p. 95.

tribe (trīb). Group of people held together by family and social ties, geography, or custom. p. 23.

tributary (trib′ yə ter ē). Stream that flows into a larger stream or body of water. p. 6.

Truman Doctrine (trü′ mən dok′ trən). Declaration in 1947 that the United States would help free peoples resist communism. p. 634.

trust (trust). Organization that controls several different companies or corporations. p. 439.

tsar (zär). Title of the rulers of the Russian empire. p. 56.

Tweed Ring (twēd ring). Corrupt group led by New York political boss, William Tweed; the ring robbed the New York City treasury of millions of dollars. p. 378.

tyranny (tir′ ə nē). Harsh and unfair government. p. 119.

Uncle Tom's Cabin (ung′ kəl tomz kab′ ən). Famous antislavery novel written by the American writer Harriet Beecher Stowe. p. 335.

Underground Railroad (un dər ground′ rāl′ rōd). System by which people opposed to slavery secretly guided fugitive slaves to safety in free states or Canada. p. 324.

Union party (yün′ yən pär′ tē). Name used for the Republican party during the presidential election of 1864. p. 360.

unit (yü′ nit). Special part or section, as in a book. p. 14.

United Nations (yü nī′ tid nā′ shənz). Worldwide organization formed after World War II to promote peace and social and economic welfare. p. 630.

vaquero (vä kär′ ō). Spanish word for "cowboy." p. 49.

vaudeville (vô′ də vil). Type of show that featured a variety of acts. p. 487.

veto (vē′ tō). Right of a person such as a President or governor to refuse to approve bills passed by the legislature. p. 123.

Vietnamization (vē et nə mi zā′ shən). United States plan to train and equip South Vietnamese troops to take over the fighting in their country. p. 679.

vigilante (vij ə lan′ tē). Member of a group that captures and punishes criminals without the sanction of the law. p. 412.

Vikings (vī′ kingz). Bold seafaring people from the Scandinavian countries who raided European coastal towns and explored distant lands. p. 43.

Vinland (vin′ lənd). Place along the coast of North America visited by the Vikings, and named after the many wild grapes they found there. p. 43.

Virginia Dynasty (vər jin′ yə dī′ nəs tē). Virginians who headed the United States government during the first quarter of the nineteenth century. p. 249.

Virginia Plan (vər jin′ yə plan). Large State plan, or the proposal that states should be represented in Congress according to population. p. 169.

War Democrat (wôr dem′ ə krat). Northern Democrat who supported the war effort. p. 359.

War Hawk (wôr hôk). Person, especially a member of Congress, who supported the War of 1812. p. 243.

warrant (wôr′ ənt). Written order issued by a judge or other authorized person that gives an official the right to make a search or an arrest or to carry out other acts. p. 118.

Western civilization (wes′ tərn siv ə lə zā′ shən). High-level culture beginning in Europe in the fifteenth century and characterized by a strong emphasis on technology. p. 37.

Western Front (wes′ tərn frunt). Line of the battlefront across Belgium and France during World War I. p. 538.

western land claims (wes′ tərn land clāmz). Land west of the Appalachian Mountains that was claimed by eastern states. p. 164.

Whig (hwig). Member of a political party that was formed in the United States in the early 1830s in opposition to President Andrew Jackson and the Democratic party. p. 262.

Whiskey Rebellion (hwis′ kē ri bel′ yən). Rebellion in 1794 of Pennsylvania farmers against paying taxes on whiskey. It was put down by federal troops. p. 211.

White House (hwīt hous). Official residence of the President of the United States, in Washington, D.C. p. 217.

Wilderness Trail (wil′ dər nis trāl). Path cleared and marked by Daniel Boone that ran from eastern Virginia through the Cumberland Gap into Kentucky. p. 232.

Women's Liberation movement (wi′ mənz lib ə rā′ shən müv′ mənt). Group organized to promote equality for women. p. 695.

women's rights (wi′ mənz rīts). Movement for equality between men and women. p. 271.

work week (wėrk wēk). Part of the week during which work is done. p. 624.

writ of assistance (rit ov ə sis′ təns). Document that gave a British official looking for smuggled goods the right to enter and search a ship or building. p. 122.

XYZ affair (eks wī zē ə fär′). Incident that occurred during negotiations to end a dispute between France and the United States during the Adams administration. p. 216.

yellow journalism (yel′ ō jėr′ nə liz əm). Writing that makes use of sensational headlines and exaggerated news stories. p. 518.

INDEX

CREDITS

1 2 3 4 5 6 7 8 9 10—RRD—92 91 90 89 88 87 86 85 84

TEACHER'S ANSWER KEY

ONE FLAG, ONE LAND

CONTENTS

ANSWER KEY

Where possible answers for Activities in Chapter Reviews are provided. Some Activities require individualized responses for which specific answers are not appropriate.

UNIT 1 A NEW WORLD IS ADDED TO THE OLD

CHAPTER 1 The United States Today

ANSWERS FOR CHECKUP QUESTIONS

PAGE 9

1. A political map of the United States shows national and state boundaries and the names and locations of towns and cities. A relief map shows the elevation of the earth's surface.

2. At first, mountain ranges, rivers, and lakes were barriers that slowed the movement of the American people. However, these barriers were overcome as the United States spread from the Atlantic to the Pacific.

3. The Mississippi River, its tributaries, and the Great Lakes are waterways that provide a natural system of transportation in the United States.

4. Americans added to the natural transportation system by building canals and railroads.

5. In everyday life, people use a variety of maps, such as road maps, state and city maps, seating plan maps for theaters and ballparks, and world maps.

PAGE 13

1. Tables can present many facts and statistics in rows and columns. Graphs can present the same information using circles, bars, and lines.

2. There are four kinds of graphs—pictographs, bar graphs, pie graphs, and line graphs. The pictograph is not shown in this chapter.

3. The graphs in this chapter give the following information about the American population: the population by sex, the size of different age groups, the racial makeup, and the percentages of women in the labor force from 1890 to 1980.

4. The formula leading to understanding in history is *facts + explanation = understanding.*

PAGE 16

1. This book is divided into chapters and units.

2. The Declaration of Independence and the Constitution are printed in full and are annotated in this book.

3. The Skills Development page at the end of each chapter offers additional facts about American history and serves to sharpen skills.

4. The feature Benchmarks is a reference point by which to compare facts at different periods in history. The boxes on the Presidents give facts about the life of each President. The feature What's in a Name gives interesting information and facts about names.

5. The following learning aids are found near the end of the book: The Biographical Dictionary, the Glossary, the Atlas, and the Index.

ANSWERS FOR CHAPTER REVIEW

PAGE 18
Vocabulary Quiz
1. e 2. a 3. b 4. c 5. d 6. j 7. f 8. h 9. i
10. g

Review Questions
1. Some things maps can show that cannot be seen by astronauts in space are state and national boundaries, and names and locations of towns, cities, and state capitals.

2. Political maps show things such as state and national boundaries and the names and locations of towns and cities. Relief maps show landforms, such as mountain ranges and the elevation of the earth's surface.

3. Contour lines would appear on a relief map. The location and name of a city would appear on a political map.

4. Maps can show yearly precipitation, climate, rivers and lakes, highways, and the way things were in the past.

5. Tables and graphs can show statistics and facts about the American people.

6. Answers will vary but should include six of the following and a reasonable description of each. Content pages, units, historical documents, Vocabulary, Checkup, Skills Development, How Americans Lived, captions, What's in a Name, Benchmarks, the Atlas, and the Index are all parts of this book.

Activities
Answers will vary.

ANSWERS FOR SKILLS DEVELOPMENT

PAGE 19
Skills Practice

1. Titles of both Unit 1 and Unit 2 are on the Contents page.

2. An account of World War II can be found in Unit 7.

3. Unit 7 covers from approximately 1920 to 1945.

4. Chapter 11 deals with Andrew Jackson's presidency. The rise of industry is discussed in Chapter 19. Chapter 25 deals with the 1920s.

5. A map showing all of the English colonies is on page 79.

6. A graph showing estimated Native American population in 1492 is found on page 28.

7. The Constitution is longer than the Declaration of Independence.

8. The Declaration of Independence begins with the words "When, in the course of human events . . .."

9. There are 26 amendments to the Constitution.

10. There are four terms in the vocabulary box at the beginning of Chapter 14.

11. There are two other vocabulary boxes in Chapter 14.

12. Key Facts, on the chapter review page, tells some of the main ideas of the chapter.

13. According to the time line the convention at Seneca Falls took place in 1848.

14. The Benchmarks charts are found in the sections titled How Americans Lived.

15. There are five sections titled How Americans Lived in the book.

16. The United States population was closest to 75 million in 1900.

17. There are 39 presidential boxes in the book.

18. A map of the world can be found on pages 714–715.

19. John C. Calhoun's home state is South Carolina. Henry Cabot Lodge's home state is Massachusetts. Belva Lockwood's home state is New York.

20. In the Index, the siege of Vicksburg is found on page 353. The impeachment of President Andrew Johnson is found on pages 369–370. The appointment of Sandra Day O'Connor to the Supreme Court is found on pages 695 and 705.

CHAPTER 2 The Earliest Americans

ANSWERS FOR CHECKUP QUESTIONS

PAGE 25

1. Three points that are used as evidence that the first people in America came from Asia are (a) Asia was once connected to North America by a narrow strip of land. (b) The American Indians and the people of China are both of the Mongoloid race. (c) The American Indians and the people of China have some similar physical characteristics.

2. The first Americans met their daily needs by hunting for animals.

3. The discovery of Folsom man helped to prove that early people had lived and hunted in New Mexico during the Ice Age.

4. Prehistoric bones are dated by a process known as carbon dating.

PAGE 29

1. After the Ice Age ended, many animals became extinct. Early Americans turned to plants as a source of food.

2. Agriculture in the Americas probably originated in the Andes Mountain region of South America. Some of the crops that were grown were potatoes, peanuts, kidney beans, peppers, and tomatoes.

3. Three early American civilizations south of the present-day United States are (a) the Incas, whose empire included all the tribes in the area of present-day Peru and Ecuador and parts of Chile, Bolivia,

and Argentina; (b) the Mayas, who built large cities in the jungles of Central America and southern Mexico; and (c) the Aztecs, whose capital stood on the site of Mexico City today.

4. The main features of the Pueblo Indian civilization were that its system of agriculture was well developed and that most of the population lived in pueblos or apartment houses.

PAGE 33

1. Little is known about the Mound Builders' civilization because no European ever saw the Mound Builders at the high point of their civilization, and the Mound Builders left no written records.

2. Burial mounds are small and round and were nearly always used to bury the dead. Temple mounds were flat on top but sometimes had terraced sides. They were used as a foundation for a wooden building or temple. Geometric mounds were built in the form of circles, squares, or parallel lines and enclosed large areas of land. Effigy mounds were built in the shape of a bird, snake, animal, or human being.

3. The Cahokia Mounds are remarkable because they are like a city. They include a great number of different mounds that covered 14 acres (6 ha) of land. The site was surrounded by a 50,000-log stockade. Had the Mound Builders known about the wheel, their work would have been made much easier.

4. The Mound Builders may have been invaded by warlike people, causing their civilization to decline and finally disappear.

PAGE 37

1. Environment shaped the culture of the North American Indians. Since they had no way of changing their physical surroundings, the Indians' way of life was determined by their environment.

2. The way of life of the Indians on the western plains was changed by the increased number of buffalo herds.

3. In their clash with Western civilization, Indian civilizations lacked the technology of Europeans.

4. The Indian cultures had the skill and knowledge to survive in the Americas. Contributions and Indian influences are seen today in place-names, words, jewelry design, woodcraft, and the ideas of the relationship between human beings and nature.

ANSWERS FOR CHAPTER REVIEW

PAGE 38
Vocabulary Quiz
1. T **2.** T **3.** F, carbon 14 **4.** T **5.** F, Mexico
6. F, Indian Mounds **7.** F, Illinois **8.** F, way of life **9.** T **10.** F, agriculture

Review Questions
1. The imaginary characters in this chapter are associated with the following event, fact, or achievement: (a) Amuk the Leader and his small band were the first people to enter America. (b) Leel the Clever One started the practice of agriculture in North America. (c) Aru the Strong and people like him built large earthen mounds long before the wheel was invented. (d) Salma the Priest Woman showed how the environment shaped a tribe's culture.

2. Carbon dating, a method used to time-date something, has helped scientists contribute to the study of ancient human life.

3. Agriculture has been important to the rise of concentrated populations and complex civilizations by making it possible for large populations to remain in one place.

4. The Pueblo Indians lived in the Southwest, where there were not many trees. They built their pueblos along the sides of steep cliffs. They also built their homes to accommodate many people. The Pueblos farmed and raised cotton. The Indians of the Northeast lived in wooded land. Their homes were built from trees and bark. They farmed, fished, hunted, and grew tobacco.

Activities
Answers will vary.

ANSWERS FOR SKILLS DEVELOPMENT

PAGE 39
Skills Practice
1. California

2. 114,400

3. Washington, Oregon, Idaho

4. 1680

5. Central mountain

6. Northern

7. Central mountain

8. 1740

ANSWER KEY

ANSWERS FOR CHECKUP QUESTIONS

PAGE 45

1. Columbus's goal was to reach the Indies by sailing west from Europe.

2. When Columbus landed in the Americas, he called the people there Indians because he thought he was in the Indies.

3. Columbus is called the discoverer of America because his voyage led directly to its exploration and colonization. Others who might be called America's discoverers are the Vikings, Cabral, Balboa, Ponce de Leon, Magellan, and Amerigo Vespucci.

4. Cabral landed on the coast of South America and claimed for Portugal the land that is now Brazil. Balboa was the first European to see the Pacific Ocean from the shores of the New World. Ponce de Leon discovered Florida. Magellan was the first European to sail the ocean he named the Pacific.

PAGE 50

1. The empires of the Aztecs and the Incas came to an end because both were conquered by the Spaniards.

2. De Soto's expedition made it possible for Spain to add the southeastern part of what is now the United States to its empire. Coronado's contribution to Spain's empire was the exploration of the American Southwest. Cabrillo explored for Spain the Pacific coast as far north as present-day Oregon.

3. Spanish influence can be seen in the American Southwest, in southern Florida, and in other parts of the United States.

4. Spanish influence is shown in the colonial architecture of the houses, churches, and public buildings. Other influences are cowboy equipment, Longhorn cattle, rodeos, and the Spanish language.

PAGE 53

1. Early French explorers were looking for a northwest passage to the Indies.

2. Verrazano explored the eastern coast of North America from North Carolina up to Newfoundland. Champlain started the first French colony along the St. Lawrence River. He explored as far west as Lake Huron and as far south as New York State. Marquette and Joliet explored part of the Mississippi River. Cartier discovered the Gulf of St. Lawrence and sailed up the St. Lawrence River as far as Montreal. Nicolet explored as far west as Wisconsin. La Salle explored the Mississippi River down to the Gulf of Mexico. Earlier La Salle had explored the Ohio River country.

3. Water highways contributed to the French empire by connecting the vast unsettled lands. These waterways made it easy to transport furs by fishing boats.

4. The French empire was sparsely settled because landowners wanted to rent their land and settlers wanted to own the land they lived and worked on. Also, the French government allowed only Roman Catholics to settle in New France.

5. Place-names are reminders today that France once claimed large parts of the United States.

PAGE 57

1. Dutch merchants hired Henry Hudson to find a shorter route from the Netherlands to the Spice Islands.

2. The Dutch promoted settlement of their colony by offering large grants of land. The patroons of the land grants were supposed to rent the land to settlers. The Dutch were unsuccessful because farmland was easy to get in North America, and most people wanted to own rather than rent land.

3. Swedish colonists may have built the first log cabins in America.

4. Vitus Bering's explorations gave Russia claims to Alaska.

5. The tsar required the Russian American Company to trade furs, promote settlement, and teach Christianity to the Indians.

6. Hawaii's history makes it unique among American states because no European country ever planted a colony on its islands.

PAGE 59

1. Africans helped build New World empires for European powers by exploring and opening up part of the New World. They accompanied most European explorers to North America and many worked as sailors, guides, and fur traders.

2. Estevanico was an advisor to Cortes. He was also a guide who traveled through Florida, Mexico, and parts of the Southwest. His travels spurred other explorers to search for the Seven Cities of Gold. Du Sable started a trading post in what is today the city of Chicago.

3. About 10 million Africans were brought to the New World as slaves.

4. The majority of Africans brought to the New World as slaves were sent to Brazil and the Caribbean Islands.

ANSWERS FOR CHAPTER REVIEW

PAGE 60
Vocabulary Quiz
1. e **2.** c **3.** a **4.** j **5.** d **6.** i **7.** b **8.** h **9.** f **10.** g
Review Questions
1. Columbus died a bitter man because he did not get the profits promised to him by Spanish rulers and businessmen.

2. The Spanish were able to build a rich empire in the New World because they conquered two powerful Native American civilizations and took their land and riches.

3. The French empire stretched from the St. Lawrence River in the north to the Gulf of Mexico. Also, the French claimed vast unsettled land between the Appalachians and the Rocky Mountains.

4. France had little success in attracting settlers to North America because the French king granted land to aristocrats, who in turn wanted settlers to rent the land from them. However, settlers wanted to own land, not rent it. In addition, the French government allowed only Roman Catholics to settle in New France.

5. There were conflicting claims down the west coast of North America between the Russians and the Spanish. Spain and France clashed over settlement in Florida and the Carolinas. Almost every part of the United States, except Hawaii, was claimed by one or more European powers.

6. Estevanico is remembered for having led the search for the Seven Cities of Gold.

7. Africans contributed to building European empires in the New World because they were among the early explorers of the Americas. They not only joined explorations but also helped to build cities. They worked as skilled and unskilled laborers.

Activities
Answers will vary.

ANSWERS FOR SKILLS DEVELOPMENT

PAGE 61
Skills Practice
Answers are shown as annotations on page 61.

CHAPTER 4 England Plants Colonies

ANSWERS FOR CHECKUP QUESTIONS

PAGE 69
1. John Smith helped make Virginia a success because he took over leadership in Jamestown. Smith forced the colonists to do their share of the work. He was also able to get food from nearby Indians, enabling the colonists to survive the first winter.

John Rolfe helped make Virginia a success by raising and selling tobacco. Other farmers followed his example, and tobacco became Virginia's cash crop.

2. The defeat of the Invincible Armada was important to English colonization because Spain could no longer prevent other European countries from colonizing the east coast of North America.

3. Some known facts about the colony set up by Sir Walter Raleigh are that it was located on Roanoke Island; Virginia Dare, the first English child born in the United States, was born there; and the people disappeared and left no trace except for the word *Croatan* carved on a post.

Still unknown is what happened to the colony and to Virginia Dare.

4. Joint-stock companies were helpful in planting English colonies in America because many people shared in the cost of starting a colony. If the colony was successful, people of the joint-stock company shared in the wealth.

5. The Virginia House of Burgesses was important because it was the first step toward self-government for the colonists.

ANSWER KEY

6. King James I took back the charter and made Virginia a royal colony. He also planned to do away with the House of Burgesses, but he died before he could do so.

PAGE 75
1. The Indians helped the Plymouth colonists survive by offering their friendship, by showing the colonists where to hunt and fish, and by teaching them to raise corn.

2. The Pilgrims were mostly poor people who came to North America because they wanted to separate from the Church of England yet keep their English way of life.

The Puritans on the other hand were prosperous and well-educated. They wanted to stay within the Church of England but wanted a more simple church organization.

3. Massachusetts Bay took over settlements in New Hampshire, Maine, and the older Pilgrim colony at Plymouth.

4. Other New England colonies grew out of Massachusetts because most of them were started by Puritans who disagreed with the church. These people left Massachusetts and built settlements.

PAGE 78
1. The Dutch colony of New Amsterdam was renamed New York when it was taken over by the English.

2. The three English colonies that grew from former Dutch possessions were New York, New Jersey, and Delaware.

3. The colony of Pennsylvania was started by William Penn when he received a large land grant from the king as payment for a debt owed to Penn's father.

4. Some of the reasons that settlers were attracted to Pennsylvania were that it offered religious freedom, fertile soil, good government, peaceful Indians, and a healthful climate.

5. The four middle colonies were New York, New Jersey, Pennsylvania, and Delaware. They were called the middle colonies because they were located between the New England and the southern colonies.

PAGE 81
1. Proprietors of colonies hoped to profit from their holdings by selling the land to settlers.

2. Maryland was founded because Lord Baltimore wanted to make money selling the land to settlers, and he wanted the colony to be a refuge for Roman Catholics from England.

3. The colonists in South Carolina were mostly English aristocrats, but the colonists in North Carolina were mostly poor squatters who had drifted down from Virginia.

4. Georgia was founded in 1733 to protect South Carolina from raids by Spaniards and Indians in Florida. It also served as a home for imprisoned English debtors, who agreed to become part-time soldiers in return for their freedom.

5. The five southern colonies were Virginia, Maryland, North Carolina, South Carolina, and Georgia.

ANSWERS FOR CHAPTER REVIEW
PAGE 82
Vocabulary Quiz
1. d **2.** i **3.** a **4.** j **5.** h **6.** b **7.** e **8.** g **9.** c **10.** f

Review Questions
1. England was slow in starting colonies in North America because it did not have the energy or wealth to follow up on discoveries and because it did not want to provoke Spain.

2. Virginians overcame difficulties and became the first successful English colony by raising and selling tobacco.

3. The Puritans were important in New England colonies because there was close relationship between the Puritan church and the colonial government. Only members of the Puritan church could vote and hold office.

4. The colony of New York was a former Dutch possession taken over by the English, who did not want a Dutch colony between the New England and the southern colonies.

The English colony of Pennsylvania was started by William Penn, who was given the land by King Charles II. Penn wanted to further the Quaker way of life.

5. The four New England colonies were Massachusetts, New Hampshire, Rhode Island, and Connecticut.

New York, New Jersey, Pennsylvania, and Delaware were the four middle colonies.

The five southern colonies were Maryland, Virginia, North Carolina, South Carolina, and Georgia.

Activities

1. The table provides the answers for (a) and (b). For (c) answers will vary, accept all reasonable answers.

Colony	Date	Type	Person or Group (answers will vary.)
Virginia	1607	Southern	John Smith, John Rolfe
Massachusetts	1620	New England	Pilgrims
New Hampshire	1623	New England	Pilgrims
New York	1624	Middle	Peter Stuyvesant
Connecticut	1633	New England	Thomas Hooker
Maryland	1634	Southern	Catholics
Rhode Island	1636	New England	Anne Hutchinson
Delaware	1638	Middle	Swedes
New Jersey	about 1640	Middle	Sir George Carteret
Pennsylvania	1643	Middle	William Penn
North Carolina	about 1653	Southern	Lords
South Carolina	1670	Southern	Proprietors
Georgia	1733	Southern	James Oglethorpe

2. Virginia: Elizabeth I, the virgin Queen
Massachusetts: Indian tribe
New Hampshire: the country of Hampshire, England
New York: the Duke of York
Connecticut: Indian word meaning "on the long tidal river"
Maryland: Henrietta Maria, wife of King Charles I
Rhode Island: Island of Rhodes in the Mediterranean Sea
Delaware: Lord De La Warr
Pennsylvania: William Penn
North and South Carolina: King Charles II
New Jersey: English island of Jersey
Georgia: George II

3. Answers will vary.

ANSWERS FOR SKILLS DEVELOPMENT

PAGE 83
Skills Practice
Answers will vary.

CHAPTER 5 The 13 Colonies Grow Stronger

ANSWERS FOR CHECKUP QUESTIONS

PAGE 88

1. After quarreling with his half brother, Benjamin Franklin decided to strike out on his own, and he moved to Philadelphia.

Franklin was very successful in Philadelphia. He married and became the sole owner of a prosperous printing business and a newspaper.

2. The purpose of promotional literature was to attract people across the Atlantic to come to the English colonies. The literature reflected the people's hopes and dreams of what they might find in the colonies.

3. According to Gabriel Thomas, some attractions in Pennsylvania were plentiful food, inexpensive land, a just government, good schools, peaceful Indians, and healthful air and climate. Also, people were able to worship as they pleased, and wages were up to 3 times higher.

4. Some of the hardships of coming to America by ship were sickness, bad food, foul water, heat, and stench.

ANSWER KEY

5. The indenture system was a plan whereby a poor person who wanted to come to the colonies signed a contract with the ship's captain. The contract pledged the person to work as a servant for a certain number of years. Upon reaching the colonies, the captain would sell the contract to someone who wanted a servant.

Many people came to the colonies as indentured servants because they were too poor to pay their way. Also, at the end of their service, an indentured servant might receive new clothes, tools, money, or land.

PAGE 92

1. Groups of non-English people who came to the colonies in large numbers in the 1700s were Germans, Scots and Scots-Irish, and Africans.

2. Most newcomers to the colonies generally went to the frontier because good land near the coast was expensive, and the frontier had fewer people.

3. The number of slaves increased rapidly during the 1700s because, unlike indentured servants, slaves did not have to be released after a certain time; children of slaves were born into slavery, automatically increasing the number of slaves; growth of the plantation system created a need for laborers; and large profits could be made from the slave trade.

PAGE 97

1. Some occupations available to colonial workers: farmer, blacksmith, carpenter, bricklayer, mason, shoemaker, tailor, sawyer, weaver, wool comber, potter, tanner, currier, brickmaker, hatmaker, glazier, cooper, baker, butcher, brewer, silversmith, plasterer, wheelwright, millwright, brazier, gunsmith, locksmith, watchmaker and clockmaker, saddler, barber, printer, bookbinder, rope maker, lawyer, and physician.

2. The products most typical of the southern colonies were tobacco, rice, and indigo. In the middle colonies, grain, beer, beef, pork, and furs were the most typical products.

3. Shipbuilding, fishing, and trade were the ways most New Englanders made their living.

4. A triangular trade route was a trade system carried on by colonial merchants. This is how the system worked: Rum made in New England was carried to Africa, where it was traded for slaves.

The slaves were carried to the West Indies and traded for molasses. Then the molasses was brought back to New England and used to make more rum.

Mercantilism was a system adopted by England for use in the colonies. In such a system, colonies existed for the benefit of the country that held them. England wanted its colonies to produce raw materials and send them back to England. There the materials would be made into manufactured goods and sold back to the colonies.

5. Colonial women cooked, cleaned, and took care of the children. Many helped their husbands in their craft or trade. On southern plantations, women supervised the housework, spinning, weaving, and food preserving. In addition, women had the role of doctor-nurse.

PAGE 101

1. In each of the three colonial wars that took place between 1689 and 1750, the colonists fought with the British troops against the French.

2. The French government attempted to protect Louisiana by building a string of forts along the water routes that held the vast territory together. In addition, the French government sent colonists from Canada to settle in Louisiana.

3. Some West Indian islands were considered valuable because of their sugar plantations.

ANSWERS FOR CHAPTER REVIEW

PAGE 102

Vocabulary Quiz
1. f **2.** a **3.** c **4.** i **5.** d **6.** j **7.** b **8.** e **9.** h
10. g

Review Questions
1. As a youth, Benjamin Franklin was an apprentice to his half brother, who was a printer and newspaper owner. This prepared Franklin for the occupation he followed in Philadelphia.

2. Life in the English colonies was more attractive than life in Europe because the colonies offered employment, plenty of land, freedom from religious persecution, and better opportunities for getting ahead in life.

3. There was a population explosion in the colonies during the 1700s because more immigrants came to the colonies. Families were large, so there were many native-born Americans. And increased numbers of African people were brought to the colonies as slaves.

4. Slavery became fastened on the colonies because slaves were considered more desirable than indentured servants.

5. Between 1689 and 1750 the colonists were drawn into three wars between France and Great Britain. In each of the wars the colonists fought alongside the British. In two of the wars, France and Spain were allies against Great Britain. Both France and Great Britain had Indian allies.

6. To strengthen their control over lands they claimed in North America, the French built forts along the water routes that held the territory together. They also transported colonists from Canada to settle in Louisiana.

Activities
Answers will vary.

ANSWERS FOR SKILLS DEVELOPMENT

PAGE 103
Skills Practice
1. major city

2. city

3. take care of

4. part

5. increasing rapidly

6. coastal area

7. touching each other

8. entered

9. highest ridge

10. warlike action

11. stirred up

12. Philadelphia

13. twelve, counting Philadelphia

14. in South Carolina

15. Hudson River valley

16. the crest of the Appalachians

17. the hostility of Indian tribes

18. French and Spanish agents

How Americans Lived, 1750

ANSWERS FOR CHECKUP QUESTIONS

PAGE 109
1. In 1750, education was left to parents and to dame schools—private schools taught by women in their homes. At dame schools, children were taught the alphabet and the simplest addition and subtraction. Boys went on to grammar school where they learned Latin, Greek, and advanced mathematics, in preparation for college.

Schoolhouses in 1750 were freezing cold in winter. Students sat for 8 hours on narrow, backless benches. Failure to recite correctly or the slightest disorder could result in a whipping.

Girls received little formal education because they were expected to become wives and mothers, and it was felt that they did not need much book learning to fill those roles.

2. The Boone family's house was built of logs, with a clapboard roof and puncheon floor. The one room cabin had a fireplace that provided heat and was also used for cooking.

3. George Mason's house—Gunston Hall—was started in 1755 and completed in 1758. It was built by skilled craftworkers from England.

4. Prior to her marriage, Eliza Lucas set out to learn all she could about managing a plantation. She ordered the planting of oak trees, and experimented with growing indigo. After her marriage, she kept up her agricultural experiments and found better ways to raise hemp and flax. Lucas also became interested in using silkworms to produce threads to be woven into silk cloth.

ANSWERS FOR UNIT REVIEW

PAGE 110
Reading the Text
1. Technology is the amount of scientific knowledge and the kinds of tools a people have.
2. Western civilization put a very high value on technology.
3. Western civilization grew up in Europe.
4. Answers will vary.
5. Answers will vary.

ANSWER KEY

Reading a Map
1. Massachusetts
2. Georgia
3. North
4. East
5. South

Reading a Picture
1. The two Indians on the far left are fishing.
2. They are fishing with spears.
3. The Indian standing by the tree has made notches on the tree in preparation for cutting it down.
4. Answers will vary. The Indian is probably burning out the log to make a canoe.
5. Answers will vary.

Reading a Table
1. T 2. F 3. F 4. F 5. F

UNIT 2 FOUNDING A NEW NATION

CHAPTER 6 The Road to Independence

ANSWERS FOR CHECKUP QUESTIONS

PAGE 119

1. The French and Indian War began near the headwaters of the Ohio River. The war was started when Washington ordered an attack on a group of French soldiers in the wilderness near Fort Duquesne.

2. France gave all of Canada and the part of Louisiana east of the Mississippi River to Great Britain. France also gave the port of New Orleans and all of Louisiana west of the Mississippi to Spain. Spain in turn was forced to give up Florida to the British.

3. Prime Minister Grenville wanted Britain to have tighter control over the colonies and wanted the colonies to pay a share of the war debt.

4. The colonists objected to (a) the Proclamation of 1763 because it prohibited them from moving to land west of the Appalachians; (b) the trade and navigation laws because they regulated where the colonists could sell and ship their products and prevented free trade with the Indians; (c) the Quartering Act because it ordered the colonial governments to pay for keeping British troops in America after the war; (d) the Stamp Act because it was an internal tax—a type that had not been previously collected—and because it taxed all printed matter and therefore affected nearly everyone in the colonies.

PAGE 124

1. The colonists resisted the Stamp Act in several ways. One way was by organizing secret societies called Sons of Liberty. Some of their members tarred and feathered stamp-tax collectors. Another way the colonists resisted was by sending delegates to a Stamp Act Congress meeting. Delegates urged colonial merchants to stop all imports from England.

2. A drop in the sale of British goods in the colonies and pressure from British merchants and ship captains caused Parliament to repeal the Stamp Act.

3. Each of the 13 colonies had a governor. The governor could appoint people to certain jobs in the colony, could command the armed forces of the colony, was responsible for seeing that laws were enforced, and could veto acts that had been passed by the legislature. The legislature in each colony was divided into two parts—the upper house and the lower house. The members of the upper house were appointed by the governor. Members of the lower house were elected by voters. The lower house, or assembly, as it was called, had control over taxes within each colony.

In some colonies the governor's salary was paid from the taxes. If a governor did something to displease the assembly, its members could vote to withhold the governor's pay.

4. The years between 1767 and 1770 were years of turmoil because Americans started to disagree among themselves about new British policies.

PAGE 131

1. The circumstances of the Boston Massacre were as follows: A crowd, gathered in front of the Boston Customs House, began to jeer, hoot, and wave clubs at a British soldier standing guard. As the crowd became more threatening, the soldier called for help. Soon the colonists and soldiers were separated by no more than an arm's length. Suddenly, a shot rang out. The other soldiers fired into the crowd. The result was that four colonists were dead and one was seriously wounded and later died.

2. Colonial leaders kept in touch about their plans for resisting the British policies after 1770 by sending letters through the well-organized Committees of Correspondence.

3. Tea became important to the road toward independence because when the British government repealed the Townshend Acts, it kept the tax on tea sold to the colonies. The colonists continued to resent the tea tax. In addition, Parliament gave the British East India Company a monopoly on the sale of tea in the American colonies. This further angered the colonists and marked another step along the road to war.

4. The Intolerable Acts were four laws passed by the British to punish the people of Massachusetts in response to the Boston Tea Party.

Americans called the four laws the Intolerable Acts because the laws angered them.

5. Fighting broke out at Lexington and Concord as follows: One night, British troops set out from Boston to seize military supplies stored at Concord. As the troops marched, Paul Revere and others rode ahead of them, warning that the British were coming. When the troops reached Lexington, they found about 70 militiamen on the village green. The British commander ordered the militiamen to disperse. The commander of the militia told his men to stand their ground. Suddenly the sound and smoke of musket fire filled the air. After a brief skirmish the militiamen withdrew and the British troops marched on to Concord.

When the British arrived, militiamen in large numbers were gathered at Concord. After a small battle, the outnumbered British force marched back to Boston.

ANSWERS FOR CHAPTER REVIEW

PAGE 132

Vocabulary Quiz
1. F, closed **2.** T **3.** T **4.** F, Great Britain or England **5.** T **6.** F, tea **7.** T **8.** F, Lexington **9.** T **10.** F, assembly

Review Questions
1. Paul Revere's activities contributed to the movement for independence because he was able to warn the militia and the minutemen about the British troops that were coming.

2. Three ways in which the colonists opposed the Stamp Act and the Grenville Acts were that they made speeches against the Stamp Act and what they considered to be illegal acts of the British government; they formed secret societies known as the Sons of Liberty; and delegates from nine colonies united in opposition to the British policies and formed the Stamp Act Congress.

3. The British response to the Boston Tea Party was to pass four laws—the so-called Intolerable Acts—to punish the people of Massachusetts.

4. Evidence that the colonies were becoming more united between 1753 and 1775 is that the colonies organized resistance to the new British policies.

Activities
Answers will vary.

ANSWERS FOR SKILLS DEVELOPMENT

PAGE 133

Skills Practice
Answers will vary.

CHAPTER 7 The War for Independence

ANSWERS FOR CHECKUP QUESTIONS

PAGE 140
1. Delegates from all 13 colonies attended the Second Continental Congress in Philadelphia. During the War for Independence, the Second Continental Congress acted as a central government.

2. Three accomplishments of the Second Continental Congress were that they acted as a central government for the colonies; they chose George Washington to command the Continental army; and they wrote the Declaration of Independence.

3. The big battle fought before Washington took command of the Continental army was the battle of Bunker Hill.

4. Thomas Paine contributed to the drive for independence by writing the pamphlet *Common Sense*. The pamphlet convinced thousands of colonists that independence from Great Britain was proper and logical.

5. Americans celebrate on July 4 because it is the date the Declaration of Independence was approved.

6. Answers will vary.

PAGE 152
1. After its defeats in New York, Washington took the Continental army across the Hudson River into New Jersey.

2. The victories at Trenton and Princeton were important because they encouraged many of Washington's men to reenlist, thus saving the Continental army.

3. Burgoyne's surrender at Saratoga might be considered the turning point of the war because with this victory the Americans had a good chance of winning. It also convinced France to openly help the Americans.

4. The main achievements of American naval vessels in the War for Independence were that single ships were able to sink or seize British merchant ships in their own waters, and privateers could be used to attack and capture British merchant ships on the high seas.

5. The winter of 1777–1778 was a hard time for the Continental army because the camp was on a low, windswept plateau. Ice and snow covered the ground at Valley Forge. The soldiers lived in tents and small huts that were drafty, sunless, and damp. Food was in short supply. The soldiers had no soap to wash with, and there was much sickness and infection among the troops.

PAGE 159
1. George Rogers Clark's campaign in the west was important for the United States because it left Americans in control of the territory north of the Ohio River.

2. The disastrous defeat the Americans suffered in South Carolina was the surrender of Charleston to the British. After that defeat the Patriots in South Carolina fought back by conducting surprise attacks on the British from secret bases in the Carolina swamps.

3. The two pieces of bad news that came to George Washington from West Point and Morristown, New Jersey, were that Benedict Arnold had committed treason, and Pennsylvania soldiers had mutinied.

4. The events that brought about the surrender of Cornwallis at Yorktown were as follows: A French fleet sailed from the West Indies to drive the British from Chesapeake Bay. Washington and Rochambeau brought their armies southward to join other troops already in Virginia. The combined armies surrounded Yorktown on land and the French fleet blocked the mouth of Chesapeake Bay, trapping Cornwallis.

5. The provisions of the Treaty of Paris stated that the new country's boundaries were the Mississippi River on the west, Florida on the south, and the Great Lakes on the north.

ANSWERS FOR CHAPTER REVIEW

PAGE 160
Vocabulary Quiz
1. f **2.** no answer **3.** b **4.** h **5.** e **6.** i **7.** a
8. d **9.** c **10.** j **11.** g **12.** no answer

Review Questions
1. George Washington was the "indispensable man" in the American Revolution because he remained the commanding general of the Continental army throughout the long years of the War for Independence.

2. Even though the colonists were defeated, the battle of Bunker Hill was a valuable experience for the Continental troops because it gave them the confidence they needed to continue to fight.

3. The seizure of Fort Ticonderoga helped the Continental cause because the colonies gained a key fort and captured valuable supplies.

4. The immediate effects of the Declaration of Independence were that the undecided had to choose between loyalty to the revolution and loyalty to Great Britain, and foreign nations that were enemies of Great Britain had a chance to harm Britain by helping the new country gain independence.

The long-term effects are the Declaration of Independence is the best-known American document, and colonial people everywhere have used the document's ideas in their own movements toward independence. In the United States the Declaration of Independence is a source of inspiration for people fighting for equal rights for all Americans.

5. Foreign countries helped the United States in its struggle for independence because by helping the colonies they were harming Britain.

6. The War for Independence was finally brought to an end because the British government and the British people were growing tired of war.

Activities
Answers will vary.

ANSWERS FOR SKILLS DEVELOPMENT
PAGE 161
Skills Practice
1. P **2.** S **3.** P **4.** S **5.** P **6.** P **7.** S

CHAPTER 8 Confederation and Constitution

ANSWERS FOR CHECKUP QUESTIONS
PAGE 167
1. It took a long time for the states to adopt the Articles of Confederation because some delegates felt that a central government would limit the powers of the individual states. In addition, the Articles of Confederation provided that the new government

should control land west of the Appalachians, and some states were reluctant to give up their western land claims.

2. The main powers of the government under the Articles of Confederation were that Congress could wage war and make peace; it could conduct negotiations between the United States and foreign countries; it could control trade with Indian tribes; it could organize mail service; and it could borrow money in the name of the United States.

3. The weaknesses of this government were that it lacked power to regulate trade and commerce among the states, and it had no power to compel payment of taxes.

4. The Northwest Ordinance is considered a major accomplishment of the Confederation government because it set up a system for governing the Northwest Territory.

5. Alexander Hamilton and James Madison led the movement for a stronger central government.

PAGE 171

1. The delegates to the Constitutional Convention were distinguished and experienced men. Most were prosperous lawyers, merchants, bankers, or plantation owners. The delegates hoped to write a new constitution for the government of the United States.

2. The three important compromises that were written into the Constitution were the Virginia Plan, the New Jersey Plan, and the Great Compromise.

3. Under the United States Constitution the legislative branch would pass national laws. The executive branch would carry out the laws. The judicial branch would try those who disobeyed the laws.

4. The issue of slavery was not mentioned in the Constitution.

PAGE 175

1. The Federalist papers were a total of 85 newspaper articles written mostly by Alexander Hamilton and James Madison supporting the Federalist arguments in favor of the Constitution.

2. Those who opposed the new Constitution argued that it had no guarantees of certain rights or freedoms for the people of the United States. They believed it would destroy the states by not sharing power with them. They felt the new government

would favor the rich, setting up a ruling class of wealth and power.

These arguments appealed to the people living on the frontiers, to poorer people living in towns and cities, and to people with small businesses. They also appealed to some wealthy plantation owners who were powerful within their states and several state officials who feared that the central government would overshadow state governments.

3. Smaller states approved the Constitution because it gave them equal representation in the Senate.

4. Alexander Hamilton persuaded the New York convention to approve the Constitution by delaying their vote until after Massachusetts and Virginia had voted. Then, Hamilton argued that New York could not afford to stay out of the new government.

5. Some of the ways the new government was stronger than the old Confederation government were that the new government had an executive branch headed by a strong President; a federal court; a Congress with powers to regulate foreign and interstate commerce and to levy taxes; extensive executive and judicial powers; a central government to coin money; two votes in the Senate for each state; membership in the House based on population; a simple majority in both houses of Congress required to pass legislation, subject to presidential veto; and a less difficult amending process.

ANSWERS FOR CHAPTER REVIEW

PAGE 176

Vocabulary Quiz

1. confederation
2. Shays's Rebellion
3. Northwest Ordinance
4. Virginia Plan
5. electors
6. judicial
7. slaves
8. Federalists
9. Bill of Rights
10. states

Review Questions

1. Answers will vary.

2. Three accomplishments of the Confederation government were that it directed the War for Independence to a successful conclusion; it held the country together for 6 years following the war; and it passed the Northwest Ordinance. (Answers will vary for the second part of the question.)

3. The major difference between the central government under the Articles of Confederation and the central government under the Constitution was that under the Constitution the new government was a federal republic. It was federal because powers were shared by the states and the central government. It was a republic because it was based on the consent of the people, acting through their elected representatives.

Activities
Answers will vary.

ANSWERS FOR SKILLS DEVELOPMENT

PAGE 177
Skills Practice
1. The legislative branch passes laws.

2. By deciding whether a law is constitutional, the federal courts can check the power of Congress.

3. The executive branch appoints justices to the federal courts.

4. The Congress can override the President's veto.

5. The President can check the power of Congress by vetoing bills.

6. The legislative branch has the power to impeach federal officials.

7. The Congress may override decisions of the Supreme Court.

8. The executive branch grants pardons.

CHAPTER 9 The Federalist Period

ANSWERS FOR CHECKUP QUESTIONS

PAGE 209
1. The tariff of 1789 raised money for the new government by putting a tax on about 80 manufactured articles imported into the United States.

2. The purpose of the President's Cabinet was to help the President run the executive branch of the government.

3. The Judiciary Act of 1789 established a federal courts system by providing for a Supreme Court with a chief justice and five associate justices. It also set up 3 circuit courts and 13 district courts.

4. Hamilton's debt plan was adopted because southerners wanted the capital of the United States to be located in the South. Hamilton had enough influence to put it there provided southerners accepted his debt plan.

5. Hamilton and Jefferson disagreed on how to interpret the Constitution. Hamilton believed in a loose interpretation. That is, the Congress had the power to create whatever agencies were necessary and proper to carry out the functions of government.
Jefferson believed in a strict interpretation of the Constitution. He felt the federal government could do only what the Constitution specifically gave it the power to do.

PAGE 212
1. The first two political parties in the United States were the Federalist party and the Democratic-Republican party.

2. The main differences between the two parties were that the Federalist party believed in a strong central government and had worked to get the Constitution ratified. The Democratic-Republican party had been against the ratification of the Constitution.

3. The main functions of political parties in the United States are to work to elect people of their choice to office and to shape government policies.

4. The presidential election of 1796 showed the growing strength of the Democratic-Republican party because Thomas Jefferson, chosen as the party's presidential candidate, became Vice President since he had the second highest number of electoral votes.

PAGE 216
1. President Washington issued a proclamation of neutrality because he knew the United States was too weak to get involved in another war so soon after the War for Independence.

2. Jay's Treaty provided that Great Britain move out of the forts and trading posts on America's western lands. Pinckney's Treaty granted Americans the right to travel on the Mississippi River and to ship goods through the port of New Orleans, and it also cleared up the disputed boundary between American and Spanish territory in the southeastern United States.

Pinckney's Treaty was more popular with Americans than Jay's Treaty because Pinckney's Treaty allowed Americans the right to travel on the Mississippi River.

3. Some of the troubles that disturbed relations between the United States and France in the 1790s were Washington's proclamation of neutrality and the XYZ affair.

4. Peaceful solutions to the troubles between the United States and France were worked out when Napoleon Bonaparte came to power in France. The United States canceled the Treaty of Alliance of 1778, and the two countries signed a trade treaty.

PAGE 221

1. The contributions of the Federalist party during the 12 years it controlled the federal government were the setting up of a system of American coins; the issuing of patents to inventors; and the arrangement of treaties that solved problems existing between the United States and foreign countries.

2. The Alien and Sedition Acts were laws supported by the Federalists and aimed at curbing opposition to President Adams.

3. The Alien and Sedition Acts contributed to the defeat of the Federalists in 1800 because naturalized citizens thought the Federalists were questioning their loyalty by passing the Alien Act.

4. The election of 1800 might be called a peaceful revolution because the Federalists accepted their defeat and gave up control without a fight.

ANSWERS FOR CHAPTER REVIEW

PAGE 222
Vocabulary Quiz
1. Cabinet
2. loose
3. Pennsylvania
4. Democratic
5. caucus
6. electors
7. neutrality
8. France
9. patent
10. Florida

Review Questions
1. Congress added the first ten amendments to the Constitution because in Massachusetts, Virginia,

and other states, Federalist leaders had promised to add a bill of rights to the Constitution.

2. The President's Cabinet helps the President run the executive branch of the government.

3. The chief differences between the Federalists and Democratic-Republicans were that the Federalists held views similar to Hamilton's, and the Democratic-Republicans sided with Jefferson. The Federalists were for ratification of the Constitution and the Democratic-Republicans were against it.

4. In what became known as Jay's Treaty, Britain agreed to move out of the forts and trading posts on America's western lands. Pinckney's Treaty granted Americans the right to travel on the Mississippi River and to ship goods through the port of New Orleans, and cleared up the disputed boundary between American and Spanish territory in the southeastern United States.

5. Federalist leaders forced the Alien and Sedition Acts through Congress because they thought these acts would weaken the Democratic-Republican party.

Activities
1. Some of the good things the Federalists did were they kept the country out of war; arranged treaties that solved problems existing between the United States and foreign countries; worked wonders for the credit of the United States government; achieved a decent prosperity at home.

Some of the mistakes the Federalists made were they had the reputation of being a party for the wealthy; the treaty John Jay worked out with Great Britain was unpopular; the whiskey tax, and the way the government crushed the Whiskey Rebellion; and the Alien and Sedition Acts.

2. Answers will vary.

ANSWERS FOR SKILLS DEVELOPMENT

PAGE 223
Skills Practice
1. hitherto
2. favorable
3. breeze
4. pieces
5. violent
6. cabins
7. closing
8. sun
9. dispelled

How Americans Lived, 1800

ANSWERS FOR CHECKUP QUESTIONS

PAGE 229

1. Answers will vary.

2. Calhoun, Webster, and Clay prepared themselves for a career in politics by first becoming lawyers.

3. Factors that led to the rise of textile mills in New England: The British government passed laws against letting spinning and weaving machines out of their country. Before leaving England, Samuel Slater memorized all the details of the spinning machines, and after settling in Rhode Island, Slater built the machines from memory.

4. The invention of the cotton gin caused the production of cotton to increase and caused the possibility of freedom for slaves to become remote. Whitney's idea of interchangeable parts made it possible to mass-produce by replacing worn-out parts.

ANSWERS FOR UNIT REVIEW

PAGE 230

Reading the Text

1. One problem faced by the delegates was how states should be represented in the law-making body of the new central government.

2. The Virginia Plan proposed that states should be represented in the Congress according to population.

3. The New Jersey Plan proposed that states should be represented equally in Congress.

4. Roger Sherman played a part in solving the problem by helping to work out the Great Compromise.

5. The Great Compromise suggested that the states be represented according to population in the House of Representatives. In the Senate, each state would be represented equally.

Reading a Map

1. green—Spain; brown—Britain

2. France

3. Britain

4. Spain and Russia

5. Spain

Reading a Picture

1. The uniformed men on the right are British troops.

2. The people on the left are American civilians.

3. The picture does not totally agree with the account given in the text.

4. Answers will vary.

5. Answers will vary.

Reading a Table

1. Appointed by king

2. 9

3. Delaware and Pennsylvania had the same governor.

4. Pennsylvania and Delaware

5. Connecticut and Rhode Island

ANSWER KEY

CHAPTER 10 **The Frontier Move West**

ANSWERS FOR CHECKUP QUESTIONS

PAGE 234

1. Tecumseh wanted Indians to unite to prevent invasion of the western lands by whites.

2. It was hard for Indians to stop settlers from moving onto Indian lands because settlers came by the thousands once a trail was blazed.

3. The treaty of Greenville was typical of the agreements signed by the American government and Indian tribes because in time it was broken by the settlers who invaded the Indian lands.

4. Rivers and streams were important in the settlement of the western lands because they were used for traveling, for shipping crops to market, as a source of waterpower, and as a place around which a town could grow.

PAGE 240

1. To keep New Orleans open to American goods, Jefferson offered to buy the port for $10 million. France needed money for new wars and was willing to sell all of Louisiana for $15 million.

2. The Lewis and Clark Expedition traveled up the Missouri River to Indian villages near the site of present-day Bismarck, North Dakota. After the winter they moved west toward the Rocky Mountains.

3. Sacagawea helped the expedition by serving as a peacemaker among the Indian tribes that were encountered.

4. Lands in the Old Northwest were surveyed and sold in accordance with an ordinance passed by the Confederation Congress in 1785. In the Old Southwest there was not such an orderly land policy. The status of slavery marked another important difference. Slavery was illegal in the Old Northwest but not in the Old Southwest.

5. The Adams-Onis Treaty gave the United States all of Florida in return for a $5 million payment to Spain. The treaty also fixed the boundary between the United States and Spanish territory in the New Southwest. In the north, the boundary of the Louisiana Purchase was worked out between Great Britain and the United States.

PAGE 248

1. Foreign trade was vital to the United States in the early nineteenth century because poor transportation made it hard to trade by land within the boundaries of the United States, and the United States had few factories to manufacture necessary items.

2. Presidents Jefferson and Madison tried to defend the neutral rights of the United States with the embargo policy and other peaceful means of protection.

3. The War Hawks were young Democratic-Republicans from the South and West in the House of Representatives. The War Hawks believed that by declaring war on Great Britain and then invading Canada, the United States could add more territory into which American settlers could expand. They also believed an invasion of Canada might destroy bases from which Indians had been raiding frontier settlements in the Northwest Territory.

4. It can be said that the Treaty of Ghent was a peace without victory because even though the United States failed to gain territory, it had not lost any.

5. The most important results of the War of 1812 were that the Federalist party was badly weakened; the war convinced European countries that the United States could defend itself; it created an increasing spirit of nationalism among Americans; it broke the power of the Indians in the Northwest Territory; and it made heroes of Andrew Jackson and William Henry Harrison.

PAGE 251

1. Four leaders who might be considered members of the Virginia Dynasty are Thomas Jefferson, James Madison, James Monroe, and Alexander Hamilton.

2. Alexander Hamilton was the guiding light of the Federalist party. As a result of his death from the Burr-Hamilton duel, the Federalist party disappeared.

3. The Hamiltonian policies that came to be adopted by the Democratic-Republicans were chartering a Bank of the United States and the approval of a protective tariff.

4. The Monroe Doctrine promised European nations that they could keep whatever possessions they had in the Western Hemisphere as of 1823. However, they must not claim any additional territory in this hemisphere. The United States would oppose any effort to extend the European system of rule by kings and queens to the Western Hemisphere. In return, the United States promised not to interfere in events that might take place inside any European country.

5. By means of the Missouri Compromise, the North and the South each gave up the majority vote in the Senate. This was a gain for the whole nation because Congress avoided a dangerous confrontation between the North and the South.

ANSWERS FOR CHAPTER REVIEW

PAGE 252
Vocabulary Quiz
1. F **2.** F **3.** T **4.** F **5.** F **6.** T **7.** F **8.** T **9.** T **10.** T

Review Questions
1. Rivers and streams were used by frontier settlers for travel, as sources of waterpower, and to get their surplus farm crops to market.

2. Lands in the Old Northwest were surveyed and sold in accordance with an ordinance passed by the Confederation Congress in 1785. In the Old Southwest there was not such an orderly land policy. The status of slavery marked another important difference. Slavery was illegal in the Old Northwest but not in the Old Southwest.

3. Two complaints against Great Britain that helped bring on the War of 1812 were that Great Britain violated the neutral rights of the United States and had impressed American sailors.

4. President James Monroe issued the doctrine that bears his name as a warning to European countries. The Monroe Doctrine promised European nations that they could keep whatever possessions they had in the Western Hemisphere as of 1823. However, they must not claim any additional territory in this hemisphere. Moreover, the United States would oppose any effort to extend the European system of rule by kings and queens to the Western Hemisphere. In return, the United States promised not to interfere in events that might take place inside any European country.

5. The Missouri Compromise avoided a dangerous confrontation by preserving the balance between slave states and free states in the Senate.

Activities
1. Kentucky: 1792 S
Tennessee: 1796 S
Ohio: 1803 N
Louisiana: 1812 L
Indiana: 1816 N
Mississippi: 1817 S
Illinois: 1818 N
Missouri: 1821 L

2. Answers will vary.

3. Answers will vary.

ANSWERS FOR SKILLS DEVELOPMENT

PAGE 253
Skills Practice
1. a **2.** c **3.** c **4.** a **5.** c

CHAPTER 11 **The Jacksonian Era**

ANSWERS FOR CHECKUP QUESTIONS

PAGE 258
1. Andrew Jackson was a "new kind of President" because he was not a descendant of an old colonial family. He was the son of an immigrant, raised on the frontier and grown to manhood in the newly opened lands west of the Appalachians.

2. Jackson's supporters charged that a "corrupt bargain" had been made because Clay gave Adams his support in return for the office of secretary of state.

3. John Quincy Adams's administration was generally unsuccessful because he entered office under the handicap of the "corrupt bargain" charges. He was a "minority President," having received fewer than one third of the popular votes in the election. He lacked political skill and had to combat increasing sectionalism, which was dividing the country. He also proposed to raise money for internal improvements by raising the tariff and by increasing the price of public land.

4. The reasons for Jackson's easy victory in the 1828 election were the hard work by his campaign managers; his standing as a war hero; and the fact that John Quincy Adams was not popular.

PAGE 264

1. Higher tariffs meant that southerners had to pay more for manufactured products. The legislature of South Carolina protested this action by Congress. The legislature supported a statement issued by John C. Calhoun. Calhoun said that a state could nullify—that is, cancel or veto—a national law within its own boundaries. The belief that a state could do this was called the nullification doctrine.

2. The nullification controversy between South Carolina and the national government resulted in a compromise. The Compromise Tariff of 1833 was passed, lowering tariff rates over a period of 10 years. At the same time, Congress passed the Force Bill. This authorized the President to use the army and navy, if necessary, to collect tariff duties.

3. Jackson vetoed the Bank Charter Bill because he thought it was unconstitutional, a monopoly, and un-American, since many of the stockholders were British.

4. The Whigs won the presidential election of 1840 by agreeing on one candidate and by using slogans, parades, and shouting, which drowned out any serious discussion of the issues.

PAGE 269

1. The presidential nominating conventions helped to give people more political rights by allowing the people to have a voice in choosing their party's candidates for the country's highest office.

2. New constitutions in some states permitted all white men over 21 years of age to vote. Property requirements for voting and holding office were removed from most states, as were all religious requirements.

3. After Jackson was defeated in 1824, those who had backed him started planning for victory in 1828 by forming political organizations. Full-time workers were paid through dues or gifts from party members. Or they were given government jobs while still spending much of their time working for their political party.

4. The official Cabinet and the Kitchen Cabinet gave advice to Andrew Jackson. Jackson paid more attention to the Kitchen Cabinet because he knew its members were in close touch with ordinary people, and he wanted to know what ordinary voters were thinking.

PAGE 271

1. Indians, blacks, and women did not gain equality during the Jacksonian era.

2. Eastern Indians were removed to lands west of the Mississippi because many white people wanted to take this land away from the Indians.

3. By the time of the Jacksonian era, abolitionists—people who wanted to abolish slavery—were active in all parts of the nation. An antislavery petition was sent to Congress. A group of northerners became extreme abolitionists; they wanted slavery ended immediately. A paper was published in Boston that carried the views of the extreme abolitionists. In 1833 abolitionist leaders organized the American Anti-Slavery Society.

4. Women were denied equality during the Jacksonian era by not being allowed to vote or hold office. Most states refused women the right to own property. Women were also denied entry into the professions of law, medicine, and the ministry.

ANSWERS FOR CHAPTER REVIEW

PAGE 272

Vocabulary Quiz

1. c **2.** c **3.** c **4.** b **5.** b

Review Questions

1. Favorite-son candidates were nominated by the Democratic-Republicans in 1824 and the Whigs in 1836 because the parties failed to agree on a single candidate.

2. (a) Jackson thought that the Second Bank of the United States was unconstitutional because Congress had no power to charter a bank. He said the Second Bank was a monopoly and that it was un-American because many of the stockholders were British.
(b) Jackson strongly opposed the nullification doctrine.

3. Permanent political organizations and the spoils system were linked together because many employees of the national government held their jobs for long periods of time.

4. Women were denied the right to vote, to hold public office, to own property, and to enter the professions of law, medicine, and the ministry.

Activities
Answers will vary.
ANSWERS FOR SKILLS DEVELOPMENT

PAGE 273

Skills Practice: Part I
1. Large 2. fight 3. kept 4. collapsed 5. stop

Skills Practice: Part II
Answers will vary.

CHAPTER 12 An American Spirit Grows

ANSWERS FOR CHECKUP QUESTIONS

PAGE 282

1. Reform brought about the first organized Women's Rights Convention in 1848. Reform is improving conditions by changing them. Both men and women reformers attended the convention.

2. Some men and women of the time could be described as "all-purpose reformers" because they were generally interested in more than just one reason for reform.

3. The reformers used methods such as working inside the existing bodies of government. Those working for women's rights set out to bring about changes in state laws that discriminated against women. Abolitionists hoped to do away with slavery in the South by state action. Temperance advocates petitioned for laws limiting the sale of liquor or prohibiting it completely.

4. Better educational opportunities were made available in the 1830s and 1840s by providing children with free public elementary education. Thus this new interest in education brought about the growth of high schools, colleges, and universities. Educational opportunities for girls and women increased during this time.

5. There was opposition to reform because most people were against change.

PAGE 286

1. Ralph Waldo Emerson urged Americans to create stories, pictures, statues, and songs based on American ideas and American scenes.

2. Subjects of each of the following painters: (a) Asher Durand painted scenes along the Hudson River in a distinctive style. (b) George Caleb Bingham painted scenes of American frontier life. (c) George Catlin painted American Indians of the early nineteenth century. (d) John James Audubon painted American birds and animals.

3. Nathaniel Currier and James M. Ives were noted for their reproductions of pleasant scenes of American life.

4. Artistic creations that come from the common people are known as folk art. Much of nineteenth-century folk art was made of wood because it was readily available.

5. The members of the Concord group were known for their distinctly American writings. They borrowed some European ideas, mixed them with their own thoughts, and then based their work in American locations.

PAGE 291

1. The Erie Canal set off a canal boom in the United States because it took less time for the canal boat to travel on a canal and freight rates dropped within a few years. Before the completion of the Erie Canal, there were fewer than 100 miles (160 km) of canals in the United States. Within 15 years, more than 3,300 miles (5,310 km) of canals had been built.

2. Railroads had several advantages over canals. Trains were faster than canal boats. Railroad tracks could be laid where it was difficult or even impossible to dig canals. During cold weather, canals might freeze over, while railroads could continue to operate.

3. Steamboats were used widely in the early nineteenth century on the Hudson, Ohio, and Mississippi rivers.

4. The effects of the transportation revolution in the United States speeded up the westward movement of the American people and increased economic specialization in major sections of the country.

5. The factory system developed first in New England because of an abundance of waterpower. The small, swift rivers of southern New England proved ideal for this purpose.

6. The spirit of American enterprise revolutionized farming methods between 1825 and 1850 by the invention of a mechanical reaper, a steel-bladed plow, an improved grain drill, a threshing machine, and a mechanical binder, all of which proved to be a great help to farmers.

ANSWER KEY

ANSWERS FOR CHAPTER REVIEW

PAGE 292

Vocabulary Quiz
1. T 2. F 3. T 4. F 5. F 6. T 7. F 8. T
9. T 10. F

Review Questions

1. A Declaration of Sentiments was issued at the Seneca Falls Convention of 1848. The declaration listed ways in which society discriminated against women and demanded that women be given suffrage, or the right to vote.

2. To accomplish their goals, reformers used methods such as working inside the existing bodies of government. Those working for women's rights set out to bring about changes in state laws that discriminated against women. Abolitionists hoped to do away with slavery in the South by state action. Temperance advocates petitioned for laws limiting the sale of liquor or prohibiting it completely. Sometimes reformers organized tiny political parties made up of those who believed reforms were needed.

3. Educational opportunities for girls and women improved in some states during the 1830s and 1840s as girls studied alongside boys in free public elementary schools. Four girls were allowed to enroll in an Ohio college along with male students. Other western colleges and universities admitted women as well as men, and separate colleges for women were established.

4. Jacksonian democracy and religious beliefs acted as sources for reform ideas because they were both based on ideas of dignity and equality of individuals.

5. The first American authors to use American themes in their work were Ralph Waldo Emerson, Washington Irving, and James Fenimore Cooper. The first American painters to use American themes in their work were Thomas Cole, Thomas Doughty, and Asher Durand.

6. During this period, advances made in transportation and manufacturing included the growth of canals, railroads, steamboats, and factories.

Activities
Answers will vary.

ANSWERS FOR SKILLS DEVELOPMENT

PAGE 293

Skills Practice
Answers will vary.

CHAPTER 13 **Spanning the Continent**

ANSWERS FOR CHECKUP QUESTIONS

PAGE 299

1. Major Stephen Long led an exploring expedition in the lands between the Missouri River and the Rocky Mountains. The official maps of the expedition labeled the region the Great American Desert. Long claimed this region to be wholly unfit for cultivation and uninhabitable by people depending on agriculture for their subsistence. The effect of this name was that for 50 years, mapmakers copied Long's maps with misleading labels. Settlers on their way west crossed the "desert" without stopping. Today these plains support millions of people.

2. The mountain men guided exploring expeditions, led parties that had goods to trade with the Indians for furs, and hired out as guides to the wagon trains. The missionaries established missions that attracted settlers.

3. The Oregon Trail covered nearly 2,000 miles (3,200 km) and took about 6 months to complete. The trail traveled northwest to the Platte River, followed the river to Fort Laramie, and then continued through the Rockies by way of South Pass to the Snake River. Here the settlers made a choice to either turn southwest toward California or continue following the Snake and Columbia rivers to their destinations. The settlers traveled over the Oregon Trail in huge covered wagons pulled by oxen. Sometimes they rode on the wagons, but most of the time they walked alongside.

4. The Willamette Valley was the favored destination of many early pioneers in the Oregon country because the valley had rich farmland.

5. The "Oregon question" arose because Americans were dissatisfied with joint ownership of the Oregon country between Great Britain and the United States.

The Oregon question was settled by a treaty that set the boundary at the 49th parallel north latitude, an extension of the eastern boundary between the United States and British-controlled Canada. The northern boundary of the United States was now fixed from the Atlantic to the Pacific.

PAGE 303

1. Moses Austin received permission from the Spanish government to bring Americans to Texas. However, he died before any settlers came. His son, Stephen Austin, led in the development of an American settlement along the Brazos River. The settlers were able to buy good land for 12½ cents an acre.

2. Texas wanted independence from Mexico because Americans outnumbered the Mexicans living there and the Mexican government forbade any more Americans to settle in Texas. Some land grants were canceled.

3. James K. Polk's campaign of 1844 was based on the annexation of Texas.

4. The annexation of Texas by the United States brought on a war with Mexico because Americans and Mexicans differed over the boundary between Mexico and the new American states. President Polk angered the Mexican government by sending American troops into the disputed border area. He also sent gunboats to patrol Mexico's eastern coast.

PAGE 309

1. The major provisions of the Treaty of Guadalupe Hidalgo were that Mexico accepted the Rio Grande as the boundary of Texas, and that Mexico ceded to the United States the rest of the territory between Texas and the Pacific. The United States agreed to pay Mexico $15 million for this land and the American government agreed to pay claims of American citizens against Mexico up to a total of $3.5 million.

2. When Americans spoke of manifest destiny, they meant that fate had clearly intended for the country to stretch from ocean to ocean.

3. The Mormons originated in western New York State. They were unpopular with many neighbors and were forced to move. Their leader led them to the area of the Great Salt Lake, which at that time was outside the western boundaries of the United States.

4. Americans wanted California to be part of the United States and took the lead in a revolt against Mexican rule. When the Mexican War began, a small American army brought all of Upper California under American control. They then worked to establish an American territorial government for California.

5. The discovery of gold in California brought thousands of people to that region and hastened its development.

ANSWERS FOR CHAPTER REVIEW

PAGE 310
Vocabulary Quiz
1. f 2. extra description 3. b 4. a 5. c 6. extra description 7. d 8. e 9. g 10. h 11. j 12. i

Review Questions
1. Pioneers in the West first settled along the Pacific coast rather than in the Great Plains area because they were led to believe by Stephen Long that the region was "wholly unfit for cultivation and uninhabitable to people depending on agriculture for their subsistence."

2. The main routes to the Pacific coast were by way of the Oregon Trail.

3. Texas won its independence of Mexico following the victory at the battle of San Jacinto. A treaty was signed that later the Mexican congress refused to approve.

4. Faced with a serious dispute that seemed likely to lead the United States to war with Mexico, Polk decided to compromise on the Oregon question. A treaty set the boundary at the 49th parallel north latitude.

5. The war with Mexico resulted in the United States gaining a vast expanse of land in the Southwest.

Activities
Answers will vary.

ANSWERS FOR SKILLS DEVELOPMENT

PAGE 311
Skills Practice
Answers will vary.

ANSWER KEY

How Americans Lived, 1850

ANSWERS FOR CHECKUP QUESTIONS

PAGE 317

1. Between 1849 and 1850, life changed for Harriet Tubman. With the death of the plantation master, Harriet Tubman escaped to Philadelphia and got a job in a hotel. Later in 1850 she returned to Maryland and helped her sister and two children to escape to freedom.

2. In 1850, life for the owner of a cotton plantation in Mississippi was leisurely and elegant. Overseers were hired to manage the slaves and the business matters. Tutors were brought in to educate the children. The children were also taught to ride. Once they became adults, they engaged in fox hunting, which was a social occasion.

3. Answers will vary.

4. Answers will vary.

ANSWERS FOR UNIT REVIEW

PAGE 318

Reading the Text

1. From 1824 to 1840

2. By caucus

3. Nominating convention

4. Every 4 years

5. 1832

Reading a Map

1. Scott's army left from New Orleans.

2. Scott's final destination was Mexico City.

3. Doniphan and Taylor were the leaders of the two forces that reached Monterrey.

4. The area between the Nueces River and the Rio Grande River was claimed by both the United States and Mexico.

5. New Mexico, California, Arizona, Nevada, Utah, and Colorado were carved out, in whole or in part, from the Mexican Cession.

Reading a Picture

1. Francis Scott Key

2. British warship

3. Baltimore

4. Fort McHenry

5. Dawn

Reading a Time Line

1. 1775 to 1825   **2.** 5   **3.** 10   **4.** F   **5.** F   **6.** F
7. F   **8.** T

UNIT 4 THE NATION DIVIDES AND REUNITES

CHAPTER 14 Rising Tensions

ANSWERS FOR CHECKUP QUESTIONS

PAGE 325

1. In 1850, Clay presented his compromise plan to the Senate. It was an attempt to deal with several unsolved issues between the North and the South. Calhoun agreed with the purpose of Clay's bill but insisted that it should give even more protection to the South. He demanded that the government bring back the political balance between the North and the South and stop tampering with the slavery question. Webster approved the compromise and asked the whole country to do the same.

2. The six provisions of the Compromise of 1850 were as follows:
(1) California would be admitted as a free state.
(2) The remainder of the Mexican Cession would be organized into two territories, Utah and New Mexico. Presumably the people of these territories could decide whether they wanted slavery when they applied for admission as a state.
(3) Some land in dispute between Texas and New Mexico would be awarded to New Mexico.
(4) Texas would receive $10 million from the national government for giving up its claims to this land.
(5) The buying and selling of slaves, but not slavery itself, would be prohibited in the District of Columbia.
(6) Congress would enact a strict law requiring that runaway slaves be returned to their masters.

3. Blacks considered the Compromise of 1850 no compromise at all for several reasons. White families living in the District of Columbia could keep slaves, and Southern officeholders could bring slaves to serve them in the capital city. The passing of the Fugitive Slave Law, one part of the Compromise of 1850, was a chief threat for black people. Slaves who escaped to free soil in the North were no longer safe. They were to be picked up and returned to their masters. The new law provided bounties, or rewards, for the capture of escaped slaves. The law

stated, too, that officials in Northern towns and cities had to help in the return of fugitive slaves when asked to do so. Also, those who knew of escaped slaves and did not report what they knew could be fined or even jailed, according to the law.

4. The Fugitive Slave Law caused many more people in the North to become abolitionists. The Northern reaction convinced many Southerners that people in the North did not intend to obey the law.

PAGE 333

1. Some people believe that Senator Douglas sponsored the Kansas-Nebraska bill to attract Southern support for another try at the presidency in 1856. Others thought that Douglas put forth the bill because it would help in a plan to build a railroad from Chicago to the West Coast. Such a railroad would encourage settlement of the sparsely settled lands north and south of the Missouri River and enable Douglas to profit from his landholdings along the proposed railway route.

2. The main provisions of the Kansas-Nebraska bill were that two territories, Kansas and Nebraska, would be formed from the Louisiana Purchase land. The people of Kansas and Nebraska could decide whether they wanted to allow slavery in their territory.

3. One result of the Kansas-Nebraska Act was the opposition that caused the formation of the Republican party. Another result was open warfare in Kansas. Men favoring slavery formed one territorial government in Kansas, while men opposed to slavery formed another.

4. Southern and Northern Democrats reacted differently to the Dred Scott decision because it seemed to mean that all the territories of the national government were open to slavery and that not even a vote of the residents could keep slavery out. The decision pleased the Southern Democrats but angered the Northern Democrats.

5. The Lincoln-Douglas debates widened the split in the Democratic party because Lincoln forced Douglas to admit he was not wholly in favor of the Dred Scott decision. This admission lost Douglas some Southern support in his campaign for the presidency 2 years later.

6. The candidates in the presidential election of 1860 were Stephen A. Douglas for the Northern Democrats, John Breckenridge for the Southern Democrats, John Bell for the Constitutional Union party, and Abraham Lincoln for the Republicans. Abraham Lincoln won the election. Soon after Lincoln's election, seven Southern states seceded and formed the Confederate States of America.

PAGE 337

1. The major differences between the Southern and Northern people in 1860 were that there were more blacks in the South and more foreign-born in the North. Also, most people in the South farmed for a living, while most Northerners worked in factories.

2. Southern farmers without slaves were like Northern farmers in many ways. They often raised some corn and wheat, as Northern farmers did. Most Southern and Northern farmers lived in simple frame or log houses.

3. Plantation owners as a group had most of the political power in the South. They also had great economic power. They provided the money that supported shopkeepers, warehousemen, lawyers, and cotton merchants.

4. Slaves showed they were unhappy with their existence by escaping to the North, staging slave revolts and work stoppages, and destroying tools and other property of their masters.

5. *Uncle Tom's Cabin* was an important book because many who had been unconcerned about slavery began to oppose it strongly.

ANSWERS FOR CHAPTER REVIEW

PAGE 338
Vocabulary Quiz
1. T **2.** F, harder **3.** F, Harriet Tubman **4.** F, was not in agreement **5.** T **6.** T **7.** T **8.** F, John Brown **9.** F, after **10.** F, North

Review Questions
1. In 1850, Clay presented his compromise plan to the Senate. It was an attempt to deal with several unsolved issues between the North and the South. Calhoun agreed with the purpose of Clay's bill but insisted that it should give even more protection to the South. He demanded that the government bring back the political balance between the North and the South and stop tampering with the slavery question. Webster approved the compromise and asked the whole country to do the same.

2. The Fugitive Slave Law was a disaster for black Americans because escaped slaves were no longer safe anywhere in the United States. The new law also made it necessary for free blacks in the North and the South to carry "freedom papers" proving they were not escaped slaves.

3. The Kansas-Nebraska Act hindered Douglas's chances of becoming President.

4. Although Douglas won the election to the Senate, the debates brought Lincoln national attention.

5. Dred Scott, a slave, had been taken by his master back and forth from slave to free states. Some antislavery people helped Dred Scott sue for his freedom on the grounds that he had been taken to live in a territory where slavery was prohibited. The Supreme Court said that a black person was not a citizen and did not have the right to sue in a federal court. The court ruled that slaves were property, and the Fifth Amendment to the Constitution protected property. Therefore, Congress could not prohibit slavery in any of the territories, and the Missouri Compromise was unconstitutional. The Dred Scott decision pleased the Southern Democrats but angered the Northern Democrats. Republicans and other opponents of slavery attacked the Dred Scott decision. Also, Northerners refused to obey the Fugitive Slave Law.

6. Answers will vary.

Activities
1. Clay Submits Compromise Plan
Senator Calhoun Dies
Stowe's Book a Sensation
Douglas Introduces Kansas-Nebraska Bill
Buchanan Elected President
Dred Scott Decision Announced
John Brown Hanged for Treason
Lincoln Wins Presidency
South Carolina Secedes
Confederacy Organized

2. Answers will vary.

ANSWERS FOR SKILLS DEVELOPMENT

PAGE 339
Skills Practice
1. The abolitionists are helping the slaves escape to freedom by supplying them with transportation.

2. The escaping slaves used a horse-drawn wagon to get to Coffin's farm.

3. Answers will vary.

4. If escaping slaves were caught, they would be severely punished or even shot. The abolitionists who helped them would be fined or jailed.

5. Answers will vary.

CHAPTER 15 **The Civil War**

ANSWERS FOR CHECKUP QUESTIONS

PAGE 349

1. When the war began, Jefferson Davis was President of the Confederacy and Abraham Lincoln was President of the Union.

2. Fighting between the Union and Confederacy began with the bombardment of Fort Sumter by the Confederates in the harbor of Charleston, South Carolina.

3. The war goal of the Confederacy was to fight for their independence. The war goals of the Union were foremost to preserve the Union and second to abolish slavery.

4. The Army of Northern Virginia, which had a strong army and steady leadership, won a series of victories over the Army of the Potomac. The Union army was untrained and without strong leadership in the early years of the war.

5. As a result of Lincoln's Emancipation Proclamation, thousands of slave families left the plantations to seek freedom behind Union lines. Former slaves joined the Northern armies. Most antislavery people in the North welcomed the long-awaited proclamation of freedom. In Great Britain the common people greeted the news with joy. Now there was little chance that aristocratic British leaders would risk giving aid to the Confederacy.

PAGE 356

1. The battle of Gettysburg is often looked upon as the turning point of the war. It is also remembered for Abraham Lincoln's Gettysburg Address, which has been called the perfect expression of the democratic faith of the American people.

2. The Union divided the Confederacy by capturing control of the Mississippi River.

3. Sherman's march to the sea divided the Confederacy a second time because the Union army forced its way through the gap that led through the southern mountains into Georgia. This made it possible to divide the eastern half of the Confederacy by capturing Atlanta and Savannah.

4. The Anaconda Plan had four goals:
(1) To blockade the ports of the Confederacy to prevent trade with Europe
(2) To cut the Confederacy in two by capturing control of the Mississippi
(3) To cut the eastern half of the Confederacy in two by advancing up the Tennessee River and then southward into Georgia
(4) To capture Richmond

5. The four parts of the Anaconda Plan were completed by the spring of 1865 as follows:
(1) The Union army captured New Orleans.
(2) The Union divided the Confederacy by capturing control of the Mississippi River.
(3) The eastern half of the Confederacy was cut in two by capturing Atlanta and Savannah.
(4) The Union captured and took control of the Confederate capital, Richmond.

PAGE 361

1. Both the Union and Confederacy objected to the draft laws because men with money could buy exemption from the draft or hire men to go in their place. Owners of more than 15 slaves and those who supervised the work of that number could claim exemption.

2. In filling the ranks of the army, the two sources that the Union used but the Confederacy would not were immigrants and slaves.

3. Northern women assisted in the war effort by working in factories, on farms, and in hospitals. Southern women assisted in the war effort by managing plantations, planting crops, and working in war factories and hospitals. Women on each side acted as spies.

4. The chief economic problem in the North by 1864 was rising prices and in the South, shortages in practically everything.

5. The Union party was formed for the presidential election of 1864 to take the place of the Republican

ANSWER KEY

party. The presidential candidate was Abraham Lincoln and the vice presidential candidate was Andrew Johnson.

ANSWERS FOR CHAPTER REVIEW

PAGE 362
Vocabulary Quiz
1. c 2. a 3. a 4. b 5. d

Review Questions
1. At the beginning of the war, the goal of the Union was to preserve the Union, while the goal of the Confederacy was to gain independence.

2. The Union completed the four parts of the Anaconda Plan by capturing New Orleans, capturing control of the Mississippi River, capturing Atlanta and Savannah, and taking control of Richmond.

3. The draft used by both the Union and the Confederate armies was unfair because men with money could buy exemption from the draft or hire men to go in their place. Owners of more than 15 slaves and those who supervised the work of that number could claim exemption.

4. The economic problem in the North during the war was rising prices, and in the South it was shortages in practically everything.

5. The new Union party took the place of the Republican party. This party was made up of the War Democrats and the Republicans. Their candidate for President was Abraham Lincoln, and their candidate for Vice President was Andrew Johnson.

   The majority of Northern Democrats, who favored an immediate end to the war, were known as Peace Democrats. Their choice for President was George B. McClellan. Abraham Lincoln won the election.

ANSWERS FOR SKILLS DEVELOPMENT

PAGE 363
Skills Practice: Part I
1. T 2. T 3. F 4. T

Skills Practice: Part II
1. F 2. T 3. F 4. T

Skills Practice: Part III
1. T 2. F 3. T 4. T

CHAPTER 16 Reconstruction

ANSWERS FOR CHECKUP QUESTIONS

PAGE 370
1. The main features of the Lincoln-Johnson plan for Reconstruction were that 10 percent of the voters in a Confederate state must take an oath of allegiance pledging themselves to support the Constitution of the United States. They must agree to obey laws passed by the United States Congress and to honor the President's proclamations on slavery. Then they could organize a state government. The state governments had to repeal their secession acts, promise they would not pay the Confederate war debt, and ratify the Thirteenth Amendment to the Constitution.

2. The Radical Republicans gained allies after the election of the first postwar Congress because Northerners were alarmed by the presence of these former Confederates in the nation's Congress.

3. The Radical Republicans failed in their attempt to impeach President Johnson. The effect of the trial was that the weapon of impeachment would not be freely or easily used in future conflicts between Congress and the President. Johnson's fight to save his presidency also helped to insure the future independence of the executive branch of government.

4. The Thirteenth, Fourteenth, and Fifteenth Amendments were added to the Constitution with the goal of giving black Americans the same rights enjoyed by white citizens.

PAGE 376
1. The future for white Southerners appeared bleak. For most of them the South was a land of war ruin and war cripples—poor and defeated. The future of black Southerners was even more hopeless. With Lincoln's assassination came sadness and fear, for he had represented the end of slavery and great hope for future progress.

2. The Freedmen's Bureau helped Southern blacks by furnishing food and supplies. It also found jobs and homes for poor people and organized efforts for the education of freed slaves.

   The black codes hindered them by putting restrictions on freed blacks that were not applied to Southern whites. They forbade former slaves from moving freely from one place to another and made it illegal for freedmen to possess firearms, to sit on juries, to vote, or to hold office. In some states, blacks were forbidden to own land or to testify against whites in court, and more severe penalities were applied to blacks than to whites guilty of the same crimes.

3. The crop lien system and sharecropping were two systems used to get Southern agriculture back into production after the war. Through the crop lien system, landowners got seeds, tools and other necessities from a local merchant. In return, farmers gave the merchant a first lien on their crop, usually cotton. This meant repaying the merchant first when the year's crop was sold. By sharecropping, landowners would get people to farm the land in return for a share of the crop that was produced.

PAGE 379
1. Northern soldiers returned to a prosperous land that was almost wholly unscarred by war. They were given money and clothing by the government, and they found jobs available nearly everywhere.

Southern soldiers returned to a land of ruin, penniless and dressed in rags. Their hopes and fortunes were gone.

2. The Republicans were able to remain the dominant party for a generation following the war because they were honored as the party that saved the Union, the party that freed the slaves, and the party of Abraham Lincoln.

3. Answers will vary.

4. The presidential election of 1876 was disputed because of 20 electoral votes—19 in three Southern states and 1 in Oregon. The three Southern states were still under military occupation as part of the Radical Republican Reconstruction plan. Each of these states sent two sets of electors for the final count. One set favored Tilden, the other favored Hayes.

5. Congress appointed an electoral commission to settle the dispute. The Republicans made up the majority on this commission. They decided all of the disputed electoral votes should be awarded to Hayes. This gave Hayes the necessary number of electoral votes to become President.

The terms and results of the settlement were that soldiers would be withdrawn from those Southern states where they still remained; Hayes promised to

pick at least one Southerner for his Cabinet; and leaders of the Republicans in Congress promised to supply money for internal improvements in the South. The Compromise of 1877 meant the end of Reconstruction under the Radical Republican plan.

ANSWERS FOR CHAPTER REVIEW
PAGE 380
Vocabulary Quiz
1. h **2.** d **3.** i **4.** g **5.** a **6.** extra definition
7. c **8.** j **9.** f **10.** b **11.** extra definition
12. e

Review Questions
1. The Lincoln-Johnson plan for Reconstruction stated that 10 percent of the voters in a Confederate state must take an oath of allegiance pledging themselves to support the Constitution of the United States. They must agree to obey laws passed by the United States Congress and to honor the President's proclamation on slavery. Then they could organize a state government. The state governments had to repeal their secession acts and promise they would not pay the Confederate war debt. They also had to ratify the Thirteenth Amendment to the Constitution.

The Reconstruction Act of 1867 divided the former Confederate States of America, except for Tennessee, into five military districts. In each one a United States Army general was in charge, with soldiers to carry out his orders. To get out from under military rule, a state had to accept the Fourteenth Amendment and had to guarantee black men the right to vote. Only then would Congress agree to accept that state's senators and members of the House of Representatives.

2. The purpose of the Thirteenth Amendment was to declare slavery nonexistent in the United States. The Fourteenth Amendment was designed to make black people United States citizens if they were born there. The Fifteenth Amendment forbade any state to deny a person the right to vote because of race, color, or previous condition of servitude.

3. Many leaders of Southern state governments were carpetbaggers. Carpetbaggers were Northerners who came south after the war, carrying their belongings in luggage made of carpeting. The carpetbaggers came for various reasons. Some sincerely wanted to help in the rebuilding of the South. Others were out to profit from the unsettled conditions.

Others who gained influence in the state governments were certain white Southerners who co-operated with the carpetbaggers. These people were known as scalawags. Some of these Southerners had the best of intentions. Others simply aimed to gain power for themselves.

The carpetbag governments created a public education system for the South, which was a good point. A bad point was that the governments seemed to spend a great deal of money, sometimes frivolously.

4. A compromise was necessary in order to settle the disputed presidential election of 1876 because tempers in the North and the South had become heated. Tensions between Republicans and Democrats had risen to the point that some people feared civil war might break out again.

Activities
Answers will vary.

ANSWERS FOR SKILLS DEVELOPMENT
PAGE 381
Skills Practice
1. Tweed is giving the people money in order to get them to vote a certain way.

2. The Public Treasury sign tells you the money belongs to the taxpayers.

3. Tweed is guarding the ballot box to make certain the voters cast their ballots as instructed.

4. The phrase "in counting there is strength," means that the person or group who controlled the ballot boxes could falsify the count of votes in favor of their candidate.

CHAPTER 17 The Gilded Age

ANSWERS FOR CHECKUP QUESTIONS
PAGE 386
1. The Gilded Age got its name from a novel titled *The Gilded Age* by Mark Twain and Charles Dudley Warner. Something that is gilded is attractive and shiny on the surface, but underneath the object may be ugly and cheap. That is the way the two writers looked at the years following the Civil War. Their novel described the flashy, get-rich-quick society of the United States after the war. *The Gilded Age*

pointed out that underneath the glittering surface lay corruption and false ideals.

2. There was little difference between the two political parties during the 1870s and 1880s. Both parties lived up to the compromise that settled the election of 1876. Both parties became and remained white men's parties. Black men were kept from voting and holding office in the southern states in all of which white Democrats held control. Women were still denied political rights.

3. The Republican Presidents during the Gilded Age were Rutherford B. Hayes, James A. Garfield, and Chester A. Arthur.

4. Grover Cleveland differed from the other Presidents of the Gilded Age because he was a Democrat.

PAGE 390
1. The main features of the Atlanta Compromise were that blacks should give up temporarily their attempts for social equality with whites and develop their work skills. Washington also asked southern whites to provide economic opportunities for blacks to aid mutual progress.

2. The decisions in the *Plessy* v. *Ferguson* case and the civil rights cases fastened racial segregation on the country. By law and by custom, public facilities were segregated according to race. All this was accepted as legal if the separate facilities were "equal."

3. More political and social restrictions were being placed on black Americans, and by the end of the Gilded Age some southern states were considering laws that would keep blacks from voting. The Fourteenth and Fifteenth Amendments had little meaning for black Americans.

PAGE 394
1. The two women who ran for President during the Gilded Age were Virginia Woodhull and Belva Lockwood.

2. Suffrage, temperance, and improving conditions for the Indians were reforms that occupied the attention of women's organizations during the Gilded Age.

3. Some colleges and universities began to allow women to enter for advanced education during the Gilded Age. By the beginning of the 1870s there were three medical schools for women. However, after graduation, women had great difficulty in practicing medicine. No established hospital would

take them as students, interns, or staff members. Most women lawyers in the Gilded Age were the wives of lawyers. After passing the bar exams, they joined their husbands in practice.

4. During the Gilded Age, hundreds of thousands of women were employed as teachers, typists, stenographers, switchboard operators, sales clerks, and factory workers.

PAGE 399

1. Walt Whitman's poems focus on being involved with the world, while Emily Dickinson's focus on the inner self.

2. George Inness was a follower of the Hudson River school in his early career, painting American scenes. He later went beyond these painters and developed his own realistic style.

Winslow Homer first became known as an illustrator and painter of Civil War scenes. After the war, he shifted to landscapes and pictures of rural people working and playing. His third type of painting included scenes showing the drama of the sea.

Thomas Eakins was a third great American artist painting during the Gilded Age. He was a master at drawing the human figure at rest or in action.

3. Mark Twain could be considered a local colorist because his stories reflected the scenes, characters, and dialogue typical of the area along the Mississippi River, where he grew up, and of life in the West, where he lived most of his life.

4. John Philip Sousa is chiefly remembered as a composer of marches. His marches are played today.

ANSWERS FOR CHAPTER REVIEW

PAGE 400

Vocabulary Quiz
1. c **2.** d **3.** d **4.** c **5.** a

Review Questions
1. The main features of the Atlanta Compromise were that blacks should give up temporarily their attempts for social equality with whites in return for economic opportunities. He asked that southern whites provide these economic opportunities by making use of the 8 million southern black people. Booker T. Washington accepted the Atlanta Compromise to help black Americans achieve economic opportunities.

2. Most black Americans lived in the South during the Gilded Age and because of law, custom, and the

separate but equal system, they gradually were pushed into the status of second-class citizens.

3. During the Gilded Age, women were employed as teachers, typists, stenographers, switchboard operators, sales clerks, and factory workers. Medical schools began to accept women and some women became lawyers.

4. (a) Emily Dickinson contributed her poems focusing on the inner self. (b) Thomas Eakins's contribution to the arts were his paintings of human figures at rest or in action. (c) John Philip Sousa was a composer of marches. He contributed popular marches that are still played today, such as *Semper Fidelis* and *Stars and Stripes Forever*.

Activities
Answers will vary.

ANSWERS FOR SKILLS DEVELOPMENT

PAGE 401

Skills Practice
1. F **2.** O **3.** O **4.** F **5.** O **6.** F **7.** O **8.** O **9.** O **10.** F

ANSWERS FOR UNIT REVIEW

PAGE 402

Reading the Text
1. Henry Clay **2.** California **3.** Free **4.** The people **5.** Yes **6.** No **7.** D.C. **8.** Stephen Douglas **9.** Daniel Webster **10.** John C. Calhoun

Reading a Map
1. F **2.** F **3.** T **4.** F **5.** F

Reading Pictures
1. The painting shows a farm scene on a summer afternoon with heavy storm clouds overhead.

2. The dark clouds suggest that a storm is coming.

3. Two men on the deck of a ship are using an instrument to determine the ship's location.

4. The water and parts of the ship tell us that the painting shows a scene aboard ship.

5. Answers will vary.

Reading Presidential Boxes
1. T **2.** F **3.** T **4.** T **5.** F **6.** F **7.** F **8.** F **9.** T **10.** F

CHAPTER 18 **The Last Frontier**

ANSWERS FOR CHECKUP QUESTIONS

PAGE 410

1. The United States government decided to make room for white settlers by requiring various Indian tribes of the Northwest to move onto reservations. The Nez Percé agreed to accept a reservation of 10,000 square miles (25,900 sq km). In just 8 years the United States government decided that the reservation must be cut down to 1,000 square miles (2,590 sq km). A band of Nez Percé then murdered 18 white settlers. To save their own lives, Chief Joseph and his tribe of Nez Percé started their long fight. The reason Chief Joseph surrendered is that he knew his situation was hopeless.

2. Broken treaties and settlers' demands for more and more of the Indian lands brought about the years of warfare between Indians and the United States Army on the Great Plains.

3. The development of new weapons like the repeater rifle and the Colt six-shooter revolver and the destruction of the buffalo herd weakened the Plains Indians' ability to resist.

4. The Dawes Act aimed to make Indians accept the ways of white Americans. The law made it possible for each head of a reservation family to own land on which the family could farm.
   The plan did not work out well because it tried to force Indians to give up their tribal ways. Most Indians were ill-prepared for farming.

PAGE 413

1. The phrase "Pikes Peak or Bust!" is connected with the discovery of gold near Pikes Peak in the Colorado Territory.

2. The Comstock Lode became known as the richest silver discovery in western history.

3. Answers will vary, but pupils should note that the population grew rapidly in mining areas; new businesses to serve the miners were developed; fron-

tier justice was the form of law and order; and many mining areas were settled by enough people that they eventually became states.

4. A gold or silver rush helped to settle the West. It brought men and women to run stores, farm the land, and start schools, churches, and newspapers. When the mining frontier passed on, many people stayed to raise families and build up the country.

PAGE 418

1. The problem of getting the cattle to the East for market had to be overcome before cattle ranching could be profitable.

2. The long drive was the process of bringing the herds of cattle together in the autumn and driving them northward to the railroad in Sedalia, grazing them along the way.

3. Cow towns grew up across Kansas because cattle were driven to the cow towns to be shipped by railroad to eastern cities.

4. Answers will vary, but pupils should note the dull routine of riding along the boundary of a ranch, the roundup, branding newborn calves, getting cattle ready for market, and enduring the hardships of the long drive. They should also note the satisfaction of many cowboys.

5. The prosperous days of the cattle kingdom came to an end because soon there were more cattle than the market demanded. Prices fell sharply. Then came a spell of bad weather. Most of the cattle died in the bitter winters of 1886 and 1887. Ranchers were ruined, and the cattle kingdom tumbled down.

PAGE 421

1. Large numbers of farmers moved onto the Great Plains in the 1870s because there was a change in the weather pattern, bringing above-average rainfall; private land companies and the railroads that owned land in the West advertised to attract settlers; and the Homestead Act encouraged settlement.

2. The problems that the newcomers to the Great Plains encountered were summer temperatures of 110°F; little rainfall; scarce water supplies; no wood for buildings, fencing, and fuel; and tough sod that would not yield to the old plows.

3. The farmers dealt with these problems by adopting a method of farming called dry farming, by using new farming machines, and by building sod houses.

4. The settlement of Oklahoma was different from that of other states because of the land rush. Homesteaders lined up at the Oklahoma border on April 22, 1889, to claim the 2 million acres that were divided into 160-acre homesteads.

ANSWERS FOR CHAPTER REVIEW

PAGE 422
Vocabulary Quiz
1. F—Indians **2.** F—sod house **3.** T **4.** F—Colorado **5.** T **6.** F—Colorado **7.** T **8.** F—cow town **9.** F—Dawes Act **10.** T

Review Questions
1. The discovery of gold and silver in the West caused the Indians to lose land that treaties were supposed to protect. Their land was claimed by the miners.

2. The Plains Indians were forced to change their way of life after 1887 by the passing of the Dawes Act. The Dawes Act was aimed at making Indians accept the ways of white Americans. The law made it possible for each head of a reservation family to own land on which the family could farm. The plan did not work out because the Indians did not want to give up their tribal ways.

3. Chief Joseph said "I will fight no more forever" when he surrendered to the army.
   Miners who set out to Pikes Peak in the Colorado Territory did so with the cry "Pikes Peak or Bust!"
   Major Stephen Long called the Great Plains region the Great American Desert many years before the land was settled.

4. Bad weather and more cattle than the market demanded led to the downfall of the cattle kingdom.

5. By the 1880s the cattle ranchers no longer had the open range to themselves because farmers moved in to benefit from the free use of the government's grasslands. Before long the cattle owners were battling with these newcomers for the right to use the land.

6. Some of the hardships of the farming family on the Great Plains included extremely hot summers; lack of water; no wood for buildings, fencing, and fuel; and tough sod that was hard to plow.

Activities
Answers will vary.

ANSWERS FOR SKILLS DEVELOPMENT
PAGE 423
Skills Practice
1. 6, 51, 116–117
2. 134–136, 146–148, 151–153
3. 49, 405, 415–417
4. 27, 36, 46
5. 634
6. 301
a. Arapaho and Cheyenne
b. Colorado Territory
c. Colonel Chivington
d. 1864

CHAPTER 19 The Rise of Industry

ANSWERS FOR CHECKUP QUESTIONS
PAGE 428
1. The Carnegie family left Scotland to seek new opportunities in America.

2. Answers will vary.

3. Carnegie shifted from making iron to steel because after a visit to a Bessemer furnace in England, he became convinced that the future of industrial growth lay with steel.

4. The four factors that led to success for Carnegie in the steel industry were efficiency, reinvesting profits, skilled management, and foresight and imagination.

PAGE 432
1. The federal and state governments helped railroad builders with loans and with gifts of land or money called subsidies.

2. The builders of the first transcontinental railroad were confronted with problems such as building around and sometimes through the mountains, using only pickaxes and shovels; suffering Indian attacks in the plains region; and working under the blazing summer sun and in below-zero cold and snows of winter.

3. Railroads contributed to the settlement of the West by promoting the western region through advertisements and by making travel and the shipping of crops faster and safer.

4. Railroads helped bring about the growth of an industrial economy by being the largest employer in the United States; by creating a demand for other goods, such as steel; and by carrying raw materials and finished goods cheaply from one part of the country to another. They also helped some businesses to become very large.

PAGE 433

1. The Civil War gave a boost to manufacturing. Iron was needed for weapons and there was a great demand for uniforms, boots, and other supplies. By the end of the war the United States was ready to embark on its great industrial expansion.

2. Coal, iron ore, gold, silver, copper, lead, zinc, and oil were natural resources found in the United States that were important for industrial expansion.

3. The increased population helped industrial expansion because there were more people to buy the products produced by the factories and a growing supply of labor to produce them.

4. Capital is an important factor in industrial growth because it takes a great deal of money to start and build businesses.

PAGE 439

1. Answers will vary but could include the air brake, telephone, typewriter, light bulb, and the oil refinery.

2. Three inventions of Thomas Edison's that led to new industries were the phonograph, the electric light bulb, and the motion-picture machine.

3. John D. Rockefeller gained control of the oil industry by being an efficient producer. He plowed back profits into the business to pay for expansion. He used the latest methods and machinery. He saved money by manufacturing his own barrels, building his own warehouses, and buying his own pipelines. He was able to ship and sell oil for less than his competitors.

4. Big business brought important benefits to the American people by making goods more efficiently. Because of this, American-made goods could compete in foreign markets against goods made in other countries. Selling more goods abroad meant more jobs for American workers. At home, some large

businesses sold their goods to American consumers for less.

Americans became concerned about the growth of big business because big corporations threatened to put an end to both competition and opportunity in business. People also feared big business's growing power in politics.

ANSWERS FOR CHAPTER REVIEW

PAGE 440
Vocabulary Quiz

1.	inventors	6.	stock
2.	rebates	7.	patent
3.	steel plant	8.	monopoly
4.	subsidy	9.	trust
5.	capital	10.	corporation

Review Questions

1. A patent encourages inventions. To make even a minor adjustment to an invention, a new patent is required.

2. The government encouraged the building of railroads by helping the railroad companies with loans and with gifts of land or money called subsidies.

3. Rockefeller gained control of the oil-refining business by being an efficient producer. He plowed back profits into the business to pay for expansion. He used the latest methods and machinery. He saved money by manufacturing his own barrels, building his own warehouses, and buying his own pipelines. He was able to refine and ship oil for less. He also could sell oil for less than his competitors. He gave other companies the choice to either sell out to him at a fair price or be driven out of business. With methods such as these, Rockefeller created a monopoly.

4. Railroads contributed to the growth of an industrial economy. The railroad industry was the largest employer in the United States. Railroads created a demand for other goods. For example, three fourths of all the steel made in the United States in 1880 was used to make steel rails. Thus the steel industry was given a great boost by the railroads. Railroads carried raw materials and finished goods cheaply from one part of the country to another. They helped some businesses grow to be very large by transporting their goods at lower prices.

Activities
Answers will vary.

ANSWERS FOR SKILLS DEVELOPMENT

PAGE 441
Skills Practice
Answers will vary.

CHAPTER 20 Cities and Immigrants

ANSWERS FOR CHECKUP QUESTIONS

PAGE 446
1. Skeletons of iron and steel made it possible to have taller office buildings with ample window space.

2. During the 1800s, American cities changed as a result of the development of the skyscraper, improvements in transportation, and rapid population growth.

3. Three reasons why cities grew rapidly in the late nineteenth century were the location on important water routes, which increased trade; the development and growth of railroads, and the industrial revolution.

4. Transportation developments such as the streetcar made it possible for cities to spread out.

PAGE 454
1. The two main sources of new city dwellers in the late nineteenth century were farmers from America's countryside and immigrants from Europe's farms and villages.

2. Farmers settled in the city because during the last three decades of the 1800s, low farm prices made it difficult for them to make a living. Some lost their farms. Some hoped to escape the long hours, hard work, and loneliness of farm life.
   Irish immigrants were fleeing the potato famine as well as harsh British rule. Most of the European immigrants were farming people hoping to find land and a good life for farming in America. But the majority of these people wound up in the cities because they were too poor to buy farmland. They had to find work quickly, and they could find jobs in the cities.

3. Immigration from the countries in northern and western Europe was called the Old Immigration. Immigration from eastern and southern European countries was called the New Immigration.

4. Most jobs filled by immigrants were building railroads; working in steel mills, meat-packing plants, textile mills, and clothing factories; and doing domestic work. Immigrants provided much of the physical labor that built modern America.

5. Some Americans worried about the large number of immigrants entering the United States because they believed these new immigrants would change the character of America by not adopting American ways and values. They were worried about the different religions of the immigrants, and they complained that the immigrants worked for low pay and would either take jobs away from Americans or lower the wage level for all.

6. Chinese people were excluded from immigration in 1882.

PAGE 459
1. Four problems that faced growing cities by the late nineteenth century were dusty, unpaved streets; crowded buildings; increased crime; and sanitation.

2. The cities attempted to meet these problems by organizing professional fire departments, training fire fighters, and buying fire engines that could pump water to the roofs of most city buildings. They organized professional police departments to protect citizens. They arranged to collect garbage on a regular schedule and to burn or bury the garbage outside the city.

3. Jacob Riis wrote articles and books about the life of the poor. Through his writings he got the tenement block known as Mulberry Bend torn down.
   Jane Addams opened a settlement house in Chicago. In this building, services of various kinds were provided for the poor of the neighborhood.

4. The political machine was good in the sense that it helped the immigrants to find jobs, provided them with food and coal in hard times, and helped their children who had brushes with the law. It also joined their ethnic celebrations and helped them with their citizenship papers.
   The political machine was bad because it elected its friends—not always in the best interest of the citizens. In awarding contracts for paving roads, constructing city buildings, and providing public

ANSWER KEY

utilities, the city officials acted as the machine boss told them to. Those who received the contracts paid the machine and the boss handsomely.

ANSWERS FOR CHAPTER REVIEW

PAGE 460
Vocabulary Quiz
1. F—skyscraper 2. F—architects 3. T 4. F—New immigration 5. T 6. T 7. F, nativists 8. T 9. T 10. F—urban or city.

Review Questions
1. Health and safety problems such as fires, poor and crowded housing, crime, and sanitation needed to be solved in the late years of the nineteenth century. People tried to solve these problems by forming professional fire departments, training fire fighters, and buying adequate fire engines. Professional police departments to protect citizens were organized. Garbage collection on a regular schedule was arranged. Settlement houses were formed to help the poor, but crowded housing remained a problem for a long time. We still have the same problems today in our cities.

2. Immigrants from eastern and southern Europe were called the New Immigration; and immigrants from northern and western Europe were called the Old Immigration. The New Immigrants eventually exceeded the Old Immigrants in number. The New Immigrants came from more oppressive countries than the Old Immigrants.

3. Immigrants sought the comfort and security of living with their own kind. The advantages of settling in neighborhoods with their own kind were that they could continue to speak their own language, follow their familiar customs, and wear their traditional dress. The disadvantages were that few could speak English and most were unskilled workers; therefore, they often wound up with the hardest and lowest-paying jobs.

Activities
Answers will vary.

ANSWERS FOR SKILLS DEVELOPMENT

PAGE 461
Skills Practice
Answers will vary.

CHAPTER 21 Workers and Farmers Seek Reforms

ANSWERS FOR CHECKUP QUESTIONS

PAGE 466
1. Striking, being fired, and being blacklisted were early experiences that taught Samuel Gompers about labor unions.

2. Machines began to do the jobs that skilled workers had done before the growth of industrialism. Machines were run by young boys and girls, women, and unskilled immigrants. All were paid very low wages. Skilled workers could not compete with goods made by lower-paid workers in factories, and many had to give up their trades. Some became factory hands themselves.

3. Increasing use of machines affected safety conditions because wage earners were not protected from the dangerous machinery.

4. Children between 10 and 14 years of age worked between 10 and 12 hours a day. In some southern cotton mills, children under 10 years old worked the 12-hour night shift. Their bosses kept the children from falling asleep at their machines by throwing cold water on them from time to time.

PAGE 471
1. Trade unions were formed by workers to make employers listen to the workers' demands for better wages and working conditions.

2. Terence Powderly favored the use of boycotts to advance the cause of labor.

3. The Knights of Labor suffered a crippling blow as a result of the Haymarket Riot. They had nothing at all to do with the rally at Haymarket Square, but they became connected with violence in the minds of many Americans. Public opinion turned against the union, and members dropped out.

4. The McCormick Harvesting and Pullman strikes were regarded as setbacks to labor unions because violence resulted and the strikes were broken.

PAGE 481
1. Industrialism caused farmers to change from small self-sufficient farms to large farms with single cash crops. This change became necessary because of the size and cost of the time-saving farm machines

produced by industrialists. The change resulted in larger crops that had to be taken to market. The costs for the farm equipment and crop transportation were high, while the prices for farm products dropped.

2. To improve the lot of farmers, the Grange pooled their money and formed cooperatives. They set up factories to make machinery, built their own warehouses, and formed their own insurance companies. Grangers also got the legislatures in some states to pass laws regulating railroad rates.

3. Answers will vary but should include items listed on page 477.

4. In the election of 1896 the Republican party came out firmly against the free coinage of silver. It favored the gold standard—basing the money supply of the country on gold. The Democratic party favored free coinage of silver.

5. The Republican candidate in the election of 1896 was William McKinley. The Democratic candidate was William Jennings Bryan. McKinley won the election.

ANSWERS FOR CHAPTER REVIEW

PAGE 482

Vocabulary Quiz
1. extra description **2.** b **3.** f **4.** i **5.** e **6.** c
7. g **8.** j **9.** d **10.** extra description **11.** a **12.** h
Review Questions
1. **(a)** The Sherman Antitrust Act attempted to stop the growth of trusts and monopolies. **(b)** The Interstate Commerce Act forbade railroads to charge unfair rates, to give rebates to favored shippers, and to charge more for short distances than for long ones. **(c)** The Granger laws regulated railroad rates.

2. Industrialism changed the way that people worked in many ways. Small workshops gave way to factories. Machines began to do the jobs of skilled workers. At the start of the century, 9 of every 10 Americans made their living by farming, and many of the others were self-employed. By the end of the century, half of all Americans worked for wages.

Some advantages of industrialism were that unskilled workers could make money and that goods could be produced faster. Problems created by industrialism included poor and dangerous working conditions and forced child labor.

3. Answers will vary but should include items listed on page 477.

4. In the late 1800s the amount of wheat grown in other countries affected wheat farmers in the United States because price was now determined by supply and demand in the whole world, not just the United States. United States production increased world supply, and prices fell still more.

5. Initially the Haymarket Riot and the Pullman strike turned public opinion against unions. When people began to associate violence with unions, union membership was reduced.

Activities
Answers will vary.

ANSWERS FOR SKILLS DEVELOPMENT

PAGE 483

Skills Practice
early, young, wearily, badly, ventilated, large, noisy, another, exhausted, about, cold
a. Who—young lad, exhausted boy
b. When—early morning
c. Where—badly ventilated factory
d. How—trudges wearily
e. Why—because his family needs his income

How Americans Lived, 1900

ANSWERS FOR CHECKUP QUESTIONS

PAGE 489

1. Answers will vary, but pupils' answers should include swimming, fishing, hunting, ice skating, and sledding. In addition, there were touring professional entertainers so that people living in rural areas could watch a play, listen to a lecture, hear a dramatic reading, attend a concert, or watch a circus. Moreover, residents of small towns frequently had dances, picnics, fairs, gun-shooting contests, and baseball games.

2. City dwellers' leisure-time activities consisted of skating and sledding in winter and baseball games in summer. As vacant lots became filled, playgrounds were created. However, the most popular sport was bicycling. For entertainment, city dwellers could see professional baseball games, stage plays, musical comedies, concerts, and moving pictures.

ANSWER KEY

3. In 1900, doctors in rural and urban areas had a number of things in common. They were mainly family doctors and had similar kinds of medicines. They differed in that country doctors visited all their patients in their homes. (For house calls less than 3 miles away, doctors walked. For those more than 3 miles, they rode on horseback.) Although city doctors treated many patients in their homes, a growing number kept office hours.

The doctors were different in that country doctors rarely used mercury thermometers. City doctors had new medical equipment such as X-ray machines. Eventually city doctors started to specialize, while country doctors remained family doctors.

4. The life expectancy in 1900 was so much different from what it is today because today we have better medical knowledge and vaccines and cures for many common diseases.

ANSWERS FOR UNIT REVIEW

PAGE 490
Reading the Text
1. "A strong foundation" is a phrase that describes the United States' success in the industrial revolution. American industry had been established before the Civil War. The war gave a boost to manufacturing, and as a result American industry was ready for expansion.

2. Answers will vary, but pupils should include some of the following resources: coal, iron ore, copper, zinc, gold, silver, and a large labor force.

3. The increase in population contributed to industrial growth because more people meant more consumers and a larger labor force.

4. A corporation was a favorite form of business organization because it allowed individuals to pool their money together and share in the profits while at the same time protect themselves from any losses greater than their initial investment.

5. Answers will vary, but pupils should include some of the following factors that led to America's industrial growth: steel industry, railroads, natural resources, the Civil War, increase in population, new inventions, greater availability of capital, and great business leaders.

Reading a Map
1. F **2.** F **3.** T **4.** T **5.** T **6.** F **7.** F **8.** T **9.** F **10.** F

Reading a Picture
1. The people at the upper right are laying rails for a railroad.

2. The buildings are on wheels so that they can be pulled along the rails as the workers move ahead.

3. The buildings were probably used to store supplies and as living quarters for the workers.

4. The wagons at left center were probably used for hauling supplies.

5. The soldiers were probably there to protect the railroad workers and to maintain order.

Reading Time Lines
Homestead Act, 1862
Oklahoma land rush, 1889
Transcontinental railroad line completed, 1869
Peak year of immigration, 1907
Haymarket Riot, 1886
Decade of great city growth begins, 1880
Bryan's "cross of gold" speech, 1896
First modern skyscraper, 1885

UNIT 6 BECOMING A WORLD LEADER

CHAPTER 22 **The Progressive Movement**

ANSWERS FOR CHECKUP QUESTIONS

PAGE 498

1. Answers will vary but could include the following:

(a) the direct primary—In a direct primary, voters in each party choose the party's candidates directly, instead of having a convention of delegates choose them.

(b) the recall—By using the recall, voters may remove an official from office.

(c) a workmen's compensation law—This law made payments to those hurt while working on the job.

(d) the regulation of railroads—This reform taxed the railroads on the value of their properties so that they paid a fair share of taxes.

(e) a state income tax—The taxpayers paid a tax on their income.

2. Florence Kelley worked for reforms such as ending child labor and limiting working hours for women.

3. The Progressives were city dwellers. They focused on problems of urban and industrial life. Some were mainly concerned with improving housing or health. Others sought to get rid of sweatshops. Some worked to give the people a greater say in government and to make government more honest and efficient. There were Progressives who concentrated on protecting natural resources, attaining woman suffrage, and getting rid of liquor. Others wanted to limit the power of great corporations and regulate them in the public interest.

The Populists were from farms and small towns. Their programs reflected the interests of rural America.

4. Lincoln Steffens exposed the corruption of governments in many American cities in his writings. Ida Tarbell spent 5 years gathering facts on the methods John D. Rockefeller used to drive out competition and create the Standard Oil monopoly. As mayor of Cleveland, Tom Johnson opened up government to the people. He held public meetings so that the citizens and city officials could discuss ways of dealing with problems. He put a stop to those people who were paying lower taxes than other citizens because they were friends of government officials. He got the city council to tax the utility companies and to lower the fares charged by the street-railway companies. In addition, Johnson brought in experts to run city departments.

PAGE 505

1. President Roosevelt took action against the Northern Securities Company, which controlled all the long-distance railroad lines in the northwestern part of the country. Roosevelt said the company violated the Sherman Antitrust Act. The Supreme Court agreed and ordered that the company be broken up. Roosevelt later brought action against Standard Oil, the American Tobacco Company, and more than 40 other large business combinations.

2. Roosevelt called representatives of both sides of the coal-mining industry to the White House and asked them to settle their differences. The miners were willing, but the owners were not. Roosevelt eventually succeeded in getting the two sides to agree to arbitration. The strike then ended.

3. Roosevelt set aside 150 million acres of land to add to the national forests. He also saw to it that the government held on to millions of acres of mineral-rich land for the future. And he created five new national parks. He brought the need for conserving natural resources to the attention of the people.

4. The split between Taft and Roosevelt in the election of 1912 gave supporters of the Democratic party a golden opportunity. The party nominated Governor Woodrow Wilson of New Jersey for President, and Wilson easily won the election.

PAGE 509

1. Roosevelt did not believe that a company was automatically bad because it was big. He felt that large business combinations were a natural development of modern business. The correct way for the federal government to deal with them was to accept them but regulate them so they would serve the public interest.

Woodrow Wilson believed that all trusts were bad because they shut out competition. He said that government should break up trusts and prevent new ones from forming. His strong belief in competition also led Wilson to favor lowering the tariff.

2. Heading the Federal Reserve System was a Federal Reserve Board in Washington, D.C. Its members were appointed by the President. Through their decisions they could affect the supply of money in circulation and the rate of interest that borrowers would pay. Thus they had a large influence on the economy.

3. The Clayton Antitrust Act prohibited companies from gaining control of other companies in the same industry. It also stopped them from engaging in certain business practices if these practices reduced competition.

The Federal Trade Commission Act created a federal commission to regulate big business. The President appointed five commissioners. They had the power to investigate businesses. They could order businesses to stop harmful practices such as false advertising.

4. The Progressive movement brought about important changes to American life. It showed how experts could make government better and more efficient. It ended forever the idea that government had no responsibility to deal with large social problems. It established the principle that business had responsibilities to the public. And it established the idea that the federal government should play an active role in improving American life.

ANSWERS FOR CHAPTER REVIEW

PAGE 510
Vocabulary Quiz
1. direct primary
2. Progressive
3. public utility
4. recall
5. banking
6. commission
7. conservation
8. muckraker
9. arbitration
10. city manager

Review Questions
1. Answers will vary.

2. Progressives and Populists sought some of the same changes, like the initiative, referendum, and direct election of senators. But the two movements were quite different. Populists were from farms and small towns. Their programs reflected the interests of rural America. Most Progressives were city dwellers. They focused on problems of urban and industrial life.

3. Answers will vary.

4. (a) The direct primary was meant to give more power to the people by letting voters in each party choose the party's candidates directly, instead of having a convention of delegates choose them.
(b) The recall gave voters the power to remove an elected official from office.

Activities
Answers will vary.

ANSWERS FOR SKILLS DEVELOPMENT

PAGE 511
Skills Practice
Answers will vary.

CHAPTER 23 Expansion Overseas

ANSWERS FOR CHECKUP QUESTIONS

PAGE 517
1. American thinking about an overseas empire changed in the late 1800s. The great production of America's farms, factories, and mines were attracting the interest of some Americans toward the rest of the world. Some people came to believe that the United States was producing more goods than its people could consume. If Americans were to continue to be employed and if farms and businesses were to keep on making profits, the United States would have to find markets in other lands for its goods. Bankers and investors also looked for opportunities to invest in railroads, mines, and factories in other countries.

2. (a) The United States came into contact with China through its merchants and their trading ships. (b) In 1853, Commodore Matthew Perry arrived in Japan with a fleet of four warships and carried a letter from the President of the United States asking that trade be opened between the two countries. One year later a trade treaty was signed and the Japanese agreed to open several ports to American trading ships. **(c)** In 1878, local rulers of Samoa gave the United States the right to build a naval base in Samoa. Britain and Germany also had claims in the islands. Arguments among the three countries almost led to war. In 1899 it was agreed that Samoa would be divided between the United States and Germany, with Great Britain receiving land elsewhere.

3. The Americans in Hawaii wanted the United States to annex Hawaii, a move that would lift the sugar tariff. The queen of Hawaii disagreed and announced a new constitution that gave her complete power. The sugar planters with the help of American marines decided to overthrow the queen. They were successful and asked that Hawaii be made part of the United States. Although President Cleveland refused to go along with annexation at that time, Hawaii was finally annexed during the war with Spain in 1898.

4. The United States played the part of arbitrator in a boundary dispute in South America. The Monroe Doctrine gave the United States the right to step into any dispute between European and South American countries when the peace of the Western Hemisphere was threatened.

PAGE 523

1. Spanish cruelty to the Cubans aroused the sympathy of Americans in the mid-1890s.

2. The United States was pushed toward war with Spain in February 1898 by the public reaction to the sinking of the American battleship *Maine*.

3. **(a)** Commodore George Dewey and his navy fleet defeated the Spanish fleet in Manila Bay. **(b)** Colonel Theodore Roosevelt led a cavalry regiment known as the Rough Riders up San Juan Hill to victory.

4. By the terms of the peace treaty ending the Spanish-American War, Spain agreed to leave Cuba and to hand over Puerto Rico to the United States. The United States also acquired the Philippine Islands and Guam.

5. Some Americans opposed the building of an overseas empire because they thought that ruling other peoples without the peoples' consent went against the ideas of the Declaration of Independence.

PAGE 531

1. John Hay promoted the Open Door policy to keep the United States from being shut out of China. It was believed that China would become a great market for American goods and investments. The Open Door policy would give all nations an equal opportunity to trade with China, even within another country's sphere of influence.

2. President Theodore Roosevelt tried to improve relations between Japan and the United States by the Gentlemen's Agreement. He invited San Francisco's mayor and members of its school board to the White House and convinced them to cancel their order to segregate Asian children. At the same time, he got Japan to agree not to let more workers leave Japan for the United States.

3. The Roosevelt Corollary helped turn the Caribbean Sea into an American lake by controlling the actions of many countries in the region. The corollary allowed the United States to intervene in the affairs of these countries, assuring that they paid their debts, preserved order, and protected life and property.

4. The United States was able to get control of land for a canal across Central America by protecting the Panamanians from a Colombian invasion. Protection by United States warships allowed the Panamanians to gain their independence from Colombia. Then the new Panamanian government signed a treaty with the United States allowing it to rent forever the strip of land for the canal.

5. Colombia's refusal to let the United States rent a strip of land across Panama to build a canal was the main difficulty that had to be overcome in the building of the Panama Canal. The other major obstacle was to rid the area of the mosquito—the carrier of yellow fever and malaria.

ANSWERS FOR CHAPTER REVIEW

PAGE 532

Vocabulary Quiz
1. F, Imperialists were in favor of extending control over distant lands.

2. T

3. T

4. F, "Remember the Maine!" became a slogan after the battleship was blown up at Havana.

ANSWER KEY

5. F, The Boxer Rebellion came about as an effort to get foreigners out of China.

6. F, Theodore Roosevelt led a cavalry regiment known as the Rough Riders into battle at San Juan Hill in Cuba.

7. T

8. T

9. F, The Roosevelt Corollary discouraged European countries from coming into the Western Hemisphere.

10. T

Review Questions
1. Imperialists were in favor of overseas expansion because they were envious of European countries that had created overseas empires. They declared that America should also have colonies. They also favored overseas expansion for the economic benefits. Anti-imperialists opposed the building of an overseas empire because they thought that ruling other peoples without the peoples' consent went against the ideas of the Declaration of Independence.

2. The sugar planters in Hawaii wanted the United States government to annex Hawaii because then the sugar tariff would no longer apply. The tax made Hawaiian sugar more expensive than sugar grown in the United States. As a result, sales dropped and the islands faced hard times.

3. American anger over Spanish cruelty in Cuba, combined with the sinking of the *Maine*, led America into war with Spain in 1898.

4. The Open Door policy meant that all nations should have an equal opportunity to trade with China, even within another country's sphere of influence. The United States was in favor of the Open Door policy to preserve trading opportunities between the United States and China and to keep that country from being carved up by other powers.

5. The Roosevelt Corollary led to a great deal of ill toward the United States by the small nations in the Caribbean.

6. The building of the Panama Canal was important to the United States because such a canal would allow the United States Navy to travel quickly from one ocean to another.

Activities
Answers will vary.

ANSWERS FOR SKILLS DEVELOPMENT
PAGE 533
Skills Practice
Pupil's outlines will vary, but might look something like the following:
II. Hawaii is Annexed
  A. Hawaiian Revolution
    1. Sugar planters organize against Queen
    2. American marines sent in
    3. Queen Liliuokalani removed from power
  B. Hawaii comes under American control
    1. Sugar planters form republic
    2. President Cleveland opposes imperialism
    3. American planters control Hawaii
    4. Hawaii annexed during war with Spain

CHAPTER 24 World War I

ANSWERS FOR CHECKUP QUESTIONS
PAGE 539
1. In Sarajevo in June 1914, Archduke Franz Ferdinand and his wife were shot and killed. Those two shots set off a chain of events that led to one of the most destructive wars in history. Nearly every country in Europe became involved in what soon was called the Great War. It is known today as the First World War.

2. European countries were competing for colonies at this time because colonies provided a supply of raw materials for those countries' expanding industries as well as markets for manufactured goods. Bankers could invest in colonies and get a good, safe return on their money. Controlling others gave a satisfying feeling of power and pride to the peoples and governments of the imperialist countries.

3. The rise of nationalism and the drive for colonies resulted in rivalry and militarism among the European powers. Each country believed that a large army was an expression of national greatness and provided protection. The European countries also sought protection by forming alliances.

4. Warfare of World War I was different from earlier wars because of a new weapon, the machine gun. Each side dug trenches for protection against the new weapon.

ANSWER KEY

PAGE 544

1. Most Americans leaned toward the Allies from the very outbreak of the Great War because many Americans were of British origin and spoke the same language and shared many traditions. Also, Germany's invasion of neutral Belgium turned many Americans against Germany.

2. The British violated America's neutral rights on the seas by blocking all German ports. The British navy stopped and searched American ships on the high seas for war goods. They sometimes forced American cargo ships into British ports for weeks at a time.

3. German submarine warfare made it more difficult for the United States to stay neutral because the German government torpedoed neutral ships that entered the war zone. Shortly after, the British passenger liner *Lusitania* was torpedoed without warning, and 128 Americans were killed. Soon after the sinking of the *Lusitania*, a German submarine torpedoed the French passenger ship *Sussex*, injuring several American passengers. Then, in 1917, German submarines sank three American ships.

4. The Zimmerman telegram helped bring the United States into the war because the telegram instructed the German diplomat to offer Mexico the opportunity to ally itself with Germany if the United States declared war on Germany. In exchange for Mexico's support, Germany would help Mexico to reconquer territory in Texas, New Mexico, and Arizona.

PAGE 550

1. To increase industrial production and cut down waste, the government created the War Industries Board. The War Industries Board decided how much of something should be produced, which companies should make the products, and how much the price would be. Urged on by the War Industries Board, factories ran day and night. Shells, rifles, uniforms, and other military supplies poured out of America's factories.

2. To increase production of food and also to cut down consumption at home, the government created the Food Administration. The Food Administration encouraged farmers to grow more food by offering a high price for all the wheat they could produce. Americans were urged to cut down consumption of food by observing "wheatless Mondays" and "meatless Tuesdays." Certain goods, such as sugar, were rationed, and Congress passed a law prohibiting the use of grain for making alcohol.

3. The threat of submarine warfare in getting goods and troops to Europe was met by using the convoy system. In a convoy, freighters and troop carriers travel in a large group, escorted on all sides by destroyers.

4. The American Expeditionary Force helped win the Great War by adding men to a depleted Allied army, by giving new hope to the Allied forces, and by successfully resisting and then attacking the Germans.

PAGE 553

1. Answers will vary. Refer to page 551 to check pupils' responses.

2. Europe's victorious powers burned with revenge and wanted to punish Germany. Each country, fearing for its future security, wanted to leave Germany too weak ever to make war again. In the peace terms the victorious powers wanted to take over territory that was part of Germany or Austria-Hungary, to take over Germany's colonies, or do both. And each wanted to make Germany pay for the entire cost of the war.

3. The Treaty of Versailles might be called a victor's peace because it was a peace that dictated terms to the defeated Germany.

4. The task of winning United States approval of the peace treaty awaited Wilson upon his return from Paris.

5. Wilson failed to win approval for the peace treaty because the Senate was strongly opposed to United States entry into the League of Nations. Once Wilson became ill, all hopes of his changing the Senate's position vanished.

ANSWERS FOR CHAPTER REVIEW

PAGE 554
Vocabulary Quiz
1. d **2.** e **3.** c **4.** j **5.** h **6.** extra definition **7.** b **8.** i **9.** extra definition **10.** a **11.** g **12.** f

Review Questions
1. (a) Alliances helped bring on the Great War because countries did not depend only upon their own armies and navies to protect themselves. They formed alliances with others. The web of alliances helped to polarize the European countries.

(b) Nationalism is a very strong feeling of loyalty toward one's country. Strong feelings combining with old grudges and hatreds helped to bring on the Great War.

(c) Militarism helped bring on the Great War because militarism emphasizes armies, navies, and military power. Each country believed that a large army was an expression of national greatness as well as a means of protection. Europe became an armed camp.

2. When the United States government released the Zimmerman telegram to the newspapers, Americans were furious and turned against the Germans.

3. Pupils should include these three agencies: the War Industries Board, the War Labor Board, and the Food Administration.

4. The convoy system was devised to combat submarine warfare.

5. The Big Four were President Wilson and the prime ministers of Great Britain, Italy, and France. Wilson called for a "peace without victory." He felt such a settlement would not leave hatreds and the desire for revenge that could breed future wars. But Europe's victorious powers burned with revenge and wanted to punish Germany.

Activities

1. In 1919, President Woodrow Wilson proclaimed November 11 as Armistice Day to remind Americans of the tragedies of war. Today Armistice Day is known as Veterans Day.

2. Answers will vary.

3. Answers will vary.

4. The Tomb of the Unknown Soldier is in Arlington National Cemetery, Arlington, Virginia.

The Tomb of the Unknown Soldier was built as a memorial to American soldiers killed in battle in World War I, whose bodies could not be identified.

ANSWERS FOR SKILLS DEVELOPMENT

PAGE 555
Skills Practice
1. Answers will vary.

2. Patriotism

3. Answers will vary.

ANSWERS FOR UNIT REVIEW

PAGE 556
Reading the Text
1. European nations competed for colonies in the late nineteenth century because colonies were a source of raw materials, a marketplace for manufactured goods, offered places for safe investments, and a way of exercising power.

2. Nationalism is a good feeling when it does not become more than a peaceful expression of pride and loyalty for one's country. It becomes a bad feeling when it provokes people to carry grudges and make war.

3. The big nations in Europe at this time built large armies because they felt that military power was an expression of national greatness.

4. Alliances increased the threat of war because nations were bound to protect and rely on each other. Therefore if one country suffered an attack the whole continent automatically became involved.

5. Europe could be compared to a powder keg because it could at any moment explode into a battlefield.

Reading a Map
1. Guatemala, Honduras, El Salvador, Nicaragua, Costa Rica, Panama

2. Virgin Islands, Puerto Rico, Canal Zone in Panama

3. Veracruz

4. Approximately 900 miles, about 1,450 kilometers

5. Haiti

Reading a Cartoon
Answers will vary.

Reading Presidential Boxes
1. Taft
2. Wilson
3. Taft
4. Roosevelt
5. Wilson
6. Roosevelt
7. Wilson
8. Roosevelt
9. Roosevelt
10. Wilson

UNIT 7 PROSPERITY DEPRESSION, AND WAR

CHAPTER 25 The Golden Twenties

ANSWERS FOR CHECKUP QUESTIONS

PAGE 563

1. More efficient factories with each worker doing a separate step and the moving assembly line were two methods used by Henry Ford that led to his success in making automobiles.

2. The automobile changed the way people worked and played. People could live farther from their places of work. This speeded the growth of suburbs around large cities. People could shop in places far from their own neighborhoods. They could travel long distances or just take a ride. The automobile gave people a feeling of independence and freedom.

3. Advertising and consumer credit were used widely in the 1920s to increase the sale of goods.

4. In the 1920s many workers in the coal mining, cloth manufacturing, and shipbuilding industries were laid off. These workers, farmers, and unskilled workers such as blacks, Mexican Americans, and recent immigrants did not share in the prosperity of the 1920s.

PAGE 571

1. After World War I, racial prejudice showed itself by the lynching of blacks in the South; blacks who went north met with racial prejudice as they competed with whites for jobs and housing; racial riots occurred throughout many cities.

2. (a) The Red Scare contributed to tension in the early 1920s because many Americans took the scattered acts of terrorism by the American Communists to be the start of a campaign to overthrow the government.
(b) Strong feelings against foreigners and radicals continued after the Red Scare died out. In 1920, Sacco and Vanzetti were accused of killing a man carrying a factory payroll. Both men were Italian immigrants and anarchists. The evidence against them was not very strong, but they were found guilty and sentenced to death.

(c) The Ku Klux Klan contributed to tension in the early 1920s by the desire to "save" America from foreign influences and radical ideas. The Klan used threats and acts of violence to drive blacks, Catholics, Jews, and immigrants from their communities.

3. New inventions cut down the time needed for housework, so more women were free to take jobs outside the home. They worked as schoolteachers, nurses, office workers, and sales clerks at department stores. Some cut their hair short, wore knee-length skirts, took up smoking, and learned to drive cars.

4. (a) Sporting events enabled people to watch their favorite professional baseball and college football teams, heavyweight boxing champions, and golf and tennis pros.
(b) The radio promoted family togetherness. Families gathered around the radio to listen to their favorite programs—music, comedy shows, adventure programs, sporting events, and the evening news.
(c) Prohibition resulted in a decline in drinking but it also led to bootlegging, speakeasies, and the growth of organized crime.

PAGE 577

1. Proof that Harding was a poor judge of people is that he chose many of his old Ohio pals and card-playing friends for many posts of government. They turned his administration into one of the most corrupt in American history by taking bribes and giving pardons, paroles, and liquor permits. The biggest of the Harding scandals involved Teapot Dome.

2. President Coolidge followed Harding's policies on government economy, taxes, and business. He kept government spending down and vetoed a number of spending bills. He favored cutting taxes on high incomes and believed that government should not interfere with the dealings of business.

3. The United States promoted steps to maintain world peace in the 1920s by holding a conference in Washington, D.C., with the leading naval powers and urging the nations to sign a treaty to reduce the size of navies. Then 62 countries signed the Kellogg-Briand Pact, in which the nations agreed not to use war as an instrument of national policy. This meant that they agreed to settle disputes by peaceful means only. The United States also took steps to improve its relations with Latin American countries.

4. The presidential candidate for the Republican party in the election of 1928 was Herbert Hoover, and the Democratic candidate was Alfred E. Smith.

ANSWER KEY

Hoover was raised on an Iowa farm and had a career as a mining engineer and businessman. He was a Protestant and he believed in prohibition. Smith grew up in New York City. He was a career politician and the first Catholic to run for the presidency. He favored repeal of the prohibition amendment. He seemed to stand for everything that rural and small-town Americans were against. Hoover won the election of 1928.

ANSWERS FOR CHAPTER REVIEW

PAGE 578
Vocabulary Quiz
1. Harlem Renaissance

2. Teapot Dome

3. assembly line

4. consumer goods

5. consumer credit

Review Questions
1. Consumer credit made it possible for buyers to enjoy the use of a product immediately while paying only part of its price at the time of purchase. The rest was paid for in small monthly installments.

2. The mass production of inexpensive automobiles affected American life by changing the way people worked and played. People could live farther from their places of work. This speeded the growth of suburbs around large cities. People could shop in places far from their own neighborhoods and travel long distances to places of interest.

    The automobile helped make the 1920s a decade of prosperity. Auto factories employed hundreds of thousands of workers. Hundreds of thousands more worked to make materials that went into making cars, and new businesses sprang up. Also, governments spent billions of dollars on roads.

3. In the 1920s many workers in the coal mining, cloth manufacturing, and shipbuilding industries were laid off. These workers, farmers, and unskilled workers such as blacks, Mexican Americans, and recent immigrants missed out on the prosperity of the 1920s.

4. (a) Because of the Red Scare, Americans thought labor strikes were the work of Communist plotters.
(b) Groups of foreigners who met together were thought to be Communists and a danger to the country. Some were sent back to the countries they came from.
(c) Congress limited the number of immigrants from Europe in any given year in the 1920s. Each country in Europe was assigned a quota.

5. Prohibition did result in a decline in drinking, but it also led to some undesirable effects, such as bootlegging, speakeasies, and the growth of organized crime.

6. Presidents Harding and Coolidge believed that government should not interfere with the dealings of business.

Activities
1. Admiral Byrd—Explorer of the Arctic and Antarctic
  Babe Ruth—Baseball player famous for hitting home runs
  Al Capone—Head of the Chicago underworld
  Ty Cobb—Famous baseball player
  Gene Tunney—World heavyweight boxing champion
  Rudolph Valentino—Star of silent motion pictures
  Sacco and Vanzetti—Defendants in a famous trial
  Gertrude Ederle—First woman to swim the English Channel
  Charles Lindbergh—An aviator who made the first solo nonstop flight across the Atlantic
  Ernest Hemingway—Famous American writer
  Bobby Jones—Famous golfer
  Rudy Vallee—Famous radio singer

2. Answers will vary.

3. Answers will vary.

ANSWERS FOR SKILLS DEVELOPMENT

Skills Practice

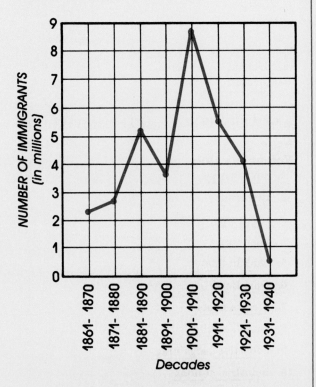

Decades

NUMBER OF IMMIGRANTS (in millions)

CHAPTER 26 **The Great Depression and the New Deal**

ANSWERS FOR CHECKUP QUESTIONS

PAGE 585

1. The stock market crash of 1929 was caused by excessive speculation, buying stocks on margin, and panic selling when the stock prices began to fall.

2. Weaknesses in the American economy that helped bring on the Great Depression were that Americans could not consume as much as they produced, nor could all the goods be sold abroad. Factories cut down production and laid off workers. Banks that had loaned money or invested in stocks lost a great deal of money. When people asked for all their savings at once, the banks were in trouble and many depositors lost all their savings.

3. Businesses were affected by the depression by having to lay off workers and cut wages of other workers. Workers without jobs could not buy goods, so more factories had to cut their output. Thousands of firms, large and small, went out of business.

Farm prices collapsed altogether as a result of the depression. Wheat, cotton, and corn brought such low prices that farmers could not pay their debts, and they lost their farms.

4. President Hoover tried to fight the depression by the Reconstruction Finance Corporation (RFC). The RFC made loans to banks, insurance companies, and railroads to keep them going. The federal government also helped farmers by buying and storing some of their crops.

PAGE 593

1. President Roosevelt dealt with the banking crisis by declaring a bank holiday to close all banks in the country and calling Congress into a special session to pass an emergency banking bill. Only the healthy banks were allowed to reopen. Congress also created the Federal Deposit Insurance Corporation (FDIC). This insured deposits up to a certain amount. Even if banks should fail, depositors would get their money back.

2. The Civilian Conservation Corps (CCC) combined unemployment relief and conservation. The CCC hired men between the ages of 18 and 25 from needy families to work on conservation projects in rural areas.

The Public Works Administration (PWA) spent $3 billion over several years for hiring unemployed people to build roads, bridges, dams, and government buildings.

The Agriculture Adjustment Act (AAA) was the main effort to help the farmer. The government paid farmers to plant crops on only a part of their fields to help prices rise again. They also helped farmers get low-interest loans to meet their mortgage payments.

The National Industrial Recovery Act (NIRA) was the main effort to bring about recovery in industry. The NIRA gave business the right to hire back workers and start up production by ignoring the antitrust laws. In exchange, business was required to do certain things for its workers. Companies had to pay a fair minimum wage, agree on maximum hours, end child labor, and allow their workers to form unions.

ANSWER KEY

The Tennessee Valley Authority (TVA) attempted to plan the economic development of a whole region. The TVA built dams to control flooding, produced electricity, and planted trees to hold the soil during heavy rains.

3. The Social Security Act provided help for people in their old age. During their working years, workers paid a tax into a special fund. This tax was matched by their employers. When the workers retired, they would receive monthly payments from this fund. The law also provided help for workers who became blind, crippled, or handicapped in other ways and could no longer work. It also helped children with no means of support. The second part of the act provided for unemployment insurance.

4. Falling farm prices and climbing unemployment brought about the decline of the New Deal.

PAGE 597

1. The western part of the Great Plains was so hard-hit during the depression because of the terrible droughts that lasted several years in this region. The soil turned to dust. High winds swept the dust across the open plains. Dust storms continued for several years, giving to the region the name Dust Bowl. With their farms gone, thousands headed west, hoping to make a fresh start.

2. Relief and welfare programs of the New Deal helped millions of black people. President Roosevelt appointed a number of blacks to important positions in government. These officials came to be known as the Black Cabinet. They often met together and spoke up for the interests of black people. Eleanor Roosevelt also worked to end discrimination against blacks and other minorities.

3. Mexican Americans fared poorly under the New Deal because some federal and state officials tried to reduce the number of people seeking jobs by sending Mexicans back to Mexico. But Native Americans had the hardest time of all minorities. Their unemployment rate was high, they had lower income, less schooling, and died younger than other Americans. Most New Deal relief and recovery programs did not help them. However, under the New Deal the Indian Reorganization Act of 1934 ended the breakup of Indian reservations into small pieces of land. It also allowed the tribes to have more say over their own future. The new policy brought greater freedom and cultural pride to Indians.

4. During the 1930s, labor unions changed. The American Federation of Labor had long represented the skilled workers. However, there were many other workers in the industries who were not represented by unions. In 1935, John Lewis and others formed the Congress of Industrial Organizations (CIO). The CIO organized workers in America's basic industries. By the end of the 1930s, union membership by American workers had increased 100 percent.

ANSWERS FOR CHAPTER REVIEW

PAGE 598
Vocabulary Quiz
1. stock market
2. dividends
3. inventory
4. New Deal
5. bank holiday
6. Dust Bowl
7. fireside chats
8. social security
9. collective bargaining
10. industrial unions

Review Questions
1. (**a**) Speculation helped bring on the Great Depression because people, hoping to gain a quick profit, kept buying stocks on borrowed money. When stock prices fell, many people tried to get rid of their stocks quickly. These speculators and their bankers went broke. (**b**) Overproduction of goods forced factories to reduce production and lay off workers. (**c**) A high tariff prevented Europeans from selling many goods in the United States. So Europeans, in turn, could not afford to buy American goods. This led to excess inventories, factory slowdowns, and layoffs. (**d**) Surplus farm crops forced prices so low that farmers could not make money. Without money they could not purchase goods produced by factories.

2. Hoover did not believe that the government should give money and jobs directly to the people during the depression. He left that responsibility to private charities and local and state governments. Roosevelt, on the other hand, believed the federal government should directly aid the American people through money and jobs. His beliefs became realities through programs such as the CCC, the FERA, and the PWA.

3. Five major laws that were passed during the New Deal were (**a**) the FDIC, which insured depositors' money up to a certain amount; (**b**) the CCC program, which provided jobs on conservation projects for people; (**c**) the FERA, which provided money for the needy; (**d**) the PWA, which hired people to build bridges, roads, dams, and government buildings; and (**e**) the AAA, in which the government paid farmers not to grow crops.

4. Roosevelt wanted to change the number of Supreme Court justices because they declared many New Deal laws unconstitutional. Roosevelt felt that younger, more progressive justices would give more support to his programs. His proposal led to a storm of protest from those who thought he had become power-hungry. He lost much public support over this issue.

5. Farmers who lived in the Dust Bowl were forced to gather whatever belongings they could carry with them and head west to California. They became migrant workers and lived in roadside camps.

6. The CIO differed from the AFL because it represented the millions of industrial workers who worked the factory assembly lines and other unskilled jobs. The AFL restricted its membership to skilled workers.

Activities
1. The Twentieth Amendment moved the date newly elected Presidents and congressmen take office closer to election time.

2. Answers will vary.

3. Answers will vary.

ANSWERS FOR SKILLS DEVELOPMENT

PAGE 599
Skills Practice: Part I
Answers for the number of dictionary definitions may vary depending on the dictionary used. Accept all reasonable answers for correct definitions of the terms.

Skills Practice: Part II
Answers will vary.

CHAPTER 27 World War II

ANSWERS FOR CHECKUP QUESTIONS
PAGE 606
1. Totalitarian governments were governments with total power over the people. In a democracy, government is the servant of the people. Under a totalitarian government, the people exist to serve the state.

2. Japan was the first to break the peace by invading and taking control of Manchuria in 1931. In 1935, Mussolini invaded and conquered the North African country of Ethiopia. In 1936, Hitler sent German troops into the Rhineland.

3. Congress passed the Neutrality Acts to try and keep America out of the war. One law prohibited the sale of arms to countries at war. Another forbade Americans to lend money to warring countries or to travel on their ships. A third law said that countries at war could not buy goods from the United States on credit.

4. War was brought on in Europe by the following series of events: (**a**) When Hitler took the Sudetenland and Czechoslovakia without firing a shot, Britain and France became alarmed. They promised to come to Poland's aid if Germany attacked that country. (**b**) In August of 1939 Germany and the Soviet Union signed a treaty not to attack one another and secretly to divide Poland. (**c**) On September 1, Germany invaded Poland and on September 3, Britain and France declared war on Germany.

PAGE 617
1. Prior to entering the war, the United States helped Great Britain by lending them the weapons they needed. This program was known as lend-lease. Shortly after, the United States was also sending lend-lease aid to Russia. American naval vessels were protecting American and British merchant ships as they carried war goods across the Atlantic Ocean. In addition, Roosevelt and Churchill drew up the Atlantic Charter opposing Nazi tyranny.

2. The outlook for America was grim for the first year after it entered the war because Japan was having great success in the Pacific. In addition, German armies had taken Greece and Yugoslavia, and German and Italian armies in North Africa pushed British forces back across the desert into Egypt.

3. The Allied strategy in Europe was first to bring German submarines under control, and then to take the offensive position. This offensive position was supported by bombers.

In the Pacific the Japanese tide was first checked and then reversed in two big naval battles in 1942. Aircraft carriers and bombers had a major role in the Allied offense against Japan.

4. British general Bernard Montgomery won a brilliant victory at El Alamein in Egypt in 1942. This victory helped turn the tide in Africa.

The invasion of western Europe called D-Day took place on the beaches of Normandy, France. American, British, Canadian, and French forces were supported by 4,000 ships and 11,000 planes overhead —one of the greatest military operations in history.

The Russians held firm at Stalingrad, and then counterattacked. Hitler's armies were defeated with great losses. The battle of Stalingrad was a major turning point in the war.

In the Battle of the Bulge the Germans attacked westward into Belgium and Luxembourg with the aim of splitting the Allied armies. Though German troops created a bulge 60 miles deep in the Allied line, they could not break through.

In the battle of the Coral Sea, British and American forces checked the advancement of the Japanese. This battle introduced fighting done by planes launched from aircraft carriers.

The battle of Leyte Gulf was the largest battle in naval history. Japan's navy was crushed, and with that defeat Japan was through as a naval power.

Hiroshima, Japan, was where the first atomic bomb was dropped. It wiped out nearly the whole city and killed thousands of people.

PAGE 621
1. World War II differed from earlier wars because America's whole population was fully involved. The country's material resources were completely devoted to the goal of victory. People everywhere sacrificed willingly.

2. American industry held one of the keys to victory in World War II. A government agency, the War Production Board (WPB), helped organize the changeover from peacetime manufacturing to making goods for war. The WPB also saw that war industries received the raw materials they needed. World War II was won on the production lines as well as on the battlefields.

3. The government met the problem of shortages of many kinds of goods by rationing with ration stamps. To make sure that everyone got a fair share of these scarce goods, the government limited the amount of goods each person could buy.

4. In World War II many blacks left the South for jobs in the war factories in the North. Blacks made their contribution to the war effort on the home front and in battle. Charles Drew, a black doctor, developed the blood bank, in which blood was collected and stored for those wounded in battle.

Thousands of Japanese Americans enlisted in the service in 1943. One of their units was the most decorated combat force in the army.

Blacks met with discrimination in northern cities as well as in the military. Most Japanese Americans lived on the West Coast, where many residents held a prejudice against them. They were moved to relocation centers further inland. These centers were crowded, hastily built camps where the residents lived behind barbed wire and under armed guard during the war. Some Japanese Americans who were forced to give up their homes, businesses, and jobs had been born in the United States and were American citizens.

ANSWERS FOR CHAPTER REVIEW

PAGE 622
Vocabulary Quiz
1. j 2. d 3. c 4. g 5. a 6. f 7. b 8. h 9. i
10. e

Review Questions
1. The Good Neighbor policy was President Roosevelt's plan for improving relations with other countries in the Western Hemisphere. It affected all the Latin American countries but it especially affected Nicaragua and Haiti as well as Cuba.

2. (a) Economic conditions helped lead to the rise of dictatorship in Europe because after World War I, there was depression and unemployment. The dictators promised jobs to the people. **(b)** Nationalism helped lead to the rise of dictatorships in Europe because some countries were left with weak governments after World War I. In Germany and Italy the people felt that they did not receive all they should have from the peace treaty. Mussolini and Hitler gained power by playing on the nationalistic pride of the citizens of their respective countries.

3. Hitler signed a pact with Russia in 1939 because if Britain and France went to war against Germany, he did not want to have to fight Russia at the same time. In addition, Germany and Russia made a secret pact to divide Poland between them. Hitler, however, did not keep the treaty. He attacked the Soviet Union in June 1941.

4. After the fall of France, America spent billions of dollars to build up its military strength. It also passed the first peacetime draft law and sent military aid to Great Britain.

5. The United States government moved Japanese Americans living on the West Coast to relocation centers further inland. This action was taken because many people on the West Coast felt that the people of Japanese ancestry might help Japan in an attack upon the Pacific coast.

6. After he warned the Japanese to surrender but received no reply, President Truman dropped the atomic bomb on Japan. Some of his advisers opposed this action because they felt that unleashing this new force might have terrible consequences for the future of humankind.

Activities
Answers will vary.

ANSWERS FOR SKILLS DEVELOPMENT

PAGE 623
Skills Practice
Answers will vary.

How Americans Lived, 1950

ANSWERS FOR CHECKUP QUESTIONS

PAGE 627
1. Between 1900 and 1950 the average workweek changed from 60 hours to 40 hours.

2. Television affected a family life by changing the entertainment habits of Americans. People spent their leisure time watching television instead of going out. It also affected family mealtime conversation. In many homes, family members sat in front of the television, eating their separate dinners and hardly exchanging a word.

3. By 1950, Americans spent their vacation time going someplace instead of relaxing at home.

4. American's vacation activities caused the hotel, motel, gas station, and restaurant businesses to grow.

ANSWERS FOR UNIT REVIEW

PAGE 628
Reading the Text
1. F **2.** F **3.** F **4.** T **5.** F **6.** T **7.** T **8.** T **9.** F **10.** T

Reading a Map
1. Stalingrad—Soviet Union
The Bulge—Belgium   Salerno—Italy
Normandy—France   El Alamein—Egypt

2. Germany   **3.** Sicily

4. Norway and Finland

5. Spain, Portugal, Ireland, Sweden, Switzerland, Turkey (partly in Europe)

Reading Pictures
Answers will vary.

Reading Charts
1. 75 million   **2.** 3

3. Became more urban

4. Texas, in both years

5. New York State and New York City, in both years

ANSWER KEY

CHAPTER 28 The Cold War

ANSWERS FOR CHECKUP QUESTIONS

PAGE 636

1. The main bodies of the United Nations are the General Assembly and the Security Council.

2. The Big Three leaders agreed at Yalta that until a final peace treaty was made with Germany, they would divide the country into four parts, or zones. They also agreed on free elections in the countries of Eastern Europe.

3. Cooperation between the United States and the Soviet Union ended after World War II because the Soviets placed Communist governments in surrounding countries.

4. (a) The Truman Doctrine was founded to give military aid to countries who were resisting Communist take-over. (b) The Marshall Plan was proposed to give economic help to countries of Western Europe that had not recovered from the ruin of war. (c) The Berlin airlift was organized to get food, fuel, and other supplies into Berlin because the Soviets had blocked all land entries into Berlin. (d) The North Atlantic Treaty Organization (NATO) was formed to help defend Western Europe. The NATO countries agreed that an attack on any one of them would be considered an attack on all.

PAGE 643

1. Serious military mistakes made by Chiang, the Nationalist leader, and corruption in the government caused much of the population in China to turn against the party in power, the Nationalists. The Communists made promises of land reform and drove the Nationalists off the mainland of Asia. A new Chinese government, the People's Republic of China, was proclaimed by the Communist leader, Mao.

2. After the North Korean army invaded South Korea, the United States sent naval and air forces to help South Korea. President Truman asked the United Nations to take action. The Security Council did, calling upon member nations to come to South Korea's aid. Nineteen UN members sent troops.

3. During the 1950s, cold war tensions relaxed somewhat because of the end of the fighting in Korea; the death of the Russian dictator, Joseph Stalin; and the development of the hydrogen bomb by the Soviet Union.

4. The United States became involved in the Middle East in the 1950s by adopting the Eisenhower Doctrine. It said that the United States would defend countries in the Middle East against armed attack by Communist countries. The United States also offered economic help to the countries of the region.

PAGE 647

1. President Kennedy brought new ideas to American foreign policy such as the Peace Corps and the Alliance for Progress.

2. The Bay of Pigs affair was a setback for the United States because it drove Castro more firmly into the Soviet camp.

3. The Berlin wall was built by the Communists to make escape from East Berlin impossible. It reminded the world of the differences between a Communist state and a free society.

4. The Cuban missile crisis was resolved as follows: President Kennedy demanded that Khrushchev remove the missiles already in Cuba and tear down the missile bases. Khrushchev decided not to challenge the United States blockade and the Soviet ships turned back. Russia removed the missiles and bases. The United States promised not to invade Cuba.

ANSWERS FOR CHAPTER REVIEW

PAGE 648

Vocabulary Quiz

1. United Nations

2. iron curtain

3. cold war

4. containment

5. Truman Doctrine

6. Marshall Plan

7. North Atlantic Treaty Organization

8. summit conference

9. Peace Corps

10. Alliance for Progress

Review Questions

1. (a) The Truman Doctrine affected the eastern Mediterranean. (b) Countries of Western Europe were affected by the Marshall Plan. (c) The Alliance for Progress affected all the countries of the Western Hemisphere except Cuba. (d) The Eisenhower Doctrine affected the Middle East.

2. After World War II, Japan adopted a new constitution, which made the country a democracy. The new constitution promoted civil rights and gave women the right to vote.

3. Nineteen UN member nations sent troops to the aid of South Korea during the Korean War.

4. (a) The invasion of the Bay of Pigs came about when exiled Cubans living in the United States decided to return to Cuba and overthrow Fidel Castro, the Cuban dictator. Trained and armed by the United States under President Eisenhower, the exiles landed at the Bay of Pigs in 1961. Within a few days all the invaders were killed or captured. This adventure was a serious setback for the United States in Latin America and drove Castro firmly into the Soviet camp. (b) The Cuban missile crisis came about when an American spy plane photographed the Soviets secretly building missile bases in Cuba. President Kennedy, concerned that these bases could carry nuclear bombs to reach the eastern and southern United States, ordered the United States Navy to blockade any ships bound for Cuba with weapons. He also demanded that Khrushchev remove the missiles already in Cuba and tear down the missile bases. As Russian ships neared the blockade, Khrushchev decided not to challenge the United States. The ships turned back. After Russia removed the missiles and bases, the United States promised not to invade Cuba.

Activities

1. Belgium, Canada, Denmark, Spain, Great Britain, Iceland, Italy, Luxembourg, The Netherlands, Norway, Portugal, Greece, Turkey, West Germany, and the United States

2. (a) UNESCO—United Nations Educational, Scientific and Cultural Organization

(b) UNICEF—United Nations Children's Fund, originally titled United Nations International Children's Emergency Fund
(c) WHO—World Health Organization

3. UNESCO works for understanding and cooperation among people all over the world. UNICEF aids children in more than 100 countries by helping to solve problems of health, hunger, and education. WHO works to promote the health of all people.

ANSWERS FOR SKILLS DEVELOPMENT

PAGE 649
Skills Practice: Part I
June 25, 1950; eventually; at first; finally; August; then; mid-September; at the same time; by fall

Skills Practice: Part II
1. 3 2. 4 3. 1 4. 2

CHAPTER 29 A Changing Nation

ANSWERS FOR CHECKUP QUESTIONS

PAGE 655
1. There was a building boom after World War II because of a great increase in population, great shifts of population within the United States, and the period of prosperity that the United States experienced from 1945 to 1970.

2. Four population shifts that occurred in the postwar years were as follows:

The first shift was farm to city. In 1940 nearly 1 in every 4 Americans lived on a farm. Thirty years later, fewer than 1 in 20 did. This shift resulted mainly from advances in agriculture known as the Green Revolution. With better fertilizers, better insect control, and more efficient farm machinery, production increased dramatically. Fewer people were now needed on farms, and millions left.

A second great shift was from city to suburb. Cars and new roads made it possible for people to live in the suburbs and work in the city. Eventually, business and industry moved to the suburbs. Shopping centers were built. Soon many people were working in the suburbs as well as living there.

ANSWER KEY

A third population shift was from the northern and eastern parts of the United States to the West and the South. This area is known as the Sunbelt. People moved to the Sunbelt because of the sunny and warm climate much of the year and the mild winters. They were attracted by the different style of living in this region and by job opportunities, which increased as the textile industry moved south. Also, the oil, gas, space, and defense industries in the Sunbelt states grew. As a result new cities and towns sprang up.

The fourth shift was the movement of black Americans from the South to the North. The migration of the black population to the northern states was great during and after World War II. By 1960 half of the black population lived outside the South.

3. The postwar period was a time of prosperity because of the demand for consumer goods. Americans made good money during the war but found few things to spend it on. They either saved their money or bought war bonds. When the factories began to make consumer goods once again, consumers bought them as fast as they were being made. This postwar demand for goods provided high employment and good wages. The baby boom also created a demand for consumer goods. In addition, the United States found a large market for its goods overseas.

PAGE 662
1. Inflation caused workers to want wage increases. There were many strikes. When employers agreed to raise wages, they covered their higher costs by charging more for their products. This raised the cost of living, leading to still more demands for higher wages.

2. Senator McCarthy came into prominence in the early 1950s by taking advantage of the fears of the American people that communism was spreading at home. He claimed that there were over 200 known Communists in the State Department as well as universities, in business, and in the military. After a Senate committee investigated his charge of Communist influence in the army, McCarthy was censured by the Senate for his behavior.

3. (a) President Kennedy's New Frontier program urged Congress to provide funds to retrain unemployed workers and to help depressed areas. He called for a space program that would "land a man on the moon" before 1970. He proposed plans for medical care for the aged, greater protection of civil rights, and federal aid to education.

(b) Eisenhower called his program Modern Republicanism. Congress raised the minimum wage and brought millions of workers into the social security system. The Department of Health, Education, and Welfare was created and more funds were provided for medical research, hospitals, and urban renewal. The Highway Act of 1956 was proposed.

(c) President Truman's Fair Deal extended social security coverage to more workers and raised the minimum wage. It also passed a housing act under which the federal government cleared slums and built housing for low-income families.

4. The launching of Sputnik was a blow to American prestige because it appeared that the Russians had beaten America at its own game—science and technology. It also increased concern for America's security against attack.

The United States government reacted by providing more funds for America's own space program, and by setting up the National Aeronautics and Space Agency (NASA) to direct it. They also adopted the National Defense Education Act (NDEA). One aim of this act was to produce more scientists and science teachers by providing funds for their study.

PAGE 667
1. In 1954 the Supreme Court gave its decision that desegregation of public schools should begin promptly.

2. Following the Supreme Court decision, some states and cities promptly ended school segregation. Most of the white South resisted any change in its ways. While Citizens Councils fought desegregation and threatened blacks and whites who challenged segregation with the loss of their jobs. The Ku Klux Klan came to life again, threatening violence to stop desegregation. Southern leaders and officeholders threw up roadblocks.

3. Black people turned to more direct ways to end segregation since change was slow through the courts. In Montgomery, Alabama, a black woman boarded a bus at the end of a day's work and sat in the front. At that time, whites sat in the front, and blacks were required to sit in the back. When a white man entered the bus, the driver ordered the woman to give her seat up and move to the back. The woman refused, and the driver had her arrested. As a result, blacks began a boycott of the city's buses.

4. The struggle for civil rights for black people was also pursued by sit-ins. Blacks took seats in reserved sections for whites. They were committed to nonviolence. They would stage sit-ins to force department stores to desegregate their lunch counters. They held demonstrations for the desegregation of hotels, theaters, beaches, pools, waiting rooms, water fountains, and toilets.

ANSWERS FOR CHAPTER REVIEW

PAGE 668
Vocabulary Quiz
1. agriculture
2. war veterans
3. South and the West
4. rises
5. union
6. condemned
7. space satellite
8. sit-ins
9. public schools
10. nonviolent resistance

Review Questions
1. During the postwar years American scientists developed new varieties of rice, wheat, soybeans, and corn that produced many times more food than older varieties.

2. The country's rapid growth in population contributed to new job opportunities and economic growth because city and state governments had to spend more for schools, roads, hospitals, and police and fire services. This meant more jobs. More jobs meant more people could afford homes. Thus the demand for and sale of more consumer goods was created.

3. Following World War II, prices rose because factories could not keep up with the demand for consumer goods. Workers wanted wages increased. When employers agreed to raise wages, they covered their higher costs by charging more for their products.

4. Reforms in social security and in the minimum wage were proposals in President Truman's Fair Deal program that were passed into law.

5. Harry Truman helped to end segregation by seeking laws to protect the civil rights of blacks and other minorities and by ending segregation in the armed forces.

Activities
Answers will vary.

ANSWERS FOR SKILLS DEVELOPMENT

PAGE 669
Skills Practice
1. 1295
2. Seattle
3. Boston and New York
4. Miami and Seattle
5. 510 miles

CHAPTER 30 **A Time of Shocks**

ANSWERS FOR CHECKUP QUESTIONS

PAGE 674
1. The Civil Rights Act of 1964 provided for the end of racial discrimination in hotels, restaurants, theaters, and other businesses that served the public. It prohibited race and sex discrimination in hiring and attempted to protect the voting rights of blacks. The act also gave the federal government more power to speed up desegregation of public institutions.

2. Five of the Great Society programs were (a) the war on poverty, which supplied money to local communities to provide relief and jobs for the poor; (b) Medicare, which provided health care for the aged through the social security system; (c) The program of aid to education, which provided federal funds to schools for the first time; (d) Volunteers in Service to America (VISTA), which was a kind of Peace Corps at home; and (e) the Voting Rights Act of 1965, which protected the rights of all Americans to register to vote. (Note that pupils may also select and describe the Job Corps; food stamps; Head Start; rent and housing aid; money for local improvements of buildings, transportation, and hospitals; and the new immigration law.)

ANSWER KEY

3. Immigration quotas were changed by the 1965 law. The law allowed more immigrants to come from Mexico and Asian countries than in the past.

4. Riots occurred in many cities in the middle years of the 1960s because blacks living in ghetto areas felt they were treated unfairly by white landlords, merchants, and the police.

PAGE 680

1. Vietnam was divided along the 17th parallel north as a result of an agreement among European powers and representatives of the peoples of Indochina. In the agreement, Communists led by Ho Chi Minh would control North Vietnam, and anti-Communists led by Ngo Dinh Diem would control South Vietnam until a national election could be held.

2. The United States became involved in Vietnam because the government leaders wanted to contain Soviet communism. Millions of dollars in military aid and supplies were sent to South Vietnam by the United States. Even American soldiers were sent to train the South Vietnamese.

3. The war in Vietnam divided the American people because many Americans believed we should not participate in another country's civil war. Other Americans objected to the South Vietnamese dictatorship. Opposition to the war grew as more American soldiers died and young people protested being drafted.

4. As a result of the war in Vietnam, 57,000 American soldiers' lives were lost, and 300,000 were wounded or maimed; the North Vietnamese troops overtook South Vietnam soon after the American troops left; and many South Vietnamese fled to the United States.

PAGE 687

1. President Nixon brought about a change in the originally hostile United States policy toward China by supporting, for the first time, the People's Republic in obtaining China's United Nations seat, by visiting China and meeting with the Chinese leaders, and by restoring limited trade and cultural exchanges.

2. Although the United States attempted to follow an evenhanded policy toward the Arabs and Israelis, it stepped in and aided the Israelis with an emergency shipment of arms to use against the Arabs, who had unexpectedly attacked Israel on October 6, 1973.

Some Arab countries placed an embargo on oil shipments to punish the United States for helping Israel.

3. (a) The purpose of the revenue sharing program was to share federal funds with the states so that officials could use the funds to solve pressing problems. (b) The purpose of the busing program was to help desegregate schools.

4. The Watergate affair was touched off when five burglars were caught breaking into the offices of the Democratic National Committee in the Watergate building. It was compounded when Nixon tried to cover up the affair.

5. President Nixon resigned because the House Judiciary Committee demanded that he hand over tape recordings of meetings in his office and then recommended that he be impeached for obstructing justice and misusing presidential power. Nixon was forced to admit that he had been part of the cover-up.

ANSWERS FOR CHAPTER REVIEW

PAGE 688

Vocabulary Quiz
1. c 2. h 3. b 4. i 5. extra definition 6. f
7. a 8. e 9. extra definition 10. d 11. j 12. g

Review Questions
1. The Voting Rights Act of 1965 let local officials know that if they would not register voters fairly, federal officials would step in and do it. As a result of the law, the number of registered southern blacks jumped by 40 percent and blacks began to run for office.

2. The continuing war in Vietnam raised opposition to President Johnson and led to the end of his political career.

3. (a) OPEC stands for Organization of Petroleum Exporting Countries. (b) SALT stands for Strategic Arms Limitation Talks. (c) VISTA stands for Volunteers in Service to America.

4. The oil embargo forced Americans to conserve gasoline by driving more slowly and to conserve heating oil by turning down their thermostats. It also contributed to inflating the American dollar.

5. (a) Executive privilege was the right that Nixon claimed he had as President to keep his records confidential. He used this excuse to keep his tapes

away from the special prosecutor. **(b)** Hush money was money Nixon approved for payment to the burglars so that they wouldn't talk. **(c)** Nixon instructed his staff to stonewall the investigators, which meant that they were to say nothing. **(d)** "Third-rate burglary" was the term Nixon used to publicly dismiss the break-in. **(e)** The 18½-minute gap was discovered when Nixon finally handed over some of the tapes. The special prosecutor knew, through experts, that the tapes had been deliberately erased.

Activities
1. Answers will vary.

2. Answers will vary.

3. The Twenty-fifth Amendment was proposed on July 6, 1965 and ratified on February 10, 1967. This Amendment was added to the Constitution to clarify the problem of presidential succession. This problem was fresh in the minds of Americans because of the numerous illnesses of President Dwight Eisenhower in the 1950s and the tragic death of President J.F. Kennedy in 1963.

4. Answers will vary.

ANSWERS FOR SKILLS DEVELOPMENT
PAGE 689
Skills Practice
a. Space Program—1,7,8,12,14
b. Vietnam War—4,9,10
c. Watergate—3,10,5
d. Civil Rights Movement—5,13,16
e. Johnson's "Great Society"—2,6,11

CHAPTER 31 America Today and Tomorrow

ANSWERS FOR CHECKUP QUESTIONS
PAGE 697
1. The two large Hispanic groups that are included in the United States population today are Mexican Americans and Puerto Ricans.

2. Mexican Americans and Puerto Ricans are similar because they live in barrios, cling to their native language and culture, come to the United States for job and educational opportunities, are part of the fastest growing minority in the United States, and are gradually gaining political power and some political offices. They differ because most Mexican Americans have migrated to America before gaining citizenship, whereas Puerto Ricans are already American citizens. Also, most Mexican Americans are found in the southwestern portion of the United States, whereas Puerto Ricans have generally settled in the cities of the Northeast.

3. In recent years women have made gains in finding job opportunities, receiving equal pay for equal work, and serving in public office.

4. The goals of Indian leaders for improving the lot of their people include preserving their cultural heritage and choosing their own local governments on the reservations.

5. The position of black people in American society improved in the 1970s through better job opportunities and better pay. This allowed them to work their way into the middle class.

PAGE 703
1. The problems inside the United States that confronted President Carter included energy conservation efforts, inflation, unemployment, and potential disaster at nuclear power plants.

2. The status of the Panama Canal was changed from United States control to joint control with Panama until the year 2000. After that, Panama would have total control of the canal, but the United States would retain the right to defend it.

3. To bring peace to the Middle East, President Carter offered to help President Sadat and Prime Minister Begin develop a peace plan in the quiet environment of Camp David in Maryland.

4. Unrest in Central America presented a difficult problem for the United States because on one hand Carter did not want to support governments that denied their people human rights. On the other hand rebel victory might lead to the spread of communism in the region.

5. Americans were taken hostage in Iran because Carter allowed the Shah of Iran to enter a United States hospital. The Iranians wanted the Shah returned to Iran to stand trial for his crimes against the people. The Iranians took the Americans hostage as leverage to convince the United States to hand over the Shah and all his wealth.

ANSWER KEY

1. President Reagan's approach to (**a**) taxation was to give Americans a 25 percent tax cut over 3 years and businesses a tax cut so that they could reinvest in factories and equipment; (**b**) military spending was to increase it so that the United States could catch up to the Soviet Union in several kinds of weapons; (**c**) regulation of business was to relax the regulations, to reduce government spending, and to cut regulatory costs for businesses.

2. The proposals made under the New Federalism program included shifting some federal welfare and health-care programs to the states along with federal revenue supports.

3. There was a worsening of relations between the United States and the Soviet Union because President Reagan believed that the Soviet Union was behind the conflicts in Central America and the Middle East. He restricted the sale of goods that would add to the Soviet Union's military strength. The United States denounced the imposition of martial law in Poland and Reagan subsequently called the Soviet Union an "evil empire." In addition, the United States built a new kind of missile, and several of those missiles were installed in NATO countries amidst protest from the Soviet Union and other countries. Then in September 1983 the Soviet Union shot down a Korean airliner that had strayed into Soviet airspace. The Soviets were condemned by the United States and other free nations for this act.

4. The United States became involved in (**a**) Central America because President Reagan felt it was necessary to stop the spread of communism and (**b**) Lebanon because the Lebanese government requested the United States, France, and Italy to send peacekeeping forces into Beirut after civil war broke out between the Moslems and Christians and international war broke out on Lebanese land between the Syrians, the PLO, and the Israelis.

ANSWERS FOR CHAPTER REVIEW

Vocabulary Quiz

1. F, Migrant workers are usually employed on farms, planting, cultivating, and harvesting crops.

2. T

3. F, The plan of termination ended special health and education services for Native Americans.

4. T

5. F, The Camp David accords, which were signed by Carter, Sadat, and Begin, established peace between Israel and Egypt.

6. T

7. F, The Iranians agreed to return the American hostages on President Carter's last day in office.

8. F, If the federal budget has a deficit, it means that the government has spent more than it took in.

9. F, Under Reagan's New Federalism, welfare and health-care programs were to be shifted from the federal government to the states.

10. F, Under martial law, the government of Poland arrested many Solidarity leaders.

Review Questions

1. It can be said that it is both an advantage and a disadvantage for Mexican Americans and Puerto Ricans to hold onto their native Spanish language because although the language enhances their Spanish heritage and may be useful to them in some careers, many American schools do not have Spanish-speaking teachers or Spanish textbooks for all subject areas. This situation makes it difficult for Spanish-speaking children to learn. In addition, many jobs require the use of the English language. Mexican Americans and Puerto Ricans who have not learned English will be very limited in their job opportunities.

2. The arguments for the Equal Rights Amendment included providing opportunities for women in public office, equal pay for equal work, job opportunities for women, and equal opportunities for women in all areas of life. The women who were against the ERA argued that women already had equal rights under the law. They felt the law would weaken marriages and family life, they feared that it would wipe out legal protections women had won over the years, and they also feared that women would be drafted.

3. The Middle East was the scene for success for President Carter because he significantly aided President Sadat of Egypt and Prime Minister Begin of Israel in achieving peace agreements, which were spelled out in the Camp David accords. The Middle

East was also the scene of failure for President Carter because Americans in the embassy in Iran were taken hostage when Carter allowed the Shah to enter an American hospital. A daring rescue attempt failed, and negotiations were unsuccessful until the last day of Carter's presidency.

4. President Reagan's domestic programs differed from those of President Carter in the following ways: (a) President Reagan was able to get Congress to deregulate the prices of oil and gas; Carter tried, but Congress resisted. (b) President Reagan brought inflation down during his administration. Inflation had risen during Carter's administration. (c) President Reagan was less conscious of providing opportunities for women and minorities than was President Carter.

5. Under President Carter the United States policy in Central America was to provide military and economic aid to the non-Communist governments while trying to stop their violations of human rights. President Reagan's policy in Central America saw an increase in military aid to the area to stop the spread of communism. Reagan felt it was most important to stop communism, even at the expense of human rights.

Activities

1. Affirmative Action is the action taken by employers to remedy the effects of job discrimination and to stop such discrimination. In certain jobs, blacks, Hispanics, and women have not been employed in sufficient numbers in comparison to their number in the available labor force.

2. (a) Before becoming President, Carter was a Naval officer and a farmer; Reagan was a radio announcer and a motion picture actor. (b) Both were governors before becoming President. (c) Carter was not very successful in winning support in Congress; Reagan was very successful.

3. Answers will vary.

ANSWERS FOR SKILLS DEVELOPMENT

PAGE 712
Answers will vary.

ANSWERS FOR UNIT REVIEW
PAGE 713

Reading the Text

1. The postwar building boom was connected to an increase in population, great shifts in population, and demands for consumer goods.

2. The four great population shifts that occurred in the United States between 1940 and 1970 were: the shift from farm to city; from the city to the suburbs; from the northern and eastern parts of the country to the west and south; and the migration of black Americans from the south to the north.

3. The population shift from the farm to the city resulted from the Green Revolution.

4. The southern third of the United States is known as the Sunbelt.

5. Five of the nation's largest cities in the Sunbelt in 1980 were San Antonio, Houston, Dallas, Los Angeles, and San Diego.

Reading a Map

1. NATO and Warsaw Pact nations

2. 13

3. 7

4. West Germany, Norway, Greece, Turkey

5. Switzerland, Ireland, Sweden, Finland, Austria, Yugoslavia

Reading a Picture
Answers will vary.

Reading a Chart

1. General Assembly

2. Secretariat, Economic and Social Council, Trusteeship Council

3. Security Council, International Court of Justice

4. 15

5. Trusteeship Council

Teacher's Notes

1 2 3 4 5 6 7 8 9 10—RRD—90 89 88 87 86 85 84